THE ENGLISH DUDEN

The English Duden

A Pictorial Dictionary with English and German Indexes

Edited by the Fachredaktionen of the
Bibliographisches Institut, Mannheim,
and the Modern Languages Department
of George G. Harrap & Company Ltd,
London

2nd revised edition

GEORGE G. HARRAP AND CO. LTD
LONDON · TORONTO · WELLINGTON · SYDNEY

Containing 25,000 words
Illustrated by Line Drawings and
8 Plates in Full Colour

PUBLISHERS' NOTE

Some of the illustrations may seem unfamiliar to English readers, but they have been retained from the German edition in order that the two books can be used side by side. Users of *The English Duden* will find it interesting to compare the Germany of the pictures with their own country. They may be surprised to see a chimney-sweep climbing onto the roof of a house, a ticket-collector creeping from door to door along the outside of a train, a water-meter for measuring the water consumption of a household (so that it can be charged to the householder, of course), or a billiard-table with no pockets. These are, however, common enough sights in Germany and the reader might like to reflect that though the way of cutting up carcases or of numbering the registration plate of a car may differ from country to country, atomic power stations (like parts of the body) are much the same wherever they are found.

We would like to thank all those firms, libraries, institutes, and specialists who have co-operated in the production of this work, and whose names are listed at the end of the book. A special word of thanks is due to Anabel Dapurkar B. A., Arethusa Ewbank B. A., Licenciée ès Lettres, Elise Hurd B. A., William Bainbridge and Peter Collin B. A. for their assistance in checking translations. For the editorial work we extend our gratitude to Fräulein Dipl.-Phil. Gisela Preuß and Herrn Dr. phil. Otto Weith.

SBN 245 559 00 0

Alle Rechte vorbehalten
© Bibliographisches Institut AG · Mannheim 1960
First published in Great Britain 1960
by George G. Harrap & Co. Ltd, 182 High Holborn, London, W. C. 1
Printed in Germany

PREFACE

The English Duden has been adapted from the German *Duden Bildwörterbuch* published in 1958, and, like its original, groups by subjects words which can be represented pictorially. A first edition of *The English Duden* was adapted from the *Duden Bildwörterbuch* of 1936, but since then the vocabulary of almost every subject which these books covered has undergone so great a change that a complete revision of both editions was necessary. The revised *Duden Bildwörterbuch* was published in 1958 and its success has encouraged the compilation of this companion volume.

Here, as in the German edition, the words are grouped by their subject-matter into 368 sections, each with a picture and a word list. The table of contents on page 6, divided into fifteen main headings, lists all the 368 plates and their numbers, while the indexes at the back of the book give after each word the reference number of the word itself and the number of the plate in which it appears. The English index (pp. D 1-112) includes in alphabetical order all the words in the lists accompanying the plates. The German index (pp. E 1-128) is reproduced from the *Duden Bildwörterbuch.* Thus to identify a German or English word the user should look it up in the appropriate index which will refer him to the picture. On the other hand, by referring directly to the pictures and their word-lists unknown objects can be named or the complete vocabulary of a particular subject can be found. By comparing *The English Duden* with the *Duden Bildwörterbuch* (the numbering of pictures and words is identical in both books), a translation from English into German can be obtained. *The English Duden* can thus serve three purposes. It can stand alone as an English glossary, it can provide a translation from German to English, and, in conjunction with the *Duden Bildwörterbuch*, it will give an English-German translation for each word.

Contents

Crafts and Trade

Industry

Printing and Allied Trades

Transport and Communications

Office, Bank, Stock Exchange

State and City

Travel and Recreation

Sport

Entertainment and Music

Science, Religion, Art

Animals and Plants

1 Atom I

1-4 model of an atom,
1 and 2 the atomic nucleus:
1 the proton [positive]
2 the neutron [non-electric, neutral];
3 the electron [negative]
4 the electron orbit [forming the electronic shell];

5-8 model of an isotope appertaining to 1-4 [radioactive]:
5 the proton
6 the neutron
7 the electron
8 the electron orbit;

9-12 spontaneous disintegration of an atom [radioactivity]:
9 the atomic nucleus
10 the alpha radiation (alpha particle emission) [helium nucleus]
11 the beta radiation (beta particle emission) [electrons]
12 the gamma radiation (X-rays);

13-17 the nuclear fission (atomic fission):
13 the atomic nucleus
14 the bombardment by neutron
15 two new atomic nuclei
16 the neutrons being released [generation of heat]
17 X-ray-like (roentgen-like) radiation (gamma radiation);

18-21 the chain reaction (nuclear chain reaction):
18 the neutron splitting the atomic nucleus
19 the atomic nucleus before fission
20 the fragments of the split nucleus (fission fragments)
21 neutrons released by the fission and splitting further atomic nuclei;

22-30 the controlled (governed) **chain reaction:**
22 the atomic nucleus of a fissionable element
23 the bombardment by neutron
24 the neutron released and splitting another atomic nucleus
25 two new atomic nuclei
26 the moderator, a slowing-down layer of graphite
27 the neutrons being released [generation of heat]
28 the extraction of heat [production of energy]
29 the X-ray-like (roentgen-like) radiation
30 the protective concrete or lead wall;

31-46 the atomic pile (atomic reactor, nuclear reactor, reaction pile, graphite pile):
31 the protective concrete wall
32 the air layer
33 the air shaft (air duct)
34 the moderator
35 the cooling tube
36 the tube for radio-isotopes
37 the loading side
38 the loading aperture
39 the uranium rod (filling rod) [the fuel of the pile]
40 the atomic physicist (nuclear physicist)
41 the technician
42 the gallery, a lifting platform for loading the pile
43 the ladder
44 the aperture for radio-isotopes
45 the control rod of a cadmium or boron compound
46 the control rod motor;

47 the atomic bomb (atom bomb, A-bomb):
48 the plutonium or uranium isotopes
49 the timer
50 the reflector (tamper) of beryllium

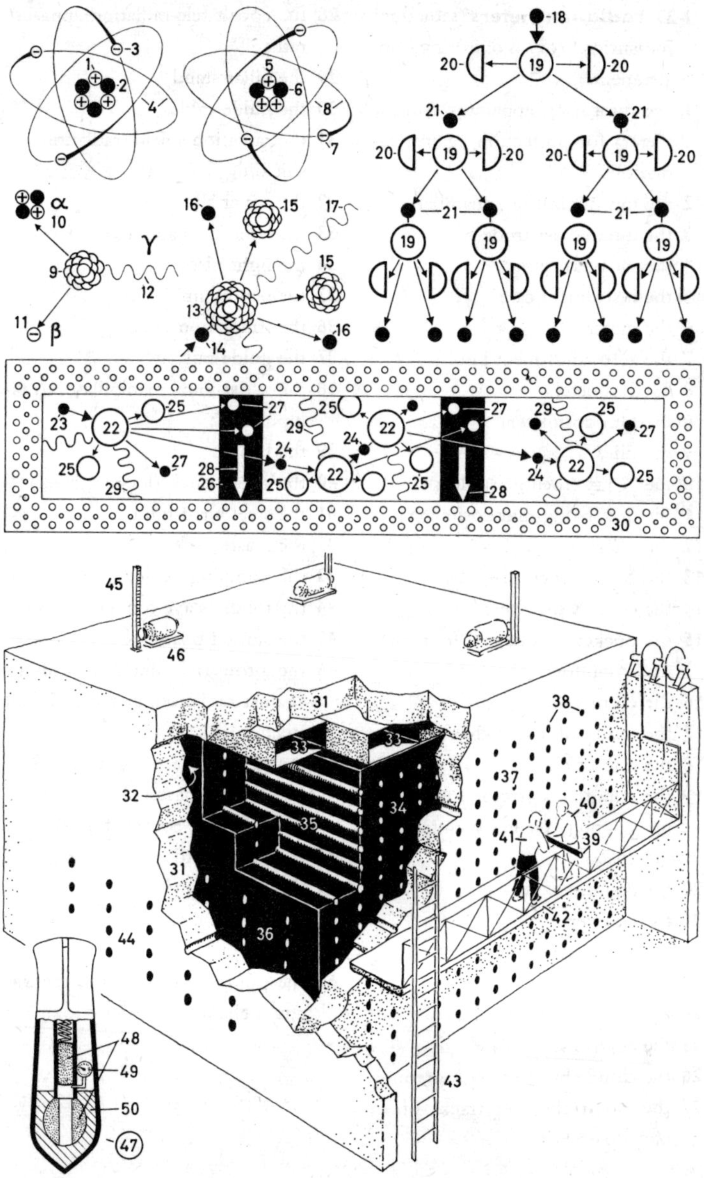

1-23 radiation meters (radiation-measuring, or monitoring, instruments),
1 the measuring apparatus (survey meter) for protection against radiation:
2 the ion (ionization) chamber
3 the internal electrode
4 the range selector
5 the instrument case
6 the meter
7 the zero adjustment knob;
8–23 dosimeters,
8 the film dosimeter:
9 the filter
10 the X-ray (roentgen) film;
11 the finger-ring film dosimeter:
12 the filter
13 the X-ray (roentgen) film
14 the cover with filter;
15 the pocket dosimeter ('fountain-pen' monitor):
16 the eyepiece
17 the ion (ionization) chamber
18 the pocket clip;
19 the counting detector tube (Geiger counter, Geiger counter survey meter):
20 the counter envelope
21 the counter
22 the instrument case
23 the range selector;
24 the Wilson cloud chamber:
25 the compression plate;
26 the cloud chamber photograph:
27 the cloud chamber tracks of an alpha particle;
28 the cobalt tele-radiation apparatus:
29 the pillar stand
30 the guide cables
31 the radiation shield (radiation shielding)
32 the cover slide
33 the lamellar diaphragm
34 the light visor
35 the pendulum device
36 the irradiation table
37 the guide rail;
38 the wrist-joint manipulator (manipulator):
39 the handle
40 the safety catch (locking lever)
41 the steel wrist joint
42 the master arm
43 the clamping device
44 the tongs (slave tongs)
45 the slotted board
46 the protective shield (shielding) against radiation, a lead-seal wall [section];
47 the gripping arm of a twin manipulator (master-slave manipulator, remote-control tongs):
48 the dust guard;
49 the cosmotron:
50 the danger area
51 the magnet
52 the pumps for emptying the vacuum chamber

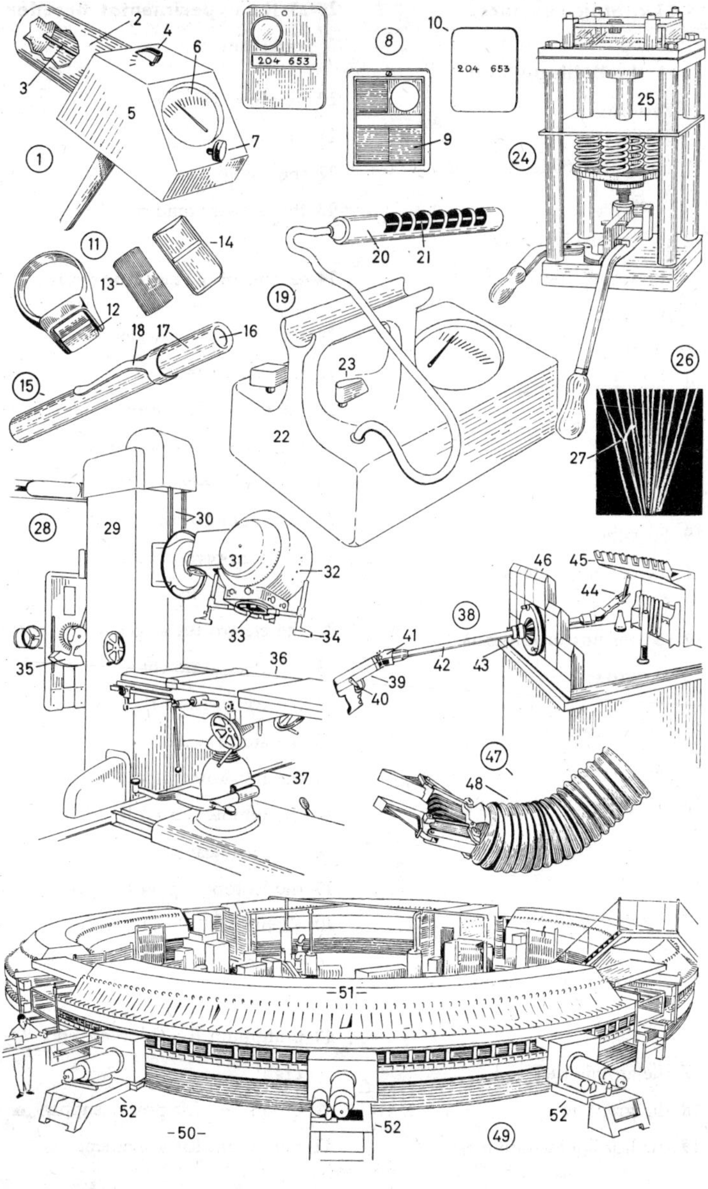
1
2
3
4
5
6
7
204 653
8
9
10
204 653
11
12
13
14
15
16
17
18
19
20
21
22
23
24
25
26
27
28
29
30
31
32
33
34
35
36
37
38
39
40
41
42
43
44
45
46
47
48
49
-50-
-51-
52
52
52

1-23 atomic reactors,

1-11 the boiling-water reactor:

1 the shield (shielding) against radiation
2 the water-filled tank
3 the atomic fuel
4 the control rods
5 the steam
6 the turbo-generator
7 the heat-exchanger
8 the steam inlet
9 the cold-water entry
10 the condenser
11 the cooling-water inlet;

12-16 the homogeneous reactor:

12 the reactor
13 the reflector
14 the reactor liquid, a liquid metal
15 the boiler
16 the heated fuel;

17-19 the sodium graphite reactor:

17 the atomic fuel rod
18 the graphite
19 the hot liquid sodium;

20-23 the experimental breeder reactor:

20 uranium 238
21 uranium 235
22 the hot liquid metal
23 the cooled liquid metal;

24-42 the ideal reactor cycle:

24 the compressed-water reactor
25 the reactor tank
26 the uranous solution
27 the cooling-water system
28 the cooling-water inlet
29 the cooling-water outlet
30 the high-pressure steam
31 the water inlet
32 the electro-turbo-generator
33 the electric power station
34 the steam from the turbine
35 the steam outlet
36 the hot-water pipe
37 the remote-heated building
38 the chemical plant
39 the isotope-separating plant
40–42 further utilization of the plutonium gained for generation of energy:
40 plutonium for shipping and aircraft
41 plutonium for power supply
42 plutonium for armament

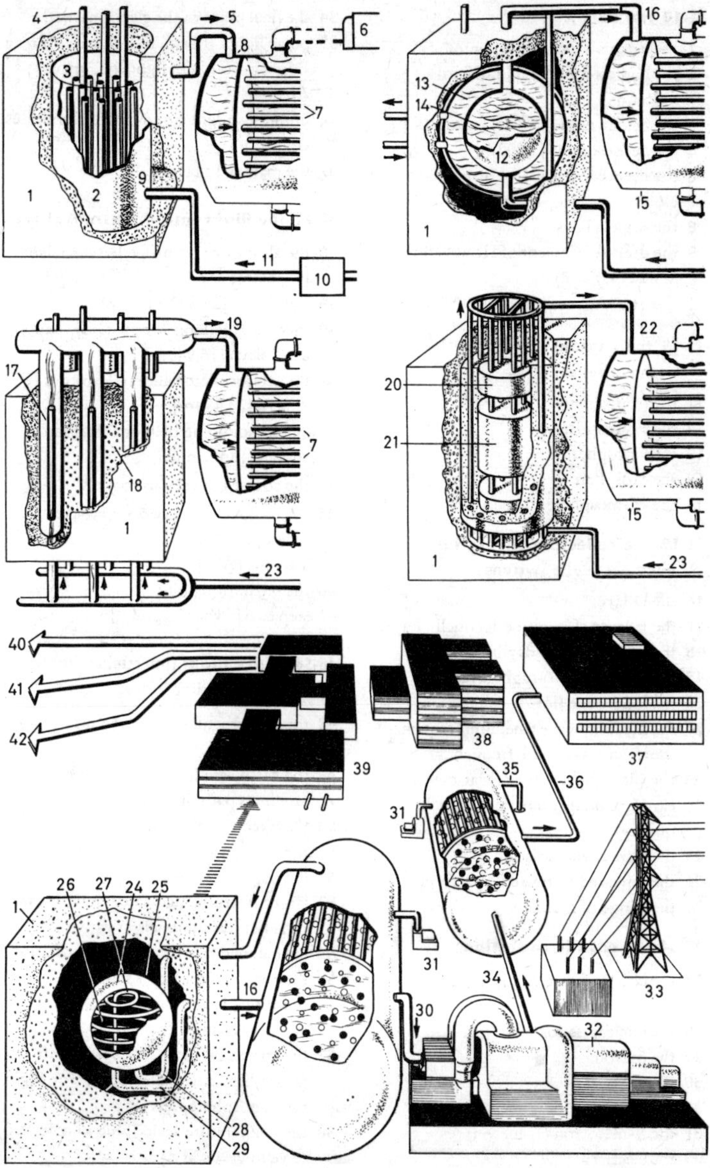
4
5
6
3
8
7
2
9
1
10
11
16
13
14
12
15
19
17
18
7
23
20
21
22
15
23
40
41
42
39
38
37
35
36
31
26 27 24 25
16
31
34
30
32
33
28
29

4 The Atmosphere

1-10 the earth:

1 the earth's crust (lithosphere)
2 the highest mountain [8,882 m]
3 volcano
4 the smoke cloud of Krakatoa [30 km]
5 the deepest mine [2,800 m]
6 the deepest oil well [6,170 m]
7 clouds
8 the sea level
9 the deep-sea descent of Houot and Willm [4,050 m]
10 the greatest ocean depth [10,899 m];

11-15 the regions (layers) **of the atmosphere:**

11 the troposphere
12 the stratosphere
13 the ionosphere
14 the exosphere
15 the chemosphere;

16-19 the reflecting layers for wireless (radio) **waves:**

16 the D-layer
17 the E-layer (Heaviside-Kennelly Layer)
18 the F*1* (Appleton)-daytime layer
19 the F*2* (Appleton)-night layer;
20 the long wave (low frequency)
21 the medium wave (medium frequency)
22 the short wave (high frequency)
23 the ultra-short wave (radar connection earth-moon through very high frequency)
24 the ultraviolet radiation
25 the infra-red (ultra-red) radiation
26 the fringe of darkness

27-34 the cosmic radiation:

27 the cosmic particle (cosmic ray particle)
28 the nuclear fission
29 the proton
30 the neutron
31 the π-mesotron (π-meson)
32 the μ-mesotron (μ-meson)
33 the electron
34 the final point of the electrons' path;
35 polar lights (northern lights or Aurora Borealis, southern lights or Aurora Australis)
36 luminous night clouds (night-luminous clouds)
37 the meteor (meteorite)

38-47 the flight into the atmosphere:

38 the altitude of jet-propelled aeroplanes [16,000 m]
39 Bell X-1A [27,500 m]
40 Piccard's balloon ascent (*Am.* balloon ascension) [16,940 m]
41 the stratosphere balloon 'Explorer II', U.S.A. [23,490 m]
42 and 43 sounding balloons (balloon sondes) [unmanned]
44 the courses of various rockets
45–47 the ascent of a two-step rocket ['Bumper-Wac']:
45 step one ['V2']
46 the separation point
47 step two ['Wac Corporal'];

48-58 space flight (interstellar flight, astronautical flight):

48 the instrumented earth satellite (Sputnik)
49 the earth satellite's line of flight (earth satellite's path or course)
50 the direction of flight
51 the centrifugal force
52 the centripetal force
53 larger instrumented satellite with experimental (test) animals
54 the manned space station (outer station)
55 the course of the outer station
56 the winged end stage of a manned, multi-stage satellite rocket
57 the structural parts of a space craft (spaceship, interstellar craft), for flight the atmosphere only
58 the temperature scale [blue = cold, red to yellow = warm]

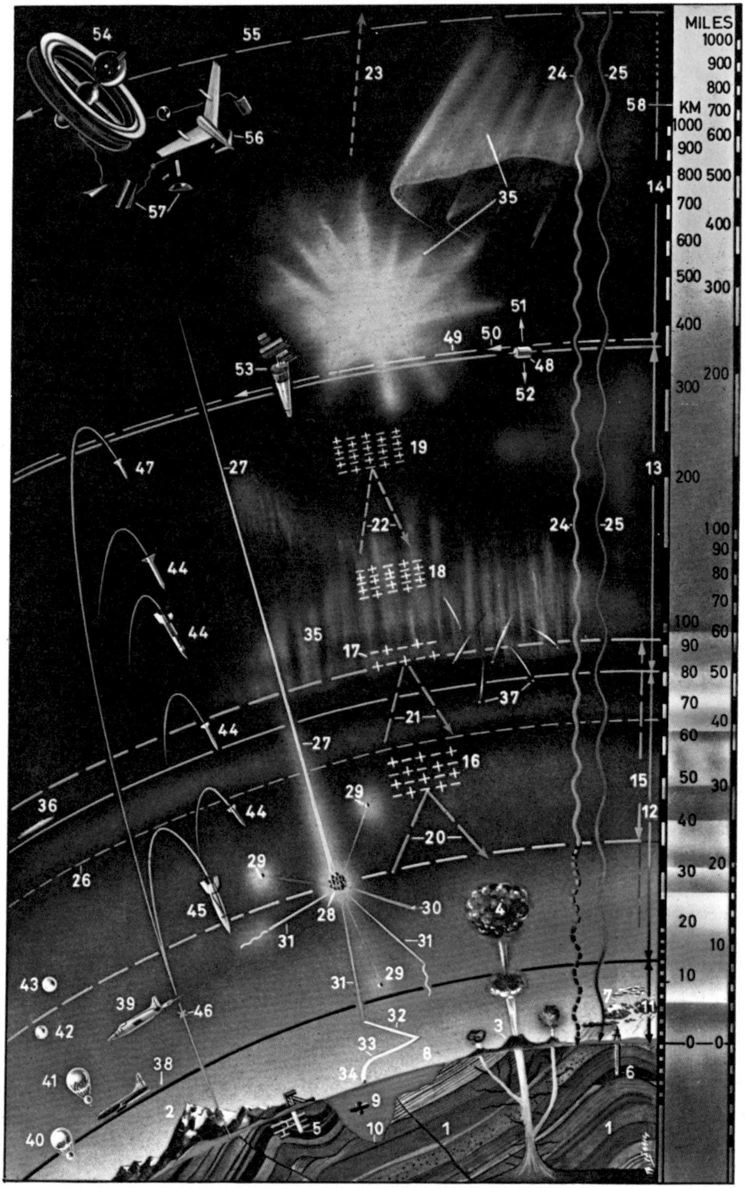

MILES
KM
1000
900
800
700
600
500
400
300
200
100
90
80
70
60
50
40
30
20
10
0

5 Astronomy I

1-35 star map of the Northern sky or heavens (Northern hemisphere), a celestial chart, a planisphere,

1–8 divisions of the sky:

1 the celestial pole with the north star (pole star, polaris)

2 the ecliptic (apparent yearly orbit, or path, of the sun)

3 the celestial equator (equinoctial)

4 the tropic of Cancer

5 the circle enclosing the circumpolar stars [which never set]

6 and **7** the equinoxes:

6 the first point of Aries (vernal equinox)

7 the first point of Libra (autumnal equinox)

8 the summer solstice (solstice);

9-48 constellations (grouping of fixed stars into figures)

and names of stars:

9 Aquila (Eagle) with chief star Altair

10 Pegasus

11 Cetus (Whale) with Mira, a variable star

12 Eridanus (River Eridanus)

13 Orion (Hunter) with Rigel, Betelgeuse, and Bellatrix

14 Canis Major (Great Dog) with Sirius, a star of the first magnitude

15 Canis Minor (Little Dog) with Procyon

16 Hydra (Water Snake)

17 Leo (Lion) with Regulus

18 Virgo (Virgin) with Spica

19 Libra (Balances, Scales)

20 Serpens (Serpent)

21 Hercules

22 Lyra (Lyre) with Vega

23 Cygnus (Swan) with Deneb (Aridad)

24 Andromeda

25 Taurus (Bull) with Aldebaran

26 the Pleiades (Pleiads), an open cluster of stars

27 Auriga (Waggoner, Charioteer) with Capella

28 Gemini (the Twins) with Castor and Pollux

29 Ursa Major (the Plough; Great, or Greater, Bear; Charles's Wain; *Am.* Big or Great Dipper) with double star (binary stars) Mizar and Alcor

30 Boötes (Bear Driver, Herdsman) with Arcturus

31 Corona Borealis (Northern Crown)

32 Draco (Dragon)

33 Cassiopeia

34 Ursa Minor (Little, or Lesser, Bear, *Am.* Little Dipper) with the north star (pole star, polaris)

35 the Milky Way (Galaxy);

36–48 the Southern stellar heavens:

36 Capricornus (Capricorn, Goat, Sea-Goat)

37 Sagittarius (Archer)

38 Scorpio (Scorpius, Scorpion)

39 Centaurus (Centaur)

40 Triangulum Australe (Southern Triangle)

41 Pavo (Peacock)

42 Grus (Crane)

43 Octans (Octant)

44 Crux (Southern Cross, Cross)

45 Argo (Ship Argo)

46 Carina (Keel)

47 Pictor (Painter)

48 Reticulum (Net)

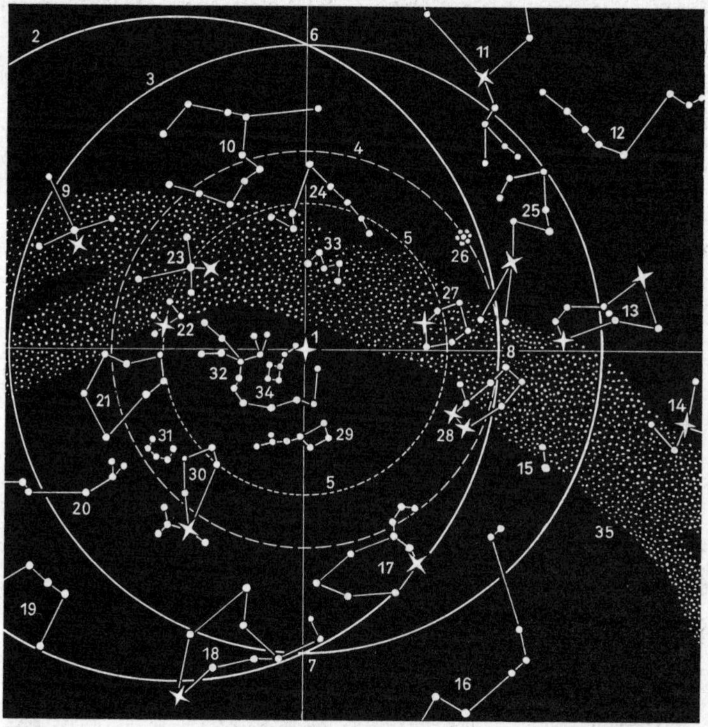

1
2
3
4
5
6
7
8
9
10
11
12
13
14
15
16
17
18
19
20
21
22
23
24
25
26
27
28
29
30
31
32
33
34
35

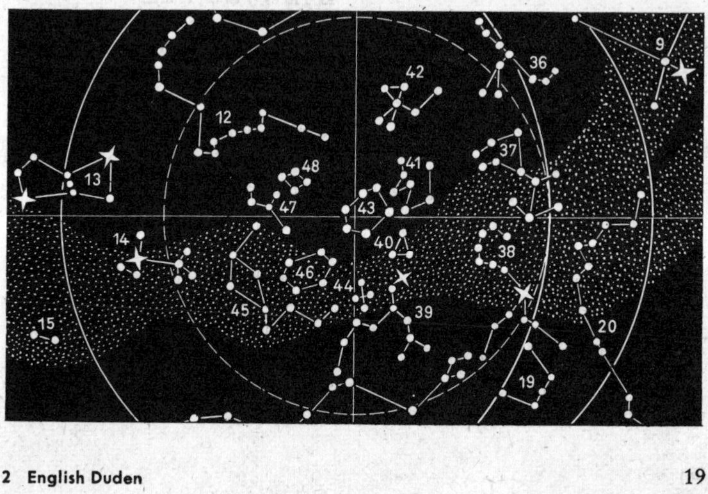

9
12
13
14
15
19
20
36
37
38
39
40
41
42
43
44
45
46
47
48

6 Astronomy II

1-51 uranology (uranography):
1 the firmament (starry sky, heavens, canopy of heaven, vault of heaven)

2-11 the astronomical observatory,
2–7 the reflecting telescope (reflector):
2 the trellis tube (lattice tube)
3 the ocular, sometimes a camera for astrophotography
4 the concave mirror (parabolic reflector or mirror)
5 the polar axis
6 the declination axis
7 the foundations (bearings);
8 the revolving dome
9 the observing aperture
10 the astronomer's observing position
11 the guide rails;

12-14 the planetarium (orrery):
12 the stationary cupola
13 the artificial firmament
14 the projection apparatus;

15-20 the Einstein tower [at Potsdam],

15-18 the coelostat:
15 the mirrors
16 the wooden tower
17 the light shaft
18 the lower mirror;
19 the thermostable room
20 laboratories for testing sunlight and starlight (for solar physics, astrophysics, spectral analysis) and concerning Einstein's theory of relativity;

21-31 the solar system (planetary system) **and the signs** (symbols) **of the planets:**
21 the sun

22-31 the planets (wandering stars):
22 Mercury
23 Venus
24 the Earth and the moon, a satellite
25 Mars and 2 satellites
26 the asteroids (minor planets, remnants of a planet)
27 Jupiter and 12 satellites
28 Saturn and 9 satellites
29 Uranus and 5 satellites
30 Neptune and 2 satellites
31 Pluto;

32-43 the signs (symbols) **of the zodiac** (zodiacal signs):
32 Aries (Ram)
33 Taurus (Bull)
34 Gemini (the Twins)
35 Cancer (Crab)
36 Leo (Lion)
37 Virgo (Virgin)
38 Libra (Balance, Scales)
39 Scorpio (Scorpion)
40 Sagittarius (Archer)
41 Capricornus (Capricorn, Goat)
42 Aquarius (Water-carrier, Water-bearer)
43 Pisces (Fishes, Fish);

44-46 a spiral nebula:
44 the nucleus of the spiral nebula
45 the spiral arm
46 the diameter of the spiral nebula;
47–50 schematic edge-on view of the Milky Way:
47 the nucleus of the galactic system
48 the approximate position of our solar system
49 the border zone consisting of dark nebulae
50 the depth;
51 the great **Orion nebula,** a gaseous nebula

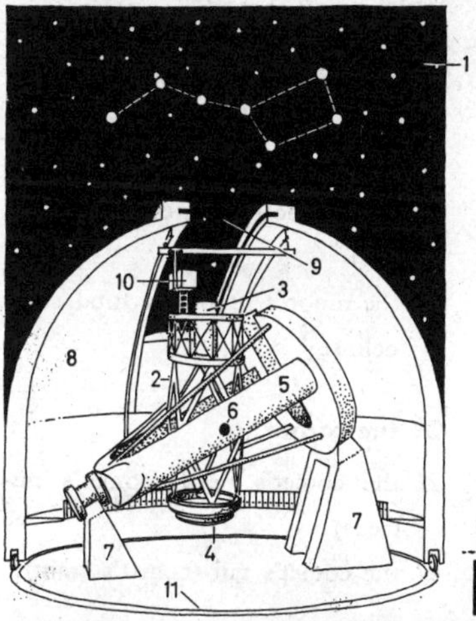
1
2
3
4
5
6
7
7
8
9
10
11

12
13
14

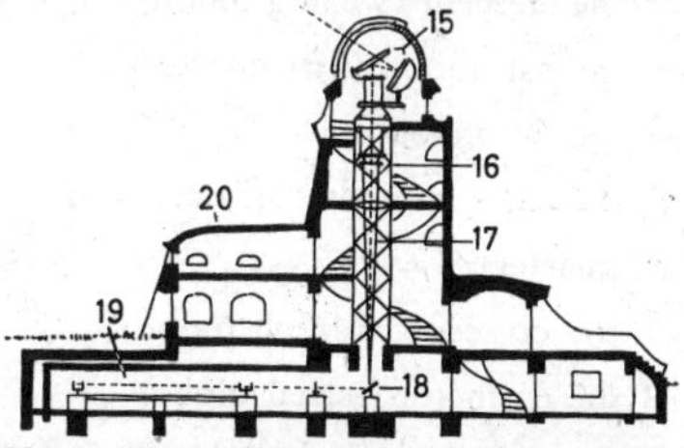
15
16
17
18
19
20

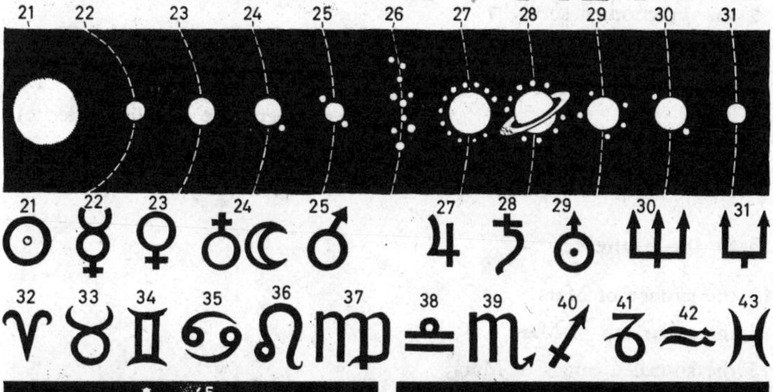
21
22
23
24
25
26
27
28
29
30
31

21
22
23
24
25
27
28
29
30
31

32
33
34
35
36
37
38
39
40
41
42
43

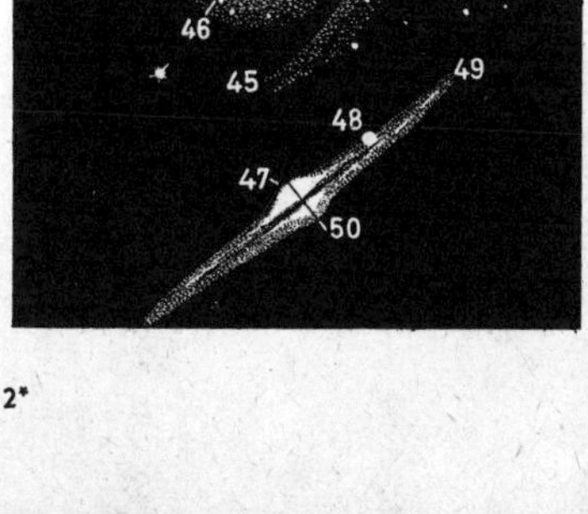
44
45
46
46
45
47
48
49
50

51

7 Astronomy III

1-12 the moon:

1 the moon's orbit (revolution of the moon round the earth)

2–7 the lunar phases (moon's phases, lunation):

2 the new moon

3 the crescent (waxing moon)

4 the half-moon (first quarter)

5 the full moon

6 the half-moon (last quarter, third quarter)

7 the crescent (waning moon);

8 the earth (terrestrial globe)

9 the direction of sunlight

10 the surface of the moon:

11 a lunar sea, a barren level area

12 a lunar crater (moon crater);

13-18 the planets,

13 the surface of Mars:

14 the polar cap of Mars

15 the so-called canals of Mars;

16 Saturn:

17 the rings of Saturn

18 belts in Saturn's atmosphere;

19-23 the sun:

19 the solar disc (solar globe, solar sphere)

20 sunspots

21 eddies in the surroundings of sunspots

22 the corona (corona of the sun), the sun's limb (sun's halo), observable during total solar eclipse or by means of special instruments

23 prominences (erupting clouds of gas);

24 the moon's limb at a total solar eclipse

25 the comet:

26 the comet's head (comet's nucleus)

27 the comet's tail (comet's train);

28 the shooting star (falling star, meteor, bolide, fire ball):

29 the meteorite (aerolite, siderite)

30 the meteoric crater

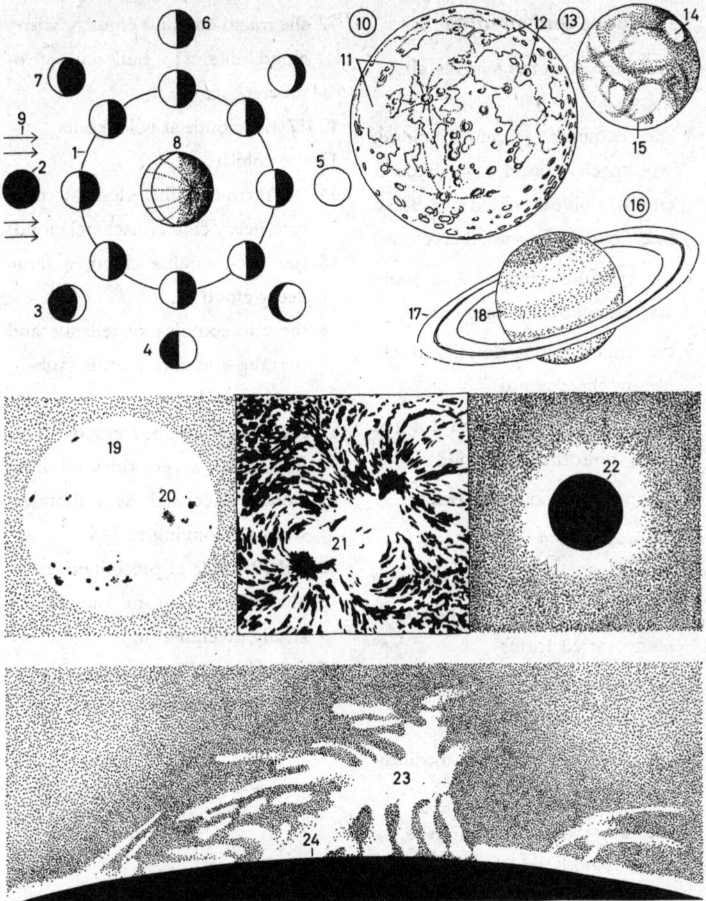
1
2
3
4
5
6
7
8
9
10
11
12
13
14
15
16
17
18
19
20
21
22
23
24
25
26
27
28
29
30

1-19 clouds and weather,

1–4 clouds of homogeneous air masses:

1 the cumulus (cumulus cloud, wool-pack cloud, cauliflower cloud), a billowy cloud (flat-based heap cloud, fair-weather cloud)

2 the cumulus congestus, a more actively billowing heap cloud

3 the stratocumulus cloud, a thick, lumpy sheet cloud

4 the stratus cloud (high fog), a thick, uniform sheet cloud;

5–12 the clouds at warm fronts:

5 the warm front

6 the cirrus cloud, a high to very high ice-crystal cloud, thin, with many varied forms

7 the cirro-stratus cloud, an ice-crystal haze cloud

8 the alto-stratus cloud, a medium-high sheet cloud

9 the alto-stratus praecipitans, a sheet cloud with precipitation (rain streaks) from above

10 the nimbo-stratus or nimbus cloud, a rain cloud, very thick sheet cloud, from which precipitation (rain or snow) falls

11 the fracto-stratus cloud, a wispy cloud below the nimbo-stratus cloud

12 the fracto-cumulus cloud, a wispy cloud like 11, but with protuberances;

13–17 the clouds at cold fronts:

13 the cold front

14 the cirro-cumulus cloud, a delicate, fleecy cloud (mackerel cloud)

15 the alto-cumulus cloud, a large fleecy cloud

16 the alto-cumulus castellanus and the alto-cumulus floccus, subspecies of 15

17 the cumulo-nimbus cloud (thunder cloud), a very thick swelling cloud; associated with thunderstorms belonging to 1–4;

18 and 19 kinds of precipitation:

18 the steady rain or snowfall, a steady precipitation

19 the shower, a sudden (local, passing) precipitation

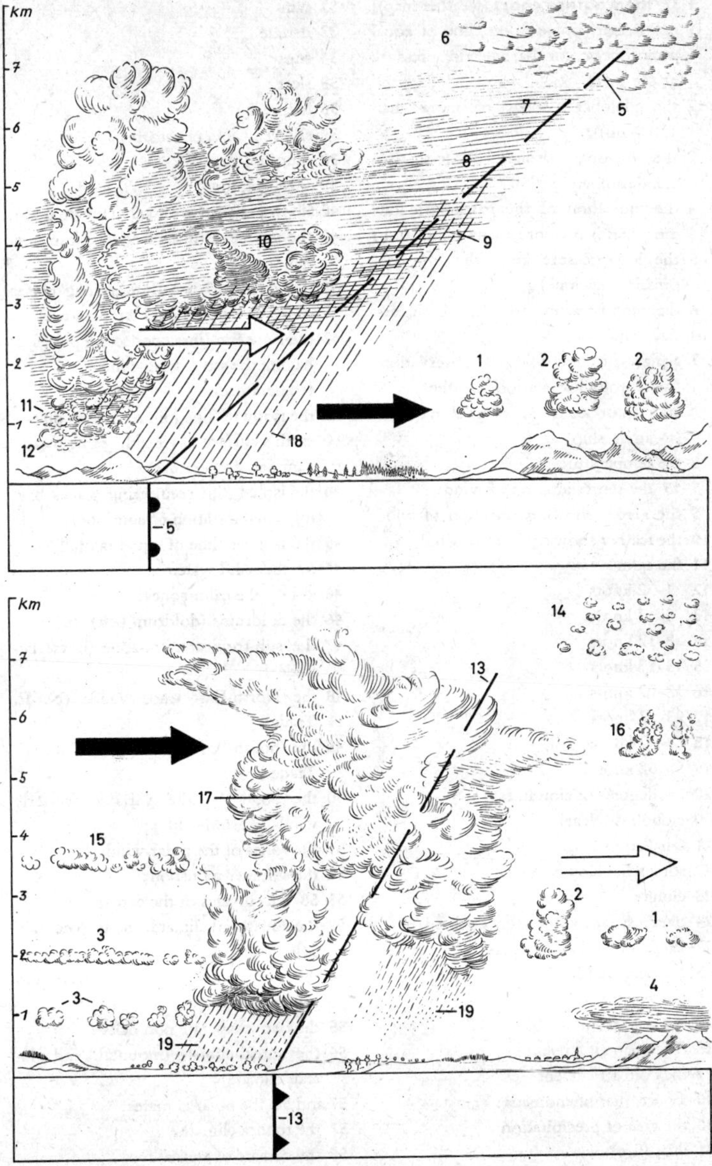
km
7
6
5
4
3
2
1
1
2
2
5
6
7
8
9
10
11
12
18
-5
km
7
6
5
4
3
2
1
13
14
15
16
17
3
3
2
1
4
19
19
-13

9 Meteorology II and Climatology

1-39 the weather chart (weather map):
1 the isobar (isobaric line, line of equal atmospheric, or barometric, pressure at sea level)
2 the pleiobar (isobar of more than 1,000 mb)
3 the meiobar (isobar of less than 1,000 mb)
4 the indication of the barometric (atmospheric) pressure in millibars (mb)
5 the low-pressure area (the low, depression, cyclone)
6 the high-pressure area (the high, anticyclone)
7 a place of meteorological observation (meteorological station, weather station) or an observation ship (weather ship)
8 the temperature
9–19 the representation of wind:
9 the arrow showing direction of wind
10 the feather showing force of wind
11 the calm
12 1– 2 knots
13 3– 7 knots
14 8–12 knots
15 13–17 knots
16 18–22 knots
17 23–27 knots
18 28–32 knots
19 58–62 knots;
20–24 degrees of cloudiness:
20 cloudless (clear)
21 fair (bright)
22 somewhat cloudy
23 cloudy
24 overcast (sky completely covered);
25–29 fronts and air currents:
25 the occluded front
26 the warm front
27 the cold front
28 the warm air current
29 the cold air current;
30–39 weather phenomena:
30 the area of precipitation
31 mist (fog)
32 rain
33 drizzle
34 snow
35 sleet
36 hail
37 shower (*Am.* rainstorm)
38 thunderstorm
39 sheet-lightning;

40-58 the climatic chart (climate map):
40 the isotherm (line of equal mean temperature)
41 the zero isotherm (line joining places of 0° C. mean annual temperature)
42 the isocheim (line connecting places having the same mean winter temperature)
43 the isothere (line joining points on earth's surface having the same mean summer temperature)
44 the isohel (line connecting places having equal duration of sunshine)
45 the isohyet (line of equal rainfall);
46–52 the wind systems,
46 and 47 the calm-zones:
46 the doldrums (doldrum belt)
47 the sub-tropical calm-zone (horse latitudes);
48 the North-East trade winds (N. E. Trades)
49 the South-East trade winds (S. E. Trades)
50 the zones of the variable westerly winds (westerlies)
51 the zones of the polar winds
52 the summer monsoon;
53–58 the climates of the earth:
53 the equatorial climate: the tropical rain belt
54 the two desert belts: the desert and steppe zones
55 the two temperate rain belts
56 the boreal climate (mountain and plateau climate)
57 and 58 the polar climates:
57 the tundra climate
58 the climate of eternal frost

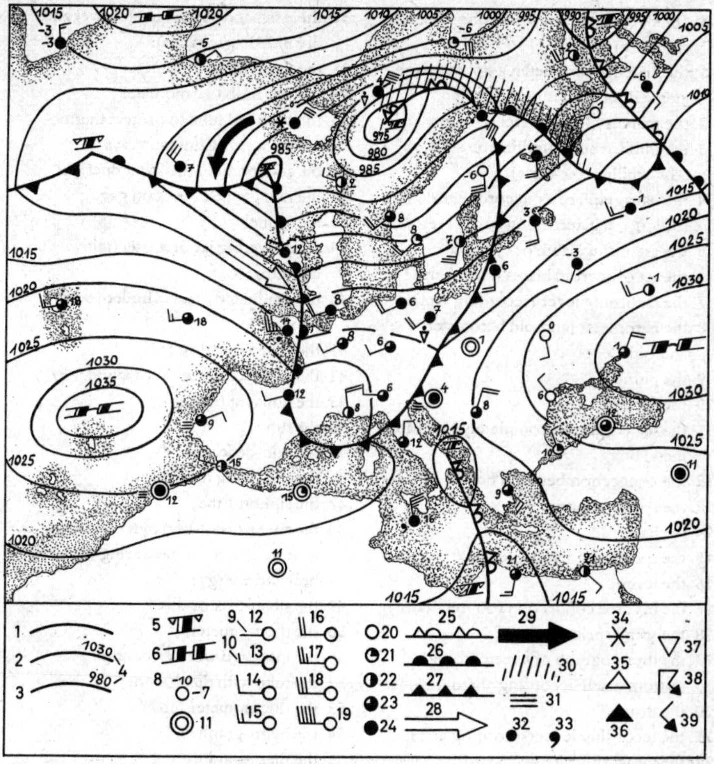
1
2
3
1030
980
4
5
6
8
10
-7
11
9
10
12
13
14
15
16
17
18
19
20
21
22
23
24
25
26
27
28
29
30
31
32
33
34
35
36
37
38
39

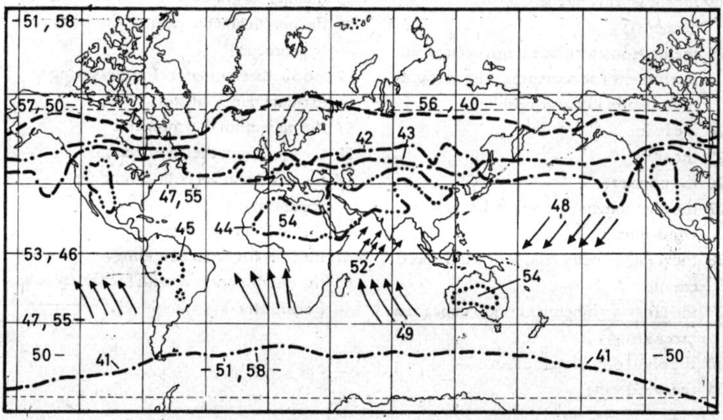
51, 58
57, 50
56
40
42
43
47, 55
45
44
54
53, 46
52
48
49
41
50

10 Meteorological Instruments

1–18 instruments for measuring atmospheric pressure,
1 the mercury barometer, a siphon barometer, a liquid-column barometer:
2 the mercury (quicksilver) column
3 the millibar scale (millimetre scale, *Am.* millimeter scale);
4 the barograph of a meteorological station, a self-recording barometer:
5 the recording drum or cylinder
6 the set of aneroid boxes (chambers)
7 the recording lever (recording arm);
8 the barometer (aneroid barometer, aneroid):
9 the pointer
10 the spring
11 the sealed, almost completely evacuated metal box
12 the connection between box and spring
13 the spring support
14 the base plate
15 the spring-regulating device
16 the lever
17 the pivoted connection rod (regulator)
18 the spiral spring;
19 the thermograph of a meteorological station, a self-recording thermometer:
20 the drum
21 the recording lever (recording arm)
22 the measuring element (sensitive element);
23 the hygrometer (hair hygrometer), an instrument for measuring the amount of moisture in the atmosphere:
24 the hair
25 the scale
26 the pointer;
27 the anemometer (wind gauge, *Am.* wind gage):
28 the wind velocity counter (wind speed counter)
29 the cross with hemispherical cups (*Am.* cross arms)
30 the wind direction indicator
31 the wind vane;
32 the Assmann psychrometer (wet and dry bulb hygrometer):
33 the dry bulb thermometer
34 the wet bulb thermometer
35 the polished tube to protect thermometer bulbs against sun rays
36 the suction tube (main air duct);
37 the rain gauge (*Am.* rain gage):
38 the funnel
39 the collecting jar or vessel (rain collector)
40 the graduated glass cylinder (rain measure)
41 the insert for snow;
42 the self-recording rain gauge:
43 the housing (casing)
44 the funnel
45 the rain-deflector
46 the recording mechanism
47 the siphon-tube;
48 the silver-disk (disc) pyrheliometer, an instrument for measuring the sun's heat and energy:
49 the silver disk or disc
50 the thermometer
51 the insulated wooden casing
52 the tube with diaphragm;
53 the thermometer screen:
54 the hygrograph
55 the thermograph
56 the psychrometer (wet or dry bulb hygrometer)
57 and **58** thermometers for measuring extreme temperatures:
57 the maximum thermometer
58 the minimum thermometer;
59 the radio-sonde (radio-sounding apparatus):
60 the hydrogen balloon
61 the foils for radar sounding
62 the instrument box with the short-wave transmitter

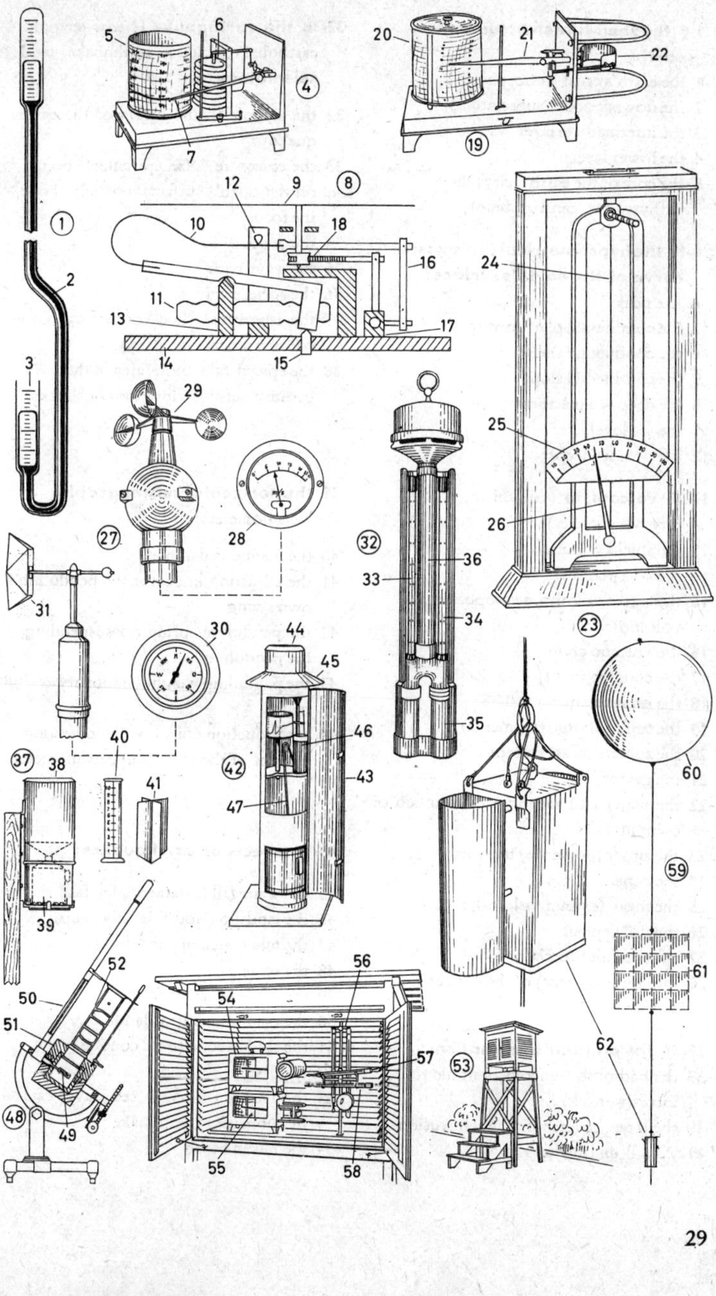
1
2
3
4
5
6
7
8
9
10
11
12
13
14
15
16
17
18
19
20
21
22
23
24
25
26
27
28
29
30
31
32
33
34
35
36
37
38
39
40
41
42
43
44
45
46
47
48
49
50
51
52
53
54
55
56
57
58
59
60
61
62

11 General Geography I

1-5 the shell-like structure of the earth:
1 the earth's crust (lithosphere)
2 the flowage zone (substratum)
3 the intermediate layer
4 the lower layer
5 the core of the earth (barysphere bathysphere, centrosphere);

6-12 the hypsometrical (hypsographic) **curve of the earth's surface:**
6 the peak
7 the continental platform
8 the continental shelf
9 the continental slope
10 the deep-sea platform
11 the sea level
12 the oceanic deeps;

13-20 volcanism (vulcanism, volcanicity, vulcanicity):
13 the shield volcano
14 the lava plateau
15 the active volcano, a composite volcano:
16 the volcano crater
17 the conduit (vent)
18 the lava stream
19 the tuff (volcanic fragments)
20 the subterranean volcano;
21 the geyser:
22 the water and steam jet or fountain or column
23 the sinter (geyserite) terraces;
24 the cone
25 the maar (extinct volcano):
26 the tuff deposit
27 the conduit breccia
28 the conduit (vent) of the extinct volcano;

29-31 the plutonic magmatism:
29 the batholith (igneous plutonic rock, intrusive rock)
30 the laccolite (laccolith), an intrusion
31 the sill, an ore deposit;

32-38 the earthquake [*kinds:* tectonic earthquake, volcanic earthquake] **and seismology:**

32 the seismic focus (origin of the earthquake)
33 the epicentre (*Am.* epicenter); point on the earth's surface vertically above the focus)
34 the depth of focus
35 the wave path
36 the surface waves
37 the isoseismal (line connecting places of same seismic intensity)
38 the epicentral region (area of the greatest seismic vibrations or shocks);

39 the horizontal seismograph (seismometer):

40 the magnetic damper
41 the adjusting knob for the pendulum's own swing
42 the pendulum spring for suspending the pendulum
43 the pendulum weight (stationary mass)
44 the induction coils for the indicating current of the recording galvanometer;

45-54 effects of earthquakes:

45 the waterfall (cataract, *Am.* fall)
46 the landslip (landslide, *Am.* slip):
47 the talus (area of deposition)
48 the scar;
49 the funnel-shaped fissure
50 the displacement of land
51 the sludge cone (mud cone)
52 the fissure
53 the tsunami (seismic sea wave) caused by submarine earthquake
54 the raised beach

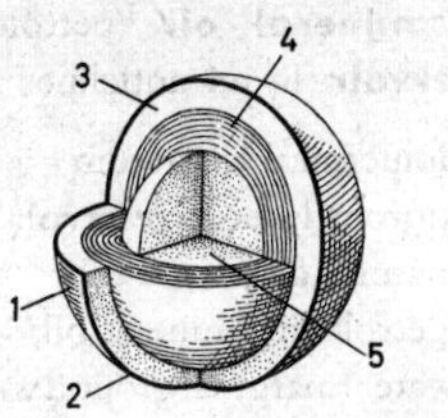
1
2
3
4
5

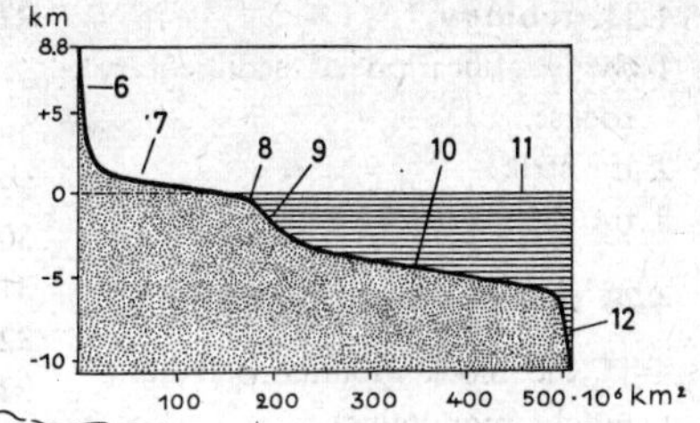
km
8.8
+5
0
-5
-10
6
7
8
9
10
11
12
100
200
300
400
500 · 10⁶ km²

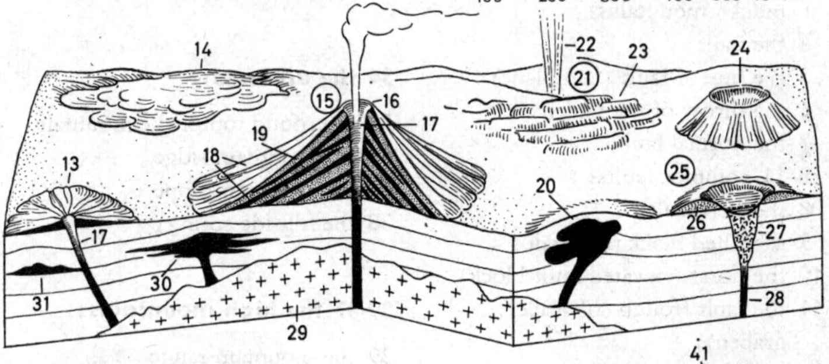
13
14
15
16
17
18
19
20
21
22
23
24
25
26
27
28
29
30
31

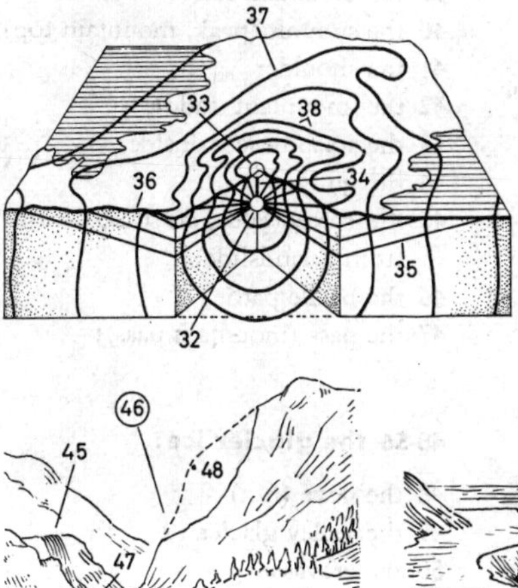
32
33
34
35
36
37
38

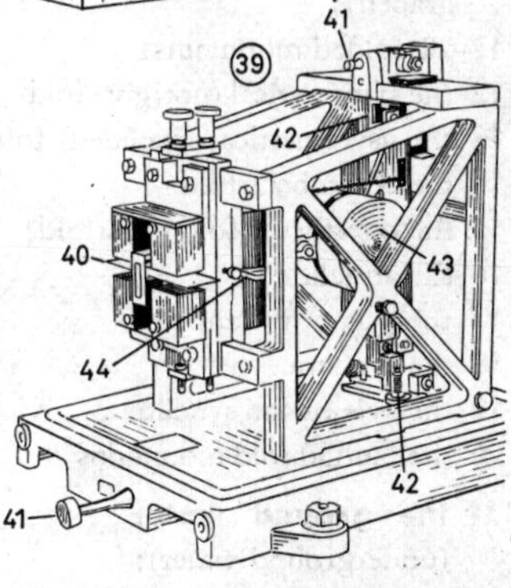
39
40
41
42
43
44

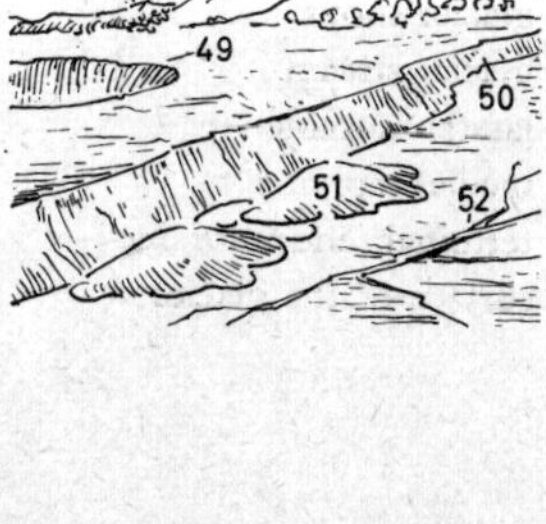
45
46
47
48
49
50
51
52

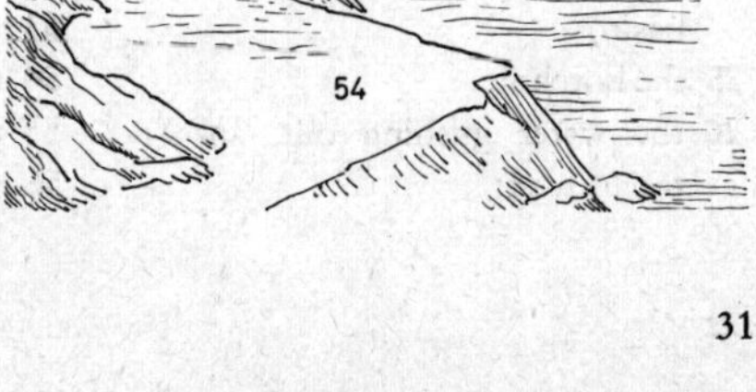
53
54

1-33 geology,

1 the stratification of sedimentary rocks:

2 the strike

3 the dip;

4-20 the mountain building,

4–11 the block mountains fault block mountains),

4 the fault:

5 the line of fault (faultplane)

6 the throw of the fault;

7 the normal fault

8–11 complex faults:

8 the step faults

9 the tilted block mountains

10 the horst (elevated fault block)

11 the fault trough (rift valley, graben);

12–20 folded mountains:

12 the symmetrical (upright) fold

13 the asymmetrical (inclined) fold

14 the recumbent fold

15 the overthrust fold (overfold)

16 the anticline

17 the axis of the anticline

18 the syncline

19 the axis of the syncline

20 the faulted fold mountains;

21 the ground water (underground water):

22 the aquifer (water-bearing stratum or layer)

23 the impermeable (watertight, impervious) stratum or layer or bed

24 the catchment area (catchment basin)

25 the borehole

26 the water gushing out, an Artesian well;

27 the mineral oil (petroleum) **reservoir** in an anticline:

28 the impermeable stratum

29 the porous layer as reservoir rock

30 the natural gas, a gas cap

31 the petroleum (mineral oil)

32 the water (marginal ground water)

33 the derrick;

34 the uplands:

35 the round top of the mountain

36 the mountain ridge

37 the mountain slope

38 the hillside spring;

39-47 the high mountains:

39 the mountain range

40 the summit (peak, mountain top)

41 the shoulder

42 the mountain saddle

43 the steep mountainside

44 the gully

45 the scree (talus, detritus, debris from a landslide)

46 the bridle path

47 the pass (mountain pass);

48-56 the glacier ice:

48 the névé (firn)

49 the valley glacier

50 the crevasse

51 the glacier snout

52 the glacier stream

53 the lateral moraine

54 the medial moraine

55 the terminal (end) moraine

56 the surface of the glacier

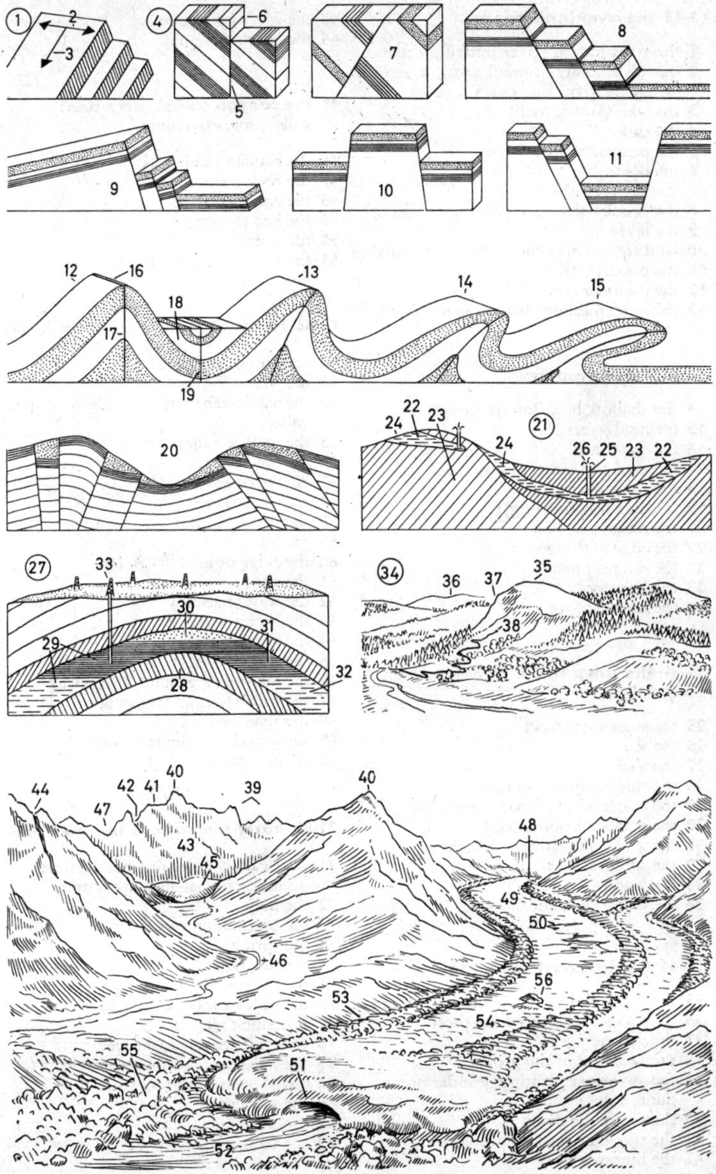
1
2
3
4
5
6
7
8
9
10
11
12
13
14
15
16
17
18
19
20
21
22
23
24
25
26
27
28
29
30
31
32
33
34
35
36
37
38
39
40
41
42
43
44
45
46
47
48
49
50
51
52
53
54
55
56
40

13 General Geography III

1-13 the river landscape:

1 the river mouth (river outfall), a delta
2 the distributary (outfall arm), a river arm (*Am.* river branch)
3 the lake (*Scotch:* loch)
4 the shore
5 the peninsula (*Am.* neck)
6 the island
7 the bay (bight)
8 the brook (stream, rivulet, *Am.* creek)
9 the levee
10 land from which the water has receded
11 the meander (bend)
12 the meander core
13 the water meadow (low-lying meadow);

14-24 the swamp (bog),

14 the shallow bog (lowland bog):
15 the mud layers
16 the water cap
17 the reed and sedge peat
18 the alder-fen peat;
19 the high bog (hill bog):
20 the recent peat bed
21 the edge of the layer
22 the old peat bed
23 the bog pool
24 the saturated zone;

25-31 the steep coast (high coast, high coastline):

25 the stack (sea stack)
26 the sea
27 the surf
28 the cliff (steep face of rock)
29 the beach rubble (beach debris)
30 the wave-cut notch (cliff notch)
31 the wave-cut platform (bench);
32 the atoll, a coral reef:
33 the lagoon
34 the entrance to the lagoon;

35-44 the flat coast (flat beach):

35 the high-tide limit (*Am.* tidewater limit)
36 the waves breaking on the shore
37 the groyne
38 the land end of the groyne
39 the migratory (drifting, wandering) dune, a dune
40 the crescentic dune
41 the ripple marks (wind ripples)
42 the hummock
43 the wind-swept tree
44 the beach lagoon;

45 the canyon (cañon, steep-sided valley, *sim. Am.* coulee):

46 the plateau (tableland)
47 the rock terrace
48 the stratified rock
49 the bed terrace
50 the cleft
51 the canyon (cañon) river;

52-56 forms of valleys [cross sections]:

52 the gorge (ravine, glen)
53 the young V-shaped valley
54 the adolescent valley (wide V-shaped valley)
55 the mature valley
56 the old valley;
57–70 the river valley:
57 the steep slope
58 the gentle slope
59 the mesa
60 the ridge of hills
61 the river
62 the water meadow
63 the rock terrace
64 the gravel terrace
65 the valley slope
66 the hill (rising ground, eminence)
67 the valley bottom (valley floor)
68 the river bed
69 the deposits (sedimentation)
70 the bedrock;

71-83 karst formations in limestone:

71 the swallow hole (sink hole, doline, dolina), a funnel-shaped cavity
72 the polje
73 the percolation of a river
74 the spring
75 the dry valley
76 the system of caves
77 the water level (water table) in a karst formation
78 the impermeable rock layer
79 the stalactite cavern (karst cave),
80 and **81** stalactic structures:
80 the stalactite
81 the stalagmite;
82 the column or pillar
83 the subterranean river

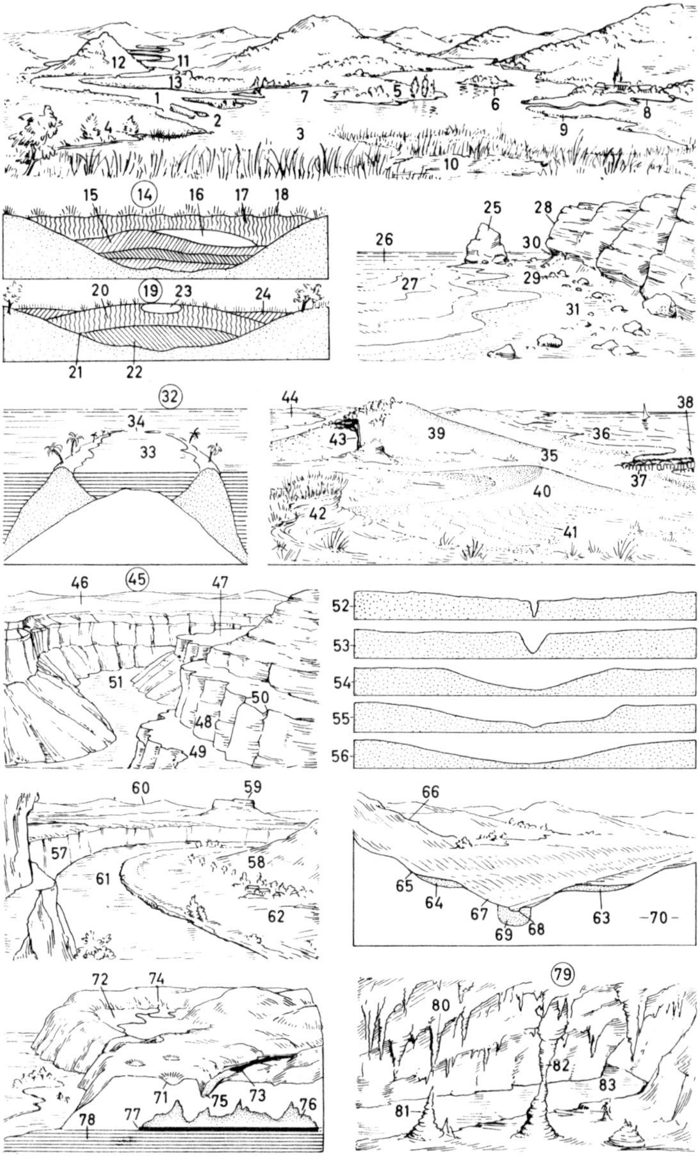
12
11
13
1
2
4
3
7
5
6
8
9
10
15
14
16
17
18
20
19
23
24
21
22
25
28
26
30
27
29
31
32
34
33
44
38
43
39
36
35
37
40
42
41
46
45
47
51
50
48
49
52
53
54
55
56
60
59
57
58
61
62
66
65
64
67
63
-70-
69
68
72
74
71
75
73
76
77
78
79
80
82
83
81

14

1 2 3 4 5
6 7 8 9 10
11 12 13 14 15
16 17 18 19 20
21 22 23 24 25
26 27 28 29 30
31 32 33 34 35
36 37 38 39 40
41 42 43 44 45
46 47 48 49 50
51 52 53 54 55

1–26 Europe:
1 Albania
2 Belgium
3 Bulgaria
4 Denmark
5 Germany
6 Finland
7 France
8 Greece
9 Great Britain
10 Eire (The Republic of Ireland)
11 Iceland
12 Italy
13 Yugoslavia
14 Netherlands; Luxembourg (Luxemburg)
15 Norway
16 Austria
17 Poland
18 Portugal
19 Rumania
20 Sweden
21 Switzerland
22 Union of Soviet Socialist Republics (Soviet Union, U.S.S.R.)
23 Spain
24 Czechoslovakia (Czecho-Slovakia)
25 Hungary
26 Vatican State;
27 Australia
28 New Zealand
29–34 America,
29 and **30** North America:
29 Canada
30 United States of America (U.S.A.);
31 Mexico [Central America]
32–34 South America:
32 Argentina (The Argentine Republic)
33 Brazil
34 Chile;
35–38 Africa:
35 Egypt
36 Ethiopia
37 Liberia
38 Union of South Africa;
39–54 Asia,
39–45 Western Asia (the Near East):
39 Israel
40 Turkey
41 Lebanon
42 Jordan (Transjordan)
43 Syria
44 Iran (Persia)
45 Iraq (Irak);
46 India
47 Pakistan
48 China (People's Republic)
49 China (Nationalist China)
50 Japan
51 Korea (North Korea)
52 Korea (South Korea)
53 Indonesia
54 Philippine Islands (Philippines);
55 United Nations

15 Map I

1-7 the network (grid) of parallels and meridians on the surface of the earth:

1 the Equator
2 a line of latitude (a line of terrestrial latitude, a line of geographical latitude, a parallel)
3 the pole, a terrestrial pole (geographical pole)
4 a line of longitude (a line of terrestrial longitude, a line of geographical longitude, a meridian)
5 the prime meridian (standard meridian)
6 the angle of latitude (angle of geographical latitude, angle of terrestrial latitude
7 the angle of longitude (angle of geographical longitude, angle of terestrial longitude);

8 and 9 map projections:

8 the conical (conic) projection
9 the cylindrical projection;

10-45 the map of the world:

10 the tropics
11 the polar circles
12–18 the continents,
12 and **13** the Americas:
12 North America
13 South America;
14 Africa
15 and **16** Eurasia:
15 Europe
16 Asia;
17 Australia
18 the Antarctic (Antarctic Continent, Antarctica);
19–26 the ocean (seas):
19 the Pacific Ocean
20 the Atlantic Ocean
21 the Arctic Ocean
22 the Antarctic Ocean (the South Polar Ocean, Southern Ocean)
23 the Indian Ocean
24 the Straits of Gibraltar, a strait
25 the Mediterranean Sea (Mediterranean)
26 the North sea, a fringing sea (marginal sea, epicontinental sea)
27–29 the key [to symbols on the map], an explanation of symbols [on the map]:
27 the cold ocean current
28 the warm ocean current
29 the scale;
30–45 the ocean currents (oceanic currents):
30 the Gulf Stream (North Atlantic Current, Gulf Stream Drift)
31 the Kuro Shio
32 the North Equatorial Current
33 the Equatorial Counter Current
34 the South Equatorial Current
35 the Brazil Stream
36 the North East Monsoon Drift
37 the Agulhas Current
38 the East Australian Current
39 the California Current
40 the Labrador Current
41 the Canaries Current
42 the Peru Current
43 the Benguela Stream
44 the Antarctic Drift (Antarctic Current, West Wind Drift, Cirumpolar Current)
45 the West Australian Current;

46-62 surveying (land-surveying, survey, geodesy, geodetic surveying),

46 levelling (*Am.* leveling; geometrical measurement of height):
47 the levelling (*Am.* leveling) staff
48 the level, a telescope level (*Am.* aiming telescope);
49 the trigonometrical point:
50 the supporting scaffold
51 the signal tower;
52–62 the theodolite, an instrument for measuring angles:
52 the micrometer knob
53 the microscope eyepiece
54 the screw for remote control of elevation
55 the elevation lock nut
56 the screw for remote control of lateral movement
57 the lateral lock nut
58 the adjusting knob for the illuminating mirror
59 the illuminating mirror
60 the telescope
61 the transverse level
62 the circular adjustment;
63–66 the aerial photogrammetry (photogrammetry, phototopography):
63 the series topographic camera (*Am.* automatic camera)
64 the stereotope:
65 the pantograph;
66 the stereoplanigraph

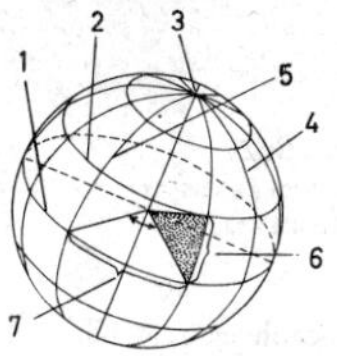
1
2
3
4
5
6
7

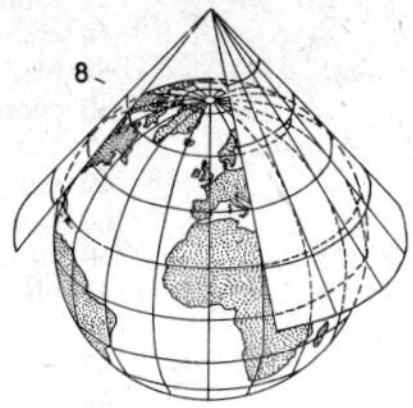
8

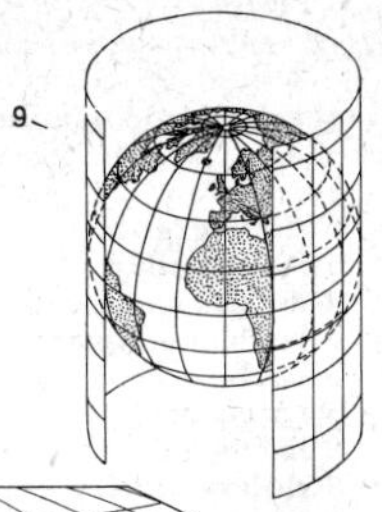
9

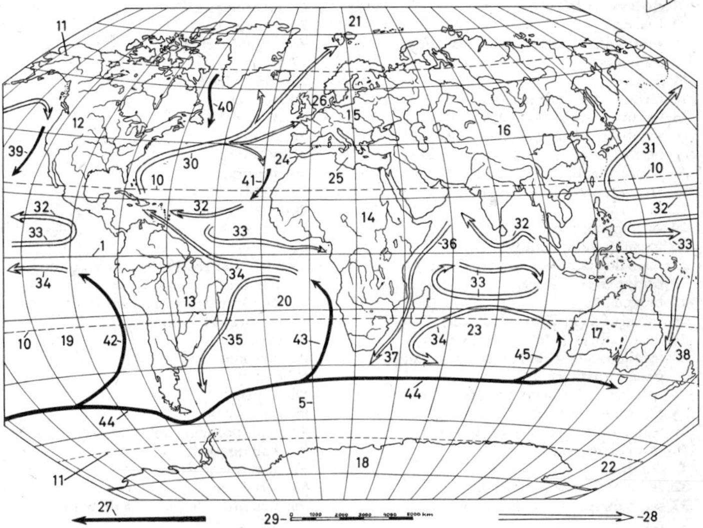
11
21
12
26
15
16
40
39
30
24
25
31
10
41
10
32
32
14
32
33
32
36
33
1
34
33
34
13
20
10
19
42
35
43
37
34
23
17
45
38
44
5
44
18
11
22
27
29 0 1000 2000 3000 4000 5000 km
28

63

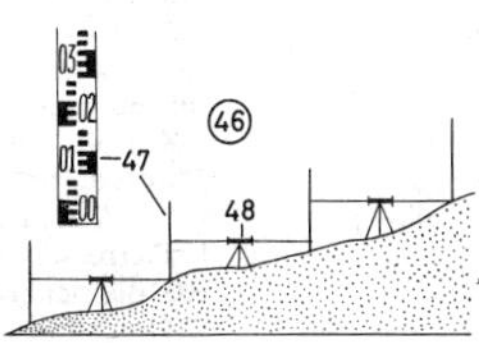
46
47
48

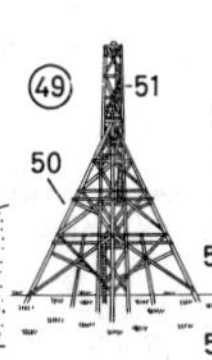
49
51
50

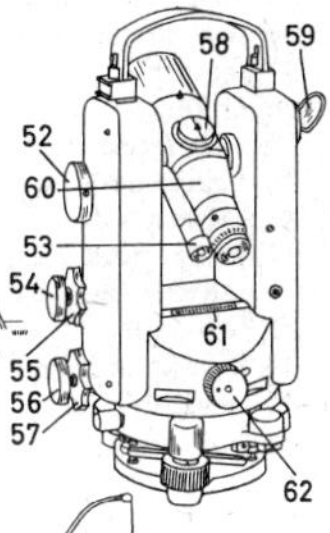
58
59
52
60
53
54
61
55
56
57
62

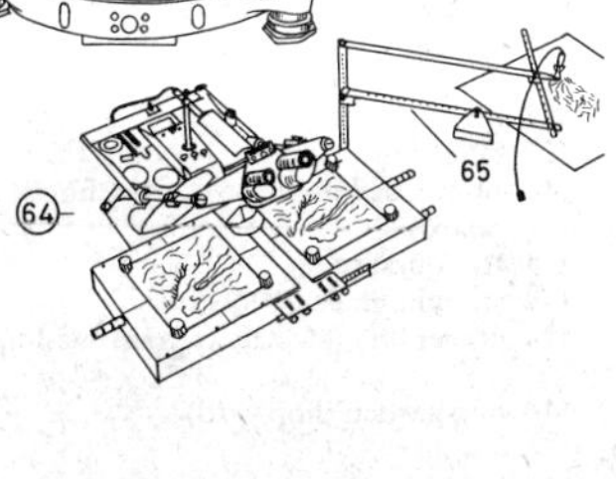
64
65

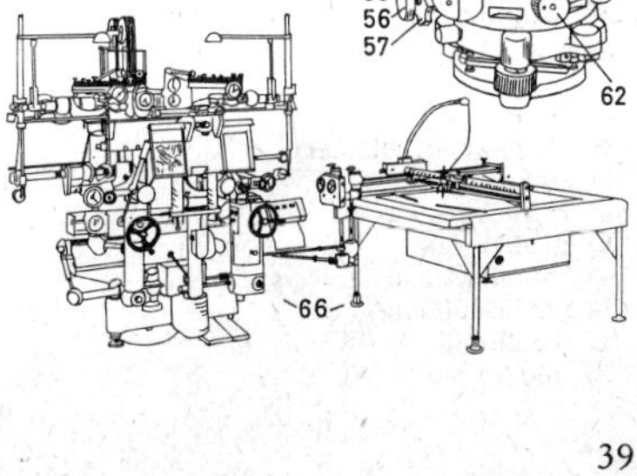
66

Engl. railway = *Am.* railroad

1–114 the map signs (map symbols), scale 1:25,000:
1 coniferous (fir, pine) wood or forest
2 clearing (glade)
3 forestry office
4 deciduous wood (deciduous forest)
5 heath (heathland, moor, moorland)
6 sand
7 lyme-grass
8 lighthouse
9 shallows limit
10 beacon
11 submarine contours (isobathic lines)
12 train ferry
13 lightship
14 mixed wood (mixed forest)
15 brushwood (thicket, *Am.* brush)
16 autobahn (dual carriageway, super-highway, motorway, *Am.* speedway) with approach (slip road)
17 arterial road (trunk road)
18 meadow
19 swampy meadow
20 marsh (swamp, bog)
21 main line railway (*Am.* trunk line)
22 bridge over railway
23 branch line
24 signal box (*Am.* switch tower)
25 local railway (*Am.* spur, spur line)
26 level crossing (*Am.* crossing at grade, grade crossing)
27 halt (stop, *Am.* way station, point)
28 garden suburb
29 water gauge (*Am.* water gage)
30 third-class road
31 windmill
32 salina (salt works, thorn house)
33 radio mast (*Am.* radio tower)
34 mine
35 abandoned mine
36 second-class road
37 factory
38 chimney
39 wire fence
40 bridge over railway
41 railway station (*Am.* railroad depot)
42 bridge under railway (railway bridge, railway viaduct)
43 footpath
44 bridge under railway
45 navigable river
46 pontoon (floating) bridge
47 car ferry
48 stone mole
49 beacon (*Am.* blinker)
50 stone bridge
51 town (*Am.* city)
52 market place
53 church with two towers
54 public building
55 road bridge
56 iron bridge
57 canal (waterway)
58 chamber lock
59 pier
60 passenger ferry
61 chapel
62 contour (contour lines)
63 convent (monastery, cloister)
64 church visible from afar
65 vineyard
66 weir
67 cableway (*Am.* cable car)
68 outlook tower
69 retaining lock
70 tunnel
71 trigonometrical point
72 ruin
73 wind wheel
74 fortress
75 ox-bow lake
76 river
77 watermill
78 footbridge
79 pond
80 brook (*Am.* creek)
81 water tower
82 spring
83 first-class road (*Am.* auto highway, arteria)
84 narrow pass (defile; *man-made:* cutting; *Am.* notch)
85 cave
86 lime kiln
87 quarry
88 clay pit
89 brickworks
90 field (portable, light) railway
91 loading yard
92 monument
93 battlefield
94 estate (country seat), a domain (demesne)
95 wall
96 palace
97 park
98 hedge
99 maintained carriageway (private road, drive, *Am.* driveway)
100 draw well
101 solitary farm (isolated farm)
102 cross-country path (*Am.* dustroad)
103 district border
104 embankment (*Am.* levee)
105 village
106 cemetery (graveyard)
107 village church
108 orchard
109 milestone
110 sign post (finger post, *Am.* finger board)
111 tree nursery
112 straight glade
113 power line (electricity transmission line)
114 hop garden (hop yard)

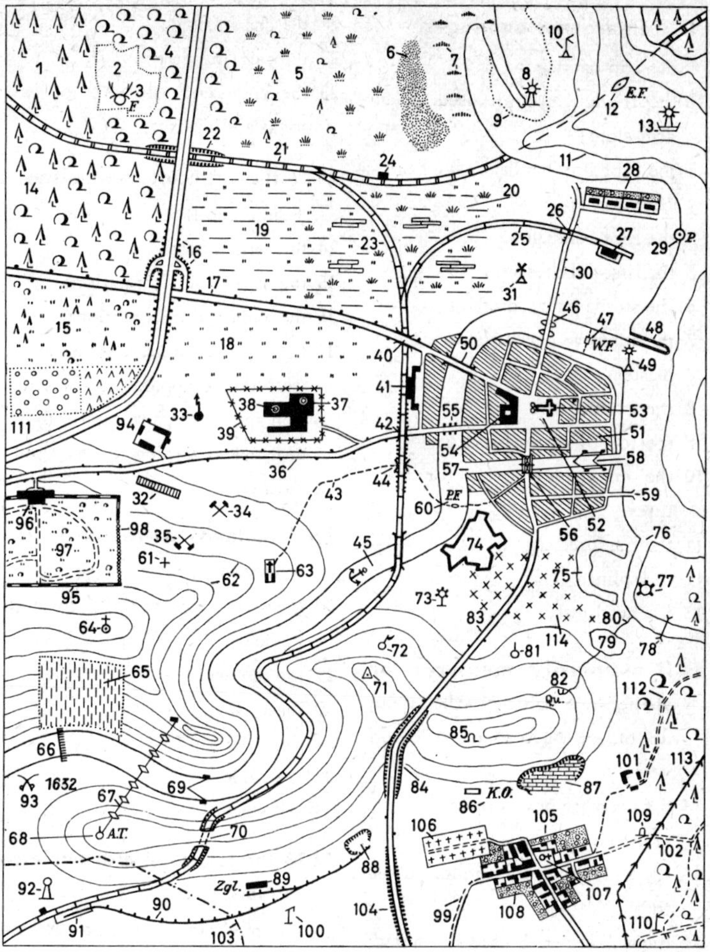
E.F.
P.
W.F.
P.F.
Qu.
K.O.
A.T.
Zgl.
1632

in England:

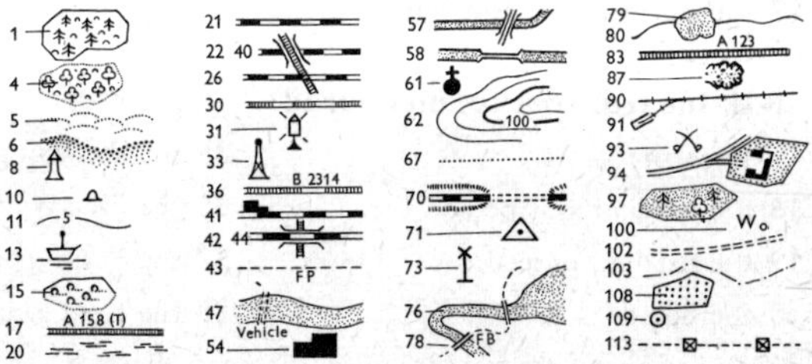
5
A 158 (T)
B 2314
FP
Vehicle
100
A 123
W
FB

1-13 emergency bandages,

1 the arm bandage:

2 the triangular cloth used as an arm sling;

3 the capelline bandage (the head bandage)

4 the foot bandage

5 the first-aid dressing;

6 the sterile gauze dressing

7 the adhesive plaster (sticking plaster)

8 the wound

9 the roll of gauze bandage

10 the emergency splint for fractures:

11 the fractured leg

12 the splint;

13 the head-rest;

14-17 temporary measures for stanching blood (the tying up of, or ligature of, a blood vessel):

14 the pressure points of the arteries

15 the emergency tourniquet on the thigh:

16 the walking-stick used as a screw;

17 the compression bandage;

18-23 the transport of an injured person:

18 the unconscious person

19 the first-aid official

20 the helper

21 the chair grip

22 the carrying grip

23 the emergency stretcher of two sticks and a jacket;

24-27 the artificial respiration (reanimation):

24 the tongue hitch

25 the inhalation (inspiration)

26 the exhalation (expiration)

27 the electric lungs, a resuscitator (respiratory apparatus, resuscitation apparatus), a respirator (*Am.* artificial breathing device, pulmotor);

28-33 methods of rescue in ice accidents:

28 the person who has fallen through the ice

29 the rescuer

30 the rope

31 the table

32 the ladder

33 self-rescue;

34-38 the rescue of a drowning person,

34 the method of release (release grip, release) to liberate rescuer from the clutch of a drowning person:

35 the drowning person

36 the life-saver

37 the chest grip, a towing grip

38 the tired swimmer grip (hip grip)

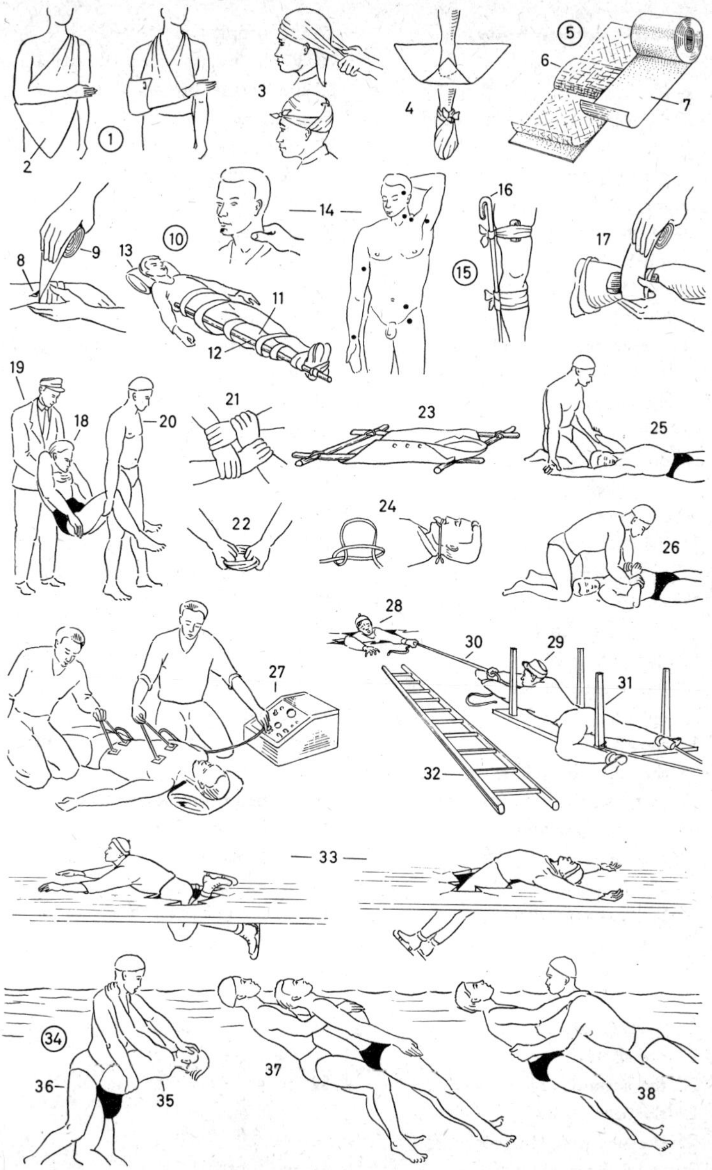
1
2
3
4
5
6
7
8
9
10
11
12
13
14
15
16
17
18
19
20
21
22
23
24
25
26
27
28
29
30
31
32
33
34
35
36
37
38

1-54 the human body,

1–18 the head:
1 the top (crown) of the head (vertex)
2 the back of the head
3 the hair
4–17 the face,
4 and **5** the forehead:
4 the frontal eminence (frontal bump)
5 the superciliary arch (*pop.* bulge of the forehead);
6 the temple
7 the eye
8 the cheekbone (zygomatic bone)
9 the cheek
10 the nose
11 the line (furrow) from the nose to the corner of the mouth
12 the groove at the median line of the upper lip (philtrum)
13 the mouth
14 the dimple at the corner of the mouth
15 the chin
16 the dimple (cleft) in the chin (dimple, fossette, fossula)
17 the jaw (jawbone);
18 the ear;
19–21 the neck:
19 the throat (gullet)
20 the hollow of the throat
21 the nape (scruff) of the neck;
22–41 the trunk,
22–25 the back:
22 the shoulder
23 the shoulder blade
24 the loin (loins)
25 the small of the back;
26 the armpit
27 the armpit hair
28–30 the breast (chest, thorax),
28 and **29** the breasts (breast, mammae):
28 the nipple (teat, mamilla)
29 the areola;
30 the bosom (bust);
31 the waist
32 the flank (side)
33 the hip (haunch)
34 the navel
35–37 the belly (abdomen; *in polite usage:* stomach):
35 the upper abdomen
36 the abdomen
37 the lower abdomen;
38 the groin
39 the pudenda
40 the seat (bottom, backside, hind quarters, posterior, buttocks)
41 the posterior ruga;
42 the bend of the upper thigh
43–54 the limbs (extremities, members),
43–48 the arm:
43 the upper part of the arm (upper arm)
44 the bend (crook) of the arm
45 the elbow
46 the forearm
47 the hand
48 the fist (clenched hand);
49–54 the leg:
49 the thigh
50 the knee
51 the hollow of the knee (back of the knee)
52 the shank (lower part of the leg)
53 the calf
54 the foot

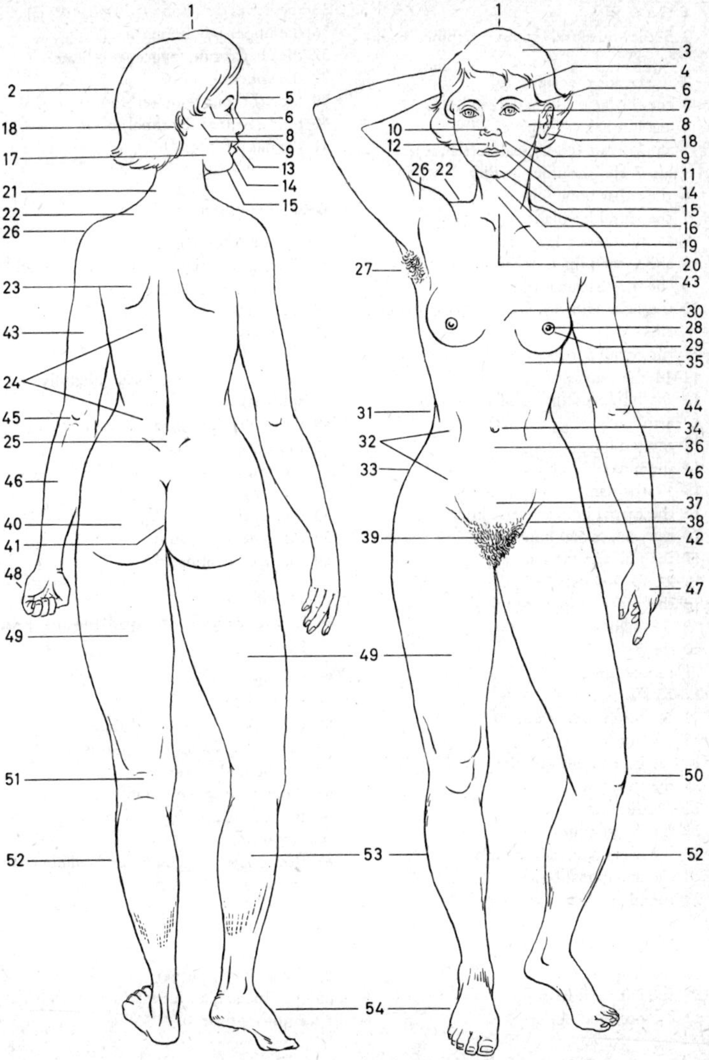
1
2
5
6
18
8
9
17
13
14
21
15
22
26
23
43
24
45
25
46
40
41
48
49
51
52
1
3
4
6
7
10
8
18
12
9
11
26 22
14
15
16
19
27
20
43
30
28
29
35
31
44
34
32
36
33
46
37
38
39
42
47
49
50
53
52
54

1-29 the skeleton (osseous framework, bones):
1 the skull
2–5 the vertebral column (spine, backbone):
2 the cervical vertebra(e)
3 the thoracic (dorsal) vertebra(e)
4 the lumbar vertebra(e)
5 the coccyx (coccygeal vertebrae);
6 and 7 the shoulder girdle:
6 the collar bone (clavicle)
7 the shoulder blade (scapula);
8–11 the chest (thorax):
8 the breastbone (sternum)
9 the true (sternal) ribs
10 the false and the floating (two lowest) ribs
11 the costal cartilage;
12–14 the arm:
12 the humerus (bone of the upper arm)
13 the radius
14 the ulna;
15–17 the hand:
15 the carpal bones (wrist bones)
16 the metacarpal bone(s)
17 the phalanx (phalange);
18–21 the pelvis:
18 the ilium (hip bone)
19 the ischium
20 the pubis
21 the sacrum;
22–25 the leg:
22 the thigh bone (femur)
23 the kneecap (patella)
24 the splint bone (fibula)
25 the shin bone (tibia);
26–29 the foot:
26 the tarsal bones
27 the heel bone (calcaneum)
28 the metatarsal bones
29 the phalanges (toe bones);

30-41 the skull (cranium):
30 the frontal bone
31 the left parietal bone
32 the occipital bone
33 the temporal bone
34 the external auditory meatus or canal
35 the lower jaw bone (jaw, mandible)
36 the upper jaw bone (maxilla)
37 the cheekbone (zygomatic bone)
38 the sphenoid bone
39 the ethmoid bone (ethmoid)
40 the lachrimal (lacrimal) bone
41 the nasal bone;

42-55 the head [section]:
42 the brain (cerebrum)
43 the hypophysis cerebri (pituitary gland)
44 the corpus callosum
45 the cerebellum
46 the pons
47 the medulla oblongata
48 the spinal cord (marrow, medulla spinalis)
49 the gullet (oesophagus, esophagus)
50 the windpipe (trachea)
51 the epiglottis
52 the tongue
53 the nasal cavity
54 the sphenoidal sinus
55 the frontal sinus;

56-65 the organ of equilibrium and hearing,
56–58 the external ear:
56 the auricle
57 the lobe of the ear (lobule)
58 the external auditory meatus or canal;
59–61 the middle ear:
59 the tympanic membrane
60 the ear drum (tympanic cavity, tympanum)
61 the ossicles: the hammer (malleus), the anvil (incus), the stirrup (stapes);
62–65 the inner ear (internal ear):
62 the labyrinth
63 the cochlea
64 the auditory nerve
65 the Eustachian tube (Eustachian canal, auditory tube)

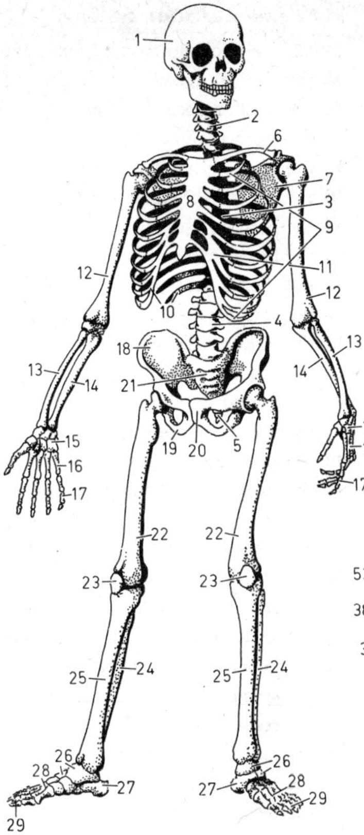
1
2
6
7
8
3
9
11
12
10
4
13
14
18
21
15
16
17
19
20
5
22
23
24
25
26
28
27
29

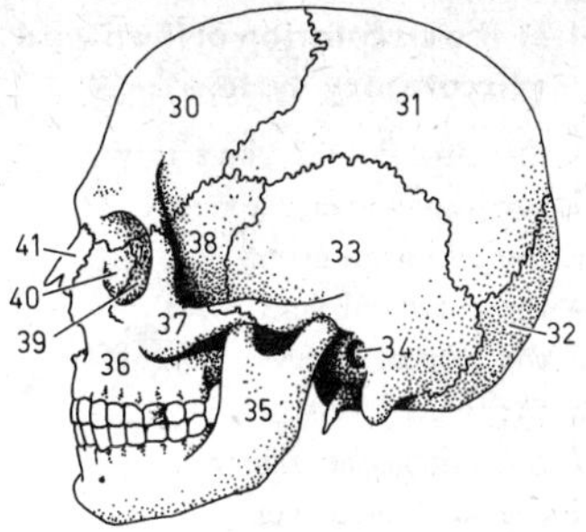
30
31
41
40
39
38
33
37
36
34
32
35

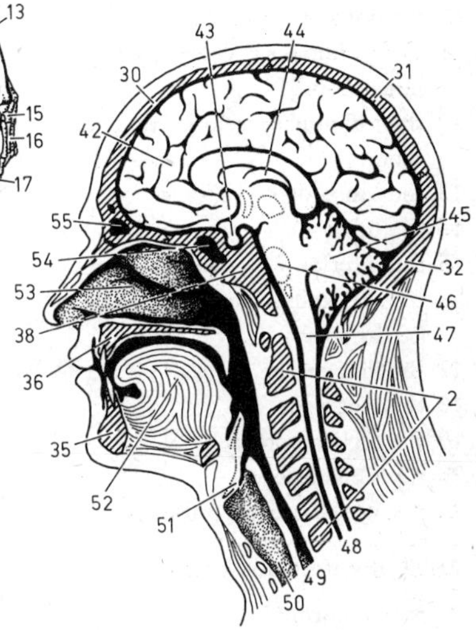
43
44
30
31
42
55
54
53
38
36
35
52
51
45
32
46
47
2
48
49
50

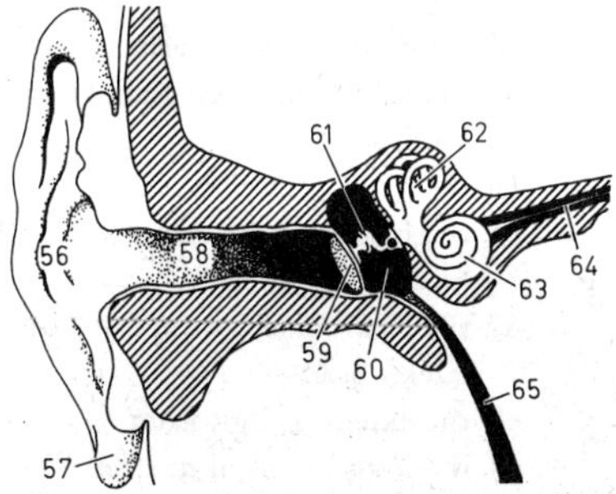
61
62
56
58
64
63
59
60
65
57

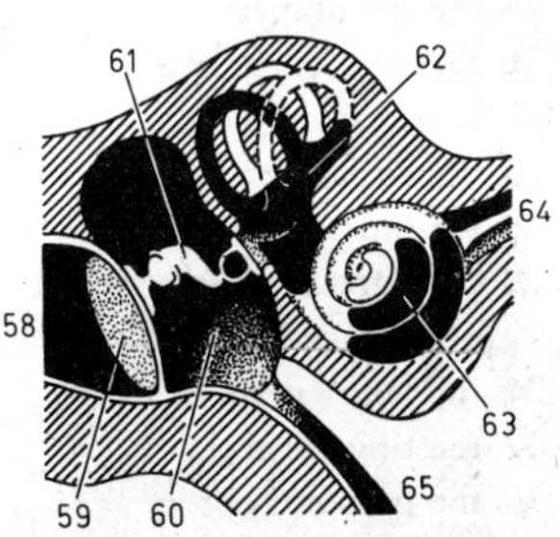
61
62
64
58
63
59
60
65

1-21 the circulation of the blood (circulatory system):

1 the carotid artery, an artery
2 the jugular vein, a vein
3 the temporal artery
4 the temporal vein
5 the frontal artery
6 the frontal vein
7 the subclavian artery
8 the subclavian vein
9 the superior vena cava
10 the aortic arch (aorta)
11 the pulmonary artery [with venous blood]
12 the pulmonary vein [with arterial blood]
13 the lungs
14 the heart
15 the inferior vena cava
16 the abdominal (descending branch of the aorta)
17 the iliac artery
18 the iliac vein
19 the femoral artery
20 the tibial artery
21 the radial artery ('pulse');

22-33 the nervous system:

22 the cerebrum
23 the cerebellum
24 the medulla oblongata (cone)
25 the spinal marrow
26 the thoracic nerves
27 the brachial plexus
28 the radial nerve
29 the ulnar nerve
30 the great sciatic nerve [lying posteriorly]
31 the femoral nerve
32 the tibial nerve
33 the peroneal nerve;

34-64 the muscular system:

34 the sternocleidomastoid (annuent muscle)
35 the deltoid muscle
36 the greater pectoral muscle (pectoris major)
37 the biceps (brachial biceps)
38 the triceps (brachial triceps)
39 the brachio radialis
40 the flexor carpi radialis
41 the thenar muscles
42 the serratus anterior
43 the oblique abdominal muscle (oblianus abdominis)
44 the straight abdominal muscle (transversus abdominis)
45 the sartorius
46 the vastus lateralis and vastus medialis
47 the anterior tibial muscle
48 the heel string (Achilles' tendon, calcaneal tendon)
49 the great-toe flexor, a foot muscle
50 the posterior head muscles
51 the splenius
52 the trapezius
53 the fascia infraspinata
54 the teres minor
55 the teres major
56 the extensor carpi radialis longus
57 the extensor digitorum communis
58 the flexor carpi ulnaris
59 the latissimus dorsi (latissimus of the back)
60 the great gluteal muscle
61 the biceps of the thigh (femoral biceps)
62 the gastrocnemius medial and lateral head
63 the extensor digitorum
64 the long peroneal muscle

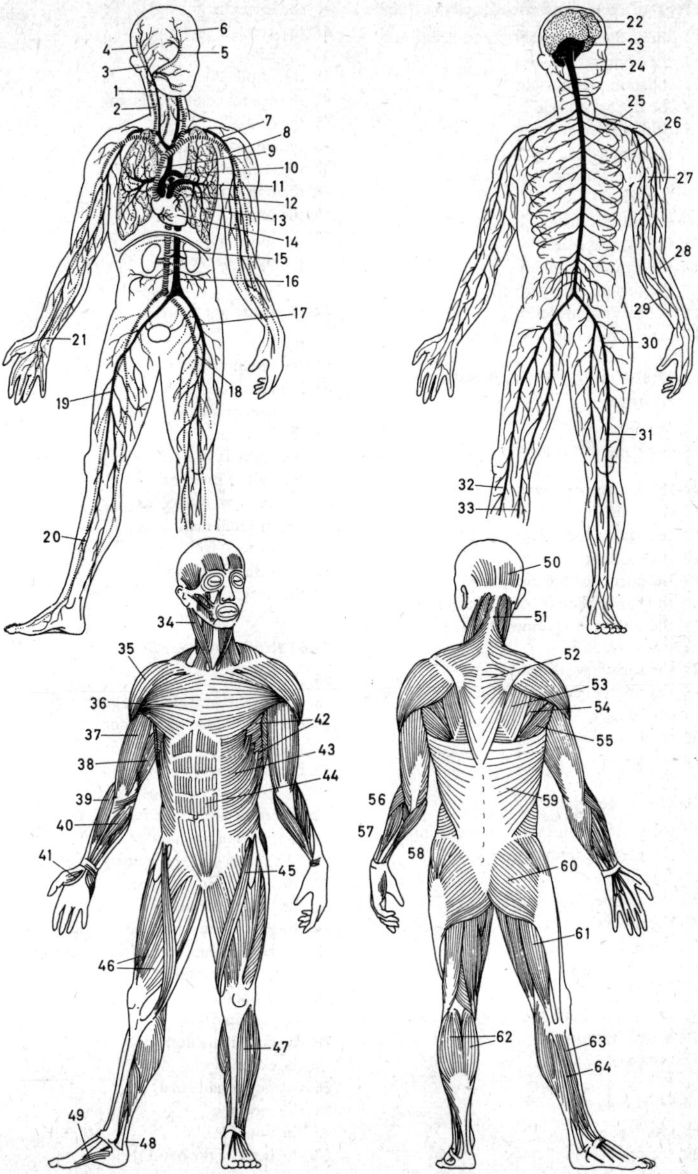
1
2
3
4
5
6
7
8
9
10
11
12
13
14
15
16
17
18
19
20
21
22
23
24
25
26
27
28
29
30
31
32
33
34
35
36
37
38
39
40
41
42
43
44
45
46
47
48
49
50
51
52
53
54
55
56
57
58
59
60
61
62
63
64

21 Man IV

1-13 muscles and glands of the head:

1 the annuent muscle (sterno-mastoid)
2 the occipital muscle
3 the temporal muscle
4 the frontal muscle
5 orbicularis oculi
6 facial muscles
7 the great masticatory muscle (masseter)
8 orbicularis oris
9 the parotid gland
10 the lymphatic gland
11 the sub-maxillary gland
12 the cervical muscles
13 the Adam's apple [with men only];

14-37 the cavity of the mouth and the pharynx:

14 the upper lip
15 the gum

16-18 the set of teeth:

16 the incisors
17 the canine tooth (eye tooth)
18 the molars;
19 the corner of the mouth
20 the hard palate (roof of the mouth)
21 the soft palate (velum)
22 the uvula
23 the tonsil (palatine tonsil)
24 the pharyngeal cavity (pharynx)
25 the tongue
26 the lower lip
27 the upper jaw

28-37 the tooth:

28 the periodontium (pericementum)
29 the cement (crusta petrosa, toothbone)
30 the enamel (encaustum)
31 the dentine
32 the pulp (dental pulp)
33 the nerve fibres and blood vessels
34 the incisor (front tooth)
35 the molar (back tooth, double tooth)
36 the root (fang)
37 the crown;

38-51 the eye:

38 the eyebrow
39 the upper lid
40 the lower lid
41 the eyelash
42 the iris
43 the pupil
44 the eye muscles (eye strings)
45 the eyeball
46 the vitreous humour
47 the cornea
48 the lens (crystalline lens)
49 the retina
50 the blind spot
51 the optic nerve;

52-63 the foot:

52 the big (great) toe
53 the second toe
54 the third toe
55 the fourth toe
56 the little toe
57 the toe nail
58 the ball of the foot
59 the external malleolus
60 the internal malleolus
61 the instep (arch)
62 the sole of the foot
63 the heel;

64-83 the hand:

64 the thumb
65 the forefinger (index finger)
66 the middle (second) finger
67 the ring finger
68 the little finger
69 the radial side of the hand
70 the ulnar side of the hand
71 the palm of the hand (thenar)
72–74 the lines of the hand:
72 the line of life (life line)
73 the line of the head (head line)
74 the line of the heart (heart line);
75 the ball of the thumb (thenar eminence thenar prominence)
76 the wrist (carpus, carpal joint)
77 the phalanx
78 the finger cushion
79 the finger tip
80 the finger nail (nail)
81 the moon
82 the knuckle
83 the back of the hand

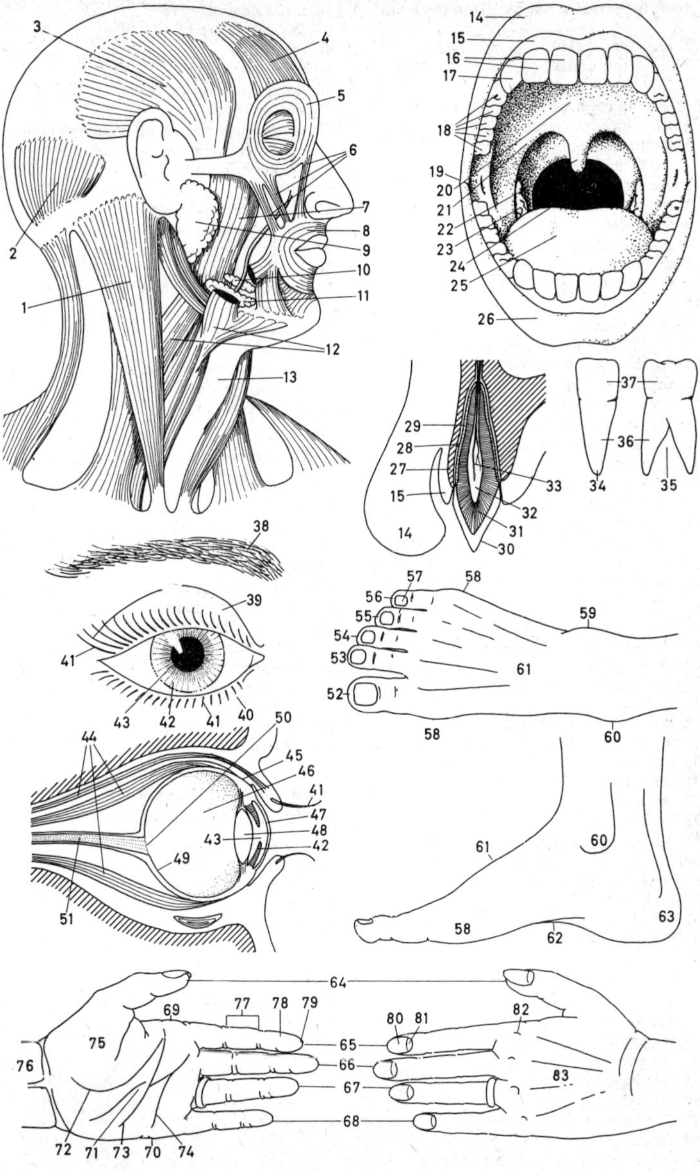
1
2
3
4
5
6
7
8
9
10
11
12
13
14
15
16
17
18
19
20
21
22
23
24
25
26
27
28
29
30
31
32
33
34
35
36
37
38
39
40
41
42
43
44
45
46
47
48
49
50
51
52
53
54
55
56
57
58
59
60
61
62
63
64
65
66
67
68
69
70
71
72
73
74
75
76
77
78
79
80
81
82
83

1-57 internal organs [from the front]:

1 the thyroid gland
2 and 3 the larynx:
2 the hyoid bone
3 the thyroid cartilage;
4 the windpipe (trachea)
5 the bronchus
6 and 7 the lungs:
6 the right lung
7 the upper lobe of the lung [section];
8 the heart
9 the diaphragm
10 the liver
11 the gall bladder
12 the spleen
13 the stomach
14–22 the intestines (bowels),
14–16 the small intestine:
14 the duodenum
15 the jejunum
16 the ileum;
17–22 the large intestine:
17 the caecum
18 the vermiform appendix
19 the ascending colon
20 the transverse colon
21 the descending colon
22 the rectum;
23 the gullet (oesophagus, esophagus)
24 and 25 the heart:
24 the auricle
25 sulcus longitudinalis anterior;
26 the diaphragm
27 the spleen
28 the right kidney
29 the suprarenal gland
30 and 31 the left kidney [section]:
30 the renal calyx
31 the renal pelvis;
32 the ureter
33 the bladder
34 and 35 the liver [from beneath]:
34 the lateral ligament [of liver]
35 the lobe of the liver;
36 the gall bladder
37 and 38 the common bile duct:
37 the hepatic duct
38 the cystic duct;
39 the portal vein
40 the gullet
41 and 42 the stomach:
41 the orifice of the stomach
42 the pylorus;
43 the duodenum
44 the pancreas
45–57 the heart [section]:
45 the atrium
46 and 47 the valves of the heart:
46 the tricuspid valve
47 the mitral valve;
48 the cuspis
49 the aortic valve
50 the pulmonary valve
51 the ventricle
52 the septum musculare ventriculorum cordis (ventricular septum)
53 the superior vena cava
54 the aorta
55 the pulmonary artery
56 the pulmonary vein
57 the inferior vena cava;
58 the peritoneum
59 the rump bone (chine bone, sacrum)
60 the coccyx
61 the rectum
62 the anus
63 the sphincter of the anus
64 the fork (perineum)
65 symphysis pubis

66-77 the male sexual organs [longitudinal section]:

66 the penis
67 corpus cavernosum and spongiosum
68 the urethra
69 glans penis
70 the foreskin (prepuce)
71 the scrotum (purse)
72 the right testicle (testis)
73 the epididymis
74 the spermatic duct
75 Cowper's gland
76 the prostate
77 the seminal vesicle;
78 the bladder

79-88 the female sexual organs [longitudinal section]:

79 the uterus (womb, matrix)
80 the uterine cavity
81 the Fallopian tube
82 the fimbria
83 the ovary
84 the follicle with the ovum (egg)
85 os uteri
86 the vagina
87 the lips of the vulva
88 the clitoris

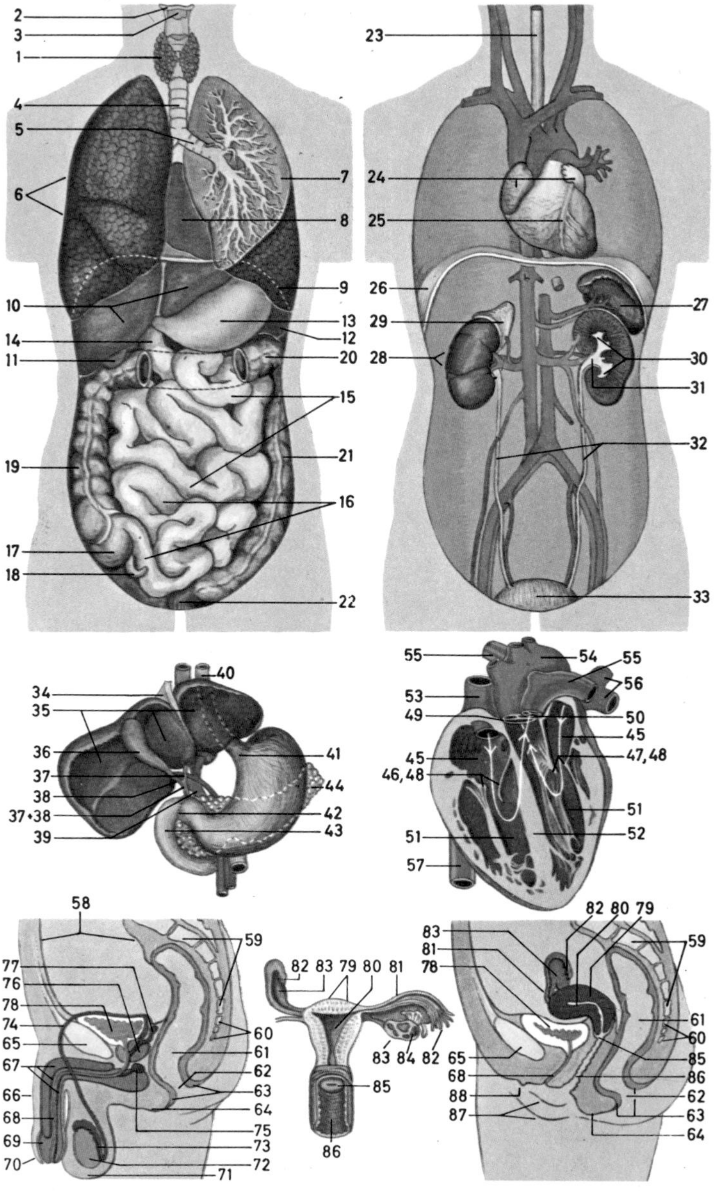
2
3
1
4
5
6
7
8
9
10
13
12
14
11
20
15
19
21
16
17
18
22
23
24
25
26
27
29
28
30
31
32
33
40
34
35
36
41
37
38
44
37+38
42
39
43
55
54
55
56
53
49
50
45
45
47,48
46,48
51
51
52
57
58
59
77
76
78
74
60
65
61
67
62
66
63
68
64
75
69
73
70
72
71
82 83 79 80 81
83 84 82
85
86
82 80 79
83
81
78
59
61
60
65
85
68
86
88
62
87
63
64

1 the sphygmomanometer (instrument for measuring the blood pressure):
2 the screw for outlet of air
3 the rubber-bulb blower
4 the rubber bandage (rubber arm bandage)
5 the mercury manometer;
6 the prescription
7 the suppository
8 the pill box
9 the pill
10 the tablet tube
11 the tablet (tabloid, lozenge)
12 the packet with sugar-coated pills (drageoir)
13 the sugar-coated pill (dragée)
14 the hot-water bottle (metal hot-water bottle)
15 the wet compress
16 the hand spittoon (sputum mug):
17 the snap lid;
18 the bell push
19 the wet pack (packing for whole body):
20 the wet pack sheet
21 the blanket
22 the rubber sheet;
23 the nurse, a lay sister
24 the bed pan
25 the night stool (close stool, night commode, chair commode)
26 the room thermometer
27 the rubber hot-water bottle
28 the air cushion
29 the ice bag
30 the finger stall (thumb stall)
31 the finger stall with fastening ribbon
32 the pocket spittoon (sputum container)
33 the inhaler (inhaling apparatus):
34 the vaporizer (atomizer)
35 the drug for inhalation, an inhalant
36 the electric air pump

37 the eye shield (eye patch)
38 the truss:
39 the pad;
40 the eye bath
41 the extension (pulley) apparatus:
42 the stretching weights
43 a Braun splint
44 the wire [through the perforated bone]
45 the caliper;
46 the irrigator (douche, fountain syringe) for administering an enema
47 the elastic (crepe) bandage, a bandage
48-50 prosthesis (prothesis, artificial limbs):
48 the artificial leg (leg prosthesis)
49 the artificial arm (arm prosthesis):
50 the interchangeable prehensile tool;
51 the invalid chair (wheel chair, Bath chair)
52 the electric warming pad (heating pad):
53 the switch, a three-way switch (three-point switch);
54-63 the family medicine chest (medicine cupboard):
54 the sticking plaster (adhesive tape)
55 the cotton (muslin) bandage
56 the drop-bottle
57 the valerian essence
58 the tincture
59 the rectal syringe (enema syringe) for a baby
60 the styptic powder in the sprinkling box
61 the laxative (purgative) pills
62 the headache tablets
63 the sanitary towels (*Am.* sanitary napkins, napkins)

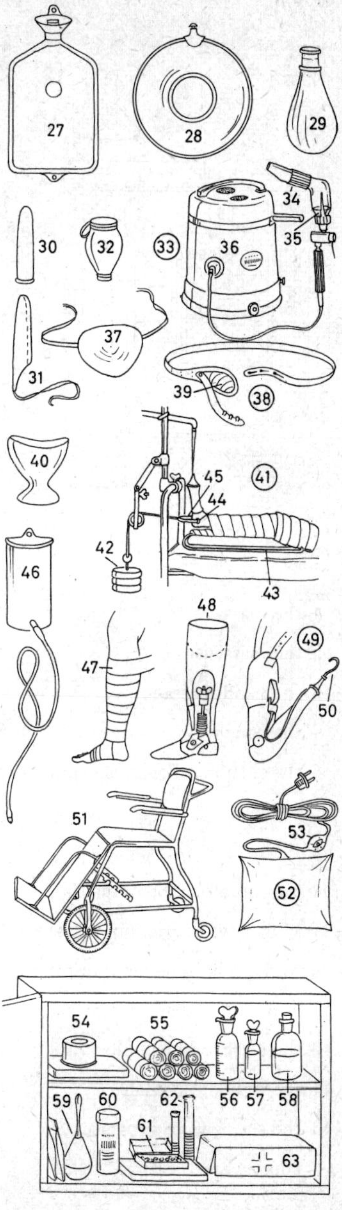

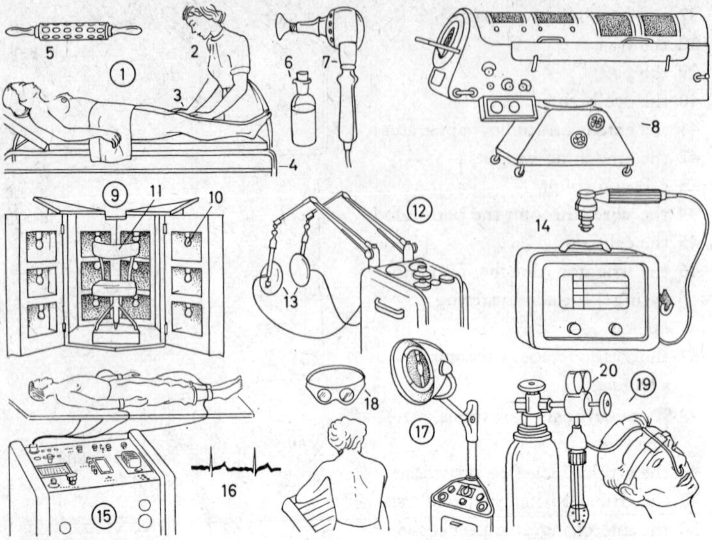

1 the massage:
2 the masseuse
3 the hand massage
4 the couch for massage
5 the suction roller (rubber puncture roller)
6 the oil for massage
7 the vibrator (apparatus for vibratory, or friction, massage);
8 the iron lung (cabinet respirator)
9 radiant-heat bath cabinet:
10 the electric light bulb
11 the irradiation chair;
12 the short-wave apparatus for short-wave therapy:
13 the electronic pads;
14 the ultrasonic (supersonic, *Am.* transsonic, transonic) wave apparatus for ultrasonic (supersonic) wave treatment
15 the electrocardiograph:
16 the electrocardiogram;
17 the ultraviolet lamp (artificial sun, mercury-vapour lamp, quartz lamp, irradiation lamp) for treatment with ultraviolet rays:
18 the goggles;
19 the oxygen respirator (apparatus for inhalation of oxygen):
20 the oxygen meter

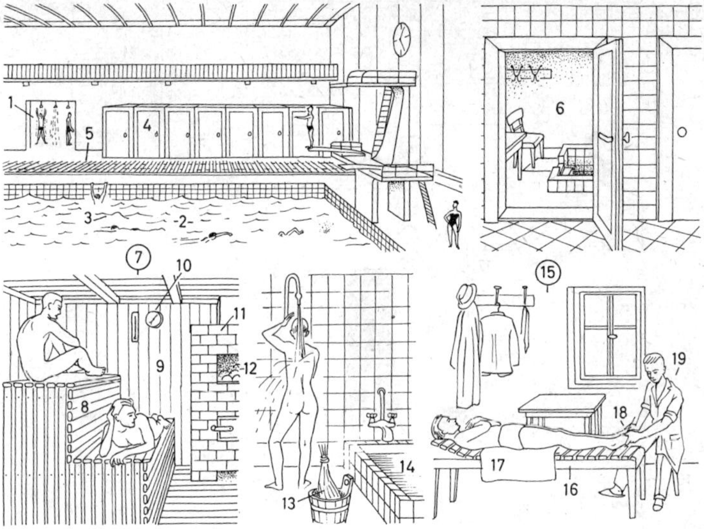

1-6 the public baths,

1–5 the indoor swimming pool (swimming bath):

1 the showers (shower baths, douches)

2 the swimming pool (basin, *Am.* natatorium, *form.* natatory)

3 the artificial waves

4 the dressing cubicle (cubicle, dressing cabin, cabin)

5 the duckboards (grating of wooden slats);

6 the bath;

7-16 the sauna (Finnish hot-air bath); *sim. with hot, damp air :* vapour bath (*Am.* vapor bath), Turkish bath, Russian bath,

7 the hot room:

8 the benches (steps) to sit or lie on

9 the wooden partition

10 the hygrometer

11 the sauna stove

12 the stones;

13 the birch twigs (birch rods) for beating the skin

14 the cold-water bath

15 the rest room:

16 the bench for taking a rest;

17 the Turkish towel (bath towel)

18 the pedicure (chiropody)

19 the chiropodist

26 The Doctor

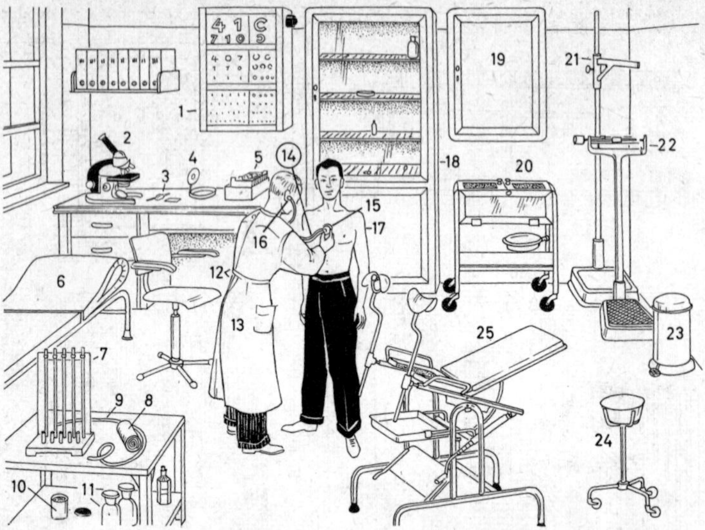

1-25 the surgery (consulting room, *Am.* physician's office):

1 the sight-testing chart (chart for testing the eyesight)

2 the microscope

3 the specimen on the glass slide

4 the forehead mirror

5 the card index of patients

6 the examination couch

7 the apparatus for hypostasis

8 the plaster-of-Paris bandage

9 the gastric (intestinal) tube

10 the ointment tin with ointment

11 the medicine bottle with medicine (with remedy)

12 the doctor (physician), a medical man (general practitioner, G. P., or specialist)

13 the doctor's coat (doctor's overall)

14 the stethoscope (membrane stethoscope, phonendoscope), an auscultation apparatus:

15 the membrane-covered chestpiece

16 the olive-shaped ear nibs;

17 the patient under medical treatment

18 the instrument cabinet

19 the medicine cupboard (medicine cabinet)

20 the instrument trolley or table

21 the height-measuring gauge (*Am.* gage) for measuring the height of the body

22 the weighing-machine standard (scales)

23 the refuse bin (pail for used dressings)

24 the basin stand

25 the gynaecological examination chair;

26-62 medical instruments:

26 Piorry's wooden stethoscope

27 the percussor

28 the hypodermic syringe (hypodermic):
29 the plunger
30 the barrel (glass cylinder)
31 the cannula (hypodermic needle);
32 the ampoule (ampulla, phial, vial) with serum or vaccine (lymph)
33 the ophthalmoscope:
34 the magnifying lens;
35 the tweezers (non-toothed forceps)
36 surgical needles
37 the needle-holder
38 the surgical clip
39 the scalpel (surgical knife, dissecting knife)
40 the bone cutting forceps
41 and **42** trocars (trochars):
41 the straight trocar
42 the curved trocar;
43 the probe
44 the glass dropper (pipette):
45 the rubber cap
46 the glass tube
47 the ball-shaped nozzle;
48 the cautery burner (cautery):
49 the cautery cords;
50 the cystoscope:
51 the small lamp
52 the eyepiece;
53 the catheter:
54 the beak
55 the eye;
56 the cupping glass (cupping instrument):
57 the suction pump;
58 the ear syringe
59 the auriscope (aural syringe)
60 the curette
61 the laryngoscope (laryngeal mirror)
62 the kidney-shaped bowl (kidney dish)

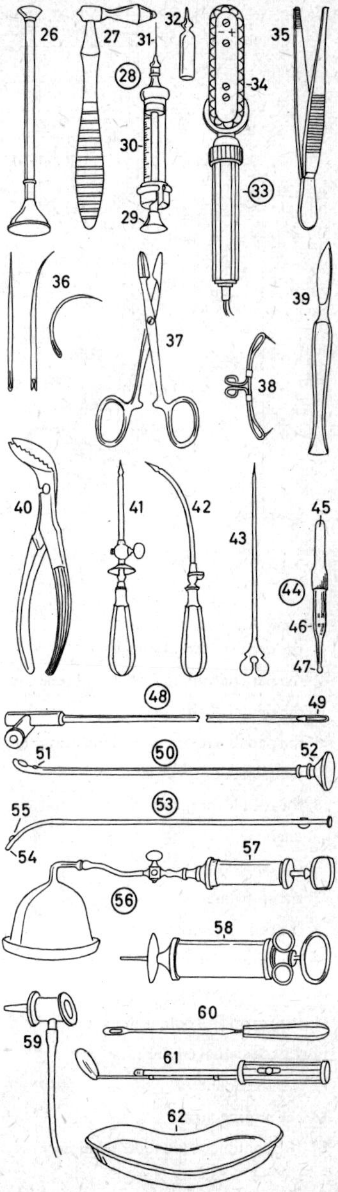

27 The Dentist

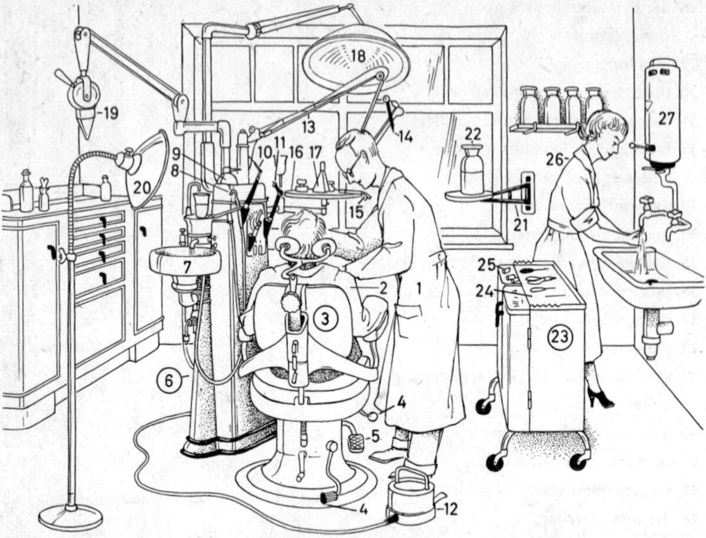

1 the dentist (dental surgeon)
2 the patient undergoing dental treatment
3 the dental chair;
4 the pedals for raising and lowering the dental chair
5 the foot lever for tilting the dental chair;
6 the dental unit:
7 the spittoon
8 the saliva ejector
9 the spray (spraying apparatus)
10 the hot-air syringe
11 the warm and cold water syringe
12–15 the dental engine:
12 the foot control
13 the engine arm
14 the handpiece (straight handpiece)
15 the handpiece (contra or right angle handpiece);
16 the bracket table
17 the amalgam
18 the operating lamp
19 the X-ray apparatus
20 the radiation lamp
21 the swivelling wall bracket
22 the bottle of liquid disinfectant
23 the instrument cabinet:
24 the instrument table
25 the cotton-wool roll;
26 the dentist's assistant
27 the rapid water-heater, a non-storage heater

28 the upper denture
29 the dental bridge:
30 the prepared stump of the tooth
31 the crown; *kinds:* gold crown, jacket crown
32 the porcelain tooth (porcelain pontic);
33 the filling
34 the post crown:
35 the facing
36 the diaphragm
37 the post;
38 the carborundum or diamond disc
39 the carborundum or diamond wheel
40 burs
41 the flame shaped finishing bur
42 fissure burs
43 the mouth mirror
44 the mouth lamp
45 the cautery:
46 the platinum-iridium electrode;
47 the tooth scalers
48 the extraction forceps
49 the tooth-root elevator
50 the bone chisel
51 the spatula
52 the mortar
53 the pestle
54 the hypodermic syringe for injection of local anaesthetic
55 the matrix-holder
56 the impression tray
57 the spirit lamp

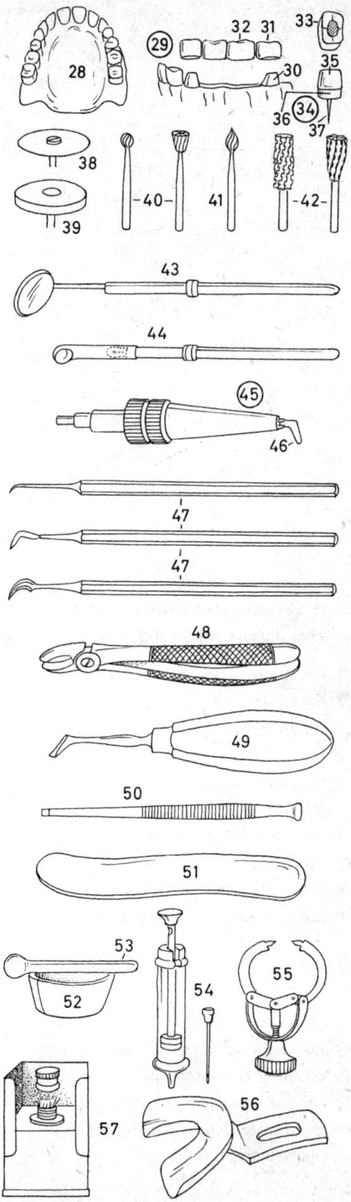

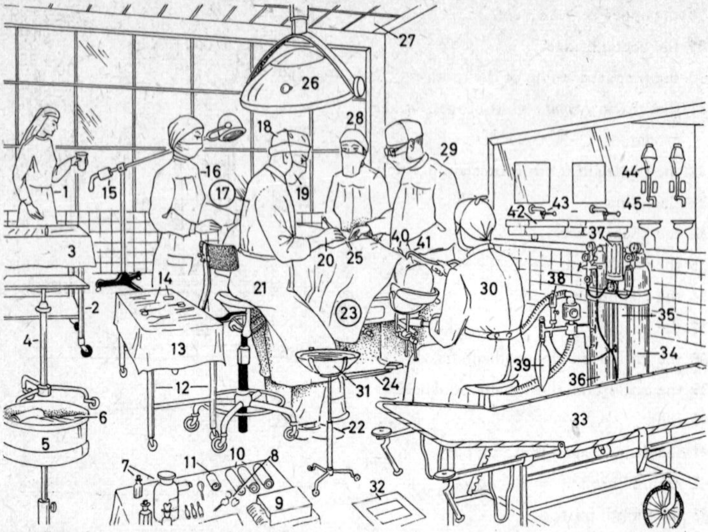

1-45 the operating theatre (*Am.* operating theater; operating room):

1 the theatre (*Am.* theater) nurse

2 the suture table

3 the rubber sheet

4 the small operating table

5 the sterilizing drum

6 the surgical dressing

7 the medicines (remedies)

8–11 bandages:

8 the swab (tampon, pledget)

9 the cotton-wool (surgical cotton, *Am.* absorbent cotton)

10 the roll of sterile bandage

11 the roll of gauze;

12 the instrument table

13 the sterile (sterilized) cloth

14 the sterilized instruments

15 the standard lamp (scialytic light)

16 the theatre sister (*Am.* theater sister; operating sister)

17 the surgeon (operating surgeon):

18 the operating cap

19 the mask (operating mask)

20 the rubber operating glove

21 the operating overall (operating gown, surgeon's overall, *Am.* overalls)

22 the rubber shoe;

23 the operating table:

24 the lever for raising and lowering the table top;

25 the operation area (area to be operated)

26 the operating lamp

27 the skylight (glass roof)

28 the woman (lady) assistant surgeon

29 the assistant surgeon (house surgeon, *Am.* intern, interne)

30 the anaesthetist (anesthetist)

31 the sublimate bowl

32 the waste outlet (drain)

33 the wheeled stretcher

34-41 the anaesthetizer (anesthetizer, anaesthetizing apparatus, anesthetizing apparatus):

34 the laughing gas (nitrous oxide) cylinder
35 the carbonic acid container
36 the oxygen cylinder
37 the anaesthesimeter (anesthesimeter, flowmeter)
38 the ether bottle
39 the pressure gauge
40 the pilot balloon
41 the tube;

42-45 the wash room:

42 the wash-basin
43 the tap (*Am.* faucet) with elbow lever (elbow-operated tap, tap operated by elbow)
44 the alcohol container
45 the alcohol tap;

46-59 surgical instruments:

46 the olive-pointed (bulb-headed) probe
47 the hollow sound
48 the curved scissors
49 the lancet
50 the ligature-holding forceps
51 the silk suture
52 the sequestrum forceps
53 the drainage tube
54 the surgeon's tourniquet (torcular)
55 the non-toothed artery forceps (artery tweezers)
56 the blunt hook
57 the bone nippers (bone cutting forceps)
58 the scoop (curette) for erasion (for curettage)
59 the obstetrical forceps (midwifery forceps);
60 the sterilizer (sterilizing apparatus, autoclave)
61 the dry sterilizer
62 the syringe-scalder
63 the water-distilling apparatus (water-distiller)

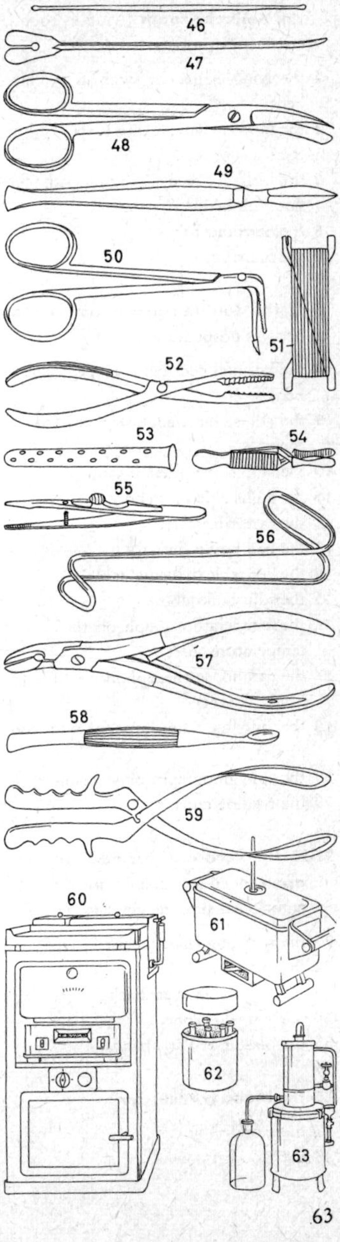

29 The Hospital II

1 **the delivery room** (lying-in room, confinement room):

2 the lying-in patient (woman in childbed)
3 the obstetrician
4 the leg support
5 the delivery bed (lying-in bed, confinement bed)
6 the newborn baby
7 the midwife;

8-20 the double room (room with two beds), a hospital room,

8 the hospital bed (patients' bed, wheel bed):
9 the adjustable wedge-shaped head rest
10 the stop screw (detent screw)
11 the adjustable foot end
12 the castor (caster);
13 the bed bottle (urinal)
14 the bed table (patients' table):
15 the adjustable table top;
16 the temperature graph on the temperature chart
17 the earphones (headphones, head receiver)
18 the nursing sister (nun of a nursing order)
19 the sphygmograph (pulse-counter)
20 the feeding cup;

21-25 the veranda (verandah) **in the open** (open-air veranda) for the rest cure (open-air cure, convalescence),

21 the reclining chair (chaise longue):
22 the ratchet
23 the adjustable chair back;
24 the convalescent
25 the plaster-of-Paris bandage;

26 the blood transfusion:

27 the blood-donor
28 the blood recipient
29 the blood transfusion apparatus with three-way tap (*Am.* faucet);

30-38 the radio therapy (X-ray therapy, roentgen therapy, X-ray treatment),

30 the X-ray apparatus:
31 the X-ray tube casing
32 the tube
33 the overhead support
34 the electric cable (electric flex);
35 the X-ray table (X-ray couch)
36 the upholstery
37 the control room
38 the assistant radiographer, a radiographer;

39-47 the X-ray examination (X-ray),

39 the X-ray apparatus (roentgen apparatus, apparatus for radioscopy, for skiagraphy):
40 the control panel
41 the fluorescent screen
42 the X-ray table with tilting action
43 the protective screen
44 the mobile platform;
45 the radiologist
46 the adaption goggles
47 the protective gloves;

48-55 the radium therapy (radium treatment; gamma-ray treatment of skin diseases and cancer, of dermal and cancerous diseases):

48 the Geiger-Müller counter
49 the integrating meter (integrator)
50 the Geiger tube
51 the radium cupboard, a lead cupboard, a lead safe
52 the radium container, a platinum tube
53 the forceps
54 the radium-packing table with the instruments
55 the plastic material with radioactive cobalt

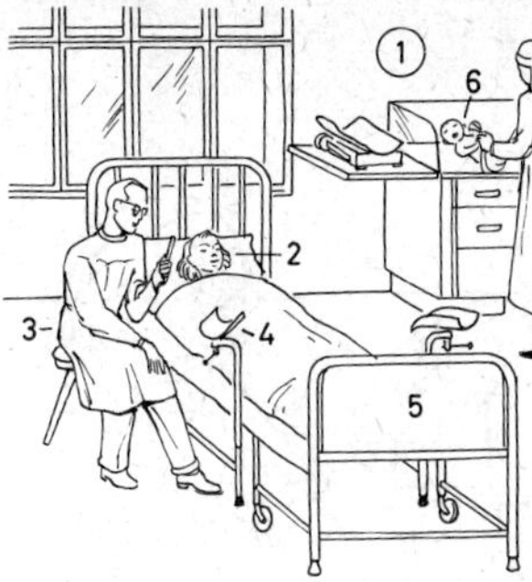
1
2
3
4
5
6
7

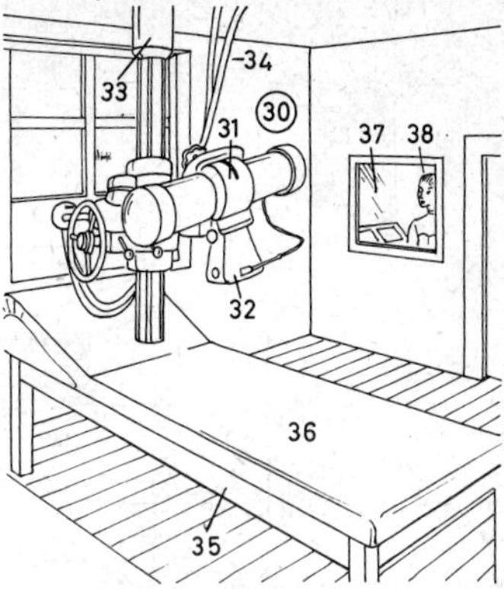
30
31
32
33
34
35
36
37
38

8
9
10
11
12
13
14
15
16
17
18
19
20

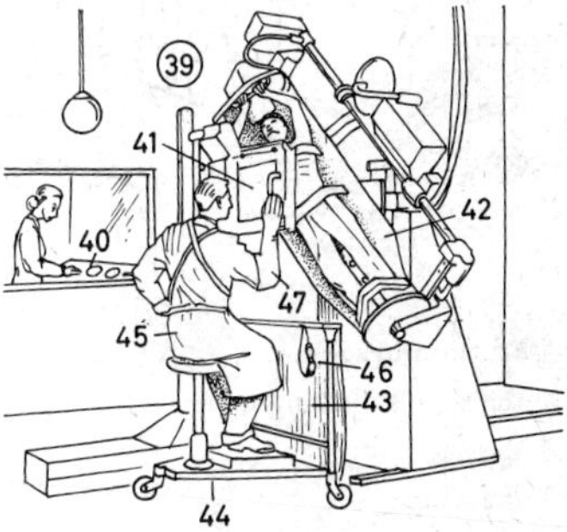
39
40
41
42
43
44
45
46
47

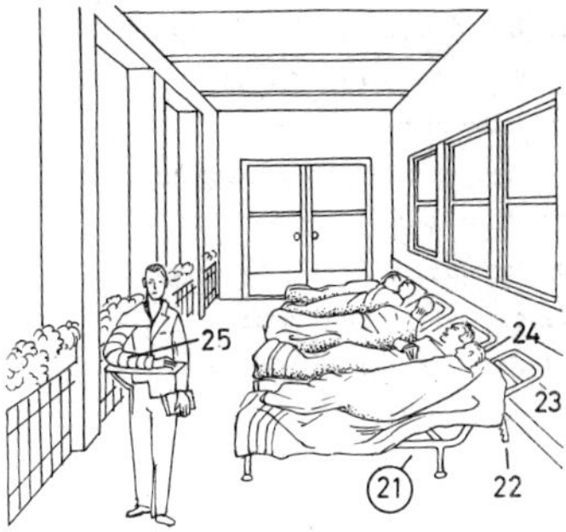
21
22
23
24
25

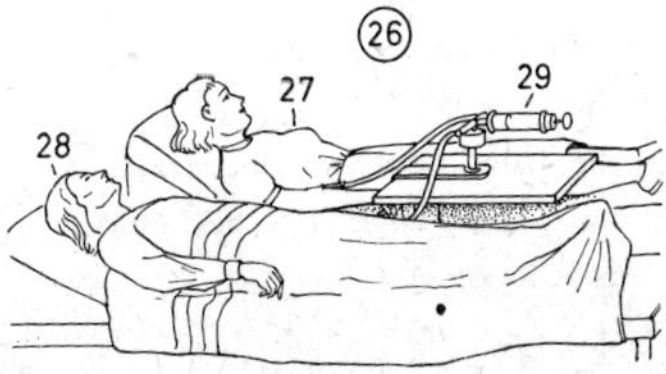
26
27
28
29

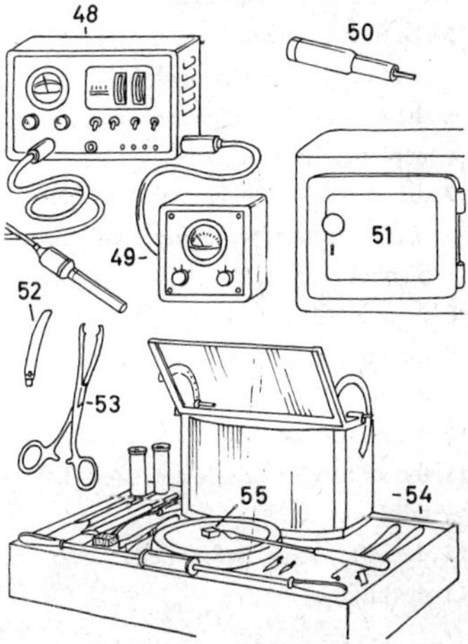
48
49
50
51
52
53
54
55

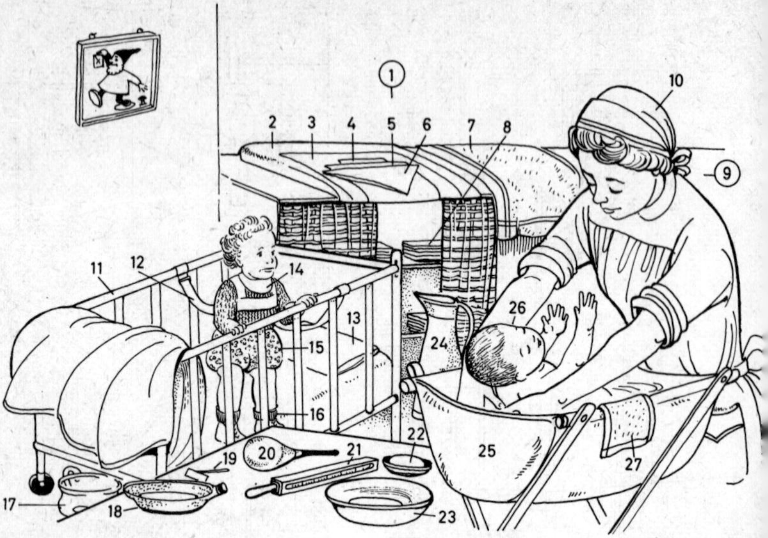

1-52 the nursery,

1 the baby's dressing-table:

2 the pad

3 the wrap

4 the rubber sheet (rubber square)

5 the flannel square (flannel napkin; *fam.* nappy; *Am.* flannel diaper)

6 the muslin square (gauze square, napkin, *Am.* gauze diaper)

7 the woollen (*Am.* woolen) blanket (frieze blanket, wrapping blanket), a blanket

8 the under-blankets;

9 the nurse (children's trained nurse, nanny):

10 the nurse's cap;

11 the adjustable baby's cot (*Am.* baby's crib)

12 the safety strap (safety belt)

13 the pillow

14 the bib

15 the rubber panties

16 the baby's socks

17 the chamber-pot, a glass, or earthenware, chamber-pot ('chamber', *fam.* pottie)

18 the pap plate, a warming dish

19 the pusher

20 the enema, a rubber syringe

21 the bath thermometer

22 the soap dish and the piece (cake) of soap (soap)

23 the wash-basin (wash-bowl)

24 the water jug (*Am.* water pitcher)

25 the folding rubber bath (baby's bath, *Am.* baby bathtub, folding tub), a bath

26 the baby (suckling, little one, newborn child, child in arms, infant, babe in arms)

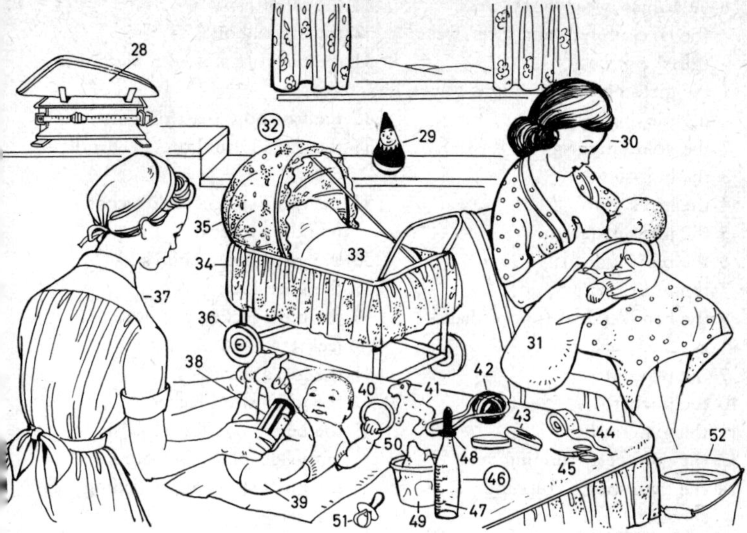

27 the face-flannel (face-cloth, *Am.* wash-rag, washcloth, facial cloth)

28 the baby scales

29 the tumbler (tumbling clown)

30 the mother (or a wet-nurse) feeding (nursing, wet-nursing) the baby (the nursing mother)

31 the 'kicking-sack', a tunic-like garment with shoulder straps, sewn up at the bottom

32 the bassinet on wheels (basket crib on wheels):

33 the feather quilt

34 the lace flounce (lace frill)

35 the hood

36 the rubber tyre (*Am.* rubber tire);

37 the nurse changing the baby (changing the baby's napkin)

38 the powder tin (dredging tin) with baby powder

39 the child's buttocks (*fam.* bottom)

40 the teething ring

41 the rubber animal

42 the baby's rattle (child's rattle)

43 the tin of ointment (tin of vaseline), a tin

44 the binder

45 the baby's nail-scissors

46 the bottle (feeding bottle, feeder, baby's bottle, *Am.* nurser, nursing bottle):

47 the scale;

48 the teat, a rubber cap for the feeder (*Am.* nipple)

49 the pot for cotton-wool (container for cotton-wool)

50 the cotton-wool (*Am.* cotton)

51 the dummy (comforter)

52 the water pail

31 Children's Wear (Children's Clothing)

1–60 babies' wear, boys' wear (boys' clothing), and girls' wear (girls' clothing),
1 the girl's nightdress (night-gown, nightie, nighty):
2 the yoke (night-gown top);
3 the hair-slide
4 the girl's vest
5 the playsuit (sunsuit):
6 the bib (bodice);
7 the tuft of hair (quiff)
8 the handkerchief (pocket handkerchief; *fam.* hanky
9 the playsuit:
10 the pocket;
11 the gym outfit:
12 the gym vest (running vest)
13 the gym shorts (running shorts);
14 the boy's sleeping-suit (*Am.* sleeper):
15 the fly front (button tab);
16 babies' wear (babies' clothes, layette, infant's outfit):
17 the baby's vest
18 the baby's bootee
19 the baby's rompers
20 the baby's jacket (baby's coat)
21 the baby's bonnet (baby's cap);
22 the child's dress (child's frock):
23 the sleeve
24 the collar;
25 the rain-cape:
26 the hood;
27 the leggings
28 the sailor-suit:
29 the sailor-blouse (blouse)
30 the sailor-collar (collar)
31 the sailor-knot (sailor tie);
32 the sailor-cap:
33 the cap ribbon;
34 the pinafore slip with pleated skirt
35 the hair bow (hair ribbon)
36 the girl's Dirndl dress (Dirndl dress)
37 the girl's coat, a child's coat (child's overcoat)
38 the girl's hat, a child's hat
39 the knee-sock
40 the girl's jacket, a sports jacket
41 the girl's slacks
42 the girl's wind-jacket
43 the beret; *sim.* the Scottish tam-o'-shanter (*fam.* tammy)
44 the girl's ski trousers (skiing trousers)
45 the child's boot
46 the boy's wind-jacket
47 the cap with ear-flaps
48 the girl's pinafore
49 the cricket shirt (sports shirt)
50 the boy's leather shorts (Lederhosen, leathers, Bavarian leathers):
51 the trouser fly
52 the braces (*Am.* suspenders);
53 the boy's suit
54 the shorts
55 the bush-shirt
56 the sock
57 the lad's duffle-coat
58 the cricket-cap (English school cap)
59 the German school cap
60 the girl's blouse (spotted blouse);
61 the chain with pendant
62 the pony-tail hair-style

1
2
3
4
5
6
7
8
9
10
11
12
13
14
15
16
17
18
19
20
21
22
23
24
25
26
27
28
29
30
31
32
33
34
35
36
37
38
39
40
41
42
43
44
45
46
47
48
49
50
51
52
53
54
55
56
57
58
59
60
61
62

32 Ladies' Wear (Women's Clothing)

1 the tailored costume (tailor-made suit, tailored suit):
2 the costume jacket (jacket)
3 the patch pocket
4 the costume skirt
5 the inverted pleat;
6 the shirt blouse (tailored blouse, blouse, *Am.* shirtwaist):
7 the edging;
8 the coat-dress (tailored dress, button-through dress)
9 the two-piece:
10 the box pleat;
11 the pinafore dress
12 the pullover (jumper, sweater, *Am. pop.* knittie):
13 the polo neck
14 the long sleeve;
15 the house-dress (house-frock):
16 the three-quarter sleeve;
17 the pinafore (apron, *fam.* pinny):
18 the apron pocket;
19 the overall:
20 the shawl collar;
21 the Dirndl dress:
22 the puff sleeve;
23 the Dirndl apron, a fancy apron:
24 the apron string;
25 the evening dress, an evening gown:
26 the decolletage (lowcut and V-shaped neckline)
27 the sash;
28 the cocktail dress, an afternoon dress:
29 the bolero (bolero jacket)
30 the tiered flounces (volants);
31 the summer dress:
32 the short sleeve (cap-sleeve)
33 the permanent pleating (permanently pleated skirt);
34 the parasol
35 the dress with jacket to match (dress and jacket ensemble, two-piece):
36 the coat, a woollen jacket (*Am.* woolen coat)
37 the woollen dress (*Am.* woolen dress)
38 the fold;
39 the twin-set
40 the fancy pullover with round neck (with round neckline)
41 the edge-to-edge cardigan
42 the poplin (*Am.* broadcloth) coat a rain-coat or dust-coat (*Am.* duster):
43 the hood;
44 the fur jacket with accessories:
45 the fur jacket
46 the fur bonnet (fur cap, fur hat)
47 the muff;
48 the fur scarf
49 the fur coat (fur):
50 the wide sleeve
51 the button;
52 the winter coat (overcoat), a fitted coat:
53 the fur trimming (fur collar, fur cuffs, and pocket trimming);
54 the summer coat, a loose coat:
55 the stitching;
56 the holiday outfit:
57 the jeans;
58 the casual suit, a tweed suit:
59 the inset pocket

1
2
3
4
5
6
7
8
9
10
11
12
13
14
15
16
17
18
19
20
21
22
23
24
25
26
27
28
29
30
31
32
33
34
35
36
37
38
39
40
41
42
43
44
45
46
47
48
49
50
51
52
53
54
55
56
57
58
59

33 Underclothing and Indoor Clothing

Engl. pyjama = *Am.* pajama

1-34 ladies' (women's) **underclothing** (underclothes, underwear, undergarments, *fam.* undies), linen, and indoor wear,

1 the sleeveless nightdress (night-gown, *fam.* nightie, *Am.* nightrobe):
2 the night-gown lace (night-gown frill), a trimming (yoke);
3 the lady's pyjamas:
4 the pyjama jacket
5 the pyjama trousers;
6 the high-necked dressing-gown (housecoat, *Am.* bathrobe, *coll.* slumber robe)
7 the casual clothes:
8 the tapered slacks or trousers
9 the blouse (*Am.* shirtwaist)
10 the house jacket;
11 the lady's chemise (lady's vest):
12 the shoulder-strap;
13 the cami-knickers (*Am.* union suit)
14 the brassière (*fam.* bra)
15 the strapless brassière
16 the girdle (suspender girdle):
17 the busk (bone);
18 the suspender belt (*Am.* garter belt):
19 the suspender (stocking-suspender, *Am.* garter);
20 the panties (briefs)
21 the knickers (bloomers):
22 the elastic top (elastic);
23 the foundation garment:
24 the elastic (elastic inset)
25 the lacing;
26 the waist petticoat (half petticoat):
27 the waistband;
28 the slip (petticoat):
29 the lace top;
30 the bed-jacket
31 the dress-shield (dress-preserver)
32 the rayon stocking (stocking of artificial silk) or silk stocking, nylon stocking, perlon stocking, a lady's stocking
33 the net stocking
34 the figured woollen (*Am.* woolen; worsted) stocking (Jacquard stocking);

35-65 gentlemen's (men's) **underclothing** (underclothes, underwear, undergarments) **and linen:**

35 men's pyjamas (pyjamas)
36 the shirt (man's shirt):
37 the detachable collar, a soft collar
38 the cuff;
39 the sports shirt:
40 the attached collar;
41 the dress shirt (starched shirt, stiff shirt, *coll.* boiled shirt):
42 the shirt front (*Am.* shirt bosom)
43 the shirt sleeve;
44 the bow-tie
45 the tie (neck-tie; *sim. Am.* string tie):
46 the knot of the tie (knot);
47 the braces (*Am.* suspenders)
48 the vest (*Am.* undershirt)
49 the cellular vest
50 the man's nightshirt:
51 the shirt collar
52 the shirt button
53 the cuff;
54 the belt
55 the stiff (starched) wing collar
56 the pants (short pants, *Am.* underpants)
57 men's pants, men's short pants (briefs)
58 the long pants (drawers):
59 the leg of the pants;
60 the cuff-link
61 the one-piece and the lever-top collar stud (*Am.* collar-button)
62 the sock
63 the suspender (sock-suspender, *Am.* garter)
64 the ankle-sock:
65 the elastic sock top (elastic top)

1
2
3
4
5
6
7
8
9
10
11
12
13
14
15
16
17
18
19
20
21
22
23
24
23
25
26
27
28
29
30
31
32
33
34
35
36
37
38
39
40
41
42
43
44
45
46
47
48
49
50
51
52
53
54
55
56
57
58
59
60
61
62
63
64
65

34 Men's Clothing (Gentlemen's Wear)

1 the sports jacket and trousers (informal wear):
2 the sports jacket (sports coat, *Am.* sack coat)
3 the trousers (slacks, flannels);
4 the double-breasted suit, a lounge suit (*Am.* business suit):
5 the jacket
6 the jacket button
7 the buttonhole
8 the breast pocket
9 the pocket flap;
10 the trousers (long trousers; *fam.* bags):
11 the trouser-leg
12 the crease of the trousers (crease);
13 the single-breasted suit:
14 the side pocket
15 the jacket collar (collar)
16 the lapel
17 the sleeve
18 the jacket lining (lining)
19 the inside breast pocket (inside pocket, inner pocket);
20 the golfing outfit:
21 the sports coat
22 the plus-fours (*form.* knicker-bockers; *sim.* knee breeches);
23 the lumber jacket:
24 the zip (zip-fastener)
25 the knitted waistband (elastic waist-band);
26 the national-costume jacket
27 the breeches (riding breeches):
28 the waistband
29 the trouser button
30 the fly (slit, opening) of the trousers (*fam.* flies)
31 the trouser pocket
32 the double seat (reinforcement for riding);
33 the hip pocket (back trouser pocket)
34 the seat of the trousers
35 the transparent plastic rain-cape (cape)
36 the duffle-coat:
37 the patch coat pocket (sewn-on coat pocket)
38 the toggle button;
39 the rain-coat (mackintosh, waterproof, *Am.* slicker)
40 the man's trench coat
41 the raglan, a sports coat, storm coat (waterproof coat)
42 the fancy waistcoat (ornamental waist-coat), a waistcoat (*Am.* vest):
43 the waistcoat (*Am.* vest) lining
44 the waistcoat (*Am.* vest) pocket
45 the waistcoat (*Am.* vest) button;
46 the dressing-gown (*Am.* bathrobe)
47 the smoking jacket
48 the overcoat (top-coat, greatcoat):
49 the coat collar
50 the coat button
51 the coat pocket;
52 the light overcoat
53 the frock-coat (*Am.* Prince Albert coat, Prince Albert):
54 the lapel;
55 the morning coat (cut-away):
56 the striped trousers;
57 the dress suit (*fam.* tails), an evening suit:
58 the coat-tail (swallow-tail)
59 the white waistcoat (*Am.* evening-dress vest)
60 the white bow-tie;
61 the dinner suit (*Am.* tuxedo, tux), an evening suit:
62 the dinner jacket (*Am.* tuxedo jacket, tuxedo)
63 the fancy handkerchief
64 the black bow-tie for wear with the dinner suit (*Am.* black tuxedo bow tie);
65 the long fur coat (man's winter coat, greatcoat):
66 the fur lining (furring);
67 the wind-jacket (hooded jacket, wind-breaker):
68 the fur collar

1
2
3
4
5
6
7
8
9
10
11
12
13
14
15
16
17
18
19
20
21
22
23
24
25
26
27
28
29
30
31
32
33
34
35
36
37
38
39
40
41
42
43
44
45
46
47
48
49
50
51
52
53
54
55
56
57
58
59
60
61
62
63
64
65
66
67
68

1-26 beards and men's hair fashions:

1 long, loose hair
2 the full-bottomed wig (full-dress wig) with flowing ringlets, a wig; *shorter and smoother:* bob wig, toupee (toupet):
3 the curls;
4 the bag wig
5 the pigtail wig:
6 the pigtail
7 the tie (ribbon) of the pigtail;
8 the Henri Quatre beard, a combined pointed and Vandyke beard
9 the pointed beard (goatee), a goatee beard
10 the hair à la brosse (bristly hair) (*Am.* crew haircut)
11 the whiskers (side-whiskers)
12 the Vandyke beard and the waxed moustache
13 the side parting
14 the full beard
15 the trimmed beard (square beard)
16 the imperial
17 the curly hair
18 the long moustache (handlebars)
19 the centre parting (*Am.* center parting)
20 the partly bald head:
21 the bald part;
22 the bald head (bald pate)
23 the stubbly beard (bristly beard, bristles)
24 the side-whiskers (*fam.* sideboards, *Am.* sideburns)
25 the clean shave (the clean-shaven face, smooth-shaven face)
26 the short moustache (clipped moustache, *fam.* toothbrush moustache);

27-38 women's hair styles (coiffures, ladies' and girls' hair styles):

27 long, loose hair (shoulder-length hair)
28 swept-back hair:
29 the bun (knot, chignon);
30 the plaits (pigtails, braids)
31 the chaplet hair-style:
32 the chaplet of plaited hair;
33 curly hair
34 bobbed hair (shingled hair)
35 the page-boy style:
36 the fringe; *sim.* bang;
37 the earphone style (earphones):
38 the earphone

1
2
3
4
5
6
7
8
9
10
11
12
13
14
15
16
17
18
19
20
21
22
23
24
25
26
27
28
29
30
31
32
33
34
35
36
37
38

36 Headwear (Headgear)

1-26 the gentlemen's hat shop (hatter's, hatter's shop):

1 the cloth hat

2 the jelly-bag cap (night cap); *sim.* the French Jacobin cap (liberty cap, Phrygian cap):

3 the tip (point) with tassel;

4 the high fur cap; *sim.* astrakhan cap (Cossack cap)

5 the smoking-cap (grandfather's cap)

6 the Panama hat, a straw hat

7 the hard felt hat (bowler hat, bowler, pot-hat, *Am.* derby); *sim.* billy-cock

8 the ramie hat, a bast hat

9 the slouch hat (floppy hat, squash hat, artist's hat)

10 the velour (velours, Homburg) of hare fur

11 the trilby, a man's hat:

12 the hat crown

13 the dent

14 the hatband

15 the brim

16 the edge of the hat brim;

17 the Spanish hat, a broad-brimmed hat

18 the sports cap, a tweed cap (cloth cap)

19 the soft felt hat

20 the top hat (silk hat; *joc.* stove-pipe hat, topper, *Am. coll.* chimney-pot, tile, *sl.* plug hat) of taffeta; *when collapsible:* crush hat (opera hat, top hat)

21 the hat-box

22 the boating straw hat (boater; *fam.* basher)

23 the yachting cap (yachtman's cap, naval cap), a cap:

24 the flat crown

25 the cap peak;

26 the mountaineer's cap (skiing cap);

27-57 the milliner's shop:

27 the toque
28 the small soft hat
29 the bonnet
30 the milliner
31 the hood (forme)
32 the hat block (hat mould, *Am.* hat mold)
33 the felt cloche
34 the evening hat, a brocade hat:
35 the heron's feather;
36 the artificial flower
37 the straw braiding
38 the nape band
39 the picture hat (Gainsborough hat), a wide-brimmed straw hat
40 the half-veil (face veil)
41 the velvet ribbon (velvet band) or silk ribbon (silk band), moiré ribbon (tabby ribbon)
42 the cock's feather (cock's plume)
43 the feather shape
44 the suède cap:
45 the knitted band;
46 the mourning hat
47 the half-veil
48 the lady's hat, a covered silk, or tulle, hat:
49 the hat trimming
50 the hat-pin;
51 the hat-stand
52 the wing (bird's wing)
53 the knitted hat, a versatile hat
54 the beret
55 the baker-boy beret
56 the pheasant's feather
57 the beach hat, a chip-hat

37 Clothing Requisites

1–27 clothing requisites (clothing accessories and haberdashery, *Am.* notions):
1 the wristlet
2 the handkerchief (pocket handkerchief, *fam.* hanky):
3 the fancy edge, a fancy lace
4 the linen initials (linen monogram), a mark of ownership;
5 the linen stencil (stencil for marking the linen)
6 the fancy collar, a lace collar
7 the fancy cuff, a lace cuff, a gauntlet cuff
8 the draw-string bag
9 the square (scarf, neckerchief)
10 the lady's hand-bag (lady's bag, bag):
11 the handle
12 the clasp;
13 the plaited (braided) belt:
14 the belt buckle
15 the belt loop;
16 the leather belt:
17 the button-fastening;
18 the ruche (ruffle, *Am.* ruching)
19 the collar-stiffener, a plastic stiffener; *form.* baleen bone
20 the snap-fastener (snap)
21 the zip fastener (zip):
22 the sliding cam (slider, slide);
23 the hook
24 the eye
25 the safety-pin
26 the linen button
27 the trouser button, a button

1–33 jewellery (jewelry, jewels, trinkets, bijouterie):

1 the decorative paillette, a belt decoration

2 the earring:

3 the clip (screw);

4 the hair clasp, a hair ornament

5 the coin bracelet

6 the jewelled tiara (diadem, coronet)

7 the ear pendant (earring)

8 the diamond necklace or necklet

9 the clip (clasp)

10 the shoe clasp, a shoe ornament

11 the jewel-case (jewel-casket)

12 the string of pearls (set of pearls, pearl necklace)

13 the Spanish back-comb

14 the locket pendant

15 the slave bangle, a bangle

16 the bangle, filigree work

17 the brooch (scarf-pin)

18 the chain bracelet:

19 the safety chain;

20 the ring, a finger ring (ring)

21 the link bracelet

22 the cameo brooch

23 the armlet or bracelet

24 the diamond ring:

25 the claw setting

26 the cut diamond (brilliant), a facet(t)ed (cut) precious stone (stone);

27 the facets

28 the signet ring:

29 the engraving

30 the hall mark (plate mark, carat mark);

31 the tie-pin (scarf pin, *Am.* stick pin)

32 the watch charm (trinket, fancy pendant)

33 the watch chain

39 The Dwelling House and Types of Houses

1–53 the detached house (self-contained house, *Am.* home, homestead):
1 the basement (cellar)
2 the ground floor (*Am.* first floor, street floor, main floor)
3 the first floor (first storey, upper story, *Am.* second floor)
4 the loft
5 the roof, an unsymmetrical pitched roof
6 the eaves
7 the ridge
8 the barge course and barge board
9 the cornice, a rafter cornice
10 the chimney
11 the gutter
12 the rain-water head
13 the rain-water downpipe
14 the gully, a cast-iron pipe
15 the gable (gable end)
16 the wind-breaking wall (wind break)
17 the base wall of the house
18 the balcony (*Am.* piazza)
19 the parapet
20 the balcony flower box
21 the French window
22 the double-light window
23 the single window:
24 the window ledge with window sill
25 the window lintel
26 the window jamb;
27 the cellar window (basement window)
28 the sliding shutter (blind, *Am.* shade):
29 the sliding shutter guide (*Am.* shade guide);
30 the window shutter (folding shutter, *Am.* shade):
31 the shutter (*Am.* shade) catch;
32 the garage with tool room
33 the espalier
34 the wooden door
35 the fanlight with mullion and transom
36 the terrace
37 the garden wall with coping
38 the garden lamp
39 the steps into the garden
40 the rockery (rock garden)
41 the hose tap (*Am.* hose faucet)
42 the garden hose
43 the lawn-sprinkler
44 the paddling pool
45 the stepping stones
46 the sunbathing lawn
47 the deck chair
48 the garden umbrella
49 the garden chair
50 the garden table
51 the frame for carpet-beating
52 the garage approach (*Am.* garage driveway)
53 the paling, a wooden fence;
54–57 the workers' settlement (housing estate, *Am.* cabin colony),
54 the house on a housing estate:
55 the pentroof (lean-to roof)
56 the dormer;
57 the back garden (*Am.* dooryard);
58–63 the terrace houses, stepped:
58 the front garden (*Am.* frontyard)
59 the hedge
60 the pavement (*Am.* sidewalk, walkway, banquette, *Austral.* footpath)
61 the street
62 the street lamp
63 the litter bin (*Am.* waste-basket);
64–68 the house for two families (house with two maisonettes, *Am.* duplex house):
64 the hip roof
65 the entrance (front door)
66 the doorsteps (*Am.* stoop)
67 the porch roof (canopy)
68 the sun window;
69–71 the four-family house, a semi-detached house:
69 the balcony
70 the sun parlour (sun trap, *Am.* sun parlor)
71 the awning (sun blind, sunshade);
72–76 the block of balcony flats (*Am.* of balcony apartments):
72 the staircase (*Am.* stairway)
73 the covered way
74 the studio flat (penthouse, *Am.* studio apartment)
75 the flat roof, a sun roof
76 the grass plot (*Am.* grass lot);
77–81 the multi-storey (multi-story) block of flats (*Am.* block of apartments):
77 the flat roof
78 the pentroof
79 the garage
80 the pergola (*Am.* arbor)
81 the staircase window;
82 the multi-storey building:
83 the lift (*Am.* elevator) room and staircase exit;
84–86 the weekend house, a wooden house (timber house, *Am.* frame house, cottage, cabin):
84 the horizontal boarding
85 the stone base wall (plinth)
86 the mullioned window (four-light window)

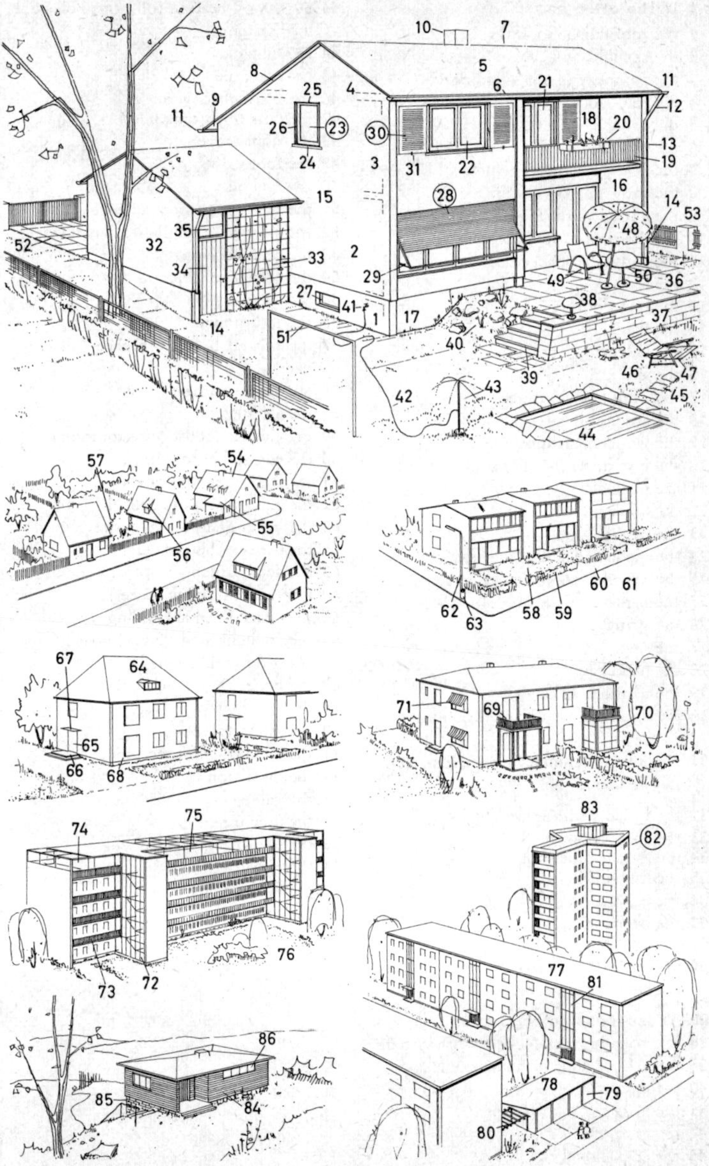

1
2
3
4
5
6
7
8
9
10
11
12
13
14
15
16
17
18
19
20
21
22
23
24
25
26
27
28
29
30
31
32
33
34
35
36
37
38
39
40
41
42
43
44
45
46
47
48
49
50
51
52
53
54
55
56
57
58
59
60
61
62
63
64
65
66
67
68
69
70
71
72
73
74
75
76
77
78
79
80
81
82
83
84
85
86

1-29 the attic (garret, loft):
1 the roof finish (roofing)
2 the skylight
3 the gangway (gang boarding)
4 the roof ladder
5 the chimney
6 the roof hook
7 the dormer (dormer window)
8 the snow guard
9 the gutter (guttering)
10 the drain pipe (down pipe)
11 the cornice (roof cornice)
12 the loft
13 the trap door
14 the hatch
15 the ladder:
16 the side rail
17 the rung (spoke, round);
18 the attic:
19 the wooden partition
20 the box room (lumber room) door
21 the padlock
22 the hook
23 the clothes line;
24 the expansion tank of the heating system
25 the wooden stairs (wooden steps) and the banisters (balustrade):
26 the string
27 the step
28 the hand-rail
29 the banister (baluster);
30 the lightning conductor (lightning rod)

31 **the sweep** (chimney sweep, *Am.* chimney cleaner):
32 the brush with the weight
33 the shoulder iron
34 the sack for the soot
35 the flue brush
36 the broom
37 the broomstick;

38-81 hot-water heating, a central heating installation,
38–43 the furnace room,
38 the coke-heating (coke-firing) system:
39 the ash pit door (ash box door)
40 the uptake (flue)
41 the poker
42 the rake
43 the coal shovel;
44–60 the oil-heating (oil-firing, oil-burning) system,
44 the oil tank:
45 the manhole
46 the manhole cover
47 the tank filler (tank inlet)
48 the dome cover
49 the foot valve
50 the fuel oil
51 the vent pipe (breather tube)
52 the vent cap (ventilation jacket)
53 the oil level pipe
54 the oil gauge (*Am.* oil gage)
55 the suction pipe
56 the return pipe;
57 the central heating furnace (oil furnace),
58–60 the oil burner:
58 the air injector
59 the electric motor (electromotor)
60 the encased burner jet;
61 the feed door (firebox door)
62 the glass observation panel
63 the water gauge (*Am.* water gage)
64 the furnace thermometer
65 the feed tap and emptying cock (*Am.* feed and emptying faucet)
66 the furnace bed or bedding;
67 the switchboard (switchboard panel, control panel, panel)
68 the boiler (hot-water tank):
69 the overflow pipe (vent pipe)
70 the safety valve;
71 the main distributing pipe:
72 the insulation
73 the valve;
74 the flow pipe
75 the regulating valve
76 the radiator
77 the radiator rib
78 the room thermostat
79 the secondary return
80 the primary return
81 the flue

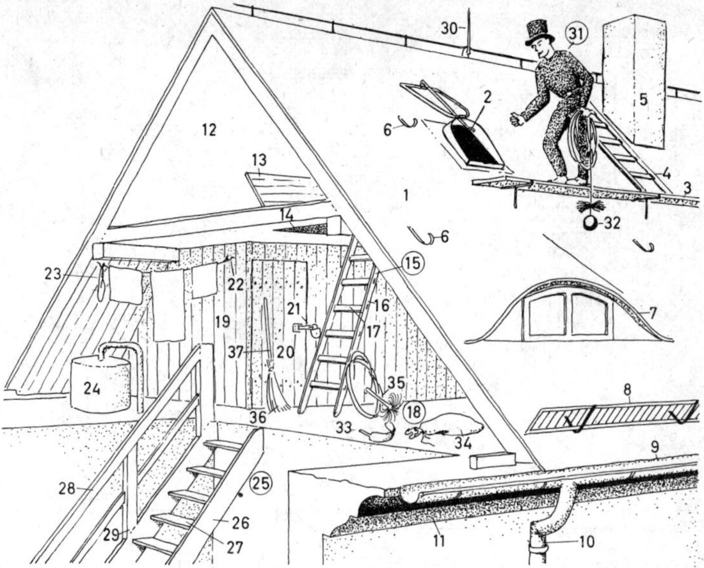
30
31
2
5
6
12
13
4
3
1
14
32
6
23
22
15
21
16
19
17
7
37
20
24
35
8
18
36
33
34
9
28
25
26
29
27
11
10

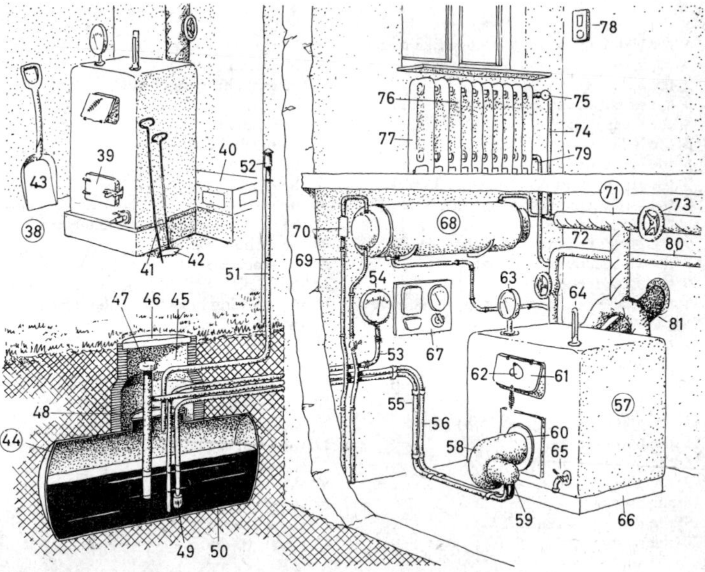
78
76
75
77
74
39
40
79
52
43
71
73
70
68
38
72
80
69
42
41
51
54
63
64
47
46
45
81
53
67
62
61
48
55
56
57
44
58
60
65
59
66
49
50

1 the wall cupboard (*Am.* closet), a china cupboard
2 the skimmer
3 the potato-masher
4 the meat-beater
5 the ladle
6 the bread-bin
7 the cookery book (*Am.* cook-book)
8 the kitchen cupboard (kitchen cabinet):
9 the cutlery drawer (*Am.* flatware drawer, silverware drawer)
10 the spice rack;
11 the refuse-bin (waste-bin, *Am.* garbage can, waste-can):
12 the foot (step-on) lever;
13 the kitchen window curtain
14–16 tea-cloths (tea-towels, drying-up cloths):
14 the glass-towel (glass-cloth)
15 the cutlery cloth
16 the crockery cloth;
17 the sink:
18 the crockery board
19 the draining-board
20 the rinsing sink
21 the rinsing water
22 the washing-up sink
23 the swivelling water tap (*Am.* swiveling faucet);
24 the scourer
25 the bottle-brush
26 the dish-washer
27 the sand
28 the soda
29 the washing-up powder (detergent)
30 the dish-cloth
31 the soft soap
32 the cook
33 the working board, a corner board
34 the kitchen waste
35 the gas-cooker (gas-stove, *Am.* gas-range):
36 the gas-burner (gas-ring)
37 the gas-tap (gas-cock)
38 the oven;
39 the kitchen range (cooking range, *Am.* cookstove):
40 the water-heater
41 the stove-plate (stove-top)
42 the stove-rings
43 the stove-door

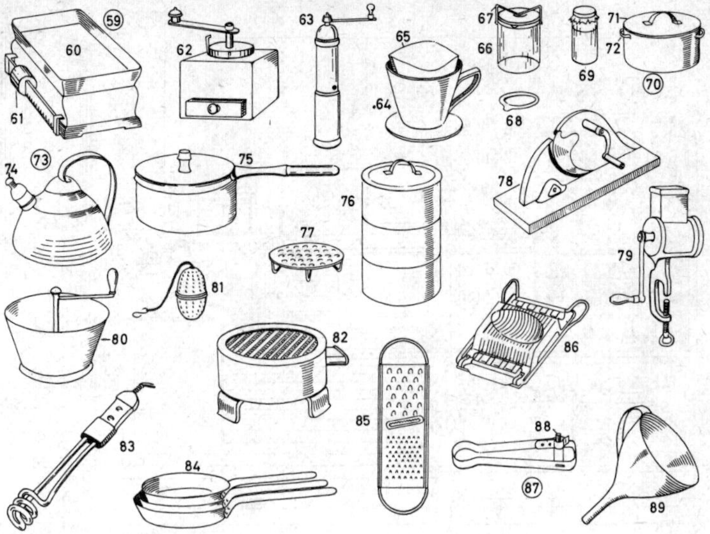

44 the draught-door (*Am.* draft-door)
45 the ash-pan;
46 the coal-box (*Am.* coal-hod)
47 the coal-shovel
48 the fire-tongs
49 the poker
50 the stovepipe
51 the wall-tile
52 the kitchen chair
53 the kitchen table
54 the bread-knife
55 the potato-peeler
56 the kitchen-knife
57 the mincing (chopping) board
58 the mincing knife
59 the kitchen (household) scales, a sliding-weight balance:
60 the scale pan (scale)
61 the sliding weight (slider);
62 the coffee mill (coffee-grinder)
63 the mocha mill (mocha-grinder)
64 the coffee filter (percolator, *Am.* drip coffeemaker, dripolator)
65 the filter paper
66 the preserving jar
67 the spring clip
68 the rubber ring
69 the preserving bottle
70 the pan (pot):
71 the pan-lid
72 the handle;
73 the kettle:
74 the whistle;
75 the saucepan (stewpan)
76 the steamer
77 the perforated rack
78 the bread-slicer (bread-slicing machine)
79 the grating machine
80 the food mill
81 the tea infuser
82 the electric boiling-ring
83 the immersion heater
84 the set of frying-pans
85 the grater
86 the egg-slicer
87 the gas-lighter (gas-igniter):
88 the flint;
89 the funnel

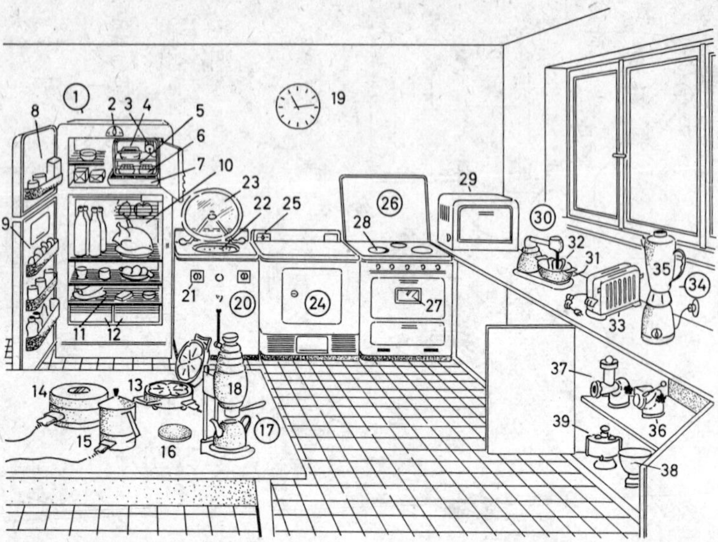

1-66 kitchen machines and kitchen implements (kitchen utensils, kitchen appliances, kitchen gadgets),

1 the refrigerator (compressor-type refrigerator):

2 the temperature control switch

3 the evaporator, a cooling box (froster)

4 the deep-freezing compartment

5 the freezing compartment (freezer)

6 the ice-tray

7 the drip-tray (drip-pan)

8 the door shelf

9 the egg rack

10 the bottle compartment

11 the rack

12 the vegetable compartment;

13 the electric waffle-iron

14 the boiling-plate (hot-plate)

15 the electric saucepan

16 the asbestos mat

17 the espresso machine, a mocha machine (mocha urn, mocha per colator):

18 the filter;

19 the kitchen clock

20 the washing-machine:

21 the preselector

22 the washing drum

23 the safety glass lid;

24 the automatic dryer:

25 the safety switch;

26 the electric cooker (electric stove):

27 the observation panel

28 the boiling-plate (hot-plate);

29 the electric grill (electric roaster)

30 the stirring and kneading machine (mixer):

31 the mixing bowl

32 the whisk;

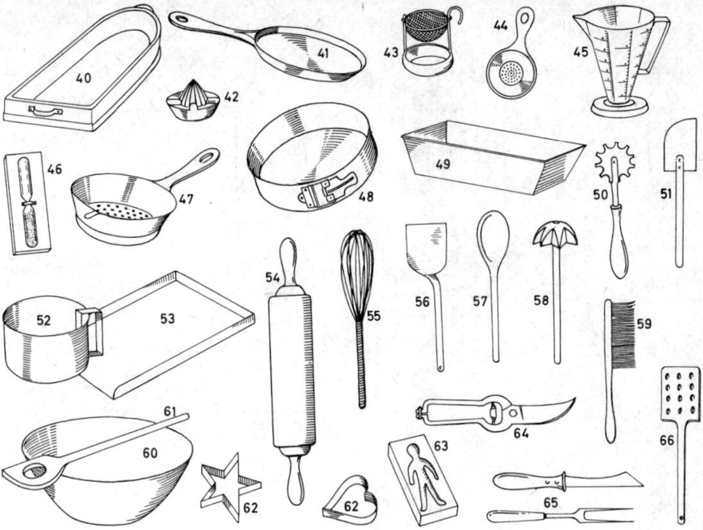

33 the toaster
34 the mixer (mixing machine):
35 the top;
36 the vegetable-chopper (vegetable-cutter)
37 the electric meat-mincer (mincing machine)
38 the electric cream-maker
39 the juice-extractor
40 the baking-dish (baking-tin)
41 the frying-pan
42 the lemon-squeezer
43 the tea-strainer
44 the coffee-strainer (strainer)
45 the measuring jug (*Am.* pitcher)
46 the egg-timer
47 the colander (cullender)
48 and **49** cake-tins (cake-moulds, *Am.* cake molds):
48 the round cake tin with spring clip
49 the cake-tin;
50 the fluted pastry wheel
51 the dough-scraper (baker's scraper)
52 the flour-sifter
53 the baking-sheet
54 the rolling-pin
55 the whisk (egg-whisk)
56 the slice
57 the wooden spoon
58 the quirle
59 the cake-brush
60 the mixing bowl
61 the perforated spoon, a stirring spoon
62 the pastry-cutter
63 the wooden form or mould (*Am.* mold)
64 the poultry shears
65 the pair of carvers (carving knife and fork)
66 the fish-slice

43 The Hall

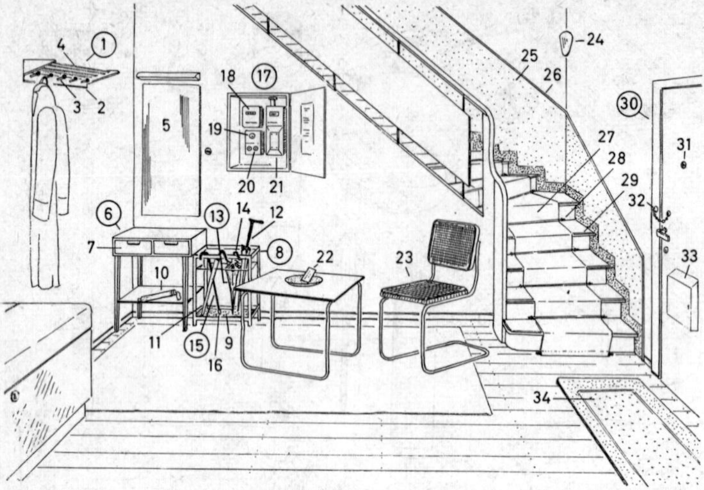

1–34 the hall (entrance hall, vestibule, hallway, *Am.* entry),
1 the clothes-rack (coat rack):
2 the rack
3 the peg (coat hook)
4 the hat rack;
5 the hall mirror, a long mirror
6 the hall table:
7 the glove drawer;
8 the hall stand for umbrellas and walking sticks:
9 the drip-tray;
10–14 umbrellas:
10 the collapsible (folding, telescopic) umbrella; *sim.* motorcar umbrella
11 the walking-stick umbrella
12 the lady's umbrella, an umbrella
13 the gentleman's umbrella:
14 the umbrella handle (crook handle);
15 the walking-stick (stick, *Am.* cane):
16 the ferrule (ferrel);
17 the meter cupboard:
18 the electricity meter
19 the main switch
20 the fuse
21 the gas meter;
22 the visiting cards (*Am.* calling cards)
23 the tubular-steel chair with cane seat and back, a unit of tubular-steel furniture
24 the stair lamp, a corner bulkhead fitting
25 the wainscoting (wainscotting)
26 the edging (border; *rare:* reglet)
27 the stair carpet (stair runner)
28 the stair rod
29 the rubber nosing, a strip of rubber
30 the front door:
31 the peep hole (spy hole)
32 the safety door chain
33 the letter box (*Am.* mailbox);
34 the door mat

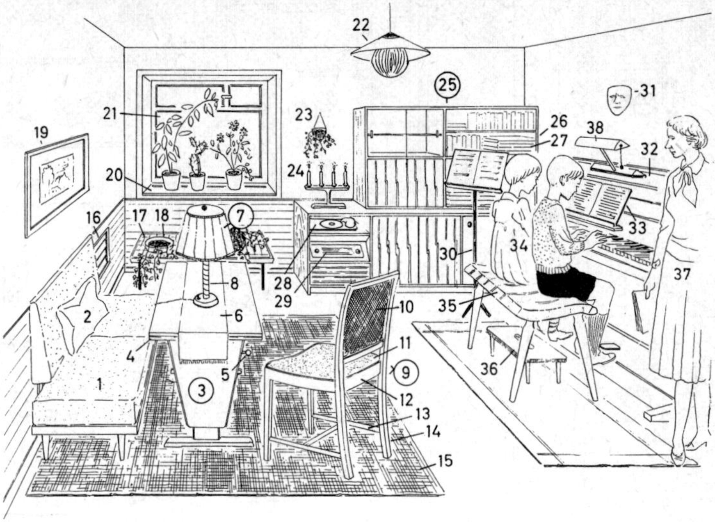

Engl. sitting room = *Am.* parlor

1 the upholstered settee
2 the (sofa) cushion
3 the all-purpose (general-purpose) table:
4 the pull-out leaf
5 the height-adjustment handle;
6 the table runner
7 the table lamp:
8 the lamp stand;
9 the chair:
10 the wickerwork back
11 the seat (upholstered seat)
12 the frame
13 the cross bar
14 the chair leg;
15 the sisal mat
16 the outlet terminal of the flat's heating system
17 the flower table
18 the flower bowl (plant bowl)
19 the aquarelle (water colour, *Am.* watercolor)
20 the window ledge (window sill)
21 the flower window
22 the pendant, a cord-grip pendant
23 the wall vase (vase); *sim.* a wall or hanging plant holder
24 the candelabra, a type of candlestick
25 the multi-purpose cupboard, a piece of unit furniture:
26 the music shelf;
27 the book of music
28 and 29 the radiogram:
28 the record-player
29 the wireless (wireless set, radio);
30 the music stand
31 the death mask (mask)
32–37 the piano lesson:
32 the upright piano
33 the book of music
34 the pupils, playing a piano duet
35 the music stool
36 the foot stool
37 the piano teacher;
38 the picture light (music light) a strip light

45 The Dining Room

1–29 the table set for coffee,
1–4 the family,
1 and **2** the parents:
1 the father (daddy, dad)
2 the mother (mummy, mum);
3 and **4** the children:
3 the boy (lad, *Scot.* laddie)
4 the girl (lass, *Scot.* lassie);
5 the dining table
6 the table cloth
7–21 the coffee set:
7 the cup (coffee cup)
8 the saucer
9 the side-plate (tea plate)
10 the tartlet (small tart)
11 the coffee spoon; *sim.* tea spoon
12–17 the coffee pot:
12 the belly
13 the lid
14 the knob
15 the spout
16 the tip of the spout
17 the handle;
18 the stand
19 the cream jug
20 the milk-server
21 the sugar basin (sugar bowl);
22 the lump of sugar
23 the sugar tongs
24 the sugar-server
25 the coffee-strainer
26 the cake plate
27 the fruit tart (fruit flan)
28 the cake slice (cake shovel)
29 the ring cake (tall ring cake);
30 the multi-light pendant fitting, a hanging lamp fitting:
31 the inverted bowl fitting (the dish fitting);

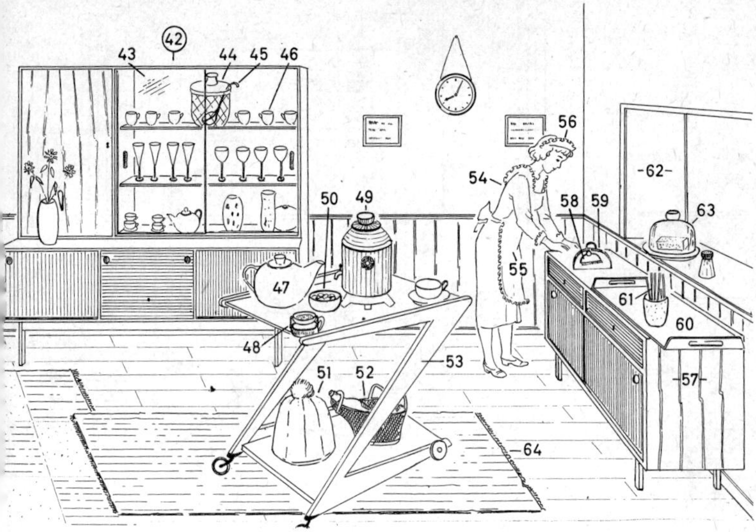

32 the cocoa jug:
33 the drip-catcher
34 the drop;
35 the biscuit barrel
36 the cake tongs
37 the salt pot (salt shaker)
38 the egg cup
39 the egg cosy
40 the egg spoon
41 the coffee cosy (cosy)
42 the sideboard:
43 the sliding door;
44 the punch bowl
45 the punch ladle
46 the punch cup
47 the teapot
48 the tea-strainer
49 the tea urn (samovar, *Am.* tea-kettle)
50 the salted almonds
51 the tea cosy (cosy)
52 the bottle basket
53 the tea trolley (dumb-waiter)
54 the domestic (servant, maid, domestic help, *Am.* hired girl, help, chambermaid)
55 the maid's apron, a fancy apron
56 the maid's cap
57 the sideboard (buffet)
58 and 59 the crumb set:
58 the crumb brush
59 the crumb tray;
60 the tray
61 the cheese and salt straws (*Am.* cheese and salt sticks)
62 the serving hatch
63 the cheese dish cover
64 the mat

46 The Table (Set Table)

1 the dinner table
2 the table cloth, a damask cloth
3–12 the cover:
3 the under plate
4 the dinner plate (flat plate)
5 the soup plate (deep plate)
6 the pudding plate (plate for the dessert, *Am.* for the sweet course)
7 knife and fork
8 fish knife and fork
9 the napkin (table napkin, serviette)
10 the napkin (serviette) ring
11 the knife rest
12 the wine glasses;
13 the place card
14 the soup ladle
15 the soup tureen
16 the candlestick
17 the sauce (gravy) boat
18 the sauce (gravy) ladle
19 the table decoration
20 the bread (roll) basket
21 the roll
22 the slice of bread
23 the salad bowl
24 the salad-servers (salad set)
25 the vegetable dish [for hot vegetables]
26 the meat dish (platter for the roast, *Am.* joint platter)
27 the roast meat
28 the compote (stewed-fruit) bowl
29 the compote dish
30 the compote (stewed fruit)
31 the potato dish
32 the serving trolley
33 the vegetable dish (vegetable platter) [for cold vegetables or hors d'œuvre]
34 the toast
35 the cheese dish
36 the butter dish
37 the open sandwich
38 the comestible
39 the sandwich
40 the fruit bowl
41 the almonds
42 the oil and vinegar bottle
43 the ketchup (catchup, *Am.* catsup)
44 the sideboard
45 the electric plate-warmer
46 the corkscrew
47 the crown-cork bottle-opener, a bottle-opener

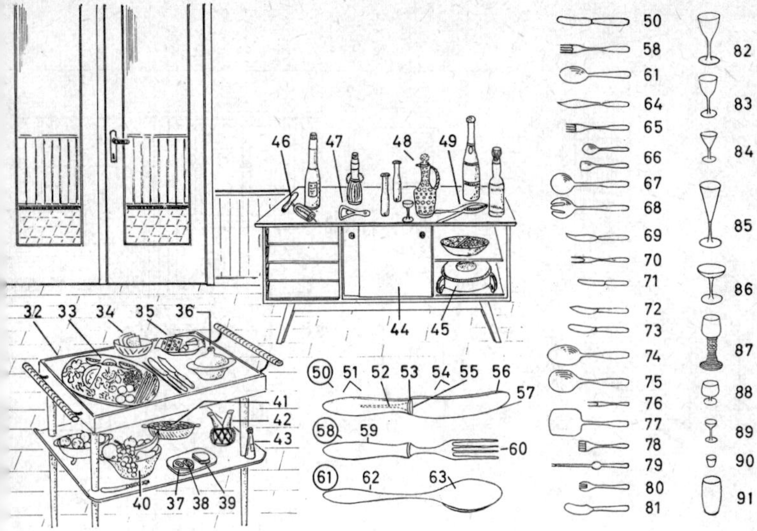

48 the liqueur decanter
49 the nut-crackers
50 the knife:
51 the handle
52 the tongue
53 the bolster
54 the blade:
55 the end
56 the back
57 the edge;
58 the fork:
59 the handle
60 the prong (tine, tang);
61 the spoon (soup spoon):
62 the handle
63 the bowl;
64 the fish knife
65 the fish fork
66 the dessert spoon (pudding spoon)
67 the salad spoon
68 the salad fork
69 and 70 the set of carvers:
69 the carving knife
70 the carving fork;
71 the fruit knife
72 the cheese knife
73 the butter knife
74 the vegetable spoon, a table spoon (serving spoon)
75 the potato spoon
76 the sandwich fork
77 the asparagus-server (asparagus slice)
78 the sardine-server
79 the lobster fork
80 the oyster fork
81 the caviar knife
82 the white-wine glass
83 the red-wine glass
84 the sweet-wine glass
85 and 86 champagne glasses:
85 the tapering glass
86 the shallow-bowled champagne glass, a crystal glass;
87 the rummer
88 the brandy glass
89 the liqueur glass
90 the gin glass
91 the tumbler, a beer glass

47 The Study

1–61 the study (*fam.* den),

1 the hot-air stove:

2 the hot-air outlet

3 the air intake (air inlet) duct;

4 the bookcase

5 the row of books

6 the oil painting, a landscape

7 the newspaper and magazine rack or stand

8 the daily newspaper (journal)

9 the magazine, a monthly

10 the illustrated paper (picture paper), a weekly

11 the writing table (desk)

12 the desk telephone

13 the fountain pen stand

14 the photograph album (photo album)

15 the photograph (photo)

16 the photograph frame

17 the desk lamp, an adjustable reading lamp

18 the desk chair:

19 the leather upholstery;

20 the hassock

21 the smoking table, a tiled table:

22 the table-leg

23 the table-top;

24 the candle (light):

25 the wick

26 the candle flame;

27 the candlestick

28 the fumigating candle (fumigation pastil or pastille)

29 the snuffers

30 the smoke-consumer

31 the ash-tray

32 the cigarette-box

33 the cigar-box

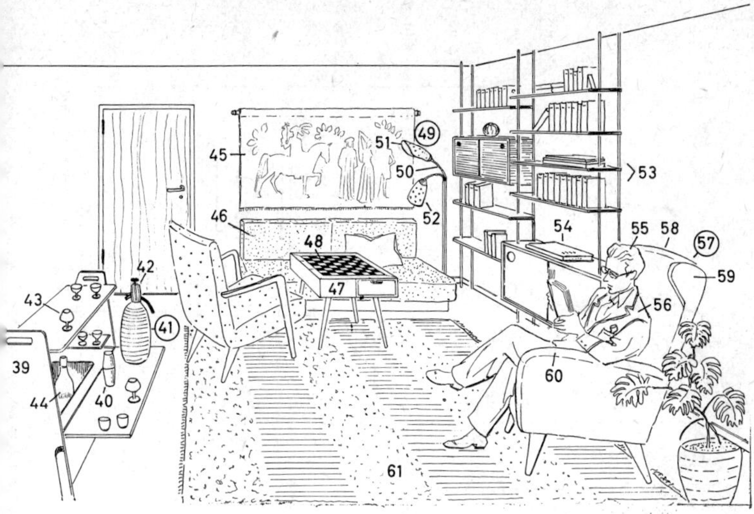

34–36 the natural history collection:
34 the butterfly collection
35 the insect and beetle collection
36 the mineral collection;
37 the collection of photographs
38 the coin collection
39 the cocktail cabinet
40–43 the mixing set (cocktail set):
40 the shaker
41 the siphon (syphon; siphon bottle) with the soda water (aerated water):
42 the oxygen capsule;
43 the cocktail glass;
44 the bottle of whisky (of whiskey)
45 the Gobelin tapestry (hand-woven tapestry)
46 the couch, a sofa-bed (settee-bed, studio couch)
47 the chess table
48 the inlaid work (wood mosaic, marquetry), a chessboard
49 the reading lamp, a standard lamp (floor lamp):
50 the flexible arm (gooseneck)
51 the bullet-shaped shade
52 the lamp-shade;
53 the book-shelves, a sectional bookcase, a piece of combination furniture (unit furniture)
54 the art album
55 the master of the house
56 the smoking jacket
57 the high-backed armchair (wing chair, upholstered armchair, easy chair), an armchair:
58 the back of the chair
59 the head-rest (wing)
60 the arm (arm-rest);
61 the pile carpet

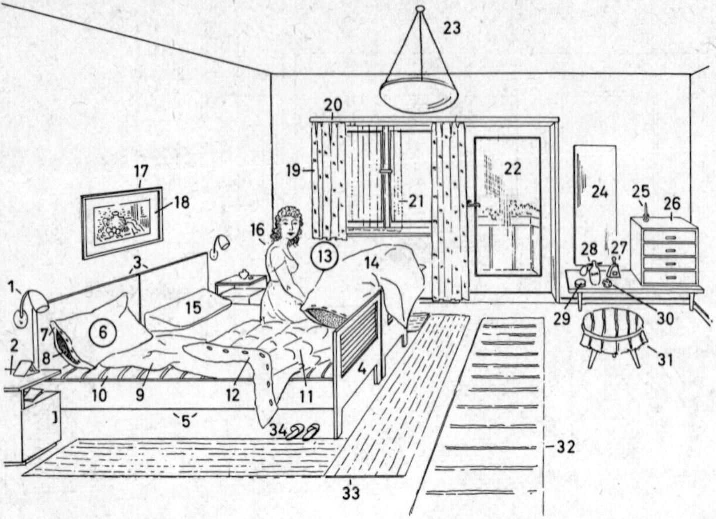

1 the bedside reading lamp, a wall lamp
2 the bedside or night table (night com-
3–15 the bed, a double bed, ⌊mode)
3–5 the bedstead:
3 the head of the bed
4 the foot of the bed
5 the side of the bed;
6 the pillow (feather pillow):
7 the pillow slip
8 the tick (ticking);
9 the bottom sheet, a linen sheet (sheet)
10 the mattress with tick (ticking) cover
11 the quilt (*Am.* comfortable, comforter), an eiderdown (down), or sheeps-wool quilt
12 the quilt cover (turn-down sheet)
13 the feather bed:
14 the feather-bed cover;
15 the wedge-shaped bolster;
16 the lady in nightdress (*fam.* nightie; in négligé, deshabille, dishabille)
17 the picture frame
18 the interchangeable mount
19 the curtain
20 the curtain-rod
21 the window curtain, a drawable curtain
22 the balcony door
23 the bedroom lamp
24 the dressing mirror (dressing table
25 the ring stand ⌊mirror)
26 the dressing table (toilet table, *Am.* dresser, vanity)
27 the scent bottle (perfume flacon)
28 the scent spray (perfume spray, *Am.* atomizer)
29 the powder box (powder bowl, *Am.* compact)

30 the powder puff

31 the dressing pouffe (dressing pouf), a fancy tabouret

32 the carpet runner

33 the bedside carpet runners

34 the slipper (mule), a pabouch (pabouche, papoosh, babouche, *Am. coll.* softies)

35 the bedside rug (*Am.* throw rug)

36 the curtain on runners

37 the ceiling slat

38 the rod for drawing the curtain

39 the washing niche (washing recess)

40 the bedroom cupboard (combined wardrobe and linen cupboard):

41 the cupboard shelf (linen shelf)

42 the stack (pile) of linen (linen)

43 the wardrobe mirror;

44 the air-tight, dustproof, and moth-proof storage bag or sack

45 the wardrobe rod

46 the trouser-hanger

47 the screen (folding screen)

48 the lady's maid (*Am.* chambermaid)

49 the dirty-linen basket (laundry basket)

50 the curved stool, a stool

51 the electric blanket (heating blanket):

52 the temperature regulator for controlling the heat;

53 the couch (divan):

54 the neck cushion (bolster, couch roll, divan roll);

55 the travelling (*Am.* traveling) rug (rug, *Am.* lap robe, car rug, steamer rug), a blanket

56 the kimono, a dressing gown (*Am.* bathrobe, slumber robe)

49 The Day-Nursery

1-29 the day-nursery (nursery, children's play-room):

1 the nursemaid (nursery maid)

2 the child's cot (*Am.* baby's crib)

3 the go-cart (*Am.* baby-walker, walker)

4 the play-pen

5-29 toys (playthings):

5 the teddy bear, a soft animal, a cuddly toy

6 the doll's house:

7 the doll's kitchen

8 the doll's kitchen range

9 the doll's room

10 the doll's furniture

11 the doll's tableware;

12 the doll's pram

13 the rocking-horse

14 the jumping jack (*Am.* supple-jack)

15 the rocking-duck, a rocking-seat

16 the toy house

17 the toy animals

18 the toy trumpet

19 the toy bricks

20 the toy train

21 the toy drum

22 the drumsticks

23 the toy motor car (toy car)

24 the humming-top

25 the tin soldier (lead soldier, toy soldier), a tin figure (lead figure)

26 the small child (infant, child under school age, toddler)

27 the child's chair

28 the child's table

29 the child's milk-beaker

1 the kindergarten teacher
2 the overall (nurse's uniform)
3 the child
4 the baby doll
5 blindman's buff
6 the bandage over the eyes
7 the hobby-horse
8 the doll's bed:
9 the canopy;
10 the toy shop
11 the child's stool
12 the toy box
13 the bricks
14 the jig-saw puzzle, a puzzle
15 the doll's cradle
16 the picture-book
17 the transfer-picture (transfer)
18 the mosaic game
19 the kaleidoscope

20-31 children's handicrafts (handwork):

20 the glass beads (beads)
21 the cut-out sheet of cardboard
22 the plasticine, modelling (*Am.* modeling) material
23 the modelling (*Am.* modeling) board
24 the coloured (*Am.* colored) pencils (crayons)
25 the painting-book
26 the paste-pot
27 the paste-brush
28 the paste-work
29 the weaving
30 the embroidery, needlework
31 the paint-box

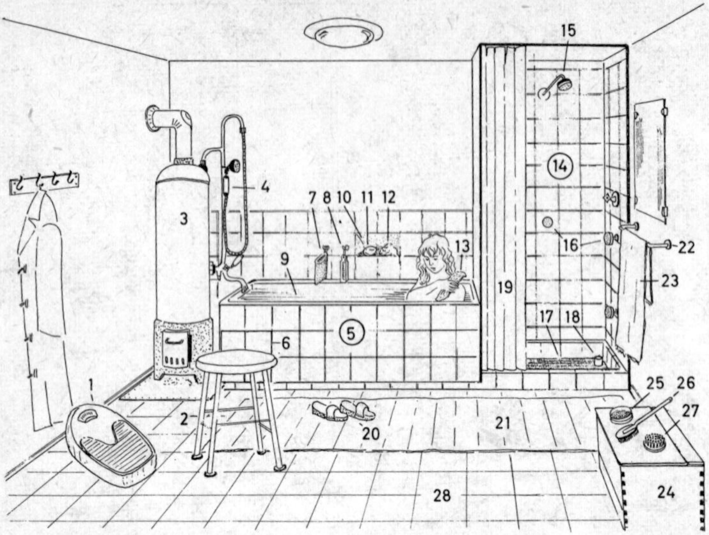

1-28 the bathroom (*Am.* bath, toilet):

1 the bathroom scales (personal weighing machine)
2 the bathroom stool
3 the coal water-heater
4 the hand shower
5 the built-in bath, a full-length bath:
6 the inspection panel;
7 the wash glove (bath mit)
8 the bath thermometer
9 the bath water
10 the soap-dish recess
11 the bath soap
12 the bath sponge
13 the loofa(h)
14 the shower cabinet:
15 the ceiling shower
16 the wall shower
17 the shower tray
18 the overflow pipe (water outlet);
19 the plastic curtain
20 the bath slipper (mule)
21 the bath mat
22 the towel rail
23 the bath towel
24 the box seat
25 the bath salts (bath crystals)
26 the back brush (bath brush, flesh brush)
27 the massage brush (body friction brush)
28 the tiled floor;

29-82 the lavatory:

29 the air-purifier (deodorant)
30 the toilet (lavatory) paper-holder
31 the toilet roll, a crepe paper product
32 the lavatory seat-cleaner
33 the lavatory brush
34 the pedestal mat
35 the closet water closet (W.C., w.c., lavatory, toilet):
36 the water-closet bowl (lavatory bowl)
37 the water-closet pan (lavatory pan)
38 and 39 the closet seat with cover:

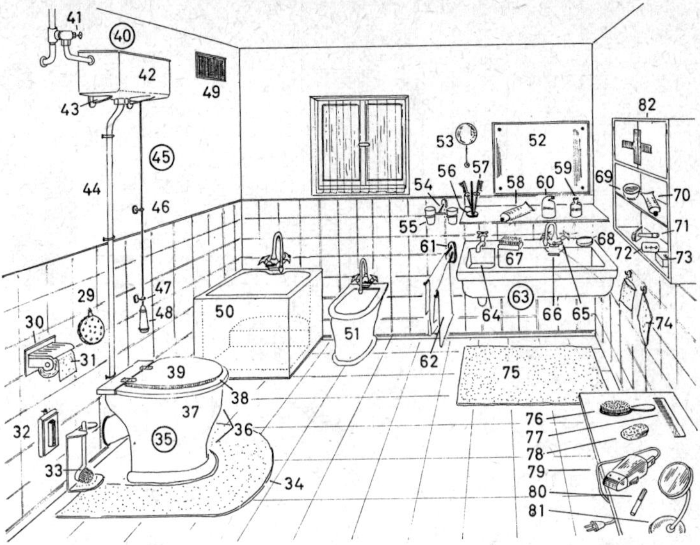

38 the lavatory seat
39 the lavatory lid (lavatory cover);
40 the flushing system:
41 the stopcock
42 the cistern (water tank)
43 the bracket
44 the flush pipe;
45 the chain pull and handle:
46 the chain
47 the bracket
48 the handle;
49 the ventilator
50 the hip bath (sit-down bath)
51 the bidet
52–68 the wash-basin, with accessories:
52 the bathroom mirror
53 the wall light
54 the tooth glass holder
55 the tooth glass
56 the tooth brush stand
57 the tooth brush
58 the tooth paste (dentifrice)
59 the tooth powder (dentifrice)
60 the mouth wash
61 the towel rail
62 the towel
63 the wash-basin (hand-basin)
64 the mouth-rinsing basin
65 the plug lever
66 the overflow;
67 the nail brush (*Am.* hand scrub, hand brush)
68 the toilet soap;
69 the shaving soap
70 the shaving cream
71 the safety razor
72 the razor blade
73 the razor blade hone or sharpener
74 the face-flannel (face-cloth, *Am.* wash rag, wash cloth)
75 the foam-rubber mat
76 the hair brush
77 the comb
78 the pumice stone
79 the electric razor
80 the styptic pencil
81 the shaving mirror
82 the family medicine chest (bathroom cabinet, toilet cabinet)

52 The Store-Room

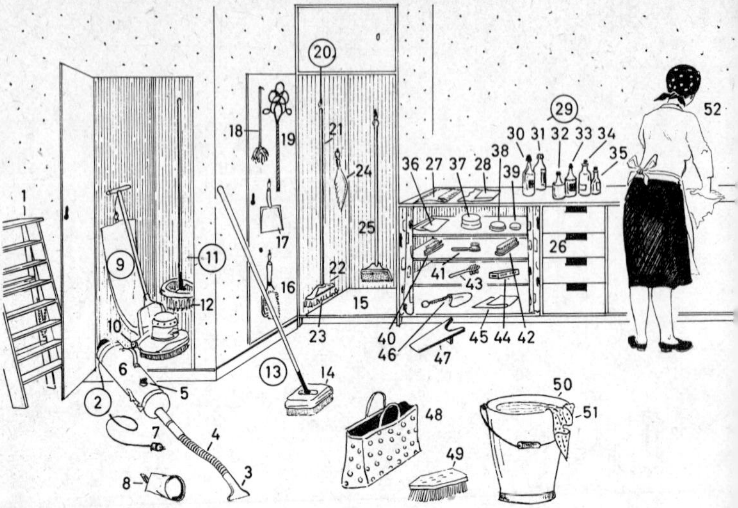

1 the pair of steps (step-ladder)
2 the vacuum cleaner (cleaner):
3 the nozzle
4 the flexible metal hose
5 the switch
6 the cylinder (tank, body)
7 the plug
8 the dust-bag;
9 the carpet-sweeper and floor-polisher:
10 the foot-operated on-off switch;
11 the mop:
12 the yarn;
13 the floor-polisher:
14 the polishing brush;
15 the broom cupboard
16 the brush
17 the dustpan
18 the feather-duster
19 the carpet-beater
20 the soft broom (*Am.* long-handled brush):
21 the broomstick
22 the broom head
23 the bristles;
24 the feather-brush
25 the scrubber (long-handled scrubbing brush, *Am.* long-handled scrub-brush)
26 the shoe-cleaning (*Am.* shoeshining) cupboard
27 the duster
28 the window leather (chamois leather, shammy)
29 cleaning materials (cleaners):
30 the cleaning petrol (*Am.* cleaning gasoline)
31 the ammonia solution
32 the spirit (alcohol)
33 the glycerine
34 the turpentine (*coll.* turps)
35 the spirits of salt (hydrochlorid acid, muriatic acid);
36 the floor-polishing cloth
37 the floor-polish (floor wax)
38 the shoe-polish (*Am.* shoeshine)

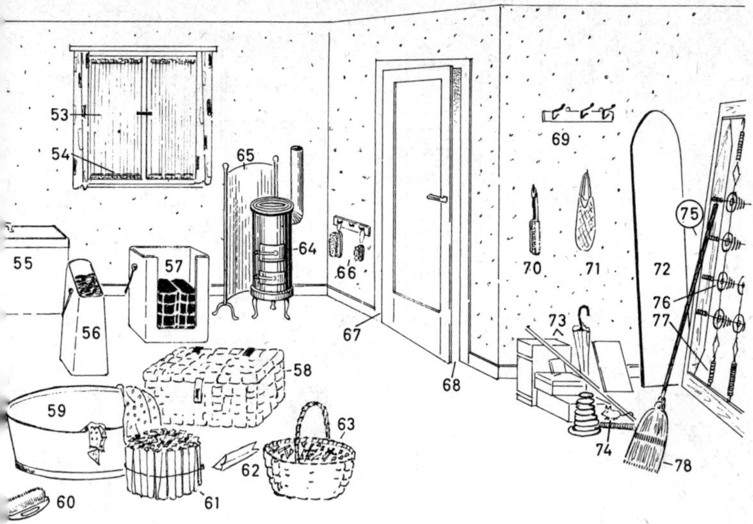

39 the dubbin (dubbing)
40–43 shoe brushes:
40 the cleaning brush
41 the brush for applying polish
42 the polishing brush
43 the rubber brush (suède brush), a brush for suède shoes;
44 the suède powder
45 the furniture-polishing cloth
46 the shoe-tree (shoe-stretcher)
47 the boot-jack
48 the shopping-bag
49 the scrubbing brush (*Am.* scrub-brush)
50 the pail (bucket)
51 the cleaning-cloth
52 the charwoman (char, cleaner, *Am.* hired woman, scrubwoman)
53 the casement curtain
54 the curtain-rod
55 the coal-box
56 the coal-hod
57 the briquette box
58 the lockable hamper
59 the tin bath
60 the carpet brush
61 the kindling wood, a bundle of firewood
62 the piece of wood
63 the wood-basket
64 the cylindrical iron stove
65 the fire-screen
66 the clothes-brush
67 the crack in the door
68 the door opening
69 the clothes-rack
70 the crumb-brush
71 the string-bag
72 the ironing-board
73 the lumber
74 the mouse
75 the spring mattress:
76 the spiral (helical) spring
77 the draw (tension) spring;
78 the birch broom (besom)

Engl. courtyard = *Am.* dooryard

1-49 the court (courtyard, backyard):

1 the side building (annex), a back building
2 the cellar door
3 the cellar steps
4 the padlock
5 the hasp
6 the saw horse (saw jack, saw buck, saw trestle)
7 the log
8 the firewood (chopped wood, kindling)
9 the chopping (hacking) block
10 the wood-cutter (wood-chopper)
11 the street children (urchins, raga-muffins, street arabs)
12 the block of flats (tenement house, *Am.* apartment house):
13 the lavatory (W.C., toilet) window
14 the staircase window
15 the back-door
16 the courtyard lamp
17 the built-in balcony (loggia)
18 the window-box
19 the passage (passageway, doorway, *Am.* driveway, thrufare):
20 the door (yard door)
21 the kerb (curb)
22 the kerbstone (curbstone);
23 the neighbouring (*Am.* neigh-boring; adjoining, next-door) house
24 the street singer (street musician)
25 the courtyard wall (party wall)
26 the barrel-organ
27 the organ-grinder
28 the caretaker (janitor, porter, con-cierge)
29 the gossip (scandalmonger, newsmon-ger, tattler)
30 the pedlar (hawker)
31 the woodpile (stack of wood, pile of wood
32 the dustbin (refuse bin, trash bin, *Am.* ashcan, garbage can):
33 the lid (hinged lid)
34 the handle;

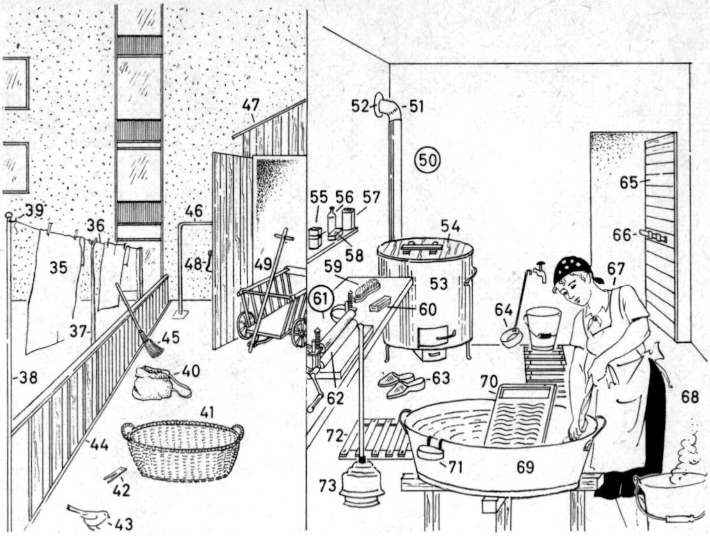

35-42 the clothes-drying place (drying yard):

35 the washing
36 the clothes-line
37 the clothes-prop
38 the clothes-line post
39 the hook
40 the clothes-peg (clothes-pin) bag
41 the clothes-basket
42 the clothes-peg (*Am.* clothes-pin);
43 the house-sparrow
44 the wooden fence
45 the birch broom (besom)
46 the carpet-beating bar
47 the shed (lean-to)
48 the hook
49 the hand-truck (small cart);

50-73 the wash-house,

50 the stovepipe, a flue (gas escape):
51 the pipe elbow (pipe bend, pipe knee)
52 the stovepipe collar or rosace;
53 the copper
54 the copper lid, a wooden lid
55 the soap-powder
56 the stain-remover (*Am.* spot remover)
57 the starch
58 the packet of blue (of washing-blue)
59 the scrubbing-brush (*Am.* scrub-brush)
60 the bar of washing-soap (*Am.* laundry soap)
61 the wringer:
62 the roller;
63 the clog (wooden shoe)
64 the ladle
65 the wash-house door
66 the door-bolt, a bolt
67 the washerwoman (laundress, *Am.* washwoman)
68 the plaster (cement) floor
69 the wash-tub
70 the scrubbing-board (*Am.* wash-board)
71 the soap-dish
72 the duckboards
73 the dolly

54 The Flower Garden (Pleasure Garden)

1 the rockery (rock garden)
2 the summer house
3 the garden furniture
4 the ornamental shrub
5 the covered walk (arbour, arboured walk; *Am.* arbor, arbored walk; pergola)
6 the round bed
7 the garden chair
8 the storm lantern
9 the tiltable sunshade (tiltable garden parasol)
10 the deck chair
11 the globular (bushy-topped) acacia
12 the screen (folding screen), a protection against the wind
13 the thuja hedge (thuya hedge)
14 the bird house (bird table)
15 the bird bath, a concrete bowl
16 the wire rake
17 the watering can (*Am.* sprinkling can)
18 the garden bench (garden seat)
19 the garden pond, a pond
20 the fountain
21 the lawn
22 the crazy paving (crazy pavement)
23 the landscape gardener (horticulturist, *Am.* landscape architect)
24 the stone steps
25 the garden swing

1–31 the small garden (garden plot, vegetable and fruit garden),

1, 2, 16, 17, 29 dwarf fruit trees (espaliers, espalier fruit trees, fruit trees trained to grow flat):

1 the quadruple cordon

2 the vertical cordon (single-stem fruit tree)

3 the garden shed

4 the water-butt (water barrel, barrel for rain-water)

5 the climbing plant (climber, creeper, rambler)

6 the compost heap

7 the sunflower

8 the garden ladder

9 the perennial (flowering perennial)

10 the garden fence (wooden fence, paling)

11 the standard berry

12 the climbing rose (rambler rose) on the trellised arch

13 the rose bush (bush rose, dwarf rose)

14 the summer house

15 the Chinese lantern (paper lantern)

16 the pyramid (pyramid-trained tree, round tree), a free-standing espalier

17 the double horizontal cordon, a wall espalier

18 the flower bed, a border bed

19 the berry-bearing bush

20 the border of concrete slabs

21 the rose standard (rose tree, standard rose)

22 the border with perennials

23 the garden path, a gravel path

24 the amateur gardener

25 the asparagus bed

26 the vegetable bed

27 the scarecrow

28 the bean stick (bean pole)

29 the horizontal cordon

30 the standard fruit tree

31 the tree stake

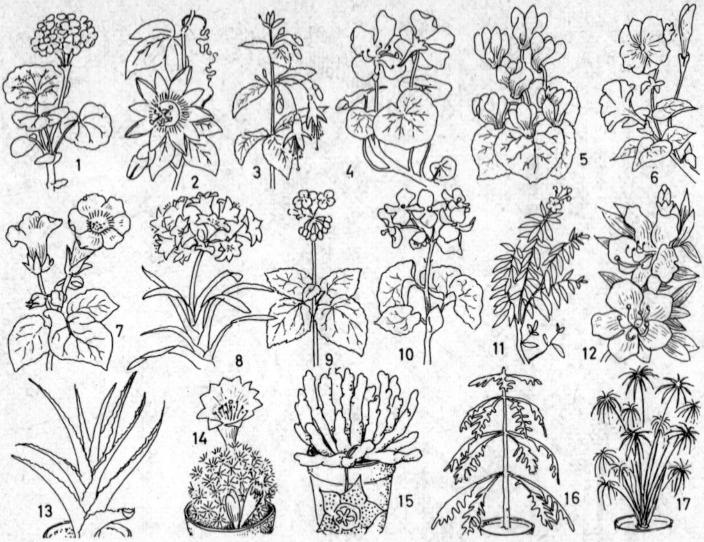

1 the geranium (pelargonium, scarlet geranium), a Geranium

2 the passion flower (Passiflora), one of the Parietales

3 the fuchsia, an evening primrose, one of the Onagraceae

4 the nasturtium (Indian cress, Tropaeolum)

5 the cyclamen (sowbread), one of the Primulaceae

6 the petunia, one of the Solanaceae

7 the gloxinia (sinningia), one of the Gesneriaceae

8 the clivia (Kaffir lily), an Amaryllis

9 the African hemp (Sparmannia), one of the Tiliaceae

10 the begonia

11 the myrtle

12 the azalea, one of the Ericaceae

13 the aloe, one of the Liliaceae

14 the globe thistle (Echinops)

15 the carrion flower (Stapelia), an asclepiad

16 the Norfolk Island Pine, an Araucaria

17 the galingale (Cyperus), one of the Cyperaceae

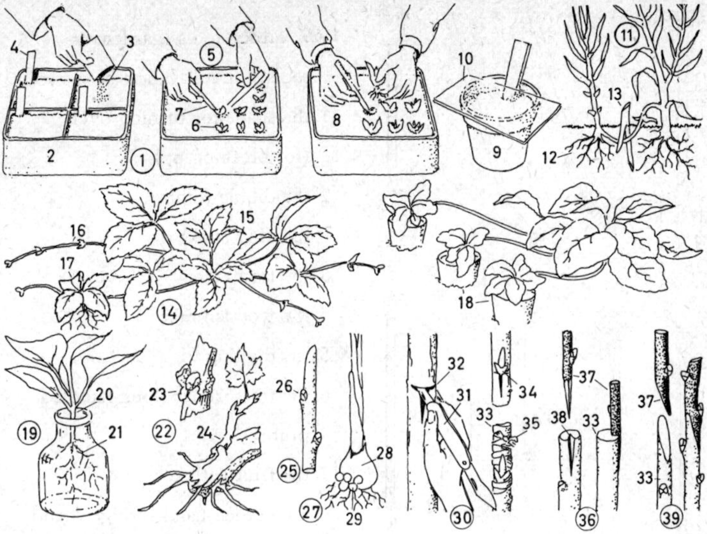

1 seed-sowing (sowing):
2 the seed pan (sowing pan)
3 the seed
4 the plant label (plant-marker, tally with the name of the plant)
5 the pricking-out (pricking-in, pricking-off) of the seedlings:
6 the seedling (young plant)
7 the dibble (dibber, planting stick)
8 the transplanting of the seedlings;
9 the flower pot, a pot for seed-sowing
10 the pane of glass;
11 the propagation by layers (layering):
12 the rooted layer
13 the forked twig for fixing;
14 the propagation by runners:
15 the parent plant
16 the runner
17 the rooted offshoot;
18 the setting of offshoots in pots
19 the cutting in water:
20 the cutting (slip, set)
21 the root;
22 the eye-cutting on the vine branch:
23 the eye (bud)
24 the sprouting (shooting) cutting;
25 the hard-wood cutting:
26 the bud;
27 the propagation by offsets:
28 the old bulb
29 the offset;

30-42 grafting,

30 budding (shield-budding):
31 the budding knife
32 the T-shaped slit
33 the stock
34 the inserted eye
35 the raffia (bast) binding;
36 the grafting (cleft-grafting):
37 the graft (scion, shoot)
38 the wedge-shaped slit;
39 the splice-grafting

58 Garden Tools

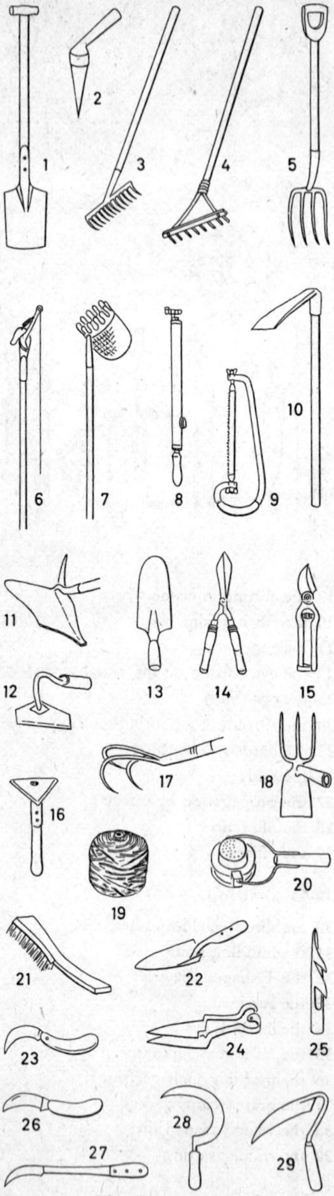

1–29 garden tools (gardening tools) for cultivation of the soil:

1 the spade for turning over (for breaking up)

2 the dibble (dibber, planting stick)

3 the iron rake

4 the wooden rake

5 the digging fork

6 the tree-pruner (long-handled pruner)

7 the fruit-gatherer

8 the garden hand-syringe (hand insecticide-sprayer, shrub-sprayer, hand-sprayer)

9 the pruning saw (saw for cutting branches)

10 the mattock

11 the triangular-bladed draw hoe

12 the draw hoe

13 the garden trowel

14 the hedge shears (hedge-clipper, garden shears)

15 the pruning-shears (secateurs)

16 the tree-scraper (bark-scraper)

17 the three-prong cultivator

18 the combined hoe and fork

19 the twine for edge-straightening

20 the caterpillar lamp
21 the tree brush (bark brush)
22 the small trowel (hand trowel)
23 the curved pruning knife
24 the border shears
25 the weeder (thistle-lifter)
26 the grafting knife
27 the asparagus-cutter (asparagus knife)
28 the sickle (reaping hook)
29 the scythe-bladed sickle;
30 the garden truck (garden cart)
31 the semi-automatic spade
32 the drill
33 the edge-trimmer
34 the lawn-mower
35 the hose reel
36 the hose reel with handle and wheels
37 the garden hose
38 the sun-couch on wheels
39 the sundial
40 the garden-sprinkler
41 the lawn-sprinkler
42 the liquid-manure scoop
43 the mole-trap
44 the vole-trap

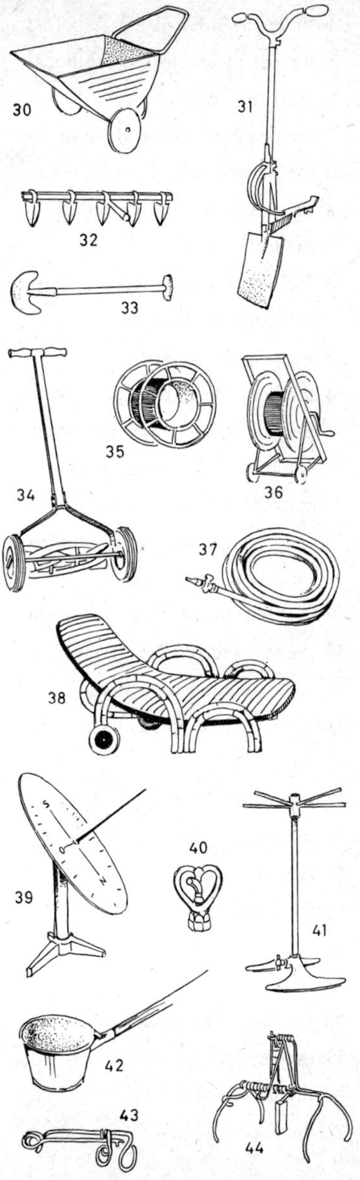

59 Vegetables (Vegetable Plants)

1–11 leguminous plants,
1 the pea plant (pea), a papilionaceous flower:
2 the pea flower (pea blossom)
3 the pinnate leaf
4 the pea tendril, a leaf tendril
5 the leafy stipule
6 the pod, a seed vessel (pericarp, fruit capsule, legume)
7 the pea, the seed;
8 the bean plant (bean), a climbing plant (climber, creeper); *kinds:* common bean (green bean); runner bean; scarlet runner (*Am.* snap bean, string bean); *smaller:* bush bean (dwarf bean):
9 the bean flower (bean blossom)
10 the twining (creeping) bean stalk (twining bean stem)
11 the bean [the pod as well as the seed];
12 the tomato (love apple, apple of love)
13 the cucumber
14 the asparagus
15 the radish
16 the large radish
17 the carrot
18 the carrot (Belgian carrot)
19 the parsley
20 the horse radish
21 the leek
22 the chives
23 the pumpkin (*Am.* squash); *sim.* melon
24 the onion
25 the onion skin
26 the kohlrabi (turnip cabbage)
27 the celeriac;
28–34 cabbage plants:
28 the mangel (mangel wurzel, mangold, mangold wurzel)
29 the spinach
30 the Brussels sprouts (sprouts)
31 the cauliflower
32 the cabbage (cabbage head, head of cabbage), a cabbage; *sorts:* white cabbage, red cabbage
33 the savoy (savoy cabbage)
34 the kale (kail, Scotch kale, borecole, winter greens, curly kale, curly greens);
35 the scorzonera (black salsify, viper's grass)
36–42 salad plants,
36 the lettuce (head of lettuce):
37 the lettuce leaf;
38 the corn salad (lambs' tongues)
39 the endive
40 the chicory plant (*Am. loosely:* endive)
41 the artichoke
42 the paprika (Spanish pepper, Hungarian red pepper)

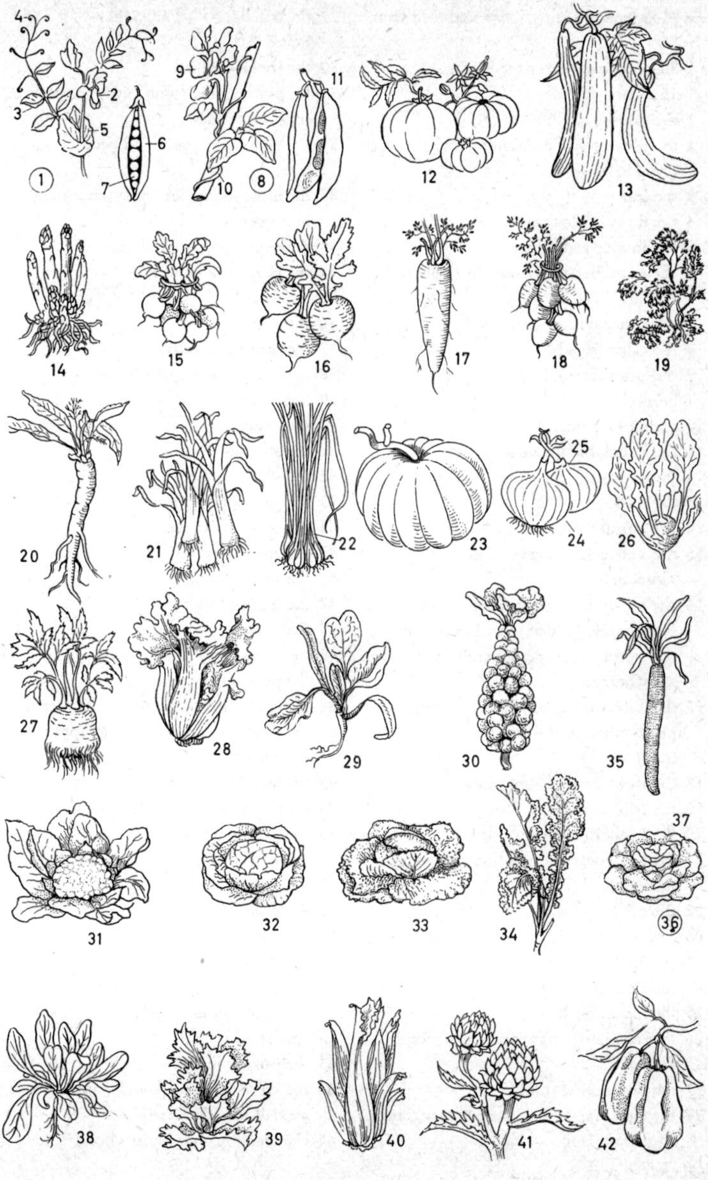
1
2
3
4
5
6
7
8
9
10
11
12
13
14
15
16
17
18
19
20
21
22
23
24
25
26
27
28
29
30
31
32
33
34
35
36
37
38
39
40
41
42

60 Soft Fruit and Pomes (Pomiferous Fruit)

Engl. kernelled fruit = *Am.* kerneled fruit

1–30 soft fruit (berry bushes),
1–15 Ribes,
1 the gooseberry bush:
2 the blossoming gooseberry twig (twig in flower)
3 the leaf
4 the flower (blossom)
5 the looper caterpillar
6 the gooseberry blossom (gooseberry flower)
7 the ovary lying inferiorly
8 the calyx (sepals)
9 the gooseberry (*fam.* goosegog), a berry;
10 the currant bush:
11 the bunch of currants
12 the currant
13 the stalk
14 the currant twig in flower
15 the cluster of flowers (of blossoms);
16 the strawberry plant; *sorts :* wild strawberry, garden strawberry (wood strawberry), perpetual-fruiting wood strawberry:
17 the blossoming and fruit-bearing plant (plant in flower and in fruit)
18 the rhizome (*err.* root stock)
19 the trifoliate leaf
20 the runner (side shoot, layer)
21 the strawberry, a pseudocarp (pseudoberry):
22 the calyx
23 the achene (akene, achaenocarp, one-seeded fruit, seed)
24 the flesh (pulp);
25 the raspberry bush:
26 the raspberry blossom (raspberry flower)
27 the flower bud (bud)
28 the fruit (raspberry, *dialect :* rasp), an aggregate fruit;
29 the blackberry (brambleberry, bramble):
30 the thorny tendril;
31–61 pomes (fruit with pips, pomiferous fruit, Pomoideae),
31 the pear tree; *also :* wild pear tree:
32 the blossoming pear twig (pear twig in flower)
33 the pear [longitudinal section]:
34 the pear stalk (stalk)
35 the flesh
36 the core
37 the pear pip (seed);
38 the pear flower (pear blossom):
39 the ovule
40 the ovary
41 the stigma
42 the style
43 the petal (flower leaf)
44 the sepal (calyx leaf)
45 the anther;
46 the quince tree:
47 the quince leaf
48 the stipule
49 the apple quince (quince)
50 the pear quince (quince);
51 the apple tree; *also :* wild apple tree:
52 the blossoming apple twig (apple twig in blossom)
53 the leaf
54 the apple flower (apple blossom)
55 the deflorate flower;
56 the apple [longitudinal section]:
57 the apple skin
58 the flesh
59 the apple core
60 the apple pip, a fruit pip
61 the apple stalk (stalk);
62 the apple moth (codling moth), a small moth
63 the burrowing passage
64 the larva (maggot, worm, apple grub), a small moth's caterpillar
65 the maggot hole (worm hole)

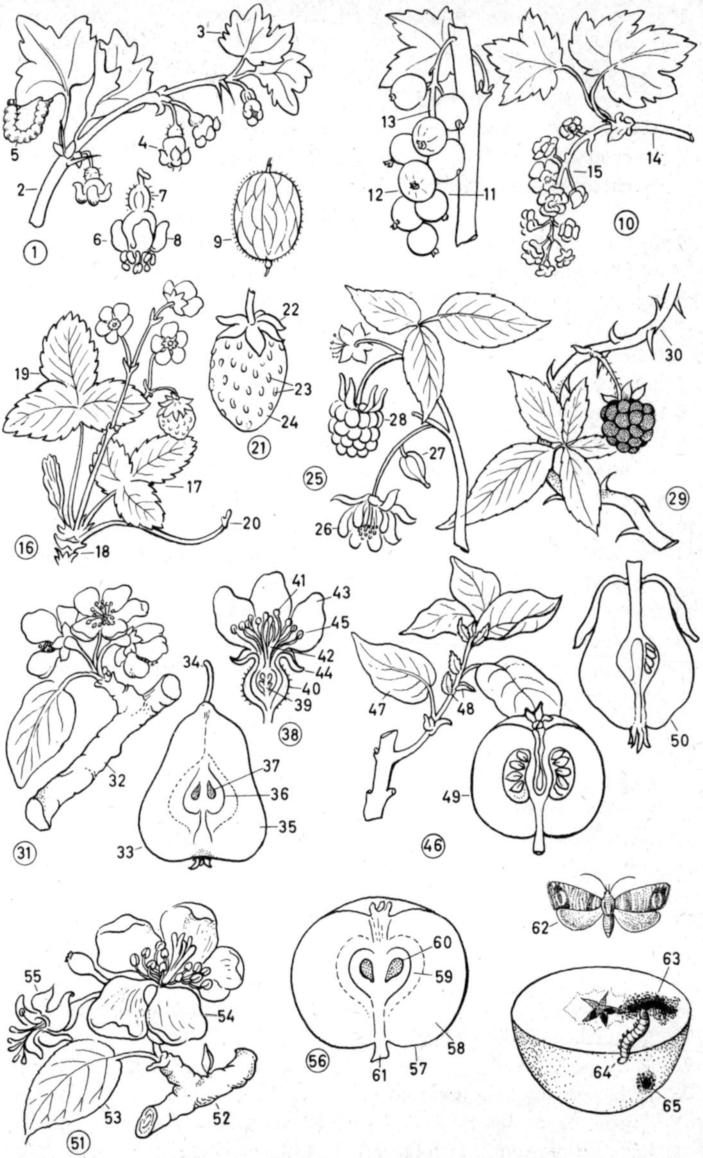
1
2
3
4
5
6
7
8
9
10
11
12
13
14
15
16
17
18
19
20
21
22
23
24
25
26
27
28
29
30
31
32
33
34
35
36
37
38
39
40
41
42
43
44
45
46
47
48
49
50
51
52
53
54
55
56
57
58
59
60
61
62
63
64
65

61 Stone Fruit and Nuts (Kernelled Fruit)

1–36 stone fruit plants (drupes, Prunoideae),
1–18 the cherry tree,
1 the blossoming cherry twig (cherry twig in flower):
2 the cherry leaf
3 the cherry blossom (cherry flower)
4 the flower stalk (peduncle);
5 the cherry; *sorts:* black heart cherry (sweet cherry), wild cherry (gean), sour (bitter) cherry (mahaleb), morello:
6 the flesh
7 the cherry stone
8 the seed (kernel);
9 the flower (blossom) [cross section]:
10 the anther
11 the petal
12 the sepal
13 the pistil
14 the ovule in the central ovary
15 the style
16 the stigma;
17 the leaf:
18 the nectary of the leaf (leaf nectary);
19–23 the plum tree,
19 the fruit-bearing twig (twig with fruit):
20 the plum
21 the plum leaf
22 the bud;
23 the plum stone;
24 the greengage
25 the mirabelle (yellow plum)
26–32 the peach tree,
26 the blossoming twig (twig in blossom or in flower):
27 the peach blossom (peach flower)
28 the flower shoot (sprout)
29 the leaf in bud (young leaf);
30 the fruit-bearing twig (twig with fruit)
31 the peach
32 the peach leaf;
33–36 the apricot tree,
33 the blossoming apricot twig (apricot twig in flower):
34 the apricot blossom (apricot flower)
35 the apricot
36 the apricot leaf;
37–51 nuts,
37–43 the walnut tree (nut tree),
37 the blossoming nut-tree twig nut-tree twig in flower):
38 the female flower
39 the male inflorescence (male flowers, catkin with the male flowers)
40 the imparipinnate leaf;
41 the fruit:
42 the pericarp (soft outer covering)
43 the walnut (nut), a stone fruit (drupe);
44–51 the hazel tree (nut tree), an anemophilous plant,
44 the blossoming hazel twig (hazel twig in flower):
45 the male catkin (lamb's-tail, male inflorescence)
46 the female inflorescence
47 the leaf bud;
48 the fruit-bearing twig (twig with fruit):
49 the hazel nut (nut, cob nut, filbert), a fruit
50 the husk (cupule)
51 the hazel leaf

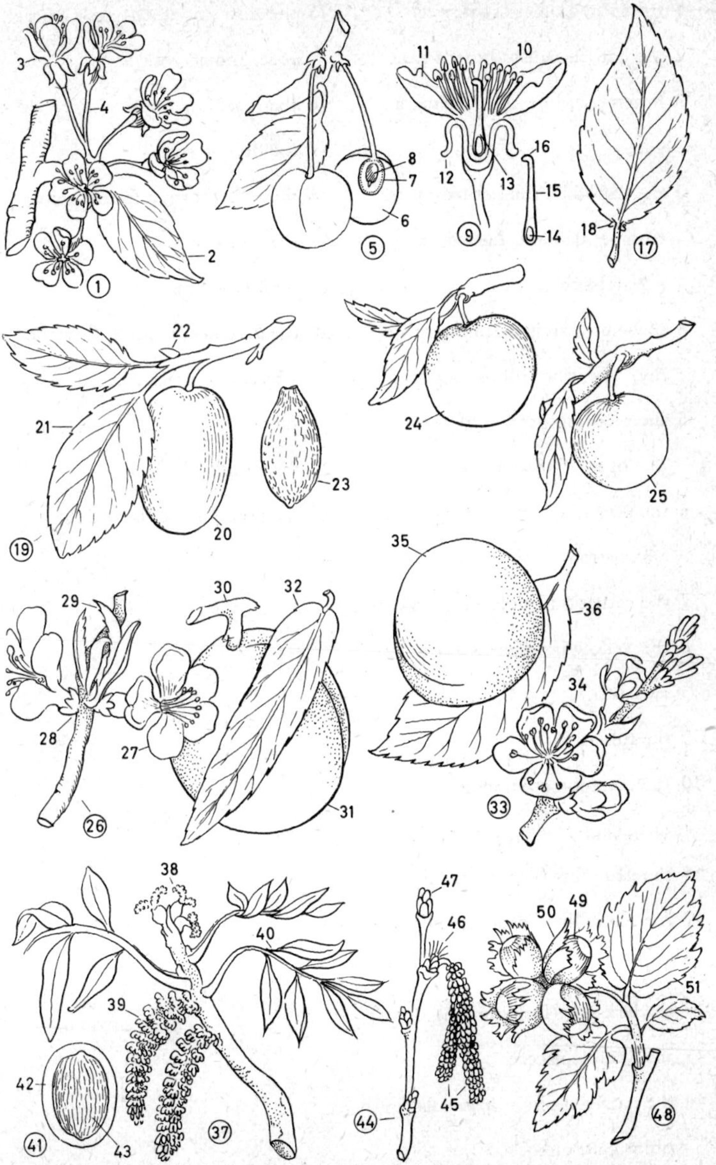
1
2
3
4
5
6
7
8
9
10
11
12
13
14
15
16
17
18
19
20
21
22
23
24
25
26
27
28
29
30
31
32
33
34
35
36
37
38
39
40
41
42
43
44
45
46
47
48
49
50
51

1 the snowdrop (snowflower)

2 the garden pansy (heart's-ease, heartsease, love-in-idleness), a pansy

3 the daffodil (trumpet narcissus, trumpet daffodil, Lent lily), a Narcissus

4 the white narcissus (pheasant's-eye lily); *sim.* polyanthus narcissus

5 the bleeding-heart (lyre flower), one of the Fumariaceae

6 the sweet-william (bunch pink), a carnation

7 the carnation (pink, gilly-flower)

8 the yellow iris (flag, sword-flag), an Iris

9 the tuberose

10 the common columbine (Aquilegia)

11 the gladiolus (*pop.* sword lily)

12 the white lily (madonna lilly), a lily

13 the larkspur (Delphinium), one of the Ranunculaceae

14 the panicled phlox (paniculate phlox), a Phlox

15 the rose (monthly rose, China rose, Indian rose):

16 the rosebud, a bud

17 the double rose

18 the rose thorn, a thorn (spine);

19 the gaillardia

20 the French marigold

21 the love-lies-bleeding (love-lies-a-bleeding, amaranth), an Amaranthus

22 the zinnia

23 the pompon dahlia, a Dahlia

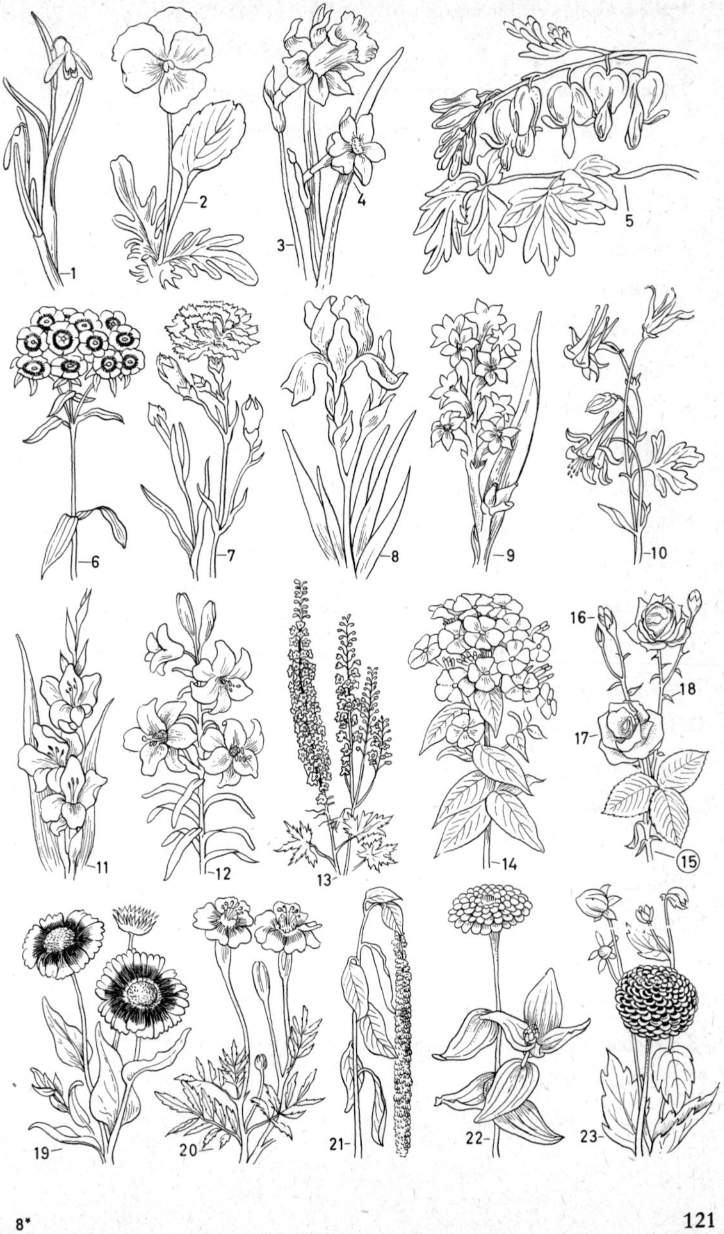
1
2
3
4
5
6
7
8
9
10
11
12
13
14
15
16
17
18
19
20
21
22
23

63 Weeds

1 the corn flower (bluebottle), a Centaurea
2 the corn poppy (field poppy, red weed, common red poppy), a poppy (Papaver):
3 the bud
4 the poppy flower (poppy blossom)
5 the seed capsule (poppy capsule, poppy head) with the poppy seed;
6 the corn cockle (cockle)
7 the yellow ox-eye daisy (corn marigold), a Chrysanthemum
8 the corn camomile or chamomile (wild chamomile, mayweed)
9 the shepherd's-purse:
10 the flower (blossom)
11 the fruit (pouch-shaped pod);
12 the common groundsel
13 the dandelion (*dial.* pissabed); *sim.* common dandelion, autumn dandelion:
14 the capitulum (head)
15 the fruit;
16 the hedge mustard, a mustard
17 the alyssum (sweet alison)
18 the charlock (wild mustard):
19 the flower (blossom)
20 the fruit, a pod (siliqua);
21 the wild radish (runch, jointed charlock):
22 the flower (blossom)
23 the fruit (pod);
24 the common orach (common orache)
25 the goose-foot (fat-hen)
26 the field bindweed, a bindweed
27 the scarlet pimpernel (red chickweed, poor man's weather glass, pimpernel)
28 the wall barley (way bent, barley grass, wild barley)
29 the perennial rye grass (red darnel)
30 the couch (couch grass, quitch, twitch, quitch grass, creeping wheat-grass); *sim.* dog's tooth grass (foxtail, dog grass, dog's grass), bent-grass, sea wheat-grass
31 the galinsoga
32 the creeping thistle (corn thistle), a thistle
33 the stinging nettle, a nettle

63

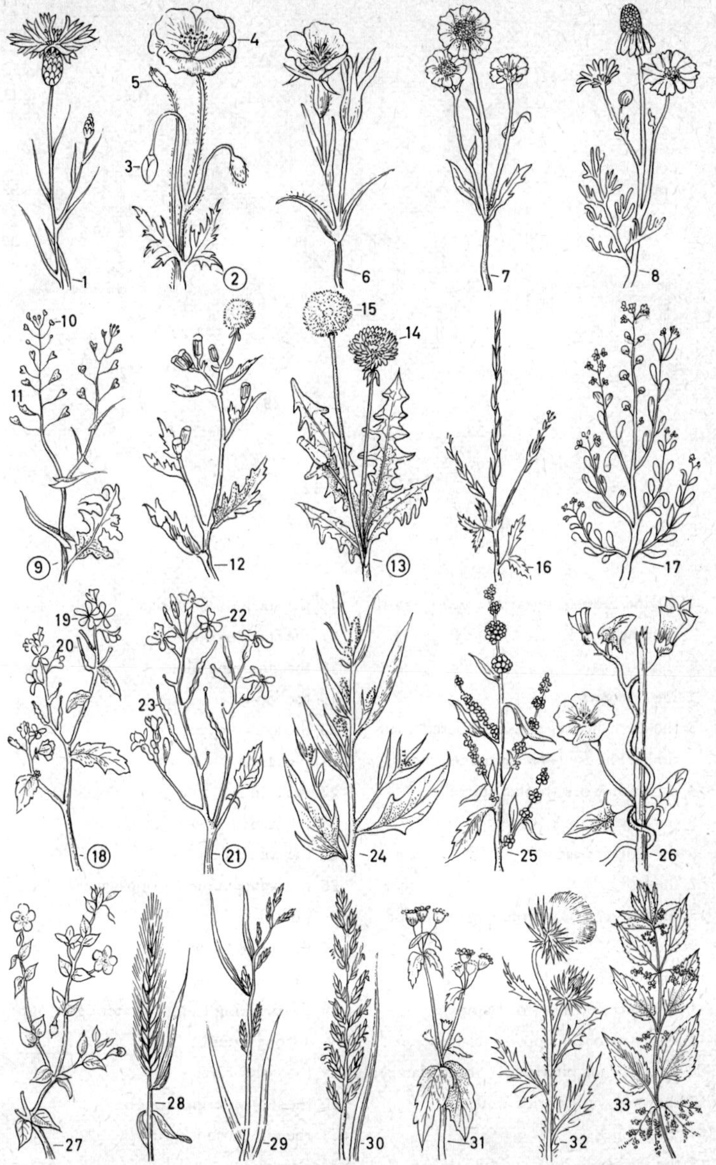
1
2
3
4
5
6
7
8
9
10
11
12
13
14
15
16
17
18
19
20
21
22
23
24
25
26
27
28
29
30
31
32
33

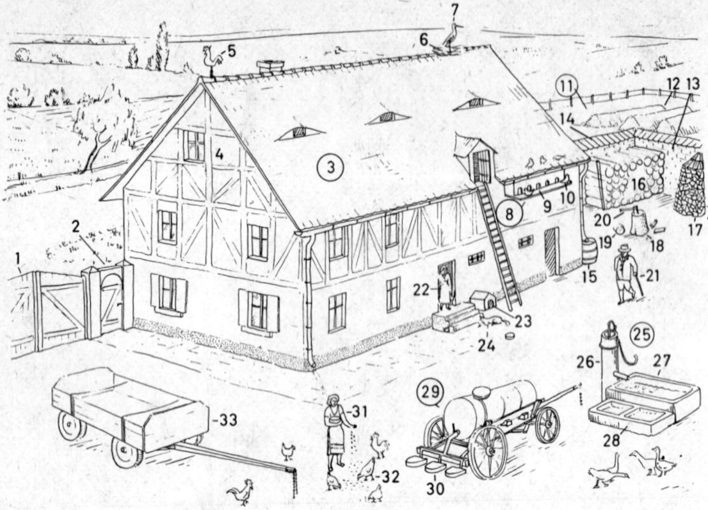

1–60 the farmstead (farm; *smaller :* small holding):
1 the yard gate
2 the side gate
3 the farm house, a half-timbered (half-timber) house (*Am.* frame building):
4 the framework (timber frame)
5 the weathercock (vane)
6 the stork's nest:
7 the stork;
8 the dovecot (dovecote, pigeon house):
9 the exit
10 the pigeon, a domestic pigeon;
11 the place for pits (for clamps):
12 the potato pit (potato clamp); *sim.* fodder roots pit (fodder roots clamp);
13 the yard wall, a brick wall:
14 the coping;
15 the rain-water butt
16 the stack (pile) of logs
17 the stack of firewood
18 the chopping block
19 the log
20 the axe (*Am.* ax)
21 the farmer
22 the farmer's wife
23 the kennel
24 the watch-dog
25 the water pump (spring-water pump):
26 the pump barrel
27 the water trough
28 the drinking trough (watering trough), a stone trough;
29 the water-cart:
30 the self-watering trough;
31 the girl (farmer's girl)
32 the poultry (fowls)

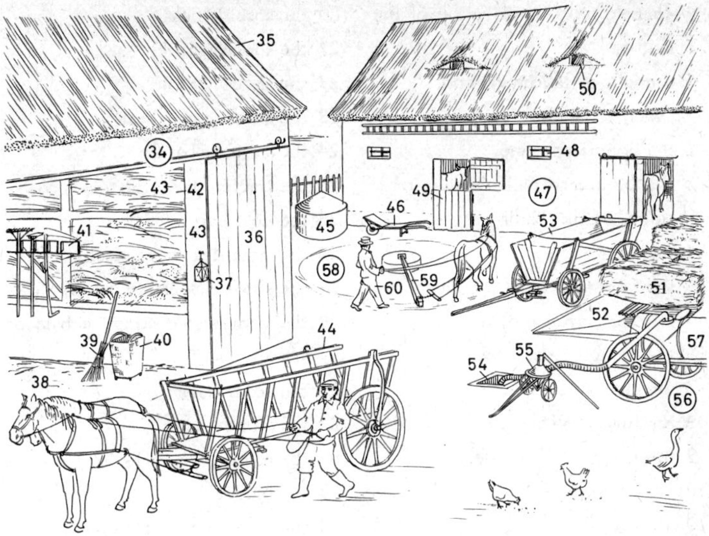

33 the rubber-wheeled farm-cart;
34 the barn:
35 the thatched roof; *here:* straw roof; *sim.* reed roof
36 the barn-door
37 the stable lantern
38 the threshing floor
39 the birch broom (besom, *Am.* brush)
40 the pannier (dosser), a wicker basket
41 the tool-rack
42 the bay
43 the corn;
44 the harvesting-wagon, a rack wagon
45 the fodder silo (silo)
46 the dung barrow (manure barrow)
47 the stables (stabling); *kinds:* stable, pigsty (*Am.* hogshed, hog pen), cow-shed, sheep pen, goat pen, shed for young cattle:
48 the stable window
49 the divided door (hatch), a stable door
50 the roof window;
51 the dung-heap
52 the dung-heap floor
53 the dung-cart, a box cart
54 the liquid-manure pit
55 the liquid-manure pump
56 the liquid-manure cart
57 the liquid-manure tank
58 the horse-gear:
59 the pole of the horse-gear;
60 the farmhand (farm labourer, *Am.* farm laborer; farmer's man)

65 Agriculture (Farming)

1–46 field work (cultivation of the land):

1 the fallow (fallow ground, *Am.* bad land)

2 the boundary stone

3 the boundary balk (baulk) or ridge, a balk (baulk)

4 the field

5 the farm labourer (*Am.* farm laborer; farmhand)

6 the plough (*Am.* plow)

7 the clod

8 the furrow slice

9 the stone (*Am.* boulder)

10–12 sowing:

10 the sower

11 the seed lip

12 the seed corn (seed);

13 the field guard

14 the artificial manure (fertilizer, *Am.* synthetic fertilizer); *kinds:* potassic (kali) manure, phosphatic manure, lime manure, nitrogenous manure

15 the load of dung (*Am.* dungload; stable dung, dung)

16 the ox team (*Am.* span of oxen)

17 the fields (stretch of open country)

18 the farm road (accomodation road, drift, *Am.* dustroad)

19–24 the harvest (harvest of corn, harvest of grain):

19 the cornfield; *kinds:* rye field, wheat field, barley field, oat field

20 the stubble field

21 the shock (stook)

22 the shock (stook)

23 the sheaf (corn sheaf):

24 the sheaf tie band;

25 the tractor (farm tractor)

26 the field barn

27 the corn rick (corn stack)

28 the straw rick (straw stack)

29 the compressed straw, a bale of straw

30 the straw baler:

31 the straw intake

32 the feeder

33 the binder

34 the compression chamber;

35–43 the hay harvest (haymaking, *Am.* haying season); *the second hay harvest:* second hay crop (aftermath, *Am.* rowen):

35 the meadow (hayfield)

36 the haystack (hayrick, hay mow)

37 the haycock

38 the hay fence

39 the hay tripod

40 the hay swath (hay swathe, windrow)

41 the hay trailer

42 the hay prop

43 the quadrupod;

44 the tile drain

45 the drainage ditch

46 the field of beet

1
2
3
4
5
6
7
8
9
10
11
12
13
14
15
16
17
18
19
20
21
22
23
24
25
26
27
28
29
30
31
32
33
34
35
36
37
38
39
40
41
42
43
44
45
46

66 Farmer's Tools (Farm Equipment)

1 the draw hoe:
2 the hoe handle;
3 the push hoe
4 the ridging hoe:
5 the hoe blade;
6 the potato hoe
7 the three-tined dung fork
8 the potato fork
9 the spade
10 the dung hoe
11 the four-tined fork
12 the scythe:
13 the scythe blade
14 the cutting edge (scythe edge)
15 the scythe heel
16 the snaithe
17 the handle;
18 the scythe sheath
19 the whetstone (hone, hone stone)
20 the whetstone (hone) sheath
21 the whetting hammer:
22 the pane (hammer edge, peen, pein);
23 the whetting anvil
24 the potato rake
25 the sickle (reaping hook)
26 the potato-planting trug
27 the flail:
28 the swingle (swipple)
29 the flail staff (flail handle, flail helve);
30 the digging fork
31 the hay rake (rake)
32 the chopping hoe
33 the weeding hoe (hoe)
34 the fodder-cutter (fodder knife)
35 the beet-lifter
36 the fodder-cutting roller
37 the fodder-cutting foot iron
38 the potato basket, a wire basket
39 the seed barrow

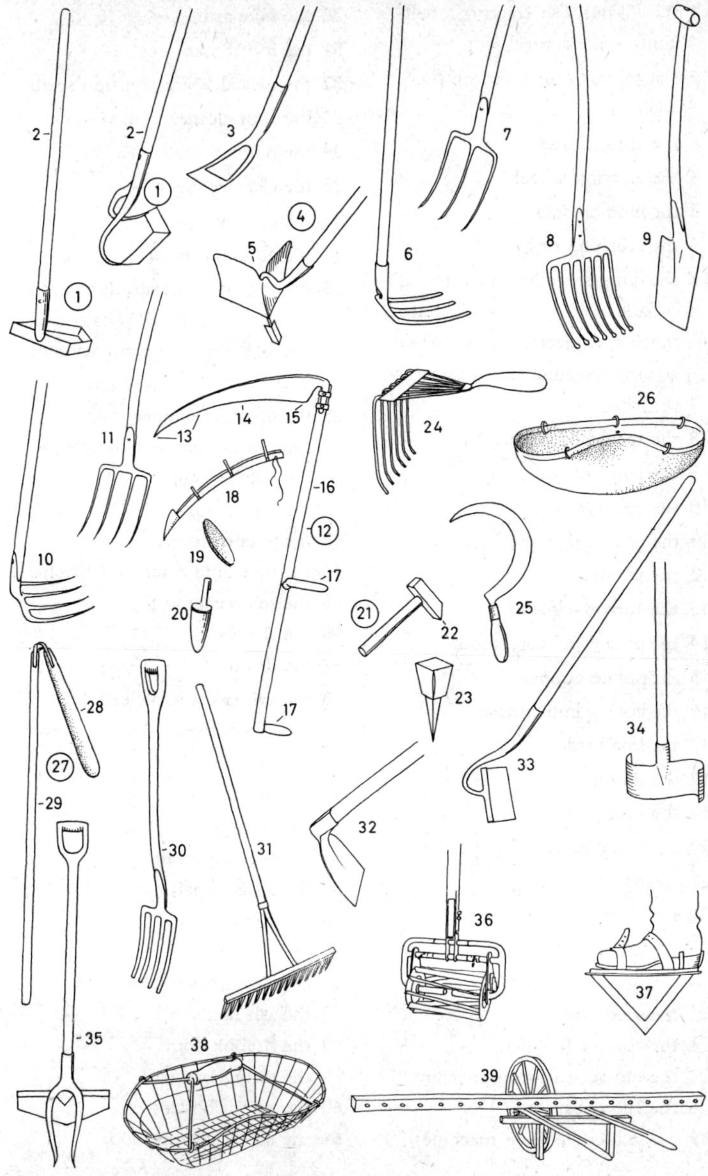
2
2
3
1
1
4
5
6
7
8
9
10
11
13
14
15
16
12
17
18
19
20
21
22
23
24
25
26
27
28
29
30
31
32
33
34
35
36
37
38
39

1 the all-purpose tractor, a self-contained tractor:
2 the tractor tyre (*Am.* off-the-road tire)
3 the sprung seat
4 the steering wheel;
5 the clod-crusher:
6 the crushing ring;
7 the dung-spreader (manure-broadcaster, manure-distributor, muck-spreader); *sim.* broadcast sowing machine (broadcast seeder):
8 the spreading box;
9 the land roller:
10 the roller;
11 the potato-planter:
12 the coulter
13 the furrow-closer
14 the potato delivery spout
15 the potato hopper;
16 the hoeing implement:
17 the hoe blade;
18 the dibbler:
19 the dibbler star
20 the fore-blade;
21 the hay rake:
22 the tines
23 the rake tine;
24 the seed drill (drill, seeder):
25 the seed box
26 the coulter (colter);
27 the mower (mowing machine):
28 the cutter bar;
29 the tedder (tedding machine):
30 the rake arm
31 the foot brake
32 the helical (spiral) tension spring;
33 the root-cleaner with root-cutter:
34 the hopper
35 the cleaning bars
36 the cutting drum
37 the cleaning drum;
38 the elevator potato-digger (potato-harvester), a potato-raiser; *sim.* beet-digger (beet-harvester, beet-lifter):
39 the drawbar connection
40 the power take-off connection
41 the delivery chute
42 the screen apron
43 the potato scoop;
44 the threshing machine (thresher):
45 the self-feeder
46 the shaker
47 the drum
48 the awner (hummeller, *Am.* hummeler, barley-bearder)
49 the dresser
50 the winnower
51 the elevator
52 the cavings spout
53 the shaker shaft
54 the straw press;
55 the fodder-steamer:
56 the jacket base
57 the ash box
58 the firebox door
59 the swing frame
60 the tilting boiler
61 the screw closure door

1
2
3
4
5
6
7
8
9
10
11
12
13
14
15
16
17
18
19
20
21
22
23
24
25
26
27
28
29
30
31
32
33
34
35
36
37
38
39
40
41
42
43
44
45
46
47
48
49
50
51
52
53
54
55
56
57
58
59
60
61

Engl. plough = *Am.* plow

1–34 ploughs,
1 the wheel plough, a single-furrow plough; *kinds:* wheel plough, ridging plough (ridge plough):
2 the handle
3 the stilt (*Am.* plow neck, plow tail)
4–8 the plough body (*Am.* plow bottom):
4 the mouldboard
5 the landside
6 the sole
7 the plough share (share)
8 the frog;
9 the beam (plough beam)
10 the coulter (colter)
11 the skim coulter (skim colter)
12 the guiding cross piece for automatic guiding by chain
13 the chain for automatic guiding
14–19 the forecarriage:
14 the adjustable bow
15 the land wheel
16 the furrow wheel
17 the hake chain
18 the draught beam (draw beam, draw-bar, *Am.* draft beam)
19 the hake;
20 the one-way plough:
21 the crank
22 the spindle
23 the draught chain (draw chain, *Am.* draft chain);
24 the swing plough:
25 the disk (disc) coulter
26 the land wheel;
27 the swing plough:
28 the furrow-width adjuster
29 the adjustable bar
30 the draught beam (draw beam, draw-bar, *Am.* draft beam);
31 the cultivator (grubber, *Am.* lister):
32 the frame
33 the carrier
34 the ducksfoot tine;
35 the disk (disc) harrow, a harrow (*Am.* soil pulverizer):
36 the disk (disc)
37 the scraper
38 the sprung seat
39 the adjusting lever
40 the road wheel;
41 the potato-spinner (potato-digger, spinner-type potato-digger):
42 the rotary wheel
43 the tine
44 the prong;
45 the stearage hoe (hoeing machine, *Am* cultivator):
46 the steering handle
47 the hoe blade;
48 the combine harvester (harvester combine, *Am.* combine) [longitudinal section]:
49 the swath board
50 the reel
51 the tine
52 the cutter bar and the ear-lifter
53 the auger feeder (screw auger)
54 the steering
55 the conveyor
56 the power unit
57 the threshing drum (threshing cylinder)
58 the beater
59 the concave
60 the grate (grating, grid)
61 the straw conveyor
62 the straw-shaker
63 the separator check flap
64 the grain conveyor (return conveyor)
65 the caving riddle (caving screen)
66 the grain collector
67 the winnower
68 the screw (auger) to the hummeller [second dressing]
69 the ear elevator screw (ear elevator auger)
70 the straw feeder
71 the straw press
72 the steering axle
73 the gear

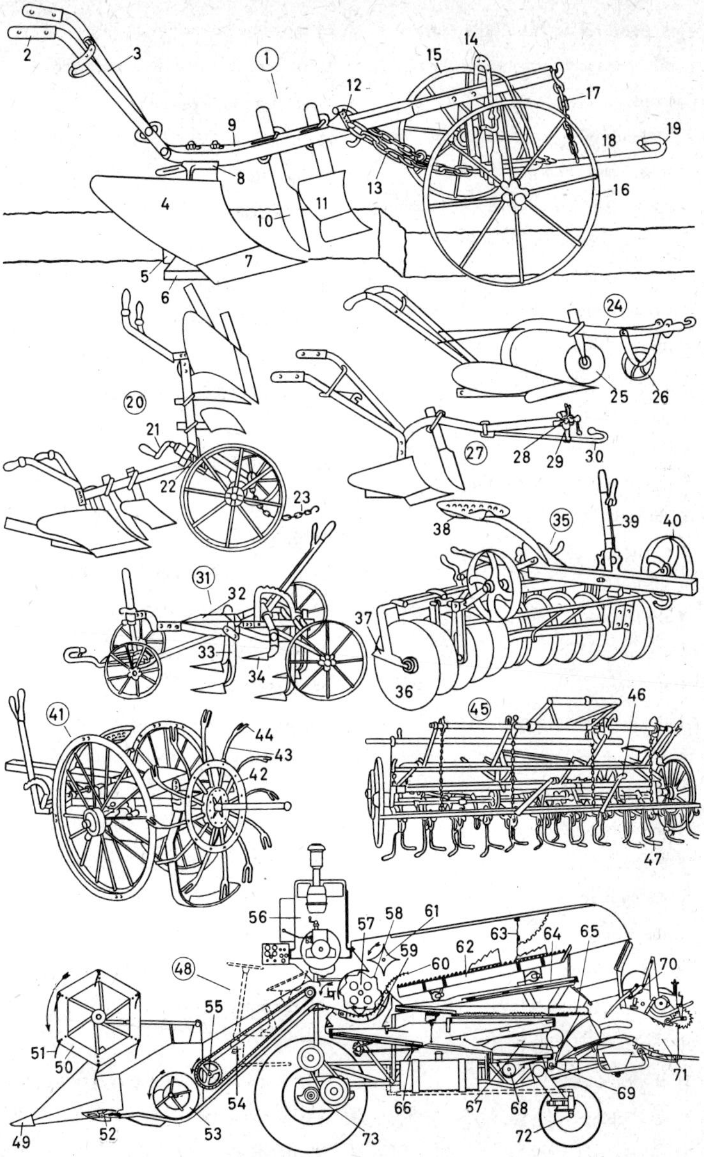
1
2
3
4
5
6
7
8
9
10
11
12
13
14
15
16
17
18
19
20
21
22
23
24
25
26
27
28
29
30
31
32
33
34
35
36
37
38
39
40
41
42
43
44
45
46
47
48
49
50
51
52
53
54
55
56
57
58
59
60
61
62
63
64
65
66
67
68
69
70
71
72
73

1-45 produce of the fields (agricultural products, farm products, farm crops),

1–37 kinds of grain (grain, cereals, bread corn, farinaceous plants, corn),

1 the rye (*also:* corn, 'corn' often meaning leading bread corn; in Northern Germany: wheat, in Sweden and Norway: barley, in Italy and North America: maize, in China: rice):

2 the ear of rye, a spike (ear)

3 the spikelet

4 the ergot, a grain deformed by a fungus;

5 the corn stem after tillering:

6 the stalk

7 the node

8 the leaf

9 the leaf sheath (sheath);

10 the spikelet:

11 the glume

12 the awn (beard, arista)

13 the seed (grain, kernel, flour-yielding grain, farinaceous grain);

14 the embryo plant:

15 the seed

16 the embryo

17 the root

18 the root hairs;

19 the corn leaf:

20 the leaf blade (blade, lamina)

21 the leaf sheath

22 the ligule;

23 the wheat

24 the common spelt or dinkel:

25 the seed (kernel); *immature*: green spelt, a soup vegetable;

26 the barley

27 the oats

28 the millet

29 the rice:

30 the rice grain;

31 the maize (Indian corn, *Am.* corn; *in South Africa :* mealies; *kinds :* popcorn, dent corn or horse-tooth, flint corn, pod corn, soft corn, sweet corn):

32 the female inflorescence

33 the husks

34 the pistil

35 the male inflorescence (tassel);

36 the maize cob (corn cob)

37 the maize kernel (grain of maize);

38–45 root crops,

38 the potato plant (potato), a tuberous (bulbiferous, bulbous) plant; *kinds :* the round, round-oval (pear-shaped), flat-oval, long, kidney-shaped, potato; *according to colour:* the white (*Am.* Irish), yellow, red, purple, potato:

39 the seed potato (seed tuber)

40 the potato tuber (potato, tuber; *fam.* spud)

41 the potato foliage

42 the flower

43 the inedible potato berry, a fruit;

44 the sugar beet, a beetroot:

45 the root (beet)

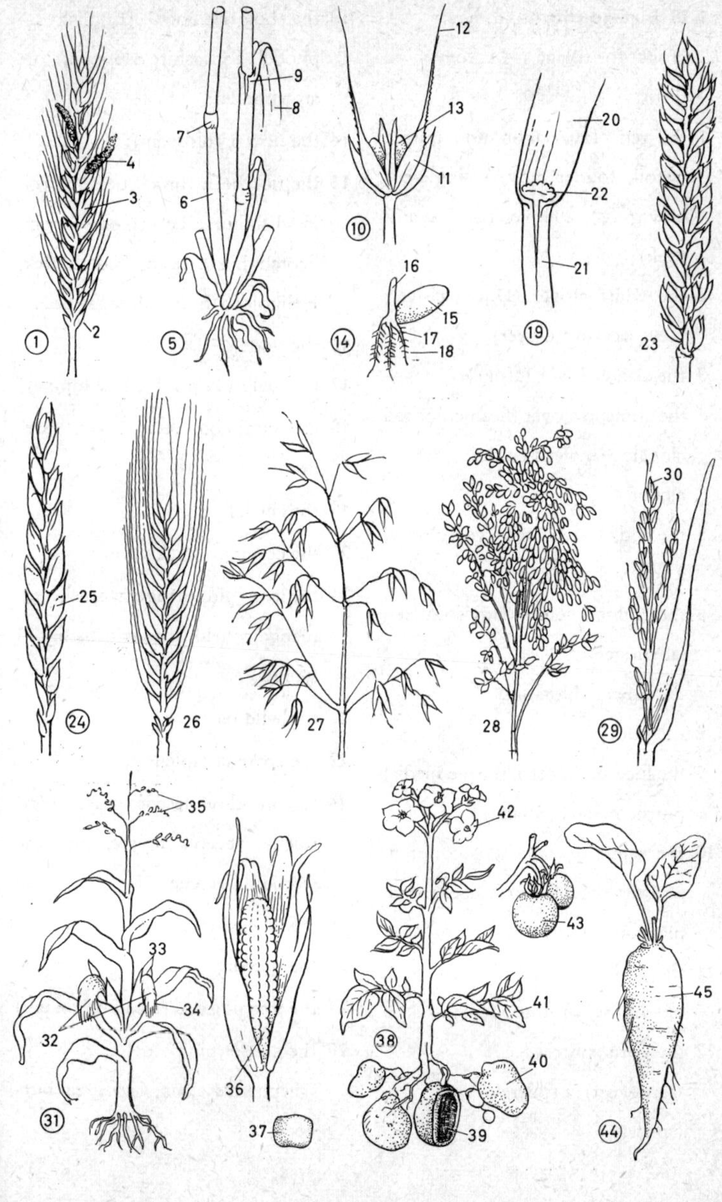
1
2
3
4
5
6
7
8
9
10
11
12
13
14
15
16
17
18
19
20
21
22
23
24
25
26
27
28
29
30
31
32
33
34
35
36
37
38
39
40
41
42
43
44
45

1-28 forage plants (forage crops) for tillage (*Am.* for tilth):

1 the red clover (common purple trefoil, fodder clover, single-cut cow grass), a clover (*Irish* shamrock)

2 the white clover (Dutch clover, New Zealand clover)

3 the alsike clover (alsike)

4 the crimson clover (flesh-coloured clover, *Am.* flesh-colored clover):

5 the four-leaf (four-leaved clover, a 'lucky charm');

6 the kidney vetch (lady's-fingers, ladyfinger):

7 the flower (blossom)

8 the pod;

9 the lucerne (lucern, purple medic, purple medick, alfalfa)

10 the sainfoin (saintfoin, common sainfoin, cock's-head, cockshead, plantain, knapweed)

11 the bird's-foot trefoil (bird-foot), one of the Ornithopoda

12 the corn spurrey, (sandwort), a spurrey (spurry)

13 the bog asphodel (English asphodel, Lancashire asphodel), an asphodel:

14 the flower (blossom);

15 the tick bean (broad bean); *sim.* English horse bean (coarse bean, Scotch horse bean, Scotch tick, Heligoland bean, Mazagai bean):

16 the pod;

17 the yellow lupin (yellow lupine)

18 the common vetch (tare, tare-fitch)

19 the chick pea

20 the common buckwheat

21 the mangold (mangel wurzel, mangel, field mangel, mangold wurzel)

22 the wild oat:

23 the spikelet (spicula);

24 the meadow fescue grass (hard fescue, sheep's fescue, meadow fescue), a fescue

25 the cocksfoot grass

26 the quaking grass

27 the foxtail grass (meadow foxtail)

28 the scarlet pimpernel (shepherd's-clock, *form.* great burnet)

70

71 Breeds of Dogs

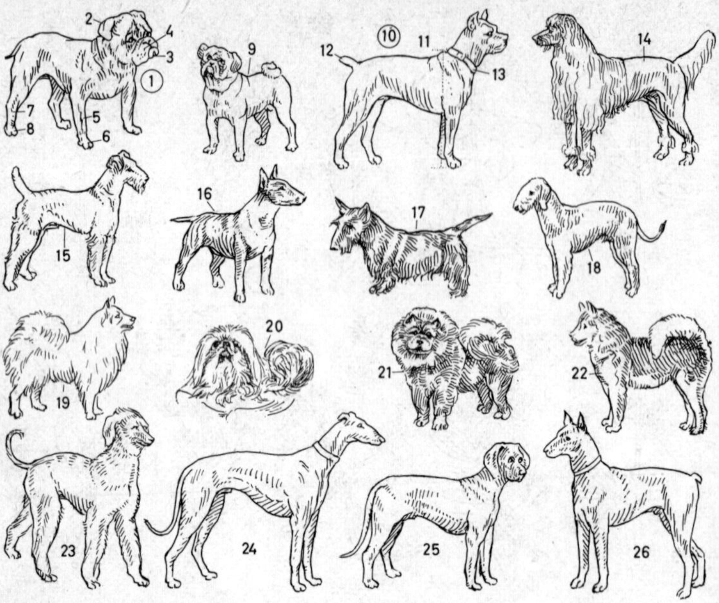

1 the bulldog:

2 the ear

3 the mouth

4 the muzzle

5 the foreleg

6 the fore-paw

7 the hind leg

8 the hind paw;

9 the pug (pug dog)

10 the boxer:

11 the withers

12 the tail (dog's tail), a docked tail;

13 the dog collar

14 the poodle; *sim. and smaller:* miniature poodle

15–18 terriers:

15 the fox terrier (wire-haired terrier)

16 the bull terrier

17 the Scotch terrier (*coll.* Scottie)

18 the Bedlington terrier;

19 the Pomeranian (Pomeranian dog, Spitz, *coll.* Pom)

20 the Pekin[g]ese dog (Pekinese spaniel, Pekinese, Pekingese)

21 the chow (chow-chow)

22 the husky (malamute, malemute, Eskimo dog)

23 the Afghan
24 the greyhound
25 the tracking hound
26 the Doberman terrier
27–30 the dog's outfit:
27 the muzzle
28 the dog brush
29 the dog comb
30 the lead (dog lead, leash), *in hunting:* leash;
31 the Alsatian (Alsatian wolf-dog, wolf dog, German sheep-dog), a police and watch dog:
32 the flews (chaps);
33 the dachshund (badger dog, badgerer, a badger-baiter)
34 the Great Dane
35 the bone
36 the dog bowl
37 the wire-haired German terrier (schnauzer)
38 the St. Bernard (St. Bernard dog)
39 the Newfoundland dog
40–43 hunting dogs (sporting dogs):
40 the German pointer
41 the setter (English setter), a setter
42 the cocker spaniel
43 the pointer, a tracking dog

1-6 horsemanship (the art of riding, High School Riding, Haute Ecole, equitation, equestrianism; riding on trained, or schooled, horses):

1 the piaffer (Spanish walk)
2 the walk (short pace)
3 the passage
4 the levade
5 the capriole
6 the courbette;

7-25 the harness (horse's harness, collar harness),

7–13 and 25 the bridle (head gear),
7–11 the headstall (headpiece, halter):
7 the nose band
8 the cheek straps (cheek piece)
9 the frontlet (brow band)
10 the headband (head strap, crown piece)
11 the throat latch (throat lash, throat band);
12 the curb chain
13 the curb bit;
14 the hook of the hame (*Am.* drag hook)
15 the horse collar (collar, hames), a pointed horse collar
16 the trappings (side trappings)
17 the pad (back pad, harness pad, saddle)
18 the belly band (girth)
19 the backband
20 the shaft chain
21 the shaft (thill, pole)
22 the trace
23 the second (emergency) belly band
24 the trace
25 the reins (driving reins, *Am.* line);

26-36 the breast harness:

26 the blinker (winker, *Am.* blinder, blinders)
27 the breast collar ring
28 the breast collar
29 the fork
30 the neck strap
31 the pad (back pad, harness pad, saddle)
32 the croup (croupon, croupe, crupper) strap
33 the reins (driving reins, *Am.* line)
34 the croup (croupe, crupper) dock (loop)
35 the trace
36 the belly band;

37-49 saddles (riding saddles),

37–44 the stock saddle:
37 the saddle seat
38 the horn (saddle bow, pommel)
39 the cantle (hind bow)
40 the flap
41 the bars (parts of the saddle tree)
42 the stirrup leather (stirrup strap)
43 the stirrup (iron)
44 the saddle blanket (horse blanket);
45–49 the pad (pad saddle):
45 the seat
46 the pommel
47 the flap
48 the roll (knee roll)
49 the pad;

50 and 51 spurs with rowels:

50 the screwed jack spur
51 the strapped jack spur;
52 the port bit (port mouth, bit)
53 the gag bit (gag)
54 the curry comb
55 the horse brush (body brush)

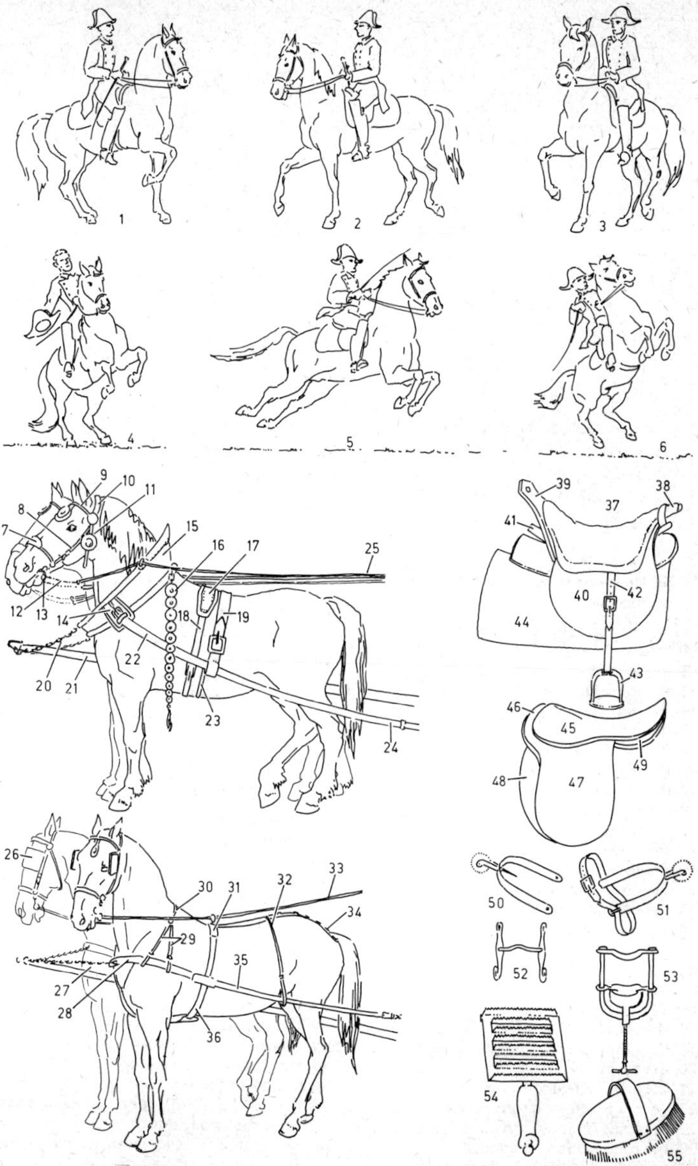
1
2
3
4
5
6
7
8
9
10
11
12
13
14
15
16
17
18
19
20
21
22
23
24
25
26
27
28
29
30
31
32
33
34
35
36
37
38
39
40
41
42
43
44
45
46
47
48
49
50
51
52
53
54
55

73 The Horse II

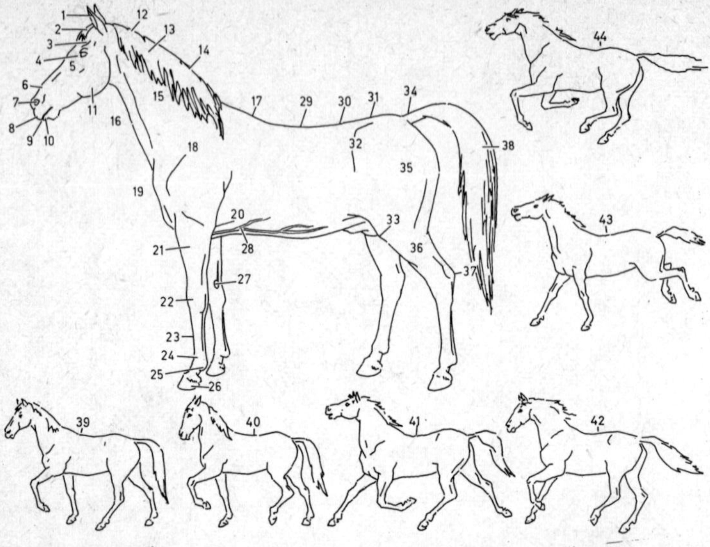

1-38 the points of the horse (exterior of the horse),

1–11 the head (horse's head):
1 the ear
2 the forelock
3 the forehead
4 the eye
5 the face
6–10 the muzzle:
6 the nose
7 the nostril
8 the upper lip
9 the mouth
10 the under lip;
11 the lower jaw;
12 the crest (neck)
13 the mane (horse's mane)
14 the crest (horse's crest)
15 the neck
16 the throat (windpipe)
17 the withers
18–27 the fore hand:
18 the shoulder (shoulder blade)
19 the point of shoulder and chest (breast)
20 the elbow
21 the arm (forearm)
22–26 the forefoot (front foot):
22 the knee (carpus, wrist)
23 the cannon bone (cannon)
24 the fetlock (pastern joint)
25 the pastern (*coll.* fetlock; *the lowest part:* coronet)
26 the hoof (foot);
27 the chestnut (castor), a callosity;
28 the spur vein
29 the back (horseback)
30 the loins (lumbar region)
31 the croup (horse's croupe, crupper, rump)
32 the hip
33–37 the hind leg:
33 the stifle (stifle bone, horse's knee pan, horse's knee cap)
34 the root of the tail or dock
35–37 the hind quarter:
35 the quarters (haunch)
36 the gaskin (second thigh)
37 the point of the hock or hough;
38 the tail (horsetail);

39-44 the gaits of the horse:

39 the walk
40 the pace (amble)
41 the trot
42 the canter (hand gallop)
43 and **44** the full gallop:
43 the gallop at the moment of descent onto the two forefeet
44 the gallop at the moment when the four feet are off the ground

Abbr.: *m.* = male, *c.* = castrated, *f.* = female, *y.* = the young animal.

1 and 2 great cattle (*Am.* stock):

1 the cow (*f.*), a bovine animal, a horned animal, a ruminant; *meat:* beef; *m.* bull (*y.* and *c.* bullock); *c.* ox; *f.* cow; *y.* calf (*m.* bull calf, *f.* cow calf, heifer); *meat:* veal

2 the horse; *m.* stallion (sire, stud horse); *c.* gelder (gelding); *f.* mare (*as a mother:* dam); *y.* foal (*m. usually:* colt, *f.* filly);

3 the donkey (domestic ass, *Scotch* cuddy, cuddie); *m.* he-ass (jackass); *f.* she-ass (jenny-ass); *as a beast of burden (sumpter animal):* packass; *y.* ass foal:

4 the pack saddle (carrying saddle)

5 the pack (burden, load)

6 the tufted tail

7 the tuft;

8 the mule, a hybrid (cross) between a male ass and a mare

9 the domestic pig (pig, hog, swine), a bristle-bearing (setiferous) animal, a cloven-hoofed animal (artiodactyl); *meat*: pork; *m.* boar; *c.* hog; *f.* sow; *y.* piglet (sucking pig; *older*, *Am.* shote, shoat):

10 the pig's snout (snout)

11 the pig's ear

12 the curly tail;

13 the sheep; *meat*: mutton; *m.* ram (tup); *c.* wether; *f.* ewe; *y.* lamb

14 the goat:

15 the goat's beard;

16 the domestic dog, a Leonberg; *m.* dog; *f.* bitch (she-dog, lady-dog); *y.* pup (puppy, whelp)

17 the cat (puss, pussy-cat, domestic cat), an Angora (Persian) cat; *m.* tom (tom cat); *y.* kitten

18–36 small domestic animals:

18 the domestic (tame) rabbit; *m.* buck; *f.* doe; *y.* baby rabbit

19–36 fowls (poultry),

19–26 chicken (domestic fowl),

19 the hen:

20 the crop (craw);

21 the cock (*Am.* rooster); *y.* cockerel; *c.* capon:

22 the comb (cockscomb, crest, caruncle)

23 the lappet (ear lobe)

24 the wattle (gill, dewlap)

25 the sickle-shaped tail (cock's tail)

26 the spur;

27 the guinea fowl; *f.* guinea-hen (pearl hen)

28 the turkey cock (gobbler); *f.* turkey hen:

29 the fan tail;

30 the peacock; *f.* peahen:

31 the peacock's feather

32 the eye (eyelet, ocellus, ocellate spot);

33 the domestic pigeon (dove); *m.* cock pigeon; *y.* squeaker (squab)

34 the domestic goose; *m.* gander; *y.* gosling

35 the domestic duck; *m.* drake; *y.* duckling:

36 the web of the webbed foot

1-46 poultry farming (breeding and rearing of poultry, keeping of fowls, *Am.* raising of poultry),

1 the laying house (laying shed):
2 the hopper window
3 the pop hole
4 the chicken ladder
5 the trap-nest stand
6 the nesting box;
7 the poultry farmer (*Am.* poultry raiser)
8 the self-feed hopper (automatic poultry feeder, hopper, self-feeder, feeder)
9 the cock (*Am.* rooster)
10 the sun shelter
11 the poultry farmer (*Am.* poultry raiser)
12 the lamp post
13 the hen house(poultry house):
14 the perch
15 the dropping board
16 the scratching ground (scratching space);
17 the broody hen (sitting hen)
18 the chicken run (poultry yard, *Am.* chicken yard, chicken run)
19 the green-stuff silo or silage
20 the hen (*loosely* chicken)
21 the dust bath
22 the trough for dry food
23 the wire netting
24 the post
25 the wire gate
26 the automatic door catch (door lock, self-locking catch)
27 the brooder house:
28 the canopied (cowled) brooder (foster mother)
29 the litter (peat-moss litter)
30 the incubator
31 the pop hole
32 the sliding door;
33 the chick
34 the chick trough
35 the watering pail
36 the egg carton (egg box) for transport (*Am.* for transportation)
37 the watering trough
38 the chick hopper
39 the egg-grader (egg-sorting machine) and egg-weigher
40 the chick box
41 the food-cutter (green-stuff cutter)
42 the leg ring
43 the fowl tally (wing tally, identification tally)
44 the bantam
45 the laying hen
46 the ovoscope (egg-testing lamp, egg-tester, egg lamp);

47 the hen's egg (egg):
48 the egg shell, an egg integument
49 the shell membrane (skin, membrana putaminis)
50 the air space
51 the albumen (white of egg)
52 the chalaza(albuminous substance)
53 the vitelline membrane (yolk sac, yolk bag)
54 the germinal disk or disc (blastodisc, blastoderm, cock's tread, cock's treadle)
55 the germinal vesicle (cicatricula, cicatricle, cicatricule)
56 the white
57 the yolk

1
2
3
4
5
6
7
8
9
10
11
12
13
14
15
16
17
18
19
20
21
22
23
24
25
26
27
28
29
30
31
32
33
34
35
36
37
38
39
40
41
42
43
44
45
46
47
48
49
50
51
52
53
54
55
56
57

Engl. rearing of livestock = *Am.* raising of stock

1-16 the stable:

1 the stable lantern, a hand lantern
2 the hay rack (rack)
3 the manger
4 the horse chain
5 the horse
6 the horse collar
7 the horse stall (stall, single box, horse box, box)
8 the horse droppings (horse manure)
9 the bundle of straw (straw bundle)
10 the stable boy (*Am.* cattleman, *on the range:* wrangler)
11 the bucket yoke (yoke)
12 the straw litter (litter)
13 the pitchfork
14 the suspended cross bar (suspended cross beam)
15 the veterinary surgeon (*pop.* vet, *Am.* veterinarian)
16 the storm lantern, a paraffin lantern (*Am.* kerosene lamp);

17-38 the cowshed (cattle shed, cow house, byre):

17 the dairymaid (milkmaid)
18 the cow:
19 the udder
20 the teat;
21 the liquid-manure gutter
22 the cow droppings (cow dung), excrement
23–29 the milking machine (automatic milking plant):
23 the teat cup (teat cup cluster) with milk and air tube
24 the milk line
25 the pulsator
26 the milk pail
27 the motor
28 the vacuum pump
29 the vacuum gauge (*Am.* vacuum gage);
30 the cleaning and milking passage
31 the cow chain
32 the manger
33 the feeding passage
34 the milk churn
35 the automatic trough:
36 the trough
37 the trough lid;
38 the cow horn;

39-47 the pigsties (sties, *Am.* hogpen):

39 the piglet creep
40 the piglet (*older, Am.* shote, shoat)
41 the sty
42 the sow
43 the feeding trough (swill trough, pig trough)
44 the liquid-manure drain
45 the liquid-manure gutter or gully or channel
46 the pig creep door
47 the dung barrow, a wheelbarrow (*Am.* pushcart)

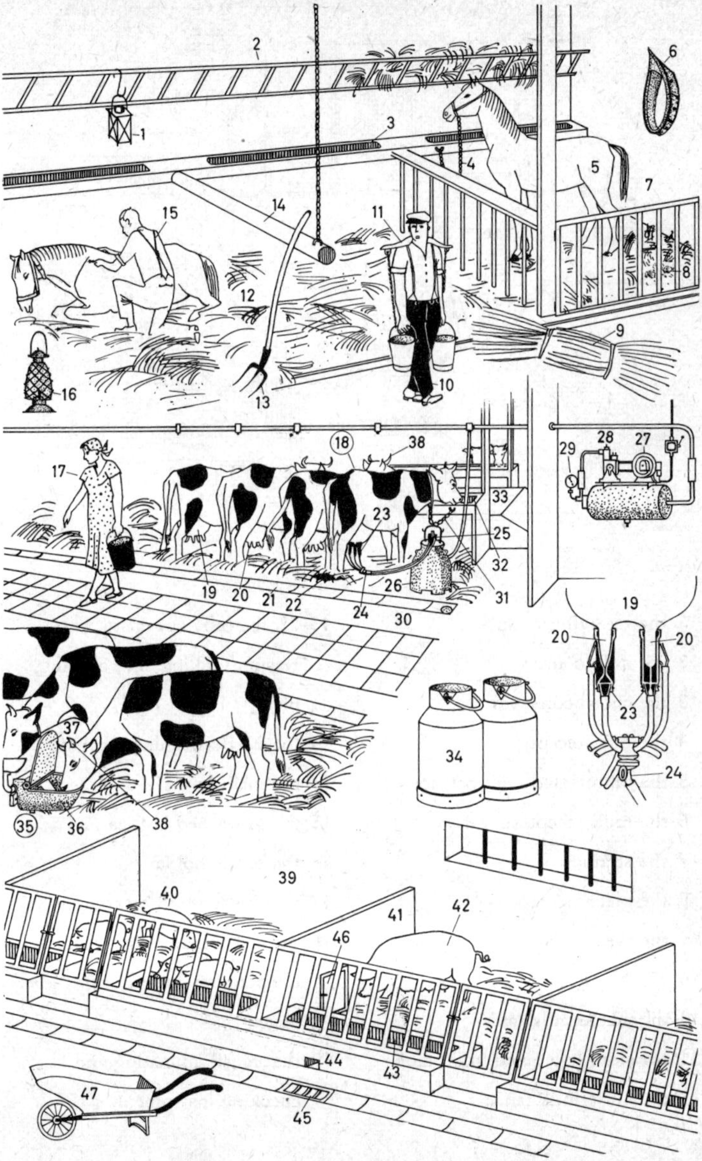
1
2
3
4
5
6
7
8
9
10
11
12
13
14
15
16
17
18
19
20
21
22
23
24
25
26
27
28
29
30
31
32
33
34
35
36
37
38
39
40
41
42
43
44
45
46
47

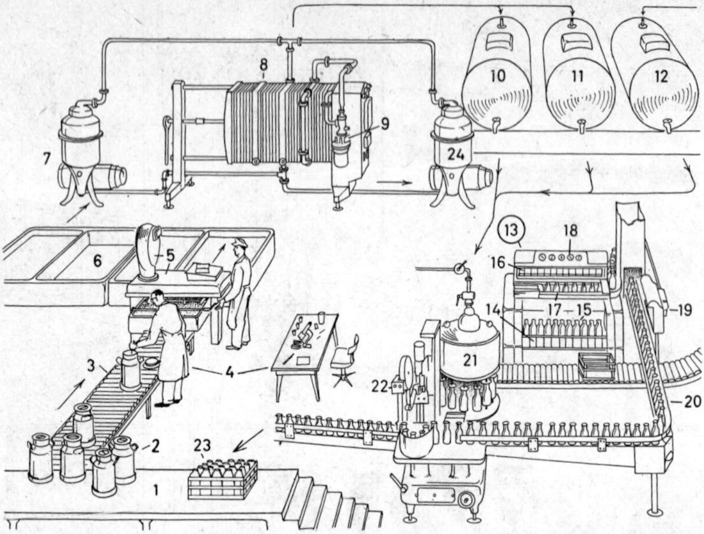

1 the receiving ramp

2 the milk churn

3 the churn conveyor

4 the milk reception

5 the illuminated milk balance

6 the milk reception vat

7 the strainer

8 the plate-heater

9 the thermostat

10–12 the milk storage tanks:

10 the whole milk tank

11 the skim (skimmed) milk tank

12 the buttermilk tank;

13–22 the fully automatic bottle-washing, filling, and capping, plant,

13 the bottle-washing machine:

14 the loading shelf

15 the unwashed bottles

16 the bottle-holder

17 the washed-bottle extractor

18 the instrument panel (gauges for temperature and pressure, *Am.* gages);

19 the transilluminating and checking instrument

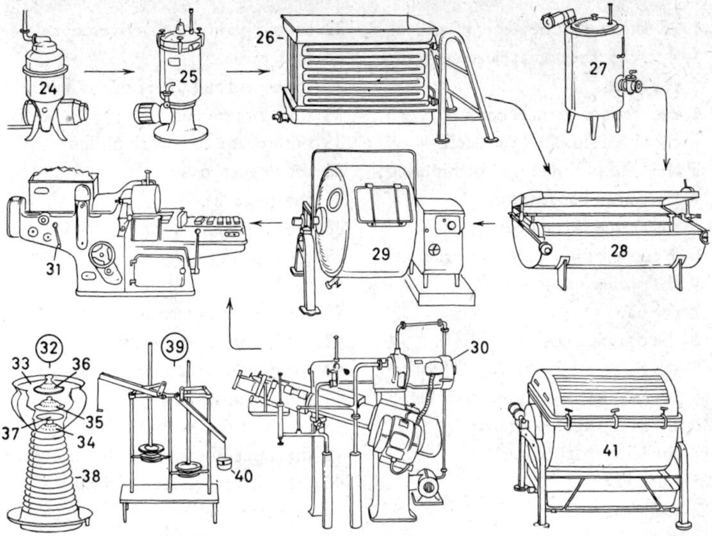

20 the bottle conveyor belt
21 the filling machine
22 the closing machine;
23 the milk-bottle crate
24 the cream-separator
25 the centrifugal cream-heater
26 the cream-cooler, a solid cooler
27 the acidifying apparatus
28 the cream-maturing vat
29 the churn, a churn for sour-cream butter
30 the butter churn
31 the butter-shaping and packing machine
32 the fresh-milk cooler:
33 the supply can [section]
34 the fine sieve
35 the medium sieve
36 the coarse sieve
37 the cotton disk or disc
38 the cooler;
39 the screw cheese-press:
40 the weights;
41 the cream-cheese machine

78 Bees and Beekeeping (Bee Culture, Apiculture)

1–25 the bee (honey-bee, hive-bee),
1, 4, and 5 the social classes among the bees,
1 the worker (female bee):
2 the three simple eyes (ocelli)
3 the load of pollen on the hind leg;
4 the queen bee (queen)
5 the drone (male bee);
6–9 the left hind leg of a worker:
6 the pollen-basket
7 the hairs
8 the double claw
9 the suctorial pad;
10–19 the abdomen (hind body) of the worker,
10–14 the stinging organs:
10 the barb (barbed dart)
11 the sting
12 the sting sheath
13 the poison sac
14 the poison gland;
15–19 the stomachic-intestinal canal:
15 the intestine
16 the stomach
17 the contractile muscle or tissue
18 the honey bag
19 the oesophagus (esophagus, gullet);
20–24 the compound eye (insect eye):
20 the facet
21 the crystal cone
22 the sensitive section
23 the fibre (*Am.* fiber) of the visual nerve
24 the visual (optic) nerve;
25 the small wax scale;
26–30 the cell (bee cell):
26 the egg
27 the cell with egg in it
28 the maggot-like larva
29 the larva
30 the pupa;
31–43 the honeycomb:
31 the brood cell
32 the capped (closed, covered) cell with pupa
33 the sealed cell with honey (honey cell)
34 the worker cells
35 the storage cells with pollen
36 the drones' cells
37 the queen's cell
38 the queen emerging
39 the cap
40 the frame
41 the distance piece
42 the artificial honeycomb
43 the pressed-in comb foundation;
44 the queen's transport box
45–50 the wooden beehive:
45 the super-hive with the honeycombs
46 the brood chamber with the breeding combs
47 the queen-excluder
48 the entrance
49 the flight (alighting) board
50 the window;
51 an oldfashioned bee shed:
52 the straw hive (skep, skip);
53 the swarm of bees
54 the swarming net
55 the hooked pole
56 a modern apiary (bee house)
57 the beekeeper (apiarist, bee man):
58 the bee veil
59 the bee smoker;
60 the natural honeycomb
61 the honey extractor (honey separator)
62 and 63 the strained honey (honey):
62 the honey pail
63 the honey jar;
64 the honey in the comb
65 the wax taper
66 the wax candle
67 the block of wax (beeswax)
68 the bee poison ointment

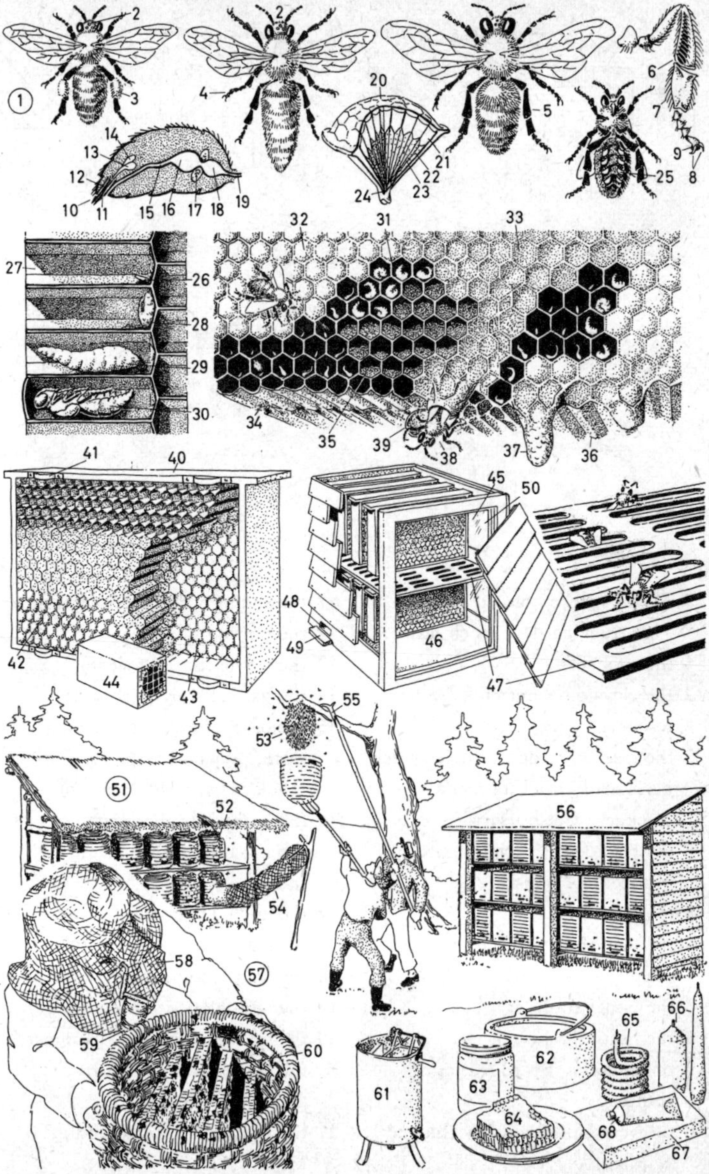
1
2
2
3
4
5
6
7
8
9
10
11
12
13
14
15
16
17
18
19
20
21
22
23
24
25
26
27
28
29
30
31
32
33
34
35
36
37
38
39
40
41
42
43
44
45
46
47
48
49
50
51
52
53
54
55
56
57
58
59
60
61
62
63
64
65
66
67
68

79 The Nursery Garden (Nursery)

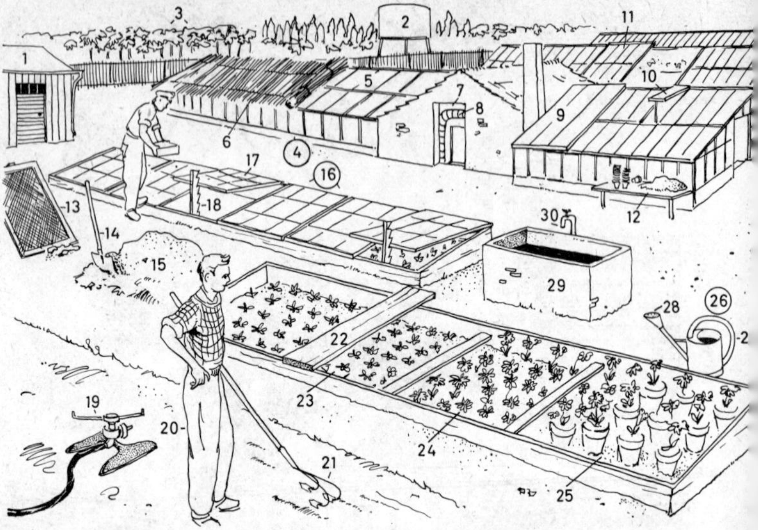

1–51 the market garden (nursery, *Am.* truck garden, truck farm):

1 the tool shed

2 the elevated water tank (water reservoir)

3 the market gardener's (*Am.* truck gardener's, truck farmer's, trucker's) tree nursery

4 the hothouse (forcing house, propagating house):

5 the glass roof

6 the roll of matting (straw mat, shader)

7 the boiler room

8 the heating pipe

9 the covering board (covering shutter)

10 the ventilation window (hinged ventilator)

11 the sliding ventilation window;

12 the potting table

13 the riddle (upright sieve)

14 the garden shovel (shovel)

15 the heap of earth (compost earth, prepared earth, garden mould, *Am.* mold; manure)

16 the hotbed (hotbed frame, forcing bed, garden frame, frame):

17 the hotbed window (frame window)

18 the ventilating prop;

19 the sprinkler (watering device)

20 the gardener (nursery gardener, market gardener, *Am.* truck gardener, trucker)

21 the hand cultivator (hand grubber)

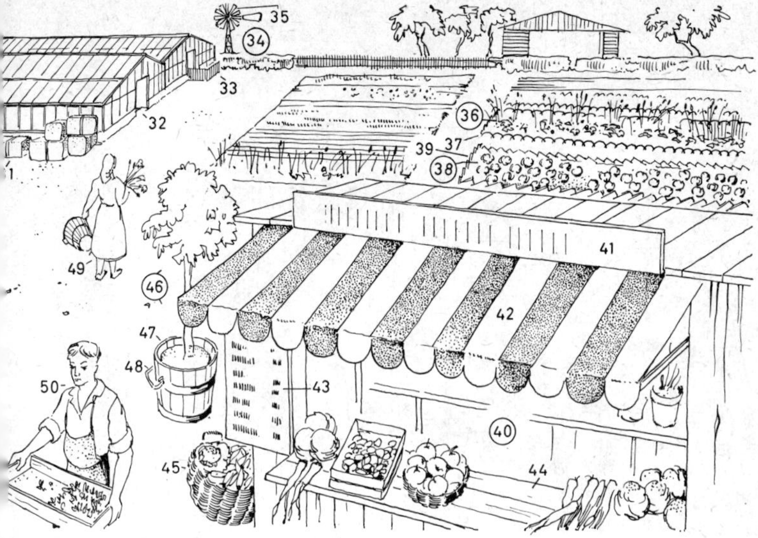

22 the plank to stand and walk on
23 pricked seedlings (pricked-out, pricked-off, seedlings)
24 forced flowers [forcing]
25 potted plants (plants in pots, pot plants)
26 the watering can (*Am.* sprinkling can):
27 the handle
28 the rose;
29 the water tank
30 the water pipe
31 the bale of peat dust (pressed peat, *Am.* peat moss)
32 the intermediate house
33 the cold-house (greenhouse), a pit house
34 the windmill motor:
35 the wind wheel;
36 the flower bed:
37 the hoop edging;
38 the vegetable bed:
39 the brick edging;
40 the vegetable stall:
41 the signboard (facia)
42 the awning
43 the board with the prices of the garden produce (*Am.* of the truck produce)
44 the shop counter (counter);
45 the basket for delivering vegetables, a vegetable basket
46 the tub plant:
47 the plant tub
48 the handle;
49 the woman gardener
50 the assistant gardener (under-gardener, *Am.* garden hand)
51 the seedling box

1–20 the wine-growing district:

1 the vineyard during the vintage

2 the wine-grower's cottage (vineyard owner's cottage, vineyard cottage)

3–6 the vine plant (vine, *Am.* grape-vine):

3 the shoot

4 the vine tendril

5 the vine leaf

6 the grapes (cluster of grapes, bunch of grapes);

7 the stake (post)

8 the tub for gathering the grapes

9 the female grape-gatherer at the vintage in the grape-harvest season

10 the pruning knife (pruning hook)

11 the vine-grower (vine-dresser, viniculturist, viticulturist)

12 the wooden dosser

13 the transport cask

14 the vineyard boy, pouring in the crushed grapes

15 the vat with the crushed grapes

16 the wine press (grape press)

17 the stone jug (stone jar)

18 the vintager
19 the wayside crucifix
20 the ruin (ruins, castle ruin);
21 the wine cellar (wine storage cellar, wine vaults):
22 the vault
23 the wine cask (wine barrel)
24 the wine tank (wine container)
25 bottling the wine
26 the bottling apparatus
27 the corking machine:
28 the cork compresser;
29 the wine cork, a bottle cork
30 the wine jug
31 the bottle cellar:
32 the bins
33 the wine bottle
34 the bottle basket
35 the cellarer's assistant;
36 wine-tasting:
37 the wine cask (wine barrel)
38 the pipette
39 the cellarman
40 the wine-taster, a wine connoisseur;
41 the wine-press shed:
42 the hydraulic wine press (grape press)
43 the press vat
44 the wheeled vat truck
45 the grape juice

81 Garden and Field Pests

1–19 fruit pests,
1 the gipsy moth (gypsy moth):
2 the egg batch (cluster of eggs)
3 the caterpillar
4 the chrysalis (cocoon);
5 the small ermine moth:
6 the larva
7 the web tent
8 the caterpillar skeletonizing the leaf;
9 the fruit surface eating tortrix moth (summer fruit tortrix moth)
10 the apple blossom weevil:
11 the capped blossom
12 the egg-laying hole;
13 the lackey moth:
14 the caterpillar
15 the eggs;
16 the winter moth:
17 the caterpillar;
18 the cherry fruit fly:
19 the maggot (larva);
20–27 vine pests,
20 the downy mildew, a disease causing leaf fall:
21 the mildew on grape fruits;
22 the grape moth :
23 the caterpillar of the 1st generation
24 the caterpillar of the 2nd generation
25 the chrysalis (pupa);
26 the root louse, a vine louse:
27 the root gall;
28 the brown-tail moth:
29 the caterpillar (larva)
30 the egg batch
31 the hibernation cocoon ('tent');
32 the woolly aphid:
33 the gall caused by the woolly aphid
34 the woolly aphid colony;
35 the San-José scale, a scale insect:
36 the adult scale insects;
37–55 field pests,
37 the click beetle, a snapping beetle:
38 the wireworm, a larva;
39 the turnip flea beetle
40 the Hessian fly, a gall midge:
41 the maggot (larva);
42 the turnip moth, an earth moth:
43 the chrysalis (pupa)
44 the cutworm, a caterpillar;
45 the carrion beetle:
46 the larva;
47 the large cabbage white butterfly:
48 the caterpillar of the small cabbage white butterfly;
49 the brown leaf-eating weevil, one of the Curculionidae:
50 the feeding site;
51 the beet eelworm, a nematode
52 the Colorado beetle (potato beetle):
53 the mature grub (larva)
54 the young grub (young larva)
55 the eggs

81

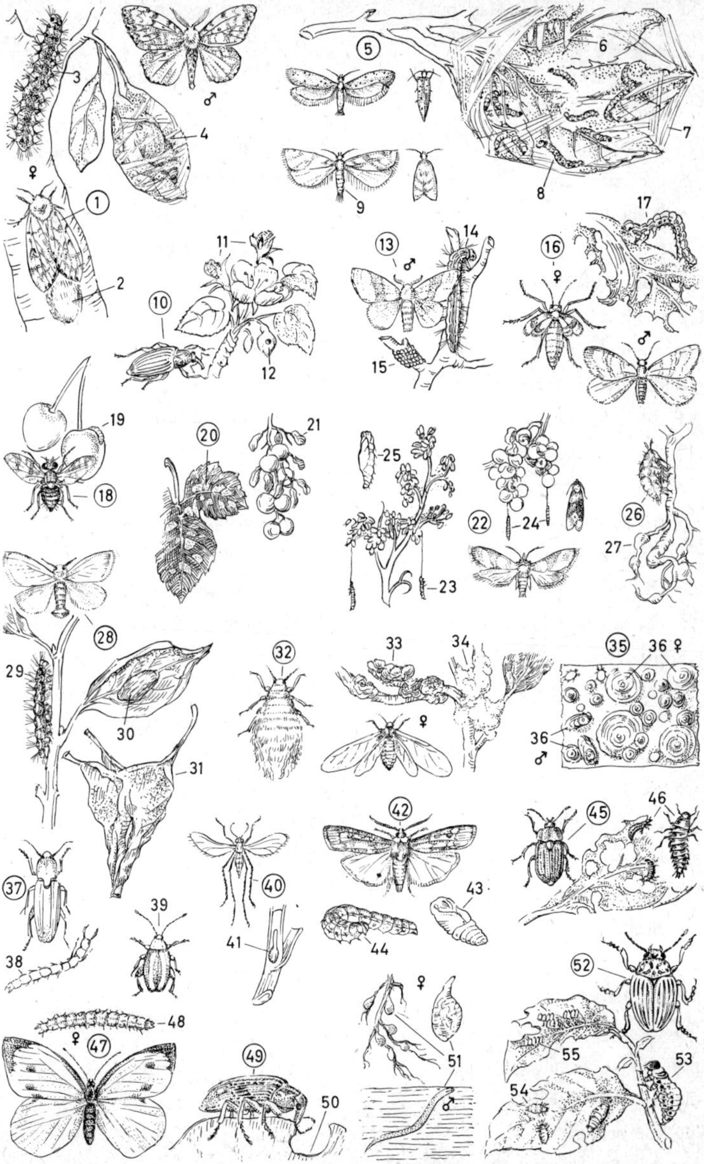

1
2
3
4
♀
♂
5
6
7
8
9
10
11
12
13
♂
14
15
16
♀
17
♂
18
19
20
21
22
23
24
25
26
27
28
29
30
31
32
33
♀
34
35
36 ♀
36
♂
37
38
39
40
41
42
43
44
45
46
47
♀
48
49
50
51
♀
♂
52
53
54
55

1 the cockchafer (May bug), a Melolontha:
2 the head
3 the antenna (feeler)
4 the prothorax
5 the scutellum
6–8 the legs:
6 the front leg
7 the middle leg
8 the hind leg;
9 the abdomen
10 the elytron (wing cover)
11 the membranous wing
12 the cockchafer grub, a larva
13 the pupa (chrysalis)
14 the processionary moth, a nocturnal moth:
15 the moth
16 the caterpillars marching in procession;
17 the black arches moth (nun moth):
18 the moth
19 the eggs
20 the caterpillar (larva)
21 the cocoon;
22 the typographical beetle, a bark beetle,
23 and **24** the galleries under the bark:
23 the egg gallery
24 the larval gallery;
25 the larva (grub)
26 the beetle;
27 the pine hawk-moth, a hawk-moth
28 the bordered white moth (pine moth):
29 the male moth
30 the female moth
31 the caterpillar (pine looper)
32 the pupa (chrysalis);
33 the cherry gall wasp, a gall wasp:
34 the gall
35 the gall wasp
36 the larva (grub) in the larval chamber;
37 the beech leaf gall
38 the spruce gall aphid:
39 the winged aphid
40 the pineapple gall;
41 the pine weevil:
42 the beetle (weevil);
43 the green oak tortrix, a leafroller:
44 the caterpillar (larva)
45 the moth;
46 the pine beauty moth:
47 the caterpillar (larva)
48 the moth

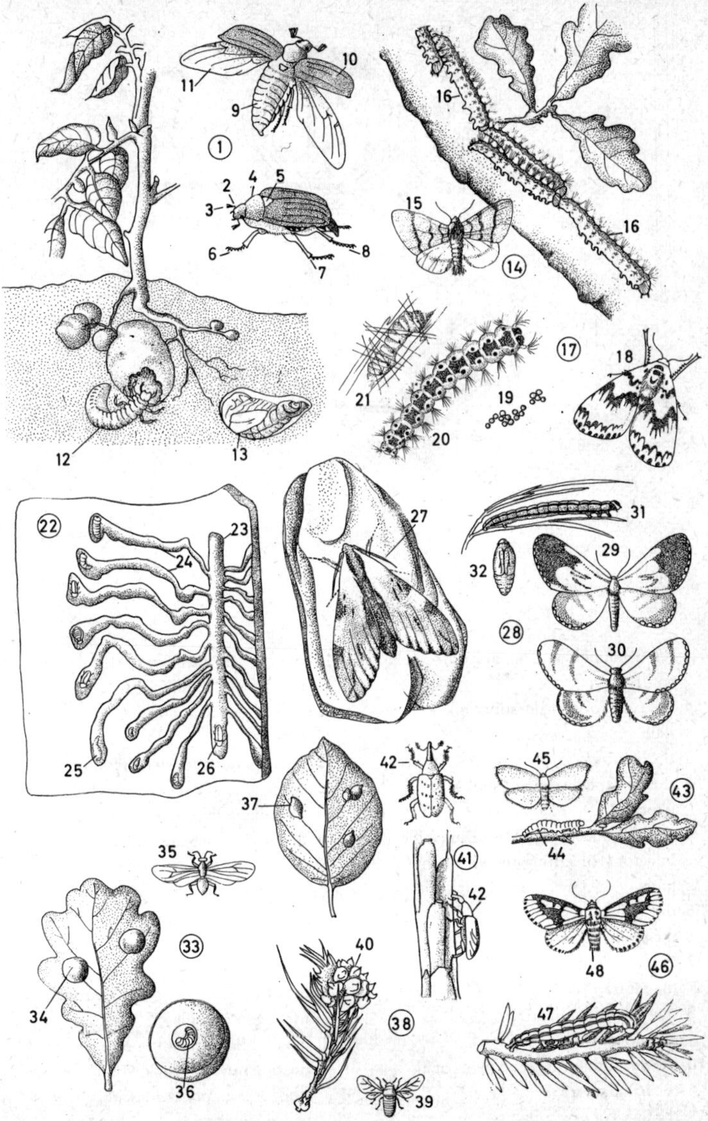

1
2
3
4
5
6
7
8
9
10
11
12
13
14
15
16
16
17
18
19
20
21
22
23
24
25
26
27
28
29
30
31
32
33
34
35
36
37
38
39
40
41
42
42
43
44
45
46
47
48

83 Pest Control and Plant Protection

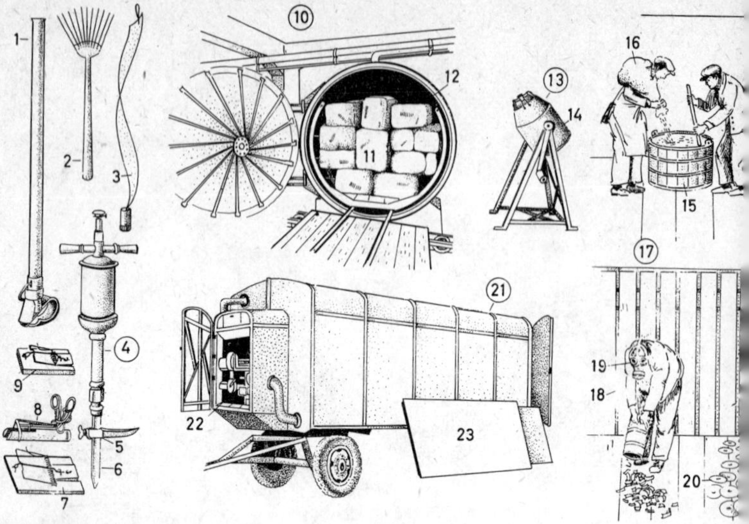

1–48 machinery and apparatus for pest control:

1 the tube for broadcasting poisoned bait

2 the fly swat

3 the fly paper, a strip of sticky paper

4 the soil injector (carbon disulphide injector) for killing the vine root louse:

5 the syringe

6 the spray outlet;

7–9 rodent traps:

7 the rat trap

8 the vole and mole trap

9 the mouse trap;

10 the vacuum fumigation plant of a tobacco factory:

11 the bales of raw tobacco

12 the vacuum chamber for the destruction of pests and mildew;

13–16 corn-dressing (cereal-dressing),

13 the apparatus for dry-dressing corn:

14 the mixing drum with the dressing;

15 the tub for wet-dressing corn

16 the sack of corn;

17 the extermination of pests:

18 the pest-exterminator (*form.* rat-catcher)

19 the gas mask

20 the disks (discs) impregnated with hydrogen cyanide;

21 the mobile fumigation chamber for treating nursery stock, young vines, seeds and empty sacks with hydrogen cyanide:

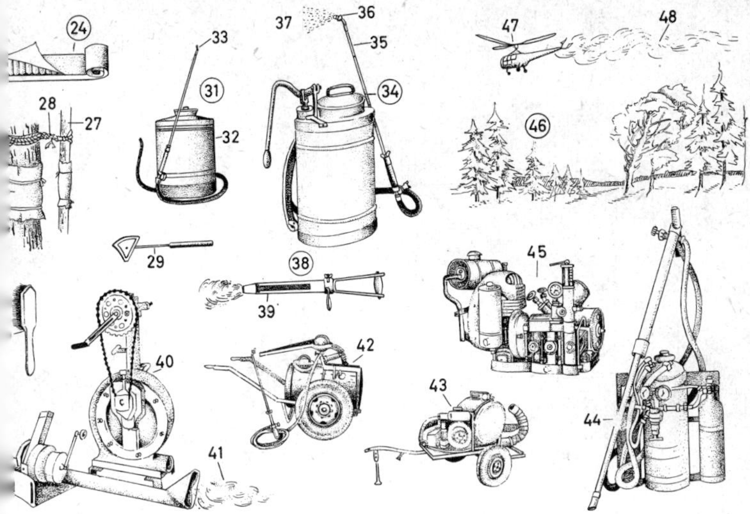

22 the gas circulation unit
23 the tray;
24–45 pest control on fruit trees,
24 the corrugated paper band:
25 the corrugated paper;
26 the sticky band
27 the tree stake
28 the tree tie;
29 the bark-scraper
30 the bark brush
31 the diaphragm knapsack sprayer:
32 the spray tank
33 the nozzle;
34–37 the piston knapsack sprayer, a piston sprayer; *also :* painting gun (paint, or impregnating agent, sprayer),
34 the lance:
35 the extension piece
36 the nozzle;
37 the spray liquid;
38 the fumigating apparatus:
39 the gas cartridge;
40 the poison gas atomiser
41 the insecticidal gas
42 the two-wheeled fruit tree spraying machine
43 the spraying, vaporising, and dusting, machine (motorised spraying machine, motorised vaporising machine, motorised dusting machine)
44 the poison foam apparatus
45 the power spraying machine;
46 forest and plantation protection (insecticide-dusting):
47 the helicopter (*Am.* direct lift machine, copter)
48 the cloud of insecticidal dust

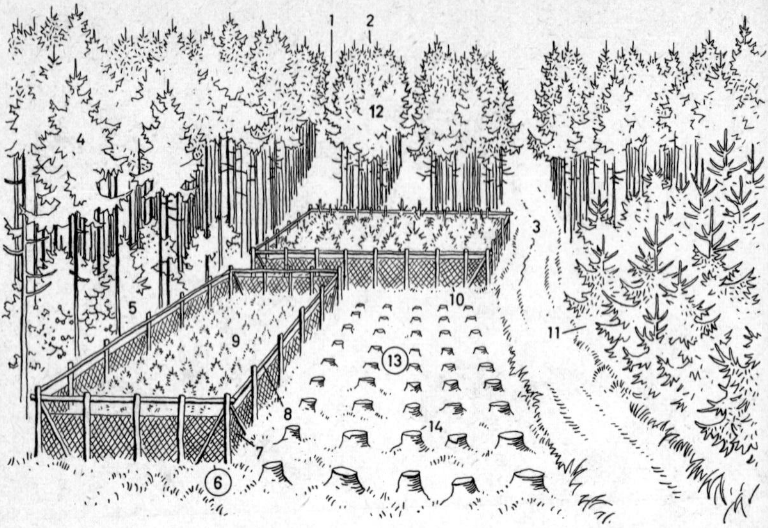

Engl. timber = *Am.* lumber or timber

1–34 the forest, a wood:

1 the ride (aisle, lane, section line, rack)

2 the forest section (compartment)

3 the wood-haulage way, a forest cart track (forest road)

4–14 the clear-felling system:

4 the standing timber, a high forest (mature timber)

5 the underwood (brushwood, shrubbery, underbrush, undergrowth, *Am.* brush)

6 the seedling nursery, a tree nursery:

7 the rabbit fence, a wire netting fence

8 the guard rail

9 the seedlings;

10 and **11** the transplants and the young plantation (saplings):

10 the tree nursery after transplanting

11 the young plantation;

12 the young plantation after clearing of the lower branches

13 the clearing:

14 the stump (stub);

15–34 the felling (cutting, *Am.* logging) and harvesting of wood (*Am. and Can.* lumbering):

15 the pole wagon (timber wagon, *Am. and Can.* lumber car, lumber wagon)

16 the heap (pile) of brushwood (of branchwood)

17 the faggot (*Am.* fagot; bundle of twigs)

18 the forest labourer (woodsman, woodman, *Am.* forest laborer, *Am. and Can.* lumberer, lumberjack, timberjack, lumberman), turning (*Am.* canting) timber

19 the cant hook (peavy)

20 the two-man team (team, *Am.* crew, buckers), sawing (cutting, *Am.* bucking)

21 the tree trunk (stem, bole)

22 the log

23 the annual ring

24 the stack of logs (pile of logs), containing a cubic metre (*Am.* meter) of wood [*in England:* a cord of wood (128 stacked cubic feet)]:

25 the post (stake)

26 the withe;

27 the feller (wood-cutter, *Am.* lumberman, lumberjack), felling

28 the drying rack:

29 the tan bark;

30 the foreman numbering the tree

31 the numbered tree

32 the timber chute (timber slide), a runway:

33 the fender

34 the log sliding down into the valley;

35 the beat forester (*Am.* ranger)

85 Forestry II

Engl. timber = *Am.* lumber or timber; *Engl.* axe = *Am.* ax

1–6 the overland timber haulage (timber transport):
1 the wheeled tractor
2 the timber carriage (timber trailer):
3 the stake
4 the pulley and the cable of the loading winch
5 the ramp
6 the log;
7 the log-walled timber slide (timber chute):
8 the sleeper (bolster)
9 the base logs
10 the fender skid
11 the side log
12 the top log;
13 the felling axe:
14 the handle (helve)
15 the edge (cutting edge)
16 the blade
17 the head
18 the eye;
19 felling with axe and saw:
20 the notch (undercut, kerf, dip, bird's-mouth)
21 the saw cut
22 the buttress (root crotch, toe, spur, claw), chopped-off
23 the wedge, driven in;
24 the felling wedge
25 the barking-iron (bark-scaler, peeling iron) for removing bark
26 the riving hammer (cleaving hammer, splitting hammer)
27 the timber bob (timber-janker) for tushing (hauling, snigging) logs:
28 the crank axle
29 the tongs;
30 the billhook for lopping
31 the lifting hook, a lever
32 the barking-spade (bark spud) for bark-peeling
33 the slide calipers, a measuring tool
34–41 the woodman's saws,
34 the two-handed cross-cut saw:
35 the saw blade
36 the saw tooth
37 the saw handle;
38 the one-man cross-cut saw
39 the bow saw (frame saw):
40 the bow (frame)
41 the grip;
42 the draw knife (peeling knife) for barking
43 the revolving die hammer (marking hammer, marking iron, *Am.* marker)
44 the one-man motor chain saw (power-driven saw):
45 the handle
46 the saw chain
47 the saw guide

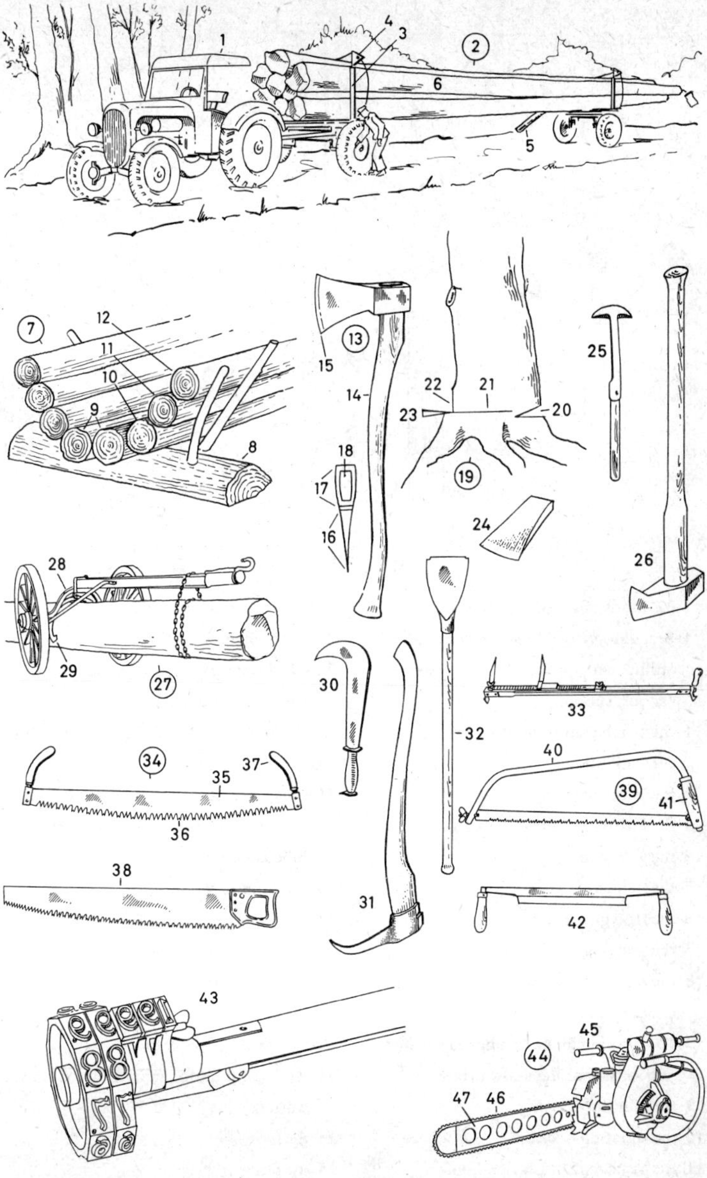
1
2
3
4
5
6
7
8
9
10
11
12
13
14
15
16
17
18
19
20
21
22
23
24
25
26
27
28
29
30
31
32
33
34
35
36
37
38
39
40
41
42
43
44
45
46
47

1–52 kinds of shooting (shooting),

1–8 stalking (to go deer-stalking, *Am.* stillhunting) in the hunting preserves (shoot, shooting),

1 the sportsman (gun, deer-stalker, *Am.* stillhunter):

2 the huntsman's suit

3 the knapsack (*Am.* carryall)

4 the shot gun

5 the huntsman's hat

6 the field glass;

7 the gun dog

8 the scent (track, trail, trace, spoor, slot; *in underwood:* abature);

9–12 shooting in the rutting season [deer] and in the pairing season [birds]:

9 the hunting screen

10 the shooting-stick

11 the blackcock displaying himself

12 the stag, roaring (belling);

13 the hind, grazing (browsing)

14–17 shooting from a high stand:

14 the high stand (shooting stand)

15 the herd of deer within range (within shooting distance)

16 the game path (*Am.* runway)

17 the roebuck, hit in the shoulder and killed by a final shot;

18 the game cart

19–27 trapping,

19 trapping beasts of prey:

20 the box fall (box trap)

21 the bait

22 the marten, a predatory beast;

23 ferreting (hunting rabbits out of their warrens):

24 the ferret

25 the ferreter

26 the burrow (*many burrows*: warren, rabbit's earth)
27 the purse net over the burrow hole;
28 the feed trough (winter feeding place)
29 the poacher
30 the carbine, a short rifle
31 the boar hunt:
32 the boar
33 the boar hound (*all of them*: the pack);
34–39 the battue (beat, hare-shooting, *Am.* surround):
34 the aim (taking aim)
35 the hare, furred game
36 retrieving
37 the beater
38 the bag
39 the cart for the game;
40 waterfowl-shooting (wildfowl-shooting, wild-fowling, duck-shooting, *Am.* duck-hunting):
41 the flight of wild duck, feathered game;
42–46 the falconry (hawking):
42 the falconer
43 the reward, a piece of meat
44 the falcon's hood
45 the jesses
46 a hawk (tiercel) stooping on a heron;
47–52 decoy-shooting from a hut:
47 the tree for the decoyed birds
48 the eagle owl, a decoy bird
49 the perch
50 the decoyed bird, a crow
51 the hut (shooting hut, shooting shelter, ambush shed)
52 the loophole

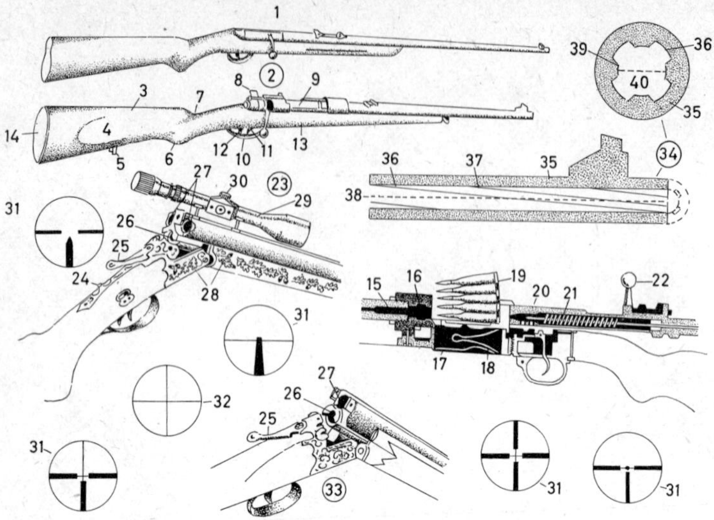

1–40 sporting weapons (sporting guns, sporting rifles):
1 the carbine
2 the repeating rifle, a small arm (fire arm), a repeater (magazine rifle):
3, 4, 6, 13 the stock of the rifle
3 the butt (rifle butt)
4 the cheek
5 the sling ring
6 the pistol grip
7 the small of the butt
8 the safety catch
9 the lock
10 the trigger guard
11 the two-pressure trigger
12 the hair trigger
13 the foregrip
14 the butt plate
15 the cartridge chamber
16 the front part of the bolt cover
17 the cartridge magazine
18 the feed spring (magazine spring)
19 the charger (cartridge clip)
20 the bolt
21 the striker (firing pin)
22 the bolt lever (bolt handle);
23 the triple-barrelled (*Am.* triple-barreled) gun, a self-cocking gun:
24 the commutating catch
25 the sliding safety catch
26 the bullet barrel
27 the small-shot barrels
28 the chasing
29 the telescopic sights (*Am.* aiming telescope)
30 the graticule-adjuster
31 and **32** the sight graticule (*Am.* cross-hair diopter):
31 various graticule systems
32 the cross wires (*Am.* cross hairs);
33 the over-and-under rifle-shotgun, a twin-barrel (double-barrel) gun
34 the rifled gun barrel:
35 the barrel casing
36 the rifle (rifling)
37 the land

38 the bore axis
39 the bore surface
40 the calibre (*Am.* caliber; bore);
41–48 hunting implements:
41 the double-edged hunting knife
42 the single-edged hunting knife
43–47 calls for luring game (calling game, the imitation of animal calls):
43 the roe call
44 the hare call
45 the quail call
46 the stag call
47 the partridge call;
48 the bow trap (bow gin), a jaw trap;
49 the small-shot cartridge (small-shot round):
50 the cardboard case
51 the small-shot charge
52 the felt wad
53 the smokeless powder;
54 the ball cartridge:
55 the full-jacket bullet or projectile or ball
56 the soft-lead core
57 the powder charge
58 the detonator cap
59 the percussion cap;
60 the hunting horn [continental type]
61–64 the weapon-cleaning kit:
61 the cleaning rod
62 the barrel-cleaning brush
63 the cleaning tow
64 the pull-through (*Am.* pull-thru);
65 the sights (sighting arrangement):
66 the notch
67 the backsight leaf
68 the sight-scale division
69 the backsight slide
70 the notch to hold the spring
71 the foresight
72 the blade of the foresight;
73 ballistics:
74 the line of azimuth
75 the angle of departure
76 the angle of elevation
77 the zenith (apex)
78 the angle of descent
79 the ballistic line

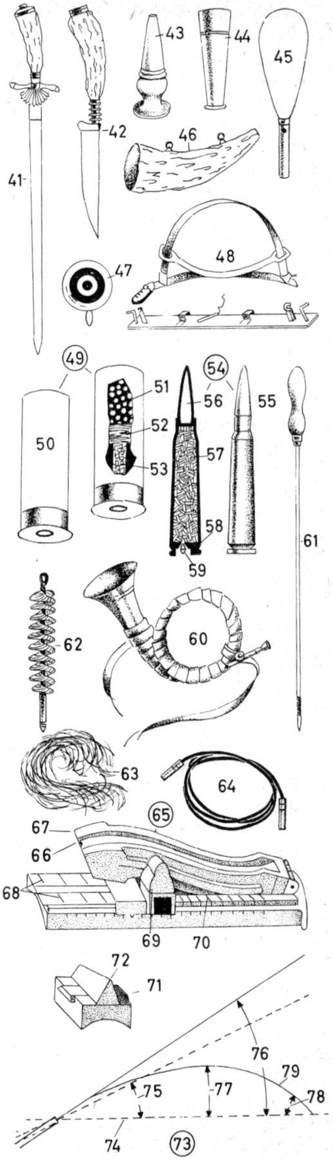

1–27 deer (red deer),
1 the hind (red deer), a young hind or a dam (mother); *several together :* a parcel; *a young deer of either sex :* fawn:
2 the tongue
3 the neck;
4 the stag (male, hart, red deer),
5–11 the antlers:
5 the burr (rose)
6 the brow tine (brow antler, brow point, brow snag)
7 the bez tine (bes tine, bay antler)
8 the trez tine (tray)
9 the surroyals
10 the tine (point, *Am.* snag)
11 the beam (*Am.* main stem, main trunk);
12 the gullet
13 the mouth
14 the larmier (tear bag)
15 the eye
16 the ear
17 the shoulder
18 the loin
19 the scut (tail)
20 the rump
21 the leg (haunch)
22 the hind leg
23 the dew claw
24 the hoof
25 the foreleg
26 the flank
27 the collar (rutting mane);
28–39 roe (roe deer),
28 the roebuck (buck),
29–31 the antlers (horns):
29 the burr
30 the beam with the beads
31 the tine (branch, point, snag);
32 the ear
33 the eye;
34 the doe (female roe), a young roe or a dam (mother):
35 the back
36 the rump
37 the leg (haunch)
38 the shoulder;
39 the fawn, a young buck or a young doe
40 the fallow buck (buck of the fallow deer), a buck with palmate antlers (*Am.* with shovel); *fem. :* doe:
41 the palm;
42 the red fox (fox); *male:* fox, *fem.:* vixen (bitch fox, she-fox):
43 the eyes
44 the ear
45 the muzzle
46 the pads
47 the brush;
48 the badger (brock):
49 the tail
50 the paws;
51 wild boar; *here:* the wild boar (wild pig, wild swine); *fem.:* wild sow, *both:* pigs (swine), *the young:* young boars:
52 the bristles
53 the snout
54 the tusk
55 the shield (thick skin on the shoulder)
56 the hide
57 the dew claw
58 the tail;
59 the hare; *fem.:* doe, *the young:* leverets:
60 the eye
61 the ear
62 the scut
63 the hind leg
64 the foreleg;
65 the rabbit
66 the black grouse (black game, heath bird); *male:* blackcock (heath cock), *fem.:* heath hen (grey hen):
67 the tail
68 the forks;
69 the hazel grouse (hazel hen)
70 the partridge:
71 the breast spot (horseshoe);
72 the capercaillie (capercailzie, wood-grouse); *the male also called* mountain cock (cock of the woods):
73 the beard
74 the breast spot
75 the tail (fan)
76 the wing (pinion);
77 the common pheasant, a pheasant:
78 the feathered ear
79 the wing
80 the tail
81 the leg
82 the spur;
83 the snipe:
84 the bill

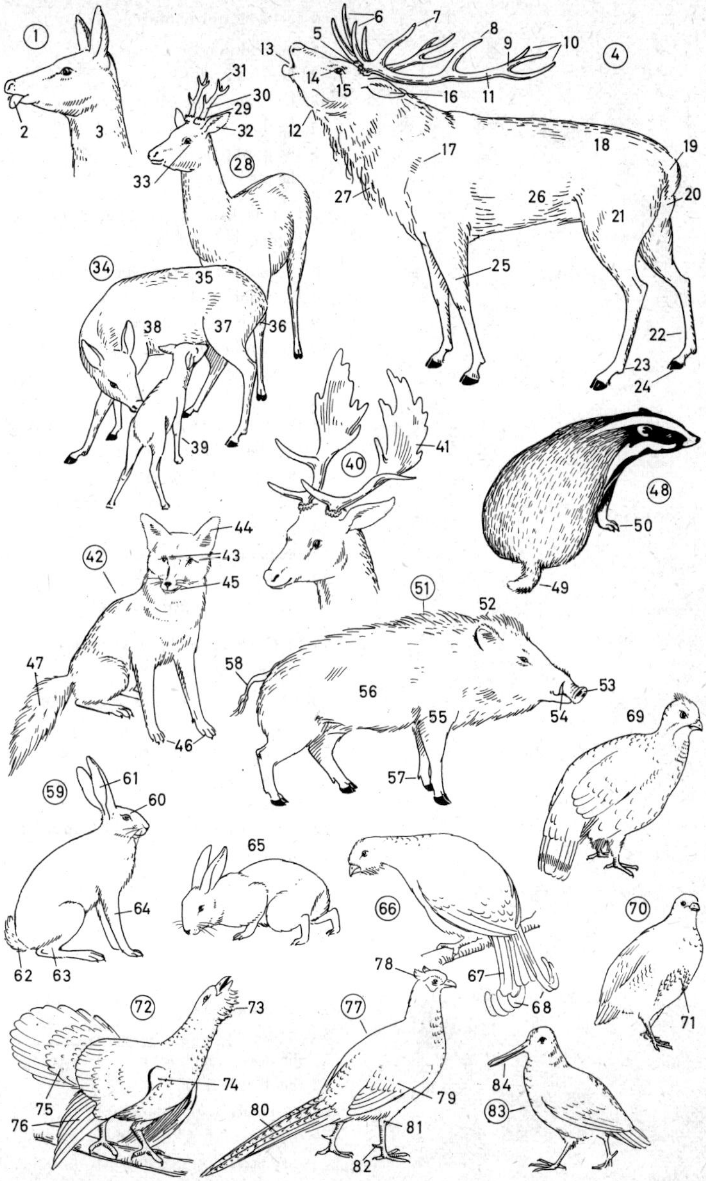
1
2
3
4
5
6
7
8
9
10
11
12
13
14
15
16
17
18
19
20
21
22
23
24
25
26
27
28
29
30
31
32
33
34
35
36
37
38
39
40
41
42
43
44
45
46
47
48
49
50
51
52
53
54
55
56
57
58
59
60
61
62
63
64
65
66
67
68
69
70
71
72
73
74
75
76
77
78
79
80
81
82
83
84

89 Freshwater Fishing (Fishery) and Sport Fishing

1-6, 13-19 net fishing:

1 the fishing boat
2 the fisherman
3 the sweep seine (sweep net, fishing net)
4 the float
5 the punt pole
6 the casting net;

7-12 line fishing (angling, rod fishing, fishing with rod and line):

7 the angler (rod fisher, line fisher)
8 the trout stream
9 the creel (fishing basket)
10 the landing net (hand net)
11 the rod rest
12 the gaff;
13 the fish ladder for fishes (fish) ascending the river (for anadromous fishes)
14 the stake net (bag net)
15 the crayfish net (*Am.* crawfish net)
16 the fish trap
17 the flat net
18 the bait tin (bait can)
19 the worm tin (worm box);

20-54 freshwater fishing tackle for sport fishing,

20–23 the jointed fishing rods (fishing rods),
20 the spinning rod, a single-handed fishing rod:
21 the ring;
22 the bottom rod, a double-handed rod
23 the fly rod, a casting rod;
24 the glass rod:
25 the pistol-type handle;
26 the fishing rod of bamboo, or pepper tree, cane
27 the spinning reel
28 the fly reel
29 the fishing line
30 the trace (*Am.* leader)
31 the hook (fish hook)
32 the double hook
33 the treble hook (triangle)
34 the set of hooks, a tackle for predatory fish [mounted in bait]:

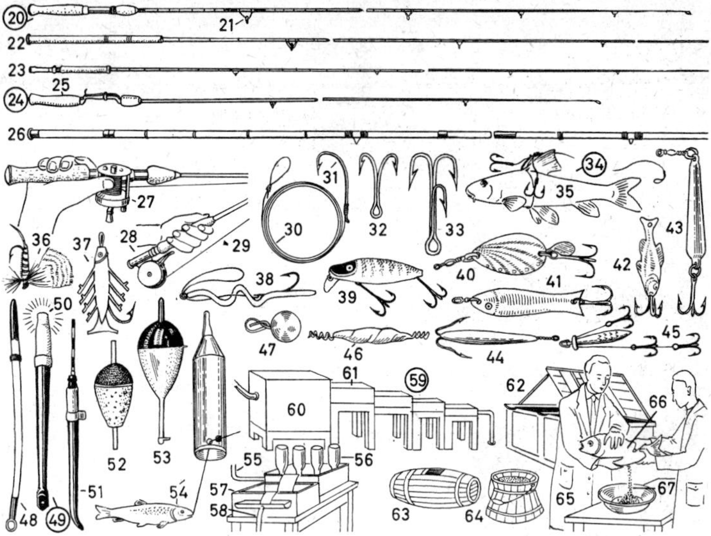

35 the live-bait fish (lure);
36–43 artificial baits:
36 the artificial fly
37 the artificial shrimp
38 the artificial maggot
39 the wobbler (plug)
40 the spinner (spoon)
41 the spoon bait (minnow)
42 the diving plug
43 the mount;
44 the troll, or gorge, hook
45 the spinner system
46 and **47** leads (sinkers):
46 the spiral lead
47 the lead ball (shot);
48 the quill float
49 the luminous quill:
50 the luminous paint;
51 the floating quill with cap
52 the cork float (float)
53 the trailing float
54 the floating tube for live-bait;

55-67 the hatchery (fish-breeding, *Am.* fish raising establishment):
55 the water-inlet (water-inflow) pipe
56 the hatching (breeding, rearing, *Am.* raising) jar
57 the fry tank
58 the water discharge (water-outflow) pipe
59 the hatching (breeding, *Am.* raising) apparatus:
60 the filter
61 the hatching (breeding, *Am.* raising) tank;
62 the fish tank
63 the fish keg, a fish cask
64 the vessel (bucket) for transporting fish
65 the pisciculturist
66 the female fish (spawner, seeder, seed fish); *the male fish:* milter; the soft roe (seed) of the male fish: milt
67 the fish spawn (spawn, roe, hard roe, fish eggs, fish ova)

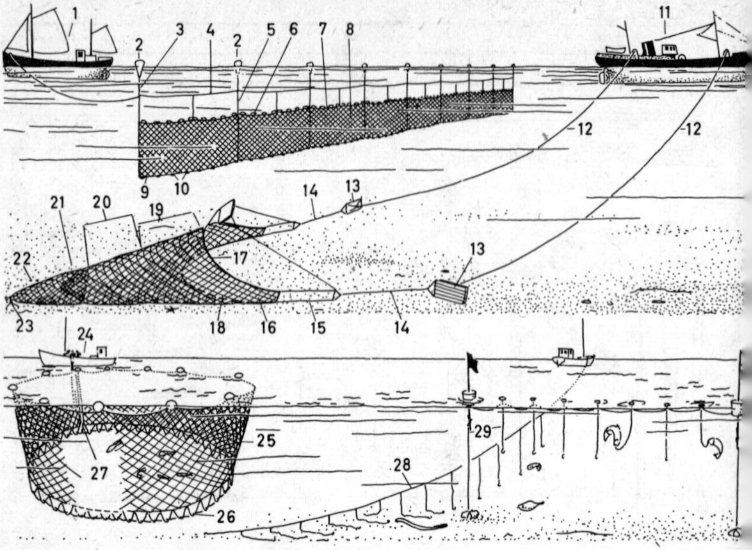

1-23 the deep-sea fishery,
1–10 the drift-net fishery:
1 the herring drifter (fishing lugger, lugger)
2–10 the herring drift-net:
2 the buoy
3 the buoy rope
4 the floating rope
5 the seizing
6 the float
7 the head (top) rope
8 the net (wall of netting)
9 the foot (bottom) rope
10 the bottom weights;
11–23 the trawling fishery (trawling):
11 the trawler, a large motor-driven fishing vessel
12 the warp
13 the otter boards
14 the bridle
15 the wire warp
16 the net wing
17 the head rope
18 the foot rope
19 the square mesh
20 the belly
21 the flap
22 the cod end
23 the cod line for closing the cod end;

24-29 the coastal fishery (inshore fishery):
24 the fishing boat
25 the ring net, a drift net set in a circle
26 the wire rope for closing the net
27 the closing gear
28 and 29 long-line fishing:
28 the long line (sea-fishing line)
29 the suspended fishing tackle (short line), a cotton line;

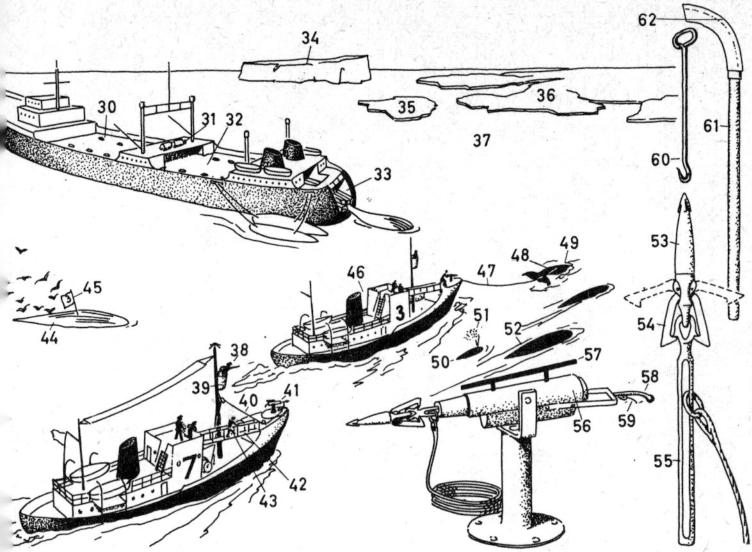

30-43 whaling (whale-fishing, whale fishery),
30–33 the factory-ship:
30 the fore plan (butcher's deck)
31 the whale winch
32 the flensing deck
33 the ramp (slipway);
34 the iceberg
35 the ice floe (ice raft, ice drift, floating ice)
36 the ice field
37 the Antarctic Sea
38–43 the whaler:
38 the lookout
39 the crow's-nest
40 the whaleline
41 the harpoon gun
42 the catwalk
43 the gunner (harpooner);
44–62 whaling:
44 the flagged whale, a killed whale, a finback (rorqual)
45 the flag with the boat's number
46 the whaler
47 the first line
48 the fluke
49 the whale held fast (whale harpooned)
50 the whale blowing (whale spouting)
51 the spout
52 the school of whales
53–59 the harpoon gun,
53–55 the harpoon:
53 the grenade
54 the barb
55 the shaft;
56 the gun barrel
57 the sights
58 the aiming grip
59 the trigger;
60 the blubber hook
61 the flensing knife
62 the cutting edge

91 Mills

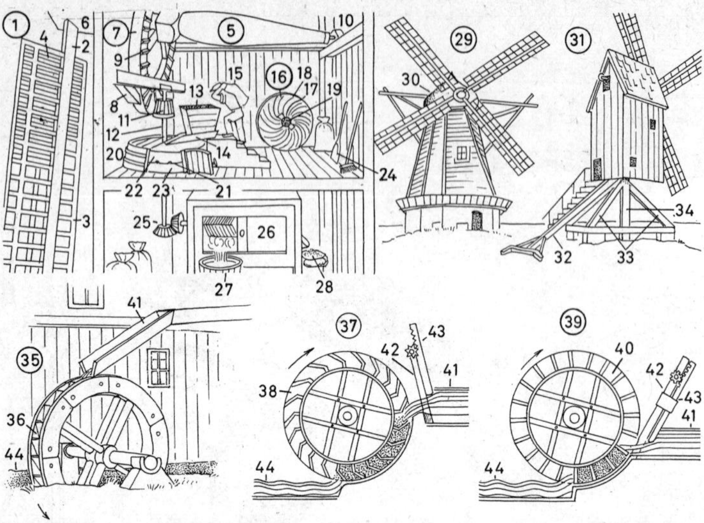

1-34 the windmill,

1 the windmill vane (windmill sail, windmill arm, windmill sail arm):
2 the stock (middling, back, radius)
3 the frame
4 the shutters;
5 the wheel shaft (sail axle, vane spindle):
6 the sail top;
7 the head wheel:
8 the brake
9 the wooden cog;
10 the pivot bearing
11 the windmill gearing
12 the stone spindle
13 the hopper
14 the shoe (trough)
15 the miller
16 the millstone:
17 the furrow flutes
18 the master furrow
19 the millstone eye;
20 the hurst (millstone casing)
21 the set of stones (milling course)
22 the runner (upper millstone)
23 the bedstone (bedder, nether millstone, lower millstone, bottom stone)
24 the wooden shovel
25 the bevel gear (angle drive, bevel wheels)
26 the bolter (sifter)
27 the wooden tub (tun)
28 the flour
29 the smock windmill:
30 the rotating windmill cap;
31 the post windmill:
32 the tailpole (pole)
33 the quarter bars
34 the main post;

35-44 the watermill,

35 the overshot (high-breast) bucket wheel, a mill wheel (water wheel):
36 the bucket;
37 the middleshot mill wheel (breast wheel):
38 the curved vane;

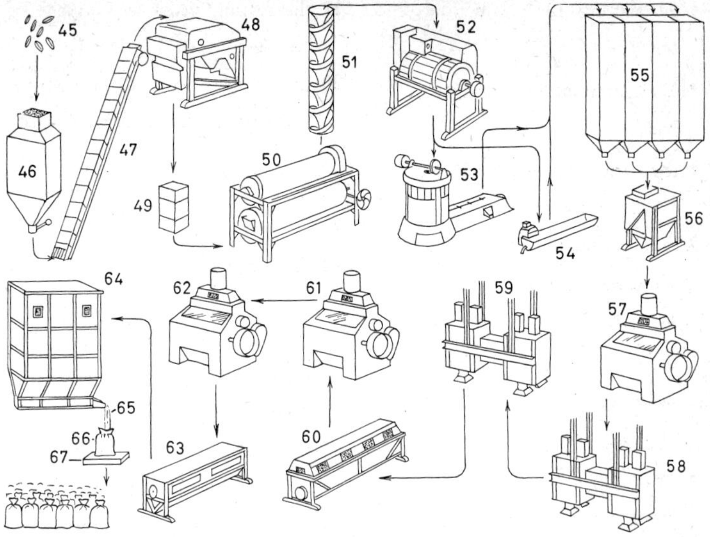

39 the undershot (impact, impulse) mill wheel:
40 the flat vane;
41 the headrace (discharge flume)
42 the mill weir (*Am.* trashrack)
43 the water overfall
44 the mill brook (mill race, *Am.* raceway);

45-67 the flour mill (corn mill, *Am.* gristmill),

45–56 grain-cleaners:
45 the grain
46 the automatic grain-weighing machine
47 the elevator
48 the aspirator (preliminary cleaner)
49 the magnet for removing iron particles
50 the cylinders for removing weed seeds
51 the spiral separator
52 the grain (corn) husker (husking machine)
53 the scourer
54 the damper
55 the conditioner
56 the brushes (grain, or corn, polisher; grain, or corn, polishing machine);
57–67 flour milling machines:
57 the brake roller mills, a double-roller mill for crushing (granulating, rough-grinding) the grain (corn)
58 the plansifter
59 the grading (sizing, sorting) plansifter
60 the purifier (groats (grits) and pollard cleaner)
61 the first reduction roller mill (groats (grits) and pollard reducing rollers)
62 the second reduction roller mill
63 the flour sieve for removing bran particles
64 the flour-mixer (flour-mixing machine)
65 the finished product
66 the flour sack
67 the sacking (sack-filling) and sack-weighing plant

1–21 malting (the production of malt),

1–7 cleaning and steeping the barley:

1 the barley-cleaning machine (barley-cleaner)

2 the steeping tank (steeping cistern)

3 the water pipe

4 the rails

5 the wheeled automatic barley-weighing machine (*Am.* weight-ometer)

6 the barley inlet

7 the drain outlet;

8–12 the germination of the barley:

8 the germination box

9 the green-malt turner:

10 the runner (rail);

11 the green malt (germinating barley)

12 the maltster (maltman);

13–20 the drying kiln (malt kiln):

13 the drying malt

14 the drying floor

15 the curing floor (finishing floor)

16 the malt-turner

17 the running chain

18 the hot-air chamber:

19 the heating system, a heating chamber

20 the air shaft for cold-air supply;

21 the malt-cleaning machine (malt-cleaner);

22–36 the extraction of the wort:

22 the malt mill

23 the miller

24 the grist

25–36 the brewing process (beer-brewing) in the brewing house (*Am.* brewhouse):

25 the masher (mashing machine) for mixing grist and water

26 the mash tun for mashing the malt

27 the mash copper (mash boiler) for boiling the mash:

28 the boiler lid

29 the rakes

30 the sliding door

31 the water supply pipe;

32 the brewer

33 the lauter tun (clarifying tank) for settling the draff, or brewer's grains, and filtering off the wort

34 the clear wort taps for draining the wort from the grain

35 the hop copper (wort boiler) for boiling the wort

36 the ladle-shaped thermometer

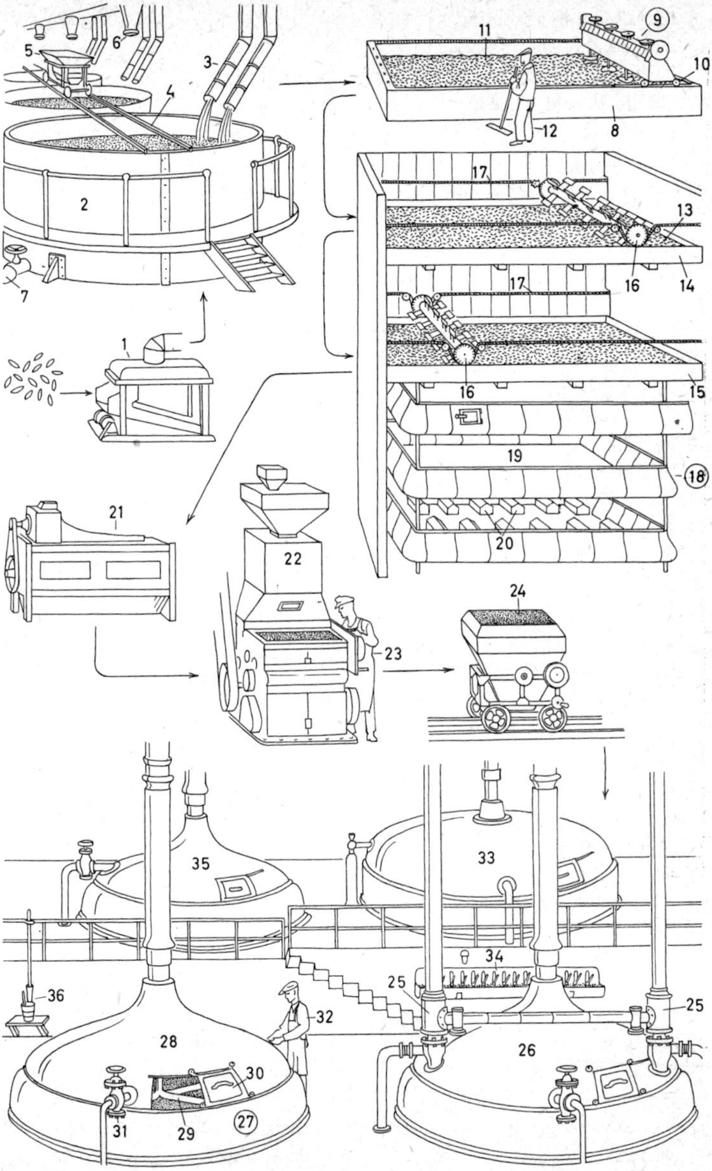
1
2
3
4
5
6
7
8
9
10
11
12
13
14
15
16
17
18
19
20
21
22
23
24
25
26
27
28
29
30
31
32
33
34
35
36

1 the cooling tray (cooling pan, surface cooler) for pre-cooling the wort and precipitation of the cloudy (turbid) deposit:
2 the support (cooler feet)
3 the pump pipe
4 the shutters (louvres, louvers) for ventilation
5 the wort;
6 the wort refrigerator (wort-cooling apparatus):
7 the wort supply pipe (wort inlet)
8 the cooling-water supply and discharge pipes
9 the collecting trough
10 the sampling of the beer (taking of a sample)
11 the wort outlet;
12–19 the fermentation of the wort,
12 the fermenting vessel:
13 the cooling pipes;
14 the fermentation cellarer skimming off the head (the eliminated substances)
15–18 the pure-yeast culture (production of biologically pure yeast),
15 the pure-yeast culture apparatus:
16 the observation hole
17 the pipe for blowing away the carbon dioxide
18 the air filter for sterilizing the air (for freeing the air of bacteria);
19 the yeast press;
20–28 racking back (drawing off) the beer and the secondary fermentation of the beer,
20 the storage cask:
21 the manhole (opening for cleaning purposes);
22 the broaching tap for drawing off beer
23 the tap (*Am.* faucet) for filling the casks
24 the cellar foreman
25 the cooling pipe
26 the beer filter:
27 the glass cylinder for observing the beer
28 the manometer;
29 the racking apparatus (drawing-off plant, cask-filler, barrel-filler; cask, or barrel, filling machine)
30 the rail
31 the bottle-cleaning machine
32 the beer-bottling machine (bottle-filling machine) and bottle-closing machine
33 the labelling (*Am.* labeling) machine
34–38 beer transport (*Am.* transportation of beer):
34 the beer barrel (trade cask) with draught beer (beer on draught)
35 the beer case
36 the dray (beer cart, brewer's dray)
37 the drayman
38 the beer lorry (*Am.* beer truck);
39 the beer tin (*Am.* can of beer)
40 the beer bottle with bottled beer; *beer sorts :* pale ale (lager, light ale, light beer, bitter beer), brown ale (mild beer); Pilsen beer, Munich (Bavarian) beer, malt (malted) beer, bock beer (bock), porter, ale, stout, Salvator (strong beer), Goslar beer, wheaten beer, small beer (swipes, *Am.* near beer):
41 the beer bottle lever-stopper
42 the bottle label (label);
43 the bottle crown cork (crown cork)
44 the tinfoil capsule
45 the trade barrel (trade cask) with export beer

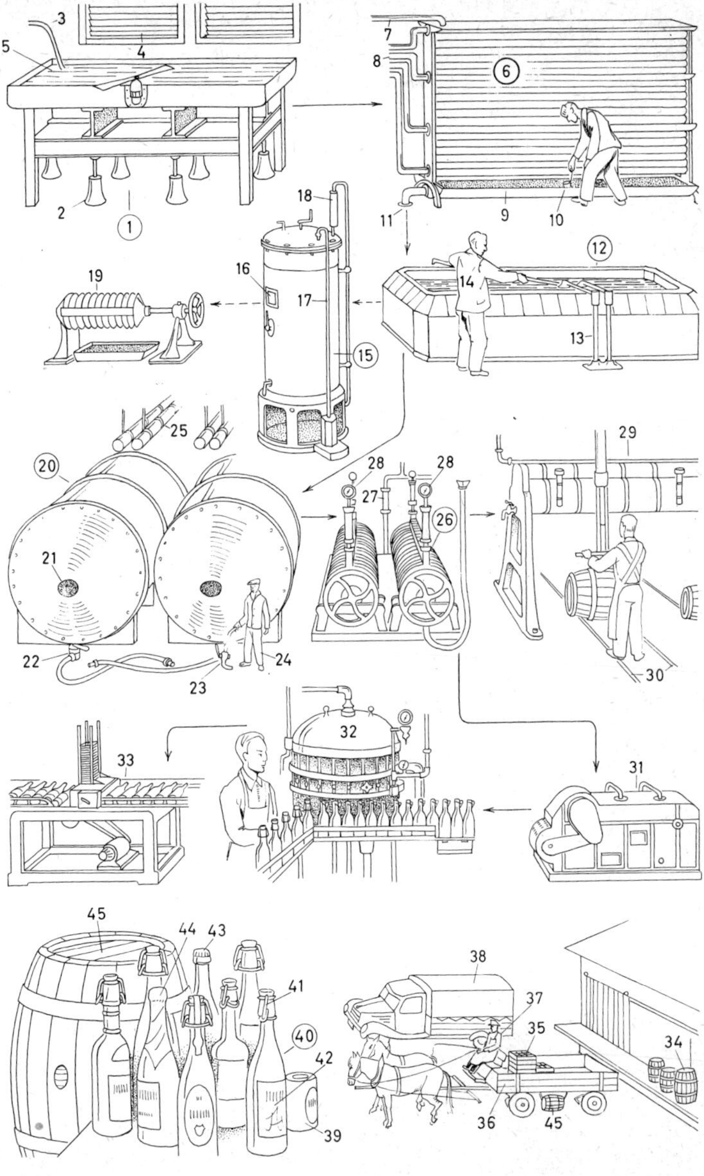
1 2 3 4 5 6 7 8 9 10 11 12 13 14 15 16 17 18 19 20 21 22 23 24 25 26 27 28 28 29 30 31 32 33 34 35 36 37 38 39 40 41 42 43 44 45 45

94 The Slaughter House

1 the slaughterman

2 the animal awaiting slaughter (*Am.* killer), an ox

3 the slaughterman's assistant

4–10 the slaughterman's tools (*Am.* findings; slaughtering tools),

4 the slaughtering mask [prohibited in the United Kingdom]:

5 the bolt (spike) [prohibited in the United Kingdom];

6 the electrolethaler

7 the slaughtering hammer (slaughtering mallet) [prohibited in the United Kingdom]

8 the slaughtering club or cudgel [prohibited in the United Kingdom]

9 the slaughtering knife

10 the slaughtering hatchet;

11–15 the slaughter house (shambles; *the public slaughter house:* abattoir),

11–14 cutting up the carcass of the pig:

11 the gambrel

12 the stretcher

13 the trichina control stamp or mark

14 the meat inspector's grade stamp (grade mark);

15 the bleeding-out;

16–18 the cold-storage chamber (cold-air store, cooling chamber):

16 the butcher's hook

17 the sprayer for disinfection

18 the spraying tube with the jets

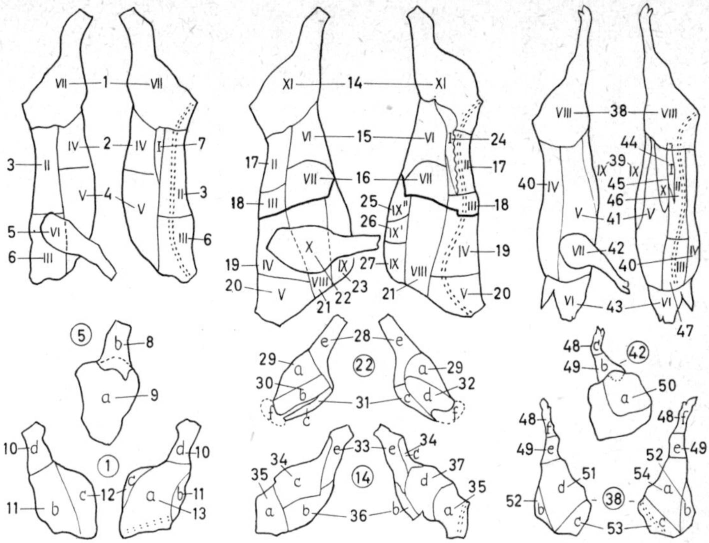

[left: meat side; right: bone side]

1–13 the calf (veal):
1 the leg with hind knuckle
2 the flank (ventral part of loin and back part of breast)
3 the loin and best-end or neck of veal
4 the breast of veal
5 the shoulder with fore knuckle
6 the scrag and neck
7 the best-end of loin of veal
8 the fore knuckle
9 the shoulder
10 the hind knuckle
11, 12, 13 parts of the leg;
14-37 the ox (beef):
14 the round (buttock) of beef with shank
15 and **16** the thin flank:
15 the hind flank
16 the fore flank;
17 the sirloin (*Am.* tenderloin, porterhouse steak, porterhouse)
18 the prime ribs (fore ribs, wing end)
19 the chuck and middle ribs
20 the neck (sticking)
21 the fore ribs (top ribs, flat ribs, clod)
22 the leg of mutton piece, bladebone, part of top ribs with shin
23 the brisket (brisket of beef, clod)
24 the fillet (fillet of beef)
25 the hind brisket
26 the middle brisket
27 the breastbone
28 the shin
29 the leg of mutton piece
30 the part of bladebone
31 the part of top ribs
32 the part of bladebone
33 the shank
34 the silverside
35 the rump
36 the thick flank
37 the top side;
38–54 the pig (pork):
38 the leg and trotter or pettitoe
39 the ventral part of belly (of spring)
40 the back fat
41 the belly (spring)
42 the bladebone with hand, spring, and trotter
43 the pig's head
44 the fillet (fillet of pork)
45 the leaf fat (flare fat)
46 the loin (pork loin)
47 the spare rib (pork spare rib)
48 the trotter (pettitoe)
49 the part of the leg near the knuckle
50 the butt
51–54 parts of the leg

1–28 the butcher's shop (*Am. coll.* meat market):
1 the counter
2 the open freezer:
3 the cooling plate;
4 the shop mincer, a mincing machine
5 lard in packets (lard)
6 the beef fat, tallow
7 the sausage ring (unlinked sausages)
8 the soup bone (marrow bone, bone)
9 the butcher
10 the long arm, a hooked pole for reaching down sausages
11 the side (flitch) of bacon (bacon)
12 the smoked meat
13 the hard sausage (salame, salami, continental sausage, *Am.* summer sausage)
14 the cooked sausage; *sorts:* Vienna sausage, Frankfurter (Frankfort sausage, *Am.* frankfurter, *coll.* franks)
15 the sausage boiler (steam cooker)
16 the liver paste, a meat paste
17 the course cut sausage, a sausage of unminced meat
18 the boiled ham
19 the bacon-slicer (sausage-slicing machine)
20 the rump steak (*Am.* porterhouse steak); *sim.* beef steak, a fillet of beef
21 the meat salad
22 the collared beef
23 the frying sausage
24 the pickled pork trotters
25 the mince (minced meat)
26 the bacon (uncooked ham)
27 the bacon (rolled ham)

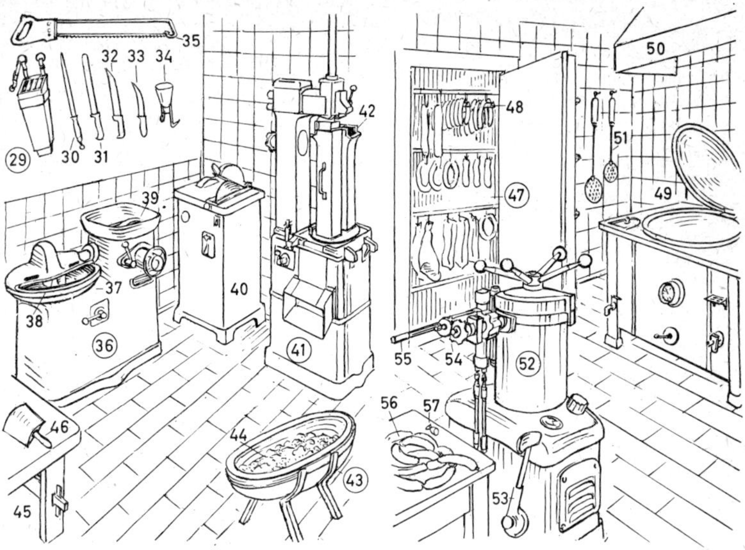

28 the pig's liver;
29–57 the manufacturing room,
29–35 the butcher's tools (*Am.* butcher's findings),
29 the wooden case for the butcher's tools:
30 the steel (sharpening steel, grinding steel)
31 the sausage knife
32 the butcher's knife
33 the skin knife;
34 the pig-bristle and ox-stomach scraper
35 the bone saw;
36 the combination, a two-purpose (twin) meat machine:
37 the cutter (mincing machine, sausage machine)
38 the cutter bowl
39 the meat-chopper (meat-shredder);
40 the electric saw
41 the pork-fat cutter:
42 the feed hole;
43 the meat-mixing trough:
44 the sausage meat;
45 the chopping board
46 the cleaver (chopper)
47 the smoking chamber:
48 the spit;
49 the sausage boiler
50 the air duct
51 the skimmer
52 the sausage-filler:
53 the knee lever
54 the automatic linker
55 the divider;
56 the filled sausage
57 the sausage end

97 The Bakery

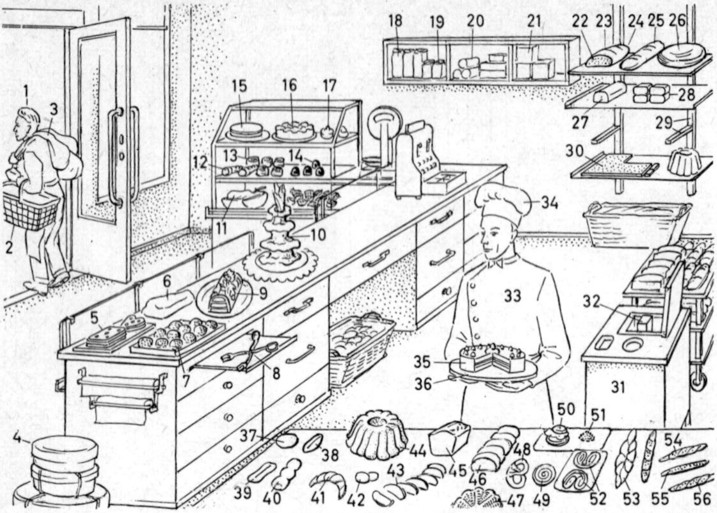

1–56 the bakery (*Am.* breadery), fancy bakery, confectionery:
1 the baker's boy
2 the basket of rolls
3 the bag of rolls
4 the cake box
5 the gingerbread (spice biscuit)
6 the currant cake, a Christmas cake
7 the doughnut (*Am.* flapjack, sinker), a deep-fried yeast cake mixture
8 the cake tongs
9 the layer cake
10 the tree-shaped Madeira cake
11 the whipped cream
12 the cream roll
13 the patty (vol-au-vent)
14 the chocolate-iced round sponge cake
15 the tart (flan) case of short pastry
16 the fruit flan (*Am.* fruit pie, pie)
17 the meringue
18 and **19** flour:
18 wheaten flour
19 rye flour;
20 the Savoy biscuit(s) (*Am.* cookie)
21 the crisp bread, a whole-meal bread
22–24 the bread (loaf):
22 the crumb
23 the bread crust
24 the end crust (crust);
25–28 sorts of bread:
25 the long loaf (bloomer loaf), wheat and rye bread
26 the round loaf, black bread
27 the tin (sandwich) loaf, a white loaf
28 the pumpernickel (whole-meal rye bread) in the air-tight wrapping;
29 the bread shelves
30 the flat (griddle) cake
31 the ice-cream machine (ice maker, ice-cream freezer)
32 the server
33 the pastry cook (confectioner, fancy baker):
34 the confectioners' (baker's) cap;
35 the iced cream cake
36 the cake plate
37–40 rolls:
37 the roll
38 the baton roll
39 the French roll

40 the Vienna roll;
41 the croissant (crescent-shaped roll, *Am.* crescent)
42 the biscuit
43 the rusk (*Am.* cracker)
44 the pyramid fruit cake (*sim. Am.* angel cake, ashcake)
45 the oblong cake
46 the soft rusk
47 the wafer
48 the pretzel (bretzel)
49 the Chelsea bun
50 the cream puff
51 the macaroon
52 the pig's-ear [of puff pastry]
53 the plaited bun
54 the salted roll (salted stick)
55 the poppy roll (poppy stick)
56 the caraway roll (caraway stick);
57–80 the bakehouse,
57–63 the oven:
57 the prooving (fermenting) and drying cabinet
58 the furnace
59 the escape hood (air duct)
60 the air duct handle
61 the baker's oven
62 the draw plate
63 the pyrometer (*Am.* thermo gage);
64 the electric dividing and moulding machine (divider)
65 the electric flour-sifting machine
66 the peel (baker's shovel)
67 the rolling-pin
68 the flour sieve
69 the deep fryer
70 the butter brush
71 the kneading table:
72 the kneading trough
73 the flour bin;
74 the electric dough machine:
75 the kneading arm;
76 the kneading pan
77 the dough scales, a beam balance
78 the dough brake (noodle machine)
79 the beating machine (mixing machine
80 the bread mould (*Am.* mold) of ratan (rattan) cane

Engl. tinned = *Am.* canned

1–87 the grocer's shop (grocer's, delicatessen shop; *Am.* grocer's store, delicatessen store; *less pretentious:* general merchandise store; *with self-service:* groceteria):
1 the show of goods in the show window (shop window, *Am.* store window)
2 the poster (placard)
3 the deep-freezer showcase
4 the sausages
5 the cheese
6 the capon, a fattened cock
7 the poulard, a fattened hen
8 the raisins; *sim.* sultanas
9 the currants
10 the candied lemon-peel
11 the candied orange-peel
12 the dial balance, a quick balance
13 the grocer's assistant (*Am.* salesclerk, store clerk)
14 the goods shelves
15–20 tinned food:
15 tinned milk
16 tinned fruit
17 tinned vegetables
18 the fruit juice
19 the sardines in oil, tinned fish
20 tinned meat;
21 the margarine
22 the butter
23 the coconut fat, a vegetable fat (*Am.* shortening)
24 the oil (olive oil, salad oil)
25 the vinegar
26 the soup cube
27 the broth cube
28 the mustard
29 the gherkin (pickled cucumber)
30 the soup flavouring (*Am.* soup flavoring)
31 the shop assistant (saleswoman, salesgirl, *Am.* sales-lady)
32–34 paste foods:
32 the spaghetti
33 the macaroni
34 the noodles;
35–39 cereals:
35 the pearl-barley
36 the semolina
37 the rolled oats
38 the rice
39 the sago;
40 the salt
41 the grocer (tradesman, shopkeeper, retailer, *Am.* storekeeper, *Scotch and Am.* merchant)

42 the capers
43 the vanilla
44 the cinnamon
45 the customer
46–49 wrapping material:
46 the wrapping paper
47 the string
48 and **49** paper bags;
50 the blancmange powder
51 whole-fruit jam (preserve)
52 jam
53–55 sugar:
53 the lump (cube, loaf) sugar
54 the icing sugar (*Am.* confectioner's sugar)
55 the granulated sugar, refined sugar;
56–59 alcohol (alcoholic liquors, spirits):
56 schnaps (schnapps)
57 the rum
58 the liqueur
59 the brandy (cognac);
60–64 wine in bottles (bottled wine):
60 the white wine
61 the chianti
62 the vermouth
63 the champagne (sparkling wine, *coll.* fizz)
64 the red wine;
65 the coffee substitute (ersatz coffee)
66–68 tea, coffee, etc.:
66 the cocoa
67 the coffee
68 the tea;
69 the electric coffee-mill (electric coffee-grinder)
70 the coffee-roaster:
71 the roasting drum
72 the sample scoop;
73 the price-list
74 the freezer
75–86 sweets (confectionery, *Am.* candies):
75 the sweet (bonbon, *Am.* candy)
76 the drops
77 the toffees (*Am.* taffy; caramels)
78 the bar (slab) of chocolate
79 the chocolate box:
80 chocolates;
81 the fudge
82 the marzipan
83 the chocolate liqueur
84 the cat's tongue
85 the nut crunch
86 the truffle;
87 the soda-water

99 The Shoemaker

1–37 the shoemaker's (bootmaker's) workshop:

1 the journeyman shoemaker

2 the stitching machine

3 the stitching thread

4 shoe socks (insoles):

5 the straw sock

6 the felt sock

7 the rubber-foam sock

8 the cork sock

9 the woven lime-wood sock;

10 the last

11 the last-hook

12 the foot tape-measure (foot-measuring tape)

13 the shoemaker's apprentice (cobbler's boy)

14 the shoemaker's stool

15 the knee strap

16 the sewing wax (cobbler's wax)

17 the nail box, an outfit box for wooden rivets, brads, tacks (tingles) and hobnails

18 the channel-cutter

19 the twine (waxed thread, cobbler's thread)

20 the shoe-stretcher

21 the finisher's (finishing) spirit lamp

22 the flat rasp

23 the shoemaker (master shoemaker, bootmaker, cobbler), repairing shoes

24 the clumping machine

25 the shoemaker's globe, a water-filled glass globe

26 the petroleum (paraffin) lamp

27 the cobbler's stand, a double stand with iron lasts

28 the platform

29 the orthopaedic (orthopedic) instep support

30 the iron sleeker (slicker, sleeking iron)

31 the wooden sleeker (slicker, sleeking stick)

32 the triple last (hobbing foot)

33 the nailing (nails)

34 the orthopaedic (orthopedic) shoe

35 the nippers (pair of pincers)
36 the spoon-shaped rasp
37 the barred rubber sole or tread;
38–55 the boot,
38–49 the upper (uppers, upper leather):
38 the toe cap (*Am.* toe box)
39 the counter
40 the vamp (upper)
41 the quarter
42 the pull-on strap (back strap, *Am.* boot strap)
43 the lining
44 the eyelet reinforcement
45 the hook
46 the eyelet
47 the bootlace (shoelace, *Am.* bootstring, shoestring)
48 the tongue; *when attached to the uppers*; tongue gusset (half-bellows tongue)
49 the leather patch;
50–54 the bottom,
50 and **51** the sole (shoe sole), a leather sole:
50 the outsole of bend leather (bend, sole leather)
51 the insole, an inner sole;
52 the welt
53 the shank (waist)
54 the heel;
55 the upper;
56 the rubber heel (heel)
57 the heel iron (iron heel-protector, horseshoe)
58 the toe plate (steel tip)
59 the hobnail
60 the shoe knife (cobbler's knife)
61 the heel-parer (paring knife)
62 the sewing awl
63 the bradawl (sprig bit)
64 the heel-glazing iron
65 the welt-cutter
66 the groover
67 the welt pincers (leather pincers)

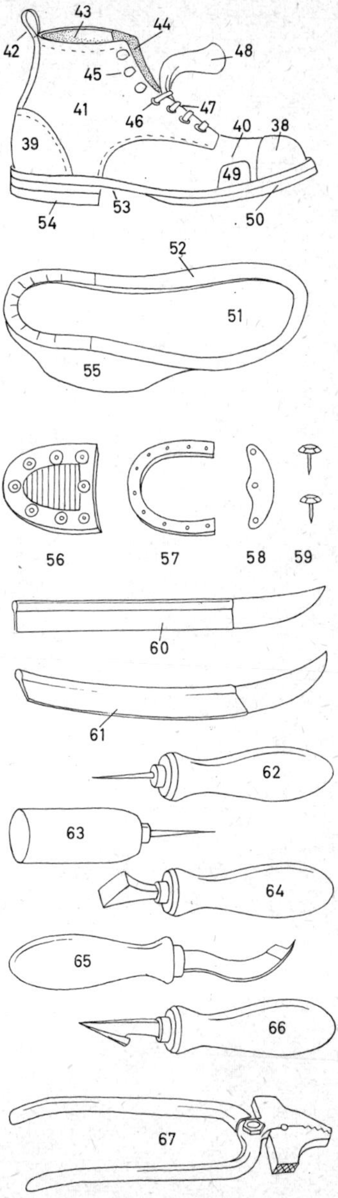

1 the leather shoe, a low shoe (Derby tie, *Am.* ties, oxford)
2 the gentleman's shoe, a suede shoe (Derby brogue, deerskin shoe, buckskin shoe):
3 the crepe rubber sole;
4 the fabric shoe
5 the rubber overshoe, a rubber shoe (*Am.* rubbers)
6 the wooden-soled shoe, a wooden-soled sandal
7 the rope sandal (bast shoe); *sim.*: straw shoe
8 the boot
9 the button shoe, a child's shoe
10 the shoe-button hook
11 the felt shoe, a felt casual
12 the slip-on casual
13 the Derby casual
14 baby's shoe
15 the high boot (high leg boot)
16 the boot tree (boot-stretcher)
17 the long shoehorn
18 the heel protector
19 the shoehorn
20 the walking shoe (men's Oxford tie-shoe)
21 the working boot (heavy-duty boot, *Am.* stogy)
22 the sports shoe
23 the hiking shoe (brogue) with fringed tongue, a girl's shoe
24 the gym shoe (tennis shoe, Plimsoll)
25 the golf shoe
26 the elastic-sided boot (*Am.* congress boot)
27 the galosh (golosh, overshoe, *Am. coll.* rubber)
28 the top boot
29 the sandal
30 the leather gaiter (leather spat)
31 the cloth spat (short cloth gaiter)
32 the evening shoe (dancing shoe)
33 the snakeskin shoe, a luxury shoe
34 the beach sandal:
35 the wedge heel
36 the cork sole;
37 the buckled shoe:
38 the shoe buckle;
39 the strap shoe
40 the court shoe (pumps):
41 the high heel;
42 the moccasin
43 a light lady's shoe the upper of which is plaited to the sole
44 the evening sandal, a lady's shoe
45 the slipper:
46 the collar
47 the pompom (pompon);
48 the mule (bath slipper)

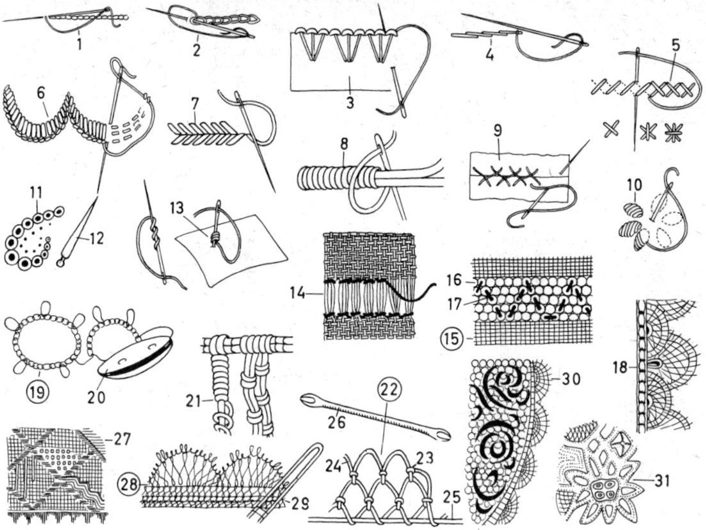

1 the backstitched seam (quilting seam)
2 the chain stitch
3 the ornamental stitch
4 the stem stitch
5 the cross stitch, double cross stitch
6 the buttonhole stitch (buttonholing, scalloping)
7 the fishbone stitch
8 the couching stitch
9 the herring-bone stitch
10 satin stitch (flat stitch work)
11 the eyelet embroidery (broderie anglaise)
12 the stiletto
13 the twisted knot stitch (French knot)
14 drawn-thread work (hemstitch)
15 tulle work (tulle lace):
16 the tulle background (net background)
17 the darning stitch;
18 the pillow lace (bobbin lace, bone lace); *kinds:* Valenciennes, Brussels lace
19 tatting:
20 the tatting shuttle;
21 macramé work (knotted work)
22 netting (filet):
23 the netting loop
24 the netting thread
25 the mesh pin (mesh gauge)
26 the netting needle;
27 openwork (à-jour-work)
28 hair-pin work (gimping):
29 the gimping needle (hair pin);
30 needle-made lace (point lace, lace work); *kinds:* reticella lace (Greek lace, Greek point, Roman lace, Roman point), Venetian lace, Alençon lace; *sim.* with metal thread: filigree work (filagree work)
31 the braid embroidery

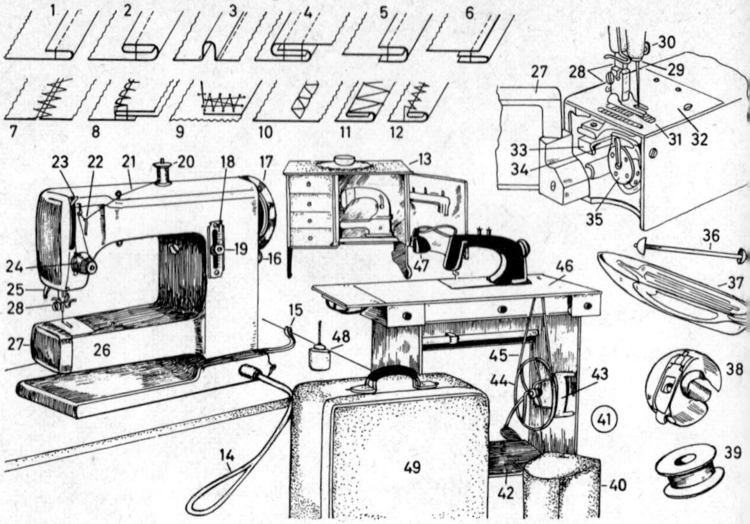

1–12 machine-stitched seams:
1 the fold
2 the hem
3 the tuck (pleat held by stitching)
4 the machine fell, flat seam
5 the trimming (binding)
6 the braid (piping, edging)
7 the zigzag stitch (selvage to selvage, selvedge to selvedge)
8 the angle stitch
9 the criss-cross stitch
10 the hemstitch
11 hemming in zigzag stitch
12 the zigzag hem stitch;
13 the sewing machine cabinet
14–47 the sewing machine,
14–40 the electric sewing machine:
14 the knee lever
15 the connecting flex
16 the bobbin-winder
17 the balance wheel
18 the stitch scale
19 the regulator for setting the stitch length
20 the reel of thread (reel of cotton, *Am.* spool of thread)
21 the upper thread (needle thread), a sewing thread
22 the thread hook
23 the thread take-up lever
24 the tension disk or disc
25 the presser foot lifter
26 the darning arm
27 the hinged cap
28 the presser bar (presser) with the presser foot
29 the needle bar
30 the needle clamp screw (thumb)
31 the feed point
32 the feed plate
33 the feed bar
34 the clip (latch)
35 the bobbin (*Am.* spool)
36 the empty bobbin for the under-thread (for the bobbin thread, *Am.* spool thread)
37 the sliding shuttle
38 the rotating shuttle

39 the under-thread spool or bobbin
40 the sewing machine cover;
41 the treadle frame (stand):
42 the treadle
43 the dress guard
44 the driving wheel
45 the driving belt;
46 the sewing table
47 the sewing machine light;
48 the oil can, a squirt oiler with sewing machine oil
49 the sewing machine case
50 the spool of sewing silk
51 the card of darning (mending) yarn or wool
52 the tacking (basting) thread
53 the thimble
54 the reel with selvage (selvedge) tape (with list)
55 the sewing machine needle
56 the sewing needle
57 the darning needle (darner)
58 the eye of the needle
59 the bodkin for elastic
60 the safety-pin
61 the ladder-mender (stocking repairer)
62 the dot (tracing) wheel (tracer)
63 the darning egg (darning ball, darning last)
64 the darning mushroom
65 the dressmakers' shears (cutting out shears)
66 the buttonhole scissors
67 the backing (buckram)
68 the pattern
69 the lining
70 the trimmers (cutting-out scissors)
71 the fashion magazine (*Am.* fashion journal)
72 the pattern sheet (pattern book)
73 the tape measure (measuring tape), an inch tape
74 the sewing box or work box with hinged compartments
75 the seamstress (sempstress, dressmaker); *sim.* cutter
76 the dressmaker's dummy or dress form
77 the pin cushion
78 the pin
79 the pin head
80 the shoulder pad
81 the snippet (scrap of cloth)
82 the dressmaker's chalk

103 Ladies' Hairdresser

1–34 ladies' hairdresser's (hair stylist's, *Am.* hairdresser shop) and beauty salon (*Am.* beauty parlor, beauty shop),

1–18 manicure:

1 the manicurist (manicure)

2 the finger bowl

3 the cuticle-remover (*Am. coll.* hangnail remover)

4 the cosmetics trolley:

5 the nail scissors

6 the cuticle scissors

7 the nail file

8 the nail-cleaner;

9 the mascara with eyelash brush

10 the tissues for facial compresses

11 the beauty cream; *sim.* day cream, night cream

12 the nail varnish (nail polish, *Am.* nail laqueur, nail enamel)

13 the varnish remover (polish remover, *Am.* laqueur remover, enamel remover);

14 the skin lotion (the astringent lotion; *Am.* skin freshener lotion)

15 the make-up

16 the eyebrow pencil

17 the face powder (powder)

18 the sulphurous (*Am.* sulfurous) powder;

19 the lipstick

20 Eau de Cologne (Cologne, *Am.* cologne, Cologne water)

21 the lavender water

22 the glycerine;

23 the drier

24 the hair net

25 the permanent wave (perm) machine

26 the gown (*Am.* cape)

27 dandruff (scurf)

28 the female hairdresser (coiffeuse)

29 the setting lotion

30 the hand-drier

31 the cold-wave lotion (waving lotion)

32 the hair dye

33 the beauty specialist (*Am. coll.* beautician), giving a face massage (*Am.* a facial massage, a facial treatment, a facial)

34 the massage chair;

35 the hair-curler (curler)

36 the hair-comb (back-comb, side-comb)

37 the flare brush for brush waving

38 the curling tongs (curling irons)

39 the thinning scissors

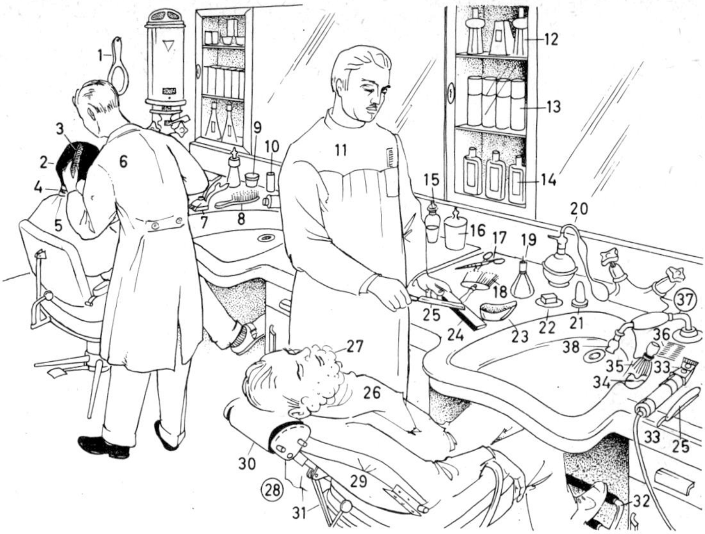

1–38 the hairdresser's shop (barber's shop, *Am.* hairdresser shop, barber shop):
1 the hand mirror
2 the haircut
3 the hairdresser's comb (comb for hair-cutting and trimming)
4 the roll of crepe paper
5 the cape (hair-dressing cloak)
6 the hairdresser's (barber's) assistant, cutting hair
7 the hair-clipper
8 the hair brush
9 the hair cream
10 the brillantine
11 the hairdresser (barber), shaving
12 the hair oil
13 the hair tonic (tonic for the scalp)
14 the after-shave lotion
15 the shampoo
16 the antiseptic
17 the hair scissors
18 the neck brush (neck-duster)
19 the powder spray
20 the scent spray (perfume spray, *Am.* atomizer)
21 the shaving soap
22 the styptic pencil, a stick of alum
23 the lathering dish (shaving dish)
24 the strop (razor strop)
25 the razor
26 the napkin as protective cloth
27 the lather
28 the hairdresser's (barber's) chair:
29 the chair back
30 the head-rest
31 the adjusting rod;
32 the foot-rest
33 the electric clippers (electric shears)
34 the soap dish
35 the shaving brush
36 the fine-tooth comb
37 the basin shower (hand shower):
38 the rose (shower rose, spray head)

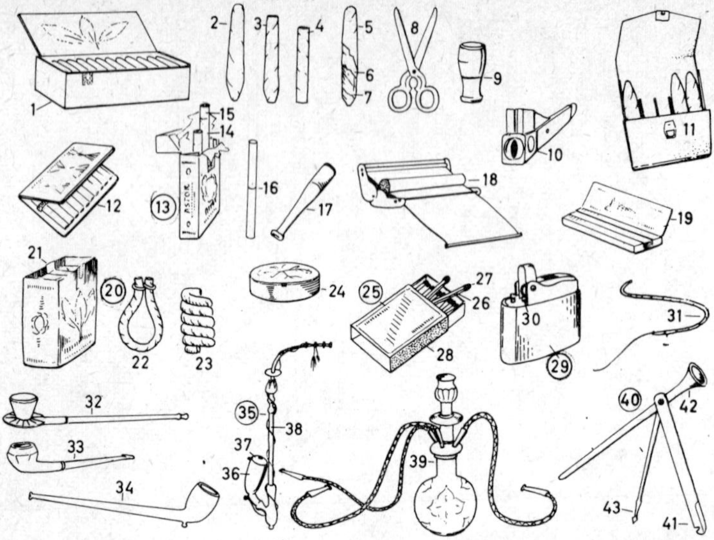

1 the box of cigars
2 the cigar; *kinds :* Havana cigar, Brazilian cigar, Sumatra cigar
3 the small cigar
4 the cheroot (*Am.* stogie)
5 the wrapper
6 the binder
7 the filler (filling)
8 the cigar scissors
9 the cigar-holder
10 the cigar-cutter
11 the cigar case
12 the cigarette case
13 the cigarette packet (*Am.* pack of cigarettes):
14 the cigarette (*sl.* fag, smoke, *Am. pop.* gasper)
15 the cigarette tip; *kinds :* gold tip, cork tip, filter tip;
16 the Russian cigarette
17 the cigarette-holder
18 the cigarette machine
19 the packet of cigarette papers
20 the packet of tobacco; *kinds :* fine cut, medium cut:
21 the revenue stamp;
22 the pigtail (twist of tobacco)
23 the chewing tobacco; *a piece :* plug (quid, chew)
24 the snuff box with snuff
25 the match-box:
26 the match
27 the sulphurated (*Am.* sulfurated) head or tip
28 the striking surface;
29 the lighter:
30 the flint;
31 the wick
32–39 pipes:
32 the chibouk (chibouque)
33 the short pipe
34 the clay pipe (Dutch pipe)
35 the long pipe:
36 the pipe bowl
37 the bowl lid
38 the pipe stem;
39 the hookah (narghile, narghileh, hubble-bubble), a pipe in which the smoke is passed through water;
40 the set of smokers' requisites (*fam.* smoker's companion, trinity):
41 the pipe-scraper
42 the tobacco-presser
43 the pipe-cleaner

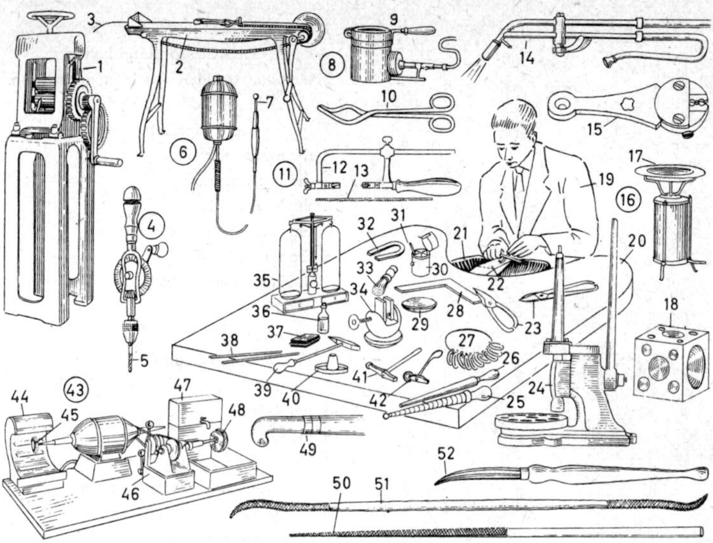

1 the wire and sheet roller
2 the draw bench
3 the wire [gold, or silver, wire];
4 the hand brace (*Am.* hand gun drill):
5 the drill;
6 the suspended (pendant) electric drilling machine:
7 the spherical cutter (cherry);
8 the melting pot:
9 the melting pot (crucible);
10 the crucible tongs
11 the piercing saw (frame saw):
12 the piercing-saw frame
13 the piercing-saw blade;
14 the soldering blowlamp
15 the die
16 the treadle (foot) blower:
17 the soldering disk or disc;
18 the swage block
19 the goldsmith
20 the work bench
21 the bench pan
22 the filing pin
23 the metal shears
24 the wedding-ring sizing machine
25 the ring gauge (*Am.* gage)
26 the ring-rounding tool
27 the ring size gauge (*Am.* gage)
28 the steel set-square
29 the leather pad (leather bag)
30 the box of punches
31 the punch
32 the magnet
33 the bench brush
34 the engraving ball (joint vice)
35 the gold and silver scales (assay balance)
36 the soldering flux
37 the plate of charcoal
38 the stick of solder
39 the soldering iron (soldering bit)
40 the soldering borax
41 the shaping hammer
42 the chasing (enchasing) hammer
43 the polishing and burnishing machine:
44 the dust-catcher (dust collector)
45 the polishing brush (polishing mop)
46 the revolution regulator
47 the burnishing box
48 the burnishing brush;
49 the bloodstone (red haematite, *Am.* hematite)
50 the tapered file
51 the channelling file (*Am.* channeling file; fluting file)
52 the polishing steel

107 The Watchmaker and Clocks

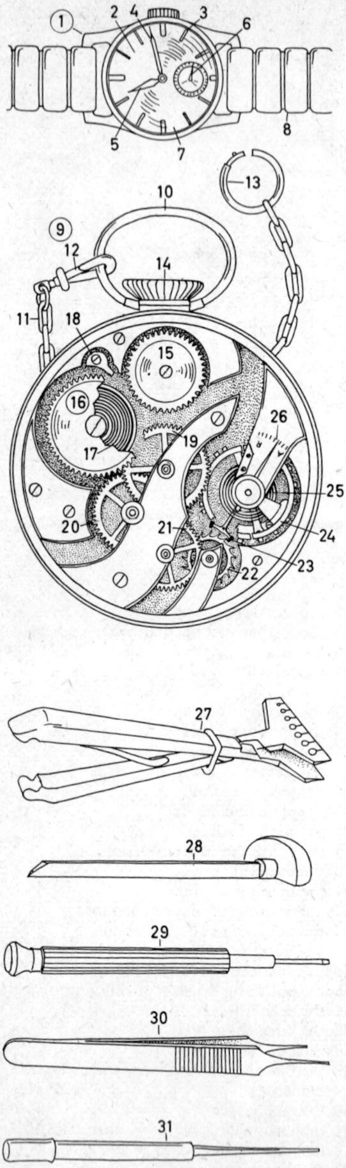

1 the self-winding wrist watch (wrist watch with self-winding device):
2 the dial (face, dial plate, dial piece, hour plate)
3 the figures (chapters)
4 the minute hand
5 the hour hand
6 the seconds hand
7 the watch glass (*Am.* crystal)
8 the watch bracelet, a watch strap;
9 the pocket watch (*Am.* stem winder):
10 the ring (bow)
11–13 the watch chain (watch guard):
11 the link
12 the swivel
13 the boltring;
14–26 the movement,
14–17 the motion work (*Am.* stem winding gear):
14 the button (crown)
15 the winding wheel (transmission wheel)
16 the barrel:
17 the mainspring (watch spring);
18 the click (pawl)
19–21 the gearing:
19 the minute wheel
20 the third wheel
21 the seconds wheel;
22 and **23** the escapement:
22 the escape wheel
23 the pallets;
24–26 the regulator:
24 the balance
25 the balance spring (hair spring)
26 the index lever (regulator lever);
27-31 watchmaker's tools (*Am.* findings):
27 the hand pliers
28 the graver
29 the screwdriver
30 the tweezers
31 the oiler;
32 the hall clock (grandfather clock):

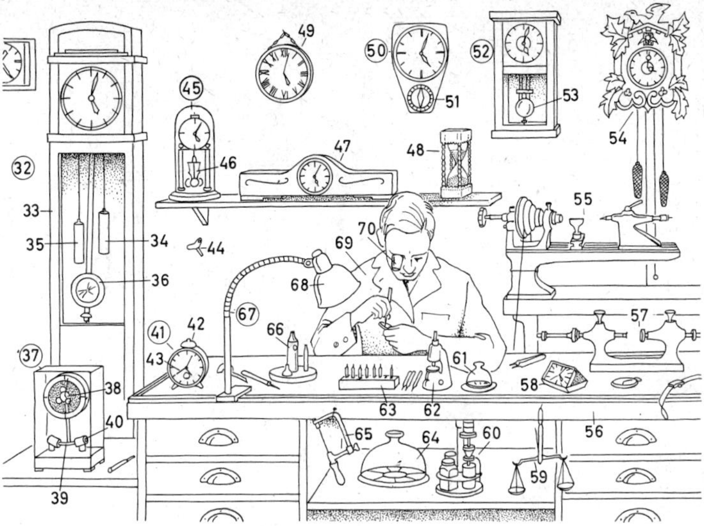

33 the clock case
34 the striking weight
35 the movement weight
36 the pendulum;
37 the electric clock:
38 the hour wheel
39 the nickel steel pendulum
40 the permanent magnet;
41 the alarm clock (alarm):
42 the alarm bell (bell)
43 the hand;
44 the clock key (key)
45 the four-hundred-day clock (annual clock):
46 the torsional pendulum;
47 the mantel clock with striking mechanism (bracket clock)
48 the hour glass (sand glass)
49 the plate clock
50 the kitchen clock:
51 the timer;
52 the wall clock (regulator):
53 the compensation pendulum;
54 the cuckoo clock
55 the watchmaker's lathe (precision lathe)
56 the work bench
57 the pivot-buffing machine (polishing lathe, polishing head)
58 the travelling (*Am.* traveling) alarm
59 the gold-scales
60 the cleaning apparatus for clocks and watches
61 the bell jar for precision instruments
62 the riveting stand
63 the punch for riveting
64 the work tray
65 the watchmaker's saw
66 the watchmaker's anvil
67 the work table lamp:
68 the reflector;
69 the watchmaker
70 the watchmaker's eye glass (watchmaker's magnifying glass)

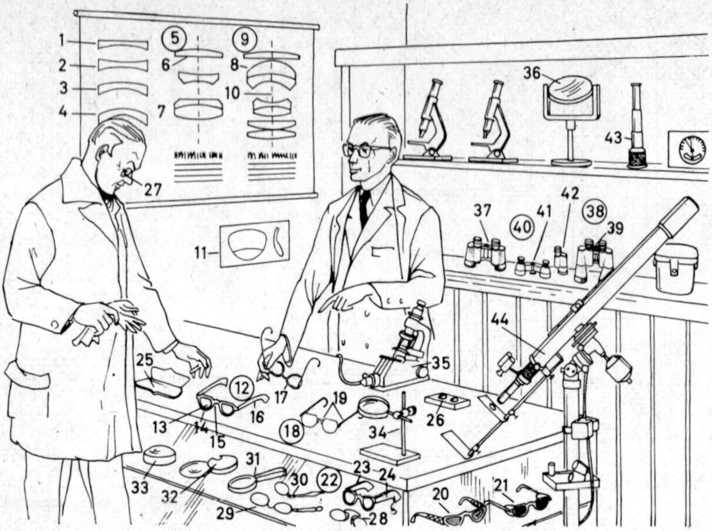

1–8 spherical lenses,
1–4 concave lenses (divergent lenses):
1 the plano-concave lens
2 the biconcave (double-concave) lens
3 the convexo-concave lens
4 the meniscus lens;
5–8 convex lenses (convergent lenses),
5 the plano-convex lens:
6 the plane surface;
7 the biconvex (double-convex) lens
8 the concavo-convex lens;
9 the optical system (system of lenses):
10 the axis;
11 the bifocal glass (two-strength glass)
12–24 spectacles (glasses, *coll.* specs),
12 the horn-rimmed glasses (horn rims):
13 the spectacle lens (spectacle glass)
14–16 the spectacle frame:
14 the rim of the lenses
15 the bridge
16 the side (*Am.* bow);
17 the metal rim
18 the rimless spectacles:
19 the bridge and sides;
20 the sun glasses
21 the blind person's glasses
22 the combined glasses and hearing aid:
23 the microphone leg (*Am.* microphone bow)
24 the battery leg (*Am.* battery bow);
25 the spectacle (glasses) case
26 the contact lens
27 the monocle (eye glass)
28 the pince-nez
29 the lorgnette
30 the lorgnon
31–34 magnifying glasses (magnifiers):
31 the magnifying glass with handle
32 the folding lens
33 the contact magnifier
34 the stand magnifying glass;
35 the vertex refractionometer
36 the concave mirror
37–44 telescopes and field glasses:
37 the field glass, binoculars
38 the hunting binoculars, a night glass:
39 the central focus(s)ing wheel;
40 the opera glass(es):
41 the bending bar;
42 the monocular field glass
43 the telescope
44 the amateur observation telescope

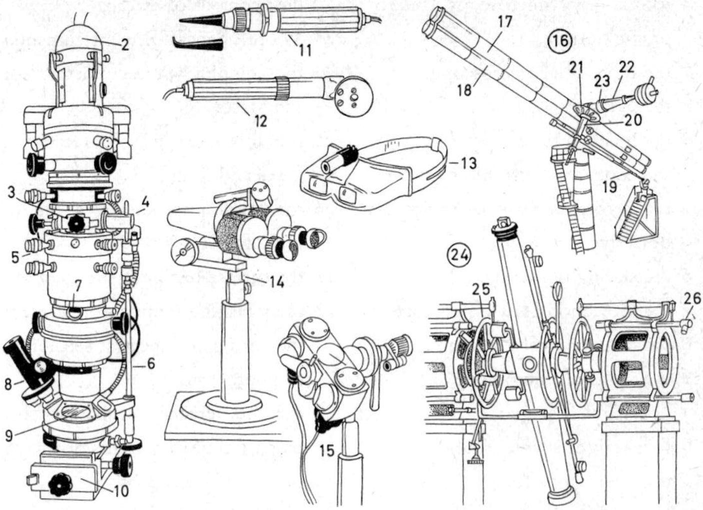

1 the electron microscope,
2–10 the microscope tube:
2 the cathode-ray discharge head
3 the door of the object chamber
4 the object chamber handle
5 the aperture diaphragm knob
6 the object stage adjustment
7 the intermediate screen-viewer
8 the final screen-viewer
9 the telescopic magnifier
10 the photographic chamber;
11–15 ophthalmic instruments:
11 the sclera lamp
12 the skiascope (retinoscope)
13 the binocular head-band magnifier
14 the cornea microscope
15 the ophthalmometer;
16–26 astronomical instruments,
16 the refracting telescope (refractor):
17 the photographic tube
18 the visual tube
19 the finder
20 the hour axis
21 the hour circle
22 the declination axis
23 the declination circle;
24 the meridian circle (transit circle):
25 the graduated scale
26 the reading microscope

1–23 instruments for microscopic technology (microscopy, microscopic optics),
1 the monocular microscope:
2 the eyepiece
3 the inclined tube
4 the condenser with filter holder
5 the revolving nosepiece with the objectives
6 the sliding object stage
7 the projection drawing mirror;
8 the phase contrast attachment
9 the surgical microscope, a binocular microscope:
10 the straight eyepiece tube;
11 the colposcope for gynaecological examinations:
12 the inclined eyepiece tube;
13 the incident-light microscope:
14 the epi-condenser
15 the tube socket
16 the objective slide changer;
17 the stereo test microscope for microstereoscopic examinations:
18 the binocular inclined twin tube;
19 the camera microscope for microphotography:
20 the vertical illuminator for bright-field, black-ground, and polarisation, photography
21 the microscope camera
22 the microscope lamp;
23 the konimeter for measuring the dust content of the air;
24–29 optical measuring instruments:
24 the dipping refractometer for food tests
25 the interferometer for tests on gases and liquids
26 the rapid photometer, a microphotometer
27 the surface-testing instrument
28 the reflecting monochromator for measuring the spectral sensibility of photoelectric cells
29 the interference comparator for precision measurements by means of light wavelengths;
30–38 geodetic (geodesic, topographic) instruments,
30 the reduction tacheometer or tachymeter (double-image rangefinder) for optical distance measurement:
31 the scale microscope
32 the reading eyepiece
33 the height-index level with coincidence-setting device
34 the optical plummet
35 the centering rod
36 the determinant triangle
37 the distance staff (base);
38 the plane-table micrometer for precision height measurements in building above and below ground

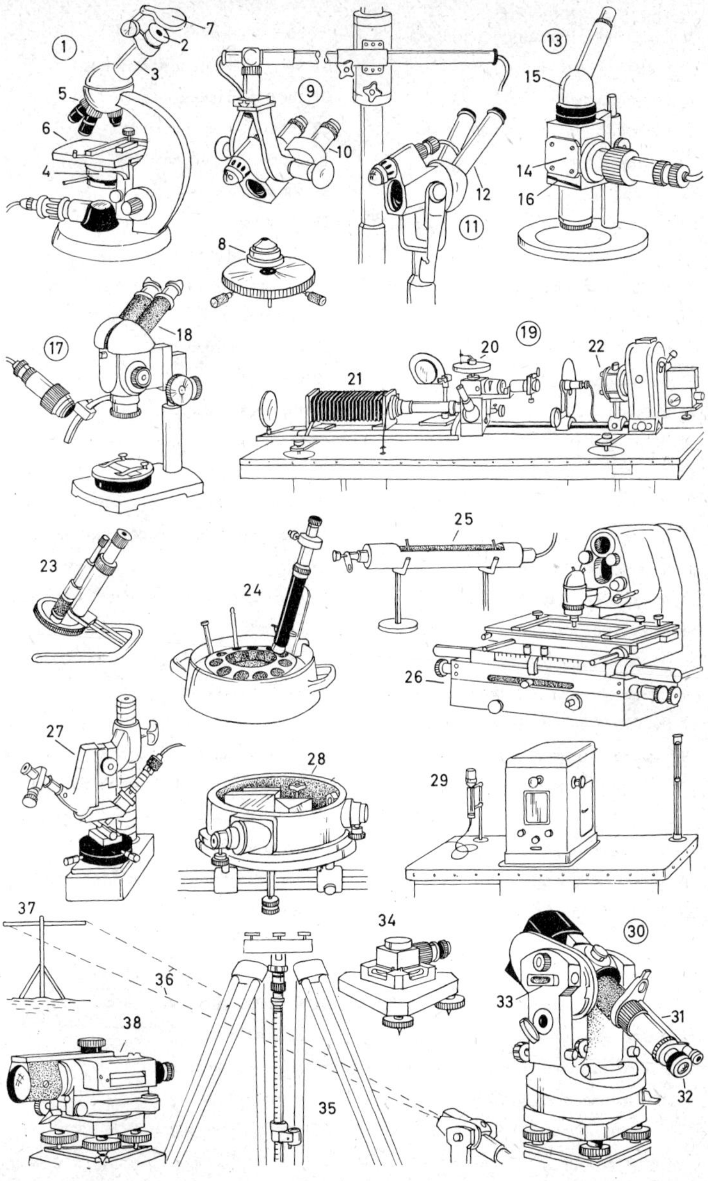
1
2
3
4
5
6
7
8
9
10
11
12
13
14
15
16
17
18
19
20
21
22
23
24
25
26
27
28
29
30
31
32
33
34
35
36
37
38

111 Photography I

1–27 cameras (photographic apparatuses or apparatus):
1 the box camera
2 the folding camera (camera with bellows):
3 the body
4 the film-winder (winding knob, roll-film-winder)
5 the shutter release (release, *Am.* push-button release)
6 the viewfinder
7 the bellows
8 the strut
9 the baseboard;
10–14 the lens (lens mount):
10 the lens
11 the exposure scale
12 the shutter setting scale
13 the focusing scale
14 the cocking lever;
15 the reflex camera:
16 the viewfinder hood (reflex hood)
17 the focusing lens (finder lens);
18 the miniature camera, a tube camera:
19 the exposure-counter
20 the timing knob
21 the socket for accessories (accessory shoe)
22 the viewfinder
23 the re-winding knob
24 the self-timer (autotimer)
25 the interchangeable lens
26 the removable base;
27 the stereoscopic camera (stereo camera, stereo) for stereophotography (three-dimensional photography);
28 the stereoscope:
29 the stereo slide
30 the milled wheel;
31–59 photographic accessories,
31 the tripod (stand):
32 the tripod bush or socket
33 the ball-and-socket joint
34 the tripod head or top
35 the set screw
36 the tripod leg;
37 the self-timer (self-timing release, autotimer)
38 the exposure meter:
39 the knob;
40 the range-finder:
41 the bracket for fitting into the accessory shoe
42 the cable release
43 the telephoto lens for telephotographs
44 the synchronised diaphragm shutter (diaphragmatic shutter), an instantaneous shutter; *other kind:* focal-plane shutter:
45 the diaphragm leaf or blade
46 the flash contact
47 the winder for the self-timer;
48 the filter (colour filter, *Am.* color filter)
49–59 flash units (flash-lights, flash lamps, flash guns),
49 the bulb flash-light:
50 the battery case
51 the connecting cord or flex (connector)
52 the reflector, a concave mirror
53 the flash bulb (vacuum flash);
54 the electronic flash unit:
55 the accumulator and the charging apparatus
56 the attachment bracket
57 the flash stick
58 the flash tube, a gas-discharge valve
59 the strap

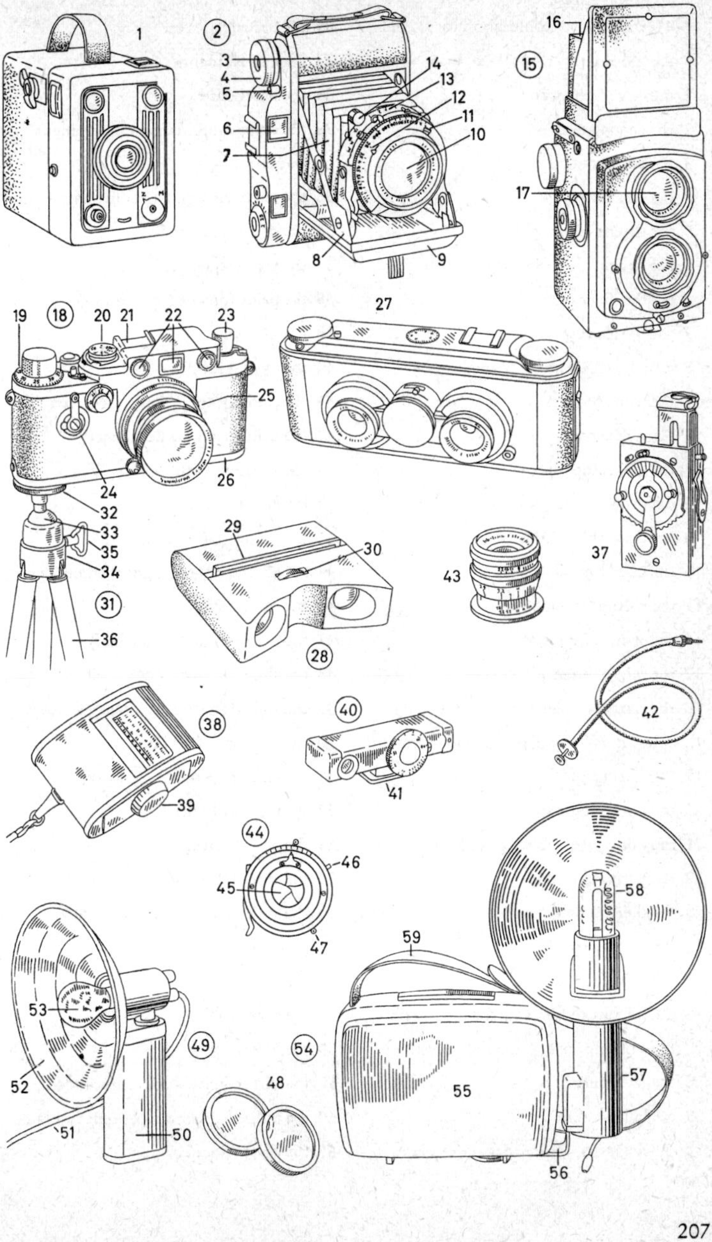
1
2
3
4
5
6
7
8
9
10
11
12
13
14
15
16
17
18
19
20
21
22
23
24
25
26
27
28
29
30
31
32
33
34
35
36
37
38
39
40
41
42
43
44
45
46
47
48
49
50
51
52
53
54
55
56
57
58
59

1–61 the photographic laboratory; *also:* darkroom:

1 the developing tank
2 the rinsing tank
3 the fixing tank
4 the washing tank
5 the drying cabinet
6 the drying clip (film clip), a metal clip for the negative
7 the bottom clip
8 the film clip, a wooden clip
9 the print (positive)
10 the bottle of chemicals
11 the glass stopper
12 the drop-bottle
13 the developing tank
14 the glass funnel
15 the natural sponge
16 the artificial sponge
17 the fan (ventilator)
18 the darkroom lamp with interchangeable filters for red, green, and orange, light
19 the alarm clock
20 the photographer
21 the miniature-film strip, a film strip
22 the masking frame
23 the thermometer
24 the printing paper
25 the printing frame
26 the miniature-film case for the roll film (cassette)
27 the printing-box (printer, *Am.* photo copier)
28 the enlarger:
29 the lamp-house
30 the negative-holder (negative-carrier)
31 the focusing lever
32 the exposure timer
33 the baseboard
34 the composing frame (enlargement frame);
35 the measuring glass (graduated measure)
36 the developing dish
37 the roller squeegee
38 the print forceps (print tongs)
39 the film-wiper
40 the drying rack
41 the photographic plate, a negative
42 the print-trimmer (trimmer)
43 the washing basin
44 the electric print dryer
45 the photograph (photo)

46 and 47 the interchangeable mount:

46 the plate-mark
47 the board (mount, *Am.* mat);
48 the slide (transparency)
49 the slide frame (transparency frame)
50 the photograph frame
51 the enlargement
52 the photo album:
53 the album cover
54 the album leaves (loose leaves);
55 the slide projector (transparency projector), a projector:
56 the lamp-house
57 the slide-holder
58 the lens;
59 the direct-light lamp, a studio lamp
60 the indirect-light lamp, a reflector lamp:
61 the photo floodlamp

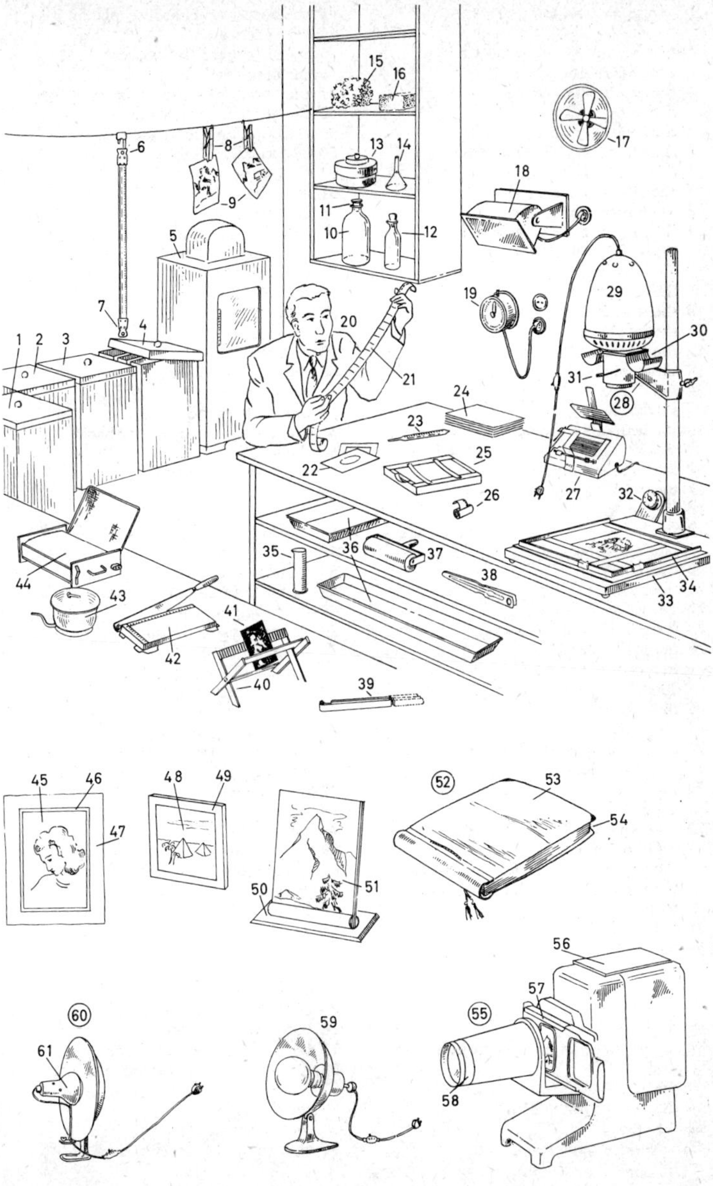
1
2
3
4
5
6
7
8
9
10
11
12
13
14
15
16
17
18
19
20
21
22
23
24
25
26
27
28
29
30
31
32
33
34
35
36
37
38
39
40
41
42
43
44
45
46
47
48
49
50
51
52
53
54
55
56
57
58
59
60
61

113 The Building Site (Site) I

Engl. site = *Am.* lot

1–49 the carcass [building a house, house construction]:
1 the basement of tamped (rammed) concrete
2 the concrete plinth
3 the basement (cellar) window
4 the outside cellar steps
5 the utility room window
6 the utility room door
7 the ground floor (*Am.* first floor, street floor, main floor)
8 the brick wall
9 the lintel (window head)
10 the reveal (revel)
11 the inner jamb
12 the window sill (window ledge)
13 the reinforced concrete lintel
14 the upper floor (upper storey, *Am.* second floor)
15 the wall of hollow building (concrete) blocks
16 the solid ceiling
17 the working platform
18 the bricklayer
19 the labourer (unskilled workman, *Am.* laborer, hired man, hand)
20 the mortar trough
21 the chimney
22 the staircase cover boards
23 the scaffold pole
24 the platform railing
25 the scaffold angle brace (diagonal stay)
26 the ledger
27 the putlog
28 the plank platform (board platform)
29 the guard board
30 the tie bar joint with chain, or rope, lashing
31 the builder's hoist (builder's lift, *Am.* building elevator)
32 the mixer-driver (*Am.* machinist)
33 the concrete-mixer (concrete-mixing machine), a gravity mixer:
34 the mixing drum
35 the loading skip;
36 the concrete aggregate [sand and gravel]
37 the wheelbarrow
38 the water hose
39 the mortar pan (mortar trough, mortar tub)
40 the pile of bricks
41 the stacked lining boards
42 the ladder
43 the bag of cement
44 the hoarding (boarding, planking), a plank fence
45 the signboard (billboard)
46 the hingless door
47 the firm's name-plates (fascia boards)
48 the hut (shed, site office)
49 the building site latrine;
50–57 bricklayer's tools:
50 the plumb-bob
51 the thick pencil
52 the trowel
53 the tiling hammer (bricklayer's hammer)
54 the lump hammer
55 the level
56 the float
57 the patter;
58–68 bonding:
58 the common brick
59 the sretcher (stretching) bond
60 the header bond:
61 the setting back (racking back);
62 the English bond:
63 the stretcher course
64 the header course;
65 the cross bond
66 the chimney bond:
67 the first course
68 the second course;
69–82 the foundation trench:
69 the profile board
70 the crossing of the cords
71 the plumb line
72 the side of the excavation
73 the upper edge board
74 the lower edge board
75 the foundation trench
76 the navvy (*Am.* excavator, construction laborer)
77 the belt conveyor
78 the excavated earth
79 the plank roadway
80 the tree guard
81 the dragline excavator (*Am.* steam shovel):
82 the scoop bucket (*Am.* shovel);
83–91 plastering:
83 the plasterer
84 the mortar trough
85 the screen
86–89 the ladder scaffold:
86 the standard ladder
87 the boards (planks, platform)
88 the diagonal stay (diagonal brace, *Am.* X-brace)
89 the railing;
90 the protective screen
91 the rope-pulley (roller) hoist or lift

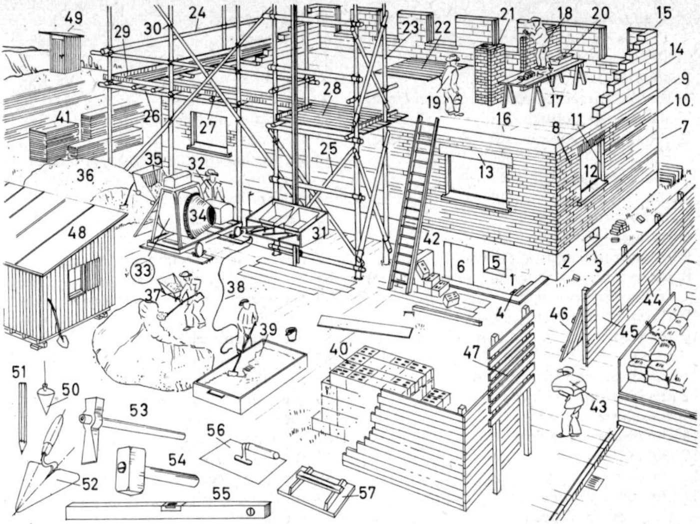
1
2
3
4
5
6
7
8
9
10
11
12
13
14
15
16
17
18
19
20
21
22
23
24
25
26
27
28
29
30
31
32
33
34
35
36
37
38
39
40
41
42
43
44
45
46
47
48
49
50
51
52
53
54
55
56
57

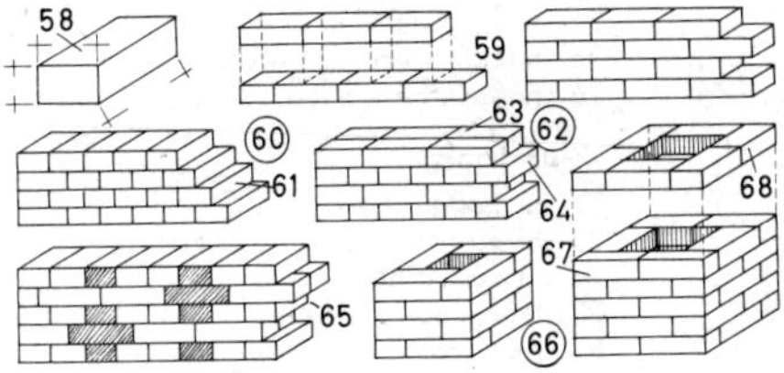
58
59
60
61
62
63
64
65
66
67
68

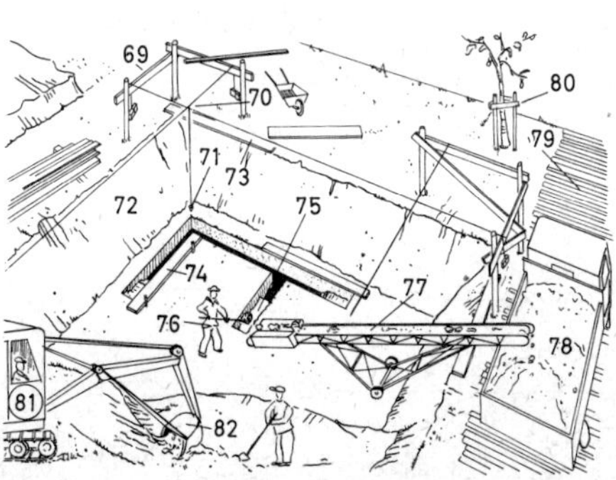
69
70
71
72
73
74
75
76
77
78
79
80
81
82

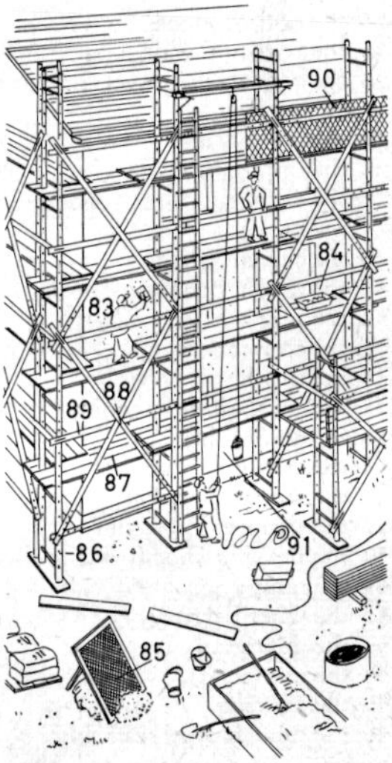
83
84
85
86
87
88
89
90
91

Engl. site = *Am.* lot

1–89 the reinforced-concrete (ferro-concrete) construction,
1 the reinforced-concrete (ferroconcrete) skeleton structure:
2 the reinforced-concrete (ferroconcrete) frame
3 the inferior purlin (beam)
4 the concrete purlin
5 the ceiling joist
6 the arch (flank);
7 the cast in situ concrete wall
8 the reinforced-concrete (ferroconcrete) ceiling or floor slab
9 the concretor, flattening-out
10 the reinforcement rods (reinforcement bars)
11 the shuttering (formwork)
12 the joist shuttering
13 the shuttering strut
14 the diagonal bracing
15 the wedge
16 the plank
17 the sheet wall (pile wall, sheet piling, sheet-pile bulkhead)
18 the lining boards
19 the circular saw (*Am.* buzz saw)
20 the bending table
21 the steel-bender
22 the hand steel-cutters or shears
23 the reinforcement rods (reinforcement bars)
24 the hollow block
25 the partition wall, a partition
26 the aggregate [gravel and sand of various grades]
27 the crane track
28 the tipping truck (tipper)
29 the concrete-mixer (concrete-mixing machine)
30 the cement silo
31 the tower slewing crane:
32 the bogie (*Am.* truck)
33 the counterweight
34 the tower
35 the crane-driver's cabin
36 the jib (boom)
37 the carrying cable
38 the concrete bucket;
39 the sleepers (*Am.* ties)
40 the braking shoe (braking block)
41 the ramp
42 the wheelbarrow
43 the guard rail
44 the hut (shed)
45 the canteen
46 the tubular-steel scaffold:
47 the standard
48 the ledger tube
49 the tie tube
50 the shoe
51 the diagonal brace
52 the planking (platform)
53 the joint;
54–76 formwork (shuttering) and reinforcement:
54 the bottom shutter
55 the side shutter of a joist
56 the cut-in bottom
57 the cross piece (supporting beam)
58 the cramp iron (cramp, dog)
59 the upright member, a standard
60 the strap
61 the cross piece
62 the stop fillet
63 the diagonal board
64 the frame timber (yoke)
65 the strap
66 the wire brace
67 the cross strut
68 the reinforcement
69 the distance piece (spacing piece)
70 the cross bar
71 the connecting rod
72 the concrete (heavy concrete)
73 the sheathing of the supports
74 the bolted frame wood
75 the bolt with thumb nut
76 the sheathing board;

77-89 tools:

77 the bending iron
78 the adjustable sheeting-carrier:
79 the adjusting screw;
80 the round-bar steel:
81 the distance block (spacer);
82 the Tor steel
83 the concrete-tamper (concrete-rammer)
84 the form for sample cubes
85 the concretor's tongs (concretor's nippers)
86 the sheeting support
87 the hand iron-cutters or shears
88 the in situ concrete vibrator:
89 the vibrating cylinder

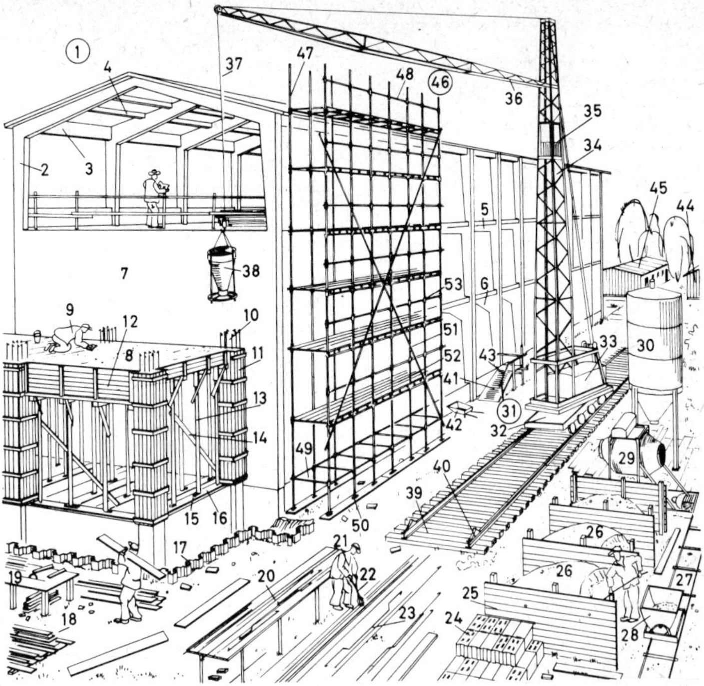
1
2
3
4
5
6
7
8
9
10
11
12
13
14
15
16
17
18
19
20
21
22
23
24
25
26
26
27
28
29
30
31
32
33
34
35
36
37
38
39
40
41
42
43
44
45
46
47
48
49
50
51
52
53

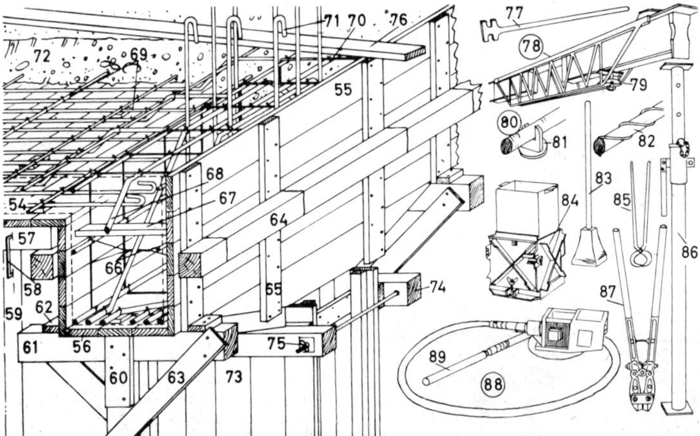
54
55
56
57
58
59
60
61
62
63
64
65
66
67
68
69
70
71
72
73
74
75
76
77
78
79
80
81
82
83
84
85
86
87
88
89

115 The Carpenter

Engl. timber = *Am.* lumber or timber

1–59 the timber yard (carpenter's yard, timber-fitting yard, fitting yard):
1 the pile of boards
2 long logs (long wood)
3 the sawing shed
4 the carpenter's workshop
5 the workshop door
6 the hand cart
7 the roof truss (principal)
8 a small tree with crown (wreath and ribbons), to celebrate erection of roof [*in Engl.* 'topping out']
9 the boarding (planking)
10 scantlings (rectangular timber, building timber)
11 the drawing floor
12 the carpenter
13 the carpenter's hat
14 the cross-cut (bucking) saw, a chain saw:
15 the traverse
16 the saw chain;
17 the mortising machine (chain cutter moulding machine, *Am.* molding machine)
18 the horse (trestle)
19 the trestled beam
20 the set of carpenter's tools
21 the electric drill
22 the dowel hole
23 the mark for the dowel hole
24 the timber to be joined
25 the stile (post, principal post, stud)
26 the corner brace
27 the brace (strut)
28 the plinth
29 the house wall
30 the window opening
31 the reveal (revel)
32 the jamb
33 the window sill (window ledge, ledge)
34 the cornice
35 the round wood
36 the floor boards
37 the hoisting rope
38 the ceiling joist (main beam)
39 the wall joist
40 the wall plate
41 the trimmer (trimming joist)
42 the tie piece
43 the inserted (intermediate, false, sound-boarded) floor
44 the floor filling of breeze, fine slag etc.
45 the fillet
46 the opening for the stairs
47 the chimney
48 the timber-framed wall:
49 the wall plate
50 the summer
51 the window jamb
52 the corner stile (corner strut, corner stud)
53 the head post (quarter post)
54 the brace with mortise (with mortice)
55 the cross bar (nogging piece)
56 the sill rail (breast rail)
57 the window lintel (window head)
58 the head
59 the filled-up pan or bay or panel;
60–82 carpenter's tools (*Am.* carpenter's findings):
60 the half-rip (hand, panel) saw
61 the bow (frame, span) saw:
62 the saw blade;
63 the compass (lock, pad, keyhole) saw
64 the plane
65 the auger (gimlet)
66 the screw clamp (cramp, hold-fast)
67 the mallet
68 the two-handled saw
69 the try square
70 the broad axe (*Am.* broad ax)
71 the chisel
72 the mortise axe (mortice axe, *Am.* mortise ax)
73 the axe (*Am.* ax)
74 the carpenter's hammer:
75 the claw head;
76 the folding rule
77 the carpenter's pencil
78 the iron square
79 the draw knife
80 the shaving
81 the bevel
82 the mitre square (*Am.* miter square, miter angle);
83–96 building timber,
83 the round trunk (unconverted timber, *Am. and Can.* rough lumber):
84 the heartwood (duramen)
85 the sap (sapwood, alburnum)
86 the bark;
87 baulk
88 half timber (*Am. and Can.* shiplapped lumber):
89 wane, waney edge;
90 quarter timber
91 the plank (board):
92 the end-grain (cross-grain) timber;
93 the heartwood plank
94 the unsquared (untrimmed) board
95 the squared board
96 the slab (outside board, paling)

1
2
3
4
5
6
7
8
9
10
11
12
13
14
15
16
17
18
19
20
21
22
23
24
25
26
27
28
29
30
31
32
33
34
35
36
37
38
39
40
41
42
43
44
45
46
47
48
49
50
51
52
53
54
55
56
57
58
59

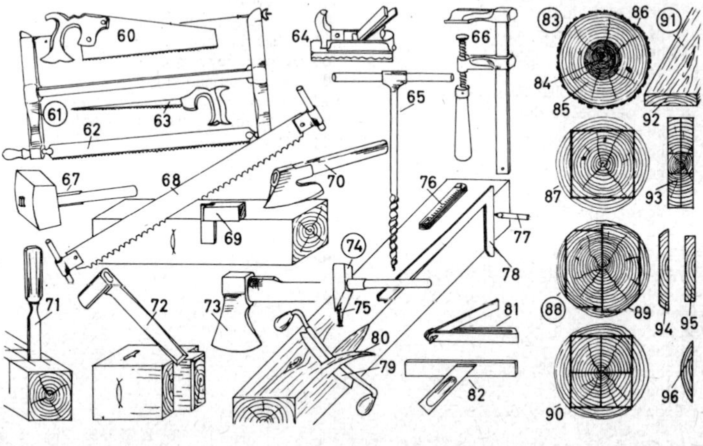
60
61
62
63
64
65
66
67
68
69
70
71
72
73
74
75
76
77
78
79
80
81
82
83
84
85
86
87
88
89
90
91
92
93
94
95
96

1–26 styles and parts of roofs,
1 the gable roof (saddleback roof, saddle roof), a ridge roof:
2 the ridge
3 the verge
4 the eaves
5 the gable
6 the dormer window;
7 the pentroof (lean-to roof):
8 the skylight (garret window)
9 the fireproof partition wall;
10 the hip roof (hipped roof):
11 the hipped end
12 the hip
13 the hipped dormer window
14 the ridge turret
15 the valley;
16 the hipped gable roof:
17 the hipped gable end;
18 the mansard roof (curb roof, French roof, gambrel roof):
19 the mansard window;
20 the saw-tooth roof:
21 the top light (north light);
22 the pavilion roof:
23 the dormer window;
24 the conical broach roof
25 the imperial roof (domed roof):
26 the vane;
27–83 wooden roofs and trusses (roof timberwork),
27 the rafter roof:
28 the rafter
29 the beam of the roof
30 the diagonal tie (cross tie)
31 the chantlate (sprocket piece)
32 the outer wall
33 the beam head;
34 the collar-beam roof:
35 the collar beam
36 the rafter;
37 the strutted collar-beam roof truss:
38 the collar beams or ties
39 the purlin
40 the post (stud)
41 the brace;
42 the king-post (unstrutted) roof truss:
43 the ridge purlin
44 the inferior purlin
45 the rafter head;
46 the queen-post (strutted) roof truss with jamb:
47 the jamb
48 the ridge board
49 the simple tie
50 the double tie
51 the purlin;
52 the strutted purlin roof truss:
53 the tie beam
54 the ceiling joist
55 the principal rafter
56 the common rafter
57 the angle brace (angle tie)
58 the brace (strut)
59 the ties;
60 the hip roof with purlin roof truss:
61 the jack rafter
62 the hip rafter
63 the jack rafter (hip jack rafter)
64 the valley rafter;
65 the queen truss:
66 the main beam
67 the summer
68 the queen post
69 the brace (strut)
70 the collar beam
71 the trimmer;
72 the solid-web wooden girder or truss:
73 the lower (bottom) member or chord
74 the upper member
75 the boarding
76 the purlin
77 the supporting outer wall;
78 the framework truss:
79 the lower member
80 the upper member
81 the post
82 the brace (strut)
83 the bearing (support);

84-98 woodwork joints (timber joints):

84 the simple mortice (mortise) and tenon joint
85 the forked mortice (mortise) and tenon joint (forked tenon)
86 the straight halved joint
87 the scarf joint
88 the oblique scarf joint
89 the dovetail halving
90 the bevel shoulder (skew) notch
91 the double bevel shoulder notch
92 the wood nail
93 the pin
94 the clout
95 the wire nail
96 the hard-wood wedges
97 the dog
98 the bolt

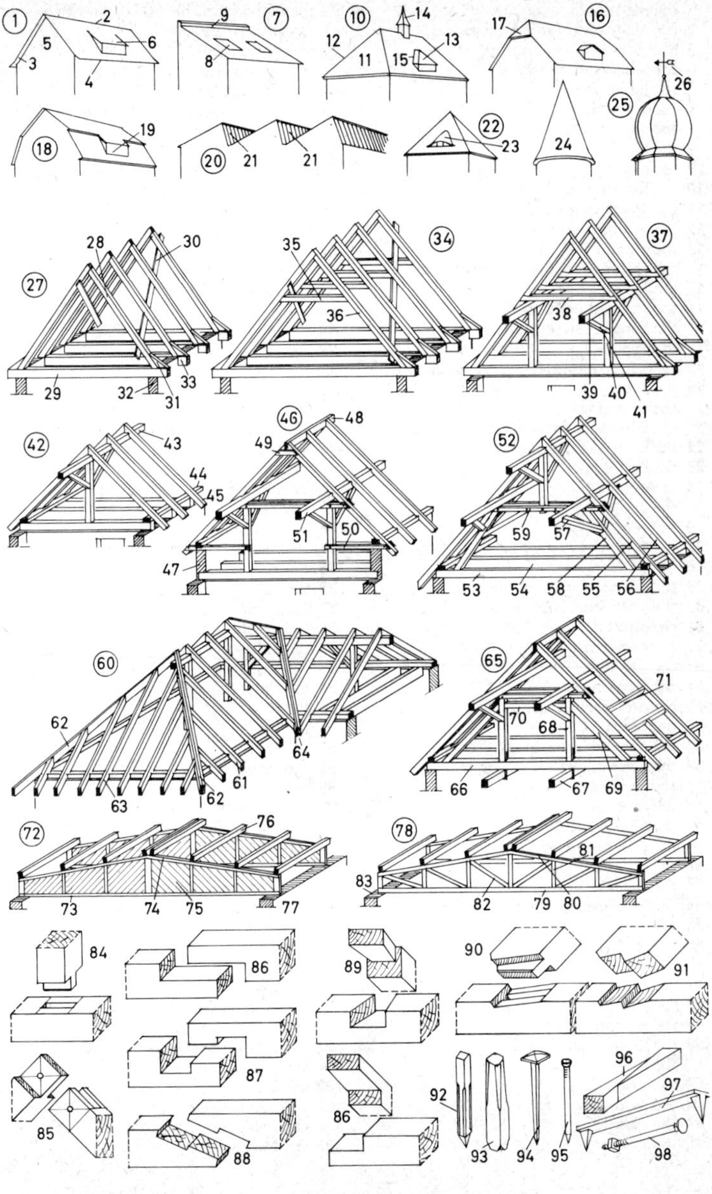
1 2 3 4 5 6 7 8 9 10 11 12 13 14 15 16 17
18 19 20 21 21 22 23 24 25 26
27 28 29 30 31 32 33 34 35 36 37 38 39 40 41
42 43 44 45 46 47 48 49 50 51 52 53 54 55 56 57 58 59
60 61 62 62 63 64 65 66 67 68 69 70 71
72 73 74 75 76 77 78 79 80 81 82 83
84 85 86 86 87 88 89 90 91 92 93 94 95 96 97 98

117 Roof and Tiler

1 the tiled roof:
2 the plain-tile double-lap roofing
3 the ridge tile
4 the ridge-course tile
5 the under-eaves tile
6 the plain tile
7 the ventilation tile
8 the hip tile
9 the hip cap
10 the hipped end
11 the valley gutter;
12 the skylight
13 the chimney
14 the chimney flashing of sheet zinc
15 the ladder hook
16 the snow guard hook
17 the battens (slating and tiling battens)
18 the batten gauge (*Am.* batten gage)
19 the rafter
20 the tile hammer
21 the lath axe (*Am.* lath ax)
22 the hod (builder's trough):
23 the hod hook;
24 the opening
25 the gable end
26 the toothed lath
27 the soffit
28 the gutter
29 the gutter pipe (rain pipe)
30 the swan's neck (swan-neck)
31 the pipe clip
32 the gutter bracket
33 the tile-cutter
34 the working scaffold:
35 the protective wall;
36 the eaves:
37 the outside (outer) wall
38 the external plaster (external rendering)
39 the built-up wall
40 the inferior purlin
41 the rafter head
42 the eaves lining
43 the double (tilting) lath
44 the insulating plates;
45–60 tiles and tile roofings,
45 the split-tiled roof:
46 the plain tile (flat tile)
47 the ridge course
48 the slip (shingle)
49 the eaves course;
50 the high-pitched roof:
51 the nib
52 the ridge tile;
53 the pantiled roof:
54 the pantile
55 the pointing;
56 the half-round tile roof (roof of convex and concave tiles):
57 the concave tile
58 the convex tile;
59 the gutter tile
60 the flap pantile;
61–89 the slate roof:
61 the roof boarding
62 the felt underlining (roofing felt, *Am.* roof paper, tar paper)
63 the roof ladder:
64 the coupling hook
65 the ridge hook;
66 the slater's plank (roof trestle):
67 the trestle rope
68 the knot
69 the ladder hook;
70 the trestle plank
71 the slater
72 the nail bag
73 the slater's hammer
74 the slate nail, a galvanized wire nail
75 the slater's shoe, a bast, or hemp, shoe
76–82 old-German method of roof-slating:
76 the eaves course
77 the corner bottom slate
78 the roof course
79 the ridge course
80 the gable slate
81 the tail line
82 the valley;
83 the trough gutter
84 the slater's shears
85 the slate:
86 the back
87 the head
88 the front edge
89 the tail;
90–103 asphalt (tarred) impregnated paper roofing and corrugated asbestos-cement roofing,
90 the asphalt impregnated paper roof:
91 the width [parallel to gutter]
92 the gutter
93 the ridge
94 the join
95 the width [at right angles to gutter];
96 the clout nail
97 the corrugated asbestos-cement roof:
98 the corrugated sheet
99 the ridge capping piece
100 the lap
101 the wood screw
102 the rust-proof zinc cup
103 the lead washer

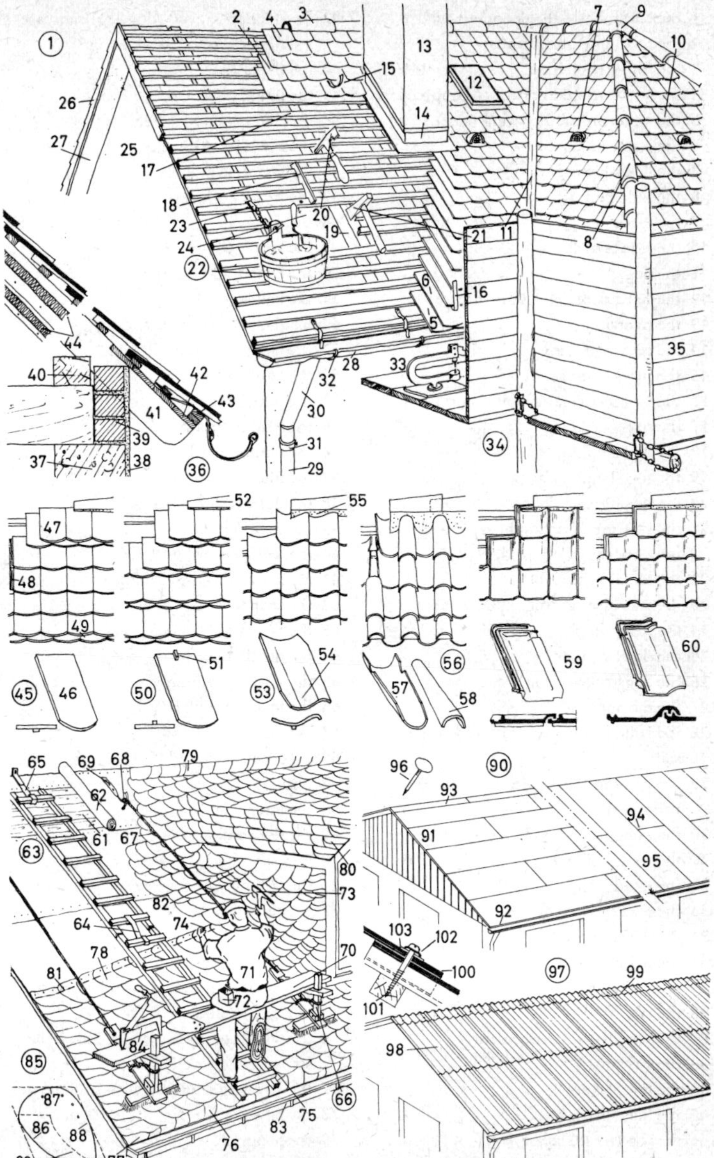
1
2
3
4
5
6
7
8
9
10
11
12
13
14
15
16
17
18
19
20
21
22
23
24
25
26
27
28
29
30
31
32
33
34
35
36
37
38
39
40
41
42
43
44
45
46
47
48
49
50
51
52
53
54
55
56
57
58
59
60
61
62
63
64
65
66
67
68
69
70
71
72
73
74
75
76
77
78
79
80
81
82
83
84
85
86
87
88
89
90
91
92
93
94
95
96
97
98
99
100
101
102
103

1 the basement wall, a concrete wall
2 the footing (foundation):
3 the foundation base;
4 the horizontal dampproof (damp) course
5 the waterproofed coating (seal)
6 the rendering
7 the brick paving
8 the sand bed
9 the earth
10 the side board
11 the peg
12 the hard core (*Am.* telford base)
13 the oversite
14 the cement paving
15 the brickwork base
16 the basement stairs, solid stairs:
17 the step
18 the first step
19 the top (landing) step
20 the nosing
21 the skirting (skirting board, baseboard, mop board, washboard);
22 the metal balustrade
23 the staircase landing
24 the front door
25 the door scraper
26 the flagstone paving
27 the mortar bed
28 the solid ceiling, a reinforced-concrete slab
29 the ground-floor (*Am.* first floor) brick wall
30 the ramp
31 the wedge step
32 the tread
33 the riser
34–41 the landing:
34 the landing beam
35 the ribbed reinforced-concrete floor:
36 the rib
37 the steel-bar reinforcement
38 the subfloor;
39 the level layer
40 the finishing layer
41 the top (tread) layer;
42–44 the dog-legged (dog-leg) staircase, a staircase without a well hole:
42 the first step
43 the newel post
44 the outer (outside) string;
45 the inner (wall) string
46 the staircase bolt
47 the tread
48 the riser
49 the string wreath
50 the balustrade:
51 the baluster
52–62 the intermediate landing:
52 the baluster (handrail) bend
53 the hand-rail;
54 the head post
55 the landing beam
56 the lining board
57 the fillet
58 the light-weight slab
59 the ceiling plaster
60 the wall plaster
61 the inserted (false) ceiling
62 the strip flooring;
63 the skirting
64 the quadrant
65 the staircase window
66 the main landing beam
67 the fillet
68 and **69** the inserted (false) ceiling:
68 the intermediate floor
69 the floor filling (pugging);
70 the laths
71 the lathing (plaster key)
72 the ceiling plaster
73 the subfloor
74 the parquet floor with pugging
75 the quarter-newelled (*Am.* quarter-neweled) stairs
76 the winding (corkscrew, spiral, well) staircase with well hole
77 the winding staircase with solid newel:
78 the newel
79 the handrail

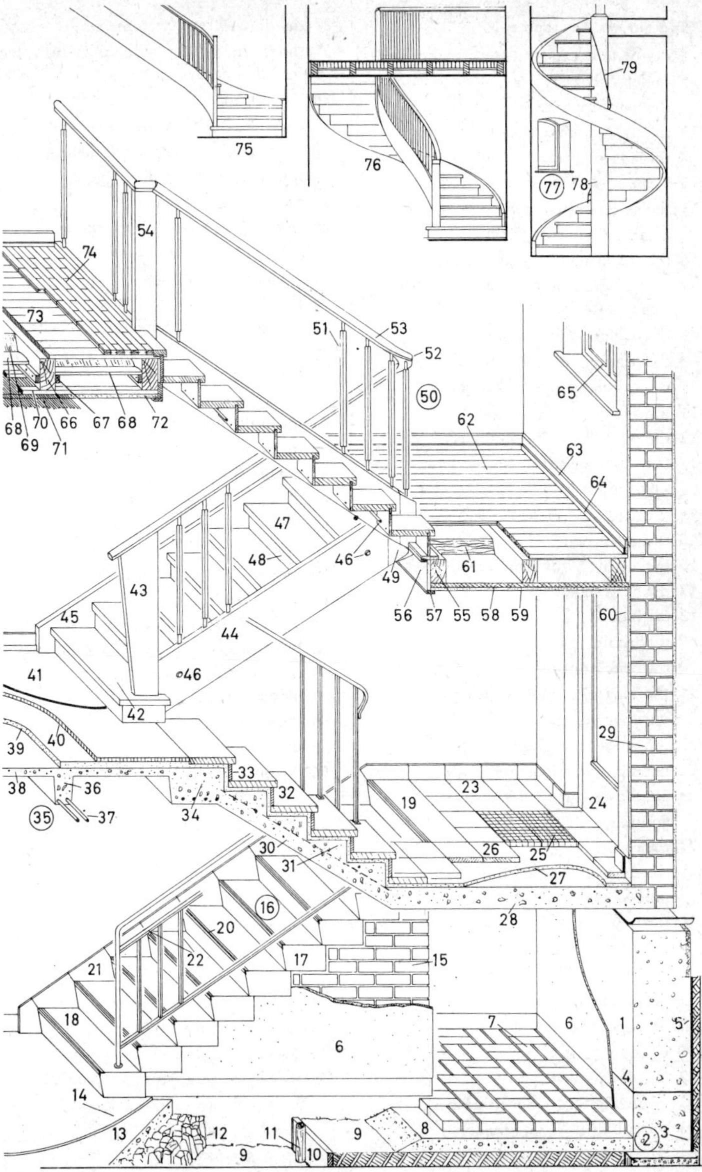
75
76
77
78
79
54
74
73
51
53
52
50
65
68
69
70
71
66
67
68
72
62
63
64
47
48
46
49
61
43
45
56
57
55
58
59
60
44
41
046
42
40
39
29
33
38
36
32
34
35
37
19
23
24
26
25
30
31
27
16
28
20
22
17
15
21
18
6
7
6
1
5
4
14
13
12
11
10
9
9
8
2
3

119 The Plumber

Engl. tap = *Am.* faucet

1 the plate shears (tinsmith's snips, *Am.* tinner's shears)
2 the bent snips (angle shears)
3 the straightening plate
4 the lapping plate
5–8 the soldering tools:
5 the spirit heated soldering iron, a hatchet soldering iron (hatchet bit)
6 the soldering iron (copper bit)
7 the soldering stone, a sal-ammoniac block
8 the soldering flux (soldering fluid);
9 the beading iron for forming rolls
10 the angular reamer, a reamer
11 the bench
12 the pipe vice (*Am.* pipe vise)
13 the plumber (tinsmith, tinman, tinker, *Am.* tinner)
14 the mallet (wooden mallet)
15 the guillotine
16 the forming iron or mandrill
17 the head stake
18 the block
19 the anvil:
20 the beck iron;
21 the flanging, beading, swaging and wiring machine
22 the funnel-forming machine
23 the pipe-fitter (gas-fitter)
24–30 the gas pipe (*Am.* gas conduit):
24 the rising gas pipe
25 the secondary pipe (distributing pipe)
26 the bracket
27 the gas plug-cock
28 the gas meter
29 the bracket
30 the pipeline;
31 the step ladder:
32 the safety chain;
33–67 fitting tools and fitting parts:
33 the snips for cutting holes, a pair of curved shears
34 the draw-off tap (water tap, bib tap, tap)
35 the special bib tap with underseat valve for rewashering
36 the raised nose pillar tap
37 the swivel outlet angle valve
38 the the swivel outlet combination fitting (hot and cold)
39 the flushing valve
40 the malleable iron pipe fittings (elbow, tee and boiler union)
41 the anti-syphon trap
42 the tread cutting stock and die
43 the stock shears (bench shears) with leverage
44 the beam compasses (trammels, *Am.* beam trammel)
45 the hollow punch
46 the beading swage (beading hammer)
47 the beading iron
48 the chamfering hammer
49 the blowlamp with soldering iron bracket
50 the gas-heated soldering iron
51 the adjustable spanner or wrench (clyburn) [Swedish form]
52 the monkey wrench, a screw-spanner
53 the shifting spanner (screw wrench, monkey wrench)
54 the wheel pipe-cutter
55 the gas pliers
56 the pipe wrench (gas-pipe tongs 'footprints')
57 the adjustable pipe wrench
58 the lead-pipe expander (turnpin)
59 the bell type flushing cistern:
60 the float
61 the bell
62 the flush pipe
63 the inlet ballvalve
64 the flushing lever;
65–67 gas-heating apparatus:
65 the radiant heater
66 the geyser (non-storage heater), an instantaneous gas water heater (multi-point)
67 the gas radiator

1
2
3
4
5
6
7
8
9
10
11
12
13
14
15
16
17
18
19
20
21
22
23
24
25
26
27
28
29
30
31
32

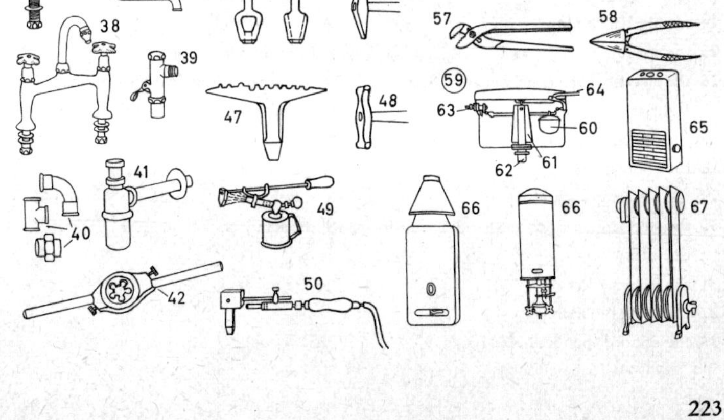
33
34
35
36
37
38
39
40
41
42
43
44
45
46
47
48
49
50
51
52
53
54
55
56
57
58
59
60
61
62
63
64
65
66
66
67

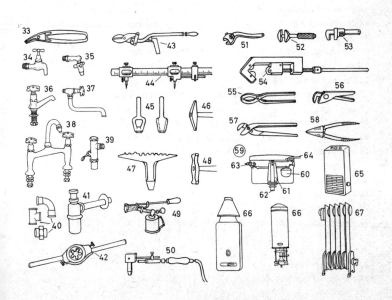

1 the electrician (wireman)
2 the light, bell, or door, button (press button, *Am.* push-button contact)
3 and 4 switches:
3 the tumbler switch
4 the rocker switch;
5 the socket (wall socket, plug point, *Am.* wall outlet, convenience outlet, outlet)
6 the three-pin socket
7 the three-pin plug
8 the switch-socket outlet
9 the four-pin plug (four-pole plug)
10 the surface rotary switch
11 the flush (panel, recessed) rotary switch
12 the pull switch (pendant switch):
13 the pull switch cord;
14 the three-way socket
15 the damp-proof junction box with hinged lid
16 the three-way multiple plug
17 the switch in cast-iron box
18 the screw-in miniature circuit-breaker:
19 the resetting button;
20 the extension cord:
21 the plug
22 the extension cord socket;
23 the flexible cord (flex) for connecting appliances:
24 the appliance plug
25 the spring;
26 the electric torch (pocket torch, flash-light):
27 the dry cell (torch battery)
28 the contact spring;
29 the two-way socket
30 the steel drawing-in tape for drawing in the wire
31 the floor socket
32 the spirit blowlamp
33 the conduit-bender (*Am.* hickey)
34 the insulating tape (*Am.* friction tape)
35 the fuse (cartridge fuse, *Am.* plug-type cut-out), a fuse cartridge with fuse link (fuse element, fusible element):
36 the indicator
37 the fuse cap
38 the fuse body
39 the fuse contact;
40 the two-way connecting block
41 the conduit sleeve
42 the voltmeter
43 the wire in flexible conduit
44 the insulating conduit (insulating tube)
45 the electrician's scissors
46 the screwdriver
47 the conduit-bending pincers (*Am.* hickey)
48 the die stock for threading solid conduit
49 the cable shears
50 the round-nose pliers
51 the insulation-stripping pliers
52 the eyelet pliers
53 the combination pliers:
54 the insulated handles;
55 the Rawlplug drill, with holder
56 the incandescent (filament) lamp or bulb (electric bulb):
57 the glass bulb
58 the coiled filament
59 the exhaust tube (exhaust tubing)
60 the lamp cap with thread
61 the seal
62 the contact;
63 the electrician's knife
64 the screw socket adapter

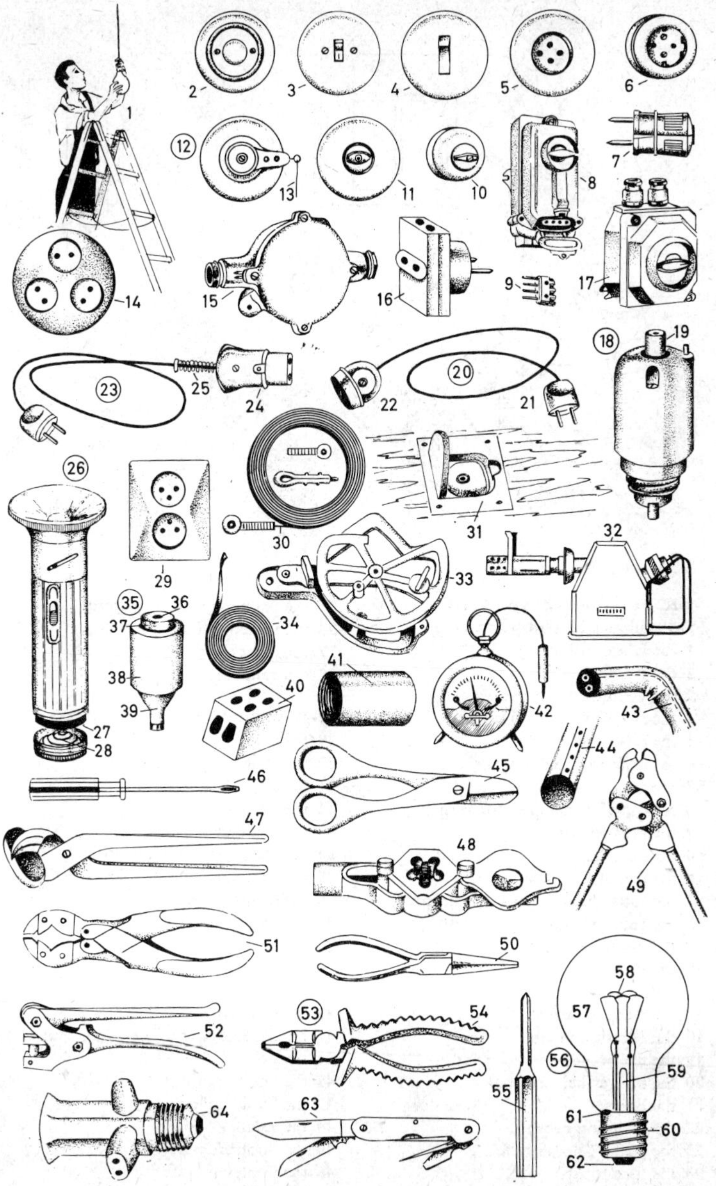
1
2
3
4
5
6
7
8
9
10
11
12
13
14
15
16
17
18
19
20
21
22
23
24
25
26
27
28
29
30
31
32
33
34
35
36
37
38
39
40
41
42
43
44
45
46
47
48
49
50
51
52
53
54
55
56
57
58
59
60
61
62
63
64

121 Painter and Paperhanger

1-28 painting walls and ceilings,
1–3 whitewashing (distempering):
1 the whitewash brush
2 the painter
3 the whitewash (distemper);
4 the double (painter's) ladder
5 the oil-painted dado
6 the distemper (whitewash) roller
7 the can of varnish
8 the can of turpentine (*coll.* turps)
9 the powder paint
10 the tin of glossy paint (top coat)
11 the pail of distemper
12 the spray gun (air brush, paint spray)
13 the painter's smoothing brush
14 the marbling brush
15 the round brush
16 the radiator brush
17 the veining brush
18 the lettering brush
19 the flat brush
20 the badger-hair softener
21 the liners
22 the stippling brush
23 the gilder's brush
24 the lime brush
25 the painter's stencil (pattern)
26 the stencil roller
27 the paint pail
28 the painter;

29-41 paperhanging:
29 the paste pot
30 the wallpaper paste
31 the size
32 the wallpaper
33 the wallpaper border
34 the skirting (skirting board)
35 the paperhanger (*Am.* decorator)
36 the length of wallpaper
37 the paste-brush
38 the smoother
39 the paperhanger's (*Am.* decorator's) hammer
40 the seam roller
41 the paperhanger's (*Am.* decorator's) trestle;
42 the linoleum (lino)
43 the linoleum lining
44 the balata
45 the linoleum putty
46 the linoleum knife

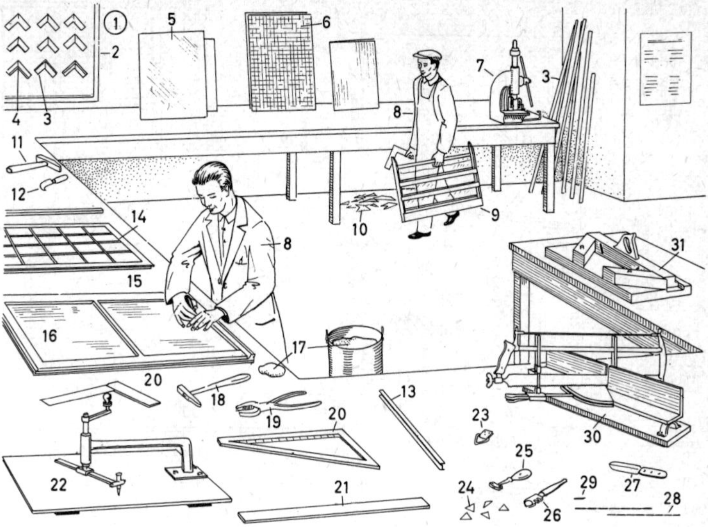

1 the glazier's workshop:
2 the samples of frame wood (samples of frames)
3 the frame wood
4 the mitre joint (mitre, *Am.* miter joint, miter)
5 sheet glass; *kinds:* window glass, frosted glass, muslin glass, crystal (flint) plate glass, thick glass, opaque (milk, alabaster) glass, compound glass, armoured (*Am.* armored) glass (safety glass)
6 cast glass; *kinds:* stained glass, ornamental glass, raw glass, bull's-eye glass, reinforced glass, line glass (lined glass)
7 the transom mitre (*Am.* transom miter)
8 the glazier; *kinds:* building glazier, art glazier
9 the glass holder (frail)
10 broken glass
11 the lead hammer
12 the lead knife
13 the came (groved rod of cast lead)
14 the leaded lights
15 the work bench
16 the pane (pane of glass)
17 the putty
18 the glazier's hammer (tack hammer)
19 the glazier's pincers (tower pincers)
20 the glazier's square
21 the glazier's lath
22 the glazier's beam compass
23 the eyelet
24 the wedge sprig
25 and 26 glass-cutters:
25 the glazier's diamond glass-cutter, a glass-cutter
26 the steel-wheel glass-cutter;
27 the putty knife
28 the sprig wire
29 the sprig (sprig pin)
30 the mitre (*Am.* miter) sawing board
31 the mitre (*Am.* miter) shooting board or block

123 The Saddler

1–33 the saddlery (harness-maker's workshop, saddler's workshop):

1 the horse collar pad

2 the leather-grooving machine for pressing grooves in belts

3 the leather skiving and paring machine

4 the horse collar form

5 the saddler's hammer

6 the round knife

7 the crescent-shaped knife

8 the leather plane

9 the edging tool

10 the leather pliers

11 the webbing-stretching pliers

12 the eyelet punch

13 the revolving punch (punch pliers)

14 the saddler's tracing wheel (saddler's roulette)

15 the pricking wheel for marking the stitches

16 the saddler (harness-maker)

17 the eyelet machine

18 the electric leather-cutting machine

19 the strap-cutting machine (strap-cutter)

20 the hand sewing iron

21 the stitching block

22 the stitching horse

23 the saddler's treadle sewing machine

24 the folding iron

25 the hollow punch

26 the round awl:

27 the awl;

28–33 saddler's (harness-maker's) needles:

28 the pin (skewer)

29 the curved sewing needle

30 the gimp (gymp) needle

31 the saddler's needle

32 the sewing awl with curved point

33 the drawing awl (collar awl, *Am.* tape needle)

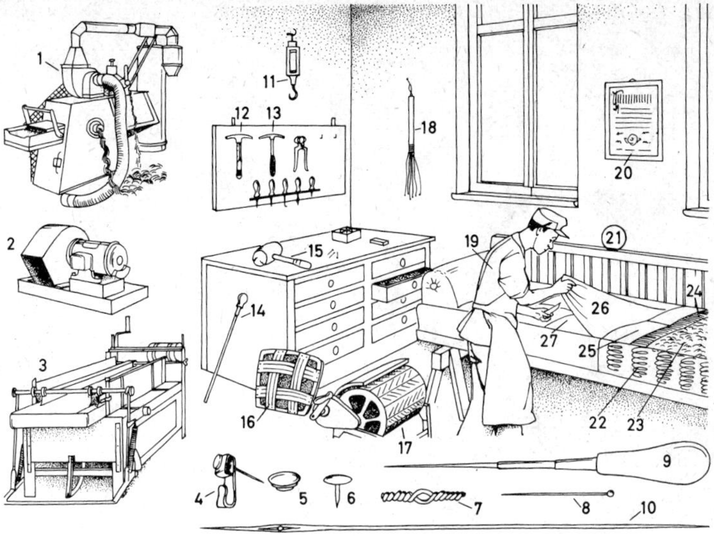

1–27 the upholsterer's workshop:

1 the combined picking and filling machine

2 the picking-machine [table model]

3 the mattress-filling and covering machine

4 the wall hook

5 the upholstery button

6 the gimp pin

7 the sewing clip

8 the pin

9 the awl (pricker)

10 the double-pointed needle

11 the horsehair-unraveller (*Am.* unraveler) for unravelling (*Am.* unraveling) curled horsehair

12 the webbing hammer

13 the upholsterer's hammer

14 the rammer

15 the round mallet

16 the webbing

17 the hand-operated teasing machine

18 the whip (cowhide whip, cat-o'-nine tails)

19 the upholsterer

20 the master's diploma

21 the couch:

22 the spiral (helical) spring

23 the padding (upholstering) material (stuffing; *kinds:* horsehair, seaweed, kapok, or rubberised hair)

24 the hessian (*Am.* burlap)

25 the filling cloth (scrim)

26 the couch covering

27 the panel

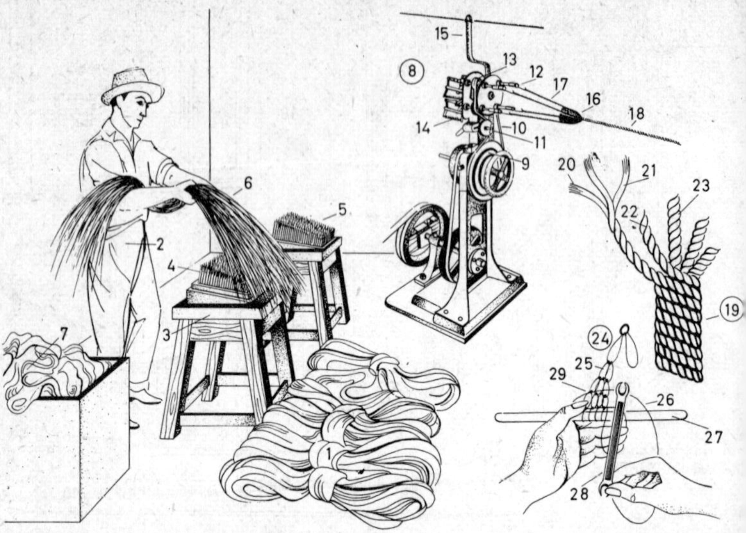

1–18 the ropemaker's workshop (rope walk; *outdoors:* rope yard),
1–7 hackling (heckling):
1 the raw hemp
2 the hackler
3 the hackling (heckling) bench
4 the coarse hackle
5 the fine hackle
6 the hackled (heckled) hemp
7 the tow (scutching tow, waste, codilla) from the coarse hackle; the hemphard (hemp tow) from the fine hackle;
8 the ropemaker's spinning machine with set of four spindles:
9 the band (strap) pulley (strap wheel)
10 the driving rope
11 the tightening device
12 the whirl
13 the driving rollers
14 the whirl pull-back springs
15 the disengaging device
16 the rope top
17 the spun yarn
18 the rope (line, cord);
19 the cable (rope):
20 the hemp fibre (*Am.* hemp fiber)
21 the single yarn (thread)
22 the strand
23 the rope core (rope heart);
24 net-making:
25 the mesh (loop)
26 the netting thread (thread, twine)
27 the mesh pin
28 the netting needle
29 the net knot (sailor's knot, knotting point)

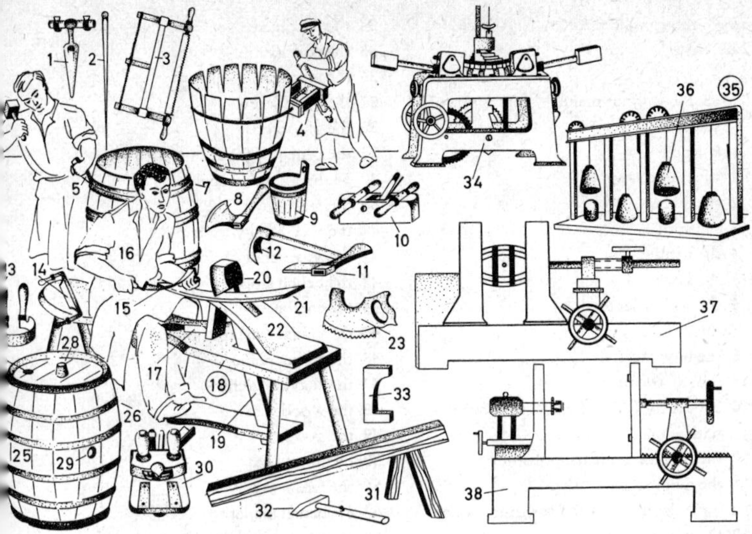

1–33 the cooper's workshop (coopery, cooperage):
1 the bung hole (*Am.* faucet hole) borer (tap-hole borer, pod auger)
2 the gauging (*Am.* gaging) rod
3 the frame (span) saw
4 the windlass for drawing the staves together
5 the mallet
6 the hoop-driver (hoop-setter, hand driver)
7 the wooden hoop
8 the round axe (*Am.* round ax)
9 the piggin
10 the two-man plane
11 the river (cleaver)
12 the hollow adze
13 the round shave
14 and **15** draw knives (draw shaves):
14 the spokeshave
15 the hollowing knife;
16 the cooper (white cooper, cask-maker, dry-cooper; *in wine-growing districts:* wet-cooper, barrel-maker)
17 the cooper's knife
18 the cooper's bench (shaving-horse):
19 the saddle post
20 the saddle post head
21 the cask stave
22 the saddle:
23 the croze saw
24 the cask:
25 the cask body
26 the hoop
27 the tap (spigot, vent) hole
28 the bung
29 the bung hole (*Am.* faucet hole);
30 the croze (crozer, chimbre, *Am.* chimber) for making the croze (groove) in the cask bottom
31 the stave-jointing bench
32 the cooper's set hammer
33 the cooper's module;
34 38 cask-making machines:
34 the stave-bending machine (hoop-bending machine)
35 the steaming cone:
36 the cone;
37 the cask-adzing machine
38 the crozing machine

127 The Cabinet-maker

Engl. mitre = *Am.* miter, *Engl.* vice = *Am.* vise

1–65 the cabinet-maker's (joiner's) workshop,
1–8 frame saws,
1 the frame saw:
2 the lever
3 the cord
4 the handle
5 the saw blade
6 the spring set teeth
7 the frame;
8 the bow saw;
9 the square mallet
10–31 the tool chest (tool cupboard) with joiner's tools:
10 the pumice stone for polishing
11 the buff pad
12 bottles with stain and furniture polish
13 the mitre square
14 the bench hammer (London hammer)
15 the try square, a back square;
16–18 brace bits:
16 the countersink
17 the twist bit
18 the centre bit (*Am.* center bit);
19 the gimlet
20 the mortise gauge (*Am.* gage) for drawing parallel lines
21 the pincers (nippers)
22 the brace:
23 the ratchet, a locking device
24 the chuck;
25 the chisels
26 the saw file, a triangular file
27 the pad saw (compass saw, keyhole saw):
28 the pad-saw handle;
29 the wood file
30 the wood rasp
31 the riffler file (riffler);
32 the veneering press:
33 the press screw;
34 and **35** the plywood:
34 the decorative veneer
35 the core (ground);
36 the large hand screw
37 the hand screw
38 the glue well
39 the glue pot for animal glue
40–44 the joiner's bench:
40 the front vice
41 the vice head with handle
42 the vice screw
43 the bench stop
44 the end vice;
45 the cabinet-maker (joiner)
46 the trying plane
47 the shavings (chips)
48 the wood screw
49 the saw set
50 the mitre box
51 the tenon saw
52–61 bench planes:
52 the smoothing plane
53 the jack plane
54 the toothing plane:
55 the handle (horn)
56 the wedge
57 the plane iron (cutter)
58 the plane stock;
59 the rabbet plane (fillister)
60 the router plane ('old woman's tooth')
61 the spokeshave;
62 the firmer chisel
63 the mortise chisel (framing chisel, heading chisel)
64 the gouge (firmer gouge)
65 the corner chisel (paring chisel)

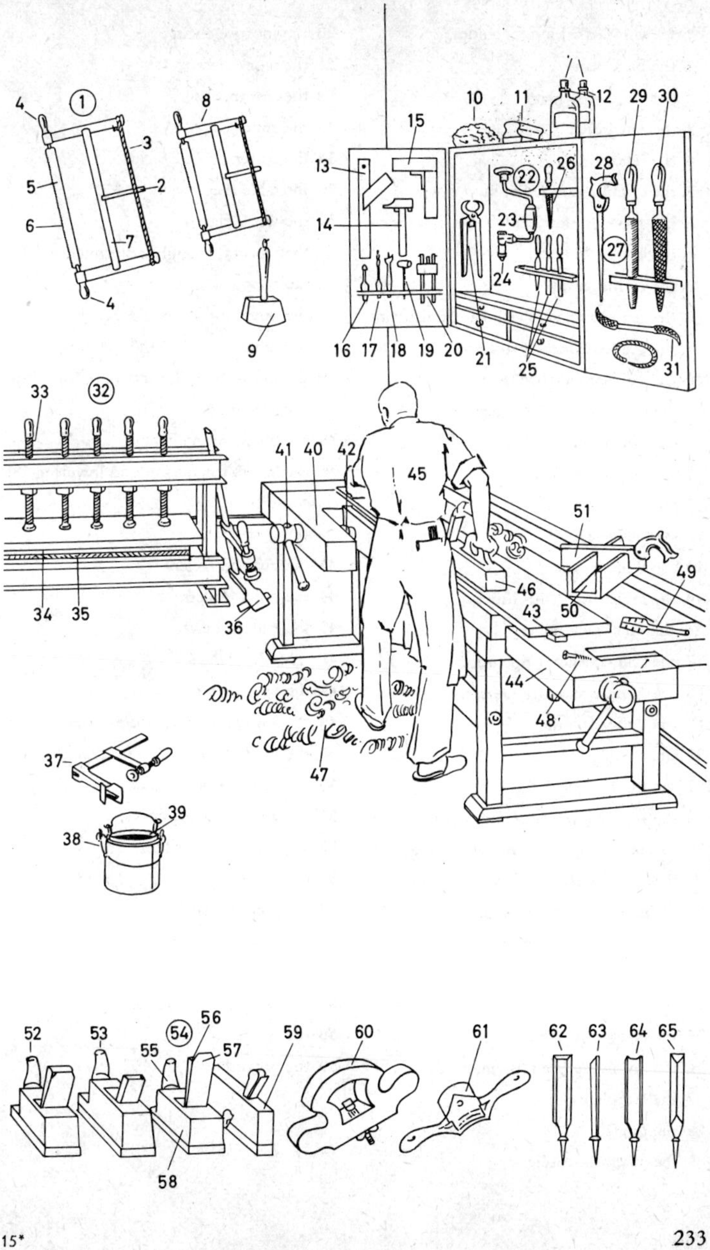
1
2
3
4
5
6
7
8
9
10
11
12
13
14
15
16
17
18
19
20
21
22
23
24
25
26
27
28
29
30
31
32
33
34
35
36
37
38
39
40
41
42
43
44
45
46
47
48
49
50
51
52
53
54
55
56
57
58
59
60
61
62
63
64
65

1–59 wood-working machines,
1 the band saw:
2 the band-saw blade
3 the saw guide
4 the fence;
5 the circular saw (*Am.* buzz saw):
6 the circular saw blade (*Am.* buzz saw blade)
7 the riving knife
8 the fence with screw thread adjustment
9 the graduated fence slide rail
10 the adjustable fence for mitres and cross-cutting (mitre fence) with graduated scale;
11 the overhead planer:
12 the cutter guard
13 the planer table;
14 the thicknesser:
15 the table (bed) with rollers
16 the kick-back fingers
17 the chip-extractor opening;
18 the spindle moulder (*Am.* molder):
19 the cutter spindle
20 the fence
21 the top bearing;
22 the router (recessing and shaping machine; copy, or profile, milling machine; surface milling and drilling machine, *Am.* die-sinking machine, tool room machine):
23 the chuck spindle
24 the router cutter (router bit)
25 the electric motor
26 the revolving head (turret head)
27 the template pin
28 the guard;
29 the chain mortiser:
30 the mortise chain
31 the work clamp;
32 the slot mortiser:
33 the chuck
34 the cutter
35 the table (bed)
36 the work clamp
37 the wheel for height adjustment of the table
38 the operating levers for positioning the table;
39 the knot-borer (knot-driller, knot-boring machine):
40 the quick-action chucks
41 the levers for raising and lowering the spindles;
42 the dowel maker:
43 the outfeed rollers
44 the guide rollers
45 the cutting head;
46 the belt sander:
47 the sanding belt
48 the sanding pad (sanding shoe)
49 the sanding table
50 the dust-extractor duct
51 the dust-extractor hood;
52 the rotary veneer lathe:
53 the thin veneer;
54 the glue spreader:
55 the spreading roller;
56 the quick-action veneer press:
57 the bottom press plates
58 the top press plates
59 the press screws

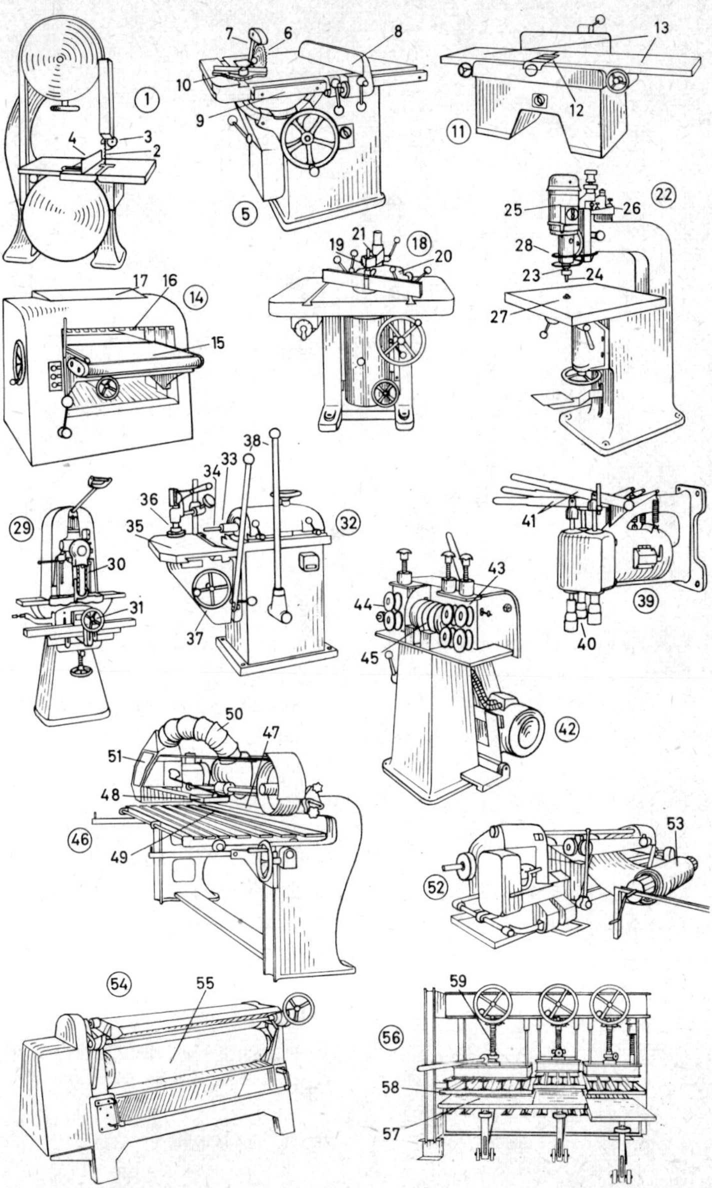
1
2
3
4
5
6
7
8
9
10
11
12
13
14
15
16
17
18
19
20
21
22
23
24
25
26
27
28
29
30
31
32
33
34
35
36
37
38
39
40
41
42
43
44
45
46
47
48
49
50
51
52
53
54
55
56
57
58
59

129 The Wood-turner

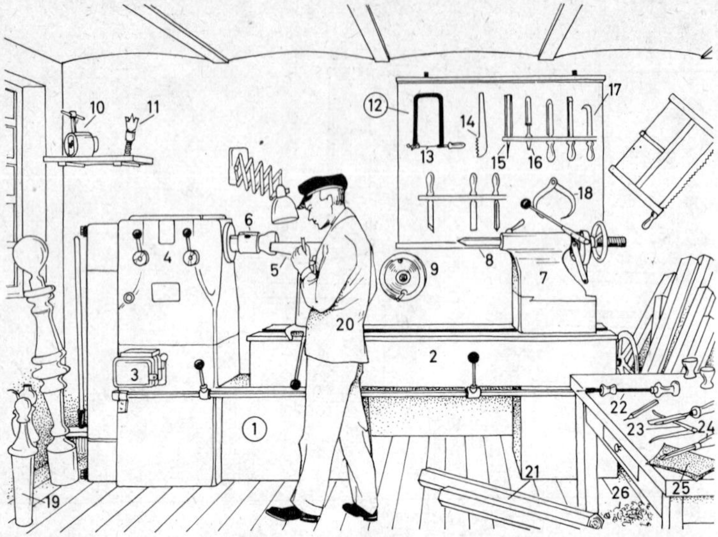

1–26 the wood-turner's workshop,
1 the wood-turning lathe:
2 the lathe bed
3 the starting resistance (*Am.* resistor)
4 the gear box
5 the hand-tool rest
6 the chuck
7 the tailstock
8 the dead centre (*Am.* dead center)
9 the driving plate with pin
10 the two-jaw chuck
11 the three-pronged centre (*Am.* center);
12 the fret saw (*Am.* scroll saw):
13 the fret saw (*Am.* scroll saw) blade;
14, 15, 24 wood-turner's tools (wood-turner's lathe, or turning, tools):
14 the thread-chaser for cutting wood threads
15 the marking gouge for preparatory cutting
16 the spoon bit
17 the hollowing tool
18 the external calipers or callipers
19 turned work (turned wooden articles)
20 the wood-turner
21 the rough wood
22 the Archimedean drill
23 the internal calipers or callipers (*Am.* inside calipers)
24 the grooving tool (parting tool)
25 the sand paper (glass paper, emery paper)
26 the chips (shavings)

1–40 basket-making (basketry, basket-work),
1–4 weaving patterns:
1 the pairing
2 the slewing
3 the oblique randing
4 randing, a piece of wickerwork (of screen work);
5 the horizontal rod (weft)
6 the stake (sail, upright rod, warp)
7 the working board:
8 the transverse ledge
9 the hole to fix the ledge in;
10 the stand
11 the chip basket:
12 the chip;
13 the soaking tub
14 the one-year willow sticks (willow twigs; osier sticks, osier twigs)
15 the three-year willow rods (osier rods)
16 the basket, a piece of wickerwork (basket work):
17 the rim (border)
18 the woven side;
19 the slath:
20 the woven bottom;
21 the bottom cross
22–24 covering a frame:
22 the frame
23 the end
24 the strut;
25 the framework
26 the grass; *sorts:* esparto grass, alfalfa grass
27 the rush (China rush string)
28 the reed (reed mace, club rush)
29 the raffia (rafia, bast)
30 the straw
31 the bamboo cane
32 the rattan (ratan)
33 the basket-maker
34 the bending tool
35 the cutting point
36 the rapping iron
37 the pincers
38 the scraper
39 the basket-maker's plane
40 the bow saw

131 The Wainwright (Cartwright)

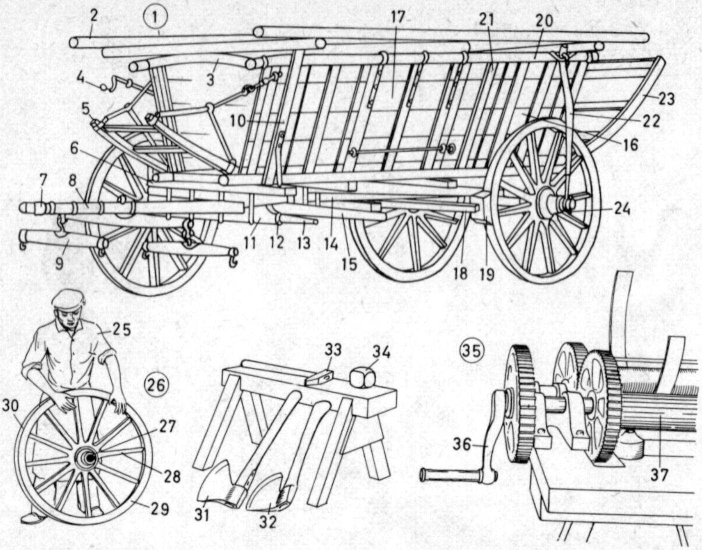

1 the farm wagon (farm-cart, *Am.* farm gear) with harvest frame:
2 the outer top rail
3 the cross bar
4 the brake handle for putting-on the brake
5 the forage ladder (hay ladder, forage frame, hay frame)
6 the bolster (axle-tree bed bolster)
7 the draught pole (*Am.* pole arm)
8 and 9 the swingle set:
8 the main swing-tree
9 the swingletree (swinglebar, swing-tree, whiffletree);
10 the stanchion (stud, stake)
11 the axle tree (axle)
12 the clout iron
13 the axle arms
14 the perch (reach, centre pole, *Am.* center pole)
15 the splinter bar (splinter)
16 the side plank
17 the body standard
18 the brake shaft
19 the brake block (brake shoe, *Am.* chock block)
20 and 21 the ladder (sparred frame):
20 the inner top rail (ladder post)
21 the spar;
22 the stake brace (stanchion brace)
23 the rear forage ladder
24 the linch pin;
25 the cartwright (wainwright, wheel-wright, wheeler)
26 the cart wheel (wheel):
27 the hub (nave)
28 the spoke
29 the wheel rim (felloes, fellies)
30 the wheel tyre (wheel tire, tyre, tire);
31 the axe (*Am.* ax)
32 the broad axe (*Am.* broad ax)
33 the scythe hammer for sharpening the scythe
34 the scythe anvil
35 the tyre bender:
36 the handle (crank)
37 the feed roller (transporting roller), a fluted roller

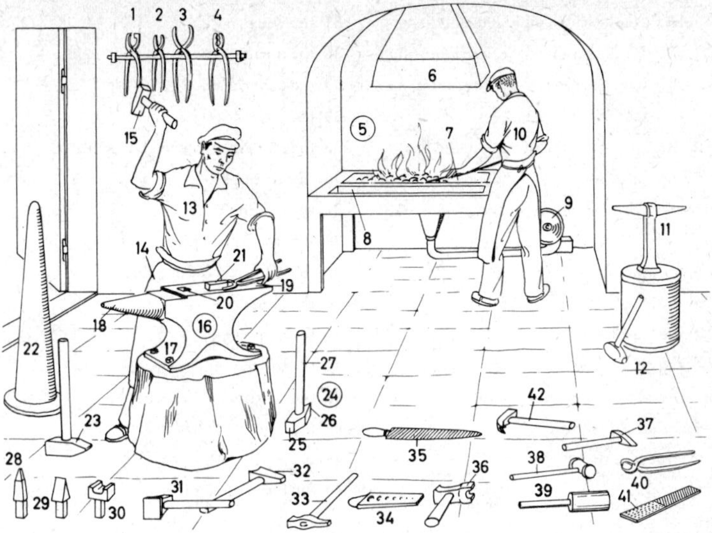

1–42 the smithy (forge, blacksmith's workshop),
1–4 blacksmith's tongs:
1 the hooked tongs
2 the forge tongs
3 the blacksmith's tongs
4 the toothed tongs;
5 the smithy chimney (smithy hearth, smithy fire, fireplace):
6 the chimney hood (smoke hood)
7 the fire pan
8 the quenching trough (quenching tank)
9 the bellows (blower) with electric motor;
10 the smith, a blacksmith
11 the beak iron (horn)
12 the snap hammer (snap set, snap head die)
13 the smith's assistant, a journeyman blacksmith
14 the leather apron (hide apron)
15 the smith's hammer (hand hammer)
16 the anvil:
17 the anvil body
18 the horn (beak iron, beck iron, bick iron, bickern, beak)
19 the tempered anvil face or plate
20 the hardy hole for the anvil tools;
21 the forged piece
22 the ring horn
23 the fore hammer (up-hand sledge, two-handed hammer)
24 the hammer, an about-sledge:
25 the tempered face
26 the pane (peen, pene, pein)
27 the hammer helve (handle, shaft);
28–30 anvil tools (anvil hardies, anvil fullers):
28 the filing block
29 the straight hardy (anvil chisel, anvil cutter)
30 the bottom swage (bottom die, bottom mould, *Am.* bottom mold);
31 the smoothing hammer (planishing hammer, set hammer)
32 the round set hammer
33 the drift hammer (hammer with projecting helve)
34 the hole gauge (*Am.* hole gage)
35 the straw file (rough file) with coarse cut
36 the top swage (top die) for moulding (*Am.* molding)
37 the blunt (caulking, calking) tool or chisel, a cold chisel or a hot chisel; *sim.:* cross chisel for nipping off rivet heads
38 the farrier's hammer
39 the mallet
40 the farrier's tongs
41 the farrier's (hoof) rasp
42 the shoeing hammer

133 The Drop Forging Works

1–61 machines for chipless machining,
1 the slot forging furnace, a pre-heating furnace, a reverberatory (puddling) furnace:
2 the air-heater, heated with waste gas
3 the gas burner
4 the working slot for heating the work (job)
5 the air duct
6 the air blast
7 the gas inlet;
8 the pneumatic power hammer (compressed-air hammer) for drop forgings:
9 the electric motor
10 the tup (ram)
11 the foot lever
12 the top die (top swage)
13 the hammer guide
14 the hammer cylinder
15 the bottom die (bottom swage);
16 the strap (belt) drop hammer (drop stamp, *Am.* lift drop hammer):
17 the disk (disc) cooler
18 the driving head
19 the frame
20 the hammer (hammer head)
21 the anvil (anvil block)
22 the anvil block insert;
23 the hydraulic forging press [up to 6,000 tons pressure]:
24 the hydraulic system
25 the piston
26 the crosshead (cross piece)
27 the top die
28 the bottom die
29 the anvil bed (stock)
30 the guide column
31 the work piece
32 the turning device
33 the crane chain
34 the crane hook;
35 the electric high-speed drop hammer:
36 the gear box
37 the coupling
38 the frame head plate
39 the lifting (hoisting) chain
40 the guide ribs
41 the hammer
42 the top die (upper swage)
43 the bottom die (lower swage)
44 the hammer column
45 the anvil (bed, stock)
46 the foot contact for electro-pneumatic control
47 the hammer stop;
48 the steam-operated forging press
49 the forging manipulator (manipulator) to handle the work for forging without dies:
50 the jaws
51 the counterweight;
52 the gas-heated forging furnace:
53 the gas burner
54 the feed opening
55 the chain curtain
56 the lifting door
57 the hot-air duct
58 the air pre-heater
59 the gas pipe
60 the electric door-lifting mechanism
61 the air blast

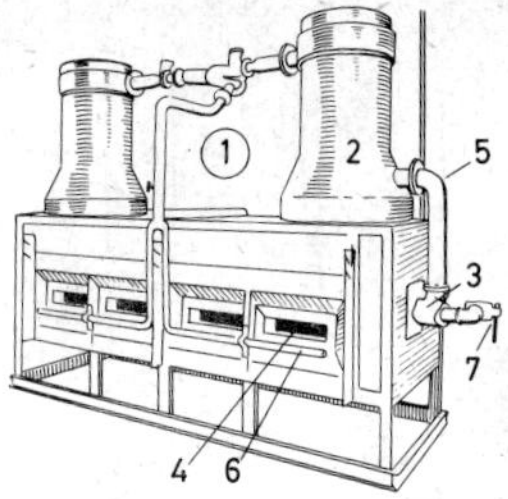
1
2
3
4
5
6
7

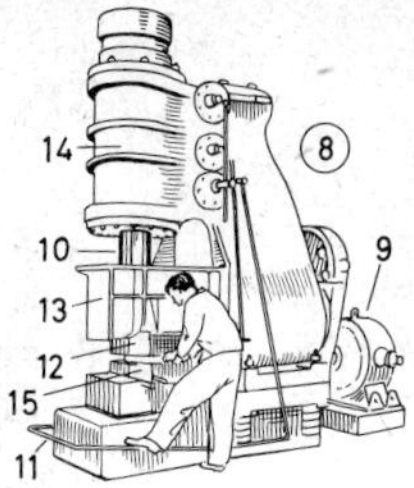
8
9
10
11
12
13
14
15

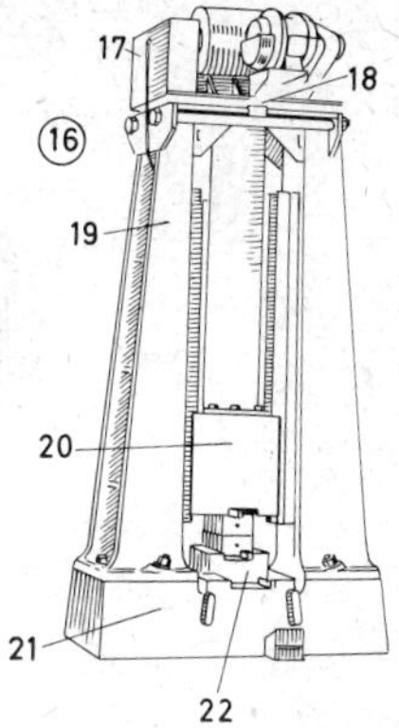
16
17
18
19
20
21
22

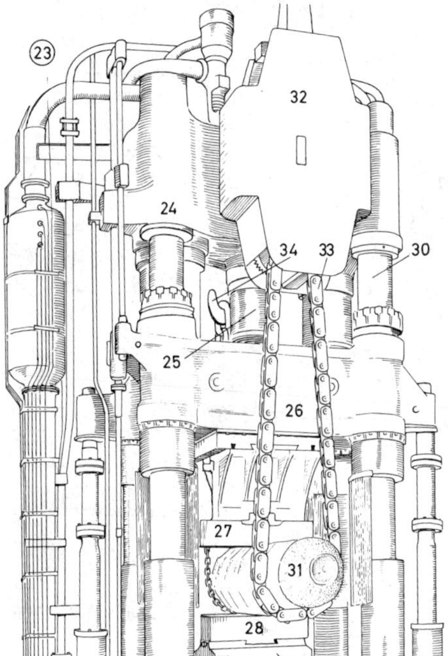
23
24
25
26
27
28
29
30
31
32
33
34

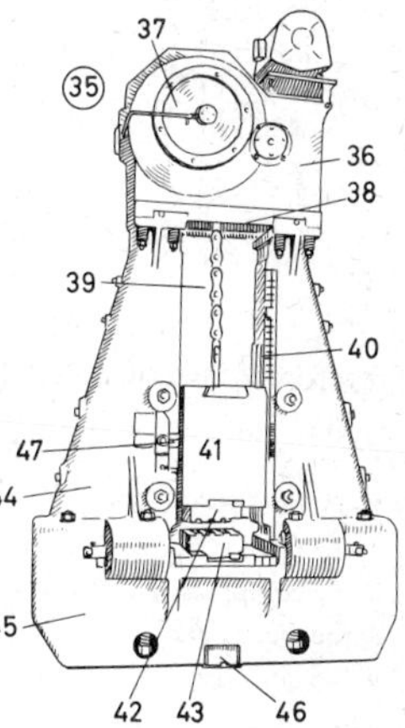
35
36
37
38
39
40
41
42
43
44
45
46
47

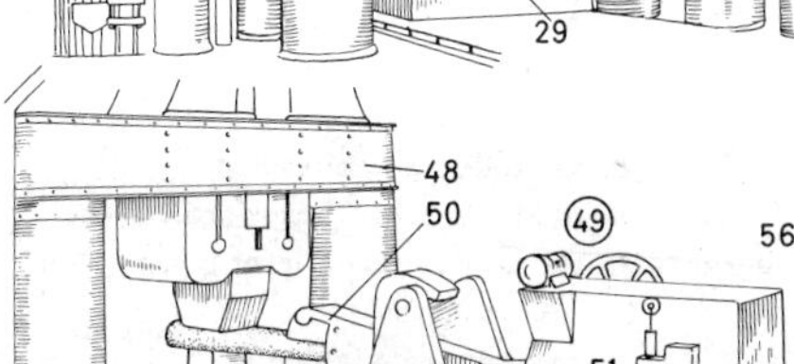
48
49
50
51

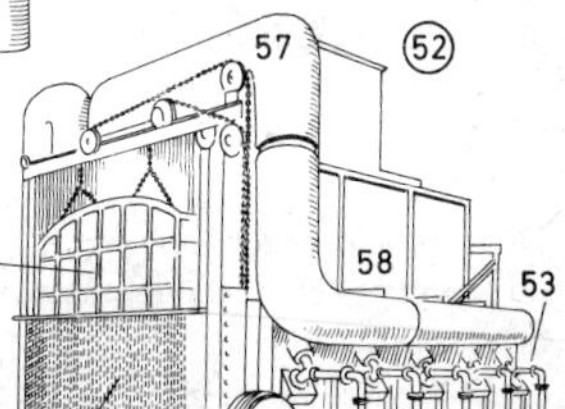
52
53
54
55
56
57
58
59
60
61

Engl. vice = *Am.* vise, *Engl.* gauge = *Am.* gage

1–34 the locksmith's shop,
1 the band-saw (filing machine):
2 the compressed air pipe
3 the file (saw);
4 the portable forge:
5 the fire pan
6 the fan (blower);
7 the locksmith (fitter)
8 the file (rough)
9 the hack saw
10 the lock pick (skeleton key, *Am.* pass key)
11 the face block for bending, straightening, and stamping
12 the parallel vice (a standard fitters vice):
13 the vice jaws
14 the vice handle;
15 the work bench (bench)
16 the hand vice (clamp)
17 the bench hammer (riveting hammer)
18 the flat chisel
19 the cross-cut chisel
20 the muffle furnace, a bench oven:
21 the gas inlet;
22 the round
23 the flat file (smooth)
24 the locksmith (keysmith) vice, a light vice
25 the reamer
26 the tap wrench
27 the die wrench
28 the solid screw chaser
29 the hand brace (breast drill)
30 the hand-operated lever punch, a lever punch
31 the grinding machine [for small tools]:
32 the felt buffing wheel

33 the guard
34 the emery wheel;
35 the mortise (mortice) lock:
36 the lock case
37 the spring bolt
38 the tumbler
39 the dead bolt
40 the keyhole
41 the guide pin for the dead bolt
42 the tumbler spring, a flat spring
43 the follower;
44 the key:
45 the bow
46 the stem (shank)
47 the bit;
48 the pin tumbler cylinder:
49 the plug and body
50 the spring
51 the pin;
52 the safety key
53 the vernier calipers
54 the vernier depth gauge:
55 the vernier scale;
56 the strap hinge
57 the flap hinge
58 the angle hinge
59 the component
60 the strip steel (brass)
61 the blanking tool
62 the feeler gauge
63 the taper hole diameter gauge
64 the plug tap
65 the halves of the screwing die
66 the screwdriver
67 the scraper
68 the centre punch (*Am.* center punch)
69 the round punch
70 the flat pliers
71 the wire cutters
72 the gas pliers (grips)
73 the pinchers

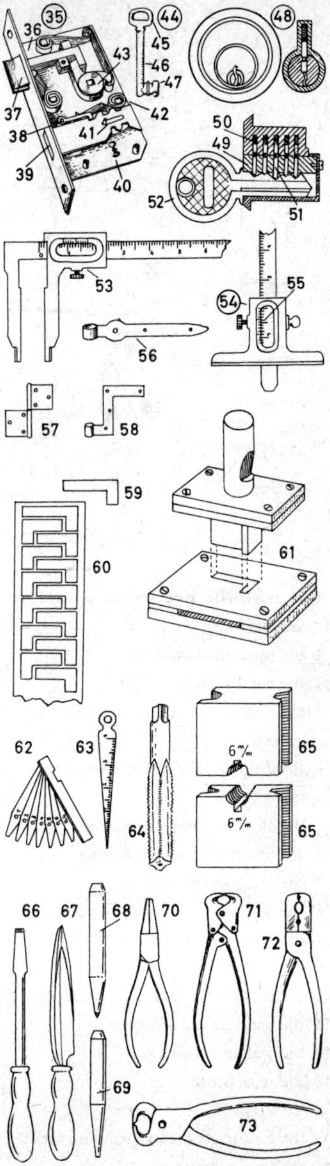

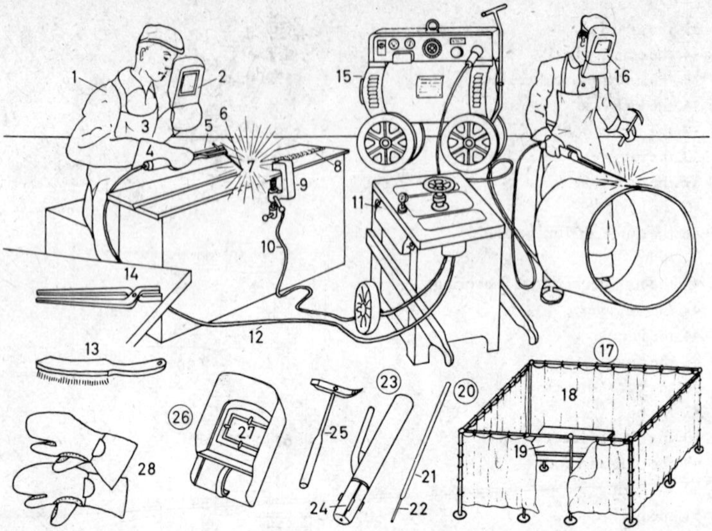

1-28 metallic arc welding (electric arc welding):

1 the operator (welder)

2 the hand shield

3 the leather apron; *sim.* asbestos apron

4 the welder's glove of asbestos or leather

5 the electrode-holder or pliers

6 the electrode (welding rod)

7 the arc (electric arc)

8 the welding bead (weld, welded joint)

9 the earth clamp

10 the earth cable (earth return lead)

11 the welding transformer

12 the welding cable

13 the wire brush

14 the tongs

15 the motor generator (welding set)

16 the head shield

17 the welding tent (welding booth):

18 the curtain

19 the work table;

20 the electrode:

21 the coating

22 the core wire;

23 the electrode-holder with insulated handle:

24 the jaws;

25 the chipping hammer

26 the hand shield:

27 the screening glass (coloured glass);

28 the welder's gauntlets (welder's gloves);

29-64 autogenous welding (gas welding, oxy-acetylene welding, acetylene welding),

29 the oxy-acetylene welding equipment:

30 the low pressure acetylene generating plant

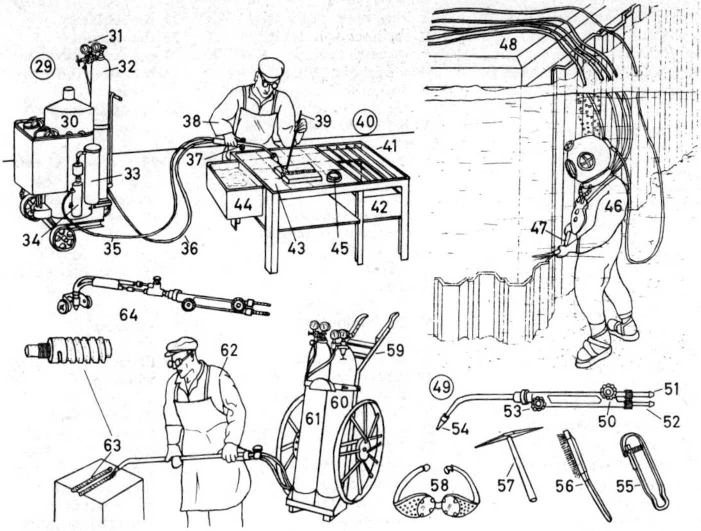

31 the pressure-reducing regulator or valve
32 the oxygen cylinder
33 the gas-purifier
34 the back pressure valve, a guard against explosion in the event of flashback
35 the gas hose
36 the oxygen hose;
37 the welding blowpipe (welding blow-lamp)
38 the gas welder (operator)
39 the filler rod
40 the work bench:
41 the cutting grating
42 the scrap-iron box
43 the table covering of chamotte slabs or fire bricks
44 the water tank;
45 the welding paste or flux
46–48 underwater-welding:
46 the diver
47 the special cutting blowpipe or torch
48 the hoses for breathing air, combustion gas, and protective gases;
49 the welding blowpipe (torch):
50 the oxygen valve
51 the oxygen connection
52 the burning-gas connection
53 the combustion gas valve
54 the nozzle tip;
55 the blowpipe-lighter
56 the wire brush
57 the chipping hammer
58 the welder's goggles
59 the cylinder trolley
60 the acetylene cylinder
61 the oxygen cylinder
62 the oxygen welder
63 the work
64 the blowpipe fitted with cutting nozzle and torch guide

[made of: iron, steel, brass, aluminium (*Am.* aluminum), plastics, etc.; in the following, iron was chosen as an example]

1 the angle (angle iron):
2 the leg (side);

3-7 rolled steel sections (girders),
3 the T-iron (tee-iron):
4 the vertical leg
5 the horizontal leg;
6 the rolled steel joist
7 the channel (U-iron, channel iron);
8 the round bar
9 the square iron (*Am.* square stock)
10 the flat bar
11 the strip steel
12 the iron wire

13-48 screws and bolts,
13 the hexagonal headed bolt:
14 the head
15 the shank (bolt, body)
16 the thread
17 the washer
18 the hexagonal nut
19 the split pin
20 the rounded end
21 the width of spanner jaw;
22 the stud:
23 the point (end)
24 the castle nut
25 the hole for the split pin;
26 the countersunk-head bolt:
27 the catch
28 the lock nut (jam nut, check nut)
29 the bolt (pin);
30 the collar bolt (collar-headed bolt):
31 the set collar (integral collar)
32 the spring washer (elastic washer, locking washer)
33 the round nut, an adjustable nut;
34 the cheese-head screw (fillister-head screw, round-headed screw, *Am.* stove bolt), a screw with slot (with slit, with groove):
35 the tapered pin (conical pin)
36 the screw slot (screw slit, screw groove);
37 the square-head bolt (square head):
38 the grooved pin, a cylindrical pin;
39 the T-head bolt:
40 the fly nut (butterfly nut, wing nut);
41 the rag bolt (rag, lewis bolt, stone bolt):
42 the barb;
43 the wood screw:
44 the countersunk head
45 the wood screw thread;
46 the threaded pin (headless screw):
47 the pin slot (pin slit, pin groove)
48 the rounded end;
49 the nail (*small:* wire nail):
50 the head
51 the shank
52 the point;
53 the roofing tack (blue-headed tack)
54 riveting (lap-riveting),

55-58 the rivet:
55 the set head (swage head, die head), a rivet head
56 the rivet shank
57 the rivet point (closing head)
58 the pitch of rivets;

59 the shaft:
60 the chamfer (bevel)
61 the journal
62 the neck
63 the seat
64 the key way
65 the conical seat (cone)
66 the thread;

67 the ball bearing (radial bearing, journal bearing, anti-friction bearing):
68 the steel ball (ball)
69 the outer race
70 the inner race;

71 and 72 the keys:
71 the feather (sunk key)
72 the gib (gib-headed key);
73 the needle roller bearing
74 the needle
75 the castle nut
76 the split pin
77 the casing (housing)
78 the casing (housing) cover
79 the grease nipple (lubricating nipple);

80-94 toothed wheels (gear wheels, cog wheels, *Am.* gears),
80 the step wheel (spur wheel):
81 the tooth (cog)
82 the space between the teeth (*Am.* gash)
83 the key way (key seat, key slot)
84 the bore;
85 the double helical spur wheel (herring-bone gear):
86 the spokes (arms);
87 the helical gearing (helical spur wheel):
88 the wheel rim (rim of the gear wheel);
89 the bevel gear wheel (bevel wheel, mitre wheel, *Am.* miter wheel)
90 and 91 the spiral toothing:
90 the pinion
91 the disk (disc, plate) gear wheel;
92 the epicyclic gear (planetary gear, sun gear, *Am.* crypto-gear):
93 the internal toothing
94 the external toothing;

95-105 brakes,
95 the shoe brake (cheek brake, block brake):
96 the brake pulley
97 the brake shaft (brake axle)
98 the brake block (brake shoe, brake cheek)
99 the pull rod
100 the brake magnet (magnetic brake, *Am.* solenoid brake, operator brake, operator)
101 the brake weight;
102 the band brake (strap brake):
103 the brake band (brake strap)
104 the brake lining
105 the adjusting screw to ensure even application of the brake

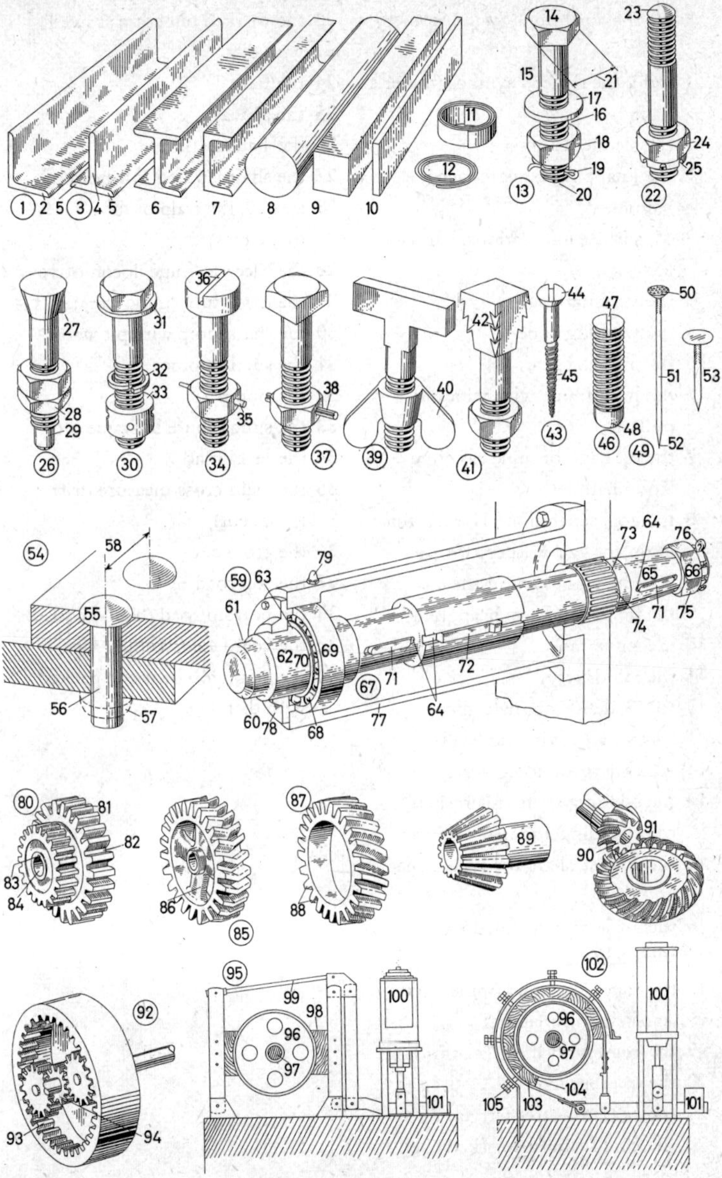
1 2 5 3 4 5 6 7 8 9 10 11 12
13 14 15 16 17 18 19 20 21 22 23 24 25
26 27 28 29 30 31 32 33 34 35 36 37 38 39 40 41 42 43 44 45 46 47 48 49 50 51 52 53
54 55 56 57 58 59 60 61 62 63 64 65 66 67 68 69 70 71 72 73 74 75 76 77 78 79
80 81 82 83 84 85 86 87 88 89 90 91
92 93 94 95 96 97 98 99 100 101 102 103 104 105

1–40 the coal mine (mine, colliery, pit),
1 and **2** the miner's symbol (miner's badge):
1 the sledge hammer
2 the knapping (square-faced) hammer;
3–11 surface installations, (surface lay-out):
3 the winding engine
4 the winding rope
5 the pit-head gear
6 the head frame with winding pulleys
7 the pit bank or mine car circulation hall
8 the coal separation plant (screening plant and washery for grading and cleaning the coal)
9 the tip heap (waste heap, bing)
10 the mine fan
11 the fan drift;
12 to **13** depth of shaft above sump or to winding level
14–40 underground lay-out:
14 the winding shaft (main shaft) for coal winding and man-riding
15 the upcast shaft for stale or bad air
16 the air lock with air doors
17 the staple pit
18 the cage with tubs (mine cars), transporting material
19 the cage with men, (man-riding)
20 the overburden
21 the coal measures (strata)
22 the coal seam (unworked coal)
23 the worked out seam stowed with dirt
24 the fault
25 the airway
26 the haulage level
27 the shaft landing (pit-bottom)
28 and **29** the train of tubs (mine cars):
28 the electric mine locomotive
29 the coal tub (mine car);
30 the shaft sump with pit water
31 the suction pipe
32 the pump
33 the spiral-chute in staple pit
34 the level road
35 the main cross measure drift (cross cut)
36 the cross cut
37 the top road
38 the bottom road (haulage road)
39 the coal face (winning face)
40 the goaf, gob or waste packed with dirt

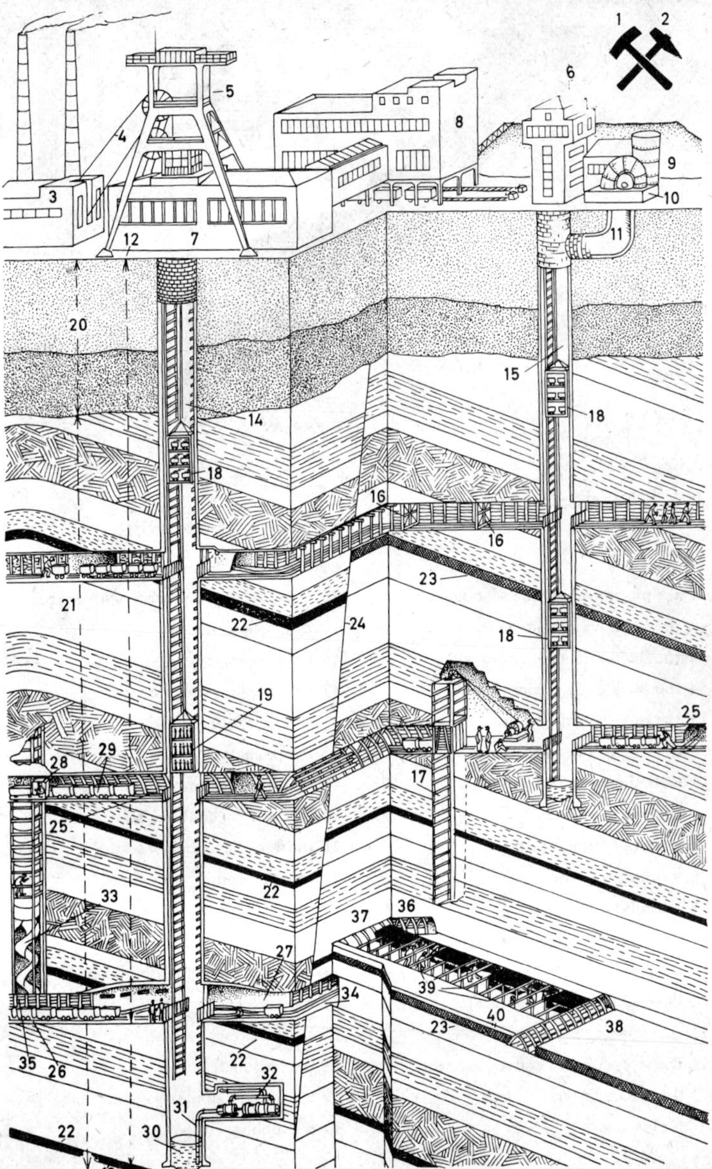
1
2
6
5
4
8
3
9
10
12
7
11
20
15
14
18
18
16
16
23
21
22
24
18
19
29
28
25
17
25
22
33
37
36
27
39
34
40
23
38
35
26
22
32
31
30
22
13

138 The Mine II

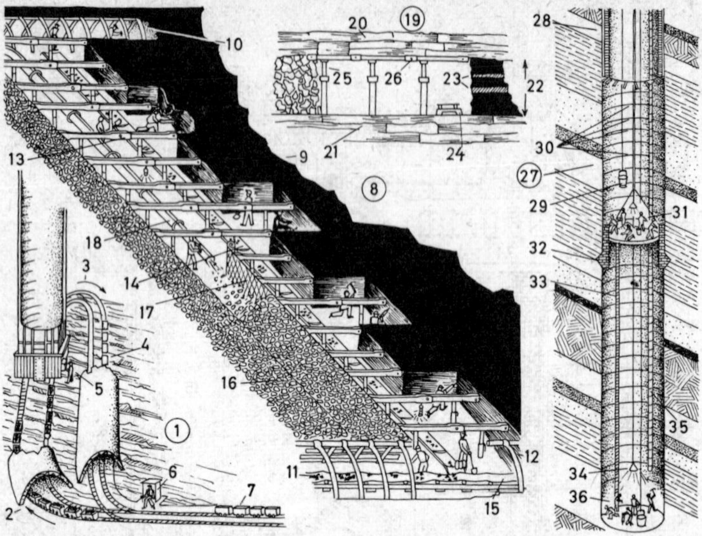

1 the pit-bottom or shaft landing:
2 the track with full tubs
3 the shaft circuit for empty tubs
4 the track with empty tubs
5 the onsetter (man controlling loading of tubs into cage and signalling)
6 the control point
7 the empty tubs return;
8 working a seam:
9 the solid coal
10 the top road (intake airway)
11 the bottom road (haulage road)
12 the coal face (winning face)
13 the working face
14 the scraper chain conveyor with double chain and scraper flights
15 the main gate conveyor with rubber or plastic belt
16 the stowed area
17 the retaining wall for stowage (*here:* wire netting)
18 the pneumatic stowing pipe;
19 the prop-free front face:
20 the roof (layer above seam)
21 the floor (layer below seam)
22 the coal seam
23 the dirt bands
24 the face conveyor
25 the steel (or light alloy) prop
26 the cantilever roof bar;
27 shaft sinking:
28 the final shaft lining
29 the sinking kibble or bucket
30 the tubbing ring

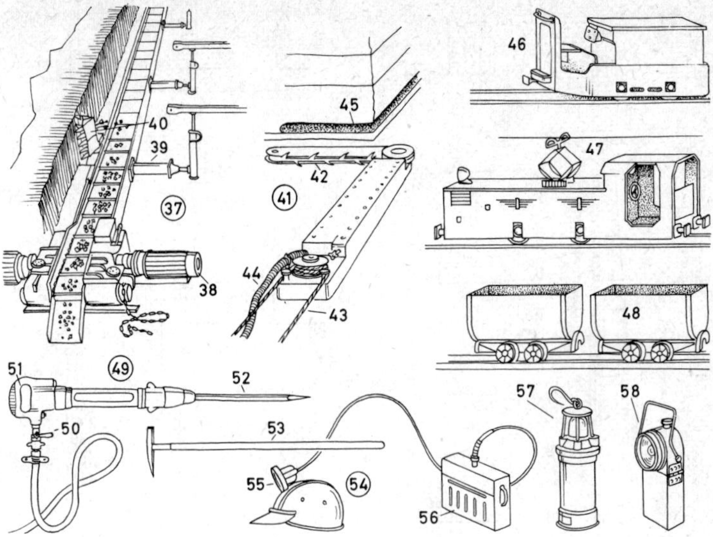

31 the sinking platform

32 the seating for the permanent lining

33 the emergency ladder

34 the floodlight

35 the ventilation duct

36 the sinking team;

37–53 mine machinery and tools,

37 the scraper chain conveyor:

38 the drive for conveyor and coal plough

39 the advancing cylinder

40 the coal plough;

41 the coal-cutting machine:

42 the cutting jib with chain and cutting picks

43 the haulage rope for coal-cutting machine

44 the compressed-air hose (compressed air supply)

45 the cut or kerf;

46 and 47 electric mine-locomotives:

46 the battery locomotive

47 the trolley-locomotive;

48 the tub (tram); *larger* : trolley

49 the pneumatic drill:

50 the air-inlet valve

51 the handle (hand-grip)

52 the pick (steel);

53 the overman's yardstick (with pick);

54–58 miner's equipment,

54 the miner's helmet:

55 the cap-lamp

56 the battery;

57 and 58 miners' lamps:

57 the electric hand lamp

58 the official's electric hand lamp

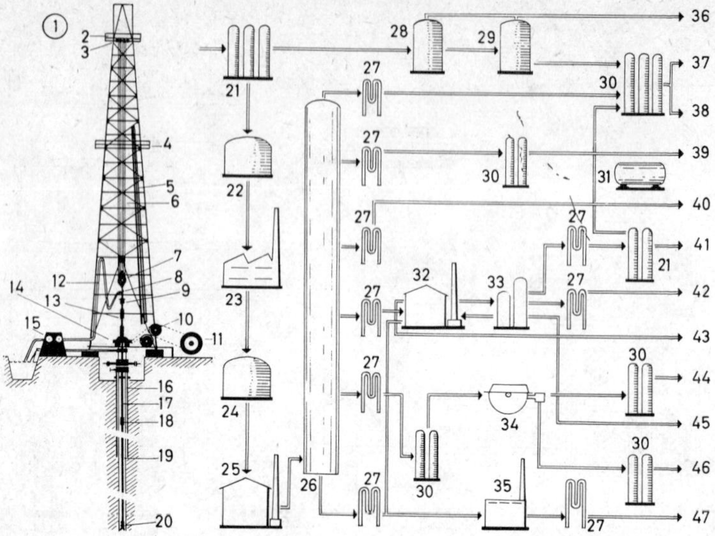

1–20 oil drilling,

1 the derrick (drilling rig):

2 the crown (safety) platform

3 the crown block

4 the safety platform (quadruple platform)

5 the stands of drill-pipe

6 the drilling cable (drilling line, block line, hoisting cable)

7 the travelling (*Am.* traveling) block

8 the hoisting hook

9 the (rotary) swivel

10 the drawworks (hoist)

11 the engine (power unit)

12 the mud hose

13 the kelly (grief stem)

14 the rotary table

15 the mud pump

16 the surface casing

17 the drill-pipe

18 the tool joint

19 the borehole

20 the drilling bit; *kinds:* fishtail (blade) bit, rock (*Am.* roller) bit, diamond (core) bit;

21–35 oil refining [diagram]:

21 the gas separator

22 the (field) storage tank

23 the pumping station

24 the (refinery) storage tank

25 the tubular heater (tubular furnace, pipe still)

26 the fractionating column (fractionating tower, distillation column)

27 the condenser (cooler)

28 the absorbtion plant

29 the stabilizer (stabilization plant)

30 the stripper

31 the alkylation plant

32 the tubular heater (tubular furnace, pipe still)

33 the cracking plant

34 the de-waxing plant

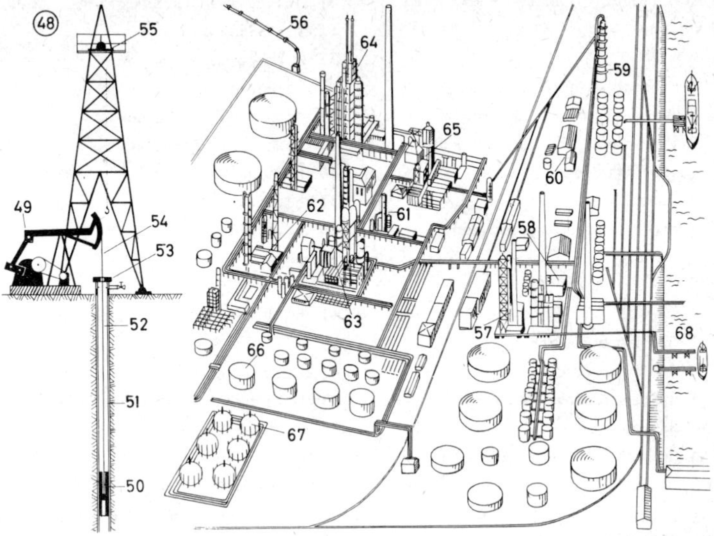

35 the bitumen plant;
36–47 crude-oil products:
36 liquefied petroleum gases (LPG)
37 aviation gasoline (aviation spirit)
38 petrol (motor spirit; *Am.* gasoline or gas)
39 paraffin (paraffin oil, kerosine; *Am.* kerosene)
40 gas oil
41 hydrocarbon gases
42 fuel oil
43 diesel oil
44 lubricating oil
45 petoleum coke
46 paraffin wax
47 bitumen (asphaltic bitumen, asphalt);
48–55 oil or crude-oil production,
48 the production (servicing) derrick:
49 the pump (pumping unit)
50 the plunger
51 the tubing
52 the sucker rods
53 the casing head
54 the polish (polished) rod
55 the pulley block;
56–67 the oil refinery:
56 the pipeline
57 the distillation plant
58 the bitumen blowing plant
59 the vacuum distillation plant
60 the lubricating oil plant (luboil plant)
61 the sulphur recovery plant
62 the gas separation plant
63 the catalytic cracker (cat cracker)
64 the catalytic reformer (hydroformer, platformer)
65 the hydrodesulphurization (hydrofining) plant
66 the storage tank (vertical storage tank)
67 the spherical tank (pressure tank);
68 the tanker terminal

Engl. mould, moulding = *Am.* mold, molding

1–19 the blast-furnace plant:
1 the blast furnace, a shaft furnace
2 the charging skip (inclined skep) for ore and flux or coke
3 the crab
4 the charging gallery (charging platform)
5 the skip bucket
6 the bell
7 the blast-furnace shaft
8 the smelting section
9 the slag and dross outlet
10 the slag ladle
11 the pig-iron (crude iron) outlet (iron tap-hole)
12 the pig-iron ladle, a ladle truck
13 the throat-gas outlet pipe
14 the dust-collector (dust-catcher)
15 the hot blast stove
16 the cold blast main
17 the gas pipe
18 the hot blast main
19 the tuyère;
20–62 the steel works,
20–29 the Siemens open hearth furnace:
20 the pig-iron ladle
21 the feed gate
22 the fixed furnace
23 the hearth
24 the furnace-charger
25 the scrap-steel feeder
26 the gas pipe
27 the gas-heating chamber
28 the air feed pipe
29 the air-heating chamber;
30 the steel-casting (steel-moulding) ladle with locking stopper [bottom discharge]
31 the ingot mould in block form
32 the steel ingot
33–43 the pig-casting machine:
33 the pouring end
34 the iron in-gate (channel)
35 the series of pig moulds
36 the mould
37 the gangway
38 the outlet chute
39 the pig
40 the travelling (*Am.* traveling) crane
41 the pig-iron ladle (casting ladle) with top discharge
42 the casting ladle lip
43 the tilting (*Am.* dumping) device;
44–47 the Siemens electric low-shaft furnace:
44 the charging mouth
45 the electrodes [arranged in a circle]
46 the ring pipe for drawing off the furnace gases
47 the tap-hole (vent) channel;
48–62 the Thomas converter:
48 the charging position for pig-iron
49 the charging position for lime
50 the blasting (operating) position
51 the discharging position
52 the tilting (*Am.* dumping) device
53 the crane-operated ladle
54 the auxiliary crane hoist
55 the lime bunker
56 the fall pipe (down pipe)
57 the trough wagon with light scrap iron
58 the scrap-iron feed
59 the control desk with switches and indicators
60 the converter chimney
61 the blast main
62 the air-jet base

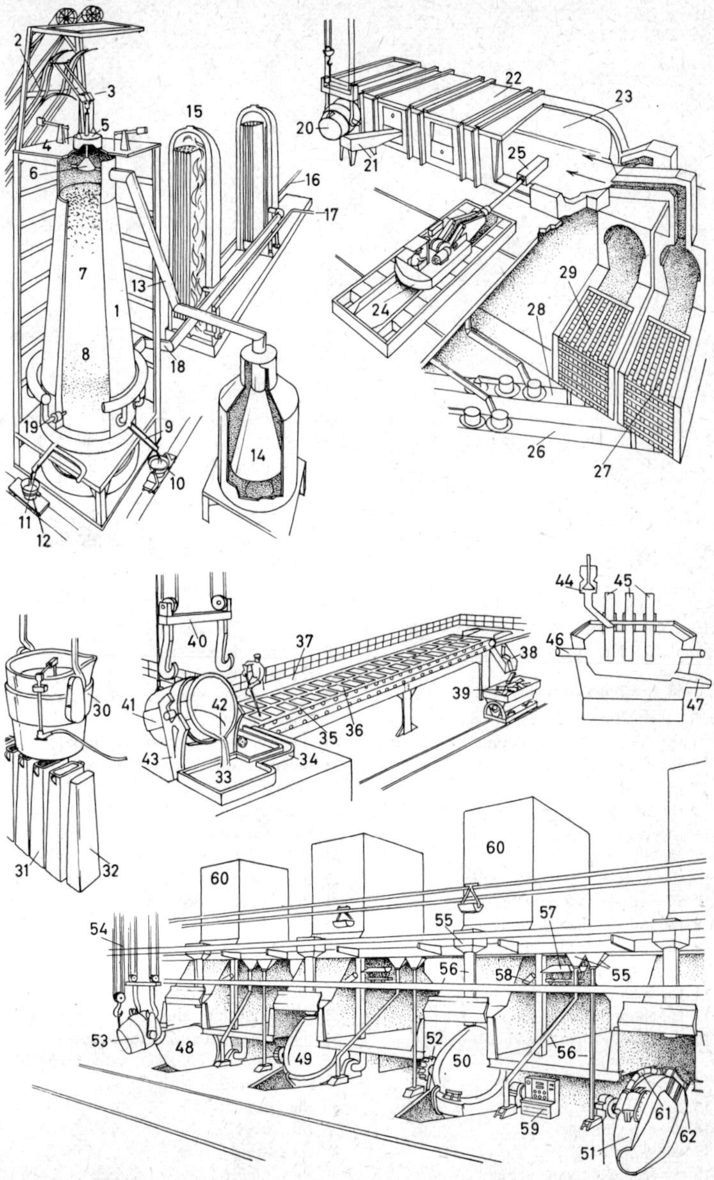
1
2
3
4
5
6
7
8
9
10
11
12
13
14
15
16
17
18
19
20
21
22
23
24
25
26
27
28
29
30
31
32
33
34
35
36
37
38
39
40
41
42
43
44
45
46
47
48
49
50
51
52
53
54
55
56
57
58
59
60
61
62

141 Iron Foundry and Rolling Mill

Engl. mould, moulder, moulding = *Am.* mold, molder, molding

1-40 the iron foundry,

1–12 smelting operations:
1 the cupola furnace (cupola), a smelting furnace
2 the blast main
3 the launder (tapping spout)
4 the inspection hole
5 the tiltable fore-hearth
6 the wheeled drum-type ladle
7 the furnaceman (smelter)
8 the foundryman (founder)
9 the tap-hole rod (tapping iron)
10 the stopper rod
11 the molten pig-iron
12 the slag runner;
13 the foundryman team (casting team, *Am.* crew):
14 the hand shank
15 the handle (support)
16 the carrying bar
17 the slag rod
18 the iron weight;
19 the closed moulding box:
20 the upper box
21 the lower box
22 the runner (runner gate, down gate, pouring gate, *Am.* sprue)
23 the riser (flow-gate, sullage pipe);
24 the hand ladle (shank)
25–32 the moulding shop (*Am.* moldery),
25 the open moulding (casting) box:
26 the moulding sand
27 the impression of the model or pattern
28 the core-print impression
29 the core;
30 the moulder
31 the pneumatic rammer
32 the hand stamper;
33–40 the cleaning shop:
33 the steel grit, or sand, feed-pipe
34 the automatic revolving table type shot blasting machine
35 the grit guard
36 the revolving table
37 the casting
38 the cleanser

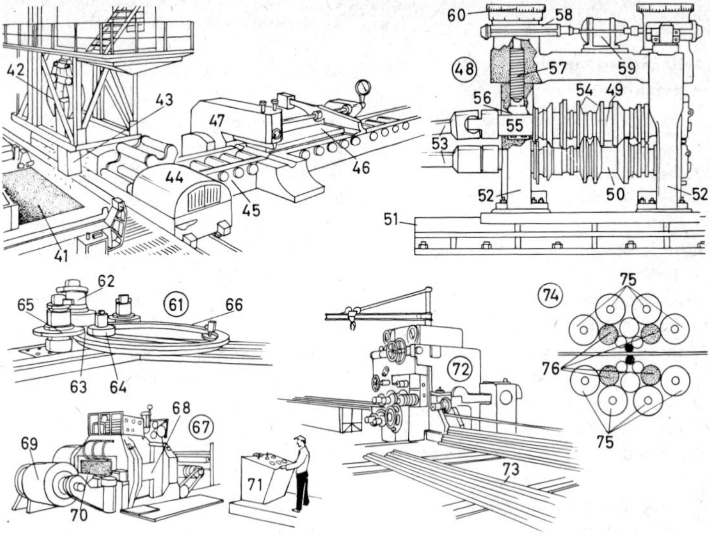

39 the pneumatic grinder (pneumatic grinding machine)
40 the pneumatic chisel;

41-76 the rolling mill:

41 the soaking pit
42 the soaking pit crane, a stripper crane
43 the slab ingot
44 the ingot chariot (*Am.* dumper)
45 the roller table (blooming train)
46 the piece being rolled
47 the bloom shears
48 the two-high mill
49 and 50 the set of roll(er)s:
49 the upper roll(er)
50 the lower roll(er);
51–55 the roll stand:
51 the base plate
52 the roll housing (roll standard)
53 the coupling spindle
54 the pass (groove)
55 the main roll bearing;
56–59 the adjusting equipment:
56 the chock (insert)
57 the main screw
58 the gear
59 the motor;
60 the indicator for rough and fine adjustment
61 the tyre (tire) and wheel-disk (wheel-disc) rolling mill:
62 the working roll(er)
63 the pass
64 the pressure roll(er)
65 the guide roll(er)
66 the angle (flange) ring;
67 the Sendzimir rolling mill, a cold rolling mill (*Am.* plate mill):
68 the rolling-mill case
69 the coiling drum
70 the sheet steel (coachwork sheet, *Am.* chassis sheet)
71 the control desk;
72 the roller-straightening machine:
73 the section steel;
74 the multi-roller plant:
75 the arrangement of the rollers
76 the driven rollers

Engl. gauge = *Am.* gage

1-47 cutting metal-working machines,

1 the lathe (high-speed lathe, metal-turning lathe):
2 the gear box (gear case, headstock)
3 the reduction (intermediate) gear lever
4 the lever for normal and coarse threads
5 the lead-screw reversing gear lever
6 the speed change lever
7 the change gears box with the adjustment plate (quadrant)
8 the feed gear box (quick-change gear box, quick-change gear)
9 the feed and screw-cutting change levers
10 the tumbler yoke (tumbler lever), a change lever
11 the switch lever for right and left-hand action of the lead screw
12 the lathe base (lathe stand)
13 the sliding handwheel (handwheel for carriage)
14 the lever for the tool-carrier reversing gear
15 the cross-slide handwheel with crank (with crank handle)
16 the tool-carrier with apron
17 the lever for longitudinal and cross traverse motion
18 the feed trip for engaging the feeds
19 the lever for the split nut (half nuts) of the lead screw
20 the spindle (mandrel, work spindle, headstock spindle)
21 the toolholder (tool post)
22 the top slide
23 the cross slide
24 the plain-turning slide (longitudinal slide)
25 the coolant supply pipe
26 the tailstock centre (*Am.* center)
27 the tailstock centre (*Am.* center) sleeve
28 the tailstock sleeve locking (clamping) handle
29 the tailstock (loose headstock)
30 the tailstock sleeve adjusting handwheel
31 the lathe bed
32 the lead screw with square thread for screw-cutting
33 the feed shaft
34 the reverse shaft for right and left-hand motion;

35–42 lathe accessories,

35 the face plate (face chuck):
36 the chuck slot;
37 the tension jaw
38 the three-jaw chuck (self-centering chuck)
39 the chuck key
40 the driving plate packing ring
41 the driving (driver, dog) plate
42 the dog-carrier (*Am.* driving dog);

43–47 turning (cutting) tools:

43 the rough-turning tool
44 the finishing tool
45 the parting-off (cutting-off) tool
46 the screwing (threading, thread-cutting) tool
47 the stop measure for adjusting the turning distance;

48–56 measuring tools:

48 the depth gauge
49 the calliper (caliper) gauge (standard gauge, *Am.* gap gage, snap gage), an external limit gauge:
50 the go-side
51 the not-go side;
52 the plug gauge (calibre gauge, *Am.* caliber gage)
53 the micrometer gauge:
54 the measuring scale
55 the graduated thimble
56 the ratchet stop

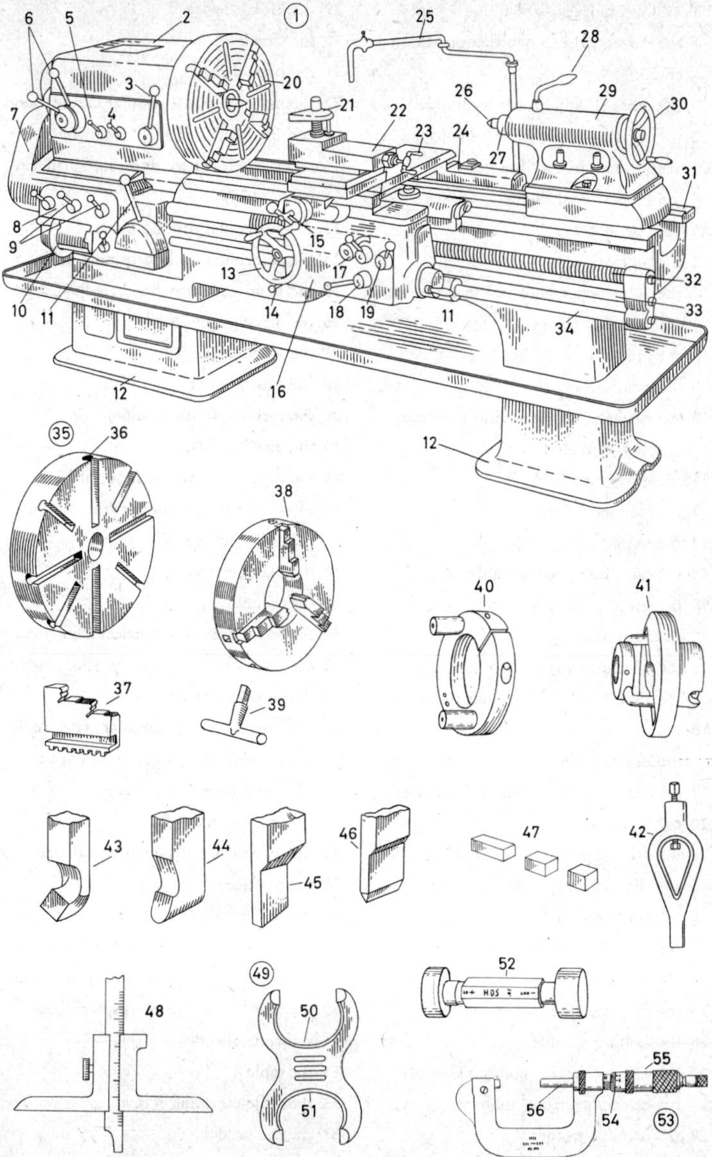
1
2
3
4
5
6
7
8
9
10
11
12
13
14
15
16
17
18
19
20
21
22
23
24
25
26
27
28
29
30
31
32
33
34
35
36
37
38
39
40
41
42
43
44
45
46
47
48
49
50
51
52
53
54
55
56

1–57 cutting metal-working machines,
1 the turret lathe, a semi-automatic machine:
2 the cross slide with the toolholder
3 the rotating turret (revolving tool box) with the multi-tool holder
4 the longitudinal slide
5 the star wheel
6 the oil trough;
7 the automatic cylindrical grinding machine (metal-grinder):
8 the grinding-wheel head
9 the work drive;
10 the surface (face) grinding machine (surface-grinder):
11 the grinding wheel
12 the magnetic chuck
13 the work table
14 the table-adjustment handwheels
15 the grinding-dust extractor (metal-dust remover);
16 the slot (groove) milling tool
17 the shank-end mill (cylindrical cutter)
18 the metal-milling machine (surface-milling machine):
19 the surface-cutter (cylindrical cutter)
20 the work table
21 the driving motor for the milling spindle (cutter spindle)
22 the table feed drive;
23 the metal-drilling machine (radial drilling machine):
24 the drilling table
25 the drilling spindle
26 the column (rotary column sleeve)
27 the hoisting (lifting) motor
28 the driving motor;
29 the Morse cone:
30 the chuck
31 the twist drill;
32 the machine tap (finishing cutter, one-cut finishing drill); *at the same time:* taper, intermediate, and plug, drill (finishing drill)
33 the horizontal drilling plant:
34 the adjustable drilling-spindle case
35 the handwheel for height adjustment
36 the drilling spindle
37 the work table
38 the steady stand
39 the carriage (bottom slide)
40 the machine base;
41 the metal-planing machine (planer, metal-planer, hydraulic twin-column planing machine):
42 the planing table
43 the column
44 the cross slide with vertical adjustment
45 the tool-carrier (planing slide) with lateral adjustment;
46 the metal-cutting circular saw (cold saw), a slide saw, a pendulum saw:
47 the metal-cutting saw blade
48 the work-holder
49 the work (*Am.* production, subject)
50 the bevel arm
51 the mitre scale (*Am.* miter scale);
52 the shaping machine (short-stroke, or high-speed, planing machine, *Am.* high-speed shaper):
53 the ram
54 the vertical slide
55 the table
56 the table-elevating screw
57 the toolholder

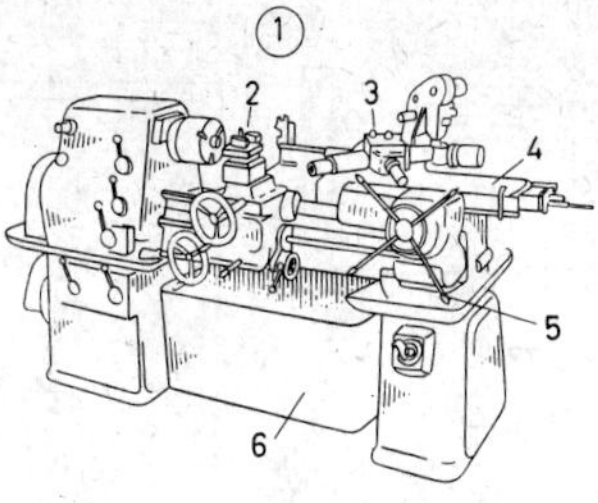
1
2
3
4
5
6

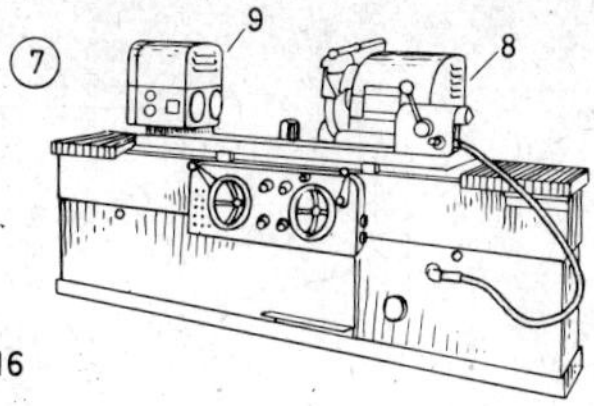
7
8
9

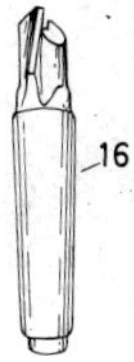
16

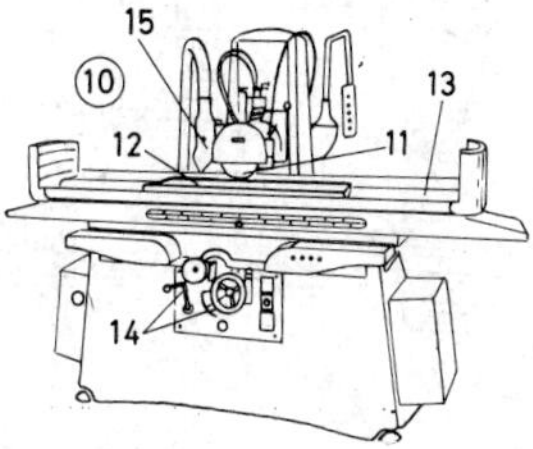
10
11
12
13
14
15

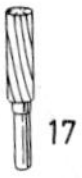
17

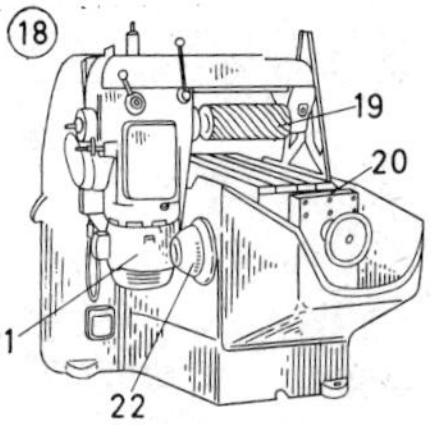
18
19
20
21
22

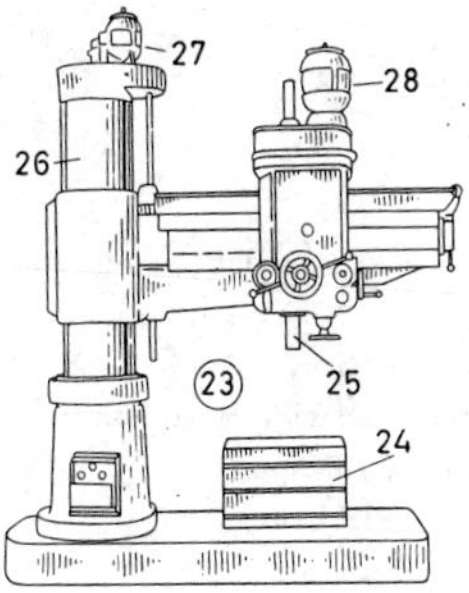
23
24
25
26
27
28

29
30
31

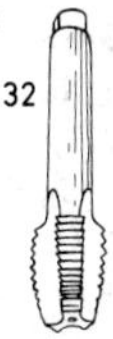
32

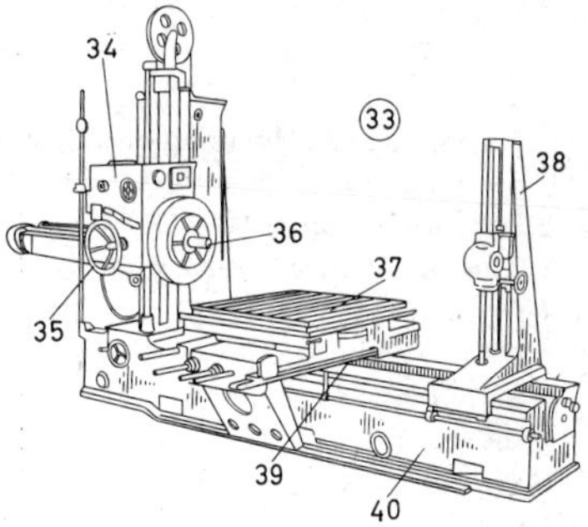
33
34
35
36
37
38
39
40

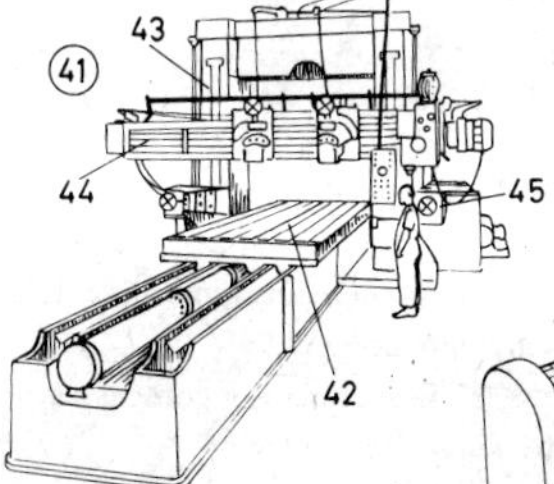
41
42
43
44
45

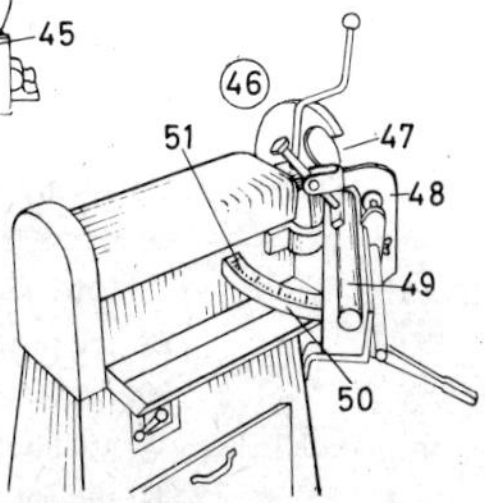
46
47
48
49
50
51

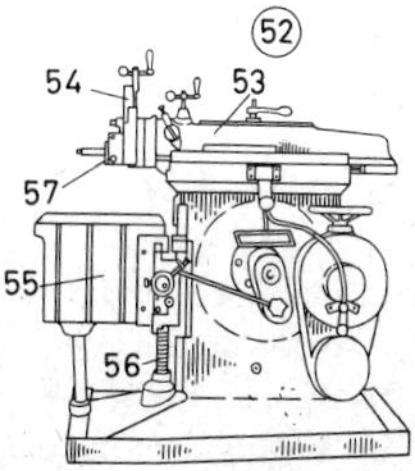
52
53
54
55
56
57

144 The Technical Office

1 the drawing table (drawing board), an upright board
2 the tracing paper
3 the value tabulation (value table)
4 the protractor
5 the set square
6 the technical drawing
7 the slide rule
8 the straight edge (straight rule) with parallel guide
9 the draftsman (draughtsman, designer)
10 the instrument box
11 the handle for adjusting the drawing board
12 the stand
13 the beam compass(es) (trammels, *Am.* beam trammel)
14 the foot lever for adjusting the hegiht of the drawing table
15 the diagram (graph, chart)
16 the drafting machine with parallelogram guide
17 the technical sectional drawing with dimensions
18 the counterweight
19 the adjustable drawing-board lamp
20 the Tee-square (T-square)
21 the drawing ruler:
22 the adjustable knob;
23 the designing engineer, a technician
24 the draftsman's (draughtsman's, designer's) overall
25 the table
26 the drawings
27 the plan-filing cabinet
28–48 the drawing instruments (drawing set, set of mathematical instruments),
28–47 drawing compasses,
28 the pair of combination compasses (*Am.* extension divider):
29 the pencil attachment
30 the tightening screw to grip the attachments
31 the joint

32 the opening joint
33 the head;
34 the large dividers
35 the extension arm:
36 the tightening screw
37 the joint;
38 the spring bow compasses:
39 the plunger
40 the regulating screw
41 the Indian-ink attachment (China-ink attachment)
42 the pencil attachment
43 the nib;
44 the hair dividers (spring bow dividers):
45 the spring
46 the adjusting screw
47 the compass needle point (compass needle);
48 the drawing pen;
49 the French curve (irregular curve, curve)
50 the propelling pencil with the refill (refill lead)
51 the triangular scale, a reduction scale
52 the drawing pin (*Am.* push pin, thumb tack)
53 the pencil rubber (pencil india rubber)
54 the Indian-ink rubber
55 the ink bottle with Indian (China) ink
56 the erasing knife (eraser)
57 the building plan (architect's plan):
58 the measurement (dimension line)
59–63 projections:
59 the section
60 the front elevation (front view)
61 the side elevation (side view)
62 the plan
63 the ground plan (foundation plan);
64 the title of the drawing with material bill;
65 the drawing nib (loose nib)
66 the writing nib for various thicknesses
67 the slip-on nib

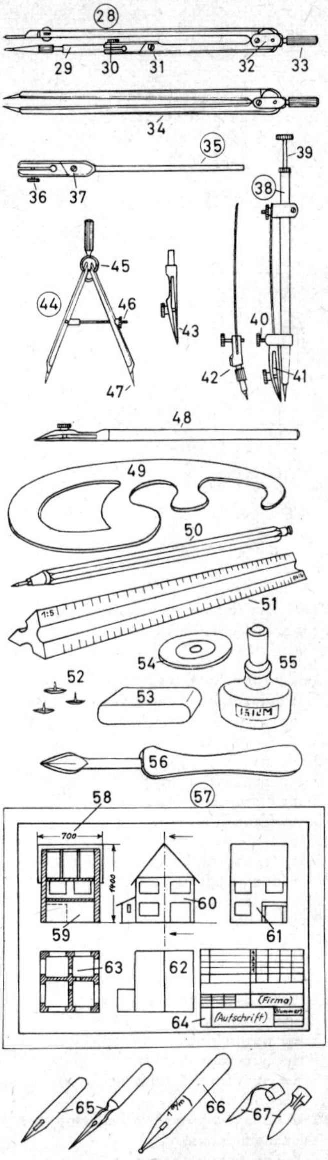

145 The Factory

Engl. gauge = *Am.* gage

1-45 the factory workshop, an assembly (erection) and testing (checking) shop,

1-19 workshop cranes,

1 the travelling (*Am.* traveling; traversing) overhead crane (shop traveller, *Am.* shop traveler):
2 the crab
3 the lifting (hoisting) gear
4 the crab-traversing gear
5 the footbridge
6 the capacity plate
7 the crane girder (main girder, crane bridge), a lattice girder
8 the crane rope
9 the pulley
10 the crane hook (load hook), a double hook
11 the operator's cabin (driver's cage)
12 the craneman (crane-driver, crane-operator)
13 the warning bell
14 the crane rail
15 the current lead, a three-pole conductor rail or contact rail;
16 the bracket crane (wall slewing crane), a slewing crane:
17 the jib (crane jib, crane arm)
18 the electro pulley blocks (electro blocks)
19 the control switch, a push-button (press-button) switch;
20 the rope block
21 the foot winch, a rack-and-pinion winch:
22 the toothed rack
23 the hand crank
24 and 25 the ratchet (stop gear, locking mechanism):
24 the ratchet wheel
25 the pawl (click);
26 the X-ray apparatus for testing metals
27 the lifting truck
28 the marking-off plate (laying-out plate, marking-out plate)

29-35 marking-out (marking-off) **implements:**

29 the height gauge
30 the sliding block (surface gauge, marking gauge, shifting gauge)
31 the prism
32 the centre punch (*Am.* center punch)
33 the scribing block
34 the scriber (drop point)
35 the back square (try square);
36 the marker-off
37 the product-checking (product-testing) table

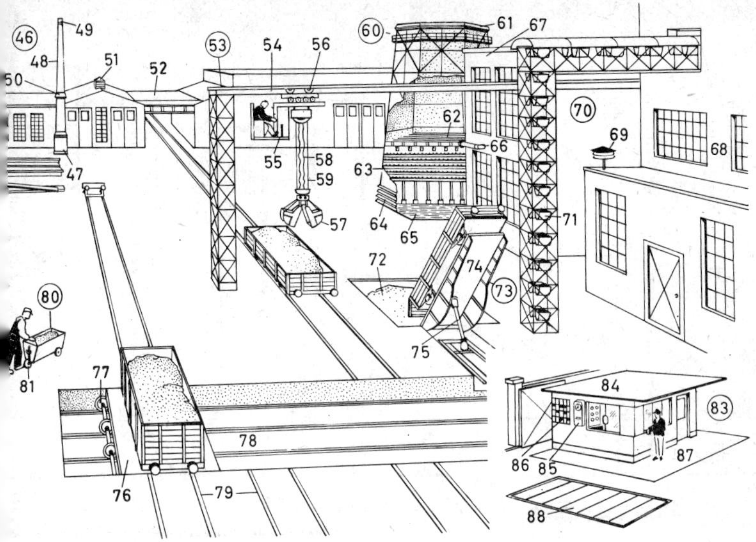

38-43 precision measuring instruments (*Am.* dial bench gages):
38 the thickness gauge
39 the precision water level
40 the meter stand
41 the screw-thread gauge (*Am.* thread pitch gage)
42 the electric precision calipers (dial indicator)
43 the tool-measuring microscope (eyepiece micrometer);
44 the chief inspector
45 the notice board (*Am.* billboard);
46 the factory chimney (chimney shaft):
47 the chimney base
48 the chimney (smoke) stack
49 the chimney top
50 the grit (dust) filter;
51 the ventilator hood (ventilation)
52 the covered bridge
53 the electric overhead monorail (telpher line, suspension monorail):
54 the rail
55 the cabin (suspended platform)
56 the crab
57 the grab (grab bucket)
58 the hauling (traction) rope
59 the load (standing) rope;
60 the cooling tower, a chimney cooler, a recooling plant:
61 the cooling chimney
62 the distributing gutter
63 the drip installation
64 the louvre (louver, shutter) opening for ventilation
65 the tank for the cooled water
66 the hot-water inlet;
67 the engine room (power station)
68 the boiler room
69 the factory siren
70 the tilting-bucket conveyor, an elevator:
71 the elevator scoop (elevator bucket);
72 the filling pit
73 the wagon tip, a platform tip:
74 the tipping (*Am.* dumping) platform
75 the pressure ram;
76 the traverser (traversing platform, *Am.* transfer table)
77 the traversing wheel
78 the traversing pit
79 the private sidings, a works' sidings
80 the three-wheeled truck, a hand barrow:
81 the steering castor;
82 the transport worker
83 the porter's lodge:
84 the checks
85 the time clock (check clock)
86 the clocking-in card;
87 the porter (gatekeeper, *Am.* janitor)
88 the weighbridge (lorry, or cart, weighing machine), a centesimal balance

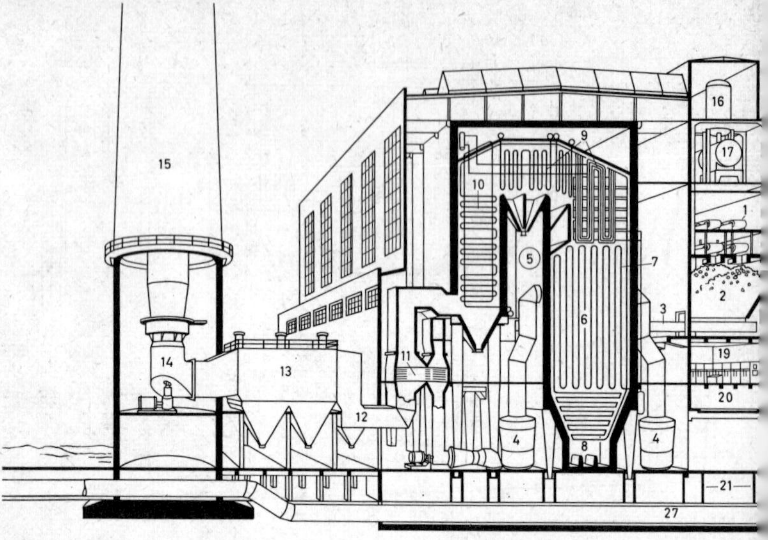

1-28 the steam power station, a generating station,

1–21 the boiler house:

1 the coal conveyor

2 the coal bunker

3 the coal conveyor

4 the coal mill (coal-grinder, coal-crusher)

5 the steam boiler, a water tube boiler:

6 the furnace (combustion chamber)

7 the water tubes

8 the ash pit (clinker pit)

9 the superheater

10 the water pre-heater

11 the air pre-heater

12 the gas duct (flue);

13 the dust collecting plant, an electrical precipitation plant

14 the induced draught fan

15 the chimney

16 the de-aerator

17 the feed water tank (hotwell)

18 the boiler feed pump

19 the switch gear

20 the cable tunnel

21 the cable cellar;

22 the turbine room:

23 the steam turbine with alternator

24 the surface condenser

25 the low-pressure pre-heater

26 the high-pressure pre-heater

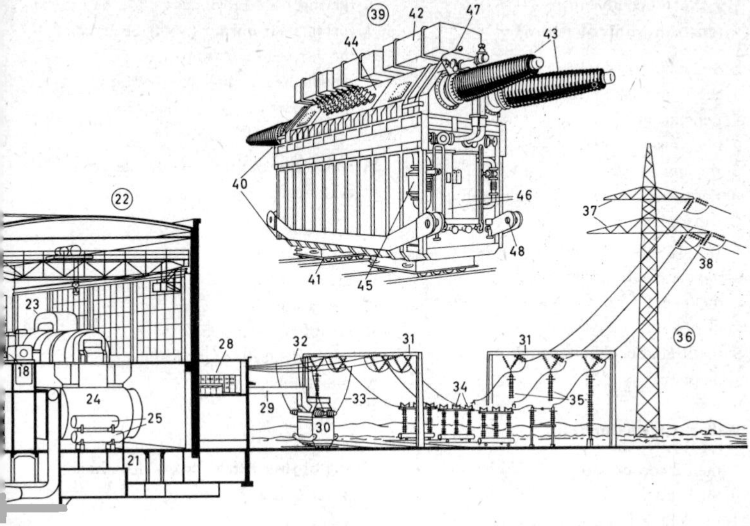

27 the circulating water pipe

28 the control room;

29-35 the outdoor substation:

29 the busbars

30 the power transformer, a transportable transformer

31 the gantry

32 the high-voltage overhead conductor

33 the high-voltage conductor

34 the air-blast circuit-breaker

35 the surge diverter;

36 the overhead line (transmission line) tower or pylon, a lattice-type tower:

37 the cross arm

38 the suspension insulator;

39 the transportable transformer (power transformer, transformer):

40 the transformer tank

41 the transport bogies

42 the oil conservator

43 the high-voltage bushings or terminals

44 the low-voltage bushings or terminals

45 the oil-circulating pump

46 the oil cooler

47 the arcing horn

48 the transport lug

1-8 the control room (station control room),

1–6 the control desk:
1 the controls for the three-phase generators
2 the control switch
3 the lamp signal
4 the control panel for controlling the high-voltage circuits:
5 the supervisory control apparatus;
6 the control buttons;
7 the panel with the measuring instruments
8 the luminous (illuminated) circuit diagram;

9-18 the transformer:

9 the oil conservator
10 the breather
11 the oil level gauge (*Am.* gage)
12 the bushing insulator
13 the tapping switch
14 the yoke
15 the primary winding (high-voltage winding)
16 the secondary winding (low-voltage winding)
17 the core
18 the tapping lead;

19 the transformer connection:

20 the star connection
21 the delta (mesh) connection
22 the neutral point;

23-30 the steam turbine (turbo-alternator set):

23 the high-pressure cylinder
24 the medium-pressure cylinder
25 the low-pressure cylinder
26 the three-phase alternator
27 the hydrogen-cooler
28 the cross-over pipe
29 the regulating valves
30 the turbine control desk with the measuring instruments (with the meters);
31 the voltage-regulator
32 the synchronizing device (automatic synchronizer)

33 the trifurcating box (cable box, cable terminal):

34 the terminal
35 the insulator
36 the stress cone
37 the casing
38 the filling compound
39 the lead sheath or covering
40 the plumbing gland
41 the cable;

42 the high-voltage cable for three-phase current:

43 the conductor
44 the metallised paper
45 the conductor insulation
46 the muslin lap
47 the lead sheath
48 the asphalted paper
49 the jute serving
50 the steel tape, or steel wire, armouring (*Am.* armoring);

51-62 the air-blast circuit-breaker:

51 the compressed-air receiver
52 the operating mechanism
53 the compressed-air connection
54 the hollow-pin insulator, a chain insulator, a cap-type insulator
55 the blast head
56 the resistor
57 the auxiliary (secondary) contacts
58 the current-transformer
59 the voltage-transformer
60 the secondary terminal box
61 the arcing horn
62 the protecting gap

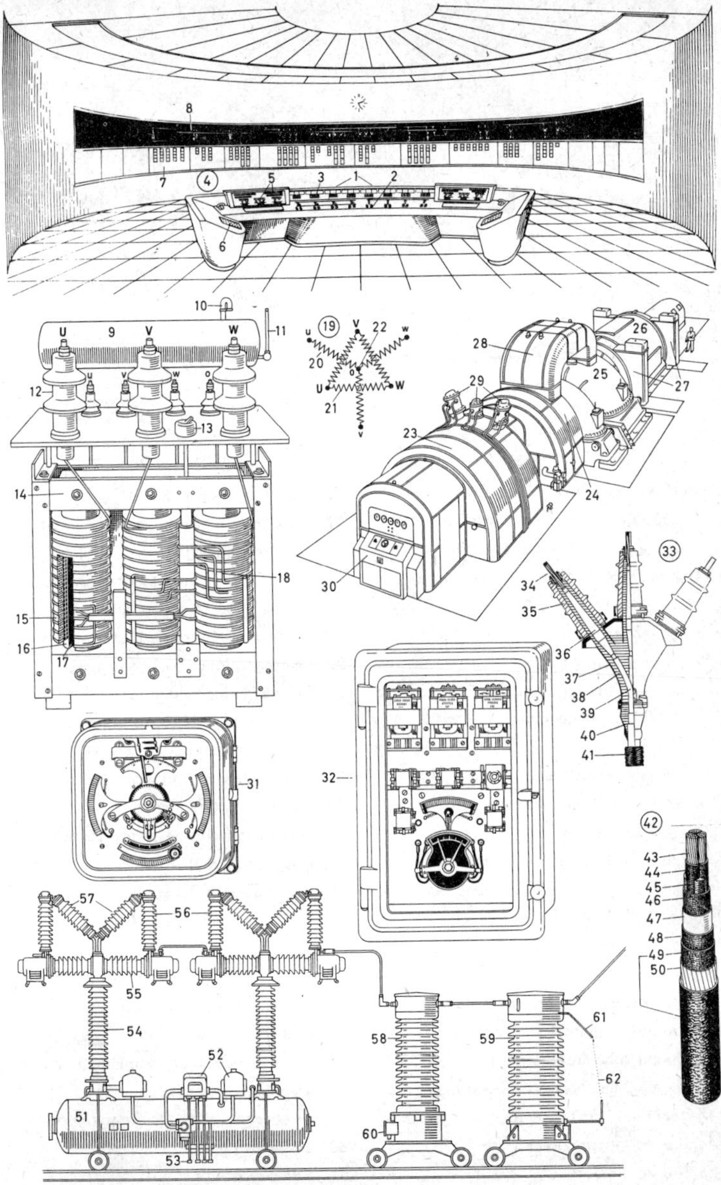
1
2
3
4
5
6
7
8
9
10
11
12
13
14
15
16
17
18
19
20
21
22
23
24
25
26
27
28
29
30
31
32
33
34
35
36
37
38
39
40
41
42
43
44
45
46
47
48
49
50
51
52
53
54
55
56
57
58
59
60
61
62
U
V
W
u
v
w
o

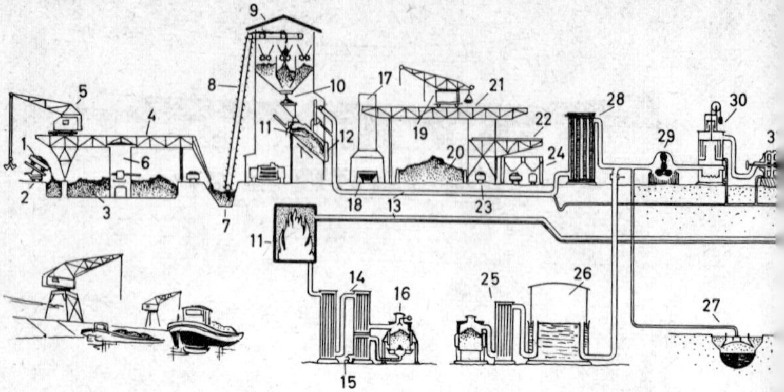

1–46 the gas production (gas manufacture, production of town gas, of lighting gas, heating gas, coal gas),

1–9 the coal haulage (transporting of coal):

1 the coal truck

2 the truck-tipper

3 the coal bunker (coal storage)

4 the sliding (travelling, *Am.* traveling) platform

5 the rotary grab crane

6 the telpher line

7 the coal-breaker

8 the inclined hoist or elevator

9 the coal-crushing and mixing plant (coal-crusher and coal-mixer);

10–12 coal-processing (coal carbonization, retort furnace house):

10 retort-charging (retort-feeding)

11 the oblique retort furnace

12 the tar tube and discharging door;

13 the raw-gas main (crude-gas main)

14–16 the producer-gas plant:

14 the secondary cooler

15 the air-blower

16 the main producer;

17–24 coke-processing (the coke plant, coke-oven plant):

17 the coke-quenching plant or tower

18 the coke-quenching truck

19 the coke-transporting unit

20 the coke bunker (coke storage)

21 the coke crane bridge

22 the coke-sorting (coke-grading) plant with graded coke bunkers

23 the coke bunker railway (*Am.* railroad)

24 the coke-loading plant;

25 and 26 the water-gas plant (carburetted water-gas plant):

25 the water-gas washer

26 the water-gas holder with water tank;

27 the waste-water purification plant

28–46 the gas purification in the refining house:

28 the raw-gas primary condenser or pre-cooler

29 the tar and gas water separator pump

30 the gas-extractor

31 the tar-separator

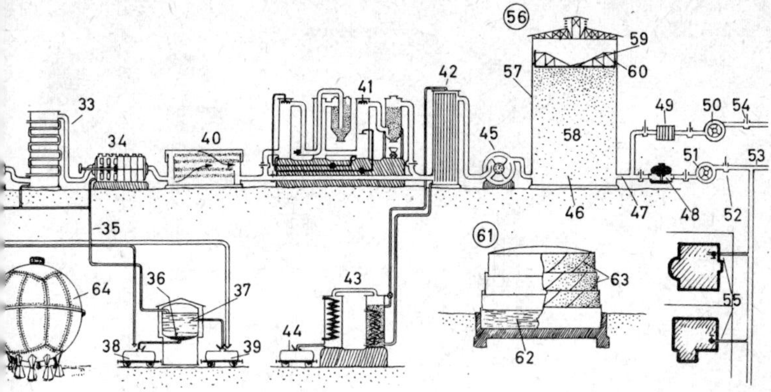

32 the naphthalene-washer

33 the raw-gas secondary condenser or cooler

34 the ammonia-washer

35 the ammonia-water waste pipe

36 and 37 the separating tank:

36 the tar tank

37 the gas water tank;

38 the tar truck

39 the gas water truck

40 the sulphur (*Am.* sulfur) purification

41 the gas de-poisoning plant

42 the benzole (*Am.* benzene) washer

43 the benzole (*Am.* benzene) recovery plant (benzole plant, *Am.* benzene plant)

44 the benzole (*Am.* benzene) truck

45 the rotary-piston gas meter (station meter)

46 the gas storage;

47–55 the gas-distributing plants:

47 the gas main

48 the station governor (town pressure regulator)

49 the gas compressor

50 the high-pressure gas meter

51 the low-pressure gas meter

52 the gas main cock

53 and 54 the town network (gas pipe network, gas pressure main, gas consumers' pipeline, gas service pipes):

53 the low-pressure gas main

54 the high-pressure gas main;

55 the consumers' lines (gas installation);

56–64 the gasometers (gasholders, *Am.* gas tanks),

56 the five-lift (five-section) waterless piston gasometer:

57 the casing

58 the gas space

59 the piston

60 the piston-edge packing with liquid seal;

61 the three-lift (three-bell, three-section) telescopic gasometer with water tank (spiral gasometer):

62 the water seal

63 the spiral guide rails;

64 the spherical high-pressure gasometer (spherical gasometer)

Engl. timber = *Am.* timber or lumber

1–59 the saw mill and planing shop:
1 the squared planks (trimmed timber, timber store, stack of planks)
2 the straight line edger (*Am.* buzz saw):
3 the set of saw blades
4 the feeding rollers
5 the breadth (width) scale
6 the recoil guard
7 the breadth (width) indicators
8 the feed scale
9 the height scale;
10 the vertical log frame (*Am.* gang mill):
11 the saw blades
12 the saw frame
13 the feed rollers (guiding rollers)
14 the fluting (grooving) on rollers
15 the oil pressure gauge (*Am.* gage; oil manometer)
16 the vertical log frame (*Am.* gang mill)
17 the mechanical dog
18 the clamping irons (clamping claws);
19 the saw mill worker (*Am.* sawyer)
20 the twin timber circular saw (*Am.* buzz saw):
21 the circular saw (*Am.* buzz saw) blades
22 the cutting-breadth regulator
23 the feeding chain
24 the saw axle;
25 the saw mill foreman
26 the light-railway track (*Am.* narrow-gage railroad track):
27 the log truck;
28 the pile of scantlings (of rectangular timber)

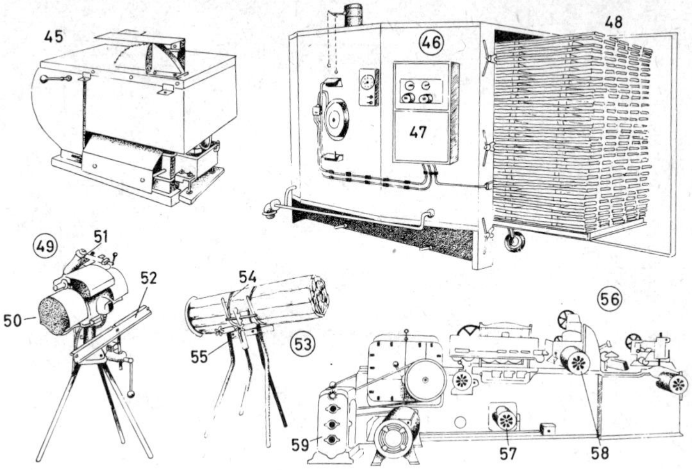

29 the sawing and planing shed
30 the log stock yard (log yard):
31 the logs;
32 the log conveyor:
33 the endless chain
34 the scraper flight
35 the engaging dogs (dogs);
36 the water channel for log-cleansing
37 the slab wood
38 the sawn log:
39 the slab
40 the heartwood side
41 the heart (duramen)
42 the side next to the heart
43 the sapwood (alburnum) side;
44 the concrete pile
45 the circular saw for cutting to length (cross-cut circular saw, *Am.* buzz saw)
46 the kiln drying chamber:
47 the control box
48 the board stack;
49 the bark-stripping (barking) machine:
50 the barking head with flat knives
51 the electric grinding machine
52 the wood rest;
53 the faggot-bundling press for pressing slabs and trimmings:
54 the tightening rope
55 the tightening device;
56 the electric planing machine:
57 the wood-shavings chipper motor
58 the cutter blocks
59 the feed control gears

150 The Quarry

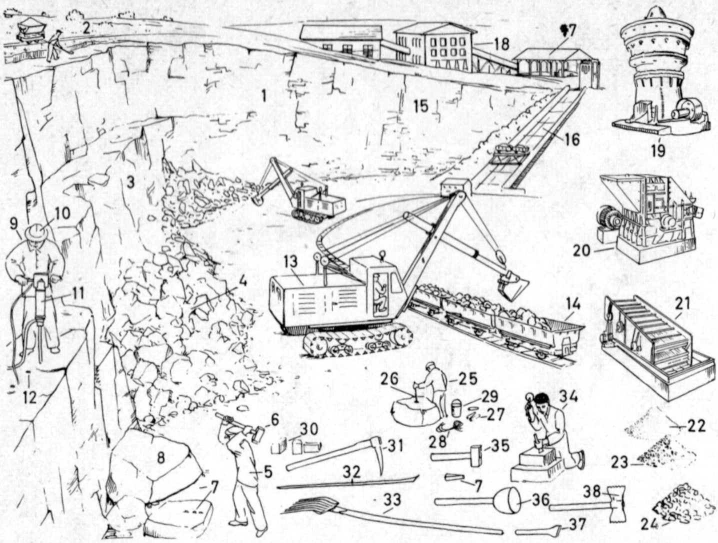

1 the quarry, an opencast working
2 the overburden
3 the working face (rock face)
4 the loose rock pile (blasted rock)
5 the quarryman (quarry labourer)
6 the sledge hammer
7 the wedge
8 the block of rock, a large rock
9 the driller
10 the safety hat (safety helmet)
11 the hammer drill (rock drill)
12 the borehole
13 the excavator (navvy)
14 the rail truck (quarry wagon)
15 the rock face (quarry face)
16 the inclined hoist
17 the primary crusher
18 the stone-crushing plant
19 the gyratory crusher (primary crusher)
20 the hammer crusher (impact crusher)
21 the vibrating screen
22 the fine screenings (dust)
23 the stone chippings
24 the crushed stone
25 the shot firer or blaster
26 the measuring rod (tamping rod)
27 the blasting cartridge
28 the fuse
29 the plugging sand (stemming sand)
30 the dressed stone (ashlar)
31 the pick
32 the crowbar (pinchbar)
33 the fork
34 the stone mason

35-38 the mason's tools:

35 the stone hammer
36 the stone mason's mawl
37 the broad chisel
38 the dressing axe

The Brickyard (Brickworks, Brick Field) 151

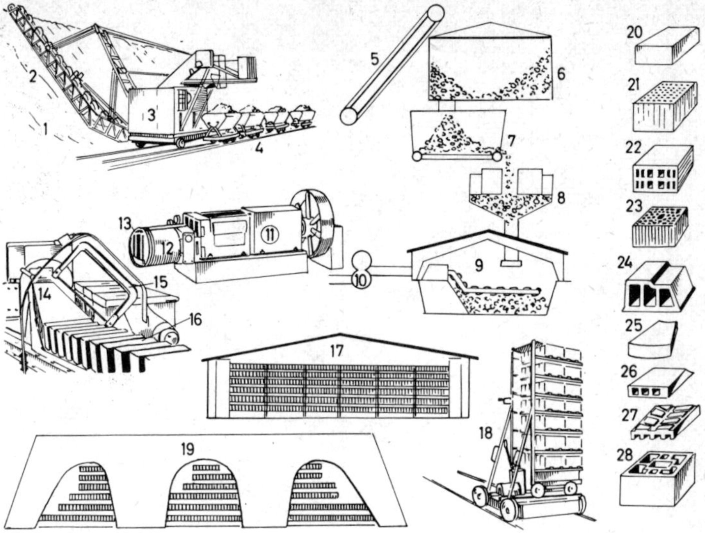

1 the clay pit

2 the loam, an impure clay (brick clay)

3 the multi-bucket excavator

4 the narrow-gauge tramway

5 the elevator

6 the ageing pits

7 the box feeder

8 the wet-pan mill (edge runner mill)

9 the rolling plant

10 the double-shaft trough mixer

11 the de-airing brick machine:

12 the vacuum chamber

13 the die;

14 the clay column

15 the cutting-off table

16 the unfired (green) brick

17 the drying shed

18 the finger car (stacker truck)

19 the kiln (brick kiln, tile kiln)

20 the solid brick (building brick)

21 and **22** perforated bricks:

21 the brick with vertical perforations

22 the hollow clay block with horizontal ports;

23 the hollow clay block with vertical ports

24 the clay floor block

25 the radial brick (for chimneys or wells)

26 the flue lining brick

27 the paving brick

28 the cellular chimney brick

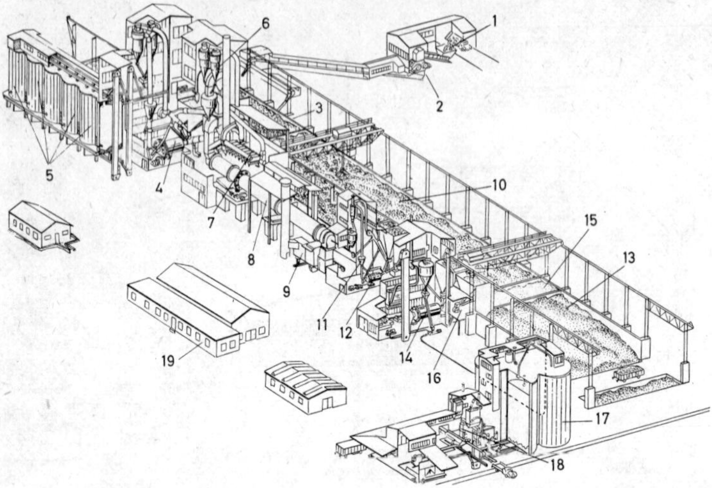

1 the raw material intake [limestone, clay and marl]

2 the hammer mill (hammer crusher)

3 the raw material store

4 the raw grinding mill and drier

5 the raw meal silos

6 the heat-exchanger

7 the dust collector

8 the rotary kiln

9 the clinker cooler (grate type cooler)

10 the clinker store

11 the primary air-blower

12 the coal pulverising plant (coal mill)

13 the coal store

14 the cement grinding mill

15 the gypsum store

16 the gypsum crusher

17 the cement silo

18 the cement packing plant

19 the power station (generating plant)

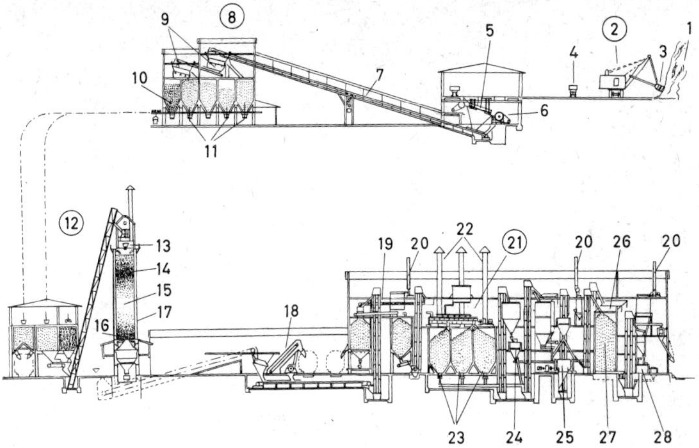

1 the quarry
2 the excavator, the navvy:
3 the excavator bucket;
4 the wagon
5 the bar screen
6 the primary crusher
7 the belt conveyor
8 the screening plant:
9 the vibrating screen;
10 the crushed limestone
11 the limestone fines (crushed stone aggregate)
12 the lime kiln (vertical kiln, shaft kiln):
13 the kiln charger
14 the kiln charge (mixture of limestone and coke)
15 the burning zone
16 the quicklime
17 the kiln shell;
18 the lime crusher and lump lime loader
19 the pulverising and screening plant
20 the dust collector
21 the lime slaking plant (hydrator):
22 the vapour vent
23 the slaked lime silo, the soaking tank
24 the air separator (sifter);
25 the pulverisor
26 the hydrated lime silo
27 the hydrated lime
28 the packing plant

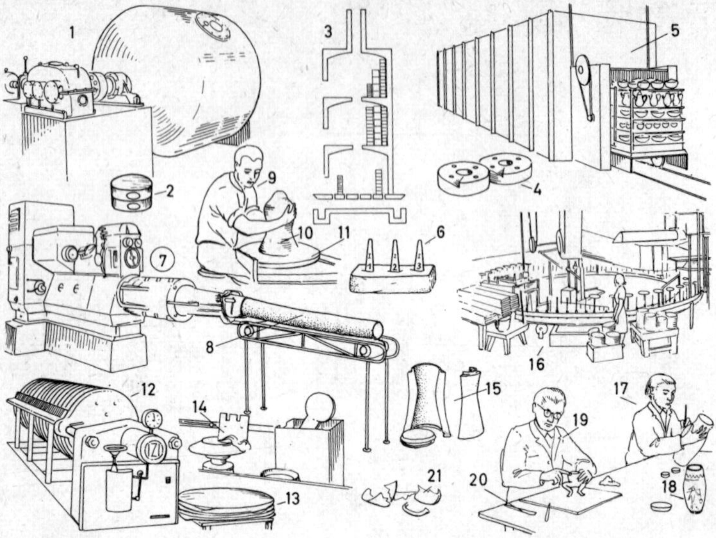

1 the grinding cylinder (ball-mill) for the preparation of the raw material in the slip state (in water)
2 the sample saggar (sample seggar) with aperture for observing the firing process
3 the bottle oven (intermittent kiln) [diagram]
4 the firing setter (*Am.* firing mold)
5 the tunnel kiln
6 the Seger cone (pyrometric cone) for measuring high temperatures
7 the de-airing pug, an extrusion press:
8 the clay column;
9 the thrower throwing a 'slug' of clay
10 the 'slug' of clay
11 the throwing wheel; *sim.* potter's wheel
12 the filter press
13 the filter cake
14 the jigger or jolley for shaping the rotating clay with a template
15 the plaster mould (*Am.* mold) for slip-casting
16 the turntable glazing machine
17 the porcelain painter (china painter)
18 the hand-painted vase
19 the burnisher
20 the blood-stone (*Am.* modeling stick)
21 the broken pottery ('shards')

1–11 the sheet-glass manufacture (flat-glass manufacture),
1 the tank furnace [diagram]:
2 the frontal feeder for feeding the mixture
3 the melting bath
4 the refining bath (fining bath)
5 the working bath
6 the working canal;
7 the glass-drawing machine:
8 the glass melt (molten glass, 'metal')
9 the drawing hearth
10 the air-cooled bending roller
11 the glass sheet;
12 Owen's bottle-blowing machine, a fully automatic machine for making bottles
13–15 glass-blowing (mouth-blowing):
13 the glass-blower
14 the blowing iron (blowing tube)
15 the parison;
16–21 piece work on glassware:
16 the glass finisher (chair worker)
17 the mouth-blown goblet
18 the implement for forming the goblet foot
19 the shape gauge (*Am.* shape gage)
20 the glass-blower's tongs
21 the glass-maker's chair or bench or stool;
22 the hooded furnace pot
23 the mould (*Am.* mold) for blowing up the pre-moulded (*Am.* pre-molded) parison

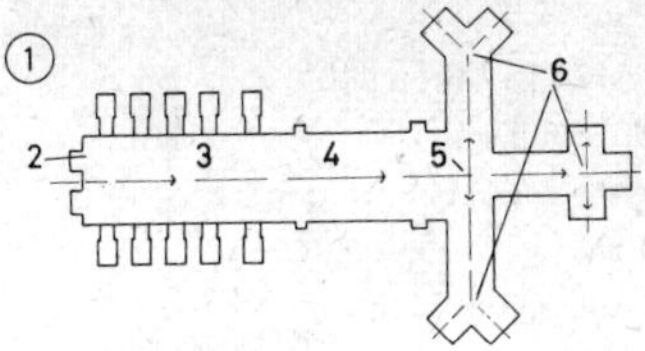

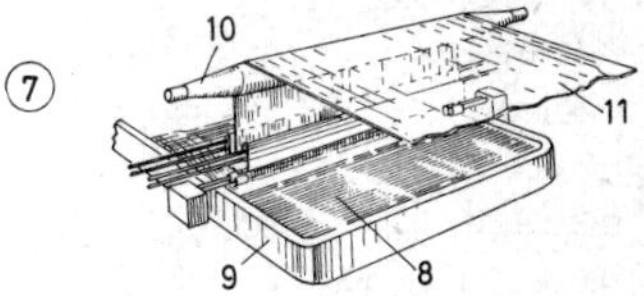

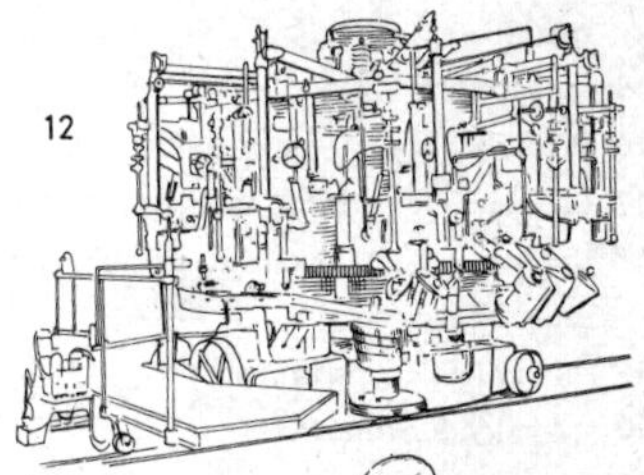

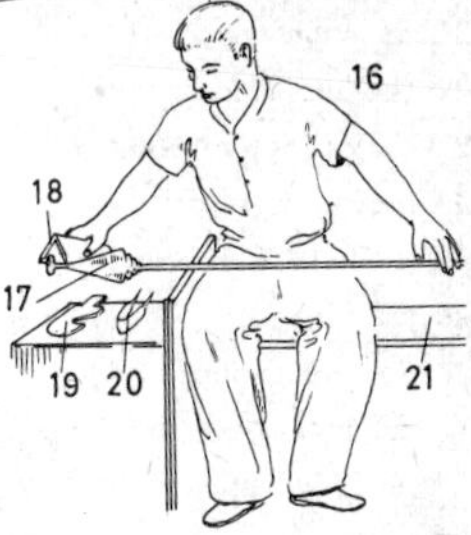

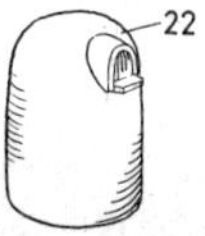

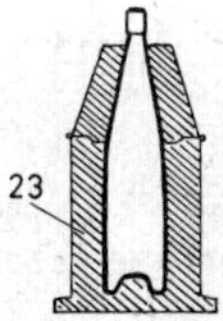

1 the ripe cotton boll
2 the full cop
3 the compressed cotton bale:
4 the jute wrapping ('tare')
5 the iron band (hoop iron)
6 the lot numbers of the bale;
7 the bale-breaker:
8 the lattice feeder
9 the feed box
10 the dust extraction fan
11 the duct to the dust chamber
12 the driving motor
13 the conveyor lattice;
14 **the double scutcher and lap machine:**
15 the lap rest
16 the rack head
17 the machine-starting handle
18 the handwheel for raising and lowering the rack head
19 the movable lap-turner
20 the calender rollers
21 the top cage cover
22 the dust chimney
23 the driving motors
24 the beater shaft;
25 the Kirschner beater
26 the grid bars
27 the pedal roller
28 the lever for regulating the feed, a pedal lever;
29 the variable change-speed gear
30 the cone drum box
31 the stop and start levers to the hopper
32 the wooden delivery roller of the hopper
33 the hopper feeder;
34 **the carding engine** (revolving flat card):
35 the card can for receiving the coiled sliver
36 the can-holder
37 the calender rollers
38 the sliver
39 the doffer comb
40 the start-stop lever
41 the grinding-roller bearing
42 the doffer
43 the cylinder
44 the flat cleaner
45 the flats
46 the supporting pulleys for the flats
47 the scutcher lap
48 the lap-holder
49 the driving motor with flat belt
50 the main driving pulley (fast and loose driving pulley);
51 line diagram of the card:
52 the feed roller
53 the licker-in (taker-in) roller
54 the taker-in under casing
55 the cylinder under casing;
56 **the comber:**
57 the gear box
58 the laps ready for combing
59 the calender rollers
60 the comber draw box
61 the counter
62 the coiler top;
63 diagram showing the principles of comber:
64 the lap
65 the bottom nipper
66 the top nipper
67 the top comb
68 the combing cylinder
69 the plain segment of the cylinder
70 the needled half-lap
71 the detaching rollers
72 the combed material

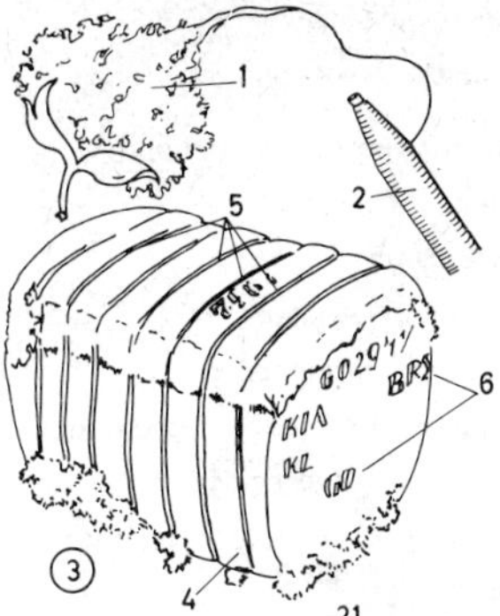
1
2
5
6
3
4
G029 1/1
BRS
KIA
KL
GO

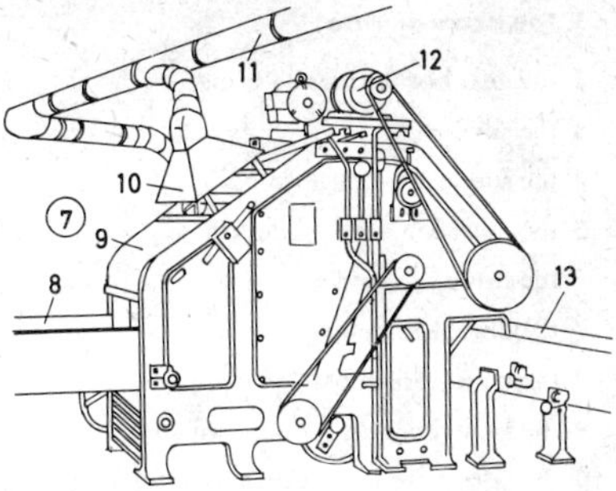
7
8
9
10
11
12
13

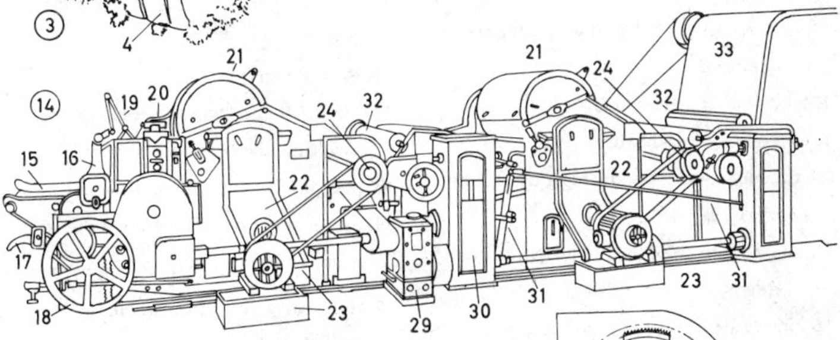
14
15
16
17
18
19
20
21
22
23
24
29
30
31
32
33

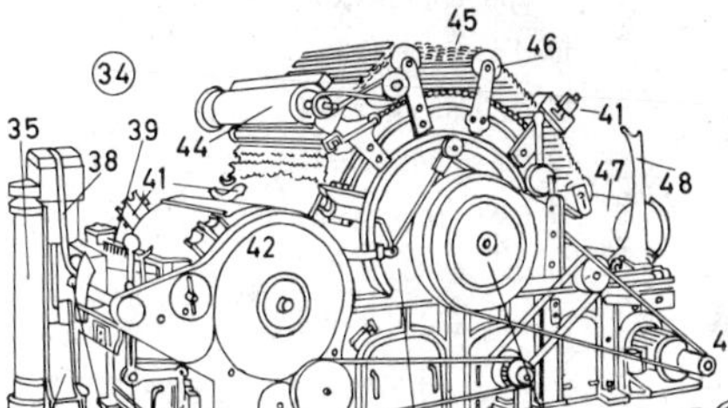
34
35
36
37
38
39
40
41
42
43
44
45
46
47
48
49
50

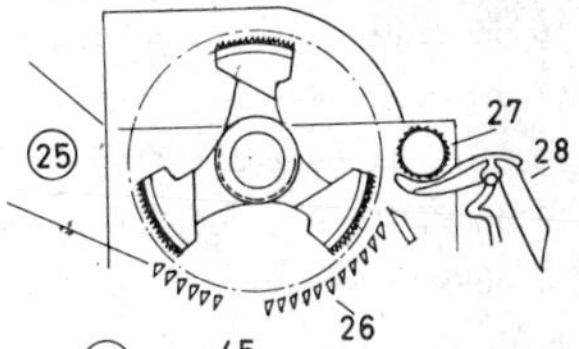
25
26
27
28

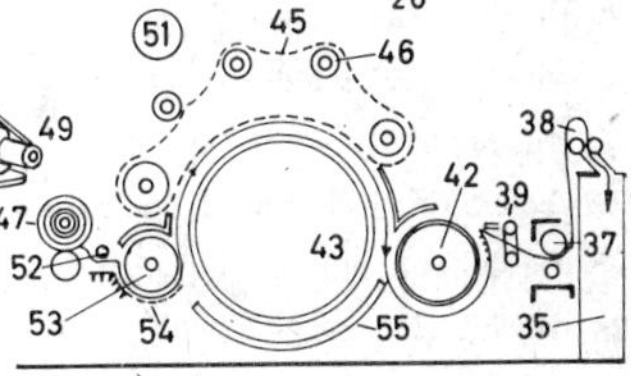
51
35
37
38
39
42
43
45
46
47
52
53
54
55

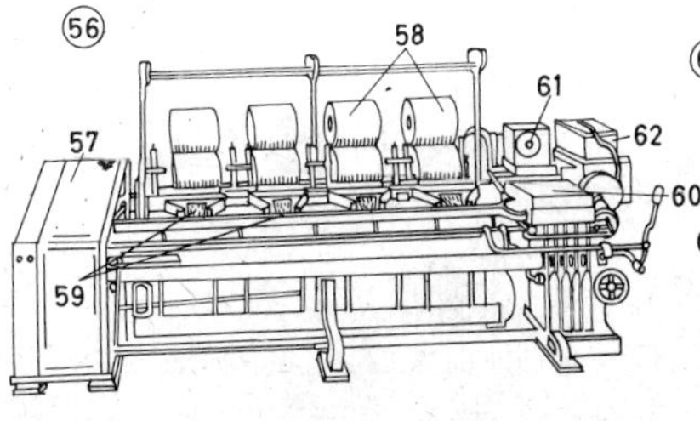
56
57
58
59
60
61
62

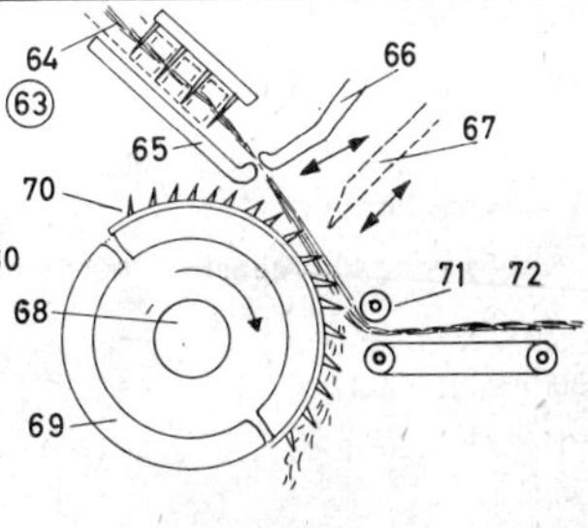
63
64
65
66
67
68
69
70
71
72

157 The Cotton-spinning Mill II

1 **the draw-frame:**
2 the gear box with built-in motor
3 the sliver cans
4 the single preventor rollers
5 the doubling of the slivers
6 the stopping handle
7 the draw-frame cover
8 the indicator lamps;
9 the four-roller draw-frame [diagram]:
10 the bottom rollers (fluted steel rollers)
11 the top rollers covered with rubber compound
12 the doubled slivers before drafting
13 the sliver after drafting;
14 the high-draft system (high-draft draw-frame) [diagram]:
15 the feeding-in of the roving through condenser
16 the leather (composition) 'apron'
17 the guide bar
18 the light top roller;
19 the high-draft speed frame (fly frame, slubbing frame):
20 the sliver cans
21 the sliver being fed to the drafting rollers
22 the drafting rollers with top clearers
23 the slubbing bobbins
24 the slubber tenter
25 the flyer
26 the frame end plate;
27 the intermediate frame:
28 the bobbin creel
29 the roving emerging from the drafting rollers
30 the lifter rail
31 the spindle drive
32 the stopping handle
33 the gear box with built-on motor;
34 **the ring frame** (ring spinning frame):
35 the three-phase motor
36 the motor base plate
37 the ring for lifting the motor
38 the control for variable-speed spindle
39 the headstock (gear case)
40 the change wheels for varying the yarn count
41 the full creel
42 the shafts and levers for raising and lowering the ring rail
43 the spindles with the separators
44 the sucting box connected to the front roller underclearers;
45 **the standard ring spindle** (*Am.* conventional spindle):
46 the spindle shaft
47 the roller bearing
48 the spindle wharve
49 the spindle catch
50 the spindle rail;
51 ring and traveller (*Am.* ring and traveler; the spinning devices):
52 the top of the ring tube or bobbin
53 the yarn
54 the ring fitted in the ring rail
55 the traveller (*Am.* traveler)
56 the yarn wound on the bobbin;
57 **the doubling frame:**
58 the creel with a set of cross-wound cheeses
59 the delivery rollers
60 the bobbins of doubled yarn

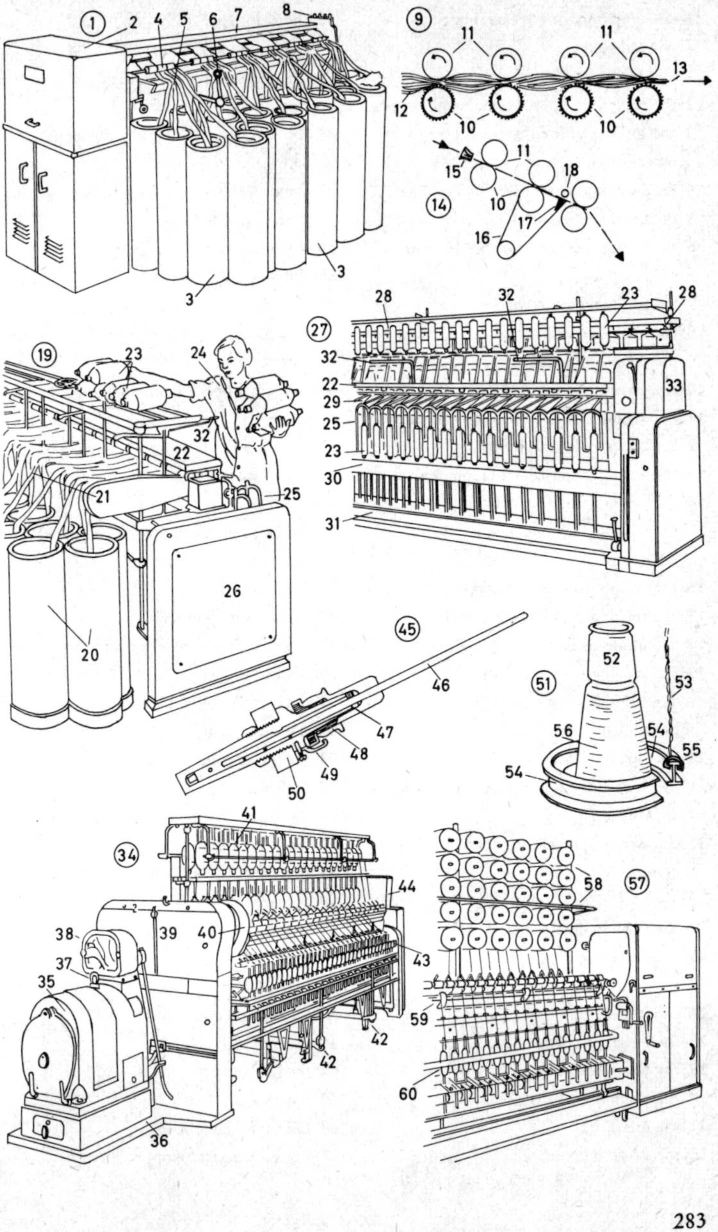
1 2 3 4 5 6 7 8
9 10 11 12 13
14 15 16 17 18
19 20 21 22 23 24 25 26 32
27 28 22 23 25 29 30 31 32 33
45 46 47 48 49 50
51 52 53 54 55 56
34 35 36 37 38 39 40 41 42 43 44
57 58 59 60

1-65 preparatory weaving machinery,

1 the cone-winding frame:
2 the travelling (*Am.* traveling) blower
3 the guide rail for the travelling (*Am.* traveling) blower
4 the blowing assembly
5 the blower aperture
6 the superstructure for the blower rail
7 the full-cone indicator
8 the cross-wound cone
9 the cone-holders
10 the grooved drum (split guiding drum)
11 the zigzag slot for crossing the threads
12 the headstock with motor
13 the tension and slub-catching device
14 the off-end framing with filter
15 the supply package, a ring tube or mule cop
16 the supply package container
17 the starting and stopping lever
18 the guide to facilitate threading
19 the automatic stop motion for stopping the machine if the thread breaks
20 the thread-clearer
21 the disk (disc) weighting for thread-tensioning;
22 the warping machine (beaming machine):
23 the fans
24 the cone in creel
25 the magazine creel
26 the adjustable comb
27 the frame side
28 the length-recorder
29 the warp beam
30 the beam flange
31 the guard rail
32 the driving drum
33 the belt drive
34 the motor
35 the release for starting the driving drum
36 the screw for adjusting the comb setting
37 the drop pins for stopping the machine when a thread breaks
38 the guide bar
39 the drop pin rollers;
40 the sizing machine (taping machine) for smoothing and strengthening the yarn:
41 the warp beam from the warping machine
42 the immersion roller
43 the squeeze rollers
44 the size
45 the size box
46 the yarn
47 the guide rollers
48 the drying cylinder
49 the fans for circulating hot air
50 the inspection panel
51 the hot-air control valve
52 the steam coils
53 the guide rollers
54 the spit rod
55 the sheet of yarn
56 the expanding comb
57 the weaver's beam with sized yarn
58 the beam bearing rollers
59 the drums controlling speed and elimination of differences in thread tension
60 the tension control
61 the belt drive
62 the belt pulley
63 the air duct
64 the drying chamber
65 the starting and stopping handle

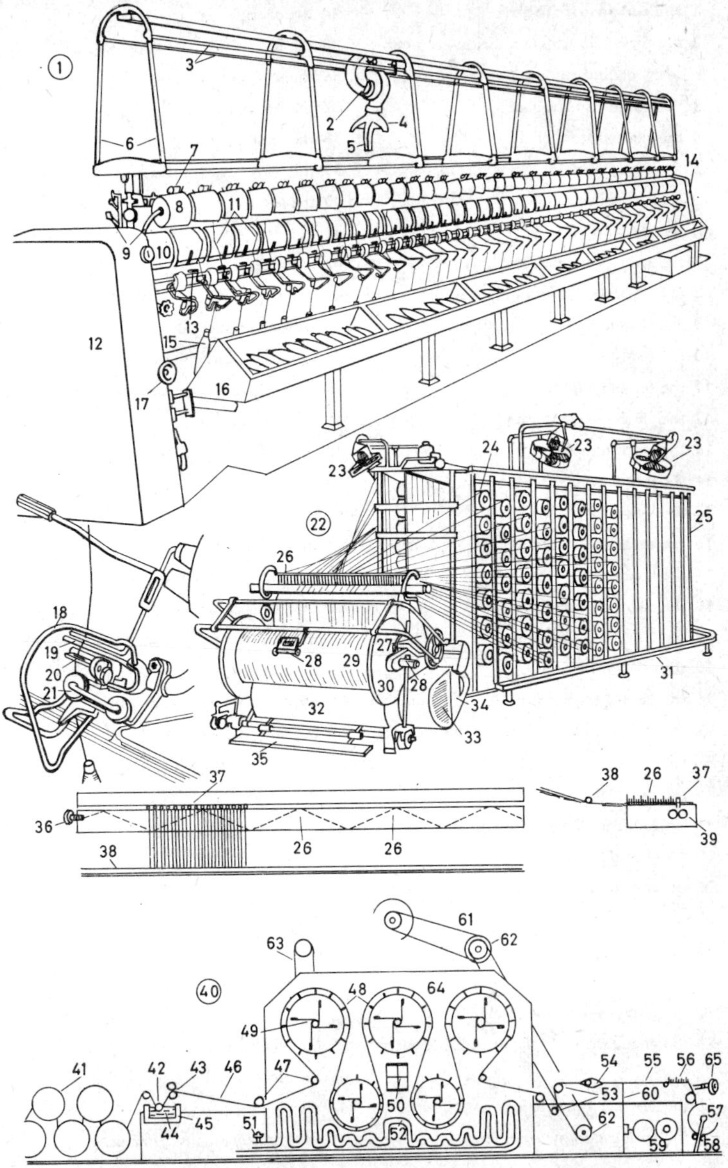
1
2
3
4
5
6
7
8
9
10
11
12
13
14
15
16
17
18
19
20
21
22
23
24
25
26
27
28
29
30
31
32
33
34
35
36
37
38
39
40
41
42
43
44
45
46
47
48
49
50
51
52
53
54
55
56
57
58
59
60
61
62
63
64
65

159 The Weaving Shed (Weaving Mill, Textile Mill) II

1 **the automatic loom:**
2 the pick-counter (revolution-counter, *Am.* reading tachometer)
3 the guides for the shafts
4 the shafts (heald shafts)
5 the rotary battery (rotary magazine) for weft pirns
6 the slay cap (sley cap)
7 the weft pirn (weft bobbin)
8 the starting and stopping handle
9 the shuttle box with shuttles
10 the reed
11 the selvedge (list)
12 the cloth (woven fabric)
13 the cloth temple
14 the electric weft feeler
15 the flywheel
16 the breast-beam board
17 the picking stick
18 the electric motor
19 the cloth take-up motion
20 the cloth roller
21 the can for empty pirns
22 the lug strap for operating the picking stick
23 the fuse box
24 the loom framing;
25 the shuttle
26 the shuttle tip
27 the heald (wire heald):
28 the heald eye
29 the shuttle eye
30 the pirn (weft bobbin)
31 the metal contact sleeve for the weft feeler
32 the slot for the weft feeler
33 the spring-clip pirn-holder
34 the drop wire;
35 the loom [side elevation]:
36 the top rollers
37 the back rest
38 the lease rods
39 the warp (warp thread)
40 the shed
41 the slay (sley)
42 the race board
43 the stop rod blade of the warp protector motion
44 the frog (bumper steel)
45 the frog (bumper steel) spindle
46 the breast beam
47 the cloth take-up roller
48 the warp beam
49 the beam flange
50 the crank shaft
51 the crank shaft wheel
52 the crank-connecting arm
53 the slay (sley) sword
54 the lam rods
55 the cam (bottom) shaft wheel
56 the cam (tappet) shaft
57 the tappets (shedding tappets)
58 the treadle lever
59 the warp let-off motion
60 the beam ruffle
61 the rope of warp let-off motion
62 the weight lever
63 the weight
64 the picker with leather, or bakelite, pad
65 the picking stick buffer
66 the picking cam
67 the picking bowl
68 the picking stick return spring

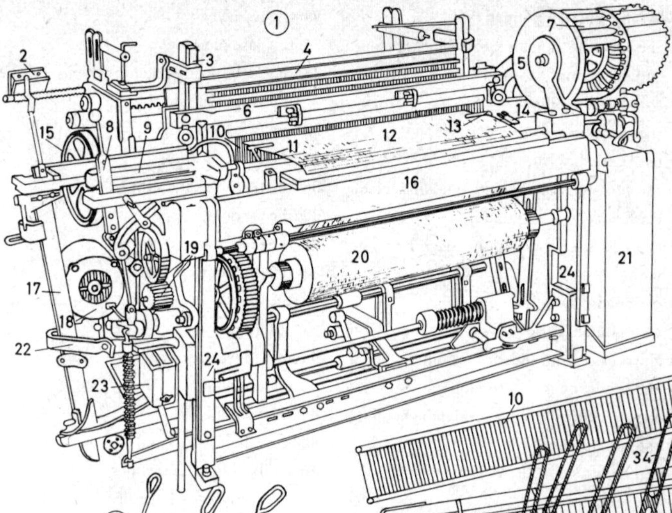
1
2
3
4
5
7
6
13
14
15
8
9
10
12
11
16
20
21
17
18
19
24
22
23
24

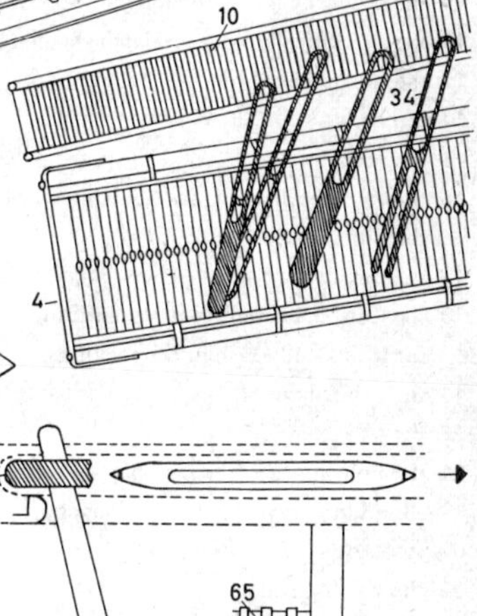
10
34
4

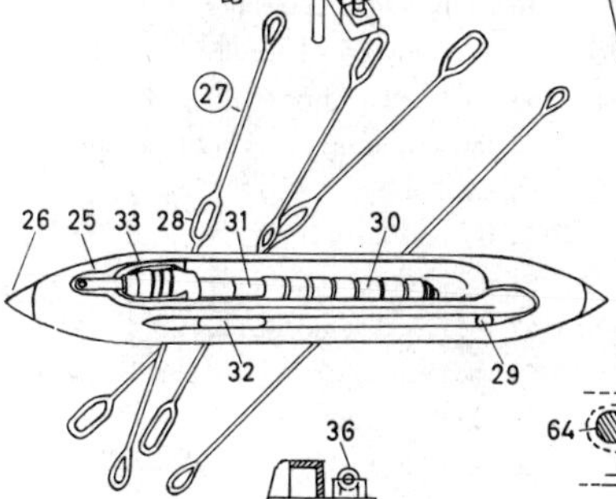
27
26
25
33
28
31
30
32
29

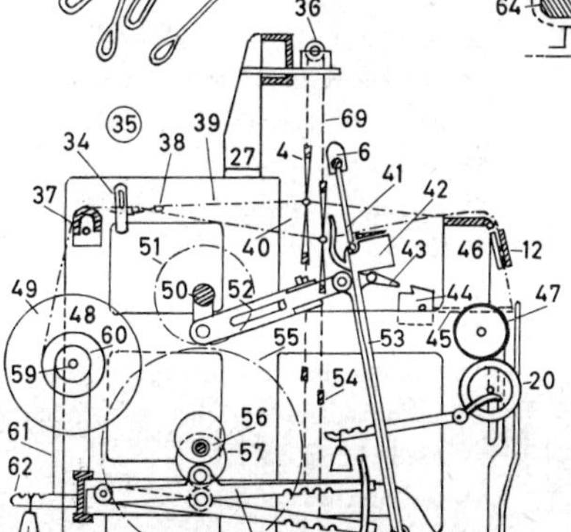
36
35
39
69
34
38
27
4
6
37
41
42
51
40
43
46
12
49
50
52
44
47
48
60
55
45
59
53
20
54
56
61
57
62
58
63

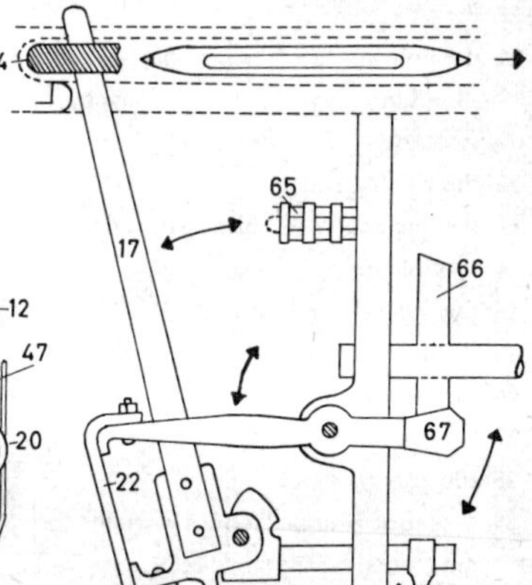
64
65
17
66
67
22
68
24

1-66 the knitting factory,

1 the knitting machine for the manufacture of tubular fabric:

2 the support pillar

3 the thread (yarn) guide

4 the bottle bobbin

5 the yarn-tensioner (yarn tension device)

6 the feeder (feeding plate)

7 the wheel for rotating the machine by hand

8 the needle cylinder

9 the tubular fabric

10 the fabric drum (fabric container);

11 the needle cylinder [section]:

12 the cylindrically arranged latch needles

13 the cam boxes

14 the cams

15 the needle tricks

16 the cylinder diameter; *also :* diameter of the tubular fabric

17 the thread (yarn);

18 the Cotton's Patent knitting machine for ladies' fully-fashioned stockings:

19 the control chain

20 the side frame

21 the knitting head; *several knitting heads :* simultaneous production of several stockings

22 the starting rod;

23 the Raschel warp-knitting machine (double rib):

24 the warp (warp beam)

25 the distributing (dividing) beam

26 the beam flange

27 the latch needles

28 the guide bar

29 the fabric (Raschel fabric) [curtains and net cloths] on the cloth beam

30 the handwheel

31 the driving wheels and the motor

32 the take-down weight

33 the frame

34 the base plate;

35 the flat-knitting machine (hand operated knitting machine):

36 the thread (yarn)

37 the thread guide

38 the thread guide support

39 the carriage

40 the feeder selecting bolt

41 the pushing handles

42 the scale for regulating the size of the stitches

43 the course-counter (*Am.* reading tachometer)

44 the control lever

45 the rail

46 the back row of needles

47 the front row of needles

48 the knitted fabric (fabric)

49 the weighting bar to hold the fabric in tension

50 the tension weight;

51 the knitting action:

52 the raised edge of tricks

53 the needles arranged in parallel order

54 the thread guide

55 the needle bed

56 the plate retaining the latch needles

57 the upper guard cam

58 the stitch cam

59 the cam for raising the needles

60 the needle butt;

61 the latch needle:

62 the fabric

63 pushing the needle through the fabric

64 the thread guide placing the yarn in the needle hook

65 the formation of a loop

66 casting off a loop

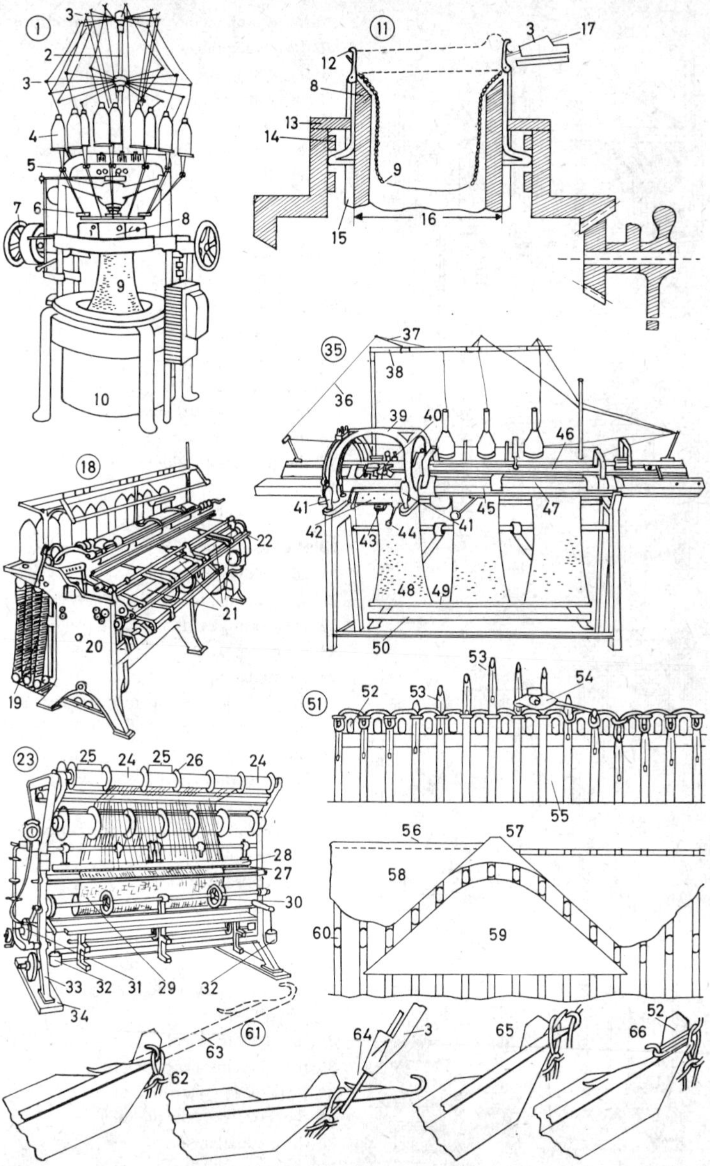
1
2
3
4
5
6
7
8
9
10
11
12
13
14
15
16
17
18
19
20
21
22
23
24
25
26
27
28
29
30
31
32
33
34
35
36
37
38
39
40
41
42
43
44
45
46
47
48
49
50
51
52
53
54
55
56
57
58
59
60
61
62
63
64
65
66

161 Textile-dyeing and Textile-bleaching

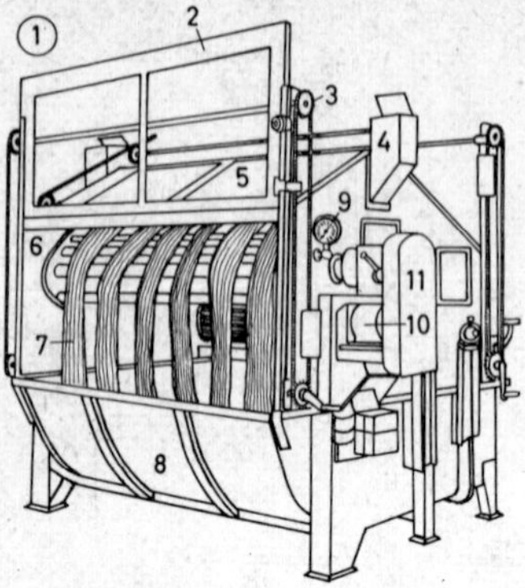

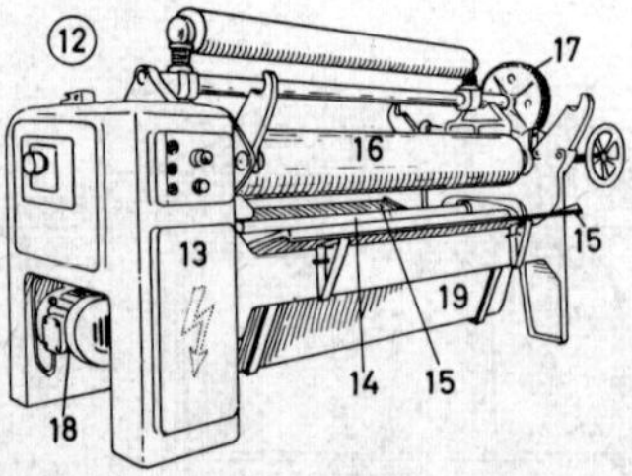

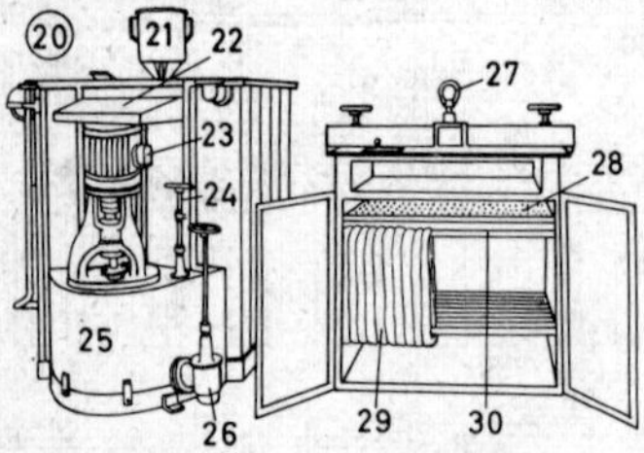

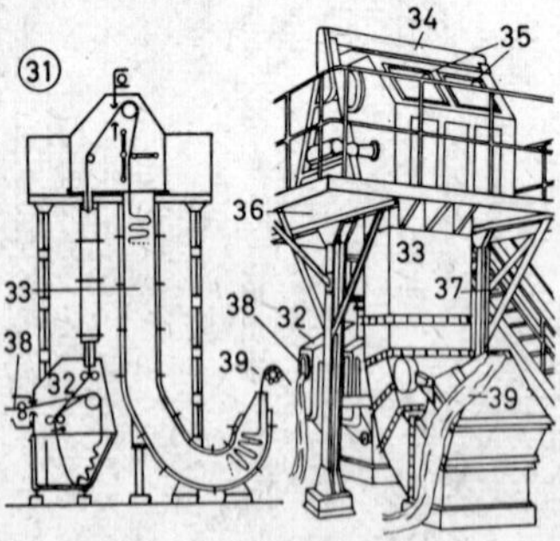

1 the winch (wince) **dying machine:**
2 the glass window
3 the window-lifting mechanism
4 the steam vent
5 the cover
6 the oval winch [may also be a round winch]
7 the material to be dyed
8 the dye vat
9 the thermometer
10 the motor
11 the belt guard;

12 the jig (jigger):
13 the control panel
14 the expander roller
15 the dye liquor drip-pan
16 the take-up roller
17 the gear wheel (*Am.* gear)
18 the motor
19 the dye beck;

20 the hank (skein) **dyeing machine,**
21–26 the dyeing unit:
21 the container for stock dye solution
22 the splash guard
23 the motor
24 the starter
25 the propeller compartment for circulating the dye liquor
26 the outlet valve;
27–30 the hank-carrier (skein-carrier):
27 the suspension ring
28 the perforated plate for distributing the dye liquor
29 the hanks (skeins)
30 the rods;

31 the continuous bleaching plant:
32 the impregnating chamber
33 the steam-heated and heat-insulated J-box (J-box)
34 the ventilation duct
35 the J-box inspection window
36 the working platform
37 the stairway to the platform
38 the material intake
39 the material delivery;

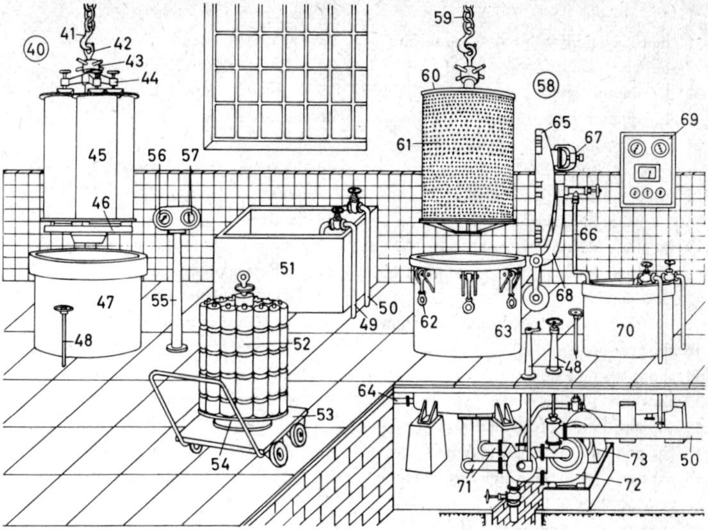

40 the beam bleaching plant for sliver or for warp yarn:
41 the crane hook
42 the suspension ring (suspension eye)
43 the capstan to tighten the clamping arms
44 the screw caps for the beams
45 the warp beams
46 the warp-beam carrier
47 the outer container (bleach vat)
48 the valve from the supply tank
49 the hard-water pipe
50 the soft-water pipe
51 the supply tank for the preparing bleaching liquor
52 the cross-wound cheeses or cones
53 the truck
54 the cross-wound cheese frame
55 the instrument stand
56 the pressure gauge (*Am.* gage)
57 the thermometer;
58 the dyeing machine for dyeing loose fibres (*Am.* fibers) or cross-wound packages (cheeses, cones, and cakes):
59 the crane chain
60 the insert
61 the perforated cage or basket
62 the clamps securing the lid
63 the outer container (dye liquor container)
64 the steam pipe
65 the lid
66 the dye liquor pipe
67 the aperture for withdrawing the samples (for withdrawing the sampling pot)
68 the support and counterweight for the lid
69 the control panel
70 the dye mixing tank
71 the liquor circulation pipes
72 the centrifugal pump
73 the pump motor

1–65 finishing,
1 the rotary milling machine for felting the wool fabric:
2 the pressure weight
3 the upper milling roller
4 the driving pulley on the shaft of the lower milling roller
5 the breast roller (guide roller)
6 the lower milling roller
7 the draft (draught) board;
8 the open-width scouring machine for finer fabrics:
9 the fabric being drawn off the machine
10 the gear box
11 the water pipe
12 the drawer roller
13 the scroll rod (scroll opener);
14 the pendulum-type centrifugal hydro-extractor for extracting water from the fabric:
15 the base of the machine
16 the case over the suspension
17 the outer casing, the rotating cage within
18 the extractor lid
19 the safety stop device
20 the starting device and the automatic brake;
21 the stenter (tenter):
22 the damp fabric
23 the operator's (operative's) platform
24 the guides feeding the fabric to the clips or pins [in case of pin stenter]
25 the electric control panels
26 the overfeed to allow shrinkage in warp direction during the drying process [pin stenter only]
27 the thermometer
28 the drying stove (drying chamber)
29 the air outlet
30 the plaiting device;
31 the wire raising machine for raising the surface of the fabric by means of rollers covered with card fillet which raise a nap on the cloth:
32 the driving gear box
33 the unraised cloth
34 the wire-covered rollers
35 the plaiting (cuttling) device
36 the raised fabric
37 the scray;
38 the rotary press for pressing the fabric:
39 the cloth
40 the push-button and wheel controls
41 the heated pressing cylinder;
42 the cloth-shearing machine:
43 the vacuum extracting duct for removing the waste loose fibres (*Am.* fibers)
44 the shearing blade (shearing cylinder)
45 the protective grid (guard)
46 the rotating brush
47 the curved scray
48 the control footboard;
49 the decatizing (blowing) machine for steaming to stabilize the finish:
50 the decatizing roller
51 the piece of cloth
52 the crank (crank handle, control handle);
53 the ten-colour (*Am.* ten-color) roller printing machine (cloth-printing machine):
54 the machine base frame
55 the motor
56 the felt, or rubber, blanket
57 the fabric after printing
58 the electric control panel;
59 the screen printing:
60 the screen on a carriage
61 the squeegee for spreading colour (*Am.* color) over the screen
62 the printing screen
63 the screen table
64 the fabric gummed down on the table and ready for printing
65 the cloth-printing operative

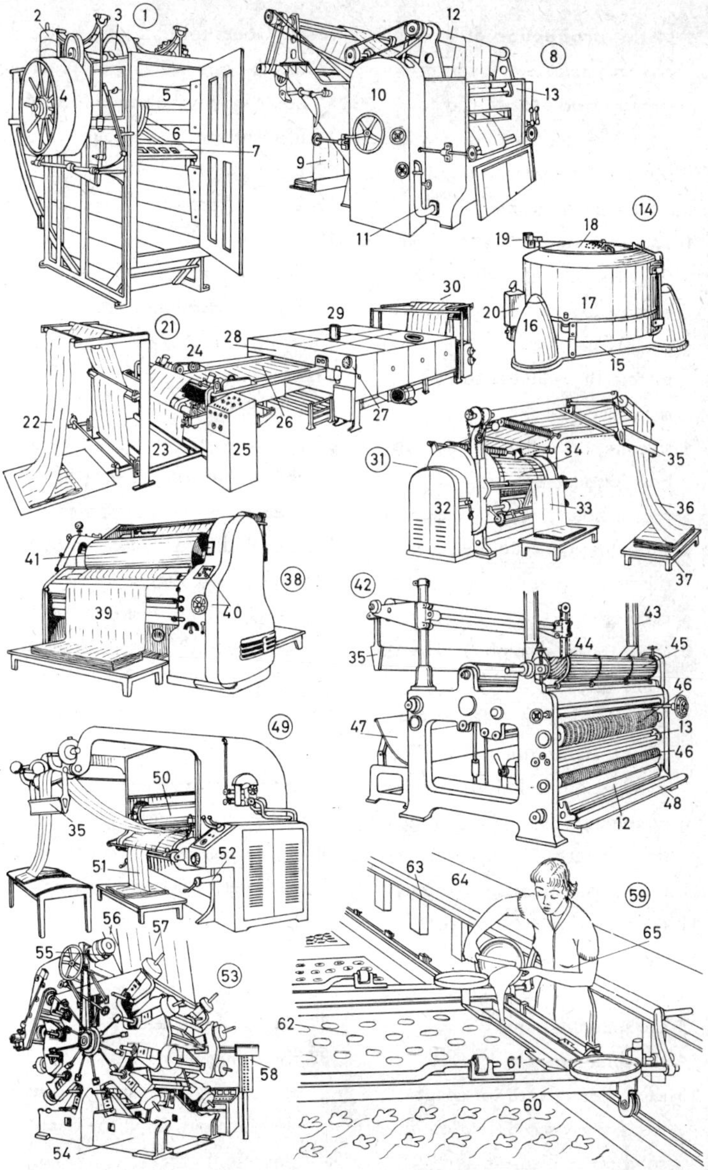
1
2
3
4
5
6
7
8
9
10
11
12
13
14
15
16
17
18
19
20
21
22
23
24
25
26
27
28
29
30
31
32
33
34
35
36
37
38
39
40
41
42
43
44
45
46
47
48
49
50
51
52
53
54
55
56
57
58
59
60
61
62
63
64
65

1-34 the production of filament rayon yarn (*Am.* rayon manufacture) **and staple** (rayon staple) by means of the viscose process (viscose rayon yarn and viscose rayon staple),

1–12 from raw material to viscose:

1 the basic material [spruce or beechwood pulp in sheets, cellulose sheets]

2 mixing the cellulose sheets

3 the caustic soda

4 steeping the cellulose sheets in caustic soda

5 pressing out thc cxcess caustic soda

6 shredding the cellulose sheets

7 the preparation of the alkali cellulose

8 the carbonic disulphide (*Am.* carbonic disulfid)

9 the sulphuration (*Am.* sulfuration; transformation of alkali cellulose into cellulose xanthate)

10 dissolving the xanthate in caustic soda for the production of the viscose-spinning solution

11 the vacuum ageing churns

12 the filter presses;

13–27 from viscose to rayon yarn:

13 the spinning pump

14 the spinning jet

15 the spinning bath for coagulating the viscose solution into solid rayon filament

16 the Godet roller, a glass roller

17 the Topham centrifugal spinning box winding the newly formed filament yarn into a cake

18 the freshly spun cake

19–27 the processing of the cake:

19 washing

20 desulphurizing (*Am.* desulfurizing; the desulphurization, *Am.* desulfurization)

21 bleaching

22 cake-finishing

23 the hydro-extracting for removing the superfluous bath liquid

24 the drying in the drying chamber

25 the winding from cake to cone

26 the cone-winding machine

27 the rayon yarn (artificial silk) on cone for further textile processing;

28–34 from viscose spinning solution to rayon staple:

28 the tows of filament

29 the washing plant

30 the cutting wheels for cutting the tow to a predetermined length [rayon staple, staple]

31 the multiple drying machine for the freshly cut staple

32 the conveyor belt

33 the baling press

34 the bale of rayon staple ready for transport (*Am.* for transportation)

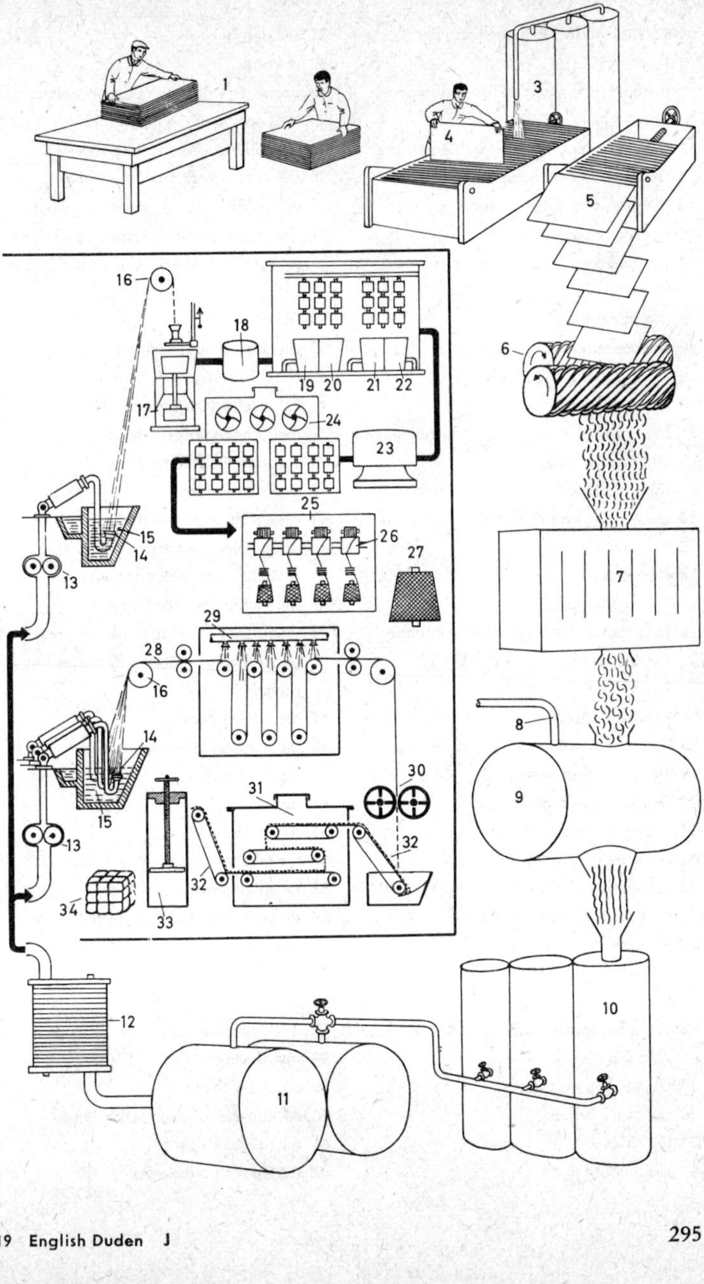
1
2
3
4
5
6
7
8
9
10
11
12
13
14
15
16
17
18
19
20
21
22
23
24
25
26
27
28
29
30
31
32
33
34

1-62 the perlon manufacture (nylon-6 manufacture):
1 the coal [raw material for perlon production]
2 the coke plant for dry coal distillation
3 the extraction of tar and phenols
4 the gradual tar distillation
5 the condenser
6 the benzene extraction and benzene dispatch
7 the chlorine
8 the benzene chlorination
9 the monochlorobenzene
10 the caustic soda
11 the evaporation of monochlorobenzene and caustic soda
12 the autoclave
13 the sodium chloride (common salt), a by-product
14 the phenol
15 the hydrogen inlet
16 the catalytic hydrogenation of phenol for the production of raw cyclohexanol
17 the distillation
18 the pure cyclohexanol
19 the oxydation (oxidation)
20 formation of cyclohexanone
21 the hydroxylamine inlet
22 the formation of cyclohexanonoxime
23 the addition of sulphuric (*Am.* sulfuric) acid for molecular re-arrangement
24 the ammonia for neutralizing the sulphuric (*Am.* sulfuric) acid
25 formation of capro lactam oil
26 the ammonium sulphate (*Am.* sulfate) solution
27 the cooling cylinder
28 the capro lactam
29 the balance
30 the melting pot
31 the pump
32 the filter
33 the polymerization in the autoclave
34 the cooling of the polyamide
35 the solidification of the polyamide
36 the paternoster lift (*Am.* endless elevator)
37 the extractor for the separation of the polyamide from the remaining lactam oil
38 the drying device (*Am.* drier)
39 the dry polyamide chips
40 the chip container
41 the smelting and spinning head for melting the polyamide and pressing it through the spinning jets
42 the spinning jets
43 the solidification of the perlon threads in the spinning tower
44 collecting the perlon thread
45 the preliminary stretching
46 the further dressing to obtain great strength and flexibility of the perlon thread
47 the final drawing
48 the package-washing
49 the drying chamber
50 re-winding
51 the perlon cone
52 the perlon cone, ready for dispatch
53 the mixing pot
54 the polymerization under reduced pressure
55 drawing
56 washing
57 tow-finishing
58 tow-drying
59 crimping the tow
60 cutting the tow into staple lengths
61 the perlon staple
62 the bale of perlon staple

164

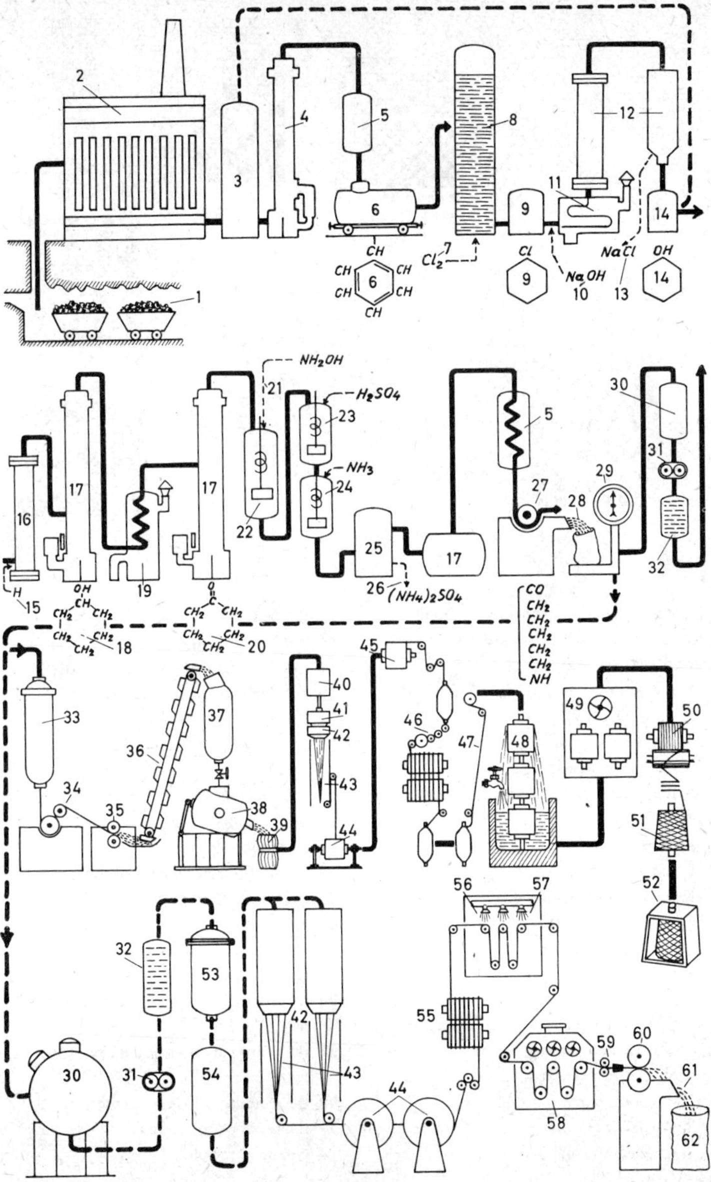
1
2
3
4
5
6
7
8
9
10
11
12
13
14
CH
CH CH
CH CH
CH
Cl2
Cl
NaOH
NaCl
OH
15
H
16
17
18
19
20
21
22
23
24
25
26
27
28
29
30
31
32
NH2OH
H2SO4
NH3
(NH4)2SO4
OH
CH
CH2 CH2
CH2 CH2
CH2
O
C
CH2 CH2
CH2 CH2
CH2
CO
CH2
CH2
CH2
CH2
CH2
NH
33
34
35
36
37
38
39
40
41
42
43
44
45
46
47
48
49
50
51
52
53
54
55
56
57
58
59
60
61
62

165 Weaves

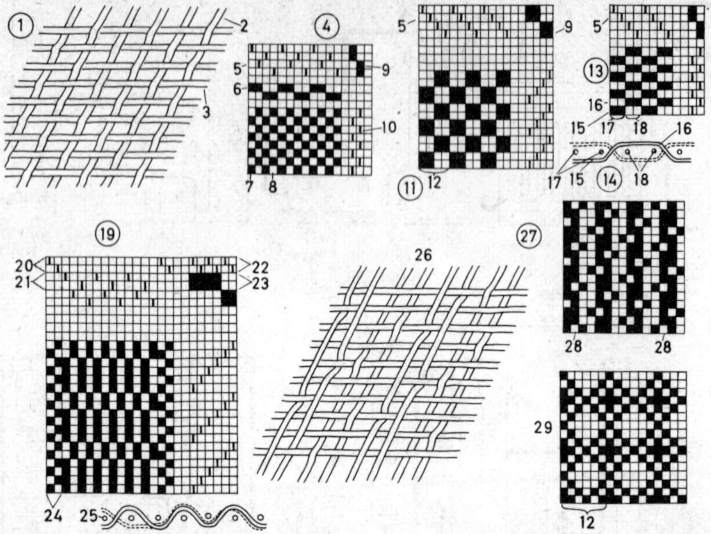

[black squares: warp thread lifted, weft thread down; white squares: weft thread lifted, warp thread down]

1 the plain weave interlacing [fabric shown from above]:
2 the warp thread
3 the weft thread;
4 the point paper design (draft, lifting plan and denting for the weaver) for plain weave:
5 the draft in the shafts
6 the denting arrangement
7 the lifted warp thread
8 the lowered warp thread
9 the tying of heald shafts in pairs
10 the treadle-lifting plan;
11 the point paper design for matt weave (for basket weave):
12 the pattern repeat;
13 the point paper design for weft rib,
14 section of weft rib fabric, a section through the warp:
15 the weft thread down
16 the weft thread up
17 the first and second warp threads [lifted]
18 the third and fourth warp threads [lowered];
19 the point paper design for modified rib weave:
20 the draft of the selvedge threads in the heald shafts (additional shafts for the selvedge)
21 the draft of the threads of the cloth
22 the tying up of the selvedge shafts
23 the tying up of the cloth shafts
24 the selvedge (list) in plain weave
25 cross section of modified rib weave;
26 thread interlacing of reversible warp-faced cord
27 the point paper design of reversible warp-faced cord:
28 the binding locking places;
29 the point paper design of honeycomb weave in the cloth

1–40 the laundry,
1 the steam washing-machine:
2 the rotating washing drum or cylinder
3 the segment compartments of the inner drum
4 the alkali (detergent, wash water) and rinsing water casing (outer drum)
5 the dirty-water outlet;
6 the tumbler, a laundry-drying machine:
7 the outer case with the drying drum
8 the loading door
9 the remote reading (distance) thermometer (telethermometer)
10 the hygrometer;
11 the wash room (laundry room),
12 the cabinet washing-machine:
13 the control lever
14 the opening for washing materials (for detergents)
15 the laundry-list holder
16 the dirty-water outlet cock (*Am.* outlet faucet);
17 the laundry trolley
18 the hydro-extractor laundry centrifuge (centrifugal hydroextractor)
19 the one-chamber laundry-dryer or drier (cabinet drier):
20 the fan for air circulation
21 the superheated-steam supply pipe
22 the condensate pipe
23 the fresh and used-air regulator
24 the fresh-air shutter;
25 the calender (ironer):
26 the heated calender roll
27 the protective grille (guard)
28 the calender operator
29 the ironing-board
30 the air outlet pipe or duct;
31 hand ironing:
32 the ironer (ironing woman)
33 the electric iron
34 the ironing-board;
35 the laundry press:
36 the polished head
37 the felt-covered buck
38 the tightening spring
39 the control treadle
40 the steam extractor

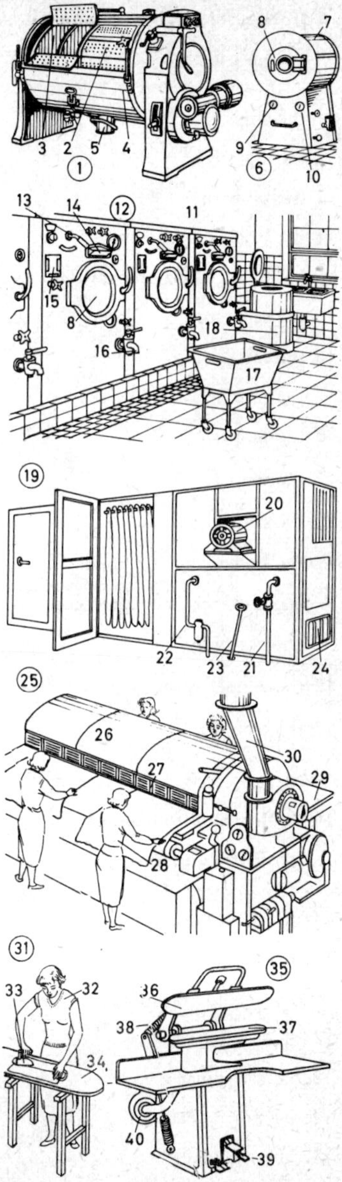

1-10 the production of chemical wood pulp:

1 the chips
2 the digester
3 the blow pit
4 the stock suspensions
5 and 6 the stock preparation:
5 the separator
6 the thickener;
7 the potcher
8 the pulper
9 the refiner
10 the conical refiner;
11 the kollergang for fiberising waste paper, sulphate pulp, and knotter pulp:
12 the runner stones
13 the trough;

14-20 the production of groundwood pulp,

14 the pocket grinder:
15 the pressure foot
16 the pressure chamber
17 the grinder shaft;
18 the caterpillar grinder:
19 the worm gear
20 the feed chain;
21 the rag boiler (rotary digester) for preparation of rag halfstuff:
22 the drive
23 the steam inlet;

24-27 the paperstock preparation,

24 the hollander (beater):
25 the raw materials, halfstuff and additives;
26 the beater roll
27 the hollander [section]
28 the bed plate

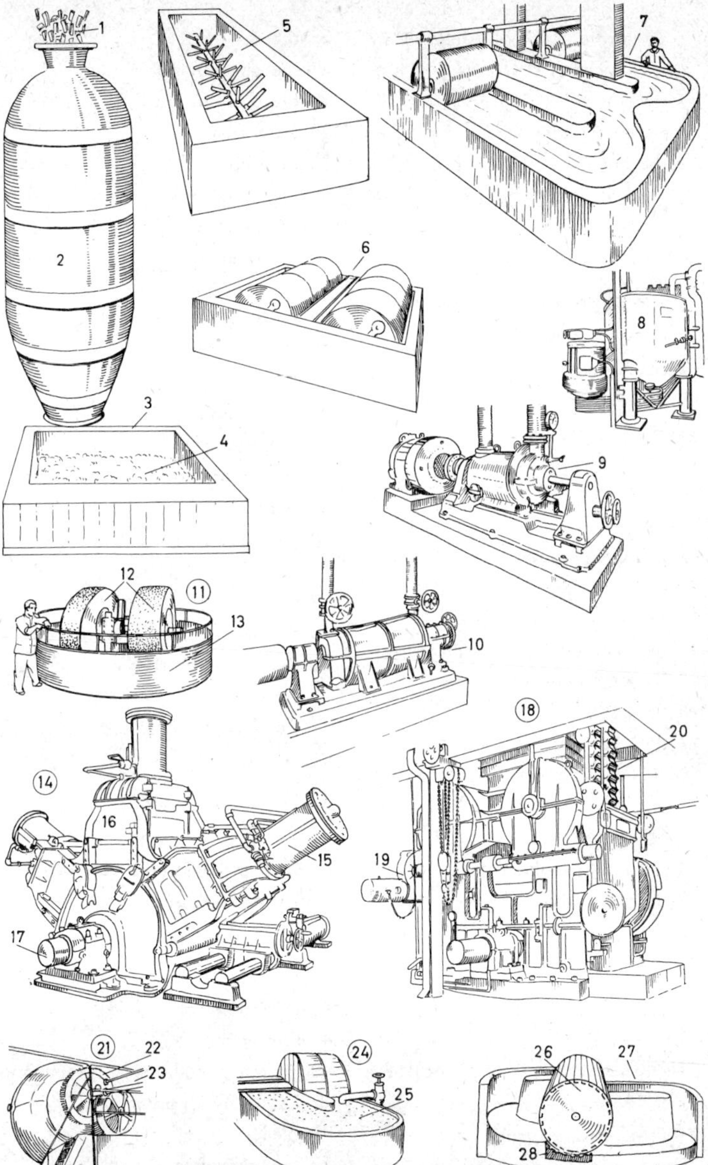
1
2
3
4
5
6
7
8
9
10
11
12
13
14
15
16
17
18
19
20
21
22
23
24
25
26
27
28

1 the stuff chest, a blending chest for stock
2 the laboratory dish:
3 the prepared stock;
4 the centrifugal cleaners ahead of stock inlet of a big paper-machine:
5 the vertical pipe;

6 the paper machine [diagram]:
7 the stock inlet
8 the riffler
9 the knotter
10–17 the wet end,
10–13 the fourdrinier section:
10 the breast roll
11 the table roll
12 the wire guide roll
13 the fourdrinier wire;
14–17 the press section:
14 the suction couch with suction box
15 the felt guide-roll
16 the wet felt
17 the wet press;
18–20 the dryer section with dryer felt, felt dryer and cooling cylinder:
18 the drying cylinder
19 the paper web
20 the guide roll for paper;
21 and **22** the finishing equipment:
21 the calender
22 the winder (reel);

23-43 the converting of paper,
23 the finishing calender, a calender:
24 the chilled iron roll
25 the paper (compressed fibre) roll
26 the web
27 the switchboard;
28 the reel cutter:
29 the cutter
30 the web;
31 the air-knife for producing art-printing- and chromo-papers, coloured (*Am.* colored) papers, chromo-board:
32 the base paper (board)
33 the pivoted unwind
34 the air-knife coater
35 the air-knife coating and smoothing equipment
36 the air supply
37 the coated paper (board)
38 the hot-air drying channel divided into sections
39 the chain conveyor
40 the hot-air blower chamber
41 the automatic web guide using photocells
42 the draw or tension control (stretching section)
43 the double rewind;

44-50 the production of hand-made paper:
44 the vatman
45 the vat
46 the mould (*Am.* mold)
47 the couchman
48 the pile of 180 sheets of paper and felt, ready for pressing:
49 the felt
50 the sheet of handmade paper

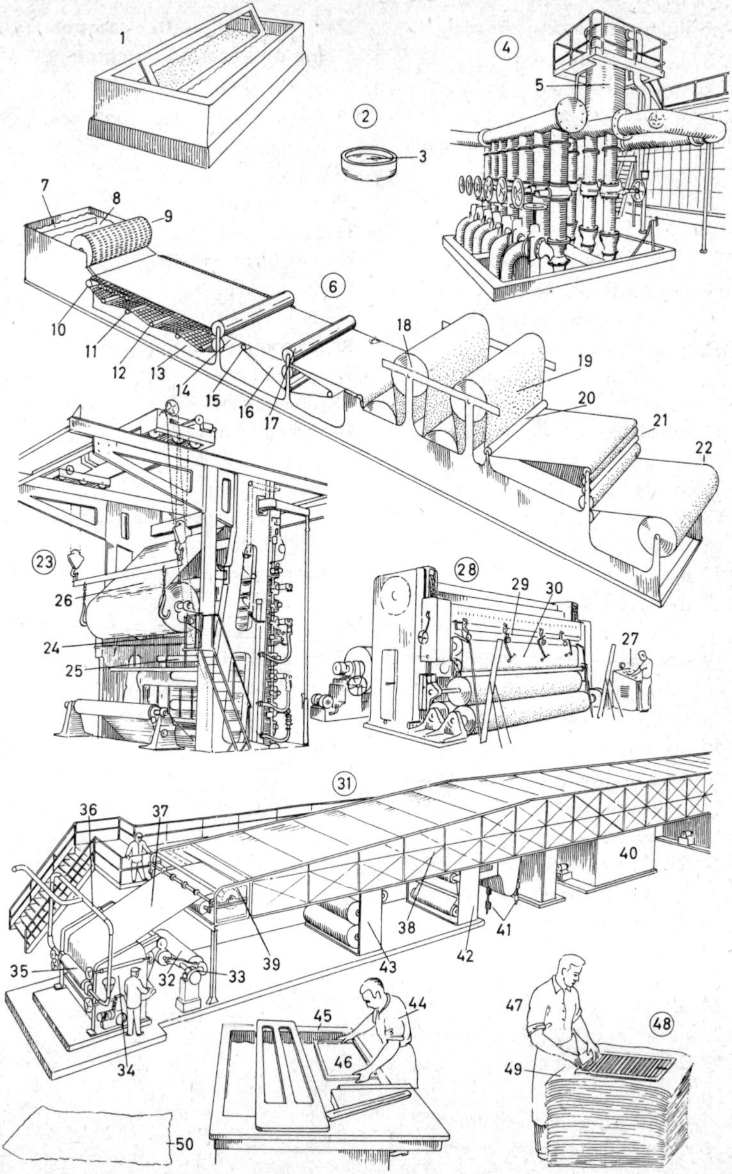
1
2
3
4
5
6
7
8
9
10
11
12
13
14
15
16
17
18
19
20
21
22
23
24
25
26
27
28
29
30
31
32
33
34
35
36
37
38
39
40
41
42
43
44
45
46
47
48
49
50

169 The Composing Department (Case Room) I

1 the hand-setting room:
2 the case stand
3 the frame (composing frame)
4 the case cabinet
5 the hand compositor (type-setter)
6 the manuscript
7 the letters (stamps)
8 the rack for furniture (leads, clumps, filling material)
9 the standing-matter rack
10 the sliding shelf for the formes
11 the standing matter
12 the make-up galley (galley, slip galley)
13 the composing stick (setting stick)
14 the setting rule (composing rule)
15 the type (lines of type)
16 the page cord
17 the bodkin
18 the tweezers;

19 the line-setting composing machine (linotype), a multi-magazine machine:
20 the distributor (dissing mechanism)
21 the type magazine with matrices (matrixes)
22 the elevator for transporting the matrices to the distributor
23 the assembler (assembler box)
24 the spaceband
25 the casting mechanism
26 the type-metal feed
27 the galley of slugs (cast lines)
28 the matrices for hand insertion;
29 the linotype matrices:
30 the teeth for the distributor
31 the type die (matrix);

32-45 the single-letter composing and casting machine (monotype),
32 the monotype standard composing machine (monotype keyboard):
33 the paper tower
34 the paper ribbon
35 the ribbon cylinder
36 the unit register
37 the keyboard
38 the compressed-air supply tube;
39 the monotype caster:
40 the automatic type-metal feed
41 the pump pressure spring
42 the matrix case
43 the paper tower
44 the galley with cast letters (cast single letters)
45 the electric heating indicator and control;
46 the matrix case:
47 the letter matrices
48 the slot for insertion into the compound slide frame

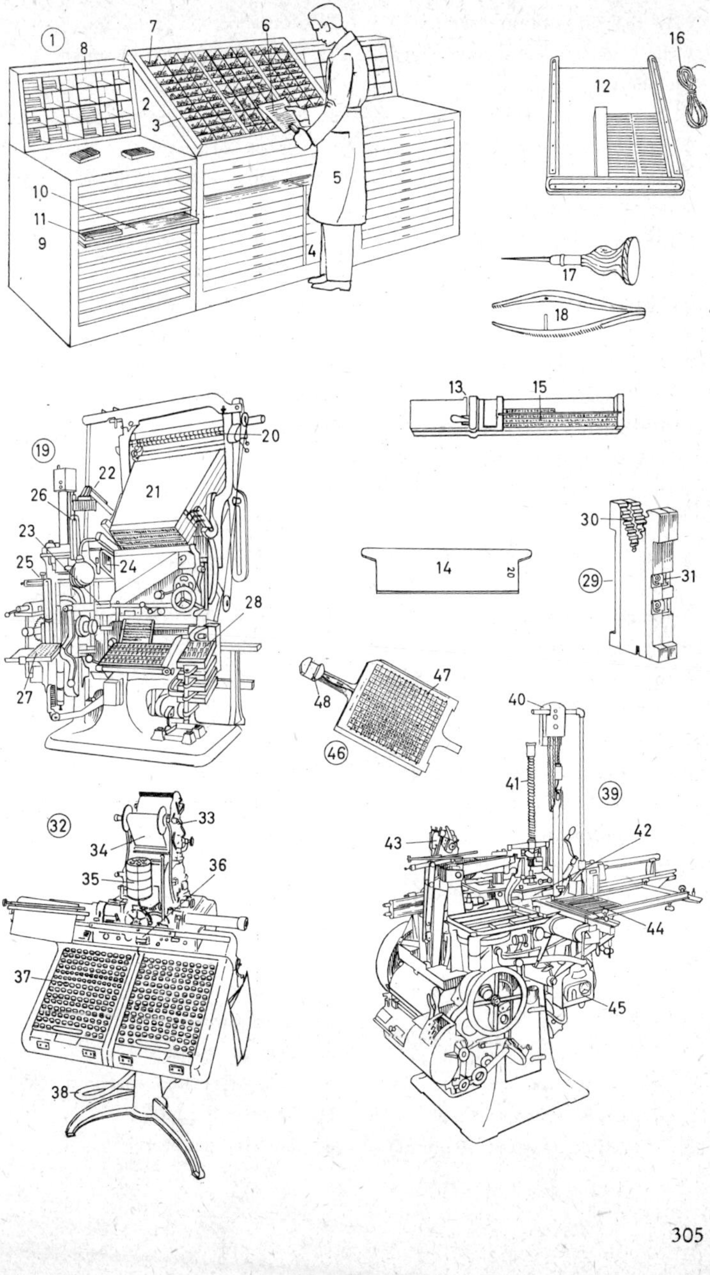
1
2
3
4
5
6
7
8
9
10
11
12
13
14
15
16
17
18
19
20
21
22
23
24
25
26
27
28
29
30
31
32
33
34
35
36
37
38
39
40
41
42
43
44
45
46
47
48

1–17 the composition (type):
1 the initial letter (capital letter, cap, cipher)
2 the heavy-faced letters (bold)
3 the semi-bold letters
4 the line
5 the interlinear space
6 the ligature (double letter)
7 the italics (italic letters)
8 the light-faced letters
9 the heavy-faced letters
10 the bold condensed letters (bold condensed)
11 the roman capital letter (cap, majuscule, upper-case letter)
12 the roman small letter (minuscule, lower-case letter)
13 the letter-spaced letters (spaced-out letters)
14 the small capitals
15 the space between two paragraphs
16 the paragraph-indention (indentation)
17 the space between words;
18 sizes of types [one typographic point = .013837 inch = 0,376 mm]:
19 'non-plus-ultra' (2 points, 2 point)
20 brilliant (approx. 3½ points; *seldom used:* excelsior, approx. 3 points)
21 diamond (approx. 4½ points)
22 pearl (approx. 5 points; ruby, *Am.* agate, approx. 5 1/2 points)
23 nonpareil (approx. 6 points)
24 minion (approx. 7 points)
25 brevier (approx. 8 points)
26 bourgeois (approx. 9 points)
27 long primer (approx. 10 points)
28 pica (approx. 12 points)
29 English (approx. 14 points)
30 Columbian (approx. 16 points)
31 paragon (two line long primer, approx. 20 points);
32–37 type-founding (type-casting):
32 the punch-cutter
33 the graver (cutter, burin)
34 the magnifying lens
35 the punch blank;
36 the finished punch
37 the stamped matrix (strike);
38 the type (piece of type, letter):
39 the head
40 the shoulder
41 the counter
42 the face
43 the bevel
44 the height-to-paper [*Engl. & Am.* 0.918 inch]
45 the shoulder height
46 the body (size of type)
47 the nick
48 the thickness;
49 the matrix-cutter, a special drilling machine:
50 the column
51 the cutter
52 the cutting table
53 the pantograph-carrier
54 the prismatic guides
55 the pattern
56 the pattern table
57 the follower
58 the pantograph
59 the matrix clamp (matrix chuck)
60 the cutting spindle
61 the driving motor

1 3 9 2

Alfred **John Dodsley,** essayist and journalist, —4
was born in Wenlock on the 5th August 1841 and
died on the 4th October 1920 in Birmingham.
His father was a journeyman thatcher and as a —5
boy Dodsley was sent to work in the fields as
a bird-scarer. Having taught himself to read
and write fluently – for many years the only —8 —6
books he possessed were a Bible and a volume
of Tillotson's sermons – he went to Shrewsbury
to study. Living in extreme poverty he began to
write for the EAST HEREFORDSHIRE GAZETTE and —14
a collection of his essays together with some poems
on country life was published in 1868 under the title
"Rural Thoughts". Among his most popular works
were *"The Diary of a Derbyshire Shepherd"* (1872), —7
"Rural Verses" (1879), *"Leaves from a Country-
man's Notebook"* (1893) and *"Memoirs of Nine-
teenth Century Shropshire"*, published posthum-
ously. Dodsley also contributed many articles on
country life to London papers and championed —13
the cause of the agricultural worker
during the depression of the 1880's. The latter —11
years of his life were embittered by controversy —12
raised by his protests against the unemployment
caused by mechanised farming. —15
16— He was for many years president of the
**Society for the Protection of the Liberties of the
Farm-worker.**
10 17

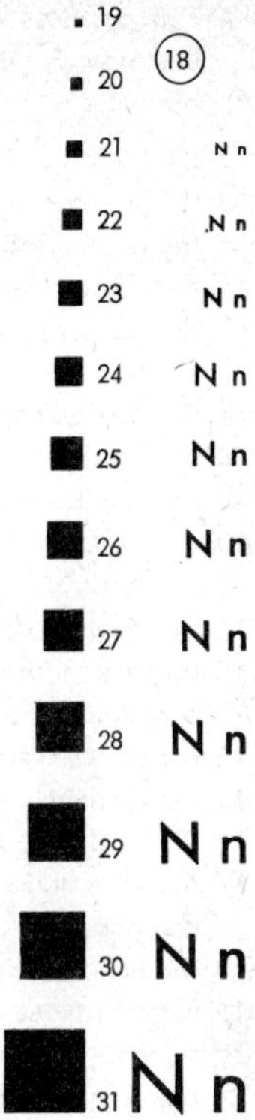

18
19
20
21 Nn
22 Nn
23 Nn
24 Nn
25 Nn
26 Nn
27 Nn
28 Nn
29 Nn
30 Nn
31 Nn

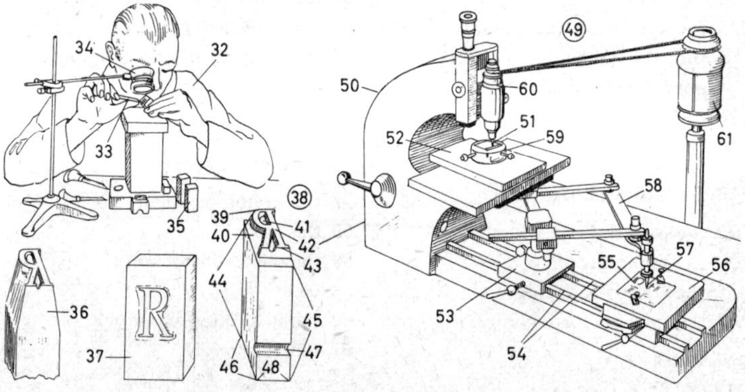

32
33
34
35
36
37
38
39
40
41
42
43
44
45
46
47
48
49
50
51
52
53
54
55
56
57
58
59
60
61

1 the process camera (copying camera, reproducing camera):

2 the focusing screen
3 the screen counterweight
4 the camera frame
5 the shutter-type dark slide
6 the transverse movement knob
7 the vertical movement knob
8 the baseboard swivel catch
9 the lens front adjustment
10 the camera frame adjustment
11 the carriage drive
12 the camera precision drive
13 the camera baseboard
14 the camera carriage
15 the carriage catch
16 the steel support
17 the vibration absorber or damper
18 the bellows
19 the lens front
20 the copy-holder frame
21 the copy-board
22 the copy-holder
23 the pivoted lamp-arms
24 the photographic arc lamp;
25 the collapsible (collapsable) thread-counter (linen-tester), a magnifying glass:
26 the measuring field or area
27 the lens;

28 the retouching desk:

29 the pattern-holder
30 the luminous plate
31 the control switches
32 the ratchets for inclining the top;

33 the super-automatic vertical process camera:

34 the focusing screen
35 the circular screen, a cross-line (reticulated) screen for breaking up the tone values of the picture
36 the bellows
37 the twin arc lamps
38 the control panel
39 the copy-holder;

40 the high-speed contact printing (contact copying) **frame:**

41 the rubber sheet
42 the control panel
43 the control clock
44 the vacuum gauge
45 the closing lever
46 the rheostat for control of light
47 the lamp for diffuse light
48 the red lamp
49 the spot light
50 the printing (copying) glass plate;

51 the spray gun (air brush), a retouching tool:

52 the jet switch
53 the nozzle
54 the hose for compressed air or carbon dioxide;
55 the scraper, an eraser (erasing knife)

56 the drying cabinet for drying films and plates:

57 the drying chamber
58 the rack
59 the thermometer and the hygrometer
60 the inspection window
61 the ventilator

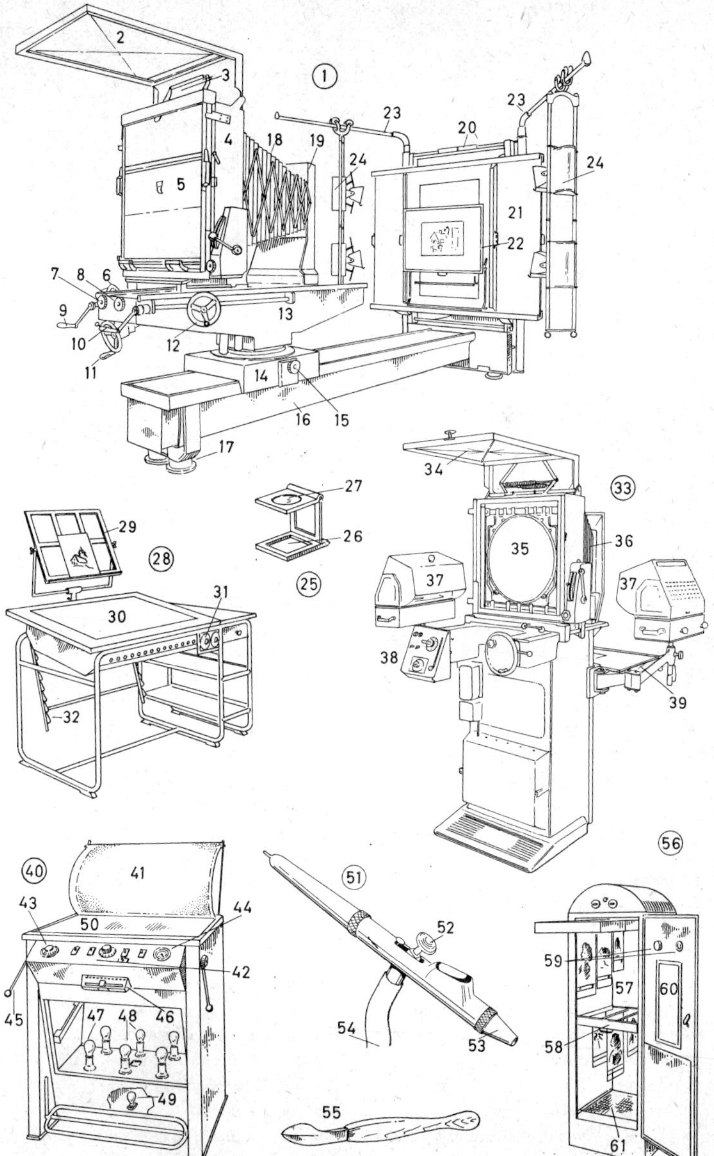
1
2
3
4
5
6
7
8
9
10
11
12
13
14
15
16
17
18
19
20
21
22
23
23
24
24
25
26
27
28
29
30
31
32
33
34
35
36
37
37
38
39
40
41
42
43
44
45
46
47
48
49
50
51
52
53
54
55
56
57
58
59
60
61

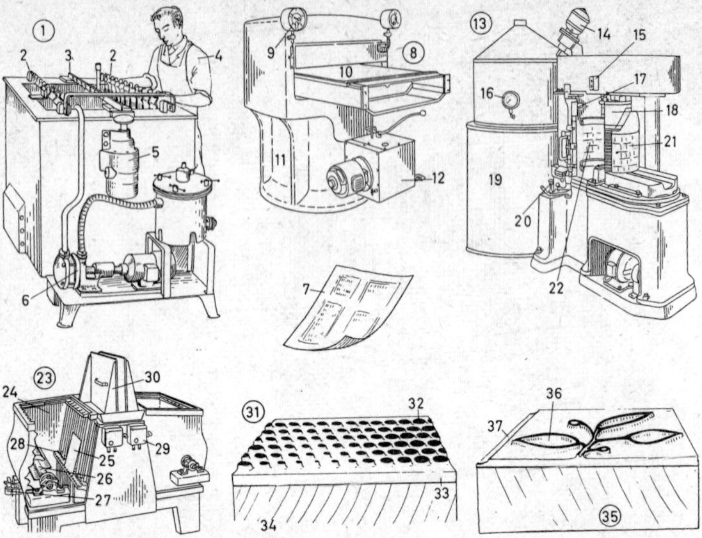

1 the electrolytic bath:
2 the anode rods (copper anodes)
3 the plate rod (cathode)
4 the stereotyper and electrotyper
5 the agitator motor
6 the set of filters;
7 the matrix or flong (*Am.* mat)
8 the hydraulic moulding press (*Am.* molding press):
9 the manometer or pressure gauge
10 the table
11 the base
12 the hydraulic press pump;
13 the curved-plate casting machine:
14 the motor
15 the control knobs
16 the pyrometer (*Am.* thermo gage)
17 the casting aperture
18 the casting chamber
19 the smelting furnace
20 the starting lever
21 the cast curved plate for rotary-press printing (for rotary printing)
22 the stationary casting mould (*Am.* mold);
23–30 block-making (photomechanical engraving, process engraving),
23 the machine for etching blocks (galvanos, cuts; block-etching machine), a twin model:
24 the etching bath [section]
25 the photo-printed zinc (or copper) plate
26 the paddle wheel
27 the outlet cock (*Am.* faucet)
28 the plate rack
29 the switch box
30 the bath lid;
31 the half-tone block, a block (printing block):
32 the screen dot, a printing element
33 the etched zinc (or copper) plate
34 the block mounting;
35 the line block:
36 the non-printing, deep-etched parts
37 the bevelled edge

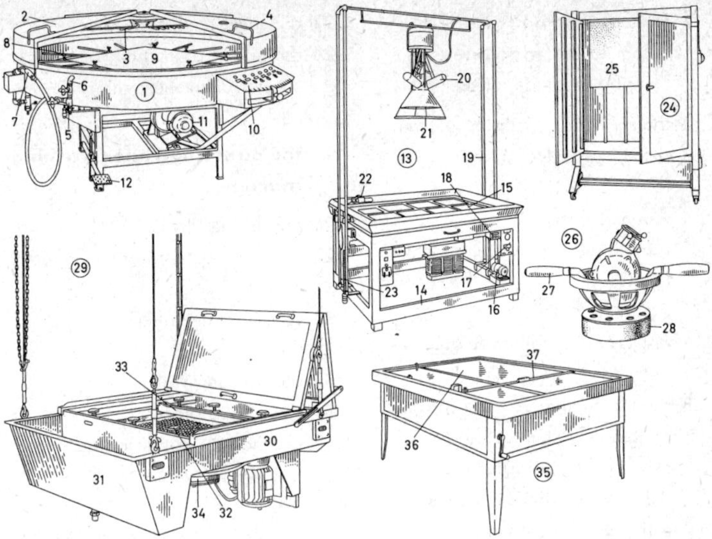

1 the plate-whirler (whirling apparatus) for coating the offset plates:
2 the sliding lid
3 the electric heating element
4 the thermometer
5 the water connection
6 the rinsing pipe
7 the hand shower
8 the rods to hold the plate
9 the zinc plate, a printing plate
10 the central control panel
11 the electric motor
12 the foot brake;
13 the pneumatic printing-down frame (vacuum frame):
14 the base of the printing-down frame
15 the glass pane
16 the vacuum pump
17 the control panel
18 the switch for lifting the glass pane
19 the frame
20 the spot-light printing arc lamp, a carbon-stick lamp
21 the ash-catcher
22 the exposure regulator
23 the spindle for lifting the glass pane
24 the drying cabinet or cupboard for offset plates:
25 the printed zinc plate;
26 the electrically driven portable apparatus for graining zinc plates:
27 the guiding handles
28 the graining disk or disc;
29 the printing-plate graining machine:
30 the graining table
31 the marble-catcher
32 the graining marbles
33 the plate clamps
34 the centrifugal drive;
35 the ruling up or checking table for checking or positioning printed matter on plate, film or paper:
36 the glass top
37 the adjustable rulers

1 the single-colour (*Am.* one-color) **offset machine** (offset printing machine, offset press):

2 the sheet pile (printing paper)
3 the sheet-feeder, an automatic feeder
4 the feed board
5 the inking rollers (ink rollers, inkers)
6 the ink fountain
7 the damping rollers (damping unit)
8 the plate cylinder (printing-plate cylinder), a steel cylinder carrying the printing-plate
9 the rubber cylinder, a steel cylinder with rubber printing blanket
10 the delivery pile board for the printed sheets
11 the gripper carriage, a chain gripper
12 the pile of sheets [printed]
13 the guard for the belt drive;
14 the diagram of the single-colour (*Am.* one-color) offset machine:
15 the ink fountain with the ink rollers
16 the damping unit with the damping rollers
17 the plate cylinder
18 the rubber-blanket cylinder
19 the impression cylinder
20 the delivery cylinder with the gripper mechanism
21 the driving wheel
22 the sheet feed board
23 the sheet feed mechanism
24 the pile of unprinted (or blank) sheets (blanksheet pile);

25 the damping-roller washing machine:

26 the drying device
27 the water-extracting roller (drier roller)
28 the damping roller
29 the water bath
30 the washing roller
31 the roller-holder;
32 the rack for conditioning the paper;

33 the 'rotaprint' sheet-fed machine (small offset sheet-fed press):

34 the ink fountain (ink unit)
35 the suction feed
36 the pile feed
37 the switchboard (control board) with counter, pressure gauge, air regulator, and sheet-feed control;

38 the flat-bed offset machine (flat-bed offset proofing press):

39 the ink fountain (ink unit)
40 the ink rollers
41 the forme bed
42 the cylinder with rubber printing blanket
43 the start-stop levers
44 the pressure adjusting wheel

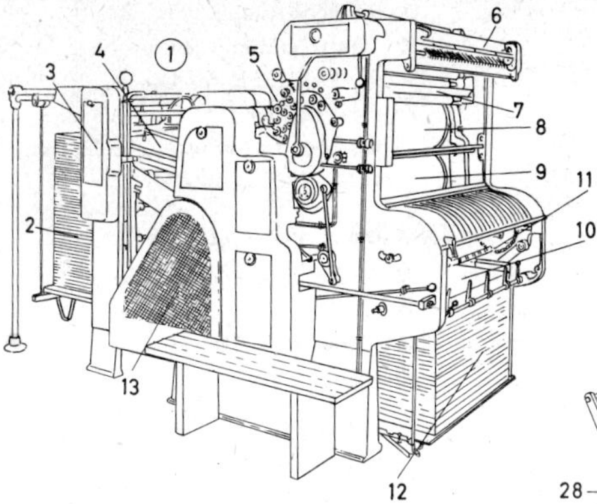
1
2
3
4
5
6
7
8
9
10
11
12
13

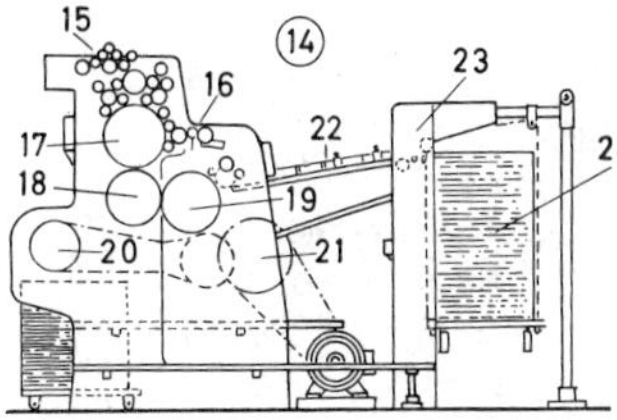
14
15
16
17
18
19
20
21
22
23
24

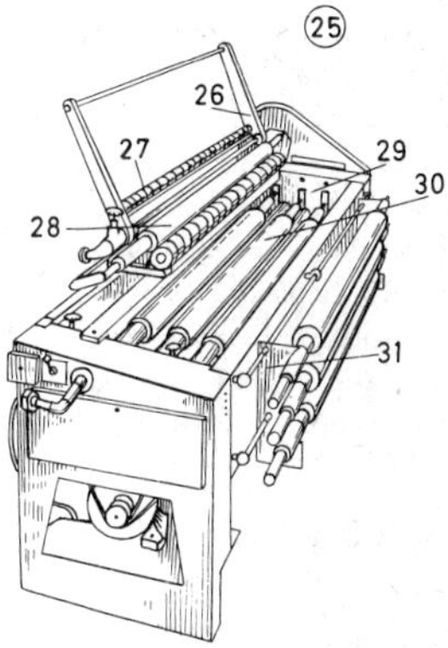
25
26
27
28
29
30
31

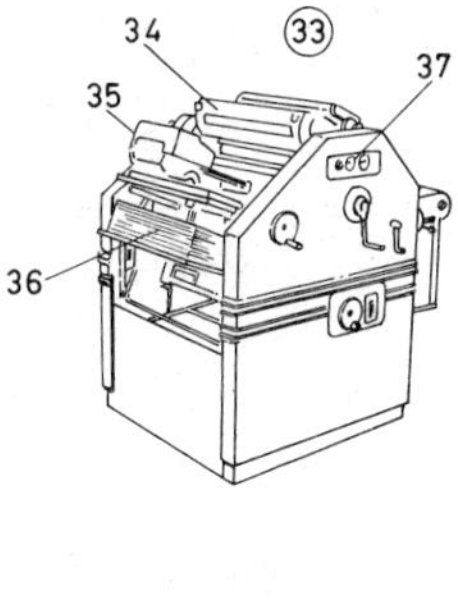
33
34
35
36
37

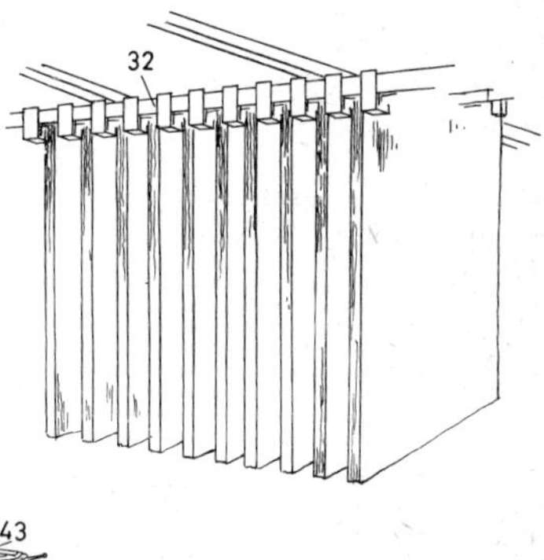
32

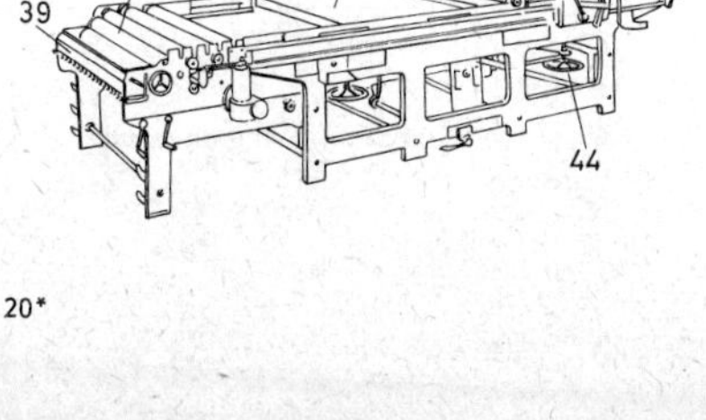
38
39
40
41
42
43
44

1–65 printing machines,

1 **the two-revolution high-speed press** or printing machine:

2 the impression cylinder
3 the cam for lifting or lowering the cylinder
4 the feed board
5 the automatic sheet-feeder, operated by suction and compressed air (by automatic sheet-feeding blowers and vacuum suckers)
6 the air pump for sucking or compressing air for feeding and delivery mechanism
7 the cylinder-inking apparatus with distributor and ink rollers
8 the ink table (ink slab)
9 the pile of printed paper
10 the anti-set-off spray
11 the interleaving paper feeder
12 the start and stop pedal;

13 **the platen machine** (platen) [section]:

14 the paper feed and delivery
15 the platen
16 the toggle-lever drive
17 the forme bed
18 the inking roller (ink roller, inker)
19 the inking unit for distributing the printing ink;

20 **the stop cylinder press:**

21 the feed board
22 the feeding apparatus
23 the pile of blank sheets
24 the paper guard
25 the pile of printed sheets
26 the control mechanism
27 the inking roller (ink roller, inker)
28 the inking unit;

29 **the platen machine** ['Heidelberg']:

30 the feed board with the pile of blank sheets
31 the delivery table
32 the start and stop device
33 the delivery blower
34 the spray gun
35 the air pump for suction, and blown, air;

36 **the locked-up forme:**

37 the type (matter)
38 the chase
39 the quoin (wedge)
40 the furniture;

41 **the letterpress rotary printing press** (rotary printing machine, rotary) for newspapers up to 16 pages:

42 the cutting rollers for cutting or slitting the web longitudinally
43 the web (roll of paper)
44 the impression cylinder
45 the tensioning roller
46 the paper reel
47 the automatic web brake
48 the first-impression printing control
49 the perfecting control
50 the inking unit (ink unit)
51 the plate cylinder
52 the cylinder for the second colour
53 the delivery to folder
54 the tachometer with sheet-counter
55 the folder (folding mechanism)
56 the folded newspaper;

57 **the ink fountain** (inking unit) for the rotary printing press [section]:

58 the web
59 the impression cylinder
60 the plate cylinder
61 the inking roller (ink roller, inker)
62 the distributor drum
63 the vibrator roller
64 the duct roller
65 the ink fountain (inking duct, ink duct)

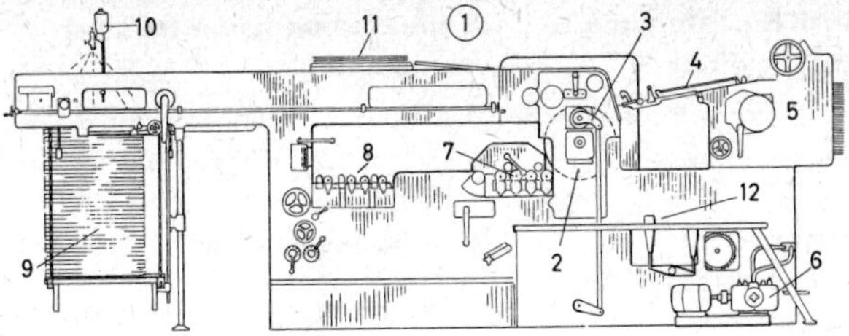
1
2
3
4
5
6
7
8
9
10
11
12

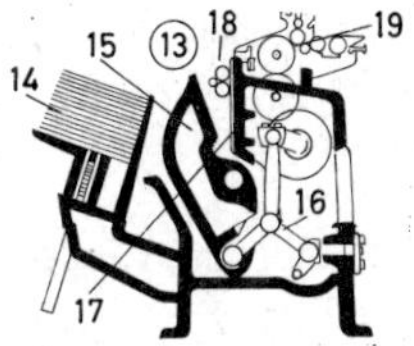
13
14
15
16
17
18
19

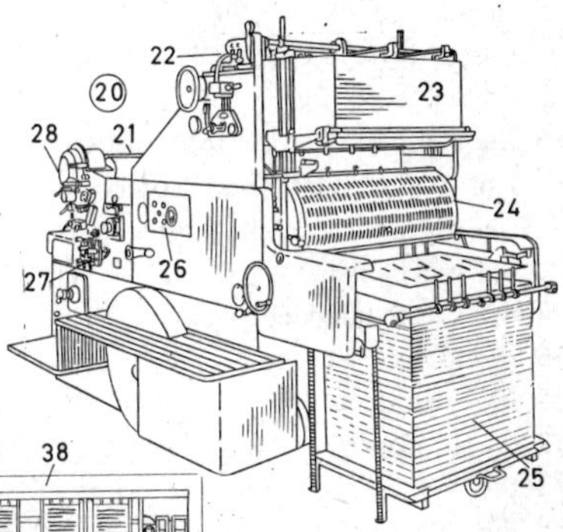
20
21
22
23
24
25
26
27
28

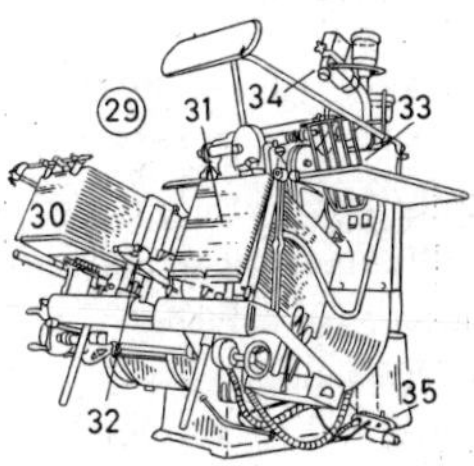
29
30
31
32
33
34
35

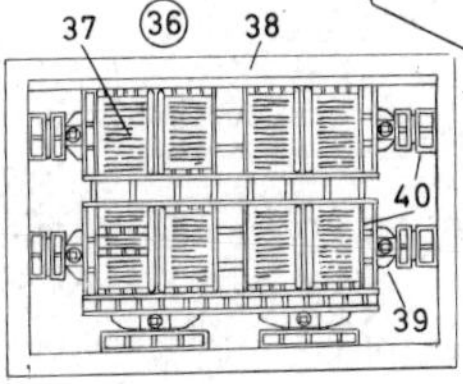
36
37
38
39
40

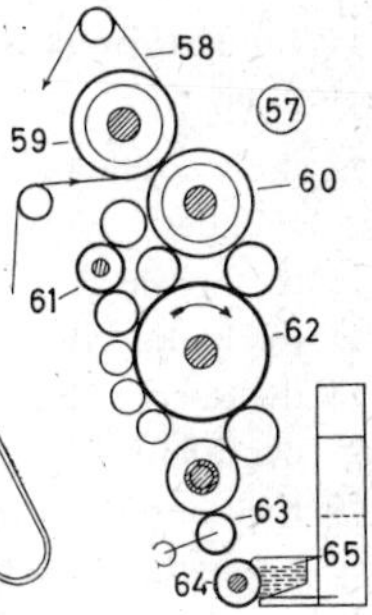
57
58
59
60
61
62
63
64
65

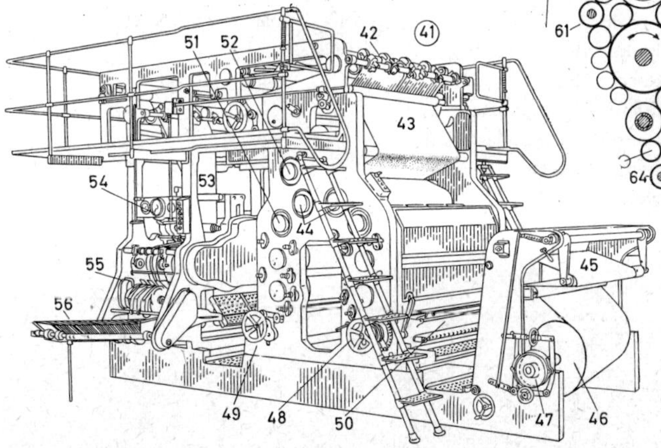
41
42
43
44
45
46
47
48
49
50
51
52
53
54
55
56

1 **the etching of the rotogravure** (photogravure) **cylinder:**
2 the copper cylinder with print (copied print) on it (rotogravure cylinder)
3 the photogravure-etcher
4 the acid solution; *here:* perchloride of iron
5 the control clock
6 the acid-proof etching bath
7 the water feed pipe;
8 the web feed for the folder of a rotogravure web press (rotary photogravure press), a turning-bar mechanism:
9 the cut or slit web
10 the turning bar
11 the cutting or slitting unit
12 the cutting or slitting rollers
13 the web coming from the printing unit [in full width];

14 **the rotogravure printing unit** [section]:
15 the rotogravure cylinder (plate cylinder)
16 the ink duct
17 the liquid gravure ink
18 the doctor blade
19 the doctor-blade adjuster
20 the impression cylinder (rubber-covered cylinder)
21 the web
22 the adjuster for the impression cylinder;

23 **the carbon tissue transfer machine:**
24 the polished copper cylinder
25 the rubber roller for pressing on the printed carbon tissue
26 the marking device;

27 **the printing unit of a multi-colour** (*Am.* multi-color) **rotogravure press:**
28 the push-button panel
29 the impression cylinder
30 the printed web
31 the blank web
32 the delivery and register roller
33 the plate cylinder
34 the doctor blade;

35 **the multi-colour** (*Am.* multi-color) **rotogravure press:**
36 the left-and-right printing unit
37 the folder (folding apparatus)
38 the outlet pipe for solvent vapours (*Am.* vapors)
39 the operating and controlling desk
40 the paper-reel holder

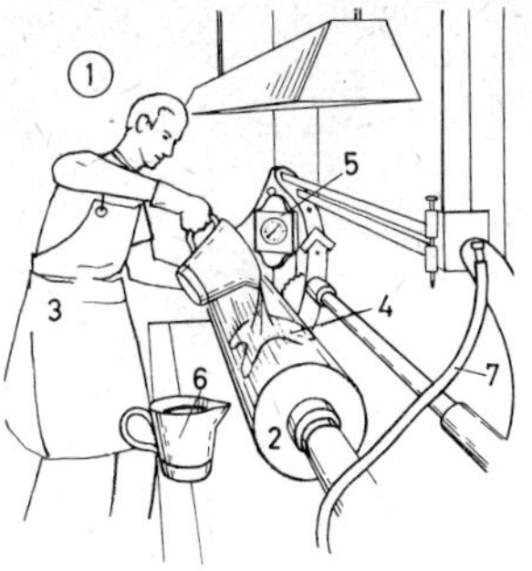
1
2
3
4
5
6
7

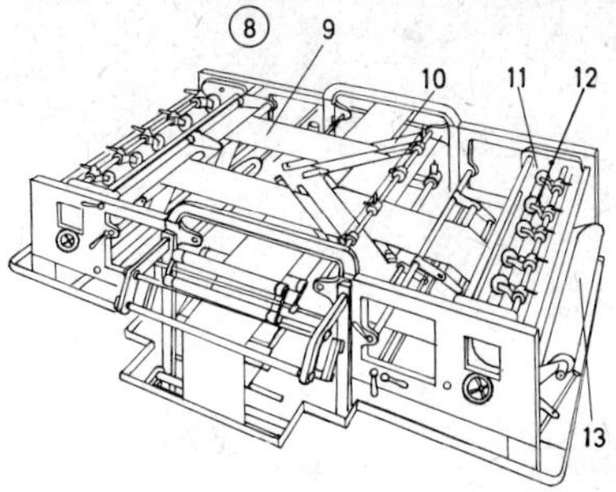
8
9
10
11
12
13

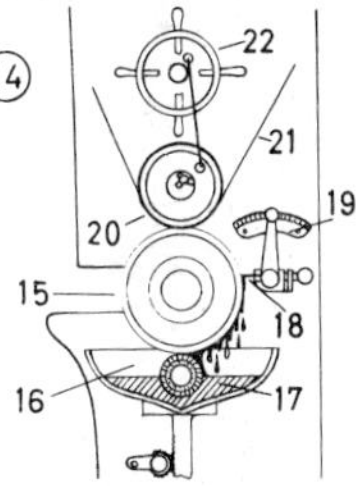
14
15
16
17
18
19
20
21
22

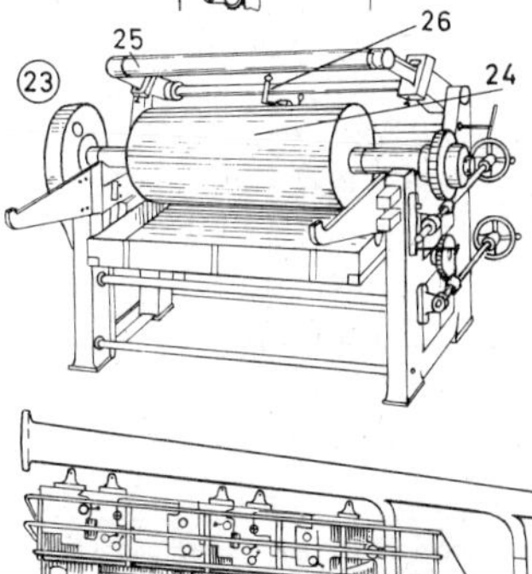
23
24
25
26

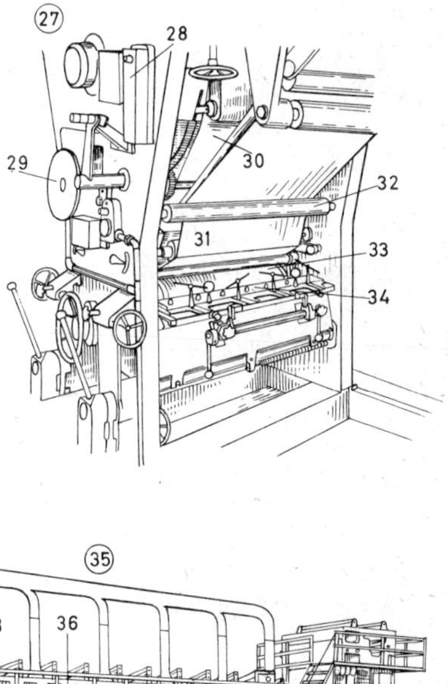
27
28
29
30
31
32
33
34

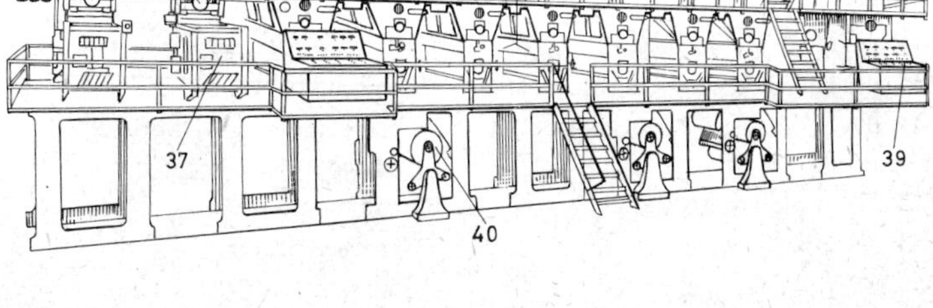
35
36
37
38
39
40

177 Bookbinding I

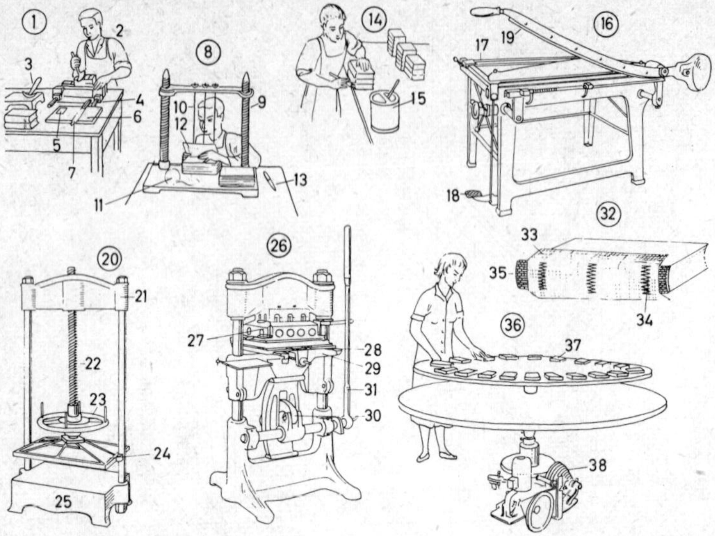

1-38 the hand bookbinding workshop (*Am.* bindery),
1 gilding (finishing) the back of the book:
2 the gilder, a bookbinder
3 the gilding tool; *here:* a palet
4 the gilding press (laying press)
5 the gold leaf (gold foil)
6 the gold-leaf cutting pad
7 the gold-leaf knife;
8 hand sewing:
9 the sewing frame
10 the sewing cord (sewing tape)
11 the ball of sewing thread
12 the book section ready for sewing
13 the bookbinder's knife;
14 book-back glueing:
15 the glue pot;
16 the chopper:
17 the back gauge (*Am.* gage)
18 the clamp with foot treadle
19 the knife beam;
20 the standing press:
21 the head beam
22 the screwed spindle
23 the pressure wheel
24 the top plate or upper platen
25 the base;
26 the gold blocking and embossing press, a hand-lever press:
27 the heated blocking or top platen
28 the sliding work-table
29 the embossing or bottom platen
30 the toggle action
31 the hand lever;

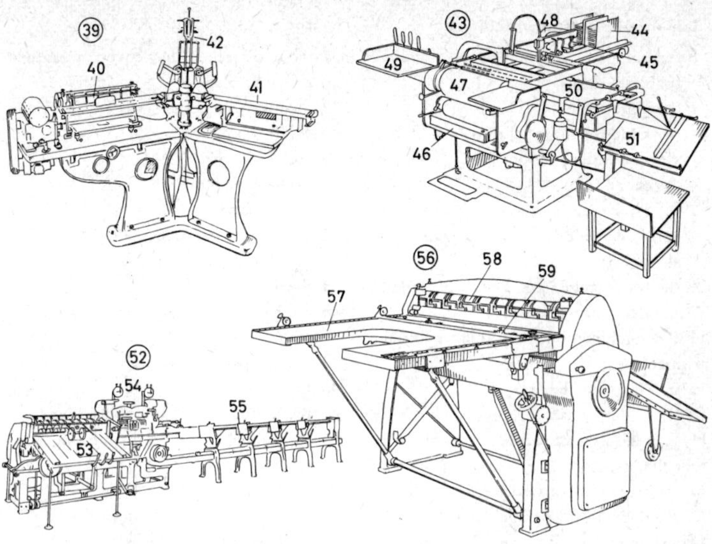

32 the book sewn on gauze or mull (sewn book):
33 the backing material (gauze or mull)
34 the sewing
35 the head band;
36 the gathering table, a rotating table:
37 the piles of signatures
38 the motor for rotating the table;

39-59 bookbinding machinery,

39 the unsewn binding machine:
40 the inserting and clamping section
41 the fanning and glueing section
42 the nipping and mull-applying section;
43 the case-making machine:
44 the board feed hopper
45 the board sucker plates
46 the glue tank
47 the cylinder for glueing the covering materials
48 the picker head (suction arm)
49 the feed table for covering materials [linen, paper, or leather]
50 the pressing mechanism
51 the delivery board;
52 the gang stitcher wire-stitching machine:
53 the delivery
54 the stitcher heads
55 the feeding stations;
56 the rotary board-cutting machine:
57 the feed table with cut-out section
58 the rotary cutters
59 the automatic cross feed bar

1-35 bookbinding machines,

1 the guillotine, a papercutting machine (paper-cutter):
2 the knife beam
3 the knife for diagonal dip-shear and vertical cutting actions
4 the clamp beam
5 the photo cell, a safety device [in England mechanically operated guards are also used]
6 the back gauge (feed gauge, *Am.* gage)
7 the clamp pressure scale;
8 the combined buckle and knife folding machine:
9 the sheet feed table
10 the folding plates
11 the register scale for the first-fold gauge (*Am.* gage)
12 the cross-fold knives
13 the delivery for parallel folded work
14 the third cross fold unit
15 the delivery box for cross-folded work;
16 the thread book-sewing machine:
17 the thread cop holder
18 the thread cop
19 the gauze-holder or mull-holder
20 the backing gauze or mull
21 the sewing needle holders
22 the sewn book
23 the book tray
24 the sewing saddle;
25 the casing-in machine:
26 the book cover or book case
27 the glue rollers
28 the uncased book
29 the book blade
30 the cased books;
31 the glueing machine for whole-surface, stencil, edge, and strip, glueing:
32 the glue tank
33 the glue roller
34 the feed table
35 the delivery;

36 the book;

37 the book jacket (dust cover), a wrapper
38 the jacket flap
39 the blurb (advertising text)
40–42 the binding:
40 the book cover (case)
41 the back (spine) of the book
42 the tailband;
43–47 the title pages or prelims (*Am.* front matter):
43 the half-title page
44 the half-title (short, bastard, or abbreviated, title)
45 the title page (inner title)
46 the title
47 the subtitle (subhead, subheading);
48 the publisher's imprint (publisher's colophon)
49 the end paper
50 the handwritten dedication
51 the book plate (ex libris);
52 the open book:
53 the printed page (page)
54 the fold
55–58 the margins:
55 the back (inner, or inside) margin
56 the head (upper) margin
57 the fore-edge (foredge, outside) margin
58 the foot (tail, lower) margin;
59 the type area
60 the chapter heading (title of the chapter)
61 the asterisk or footnote reference
62 the footnote, a note
63 the page number
64 the double-column type area
65 the column
66 the running title (title of the column)
67 the subtitle
68 the marginal (side) note
69 the signature mark
70 the bookmarker (ribbon)
71 the loose bookmarker

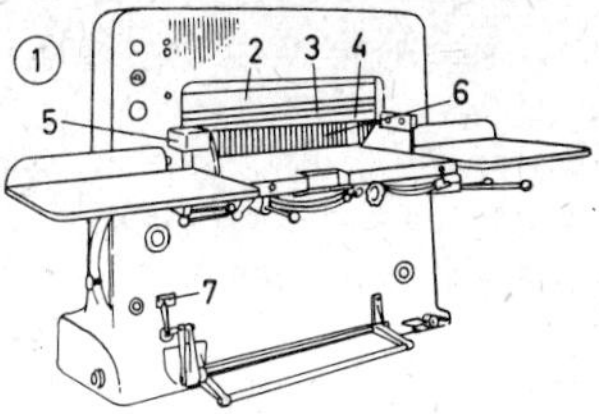
1
2
3
4
5
6
7

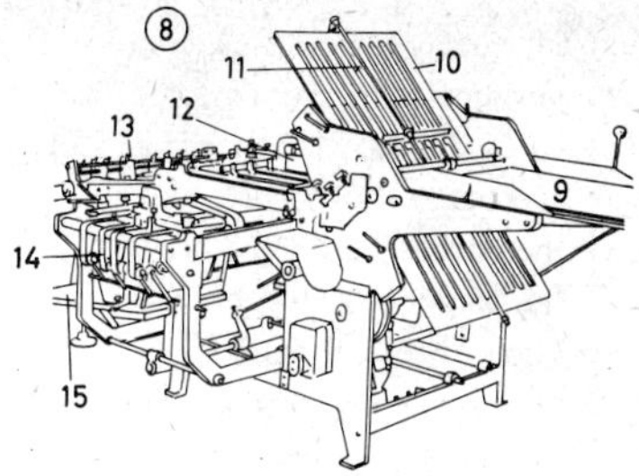
8
9
10
11
12
13
14
15

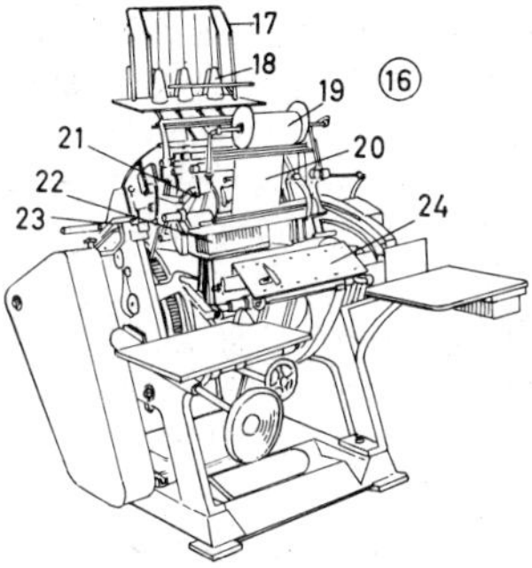
16
17
18
19
20
21
22
23
24

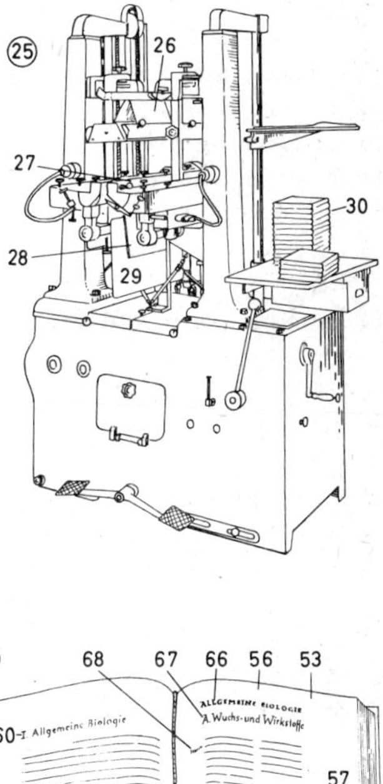
25
26
27
28
29
30

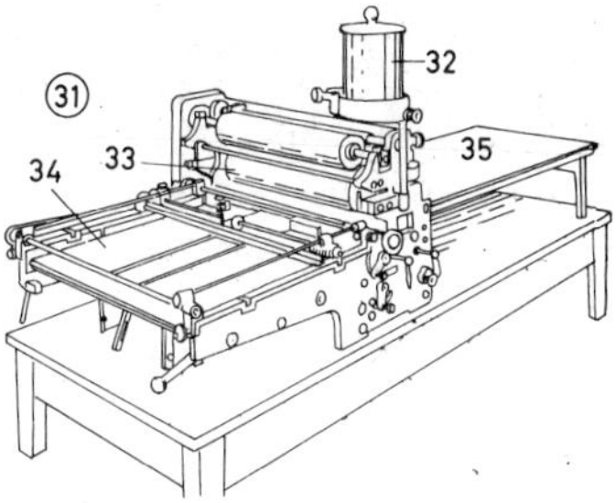
31
32
33
34
35

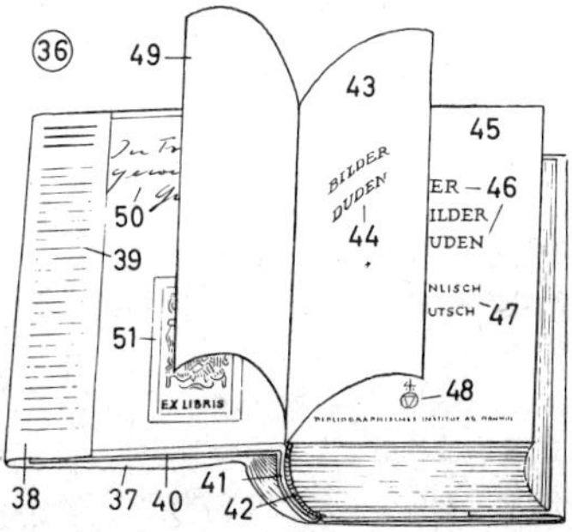
36
37
38
39
40
41
42
43
44
45
46
47
48
49
50
51
BILDER
DUDEN
ER
ILDER
UDEN
NLISCH
UTSCH
EX LIBRIS

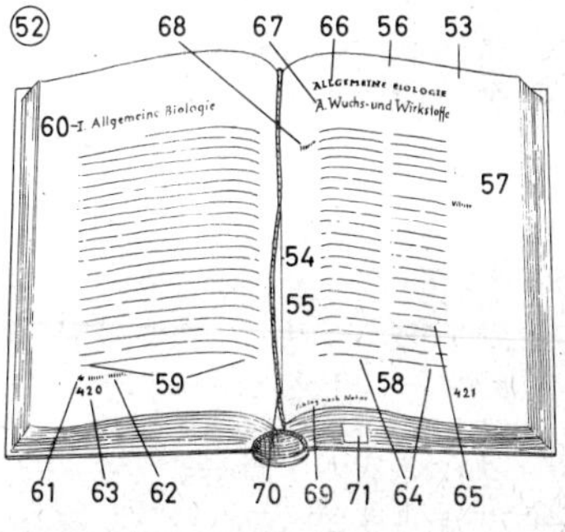
52
53
54
55
56
57
58
59
60
61
62
63
64
65
66
67
68
69
70
71
I. Allgemeine Biologie
ALLGEMEINE BIOLOGIE
A. Wuchs- und Wirkstoffe
420
421

179 Horse Carriages

1-54 carriages (vehicles, conveyances, horse-drawn vehicles),
1–3, 26–39, 45, 51–54 coaches and carriages:
1 the berlin (berline)
2 the wagonette (waggonette); *larger :* break (brake)
3 the coupé; *sim.* brougham (*Am.* town coupé):
4 the front wheel
5 the coach body
6 the splash board
7 the footboard
8 the box (coach box, driver's seat)
9 the lantern
10 the coach window
11 the door (coach door)
12 the door handle (handle)
13 the footboard (side-step, carriage step, step)
14 the fixed coach roof (fixed coach top)
15 the spring
16 the brake (brake block, brake shoe)
17 the back wheel (hind wheel);
18 the dogcart, a one-horse vehicle:
19 the shaft (thill, pole);
20 the lackey (footman, man servant, livery servant, servant):
21 the lackey's dress (livery)
22 the gallooned (braided) collar
23 the gallooned (braided) coat
24 the gallooned (braided) sleeve
25 the top hat (topper);
26 the cab (horse cab, clarence, fly, hackney carriage, hackney coach, growler, hired coach, hired carriage, four-wheeler fiacre, *Am.* hack, job carriage)
27 the stableman (groom)
28 the coach horse (carriage horse, cab horse, shaft horse)
29 the hansom (hansom cab), a cabriolet, a one-horse carriage:
30 the shafts (thills, poles);
31 the reins
32 the coachman (driver, cab-driver, cabman, *coll.* cabby) with Inverness (cloak with removable cape)
33 the covered char-à-banc (break, brake, *Am.* station car, sightseeing car), an excursion vehicle
34 the gig
35 the barouche (calash)
36 the landau, a two-horse carriage; *sim.* landaulet (landaulette)
37 the omnibus (horse omnibus, horse bus, stage coach)
38 the phaeton
39 the mailcoach (stage coach, diligence), *also :* coach for passengers:
40 the postil(l)ion (mailcoach driver, post boy, coachman)
41 the postil(l)ion's horn (post horn)
42 the hood
43 the post horses (relay horses);
44 the tilbury
45 the troika (Russian three-horse carriage):
46 the leader (wheel horse, pole horse, thill horse)
47 the near wheeler; *opp.* off wheeler;
48 the English buggy
49 the American buggy
50 the tandem
51 the victoria:
52 the collapsible hood;
53 the mailcoach (stage coach)
54 the covered (closed) chaise

1
2
3
4
5
6
7
8
9
10
11
12
13
14
15
16
17
18
19
20
21
22
23
24
25
26
27
28
29
30
31
32
33
34
35
36
37
38
39
40
41
42
43
44
45
46
47
48
49
50
51
52
53
54

180 The Bicycle I

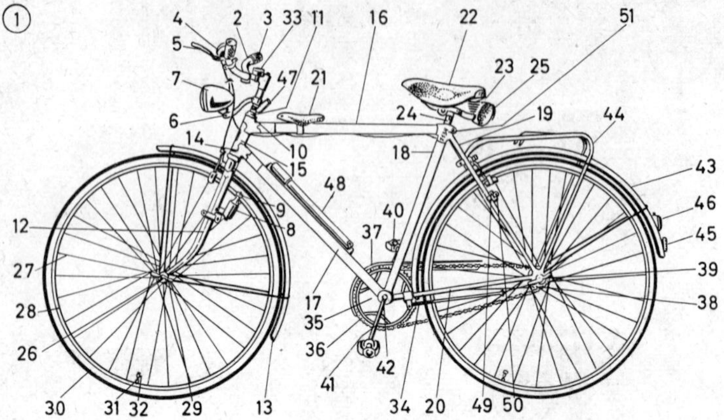

1 the bicycle (cycle, *coll.* bike, push-bike, *Am.* wheel), a gent's (man's) bicycle, a touring bicycle (roadster),
2 the handlebar (handlebars), a touring cycle handlebar:
3 the handlebar grip (grip);
4 the bicycle bell
5 the front brake
6 the lamp bracket
7 the bicycle lamp
8 the dynamo:
9 the rotor wheel;
10–12 the front forks:
10 the handlebar stem
11 the head lock ring
12 the fork blades;
13 the front mudguard (*Am.* front fender)
14–20 the bicycle frame:
14 the head tube
15 the head badge
16 the cross bar (top tube)
17 the down tube
18 the seat tube
19 the seat stays
20 the chain stays (bottom forks);
21 the child's seat (child carrier seat)
22 the bicycle saddle (spring seat saddle)
23 the saddle springs
24 the seat pillar
25 the tool bag
26–32 the wheel (front wheel):
26 the hub
27 the spoke
28 the rim
29 the wing nut (fly nut, butterfly nut)
30 the tyre (tire, pneumatic tyre or tire, high-pressure tyre or tire); *inside:* the inner tube , *outside:* the cover (outer cover):
31 the valve, an air valve with valve rubber tube, or a patent valve with ball
32 the valve cap;
33 the bicycle speedometer with cyclometer
34 the kick stand
35–42 the chain drive,
35–39 the chain transmission:
35 the chain wheel
36 the chain (roller chain, *Am.* bushed chain)
37 the chain guard
38 the rear hub sprocket (rear sprocket wheel)

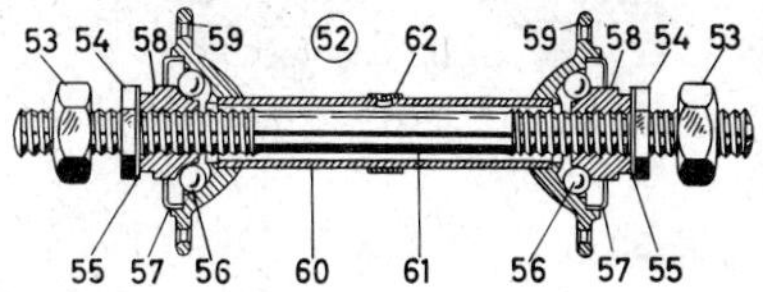

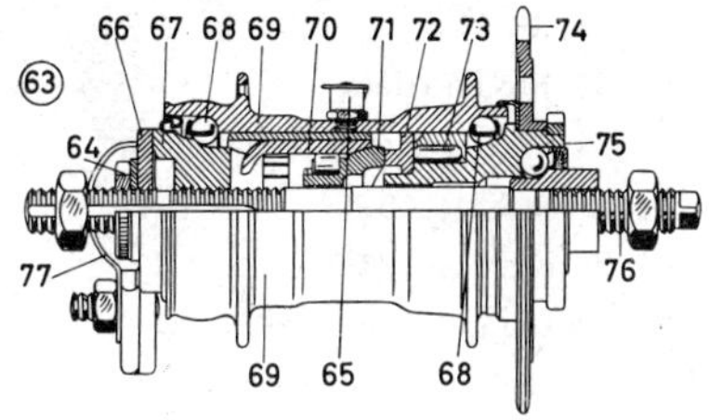

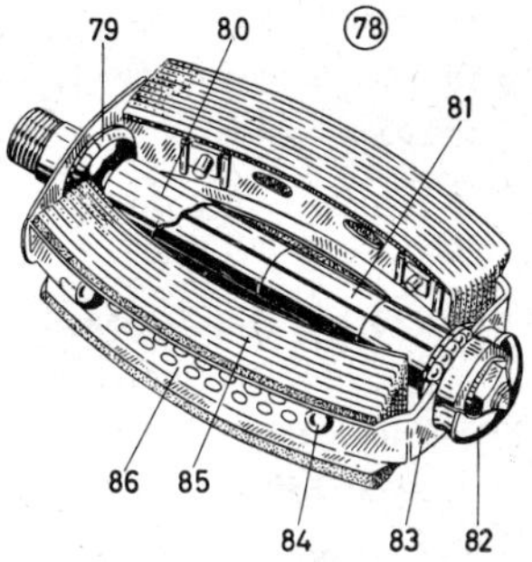

39 the chain-adjuster;
40 the pedal
41 the crank
42 the bottom bracket bearing axle;
43 the rear mudguard (*Am.* rear fender)
44 the carrier (luggage-carrier)
45 the rear reflector
46 the rear light
47 the rear (tail) light indicator lamp
48 the bicycle pump (inflator)
49 the bicycle lock
50 the patent key
51 the bicycle frame number (factory number)
52 the front-wheel hub:
53 the nut
54 the lock nut
55 the washer
56 the ball
57 the dust cap
58 the cone
59 the pedal ball-race
60 the pedal spindle
61 the axle
62 the oiler clip;
63 the free-wheel hub with back-pedal brake (with coaster brake):
64 the safety nut
65 the lubricator
66 the brake arm
67 the brake-arm cone
68 the ball housing with ball in the ball bearing
69 the hub shell (hub body, hub barrel)
70 the brake casing
71 the brake cone
72 the driver
73 the driving barrel
74 the sprocket (rim of the gear wheel)
75 the thread head
76 the axle
77 the bracket;
78 the bicycle pedal (reflector pedal, rubber pedal), block pedal:
79 the cup
80 the spindle
81 the pedal pin
82 the dust cap
83 the pedal frame
84 the rubber stud
85 the rubber block (rubber tread)
86 the glass reflectors

1 the repair kit:
2 the repair kit box
3 the rubber solution (rubber cement)
4 the oblong patch (patch)
5 the round patch
6 the gauze cover
7 the glass (sand) paper;

8 the lady's bicycle (lady's cycle), a sports bicycle (sports bike):
9 the double-tube frame
10 the semi-balloon tyre or tire, a low-pressure tyre or tire
11 the dress guard
12 the sports handlebar or handlebars;

13 the child's bicycle (child's cycle, *Am.* child's bike, kid's bike):
14 the balloon tyre or tire;

15 the carrier bicycle, a delivery bicycle, a special bicycle:
16 the front luggage-carrier
17 the small front wheel
18 the firm's name-plate;
19 the bicycle panniers
20 the bicycle trailer:
21 the ball coupling;

22 the invalid carriage (invalid tricycle, three-wheeled chair), a hand-propelled carriage:
23 the foot-rest
24 the propelling lever
25 the hand brake
26 the steering mechanism
27 the steering wheel;

28 the chain parts for moped,
29–31 the connecting link:
29 the spring clip fastener
30 and 31 the rivet and side plate unit:
30 the side-plate
31 the rivet;
32 the chain link (link);

33 the moped,
34–39 the autocycle handlebar fittings:
34 the twist grip
35 the gear twist grip
36 the clutch (clutch lever)
37 the hand brake
38 the light switch
39 the built-in speedometer (speedometer);
40 the autocycle headlight
41 the Bowden cables
42 the motif
43 the hub
44 the rear (tail) light indicator lamp
45 the fuel tank
46 the tank frame, an oval-tube frame
47 the sheet-steel casing
48 the cantilever saddle
49 the autocycle engine, a single-cylinder engine, a two-stroke (*Am.* two-cycle) engine with crankcase scavenging
50 the built-in kickstarter (starting pedal)
51 the chain guard (chain cover)
52 the driving chain
53 the chain-adjuster

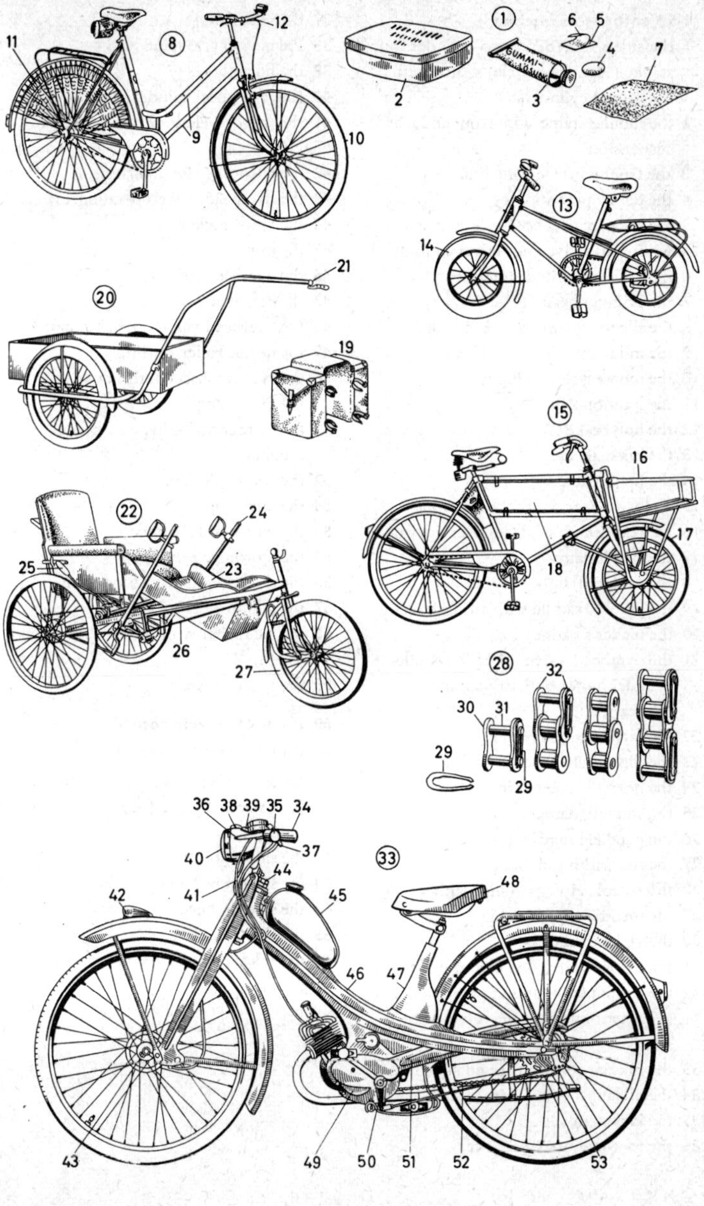
1
2
3
GUMMI-LÖSUNG
4
5
6
7
8
9
10
11
12
13
14
15
16
17
18
19
20
21
22
23
24
25
26
27
28
29
30
31
32
33
34
35
36
37
38
39
40
41
42
43
44
45
46
47
48
49
50
51
52
53

1-59 solos (solo machines),
1 the side-valve (S.V.) two-cylinder four-stroke (*Am.* four-cycle) motor with horizontal cylinders:
2 the tubular frame with front and rear suspension
3 the front-wheel leading link
4 the telescopic springing
5 the back (rear) wheel swinging arm with shaft drive and universal joint
6 the opposed-cylinder engine
7 the cylinder head
8 the silencer (exhaust box, muffler)
9 the induction pipe
10 the motorcycle headlight
11 the ignition key
12 the hub brake
13 the brake lever
14 the brake cable
15 the back (rear) wheel brake linkage
16 the rear brake pedal (*Am.* service brake)
17 the tyre inflator
18 the rear (tail) light
19 the pivoted saddle with saddle cover
20 the maker's badge;
21 the overhead-valve (O.H.V.) single-cylinder motor with dry-sump lubrication:
22 the carburettor air lever
23 the dipswitch
24 the horn (hooter) button
25 the steering damper
26 the parallel brake levers
27 the full width hub brake
28 the petrol (*Am.* gasoline) tank
29 the throttle control cable
30 the air control cable
31 the carburetter (*Am.* carburetor tickler)
32 the combined filter and petrol tap (*Am.* gasoline shut-off valve) with reserve
33 the tubular section pressed steel frame
34 the oil tank
35 the kickstarter
36 the foot-operated gear lever
37 the foot-rest
38 the motorcycle stand
39 the horn (hooter)
40 the rear wheel spindle (*Am.* axle)
41 the motorcycle tool box (*Am.* tool kit)
42 the silencer (*Am.* muffler);
43 the overhead valve operating crank:
44 the valve rocker
45 the cam
46 the overhead camshaft
47 the eccentric
48 the overhead valve operating crank
49 the needle roller bearing;
50 the vertical shaft overhead valve (O.H.V.) engine
51 the plate showing type or model number
52 the telescopic fork
53 the knee grip
54 the motorcycle battery
55 the motorcycle dual seat
56 the chain guard inspection plug
57 the pillion-rider's foot-rest
58 the handlebar windscreen (*Am.* windshield)
59 the sports model;

60 the motorcycle combination (motorcycle and sidecar):

61 the side-valve (S.V.) single-cylinder four-stroke motor (*Am.* four-cycle motor)
62 the sidecar body
63 the sidecar bumper
64 the sidecar wheel
65 the side light
66 the sidecar windscreen (*Am.* windshield)

(1)

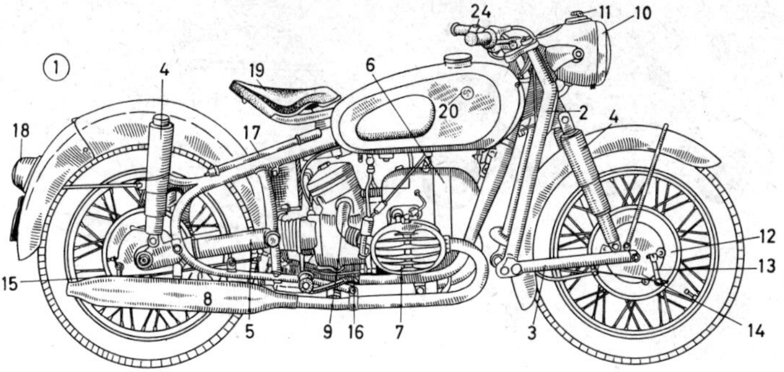
24
11
10
19
6
4
20
2
18
17
4
12
13
15
8
5
9
16
7
3
14

(21)

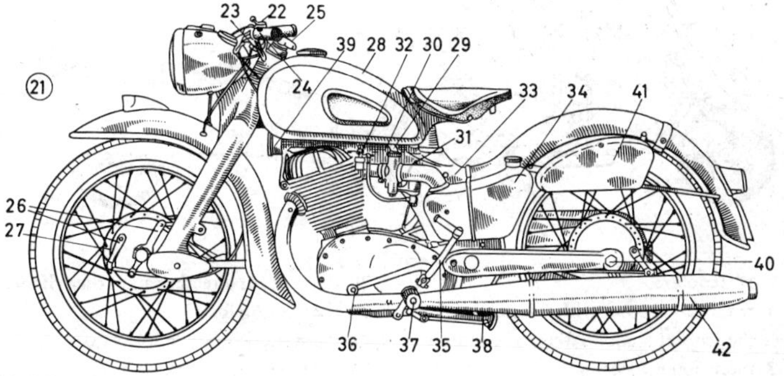
23
22
25
39
28
32
30
29
24
33
34
41
31
26
27
40
36
37
35
38
42

(43)

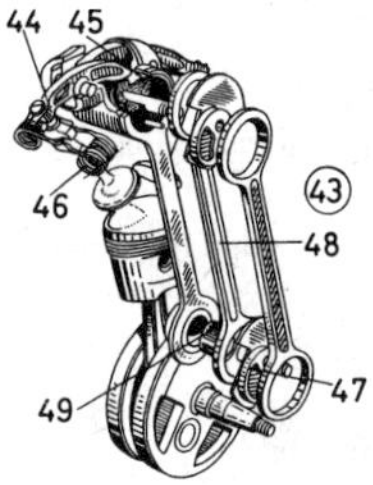
44
45
46
48
49
47

59

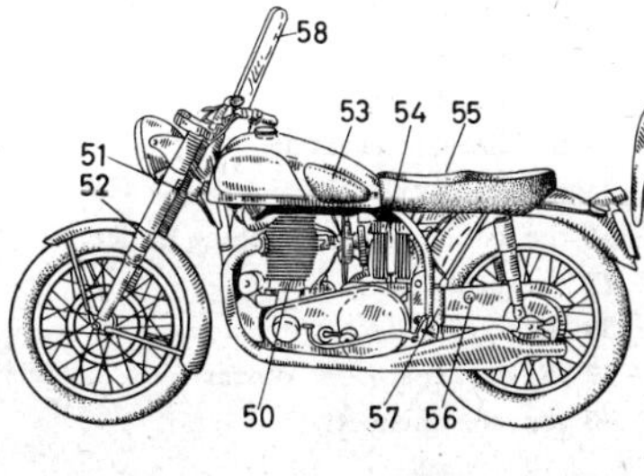
58
53
54
55
51
52
50
57
56

(60)

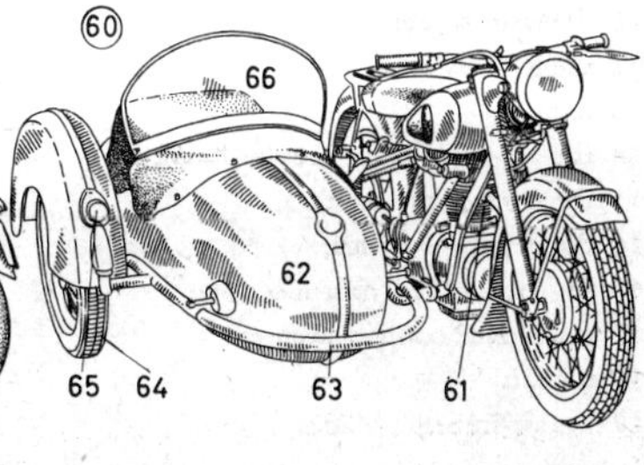
66
62
65
64
63
61

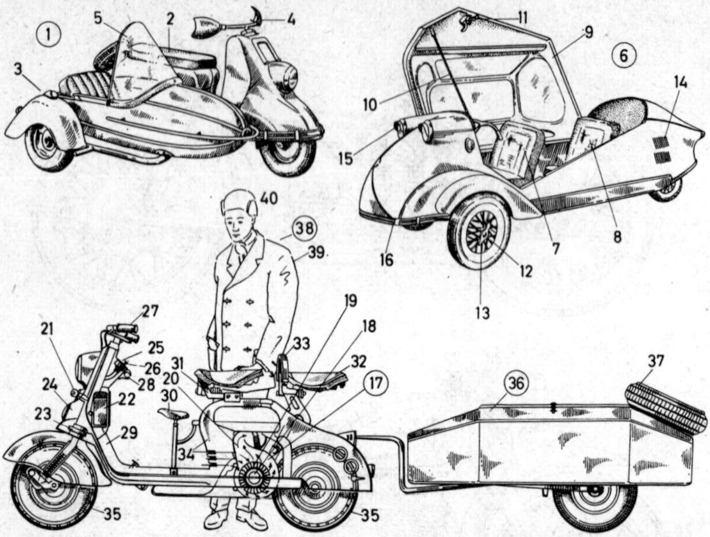

1-37 scooters,
1 the heavy scooter with sidecar:
2 the scooter combined seat and pillion
3 the scooter sidecar
4 the hand guard
5 the windscreen (*Am.* windshield);
6 the three-wheel cabin scooter (three-wheeler):
7 the front seat
8 the back (rear) seat
9 the hinged roof
10 the roof stay
11 the roof lock
12 the wire wheel
13 the wheel spindle (*Am.* axle) wing nut
14 the air-cooling louvres or louvers
15 the front lamp visor
16 the decorative fillet;
17–35 the scooter (motor scooter),
17 the engine cooling system:
18 the fan
19 the air-impeller blades
20 the duct for directing air to the cylinder;
21 the steering lock
22 the starter battery (battery case)
23 the steering head bearing
24 the fork cover
25 the instrument panel
26 the dynastarter (combined dynamo and starter)
27 the handlebār gear change (*Am.* gear shift)
28 the hook for handbag or case
29 the tubular frame
30 the scooter seat for child
31 the saddle bracket
32 the pillion (pillion seat)
33 the saddle grip
34 the sheet-metal casing
35 the scooter wheel;
36 the scooter trailer (camping trailer):
37 the spare wheel;
38 the scooter rider:
39 the dust coat (*Am.* duster)
40 the safety helmet;

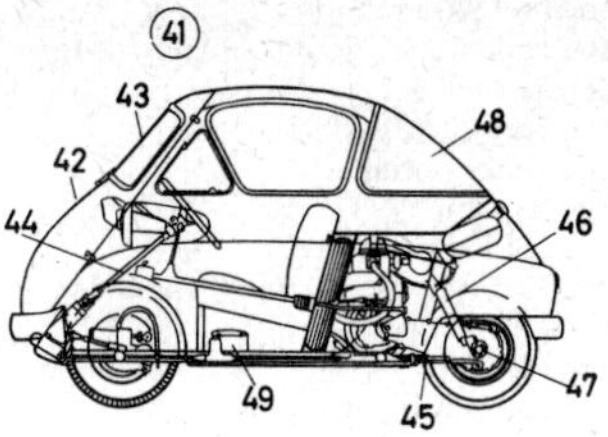

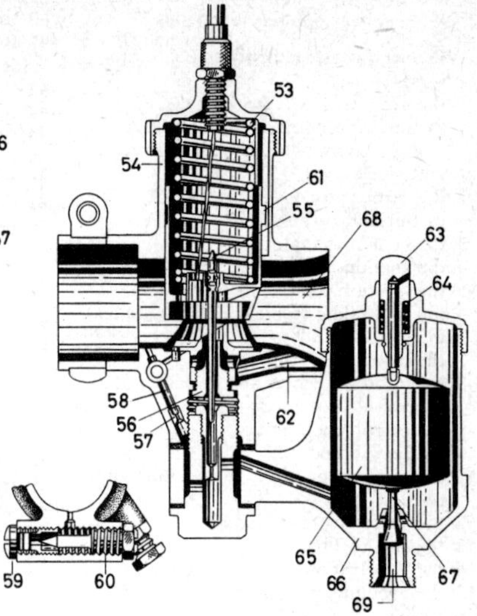

41-52 cabin vehicles,
41 the two-seater motor cabin (cabin car), a baby car (*coll.* bubble-car, *Am. coll.* runabout, flivver):
42 the front door
43 the perspex all-round-view windscreen (*Am.* windshield)
44 the forward-tilting steering column
45 the quarter-elliptic cantilever leaf (laminated) spring
46 the telescopic spring-damper
47 the rigid axle
48 the rear window
49 the hydraulic braking;
50 the four-seater motor cabin:
51 the fixed steering column
52 the half-round (semicircular) steering wheel;

53-69 the carburetter (scooter, and motorcycle, carburetter; *Am.* carburetor), a single-slide carburetter:
53 the slide spring
54 the carburetter body
55 the jet needle
56 the needle jet
57 the pilot jet (pilot)
58 the idling vent (slow-running vent)
59 the slow-running air jet
60 the air-regulating (air-adjusting) screw
61 the throttle slide; *in car engines:* throttle valve (butterfly valve, mixture throttle strangler disk or disc)
62 the atomising air-intake
63 the carburetter tickler
64 the primer (tickler) spring
65 the carburetter float
66 the float chamber (*Am.* float bowl)
67 the float needle
68 the choke tube
69 the float valve

Engl. petrol = *Am.* gasoline (gas)

1-36 carburettor engines (Otto motors),

1 the four-stroke (*Am.* four-cycle) carburettor engine, a petrol engine (*Am.* gasoline motor) with push rod and side valve:
2 the carburettor (*Am.* carburetor, carbureter, carburetter)
3 the ventilation inlet
4 the sparking plug (*Am.* spark plug)
5 the ignition cable
6 the cable shoe (cable thimble, wire terminal)
7 the distributor (timer)
8 the ignition (intensity, spark, induction) coil
9 the petrol (fuel) pump
10 the petrol pipe
11 the cool water point (water inlet connection)
12 the valve chamber cover
13 the anti-roll bar
14 the V-belt (cone belt, fan belt)
15 the vacuum fuel pipe to the induction elbow
16 the vacuum (*Am.* depression) adjustment
17 the air filter
18 the oil dip-stick
19 the fan
20 the crankcase ventilation
21 the distributor, and oil pump, shaft
22 the oil pump
23 the oil sump
24 the sump drain plug
25 the engine block (cylinder block)
26 the combustion chamber
27 the valve tappet (*also Am.* push rod)
28 the valve push rod
29 the inlet, or exhaust, valve
30 the valve stem
31 the valve head;
32 the two-stroke (*Am.* two-cycle) carburettor engine:
33 the starter pinion
34 the flywheel
35 the free wheel
36 the differential;

37-80 diesel engines (heavy-oil engines, oil engines),

37 the four-stroke (*Am.* four-cycle) diesel engine with chamber in the piston (piston chamber):
38 the injection pump
39 the atomiser (injection valve, injection nozzle)
40 the fuel feed pump
41 the centrifugal governor (centrifugal regulator)
42 the fuel filter
43 the water pump
44 the dynamo
45 the cold-start device
46 the tachometric warning appliance
47 the oil-filler pipe
48 the oil filter
49 the sump (oil pan)
50 the starter motor
51 the heat-exchanger
52 the cylinder
53 the cylinder head
54 the piston
55 the connecting rod
56 the crankshaft
57 the valve (*Am.* poppet valve)
58 the rocker arm (valve rocker)
59 the low (low-level) camshaft
60 the cam
61 the valve spring
62 the exhaust manifold;
63 the diesel engine with antechamber (pre-combustion engine):
64 the igniter (glower plug, heater plug) for pre-glowing (pre-heating)
65 the jet
66 the antechamber (pre-combustion chamber)
67 the compression chamber
68 the tappet with push rod
69 the cooling liquid
70 the cylinder bore
71 the hollow piston pin (gudgeon wrist pin (*Am.* wrist pin);
72 the two-stroke (*Am.* two-cycle) valveless diesel engine:
73 the inlet ports
74 the exhaust ports
75 the fresh air
76 the exhaust gases;
77 the diesel engine with turbulence chamber:
78 the turbulence chamber
79 the compression rings, piston rings
80 the oil scraper ring, a piston ring

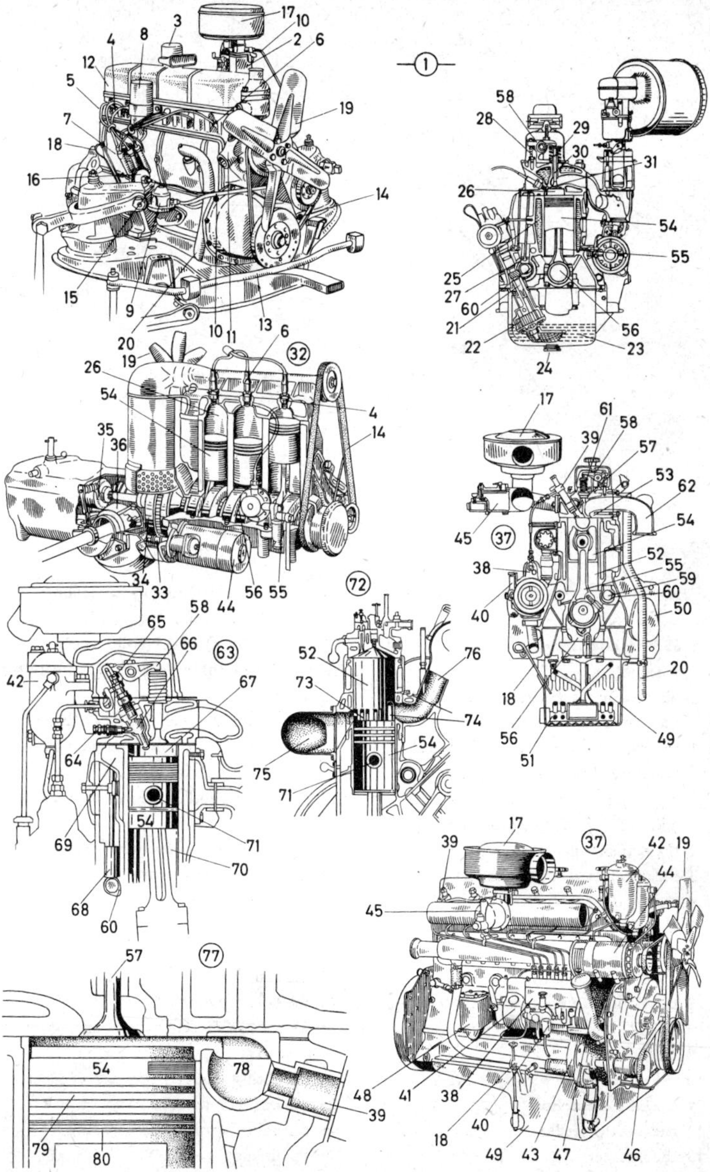
1
32
63
72
37
77
37

185 The Car (Motor-Car) I

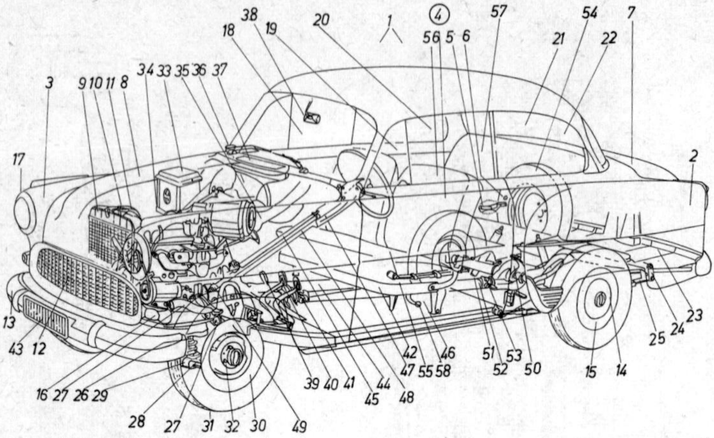

Engl. motor-car, car = *Am.* car, auto

1-65 the car (motor-car, automobile),

1–58 the car chassis and the car body (coachwork, carosserie):

1 the self-supporting welded all-steel body in chassis-less (unit, frameless) construction (integral, monocoque construction) [broken-open view]

2 the rear side-panel

3 the mudguard (wing, fender)

4 the car door:

5 the door handle

6 the door lock;

7 the boot-lid, trunk-lid

8 the bonnet (engine bonnet, *Am.* engine hood)

9 the radiator

10 the radiator cap with safety valve

11 the cool-water hose

12 the radiator grille

13 the bumper

14 the ornamental hub cap (wheel hub cover, nave plate)

15 the disk (disc) wheel (solid wheel)

16 the front blinker (*Am.* front direction indicator)

17 the headlight (headlamp) with driving light, anti-dazzle (short-range) light (dipper; *Am.* with high and low beam, with bright and dim light), and parking light

18 the windscreen (*Am.* windshield)

19 the front quarter vent

20 the door window with crank handle

21 the rear window

22 the rear quarter vent

23 the boot (*Am.* trunk)

24–29 the car suspension (car springing) system:

24 the spring shackle

25 the leaf (laminated) spring

26 the helical spring or coil spring

27 the linkage

(59)

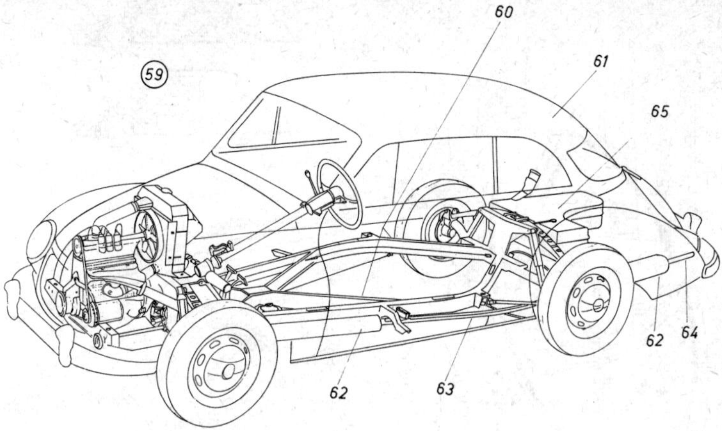

28 the stub axle bracket
29 the spring-damper (*commonly:* shock-absorber; *Am.* snubber);
30 the wheel rim
31 the car tyre (car tire)
32 the wheel bolt
33 the battery
34 the battery stand
35 the defroster hose
36 the air hose
37 the ventilator
38 the driving (driver's, rear view) mirror
39–41 the foot levers (pedals):
39 the accelerator
40 the brake (brake pedal, foot brake, *Am.* service brake)
41 the clutch (clutch pedal);
42 the seat frame
43 the front number plate (*Am.* front license plate)
44 the propeller shaft tunnel
45 the gear-change rod
46 the floor panel
47 the cowling
48 the steering column
49 the steering box
50 the differential gear (differential)
51 the rear axle
52 the Cardan shaft (propeller shaft with universal joints)
53 the Cardan joint
54 the spare wheel
55 the front seat (driving seat, driver's seat), a folding seat
56 the folding squab
57 the back seat (*Am.* rumble seat)
58 the lever for adjustment of front seat;
59 the chassis-frame construction (chassis and body as separate units):
60 the channel section
61 the fitted body
62 the silencers (*Am.* mufflers)
63 the exhaust pipe
64 the exhaust tail pipe
65 the tank (petrol tank, fuel tank, *Am.* gasoline tank)

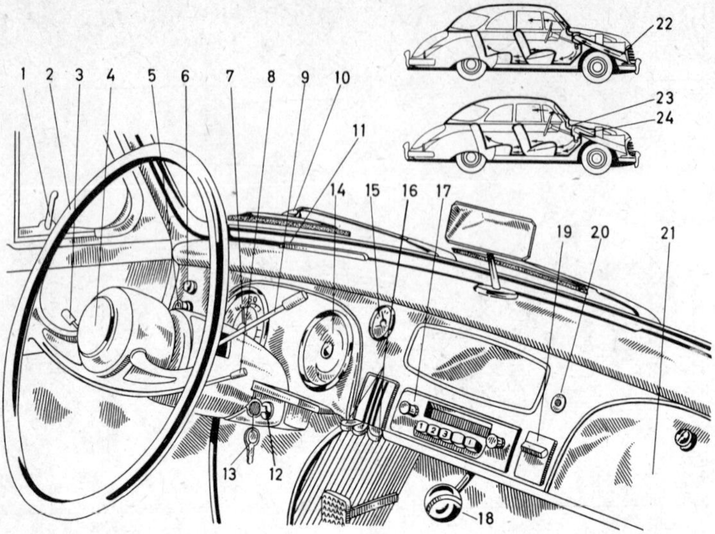

Engl. motor-car, car = *Am.* car, auto

1-21 the car dashboard (car instrument panel, *Am.* instrument board):

1 the front quarter vent handle
2 the steering wheel
3 the dipswitch (*Am.* dimswitch, dimmer)
4 the horn button (hooter button)
5 the windscreen-wiper (*Am.* windshield-wiper) button
6 the starter button (starter)
7 the speedometer with mileometer (mileage-recorder, *Am.* odometer)
8 the dash-light (*Am.* flashlight) lever
9 the gear lever
10 the windscreen (screen, *Am.* windshield) wiper
11 the defroster louvre or louver
12 the ignition switch
13 the ignition key
14 the petrol gauge (*Am.* gasoline level gage) with thermometer
15 the car clock
16 the hot, and fresh-air, levers
17 the car wireless (*Am.* car radio)
18 the hand-brake lever
19 the car ashtray
20 the socket for hand lamp or cigarette-lighter
21 the cubby-hole (*Am.* glove compartment);

22-24 the car-heating and air-conditioning system:

22 the car air-conditioning with fresh air
23 the air outlet
24 the hot-air system;

25-38 rear part of a car:

25 the boot (*Am.* trunk) lock
26 the boot (*Am.* trunk) lid handle
27 the blinker (direction indicator, 'trafficator', *Am.* direction light)
28 the stop light (stop lamp)
29 the rear (tail) light or lamp

30 the tank filler sleeve with cap
31 the rear number plate (*Am.* rear license plate)
32 the police identification mark or number:
33 the nationality sign
34 the registration number (*Am.* license number)
35 the place of registration;
36 the rear bumper
37 the bumper guard with number plate lighting
38 the reversing light;

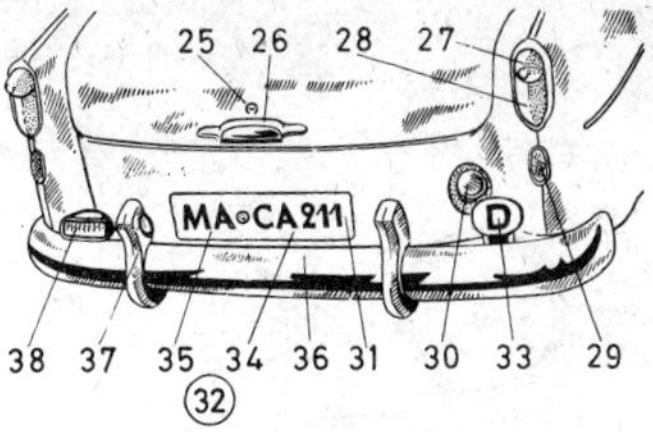

39-49 the car-steering mechanism,

39 the worm and sector steering:
40 the drop arm
41 the steering box
42 the toothed sector on the Pitman shaft
43 the worm gear with balls;
44 the steering rod (drag link)
45 the track rod adjusting screw
46 the bell-crank lever
47 the centre (*Am.* center) bolt
48 the tightening screw
49 the front suspension crossmember;

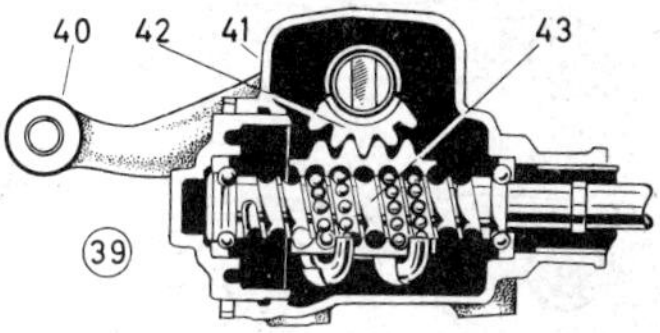

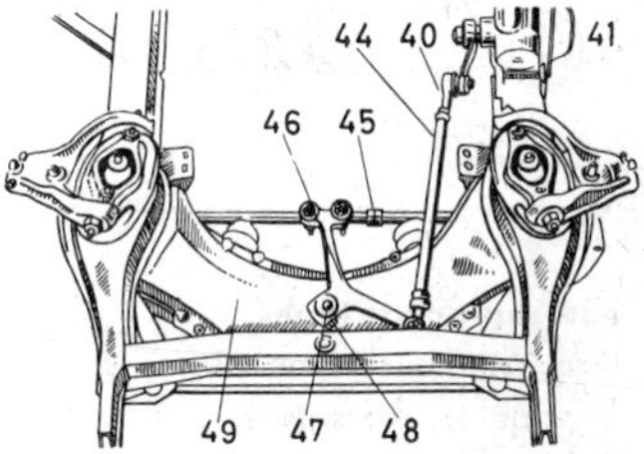

50-54 the car brakes:

50 the brake back plate
51 the brake shoe with brake lining
52 the wheel-braking cylinder
53 the pull-off spring
54 the tip of the axle;

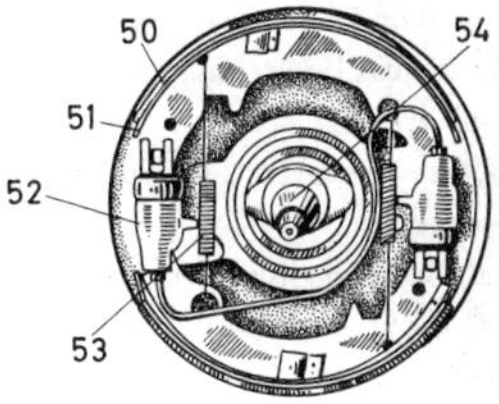

55-62 the gears (*Am.* transmission):

55 the driving shaft
56 the geared-down shaft to the Cardan shaft (propeller shaft)
57 the gear box flange
58 the oil-filler sleeve
59 the helical gear wheels
60 the synchromesh clutch hub
61 the layshaft toothed wheels
62 the gear box mounting

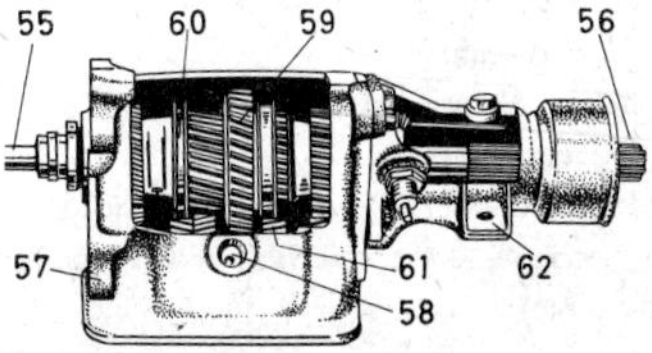

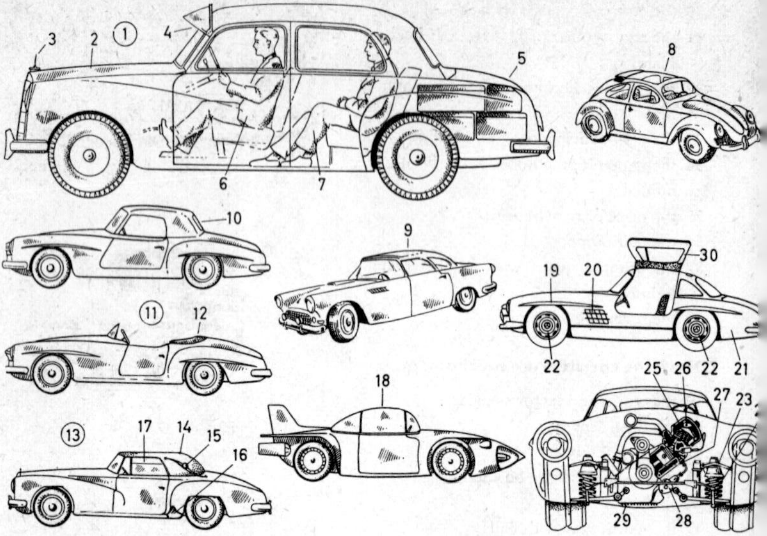

Engl. motor-car, car = *Am.* car, auto

1-30 motor-car types,

1 the two-door saloon (closed motor-car or car, *Am.* sedan):
2 the bonnet (*Am.* hood)
3 the radiator mascot
4 the sun shield (*Am.* sun visor)
5 the motor-car boot (lugagge boot, *Am.* car trunk)
6 the driver (motorist, *Am.* autoist)
7 the passenger;
8 the saloon with sliding (sunshine) roof (*Am.* convertible landau)
9 the de luxe limousine
10 the coupé
11 the roadster (two-seater sports car, two-seater):
12 the dicky (dickey) seats (*Am.* rumble seats);
13 the convertible coupé (drop-head coupé, *Am.* convertible sedan, convertible):
14 the collapsible (convertible, folding) hood or top
15 the hood stay (outside hood iron)
16 the stone fender
17 the wind-up window;
18 the rocket-driven car (rocket car)
19–30 the sports-racing car:
19 the splash form
20 the air outlet slots
21 the mudguard (*Am.* fender) sides
22 the turbo brakes to reduce braking heat
23 the upper wishbone for independent suspension
24 the coil springs
25 the overhead (overhead valve, O.H.V.), inclined Otto engine (engine in inclined position)
26 the overhead camshaft
27 the petrol (*Am.* gasoline) injector
28 the fuel injection pump
29 the cooling fins
30 the roof door with telescopic springing ('gull-wing' door)

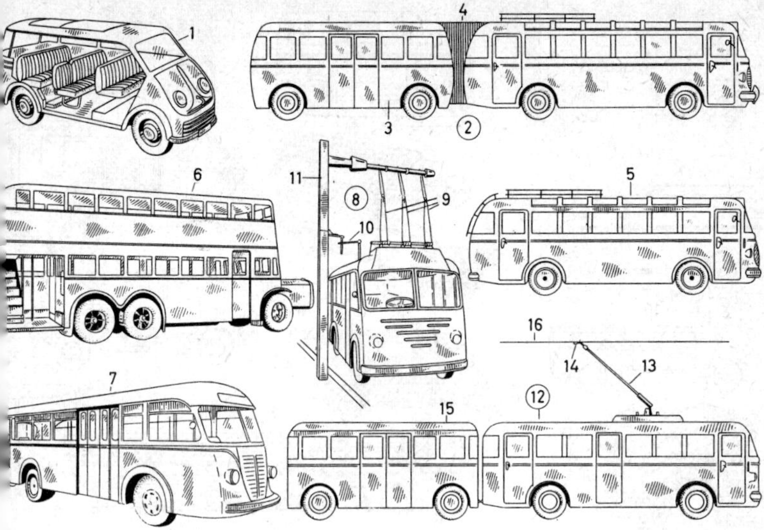

1-16 types of buses,

1–7 buses with internal-combustion engines:

1 the baby bus (small bus), a touring bus

2 the bus with trailer, a long-distance bus:

3 the bus trailer

4 the concertina (telescopic) connection;

5 the omnibus (bus, motor bus, single-decker bus, single-decker, *Am.* autobus), a rear diesel-engine bus (rear-engined bus) with rear engine

6 the double-decker bus (double-decker)

7 the town bus;

8–16 electric buses,

8 the gyro bus with electric-driven flywheel, an electro gyro:

9 the contact rods for charging the accumulator unit

10 the contact arm (bracket) for protective earthing

11 the charging pole (charging mast) at the gyro bus stop;

12-16 the trolley bus with trailer,

12 the trolley bus (*Am.* trackless trolley):

13 the slewing trolley pole or arm (contact pole or arm)

14 the trolley wheel (trolley);

15 the trolley bus trailer

16 the double-wire overhead line (two-wire overhead contact wires)

189 Motor Lorries (Lorries)

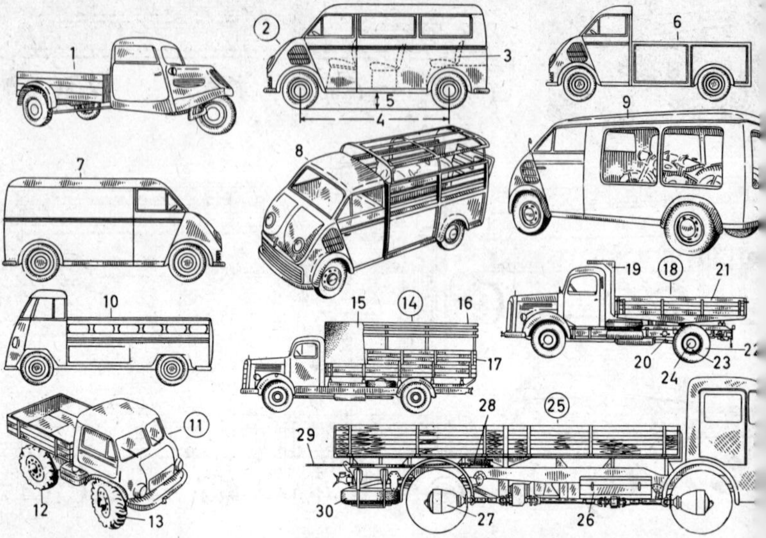

Engl. lorry (motor van, van) = *Am.* truck

1-13 small lorries and vans (small commercial motor vehicles):

1 the three-wheel delivery motor lorry (*Am.* delivery truck)

2 the station wagon (brake, shooting brake, combined passenger and commercial motor vehicle):

3 the removable seats

4 the wheel base

5 the ground clearance (road clearance, clearance above road surface)

6 the deep-loading small lorry

7 the delivery van

8 the cattle van (cattle lorry)

9 the advertising van

10 the small platform lorry

11 the universal truck cab with four-wheel drive:

12 the cross-country (*Am.* off-the-road) tyre or tire

13 the tyre (tire) tread (anti-skid tread, non-slip tread);

14-50 motor lorries (motor trucks) and vans (lorries, trucks, vans, commercial motor vehicles, industrial motor vehicles),

14 the drop-sider truck:

15 the hood (tilt, canvas cover, canvas covering)

16 the hoop (tilt-holder, hood stick)

17 the raised side;

18 the hydraulic three-way tipper (tipping lorry, tipper, *Am.* dumping truck, dump truck):

19 the cab guard (cab protector)

20 the tipping (tilting, *Am.* dumping) gear

21 the tipper body

22 the tyres (tires); *outside :* tyre (tire, cover), *inside :* inner tube

23 the tyre (tire) valve

24 the hub cap;

25 the drop-sider with enlarged loading platform:

26 the low-slung engine ('underfloor' engine)

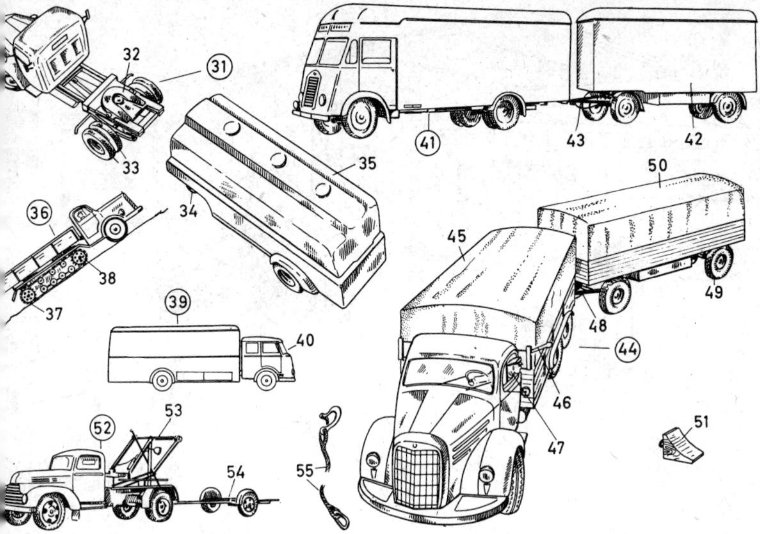

27 the differential housing
28 the cable winch
29 the cable
30 the spare wheel;
31 the tractor trailer unit:
32 the coupling unit
33 the dual wheel (double wheel; dual tyre or tire, double tyre or tire)
34 the supporting wheels [for when the trailer is unhooked]
35 the single-axle trailer, a two-wheel trailer;
36 the caterpillar motor lorry (half-track vehicle, *Am.* creeper-type truck:
37 the caterpillar track (endless track)
38 the driving wheel;
39 the large-capacity van:
40 the driver's cabin (driver's cab);
41 the furniture van (removal van, *Am.* moving van, furniture truck):
42 the furniture van trailer
43 the combination brake (trailer coupling; brake actuated by trailer pushing against lorry, and stopping trailer in the event of coupling rupture);
44 the long-distance lorry with trailer (long-distance road-train), a three-axle lorry:
45 the tractor lorry
46 the semaphore type direction indicator (trafficator)
47 the lorry-driver
48 the coupling device (coupling)
49 the cushion tyre or tire
50 the trailer;
51 the chock
52 the breakdown lorry (crane lorry, *Am.* wrecking car, trouble car):
53 the breakdown crane (*Am.* wrecking crane)
54 the breakdown trailer (*Am.* wrecking car trailer)
55 the steel cable

190 The Filling Station

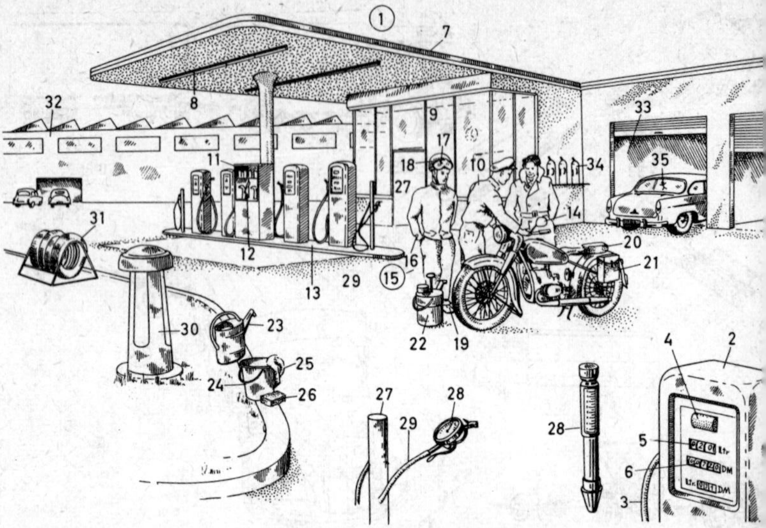

Engl. gauge = *Am.* gage; *Engl.* petrol = *Am.* gasoline (gas)

1 the filling station (petrol station):
2 the petrol pump
3 the petrol pump hose
4 the inspection glass
5 the petrol flowmeter
6 the price indicator
7 the petrol station canopy
8 the petrol station lights
9 the attendant's room
10 the petrol station attendant (*Am.* garage man)
11 the oil cabinet
12 the oil pump
13 the row of pumps;
14 the motorcycle driving mirror
15 the motorcyclist:
16 the leather jacket
17 the motoring goggles
18 the crash helmet
19 the motorcycle boots;
20 the pillion (pillion seat)
21 the pannier bag
22 the petrol dispenser
23 the water can
24 the window-cleaning pail
25 the chamois leather
26 the sponge
27 the air pump column for motor-driven air pump
28 the tyre pressure gauge
29 the air pipe
30 the traffic island lamp
31 the tyre stand
32 the garage
33 the garage compartment
34 the fire-extinguisher
35 the car mascot

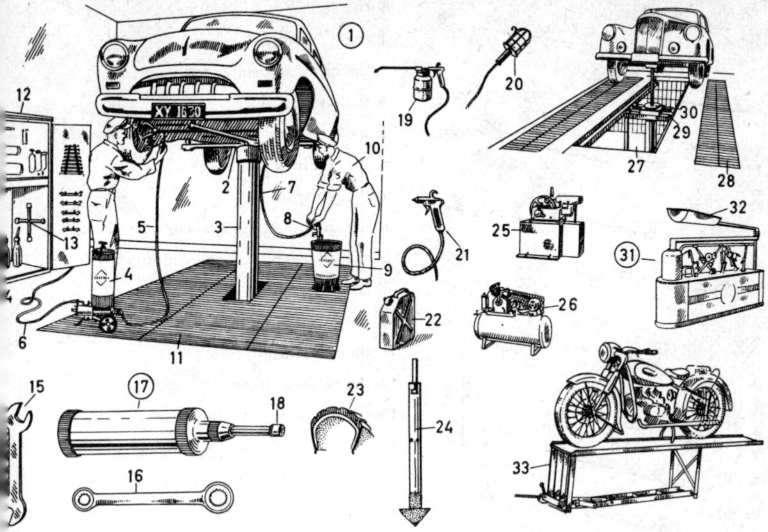

1 the lubrication workshop:
2 the hydraulic car jack
3 the lifting ramp
4 the grease compressor
5 the high-pressure grease hose
6 the compressed-air hose
7 the oil hose
8 the oil pump
9 the sump oil pail
10 the car mechanic
11 the grating
12 the tool cabinet
13 the wheel spanner
14 the engine oil container;
15 the double-ended spanner
16 the ring spanner
17 the grease gun:
18 the grease gun nipple;
19 the spray gun
20 the inspection lamp
21 the spray gun
22 the petrol can
23 the tubeless tyre
24 the vulcanizing paste press for cold vulcanization
25 the car-washing compressor machine
26 the air compressor
27 the inspection pit
28 the removable gratings
29 the guide rails
30 the pneumatic axle car jack
31 the oil stand:
32 the waste-oil collecting pan;
33 the motorcycle ramp

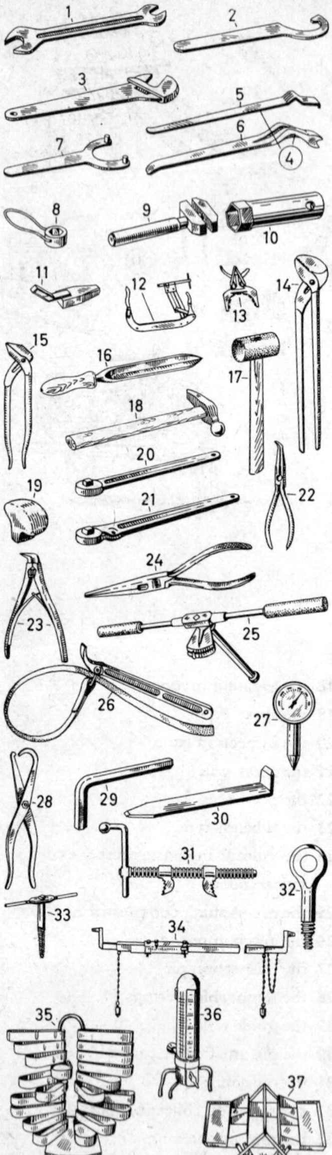

1 the double-ended spanner
2 the 'C' spanner
3 the offset adjustable spanner
4 the tyre levers:
5 the tyre lever
6 the tyre fork lever;
7 the pin spanner
8 the sparking plug spanner
9 the adjustable spanner (monkey wrench)
10 the box spanner
11 the valve-fitting tool
12 the valve spring compressor
13 the piston ring fitting tool
14 the universal pliers
15 the side cutting pliers
16 the spoon-edged scraper
17 the rubber mallet
18 the ball-pane hammer
19 the utility dolly
20 the toothed-wheel ratchet
21 the free-wheel ratchet
22 and 23 fuse pliers:
22 for inner fuses
23 for outer fuses;
24 the long-nosed pliers
25 the torque meter
26 the tank cap remover
27 the tachometer
28 the brake spring pliers
29 the socket screw hexagon wrench
30 the angle screwdriver
31 the tyre-spreader
32 the engine lifting eye bolt
33 the thread tap and wrench
34 the track gauge
35 the spare parts trays

36 the petrol consumption indicator
37 the tool box
38 the battery:
39 the battery terminal
40 the filling hole
41 the battery box;
42–45 the battery-charger:
42 the battery charger
43 the hydrometer:
44 the float;
45 the bottle of distilled water;
46 the battery cell tester
47 the car jack
48 the tyre pump
49 the footpump
50 the grease gun
51 the jet-tester
52 the boring machine
53 the honing machine
54 the hydraulic press
55 the valve-grinding machine
56 the sparking plug (plug, *Am.* spark plug) tester and cleaner
57 the tyre balancing machine
58 the headlight beam setter
59 the governor-tester
60 the hand-operated crane:
61 the crane column
62 the crane boom;
63 the repair pit
64 the repair pit cover
65 the car mechanic
66 the mobile car jack
67 the fitter's trolley
68 the tool trolley
69 the cotton waste

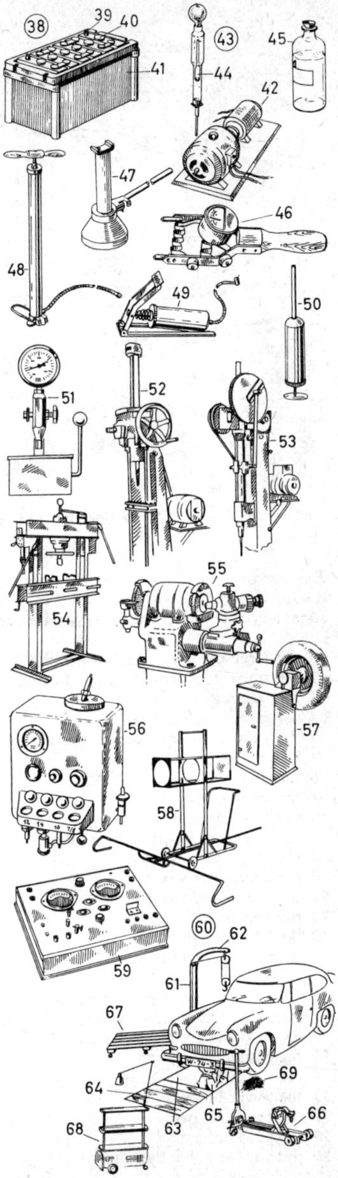

193 The Tramway (Electric Tramway, Tram)

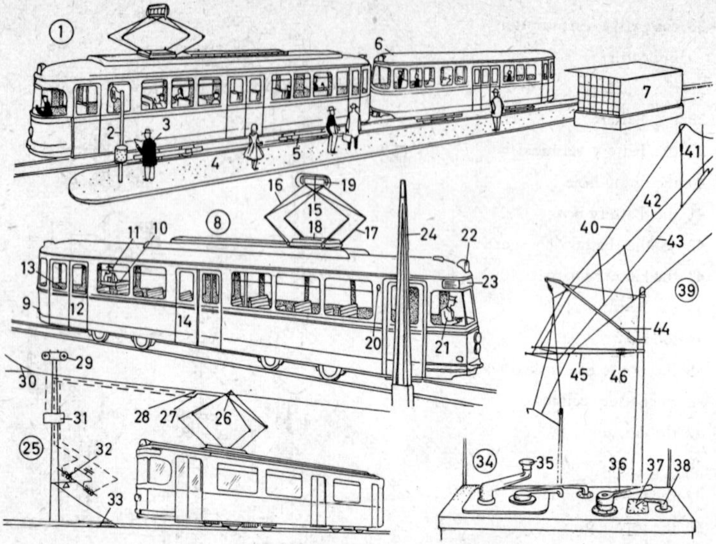

*Engl.*tramway = *Am. generally:* city traction, traction line; *Engl.* tramcar (tram) = *Am.* streetcar (trolley car, *New York:* surface car)

1 the large-capacity tram and trailer:
2 the tram stop post with the stop plate
3 the tramway passenger
4 the tram stop (tramway island)
5 the rubber-sprung (rubber suspension) bogie (*Am.* truck)
6 the tram trailer;
7 the shelter
8 the traction tramcar (front car, *Am.* bloomer), a one-direction traction car:
9 the stop light
10 the conductor's seat
11 the tram conductor
12 the rear boarding door
13 the boarding platform
14 the remote-controlled folding or sliding exit door
15–19 the pantograph (pantograph current-collector); *other system:* bow collector (bow current-collector):
15 the contact strip
16 the upper hinge
17 the lower hinge
18 the erection spring
19 the pivoted spring;
20 the blinker (*Am.* flashlight)
21 the driver (tram-driver, *Am.* motorman
22 the tramway route number (*Am.* streetcar line number)
23 the route plate;
24 the concrete post
25 the electro-magnetic tramway points
26 the contact slider
27 the sliding contact
28 the insulating contact
29 the points signal lamp
30 the aerial (overhead) contact wire frog
31 the controlling magnet
32 the drawing magnet
33 the points tongue (spring tongue);
34 the driver's cabin:
35 the controller, a cam controller, *also:* electric brake
36 the sander (sanding gear) control
37 the route timekeeper
38 the brake lever for the compressed-air brake;
39 the suspension of the overhead contact wire:
40 the carrying cable
41 the suspension wire
42 the auxiliary wire
43 the contact wire
44 the boom
45 the lateral stay
46 the suspension insulator

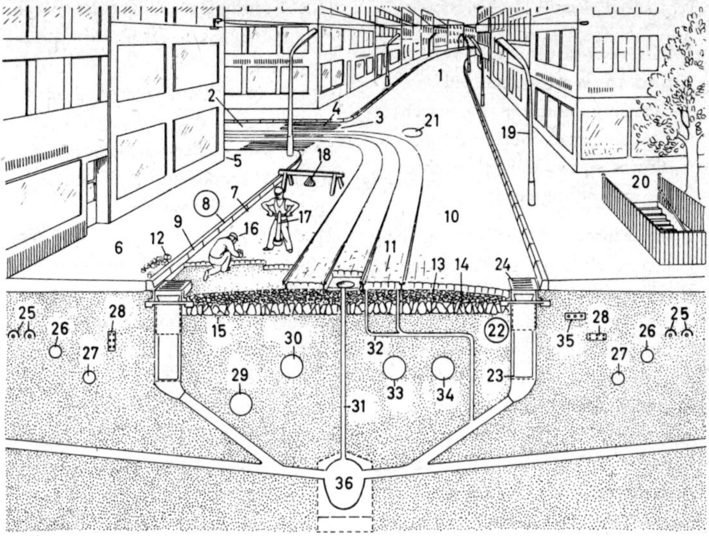

1 the street
2 the side street
3 the pedestrian crossing (zebra crossing):
4 the zebra stripes;
5 the street corner
6 the pavement (paved footpath, *Am.* sidewalk, walkway)
7 the gutter
8 the kerb (curb):
9 the kerbstone (curbstone);
10 the roadway (road, carriageway)
11 the road surface (setts):
12 the sett (paving sett), a natural stone
13 the pitching (broken-stone layer)
14 the foundation (*Am.* telford base)
15 the bed;
16 the paver (paviour, pavior)
17 the hand-rammer
18 the warning sign; *here:* Danger, Men at Work!
19 the street lamp, a neon lamp
20 the entrance to the underground public convenience (*Am.* washroom, rest room, *fam.* comfort station)
21 the manhole cover (manhole lid)
22 the gully with mud or grit trap:
23 the mud or grit trap
24 the grating;
25 the electricity cables
26 the gas main
27 the water main
28 the telephone cables (post office telephone cables)
29 the principal (leading) water main
30 the district heating main
31 the ventilation shaft
32 the rail drainage system
33 the long-distance gas main
34 the principal (leading) gas main
35 the fire brigade or police telephone cables
36 the sewer for sewage and surface waters (combined sewer)

Engl. snow plough = *Am.* snowplow

1-40 street-cleaning machines and snow ploughs (public cleansing vehicles; *Am.* street-cleansing machinery and snow-plows; snow-clearing machinery, snow-handling equipment),

1 the refuse and dustbin-emptying lorry (refuse lorry, refuse wagon, motor truck for refuse collection, *Am.* garbage truck):
2 the dustbin-tipping device (*Am.* garbage can, or ashcan, dumping device), a dust-free emptying system;
3 the small watering vehicle, a jeep
4 the pavement (*Am.* sidewalk, *Australian:* footpath) snow plough:
5 the sand (grit) spreader;
6 the three-wheeled road-sweeper
7 the road-sweeper's (road-cleaner's) barrow
8 the road-sweeper (street-sweeper, *Am.* street cleaner)
9 the broom
10 the warning armband
11 the dust pan
12 the self-loading road-sweeping machine (rotary street-sweeper, street-sweeper, mechanical road-sweeper), a tipper (tip-up lorry, *Am.* end dumping truck, dump) [in unloading position]
13 the snow-loader (snow-loading lorry, *Am.* snow-loading truck):
14 the loading vent (loading channel)
15 the side snow-sweeper (side unit);
16 the grit-spreader (sand lorry):
17 the sanding machine (grit-spreading attachment), a built-on sand hopper
18 the rotary sand-spreader (sand-spinner)
19 the sand-deflecting blade;
20 the V-shaped snow plough, a two-sided snow plough
21 the high-capacity highway snow-sweeper, a blower-type snow plough (snow-blowing machine):
22 the rotary milling drum
23 the cutter (hard-snow remover), a cutter
24 the rotating snow vents;
25 the crane gully and cesspit emptier (*Am.* truck; mechanical sludger or gully-emptier):
26 the slewing crane
27 the sludge bucket;
28 the suction gully and cesspit emptier:
29 the hose frame;
30 the hand motor snow plough, a one-sided snow plough
31 the road sweeper-collector, a combined street-watering, sweeping, and washing, lorry (*Am.* truck):
32 the rotating wire street-sweeping brush (cylindrical brush, rotary washing brush)
33 the watering nozzle (washing nozzle, horizontal jet nozzle);
34 the sewage lorry (*Am.* truck):
35 the compressor vacuum pump;
36 the watering lorry (*Am.* sprinkling truck):
37 the dome with hinged lid
38 the water tank
39 the sprinkler (sprinkling device)
40 the watering lorry (*Am.* sprinkling truck) driver

1
2
3
4
5
6
7
8
9
10
11
12
13
14
15
16
17
18
19
20
21
22
23
24
25
26
27
28
29
30
31
32
33
34
35
36
37
38
39
40

196 Road Construction (Road-making, Road Engineering) I

1-54 road machines (road-making machines),

1 the power navvy (power shovel, crane navvy, stripping shovel, *Am.* shovel-type excavator, all-purpose excavator, universal excavator, luffing-boom shovel):

2 the machine housing

3 the caterpillar mounting (caterpillar truck, *Am.* tracklaying craft, track-laying tractor)

4 the bucket arm (dipper stick, rack arm)

5 the bucket

6 the bucket teeth;

7 the end tipper (end-tip lorry, *Am.* end-dump truck, rear-dump truck), a heavy lorry (*Am.* heavy truck):

8 the tipping body

9 the reinforcement rib

10 the extended front (crab guard)

11 the driver's cabin;

12 the bulk material

13 the concrete-mixer:

14 the hoisting skip

15 the mixing drum, a mixing unit;

16 the caterpillar scraper:

17 the scraper

18 the levelling (*Am.* leveling) blade (smoothing blade);

19 the road-grader, *also:* soil-grader:

20 the ripper (road-scarifier, tynes, *Am.* roadplow, rooter plow)

21 the grader ploughshare (blade, *Am.* plow-share)

22 the blade-slewing gear;

23 the light railway (field railway, construction railway, *Am.* railroad; narrow-gage railroad):

24 the light diesel locomotive, a narrow-gauge (*Am.* narrow-gage) locomotive (field locomotive)

25 the trailer wagon (wagon truck, skip);

26 the internal-combustion punner, an earth-tamper; *heavier:* detonating rammer (*Am.* frog-type jumping rammer):

27 the guiding and controlling rods;

28 the bulldozer (angledozer):

29 the bulldozer blade

30 the pushing frame (thrust frame);

31 the road-metal spreading machine (macadam-spreader, stone-spreader, base-paver):

32 the tamping beam

33 the sole plate

34 the side stop

35 the side of the storage bin;

36 the three-wheel road roller, a road roller:

37 the road-roller

38 the all-weather roof;

39 the mobile diesel compressor (compressor unit):

40 the oxygen cylinder;

41 the chippings-spreader:

42 the spreading flap;

43 the tar-finisher (asphalt-surfacing machine):

44 the side stop

45 the material bin;

46 the tar-sprayer with tar and bitumen heater:

47 the tar tank;

48 the fully-automatic rolled-asphalt drying and mixing plant:

49 the bucket elevator feed

50 the asphalt-mixing drum

51 the filler hoist

52 the filler opening (feed opening)

53 the binder injector (binder jet)

54 the mixed-asphalt outlet;

55 typical cross section of a bituminous road:

56 the verge

57 the cross fall (straight fall, *Am.* banking)

58 the asphalt surface (bitumen layer, bituminous layer, asphalt)

59 the sub-surface

60 the bottoming (metal bed, *Am.* telford base), gravel bottoming, a frost blanket

61 the subsoil drainage (sub-drainage, sub-base drainage)

62 the perforated cement pipe

63 the drainage ditch

64 the soil (humus) covering

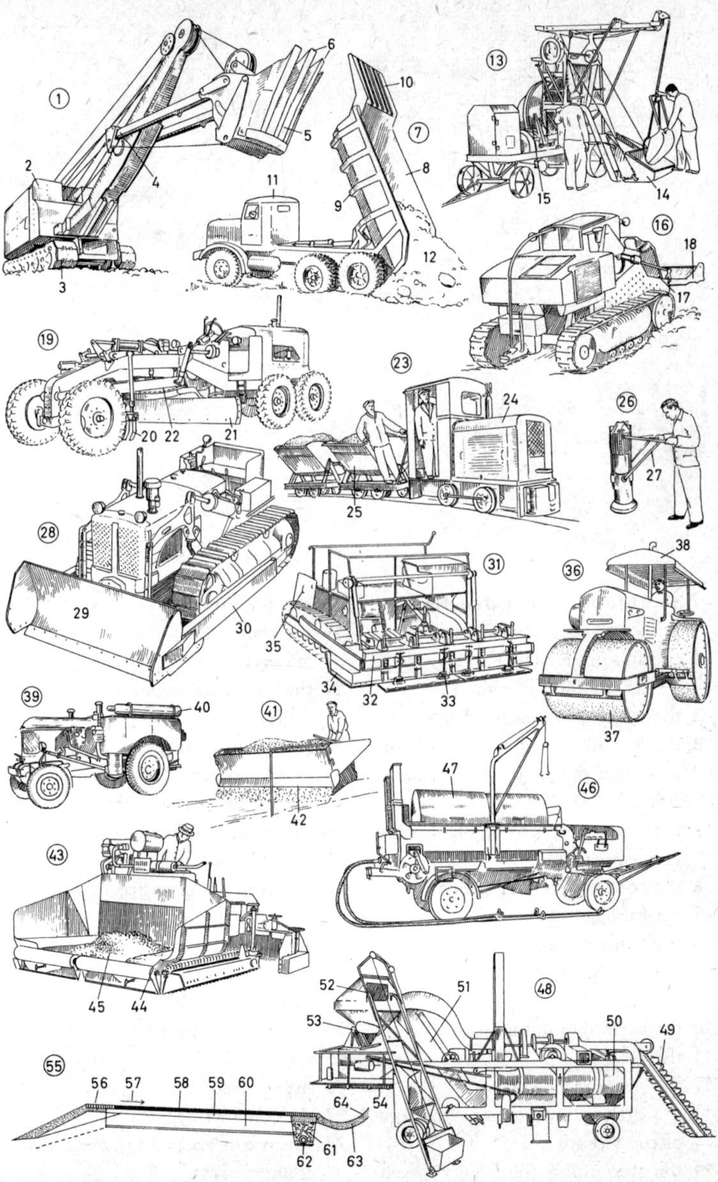
1
2
3
4
5
6
7
8
9
10
11
12
13
14
15
16
17
18
19
20
21
22
23
24
25
26
27
28
29
30
31
32
33
34
35
36
37
38
39
40
41
42
43
44
45
46
47
48
49
50
51
52
53
54
55
56
57
58
59
60
61
62
63
64

197 Road Construction (Road-making, Road Engineering) II

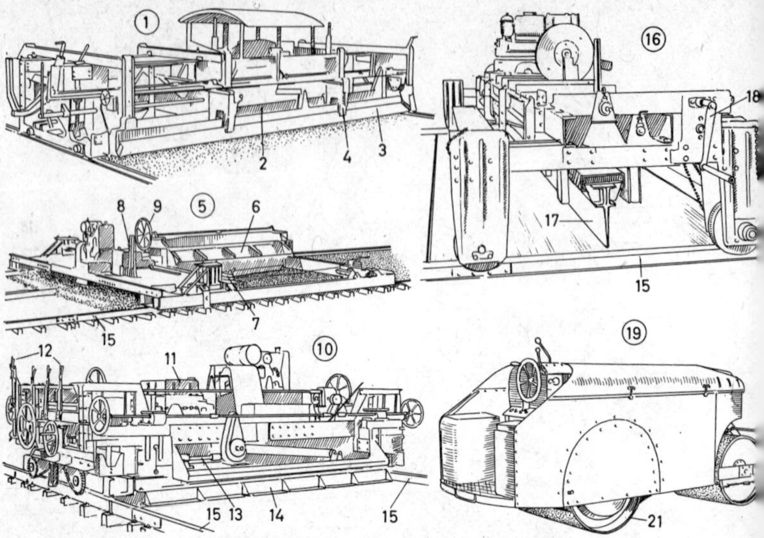

1-27 autobahn construction (concrete-road construction),

1 the sub-grader (sub-base grader), a road-building machine:

2 the tamping (consolidating) beam

3 the levelling (*Am.* leveling) beam

4 the roller guides for the levelling beam;

5 the concrete-spreading plant (concrete-spreader):

6 the concrete-spreading box

7 the cable guides

8 the control levers

9 the handwheel for emptying the boxes;

10 the surface vibrator:

11 the gearing

12 the operating levers

13 the driving axle to the vibrators of the vibration beam

14 the smoothing (finishing) screed

15 the side form;

16 the transverse-joint cutter (joint-cutter):

17 the joint-cutting knife (joint knife)

18 the crank handle for travelling (*Am.* traveling);

19 the vibrating road roller:

20 the steering roller

21 the vibrating roller;

22 the concrete-mixing plant, a central stationary mixing depot, an automatic weighing and mixing plant:

23 the collecting bin

24 the bucket elevator

25 the cement silo (cement hopper)

26 the concrete-mixer

27 the concrete bucket;

28 **the main road** (highway, *Am.* country road):

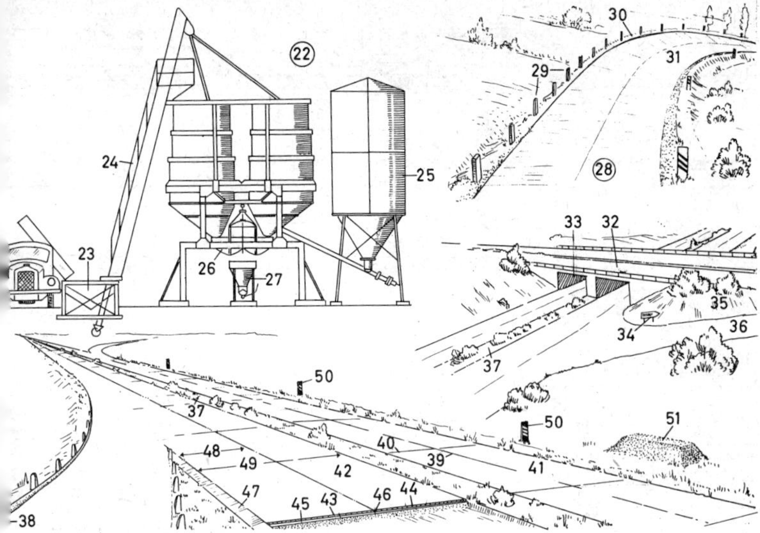

29 the bend (curve) marks (*Am.* banking indicators)

30 the superelevation of the curve (banking, cant)

31 the curve (bend);

32-50 the motorway (dual motor road, dual motor way, main arterial road, super-highway):

32 bridge over motorway (*Am.* overpass)

33 motorway under bridge (*Am.* underpass)

34 the cone of the slope, 'roundhead'

35 the road embankment

36 the motorway exit (*Am.* turn-off); *sim.* motorway approach, a feeder road

37 the central reserve

38 the guiding kerb; *kinds:* cement, or wooden, guiding kerb

39 and **40** the expansion joints (concrete joints):

39 the longitudinal joint

40 the transverse joint;

41 the concrete bay (concrete slab)

42 the concrete-road surface

43–46 cross-section of a concrete road:

43 the pavement concrete

44 the frost blanket

45 the base concrete

46 the slab junction;

47 the verge (*Am.* shoulder)

48 the width of slab

49 the width of the carriageway

50 the junction sign;

51 the store of material (heaps of materials, chippings, and sand)

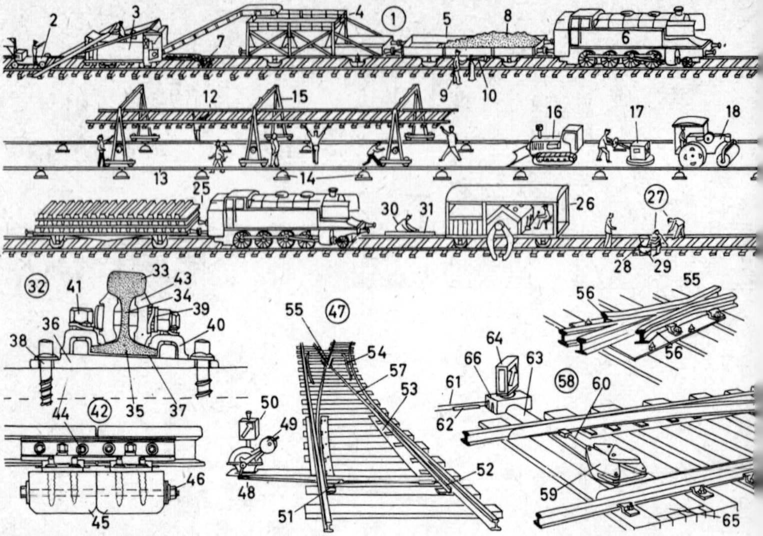

Engl. railway = *Am.* railroad;
Engl. sleeper = *Am.* tie (crosstie)

1-31 track-laying (railway construction, railway-building, track-relaying),

1 the track construction train:
2 the control truck
3 the ballast-washing machine
4 the hopper truck
5 the waste truck
6 the ballast train locomotive
7 the cleaned ballast (cleaned boxing)
8 the waste;
9 the lookout
10 the horn, a signal horn
11 the track-carrying train
12 the section of track
13 the temporary track rail
14 the gauge (*Am.* gage) rail chair
15 the travelling (*Am.* traveling) portal crane
16 the bulldozer
17 the vibratory ballast consolidator
18 the ballast-roller
19 the sleeper-layer
20 the platelayer (navvy, railway worker, *Am.* tracklayer, trackman, section hand, construction laborer, railroad laborer, jerry)
21 the rail tongs
22 the railway embankment
23 the sleeper truck
24 the sleeper conveyor truck
25 the sleeper transport (*Am.* transportation) train
26 the ballast-tamping machine
27 the welding team (*Am.* welding crew):
28 the thermite welding funnel
29 the mould (*Am.* mold)
30 the ganger (gang foreman)
31 the rail level;
32 the rail:
33 the rail head
34 the rail web
35 the rail bottom (rail foot)
36 the sole plate (base plate, *Am.* base)
37 the washer
38 the sole plate (base plate) screw
39 the spring washer
40 the clip
41 the hook bolt;
42 the rail joint:
43 the rail fish-plate (*Am.* joint bar)
44 the fish bolt
45 the coupled sleeper
46 the coupling bolt;
47 the hand-operated (manually operated) point or switch:

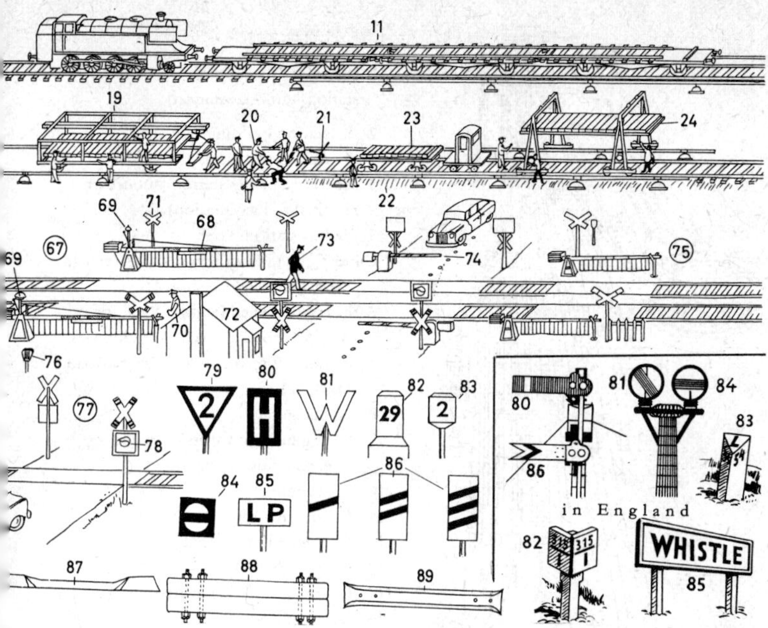

48 the hand switch box
49 the switch weight
50 the switch signal (switch lamp)
51 the stretcher bar
52 the switch toe (switch tongue, switch blade)
53 the slide chair (slide plate)
54 the inner check rail
55 the frog
56 the wing rail
57 the closure rail;
58 the remote-controlled point (remote-controlled switch):
59 the point lock (switch lock)
60 the stretcher bar
61 the wire pull
62 the turnbuckle
63 the wire pull cover
64 the electric points lamp
65 the point trough (switch trough)
66 the point drive (switch drive) with protective casing;

67-78 level crossings (*Am.* crossings at grade, grade crossings):

67 the level crossing (*Am.* crossing at grade, grade crossing)
68 the barrier, a lattice barrier (gate barrier)
69 the preliminary signal bell
70 the gatekeeper (signalman, *Am.* crossing watchman, watchman)
71 the warning cross
72 the gatekeeper's (*Am.* watchman's) cabin or box
73 the line inspector
74 the half-barrier
75 the microphone-operated barrier:
76 the electric speaking-tube appliance;
77 the unprotected crossing:
78 the traffic warning light;

79-86 running-track signs (*Am.* track targets):

79 the reduce-speed sign
80 the stop sign
81 the wait sign
82 the kilometre (*Am.* kilometer) post (railway kilometre post, *in Engl.* railway milepost, *Am.* railroad milepost)
83 the hectometre post (*Am.* hectometer post)
84 the track-closed sign
85 the bell and whistle sign
86 the distant-signal signs;
87 the concrete sleeper
88 the double sleeper (wooden sleepers, timber sleepers)
89 the steel sleeper

199 The Railway Grounds (Railway Premises)

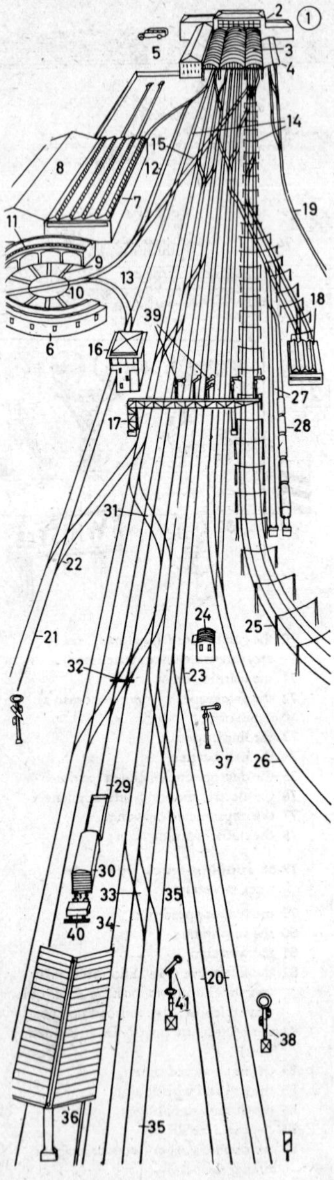

Engl. railway = *Am.* railroad

1 the terminus (terminal, dead-end station, terminal station):

2 the station building

3 the roofed platforms;

4 the local railway station (suburban terminal railway station)

5 the bus station

6 and 7 the railway repair shops (repair sheds, maintenance shops):

6 the circular shed (engine shed, locomotive shed, rotunda, *Am.* roundhouse)

7 the railway repair shop (*Am.* railroad shop);

8 the bus garage

9 the engine shed turntable roads (*Am.* roundhouse tracks)

10 the turntable

11 the smoke outlet

12 the engine line or spur

13 the triangle

14 the arrival and departure lines

15 the set of points

16 the central signal box (*Am.* main switch tower)

17 the signal gantry

18 the electric locomotive shed

19 the suburban railway, a local railway

20 the double-track main line (main line, *Am.* trunk line)

21 the engine line

22 the connection

23 the diverging junktion

24 the junction signal box (*Am.* switch tower)

25 the electrified main line

26 the single-track main line

27 the siding

28 the train of empty stock (*Am.* of cars)

29 the siding

30 the station car

31 the crossover

32 the diamond crossing

33 the connection

34 the suburban line (by-pass line)
35 the main through-line (*Am.* thru line)
36 the through station (*Am.* thru station)
37 the home signal
38 the distant signal (advance signal)
39 the stop signal
40 the buffer stop (*Am.* bumping post)
41 the block signal with outer home signal
42 the coaling plant:
43 the coaling crane
44 the coal bunker
45 the bunker wall
46 the set of floodlights
47 the travelling (*Am.* traveling) crane;
48 the elevated water tank
49 the framework substructure
50 the inspection pit
51 the ash-unloading pit
52 the water column
53 the ash bunker (slag bunker)
54 the sand-feeder
55 the railway foreman's office

56-72 signal plants,

56 the manual signal box (manual signal cabin, *Am.* switch tower):
57 the levers
58 the switch lever (points lever, change lever) [blue], a locking lever
59 the signal lever [red]
60 the trigger
61 the running-line lever
62 the block instruments
63 the block section panel;
64 the electrically operated signal box (*Am.* switch tower):
65 the switch and signal knobs
66 the interlocking board
67 the control panel;
68 the track diagram:
69 the switch table
70 the press buttons
71 the tracks
72 the two-way speaking appliance

Engl. railway station = *Am.* railroad station (station depot)

1 the parcels office:

2 the parcels

3 the parcels label;

4 the luggage (*Am.* baggage) office (luggage in-and-out counter):

5 the weighing-machine

6 the cabin trunk (*Am.* large suitcase)

7 the luggage label

8 the luggage (*Am.* baggage) receipt

9 the luggage (*Am.* baggage) clerk;

10 the appointment (*Am.* date) book

11 the shoeblack (shoe-cleaner, *Am.* bootblack, *Am. pop.* shoe-shine boy)

12 the shoe-cleaning (*Am.* shoe-shining) stool (shoe-cleaning foot-rest)

13 the station restaurant

14 the waiting room

15 the map of the town

16 the timetable (*Am.* schedule) drum

17 the hotel porter (*Am.* baggage man)

18 the train and platform indicator:

19 the arrival timetable (*Am.* arrival schedule)

20 the departure timetable (*Am.* departure schedule);

21 the luggage (*Am.* baggage) lockers for self-service

22 the platform-ticket machine

23 the platform tunnel with barrier

24 the ticket-collector's box

25 the ticket collector (*Am.* gateman, *pop.* chopper)

26 the bookstall (station book kiosk, *Am.* bookstand, news-stand)

27 the left-luggage office (cloakroom; left-luggage deposit, and withdrawal, office; *Am.* checking office, checkroom)

28 the accomodation bureau
29 the information office (inquiry office, *Am.* information bureau)
30 the station clock, a master clock
31 the exchange office
32 the wall timetable (line timetable, *Am.* wall schedule, line schedule)
33 the diagrammatic map (*Am.* railroad network map)
34 the booking office:
35 the ticket office
36 the ticket (railway ticket, *Am.* railroad ticket, one-way ticket)
37 the turning tray (money tray)
38 the speaking window membrane (speaking membrane)
39 the booking clerk (ticket clerk, *Am.* ticket agent)
40 the ticket-printing machine (ticket-stamping machine)
41 the illuminated desk scale
42 the rotating prism
43 the hand-operated ticket-printer
44 the pocket timetable (*Am.* pocket train schedule)
45 the luggage rest (*Am.* baggage rest);
46 the telephone kiosk
47 the tobacconist's kiosk (*Am.* tobacco kiosk)
48 the florist's kiosk (*Am.* flower kiosk)
49 the information official
50 the official railway guide or timetable (*Am.* train schedule, railroad schedule)
51 the board to indicate delayed trains
52 the station post box, an area letter box (*Am.* mail box)
53 the station mission
54 the first-aid station (ambulance station)

201 The Station Platform

1 the platform roofing
2 the platform stairway from the platform tunnel *(Am.* platform underpass*)*
3 the passengers
4–12 luggage *(Am.* baggage):
4 the suitcase
5 the label
6 the hotel labels
7 the travelling *(Am.* traveling) bag (hand bag, *Am.* satchel, valise, grip, gripsack)
8 the travelling (*Am.* traveling) rug (*Am.* lap robe, *also :* car rug, car wrap)
9 the dressing case (vanity bag, vanity case)
10 the umbrella with case (with umbrella case)
11 the hat box
12 the cabin trunk (*Am.* large suitcase);
13 the duty annex
14 the carriage-cleaner (*Am.* railroad car cleaner)
15 the cleaner's ladder
16 the concourse (platform next to the station building)
17 the news trolley
18 the reading matter *(Am.* transient literature) for the journey
19 the newsvender (newsvendor, *Am.* newsagent, newsdealer)
20 the level crossing
21 the platform edge
22 the railway *(Am.* railroad) policeman
23 the train indicator
24 the destination board
25 the departure indicator
26 the arrival indicator
27 the passenger train, a railcar *(Am.* power railroad train, motor railcar, diesel electric railcar)
28 the platform loudspeaker
29 the electric platform truck
30 the luggage *(Am.* baggage) official
31 the drinking fountain

32 the porter *(Am.* carrier, redcap)
33 the luggage *(Am.* baggage) barrow
34 the route and destination plate
35 the starting signal, a daylight signal
36 the carriage and wagon examiner
37 the wheel-testing hammer (long-handled hammer)
38 the travelling cleaner
39 the inspector (or foreman)
40 the signal stick [in England: signal flag]
41 the signal disk or disc [in darkness a lamp]
42 the red cap
43 the platform seat
44 the platform telephone kiosk
45 the duty room (the porters' room)
46 the platform post box (platform pillar box, *Am.* platform mail box)
47 the gangway
48 the platform refreshment stall for refreshments and food *(Am.* commissaries) for the journey
49 the refreshment trolley (*Am. pop.* dogwagon)
50 the paper cup
51 the paper plate
52 the hot-plate
53 the platform clock
54 the guard (train guard, *Am.* conductor, train conductor)
55 the book of tickets (circular-ticket book, tourist's ticket book, *Am.* round-trip ticket) with tickets
56 the ticket and date punch (ticket punch)
57 the guard's compartment
58 the compartment for women and children only
59 leave-taking
60 the kiss
61 the embrace
62 the luggage lift (*Am.* baggage elevator)
63 the driver's *(Am.* engineer's) cab
64 the winged wheel (symbol of the railways. *In Engl.* the lion)

202 The Goods Station

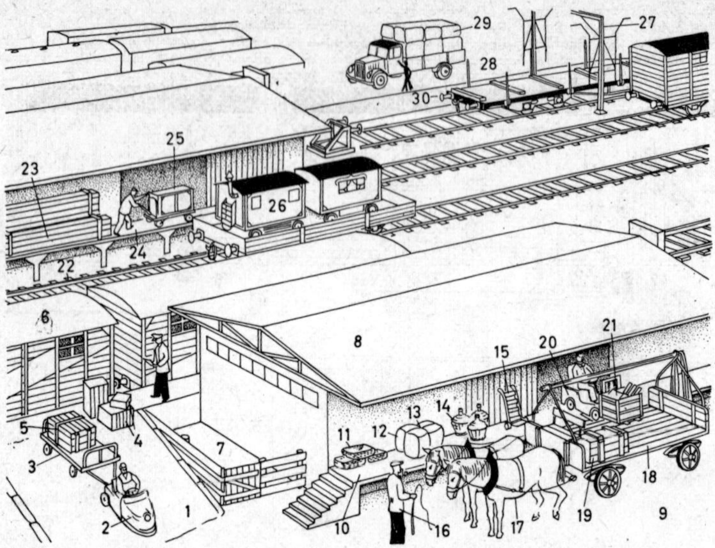

Engl. goods station = *Am.* freight depot

1 the inclined approach or ramp; *sim.* cattle ramp
2 the electric tractor
3 the electric tractor trailer
4 single consignments (*Am.* carload, C. L.); *in collective (combination) transport:* collective (combination) consignment or shipment
5 the metal strapping
6 the goods van
7 the small-cattle pen, a cattle pen
8 the goods shed (freight shed, *Am.* freight depot)
9 the loading driveway (*Am.* approach for trucks)
10 the goods-shed platform (loading platform)
11 the fruit, or vegetable, basket, a wicker basket
12 the bale
13 the roping (cording or strapping)
14 the demijohn (carboy, wicker-covered bottle)
15 the sack barrow (sack truck)
16 the carter (carrier, wagoner)
17 the draught (cart) horse (*Am.* draft horse), a draught animal (*Am.* draft animal, drafter, draughter)
18 the carrier's cart (delivery cart), a freight wagon for the goods delivery service
19 the crate
20 the fork truck (fork lift)
21 the fork carriage
22 the shed siding
23 bulky goods
24 the shed platform (side platform, loading and unloading platform)
25 the railway-owned (*Am.* railroad-owned) or supplied small container, a small wheeled container, a forwarding container (*Am.* tote box)

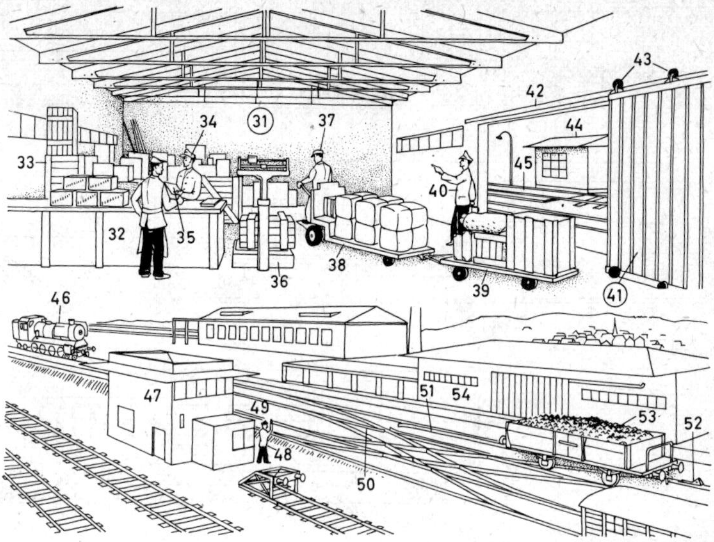

26 the showman's caravan

27 the loading gauge (*Am.* gage)

28 the loading dock

29 the bales of straw

30 the bogie bolster wagon

31 the goods shed (*Am.* freight depot):

32 the public counter (*Am.* freight agency)

33 the goods (freight)

34 the goods clerk (goods-shed foreman)

35 the waybill (consignment note)

36 the platform weighing machine

37 the goods porter

38 the electric truck, a platform truck

39 the electric truck trailer

40 the foreman;

41 the sliding door:

42 the roller rail

43 the rollers;

44-54 the marshalling yard (shunting yard, sidings):

44 the rail weighbridge office

45 the rail weighbridge

46 the shunting engine (shunting locomotive, *Am.* switcher)

47 the control cabin (*Am.* switch tower)

48 the yardmaster

49 the hump (*Am.* double incline)

50 the scissor crossing (*Am.* switching track)

51 the retarder

52 the slipper

53 the wagon load (*Am.* carload, haul)

54 the warehouse

203 Railway Vehicles (Rolling Stock) I

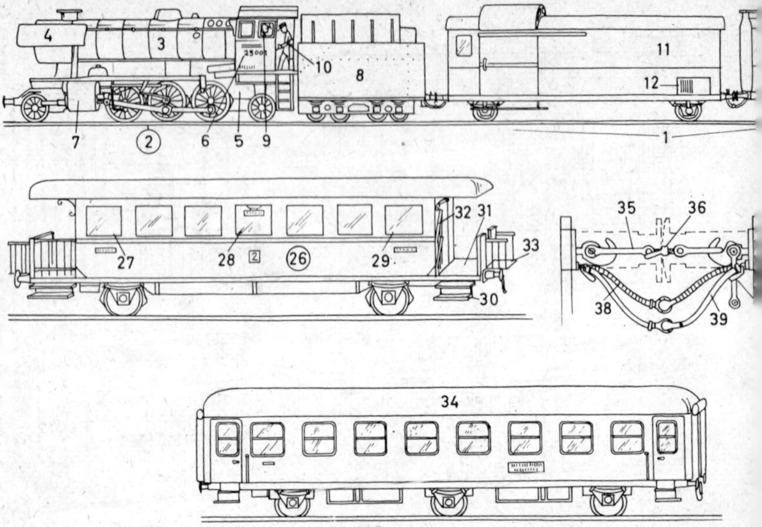

Engl. railway = *Am.* railroad; *Engl.* railway coach, railway carriage = *Am.* railroad car

1 the passenger train (slow train, stopping train, *Am.* local train, accomodation train, way train, jerkwater train),

2 the passenger train (*Am.* local train) engine or locomotive (engine, loco), a steam locomotive:

3 the boiler

4 the wind guide

5 the firebox

6 the locomotive number and series number

7 the cylinder

8 the tender;

9 and **10** the engine crew (engine staff):

9 the engine (locomotive) driver (*Am.* engineer)

10 the fireman (*Am.* stoker);

11 the passenger train luggage van (*Am.* baggage car)

12 the dog box

13 the guard (*Am.* conductor, head guard)

14 the red patent-leather strap

15 the railway cap

16 the signalling (*Am.* signaling) whistle, a trilling whistle

17 the guard (train guard)

18 the railway post:

19 the post office sorting carriage (*Am.* railroad mail car)

20 the letter slot (train letter-box slot, *Am.* train mail box slot)

21 the railway post official

22 the bag of letter mail

23 the bag of parcels mail;

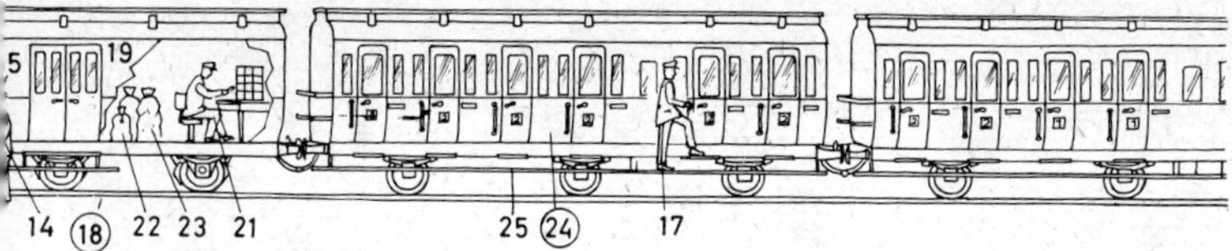

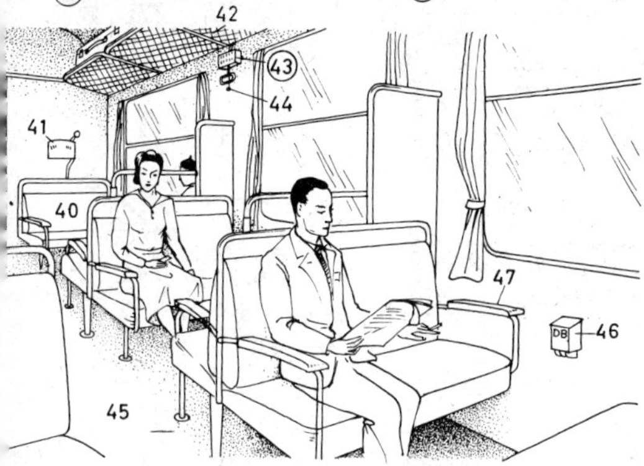

24 the non-gangwayed compartment coach:

25 the continuous footboard or step;

26 the 2nd class passenger coach (*Am.* passenger car), an open-platform coach:

27 the smoking compartment (*pop.* smoker)

28 the compartment reserved for disabled persons

29 the non-smoking compartment (*pop.* non-smoker)

30 the footboard (step)

31 the open platform

32 the folding trellis gate

33 the folding gangway plate;

34 the light-alloy (light-metal) passenger coach

35–39 pipe connection and coach coupling:

35 the coupling link

36 the tightening screw (coupling screw with turning lever)

37 the loose coupling

38 the steam heater flexible hose

39 the vacuum brake flexible hose;

40–47 the interior of the coach:

40 the seat with plastic upholstery

41 the heating regulator for regulating the temperature

42 the luggage rack (*Am.* baggage net, baggage rack)

43 the communication cord:

44 the seal;

45 the central corridor (central gangway)

46 the lidded ashtray

47 the arm-rest;

48 the ticket (railway ticket), a return ticket (*Am.* round-trip ticket)

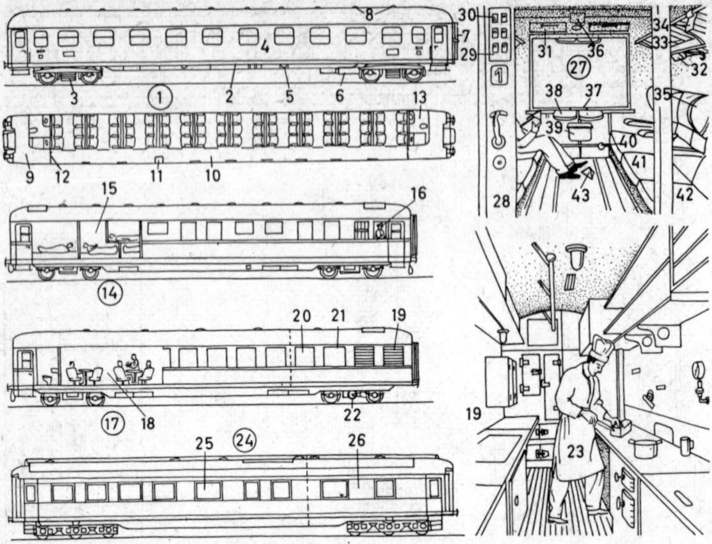

Engl. railway = *Am.* railroad; *Engl.* coach = *Am.* car

1 **the express train passenger coach** (gangwayed corridor compartment coach); *Am.* vestibule train (thru-train) passenger car (vestibule car, vestibuled car):
2 the frame (underframe)
3 the bogie (*Am.* truck)
4 the coach body
5 the pneumatic brake cylinder
6 the electric generator
7 the gangway
8 the ventilation, a ventilator
9 the vestibule
10 the side corridor
11 the tip-up seat
12 the swing door
13 the lavatory (*Am.* train toilet or washroom);
14 the sleeping car (sleeper):
15 the sleeping berth (*Am.* section; *for one person:* roomette)
16 the sleeping car (sleeper) attendant;
17 the dining car (restaurant car, *Am.* diner):
18 the dining compartment (restaurant compartment)
19 the pantry
20 the office
21 the train kitchen (coach kitchen)
22 the dynamo for generating current independently;
23 the chef (train cook)
24 the entertainment car (dancing car, cinema car):
25 the large compartment (lounge, dance floor)
26 the bar compartment (train bar);
27 the compartment (train compartment; *form.* coupé):
28 the sliding compartment door
29 the number plate for marking the occupied seats
30 the sign for the occupied seats
31 the ventilator
32 the reading light
33 the luggage (*Am.* baggage) rack
34 the label for reserved seats

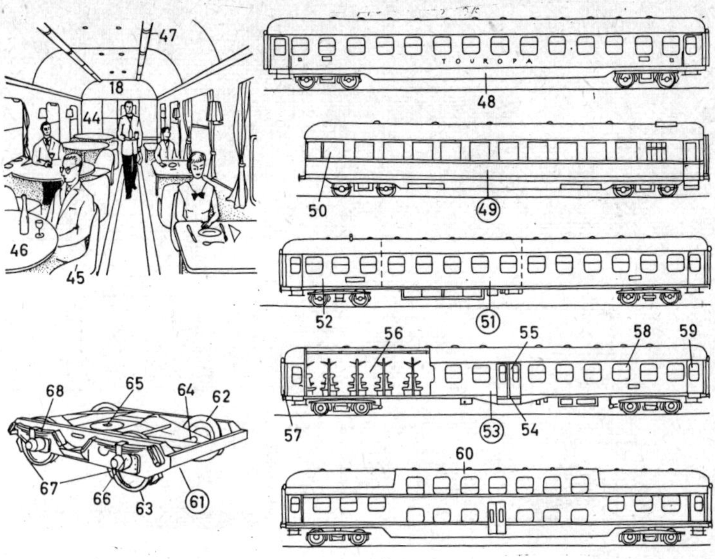

35 the adjustable head rest
36 the emergency brake
37 the warning notice ['Do not lean out of the window']
38 the collapsible table
39 the waste box
40 the heat regulator
41 the extendible upholstered seat
42 the corner seat
43 the foot rail (foot-rest);
44 the dining car (*Am.* diner) head-waiter
45 the revolving dining chair
46 the oval table
47 the fluorescent tube
48 the Touropa long-distance coach with reclining chairs, barber's (*Am.* barber) compartment, and lavatories, a reclining-chair coach
49 the saloon car (*Am.* parlor car, drawing-room car, chair car, Pullman):
50 the saloon, an observation lounge (solarium lounge) or conference room (meeting room);
51 the kitchen car:
52 the dining compartment (restaurant compartment);
53 the rapid interurban coach:
54 the rubber packing roll
55 the two-door centre (*Am.* center) entrance
56 the open compartment (high-capacity compartment)
57 the connecting gangway
58 the sash window, a draught-free (*Am.* draft-free) window
59 the single-door end entrance;
60 the double-decker passenger coach
61 the bogie (*Am.* truck),
62–64 the wheel set with axle:
62 the coach wheel
63 the wheel flange (flange)
64 the axle shaft;
65 the bogie (*Am.* truck) pin hole (bogie centre pin hole, *Am.* center pin hole)
66 the axle bearing (*Am.* journal box) with axle lubricator
67 the brake shoes
68 the axle suspension spring

205 Railway Vehicles (Rolling Stock) III

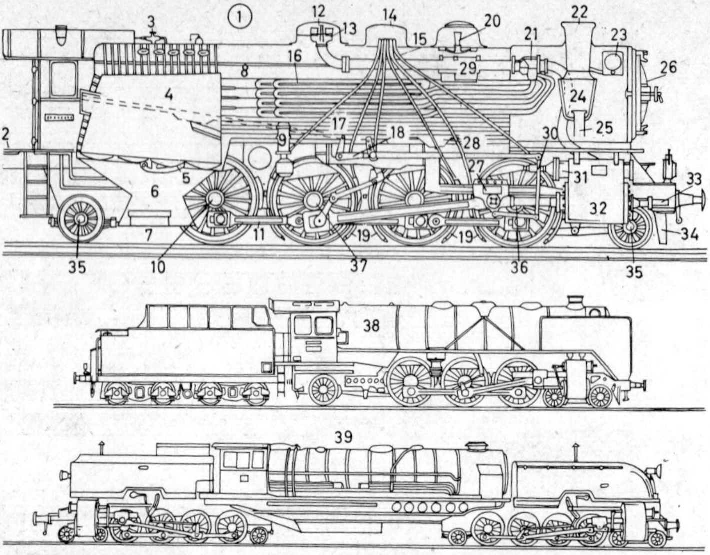

Engl. railway = *Am.* railroad, *Engl.* gauge = *Am.* gage

1 **the steam locomotive** (steam railway engine, piston engine, engine), a friction engine (adhesion engine),

2–37 the locomotive boiler and locomotive driving gear:

2 the tender fall plate with coupling

3 the safety valve for steam overpressure

4 the firebox

5 the dump (drop) fire bars

6 the ash-pan with ventilation

7 the ash pan drop bottom

8 the flue (smoke) tubes

9 the feed-water pump

10 the axle (*Am.* journal) bearing

11 the connecting rod

12 the steam dome

13 the steam regulator

14 the sand box

15 the sand tubes

16 the boiler barrel (boiler shell, boiler casing)

17 the fire (boiler) tubes

18 the steam-reversing gear

19 the pneumatic sanding gear

20 the feed valve

21 the steam collection box

22 the chimney (smoke outlet and waste-steam exhaust)

23 the feed-water pre-heater (surface preheater)

24 the spark-arrester (spark plate)

25 the blast pipe

26 the smoke box door

27 the crosshead

28 the mud collector

29 the filtering sheet of the feed-water cleaner

30 the combination lever

31 the steam chest

32 the steam cylinder (stuffing box)

33 the piston rod (extension)

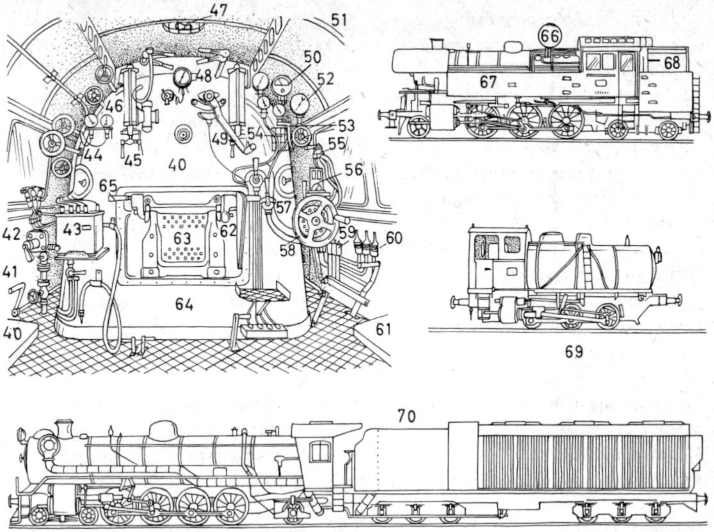

34 the rail guard (fender, life guard, cow-catcher, *Am.* locomotive pilot)
35 the carrying axle
36 the coupled axle
37 the driving axle;
38 the express tender locomotive
39 the Mallet-type (articulated) locomotive
40–65 the steam-locomotive driver's cab:
40 the fireman's seat
41 the drop fire-bars crank
42 the live steam injector
43 the automatic lubricant pump
44 the pre-heater pressure gauge or manometer
45 the heating pressure gauge
46 the water gauge
47 the light
48 the boiler pressure gauge
49 the regulator handle (steam cut-off, *Am.* steam gate valve)
50 the telethermometer
51 the locomotive-driver's cab roof
52 the brake pressure gauge
53 the steam whistle cock
54 the engine-driver's timetable (*Am.* schedule)
55 the driver's brake valve
56 the tachograph (recording tachometer, registering tachometer)
57 the cock to sand-sprayer
58 the reversing screw, *at the same time :* steering wheel
59 the emergency brake valve
60 the release (discharging) valve
61 the steam-engine driver's seat
62 the anti-dazzle shield
63 the firebox door (fire door)
64 the firebox
65 the fire door handle;
66 the tank locomotive:
67 the water tank
68 the fuel tender;
69 the steam accumulator locomotive (*Am.* steam battery locomotive; fireless works locomotive)
70 the condenser locomotive

1 **the electric locomotive** (conductor engine, electric standard-gauge locomotive, *Am.* conventional-gage locomotive):
2 the overhead contact wire (aerial line, overhead line)
3 the current collector (pantograph)
4 the main switch, an oil break switch (oil switch) or compressed-gas switch
5 the lead-in insulators
6 the roof disconnecting switch (disconnecting isolating switch)
7 the transformer (main transformer)
8 the cam-operated controls
9 the fine regulator
10 the driving motor, a frame motor
11 the axle-pressure equalizer
12 the toggle link
13 the brake motor (motor for the brake-lifter)
14 the brake-lifter
15 the sander (sanding gear)
16 the motor ventilator
17 the motor air pump (air compressor)
18 the transformer ventilator
19 the spiral oil coolers (coil oil coolers)
20 the air suction filter
21 the commutating resistors (reversing resistors, commutating rheostats, reversing rheostats)
22 the driver's brake valve
23 the locomotive coupling
24 the screw coupling
25 the draw hook (*Am.* drag hook)
26 the brake air cock;
27 the electric locomotive driver's cab or cabin;
28 the electric locomotive driver
29 the electric locomotive driver's seat
30 the electric locomotive driver's assistant
31 the controller handwheel
32 the switch step indicator (controller switch indicator)
33 the commutator switch (change-over switch)
34 the motor ventilator switch (ventilator switch)
35 the security control key (dead-man's button, dead-man's handle, safety contact)
36 the train heating system switch
37 the air compressor switch
38 the driver's pantograph valve (current collector valve)
39 the quick-acting circuit-breaker
40 the sander control (sanding gear control)
41 the heating tension gauge (*Am.* gage)
42 the contact wire tension (overhead line tension)
43 the contact wire current gauge (*Am.* gage)
44 the driving motors' traction power gauge (*Am.* gage)
45 the buzzer (warning signal)
46 the main air pipe (brake pipe) manometer
47 the auxiliary air container manometer
48 the main air container manometer
49 the locomotive brake cylinder manometer
50 the air whistle lever
51 the additional brake cock
52 the driver's brake valve for the automatic train brake
53 the main-switch hand release lever
54 the speed gauge (*Am.* speed gage; speed indicator, speedometer);
55 the electric rail coach (*Am.* railcar) with pantograph
56 the electric open-cast excavation locomotive
57 the overhead-wire examination wagon, a tower wagon
58 the battery railcar
59 the electric shunting locomotive
60 the electric three-car train

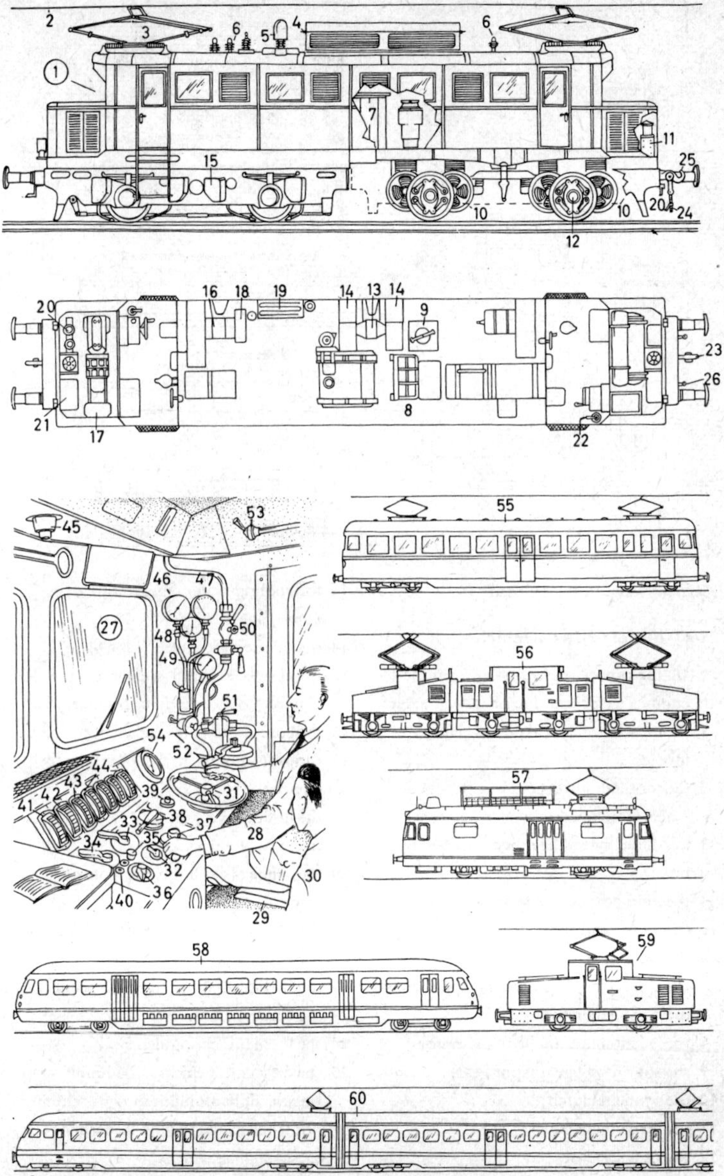
1
2
3
4
5
6
6
7
10
10
11
12
15
20
24
25
9
8
13
14
14
16
17
18
19
20
21
22
23
26
27
28
29
30
31
32
33
34
35
36
37
38
39
40
41
42
43
44
45
46
47
48
49
50
51
52
53
54
55
56
57
58
59
60

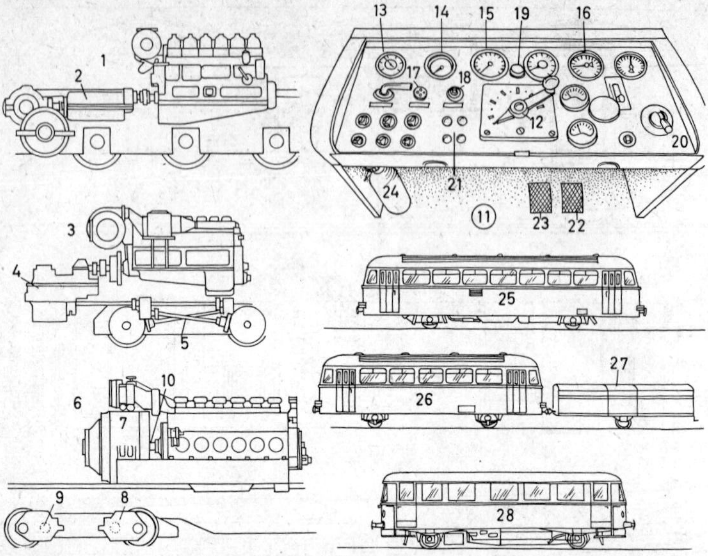

Engl. railway = *Am.* railroad

1-43 diesel railway vehicles,

1–10 the power transmission from diesel engines to locomotive or rail car axles:

1 the diesel mechanical power transmission

2 the toothed-wheel gear box (toothed-wheel clutch gear)

3 the diesel hydraulic power transmission

4 the fluid gear (turbo gear) with torque convertor and automatic gears

5 the driving axle

6 the diesel electric power transmission

7 the main generator

8 the traction motors (driving motors)

9 the spur wheel gear (spur gear)

10 the resilient clutch;

11 the instrument panel:

12 the gear selector

13 the cooling-water temperature gauge (*Am.* gage)

14 the oil pressure gauge (*Am.* gage)

15 the electric revolution-counter (rev-counter, *Am.* reading tachometer)

16 the compressed-air manometer

17 the glower plug (heater plug) control device

18 the ignition keyhole

19 the idling control knob

20 the sander (sanding gear) control lever

21 the control lamps (pilot lamps) for battery charge

22 the fuel injection pump feed pedal

23 the clutch pedal

24 the foam fire-extinguisher;

25 the diesel mechanical rail omnibus (railbus) of light aluminium (*Am.* aluminum) construction with underfloor diesel engine

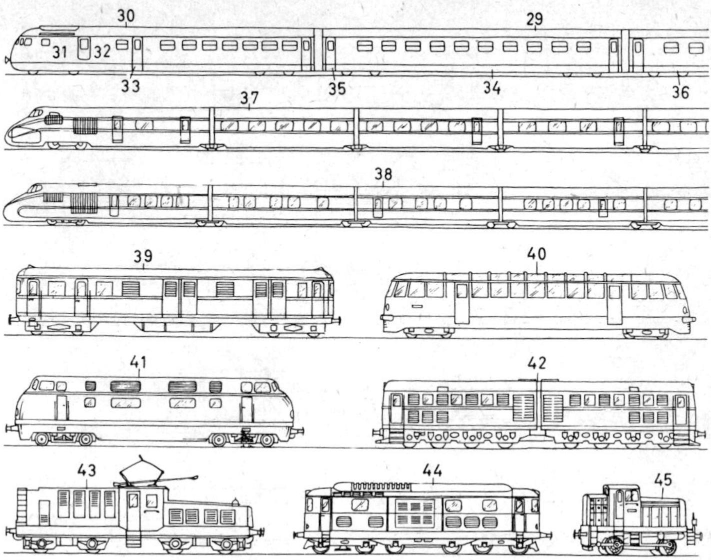

26 the railbus trailer

27 the two-wheel (one-axle) railbus luggage trailer (*Am.* baggage trailer)

28–40 diesel rail coaches (diesel railcars, *Am.* power railroad cars):

28 the diesel mechanical light-alloy (light-metal) railcar

29 the three-car diesel hydraulic long-distance railcar train (*Am.* multiple unit-car)

30 the engine car (motor-car)

31 the engine compartment

32 the luggage compartment (*Am.* baggage compartment)

33 the postal compartment (*Am.* mail compartment)

34 the second coach (middle coach)

35 the sliding swivel door

36 the control car

37 and **38** hydraulic mechanical articulated diesel trains:

37 the seven-unit day-service diesel train

38 the sleeping car train (*Am.* sleeper train);

39 the diesel goods (*Am.* freight) traction railcar, a traction and goods vehicle (*Am.* freight car) for transport of goods (*Am.* for transportation of freight) and mail

40 the glass-roof car, a diesel observation railcar (observation car, *Am. pop.* vista dome);

41 the express diesel locomotive with remote-control apparatus

42 the twin goods (*Am.* freight) diesel locomotive

43 the two-power works locomotive [electric or diesel electric];

44 the gas turbine locomotive

45 the gas engine locomotive

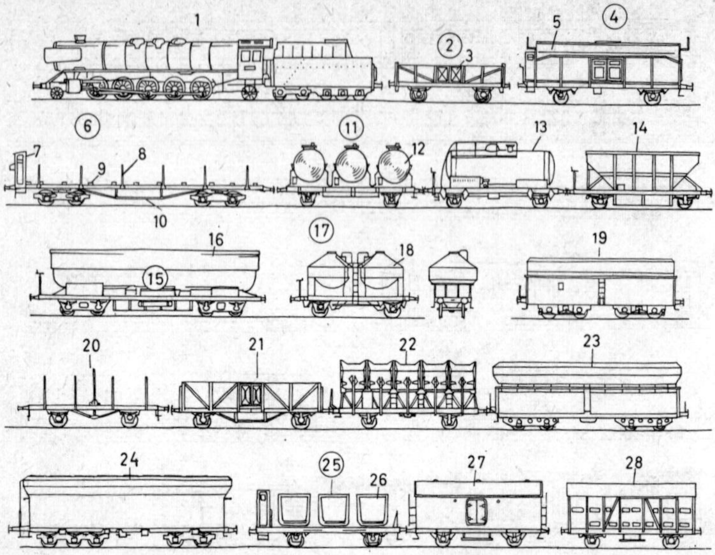

Engl. goods wagon = *Am.* freight car;
Engl. railway = *Am.* railroad

1 the goods train (*Am.* freight train) steam locomotive (goods locomotive, *Am.* freight engine) with trailing tender

2-34 goods wagons (railway wagons, railway trucks, railway vans),

2 the open goods wagon (*Am.* gondola car):
3 the side swivel doors;
4 the covered goods wagon (box goods wagon, *Am.* box freight car):
5 the sliding roof;
6 the bogie bolster wagon (*Am.* gondola car) with steel stanchions:
7 the hand-brake platform with cabin (with brakeman's cabin, with trainman's cabin)
8 the detachable stanchion
9 the bolster
10 the sole bar reinforcement (longitudinal frame reinforcement);
11 the tank wagon for chemicals:
12 the tank;
13 the all-purpose tank wagon
14 the hopper wagon (*Am.* hopper car) for boxing transport
15 the compressed-gas tank wagon for liquid gases (*Am.* tank car):
16 the sun guard;
17 the powder wagon, a self-discharger:
18 the lid;
19 the ore transport wagon, a side discharger
20 the timber transport wagon (timber wagon, *Am.* lumber car)
21 the open goods wagon
22 the trough tipper (trough-tipping wagon, *Am.* railroad V-dump car, car dumper)
23 the saddle-bottomed wagon, a two-side discharger for coke or coal

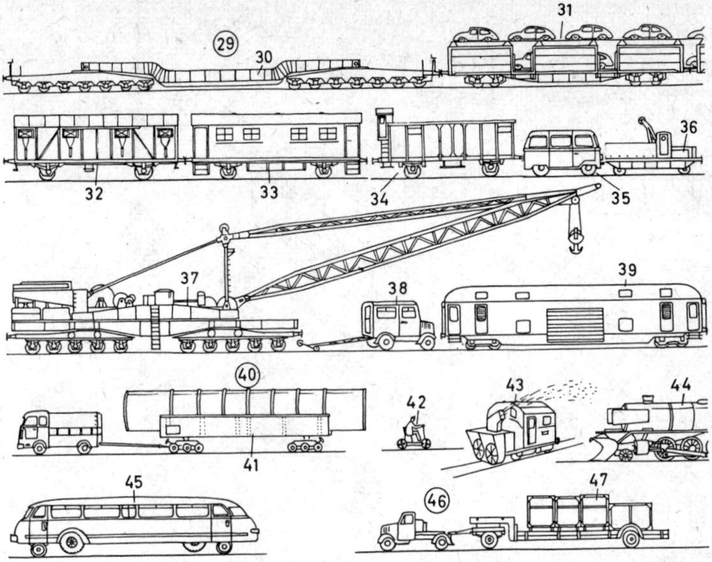

24 the covered self-discharging van (*Am.* car) for sand, ballast, etc.
25 the container flat (*Am.* tote box car)·
26 the large container (*Am.* tote box);
27 the refrigerator wagon
28 the multi-deck partitioned wagon for the transport of fowl
29 the 28-wheel (14-axle) well wagon for very heavy loads:
30 the loading well (loading surface);
31 the double-decker wagon (motorcar carrier unit)
32 the multi-purpose wagon
33 the breakdown van
34 the van (closed wagon, covered wagon, *Am.* box freight car);

35-47 special rail and road vehicles:

35 the railcar (auto railcar)
36 the platelayers' (*Am.* tracklayers', section crew's) railcar crane
37 the crane wagon for track-laying in sections and forward bridge-building
38 the track-testing trolley (line inspection trolley, *Am.* line inspection car)
39 the double-decker luggage (*Am.* baggage) van (auto railcar luggage van)
40 the 12-wheel (6-axle) road trailer:
41 the low loading platform;
42 the velocipede trolley, a rail cycle (rail bicycle) or a rail motorcycle (*Am.* inspection trolley)
43 the track rotary snow plough (*Am.* track rotary snowplow), a snow-clearing machine
44 the locomotive with ram-type snow plough (*Am.* with ram-type snow-plow)
45 the two-way vehicle (rail/road omnibus, rail/road bus)
46 the low-platform trailer:
47 the container (*Am.* tote box)

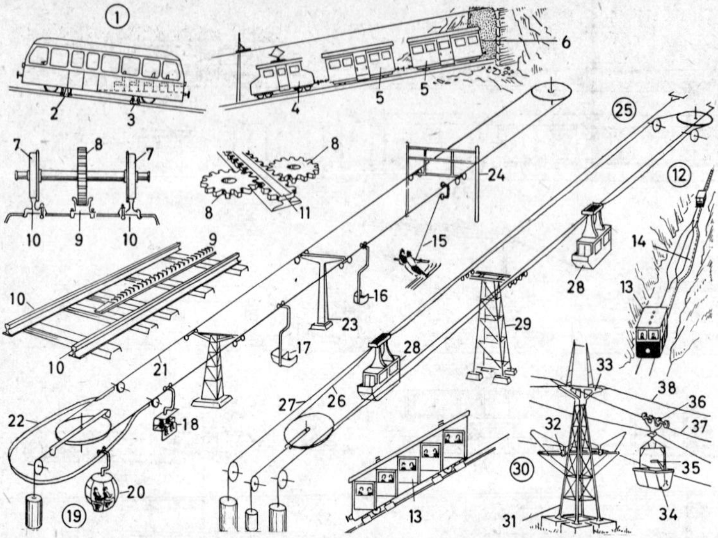

Engl. railway = *Am.* railroad; *Engl.* lift = *Am.* elevator

1-14 track mountain railways,

1 the adhesion motor rail coach (*Am.* motor railcar):
2 the drive
3 the emergency brake;
4 and 5 the rack mountain railway (rack railway, cogwheel railway):
4 the electric rack railway locomotive
5 the rack railway coach (*Am.* rack railroad car);
6 the tunnel
7–11 rack-and-pinion railways [systems]:
7 the running wheel
8 the driving pinions
9 the rack
10 the rail
11 the double rack;
12 the funicular (funicular railway):
13 the funicular railway coach (*Am.* cable car)
14 the haulage cable;

15-38 passenger cable railways (suspension cable railways, téléphériques, aerial cableways),
15–24 monocable ropeways, continuous ropeways (endless ropeways, *Am.* cable car):
15 the ski lift (ski hoist)
16–18 the chair-lift (chair-hoist):
16 the lift chair, a single chair
17 the two-seater lift chair, a double chair
18 the combinable two-seat chair;
19 the small cabin (small car) cableway, an endless cableway:
20 the small cabin;
21 the circulating rope (circulating cable), a standing (carrying) and haulage rope or cable
22 the switching rail
23 the one-mast support (one-tower support)
24 the gantry support;
25 the bi-cable ropeway (bi-cable aerial ropeway), a shuttle system (*Am.* shuttle) aerial ropeway:
26 the haulage cable
27 the standing cable (carrying cable)
28 the passenger cabin (passenger car, *Am.* shuttle car)
29 the intermediate mast (intermediate support);
30 the double cable suspension railway:
31 the lattice mast
32 the haulage-cable pulley

33 the carrying-cable bearing shoe
34 the tipping bucket (*Am.* dumping bucket)
35 the tip stop
36 the pulley cradle
37 the haulage cable
38 the carrying cable;

39 the valley station:
40 the tensioning-weight pit
41 the carrying-cable tensioning weight
42 the haulage-cable tensioning weight
43 the tension-cable plate
44 the carrying cable
45 the haulage cable
46 the lower cable
47 the emergency cable
48 the emergency-cable tensioning mechanism
49 the haulage-cable bearings
50 the spring buffer (*Am.* spring bumper)
51 the valley station platform
52 the passenger cabin (passenger car, ropeway gondola), a large-capacity cabin
53 the pulley cradle
54 the suspension gear
55 the car vibration damper
56 the guide rail;

57 the mountain station (top station):
58 the carrying-cable shoe
59 the carrying-cable anchorage
60 the haulage-rope roller battery
61 the haulage-rope guide wheel
62 the haulage-rope winding disk or disc
63 the main drive
64 the reserve drive
65 the driver's cabin;

66 the cabin pulley system:
67 the pulley cradle main carrier
68 the double cradle
69 the two-wheel cradle
70 the running wheels
71 the carrying-cable brake, an emergency brake in case of haulage-rope breakage
72 the suspension tackle bolt
73 the traction rope sleeve
74 the tail-cable sleeve
75 the derailment guard;
76 ropeway supports (cableway supports, intermediate supports):
77 the steel lattice mast (steel lattice support)
78 the tubular-steel mast, a tubular-steel support
79 the carrying-cable support shoe
80 the auxiliary scaffold for work on the cables
81 the tower base foundation

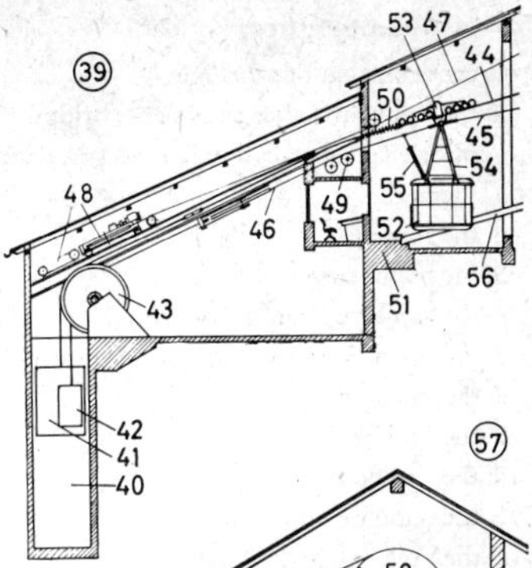

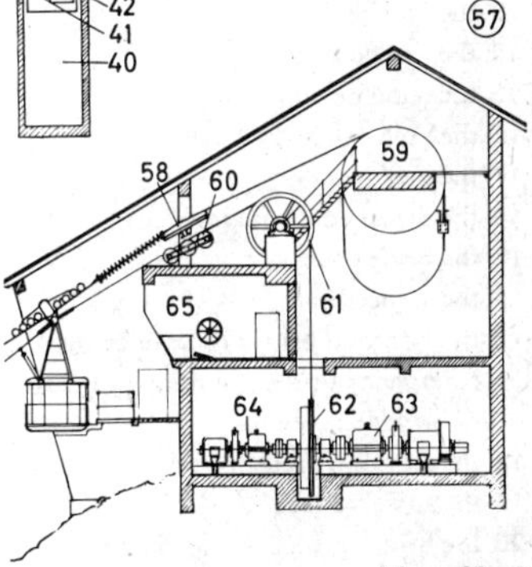

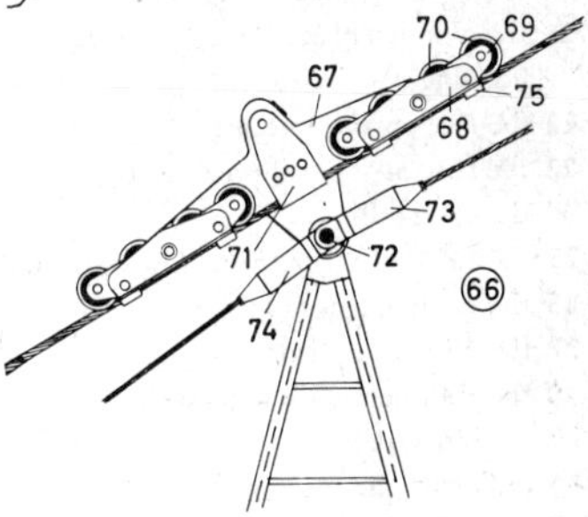

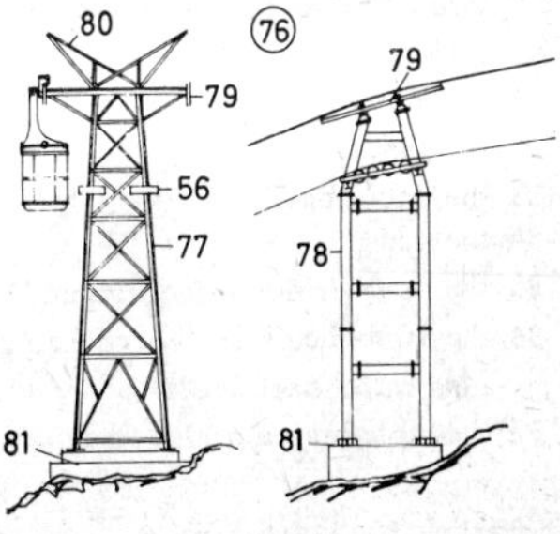

1-54 fixed bridges,

1 cross section of a bridge:
2 the roadway (*Am.* pavement; bridge floor), a steel or concrete road surfacing
3 the kerb
4 the footpath
5 the main truss
6 the cross tie (transverse girder)
7 the main (longitudinal) girder or web
8 the bracket
9 the outside girder
10 the bridge railing
11 the wind bracing;
12 the arch (arched bridge):
13 the pier
14 the detached ice guard
15 the bridge pier
16 the arched span;
17 the pontoon bridge (bateau bridge), an emergency bridge (temporary bridge) of bridge members:
18 the pontoon (bateau)
19 the anchor chain
20 the bridge girder (bridge beam, deck)
21 the wooden plank flooring (bridge flooring);
22 the suspension bridge:
23 the suspension rod (vertical tie)
24 the main cable
25 the bridge tower (*both:* bridge portal)
26 the cable anchorage
27 the stiffening girder
28 the abutment with wing wall
29 the icebreaker (cutwater);
30 the plate girder bridge (solid-web girder bridge) with plain (solid) web girders, a flat bridge:
31 the transverse stiffening
32 the pier
33 the bridge bearing
34 the span;
35 the bow-string girder bridge :
36 the parabolic girder (bow-string girder, *Am.* camel-back girder);
37 the cable-braced bridge (diagonal-cable bridge):
38 the bracing cable (diagonal cable)
39 the tower cross piece
40 the diagonal-cable anchorage;
41 the arch bridge:
42 the arch springer
43 the bridge strut
44 the arch crown;
45 the wooden (timber) bridge:
46 the bridge pile (bridge pier);
47 the lattice bridge (truss bridge, N-truss bridge, Pratt truss bridge), a steel bridge,
48–54 the bridge lattice work:
48 the top chord
49 the bottom chord, a boom
50 the strut
51 the tie
52 the system (assemblage, terminal) point
53 the upper wind bracing
54 the portal (entrance);

55-70 moving bridges,

55 the swing bridge:
56 the direction of rotation
57 the wheel race
58 the pivot pier
59 the pivot drive (turning machinery)
60 the locking pins;
61 the bascule bridge (trunnion-bascule bridge, balance bridge):
62 the bridge leaf (bascule)
63 the rack
64 the pinion;
65 the vertical lift bridge:
66 the jacking pier
67 the driving pulley
68 the lifting span (lift)
69 the counterweight
70 the lifting height

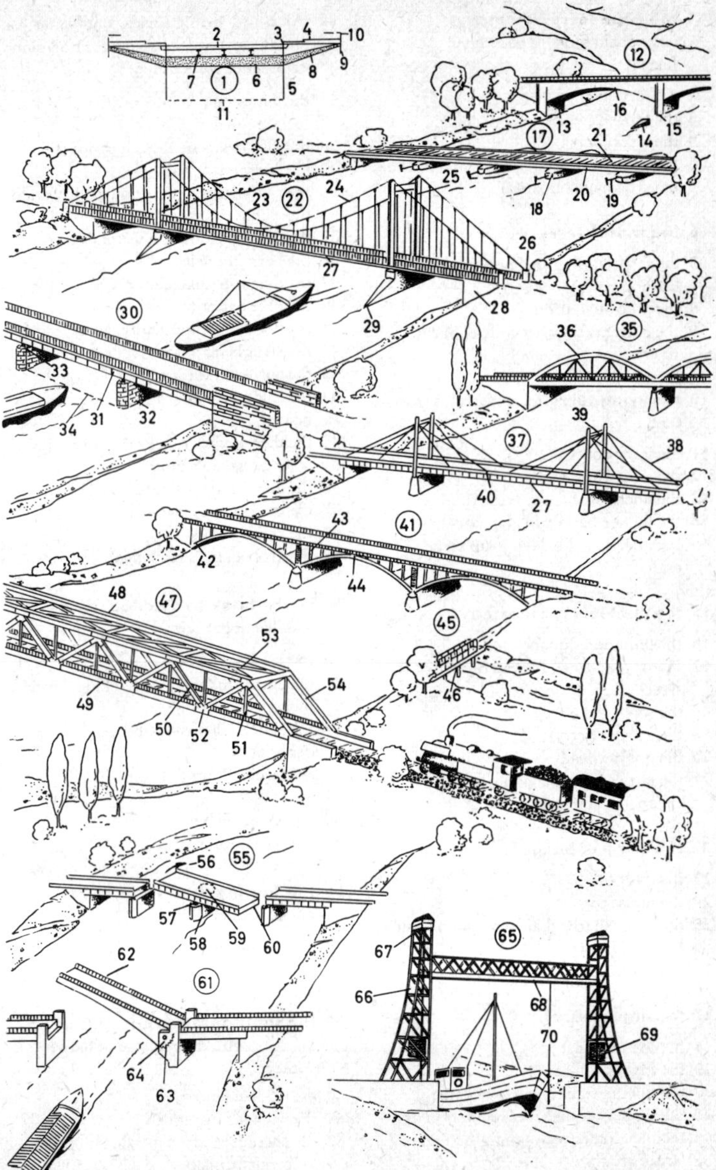
1
2
3
4
5
6
7
8
9
10
11
12
13
14
15
16
17
18
19
20
21
22
23
24
25
26
27
28
29
30
31
32
33
34
35
36
37
38
39
40
41
42
43
44
45
46
47
48
49
50
51
52
53
54
55
56
57
58
59
60
61
62
63
64
65
66
67
68
69
70

1 **the rope ferry** (cable ferry; *also :* chain ferry), a passenger ferry:

2 the ferryman
3 the ferry rope;
4 the river islet
5 the collapsed portion of the river bank, flood damage (erosion)

6 **the motor ferry:**

7 the ferry landing stage (motorboat landing stage)
8 the pile foundation;
9 the current (flow, or course, of the river)

10 **the flying ferry** (river ferry), a car ferry:

11 the ferry boat
12 the buoy (float)
13 the anchorage (*Am.* tying);
14 the winter harbour (*Am.* harbor; harbour for laying-up river craft)

15 **the punt ferry,** a boat ferry:

16 the punt pole (quant);
17 the stagnant water (dead branch of the river)
18 the stake (pile)
19 the groyne (jetty):
20 the groyne head;
21 the fairway (ship channel, navigable channel, waterway)

22 **the chain of barges:**

23 the river tug
24 the house tug
25 the barge in tow (cargo barge, freight barge, lighter)
26 the bargee (bargeman, lighterman);

27 **towing** (haulage):

28 the towing mast
29 the towing engine
30 the towing track; *form.* towpath;
31 the river after the river regulation or rectification (stream-straightening, stream-training)

32 **the flood bank** (dyke; highwater, or flood dike, or embankment; flood dam; main dike, winter dike):

33 the temporary, reinforced flood protection
34 the dike drainage lock or sluice
35 the wing (end) wall
36 the outfall ditch (drain outfall), a draining ditch
37 the drain (infiltration water drain)
38 the berm (dike ledge)
39 the dike top (dike summit);
40 the dike batter (dike slope)
41 the flood bed (inundation area)
42 the river bend in the river course
43 the current indicator
44 the kilometre board (*Am.* kilometer board)
45 the dike-keeper's (reeve's) cottage; *also :* ferryman's house
46 the dike-keeper (dike reeve)
47 the dike ramp
48 the summer dike
49 the river dam (*Am.* levee)

50-55 **the bank protection** (bank stabilization):

50 the sandbags
51 the enrockment (stone packing, stone filling)
52 the alluvial deposit (sand deposit)
53 the fascine (bundle of brushwood)
54 the wicker fences
55 the stone riprap;

56 **the floating dredger,** a multi-bucket ladder dredger:

57 the bucket chain
58 the dredging bucket;

59 **the sand-pump dredger** (suction dredger) with drag nozzle or barge sucker:

60 the pressure pump
61 the back-scouring valve
62 the suction pump, a nozzle pump with scouring nozzles

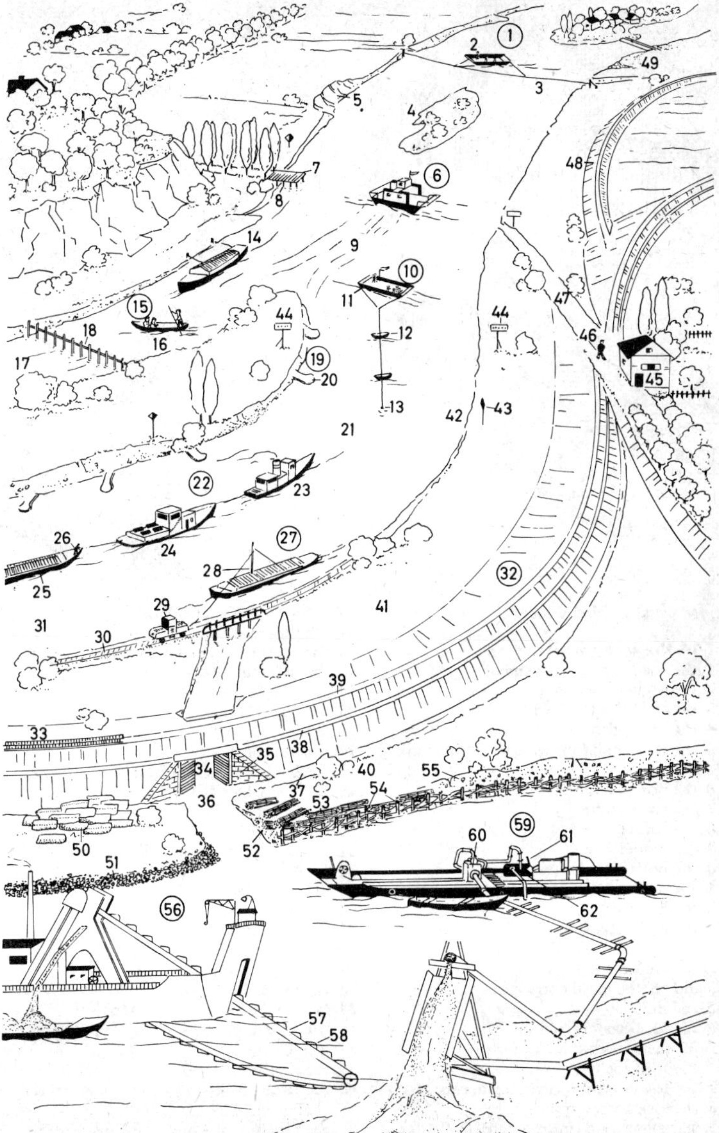
1
2
3
4
5
6
7
8
9
10
11
12
13
14
15
16
17
18
19
20
21
22
23
24
25
26
27
28
29
30
31
32
33
34
35
36
37
38
39
40
41
42
43
44
44
45
46
47
48
49
50
51
52
53
54
55
56
57
58
59
60
61
62

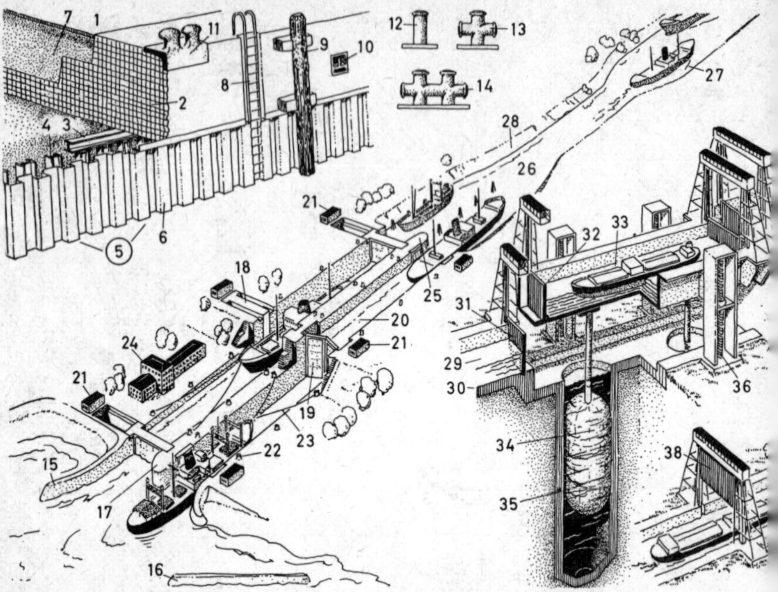

Engl. canal = *Am.* waterway

1-14 the quay wall:
1 the road surface (pavement)
2 the body of the wall
3 the steel sleeper (*Am.* steel tie)
4 the steel pile
5 the sheet wall (pile wall, sheet-pile bulkhead):
6 the box-plate pile;
7 the back filling
8 the ladder
9 the fender pile
10 the bollard niche (recess)
11 the double bollard, negro-head bollard
12 the bollard
13 the cross-shaped bollard, mooring bitt
14 the cross-head bollard;
15-28 the canal,
15 and 16 the canal entrance:
15 the mole
16 the breakwater;
17–25 the staircase locks (chain of locks, flight of locks):
17 the lower head (downstream end)
18 the lock gate, a sliding gate
19 the mitre gate (mitred gate, leaf gate; *Am.* miter, or mitered, gate)
20 the lock chamber (lock)
21 the power house
22 the hauling capstan, a capstan
23 the hauling rope, a rope
24 the canal administration
25 the upper head;
26 the lay-by
27 the passing place
28 the bank scarp (bank slope);
29-38 the ship lift (*Am.* ship elevator):
29 the lower reach
30 the canal bottom
31 the reach gate, a vertical lift gate
32 the lock-chamber gate
33 the ship chamber
34 the float, a buoyant body
35 the float shaft
36 the lifting spindle (lifting screw)
37 the upper reach
38 the vertical lift gate;
39-44 the pump storage station (pump-fed power station, water-pumping plant):
39 the reservoir (forebay)
40 the surge tank (intake chamber, water chamber)
41 the pressure pipeline
42 the sluice-valve (sluice-gate) house

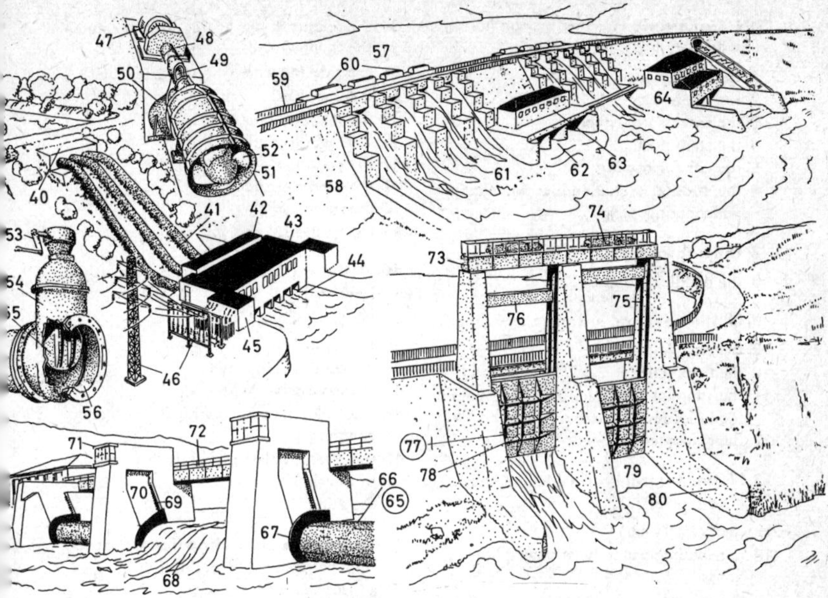

43 the turbine house (pumping station)
44 the discharge structure (headway structure, outlet structure);
45 the control station
46 the transformer station
47-52 the wing pump (vane pump, semi-rotary pump):
47 the driving motor
48 the gear
49 the driving shaft
50 the pressure pipe
51 the suction funnel
52 the impeller wing wheel (vane wheel);
53-56 the slide valve (sluice valve, gate valve):
53 the crank drive
54 the valve housing
55 the slide (gate)
56 the discharge opening (sluiceway);
57-64 the dam (barrage):
57 the storage pool (storage lake, storage reservoir, impounded lake)
58 the masonry dam
59 the dam crest (dam top)
60 the spillway (overflow)
61 the stilling basin (absorption, *Am.* stilling pool)
62 the bottom discharge tunnel (outlet tunnel, sluiceway, scour outlet)
63 the sluice-valve house (sluice-gate house)
64 the power station;
65-72 the roller dam (roller weir), a barrage; *other system :* shutter weir,
65 the roller, a barrier:
66 the roller top
67 the side-plate;
68 the submergible roller
69 the geared (toothed) rack
70 the niche (recess)
71 the hoisting gear cabin (hoisting winch cabin)
72 the weir service gangway (service bridge);
73-80 the sluice dam (sluice weir):
73 the hoisting gear bridge
74 the winding gear
75 the guide groove
76 the balance weight (counterweight, counterpoise)
77 the sluice (sluice gate, penning gate, floodgate):
78 the stiffening rib (reinforcing rib);
79 the dam sill (weir sill)
80 the side wall (wing wall, abutment)

213 Types of Historical Ships

1-6 Germanic rowing barge [about 400 A. D.], the Nydam boat:

1 the stern post
2 the steersman
3 the rowers (oarsmen)
4 the stem post
5 the oar for rowing
6 the rudder, a side rudder for steering (the steering oar);

7 **the dug-out**, a hollowed-out tree trunk
8 the paddle

9-12 the trireme, a Roman warship:

9 the ram
10 the forecastle
11 the grapnel (grapple, grappling beam) for holding the enemy ship
12 the three tiers of oars;

13-17 the Viking ship ('dragon' ship [Old Norse]):

13 the helm (tiller)
14 the awning crutch with carved horse heads
15 the awning
16 the dragon figure head
17 the shield;

18-26 the cog (Hanse cog, Hanse ship):

18 the anchor cable (anchor hawser)
19 the forecastle (fo'c'sle)
20 the bowsprit
21 the furled (brailed-up, clewed-up) squaresail
22 the town banner (city banner)
23 the after castle
24 the rudder, a stern rudder
25 the rounded stern
26 the wooden fender;

27-43 the caravel (carvel) ['Santa Maria' 1492]:

27 the admiral's cabin
28 the spanker boom
29 the spanker (driver, mizzen), a Lateen sail
30 the spanker yard (Lateen yard)
31 the mizzen mast
32 the lashings
33 the mainsail (maincourse), a squaresail
34 the bonnet, a removable strip of canvas
35 the bowline
36 the side buntline (martinet, martnet)
37 the mainyard
38 the main topsail
39 the main topsail yard
40 the mainmast
41 the foresail (forecourse)
42 the foremast
43 the spritsail;

44-50 the galley [15th to 18th cent.], a slave galley:

44 the lantern
45 the cabin
46 the central gangway
47 the slave driver with whip
48 the galley slaves (rowing slaves, galley convicts)
49 the covered platform in the fore part of the ship
50 the gun;

51-60 the ship of the line (line-of-battle-ship, battleship) [18th/19th cent.], a three-decker:

51 the jib boom
52 the fore topgallant sail
53 the main topgallant sail
54 the mizzen topgallant sail
55–57 the gilded stern:
55 the upper stern
56 the stern gallery
57 the quarter gallery;
58 the lower stern
59 the gun openings for broadside fire
60 the gun port

1
2
3
4
5
6
7
8
9
10
11
12
13
14
15
16
17
18
19
20
21
22
23
24
25
26
27
28
29
30
31
32
33
34
35
36
37
38
39
40
41
42
43
44
45
46
47
48
49
50
51
52
53
54
55
56
57
58
59
60

1-72 the rigging (rig, tackle) **and the sails of a bark** (barque),

1-9 the masts:

1 the bowsprit
2–4 the foremast:
2 the lower foremast
3 the fore topmast
4 the fore topgallant mast;
5 and 6 the mainmast:
5 the lower mainmast
6 the main topmast;
7 the main topgallant mast
8 and 9 the mizzen mast (mizen mast):
8 the lower mizzen mast
9 the mizzen topmast;

10-19 the standing rigging:

10 the fore, main and mizzen stay
11 the fore, main and mizzen topmast stay
12 the fore, main and mizzen topgallant stay
13 the fore and main royal stay
14 the jib stay
15 the bobstay
16 the shrouds
17 the topmast rigging
18 the topgallant rigging
19 the backstays;

20-31 the fore-and aft sails:

20 the fore topmast staysail
21 the inner jib
22 the outer jib
23 the flying jib
24 the main topmast staysail
25 the main topgallant staysail
26 the main royal staysail
27 the mizzen staysail
28 the mizzen topmast staysail
29 the mizzen topgallant staysail
30 the spanker (driver)
31 the gaff topsail;

32-45 the spars:

32 the fore yard
33 the lower fore topsail yard
34 the upper fore topsail yard
35 the lower fore topgallant yard
36 the upper fore topgallant yard
37 the fore royal yard
38 the mainyard
39 the lower main topsail yard
40 the upper main topsail yard
41 the lower main topgallant yard
42 the upper main topgallant yard
43 the main royal yard
44 the spanker boom
45 the spanker gaff;
46 the foot rope
47 the lifts
48 the spanker boom topping lift
49 the peak pendant (spanker gaff lift)
50 the foretop
51 the fore topmast cross trees
52 the main top
53 the main topmast cross trees
54 the mizzen top

55-66 the square sails:

55 the foresail
56 the lower fore topsail
57 the upper fore topsail
58 the lower fore topgallant sail
59 the upper fore topgallant sail
60 the fore royal sail
61 the main sail
62 the lower main topsail
63 the upper main topsail
64 the lower main topgallant sail
65 the upper main topgallant sail
66 the main royal sail;

67-71 the running rigging:

67 the braces
68 the sheets
69 the jigger sheet
70 the spanker vangs
71 the buntline;
72 the reef

214

1
2
3
4
5
6
7
8
9
10
11
12
13
14
15
16
17
18
19
20
21
22
23
24
25
26
27
28
29
30
31
32
33
34
35
36
37
38
39
40
41
42
43
44
45
46
47
48
49
50
51
52
53
54
55
56
57
58
59
60
61
62
63
64
65
66
67
68
69
70
71
72

1-5 forms of sails:

1 the gaffsail (*small:* trysail, spencer)

2 the gib

3 the Lateen sail

4 the lugsail

5 the spritsail;

6-8 single-masted sailing boats (*Am.* sailboats),

6 the gaff-rigged sloop:

7 the lee board;

8 the cutter;

9 and 10 mizzen-masted sailing boats (*Am.* sailboats):

9 the ketch

10 the yawl;

11-17 two-masted sailing vessels,

11–13 the topsail schooner:

11 the mainsail

12 the boom fore sail

13 the square fore sail;

14 the brig schooner:

15 the half-rigged mast with fore and aft sails

16 the full-rigged mast with square sails;

17 the brig;

18-27 three-masted (three-mast) **sailing vessels** (three-masters):

18 the three-masted fore-and-aft schooner

19 the three-masted topsail schooner

20 the barque schooner

21–23 the bark (barque) [cf. plans of rigging and sails on plate 214]:

21 the foremast

22 the main mast

23 the mizzen mast;

24–27 the full-rigged ship (ship):

24 the mizzen mast

25 the crossjack (cro'jack) yard

26 the crossjack sail

27 the row of ports;

28-31 four-masted (four-mast) **ships** (four-masters):

28 the four-mast fore and aft schooner

29 the four-masted barque:

30 the mizzen mast;

31 the four-masted full-rigged ship;

32-34 the five-masted bark or barque:

32 the skysail

33 the mizzen mast

34 the jigger;

35-37 the development of sailing ships over 400 years:

35 the five-mast full-rigged ship 'Preußen'

36 the British clipper 'Spindrift'

37 the caravel (caravelle, carvel) 'Santa Maria'

1
2
3
4
5
6
7
8
9
10
11
12
13
14
15
16
17
18
19
20
21
22
23
24
25
26
27
28
29
30
31
32
33
34
35
36
37

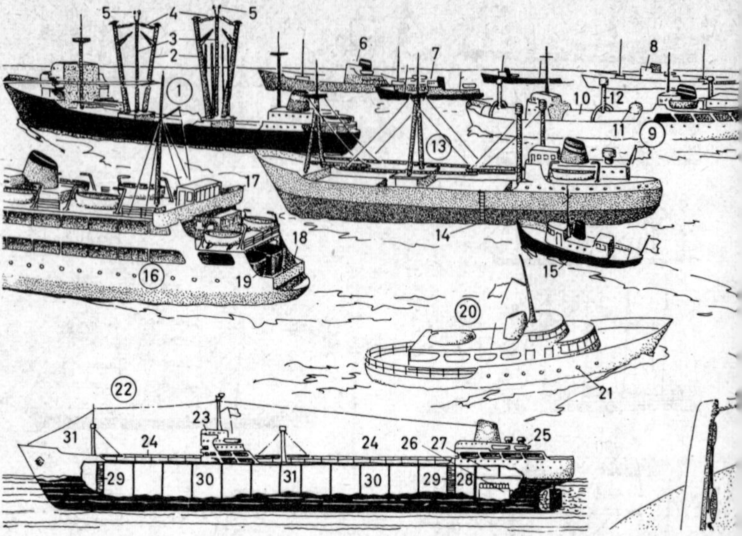

1 the heavy lift cargo ship, a cargo ship (merchant ship, merchantman, cargo boat) specially designed for foreign-going trade:
2 the heavy lift derrick
3 the heavy cargo boom (derrick)
4 the lifting tackle (purchase), a set of pulleys, a strong tackle
5 the pulley head;
6 the factory trawler
7 the trawler, a fishing vessel
8 the banana boat, a fruit-carrier
9 the liquid-gas tanker:
10 the gas tank
11 the dome
12 the gas vent for burning gas residues;
13 the motor cargo ship for intermediate trade:
14 the Jacob's ladder, a rope ladder;
15 the pilot vessel
16 the train ferry (ferry boat, ferry bridge):
17 the manoeuvring (*Am.* maneuvring) bridge
18 the ferry deck
19 the railway carriage (*Am.* railroad car);
20 the private launch, a motor launch:
21 the port hole (port);
22 the tanker (ocean tanker):
23 the navigating bridge superstructure
24 the fore-and-aft gangway (*Am.* gang plank)
25 the engine room superstructure
26 the engine room
27 the auxiliary engine room
28 the oil fuel tank
29 the coffer dam
30 the tank
31 the pump-room;
32 the passenger liner (passenger steamer, ocean steamship), an ocean-going liner (atlantic liner, transatlantic liner)

33 the motor passenger ship:
34 the gangway (*Am.* gang plank)
35 the disembarkation;
36 the seaside resort pleasure boat (excursion vessel) on her maiden trip (maiden voyage):
37 the bunting (*Am.* colors) [on a ship dressed 'over all'];
38 the coasting (home-trade) motorship (coaster, coastal craft) for coastal trade (*Am.* for cabotage)
39 the customs launch
40 the cattle boat, a special vessel:
41 the companion way (companion)
42 the ventilator
43 the side port
44 the freeing port;
45–66 the excursion boat (pleasure steamer),
45–50 the lifeboat launching gear:
45 the davit
46 the wire span
47 the man rope
48 the purchase (block and tackle):
49 the block
50 the tackle;
51 the tarpaulin
52 the passenger
53 the steward
54 the deck chair
55 the cabin boy
56 the bucket
57 the boatswain (*Am. coll.* bosun):
58 the tunic (jacket);
59 the awning:
60 the awning stanchion
61 the awning spar
62 the strop;
63 the night life buoy:
64 the patent flare;
65 the officer of the watch:
66 the duty jacket (working jacket)

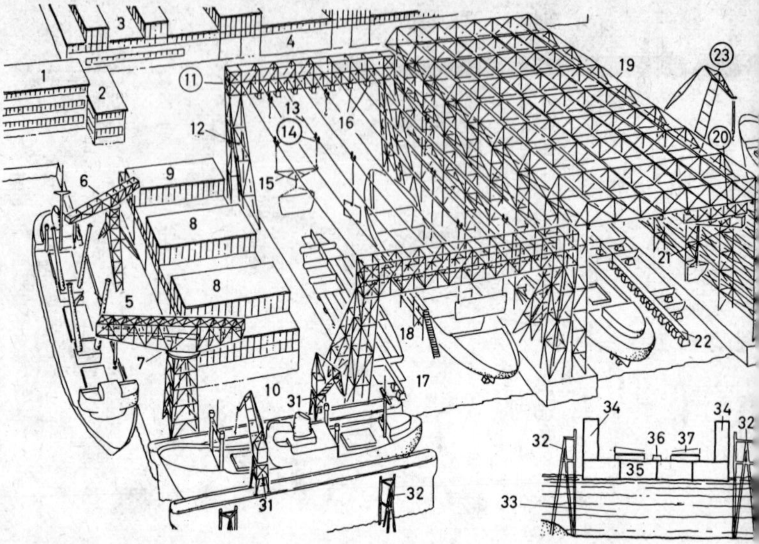

1-40 the shipyard (dockyard, *Am.* navy yard):

1 the general offices
2 the drawing office
3 and 4 the ship-building hangar:
3 the mould loft (*Am.* mold loft)
4 the erection shop;
5–9 the fitting-out quay:
5 the quay
6 the tripod crane
7 the hammer-headed crane
8 the engine workshop
9 the boiler shop;
10 the repair quay

11-26 the building slip (slip, slipway, launching way),

11–18 the cable crane berth (cable slipway),
11 the slipway portal:
12 the portal support;
13 the crane cable
14 the crab:
15 the cross piece;
16 the crane-driver's cabin
17 the slipway floor
18 the scaffolding;
19–21 the frame slipway:
19 the slipway frame
20 the overhead travelling (*Am.* traveling) crane (gantry crane):
21 the slewing crab;
22 the keel in position
23–26 the modern crane slipway,
23 the luffing jib crane, a slipway crane:
24 the crane track;
25 the hull frames in position
26 the new ship (ship under construction);

27-30 the dry dock (graving dock):

27 the dock floor
28 the dock gates (caisson, dock pontoon, closing pontoon, floodgates)
29 the cantilever crane
30 the pumping station;

31-40 the floating dry dock:

31 the dock crane, a gib crane
32 the fender dolphins
33–40 dock layout:
33 the dock basin
34 and 35 the dock structure:
34 the side tank
35 the floor tank (bottom tank);
36 the keel blocks

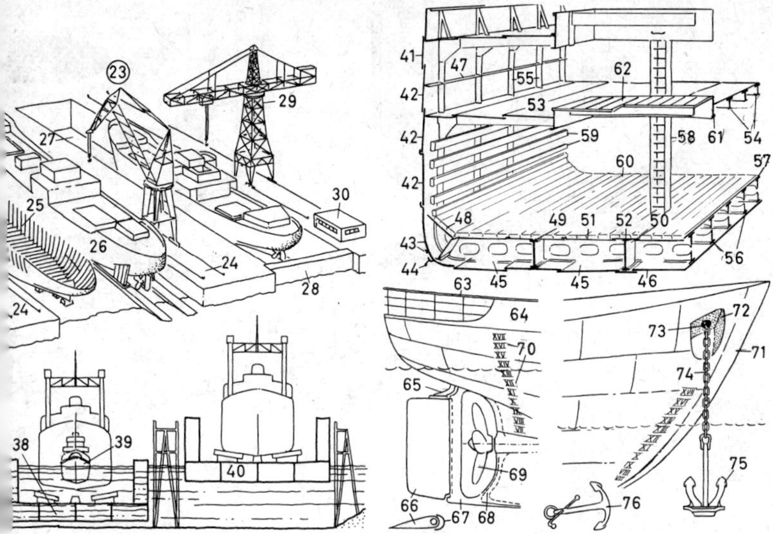

37 the bilge blocks
38–40 docking a ship:
38 the flooded (filled) floating dry dock
39 the tug towing the ship (*Am.* towboat, tugboat)
40 the emptied (pumped-out) dock;

41-58 the ship's structural parts,

41–53 the longitudinal strength,
41–46 the shell plating (outer skin):
41 the sheerstrake (sheerwale)
42 the side strake
43 the bilge strake
44 the bilge keel (rolling chock)
45 the bottom plating (garboard strake)
46 the flat-plate keel (keel plate);
47 the side stringer
48 the tank margin plate (wing girder)
49 the side girder
50 the centre (*Am.* center or through) girder (keelson, kelson, vertical centre plate)
51 the tank top plating (tank crown)
52 the centre (*Am.* center) strake
53 the deck plating;
54 the deck beam
55 the rib (frame)
56 the floor plate
57 the double bottom
58 the hold stanchion (hold pillar);
59 and 60 the dunnage:
59 the side cargo battens (spar ceiling)
60 the ceiling;
61 and 62 the hatchway:
61 the hatch coaming
62 the hatch cover;
63–69 the stern:
63 the rails
64 the bulwark
65 the rudder stock
66 and 67 the Oertz rudder:
66 the rudder blade
67 and 68 the stern frame:
67 the rudder post
68 the propeller post (screw post);
69 the ship's screw (ship's propeller);
70 the draught marks (*Am.* draft numerals)
71–73 the bow:
71 the stem
72 the hawse
73 the hawse pipe;
74 the anchor cable
75 the patent (stockless) anchor
76 the stock anchor (standard anchor, *Am.* common anchor)

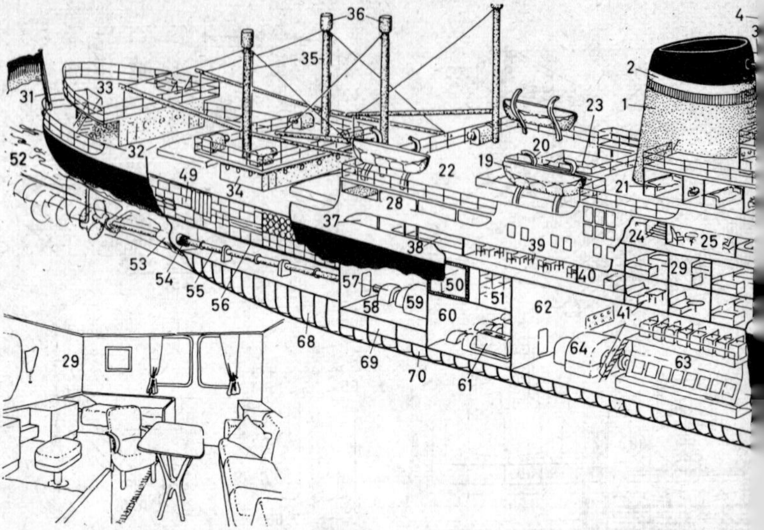

1-71 the combined passenger and cargo motorship (passenger and freight vessel or boat):

1 the funnel

2 the funnel marking

3 the ship's siren (foghorn)

4–11 the monkey island:

4 the aerial lead-in

5 the D. F. aerial or loop (*Am.* aural null loop)

6 the azimuth (standard) compass

7 the signalling (*Am.* signaling) lamp (morse lamp)

8 the radar scanner

9 the flag signal

10 the signal halyards

11 the triatic stay;

12–18 the bridge deck (navigating bridge):

12 the wireless (*Am.* radio) cabin

13 the captain's cabin

14 the chart room

15 the starboard side light [green; the port light on the other side: red]

16 the wing of the bridge

17 the wind deflecting screen (dodger)

18 the wheel house;

19–21 the boat deck:

19 the lifeboat

20 the davit

21 the officer's cabin;

22–27 the promenade deck:

22 the sun deck (lido deck, sports deck)

23 the swimming pool

24 the companion way

25 the ship's library

26 the lounge

27 the promenade;

28–30 the A-deck:

28 the semi-enclosed deck space

29 the two-berth cabin, a cabin

30 the luxury (state) cabin;

31 the ensign staff

32–42 the B-deck (main deck):

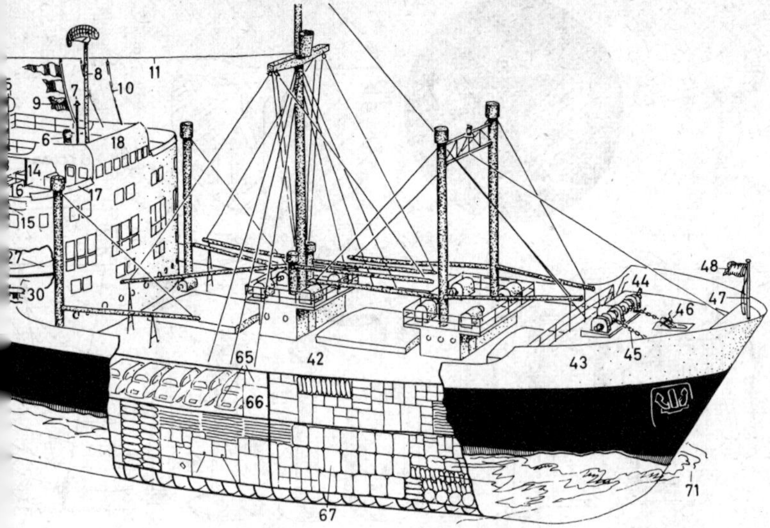

32 the after deck
33 the poop
34 the deck house
35 the samson post
36 the ventilator head
37 the galley (*Am.* caboose; cook room, ship's kitchen)
38 the pantry
39 the dining saloon
40 the purser's office
41 the one-berth (single, single-bed) cabin
42 the fore deck;
43 the forecastle (bows)
44–46 the anchor gear:
44 the windlass
45 the anchor chain (cable chain, anchor cable)
46 the chain stop;
47 the jack staff
48 the forward jack
49 the after holds
50 the refrigerating chamber (cold-storage room)
51 the store room (*Am.* commissaries)
52 the wake
53 the shaft brackets
54 the stuffing box (gland)
55 the propeller shaft
56 the shaft tunnel (shaft trunk, tail shaft passage)
57 the thrust block
58–64 the diesel electric ship drive:
58 the electric motor room
59 the electric motor
60 the auxiliary engine room
61 the auxiliary engine
62 the main engine room
63 the main engine, a marine diesel engine
64 the generator;
65 the forward holds
66 the between decks
67 the cargo ('tween decks)
68 the double-bottom tank (*Am.* container) for water ballast
69 the fresh-water tank
70 the oil fuel tank
71 the bow wave

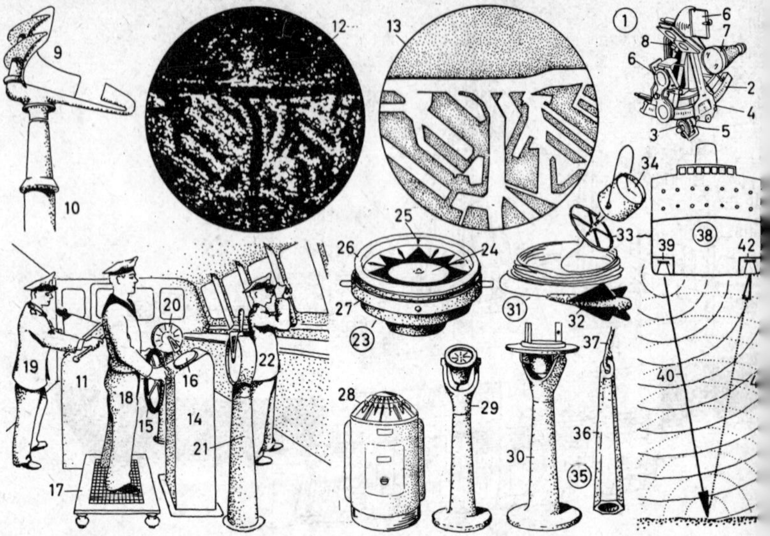

1 the sextant:
2 the graduated arc (graduated limb)
3 the micrometer drum
4 the index bar
5 the vernier
6 the index mirror and horizon glass
7 the telescope
8 the grip;

9-13 the radar unit (radio detecting and ranging apparatus):
9 the scanner
10 the scanner support
11 the radar display unit
12 the plan position indicator (P. P. I.)
13 the radar image seen on a chart (chart section);

14-22 the wheel house:
14 the steering column
15 the steering wheel
16 the steering compass
17 the quartermaster's (helmsman's, *Am.* wheelsman's) grating
18 the quartermaster (helmsman, *Am.* wheelsman)
19 the navigating officer
20 the engine room telegraph
21 the docking telegraph (*Am.* maneuvring telegraph)
22 the captain;

23-30 compasses,
23 the liquid compass, a magnetic compass:
24 the compass card
25 the lubber line
26 the compass bowl
27 the gimbals
28–30 the gyro compass unit:
28 the master compass
29 the repeater compass
30 the gyroscopic repeater with pelorus (*Am.* with bearing plate);

31 the patent log (taffrail log), a log:
32 the rotator
33 the governor
34 the log register;

35-42 leads (sounding leads, sounding lines),
35 the hand lead (*Am.* plumb bob):
36 the lead (sinker)
37 the lead line;
38 the echo sounder:

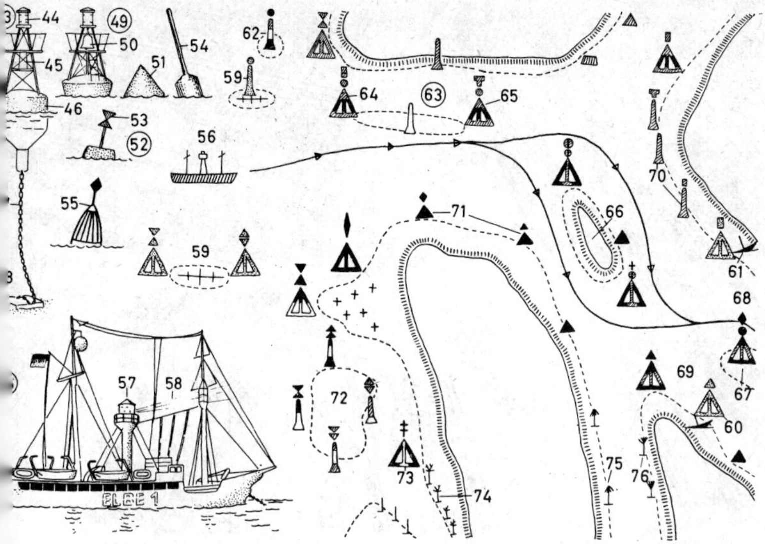

39 the sound transmitter (sound emission microphone, *Am.* impulse microphone, impulse mike)
40 the sound signal
41 the echo
42 the echo receiver;

43-76 sea marks (nautical marks) used for buoyage and lighting,
43–58 fairway marks (channel marks),
43 the light and whistle buoy:
44 the lantern
45 the buoy whistle
46 the buoy
47 the buoy chain
48 the buoy stone (sinker);
49 the light and bell buoy:
50 the buoy bell;
51 the conical buoy [black]
52 the can buoy:
53 the top mark;
54 the spar buoy [red]
55 the beacon buoy
56 the lightship (light-vessel):
57 the lantern tower, a tower mast
58 the beam of light;
59–76 marks in navigable water [German type]:
59 wreck [green buoys]
60 wreck on (to) starboard
61 wreck on (to) port
62 shallows (shallow ground, shallow water, shelves, shoals, *Am.* flats)
63 middle ground (*Am.* center bank) to port:
64 division
65 confluence;
66 middle ground (*Am.* center bank)
67 middle ground (*Am.* center bank) to starboard
68 the main fairway
69 the secondary fairway
70 port hand buoys [red]
71 starboard hand buoys [black]
72 shallows (shallow ground, shallow water, shelves, shoals, *Am.* flats) outside the fairway
73 the middle of the fairway
74 perches (pricks, *Am.* spears) on port hand
75 poles (marking posts) on starboard hand
76 poles (marking posts) on port hand

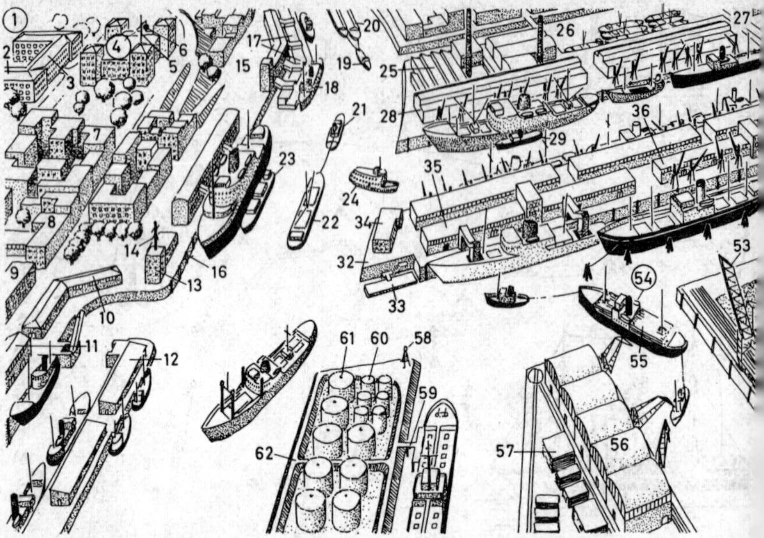

Engl. harbour = *Am.* harbor

1 the harbour hospital:
2 the quarantine station
3 the institute for tropical diseases (for tropical medicine);
4 the meteorological offices (*Am.* weather bureau), a meteorological station:
5 the signal mast
6 the storm signal (storm warning);
7 the harbour quarter

8-12 the fishing harbour (fishing port):

8 the net factory
9 the cannery
10 the packing shed
11 the fish auction market
12 the equipment shed;
13 the harbour office
14 the water level indicator
15 the quay road
16 the passenger quay
17 the landing pier (landing stage)
18 the pleasure steamer (excursion steamer)
19 the harbour launch
20 the barge (lighter)
21 the tug (steam tug, tug boat, tow boat)
22 the sea-going barge or lighter
23 the bunkering tanker
24 the harbour ferry (ferry boat)

25-62 the free port (docks):

25 the harbour industry
26 the inner harbour
27 the harbour canal
28–31 the transshipment harbour:
28 the transit shed
29 the water boat
30 the lighter
31 the warehouse;
32–36 the quay (wharf):
32 the mole (jetty)
33 the landing stage (pontoon)
34 the harbour customs house
35 the banana shed

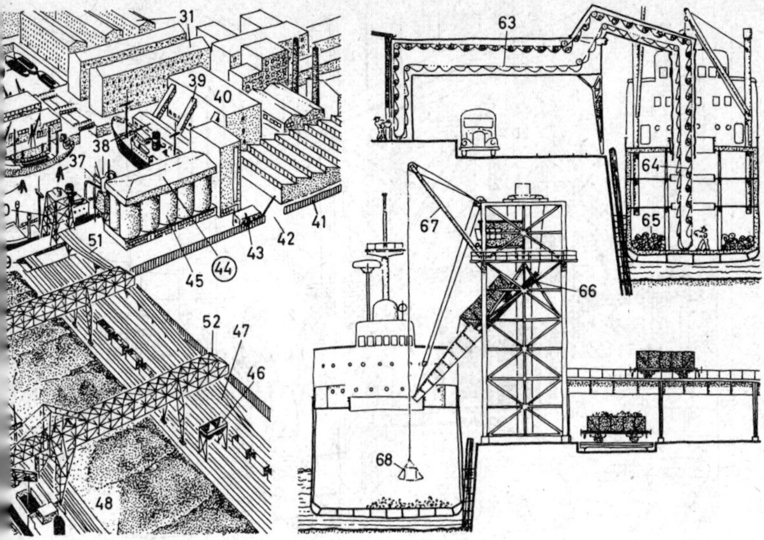

36 the fruit shed;
37 the dolphins
38 the storage shed
39 the conveyor belt
40 the cold-storage house
41–43 the free port boundary:
41 the customs fence
42 and 43 the customs entrance:
42 the customs barrier
43 the customs house;
44–53 the bulk goods wharf,
44 the silos:
45 the silo bin;
46–53 the coal wharf:
46 the elevated weighing bunker
47 the harbour railway (*Am.* harbor railroad)
48 the coal depot
49–51 the coaling station:
49 the shunting platform
50 the coal chute
51 the falling track;
52 the loading bridge (gantry)
53 the jib (boom, arm);
54 a timber ship:
55 the deck cargo (deck load);
56 and 57 the timber wharf:
56 the timber storage sheds
57 the timber stock (*Am.* lumber wharf);
58 the harbour light
59–62 the oil wharf (mineral oil wharf, petroleum wharf):
59 the pipe bridge
60 the intermediate tank
61 the storage tank
62 the safety dam;

63-68 the transshipment,

63 and 64 the banana elevator:
63 the conveyor belt
64 the conveyor bucket;
65 the banana cluster ('stick' of bananas)
66–68 the coal chute crane:
66 the lift platform (*Am.* elevator platform)
67 the boom (jib)
68 the coal distributor (coal trimmer)

221 The Harbour (Port) II

Engl. harbour = *Am.* harbor

1-36 the loading and unloading of vessels,

1–21 dockside (quayside) activity,
1–7 the slewing pillar crane (slewing portal crane):
1 the column (slewing column)
2 the jib (arm, boom)
3 the rack (gear rack)
4 the slewing gear
5 the all-round-view cabin
6 the toothed gear rim or gear ring
7 the crane portal (gantry);
8 the loading officer
9 the harbour railway (*Am.* harbor rail-road)
10 the loading wharf
11 the car slings
12 the fork truck (fork lift):
13 the lifting device;
14 the loading net
15 the trolley
16 the cargo hook
17 the two-fingered leather mitten
18 the barrow
19 the wall crane:
20 the weight
21 the crane hook;
22–36 work in the wharf shed:
22 the shed foreman (stevedore)
23 the docker (dock labourer, *Am.* dock laborer, longshoreman)
24 the water clerk
25 the bill of lading
26 the weigher
27 the tallyman (cargo-checker, tally clerk)
28 the yardstick
29 the bale gauge (*Am.* bale gage), a measuring device
30–36 the shed (wharf shed, transit shed):
30 the entrance (shed entrance)
31 the sliding door (door)
32 and **33** the weighbridge:
32 the platform scale (underfloor scale)
33 the balance column;

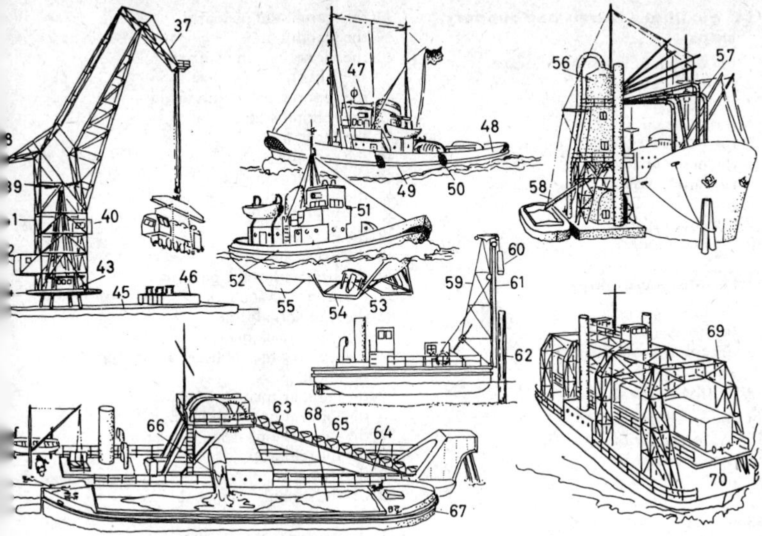

34 the bale (bale of goods)
35 the mark (identification mark)
36 the lot (stack, pile);

37-70 special harbour boats or vessels,

37–46 the floating crane:
37 the jib
38 the balance weight (counterweight)
39 the adjusting spindle
40 the crane-driver's cabin
41 the crane frame
42 the power cabin
43 the conning bridge
44 the turntable
45 the pontoon, a pram
46 the engine superstructure;
47–50 the ocean-going tug:
47 the wind dodger (splash dodger)
48 the rubbing strake
49 the port side (*form.* larboard) [port = on the left]
50 the fender;
51–55 the harbour tug, a harbour tow boat:
51 the wind-deflecting screens
52 the starboard side [starboard = on the right]
53 the Voith-Schneider propulsion
54 the propeller guard
55 the fixed deep keel;
56–58 the grain-elevator:
56 the container (silo)
57 the suction pipe
58 the loading pipe;
59–62 the pile-driver:
59 the ram framework
60 the ramming weight (ram, tup, beetle head, rammer)
61 the guide
62 the tilting (rocker, pivoting) bearing;
63–68 the bucket dredger, a dredger:
63 the bucket chain
64 the bucket conveyor
65 the bucket (scoop)
66 the chute
67 the hopper
68 the dredged material;
69 and **70** the train ferry:
69 the hoisting frame
70 the lift platform (hoisting platform)

1-8 auxilliary vessels and support ships,

1 the dock landing ship [*U.S.* type]:
2 the well deck
3 the hull
4 the crane;
5 the icebreaker [*U.S.* type]:
6 the helicopter platform
7 the lattice mast
8 the ice-breaking bows;
9 the landing craft:
10 the bow doors;

11-13 minor warships,

11 the minesweeper:
12 the boats' davits;
13 the escort vessel (frigate);

14-17 light warships,

14 the small destroyer:
15 the torpedo tubes;
16 the fleet destroyer
17 the large destroyer;

18-64 heavy warships,

18–20 submarines (*Am. coll.* sub):
18 the coastal submarine
19 the ocean-going submarine
20 the nuclear submarine;

21-30 cruisers,

21 the light cruiser:
22 the whip aerial;
23 the heavy cruiser:
24 the twin turret, a gun turret
25 the tripod mast;
26 the battle cruiser:
27 the triple turret
28 the catapult
29 the aircraft crane
30 the aircraft hanger;

31-64 heavily armoured ships (*Am.* armored ships; capital ships),

31 the battleship,
32–35 the ship's armament:
32 the main armament
33 the secondary armament (medium-calibre guns, *Am.* medium-caliber guns)
34 the light guns
35 the automatic A.A. (anti-aircraft) guns of the anti-aircraft defence (*Am.* defense);
36 the range-finder for the heavy guns
37 the range-finder for the medium and light guns
38 the searchlight platform
39 the searchlight
40 the funnel capping (*Am.* smoke stack cap)
41 the superimposed gun turret
42 the splinter screen
43 the turret mast
44 the conning tower
45 the captain's bridge
46 the breakwater
47 the boat derrick
48 the deck plan:
49 the fixed catapult
50 the aircraft storage position
51 the aircraft crane
52 the fore-and-aft line;
53 the lower deck plan:
54 the watertight bulkhead, a transverse bulkhead
55 the compartment
56 the longitudinal bulkhead
57 the side armour (*Am.* side armor)
58 the blister
59 the barbette
60–63 the propulsion machinery:
60 the engine room
61 the marine diesel engine
62 the gear room
63 the gearing;
64 the monitor;

65-77 the aircraft-carrier,

65 the bow elevation:
66 the sponson
67 the aircraft lift (*Am.* aircraft elevator)
68 the island superstructure;
69–74 the flight deck (*Am.* flying deck):
69 the landing deck
70 the landing runway
71 the arrester wires (*Am.* arresting gear, deck brake)
72 the take-off deck
73 the catapult
74 the aircraft lift (*Am.* aircraft elevator);
75 the radar unit
76 the life-saving raft
77 the counter

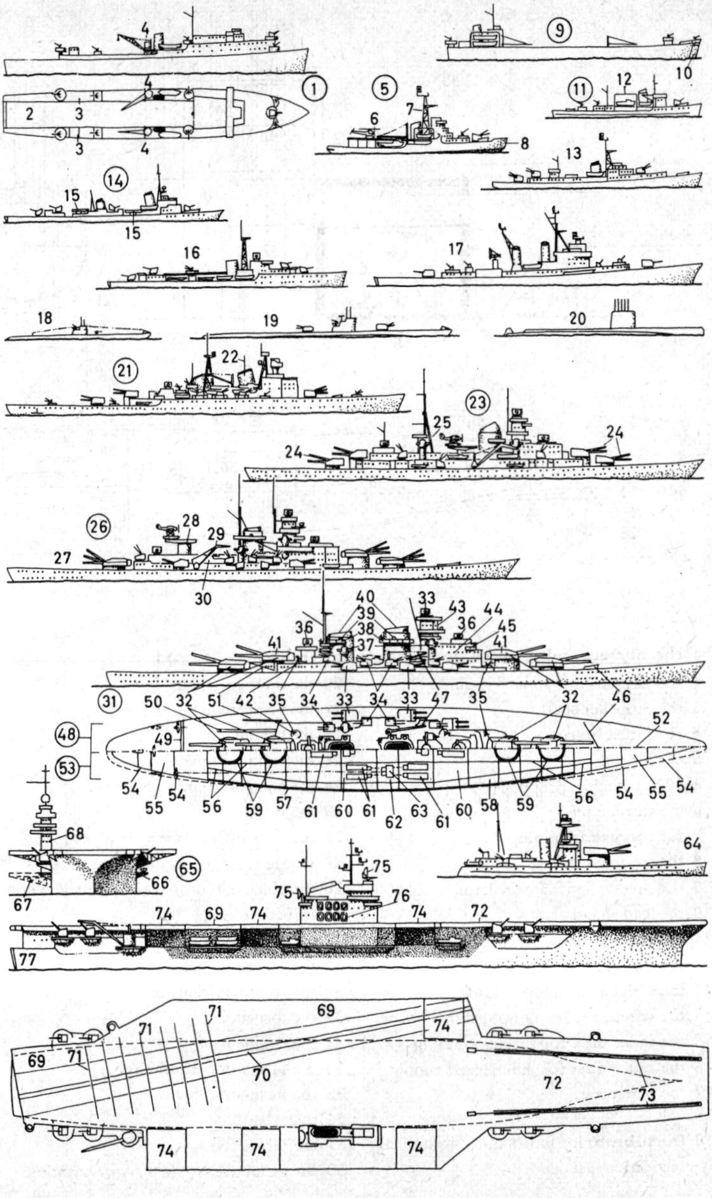
4
1
2
3
3
4
9
10
5
7
6
8
11
12
13
14
15
15
16
17
18
19
20
21
22
23
25
24
24
26
28
29
27
30
40
39
38
37
36
41
33
43
36
44
45
41
31
50
32
51
42
35
34
33
34
33
47
35
32
46
52
48
49
53
54
55
54
56
59
57
61
60
61
62
63
61
60
58
59
56
54
55
54
68
65
66
67
64
75
75
76
74
69
74
74
72
77
71
69
71
74
69
71
70
72
73
74
74
74

223 Warships (Fighting Ships, Men-of-War) II

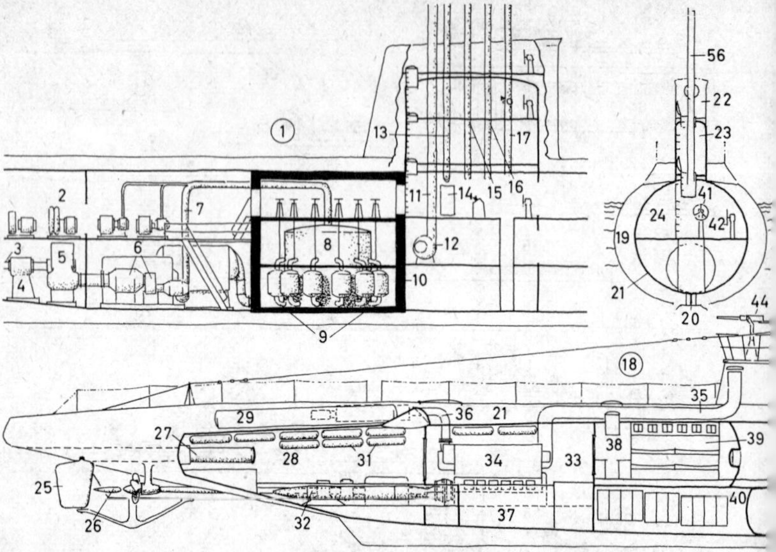

1 the nuclear submarine [midships]:
2 the auxiliary machinery room
3 the propeller shaft
4 the thrust bearing
5 the gearing
6–10 the nuclear propulsion:
6 the turbine set
7 the main steam piping
8 the steam generator
9 the pressurised water reactor
10 the lead shield;
11 the snort (schnorkel, snorkel)
12 the fresh-air blower
13 the aerial lead (antenna lead)
14 the wireless (*Am.* radio) cabin
15 the radar mast for surface running
16 the radar mast for submerged running
17 the periscope;

18 the submarine [cross and longitudinal section]:
19 the main ballast tank
20 the flooding valve
21 the pressure hull
22 the bridge
23 the conning tower
24 the control room
25 the rudder
26 the after hydroplane
27 the stern torpedo tube (stern tube)
28 the electric motor room and the stern torpedo room
29 the torpedo stowage compartment
30 the torpedo hatch
31 the compressed-air bottle
32 the torpedo
33 the engine room
34 the submarine diesel engine
35 the fresh-air inductor
36 the exhaust
37 the oil fuel tank
38 the galley; *on merchant vessels:* caboose

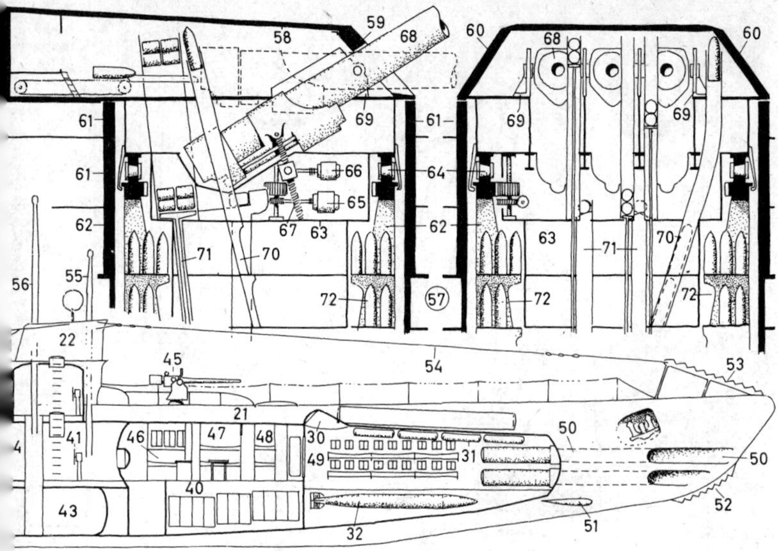

39 the petty officers' mess
40 the battery room
41 the steering wheel
42 the hydroplane control
43 the trimming tank
44 the quick-firing anti-aircraft gun (A.A. gun)
45 the quick-firing gun (*Am.* rapid-fire gun)
46 the captain's (*Am.* commanding officer's) cabin
47 the officers' cabin
48 the chief petty officer's cabin
49 the seamen's (sailors') mess and the forward (bow) torpedo room
50 the forward torpedo tube (bow tube)
51 the forward hydroplane
52 the lower net-cutter
53 the upper net-cutter
54 the aerial (antenna)
55 the low-power (attack) periscope
56 the high-power (search) periscope;
57 **the armoured** (*Am.* armored) **triple rotating turret** of the main armament,
58–60 the rotating armour (*Am.* armor):
58 the turret top
59 the front armour (*Am.* armor)
60 the side armour (*Am.* armor);
61 the barbette (stack armour, *Am.* armor)
62 the supporting cylinder
63 the turret turntable
64 the roller bearings
65 the turret training motor
66 the elevating motor
67 the elevating spindle
68 the gun barrel
69 the gun cradle
70 the shell hoist
71 the cartridge hoist
72 ammunition in readiness

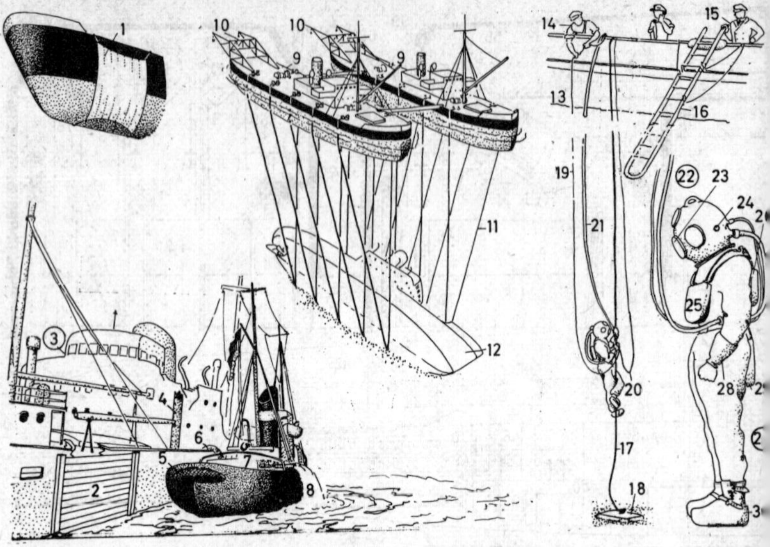

1 and 2 stopping a leak:

1 the sail over the leak, a tarpaulin

2 the patch of beams, boards, and a tarpaulin;

3 the wrecked vessel, a damaged ship:

4 the damage;

5–8 the salvage vessel:

5 the stern fender

6 the suction pipe

7 the pump-hold

8 the pumped-out water;

9-12 raising a wreck (lifting a wreck):

9 the raising ship (salvage vessel)

10 the stern crane

11 the lifting rope

12 the wreck secured below;

13-19 diving (deep-sea diving):

13 the diving boat

14 the surface crew (tender crew, *Am.* wrecking crew)

15 the salvage inspector

16 the diver's ladder

17 the descending line

18 the descending-line weight

19 the communication cord;

20-30 the diver's outfit (equipment of the deep-sea diver):

20 the telephone wire (*Am.* telephone cord)

21 the air tube

22 the diving helmet (diver's helmet):

23 the observation window

24 the air outlet valve;

25 the breast weight

26 the back weight

27 the diving suit (diver's suit):

28 the waterproof cuff

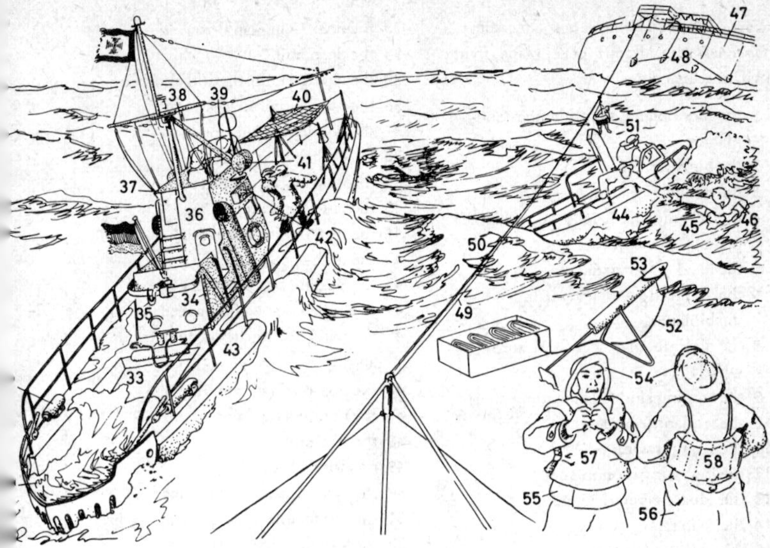

29 the lower weight
30 the diver's boots;

31-43 the lifeboat, a motor life-boat:

31 the hinged stern
32 the hoisting and lowering device
33 the well (stowage for daughter boat)
34 the towing bar
35 the towing hook
36 the wheelhouse
37 the bridge
38 the coxswain
39 the helmsman
40 the jumping net
41 the signal lamp
42 the lamp shelf
43 the watertight deck;.
44 the daughter boat
45 the life-belt (life buoy)
46 the shipwrecked man
47 the stranded (wrecked) ship (ship run aground, shipwreck)
48 the oil bag for trickling oil on the water surface
49 the life line (life rope)
50 the hauling line (whip), an endless rope
51 the breeches buoy

52 and 53 the rocket apparatus (life mortar, line-throwing gun):

52 the throwing line
53 the rocket;

54-56 the oilskins (oils):

54 the southwester (sou'wester)
55 the oilskin jacket
56 the oilskin coat;
57 the life jacket
58 the cork jacket (cork life-belt), a life-belt (*Am.* life-preserver)

Engl. aeroplane = *Am.* airplane, ship; *Engl. and Am.* aircraft, craft, plane, flying machine, machine

1 the monoplane, a high-wing monoplane:
2 the high-set wing
3 the conventional fin;
4 the sesquiplane (*Am.* one-and-a-half plane) [obsolete]:
5 the fixed undercarriage
6 the tail skid;
7 the biplane:
8 the aircraft tail-wheel (*Am.* stern wheel)
9 the landing skid (*Am.* landing sled);
10 the triplane [obsolete]:
11 the straight wing;
12 the low-wing monoplane:
13 the square tapered wing
14 the twin fins
15 the outboard tail fin
16 the torpedo-shaped fuselage;
17 the suspended fuselage
18 the round-tapered wing
19 the mid-wing aircraft (*Am.* semi-high wing monoplane):
20 the gull (cranked) wing;
21 the parasol-wing aircraft:
22 the short fin;
23 the oval wing
24 the high (tall) fin
25 the rectangular wing
26 the barrel-shaped fuselage
27 the swept-back (arrow-type) wing aircraft (*Am.* sweep-back airplane):
28 the swept-back wing (*Am.* sweep-back wing);
29 the tailless delta-type (delta-wing) aircraft ('flying wing'):
30 the delta wing
31 the tailless fin;
32 the amphibian (amphibious aircraft), a landplane and seaplane (land and sea aircraft):
33 the float (wing-tip float)
34 the deep hull
35 the tapered tailplane and elevator;
36 the canard (tail-first) aircraft:
37 the tailplane in the nose
38 the canard nose;
39 the twin-boom aircraft:
40 the tail unit bearers
41 the rectangular tailplane;
42 the high-speed aircraft:
43 the landing skid (runner)
44 the bullet-shaped fuselage;
45 the wing with marked dihedral angle
46 the box-type (square) fuselage
47 the humped fuselage
48 the triple fin
49 the nose wheel
50 the cylindrical (slim) fuselage
51 the retractable undercarriage
52 the faired-in fin and rudder
53 the delta aircraft:
54 the delta wing
55 the wing fence for boundary layer control
56 the delta tail unit
57 the delta-shaped fuselage;
58 the slotted wing
59 the T-tail unit
60 the flying boat:
61 the flying boat hull
62 the stub wing (sponson)
63 the subsidiary float (hydro stabilizer)
64 the wing-tip (outboard) float;
65 the tadpole-shaped fuselage
66 the twin tail unit
67 the crescent-wing (scimitar-wing) aircraft:
68 the crescent wing (scimitar wing);
69 the autogiro (autogyro, gyroplane)
70 the coleopter aircraft with turbojet propulsion
71 the atomic aircraft with aircraft reactor

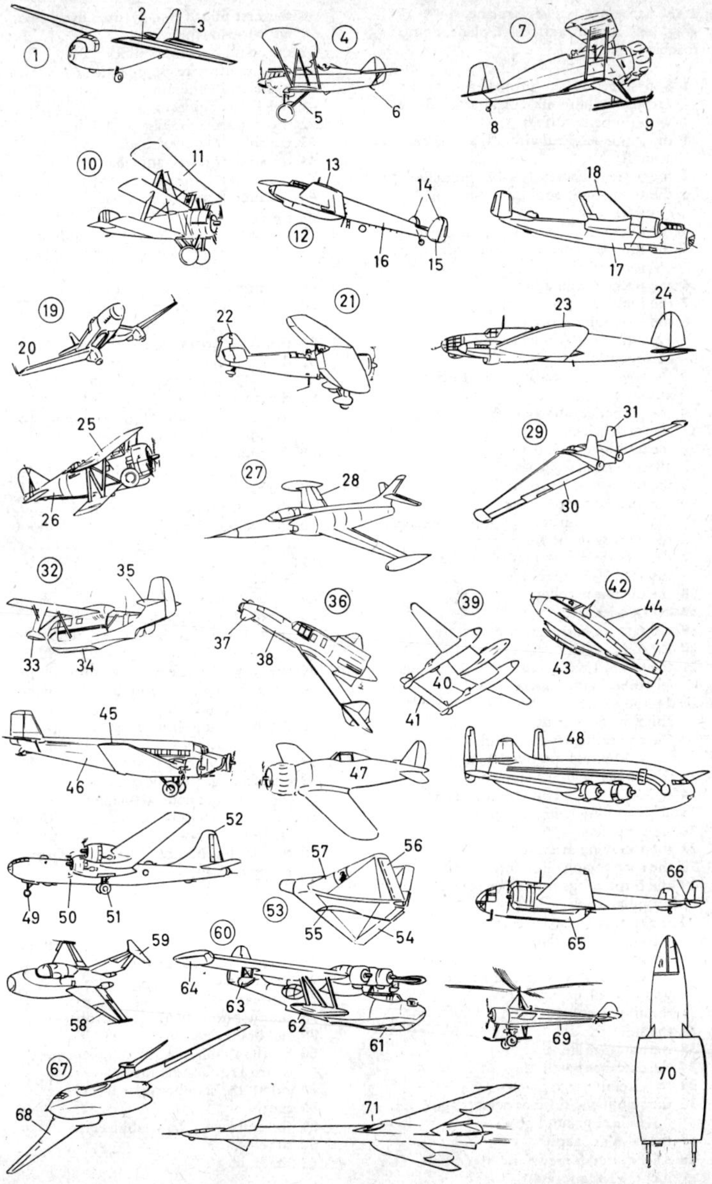

1 2 3
4 5 6
7 8 9
10 11
12 13 14 15 16
17 18
19 20
21 22
23 24
25 26
27 28
29 30 31
32 33 34 35
36 37 38
39 40 41
42 43 44
45 46
47
48
49 50 51 52
53 54 55 56 57
65 66
58 59
60 61 62 63 64
69
70
67 68
71

Engl. aeroplane = *Am.* airplane, ship; *Engl. and Am.* aircraft, craft, plane, flying machine, machine

1–8 airscrew-driven (propeller-driven) aeroplanes (aircraft with airscrew drive, with propeller drive),
1 the single-engined aircraft, a pusher aircraft:
2 the pusher airscrew (pusher propeller);
3 the twin (two) engined (bi-motor) aircraft:
4 the tractor airscrew (tractor propeller);
5 the three-engined (tri-motor) aircraft, a tractor aircraft:
6 the aircraft engine nacelle;
7 the four-engined aircraft
8 the six-engined aircraft;
9–12 turboprop (propeller-turbine) aeroplanes,
9 the single-engined propeller-turbine aircraft:
10 the propeller (airscrew)
11 the jet exhaust;
12 the multi-engined turboprop;
13–18 turbine aeroplanes:
13 the turbine air intake in the nose
14 the turbine after-burner
15 the turbine air intake on side of fuselage
16 the turbine in the wing
17 the turbine superstructure on the fuselage
18 the turbine nacelle;
19–21 ram-jet aeroplanes,
19 the ram-jet barrel-shaped aircraft:
20 the outer-wing turbine;
21 the aircraft with pulse-jet (intermitten jet) tube (with pulsojet tube);
22–24 the carrier arrangement ('parent-child' arrangement),
22 the composite ('parent-child', pick-a-back, *Am. pop.* piggyback) aircraft:
23 the carrier (parent) aircraft
24 the plane carried by another aircraft;
25 air refuelling (*Am.* air refueling):
26 the air tanker
27 the receiving aircraft;
28 the rotary wing aircraft (rotorplane):
29 the rotor wings rotated by reaction-propulsion jets;
30 the commercial (passenger) aircraft (airliner; transatlantic, or transoceanic, aircraft; stratosphere passenger aircraft; stratoliner, *Am.* oversea airplane, ocean-going seaplane):
31 the air passenger
32 the stewardess
33 the entrance steps
34 the entrance hatch
35 the aircraft cargo hatch
36 the stabilizing nose undercarriage (*Am.* nosewheel ground gear)
37 the pilot's cockpit
38–41 the aircraft crew (aircraft complement, *Am.* aircrew):
38 the first pilot (*Am.* aviator, flyer, *Am. mil.* airman; pilot)
39 the co-pilot (second pilot)
40 the aircraft wireless operator (*Am.* airplane radio operator)
41 the flight engineer;
42 the stewardess' cabin
43 the aircraft kitchen
44 the aircraft aerial (antenna) unit
45 the aircraft passenger compartment
46 the aircraft navigation light
47 the fuel tank
48 the main landing gear(main landing undercarriage, *Am.* main ground gear, main chassis)
49 the aircraft engine nacelle
50 the turbojet engine;

51 **the free balloon,** a dirigible balloon:
52 the balloon cover
53 the balloon rigging (balloon netting)
54 the rip panel with the rip cord
55 the filling (inflation) sleeve (appendix, *Am.* inflation neck)
56 the running rigging
57 the filling sleeve cord or line
58 the basket ring (load ring)
59 the basket rope or cord
60 the balloon basket (balloon car, balloon nacelle)
61 the balloon ballast [sand ballast, sand bags]
62 the balloon anchor
63 the drag (trail, guide) rope;
64 the balloon pilot (balloonist, ballooner)

65 **the airship** (Zeppelin airship, zeppelin, *coll.* zep), a dirigible rigid airship (a rigid dirigible):
66 the airship-mooring mast (airship anchor mast)
67 the mast-mooring gear
68 the passenger nacelle or gondola with the passenger compartments
69 the control nacelle or gondola with the airship pilot post
70 the landing bumper (*Am.* pneumatic bumping bag)
71 the observation platform
72 the exhaust gas shaft hood
73 the body (hull) of the airship
74 the outside covering (airship envelope)
75 the gas cells (gas bags)
76 the side nacelle
77 the rear nacelle
78 the airship screw (airship propeller)
79 the airship stern
80–83 the airship tail unit (empennage, control surfaces, controls),
80 and 81 the stabilizing surfaces:
80 the fin
81 the tailplane (*Am.* stabilizer);
82 the elevator
83 the rudder

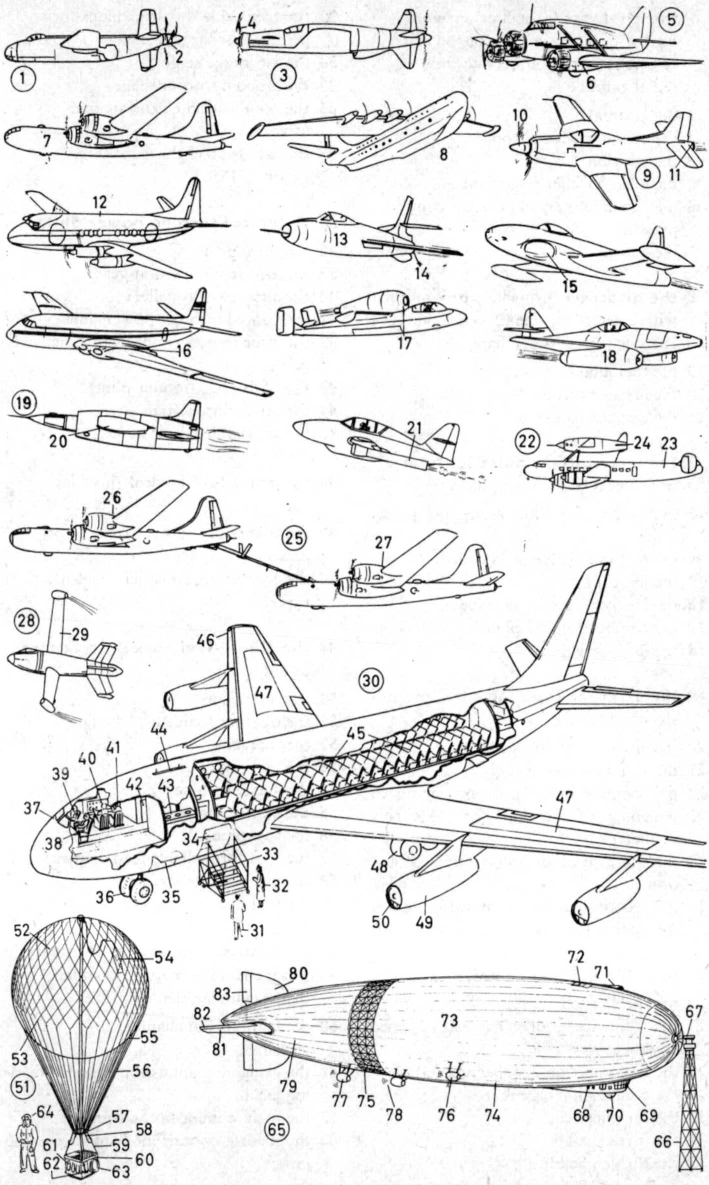
1
2
3
4
5
6
7
8
9
10
11
12
13
14
15
16
17
18
19
20
21
22
23
24
25
26
27
28
29
30
31
32
33
34
35
36
37
38
39
40
41
42
43
44
45
46
47
47
48
49
50
51
52
53
54
55
56
57
58
59
60
61
62
63
64
65
66
67
68
69
70
71
72
73
74
75
76
77
78
79
80
81
82
83

227 Aero Engines (Aircraft Engines)

1 **the airscrew** (propeller) **power unit** with piston engine (piston aero engine),a twin (double, two) row radial engine:
2 the air intake
3 the cylinder with piston
4 the ignition
5 the cylinder inlet (manifold)
6 the supercharger (blower, air compressor)
7 the exhaust;

8 **the airscrew** (propeller) **power unit** with exhaust turbine-driven supercharger (turbo-supercharger):
9 the fuel intake
10 the exhaust turbine
11 the exhaust gases;

12 **the intermittent pulse-jet tube** (pulsojet tube, V-1 propulsion):
13 the fuel piping (fuel lead, fuel manifold)
14 the fuel inlet valve, a flap valve
15 the ignition
16 the air compression chamber
17 the combustion chamber
18 the exhaust valve;

19 **the ram-jet tube** (athodyd, propulsive duct tube):
20 the air compression stage
21 the air intake (air duct)
22 the increase of air pressure owing to widening of the duct (of the tube's diameter)
23 the increase in air volume by combustion
24 the exhaust of the combustion gases (reaction gases, exhaust gases);

25 **the turbojet power unit:**
26 the turbine self-starter
27 the multi-stage air compressor (series compressors)
28 the fuel injection nozzle (fuel jet)
29 the combustion chamber
30 the turbojet
31 the drive shaft
32 the turbine bearing
33 the adjustable thrust (exhaust, propelling, discharge) cone
34 the air intake stage
35 the air compression stage
36 the combustion of the air-fuel-mixture
37 the expulsion of the exhaust gases;

38-45 **typical turbine power units,**
38 the turboprop:
39 the airscrew reduction gear
40 the airscrew (propeller)
41 the simple turbojet power unit
42 the after-burner (re-heat) turbojet power unit:
43 the flash plug (igniter plug)
44 the after-burner (ram-jet)
45 the adjustable nozzle or jet;

46 **the solid-fuel rocket** (powder rocket):
47 the rocket propulsive (rocket propulsion) charge
48 the conical nozzle or jet (venturi, tuyere);

49 **the liquid-fuel rocket** (rocket with liquid fuel):
50 the water tank
51 the oxidiser (oxidizer)
52 the fuel tank
53 the pump unit
54 the steam turbine
55 the electric starter
56 the fuel pipe
57 the fuel (propellant) feed control
58 the gas steam generator
59 the fuel nozzle (fuel jet)

60–63 the rocket combustion chambers (blast chamber, reaction chamber, thrust cylinder, flame tubes):
60 the combustion chamber for cruising
61 the cruising combustion chamber cooling jacket
62 the main combustion chamber
63 the main combustion chamber cooling jacket

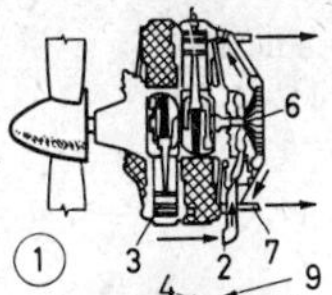
1
2
3
6
7

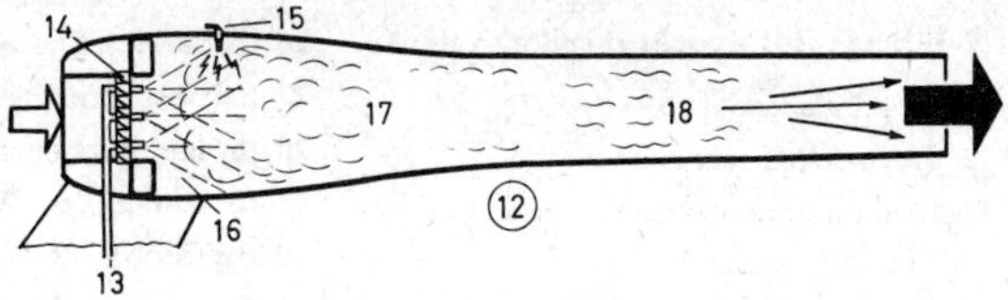
12
13
14
15
16
17
18

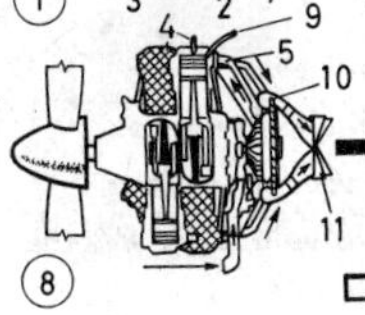
8
4
5
9
10
11

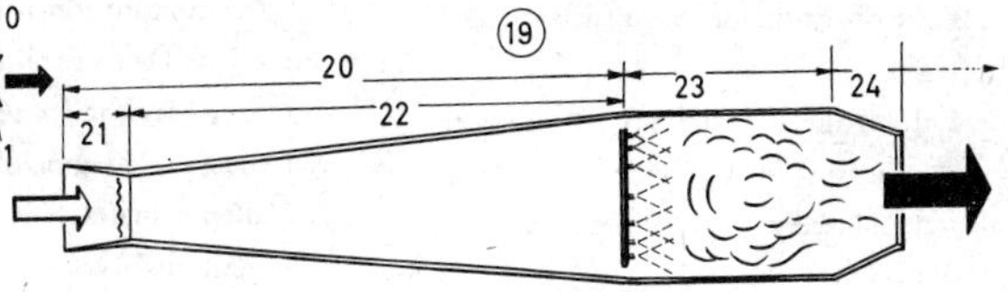
19
20
21
22
23
24

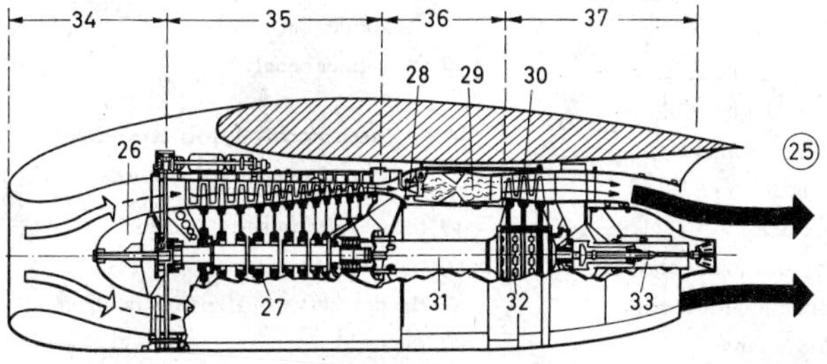
25
26
27
28
29
30
31
32
33
34
35
36
37

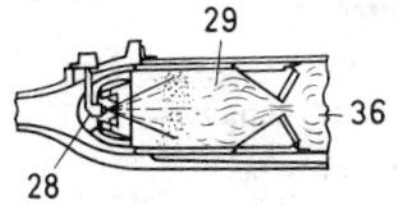
28
29
36

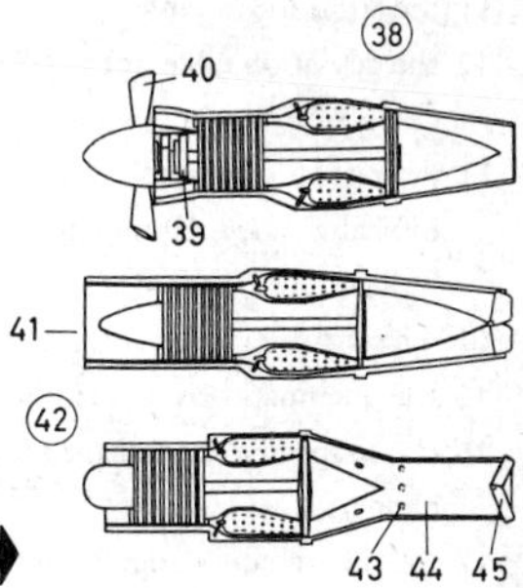
38
39
40
41
42
43
44
45

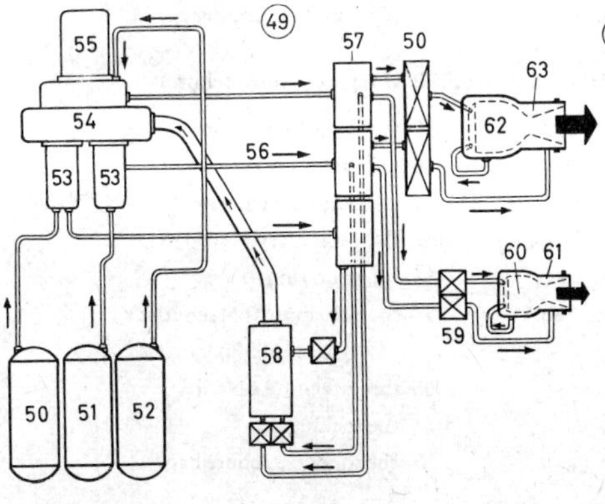
49
50
51
52
53
53
54
55
56
57
58
59
60
61
62
63

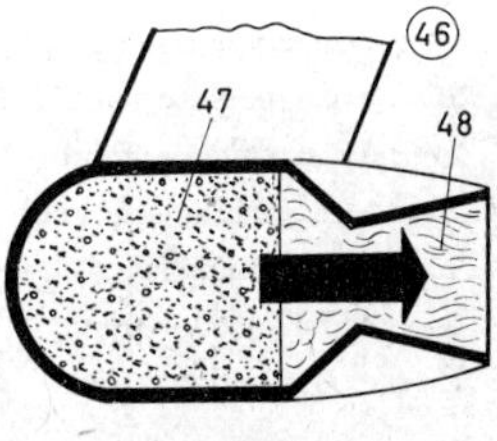
46
47
48

1-38 the pilot's cockpit (pilot's cabin):

1 the pilot's seat
2 the co-pilot's seat
3–16 the aircraft instrument panel or blind flying panel:
3 the direction indicator (directional gyro)
4 the artificial horizon (gyro-horizon indicator) for verifying the flying attitude (ascent or descent of the machine)
5 the turn-and-slip, or bank, indicator (*Am.* inclinometer) for verifying the flying altitude in turns
6 the altimeter to indicate changes in altitude (in height of flight)
7 the autopilot (automatic pilot, *Am.* navigraph)
8 the aircraft clock
9 the sensitive and coarse altimeter
10 the radio direction indicator
11 the aircraft compass
12 the deviation table or card for the corrections to the compass reading
13 the rate of climb and descent indicator (*Am.* climb and descent indicator)
14 the outside air thermometer
15 the pneumatic pressure indicator
16 the airspeed indicator (*Am.* airspeed meter);
17 the oil pressure gauge (*Am.* gage)
18 the revolutions-per-minute (rev/min) indicator (revo-counter)
19 the oil temperature gauge (*Am.* gage)
20 the fuel pressure gauge (*Am.* gage)
21 the fuel contents gauge (*Am.* gage)
22 the fire-extinguisher knob
23 the hand pump lever
24 the fuel injection pump
25 the oil injection pump
26 the fuel level visual indicator
27 the battery master switch
28 the ignition switch
29 the landing gear lever
30 the throttle lever
31 the mixture control lever
32 the fuel cock for fuel feed control
33 the nose or tail wheel release lever
34 the coupled control columns; *inside:* the aileron shafts
35 the control column (joystick, stick) for elevator and aileron control
36 the elevator push-pull rod
37 the rudder bar
38 the rudder pedal;

39-47 the aircraft flying-controls system and control surfaces:

39 the elevator push-pull rod
40 the aileron rod
41 the dorsal (vertical) fin or stabilizer
42 the rudder
43 the tailplane (*Am.* horizontal stabilizer)
44 the elevator
45 the aircraft wing unit
46 the aileron
47 the flap (auxiliary airfoil, wing flap) for reducing the landing speed;

48 the parachute (chute):

49 the parachute canopy
50 the parachute rigging line
51 the outer parachute bag
52 the main carrying rope
53 the main ring
54 the parachute (parachutist's, *Am.* parachuter's) harness
55 the parachute rip cord
56 the locking pin
57 the inner parachute bag

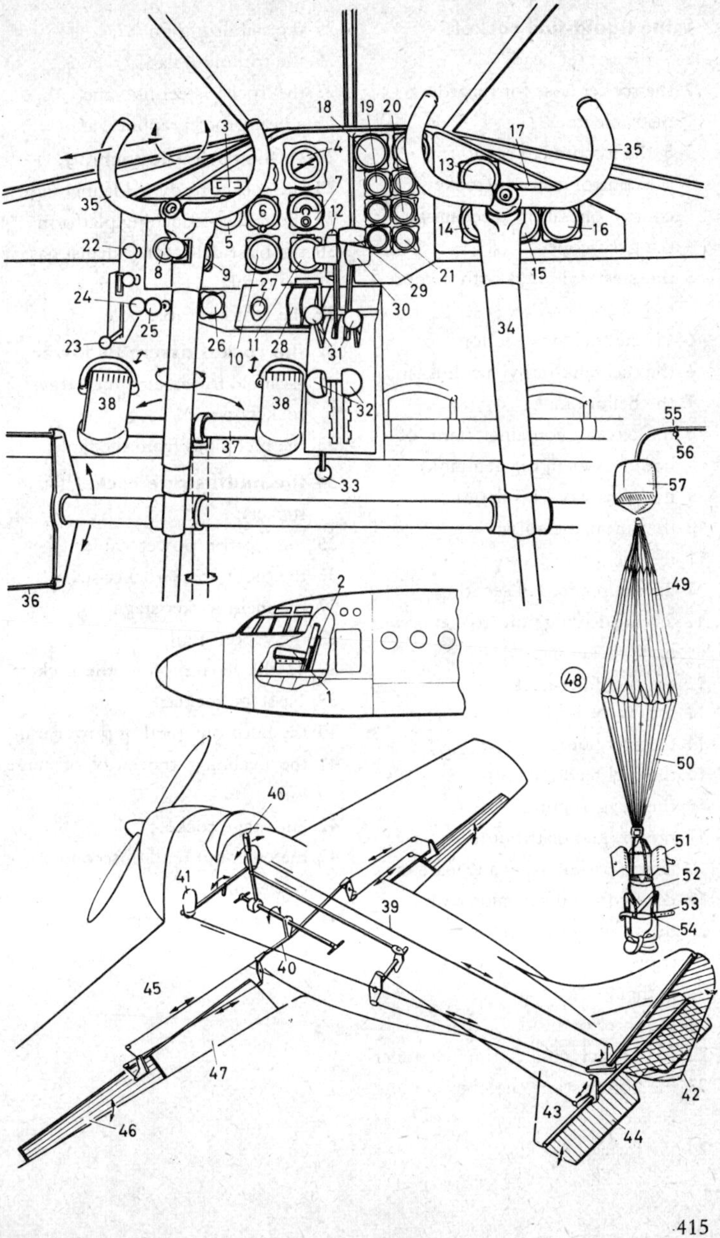
1
2
3
4
5
6
7
8
9
10
11
12
13
14
15
16
17
18
19
20
21
22
23
24
25
26
27
28
29
30
31
32
33
34
35
36
37
38
39
40
41
42
43
44
45
46
47
48
49
50
51
52
53
54
55
56
57

1 the liquid-fuel rocket,
2–5 the rocket head:
2 the rocket nose for recording instruments
3–5 the instrument section:
3 the control element (rocket control operating mechanism)
4 the gyroscope
5 the steel cylinders with compressed nitrogen;
6–11 the fuel tank section:
6 the fuel tank (ethyl-alcohol tank)
7 the helium tanks
8 the oxygen container (tank of liquid oxygen, oxygen tank)
9 the glass wool insulation
10 the automatic valve
11 the fuel pipe;
12–27 the rocket tail section,
12–24 the driving unit (rocket power unit, rocket motor):
12 the fuel-filler neck
13 the oxygen-filler neck
14 the fuel pump
15 the fuel feed-pipe
16 the oxygen pump
17 the oxygen distributor
18 the potassium permanganate tank
19 the hydrogen peroxide tank
20 the steam generator with the steam turbine for operating the pumps
21 the injector head
22 the rocket combustion chamber
23 the combustion chamber cooling jacket
24 the thrust nozzle;
25 the stabilizing fin
26 the trimming flap
27 the rocket steering vane, a heat-proof graphite vane;
28-31 the rocket-launching,
28 the rocket ready for launching:
29 the rocket-launching platform
30 the blast-deflector (exhaust gas deflector)
31 the ignition cable pole;
32 the rocket assembly tower (scaffold for assembling large rockets):
33 the fuel pipes from the tank;
34 the multi-stage rocket (stage rocket):
35 the electric power cable
36 the preliminary rocket-stage
37 the main rocket-stage
38 the vapour trail
39–42 the separation of the rockets,
39 1st-stage rocket:
40 the burn-out (end of power unit)
41 the declining trajectory of stage one;
42 2nd stage rocket;
43 the burn-out (end of second power unit)
44 the trajectory summit (summit of the rocket trajectory)

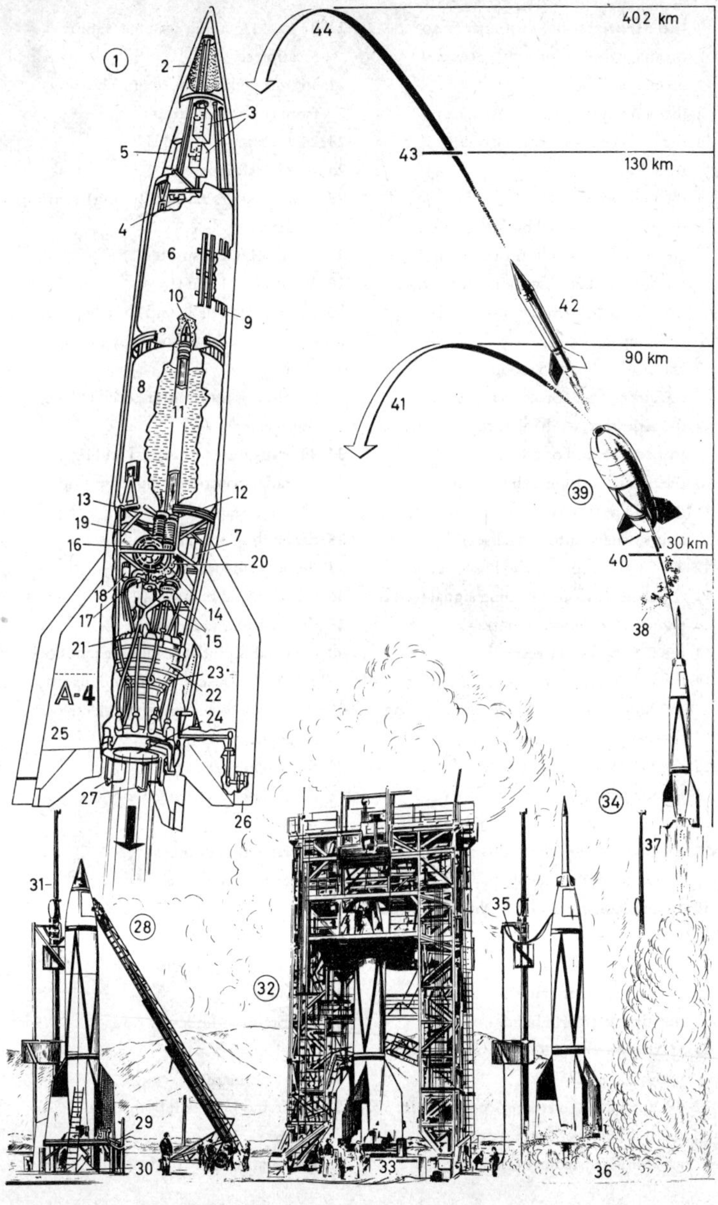

402 km
130 km
90 km
30 km
A-4
1
2
3
4
5
6
7
8
9
10
11
12
13
14
15
16
17
18
19
20
21
22
23
24
25
26
27
28
29
30
31
32
33
34
35
36
37
38
39
40
41
42
43
44

1 **the airport** [with customs] (aerodrome, aviation ground, *Am.* airdrome, airfield):
2 the runways (*Am. coll.* tarmacs)
3 the emergency (forced) landing runway
4 the radar scanner
5 the airport terminal building with airport administration offices, flight (aircraft) ticket office, airport operational control, airport restaurant
6 the hangar
7 the workshops and repair shops
8 the airport meteorological station
9 the airport repair hangar for aircraft inspections and overhauls
10 the precision approach radar set
11 the I. L. S. (instrument landing system) course-transmitter (localiser)
12 and **18** the airport radio beacons:
12 the radio beacon, a landing signal (radio signal, *Am.* landing marker)
13 the I. L. S. middle marker
14 the I. L. S. glide-path transmitter for guiding the aircraft in elevation during the last landing phase
15 the helicopter landing field
16 the telephone connections
17 the wind sock (wind cone)
18 the omni-range (omni-directional, V. O. R.) radio beacon
19 the anemometer (*Am.* hydrostatic wind gage)
20 the V. H. F. (very high frequency) radio direction finder station
21 the airport freight hangar;
22-53 **air radio** (aeronautical radio navigation service),
22–38 air traffic control procedures (air navigation aids) for bad visibility and blind (instrument) landing,
22–33 radio location systems (radio location service),
22 aircraft picking-up (fixing) bearings from two transmitters:
23, 24 transmitter I and II
25 the aircraft receiver;
26 two receivers finding (fixing) bearings of aircraft:
27 the aircraft transmitter
28, 29 receiver I and II;
30 combination of 22 and 26 (reception and reflection of I and II by aircraft):
31 the aircraft transmitter-receiver (*coll.* transceiver)
32, 33 transmitter-receiver I and II;
34 the radar-controlled blind landing:
35 the radar transmitter
36 the landing aircraft
37 the surveillance radar equipment
38 the precision radar set;
39 the scanning radar set:
40 the rotating radar scanner, a parabolic mirror for the collection and direction (beaming, focusing) of the electromagnetic waves
41 the driving unit
42 the emission (radiation) of the waves
43 the reflection of the waves
44 the transmitter-receiver case
45 the radar transmitter
46 the radar receiver
47 the controlling device;
48 the radarscope:
49 the Braun cathode-ray tube
50 the electronic map;
51 the radar map
52 the frame-built parabolic radar mirror
53 the rotational mirror tower

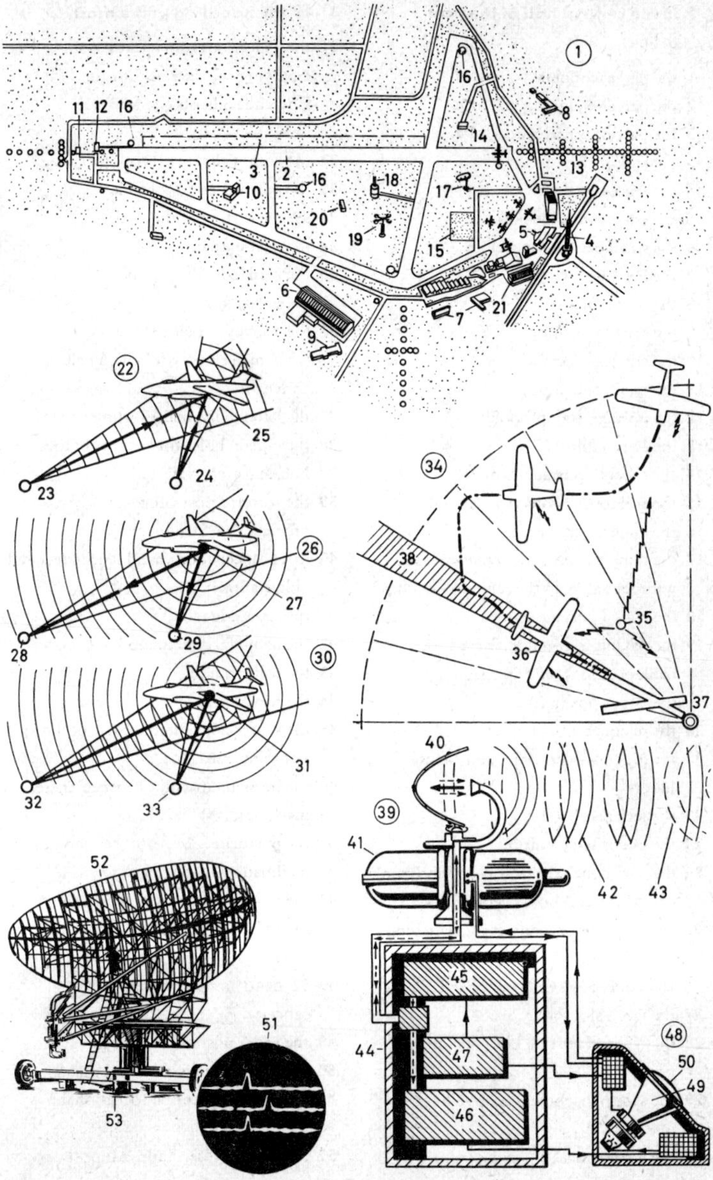
1
2
3
4
5
6
7
8
9
10
11
12
13
14
15
16
17
18
19
20
21
22
23
24
25
26
27
28
29
30
31
32
33
34
35
36
37
38
39
40
41
42
43
44
45
46
47
48
49
50
51
52
53

1-30 the central hall of the post office:

1 the parcel counter
2 the parcel-weighing machine
3 the parcel (postal parcel, *Am.* package):
4 the stick-on label;
5 the paste pot (glue pot)
6 the small parcel (packet)
7 the P. O. boxes:
8 the post-office box;
9 the stamps position
10 the counter clerk
11 the certificate of posting book
12 the postage stamp booklet
13 the stamp folio
14 the sheet of postage stamps
15 the roll top, a protective shutter
16 the counter drawer
17 the sample (*form. in Germany* sample without value) in the sample container
18 the roll of postage stamps
19 the paying-in counter (*in Engl.* savings bank position), *also* : pensions counter (pensions position)
20 the telegram position
21 the pigeon holes for poste-restante letters
22 the letter scales
23 the postmaster's office
24 the telephone call box for local and trunk calls (*Am.* call box, telephone booth):
25 the tread (floor) contact for switching on the cabin light;
26 the notice; *here* : a list of postal rates
27 the letter slot
28 the air-mail posting box (*Am.* airmail box)
29 the stamp machine (stamp selling machine)
30 the writing desk;

31-46 the handling of the mail,

31 the collection from (clearing of, emptying of) the post box [in England: pillar box, *Am.* mail box]:
32 the letter (*Am.* mail) collection bag
33 the post-office motorcycle;
34–39 the sorting of the mail:
34 the dust-extractor
35 the mail from the post box (*Am.* mail box)
36 the conveyor belt for letters (*Am.* mail conveyor belt), a belt conveyor
37 the letter (*Am.* mail) sorting frame
38 the pigeon holes for bundles of local, line, and area, mail
39 the sorter, a post-office employee or official (*Am.* mailing clerk);
40 hand cancellation (hand stamping, hand obliteration):
41 the stamping table
42 the hammer-type stamp;
43 the roller stamp
44 the hand stamp
45 the stamp cancelling (*Am.* canceling; stamping) machine
46 the franking machine (postage meter machine);
47 the postman (*Am.* letter-carrier, carrier, mailman, mail-carrier)
48 the postman's delivery pouch (postman's bag, *Am.* mail bag, mailman's bag)
49–52 hand postmarks (hand cancels):
49 the roller postmark
50 the local advertisement postmark
51 the special postmark (occasional postmark)
52 the railway (*Am.* railroad) postmark

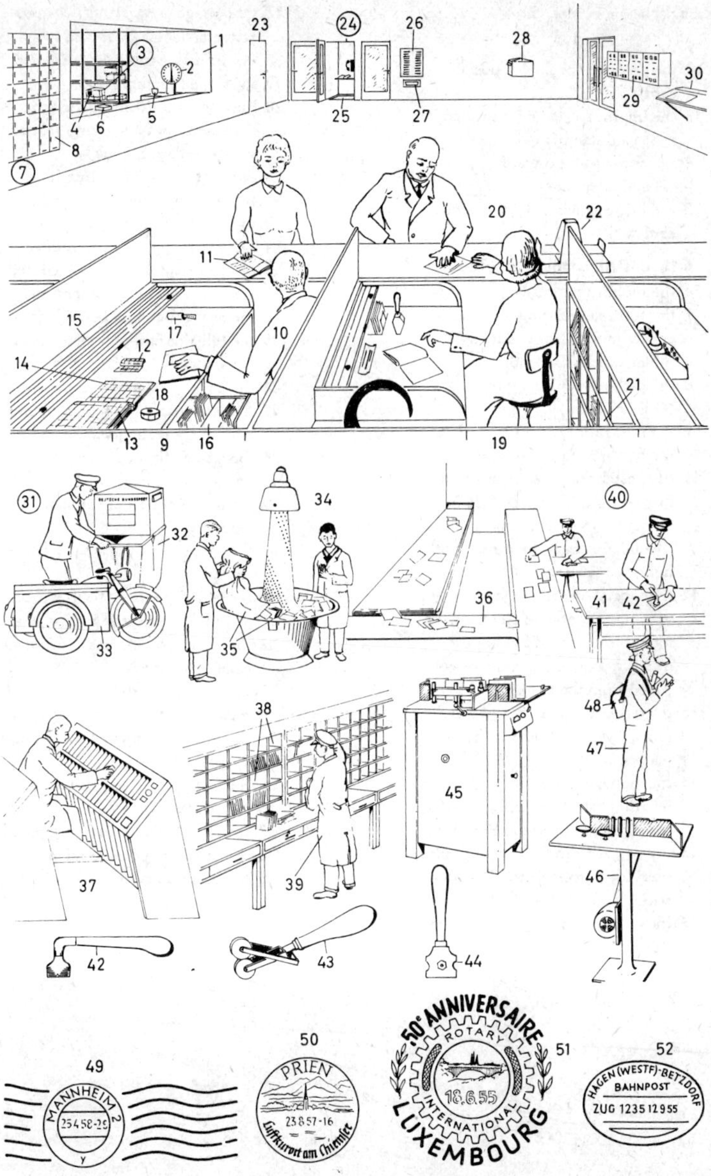
1 2 3 4 5 6 7 8 9 10 11 12 13 14 15 16 17 18 19 20 21 22 23 24 25 26 27 28 29 30
31 32 33 34 35 36 37 38 39 40 41 42 43 44 45 46 47 48
DEUTSCHE BUNDESPOST
49
MANNHEIM 2
25.4.58-29
y
50
PRIEN
23.8.57-16
Luftkurort am Chiemsee
51
50e ANNIVERSAIRE
ROTARY
18.6.55
INTERNATIONAL
LUXEMBOURG
52
HAGEN (WESTF)-BETZDORF
BAHNPOST
ZUG 1235 12.9.55

Engl. cheque = *Am.* check

1 the letter card
2 the postcard (p. c., *Am.* postal card):
3 the imprinted stamp (imprinted post-paid stamp);
4 the reply-paid postcard (*Am.* double card)
5 the picture postcard (*Am.* postal card with view)

6-15 postal forms (*Am.* blanks):
6 the receipt post card
7 the form authorizing postman to collect money from addressee [unknown in England]
8 the cash-on-delivery form (C. O. D. form)
9 the post-office receipt
10 the postal cheque envelope
11 the postal cheque for transferring money from one post-office bank account to another; *sim.* postal cheque for cash payment [both unknown in England]
12 the postal order (money order, *Am.* postal note) [in Germany the money is delivered by the postman; in England it must be collected from the P. O.]
13 the telegram (wire, telegram form, *Am.* telegraph blank; *form.* telegraph)
14 the money order for paying direct into the post-office bank account of the payee [unknown in England]
15 the parcel form [in England only used for parcels to foreign countries];
16 the printed papers (*Am.* printings, third-class matter):
17 the postage meter stamp (*Am.* postal meter stamps; post-paid stamp);
18 the air-mail letter (*Am.* air letter)
19 the air-mail stamp [U. S. A.]
20 the international reply coupon
21 the charity postage stamp (surtax stamp), a special issue,
22 and 23 the nominal value (face value):
22 the franking value
23 the charity surtax;
24 the newspaper packet, printed matter (*Am.* printings) at reduced rate (*Am.* second-class matter) in the newspaper wrapper
25 the fully insured registered letter (*Am.* money letter):
26 the envelope flap
27 the letter seal (impression of the seal on the sealing wax);
28 the label ('sticker') for registered insured mail
29 the pneumatic letter (tubular letter):
30 the pneumatic-dispatch postage stamp;
31 the label for express mail (express-mail label) [Express, By Express]
32 the label for air mail (air-mail label) [By Air Mail]
33 the label for partly insured registered mail
34 the express-delivery (special-delivery) letter
35 the partly insured registered letter:
36 the sender
37 the address (addressee, recipient)
38 the number of the postal area
39 the date stamp (postmark, cancel)
40 the postage stamp (stamp), a stamp for local, inland, or foreign, postage

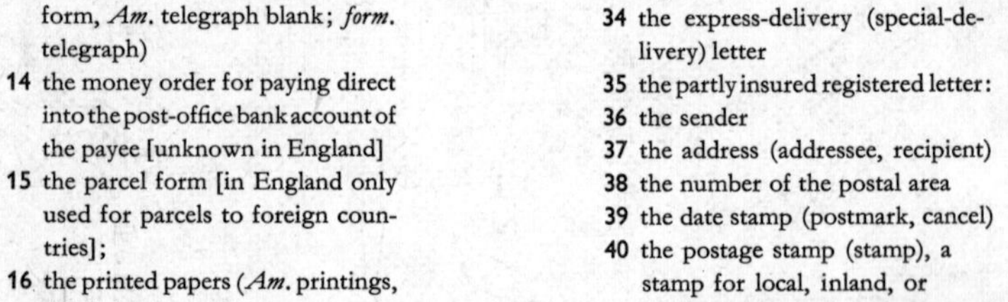

in England

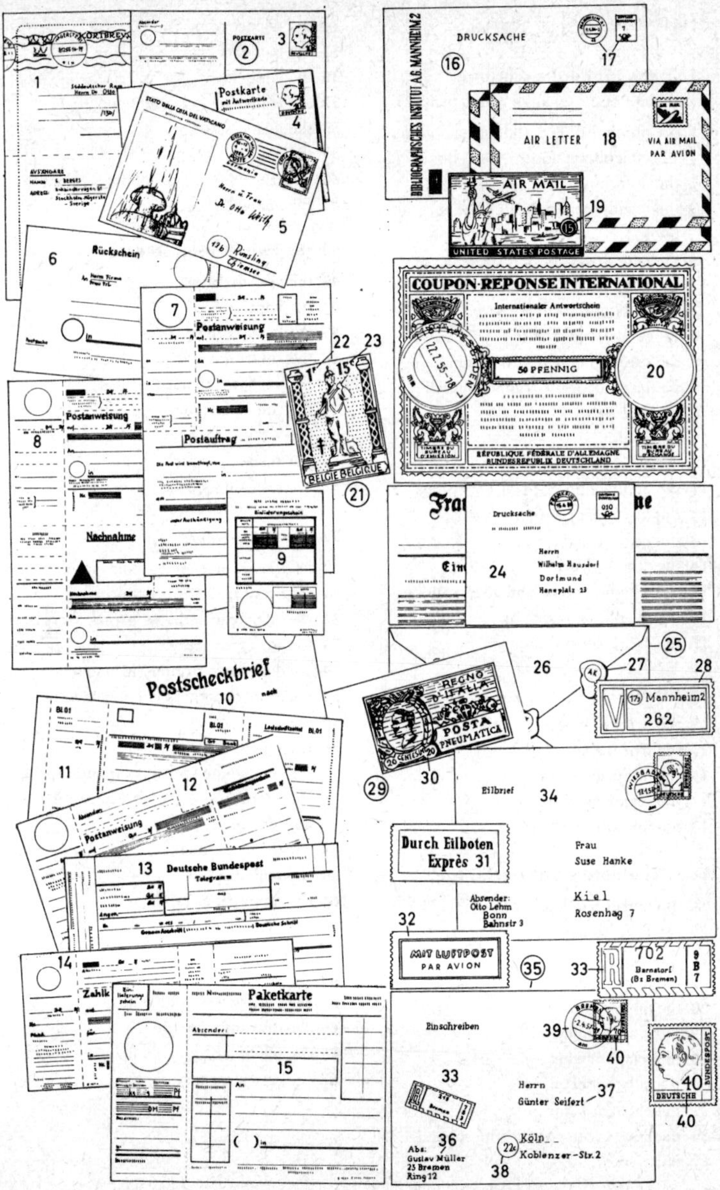

1
2
POSTKARTE
3
Postkarte mit Antwortkarte
4
STATO DELLA CITTA DEL VATICANO
5
Herrn u. Frau
Dr. Otto Wirth
17b Rimsting
Chiemsee
6
Rückschein
7
Postanweisung
8
Postanweisung
Nachnahme
Postauftrag
9
10
Postscheckbrief
11
12
Postanweisung
13
Deutsche Bundespost
Telegramm
14
Zahlk
15
Paketkarte
Absender
An
16
DRUCKSACHE
BIBLIOGRAPHISCHES INSTITUT AG. MANNHEIM 2
17
18
AIR LETTER
VIA AIR MAIL
PAR AVION
19
AIR MAIL
UNITED STATES POSTAGE
20
COUPON-REPONSE INTERNATIONAL
Internationaler Antwortschein
50 PFENNIG
RÉPUBLIQUE FÉDÉRALE D'ALLEMAGNE
BUNDESREPUBLIK DEUTSCHLAND
WIESBADEN 1
22.2.55-18
21
22
23
BELGIE BELGIQUE
24
Drucksache
Herrn
Wilhelm Hausdorf
Dortmund
Hansaplatz 23
25
26
27
28
Mannheim 2
262
REGNO D'ITALIA
POSTA PNEUMATICA
29
30
Eilbrief
34
Durch Eilboten
Exprès 31
Frau
Suse Hanke
Kiel
Rosenhag 7
Absender:
Otto Lehm
Bonn
Bahnstr 3
32
MIT LUFTPOST
PAR AVION
35
33
702
Barnstorf
(Bz Bremen)
Einschreiben
39
40
33
Herrn
Günter Seifert
37
Köln
Koblenzer-Str. 2
36
Abs:
Gustav Müller
28 Bremen
Ring 12
38
DEUTSCHE
BUNDESPOST

1–51 telephone (*coll.* 'phone),

1-17 the manual exchange,
a telephone exchange (*Am.* central),

1 the public call-box (telephone kiosk, *Am.* telephone booth), a call-box:
2 the coin box
3 the telephone directory (*Am.* telephone book);
4 the caller (telephone-user)
5 the lamp signalling switchboard; *form.* drop indicator switchboard,
6–12 the switchboard:
6 the calling lamp, a lamp signal
7 the jack, a spring-contact switch
8 the face panel
9 the plug
10 the keyshelf
11 the connecting cord of two plugs
12 the key (change-over switch);
13 the head set:
14 the mouthpiece
15 the telephone receiver, an earphone;
16 the telephone operator
17 the called telephone;

18 the dial:

19 the driving wheel
20 the worm shaft
21 the impulse cam
22 the restoring spring
23 the impulse contacts;

24-41 the automatic exchange,

24 the automatic telephone:
25 the telephone case
26 the dial
27 the finger plate
28 the finger stop
29 the rest (cradle)
30 the telephone receiver (hand set);
31 the subscriber
32 the exchange line
33 the rotary line switch (the subscriber's uniselector)
34 the wiper
35 the bank contact
36 the wiper hub
37 the trunk (*Am.* trunk lines)
38 the group selector
39 the contact banks
40 the trunk (*Am.* trunk line)
41 the final selector;

42 the two motion selector:

43 the selector shaft
44 the wiper
45 the bank contact
46 the rotary ratchet
47 the vertical ratchet
48 the rotary magnet
49 the vertical magnet
50 the release magnet
51 the restoring spring;

52-67 telegraphy,

52–64 the Morse telegraph system for transmitting and receiving:
52 the earth (earthed, *Am.* grounded) plates
53 the storage battery
54–63 the Morse printer (Morse receiver):
54 the electromagnets (*Am.* solenoids)
55 the armature
56 the armature lever
57 the restraining spring (retractile spring)
58 the recording style or stylus (ink recorder, inker)
59 the driving rollers
60 the reel of paper
61 the tape (paper tape)
62 the Morse code (signs of the Morse alphabet)
63 the tape roll;
64 the Morse key (transmitter);
65 the transmission line
66 the telegraph pole, an open-line pole
67 the porcelain insulator

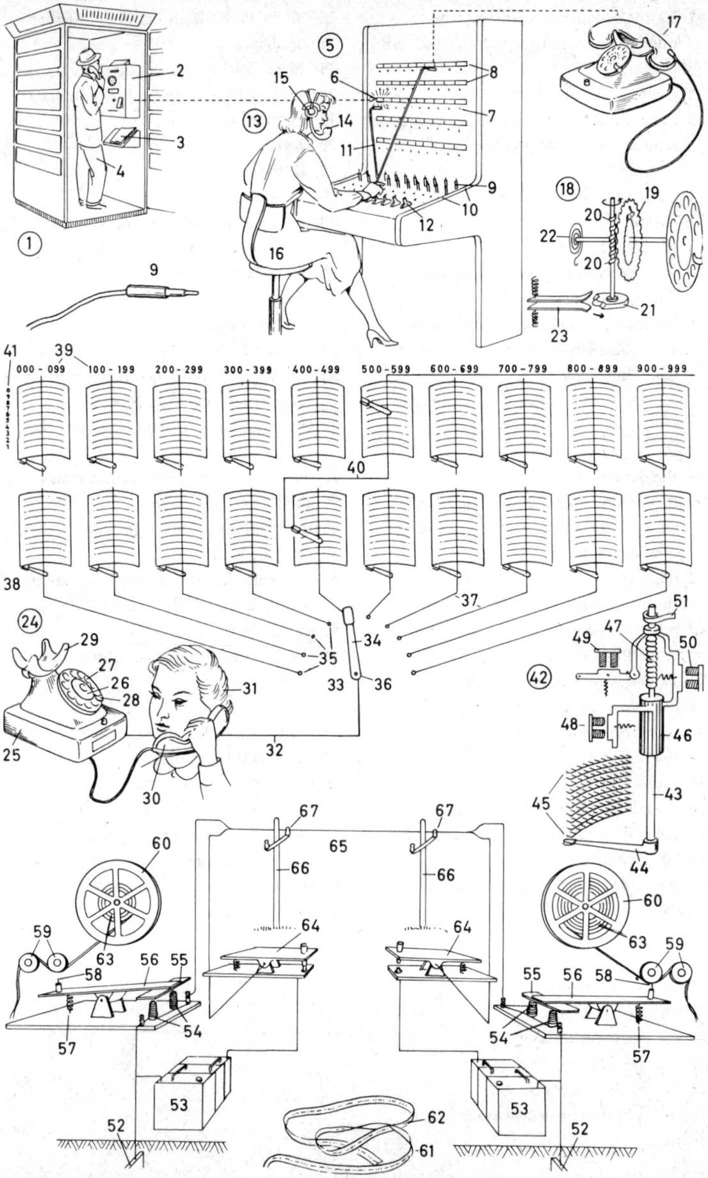
1
2
3
4
5
6
7
8
9
10
11
12
13
14
15
16
17
18
19
20
21
22
23
24
25
26
27
28
29
30
31
32
33
34
35
36
37
38
39
40
41
000 - 099
100 - 199
200 - 299
300 - 399
400 - 499
500 - 599
600 - 699
700 - 799
800 - 899
900 - 999
42
43
44
45
46
47
48
49
50
51
52
53
54
55
56
57
58
59
60
61
62
63
64
65
66
67

1–20 the broadcast (wireless transmission, radio transmission, *Am.* radio casting),
1–6 the recording room,
1 and 2 the magnetic sound-recording equipment for the production of sound effects:
1 the magnetic tape recorders
2 the mixing desk;
3 the sound engineer
4 the observation window for the producer and the studio manager
5 the monitoring (check) loudspeaker
6 the sound-absorbing wall panels or panelling (*Am.* paneling);
7–12 the news studio and the radio play studio:
7 the suspended microphone
8 the desk microphone
9 the radio announcer (*Am.* radio communicator, communicator, master of ceremonies, M. C., *coll.* emcee)
10 the script
11 the standard-time clock
12 the interchangeable wall panels for adjusting reverberation;
13–17 the radio station concert hall:
13 the microphone (*Am.* mike) suspended from three points
14 the radio stage
15 the auditorium
16 the adjustable wall panels
17 the ceiling panelling (*Am.* paneling);
18–20 the control cubicle:
18 the cables from the separate studios to the control cubicle
19 the control desk
20 the studio manager;
21–50 radio reception,
21–34 the crystal receiver:
21 the receiving aerial
22 the chain of egg insulators
23 the shackle insulator
24 the lightning protector earth connection
25–28 the H. F. (high-freqency) oscillatory circuit:
25 the oscillatory circuit coil [inductance]
26 the variable condenser [capacitance]
27 the tuning knob
28 the insulated jumper;
29–32 the detector:
29 the glass tube, a dust cover
30 the crystal [germanium, selenium, or lead sulphide, *Am.* lead sulfid]
31 the cat's whisker
32 the guide arm;
33 the banana plug
34 the earphones;
35 the wireless (wireless receiver or set, radio receiver or set, *Am.* radio):
36 the wooden or plastic receiver (*Am.* radio) cabinet
37–40 the frequency calibration scales:
37 the short-wave range
38 the medium-wave range
39 the long-wave range
40 the very high-frequency (ultra-short wave) range (V.H.F. range);
41–45 knobs:
41 the tuning knob for tuning-in the stations
42 the volume control
43 the ferrite rod antenna control
44 the bass tone control
45 the treble tone control;
46 the scale for 44 and 45
47 the push-buttons for selecting wavebands or stations
48 the magic eye, a cathode-ray tube
49 the loudspeaker aperture
50 the baffle board

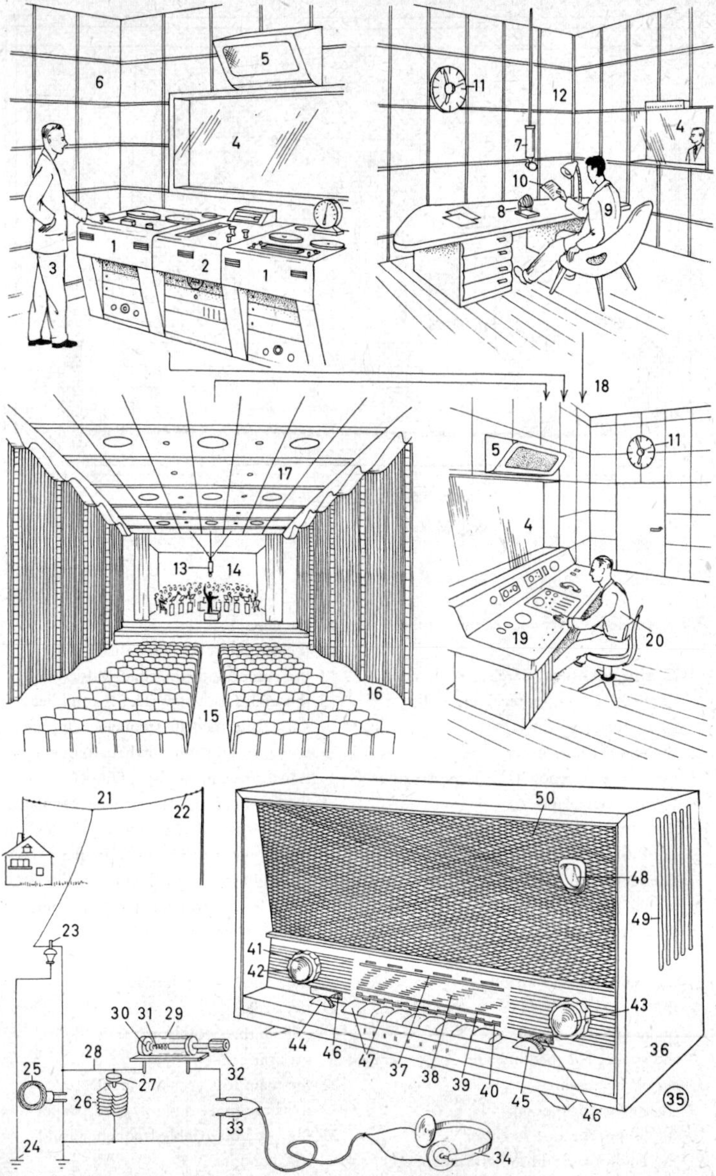
5
6
4
3
1
2
1
11
12
4
7
10
8
9
18
17
13
14
16
15
5
11
4
19
20
21
22
23
25
26
27
28
30
31
29
32
33
24
34
50
48
49
41
42
43
44
46
47
37
38
39
40
45
46
36
35

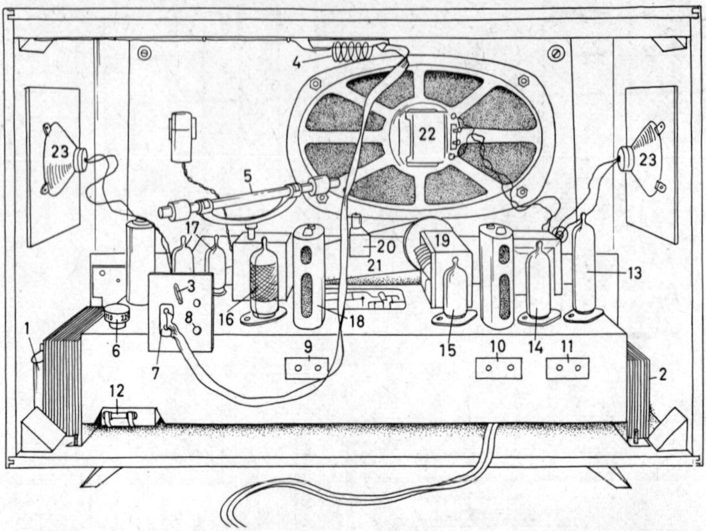

Engl. wireless valve = *Am.* radio tube

1-23 the wireless (wireless receiver, wireless set, radio receiver, radio set, *Am.* radio [interior]:

1 the mains transformer
2 the low-frequency (L.F.) transformer (output transformer)
3 the antenna switch
4 the built-in V. H. F. (very high-frequency) aerial or antenna, a dipole antenna
5 the ferrite rod aerial or antenna, a rotatable directional antenna
6 the mains-voltage switch
7 the socket for V. H. F. (very high-frequency) aerial or antenna
8 the socket for medium and long wave aerials or antenna
9 the socket for pick-up
10 the socket for tape recorder
11 the socket for additional loudspeaker;
12 the fuse
13 the output valve (*Am.* tube)
14 the compound (multiple) valve
15 the high-frequency (H. F.) amplifier valve, intermediate-frequency amplifier valve, and the intermediate-frequency transformer (a band-pass filter)
16 the frequency-changer, mixer, oscillator valve (an oscillator tube)
17 the amplifier valve, pre-amplifier valves
18 the coil assemblies (band-pass filter, intermediate-frequency filter; input, and oscillator, coil assemblies)
19 the variable condenser
20 the scale lamp, pilot lamp
21 the scale
22 and 23 three loudspeakers in 3 D-grouping:
22 the main loudspeaker, an electro-dynamic (moving-coil) loudspeaker
23 the tweeters (treble frequency loudspeakers)

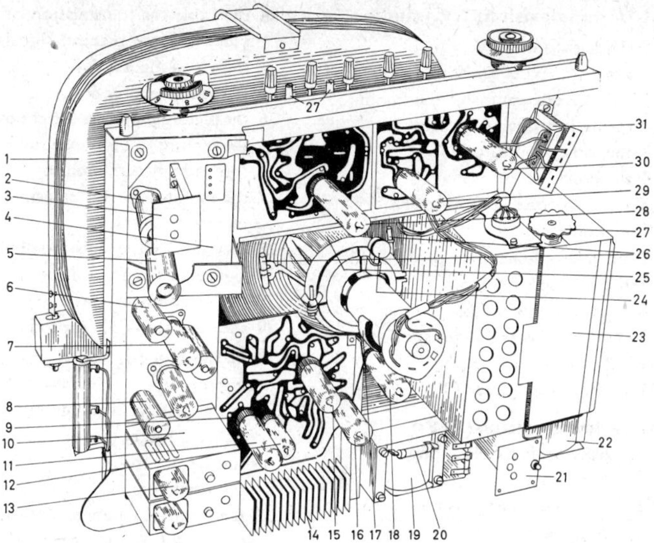

1-31 the television (T. V.) **receiver** (*coll.* telly) [interior]:

1 the picture tube

2 the H. F. (high-frequency) input (H. F. first stage, high-frequency first stage)

3 the aerial connection plate

4 the channel switch

5 the mixer stage and the oscillator

6 the vision intermediate-frequency transformer (a band-pass filter)

7 the vision intermediate frequency amplifier

8 the series resistance

9 the printed circuit

10 the vision detector

11 the video amplifier

12 the gated automatic gain control and and the black level clamp

13 the interference inverter

14 the selenium rectifier (*Am.* straightener)

15 the synchronisation separator with interference limiter

16 the sound intermediate-frequency amplifier

17 the ion trap magnet

18 the audio detector (sound demodulator) and the low-frequency input (first stage)

19 the smoothing choke

20 the hot conductor

21 the connection plate for remote control

22 the frame output transformer

23 the screening (shielding)

24 the centering magnet

25 the deflecting coil

26 the anti-distortion (equalizing) magnets

27 voltage selector

28 the frame (or vertical) blocking oscillator and the frame output stage

29 the line or horizontal line oscillator

30 the low-frequency output (end) stage

31 the sound output transformer

237 Television (T.V.) II

1-11 the television (T.V.) studio:

1 the television (T.V., *Am. coll.* tevee) camera
2 the camera cable to the monitoring instruments or sets
3 the camera operator
4 the dolly
5 the condenser (or electrostatic) microphone
6 the microphone stand or standard
7 the microphone boom
8 the microphone cable
9 the studio spot (studio spotlight)
10 the scene (set)
11 the television actor (T.V. actor);

12-39 the television (T.V.) transmission (telecasting, *Am.* telecast):

12 the sound-mixing (sound-monitoring) desk
13 the tape-recorder
14 the record-player
15 the sound engineer (control engineer)
16 the television (T.V.) sound-mixing room
17 the waveform generator for the production of horizontal and vertical deflection signals for the electron beams of the camera pick-up tubes
18 the impulse-transmitting cable
19 the monitoring apparatus

20-24 the film-scanning room:

20 the slide-scanner for the production of television signals from transparencies
21 the standard-film scanner for reproduction of talking films (*Am.* of talkies; for telefilms)
22 the narrow (sub-standard) film-scanner
23 the cable for sound transmission to the sound-mixing desk
24 the cable for transmission of the video (vision, picture) signals to the video-mixing desk;
25 the video-mixing desk
26 the picture monitors for choosing the picture to be transmitted (pre-fade picture monitors)
27 the monitor for the transmitted picture
28 the cable for transmission of video signals to the control room
29 the video-mixer
30 the television (T.V.) producer

31-34 the control room (monitoring room):

31 the television (T.V.) monitoring receiver for monitoring the video signals
32 the oscillograph
33 the terminal equipment (carrier equipment) for transposing (converting) the outgoing video frequency band to a range suitable for cable transmission to the transmitter
34 the transmission cable;
35 the demodulator
36 the modulator, part of a transmitter which converts the video frequency signals into radio frequency signals on a suitable frequency band (channel)
37 the modulator, part of the sound transmitter
38 the television (T.V.) aerial mast or antenna mast
39 the television (T.V.) transmitting aerial;

40 and 41 television (T.V.) reception:

40 the television (T.V.) receiving aerial, a foldeddipole aerial with reflector
41 the television (T.V.) receiver (television console, T.V. console)

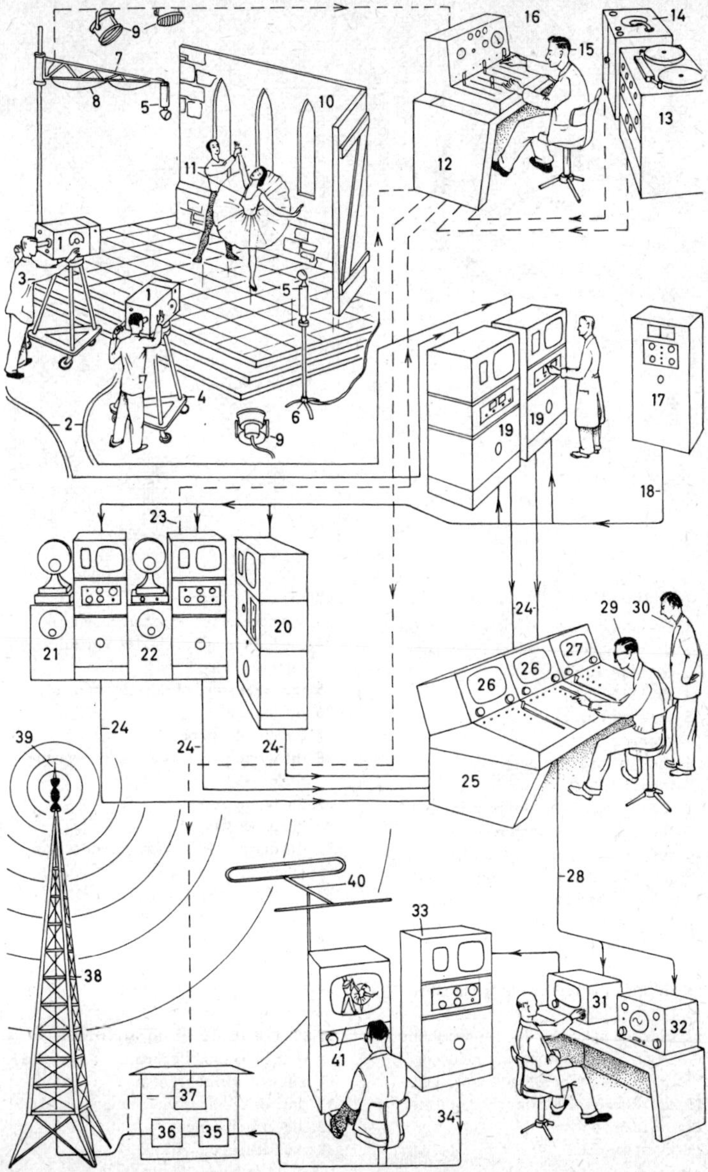
1
2
3
4
5
6
7
8
9
10
11
12
13
14
15
16
17
18
19
20
21
22
23
24
25
26
27
28
29
30
31
32
33
34
35
36
37
38
39
40
41

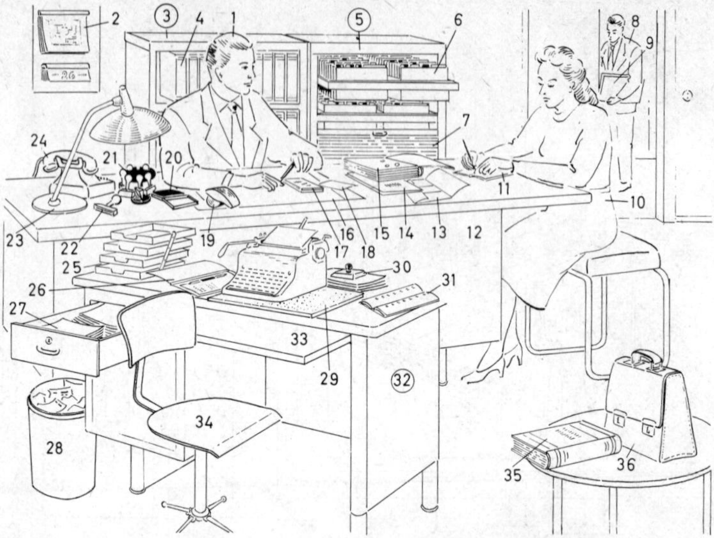

1-36 the office (*Am.* bureau):

1 the head clerk (chief clerk), an employee
2 the wall calendar (block calendar)
3 the filing cabinet:
4 the file (filer);
5 the card-index cabinet, a roll-front cabinet:
6 the card-index drawer
7 the roll front;
8 the office boy (errand boy, junior)
9 the records (file with records)
10 the female secretary, a shorthand typist (shorthand writer, stenographer)
11 the shorthand note-book
12 the desk (writing-table, bureau)
13 the folder (binder, filing case)
14 the folder
15 the file of letters awaiting signature
16 the desk pad
17 the note pad (copy block, scribbling block, *Am.* scratch pad, memo pad)
18 the slip of paper (*Am.* scrap paper)
19 the roller-type blotter (hand blotter)
20 the ink pad
21 the stamp rack
22 the rubber stamp
23 the desk lamp (*Am.* bureau lamp)
24 the desk telephone (*Am.* bureau telephone)
25 the letter tray, a four-tier letter tray
26 the letter file
27 the writing paper
28 the waste-paper basket (*Am.* waste basket)
29 the typewriter pad
30 the paper weight
31 the diary (engagement calendar, memo calendar)
32 the typewriter desk (typist desk):
33 the pull-out extension;
34 the office chair, a swivel chair
35 the directory
36 the brief case (portfolio);

37-80 the accounts department (book-keeping department) **and the record office** (registry):

37 the book-keeper (accountant)
38 the letter balance:
39 the balance weight

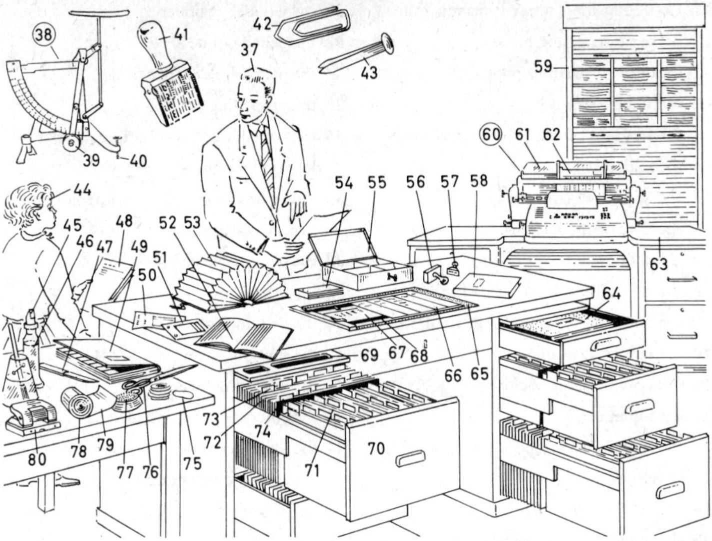

40 the adjusting screw;
41 the date stamp, an adjustable stamp
42 the paper clip
43 the paper-fastener
44 the office apprentice
45 the glue-dispenser (*Am.* mucilage-dispenser)
46 the office paste
47 the paper knife
48 the postage book
49 the postage-stamp book
50 the invoice (*Am.* bill, check)
51 the receipt; *sim.* voucher
52 the account book (book of accounts)
53 the expanding file for sorting letters, (filer)
54 the cash-report pad
55 the cash box
56 the booking stamp for stamping incoming invoices
57 the entry stamp
58 the cash book
59 the record cabinet
60 the book-keeping machine (accounting machine):
61 the holder;
62 the account sheet
63 the accounts desk
64 the ledger (balance book)
65 the desk pad for hand entries
66 the journal sheet (day sheet)
67 the account sheet
68 the carbon paper
69 the pen tray
70 the card-index drawer
71 the card index
72 the index card (record card)
73 the guide card (card-index guide card)
74 the guide-card tab (signal)
75 the rubber band
76 the paper scissors
77 the damping (moistening) sponge, a damper (moistener)
78 the roll of adhesive tape (roll of gummed tape, of Scotch tape)
79 the adhesive tape (gummed tape, *Am.* Scotch tape)
80 the letter punch (letter perforator), a perforator

1–12 the business letter (business communication, letter):
1 the sheet of writing paper (note paper)
2 the filing margin
3 the heading of the letter (letter-head)
4 the address:
5 the addressee (recipient);
6 the date of the letter (date)
7 the reference
8 the salutation (greeting), a heading
9 the contents (text, body) of the letter
10 the emphasized line
11 the complimentary close
12 the signature;
13 the stamped envelope, a window envelope:
14 the envelope flap (flap)
15 the sender's name and address
16 the envelope window (window);
17–36 writing utensils:
17 the penholder
18 the pen nib (nib), a steel nib
19 the fountain pen, a piston pen:
20 the fountain pen nib, a gold nib
21 the ink reservoir (ink barrel)
22 the piston
23 the inspection glass
24 the cap
25 the pocket clip (clip);
26 the ball point pen (ball pen):
27 the push button
28 the inner reservoir with the writing ink
29 the ball point;
30 the fountain pen holder, a holder to keep the nib moist
31 the lead pencil (pencil):
32 the wooden cylinder
33 the pencil point;
34 the pencil-holder (pencil cap)
35 the propelling pencil
36 the pencil lead (refill lead, refill, spare lead), a graphite stick;
37 the addressing machine, addressograph, a metal plate printer:
38 the plate-receiver
39 the ink ribbon
40 the printing pad
41 the stamping arm
42 the operating lever
43 the embossed printing plate
44 the plate feed;
45 the franking machine:
46 the postage stamp, a cliché
47 the ink roller
48 the levers for selecting the postage rate (franking value)
49 the hand crank (handle)
50 the ink ribbon feeder
51 the reading meter (indicating the franking-value)
52 the item-counter, a totalisator
53 the release lever

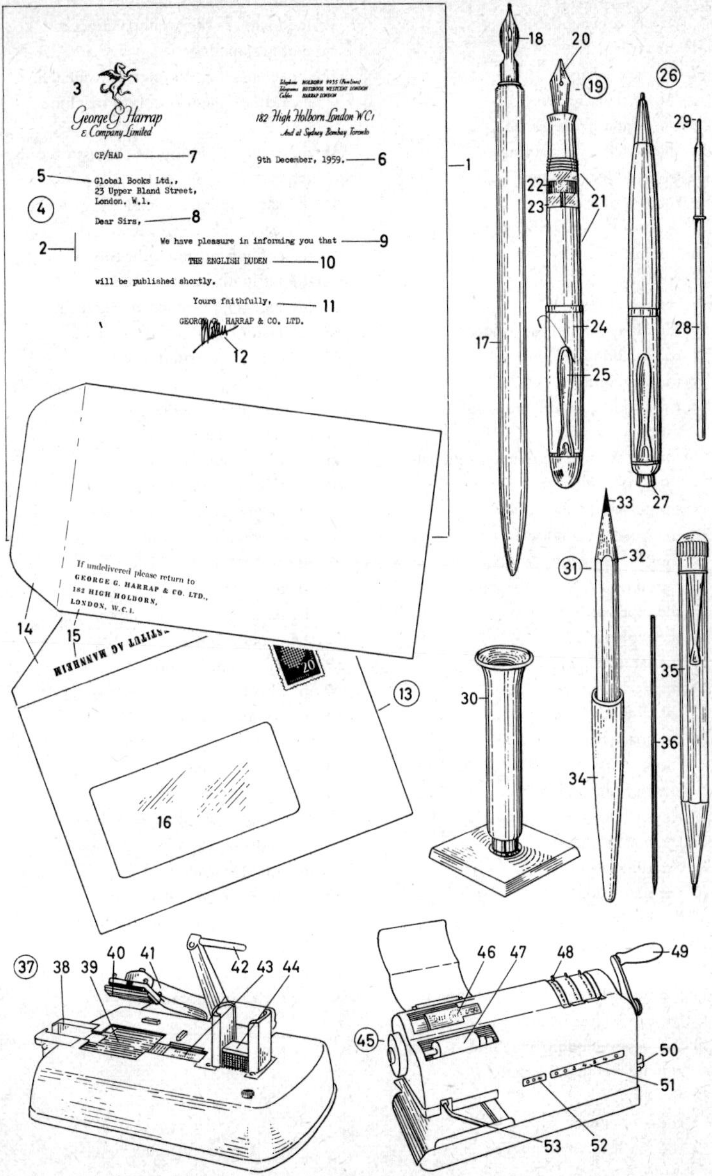
George G. Harrap
& Company Limited
182 High Holborn London WC1
And at Sydney Bombay Toronto
CP/HAD
9th December, 1959.
Global Books Ltd.,
23 Upper Bland Street,
London, W.1.
Dear Sirs,
We have pleasure in informing you that
THE ENGLISH DUDEN
will be published shortly.
Yours faithfully,
GEORGE G. HARRAP & CO. LTD.
If undelivered please return to
GEORGE G. HARRAP & CO. LTD.,
182 HIGH HOLBORN,
LONDON, W.C.1.
20
1
2
3
4
5
6
7
8
9
10
11
12
13
14
15
16
17
18
19
20
21
22
23
24
25
26
27
28
29
30
31
32
33
34
35
36
37
38
39
40
41
42
43
44
45
46
47
48
49
50
51
52
53

1–72 office machines,
1 the typewriter,
2–17 the carriage:
2 the carriage release
3 the tabulator clearance
4 the platen detent release
5 the line space gauge
6 the lateral guide
7 the front scale with margin stop
8 the paper-holder with paper guide rolls
9 the paper rest
10 the platen (roller, cylinder)
11 the card-holder
12 the type guide
13 the alignment guide (*Am.* alinement guide)
14 the typewriter ribbon (colour ribbon, *Am.* color ribbon)
15 the automatic paper feed
16 the paper feed release
17 the platen-turning knob;
18 the ribbon spool
19 the type bar with type
20 the type basket
21 the tabulator key
22 the back spacer
23 the double spacer
24 the space bar
25 the keyboard
26 the shift key, a key
27 the shift lock
28 the margin release
29 the ribbon switch
30 the line space lever
31 the line space plunger;
32 the eraser shield
33 the typewriter rubber
34 the type-cleaner, a plastic paste
35 the typewriter brush
36 the paper-stapling machine (stapler)
37 the file-stapling machine:
38 the matrix
39 the feed slide;
40 the staples (bar of staples)
41 the methods of stapling: clinching, pinning, nailing
42 the lever set hand-operated calculator, a calculating (accounting) machine (calculator):
43 the rotary counting mechanism (counter)
44 the cancelling (*Am.* canceling) lever (effacer) for the regulator
45 the column-setting indicator
46 the setting levers
47 the regulator (setting mechanism)
48 the result (product) register
49 the decimal bar with markers
50 the slide key
51 the operating handle
52 the result-effacer
53 the central effacer
54 the calculator clearance;
55 the hand-operated add listing machine with substraction, a machine for adding, subtracting, and multiplying:
56 the paper roll
57 the paper strip (paper tape)
58 the paper release
59 the tear-off plate or saw
60 the plus-minus lever
61 the column indicator
62 the error and release lever
63 the sub-total key
64 the grand total key
65 the nought (zero) keys
66 the multiplication key
67 the line space lever;
68 the pocket pencil-sharpener
69 the pencil-sharpening machine:
70 the tightener
71 the chuck
72 the shavings container

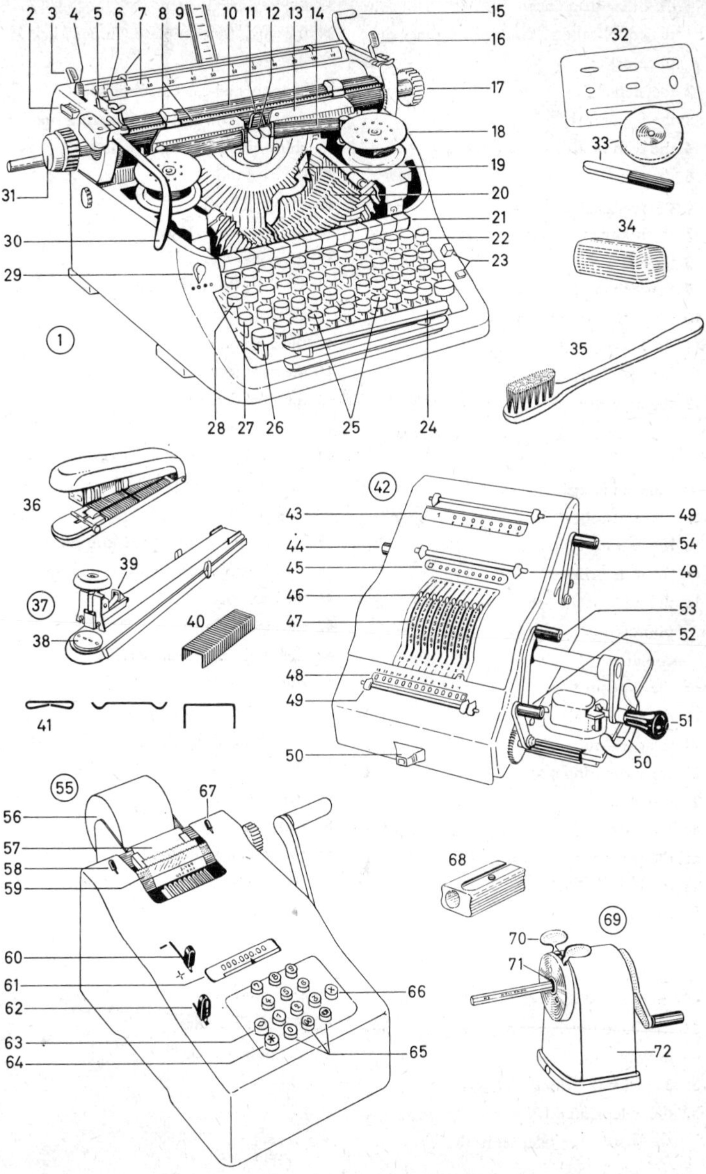
2
3
4
5
6
7
8
9
10
11
12
13
14
15
16
17
18
19
20
21
22
23
24
25
26
27
28
29
30
31
1
32
33
34
35
36
37
38
39
40
41
42
43
44
45
46
47
48
49
50
51
52
53
54
55
56
57
58
59
60
61
62
63
64
65
66
67
68
69
70
71
72
000.000,00

1–61 office machines,
1 the duplicating machine (office duplicator):
2 the stencil
3 the feed pawl
4 the feed board, a rising table
5 the clamp
6 the margin regulator
7 the ink feed button
8 the sheet-counter
9 the delivery board
10 the delivery jaw
11 the hand crank
12 the speed regulator;
13 the blue-print apparatus (copying apparatus, negative cyanotype machine):
14 the feed board
15 the feed roller
16 the exposure timer;
17 the blue print
18 the photostat (photostatic apparatus, photo-copying apparatus, *Am.* photo copier):
19 the exposure slot
20 the developing slot
21 the exposure switch
22 the measuring scale;
23 the photostat
24 the dictaphone (dictating machine):
25 the magnetic recording disk or disc
26 the index scale
27 the eraser switch
28 the tone arm switch
29 the tone control
30 the volume control
31 the hand microphone, a dynamic microphone;
32–34 the subscriber's teleprinter,
32 the teleprinter (*Am.* teletypewriter), a sheet writer, a telegraph:
33 the keyboard
34 the dial (finger plate, finger disk or disc);
35–61 punched-card machines,
35 the magnetic-barrel calculating machine, an electronic calculator:
36 the card unit
37 the barrel unit
38 the transformer unit
39 the control panel;
40–61 the group of machines (set of machines),
40 the card punch:
41 the card feed
42 the card delivery
43 the stacking table
44 the keyboard for alphabetical and numerical punching (alphabetic-numerical keyboard);
45–51 the electronic calculating punch,
45 the electronic calculator:
46 the control keys
47 the signal lamps;
48 the card punch (punch):
49 the card feed
50 the pull-out switch panel;
51 the connection cable;
52 the electronic punched-card sorting machine (card-sorter):
53 the card feed
54 the receiving magazine;
55 the punched-card accounting machine:
56 the card magazine
57 the feed
58 the printing unit
59 the type bars
60 the control keys;
61 the punched card

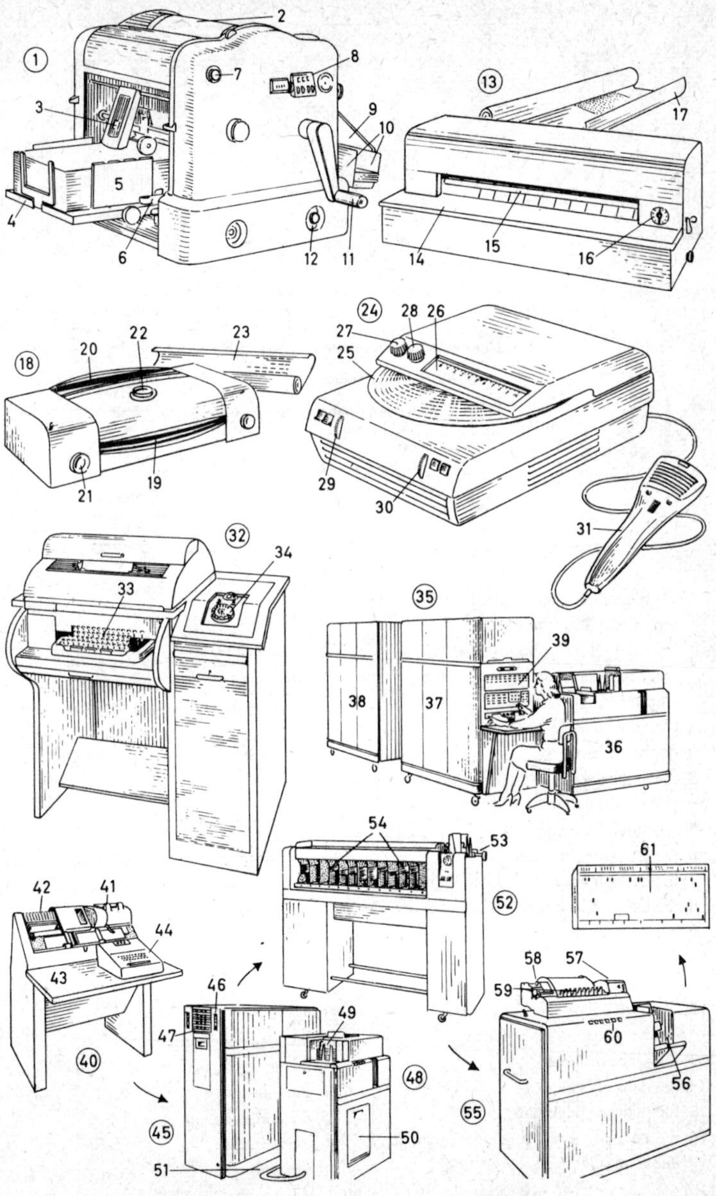
1
2
3
4
5
6
7
8
9
10
11
12
13
14
15
16
17
18
19
20
21
22
23
24
25
26
27
28
29
30
31
32
33
34
35
36
37
38
39
40
41
42
43
44
45
46
47
48
49
50
51
52
53
54
55
56
57
58
59
60
61

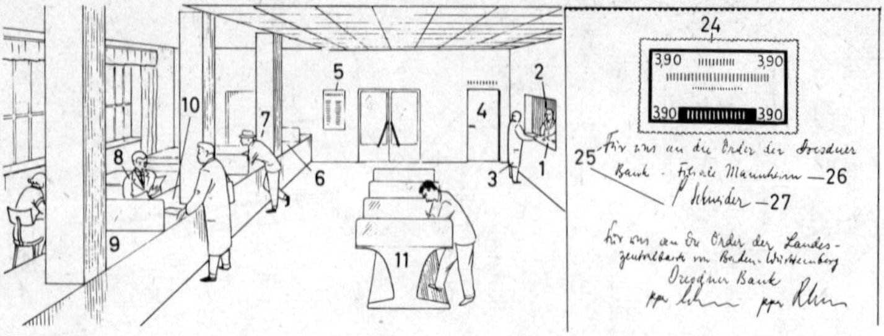

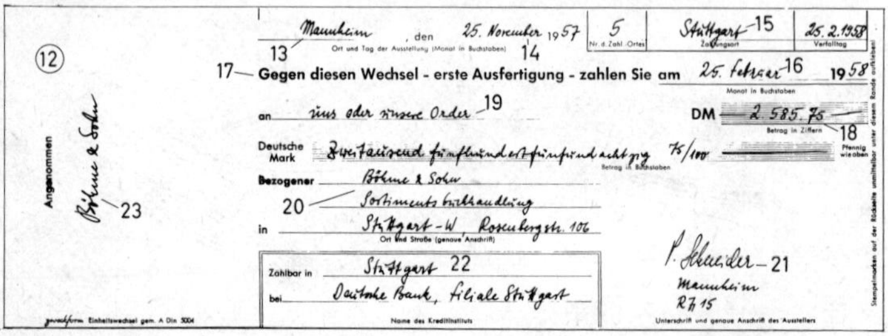

(12)

Mannheim, den 25. November 1957 — 13 — Ort und Tag der Ausstellung (Monat in Buchstaben) — 14

5 — Nr. d. Zahl.-Ortes

Stuttgart — 15 — Zahlungsort

25. 2. 1958 — Verfalltag

17 — Gegen diesen Wechsel - erste Ausfertigung - zahlen Sie am 25. Februar 16 1958

Monat in Buchstaben

an uns oder unsere Order — 19

DM 2 585.75 — 18 — Betrag in Ziffern

Deutsche Mark Zweitausendfünfhundertfünfundachtzig 75/100 — Betrag in Buchstaben — Pfennig wie oben

Bezogener Böhme & Sohn

20 — Sortimentsbuchhandlung

in Stuttgart-W, Rosenbergstr. 106 — Ort und Straße (genaue Anschrift)

Angenommen Böhme & Sohn — 23

Zahlbar in Stuttgart 22

bei Deutsche Bank, Filiale Stuttgart — Name des Kreditinstituts

P. Schneider — 21

Mannheim R 7, 15

Unterschrift und genaue Anschrift des Ausstellers

Stempelmarken auf der Rückseite unmittelbar unter diesem Rande aufkleben!

Einheitswechsel gem. A Din 5004

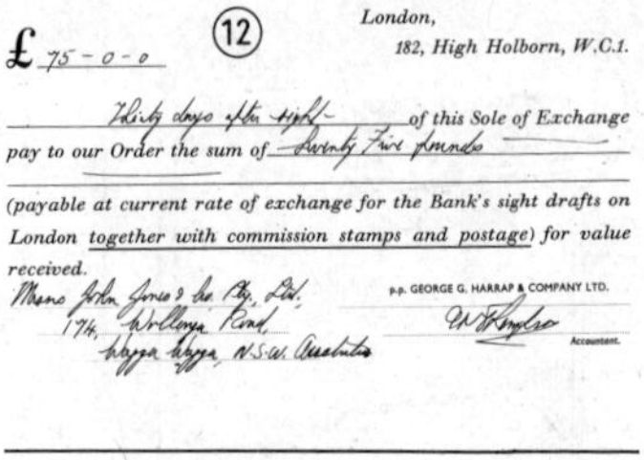

(12)

London, 182, High Holborn, W.C.1.

£ 75-0-0

Thirty days after sight of this Sole of Exchange pay to our Order the sum of Seventy Five Pounds

(payable at current rate of exchange for the Bank's sight drafts on London together with commission stamps and postage) for value received.

Messrs John Jones & Co. Pty. Ltd.
174, Wollongong Road,
Wagga Wagga, N.S.W. Australia

p.p. GEORGE G. HARRAP & COMPANY LTD.

Accountant.

1–11 the public department with counters, a hall with counters:

1 the till (teller's counter); *sim.* securities payment counter, exchange counter

2 the teller (cashier)

3 the bank customer

4 the entrance to the strong-room (to the safe vault)

5 the stock-exchange list

6 the securities counter

7 the deposit counter

8 the bank official (official at the counter)

9 the counter top

10 the foreign exchange counter

11 the writing desk, a high desk;

12 the bill (bill of exchange, B/E); *here:* a draft, an acceptance:

13 the place of issue

14 the date of issue

15 the place of payment

16 the date of payment (date of maturity, due date)

17 the 'bill (draft) clause' [an English bill does not need to have the word 'bill' or 'draft' on it]

18 the amount of the bill

19 the order (order on the bill, the payee)

20 the drawee

21 the drawer

22 the place of payment

23 the acceptance

24 the bill stamp

25 the endorsement

26 the endorsee

27 the endorser

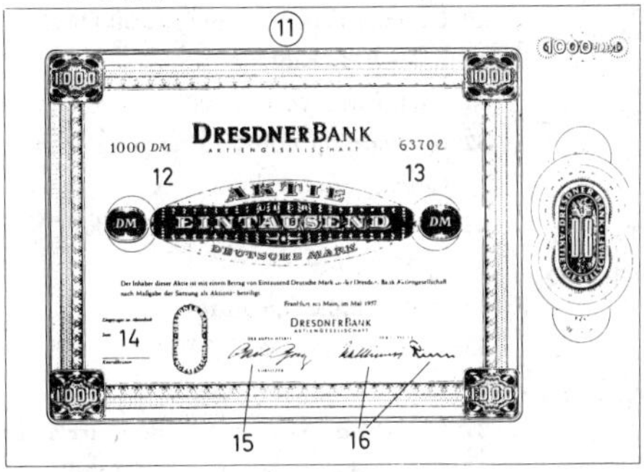

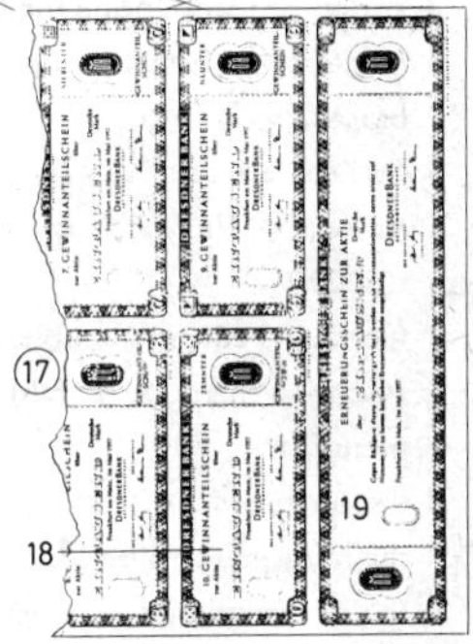

1–10 the stock exchange (stock exchange for stock, securities, or funds, *Am.* stock market),

1 the hall of the Exchange (trading floor, *Am. coll.* pit):

2 the market for securities

3 the counter for brokers (brokers' counter)

4 the sworn broker (stock broker), a broker (*Am.* stock jobber)

5 the independent broker (free stock broker, agent, *Am. coll.* pitman) for unofficial business

6 the member of the Exchange, a private person admitted for Exchange transactions

7 the jobber (dealer), a bank employee [not in Engl.]

8 the official list (board with the Exchange lists, board)

9 the Exchange usher (waiter)

10 the telephone kiosk (telephone box, *Am.* call box, telephone booth);

11–19 securities; *kinds:* shares (*Am.* common stocks), fixed-interest annuities, government and state loans, mortgage debentures, municipal (local) bonds, industry bonds (industrials), convertible loans,

11 the share warrant (bearer certificate of shares); *here:* share payable to bearer:

12 the nominal value of the share

13 the serial number of the bond

14 the page number of the entry in the bank's share register

15 the signature of the chairman of the board of directors

16 the signature of the chairman of the managing (executive) committee;

17 the coupon sheets:

18 the dividend coupon; for fixed-interest securities: the interest coupon (*Am.* share of stock)

19 the talon

1-28 coins (coinage, specie);
kinds: gold, silver, nickel, copper, or aluminium (*Am.* aluminum) coins,
1 Athens: tetradrachm (tetradrachmon, *fam.* 'owl', glauke) in the form of a nugget:
2 the owl (civic bird of Athens);
3 aureus of Constantine the Great
4 bracteate of Emperor Frederick I Barbarossa
5 France: a Louis XIV louis d'or
6 Prussia: a Frederick the Great reichst(h)aler
7 German Federal Republic: 5 D-marks (German marks); 1 DM = 100 D-pfennigs:
8 the obverse
9 the mint mark (mint letter) of the mint (place of mintage or coinage)
10 the reverse face
11 the lettered edge; the legend (inscription)
12 the coin image, a national coat-of-arms;
13 Austria: 25 schilling piece; 1 sch. = 100 groschen:
14 the armorial shield of the locality;
15 Switzerland: 5 francs; 1 franc = 100 centimes (rappens)
16 France: 100 francs; 1 franc = 100 centimes
17 Belgium: 100 francs
18 Luxemburg: 1 franc
19 Netherlands (Holland): $2^1/_2$ gulden; 1 gulden (florin) = 100 cents
20 Italy: 10 lire; 1 lira = 100 centesimi
21 Vatican City: 100 lire
22 Spain: 1 peseta = 100 céntimos = 4 reales
23 Portugal: 1 escudo = 100 centavos
24 Denmark: 1 krone = 100 öre
25 Sweden: 1 krona
26 Norway: 1 krone
27 Czechoslovakian Republic: 100 koruna; 1 koruna = 100 halerze
28 Yugoslavia: 1 dinar = 100 paras;

29-39 bank notes (paper money, soft money, notes, *Am.* bills) [*in Engl.* treasury (currency) notes],
29 German Federal Republic: 50 DM:
30 the issuing bank
31 the portrait watermark
32 the warning notice [a warning against forgery of notes];
33 United States of America: 1 dollar ($) = 100 cents:
34 the facsimile signatures
35 the control stamp
36 the designation of the series;
37 Great Britain and Northern Ireland: 1 pound sterling (£) = 20 shillings, 1 s = 12 pence, 1 penny (d), 2 s = 1 florin:
38 the guilloche pattern;
39 Greece: 1000 drachmas (drachmai); 1 drachma = 100 lepta;

40-44 the manufacture of coins,
40 and 41 the coining dies (coin stamps):
40 the upper (top) die
41 the lower (bottom) die;
42 the collar
43 the flan (blank, planchet)
44 the milling (edging, knurling) iron for milling (decorating) the coin's edge

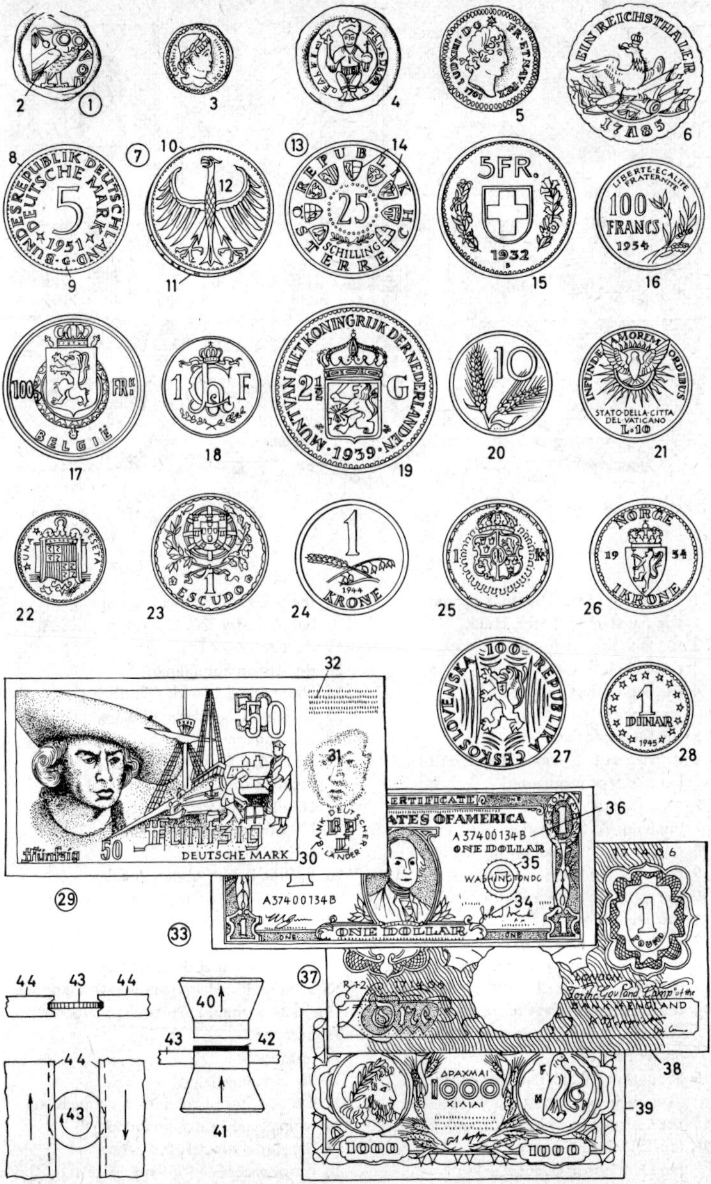
1
2
3
4
5
6
7
8
9
10
11
12
13
14
15
16
17
18
19
20
21
22
23
24
25
26
27
28
29
30
31
32
33
34
35
36
37
38
39
40
41
42
43
44

245 Flags

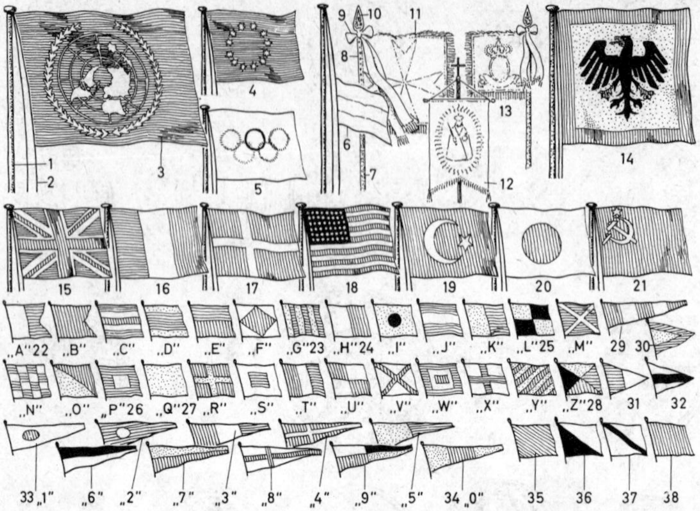

1–3 the flag of the United Nations:
1 the flagstaff with the truck
2 the tack line (halyard)
3 the flag cloth (bunting);
4 the flag of the Council of Europe
5 the Olympic flag
6 the flag at half-mast (*Am.* at half-staff); [in token of mourning]
7–11 the flag:
7 the flagpole (flagstaff)
8 the ornamental nail of the flag
9 the streamer (tail)
10 the top of the flagpole
11 the flag cloth;
12 the banner (gonfalon)
13 the cavalry standard (standard of the cavalry)
14 the standard of the President of the German Federal Republic [the ensign of head of state]
15–21 national flags (national colours, *Am.* national colors):
15 the Union Jack (Great Britain)
16 the Tricolour (France)
17 the Dannebrog (Denmark)
18 the Stars and Stripes (star-spangled banner, *Am. coll.* Old Glory; U.S.A.)
19 the Crescent (Turkey)
20 the Rising Sun (Japan)
21 Hammer and Sickle (U.S.S.R.);
22–34 signal flags, a set of flags,
22–28 alphabetical flags:
22 letter A, a burgee (swallow-tailed pennant or pendant)
23 G, pilot required signal
24 H ('pilot on board')
25 L, epidemic signal
26 P, Blue Peter ('about to sail')
27 Q, quarantine flag, a signal for a doctor
28 Z, an oblong pennant;
29 the code pennant, a pennant of the international code of signals
30–32 substitute flags (repeaters), triangular [pennants
33 and 34 numeral pennants:
33 number 1
34 number 0;
35–38 customs flags:
35 the customs pennant of revenue boats
36 'ship cleared through customs'
37 the signal for customs officer
38 the powder flag ['inflammable cargo']

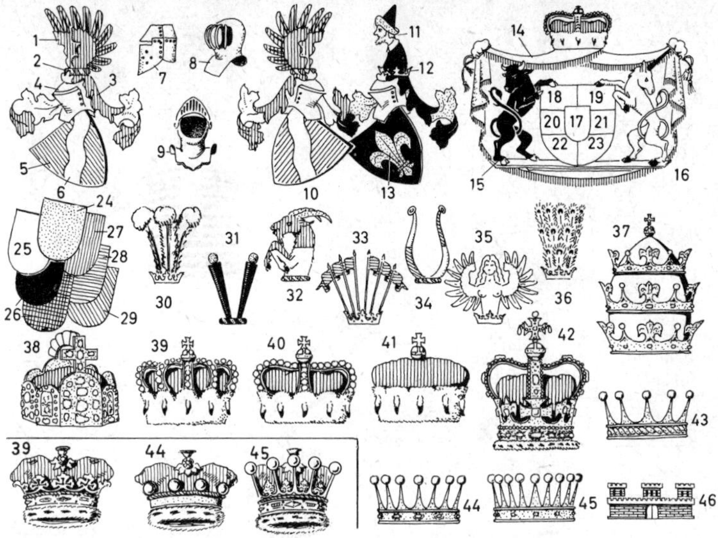

in England

1–36 heraldry (armory, blazonry),
1–6 the coat-of-arms (coat, arms, achievement, escutcheon, scutcheon, heraldic arms, armorial bearings):
1 the crest
2 the torse (twisted wreath, torque)
3 the lambrequin (mantling)
4 thè helmet (helm)
5 the shield
6 bend sinister wavy (bend sinister undee);
4, 7–9 helms:
7 the closed helmet (tilting helm)
8 the helmet with bars
9 the helmet affrontée with open visor;
10–13 the marshalled coat-of-arms:
10 the coat-of-arms
11–13 the woman's arms:
11 the bust
12 the crest coronet (crest crown)
13 the fleur-de-lis:
14 the pavilion (mantle)
15 and **16** supporters:
15 the bull (ox)
16 the unicorn;
17–23 the blazon (marshalling of coats of arms):
17 the inescutcheon; *the exact centre :* fess point (heart point)
18–23 the quarterings:
18 and **19** chief
22 and **23** base
18, 20, 22 dexter, right
19, 21, 23 sinister, left;
24–29 the tinctures (heraldic colours, *Am.* heraldic colors),
24 and **25** metals:
24 or (gold) [yellow]
25 argent (silver) [white];
26 sable (black)
27 gules (red)
28 azure (blue)
29 vert (green);
1, 11, 30–36 crests:
30 the ostrich plumes
31 the truncheons
32 the demi-goat
33 the tournament pennons
34 the buffalo horns
35 the Harpy
36 the bush (plume) of peacock's feathers;
37, 38, 42–46 crowns and coronets [continental type]:
37 the papal tiara
38 the crown of Charlemagne (of the Holy Roman Empire)
39 the ducal bonnet
40 the prince's hat or bonnet
41 the elector's hat or bonnet
42 the English Royal Crown
43–45 crowns of rank:
43 the baronet's or knight's coronet
44 the baron's coronet
45 the count's coronet;
46 the mural crown of a town's arms

247 Police

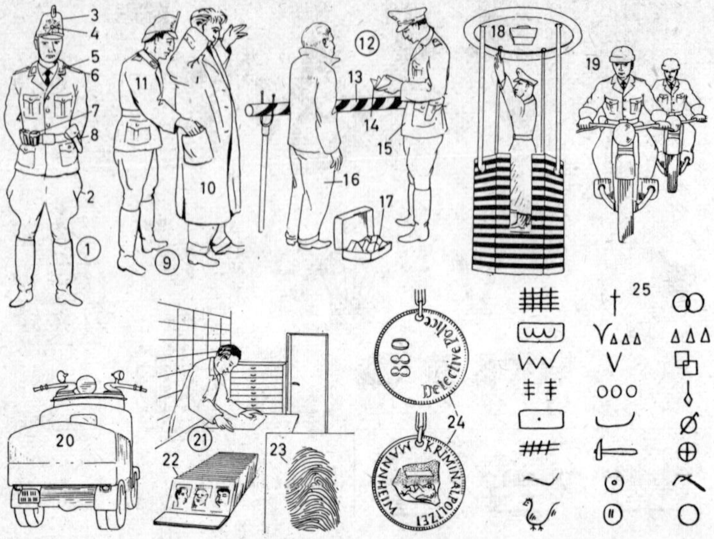

1–8 the police force (police detachment living in barracks, *Am.* platoon),

1 the policeman (police constable, constable, *pop.* bobby, *sl.* cop, copper, *Am.* patrolman, *on inspection :* roundsman):

2 the uniform (policeman's uniform)

3 the shako (cap)

4 the cockade

5 the collar badge

6 the epaulette (epaulet)

7 the cartridge pouch

8 the pistol holster;

9–11 the state police force,

9 the search:

10 the suspected person

11 the policeman;

12 frontier (border) check:

13 the turnpike; *here :* customs frontier

14 and **15** passport check (the examination of the passport):

14 the passport [with visa], a document enabling holder to cross frontiers

15 the customs officer;

16 the smuggler

17 the contraband (smuggled goods);

18 and **19** the traffic police; *other departments :* water police, police department for control of prostitution, police department for control of trading, etc.:

18 the traffic point

19 the motorised traffic patrol (*in Engl.* traffic police);

20 the water-thrower

21–24 the criminal investigation department,

21 the records department (*in Engl.* criminal records office, *pop.* rogues' gallery):

22 the criminals' photograph register

23 the fingerprint

24 the detective's badge (badge, *Am.* shield);

25 sharpers' (thieves') marks

1 the arrest:
2 the radio-equipped patrol car (*Am.* patrol wagon, squad car, prowl car)
3 the police detective (C.I.D. officer)
4 the arrest warrant
5 the arrested person (man under arrest, prisoner)
6 the policeman (police officer, *fam.* bobby, *sl.* cop, copper)
7 the pistol
8 the police dog
9 the handcuffs
10 the rubber truncheon (*in Engl.* wooden truncheon; baton, *Am.* club, blackjack, nightstick, *fam.* Billy);
11 the prison (*Am.* jail, jailhouse) **cell** (single cell, *Am.* reclusion):
12 the prisoner (convict)
13 the prison clothes
14 the prison warder (warder, *Am.* prison warden, warden, goaler, jailer, jailor, prison guard)
15 the spy hole (peep hole)
16 the service hatch
17 the barred window;
18 the trial before the Court of Law (Court of Justice, Assize Court; trial by jury):
19 the court room
20 the president of the court (presiding, or chief, judge)
21 the file
22 the assistant judge (assessor)
23 the juryman (juror, lay judge, *Am.* venireman)
24 the clerk of the court
25 the public prosecutor (*Am.* disrict attorney, prosecuting attorney)
26 the barret
27 the robe
28 the indictment
29 the accused (*Am.* defendant)
30 the defending counsel (barrister, advocate, *Am.* attorney and counselor-at-law)
31 the taking of the oath (swearing in)
32 the witness
33 the hand raised to take the oath
34 the witness stand (*Am.*; *in Engl.* witness box, *Am.* witness chair)
35 the witness barrier
36 the forensic specialist (expert, *Am. pop.* sharp)
37 the court doctor
38 the witness bench
39 the reporter
40 the Press table

249 The School

1–31 the lesson (instruction),

1 the class room (school room, form room, *Am.* grade, or recitation, room):

2 the wall blackboard

3 the blackboard frame

4 the blackboard sponge (sponge)

5 the blackboard cloth

6 the chalk

7 and **8** the writing exercise:

7 the syllable

8 the word;

9 the first-year boy

10 the teacher (schoolmaster, master, *Am.* schoolman)

11 the platform

12 the desk (teacher's desk)

13 the class register (form register)

14 the globe (terrestrial globe)

15 the reading board

16 the stuffed bird

17 the picture for object-teaching

18 the showcase with specimens

19 the boy in the corner

20 and **21** wall maps (school maps):

20 the map of the world

21 the map of Europe;

22 the pointer

23 the headmaster (*Am.* principal)

24 the ventilator

25 the class (school) cupboard

26 the class timetable (*Am.* schedule)

27 the desk (school desk)

28 the pupil (schoolboy, scholar)

29 the inkwell

30 the exercise book

31 the reader;

32–70 school materials (school utensils),

32 the slate:

33 the wooden frame

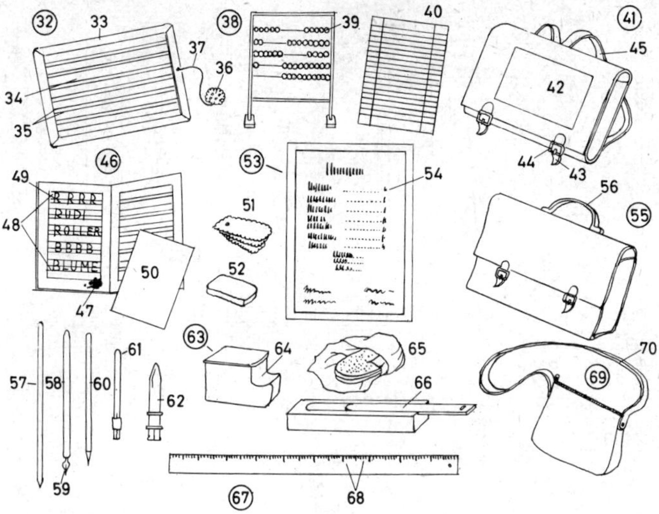

34 the slate surface (writing surface)
35 the lines
36 the slate sponge (sponge)
37 the sponge string;
38 the counting (calculating) frame (abacus):
39 the bead (counter, counting bead);
40 the sheet of lined paper
41 the satchel:
42 the satchel flap
43 the fastening strap (buckling strap)
44 the buckle
45 the shoulder-strap (carrying strap);
46 the copy book:
47 the blot (ink blot)
48 the writing
49 the letter
50 the blotting paper;
51 the pen-wiper
52 the rubber (india rubber)
53 the report:
54 the mark (*Am.* grade, point);
55 the school bag:
56 the handle;
57 the slate pencil
58 the penholder
59 the nib (pen nib)
60 the pencil
61 the pencil-holder
62 the pencil shield (point-protector)
63 the inkstand (lidded inkstand):
64 the penholder (pen) groove;
65 the sandwich for the mid-morning break (*Am.* for the intermission)
66 the pencil box
67 the ruler:
68 the centimetre and millimetre scale (*Am.* centimeter and millimeter scale);
69 the shoulder bag:
70 the shoulder-strap

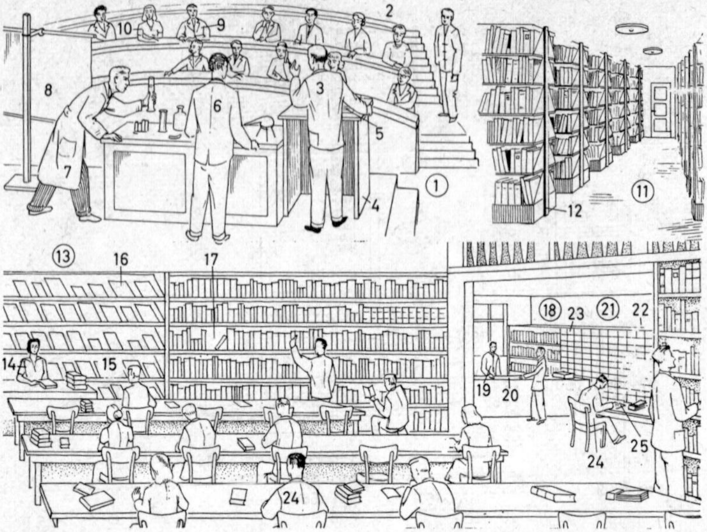

1–25 the university (*fam.* varsity),

1 the lecture:

2 the lecture room (auditorium, lecture theatre

3 the lecturer (university lecturer), a professor in ordinary (university professor) or an unsalaried private lecturer or a lector (*Am.* adjunct)

4 the lecture desk (rostrum)

5 the lecture manuscript (lecture notes)

6 the assistant

7 the assistant to the medical lecturer

8 the educational picture

9 the student

10 the woman student (*Am.* girl student);

11–25 the university library; *sim.* state library; official, or municipal (public), scientific library,

11 the stack room (room for storing books with the book stock):

12 the book shelf, a steel shelf;

13 the reading room:

14 the reading room supervisor, a lady librarian

15 the shelves for magazines. (magazine racks)

16 the newspaper racks

17 the reference library with reference books (handbooks or manuals, encyclopedias; dictionaries);

18 the lending library and the catalogue room (*Am.* catalog room):

19 the librarian

20 the issuing counter (out counter)

21 the main catalogue (*Am.* catalog)

22 the card-index cabinet

23 the index cabinet drawer

24 the visitor to the library (user of the library, library user)

25 the library ticket (borrower's ticket)

1–15 the election meeting (electors'meeting, electoral meeting, *Am.* caucus), a mass meeting (*Am.* rally),

1 and 2 the committee:

1 the chairman

2 the committee member;

3 the committee table

4 the bell

5 the election speaker (*Am. fam.* stump orator)

6 the speaker's desk, a rostrum

7 the microphone

8 the meeting (crowd, audience)

9 the distributor of pamphlets (of election leaflets)

10 the ushers (stewards)

11 the armlet

12 the election placard (poster)

13 the portable election placard (poster)

14 the proclamation

15 the heckler;

16–30 the election:

16 the polling station (*Am.* ward room)

17 the election official

18 the electoral register

19 the poll card with registration number (polling number)

20 the voting paper (ballot paper) with the names of the parties and the party candidates (*Am.* slate)

21 the ballot envelope

22 the female voter

23 the polling box (polling booth)

24 the voter with right to vote (man qualified, or entitled, to vote)

25 the election regulations

26 the poll clerk

27 the assistant with the duplicate list

28 the election supervisor

29 the ballot box:

30 the slit

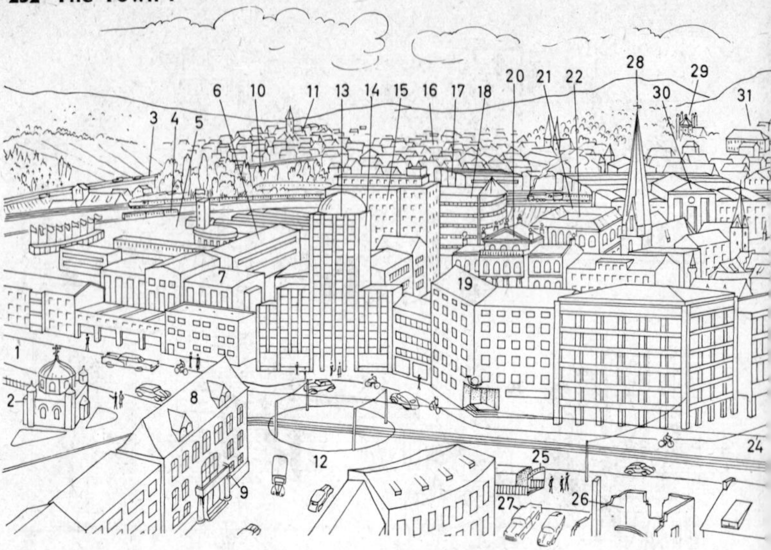

1–70 the large town (large city); *smaller :* small town, provincial town:

1 the main outlet road

2 the Greek-Orthodox church

3 the by-pass

4 the elevated railway (*Am.* elevated railroad, the elevated, El, el, L-train), a city railway (metropolitan railway, the metropolitan)

5 the exhibition grounds (*Am.* exposition grounds)

6 the exhibition hall (*Am.* exposition building)

7 the municipal hall

8 the law courts

9 the balcony

10 the municipal park

11 the suburb, a residential area (*Am.* residential section, uptown)

12 the circus (*Am.* circular place) with roundabout traffic flow

13 the multi-storey (multi-story) building

14 the advertising space

15 the office block, business premises

16 the municipal ward (quarter, district, *Am.* zone, section)

17 the tram depot (*Am.pop.* car barn)

18 the department store

19 the main post and telegraph office, a public building

20 the opera house

21 the museum

22 the glass-roofed well

23 the trolley bus (*Am.* trackless trolley)

24 the trolley bus overhead line

25 the entrance to the underground railway (to the tube, underground, *Am.* subway)

26 the bombed site

27 the parking place (parking ground, *Am.* parking lot), a car park

28 the town parish church

29 the synagogue

30 the main station (central station, railway terminus)

31 the outskirts of the town

32 the main business street, (*Am.* main street, main artery, arterial avenue)

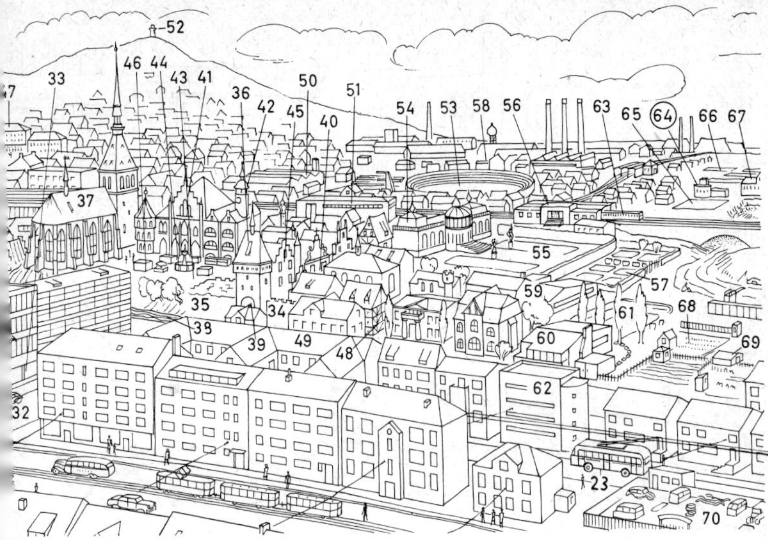

33 the business area (town centre, *Am.* center; city; the central area of the town, *Am.* downtown, business section)

34–45 the old town (centre, *Am.* center, of the old town):

34 the city wall, a circular wall

35 the rampart

36 the wall tower

37 the cathedral

38 the town moat

39 the city gate

40 the cul-de-sac (blind alley), an alley (alleyway, dead-end street)

41 the town hall (*Am.* city hall, city building)

42 the tower roof

43 the market (market place)

44 the market fountain

45 the historical building;

46 the market stalls (market stands)

47 the barracks with the parade ground

48 the half-timbered house (*Am.* frame house, frame home)

49 the block of flats (*Am.* apartment house, apartment hotel)

50 the covered market

51 the abattoir and cattle yard

52 the look-out tower (belvedere)

53 the sports stadium

54 the palace (castle)

55 the palace garden (castle garden)

56 the minor station

57 the botanical gardens

58 the industrial district

59 the residential area with detached houses (residential district, *Am.* residential section)

60 the town house

61 the garden

62 the multi-storey (multi-story) garage (*Am. coll.* carport)

63 the suburban railway (*Am.* uptown railroad)

64 the sewage works (sewage disposal works, sewage treatment works, sewage purification works):

65 the settling tank

66 the sewage farm;

67 the refuse incinerator

68 the allotments

69 the suburban estate (*Am.* cabin colony)

70 the car dump

1 the furrier's shop (*Am.* furrier store), a first-floor (*Am.* second-floor) shop
2 the street nameplate (street sign with the name of the street)
3 the bookshop (*Am.* bookstore; bookseller's shop, *Am.* bookseller's store) and second-hand bookshop (*Am.* used-book store):
4 the window display;
5 the street hawker (street vendor or vender, street seller)
6 the pavement (*Am.* sidewalk, walkway)
7 the by-street (side street); *sim.* cross street (cross road)
8 the main street (major road)
9 the crossing (cross roads, intersection)
10 the fruit barrow (fruit cart, *Am.* pashcart)
11 the fruiterer (fruit-seller, costermonger, coster, barrow boy *Am.* vender, peddler)
12 the customer (buyer, shopper)
13 the shopping bag
14 the police alarm
15 the street corner
16 the street lamp:
17 the lamp post;
18 the no-parking sign
19 the confectioner's (sweet shop, *Am.* candy store)
20 the beggar
21 the advertisement (poster) pillar:
22 the poster (placard, bill, (*Am.* sticker);
23 the druggist's shop (*Am. sim.* drugstore)
24 the florist's (flower shop):
25 the window display;
26 the coal lorry
27 the coalman
28 the chemist's shop (pharmacy, dispensary)
29 the chain barrier
30 the traffic island
31 the cyclist
32 the pedestrian
33 the pedestrian crossing

34 the road (roadway, carriageway, *Am.* pavement)
35 the taxi (taxicab, *Am.* cab) at the taxi stand (*Am.* cab stand):
36 the taximeter
37 the taxi-driver (*Am.* cab-driver);
38 the taxi passenger (*Am.* cab passenger)
39 the traffic light (*Am.* stop-go)
40 the fish shop, a corner shop (*Am.* corner store)
41 the show window (*Am.* shop window)
42 the window-cleaner
43 the bicycle stand (bicycle-rack)
44 the newsvendor (newspaper-seller, newspaper boy, newspaper man, newsboy)
45 the extra (special edition)
46 the litter (waste, garbage, rubbish) basket (bin)
47 the road-sweeper
48 the refuse (garbage)
49 the gully hole (gully drain, drain)
50 the slot machine (*Am.* vending machine)
51 the parking meter
52 the baker's shop
53 the hawker (pedlar)
54 the junk shop (second-hand shop)
55 the electric fire alarm
56 the traffic sign; *here:* Halt! Major Road Ahead!
57 the antique shop
58–69 the traffic accident (collision, smash-up),
58 the police van (*Am.* police car):
59 the blue light;
60 the damaged car
61 the overthrown motor bicycle
62 the skid mark
63 broken glass
64 the policeman, a traffic policeman
65 the motorist
66 the car documents
67 the eye witness
68 the motorcyclist; *here:* the injured person (accident victim)
69 the doctor giving first aid

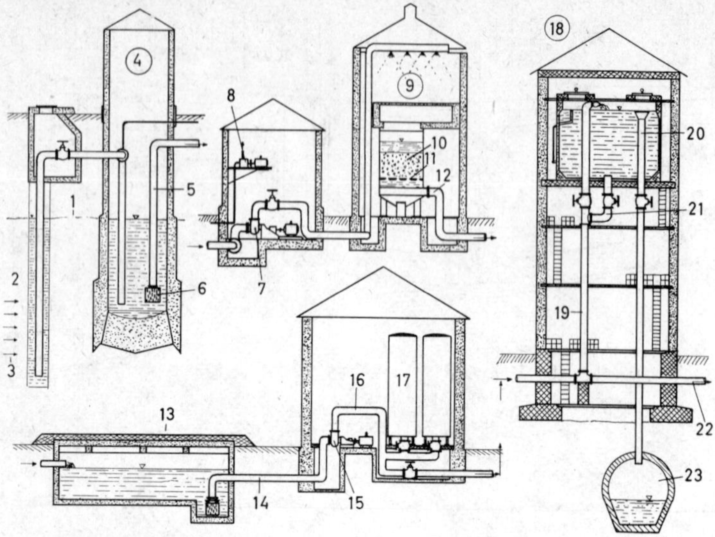

1–66 the drinking-water supply:
1 the water table
2 the water-bearing stratum (aquifer)
3 the ground-water stream (underground stream)
4 the collecting well (deep well) for the raw water:
5 the suction pipe
6 the suction rose (suction basket) with foot valve;
7 the water pump with motor
8 the vacuum pump with motor
9 the quick gravity filter plant (primary filter plant):
10 the filter gravel
11 the filter bottom, a screen plate (grating)
12 the filtered-water pipe;
13 the covered storage reservoir
14 the suction pipe with rose and foot valve
15 the main pump with motor
16 the delivery pipe
17 the air vessel
18 the water tower (service reservoir):
19 the inlet pipe
20 the overflow pipe
21 the outlet pipe
22 the distribution main
23 the excess water conduit;
24–39 tapping a spring:
24 the spring-water collecting chamber
25 the chamber wall
26 the access manhole
27 the ventilator
28 the climbing irons
29 the filling (backing)
30 the outlet control valve;
31 the bottom water outlet valve
32 the filter (strainer)

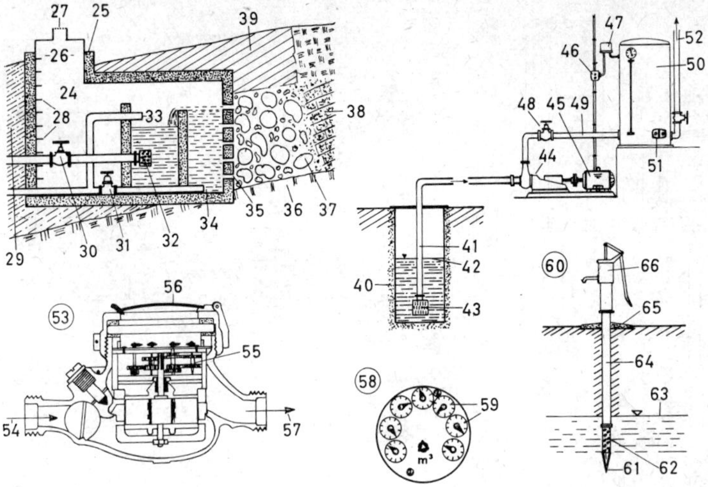

33 the overflow pipe
34 the bottom outlet
35 the earthenware pipes
36 the impermeable (impervious) stratum or layer
37 the gravel packing in front of the chamber
38 the water-bearing stratum
39 the clay or loam seal;
40–52 private water supply:
40 the well
41 the suction pipe
42 the ground-water level
43 the suction rose with foot valve
44 the centrifugal pump
45 the motor
46 the motor automatic safety switch
47 the pressure controller, a switch
48 the globe stop valve
49 the pump delivery pipe
50 the air vessel (pressure vessel)
51 the inspection manhole
52 the delivery pipe;
53 the rotary piston water meter:
54 the water inlet
55 the counter gear assembly
56 the lid with glass cover
57 the water outlet;
58 the water-meter dial:
59 the counters;
60 the pile-driven well:
61 the driving shoe
62 the filter
63 the ground-water level
64 the well pipe (seal)
65 the well head
66 the hand pump (hand feed pump)

Engl. fire brigade = *Am.* fire department

1-46 fire brigade training
(extinguishing, climbing, ladder, and rescue work),

1–3 the fire station:

1 the engine and appliance room

2 the firemen's (*Am.* fire-fighter's) quarters

3 the drill tower;

4 the fire siren (fire alarm siren)

5 the fire engine (powered pump):

6 the blue light (warning light), a flashing light (*Am.* flashlight)

7 the signal hooter (signal horn)

8 the motor pump, a centrifugal pump;

9 the motor turntable ladder:

10 the ladder, a steel ladder (automatic extending ladder)

11 the ladder mechanism

12 the jack;

13 the operator (ladder operator)

14 the extension ladder

15 the preventer (ceiling hook)

16 the hook ladder

17 the holding squad

18 the jumping sheet

19 the ambulance (ambulance car)

20 the resuscitation equipment, an oxygen cylinder

21 the ambulance attendant

22 the armband

23 the stretcher

24 the unconscious man

25 the pit hydrant:

26 the standpipe

27 the hydrant key;

28 the portable hose reel

29 the hose coupling

30 the suction hose

31 the delivery hose (high pressure)

32 the dividing breeching

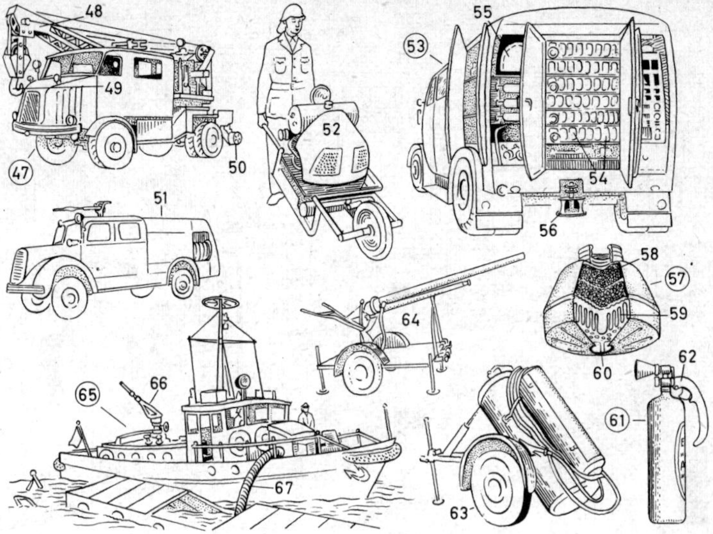

33 the branch
34 the branchmen
35 the surface hydrant (*Am.* fire plug)
36 the officer in charge
37 the fireman (*Am.* fire-fighter):
38 the fire helmet with the neck flap (neck guard)
39 the breathing apparatus
40 the face mask
41 the walkie-talkie wireless apparatus
42 the hand lamp
43 the fireman's axe (*Am.* fire-fighters ax)
44 the hook belt
45 the belt line
46 the protective clothing of asbestos (asbestos suit) or of metallic fabric;
47 the breakdown lorry (*Am.* crane truck, wrecking crane):
48 the lifting crane
49 the load hook (draw hook, *Am.* drag hook)
50 the support roll;
51 the water tender
52 the portable motor pump
53 the hose-laying and emergency tender:
54 the flaked lengths of hose
55 the cable drum
56 the windlass (winch);
57 the gas mask filter:
58 the active carbon
59 the dust filter
60 the air-inlet;
61 the fire-extinguisher:
62 the trigger valve;
63 the portable fire-extinguisher apparatus
64 the foam making branch pipe (water and air foam, *Am.* foam gun)
65 the fireboat:
66 the monitor
67 the suction hose

1 the lady cashier
2 the electric cash register (till):
3 the number keys
4 the correction button
5 the till
6 the money compartments for hard cash (specie, coins) and notes (*Am.* bills)
7 the receipted bill (bill)
8 the amount to be paid
9 the adding mechanism
10 the day's takings (turnover);
11 the glass-roofed well
12 the men's wear (gentlemen's wear) department
13 the show case (display case, indoor display window)
14 the wrapping counter (packing counter)
15 the tray for purchased articles
16 the lady customer (lady purchaser)
17 the hosiery department
18 the shop assistant (sales assistant, salesgirl, saleswoman, saleslady, *Am.* salesclerk)
19 the price card
20 the glove stand
21 the duffle-coat, a three-quarter length coat
22 the escalator (moving staircase)
23 the fluorescent light, strip light
24 the travel bureau (travel agency, *Am.* downtown ticket office)
25 the poster
26 the theatre (*Am.* theater) and concert booking agency (advance-booking office)
27 the accounts department (*Am.* installment office; *Engl.* instalment office)
28 the ladies' wear department (department for ladies' clothes):
29 the off-the-peg (*Am.* ready-to-wear, hand-me-down, store) dress
30 the dust cover
31 the clothes hanger (hanger)

32 the fitting room
33 the shop walker (*Am.* floorwalker, supervisor)
34 the dummy (tailor's dummy)
35 the easy chair
36 the fashion magazine (*Am.* fashion journal)
37 the tailor, marking the hem line:
38 the tape measure (measuring tape, metre tape, *Am.* meter tape; yard tape)
39 the tailor's chalk
40 the hem-line marker;
41 the loose-fitting coat
42 the sales counters arranged in a square
43 the warm-air curtain
44 the doorman (porter, commissionaire, *Am.* janitor)
45 the passenger lift (lift, *Am.* elevator)
46 the lift cage (lift car, *Am.* elevator car)
47 the liftboy (*Am.* elevator boy, elevator man, elevator runner)
48 the lift (*Am.* elevator) controls
49 the floor indicator
50 the automatic sliding door
51 the lift (*Am.* elevator) shaft
52 the lifting rope
53 the control cable
54 the guide rail;
55 the customer (purchaser)
56 the tricot goods
57 the linen goods (table linen and bed linen)
58 the material department (fabric department)
59 the roll of material (roll of cloth)
60 the head of the department (department manager)
61 the sales counter
62 the jewellery department
63 the novelty department sales assistant (salesgirl, saleslady, *Am.* salesclerk)
64 the bargain counter
65 the placard advertising bargains
66 the curtain department
67 the display on top of the shelves

1-40 the French park (Baroque park, ornamental park), palace gardens:

1 the grotto

2 the stone statue, a water nymph

3 the orangery

4 the bosket (bosk)

5 the maze (labyrinth of paths between hedges)

6 the natural open-air theatre (*Am.* open-air theater)

7 the Baroque castle

8 the ornamental fountains:

9 the cascade (stepped, artificial waterfall, *Am.* artificial falls);

10 the statue, a monument:

11 the monument pedestal;

12 the globe-staped tree, a round tree

13 the conical tree

14 the ornamental bush (ornamental shrub)

15 the wall fountain

16 the park bench

17 the pergola (arbour, *Am.* arbor; bower)

18 the gravel path

19 the pointed tree

20 the cupid (amoretto, amorino)

21 the fountain:

22 the jet of water

23 the overflow basin

24 the basin

25 the fountain rim (wall);

26 the person going for a walk

27 the school mistress (governess, *Am. fam.* schoolma'am)

28 the boarders (girls, pupils) of the girls' boarding school

29 the park regulations (*in Engl.* local bye-laws for parks)

30 the park keeper

31 the park gate, a wrought-iron gate:

32 the park entrance;

33 the park railings:

34 the railing;

35 the stone vase

36 the lawn (grass plot, grass lot)

37 the path border, a trimmed (clipped) hedge
38 the park path
39 the ornamental flower beds
40 the birch;

41-69 the English type of park

(landscape park, natural gardens) and park life:
41 the riding track
42 the horseman (rider), out riding (out for a ride)
43 the amateur photographer
44 the lovers (couple of lovers, pair of lovers, courting couple) at the rendezvous (date)
45 donkey-riding
46 the swan
47 the swans' house
48 the open-air meeting:
49 the soap-box orator;
50 the park pond (pond)
51 the rowing boat (boat, *Am.* rowboat)
52 the rower (oarsman)
53 the Lombardy poplar
54 the four-in-hand (carriage and four, *sim. Am.* tallyho)
55 the disabled ex-service man (disabled ex-soldier, disabled veteran), a cripple
56 the toy cart
57 the goldfish pond
58 the refreshment kiosk
59 the lollipop
60 the treadle scooter
61 the Salvation Army band:
62 the Salvation Army soldier (salvationist)
63 the female Salvation Army cadet
64 the bonnet
65 the collecting box (collection box);
66 the sleeping man (man asleep, sleeper)
67 the litter collector
68 the park-keeper, a municipal gardener
69 the waste-paper basket

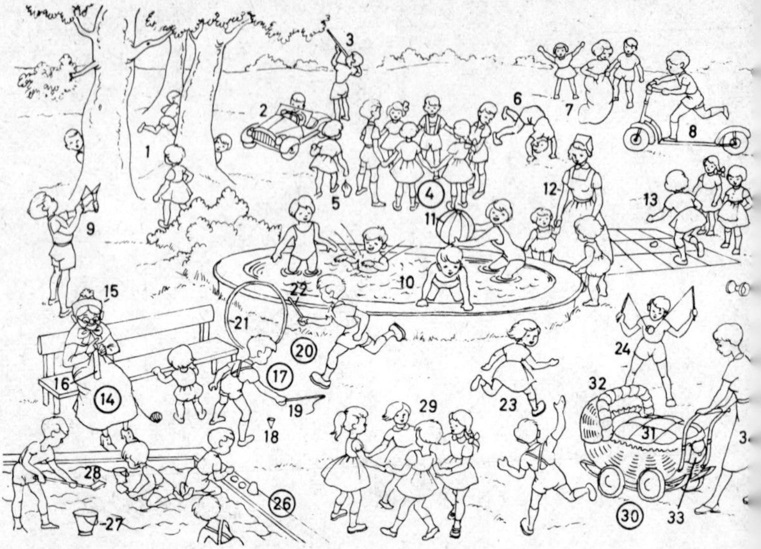

1-59 children's games (games):

1 the game of hide-and-seek (*Am.* hide-and-go-seek; *with babies and Am.* peek-a-boo)
2 the pedal car (treadle car)
3 the air gun
4 the game of drop-the-handkerchief (send a letter to my love), a round game:
5 the knotted handkerchief;
6 the somersault
7 the sack race
8 the scooter
9 the catapult (*Am.* slingshot, sling)
10 the paddling pool
11 the ball
12 the children's nurse
13 the game of hopscotch
14 the grandmother (*coll.* grandma, granny)
15 the bonnet
16 the stocking being knitted
17 whipping the top (spinning the top):
18 the top (whipping top, spinning top)
19 the whip;
20 bowling the hoop (trundling the hoop):
21 the hoop
22 the trundling stick;
23 playing at catch (at touch; the game of tig, or tag, or touch), an active game
24 the game of the devil on two sticks (diabolo), a game of skill
25 the diabolo (air top)
26 the sand pit (*Am.* sandlot):
27 the sand pail (sand bucket)
28 the sand spade;

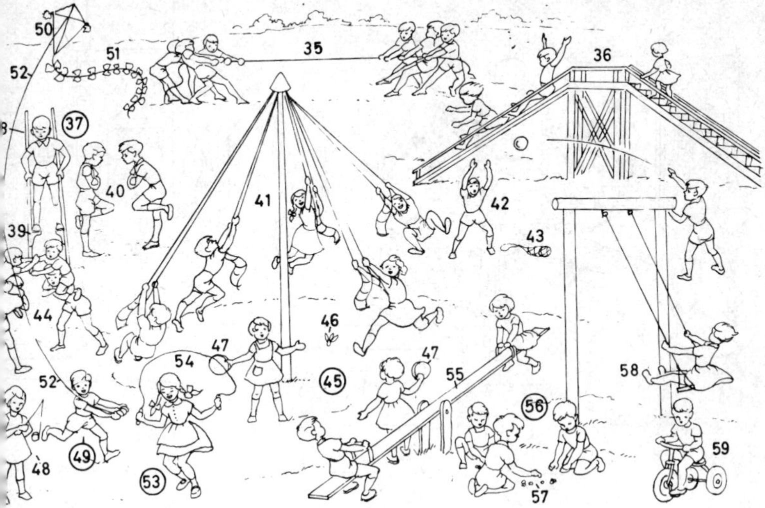

29 the round dance (*types:* here we go round the mulberry bush, ring-a-ring-a-roses)
30 the wicker pram (wicker perambulator, cane pram, wicker baby carriage, *Am. fam.* baby buggy):
31 the pram coverlet (pram rug)
32 the hood
33 the cane basket;
34 the nanny
35 the game of tug-of-war
36 the slide (chute)
37 walking on stilts:
38 the stilt
39 the bracket (foothold, step, support);
40 the cock fight (jostling)
41 the giant stride (giant's stride)
42 the game of ball
43 the ball net
44 the pick-a-back fight
45 the game of battledore and shuttlecock:
46 the shuttlecock (shuttle)
47 the tambourine (battledore);
48 the game of yo-yo
49 kite-flying:
50 the paper kite
51 the kite's tail
52 the kite string (kite cord);
53 skipping (*Am.* jumping):
54 the skipping rope (*Am.* jumping rope);
55 the seesaw (*Am.* teeter, teeter board, teetering board, teeter-totter)
56 the game of marbles:
57 the marbles;
58 the swing
59 the child's tricycle (tricycle, *Am. fam.* trike)

1–26 the hotel vestibule (hotel entrance hall), the reception hall:
1 the hall porter
2 the letter rack with pigeon holes
3 the key rack
4 the globe (ball) lamp, a frosted-glass globe
5 the indicator board (drop board)
6 the indicator light
7 the chief receptionist (chief reception clerk, *Am.* desk clerk, room clerk)
8 the hotel register
9 the room key:
10 the number tab (tag) with the room number;
11 the hotel bill (*Am.* hotel check)
12 the block of registration forms with registration forms
13 the passport
14 the hotel guest
15 the light-weight suitcase, a light suitcase for air travel
16 the wall desk
17 the boots (*Am.* baggage man);
18–26 the hotel entrance lounge (hotel lobby):
18 the page boy (boy, page, hotel boy, *Am.* bell boy, *coll.* bellhop)
19 the hotel manager
20 the dining room (hotel restaurant)
21 the lustre (chandelier), a multi-light fitting
22 the fireside corner:
23 the fireplace
24 the mantelpiece (mantelshelf, chimney piece)
25 the open fire
26 the easy chair;
27–38 the hotel room, a double room with bath:
27 the double set of doors
28 the service bell plate
29 the wardrobe trunk:
30 the clothes section (wardrobe section)

31 the linen compartment;
32 the double wash basin
33 the room waiter
34 the room telephone
35 the velour(s) carpet
36 the flower stand
37 the flower arrangement
38 the double bed;
39 the banqueting hall,
40–43 the party (guests) at table (banqueting party, private party) at the banquet:
40 the speaker proposing the toast (toasting)
41 the neighbour (*Am.* neighbor) of 42
42 the partner of 43
43 the partner of 42;
44–46 the tea dance in the hotel lounge,
44 the bar trio (bar band):
45 the violinist (fiddler);
46 the couple, dancing (pair of dancers, couple of dancers);
47 the waiter
48 the napkin
49 the cigar and cigarette boy
50 the cigarette tray
51 the hotel bar:
52 the foot rail
53 the bar stool
54 the bar
55 the bar customer (customer at the bar)
56 the cocktail glass (*Am.* highball glass)
57 the whisk(e)y glass
58 the champagne cork
59 the champagne bucket (champagne-cooler)
60 the measuring beaker
61 the cocktail-shaker
62 the barman (barkeeper, *Am.* bartender)
63 the barmaid
64 the bottle shelf
65 the glass shelf
66 the mirrored panel (panelled mirror)

1–29 the restaurant; *less pretentious:* inn, public house (*coll.* pub, *Am.* beer saloon, saloon),

1–11 the bar (buffet, counter):

1 the pressurised beer dispenser

2 the rip tin

3 the beer glass, a tumbler

4 the beer froth (head)

5 the spherical ash-tray on a stand

6 the tankard (beer mug)

7 the metal tube filled with hot water for warming beer in glass

8 the barman (*Am.* bartender, barkeeper)

9 the shelf for glasses

10 the shelf for bottles

11 the pile of plates (stack of plates);

12 the clothes rack:

13 the hat peg (hat pin)

14 the coat peg (*Am.* clothes-pin);

15 the wall ventilator

16 the bottle

17 the plate of food

18 the waitress

19 the tray

20 the lottery ticket seller

21 the menu (bill of fare, *Am.* menu card)

22 the cruet-stand

23 the tooth-pick holder

24 the match-box holder

25 the customer

26 the beer mat

27 the glass of beer (tankard of beer)

28 the flower-seller (flower girl)

29 the flower basket;

30–44 the wine restaurant (wine room):

30 the headwaiter

31 the wine list
32 the wine decanter
33 the wine glass
34 the tiled stove:
35 the stove tile
36 the stove bench;
37 the wooden panelling (wooden wainscoting or wainscotting, panelling, *Am.* paneling; wainscoting)
38 the corner bench
39 the table reserved for regular customers
40 the regular customer
41 the cutlery chest (*Am.* lowboy for silverware)
42 the wine-cooler (ice pail):
43 the bottle of wine
44 the ice cubes (pieces of ice, lumps of ice);

45–54 the snack bar (*here :* cafeteria), a self-service snack bar (*Am.* automatic restaurant, automat, quick-lunch restaurant, quick lunch):
45 the glass wall
46 the lady cashier
47 the cash register
48 the amusement machine, a slot machine (*Am.* nickel-in-the-slot machine)
49 the food compartment machine, a slot machine:
50 the coin slot
51 the food-delivery opening;
52 the drink machine, a slot machine
53 the stand-up counter (*Am.* lunch counter)
54 the partitioned plate-tray (*Am.* plate dinner, plate lunch)

261 The Café

1-26 the café (coffeehouse) and confectioner's; *sim.* espresso bar, tea room (tea shop),

1 the counter:

2 the large coffee urn

3 the tray for the money

4 the cake

5 the meringue, a sugar cake with whipped cream;

6 the confectioner's apprentice

7 the girl at the counter

8 the newspaper shelves (newspaper rack)

9 the wall lamp (wall bracket lamp)

10 the corner bench, an upholstered bench

11 the café table:

12 the marble top;

13 the waitress

14 the tray (serving tray)

15 the bottle of lemonade

16 the lemonade glass

17 the chess players, playing chess (a game of chess)

18 the coffee set:

19 the cup of coffee

20 the small sugar basin (sugar bowl)

21 the cream jug (cream-server, *Am.* creamer, cream-pitcher);

22 the admirer (escort), a young man

23 the young girl (teenager)

24 the newspaper reader, a café customer

25 the newspaper

26 the newspaper-holder;

27-44 the coffee garden, a garden café:

27 the terrace

28 the children, playing quoits:

29 the quoit

30 the catching stick;

31 the playing field

32 the veranda (verandah, glass veranda, *Am.* porch):

33 the window, a wide window;

34 the ice bomb

35 the glass of orangeade

36 the drinking straw, a natural or plastic drinking straw

37 the ice-cream dish:

38 the wafer

39 the ice-cream spoon;

40 the clip for holding the table cloth

41 the hand rail

42 the dwarf tree

43 the garden gravel

44 the foot-scraper;

45-51 the ice-cream bar and espresso bar:

45 the refrigerated container for preserving the ice-cream

46 the ice-cream

47 the electric ice-cream machine,

48 the machinery with ammonia-evaporator, compressor, and cooler:

49 the spiral mixer (mixing tool);

50 the espresso machine (Italian mocha machine)

51 the mocha cup

1–49 the spa (health resort, watering-place),
1–21 the spa park,
1–7 the salina (salt-works),
1 the thorn house:
2 the thorn branches
3 the distributing gutter for the brine
4 the brine pipe from the pumping station;
5 the salina attendant
6 and **7** the inhalation cure:
6 the open-air (outdoor) inhalatorium
7 the patient, inhaling (haling an inhalation, taking an inhalation);
8 the hydropathic (pump-room, spa hotel, assembly house) with the assembly hall (casino, Kursaal)
9 the colonnade (portico)
10 the spa promenade
11 the avenue leading to the mineral spring
12–14 the open-air (outdoor) rest cure:
12 the lawn for resting
13 the deck-chair
14 the sun canopy;
15–17 the mineral spring:
15 the pump-room (pavilion)
16 the rack for the glasses
17 the tap;
18 the visitor (patient) taking (drinking) the water
19 the bandstand
20 the spa orchestra giving a concert
21 the conductor;
22 the boarding house (*Am.* rooming house)

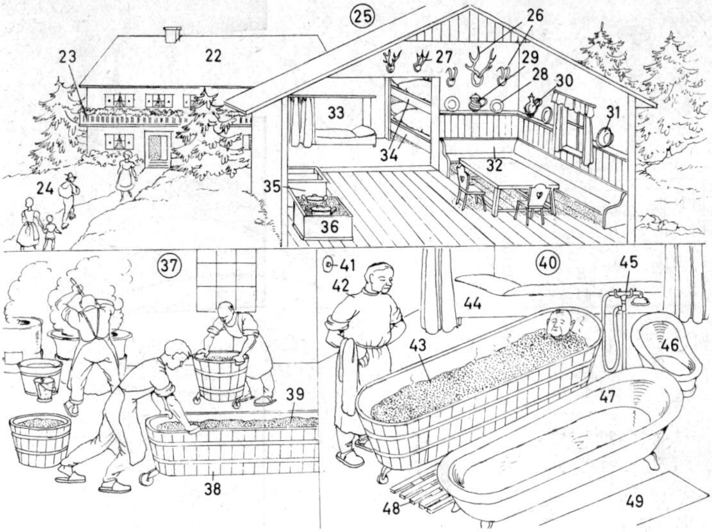

23 the continuous balcony round the house

24 the boarders (holiday-makers, summer visitors, *Am.* vacationists, summerites, summer boarders)

25 the weekend cottage, a log house (log cabin):

26 the hunting trophies (trophies of the chase)

27 the roe antlers

28–31 pewter (pewter ware):

28 the pewter plate

29 the pewter jug

30 the pewter bottle

31 the pewter bowl;

32 the corner bench

33 the folding bed (box bed)

34 the bunks (double berth)

35 the ice-box

36 the cooking-box (self-cooker; hay-box);

37–49 the mud bath,

37 the room where the mud is prepared:

38 the mud tub, a wooden tub

39 the liquid mud (therapeutic mud);

40 the bathroom:

41 the alarm bell

42 the bath attendant

43 the full-length mud bath

44 the couch

45 the hand shower

46 the hip-bath for the partial mud bath

47 the cleansing (rinsing) bath

48 the duckboards (grating of wooden slats)

49 the bath-mat

263 The Roulette

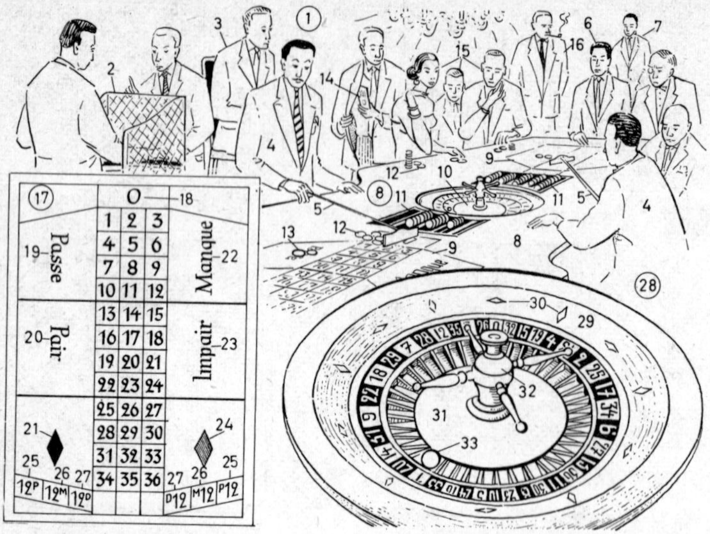

1–33 roulette, a game of chance (gambling game),
1 the gambling hall in the casino (*Am. pop.* gambling spot):
2 the cash desk
3 the chef de partie
4 the croupier
5 the croupier's rake (money rake)
6 the head croupier
7 the hall manager
8 the roulette table (gambling table):
9 the roulette plan (plan of the game)
10 the roulette
11 the bank (pool)
12 the chip (counter, fish, jetton)
13 the stake in the compartment;
14 the casino entrance-card
15 the roulette player
16 the house detective (private detective, *Am.* investigator);
17 the roulette plan (roulette table):
18 Zero (nought, 0, cipher)
19 Passe [numbers from 19 to 36]
20 Pair [even numbers]
21 Noir (Black)
22 Manque [numbers from 1 to 18]
23 Impair [odd numbers]
24 Rouge (Red)
25 Douze premier (the first dozen) [numbers from 1 to 12]
26 Douze milieu (the second dozen) [numbers from 13 to 24]
27 Douze dernier (the third dozen) [numbers from 25 to 36];
28 the roulette wheel:
29 the roulette bowl
30 the stop
31 the revolving disk or disc, showing the numbers from 0 to 36
32 the cross handle
33 the roulette ball

1–19 the game of billiards (billiards):

1 the billiard ball, an ivory or plastic ball

2–6 billiard strokes:

2 the horizontal stroke

3 the top stroke [resulting in top spin]

4 the screw shot [resulting in a back spin]

5 the spin (twist stroke)

6 the counter-spin stroke;

7–19 the billiard room (*Am.* pool-room),

7 French billiards (carambole, cannon billiards, *Am.* carom billiards, carom; carrom billiards, carrom); *sim.* German, or English, billiards (billiards with pockets);

8 the billiard player

9 the cue:

10 the cue tip, a leather tip;

11 the white (white ball, plain white ball, cue ball)

12 the red (red ball)

13 the spot (white ball)

14 the billiard table, a slate, or marble, table:

15 the bed (table-top) with green-cloth (green-baize, billiard-cloth) covering

16 the cushion (rubber ledge, top cushion);

17 the billiard clock (timer), a control clock

18 the marker

19 the cue rest

1-16 the game of chess (chess, the royal game), a combinative, or positional, game,

1 the chessboard with the chessmen in the opening position:

2 the white square (chessboard square)

3 the black square

4 the white chessmen (men, pieces) [white = W]

5 the black pieces [black = B]

6 the German system of letters and numbers for designating the squares, for notation of chess games (moves) and chess problems

7 the symbols for the chessmen used to represent chess positions:

8 the king

9 the queen

10 the bishop

11 the knight

12 the rook (castle)

13 the pawn;

14 the moves of the different pieces

15 mate (check mate), a mate by knight (knight's mate position) Kt – KB6

16 the chess clock, a double clock for chess matches (chess championships);

17-19 the game of draughts (draughts, *Scotch* dams, *Am.* checkers, chequers):

17 the draughtboard (*Scotch* dam-board, dambrod, *Am.* checker-board)

18 the white draughtsman (draught, *Scotch* dam, *Am.* checker), *also:* piece for backgammon and morris (mereles, nine-men's morris, nine-penny morris)

19 the black draughtsman;

20 the game of 'Salta' [a German game]:

21 the 'Salta' piece;

22 the board for **backgammon**

23-25 the German game 'Mühle', a kind of morris:

23 the board for 'Mühle'

24 the straight row

25 the double row;

26-28 the game of halma:

26 the halma board

27 the yard (compound, corner)

28 the halma pieces (men) of different colours;

29 the dice game (dicing); *sim. Am.* craps (crap shooting, crap game):

30 the dice box

31 the dices

32 the pips;

33 the game of dominoes (dominoes):

34 the domino brick (domino piece)

35 the double six;

36 playing cards (cards):

37 the French playing cards

38–45 the suits [42–45 only appear on German cards]:

38 and 42 clubs

39 and 43 spades

40 and 44 hearts

41 and 45 diamonds

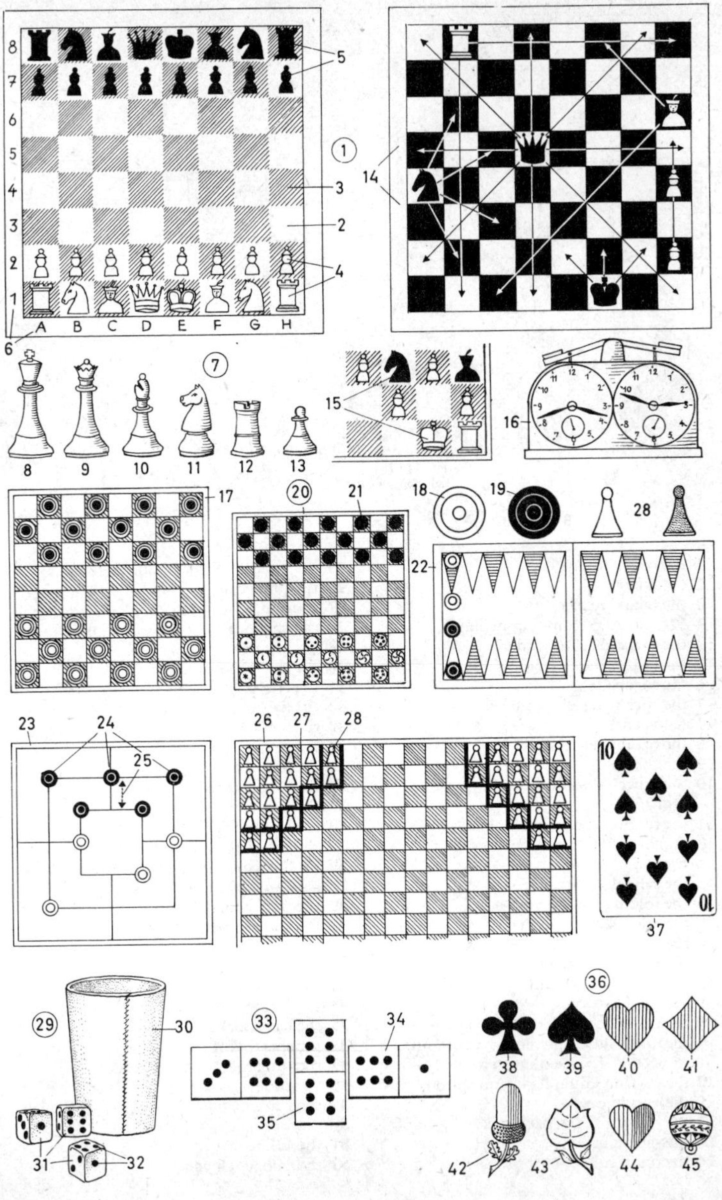
8
7
6
5
4
3
2
1
A B C D E F G H
1
2
3
4
5
6
7
8
9
10
11
12
13
14
15
16
17
18
19
20
21
22
23
24
25
26
27
28
29
30
31
32
33
34
35
36
37
38
39
40
41
42
43
44
45

266 Camping

1 the water-lily
2 the raft
3 the reeds (rushes)
4–52 the camp (camping-ground):
4 the caravan (*Am.* trailer)
5 the folding table (camp-table)
6 the sunshade
7 the spring-action camp bed (*Am.* cot)
8 the open-necked shirt
9 the shorts
10 the portable wireless (*Am.* portable radio)
11 the folding chair (camp-chair)
12 the jeans (three-quarter-length trousers)
13 the sandals
14 the folding stool (camp-stool)
15 the travelling (*Am.* traveling) first-aid chest (first-aid medicine chest)
16 the rubber water-bottle
17 the pocket-knife with corkscrew and several blades
18 the tin-opener (*Am.* can-opener)
19 the camp stove (picnic stove), a spirit, or petrol(*Am.* gasoline), stove
20 the folding knife, fork, and spoon
21 the picnic case
22 the kit-bag (*Am.* packsack)
23 the saddle bag
24 the foam-rubber cushion
25 the treadle bellows (foot bellows)
26 the toilet bag
27 the tent, a ridge tent:
28 the tent-peg (tent-pin)
29 the toggle
30 the guy-rope
31 the tent pole
32 the fly (tent fly)
33 the tent floor
34 the porch
35 the tent apse;
36 the air mattress
37 the tent awning (tent canopy)
38 the hammock
39 the lavatory (latrine, privy)
40-52 the jamboree (boy-scouts' rally; *local meeting*, *Am.* camporee),
40 the boy scout; *older member :* rover:
41 the water-bottle (canteen) with cup (with mug)
42 the knapsack (rucksack)
43 the mess kit;
44 the pennon (pennant)
45 the haversack
46 the sheath-knife
47 the scarf (neckerchief, kerchief)
48 the cooking site:
49 the cooking tripod
50 the wood fire;
51 the bell tent
52 the camp archway

1 the life-guard (beach-guard)
2 the life-line
3 the life-belt
4 the storm ball
5 the time ball
6 the warning notice board
7 the tide table, a notice board giving times of low-tide (ebb, ebb-tide, low water) and high-tide (flow, flood-tide, high water)
8 the board showing water and air temperature
9 the bathing platform
10 the pennon staff:
11 the pennon;
12 the water bicycle
13 surf-riding behind motorboat:
14 the surf-rider
15 the surf-board;
16 the water-ski
17 the inflatable beach mattress
18 the beach-ball
19–23 beach-wear,
19 the beach-suit:
20 the beach-hat
21 the beach-jacket
22 the beach-trousers
23 the beach-shoes (bathing-shoes);
24 the beach-bag
25 the bathing-wrap (bathing-gown)
26 the two-piece bathing-suit:
27 the bathing (swimming) trunks
28 the brassière (*coll.* bra);
29 the bathing-cap
30 the bather (*Am.* summerite)
31 deck-tennis (quoits):
32 the rubber ring (quoit);
33 the rubber animal, an inflatable animal
34 the beach attendant
35 the sand-castle
36 the roofed wicker beach chair
37 the underwater swimmer:
38 the diving goggles
39 the breathing tube (schnorkel, snorkel)
40 the hand harpoon (fish spear, fish lance)
41 the diving flipper for diving (underwater-swimming);
42 the bathing-suit:
43 the bathing (swimming) trunks
44 the bathing (swimming) cap;
45 the beach tent, a large tent
46 the life-guard station

1-32 the swimming pool (lido, pool, swimming baths, baths), an open-air pool:

1 the dressing cubicle (dressing cabin, cubicle, cabin)
2 the shower (shower bath)
3 the dressing (changing) room
4 the meadow (lawn) for sun bathing or lying in the fresh air

5-10 the diving arrangements:

5 the fancy diver (acrobatic diver)
6 the diving tower (tower for high diving):
7 the ten-metre (*Am.* meter) platform (stage, board)
8 the five-metre (*Am.* meter) platform (stage, board)
9 the three-metre (*Am.* meter) springboard (diving board)
10 the one-metre (*Am.* meter) board, a springboard;
11 the diving pool
12 the straight header; *sim.* swallow dive (*Am.* swan dive)
13 the jump
14 the crouched jump (*fam.* honeypot)
15 the superintendent of the baths

16-20 the swimming lesson (swimming instruction):

16 the swimming instructor (swimming teacher)
17 the learner, swimming
18 the water wings (*coll.* Mae West)
19 the swimming belt (cork belt, cork ring)
20 land practice (stroke exercises);
21–23 the swimming pools (swimming baths):
21 the non-swimmers' pool (shallow pool for non-swimmers)
22 the foot bath
23 the swimmers' pool (deep pool for swimmers);

24-32 the free-style swimming race (relay race) of a relay team:

24 the timekeeper
25 the touch umpire
26 the turn umpire
27 the starting block (starting place)
28 a competitor touching the side
29 the racing dive (racing plunge)
30 the starter
31 the swimming lane
32 the rope with cork floats;

33-40 swimming strokes (styles of swimming strokes):

33 the breast stroke
34 the butterfly stroke
35 the dolphin stroke
36 the back stroke
37 the side stroke
38 the crawl (crawling); *sim.* trudgen stroke (trudgen, *err.* trudgeon; hand-over-hand swimming, double overarm stroke)
39 diving (underwater-swimming)
40 treading water;

41-46 diving (high diving, dives, acrobatic dives):

41 the front jack knife (pike dive), from standing position
42 the isander (reverse dive)
43 the double backward somersault
44 the running twist (twist dive)
45 the screw dive (screw)
46 the handstand dive;

47-51 water polo:

47 the water polo goal
48 the goalkeeper
49 the water-polo ball
50 the back
51 the forward

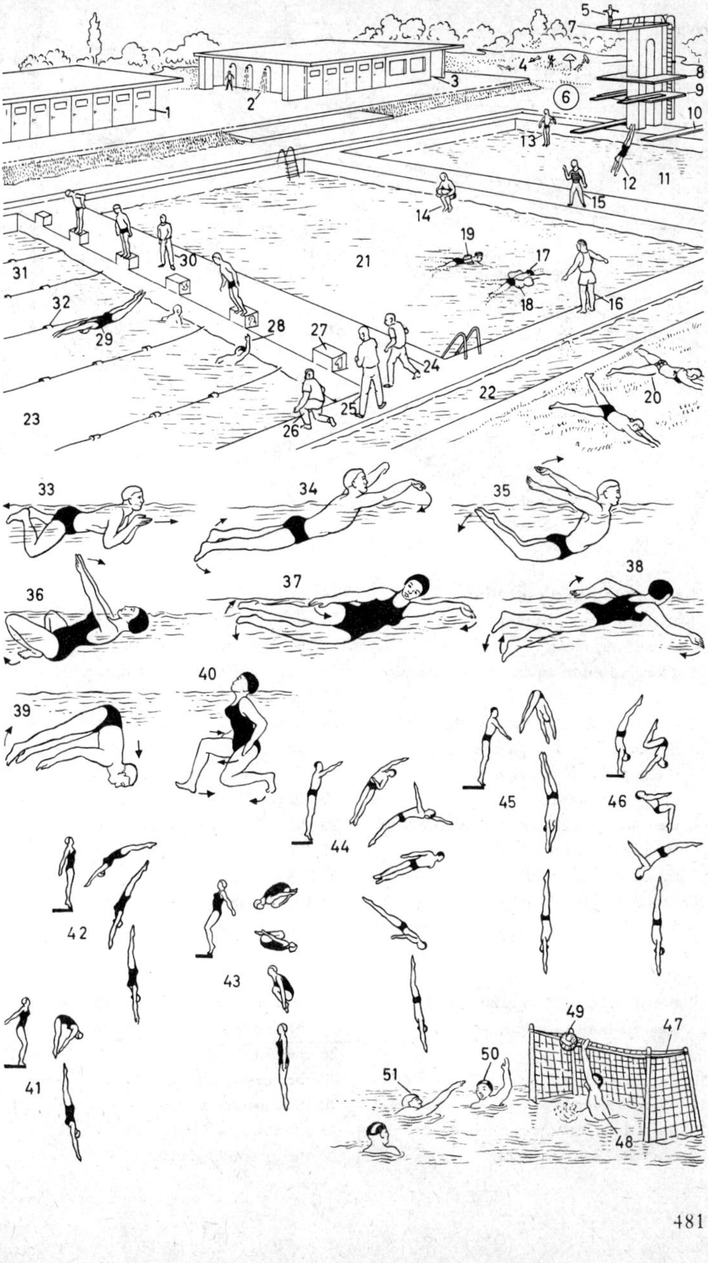
1
2
3
4
5
6
7
8
9
10
11
12
13
14
15
16
17
18
19
20
21
22
23
24
25
26
27
28
29
30
31
32
33
34
35
36
37
38
39
40
41
42
43
44
45
46
47
48
49
50
51

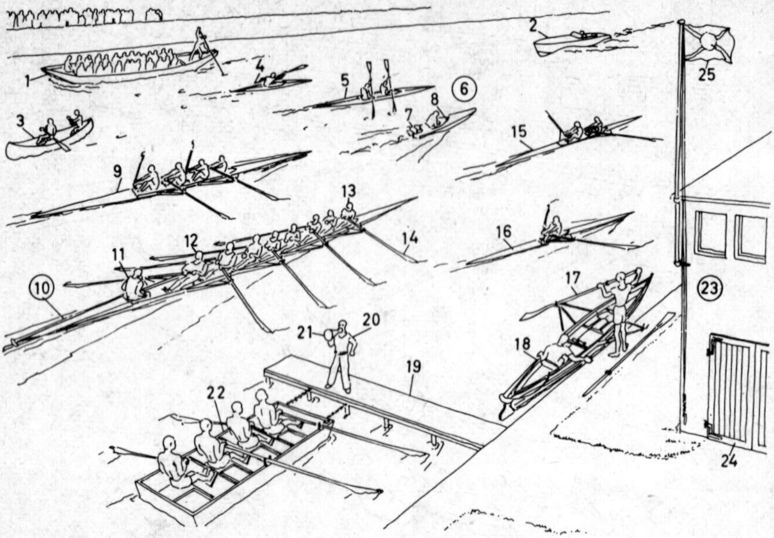

1-66 rowing and paddling,

1–18 taking up positions for the regatta (boat race, race):

1 a kind of punt, an excursion (pleasure) boat

2 the motorboat (motor launch)

3 the Canadian canoe, a canoe

4 the kayak (Rob Roy), a canoe

5 the tandem kayak

6 the outboard motorboat, a speedboat (racing motorboat):

7 the outboard motor

8 the cockpit (open well);

9–16 racing boats (sports boats, outriggers),

9–15 rowing boats (*Am.* rowboats):

9 the light four (coxswainless four), a carvel-built boat (shell-built boat)

10 the eight (racing-eight):

11 the coxswain (cox)

12 the stroke, an oarsman (rower)

13 the bow (bow oarsman)

14 the oar;

15 the pair-oar;

16 the single sculler (racing sculler, *Am.* racing shell, shell);

17 the scull

18 the single skiff with coxswain (clinker-built skiff);

19 the landing stage

20–22 rowing practice:

20 the coach (rowing instructor)

21 the megaphone (*Am. coll.* meg, megger)

22 the fixed tub (tank);

23 the club house:

24 the boat house

25 the club's flag;

26–33 the four-oared gig, a gig, a boat with tholes (in-rigged rowlocks), a touring boat:

26 the rudder

27 the coxswain's seat (thwart)

28 the oarsman's seat (oarsman's thwart)

29 the rowlock (thole, *Am.* oarlock)

30 the gunwale (gunnel)

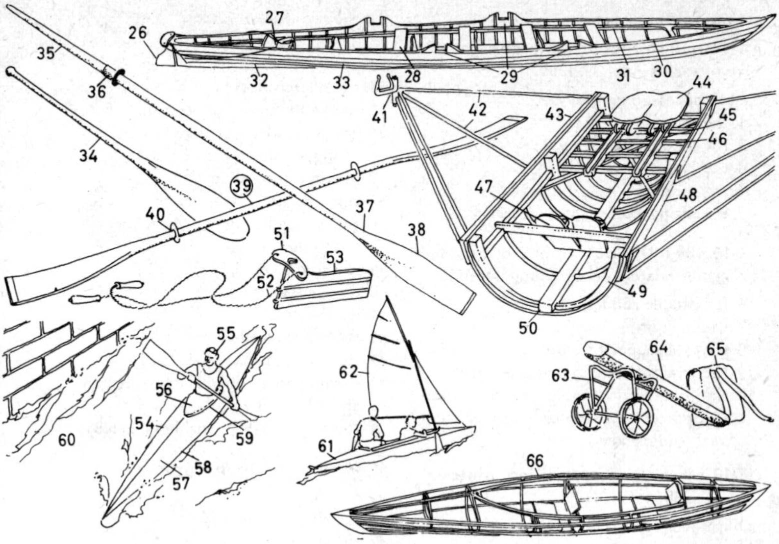

31 the scarboards (inner lining)
32 the keel (outside keel, outer keel)
33 the outer skin [clinker-built, clincher-built];
34 the single paddle
35–38 the oar (scull):
35 the shaft (oar shaft)
36 the button
37 the oar neck
38 the blade (oar blade);
39 the double-bladed paddle:
40 the drip cup;
41–50 the sliding seat:
41 the rowlock (*Am.* oarlock; swivel rowlock, outrigged rowlock)
42 the outrig
43 the saxboard
44 the sliding seat
45 the runner
46 the shoulder
47 the stretcher
48 the outer skin
49 the rib
50 the keel (inner keel, inside keel, kelson);
51–53 the rudder:
51 the rudder yoke
52 the yoke lines
53 the blade (rudder blade);
54–66 folding boats (collapsible boats, canoes):
54 the single-seater folding boat, a sporting single
55 the canoeist
56 the canvas (splasher, spray screen)
57 the deck
58 the rubberized canvas hull (outer hull, boat skin)
59 the sill
60 the raft chute (raft channel)
61 the two-seater folding boat, a touring double-seater
62 the sail for folding boat
63 the two-wheeled boat carriage
64 the bag for the rods
65 the rucksack for the hull (skin, shell)
66 the frame of the folding boat

1-60 sailing (yachting),

1-10 hull shapes of sailing boats (of yachts; *Am.* sailboats),

1–4 the sea-going keel yacht:
1 the stern
2 the spoon-shaped bow
3 the keel (ballast keel)
4 the rudder;
5 the racing keel-yacht with lead keel

6-10 the jolly boat, a centre-board (*Am.* center board) yacht (sailing dinghy):
6 the liftable rudder
7 the cockpit
8 the cabin superstructure
9 the straight stem (up-and-down stem)
10 the liftable (movable) centre board (drop keel; *Am.* center board, shifting keel, sliding keel);

11-18 stern shapes of sailing boats (of yachts):
11 the yacht stern
12 the yacht's square stern (transom stern)
13 the canoe stern
14 the cruiser stern (double-end stern)
15 the deadwood
16 the name-plate
17 the square stern
18 the transom;

19-26 the planking,
19–21 the clinker (clincher, clencher) planking:
19 the outside plank
20 the frame (rib), a transverse frame
21 the clinch (clinched, clenched) nail;
22 the carvel planking
23 the seam-frame construction
24 the seam frame, a longitudinal frame
25 the diagonal carvel planking
26 the inner planking;

27-50 types of yachts:
27 the schooner yacht 'America' [1851]
28–32 the schooner yacht, a two-master:
28 the mainsail
29 the schooner foresail
30 the jib topsail
31 the jib header rig, a schooner with triangular mainsail
32 the staysail schooner;
33–36 the yawl:
33 the mizzen sail
34 the mizzen mast
35 the balloon jib (balloon sail, Genoa jib)
36 the jib header rig, a yawl with triangular mainsail;
37–40 the cutter yacht (cutter):
37 the topsail
38 the jib header rig, a yacht with triangular mainsail
39 the spinnaker, an extra sail
40 the spinnaker boom;
41–44 the ketch:
41 the mizzen sail
42 the mizzen mast
43 the jib header rig, a ketch with main and mizzen triangular sails
44 the staysail ketch (wishbone ketch);

45-50 types of sloop riggings:
45 the sloop
46 the sliding gunter gaff
47 the stern stay (after stay)
48 the bow stay
49 the bow stay jumper strut
50 the Baltic Sea sloop;

51-60 the regatta (regatta-sailing, the sailing regatta):
51 the start
52–54 going about (tacking, making about, putting about; change of direction when sailing to windward; *repeated tacking:* beating):
52 luffing (rounding to) [let fly foresheet, haul main sheet, luff the helm, down the helm, port the helm]
53 the sails shiver or flap
54 belay the sails;
55 the turning buoy (turning mark)
56–58 wearing (change of direction when sailing before the wind):
56 falling off
57 the foresail shivers or flaps
58 belay the sails;
59 the finish
60 the direction of wind

1
2
3
4
5
6
7
8
9
10
11
12
13
14
15
16
17
18
19
20
21
22
23
24
25
26
27
28
29
30
31
32
33
34
35
36
37
38
39
40
41
42
43
44
45
46
47
48
49
50
51
52
53
54
55
56
57
58
59
60

Engl. glider [aircraft] = *Am.* sailplane

1–23 gliding (soaring, sailplaning),

1-12 glider launching methods,

1 the motorcar-tow (*Am.* auto-tow) launch or take-off:
2 the tow rope
3 the tow motorcar;
4 the winched launch or take-off (*Am.* rope start):
5 the retrievable rope
6 the retrieving winch;
7 the aircraft-towed take-off (aero-tow flight):
8 the tug (tractor aircraft, towing aircraft)
9 the towed glider;

10 **gliding** (soaring flight, motorless flight):
11 the starting slope
12 the hill-top take-off;
13 the orographic lift (hill lift, hill up-current)
14 hill soaring
15 cloud soaring
16 the cumulus cloud ('wool-pack')
17 looping the loop, an aerobatic figure (motorless aerobatics, motorless stunt flying)
18 the gliding flight
19 the thermal lift (thermal upcurrent, warm-air current, thermal, thermal bubble)
20 thermal (thermic) soaring
21 the thunderstorm front
22 front (frontal) soaring (thunderstorm soaring)
23 wave soaring (foehn soaring, chinook wind soaring);

24-37 glider types:

24 the sea glider
25 the transport (freight-carrying) glider
26 the high-performance glider
27 the powered glider;
28 the gliding plane (glider):
29 the glider pilot (soaring pilot, glider; soaring instructor, flying instructor)
30 the glider-pilot pupil
31 the fuselage
32 the pilot's seat
33 the landing skid (*Am.* ski)
34 the strut
35 the wing
36 the elevator
37 the rudder;
38 the gliding (soaring) site, terrain, or ground (*Am.* gliding field, soaring field)
39 the glider hangars with the gliding club

40-63 model glider construction,

40–58 motorless model gliders:
40 the all-wing model (tailless model)
41 the standard model
42 the canard (tail-first) model
43 the tandem-wing model
44 the model framework:
45 the model skid
46 the nose
47 the fuselage
48 the plywood frame
49 the wing-tip former
50 the sparboom (flange, member)
51 the wing
52 the aileron
53 the spar
54 the rib
55 the cover (fabric, skin)
56 the tail unit
57 the fin and rudder
58 the tailplane (*Am.* horizontal stabilizer) and elevator:

59-63 power-driven model gliders (glider models with auxiliary motor drive):

59 the rubber-driven model powered by twisted rubber threads
60 the remote-controlled model
61 the rocket-driven model with solid-fuel rocket (with powder rocket)
62 the captive model
63 the jet-propelled model

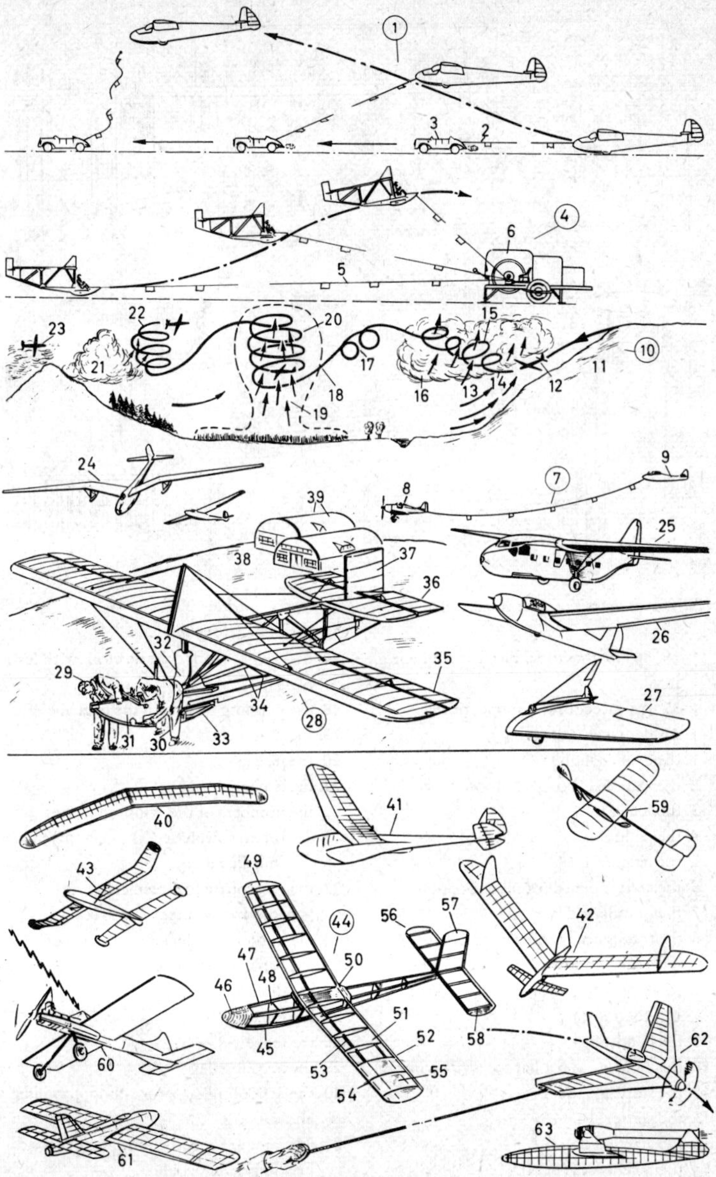

1
2
3
4
5
6
7
8
9
10
11
12
13
14
15
16
17
18
19
20
21
22
23
24
25
26
27
28
29
30
31
32
33
34
35
36
37
38
39
40
41
42
43
44
45
46
47
48
49
50
51
52
53
54
55
56
57
58
59
60
61
62
63

Engl. racecourse = *Am.* racetrack

1–29, 36–46 the horse race (horse racing, turf),
1–35 the racecourse (course, turf),
1–29 flat races (flat racing),
1 the stable (stalls):
2 the stall box (box; *sim.* loose box)
3 the scales;
4 the paddock
5 the ring
6 the starter board (number boards)
7 the grandstand
8 the totalisator (totalizator; *coll.* tote) with the windows for placing bets (making bets, laying wagers, *Am.* playing the races)
9 the bandstand
10 the racecourse for flat races (flat course)
11 the starting gate
12 the starter
13 the starting flag
14 the racehorses (field):
15 the favourite
16 the outsider;
17 the weight cloth (saddle cloth with lead plates)
18 the winning post with the mirror
19 the judges' box
20 the judges
21 the timer
22 the numbers of the winning horses
23–29 the steeplechase ('chase, hunt); *sim.* hurdle race:
23 the racecourse for steeplechasing (steeplechase course)
24 the hunter ('chaser)
25 the bank, an obstacle
26 the ditch and hedge
27 the hurdle
28 the fence
29 the marking flag;
30 the schooling lane for riding, jumping, and driving
31–34 training for show jumping or speed jumping:

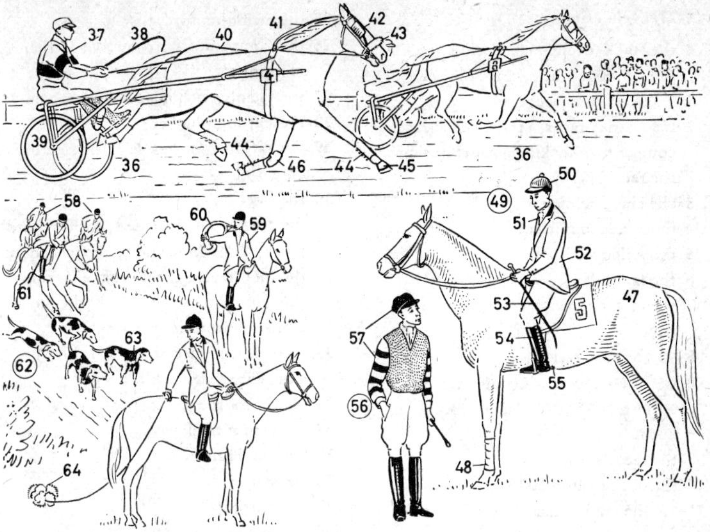

31 the water jump with hedge
32 the wall
33 the double oxer (spread fences)
34 the turning flag;
35 the course judges' box;
36–46 the trotting race:
36 the trotting course, a hard course
37 the drive r
38 the whi p
39 the sulky
40 the trotting hore (strotter)
41 the checkrein
42 the blinkers (*Am.* blinder, blinders)
43 the shadow roll
44 the tendon (brushing) boot
45 the rubber boot
46 the knee pad;
47 the saddle horse (riding horse, *Am.* saddler)
48 the bandage
49 the gentleman rider (amateur rider):
50 the riding cap (hunting cap)
51 the stock
52 the riding jacket
53 the riding whip
54 the riding boot
55 the spur;
56 the jockey, a professional:
57 the jockey dress in the colours (*Am.* colors) of the racing stud, a silk blouse and silk cap;
58–64 the hunt (hunting with hounds); *here :* a drag hunt; *sim.* paper chase:
58 the hunter (huntsman)
59 the whipper-in (hunt servant) blowing the finish of the hunt (the death)
60 the hunting horn [cotinental type]
61 the Master (*in fox-hunting :* Master of Foxhounds, M.F.H.)
62 the pack of hounds (pack):
63 the staghound (buckhound, deerhound, beagle; *in fox-hunting :* foxhounds);
64 the drag with the billet (fox droppings; *in Engl.* an aniseed trail)

1-23 cycle racing:

1 the track (cycle track, cycling track); *here:* indoor track

2–7 the six-day race:

2 the six-day racer, a track rider (racer, competitor), making a spurt during the race

3 the crash helmet

4 the race committee:

5 the judge

6 the lap-judge;

7 the racers' (riders', competitors') pavilion;

8–10 the road race:

8 the road racer, a racing cyclist; *sim.* sprinter (short-distance racer) in a sprint

9 the racer's shirt

10 the flask (water flask);

11–15 the endurance race (staying race, long-distance race):

11 the pacemaker, a motorcyclist

12 the pacemaker's machine (pacemaker's motorcycle)

13 the disk (disc), a protective device

14 the long-distance cyclist, a professional racer

15 the long-distance cyclist's bicycle, a racing bicycle;

16 the racing bicycle (racing cycle, racing machine) for road races, a road-racing bicycle (road racer):

17 the racing saddle, an unsprung saddle

18 the drop handlebars (racing handlebars)

19 the tubular tyre or tire

20 the chain

21 the racing toe cap

22 the strap

23 the spare tubular tyre or tire;

24-50 motor sports,

24–28 sand-track race, a motorcycle race; *sim.* grass-track race and road race:

24 the sand track

25 the racing motorcyclist

26 the competitor's protective leather clothing

27 the racing machine, a solo machine

28 the starting number;

29 the racing motorcycle with sidecar cornering:

30 the sidecar;

31 the completely enclosed world-record-breaking machine during the record run

32 the motorcycle gymkhana, a competition in riding ability; *here:* the motorcyclist, performing a jump

33 the cross-country race (hill climb), a capacity test

34–45 the motorcar race:

34 the racing track

35 start and finish

36 the starter

37 the starting flag

38 the racing car (racer)

39 the racing driver

40 the bale of straw

41 the pit

42 tyre-changing (tire-changing):

43 the pit mechanic;

44 the first-aid tent

45 the grandstand;

46–50 racing boats (sports boats) [section]:

46 the transversely and longitudinally stepped racing boat:

47 the motor;

48 the racing boat (stepped boat) with outboard motor; *sim.* hydroplane:

49 the outboard motor

50 the stabilizing fin

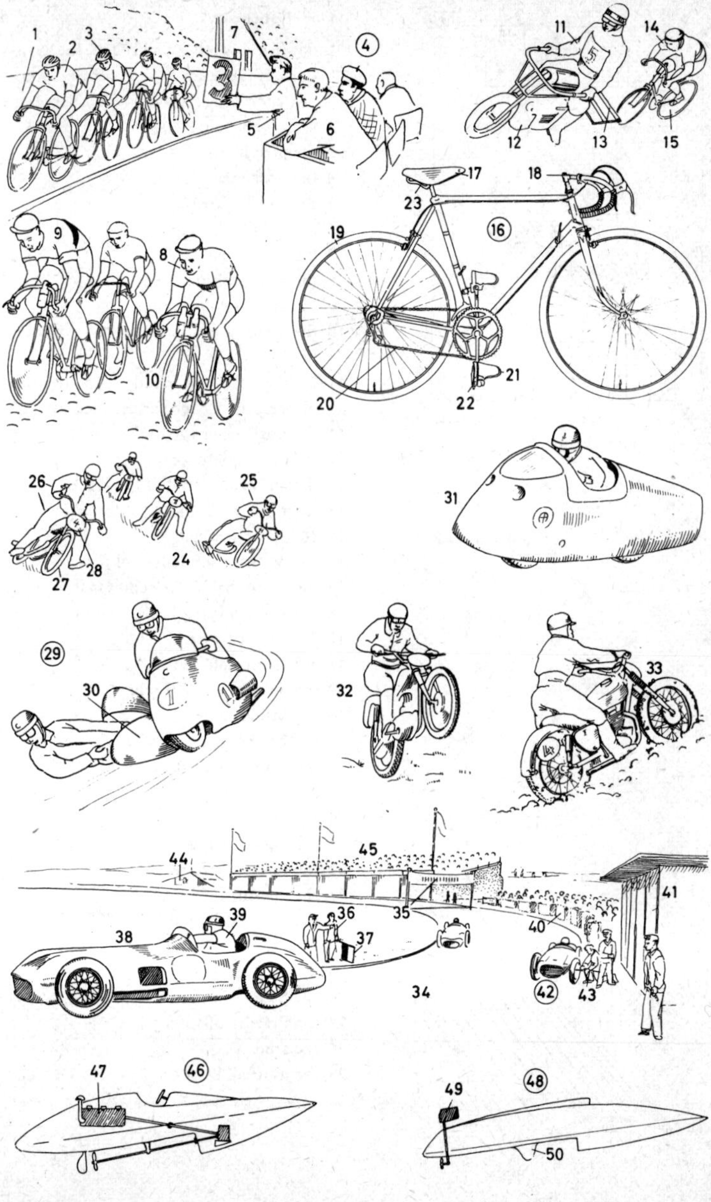
1
2
3
4
5
6
7
8
9
10
11
12
13
14
15
16
17
18
19
20
21
22
23
24
25
26
27
28
29
30
31
32
33
34
35
36
37
38
39
40
41
42
43
44
45
46
47
48
49
50

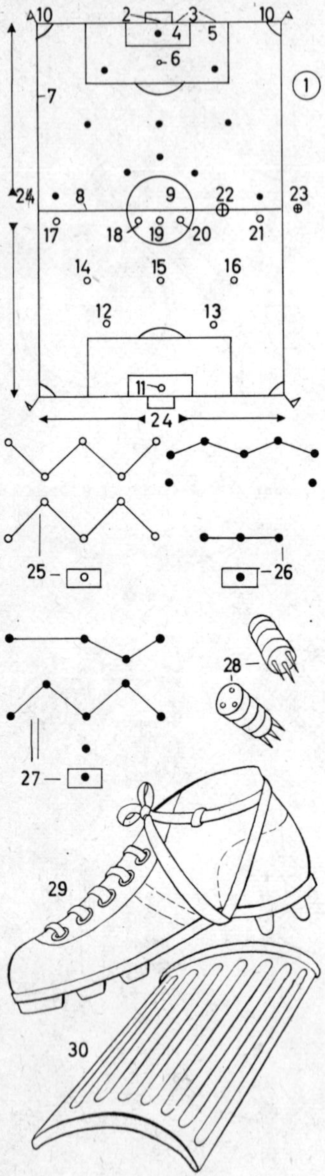

1-63 Football,

1 the field (football field) and the positions of the team for a football game or match (association football, soccer):

2 the goal

3 the goal line

4 the goal area

5 the penalty area

6 the penalty spot

7 the touch-line

8 the half-way line

9 the ten-yards' circle

10 the corner area (corner) with the corner flag;

11–21 the team (football team, football players, the eleven) at the kick-off:

11 the goalkeeper (goalie)

12 and **13** the defence:

12 the left back (left full back)

13 the right back (right full back);

14–16 the half-backs:

14 the left half (left half-back)

15 the centre half (*Am.* center half)

16 the right half (right half-back);

17–21 the forwards,

17 and **18** the left flank:

17 the outside left (left wing)

18 the inside left;

18 and **20** the inside forwards

19 the centre forward (centre)

20 and **21** the right flank:

20 the inside right

21 the outside right (right wing);

22 the referee (*coll.* ref)

23 the linesman

24 the size of the field [100-130 × 50-100 usually 115 × 75 yds]

25 the WM-system (WM-formation)

26 the Swiss formation

27 the Brazilian formation

28 the stud

29 the football boot

30 the shin guard (shin pad)
31 the grandstand (spectators' stand):
32 the terrace
33 the barrier;
34 the club flag
35 the loudspeaker mast
36 the cross bar
37 the goal post
38 the net
39 the shot at goal
40 the goalkeeper (goalie) punching the ball clear
41 the goal kick
42 the free kick
43 the wall of players
44 the trainer
45 the reserve (substitute)
46 the centre flag
47 the linesman
48 the linesman's flag
49 the throw-in
50 the ball out of play
51 the foul, a violation of the rules
52 the football (*Am. coll.* pigskin), a hollow ball with inflated rubber bladder
53 the over head kick
54 the football sock
55 the shirt (football shirt)
56 the header
57 offside
58 the corner (corner kick)
59 obstruction
60 trapping the ball with the sole of the boot
61 the pass, passing the ball along the ground
62 taking the ball on the inside of the foot
63 the break through, a dribble (dribbling the ball)

1-8 handball; *sim.* indoor handball:

1 the goal
2 the goal line
3 the goal area
4 the thirteen-metre (*Am.* meter) line
5 the free-throw line
6 the penalty corner
7 the corner
8 the handball player, one of the field team, swiping the ball;

9-18 hockey (*rare Am.* field hockey, bandy, bandyball); *sim.* shinty (shinny):

9 the side line
10 the seven-yard line
11 the goal line
12 the striking circle (circle)
13 the goal
14 the goalkeeper
15 the pad (knee, shin, and toe, pad)
16 the hockey player
17 the hockey stick (stick)
18 the hockey ball, a cork ball with leather cover;

19-27 rugby (rugby football; *coll.* rugger):

19 the scrum (scrummage, *rare:* scrimmage)
20 the oval (egg-shaped) rugby ball
21–27 the field (rugby field, *Am. coll.* gridiron):
21 the goal line
22 the in-goal
23 the touch line
24 the goal
25 the twenty-five yard line
26 the ten-yard line
27 the half-way line;

28-30 American football:

28 the football player
29 the crash helmet
30 the shoulder pad;

31-38 basket ball:

31 the ball
32 the backboard
33 the basket (elevated goal)
34–36 the basket ball court:
34 the goal line
35 the free-throw area
36 the free-throw line;
37 the basket ball player (*coll.* basket baller), scoring a goal
38 the substitutes;

39-54 baseball (the ball game, great American game); *sim.* rounders and American softball,

39–45 the baseball field (*Am.* baseball park):
39 the diamond (infield)
40 the home plate (home base) with batsman's lines
41 the batter's box
42 the field base
43 the pitching plate (pitching rubber)
44 the catcher's area
45 the player's line;
46 the batsman, a player of the batting side
47 the catcher with protective clothing and catcher's mitt
48 the umpire
49 a batsman running towards the field base
50 the baseman, a player of the fielding side
51 the base bag
52 the baseball bat
53 the pitcher
54 the baseball;

55-61 cricket:

55 the wicket (stumps) with the bails
56 the bowling crease
57 the popping (batting) crease
58 the wicketkeeper of the fielding side
59 the batsman of the batting side
60 the cricket bat, a flat wooden club
61 the fielder (fieldsman);

62-67 croquet:

62 the starting post
63 the hoop
64 the turning post
65 the croquet player
66 the croquet mallet (mallet)
67 the croquet ball (ball)

1
2
6
7
9
10
11
13
3
12
14
8
15
4
16
17
18
5
19
27
29
30
25
26
20
24
23
21
28
22
32
33
31
45
42
37
HA
38
OF
42
39
42
43
40
41
41
45
45
44
54
34
35
36
48
46
50
49
53
47
41
40
51
43
52
39
41
58
59
65
56
55
60
64
63
57
62
66
67
61

1-35 lawn tennis (tennis, the game of tennis),
1 the tennis court (court, grass court, tennis lawn), a hard court:
2 to 3 the side line for the doubles game (for doubles; men's doubles, women's doubles, mixed doubles)
4 to 5 the side line for the singles game (for singles; men's singles, women's singles)
6 to 7 the service line
8 to 9 the centre (*Am.* center) service line
3 to 10 the base line
11 the centre mark (*Am.* center mark)
12 the service court
13 the net (tennis net)
14 the net strap (net adjuster, centre band, *Am.* center band)
15 the net post
16 the tennis player; *here:* server
17 the service
18 the tennis partner
19 the receiver
20 the stance for the back-hand stroke
21 the stance for the fore-hand stroke
22 the umpire
23 the umpire's chair
24 the ball boy
25 the foot-fault judge
26 the tennis ball
27 the tennis racket (tennis racquet):
28 the racket handle
29 the striking surface (set of taut strings, catgut string);
30 the racket press:
31 the tightening screw;
32 the half volley
33 the volley
34 the smash
35 the eye shade;
36 the racket for the **game of badminton**
37 the shuttlecock (feathered ball, shuttle), a leather-covered cork ball:
38 the crown (circle) of feathers;
39-42 table tennis (ping-pong):
39 the table tennis player (ping-pong player)
40 the table tennis bat (ping-pong bat)
41 the table tennis net
42 the table tennis ball (ping-pong ball), a celluloid ball;

43-51 volley ball (the game of volley ball):
43 the back player
44 the service area
45 the server
46 the cut
47 the volley ball
48 the net player
49 the correct placing (position) of the hands
50 and 51 serving the ball:
50 the placing (position) of the hand for the drop
51 the placing (position) of the hand for the floater;

52-58 faustball ('fist ball'):
52 the base line
53 the tape
54 the 'fist ball'
55 the forward, hitting the ball over the net
56 the 'hammer' blow
57 the centre (*Am.* center)
58 the back;

59-71 golf (the game of golf),
59–62 the golf course (golf links), a part of the course:
59 the teeing ground
60 the rough
61 the bunker (*Am.* trap)
62 the putting green;
63 the golfer, driving
64 the caddie
65 the golf bag
66 putting (holing the ball) with a putter:
67 the hole
68 the flag stick;
69 and 70 golf clubs (clubs):
69 the driver, a club; *sim.* the brassie, the spoon (golf spoon)
70 the mashie, an iron; *sim.* the steel driver, the niblick
71 the golf ball

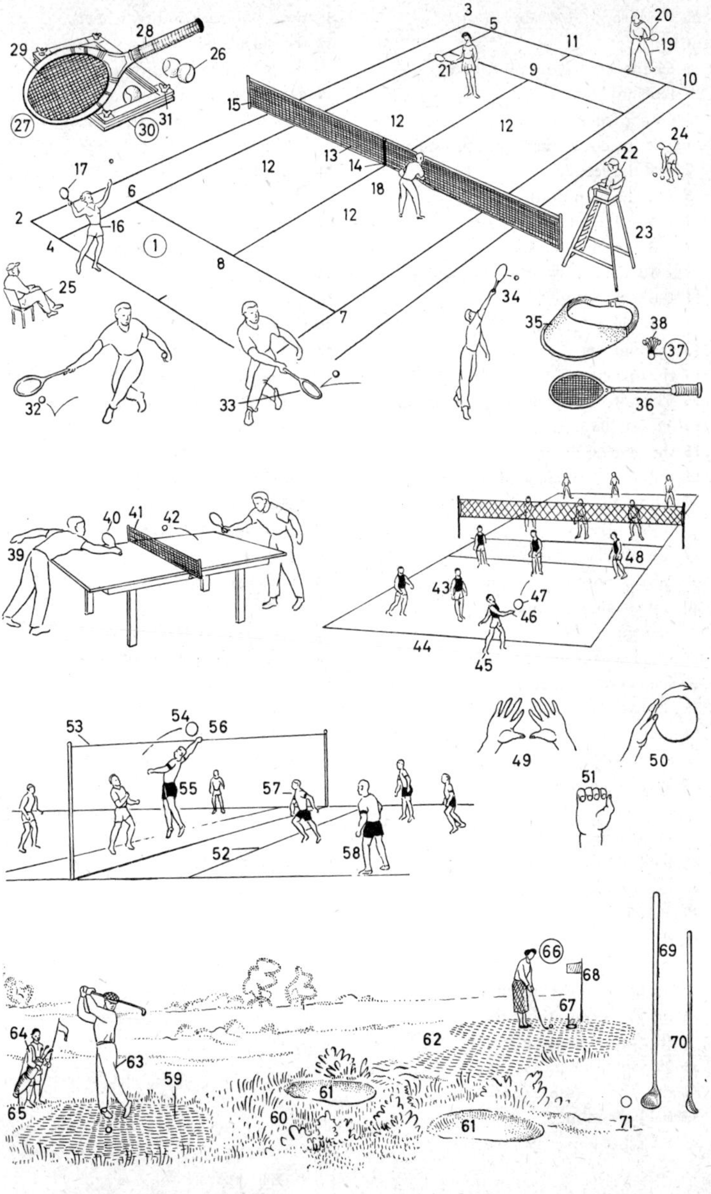
1
2
3
4
5
6
7
8
9
10
11
12
13
14
15
16
17
18
19
20
21
22
23
24
25
26
27
28
29
30
31
32
33
34
35
36
37
38
39
40
41
42
43
44
45
46
47
48
49
50
51
52
53
54
55
56
57
58
59
60
61
62
63
64
65
66
67
68
69
70
71

Engl. sabre = *Am.* saber

1–66 fencing (sword play, the art of fencing),
1–14 the fencing cuts:
1 to **2** the cut in first (first, cut-at-head)
2 to **1** the second
3 to **4** the high third
5 to **6** the low third, a cut-at-flank
7 to **8** the cut-at-cheek
9 to **10** the low fourth (cut-at-chest)
11 the side of third
12 the side of fourth
13 the high cuts
14 the low cuts;
15–43 sport (competition, piste) fencing,
15–32 foil play (foil fencing):
15 the fencing master (fencing instructor)
16 the piste (planche, fencing terrain)
17 and **18** the fencers at the assault (loose play)
19 the assailant (attacker) in the lunge (attack position; lunging)
20 the straight (direct) thrust, a movement
21 the defender in the parry (ward)
22 the parry of the tierce
23 the fixed fencing distance
24 the variable fencing distance between the fencers
25–31 fencing equipment:
25 the foil
26 the fencing glove
27 the foil mask
28 the padded neck flap (neck guard)
29 and **30** the fencing clothes:
29 the fencing jacket
30 the fencing breeches (foil breeches);
31 the heel-less fencing shoes;
32 the first position for the fencers' salute (the initial position);
33–38 sabre fencing (sabre play):
33 the sabreur (sabre fencer)
34 the light sabre
35 the sabre glove (gauntlet)
36 the sabre mask (sabre helmet)
37 the outside cut-at-head
38 the parry of fifth (fifth, quinte);
39–43 épée play (épée fencing):
39 the épée fencer (épéist, duellist)
40 the épée
41 the button (pointe d'arrêt) with electric contact
42 the sudden thrust of the head
43 the on-guard position (guard);
44 practice fencing:
45 the dummy
46 the heavy sabre
47 the mask;
48 the engagements (crossing of blades):
49 the quarte (carte) crossing
50 the tierce crossing
51 the circling crossing
52 the second crossing;
53–66 fencing weapons,
53 the Italian foil, a thrusting weapon,
54–57 the hilt:
54 the foil pommel
55 the grip
56 the cross piece (quillons)
57 the coquille (bellguard, guard, shell);
58 the foil blade
59 the button;
60 the French foil:
61 the coquille (cup guard);
62 the épée,
63 the light sabre, a cutting and thrusting weapon:
64 the guard (hilt)
65 the leather loop;
66 the dagger (stiletto)

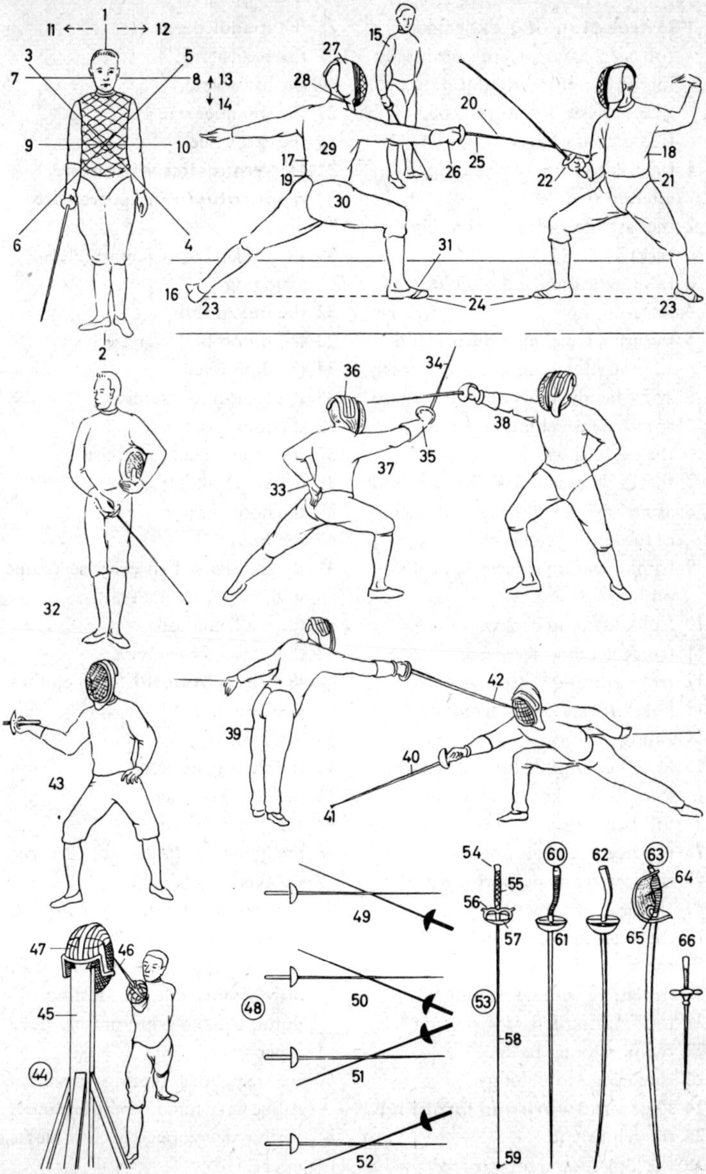
1
2
3
4
5
6
7
8
9
10
11
12
13
14
15
16
17
18
19
20
21
22
23
24
25
26
27
28
29
30
31
32
33
34
35
36
37
38
39
40
41
42
43
44
45
46
47
48
49
50
51
52
53
54
55
56
57
58
59
60
61
62
63
64
65
66

1-23 free-standing exercises (physical exercises, physical training, P. T., physical education, P.E., physical culture, *Am.* free gymnastics):

1 the basic position (standing at attention)
2 the astride position (standing at ease)
3 raising the arms and right leg forwards
4 knee-raising
5 the arm-stretching upwards (raising or stretching arms upwards)
6 arms bending upwards for sharp forward stretching and raising of the leg backwards
7 the neck grasp with heels raised
8 arms-raising sideways and raising of the left leg sideways
9 trunk bending sideways, hands on hips
10 trunk bending backwards
11 trunk bending forwards
12 trunk turning
13 knees full bend with hands on hips
14 riding position
15 knee bending, hands on hips (the knee bend, knees full bend, knee full-bending)
16 the front support position
17 the low front support position (front support with arms bent)
18 the side support position
19 the forward lunge
20 the lateral (sideways) lunge
21 foot-placing left (toe-placing left)
22 the horizontal balance
23 squatting (crouching);

24-30 ground work and tumbling:

24 the handstand
25 the long fly and forward roll:
26 the straddled legs
27 the headstand;
28 the back-bend
29 the shoulder stand
30 the cart wheel;

31-43 gymnastics with hand apparatus (hand apparatus exercises):

31 the Indian club exercise (club-swinging):
32 the Indian club;
33 the dumb-bell exercise:
34 the dumb-bell;
35 the long-pole exercise:
36 the long pole;
37 the stick (staff) exercise:
38 the stick (staff);
39 the hoop exercise:
40 the hoop;
41 the medicine ball exercise (game with the medicine ball):
42 the medicine ball;
43 the expander exercise;

44-48 the gym outfit (gym clothes, gym suit):

44 the gym vest
45 the chest band
46 the gym belt (belt)
47 the gym trousers
48 the gym shoe (plimsole; *Am. pop.* sneaker);

49 and 50 appliances for home or indoor gymnastics:

49 the spring-grip dumb-bell (Sandow's adjustable grip-testing dumb-bell), a hand-muscle developer
50 the expander (spring expander, rubber expander, chest-expander, spring developer), a chest-developer

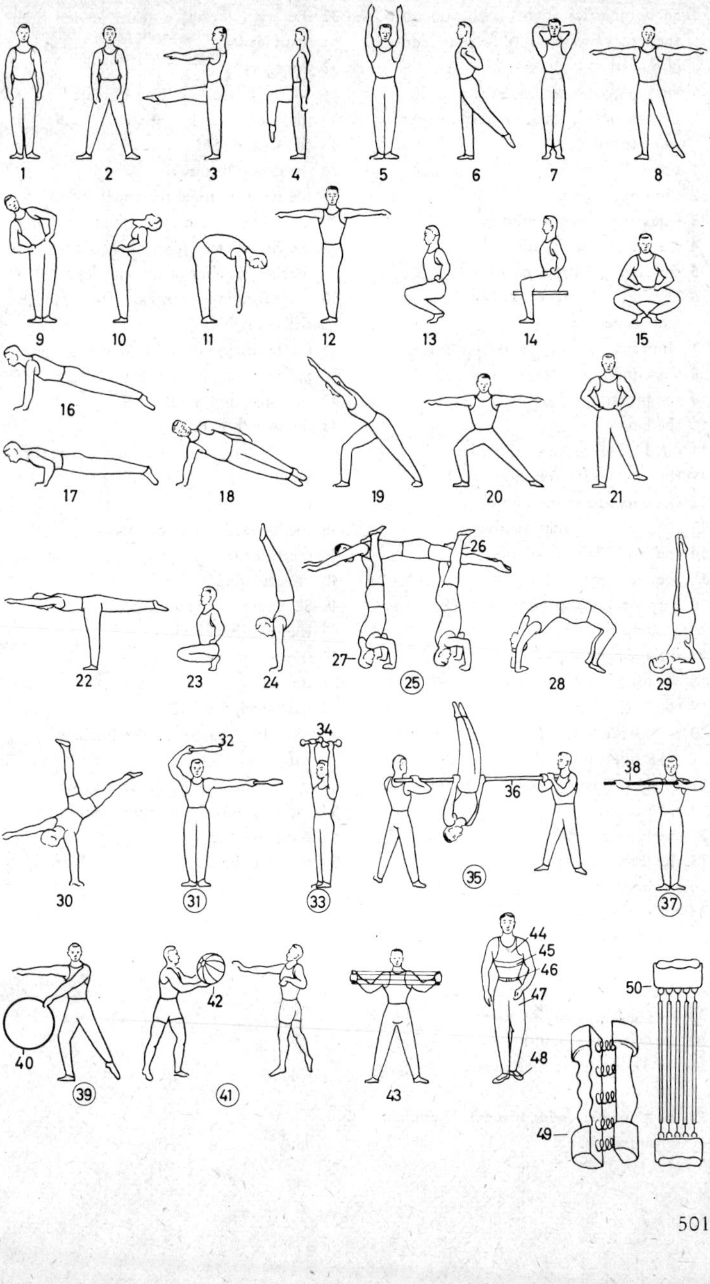
1
2
3
4
5
6
7
8
9
10
11
12
13
14
15
16
17
18
19
20
21
22
23
24
25
26
27
28
29
30
31
32
33
34
35
36
37
38
39
40
41
42
43
44
45
46
47
48
49
50

1–56 gymnastics (gym) with apparatus (heavy gymnastics) in the gym (indoor gymnastics),
1–48 the gymnastic lesson (lesson in gymnastics) in the gymnasium (gym, *Am.* armory),
1 the wall bars:
2 the rung (bar);
3 spanning (span-bending)
4 the wall ladder (ladder)
5 the climbing rope (rope)
6 climbing the rope without using the feet (rope-climbing)
7 climbing the pole (pole-climbing):
8 the climbing pole;
9 the horizontal bar:
10 the bar;
11 and **12** gymnastics on the bar:
11 the knee swing (circle)
12 the forward grand circle;
13 the mat (gym mat, mattress)
14 the table (vaulting table)
15 the handspring
16 a gymnast standing by to catch, a catcher
17 the springboard
18 vaulting over the buck:
19 the buck;
20 the astride vault (straddle vault, vertical stride vault)
21 the beat board (beating board) for the take-off
22 the jumping post
23 the jumping rope
24 the sandbag
25 the springboard
26 the bar and blocks
27 the parallel bars:
28 the bar;
29 the double shoulder stand
30 the horizontal stand
31 and **32** the team (gymnastic team, gym team):
31 the gymnast (*Am.* turner), a gymnast on apparatus
32 the gym leader, a team leader (gym team leader);
33 the scissors
34–38 the horse (vaulting horse):
34 the neck
35 the saddle
36 the croup (croupe)
37 the neck pommel (pommel)
38 the croup (croupe) pommel;
39 the instructor (gym instructor, gym teacher, teacher of gymnastics)
40 the balancing form (*sim.* the Swedish balancing form)
41 the balancing exercise (keeping the balance, keeping the equilibrium)
42 the balancing pole
43 the box (box horse)
44 the running through-vault (*Am.* thru-vault)
45 the trapeze
46 the upward circle forwards
47 the rings (hand rings)
48 the crucifix;
49–52 vaults over the horse:
49 the rear (back) vault
50 the face (front) vault
51 the side vault (flank vault)
52 the through-vault;
53–56 grips (grasps) on the horizontal bar:
53 the ordinary grip, an over grip
54 the reverse grip, an underhand grip
55 the cross grip
56 the combined grip

1
2
3
4
5
6
7
8
9
10
11
12
13
14
15
16
17
18
19
20
21
22
23
24
25
26
27
28
29
30
31
32
33
34
35
36
37
38
39
40
41
42
43
44
45
46
47
48

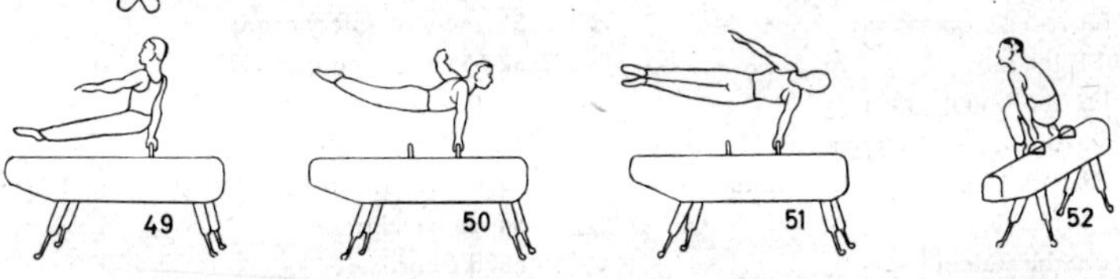
49
50
51
52

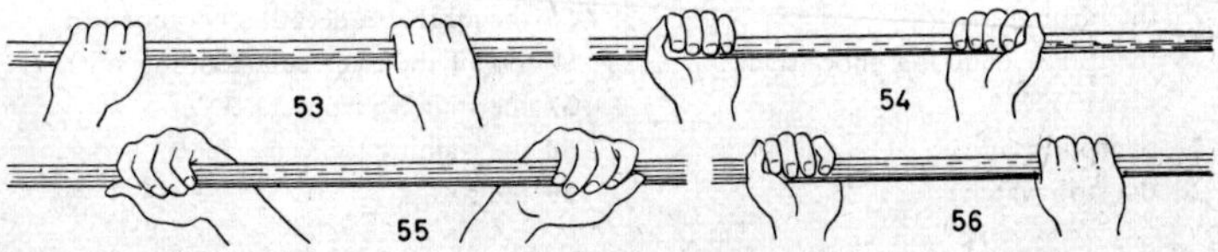
53
54
55
56

1-28 running and sprinting (the running race):
1 the starter
2 the starting hole
3 the starting line (starting mark)
4 the start for sprinting and middle-distance events
5 the lane (*all together :* cinder track, track, *Am.* cinder oval)
6 the runner, a sprinter
7 and 8 the finish:
7 the finishing line
8 the tape (finishing tape);
9 the timekeeper
10 the judge
11 and 12 the hurdle race (hurdles):
11 the hurdler
12 the hurdle;
13–16 the relay (relay race):
13 the relay runner
14 baton-changing
15 the baton (relay baton)
16 the baton-exchange area;
17–19 the long-distance race [3000 m incl.: a marathon race, marathon]:
17 the distance runner (long-distance runner)
18 the racing number
19 the lap-counting apparatus with the bell for signalling (*Am.* signaling) the last lap (last round);
20–22 the steeplechase:
20 the steeplechaser
21 and 22 obstacles:
21 the rail
22 the water jump;
23 the cross-country race
24 and 25 competitive walking, a walking race:
24 the walker
25 the turning mark;
26 the spikes (running shoe, track shoe):
27 the spike;
28 the stop watch;

29-55 jumping, throwing and putting the weight,
29–32 the long jump (*Am.* broad jump):
29 the long-jumper
30 the take-off board
31 the jumping pit (pit)
32 the record marker;
33–35 hop-step-and-jump:
33 the take-off (hop)
34 the stride (step)
35 the jump;
36 and 37 the high jump:
36 the high-jumper
37 the bar (jumping bar);
38–41 the pole vault (pole jump):
38 the pole-jumper
39 the pole (vaulting pole)
40 the jumping post
41 the take-off box;
42–44 throwing the discus (discus-throwing):
42 the discus-thrower
43 the discus, a throwing disk or disc
44 the throwing circle;
45–47 putting the weight (putting the shot):
45 the weight-putter
46 the weight (shot)
47 the putting circle;
48–51 throwing the hammer (hammer-throwing):
48 the hammer-thrower
49 the hammer (throwing hammer):
50 the steel wire;
51 the wire safety cage;
52-55 throwing the javelin (javelin-throwing):
52 the javelin-thrower
53 the throwing line
54 the javelin:
55 the cord;
56 the athlete, a decathlon competitor,
57 and 58 the track suit (training suit):
57 the training trousers
58 the training jacket;
59 the badge

1
2
3
4
5
6
7
8
9
10
11
12
13
14
15
16
17
18
19
20
21
22
23
24
25
26
27
28

29
30
31
32
33
34
35
36
37
38
39
40
41
42
43
44
45
46
47
48
49
50
51
52
53
54
55
56
57
58
59

1-6 weight-lifting:

1 the weight-lifter (lifter)

2 the one-hand snatch

3 the bar bell (barbell)

4 the two-hand jerk

5 the disk (disc) loading bar bells

6 the two-hand press;

7-14 wrestling (the wrestling match),

7–10 Graeco-Roman (Greco-Roman) wrestling:

7 the wrestler, an amateur (non-professional) wrestler

8, 9, 11 mat-wrestling (ground-wrestling);

8 the bridge, a defensive position

9 the crouch, a waiting position

10 and 12 standing wrestling:

10 the full Nelson

11 and 12 all-in wrestling (the catch-as-catch-can style, unrestricted wrestling style):

11 the arm-lock and leg-hold

12 the double leg-lock;

13 the wrestling mat (mat)

14 belt-wrestling (the Icelandic glima); *sim.* the Swiss swinging;

15-17 the ju jitsu (jiu jitsu, jiu jutsu, judo), Japanese art of self-defence (*Am.* self-defense):

15 the arm-hold

16 the strangle-hold

17 the scissors-hold;

18-46 boxing (the boxing match; pugilism, fisticuffs),

18–26 training for boxing:

18 the punch bag (punching bag)

19 the punching ball

20 the small punching ball

21 the sand bag (punching sack)

22 the boxer (pugilist), a professional boxer (professional);

23 the boxing glove

24 the sparring partner (training opponent)

25 the straight (straight punch, straight blow)

26 the duck (ducking) and the crouch (crouching);

27 infighting; *here:* clinching (the clinch)

28 the swing

29 the uppercut

30 the hook

31 the low blow (blow below the belt) [forbidden]

32 the boxing ring (price ring, ring):

33 the ropes (boxing-ring ropes)

34 the neutral corner

35 the winner

36 the boxer defeated by a knockout (knockout blow, K.O.; the floored, K.O. 'd, opponent; the loser)

37 the referee

38 the counting out;

39 the judge

40 the second

41 the manager

42 the timekeeper

43 the gong

44 the record-keeper

45 the reporter (newspaperman)

46 the press photographer

1
2
3
4
5
6
7
8
9
10
11
12
13
14
15
16
17
18
19
20
21
22
23
24
25
26
27
28
29
30
31
32
33
34
35
36
37
38
39
40
41
42
43
44
45
46

1–56 mountaineering (mountain-climbing, alpine climbing):
1 the mountain hut (alpine hut, hut)

2-14 rock-climbing (climbing) [rock technique, climbing technique]:

2 the chasm
3 the rock face (rock wall)
4 the crack
5 the ledge [of rock]
6 the climber (rock climber, mountaineer)
7 the alpine jacket
8 the breeches (climbing breeches)
9 the chimney
10 the belay (spike)
11 the belay
12 the sling (loop)
13 the rope
14 the cornice (bulge);

15-22 snow- and ice-climbing:

15 the ice (firn, snow) slope
16 the climber (ice-climber)
17 the ice axe (*Am.* ice ax)
18 the ice step
19 the snow goggles
20 the hood of the anorak
21 the snow cornice
22 the ice ridge;

23-25 roped crossing of a glacier:

23 the glacier covered with névé
24 the crevasse
25 the ice bridge (snow bridge);
26-28 the roped party (climbing party, mountaineering party, rope):
26 the leader
27 the climber (ice-climber)
28 the end man (last man);

29-34 lowering a man on the rope and **roping down** (abseiling):

29 the foot grip
30 securing by passing the rope over one shoulder and under the other
31 the descending climber
32 the thigh rappel
33 the double thigh rappel
34 the free rappel;

35-56 climbing (mountaineering) **equipment:**

35 the alpenstock:
36 the ferrule
37 the spike (point);
38 the ice axe (*Am.* ice ax):
39 the pick
40 the teeth
41 the blade
42 the gliding ring
43 the wrist strap
44 the leather toggle
45 the stop ring;
46 the nailed climbing boot:
47 the clinker (welt nail)
48 the crampon straps;
49 the Vibrams (mountaineering boot with profiled vulcanite, or ebonite, sole):
50 the reinforced counter;
51 the Kletterschuh
52 the piton hammer:
53 the wrist strap;
54 the ice piton (peg)
55 the rock piton (peg)
56 the karabiner (snaplink)

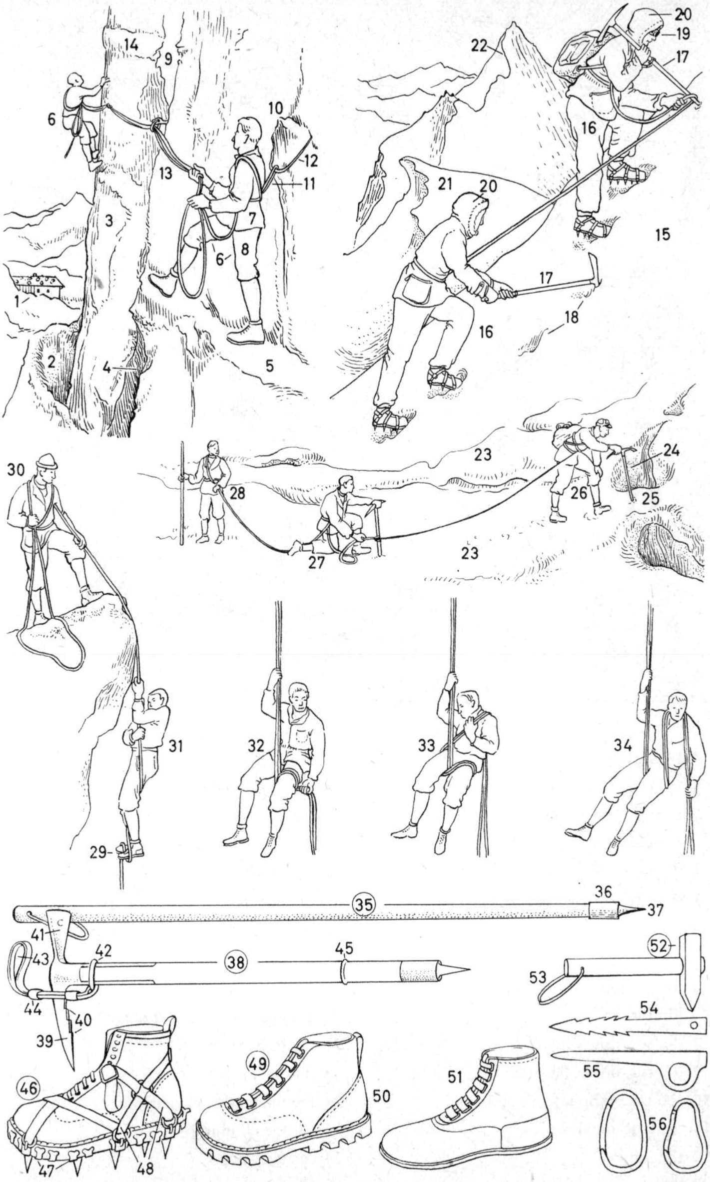
1
2
3
4
5
6
7
8
9
10
11
12
13
14
15
16
17
18
19
20
21
22
23
24
25
26
27
28
29
30
31
32
33
34
35
36
37
38
39
40
41
42
43
44
45
46
47
48
49
50
51
52
53
54
55
56

1-34 skiing:

1 the chair-lift (chair-hoist)

2 the ski-lift (ski-hoist)

3 the ski track

4 the fall

5 the ski kjoring (ski joring)

6 the ski hut

7–14 ski-jumping,

7 the ski-jump (artificial ski-jump; *form.* jumping hill):

8 the run-down tower

9 the run-down (approach)

10 the take-off platform (take-off);

11 the landing-slope

12 the finish

13 the judges' stand

14 the flight of the ski jumper, a long-distance ski jump;

15 the slalom (slalom race):

16 the finishing flag;

17 down-hill running (the run down):

18 down-hill racing, the skier leaning forward

19 the course;

20 the snow-plough (*Am.* snowplow)

21 the jump turn

22 the field jump

23 the telemark (telemark turn)

24–27 the climbing,

24 the side-step :

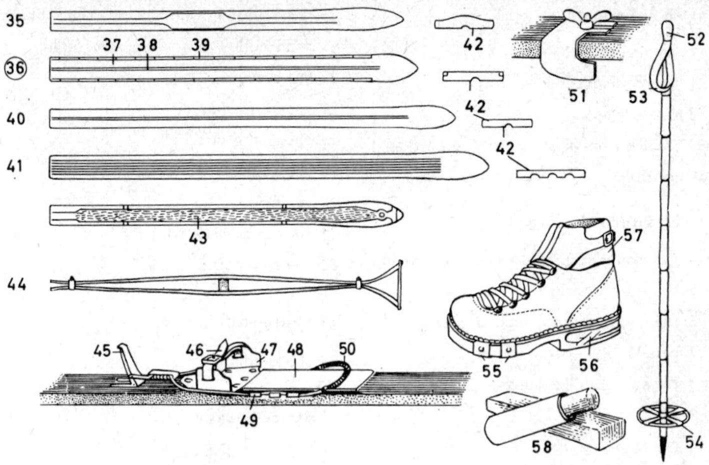

25 the upper ski
26 the lower ski;
27 the herring-bone;
28 the skating step:
29 the gliding ski;
30 the skier, a cross-country racer
31 reversing (the kick turn)
32 the christiania (christy, christie, parallel christiania), a swing turn (parallel swing)
33 the stem (stem turn):
34 canting;

35-58 skiing outfit,

35–41 the ski (skis):
35 the touring ski [from above]
36 the slalom ski (down-hill ski):
37 the running surface
38 the guiding groove
39 the steel edge;
40 the racing ski
41 the jumping ski;
42 the cross-sections of 35, 36, 40, 41
43 the sealskin (skin strapped on for climbing)
44 the ski press
45–50 the ski-binding, a Kandahar binding:
45 the fore-tightener (fore-clamp)
46 the toe-strap
47 the toe-iron
48 the foot plate
49 the down-pull
50 the spiral spring;
51 the ski crampon
52–54 the ski stick (ski pole):
52 the leather knob
53 the loop
54 the stick disk or disc (snow ring);
55–57 the ski boots (skiing boots):
55 the sole-protector
56 the heel grip
57 the ankle gaiter;
58 the ski wax

1-48 ice-sports,

1–32 skating,

1 the ice stadium (stadium):

2 the spectators

3 the ice rink (skating rink), an artificial ice rink;

4-22 figure-skating:

4 the skater (figure-skater), solo-skating

5 the spread-eagle

6 the counter-jump, a skating jump

7 pair-skating (pairs), free-skating

8 the spiral, an ice dance

9 the curve

10 the employed foot

11 the unemployed (free) foot

12 the pirouette

13–20 the elementary figures of figure-skating for school figures, compulsory figures:

13 the figure of eight

14 the serpentine

15 the figure of three

16 the double-three

17 the loop-change-loop

18 the bracket

19 the counter

20 the bracket-change-bracket;

21 the specs in free-skating

22 the beak, a braking figure in free-skating:

23 speed-skating:

24 the speed-skater;

25-32 skates (ice skates),

25 the common skate with sole- and heel-clamps:

26 the hollow-ground blade (skate blade with hollow moulding, *Am.* molding);

27 the skate key

28 the ice hockey skate

29 the racing skate

30 the sailing skate (skate for skate-sailing)

31 the figure skate with the skating boot:

32 the saw-teeth;

33 skate-sailing:

34 the hand sail;

35-41 ice hockey:

35 the ice-hockey player

36 the goal keeper (*coll.* goalie)

37 and 38 the ice-hockey stick:

37 the stick handle

38 the stick blade;

39 the puck, an ebonite (vulcanite, hard-rubber) disk or disc

40 the shin pad

41 the boards;

42 curling; *sim.* the German game of 'Eisschießen':

43 the curler

44 the curling stone (stone); *sim.* the wooden disk (disc) with handle for 'Eisschießen'

45 the tee;

46 ice-sailing,

47 and 48 the ice yacht (ice boat, *Am.* ice scooter):

47 the ice skid (ice runner)

48 the outrigger

1
2
3
4
5
6
7
8
9
10
11
12
17
19
13
14
15
16
17
18
19
20
21
22
23
24
25
26
27
28
29
30
31
32
33
34
35
35
36
41
37
38
39
40
02
45
44
42
43
46
47
47
48

1 the Nansen sledge, a sledge for polar expeditions

2 the sledge with horn-shaped runners:

3 the sledge runner (runner, sledge slip, sledge slipper)

4 the seat prop, a prop;

5-20 sledge sport, a snow sport,

5–10 bob-sleighing (bobbing),

5 the bobsleigh, a bobsleigh for two (bobsled, *Am.* bob, dirigible sledge):

6 wheel-steering; *other system :* rope-steering;

7 the steersman (bob-steerer), a bob-rider

8 the brakesman leaning out

9 the bobsleigh course (bobsleigh run, bobsleigh chute)

10 the banked bend;

11 and **12** sledging (tobogganing, coasting):

11 the sledge (toboggan, sleigh, *Am.* sled) on the toboggan slope (coasting path, coasting slide, chute, shoot, run); *sim.* racing sledge (sporting sledge)

12 the sledger (coaster);

13 the toboggan (luge), a sledge without runners:

14 the baseboard

15 the protective curved front;

16 the tobogganer's crash helmet

17 the knee pad

18 the skeleton sledge:

19 the board to lie on (slip board);

20 the spikes for steering and braking

1 the avalanche; *kinds:* wind avalanche, ground avalanche

2 the avalanche-breaker (avalanche barrier), a deflecting wall; *sim.* avalanche chock

3 the avalanche gallery

4 the snow-fall (snowstorm)

5 the snowdrift

6 the snow paling (snow fence)

7 the sprinkling machine:

8 the snow-clearing device in front (detachable snow plough, *Am.* snowplow)

9 the non-skid chain (snow chain, chain)

10 the radiator bonnet (*Am.* radiator hood)

11 the radiator shutter and the shutter opening;

12 the snowman

13 the snowshoe (racket)

14 the snowball fight:

15 the snowball;

16 the snow scooter

17 the slide (*Am.* shoot):

18 the boy, sliding

19 the icy surface (icy ground, *Am.* silver thaw);

20 the blanket of snow on the roof

21 the icicle

22 the man, shovelling away (*Am.* shoveling) snow:

23 the snow push (snow shovel);

24 the heap of snow

25 the horse sleigh (horse sledge, sleigh with bells, *Am.* cutter):

26 the sleigh bells (bells, set of bells);

27 the foot muff

28 the ear tab

29 the handsledge (tread sledge); *sim.* push sledge

287 Various Kinds of Sports

1 skittles (ninepins, *Am.* tenpins, bowls, *sim.* duckpins):
2 the skittle (ninepins) alley or yard, (*Am.* bowling alley, bowlodrome), an asphalt alley
3 the skittle ball (skittle bowl)
4 the trough fot catching the ball
5 the padded wall
6 the protective niche
7 the skittle boy
8 the skittle frame [with the skittles set up in diamond formation]
9–14 the skittles:
9 the front corner pin
10 the front row pins
11 the corner pin
12 the king (head pin)
13 the back row pins
14 the back corner pin;
15 the trough for used balls
16 the runway (return chute)
17 the score marker (score board, scorer)
18 the cushion
19 the run-up board
20 the skittle player;
21 the French game of boules; *sim.* the Italian game of boccia, the English game of bowls:
22 the boules player
23 the jack
24 the grooved bowl
25 the group of players;
26 polo; *sim.* cycle polo :
27 the polo player, a forward
28 the polo stick;
29 the cycle polo ball (two-man cycle polo):
30 the polo cycle player;
31 free-hand acrobatic (trick) cycling:
32 the trick bicycle;
33 acrobatic roller skating; *other kinds of roller skating :* speed roller skating, roller skate hockey:
34 the woman roller skater performing the splits;
35 the roller skate:
36 the metal wheel;
37–47 archery:
37 the archer (bowman)
38 the bow (long bow):
39 the bow back (belly)
40 the bow-string;
41 the arrow:
42 the arrow head (arrow point, arrow tip)
43 the arrow shaft (arrow stem)
44 the feathering (feathers)
45 the nock (notch);
46 the quiver
47 the target;
48 'hurling':
49 the 'hurling ball'
50 the throwing line;
51 the Basque game of pelota (blaid a chiestera); *sim.* jai alai:
52 the pelota player
53 the wicker racket (cesta);
54 the gyro wheel ('Rhön wheel'):
55 the handle
56 the foothold;
57 the bullfight (corrida); *sim.* the Portuguese rejonar:
58 the arena (bull ring, circus)
59, 61, 63, and 65 the bullfighters (toreros, toreadors):
59 the chulo (capeador)
60 the capa (red cloak)
61 the picador (horseman with lance)
62 the lance
63 the banderillero
64 the banderilla (barbed dart)
65 the matador (espada);
66 the muleta
67 the bull (toro)

1
2
3
4
5
6
7
8
9
10
11
12
13
14
15
16
17
18
19
20
21
22
23
24
25
26
27
28
29
30
31
32
33
34
35
36
37
38
39
40
41
42
43
44
45
46
47
48
49
50
51
52
53
54
55
56
57
58
59
60
61
62
63
64
65
66
67

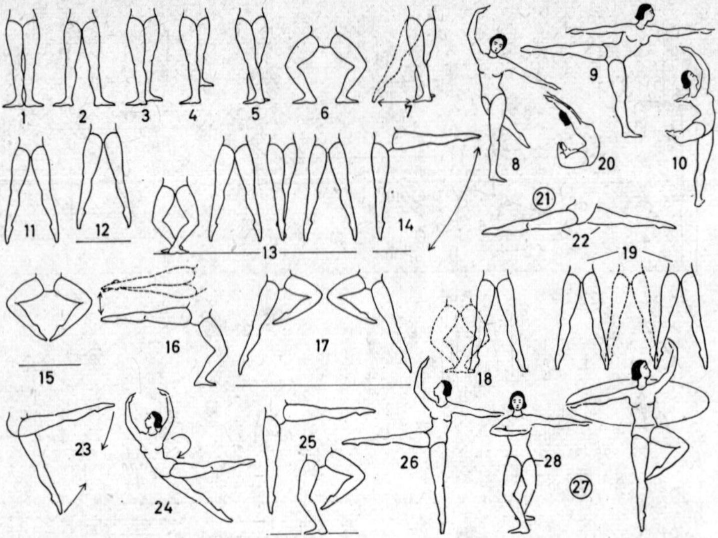

1-10 the exercise (dancing exercise) **of classical dancing,**

1–5 the foot positions:

1 first position

2 second position

3 third position

4 fourth position

5 fifth position;

6 the plié

7 the battement

8 the développé; *here:* croisé derrière

9 the arabesque

10 the attitude; *here:* attitude effacée;

11-28 the training steps:

11 échappé

12 sauté, a jump

13 entrechat; *here:* entrechat quatre with two changements (crossing of the legs) during the jump

14 assemblé

15 cambré, a passé-position

16 capriole (the cabriole)

17 pas de chat

18 glissade (the glissade, gliding step)

19 chaîné

20 soubresaut

21 jeté (jump from one foot to the other):

22 the splits;

23 jeté passé

24 grand jeté en tournant

25 fouetté; *sim.* révoltade

26 sissonne

27 pirouette (the pirouette):

28 the preparation;

29-41 the artistic dance (art of dancing),

29–34 the classical dance (classical ballet),

29 the corps de ballet (ballet groupe):

30 the ballet dancer (ballerina);

31–34 pas de trois (dance for three):

31 the prima ballerina (first ballerina, first solo dancer, first solo danseuse), a pointe danseuse (classical dancer)

32 the primo ballerino (principal male dancer, first solo dancer)

33 the tutu (ballet skirt)

34 the ballet shoe, a pointe shoe;

35 the burlesque dance, a character dance:

36 the character dancer;

37 the mime:

38 the mime (mimer);

39 the bolero, a national dance, a dance for two:

40 the dancer;

41 the modern dance (Central European dance, German dance);

42 the 'Schuhplattler' ('Plattler'), a folk dance

43 the foxtrot, a ballroom dance,

44 and **45** the dancing partners (couple, pair of dancers):

44 the male partner (dancing partner)

45 the female partner (female dancing partner)

289 The Carnival

1–48 the masked ball (fancy-dress ball, masquerade):
1 the ballroom (dance hall)
2 the dance band (jazz band), a dance orchestra
3 the jazz player, (jazz band player) a dance band player
4 the paper lantern (lampion)
5 the festoon (paper chain)
6–48 fancy dress at the masquerade,
6 the witch:
7 the face mask (mask);
8 the trapper (fur trapper)
9 the apache girl:
10 the net stocking;
11 the first prize in the raffle (in the tombola), a presentation basket
12 the pierrette:
13 the half-mask (small mask);
14 the devil
15 the domino
16 the hula-hula girl (Hawaii girl):
17 the garland (chain of flowers)
18 the grass skirt;
19 the pierrot:
20 the ruff (frill);
21 the midinette:
22 the Biedermeier dress
23 the bonnet
24 the beauty spot (patch);
25 the bayadere (Hindu Indian dancer)
26 the grandee
27 the Columbine
28 the maharaja
29 the mandarin, a Chinese notable
30 the exotic woman
31 the cowboy (*Am.* cowhand); *sim.* gaucho (*Am.* vaquero)
32 the vamp in a fanciful costume
33 the dandy (masher, exquisite, fop, buck, spark, beau, coxcomb, jackanapes, *Am.* dude), a character mask:
34 the rosette (badge for the masked ball);
35 the harlequin

36 the gipsy (gypsy) woman
37 the cocotte (demi-mondaine, *fam.* demi-rep)
38 owl-glass, a fool (wag, rogue, buffoon,
39 the fool's cap (cap and bells); [clown):
40 the rattle
41 the odalisque (oriental woman), an oriental slave or concubine:
42 the Turkish trousers;
43 the pirate:
44 the tattoo (tattooing);
45 the paper hat
46 the false nose
47 the rattle (clapper)
48 the fool's wand;
49–54 fireworks (pyrotechnical articles):
49 the cap (percussion gun cap)
50 the cracker
51 the banger
52 the jumping cracker
53 the thunderflash
54 the rocket;
55 the paper ball
56 a practical-joker's toy (jack-in-the-box, jack-in-a-box)
57–70 the carnival parade (carnival procession):
57 the carnival float (*Am.* truck)
58 the carnival prince (prince Carnival):
59 the fool's sceptre (*Am.* scepter, fool's mace)
60 the fool's badge (*Am.* scepter, carnival decoration);
61 the carnival princess (carnival queen)
62 the confetti
63 the giant figure, a satirical figure
64 the Beauty Queen
65 the fairy-tale figure
66 the paper streamer
67 the Captain of the Prince's Guards
68 the Prince's Guards
69 the clown (buffoon, jack-pudding, merry-andrew), a jester (joker, wag)
70 the lansquenet drum

1–63 the travelling (*Am.* traveling) circus (touring circus):

1 the circus tent (big top, main tent, marquee)

2 the tent pole

3 the spotlights

4 the lighting technician (electrician)

5 the platform for the artiste

6 the trapeze

7 the trapeze artiste (trapeze acrobat)

8 the rope ladder

9 the bandstand

10 the circus band

11 the ring entrance (arena entrance)

12 the circus compound

13 the tent prop (prop)

14 the jumping net, a safety net

15 the rows of seats for the spectators

16 the circus box

17 the circus director

18 the artistes' agent

19 the entrance and exit

20 the steps

21 the ring (arena)

22 the ring fence

23 the musical clown

24 the clown

25 the comedy act (comedy number), a circus act (circus number)

26 the trick riders (equestrians, circus riders)

27 the stable boy, a ring attendant

28 the pyramid:

29 the support;

30 and 31 the liberty horses (trained horses):

30 the circus horse, performing the levade
31 the ring master, a trainer;
32 the vaulter
33 the emergency exit
34 the circus caravan
35 the springboard acrobat
36 the springboard
37 the knife-thrower
38 the circus gunman (circus crack shot)
39 the girl assistant
40 the tight-rope dancer
41 the wire rope (tight rope)
42 the balancing pole
43 the throwing act
44 the balancing act:
45 the support
46 the pole (bamboo pole)
47 the acrobat;
48 the equilibrist
49 the wild-animal cage, a round cage
50 the bars of the cage
51 the passage (barred passage, passage for the wild animals)
52 the tamer (animal trainer)
53 the training whip
54 the protective fork
55 the pedestal
56 the tiger
57 the stand
58 the jumping hoop
59 the seesaw
60 the large ball
61 the camp
62 the cage caravan
63 the menagerie

291 The Fair

1–67 the fair (annual fair):
1 the fair-ground
2 the children's merry-go-round (whirligig), a roundabout (*Am.* carrousel, carousel, *err.* carousal)
3 the refreshment stall (refreshment stand)
4 the chair o'plane
5 the scenic railway, a ghost train
6 the show booth
7 the cash desk
8 the barker (tout, crier)
9 the medium
10 the showman
11 the try-your-strength machine
12 the hawker
13 the balloon
14 the paper serpent
15 the windmill, a wind wheel
16 the pickpocket (thief)
17 the vendor
18 the Turkish delight
19 the freak show
20 the giant
21 the fat woman
22 the dwarfs
23 the beer tent
24 the side-show
25–28 travelling (*Am.* traveling) artistes (travelling show people):
25 the fire-eater
26 the sword-swallower
27 the strong man
28 the escapologist;
29 the spectators
30 the ice-cream man
31 the ice-cream cornet with ice-cream
32 the broiled-sausage stand:
33 the grid (grill, *Am.* broiler)
34 the broiled (grilled) sausage
35 the sausage tongs;

36 the fortune-teller by cards, a soothsayer
37 the giant wheel (Ferris wheel)
38 the orchestrion (automatic organ), an automatic musical instrument
39 the switchback (scenic railway, *Am.* railroad, *fam.* the big dipper)
40 the toboggan slide (mat, helter-skelter, slip, chute)
41 the swing-boats
42 the waxworks
43 the wax figure (waxwork)
44 the lottery booth (tombola booth)
45 the wheel of fortune
46 the devil's wheel (typhoon wheel)
47 the quoit
48 the prizes
49 the sandwichman on stilts
50 the placard
51 the cigarette seller, an itinerant trader (street hawker)
52 the tray
53 the fruit-stall (fruit-stand)
54 the wall-of-death rider
55 the room with distorting mirrors (hall of mirrors)
56 the concave mirror
57 the convex mirror
58 the shooting gallery (miniature rifle range)
59 the hippodrome
60 the junk stalls
61 the first-aid post (ambulance station)
62 the autodrome
63 the bumper car (electric car)
64–66 the pottery stand:
64 the barker (*joc.* Cheap Jack, Cheap John)
65 the market woman
66 potter's wares (pottery);
67 visitors to the fair

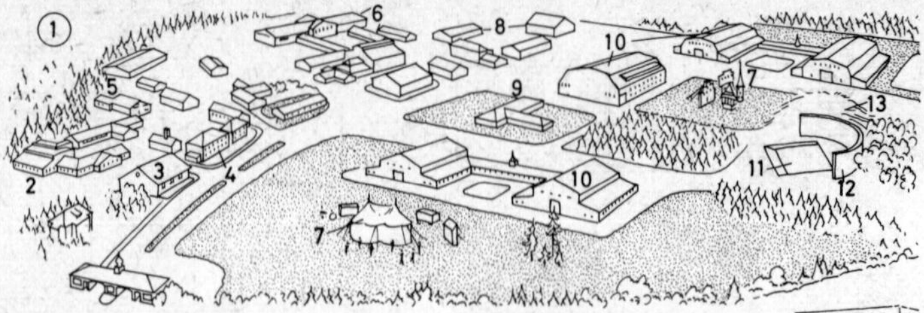

1-13 the film studios,

1 the location (lot, outdoor filming ground, studio grounds):

2 the printing (processing) laboratories

3 the cutting (editing) rooms

4 the administration building

5 the film library (film archives)

6 the workshops

7 the set (exterior construction set)

8 the power station

9 the technical and research laboratories

10 the group of stages

11 the concrete tank for water shots

12 the cyclorama

13 the horizon hill;

14-61 filming,

14 the music-recording studio (sound recording studio):

15 the 'acoustic' wall padding

16 the screen

17 the film orchestra;

18 location (exterior, outdoor) shooting:

19 the crane camera (crane dolly)

20 the trestle table

21 the microphone (*coll.* mike) on the boom ('fishpole')

22 the recording van (*Am.* truck)

23 the stills camera on wooden tripod

24 the stage hand (*here:* the dolly operator)

25 the studio manager;

26–61 floor work (stage work, interior work, indoor shooting) on the floor (sound stage, sound film studio):

26 the executive producer

27 the leading lady (actress, film star, heroine)

28 the leading man (actor, film star, hero)

29 the film extra (film super, crowd actor)

30 the microphone boom

31 the studio microphone

32 the microphone cable

33 the set and the background
34 the clapper boy
35 the clapper (clappers, takeboard) with number board for film title, scene number (take number, shot number), and take date
36 the make-up artist or expert (studio hairdresser)
37 the electrician (lighter, *Am. coll.* gaffer)
38 the colour medium
39 the continuity girl (continuity secretary, script girl)
40 the film director
41 the (chief) camera man (director of photography)
42 the camera operator
43 the art director (studio architect, studio designer)
44 the studio manager
45 the shooting script (film script, scenario)
46 the assistant director
47 the sound-proof film camera (picture camera)
48 the blimp (sound-proof metal camera cover)
49 the camera crane
50 the pump-tripod
51 the glare screen for protection from extraneous light
52 the spot (spotlight) on tripod (brightener, *sim. Am.* klieglight, kleiglight)
53 the lighting rail (gantry, catwalk)
54 the studio sound box (studio sound booth) for sound-recording:
55 the mixing console (mixing panel)
56 the sound camera
57 the sound camera table
58 the loudspeaker
59 the amplifier;
60 the sound engineer
61 the assistant sound engineer

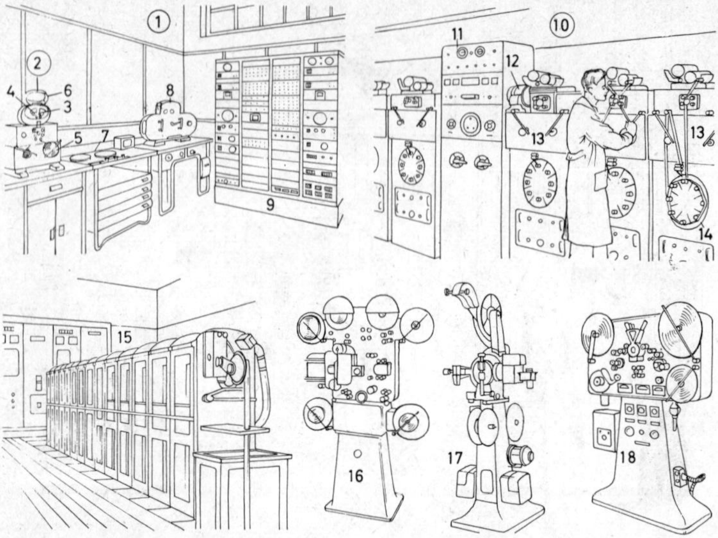

1-34 the production of sound motion pictures (of sound films, *Am.* talkies),

1 the sound-on-film recording studio (sound camera room),

2 the magnetic-sound camera for electro-magnetic sound-recording:

3 the magnetic recording head

4 the magnetic playback head

5 the magnetic film spool

6 the anti-magnetic screening hood;

7 the narrow-tape recorder (tape-recording machine)

8 the photographic sound-on-film recording camera for photographic sound-recording

9 the amplifier rack;

10 the dubbing machine room:

11 the switch panel

12 the driving and synchronizing motor

13 the sound-reproducing set (tape-reproducer) for dialogue, music, and sound tapes (playback of the dialogue, music, and sound tracks)

14 the loop attachment;

15–18 the film-processing laboratory for development and printing of the film strips:

15 the light-proof daylight film-developing machines for development of picture negatives and positives, sound negatives and positives

16–18 film-printing machines:

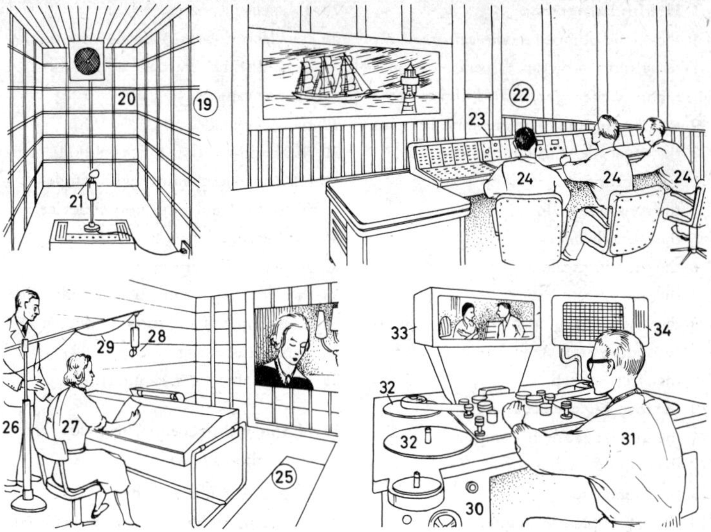

16 the contact printing machine for picture or sound, or both combined (picture-sound-printing machine)

17 the optic picture-printing machine for sub-standard film

18 the optic sound-track printing machine for sub-standard film;

19 the echo studio:

20 the echo studio loudspeaker

21 the echo studio microphone;

22–24 sound-dubbing (sound-doubling, sound-mixing, the mixing of several sound tracks),

22 the dubbing theatre (*Am.* dubbtheater; dubbing studio):

23 the mixing console (mixing desk) for one-channel sound or stereo sound

24 the dubbing mixers (dubbing editors, sound-engineers, sound-cutters), dubbing;

25–29 lip-synchronization (lip-synking, dubbing, doubling, post-synchronizing, post-synking),

25 the lip-synchronization studio:

26 the dubbing director

27 the lip-synchronist

28 the microphone and the boom

29 the sound cable;

30–34 cutting (editing):

30 the cutting and monitoring console or desk

31 the film-cutter (editor)

32 the rewind plates

33 the picture projection

34 the loudspeaker

1-35 film cameras,

1 the sound blimped studio camera (*Am.* motion-picture camera, moving picture camera), a standard-film camera:

2 the photographic camera optical system

3 the sunshade with filter holder and gauze clamp

4 the sunshade bellows

5 the variable diffuser

6 the focusing scale

7 the fine adjustment

8 the viewfinder, a traversing frosted (ground-glass) screen

9 the safety switch

10 the focusing eyepiece

11 the film magazine housing

12 the magnifier adjustment

13 the footage meter

14 the single-picture counter

15 the fade shutter adjustment

16 the sector scale

17 the side viewfinder

18 the camera housing door

19 the motor inching knob

20 the film-transporting sprocket and guide rollers

21 the eccentric lever double claw intermittent motion with register pins;

22 the light-weight picture camera (hand, or shoulder, camera)

23 the picture-sound camera (news-reel camera, reporter camera) for simultaneous picture and sound recording

24 the sub-standard (narrow-film) camera (amateur camera):

25 the viewfinder eyepiece

26 the footage-counter (film-counter)

27 the drive (clockwork spring motor);

28–35 special cameras,

28 the electron-controlled slow-motion camera (time-retarder), a high-frequency camera:

29 the switch clock;

30 the rapid-motion (quick-motion) camera (time-accelerator) with single-frame feed and stop-motion device:

31 the focusing lever;

32 the trick film camera:

33 the trick table camera, *also:* film title (*Am.* caption) and sub-title camera

34 the trick drawing

35 the film title (*Am.* caption);

36-44 the wide-screen film (wide-screen stereophonic film),

36 wide-screen film making:

37 the anamorphic (anamorphous) lens (cylindrical lens, distorting lens)

38 stereophonic sound-recording by three-channel system

39 the stereophonic camera

40 the three microphones (*Am.* mike)

41 the sound-registering strip

42 the wide-screen film projector:

43 the anamorphoscope (anamorphote front lens);

44 the three back-stage loudspeakers;

45-52 the panorama film,

45 panoramic sound-recording:

46 the five microphones (*Am.* mike)

47 the triple picture camera;

48 the triple picture projector

49 the panoramic screen (arc-shaped, curved screen)

50 the five loudspeakers

51 the effect loudspeakers in the cinema auditorium

52 the multiple sound-reproducing unit

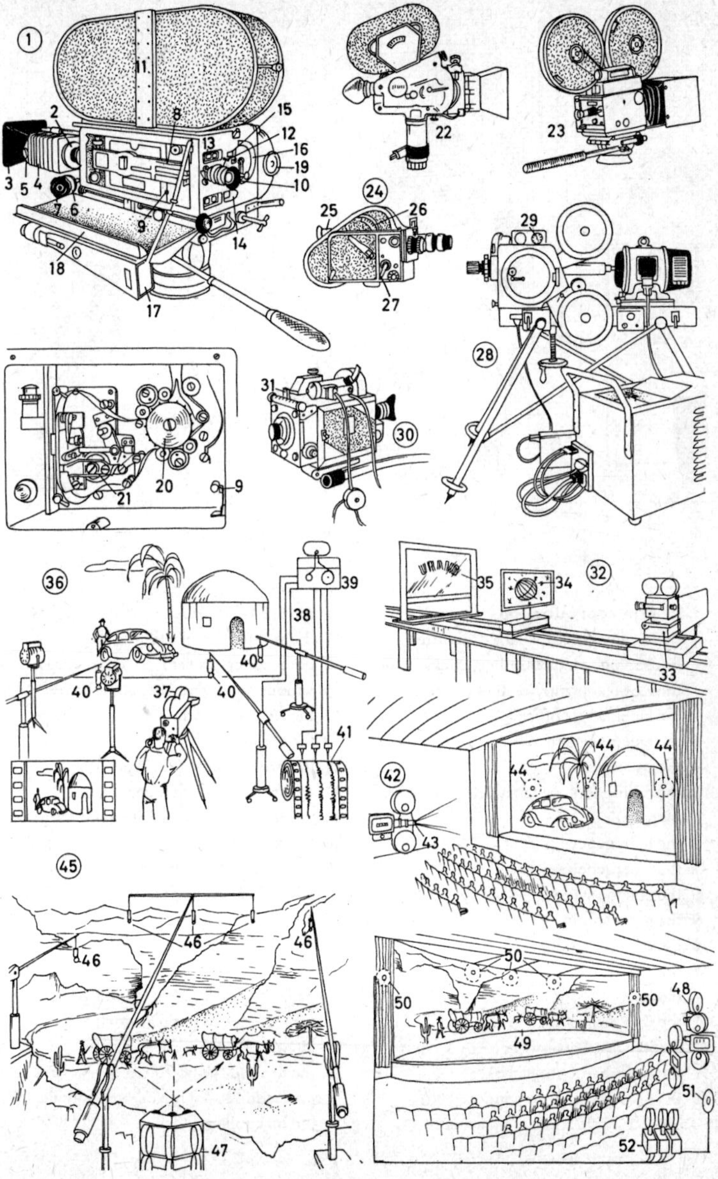
1
2
3
4
5
6
7
8
9
10
11
12
13
14
15
16
17
18
19
20
21
22
23
24
25
26
27
28
29
30
31
32
33
34
35
36
37
38
39
40
41
42
43
44
45
46
47
48
49
50
51
52

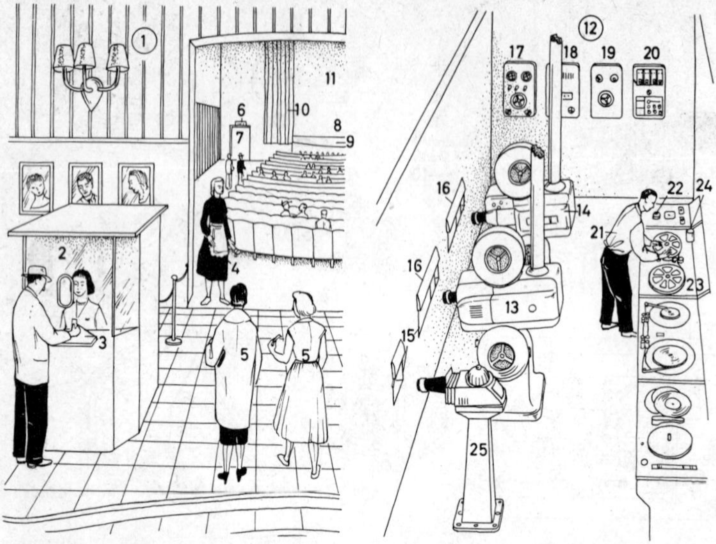

1-25 film reproduction,

1 the cinema (picture palace, picture house, *coll.* pictures, films, flicks, *Am.* movie theater, movies, flickers, *coll.* pix):

2 the cinema box office

3 the cinema ticket

4 the usherette

5 the film-goers (cinema-goers, cinema patrons)

6 the emergency light

7 the emergency exit

8 the cinema stage

9 the proscenium

10 the screen curtain

11 the screen (talking screen, *Am.* silver screen);

12 the film projection room:

13 the left-hand projector

14 the right-hand projector

15 the projection room window with projecting and observing apertures

16 the fire safety drop-shutter

17 the auditorium lighting control

18 the rectifier, a selenium or mercury vapour (rectifier, *Am.* straightener)

19 the electric curtain-drawing machine

20 the amplifier

21 the projectionist (film operator)

22 the switch for the cinema gong

23 the re-winding desk for re-winding the film

24 the film cement

25 the slide (diapositive) projector for advertisement diapositives;

26-53 film-projectors,

26 the sound-projector (sound film projector, cinema projector, exhibitor's projection unit, *Am.* talking picture projector, movie projector),

27–38 the film run mechanism:

27 the top and the bottom film box (fire protection spool boxes) with circulating oil cooling

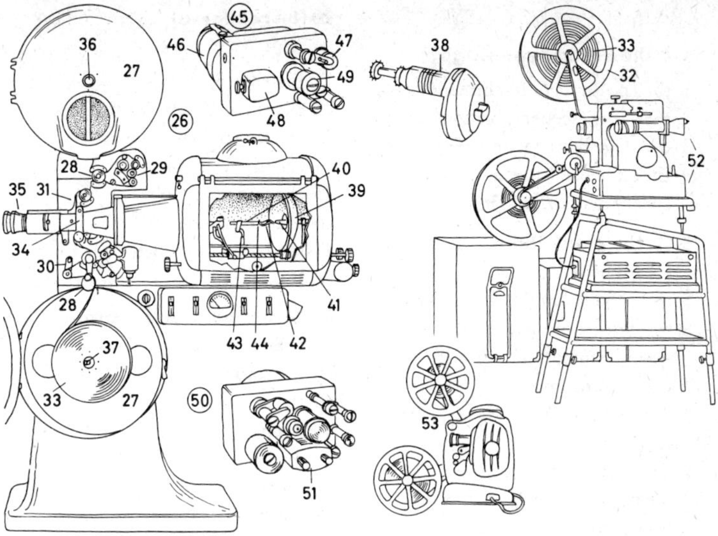

28 the take-off and take-up sprockets
29 the deflecting roller with framer control (with picture line adjustment)
30 the loop-setting device (loop compensation film, loop-absorber) for prestabilization of the film, *also* : film rupture (film break) contact
31 the picture gate
32 the film spool
33 the film roll
34 the film (picture) gate with film-cooling turbo-blower
35 the projector lens
36 the take-off spindle
37 the take-up reeling friction
38 the Maltese cross gear;
39–44 the lamp-house:
39 the reflector (mirror) arc lamp with non-spherical hollow mirror and blower magnet for arc stabilization
40 the positive carbon
41 the negative carbon
42 the arc
43 the carbon-holder
44 the crater (carbon crater);
45 the photo-electric (photographic) sound-reproducing unit [also intended for multi-channel stereo-sound reproduction and push-pull track]:
46 the photo-electric optic system
47 the sound scanning roller
48 the sound lamp in the casing
49 the photo-electric cell in the hollow axle;
50 the additional four-channel magnetic-sound reproducing unit (magnetic sound-scanner):
51 the quadruple magnetic soundhead;
52 the portable sub-standard (narrow-film) cinema projector for travelling (*Am.* traveling, itinerant) cinema
53 the home projector (home cinema, *Am.* home movies)

Engl. theatre = *Am.* theater

1-4 the arena-type stage:

1 the spotlight (*Am.* limelight) flap
2 the scene (scenery, setting)
3 the stage floor (acting area)
4 the audience (spectators, theatre spectators; *coll.* the house);

5-11 the cloakroom (*Am.* checkroom) **hall:**

5 the cloakroom (*Am.* checkroom)
6 the cloakroom attendant (*Am.* checkroom girl, check girl)
7 the cloakroom ticket (*Am.* check)
8 the playgoer (theatregoer, *Am.* theatergoer)
9 the opera glasses (glasses)
10 the commissionaire (front of house attendant)
11 the theatre ticket, an admission ticket;

12 and 13 the foyer (lobby, crush room):

12 the usher
13 the programme (*Am.* program);

14-28 the theatre:

14 the stage
15 the proscenium

16-19 the auditorium (theatre auditorium):

16 the gallery
17 the upper circle (*Am.* amphitheater)
18 the dress circle (*Am.* balcony, horseshoe, diamond horseshoe)
19 the pit (*Am.* parquet, parterre) and the orchestra stalls (stalls; *Am.* orchestra seat, orchestra chair, orchestra);

20 the rehearsal (theatre rehearsal):

21 the theatre chorus (chorus)
22 the singer (male vocalist)
23 the singer (female vocalist)
24 the orchestra pit
25 the orchestra
26 the conductor
27 the baton (conductor's baton)
28 the spectator's seat (theatre seat);

29-42 the painter's room, a theatre workshop:

29 the catwalk
30 the set piece
31 the flat
32 the built piece
33 the back-cloth
34 the portable paint box
35 the scene-painter, a scenic artist
36 the scenic artist's palette
37 the set-designer
38 the costume-designer
39 the sketch for a costume
40 the sketch for a costume
41 the model stage
42 the model set;

43-52 the theatre dressing room:

43 the dressing-room mirror
44 the make-up smock
45 the make-up table (bench)
46 the grease paint stick
47 the make-up man, a make-up artist
48 the theatre hairdresser
49 the wig
50 the hand properties (properties, props)
51 the theatrical costume
52 the call lamp

1
2
3
4
4

5
A
6
7
8
9
10
11

14
15
16
17
18
19
20
21
22
23
24
25
26
27
28

12
13

29
30
31
32
33
34
35
36
37
38
39
40
41
42

43
44
45
46
47
48
49
50
51
52

Engl. theatre = *Am.* theater

1-60 the stage with the machinery (flies and under stage machinery),

1 the control room:
2 the control desk
3 the lighting plot;
4 the grid
5 the fly floor (fly gallery)
6 the sprinkler system (sprinklers)
7 the flyman
8 the fly lines (lines)
9 the cyclorama (stage horizon, cyke)
10 the back-cloth (back-drop)
11 the cut cloth, a side drop-cloth
12 the border
13 the overhead lighting battens
14 the cyclorama floodlights
15 the acting area lamps
16 the spot bar lamps
17 the slide projectors
18 the water gun
19 the travelling (*Am.* traveling) lighting gallery
20 the electrician
21 the proscenium spotlights (pros spots)
22 the adjustable proscenium
23 the trailer curtains (theatre curtain, *coll.* tabs)
24 the safety curtain (fire curtain, *Am.* shade)
25 the forestage
26 the footlights (floats)
27 the prompt box
28 the prompter (prompt)
29 the stage manager's desk
30 the stage director (stage manager)
31 the revolving stage
32 the opening for lift
33 the hydraulic lift
34 the stage bridge (lift)
35 the pieces of scenery (*all together :* the set)
36 the scene:
37 the actor (*now rare :* player)
38 the actress
39 the supers;
40 the producer
41 the producer's script with the stage directions
42 the producer's table
43 the assistant producer
44 the prompt copy (prompt script)
45 the stage manager
46 the stage hand (scene-shifter, deck hand, *Am.* grip hand)
47 the set piece
48 the mirror spotlight:
49 the gelatine (gelly);
50 the hydraulic lifting and lowering plant:
51 the water tank
52 the suction line
53 the hydraulic press
54 the pressure line
55 the pressure chamber
56 the pressure gauge (*Am.* pressure gage)
57 the water gauge (*Am.* water gage)
58 the control lever
59 the lift operator
60 the rams

1
2
3
4
5
6
7
8
9
10
11
12
13
14
15
16
17
18
19
20
21
22
23
24
25
26
27
28
29
30
31
32
33
34
35
36
37
38
39
40
41
42
43
44
45
46
47
48
49
50
51
52
53
54
55
56
57
58
59
60

Engl. theatre = *Am.* theater

1-3 the cabaret:

1 the accompanist, a pianist

2 the compère (announcer; *Am.* master of ceremonies, *coll.* M. C.; *when a woman:* commère), a cabaret performer

3 the cabaret singer (chanson singer; diseuse), a reciter (elocutionist); *sim.* hit singer, crooner;

4-8 the variety (variety theatre, variety show, vaudeville, vaudeville theatre, music hall, revue theatre):

4 the solo dancer (première danseuse), a revue star

5 the solo dancer, a tap dancer

6 the troupe of girls (dancing troupe, line dancers):

7 the chorus girl (revue girl, girl);

8 the number girl;

9-22 art of variety and the circus:

9 the floor acrobat (acrobat, tumbler), a high-speed acrobat

10 the somersaulter

11 contortionist acts:

12 the back-bend

13 the through-bend (*Am.* thru-bend);

14 the exotic dancer

15 the strong-man act:

16 the equilibrist;

17 the juggler

18 conjurers (conjurors, magicians):

19 the sleight-of-hand artiste (legerdemainist, prestidigitator)

20 the illusionist;

21 the flying man

22 the diabolo, a catching game;

23 the Punch and Judy show (*Am. pop.* Swatchel box):

24 the devil's grandmother, a hand puppet

25 Punch (*Am. pop.* Swatchel)

26 the crocodile

27 the devil;

28 shadow puppets (Chinese shadow show)

29-40 the marionette theatre, a puppet show,

29 the marionette (fantoccino):

30 the guiding cross (manipulating cross)

31 the supporting string (head string)

32 the manipulating string

33 the hinged joint

34 the stuffed puppet body

35 the member (limb);

36 the marionette operator, a puppet man

37 the operating bridge (operating platform)

38 the miniature stage, a puppet stage

39 the stage frame (proscenium)

40 the reader

1
2
3
4
5
6
7
8
9
10
11
12
13
14
15
16
17
18
19
20
21
22
23
24
25
26
27
28
29
30
31
32
33
34
35
36
37
38
39
40

1-4 mediaeval notation (neumatic notation):

1 neumes (neums) [11th cent.]

2 and 3 plainsong notations [12th and 13th cent.]:

2 the circumflex notation

3 the square notation;

4 the mensural notation (musica mensurata, cantus mensuratus) [14th and 15th cent.];

5-9 the note:

5 the note head

6 the note stem (note tail)

7 the note hook (note crook)

8 the note bar

9 the dot, a sign of increase in length;

10-13 the clefs:

10 the treble clef (G clef, violin clef)

11 the bass clef (F clef)

12 the alto clef (C clef) for viola

13 the tenor clef (C clef) for cello;

14-21 the time values (duration) **of the notes:**

14 the breve

15 the semibreve (whole note)

16 the minim (half note)

17 the crotchet (*Am.* quarter note)

18 the quaver (*Am.* eighth note)

19 the semiquaver

20 the demisemiquaver

21 the hemidemisemiquaver;

22-29 the rests:

22 the breve rest

23 the semibreve rest

24 the minim rest

25 the crotchet rest

26 the quaver rest

27 the semiquaver rest

28 the demisemiquaver rest

29 the hemidemisemiquaver rest;

30-44 the time (measure, kinds of measure, time signatures):

30 the two-eight time

31 the two-four time
32 the two-two time
33 the four-eight time
34 the four-four (common) time
35 the four-two time
36 the six-eight time
37 the six-four time
38 the three-eight time
39 the three-four time
40 the three-two time
41 the nine-eight time
42 the nine-four time
43 the five-four time
44 the bar line;

45 and 46 the staff (stave):
45 the line
46 the space; line and space: degree;

47-50 the scales (gamuts):
47 the C major scale (natural scale); naturals: c, d, e, f, g, a, b, c
48 the C minor scale [harmonic]
49 the chromatic scale
50 the quarter-tone scale;

51-59 the accidentals (inflections),
51 and 52 the signs raising a note:
51 the sharp (the raising of the note by one semitone)
52 the double sharp (the raising of the note by two semitones);
53 and 54 the signs lowering a note:
53 the flat (the lowering of the note by one semitone)
54 the double flat (the lowering of the note by two semitones);
55 the natural
56–59 the quarter-tone accidentals:
56 the sign for raising the note by one quarter-tone
57 the sign for raising the note by three quarter-tones
58 the sign for lowering the note by one quarter-tone
59 the sign for lowering the note by three quarter-tones

300 The Musical Notation II

1-15 the keys (major keys and minor keys, parallel keys with the same key signature), each succeeding key starting a fifth above or below the previous key:

1 C major (A minor)
2 G major (E minor)
3 D major (B minor)
4 A major (F sharp minor)
5 E major (C sharp minor)
6 B major (G sharp minor)
7 F sharp major (D sharp minor)
8 C sharp major (A sharp minor)
9 F major (D minor)
10 B flat major (G minor)
11 E flat major (C minor)
12 A flat major (F minor)
13 D flat major (B flat minor)
14 G flat major (E flat minor)
15 C flat major (A flat minor);

16-18 the chord,

16 and 17 common chords (triads):
16 the major chord
17 the minor chord;
18 the dominant seventh, the chord of the seventh;
19 the unison (unison interval)

20-27 the intervals (musical intervals):

20 the major second
21 the major third
22 the perfect fourth
23 the perfect fifth
24 the major sixth
25 the major seventh
26 the perfect octave
27 the major ninth;

28-38 the ornaments (grace notes, graces):

28 the appoggiatura
29 the acciaccatura
30 the slide
31 the trill (shake) without turn
32 the trill with turn
33 the mordent (*Am.* pralltriller)
34 the inverted mordent
35 the turn
36 the ascending arpeggio
37 the descending arpeggio
38 the triplet; *corresponding groups:* duplet (couplet), quadruplet, quintuplet, sextuplet (sextolet), septuplet (septolet septimole);

39-45 the syncopation:

39 the up-beat

c' h'; c'' h''; c''' h'''; c'''' h''''; c'''''
c¹ h¹; c² h²; c³ h³; c⁴ h⁴; c⁵

in England c' b'; c'' b''; c''' b'''; c'''' b''''; c'''''
c¹ b¹; c² b²; c³ b³; c⁴ b⁴; c⁵

40 marcato, emphasised, strongly accented (a sign of accentuation)
41 the bind (tie)
42 the pause (fermata), a pause sign
43 the repeat mark
44 and **45** the octave signs:
44 ottava alta (ottava sopra; one octave higher)
45 ottava bassa (ottava sotto; one octave lower);
46–48 the canon (round):
46 the leading part (melody)
47 the imitating part
48 the indication of the tempo (of the pace);
49 crescendo (increasing gradually in loudness)
50 decrescendo (*in Engl.* diminuendo; diminishing gradually in loudness)
51 legato (smoothly)
52 portato (portando, portamento, slight glide)
53 tenuto (held to full value)
54 staccato (detached)

55-61 expression marks (signs of relative intensity):
55 piano (soft)
56 pianissimo (very soft)
57 pianissimo possibile (double pianissimo, as soft as possible)
58 forte (loud)
59 fortissimo (very loud)
60 fortissimo possibile (double fortissimo, as loud as possible)
61 forte-piano (loud attack, then continue softly);

62-70 the divisions of the compass in general use:
62 the subcontra octave (double contra-octave)
63 the contra octave
64 the great octave
65 the small octave
66 the one-line (once-marked, once accented) octave
67 the two-line (twice-marked, twice accented) octave
68 the three-line (thrice-marked, thrice accented) octave
69 the four-line (four-times marked, four-times accented) octave
70 the five-line (five-times marked, five-times accented) octave

1 the lure, a bronze trumpet
2 the Pan-pipes (Pan's pipes, Pandean pipes, syrinx), a shepherd's flute
3 the diaulos (double aulos), a double shawm (reed pipe):
4 the aulos (pipe)
5 the phorbeia (mouth-binder);
6 the cromorne (krumhorn, krummhorn)
7 the recorder (fipple flute, block flute)
8 the bagpipe; *sim.* musette:
9 the bag
10 the chanter (melody pipe)
11 the drone (drone pipes);
12 the cornett (zinke); *forms :* straight cornett, curved cornett, serpent
13 the shawm (schalmeys; *larger :* bombard pommer)
14 the lyre:
15 the arch
16 the crossbar (yoke)
17 the bridge
18 the sound board (sound chest)
19 the plectrum , a pick for plucking;
20 the pochette (kit), a pocket fiddle
21 the cittern (cither, cister, citole, a stringed instrument for plucking; *sim.* pandore (bandora):
22 the rose, a sound hole;
23 the viol (treble viol, descant viol); *larger :* tenor viol, bass viol (viola da gamba, gamba), contrabass viol (violone):
24 the viol bow (bow);
25 the hurdy-gurdy (vielle, organistrum):
26 the friction wheel
27 the cover
28 the keyboard (keys)
29 the sound body
30 the melody strings
31 the drones (bourdon strings);
32 the dulcimer; *sim.* psaltery:
33 the sound chest
34 the sound-board (sound table, sounding board)
35 the striking hammers;
36 the clavichord; *forms :* the fretted or the fretless clavichord
37 the clavichord mechanism:
38 the key (key lever)
39 the balance rail
40 the guiding pin
41 the guiding groove
42 the resting rail
43 the tangent
44 the string;
45 the harpsichord (clavicembalo, cembalo), a wing-shaped stringed keyboard instrument; *sim.* spinet, virginals:
46 the upper keyboard (upper manual)
47 the lower keyboard (lower manual);
48 the harpsichord mechanism:
49 the key (key lever)
50 the jack
51 the rack
52 the tongue
53 the crow quill (plectrum)
54 the damper
55 the string;
56 the portative organ, a portable organ; *other form :* regal; *larger :* the positive organ:
57 the pipes
58 the bellows

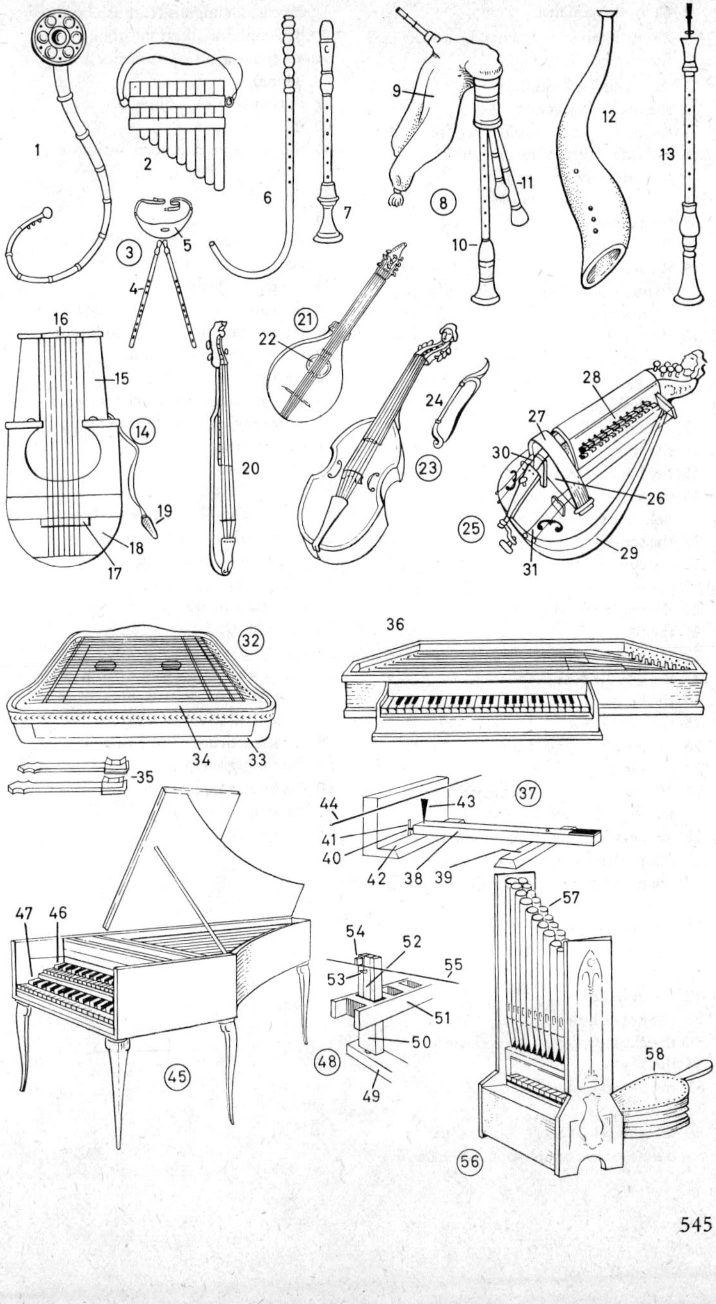
1
2
3
4
5
6
7
8
9
10
11
12
13
14
15
16
17
18
19
20
21
22
23
24
25
26
27
28
29
30
31
32
33
34
35
36
37
38
39
40
41
42
43
44
45
46
47
48
49
50
51
52
53
54
55
56
57
58

1–62 orchestral instruments,
1–27 stringed instruments, bowed instruments (strings),
1 the violin (*coll.* fiddle):
2 the neck of the violin
3 the body (belly, sound box of the violin)
4 the sides (ribs) of the violin
5 the bridge of the violin
6 the f-hole, a sound hole
7 the tailpiece
8 the chin rest
9 the strings (violin strings, fiddle strings): g-string, d′-string, a′-string, e″-string;
10 the mute (sordino)
11 the rosin (resin, colophony)
12 the violin bow (bow; *coll.* fiddle bow, fiddlestick):
13 the nut
14 the stick
15 the hair of the violin bow, horsehair;
16 the violoncello (cello), a bass violin held between the knees:
17 the scroll
18 the tuning peg
19 the nut
20 the peg box
21 the head
22 the finger board;
23 the double bass (bass):
24 the belly
25 the edge
26 the purfling (inlaid border);
27 the viola;
28–38 wood wind instruments (wood winds),
28 the bassoon; *larger :* double bassoon (contrabassoon, contrafagotto):
29 the mouthpiece with the double reed slip;
30 the piccolo (flauto piccolo)
31 the flute (German flute), a transverse flute:
32 the flute key
33 the finger hole;
34 the clarinet; *larger :* bass clarinet:
35 the key
36 the mouthpiece
37 the bell;
38 the oboe (hautboy); *kinds :* oboe d'amore; the tenor oboe: oboe da caccia, cor anglais (English horn); heckelphone (baritone oboe);
39–48 brass wind instruments (brass winds),
39 the tenor horn, a flügel horn:
40 the valve;
41 the horn (French horn, waldhorn, corno), a valve horn:
42 the bell;
43 the cornet
44 the bass tuba (tuba, bombardon); *sim.* euphonium, contrabass tuba:
45 the thumb hold;
46 the trombone; *kinds :* alto trombone, tenor trombone, bass trombone:
47 the trombone slide (slide)
48 the bell;
49–59 percussion instruments (*in the orchestra fam. called* the kitchen department):
49 the triangle
50 the cymbals
51–59 membraphonic instruments,
51 the side drum (snare drum):
52 the vellum (drum head)
53 the tightening screw;
54 the drumsticks
55 the bass drum
56 the stick
57 the kettledrum, a screw drum (timpanum); *sim.* machine drum (mechanically tuned drum):
58 the kettledrum vellum or skin
59 the tuning screw;
60 the harp, a pedal harp:
61 the strings
62 the pedals

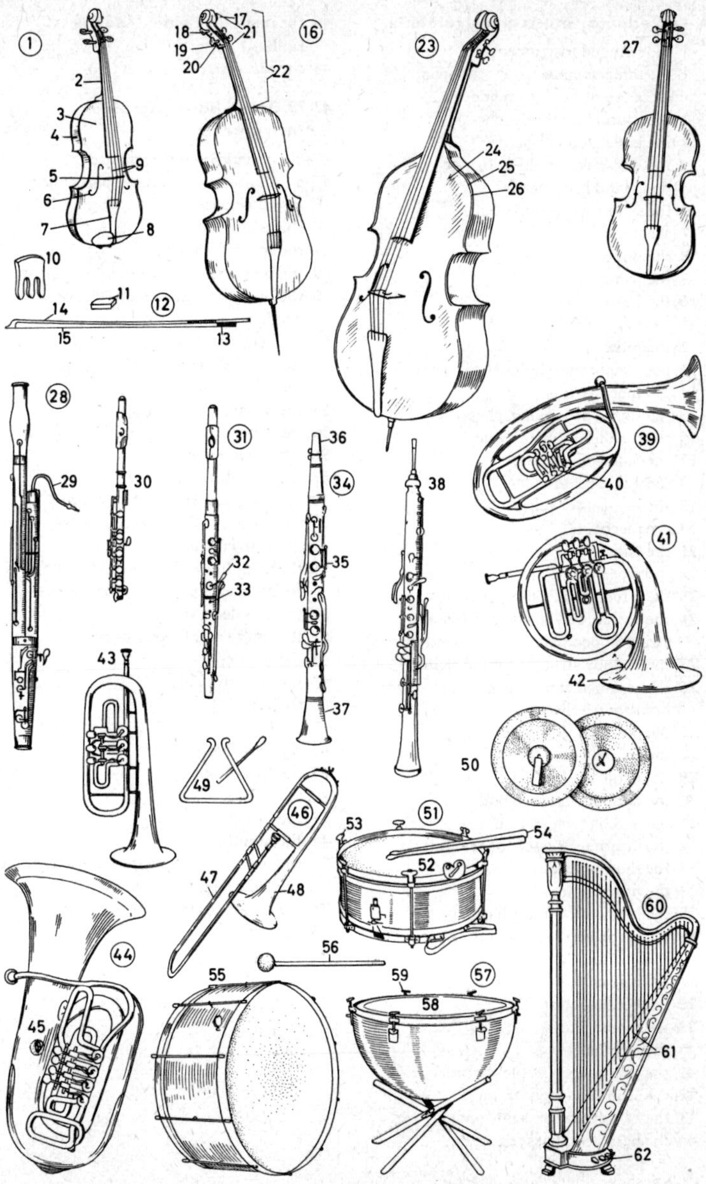
1
2
3
4
5
6
7
8
9
10
11
12
13
14
15
16
17
18
19
20
21
22
23
24
25
26
27
28
29
30
31
32
33
34
35
36
37
38
39
40
41
42
43
44
45
46
47
48
49
50
51
52
53
54
55
56
57
58
59
60
61
62

303 Musical Instruments III

1-46 popular musical instruments,

1–31 stringed instruments,

1 the lute; *older and larger:* theorbo, chitarrone; *smaller:* mandora

2 the sound box (body, chest)

3 the table (sound board)

4 the end-piece (holder, bridge)

5 the sound hole (rose)

6 the string, a catgut string

7 the neck

8 the finger board

9 the fret

10 the head (peg box)

11 the peg (pin);

12 the guitar:

13 the metal-string holder (tail piece)

14 the metal string

15 the sound box (body, chest);

16 the mandolin (mandoline):

17 the tailpiece

18 the guard plate

19 the peg-box cheek;

20 the plectrum

21 the zither:

22 the wrest plank

23 the wrest pins (tuning pins)

24 the accompanying strings (bass strings, open strings, unstopped strings)

25 the melody strings (fretted strings)

26 the rounded extension of the resonance box (sound chest);

27 the plectrum (thimble)

28 the balalaika

29 the banjo:

30 the tambourine-type body

31 the parchment (vellum);

32 the ocarina, a vessel-shaped flute:

33 the mouthpiece

34 the finger hole;

35 the harmonica (mouth organ)

36 the accordion (accordeon); *sim.* concertina:

37 the bellows

38 the bellows strap

39 the melody keys

40 the keyboard

41 the treble stop (treble register)

42 the stop key (register key)

43 the bass studs (bass buttons)

44 the bass stop (bass register);

45 the jingle tambourine (*old form:* timbrel)

46 the castanets;

47-78 dance band (jazz band) **instruments,**

47–58 percussion instruments,

47–54 the dance band (jazz) percussion instruments:

47 the bass drum

48 the snare drum (side drum)

49 the jazz tomtom (wooden-hoop drum)

50 the high-hat (Charleston) choke cymbals

51 the cymbal

52 the cymbal stand

53 the wire brush

54 the pedal mechanism;

55 the conga drum:

56 the tension hoop;

57 the timbales (side drums)

58 the bongoes (twin Cuban drums)

59 the maracas; *sim.* rumba shakers

60 the sapo cubano

61 the xylophone; *form.* 'straw fiddle'; *sim.* concert marimba, tubophone:

62 the wooden bar

63 the sound box (sound chest)

64 the beater;

65 the jazz trumpet:

66 the valve

67 the finger-hook

68 the mute (sordino);

69 the saxophone:

70 the bell

71 the detachable piece

72 the mouthpiece;

73 the struck (plectrum) guitar (jazz guitar, *sim.* Hawaii guitar):

74 the hollow to facilitate fingering;

75 the vibraphone:

76 the metal frame

77 the metal bar

78 the metal tube (resonator)

1
2
3
4
5
6
7
8
9
10
11
12
13
14
15
16
17
18
19
20
21
22
23
24
25
26
27
28
29
30
31
32
33
34
35
36
37
38
39
40
41
42
43
44
45
46
47
48
49
50
51
52
53
54
55
56
57
58
59
60
61
62
63
64
65
66
67
68
69
70
71
72
73
74
75
76
77
78

1 **the piano** (upright piano, upright pianoforte), a keyed instrument (keyboard instrument); *smaller form :* cottage piano; *earlier forms :* pantaleon; clavichord,
2–18 the piano action (piano mechanism):
2 the iron frame
3 the hammer (piano hammer); *all together :* striking mechanism
4 and 5 the keyboard:
4 the white key (ivory key)
5 the black key (ebony key);
6 the piano case
7 the strings
8 and 9 the piano pedals:
8 the right pedal (forte pedal, sustaining pedal, *coll.* loud pedal)
9 the left pedal (piano pedal, damper pedal, *coll.* soft pedal);
10 the treble strings
11 the treble bridge (treble belly bridge)
12 the bass strings
13 the bass bridge (bass belly bridge)
14 the hitch pin
15 the damper rail support
16 the pressure bar
17 the wrest pin (tuning pin, tuning peg)
18 the wrest plank;
19 the metronome
20 the tuning key (wrest)
21 the tuning wedge
22–39 the action (mechanism) of the keys:
22 the rail (middle action-rail)
23 the damper lever
24 the felt-covered hammer head
25 the hammer shank
26 the hammer rest rail
27 the check (action check head, back check)
28 the check felt
29 the check wire
30 the jack
31 the back stop (check tail)
32 the wippen (action lever)
33 the pilot (prolong, abstract)
34 the pilot wire (prolong wire)
35 the bridle wire
36 the bridle tape
37 the damper block (felt damper, damper)
38 the damper lever
39 the damper rest rail (spring rail);
40 **the concert grand** (grand, grand piano for the concert hall; *smaller :* boudoir piano, baby grand; *earlier form :* square piano):
41 the left concert grand pedal for damping tone by shifting the keyboard: 'una corda'
42 the pedal rod;
43 **the harmonium (reed organ); American Organ, melodeon:**
44 the stop (register)
45 the knee lever (knee swell)
46 the treadles (bellows pedals)
47 the harmonium case
48 the harmonium keyboard

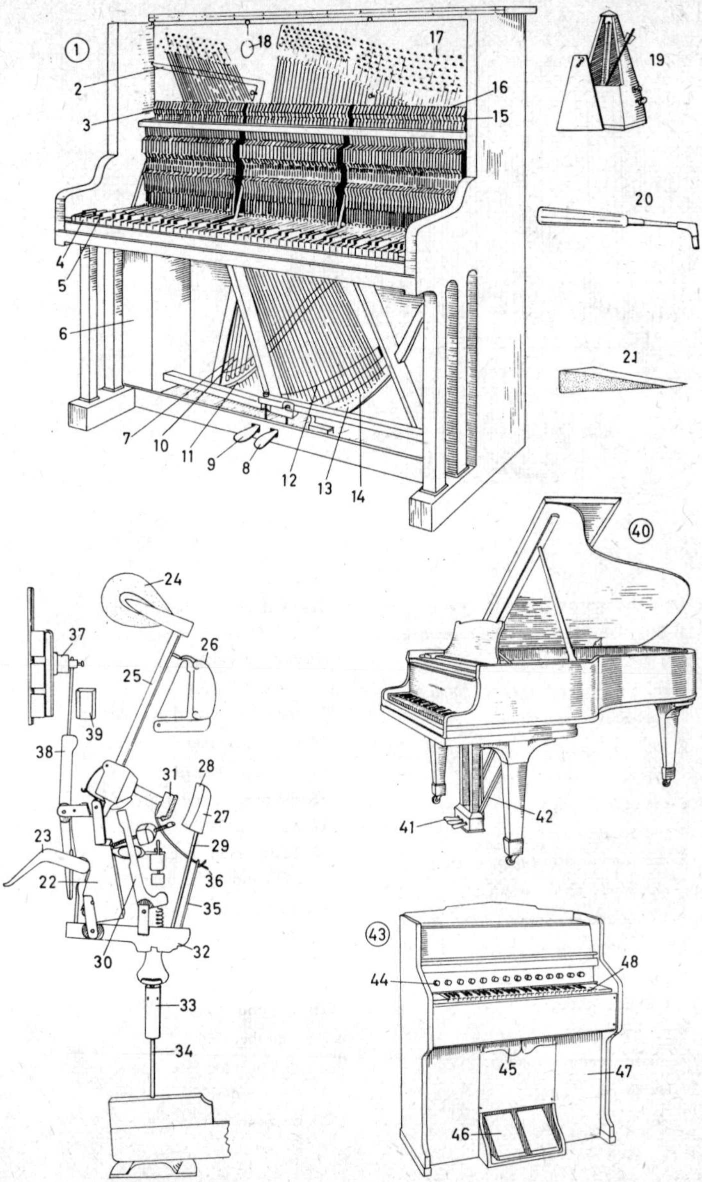
1
2
3
4
5
6
7
8
9
10
11
12
13
14
15
16
17
18
19
20
21
22
23
24
25
26
27
28
29
30
31
32
33
34
35
36
37
38
39
40
41
42
43
44
45
46
47
48

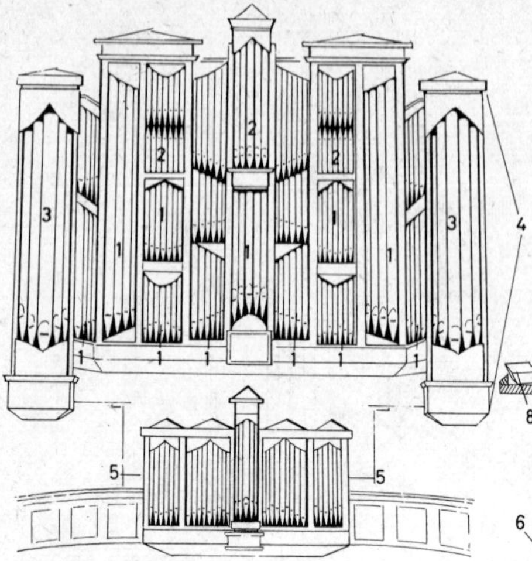

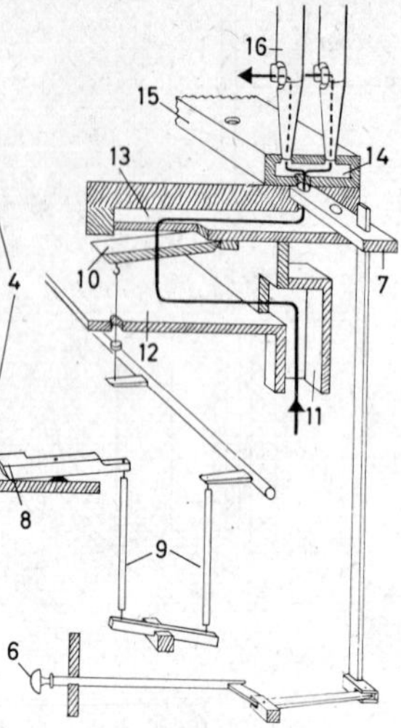

1-52 the organ (church organ),

1–5 the organ case (organ casework),

1–3 the show pipes:

1 the Hauptwerk *(approx. English equivalent :* great organ)

2 the Oberwerk *(approx. English equivalent :* swell organ)

3 the pedal pipes

4 the pedal tower

5 the Rückpositiv *(approx. English equivalent :* choir organ);

6–16 the tracker action; *other systems :* pneumatic action, electric action:

6 the draw-stop (*pop.* stop)

7 the slide (slider)

8 the key

9 the stickers and trackers

10 the pallet

11 the wind trunk

12–14 the sound-board (wind chest), a slider sound-board; *other types :* sliderless chest

12 the wind chest

13 the sound-board groove

14 the upper-board groove;

15 the upper-board(s)

16 the pipe of one stop;

17–35 the organ pipes (pipes),

17–22 the reed pipe (reed stop) of metal, a Posaune (Trumpet, Tromba, Horn)

17 the boot

18 the shallot

19 the tongue

20 the block

21 the tuning wire

22 the tube (body);

23–30 the open flue pipe of metal, a salicional:

23 the foot

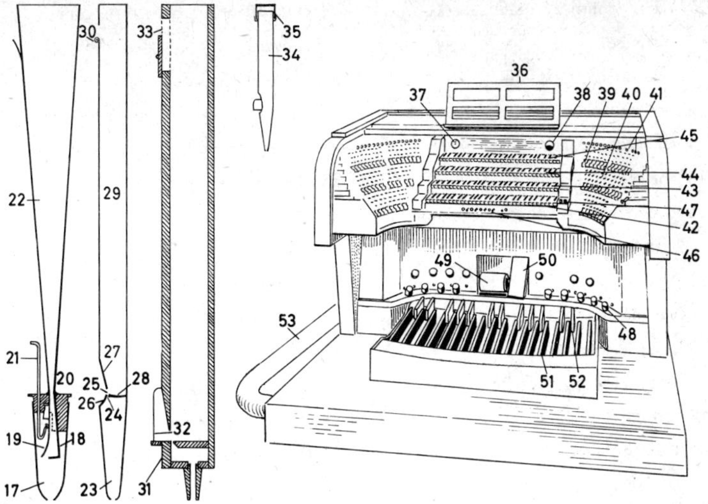

24 the flue (wind way)

25 the mouth

26 the lower lip

27 the upper lip

28 the languid

29 the body of the pipe

30 the tuning tongue (slot), a tuning device;

31–33 the open flue pipe of wood, a principal (open wood, diapason bass):

31 the cap

32 the ear

33 the tuning slot with slide;

34 the stopped flue pipe

35 the canister stopper;

36–52 the organ console (console) of an electrically controlled organ:

36 the music rest

37 the crescendo roller indicator

38 the voltmeter

39 the stops (rocking tablets)

40 the free-combination button

41 the cancel buttons for reeds, couplers, etc.

42 the Manual I, for the Rückpositiv

43 the Manual II, for the Hauptwerk

44 the Manual III, for the Oberwerk

45 the Manual IV, for the Schwellwerk *(approx. English equivalent :* for the solo organ)

46 the pistons for manual registration, free combinations, fixed combinations, and setter-combinations

47 the switches for wind and action-current

48 the toe pistons, for couplers

49 the crescendo roller

50 the swell pedal

51 the pedal key (natural)

52 the pedal key (sharp)

53 the cable

1–10 mechanical musical apparatuses,
1 the musical box:
2 the pinned barrel (reproducer)
3 the metal comb;
4 the metal reed
5 the driving mechanism (clockwork)
6 the pin
7 the adjusting device;
8 the melodeon
9 the metal disk or disc (music)
10 the case;
11 the trautonium, an electrical musical instrument:
12 the keyboard;
13 the tape-recording machine, a portable tape-recorder:
14 the recording tape
15 the tape reel
16 the winding spindle
17 the recording level control
18 the input selectors
19 the recording level indicator
20 the temporary stop button
21 the record button
22 the playback button
23 the stop bar
24 the re-wind button
25 the erase cut-out button
26 the tone control
27 the volume control and on-and-off switch
28 the microphone;
29 the automatic record-player:
30 the case
31 the record slot;
32 the record-player, an automatic record-changer:
33 the changer spindle
34 the record
35 the pick-up (tone arm)
36 and **37** the three-control key:
36 the 78 speed switch
37 the long-playing switch;
38 the repeat switch
39 the interval selector
40 the frequency correction selector
41 the turntable;
42 the audio amplifier, an amplifying device:
43 the loudspeaker
44 the remote-control panel;
45 the radiogram:
46 the radio set (wireless set; *Am.* radio)
47 the record-player

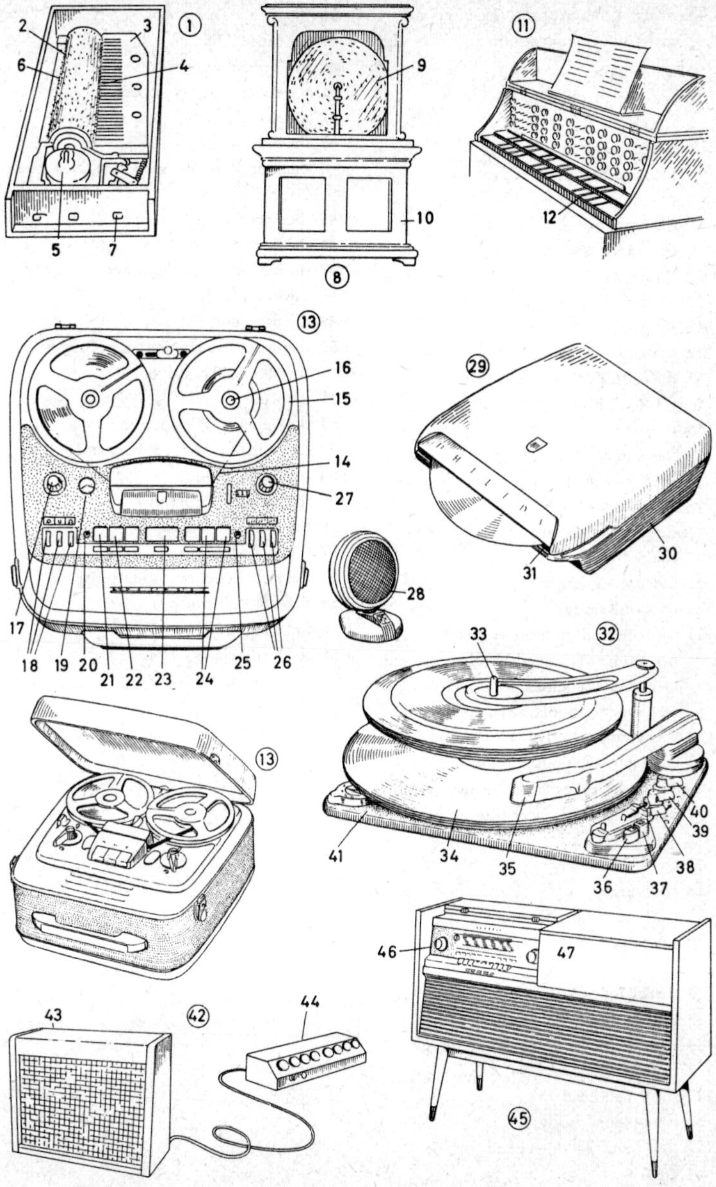
1
2
3
4
5
6
7
8
9
10
11
12
13
14
15
16
17
18
19
20
21
22
23
24
25
26
27
28
PHILIPS
29
30
31
32
33
34
35
36
37
38
39
40
41
13
42
43
44
45
46
47

307 Figures from Fable (Legend) and Myth

1–61 fabulous creatures (fabulous animals), mythological animals and beings,
1 the dragon:
2 the serpent's body
3 the claws
4 the bat's wing
5 the mouth with forked tongue
6 the forked tongue;
7 the unicorn (monoceros):
8 the spirally twisted horn;
9 Phoenix (Phenix):
10 the flames or ashes of resurrection;
11 the griffin:
12 the eagle's head
13 the griffin's claws
14 the lion's body
15 the wing;
16 the chimera (chimaera):
17 the lion's head
18 the goat's head
19 the dragon's body;
20 the Sphinx:
21 the human head
22 the lion's body;
23 the mermaid (nixie, nixy, water nixy, nix, sea maid or maiden); *sim.:* Nereid, Oceanid (sea deities, sea goddesses); *male:* merman (nix, sea man):
24 the woman's body
25 the fish's tail (dolphin's tail);
26 Pegasus ('Poets' horse', Muses' steed, winged horse); *sim.* Hippogryph (Hippogriff):
27 the horse's body
28 the wings;
29 Cerberus (the hell hound):
30 the three-headed hound's body
31 the serpent's tail;
32 the hydra of Lerna (Lernaean serpent):
33 the nine-headed serpent's body;
34 the basilisk (cockatrice) [in England usually with two legs]:
35 the cock's head
36 the dragon's body;
37 the Giant (Titan), a giant (ogre):
38 the rock
39 the serpent foot;
40 the Triton, a sea being:
41 the conch (shell trumpet)
42 the horse's foot
43 the fish's tail;
44 the hippocampus (sea horse, Neptune's horse):
45 the horse's body
46 the fish's tail;
47 the sea bull, a sea monster:
48 the bull's body
49 the fish's tail;
50 the seven-headed dragon of St. John's revelation (Apocalypse):
51 the wing;
52 the Centaur (Hippocentaur):
53 the human body with bow and arrow
54 the horse's body;
55 the harpy, a wind spirit:
56 the woman's head
57 the bird's body;
58 the Siren, a demon (daemon):
59 the woman's body
60 the wing
61 the bird's claws (talons)

1
2
3
4
5
6
7
8
9
10
11
12
13
14
15
16
17
18
19
20
21
22
23
24
25
26
27
28
29
30
31
32
33
34
35
36
37
38
39
40
41
42
43
44
45
46
47
48
49
50
51
52
53
54
55
56
57
58
59
60
61

1 Zeus (Jupiter), the father of the gods (Olympian god),
2–4 the attributes:
2 the thunderbolt
3 the sceptre (*Am.* scepter)
4 the eagle;
5 Hera (Juno):
6 the sacrificial bowl
7 the veil
8 the sceptre (*Am.* scepter);
9 Ares (Mars), god of war:
10 the crested helmet
11 the armour (*Am.* armor);
12 Artemis (Diana), goddess of hunting:
13 the quiver
14 the hind;
15 Apollo, god of light and leader of the Muses (Musagetes):
16 the bow;
17 Athene (Athena, Minerva), goddess of science and the arts:
18 the helmet plume
19 the Corinthian helmet
20 the spear;
21 Hermes (Mercury), the messenger god (herald of the gods) and god of roads and commerce:
22 the winged sandals
23 the winged hat
24 the purse
25 the caduceus (winged wand, Mercury's staff);
26 Eros (Cupid), god of love:
27 the wing
28 the arrow (Cupid's dart);
29 Poseidon (Neptune), god of the sea:
30 the trident
31 the dolphin;
32 Dionysus (Bacchus), god of wine:
33 the thyrsus (Bacchic staff)
34 the panther's skin;
35 the Maenad (Bacchante):
36 the torch;
37 Tyche (Fortuna), goddess of chance and fortune:
38 the mural crown
39 the cornucopia (horn of plenty);
40 Pan (Faunus), the shepherds' god:
41 the Pan-pipes
42 the goat's foot;
43 Nike (Victoria), goddess of victory:
44 the wreath of victory;
45 Atlas, a giant:
46 the heavens;
47 Janus, numen of the house:
48 the Janus head;
49 Medusa, one of the Gorgons:
50 the head of Medusa (of Gorgon);
51 the Erinys (Fury, one of the Eumenides), an avenging goddess:
52 the bundle of serpents;
53–58 the Moirai (Fates, Parcae), goddesses of destiny:
53 Clotho:
54 the spindle;
55 Lachesis:
56 the scroll;
57 Atropos:
58 the scissors;
59–75 the Muses (Camenae, the Nine):
59 Clio [history]:
60 the scroll;
61 Thalia [comedy]:
62 the comic mask;
63 Erato [erotic poetry]:
64 the lyre;
65 Euterpe [instrumental music]:
66 the flute;
67 Polyhymnia (Polymnia) [sacred song]
68 Calliope [epic poetry]:
69 the writing tablet;
70 Terpsichore [choral poetry and dance]:
71 the cithara;
72 Urania [astronomy]:
73 the celestial globe;
74 Melpomene [tragedy]:
75 the tragic mask

1
2
3
4
5
6
7
8
9
10
11
12
13
14
15
16
17
18
19
20
21
22
23
24
25
26
27
28
29
30
31
32
33
34
35
36
37
38
39
40
41
42
43
44
45
46
47
48
49
50
51
52
53
54
55
56
57
58
59
60
61
62
63
64
65
66
67
68
69
70
71
72
73
74
75

1-40 prehistoric finds,

1-9 the palaeolithic (paleolithic) **period** (Early Stone Age) **and the mesolithic period** (Middle Stone Age):

1 the flint axe (*Am.* ax)
2 the throwing-spear head
3 the bone harpoon head
4 the arrow head
5 the throwing stick of reindeer horn
6 the 'ancestor stone', a painted stone
7 the horse's head, a carving
8 the stone age idol, an ivory statuette
9 the bison, a cave painting (rock painting);

10-20 the neolithic period (Late Stone Age):

10 the amphora [corded ware]
11 the decorated bowl [bowl with incised ornaments]
12 the collared amphora (narrow- necked amphora) [megalithic pottery]
13 the spiral-ornamented bowl [spiral-meander ware]
14 the bell beaker [zone pottery]
15 the pile dwelling (lake dwelling), a lacustrine building (house erected on piles); *sim.* the Italian terramare, the British crannog (*err.* crannoge)
16 the dolmen, a megalithic grave (*when covered with earth:* long barrow, tumulus); *other kinds:* passage grave, gallery grave; *sim.* round barrow
17 the stone-coffin burial, a crouched burial
18 the menhir; *sim.* the Scandinavian Bauta stone, the German Hinkelstein, a standing stone
19 the boat axe, a stone axe
20 the terracotta idol, an idol;

21-40 the Bronze Age and the Iron Age; *epochs:* Hallstatt period, La Tène period (Marnean period):

21 the bronze spearhead
22 the bronze dagger
23 the hafted axe, a bronze axe
24 the belt disk (belt disc)
25 the necklace (lunula)
26 the gold neck ring
27 the brooch (clip)
28 the snake brooch; *other forms:* boat brooch, cross bow brooch
29 the ball-headed pin, a bronze pin
30 the double spiral brooch ('spectacle' brooch); *sim.* 'plate' brooch
31 the bronze knife
32 the iron key
33 the plough share (*Am.* plowshare)
34 the situla (shouldered bucket) of sheet bronze, a funerary vessel
35 the pitcher [notched-stamp pottery]
36 the kettle cart, a miniature ritual cart
37 the Celtic silver coin
38 the face urn, a cinerary urn; *other forms:* house urn, embossed urn
39 the urn burial:
40 the cone-necked urn

1
2
3
4
5
6
7
8
9
10
11
12
13
14
15
16
17
18
19
20
21
22
23
24
25
26
27
28
29
30
31
32
33
34
35
36
37
38
39
40

1 the castle (fortress, stronghold):
2 the inner bailey
3 the well
4 the keep (donjon):
5 the dungeon
6 the crenellated battlements (crenellations)
7 the battlement
8 the tower platform;
9 the guard (lookout)
10 the women's apartments
11 the dormer
12 the balcony
13 the storehouse
14 the corner tower (angle tower)
15 the outer wall, curtain wall
16 the salient
17 the guard tower (watch tower)
18 the crenel
19 the curtain wall
20 the roofed parapet walk
21 the parapet
22 the gatehouse (castle gate):
23 the machicoulis gallery
24 the portcullis;
25 the drawbridge
26 the buttress
27 the kitchen and offices
28 the wall turret
29 the castle chapel
30 the hall
31 the outer bailey
32 the outer gate
33 the outer moat
34 the approach
35 the watch tower
36 the palisade
37 the moat (foss, fosse);
38–65 the knight's armour (*Am.* armor),
38 the suit of armour (*Am.* armor),
39–42 the helmet:
39 the helmet bowl
40 the vizor (visor)
41 the beaver
42 the throat piece;
43 the gorget
44 the pass guard (passegarde, raised pauldron)
45 the pallette
46 the breastplate (cuirass)
47 the arm armour (brassarts): rerebrace (arrière-bras) and vambrace (avant-bras, vantbrace)
48 the coudière (coute)
49 the tasset (tuille)
50 the gauntlet
51 the hauberk
52 the cuisse (cuissart)
53 the genouillière (knee cop, knee piece)
54 the leg armour (jambart, jamb, jambe, jambeau, greave, leg piece)
55 the sabbaton;
56 the pavise
57 the buckler (shield):
58 the boss;
59 the iron helmet
60 the morion (burgonet)
61 the basinet (salade)
62 types of mail and armour
63 the chain mail
64 the scale armour (*Am.* armor)
65 the plate armour (*Am.* armor);
66 the accolade (knighting, dubbing):
67 the liege lord, a knight
68 the squire-at-arms (esquire)
69 the cup-bearer
70 the minstrel (troubadour);
71 the tournament (tourney, joust, just, tilt):
72 the crusader
73 the Knight Templar
74 the caparison (trappings)
75 the marshal;
76 the tilting armour (*Am.* armor):
77 the tilting helm
78 the plume
79 the tilting target
80 the lance rest
81 the tilting lance (lance)
82 the vamplate;
83–88 the horse armour (*Am.* armor):
83 the neck guard
84 the chamfron (chamfrain)
85 the poitrel
86 the flancards (flanchards)
87 the tournament saddle
88 the quarter (rump) piece

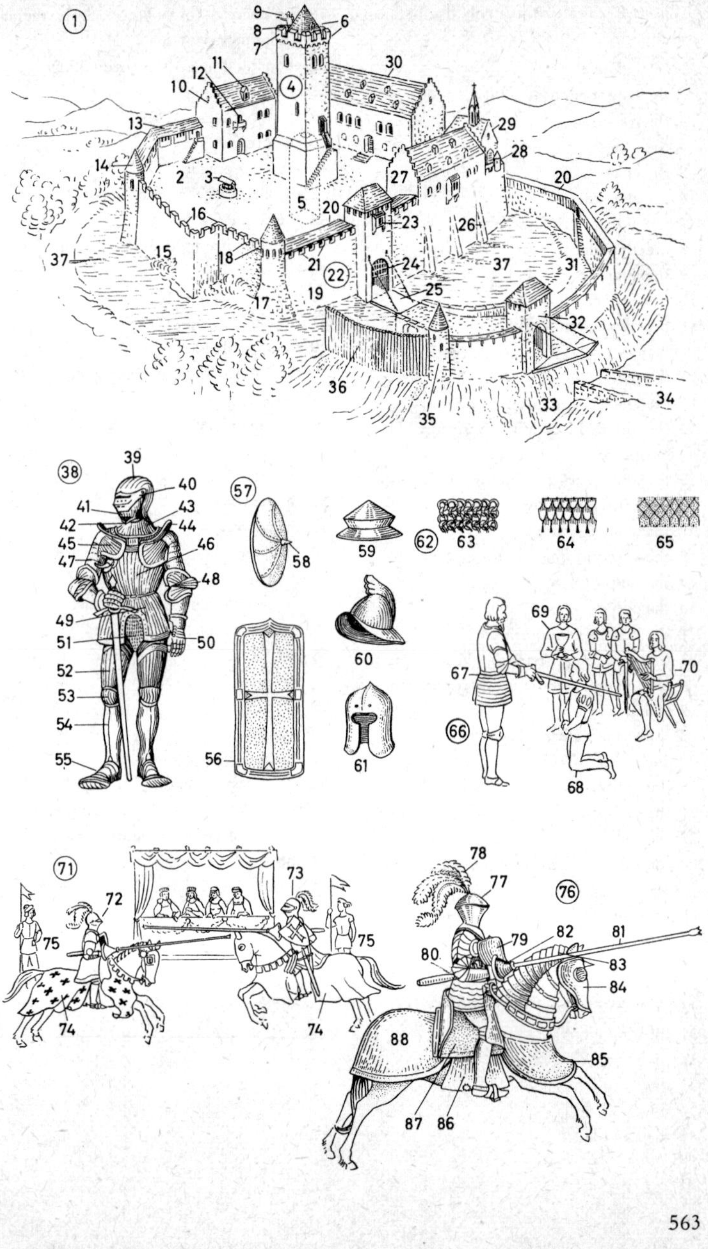
1
2
3
4
5
6
7
8
9
10
11
12
13
14
15
16
17
18
19
20
21
22
23
24
25
26
27
28
29
30
31
32
33
34
35
36
37
38
39
40
41
42
43
44
45
46
47
48
49
50
51
52
53
54
55
56
57
58
59
60
61
62
63
64
65
66
67
68
69
70
71
72
73
74
75
76
77
78
79
80
81
82
83
84
85
86
87
88

1-30 a Protestant church (Lutheran church):

1 the chancel
2 the baptismal font
3 the font basin
4 the lectern
5 the chancel chair
6 the altar carpet
7 the altar (communion table):
8 the altar steps
9 the altar cloth;
10 the altar candle
11 the pyx (box with communion wafers)
12 the paten
13 the chalice (communion cup)
14 the Bible (Holy Writ, Scripture, Holy Scripture)
15 the altar picture, a picture of Christ
16 the church window:
17 the stained glass;
18 the vestry door (sacristy door)
19 the pulpit steps
20 the pulpit
21 the canopy (sound-board)
22 the preacher (parson, vicar, rector, clergyman, pastor) in his robes (canonicals)
23 the pulpit balustrade
24 the hymn board
25 the gallery
26 the verger (sexton, sacristan, *Am.* usher)
27 the aisle
28 the pew (church pew); *all together:* the pews
29 the church-goer (worshipper); *all together:* congregation
30 the hymn book;

31-65 a Roman Catholic church:

31 the altar steps
32 the altar rails (parclose)
33 the communion bench
34 the choir stalls
35 the ambulatory
36 the chancel (presbytery, choir, sacrarium, sanctuary)
37 the altar (high altar, main altar)
38 the canon tables
39 the tabernacle
40 the crucifix
41 the altar candle
42 the altar piece (reredos with side wings):
43 the wing;
44 the altar fire (ever-burning light)
45 the side altar
46 the statue of a saint
47 the epistle side
48 the gospel side
49 the priest saying mass (Mass, Holy Mass, low Mass)
50 the missal desk with the mass-book (missal)
51 the altar cloth
52 the server
53 the pulpit
54 the angel
55 the trumpet
56 the pulpit steps
57 the station of the Cross
58 the man praying (worshipper), a believer
59 the prayer book
60 the candle
61 the alms box (poor-box)
62 the sacristan (sexton, verger, *Am.* usher)
63 the collection bag (*Am.* alms basket; *in Engl.* collection plate)
64 the alms (offering)
65 the memorial slab

1
2
3
4
5
6
7
8
9
10
11
12
13
14
15
16
17
18
19
20
21
22
23
24
123
1-4
26
25
26
27
28
29
30

31
32
33
34
35
36
37
38
39
40
41
42
43
44
45
46
47
48
49
50
51
52
53
54
55
56
57
58
59
60
61
62
63
64
65

1 **the church:**
2 the church tower; *here:* steeple
3 the weathercock
4 the weather-vane
5 the steeple ball
6 the church spire
7 the church clock
8 the sound hole (louvre, louver, belfry window)
9 the electric church bell
10 the ridge cross
11 the church roof
12 the memorial chapel
13 the vestry (sacristy)
14 the memorial tablet or plate (wall-memorial, wall-stone, *Am.* marker) with inscription (epitaph)
15 the side entrance
16 the church door (church porch);
17 the church-goer
18 the churchyard wall
19 the churchyard gate; *when deeper:* lichgate (lychgate)
20 the vicar's house (rectory, vicarage, parsonage, *Scot.* manse)

21-41 **the cemetery** (churchyard, graveyard, burial ground, God's acre, *Am.* burying ground):
21 the mortuary (dead house, lich house, lych house)
22 the grave-digger
23 the grave (tomb, burying place):
24 the grave mound
25 the cross on the tomb;
26 the tombstone (gravestone, sepulchral monument, headstone, *Am.* marker)
27 the family grave (family tomb)
28 the cemetery chapel
29 the tree of life (arbor vitae, thuya tree)
30 the child's grave
31 the urn grove (grove of urns):
32 the urn;
33 the soldier's grave
34–41 the funeral (burial, interment):
34 the open grave
35 the coffin (*Am.* casket)
36 the bowl of sand
37 the clergyman
38 the bereaved
39 the widow's veil, a mourning veil
40 the bearers (coffin-bearers, undertakers)
41 the bier;

42-50 **the procession** (ritual, or religious, procession):
42 the processional cross
43 the cross-bearer (crucifer)
44 the processional banner, a church banner (vexillum)
45 the acolyte
46 the canopy-bearer
47 the priest
48 the monstrance with the consecrated Host
49 the canopy (baldachin, baldaquin)
50 the participants in the procession;

51-61 **lying-in-state:**
51 the coffin (*Am.* casket)
52 the catafalque
53 the pall
54 the deceased (dead man, corpse, dead body, body)
55 the funerary candle
56 the candelabra, a candlestick
57 the wreath:
58 the ribbon
59 the card;
60 the laurel tree:
61 the tree tub (plant tub);

62 **the catacomb,** an early Christian subterranean burial place:
63 the niche (arched tomb recess, arcosolium)
64 the stone slab

1
2
3
4
5
6
7
8
9
10
11
12
13
14
15
16
17
18
19
20
21
22
23
24
25
26
27
28
29
30
31
32
33
34
35
36
37
38
39
40
41
42
43
44
45
46
47
48
49
50
51
52
53
54
55
56
57
58
59
60
61
62
63
64

1 **the Christian baptism** (christening):
2 the baptistery
3 the Protestant (Lutheran) clergyman:
4 the robes (vestments)
5 the bands
6 the collar;
7 the infant to be baptized
8 the christening dress (christening robe)
9 the christening veil
10 the font:
11 the font basin;
12 the godparents (sponsors);

13 **wedding** (the marriage ceremony, wedding ceremony):
14 and 15 the bridal couple:
14 the bride
15 the bridegroom (groom);
16 the ring (wedding ring)
17 the bride's bouquet (bridal bouquet)
18 the myrtle wreath (bridal wreath; *in England:* crown of orange blossom)
19 the veil (bridal veil)
20 the bridal cushion
21 the buttonhole of myrtle; *in England usually* a carnation
22 the clergyman
23 the witnesses to the marriage;

24 **the Holy Communion** (sacrament of the Lord's Supper, communion):
25 the communicants
26 the Host (holy wafer), a wafer
27 the communion cup (chalice, wine, sacramental wine);
28 the rosary:
29 the paternoster bead
30 the Ave bead; ten *beads* form a decade
31 the junction
32 the crucifix;

33-48 **liturgical vessels** (ecclesiastical vessels, sacred vessels) of the Roman Catholic Church,
33 the monstrance (sun monstrance, Venerabile, Sanctissimum):
34 the Host (large Host)
35 the lunule
36 the rays;
37 the censer (thurible) for offering incense (for incensing):
38 the thurible chain
39 the thurible cover
40 the thurible bowl;
41 the incense boat:
42 the incense spoon;
43 the Sanctus bells (altar bells)
44 the chalice
45 the holy-water basin or vessel
46 the ciborium with the small Hosts for the communion of the laity
47 the altar bell
48 the aspergillum (holy-water sprinkler);

49-66 **forms of Christian crosses:**
49 the Latin cross (Cross of the Passion)
50 the Greek cross
51 the Russian cross
52 St. Peter's cross
53 the Tau cross (St. Anthony's cross, T-cross)
54 St. Andrew's cross *(in heraldry:* saltire, saltier; Burgundian cross)
55 the Y-cross (Y-shaped cross; *in heraldry:* pall, cross pall)
56 the cross of Lorraine
57 the Tau cross with handle (crux ansata, Egyptian cross)
58 the patriarchal cross
59 the cardinal's cross
60 the papal cross (triple cross)
61 the Constantinian cross, a Christian monogram (CHR)
62 crosslet, cross crossletted *[in heraldry]*
63 cross ancrée *[in heraldry]*
64 the cross of Jerusalem; cross potent *[in heraldy]*
65 cross botonée, *[in heraldry]*
66 the fivefold cross, quintuple cross

1 2 3 4 5 6 7 8 9 10 11 12
13 14 15 16 17 18 19 20 21 22 23
24 25 26 27
28 29 30 31 32
33 34 35 36
37 38 39 40 41 42 43 44 45 46 47 48
49 50 51 52 53 54 55 56 57
58 59 60 61 62 63 64 65 66

1–12 the abbey (priory, monastery):
1 the cloisters
2 the cloister garth
3 the monk
4 the monk's cell (monastery cell, cell):
5 the bed
6 the crucifix
7 the picture of a saint
8 the monk's frock
9 the praying desk (prie-dieu, kneeling desk, faldstool)
10 the work table
11 the stool
12 the book shelf, a wall shelf;
13–24 habits and vestments of religious orders,
13 the Benedictine (Black Monk), a monk; other religious orders: Franciscans (Minorites, Friars Minor), Capuchins, Cistercians (Bernardines, White Monks), Trappists (Reformed Cistercians), Jesuits,
14–16 the monastic habit:
14 the frock
15 the scapular
16 the hood (cowl);
17 the tonsure
18 the breviary
19 the Dominican (Friar Preacher, *in England:* Black Friar, *in France:* Jacobin), a mendicant, a friar:
20 the girdle (cingulum)
21 the rosary;
22 a nun:
23 the wimple (gimp)
24 the veil;
25–58 priests in liturgical vestments,
25 the Russian Orthodox priest:
26 the sticharion
27 the epitrachelion
28 the epimanikion
29 the girdle
30 the phelonion
31 the kamelaukion;
32–58 the Roman Catholic clergy,
32 the priest in choral vestments:
33 the cassock (soutane)
34 the surplice
35 the stole (stola)
36 the biretta;
37 the priest in mass (eucharistic, sacred) vestments:
38 the alb
39 the chasuble
40 the amice
41 the chalice veil
42 the maniple;
43 the bishop:
44 the tunicle
45 the dalmatic
46 the mitre (*Am.* miter)
47 the episcopal (pontifical) ring
48 the pastoral staff (crosier, crozier, bishop's crook);
49 the cardinal in ceremonial vestments:
50 the rochet
51 the cappa magna
52 the pectoral cross
53 the zucchetto;
54 the Pope (supreme pontiff, pontifex maximus) in pontifical vestments:
55 the fanon (*form.* orale)
56 the pall (pallium)
57 the glove with the cross
58 the Fisherman's ring (Pope's ring of investiture)

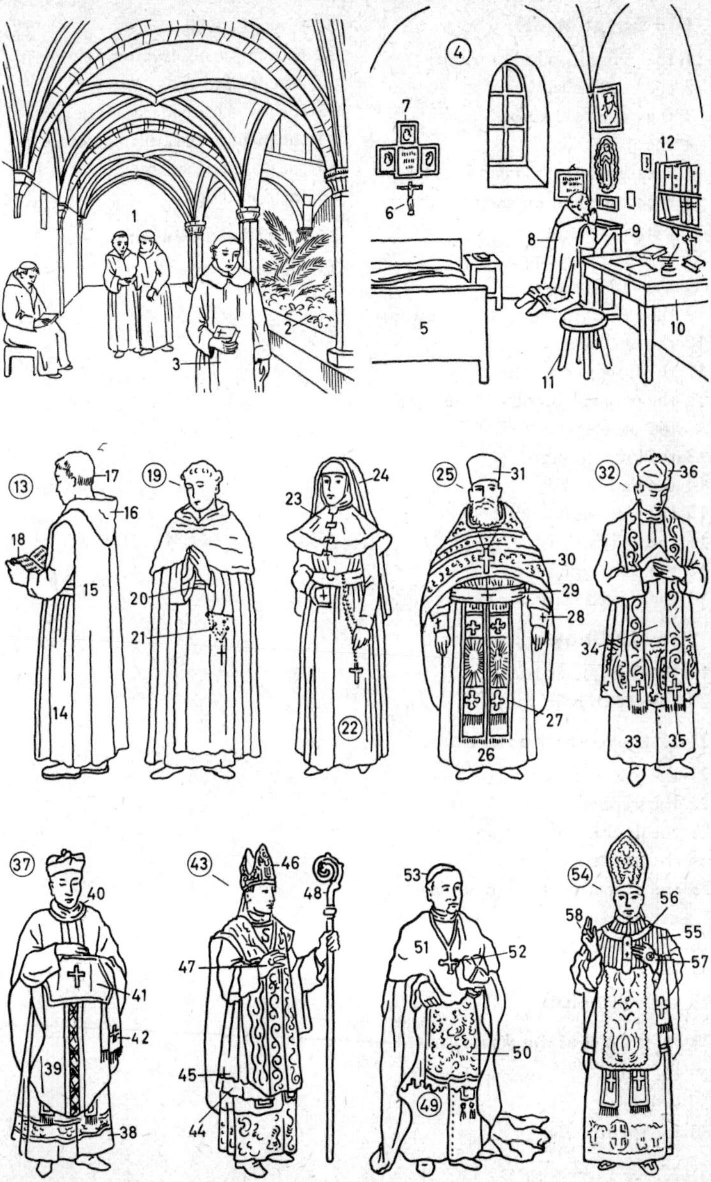
1
2
3
4
5
6
7
8
9
10
11
12
13
14
15
16
17
18
19
20
21
22
23
24
25
26
27
28
29
30
31
32
33
34
35
36
37
38
39
40
41
42
43
44
45
46
47
48
49
50
51
52
53
54
55
56
57
58

1-18 Egyptian art,

1 the pyramid, a king's tomb:
2 the king's chamber
3 the queen's chamber
4 the air passage
5 the underground chamber;
6 the general arrangement of a pyramid:
7 the funerary temple
8 the valley temple
9 the pylon (monumental gateway)
10 the obelisks;
11 the Egyptian sphinx
12 the winged sun disk or disc (solar disk or disc)
13 the lotus column:
14 the bud capital;
15 the papyrus column:
16 the bell capital;
17 the palm column
18 the carved (ornamented) column;

19 and 20 Babylonian art,

19 the Babylonian frieze:
20 the glazed relief tile;

21-28 the art of the Persians,

21 the tower tomb:
22 the stepped pyramid;
23 the double bull column:
24 the projecting leaves
25 the palmette capital (palm-leaf capital)
26 the volute (scroll)
27 the shaft
28 the bull capital;

29-36 the art of the Assyrians,

29 the Palace of Sargon, palace buildings:
30 the town wall
31 the castle wall
32 the temple observatory (ziggurat), a stepped tower
33 the flyers (outside staircase)
34 the main portal (main gateway);
35 the portal ornament:
36 the portal figure;

37 art of Asia Minor:

38 the rock tomb

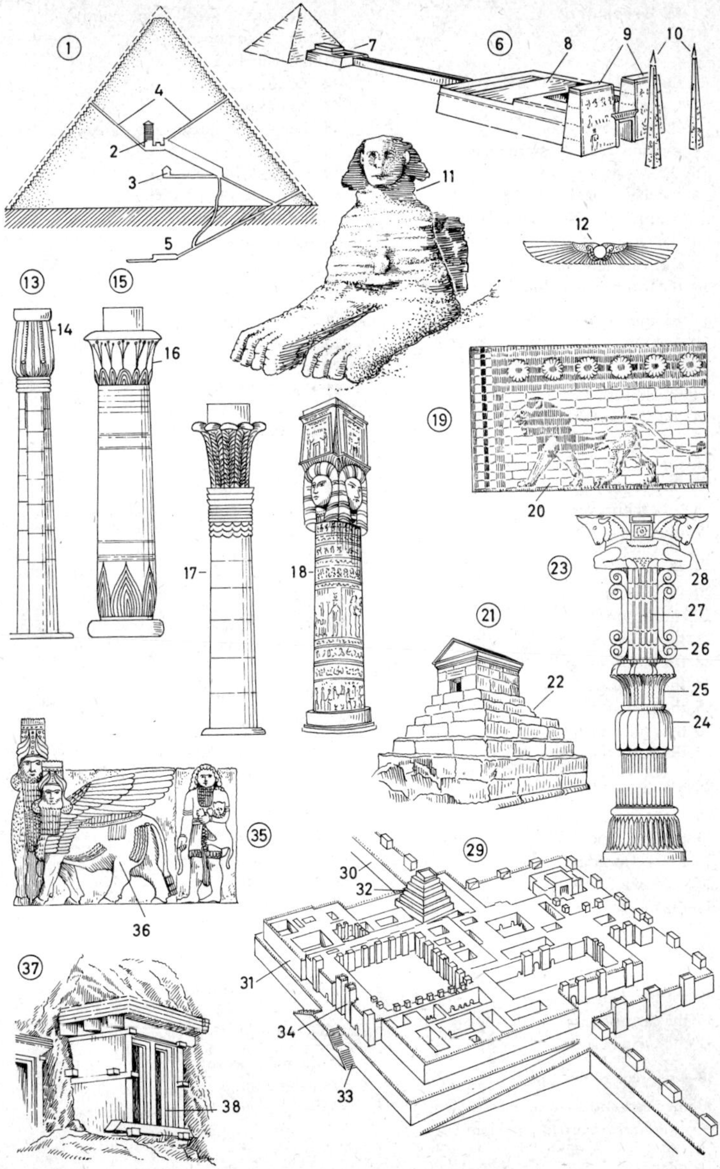
1
2
3
4
5
6
7
8
9
10
11
12
13
14
15
16
17
18
19
20
21
22
23
24
25
26
27
28
29
30
31
32
33
34
35
36
37
38

1-48 Greek art,

1–7 the Acropolis,

1 the Parthenon, a Doric temple:
2 the peristyle
3 the pediment
4 the substructure (stereobate);
5 the statue
6 the temple walls
7 the propylaea (entrance gateway);
8 the Doric column,
9 the Ionic column,
10 the Corinthian column,

11–14 the cornice:

11 the cymatium
12 the corona
13 the mutule
14 the dentils (modillions);
15 the triglyph
16 the metope, a frieze ornament
17 the regula
18 the architrave (epistyle)
19 the taenia

20–25 the capital:

20 the abacus
21 the echinus
22 the hypotrachelium (gorgerin)
23 the volute (scroll)
24 the volute cushion
25 the row of leaves;
26 the column shaft
27 the flutings (flutes)

28–31 the column base:

28 the torus
29 the trochilus (hollow moulding, *Am.* hollow molding)
30 the lower torus
31 the plinth;
32 the stylobate
33 the stele (stela):
34 the acroter (acroterium);
35 the herma (hermes)
36 the caryatid; *male :* Atlas
37 the Greek vase,

38–43 Greek ornamentation:

38 the bead-and-dart moulding (*Am.* molding), an ornamental band
39 the running scroll (wave band)
40 the leaf ornament
41 the palm leaf
42 the egg-and-dart cyma
43 the meander;
44 the Greek theatre (*Am.* Greek theater; theatron):
45 the skene
46 the proskenion
47 the orchestra
48 the thymele (altar);

49-52 Etruscan art,

49 the Etruscan temple:
50 the temple portico (temple vestibule)
51 the cella
52 the entablature;

53-60 Roman art,

53 the aqueduct:
54 the water channel (conduit);
55 the centrally-planned building (centralised building):
56 the portico
57 the reglet
58 the cupola;
59 the triumphal arch (porta triumphalis):
60 the attic storey;

61-71 early-Christian art,

61 the basilica:
62 the central nave
63 the aisle
64 the apse
65 the campanile
66 the atrium
67 the colonnade
68 the fountain
69 the altar
70 the clerestory (clearstory)
71 the triumphal arch;

72-75 Byzantine art,

72 and 73 the dome system:

72 the main dome
73 the semi-dome;
74 the pendentive
75 the eye, a lighting aperture

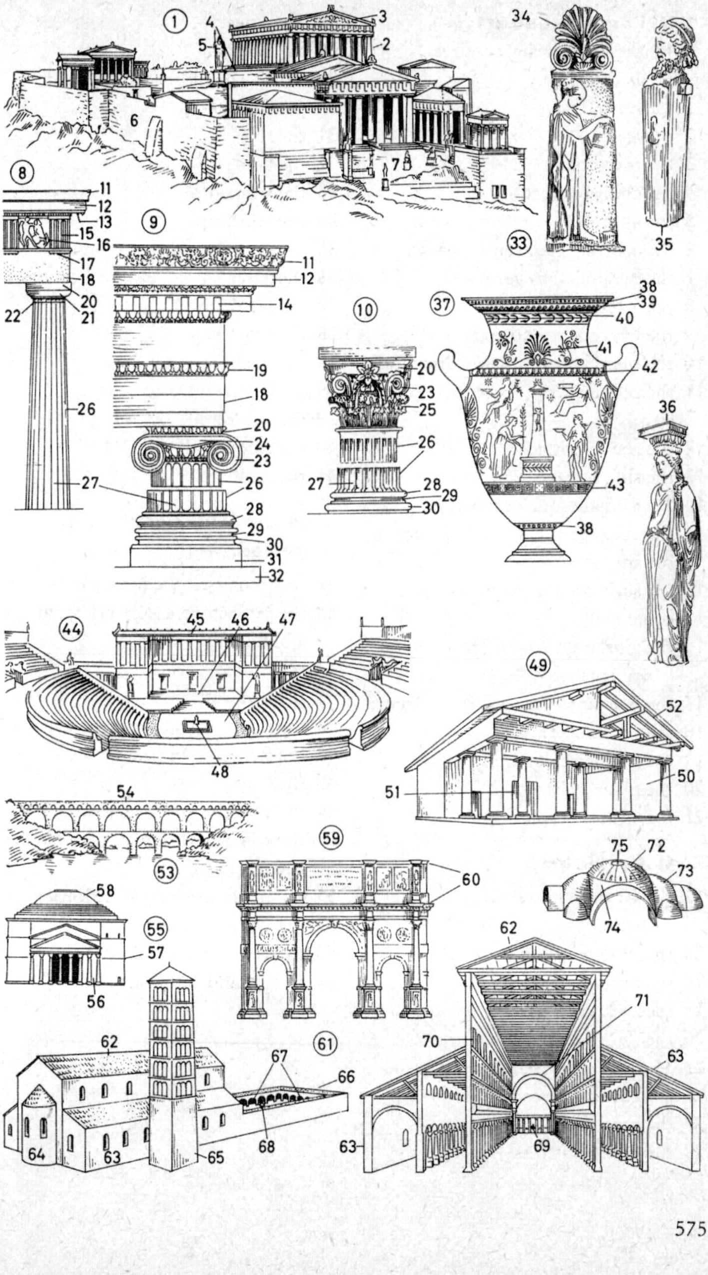
1
2
3
4
5
6
7
34
35
33
8
11
12
13
15
16
17
18
20
21
22
26
27
9
11
12
14
19
18
20
24
23
26
27
28
29
30
31
32
10
20
23
25
26
27
28
29
30
37
38
39
40
41
42
43
38
36
44
45
46
47
48
49
52
50
51
54
53
59
60
60
75
72
73
74
58
55
57
56
62
71
70
63
61
67
66
62
64
63
65
68
63
69

1-21 Romanesque art,
1–13 the Romanesque church (cathedral):
1 the central nave
2 the aisle
3 the transept
4 the choir (chancel)
5 the apse
6 the central (*Am.* center) tower:
7 the pyramidal tower roof
8 the arcading;
9 the frieze of round arcading
10 the blind arcading (wall arcading)
11 the pilaster strip, a vertical wall strip
12 the round window
13 the side entrance;
14–16 Romanesque ornaments:
14 the chequered (*Am.* checkered) ornament
15 the scale ornament (imbricated ornament)
16 the zigzag ornament (chevron ornament);
17 the Romanesque vaulting system:
18 the transverse arch
19 the semi-circular arch
20 the pillar;
21 the cushion capital;

22-41 Gothic art,
22 the Gothic church (Gothic cathedral):
23 the rose window
24 the porch
25 the archivolt
26 the tympanum;
27–35 the Gothic structural system,
27 and 28 buttresses:
27 the buttress
28 the flying buttress;
29 the pinnacle
30 the gargoyle
31 and 32 the ribbed vault (quadripartite vault):
31 the ribs
32 the boss;
33 the triforium
34 the Gothic pier
35 the shaft (engaged column);
36 the gable:
37 the finial
38 the crocket
39–41 the tracery window,
39 and 40 the tracery:
39 the quatrefoil
40 the cinquefoil;
41 the mullions;

42-54 art of the Renaissance period,
42 the Renaissance church:
43 the projection, a projecting part of a building
44 the drum
45 the lantern
46 the pilaster (wall shaft, half shaft);
47 the Renaissance palace:
48 the cornice
49 the window with pediment
50 the window with pediment (with rounded pediment)
51 the rustic work (rustication)
52 the string course;
53 the sarcophagus (tomb):
54 the garland (festoon)

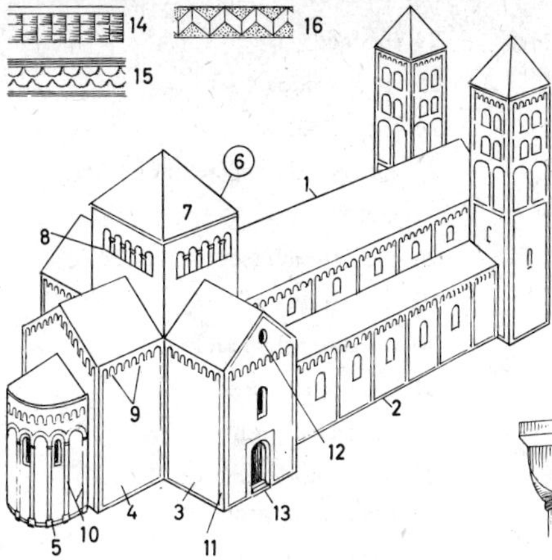
14
15
16
6
1
7
8
9
12
2
13
10
4
3
11
5

17
18
19
20

21

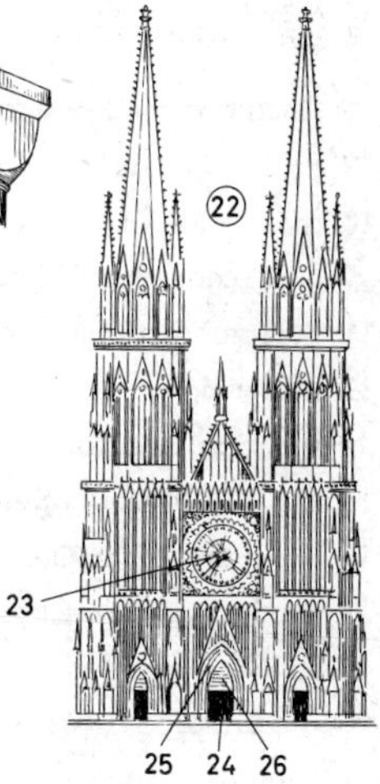
22
23
25
24
26

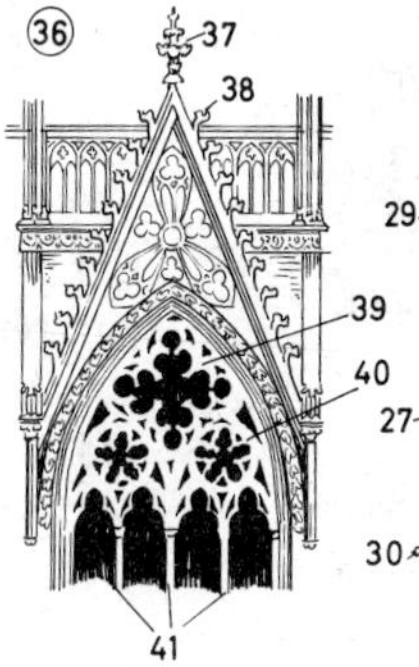
36
37
38
39
40
41

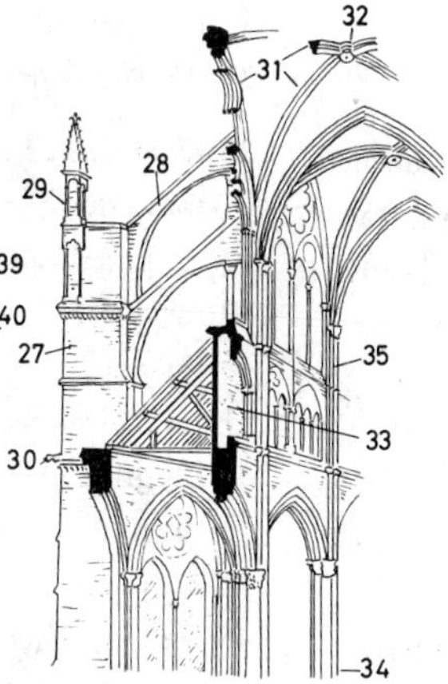
32
31
28
29
27
35
33
30
34

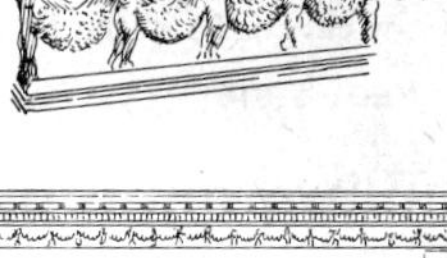
53
54

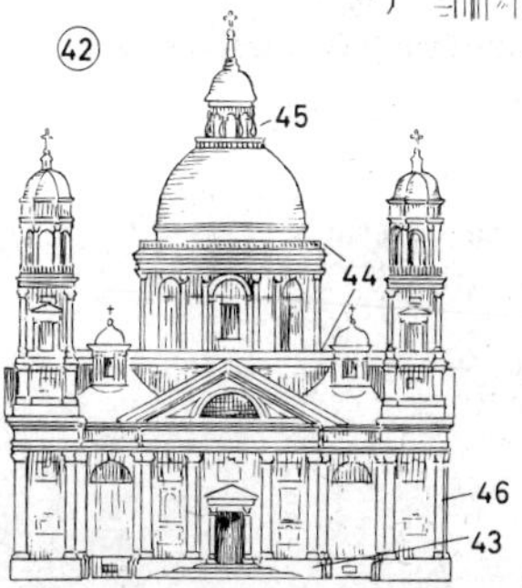
42
45
44
46
43

48
47
51
49
50
52

1-8 art of the Baroque period,
1 the Baroque church:
2 the bull's-eye
3 the lantern cupola
4 the dormer window
5 the curved gable
6 the twin columns;
7 the cartouche:
8 the cartouche work;

9-13 art of the Rococo period,
9 the Rococo wall:
10 the coving, a concave moulding (*Am.* concave molding)
11 the framing ornament
12 the headpiece;
13 the rocaille, a Rococo ornament;
14 the table in **Louis Seize style**
15 a building of the **Classic Revival period** (in Neo-Classic style), a gateway
16 the **Empire table** (table in the Empire style)
17 the **Biedermeier sofa** (sofa in the Biedermeier style)
18 the easy chair in the **Art Nouveau style**

19-37 types of arches,
19 the arch (wall arch):
20 the abutment
21 the impost
22 the springer, a wedge-shaped stone (voussoir)
23 the keystone
24 the face
25 the intrados
26 the extrados;
27 the round arch (semi-circular arch)
28 the flat arch (segmental arch)
29 the parabolic arch
30 the horseshoe arch
31 the pointed arch
32 the trefoil arch
33 the shouldered arch
34 the convex arch
35 the tented arch
36 the ogee arch
37 the Tudor arch;

38-50 forms of vaults (of vaulting),
38 the barrel vault:
39 the crown
40 the side;
41 the cloister vault
42 the groined vault
43 the ribbed vault
44 the stellar vault (lierne vault)
45 the reticulated vault
46 the fan vault (fan-tracery vault)
47 the trough vault:
48 the trough;
49 the cavetto vault:
50 the cavetto

1
2
3
4
5
6
7
8
9
10
11
12
13
14
15
16
17
18
19
20
21
22
23
24
25
26
27
28
29
30
31
32
33
34
35
36
37
38
39
40
41
42
43
44
45
46
47
48
49
50

1-6 Chinese art,

1 the pagoda (many-storied pagoda), a temple tower:
2 the superimposed roof;
3 the pailou (pailoo, pailow), a memorial archway:
4 the passage;
5 the porcelain vase
6 the incised lacquered work;

7-11 Japanese art:

7 the temple
8 the bell tower:
9 the supporting structure;
10 bodhisattva (bodhisat, bodhisattwa), a Buddhist saint
11 the torii, a gateway;

12-18 Islamic (Islamitic) **art,**

12 the mosque:
13 the minaret, a prayer tower;
14 the mihrab (prayer niche)
15 the mimbar (pulpit)
16 the mausoleum, a tomb
17 the stalactite vaulting
18 the Arabian capital;

19-28 Indian art:

19 dancing Siva (Shiva), an Indian god
20 the statue of Buddha
21 the stupa (Indian pagoda), a mound (dome), a Buddhistic sacred building:
22 the umbrella
23 the stone wall (*Am.* stone fence)
24 the entrance tower;
25 the temple buildings:
26 the sikhara (sikra, temple tower);
27 the chaitya hall:
28 the chaitya, a small stupa

1
2
3
4
7
5
6
8
9
12
13
13
11
10
16
17
15
14
18
19
20
27
22
25
26
21
22
24
23
28

Engl. colour = *Am.* color

1 red
2 yellow
3 blue
4 pink
5 brown
6 azure (sky-blue)
7 orange
8 green
9 violet
10 the additive mixture of colours (coloured light):
11 white;
12 the subtractive mixture of colours (pigments):
13 black;
14 the solar spectrum
15 the grey (gray) scale
16 the heat colours

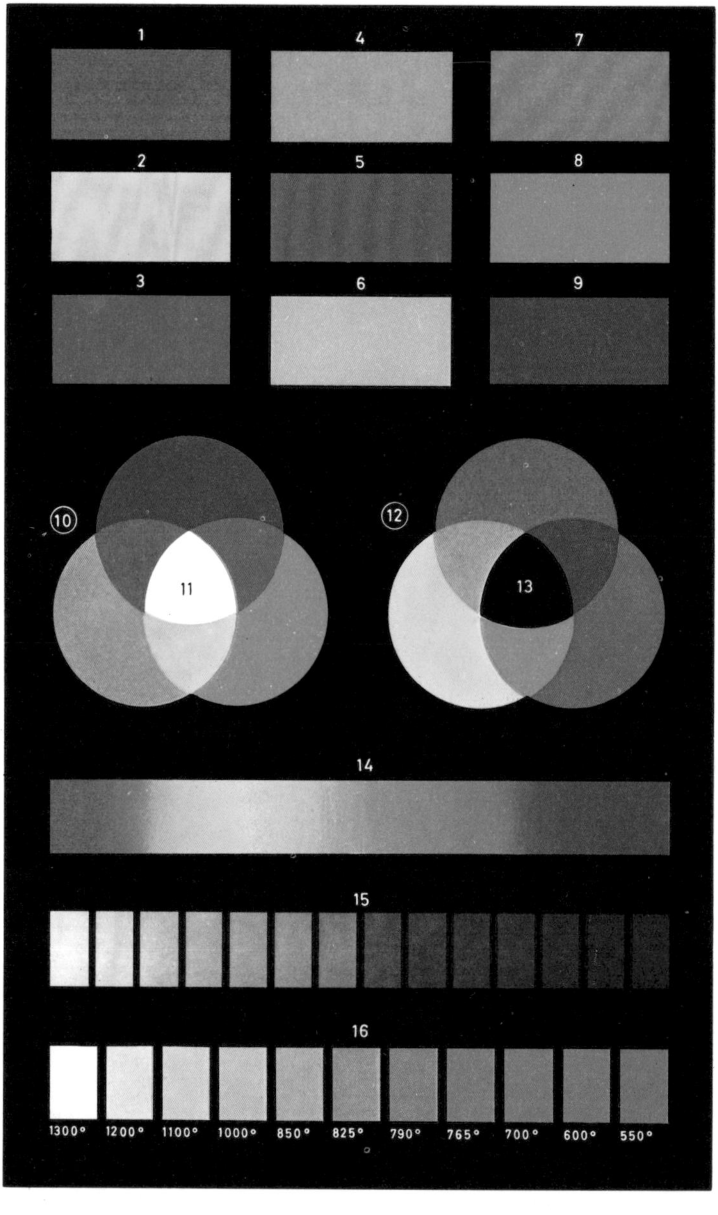
1
4
7
2
5
8
3
6
9
10
11
12
13
14
15
16
1300°
1200°
1100°
1000°
850°
825°
790°
765°
700°
600°
550°

321 The Painting, and Drawing, Studio

1–43 the studio:
1 the studio skylight
2 the painter, an artist
3 the studio easel
4 the chalk sketch with the picture in outline (composition, rough draft)
5 the chalk pencil (crayon)
6–19 painting utensils:
6 the flat brush
7 the hair brush
8 the round brush (stencil)
9 the priming brush
10 the paint (colour, *Am.* color) box:
11 the tube of oil colour (*Am.* color; oil paint)
12 the varnish;
13 the thinner (thinners)
14 the palette knife
15 the painting spatula
16 the charcoal pencil
17 the tempera (gouache) colour (*Am.* color)
18 the water colour (*Am.* water color)
19 the pastel pencil;
20 the wedged stretcher
21 the canvas
22 the piece of cardboard with the painting surface
23 the wooden board
24 the wood-fibre (*Am.* wood fiber) board (pulp board)
25 the painting table
26 the folding (collapsible, sketching) easel
27 the still life group
28 the hand palette:
29 the palette dipper;
30 the platform
31 the lay figure (manikin, mannequin)
32 the nude model (nude life model, nude)
33 the drapery
34 the drawing donkey
35 the sketching (drawing) block (*Am.* sketchblock, draft pad)
36 the study in oil
37 the mosaic (tessellation)
38 the mosaic figure
39 the mosaic tesserae
40 the fresco (mural, mural painting)
41 the graffito drawing (sgraffito drawing)
42 the plaster (glazing)
43 the cartoon

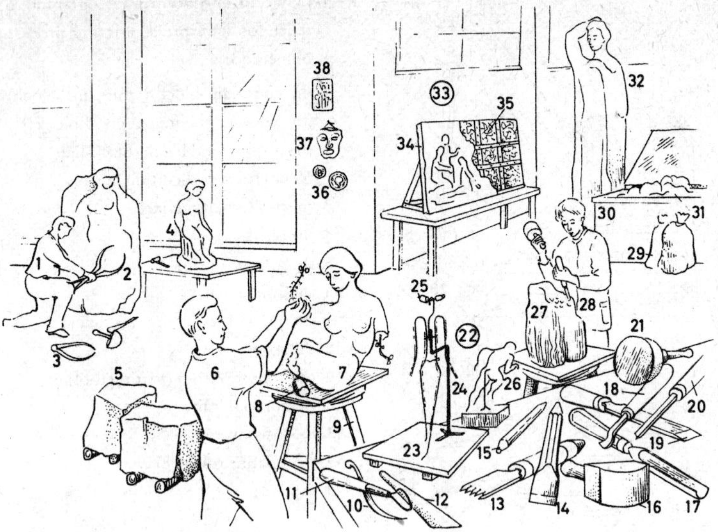

Engl. modeller, modelling = *Am.* modeler, modeling

1 the sculptor
2 the proportional dividers or compass
3 the calipers
4 the plaster model, a plaster cast
5 the block of stone (raw stone)
6 the modeller (modeller in clay)
7 the clay figure
8 the roll of clay, a modelling (plastic) substance
9 the modelling stand
10 the modelling spatula
11 the wire modelling tool
12 the beating wood
13 the claw tool
14 the bull set
15 the stippling iron (point)
16 the iron-headed hammer
17 the gouge
18 the spoon chisel (bent chisel)
19 the corner chisel, a ripping chisel
20 the straight parting tool
21 the wooden mallet (mallet)
22 the frame:
23 the stand
24 the armature support
25 the armature;
26 the wax model
27 the block of wood
28 the wood-carver (wood sculptor)
29 the sack of gypsum powder (gypsum, gesso)
30 the clay box
31 the modelling clay (clay)
32 the statue, a sculpture (work of plastic art)
33 the low relief (bas relief, basso relievo or rilievo, anaglyph):
34 the modelling board
35 the wire frame (wire netting);
36 the circular medallion (tondo)
37 the mask
38 the plaque

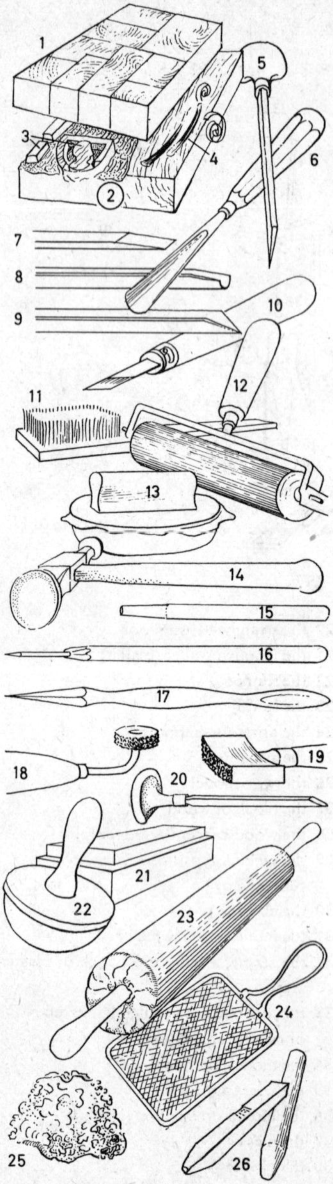

1-13 wood-engraving (xylography), a relief, or letterpress, printing process or method:

1 the end-grain block (white-line block) for wood-engraving, a wood block

2 the plank-wood block (black-line block) for wood-cutting, a woodcut:

3 the positive engraving

4 the plank cut;

5 the graver (burin)

6 the gouge

7 the flat scorper (scalper, scauper)

8 the scoop

9 the hollow V-tool (parting tool)

10 the contour knife

11 the brush

12 the gelatine roller (brayer)

13 the pad;

14-24 copper-engraving (chalcography), an intaglio-printing process or method; *kinds :* etching, mezzotint, aquatint; chalk, or crayon, method:

14 the punching hammer

15 the punch

16 the etching needle

17 the burnisher with the scraper

18 the roulette

19 the rocking tool (rocker, cradle)

20 the round-headed graver, a graving tool

21 the oilstone

22 the dabber (inking ball, tampon)

23 the leather roller

24 the splatter sieve;

25 and 26 lithography, a planographic, or surface, printing process or method:

25 the sponge for moistening the lithographic stone

26 the litho crayon (litho chalk), a crayon;

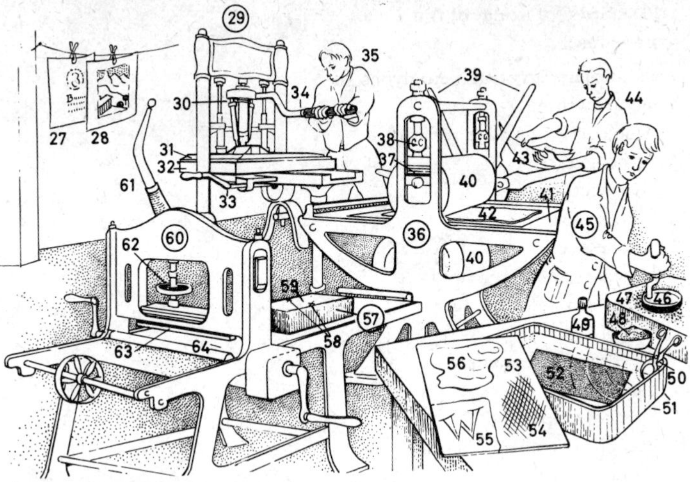

27-64 the graphic studio, a printing office (*Am.* printery):

27 the one-side print

28 the colour print (*Am.* color print; chromolithographic print)

29 the platen machine, a hand press (hand-printing machine):

30 the toggle joint

31 the platen, a press plate

32 the printing forme (printing form)

33 the drawing handle (crank)

34 the impression handle;

35 the printer

36 the copperplate press:

37 the cardboard (pasteboard) distance

38 the pressure regulator [piece

39 the star wheel

40 the cylinder (roller)

41 the bed

42 the felt cloth;

43 the proof

44 the copperplate engraver (chalcographist, calcographer)

45 the lithographer grinding the stone:

46 the grinding disk or disc (grinding stone)

47 the granulation

48 the glass sand;

49 the rubber solution

50 the tongs

51 the etching bath for etching

52 the zinc plate

53 the polished copper plate

54 the cross hatching

55 the etching ground (wax ground)

56 the covering ground (asphalt ground)

57 the lithographic stone (calcareous slate stone, *Am.* shale):

58 the fitting marks (aligning marks, *Am.* alining marks)

59 the printing surface;

60 the lithographic press:

61 the printing lever

62 the pressure screw

63 the scraper

64 the bed (bedplate)

1-20 scripts (writing) **of the peoples:**

1 the ancient Egyptian hieroglyphs, picture writing
2 Arabic script (Arabic writing)
3 Armenian script
4 Georgian script
5 Chinese script
6 Japanese script
7 Hebraic (Hebrew) script
8 cuneiform script (wedge script)
9 Devanagari (script used in Sanscrit)
10 Siamese script
11 Tamulic (Tamilian, Tamilic, Tamulian) script
12 Tibetan script
13 Sinaitic (Sinaic) script
14 Phoenician script
15 Greek script
16 Roman *(rare :* Latin) capitals (capital letters)
17 uncial script (uncials)
18 Carlovingian (Caroline, Carolingian) minuscule
19 runes (runic script)
20 Russian script;

21-26 ancient writing tools (writing instruments):

21 Indian steel style, a stylus for writing on palm leaves
22 ancient Egyptian writing stamp, a reed panicle
23 cane pen
24 writing brush (writing pencil)
25 Roman metal pen
26 quill (goose feather)

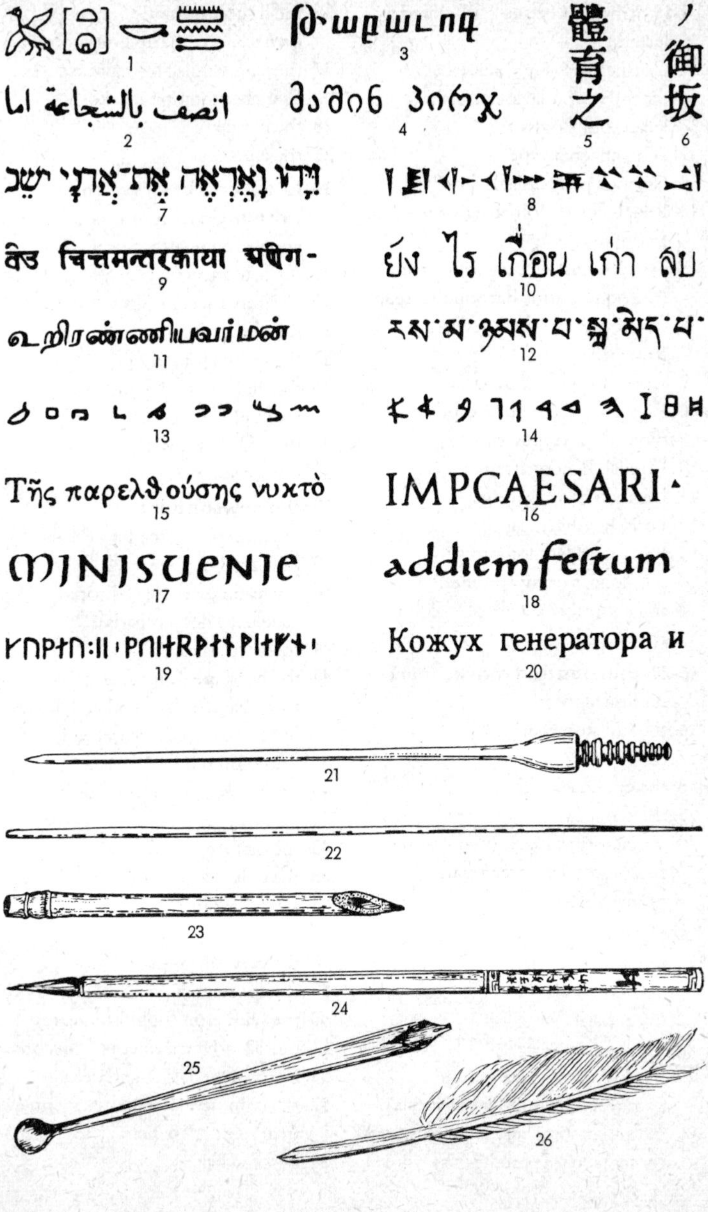
1
3
5
6
2
4
7
8
9
10
11
12
13
14
Τῆς παρελθούσης νυκτὸ
15
IMPCAESARI·
16
MINISUENIE
17
addiem festum
18
19
Кожух генератора и
20
21
22
23
24
25
26

1-15 kinds of types (of printed letters):
1 Gothic type (German text, black-letter, blackletter, black letter, old English)
2 Schwabacher type
3 German print (black-letter)
4 Renaissance Roman (Renaissance Latin, old style)
5 pre-classicistic Latin or Roman (Baroque Latin, Baroque Roman)
6 classicistic Latin (classicistic Roman)
7 sanserif (sanserif print)
8 Egyptian (Clarendon type)
9 type-script (typewriting)
10 English handwriting
11 German handwriting
12 Latin handwriting
13 shorthand (stenography)
14 phonetic writing (phonetic transcription)
15 Braille;

16-29 punctuation marks (punctuation signs):
16 the full stop (period)
17 the colon
18 the comma
19 the semicolon
20 the question mark (mark of interrogation, *Am.* interrogation point)
21 the exclamation mark (mark of exclamation, *Am.* exclamation point)
22 the apostrophe
23 the dash
24 the round brackets (round parentheses, round parenthesis)
25 the square brackets (square parentheses, square parenthesis)
26 the double quotation marks [*in Engl.* "..."] (inverted commas)
27 the single quotation marks (*Am.* French quotation marks)
28 the hyphen
29 the ellipsis;

30-35 accents of stress and pronunciation (stress accents and pronunciation accents):
30 the acute accent
31 the grave accent (grave)
32 the circumflex
33 the cedilla [under c]
34 the diaeresis (*Am.* dieresis) [over e]
35 the tilde [over n];
36 the section mark

37 the newspaper:
38 the newspaper heading (heading)
39 the imprint
40 the leading article (editorial article, leader, editorial)
41 the head rules
42 the headline (*Am., across the entire page:* banner, banner head, banner line; *sensational:* scarehead, beat)
43 the column line
44 the newspaper photograph (press photo)
45 the picture caption
46 the column heading (subheading, cross heading)
47 the column
48 the cartoon
49 the sports news
50 the feuilleton (light literature)
51 and 52 advertisements (*fam.* ads):
51 births, marriages, and deaths
52 the commercial advertisement, a firm's advertisement;
53 news in brief

Duden 1	Duden 2	Duden 3	Duden 4
Duden 5	Duden 6	Duden 7	Duden 8
Duden 9	Duden 10	Duden 11	Duden 12

13

ɔ:l pi:pl

14

15

.	:	,	;	?	!	’	—	()	[]	„“
16	17	18	19	20	21	22	23	24	25	26
» «	-	...	é	è	ê	ç	ë	ñ	§
27	28	29	30	31	32	33	34	35	36

37
38
39
40
49
51
The News
SPORT
41
42
43
44
45
46
47
48
50
53
52

①	I	II	III	IV	V	VI	VII	VIII	IX	X
②	1	2	3	4	5	6	7	8	9	10
①	XX	XXX	XL	L	LX	LXX	LXXX	XC	IC	C
②	20	30	40	50	60	70	80	90	99	100
①	CC	CCC	CD	D	DC	DCC	DCCC	CM	XM	M
②	200	300	400	500	600	700	800	900	990	1000

③ 9658 ④ 5 kg ⑤ 2 ⑥ 2. ⑦ +5 ⑧ -5

1-26 arithmetic,

1-22 the number:

1 the Roman numerals

2 the Arabic numerals

3 the abstract number, a four-figure number (number with four digits), [8 = the unit, 5 = the ten, 6 = the hundred, 9 = the thousand]

4 the concrete number

5 the cardinal number

6 the ordinal number (ordinal)

7 the positive number [with the positive sign]

8 the negative number [with the negative sign]

9 algebraic symbols

10 the mixed number [3 = the whole number (integer), $\frac{1}{3}$ = the fraction (fractional quantity)]

11 even numbers

12 odd numbers

13 prime numbers

14 the complex number [3 = the real number, $2\sqrt{-1}$ = the imaginary number]

15 and 16 vulgar fractions:

15 the proper fraction [2 = the numerator, the sign of division (horizontal line), 3 = the denominator]

16 the improper fraction, at the same time the reciprocal of 15 (the fraction inverted);

17 the compound fraction (complex fraction)

(9) a, b, c ... (10) $3\frac{1}{3}$ (11) 2, 4, 6, 8 (12) 1, 3, 5, 7

(13) 3, 5, 7, 11 (14) $3+2\sqrt{-1}$ (15) $\frac{2}{3}$ (16) $\frac{3}{2}$

(17) $\frac{\frac{5}{6}}{\frac{3}{4}}$ (18) $\frac{12}{4}$ (19) $\frac{4}{5}+\frac{2}{7}=\frac{38}{35}$ (20) 0,357

(21) $0{,}6666\ldots = 0{,}\overline{6}$ (22) (23) $3+2=5$

(24) $3-2=1$ (25) $3\cdot 2=6$ (26) $6:2=3$

18 the improper fraction [when reduced, resulting in a whole number]

19 fractions of different denominations [35 = the common denominator]

20 the proper decimal fraction with decimal point [in Engl. 0 · 357] and decimal places [3 = the tenths, 5 = the hundredths, 7 = the thousandths]

21 the recurring (non-terminating, repeating) decimal fraction

22 the recurring (non-terminating) decimal [in Engl. $0\cdot\dot{6}$];

23-26 the fundamental arithmetical operations (first rules of arithmetic):

23 addition (adding); [3 and 2 = the terms of the sum, + = the plus sign, 5 = the sum (result)]

24 subtraction (subtracting); [3 = the minuend, — = the minus sign, 2 = the subtrahend, 1 = the remainder (difference)]

25 multiplication (multiplying); [3 = the multiplicand, · = the multiplication sign (*in Engl.* ×), 2 = the multiplier, 6 = the product]

26 division (dividing); [6 = the dividend, : = the division sign, 2 = the divisor, 3 = the quotient]

① $3^2 = 9$ ② $\sqrt[3]{8} = 2$ ③ $\sqrt{4} = 2$

④ $3x + 2 = 12$

⑤ $4a + 6ab - 2ac = 2a(2 + 3b - c)$

⑥ $^{10}\log 3 = 0{,}4771$ oder $\lg 3 = 0{,}4771$

⑦ $$\frac{k[£1000] \cdot p[5\%] \cdot t[2\ \text{Years}]}{100} = z[£100]$$

1-24 arithmetics,

1-10 advanced arithmetical operations:

1 the involution (involving); [three squared (second power of three) = the power, 3 = the base, 2 = the index (exponent), 9 = the value of the power]

2 the evolution (extraction of root, *Am.* taking a root); [cube-root of eight = the cube-root, 8 = the radical quantity (radical), 3 = the index (degree) of the root, $\sqrt{\ }$ = the radical sign (radical), 2 = the value of the root]

3 the square root

4 and 5 algebra:

4 the simple equation; [3, 2 = the coefficients, x = the unknown quantity]

5 the identical equation; [a, b, c = the algebraic symbols];

6 the logarithmic calculation (taking the logarithm, log); [log = the logarithm sign, 3 = the number whose logarithm is required, 10 = the base, 0 = the characteristic, 4771 = the mantissa, 0.4771 = the logarithm]

7 the simple interest formula; [k = the principal (original sum invested), p = the rate of interest, t = the time, Z = interest (per cent, profit), % = the percentage sign]

(8) 2 Years = £50
4 Years = £x

(9) $2 : 50 = 4 : x$

(10) $x = £100$

(11) $2 + 4 + 6 + 8 \ldots$

(12) $2 + 4 + 8 + 16 + 32 \ldots$

(13) $\frac{dy}{dx}$

(14) $\int ax\,dx = a\int x\,dx = \frac{ax^2}{2} + C$

(15) ∞ (16) $\equiv$ (17) $\approx$ (18) $\neq$ (19) $>$

(20) $<$ (21) $\parallel$ (22) $\sim$ (23) $\measuredangle$ (24) $\triangle$

8–10 the rule of three (rule-of-three sum, simple proportion):

8 the statement with the unknown quantity x

9 the equation (conditional equation)

10 the solution;

11-14 higher mathematics:

11 the arithmetical series with the elements 2, 4, 6, 8

12 the geometrical series

13 and 14 the infinitesimal calculus:

13 the differential quotient (derivation); [dx, dy = the differentials, d = the differential sign]

14 the integral (integration); [x = the variable, C = the integral constant, $\int$ = the integral sign, dx = the differential];

15-24 mathematical symbols:

15 infinity

16 identically equal to (the sign of identity)

17 approximately equal

18 unequal

19 greater than

20 less than

21-24 geometrical symbols:

21 parallel (the sign of parallelism)

22 similar to (the sign of similarity)

23 the angle symbol [*in Engl.* $<$ or $\wedge$]

24 the triangle symbol

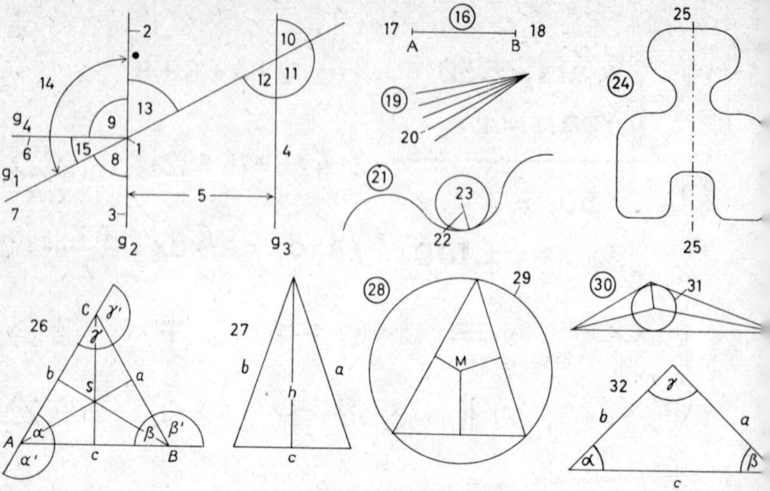

1-58 plane (elementary, Euclidean) **geometry,**

1-23 point, line, angle:

1 the point [point of intersection of g 1 and g 2], the angular point of 8
2 and 3 the straight line g 2
4 the parallel to g 2
5 the distance between the straight lines g 2 and g 3
6 the perpendicular (g 4) on g 2
7 and 3 the arms of 8
8 the angle
8 and 13 vertically opposite angles
9 the right angle [90°]
10 the acute angle
11 the obtuse angle
10, 11, and 12 the reflex angle
12 the corresponding angle to 8 and alternate to 13
13, 9, and 15 the straight angle [180°]
14 the adjacent angle; *here :* supplementary angle to 13
15 the complementary angle to 8
16 the given straight line AB:
17 the end A
18 the end B;
19 the pencil (*Am.* beam) of rays:
20 the ray;
21 the curved line:
22 a radius of curvature
23 a centre (*Am.* center) of curvature;

24-58 the plane surfaces,

24 the symmetrical figure:
25 the axis of symmetry;

26-32 plane triangles,

26 the equilateral triangle; [A, B, C = the vertices; a, b, c = the sides; α, β, γ = the interior angles; α′, β′, γ′ = the exterior angles; S = the centre (*Am.* center)]
27 the isosceles triangle: [a, b the sides (legs); c the base, h the perpendicular, an altitude]
28 the acute-angled triangle with the perpendicular bisectors of the sides:

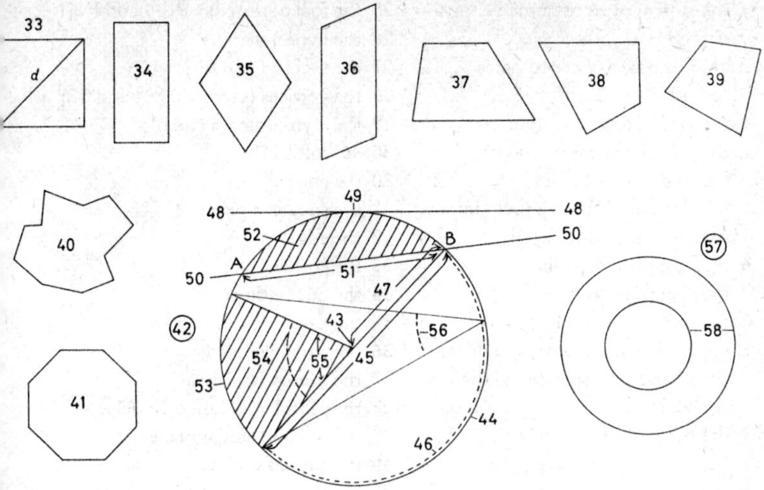

29 the circumscribed circle (circumcircle);
30 the obtuse-angled triangle with the bisector of the angles:
31 the inscribed circle;
32 the right-angled triangle and the trigonometric(al) functions of angles;
[a, b the catheti; c the hypotenuse; γ the right angle;
$\frac{a}{c} = \sin \alpha$ (sine);
$\frac{b}{c} = \cos \alpha$ (cosine);
$\frac{a}{b} = \tan \alpha$ (tangent);
$\frac{b}{a} = \cot \alpha$ (cotangent)];

33-39 quadrilaterals,

33-36 parallelograms:

33 the square [d = a diagonal]
34 the rectangle
35 the rhombus (rhomb, lozenge)
36 the rhomboid;
37 the trapezium
38 the deltoid (kite)
39 the irregular quadrilateral;
40 the polygon
41 the regular polygon

42 the circle:

43 the centre (*Am.* center)
44 the circumference (periphery)
45 the diameter
46 the semicircle (semicircumference, hemicycle)
47 the radius (r)
48 the tangent
49 the point of contact (P)
50 the secant
51 the chord AB
52 the segment
53 the arc
54 the sector
55 the centre angle (*Am.* center angle)
56 the circumferential angle;
57 the ring (annulus):
58 concentric circles

1 the system of right-angled coordinates,
2 and 3 the axes of coordinates (coordinate axes):
2 the axis of abscissae (x-axis)
3 the axis of ordinates (y-axis);
4 the origin of ordinates
5 the quadrant [I to IV: first (1st) to fourth (4th) quadrant]
6 the positive direction
7 the negative direction
8 the points [P 1 and P 2] in the system of coordinates; x 1 and y 1 [or x 2 and y 2 respectively] their coordinates
9 the value of the abscissa [x 1 or x 2 respectively] (the abscisse, abscissa)
10 the value of the ordinate [y 1 or y 2 respectively] (the ordinates);
11–29 conic sections,
11 the curves in the system of coordinates:
12 the plane curves [a the ascent of the curve, b the ordinates' intersection of the curve, c the root of curve]
13 inflected curves;
14 the parabola, a curve of the second degree:
15 the branches of the parabola
16 the vertex of the parabola
17 the axis of the parabola;
18 a curve of the third degree:
19 the maximum of the curve
20 the minimum of the curve
21 the point of inflexion (point of inflection);
22 the ellipse:
23 the transverse axis (major axis)
24 the conjugate axis (minor axis)
25 the foci of the ellipse [F 1 and F 2];
26 the hyperbola:
27 the foci [F 1 and F 2]
28 the vertices (vertexes) [S 1 and S 2]
29 the asymptotes [a and b];
30–46 solids,
30 the cube:
31 the square, a plane
32 the edge
33 the corner;
34 the quadratic prism:
35 the base;
36 the parallelepiped
37 the triangular prism
38 the cylinder, a right cylinder:
39 the base, a circular plane
40 the curved surface;
41 the sphere
42 the ellipsoid of revolution
43 the cone:
44 the height of the cone (cone height);
45 the truncated cone (frustum of a cone)
46 the quadrilateral pyramid

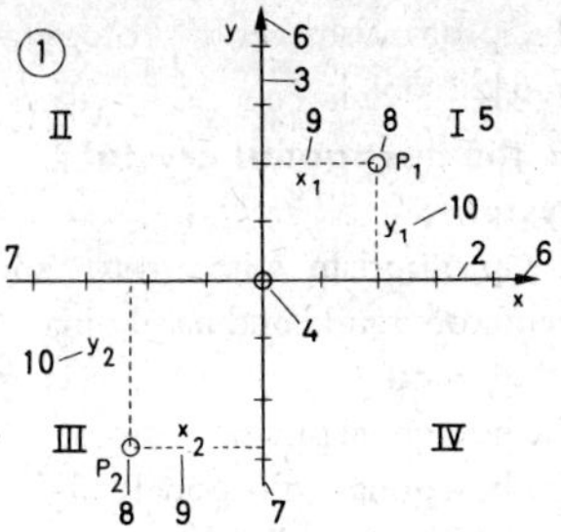
1
y
x
I
II
III
IV
2
3
4
5
6
7
8
9
10
P_1
P_2
x_1
y_1
x_2
y_2

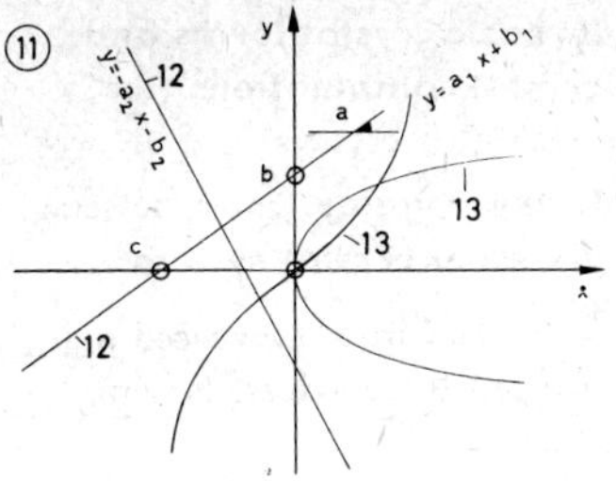
11
y
$y=a_1x+b_1$
$y=-a_2x-b_2$
a
b
c
12
13

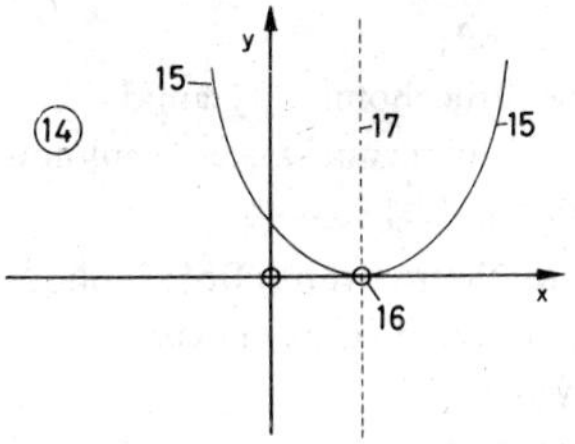
14
y
x
15
16
17

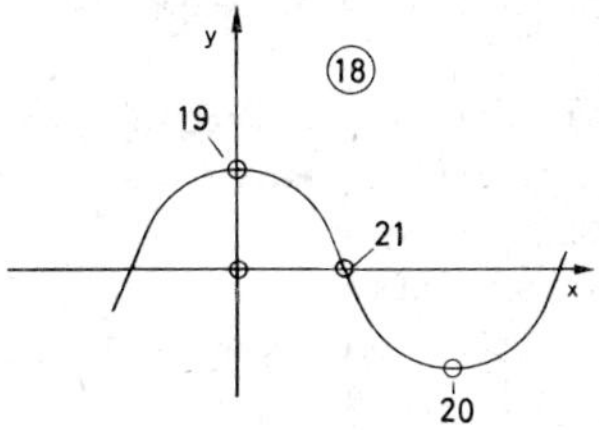
18
y
x
19
20
21

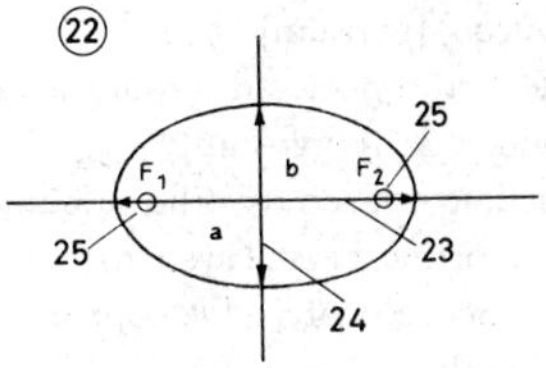
22
F_1
F_2
a
b
23
24
25

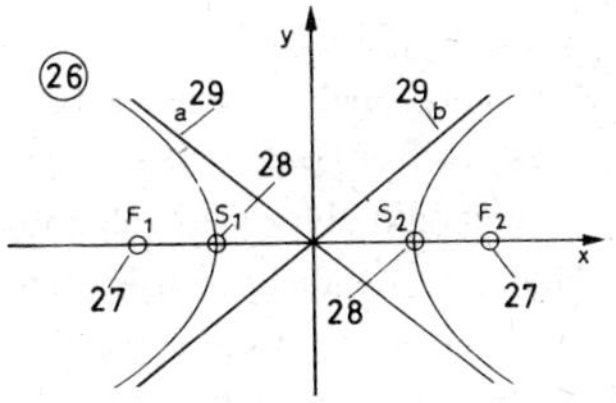
26
y
x
F_1
F_2
S_1
S_2
29_a
29_b
27
28

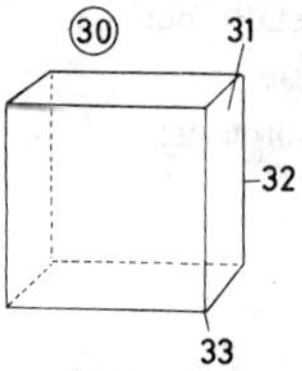
30
31
32
33

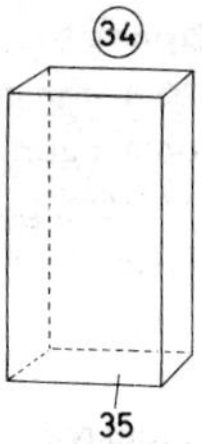
34
35

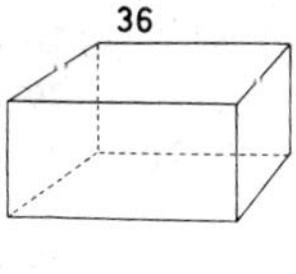
36

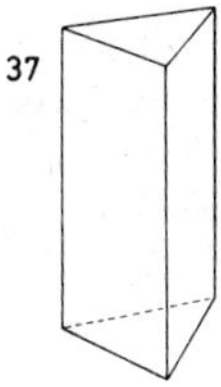
37

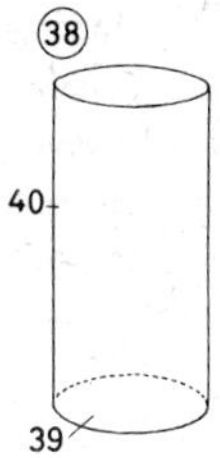
38
39
40

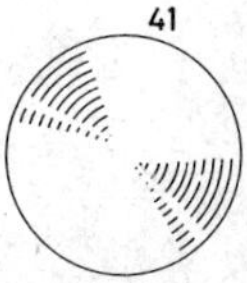
41

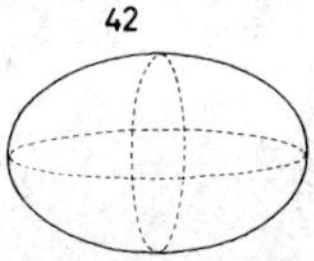
42

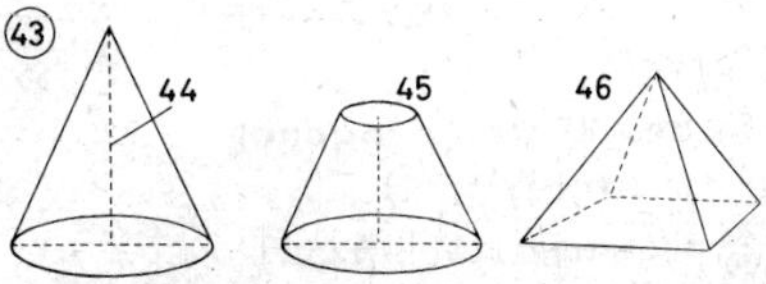
43
44
45
46

1-26 basic crystal forms and crystal combinations (the structure of crystals),

1-17 the regular (cubic, tesseral, isometric) **crystal system:**

1 the tetrahedron (four-faced polyhedron) [tetrahedrite, fahlerz, fahl ore]

2 the hexahedron (cube, six-faced polyhedron), a holohedron [rock salt]:

3 the centre (*Am.* center) of symmetry (crystal centre)

4 the axis of symmetry

5 the plane of symmetry;

6 the octahedron (eight-faced polyhedron) [gold]

7 the rhombic dodecahedron (garneto) [garnet]

8 the pentagonal dodecahedron (pyritohedron) [iron pyrites]:

9 the pentagon (five-sided polygon);

10 the triakis-octahedron [diamond]

11 the icosahedron (twenty-faced polyhedron), a regular polyhedron

12 the icositetrahedron (twenty-four-faced polyhedron) [leucite]

13 the hexakis-octahedron (hexoctahedron, fourty-eight-faced polyhedron) [diamond]

14 the octahedron with cube [galena]:

15 the hexagon (six-sided polygon);

16 the cube with octahedron [fluorspar]:

17 the octogon (eight-faced polygon);

18 and 19 the tetragonal crystal system:

18 the tetragonal bipyramid

19 the protoprism with protopyramid [zirconia];

20-22 the hexagonal crystal system:

20 the protoprism with proto- and deuteropyramid and basal pinacoid [apatite]

21 the hexagonal prism

22 the hexagonal (ditrigonal) biprism with rhombohedron [calcite];

23 the orthorhombic pyramid (rhombic crystal system) [sulphur, *Am.* sulfür]

24 and 25 the monoclinic (oblique, monosymmetric) **crystal system:**

24 the monoclinic prism with clinopinacoid and hemipyramid (hemihedron) [gypsum]

25 the ortho-pinacoid (swallow-tail twin crystal) [gypsum];

26 triclinic pinacoids (the triclinic, or anorthic, crystal system) [copper sulphate, *Am.* copper sulfate];

27-33 apparatus for measuring crystals (for crystallometry):

27 the contact goniometer

28 the reflecting goniometer:

29 the crystal

30 the collimator

31 the observation telescope

32 the graduated circle

33 the lens for reading the angle of rotation

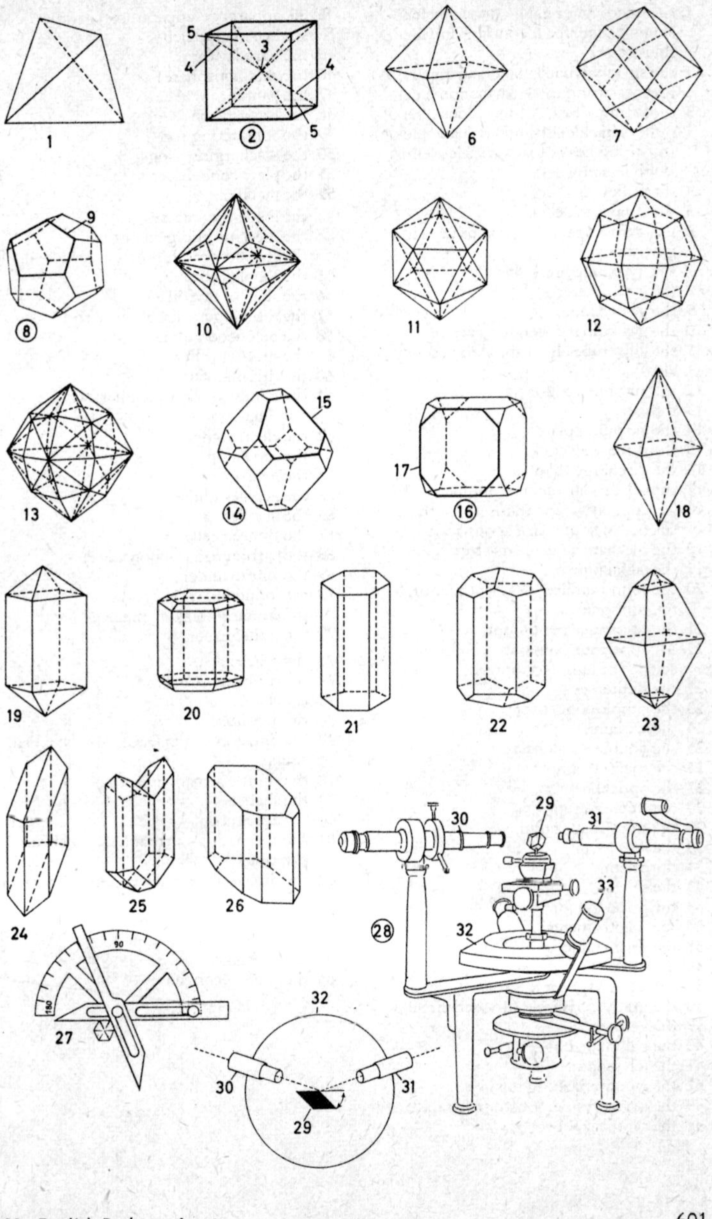
1
2
3
4
5
6
7
8
9
10
11
12
13
14
15
16
17
18
19
20
21
22
23
24
25
26
27
28
29
30
31
32
33

1 the micrometer gauge (micrometer screw gauge) for measuring small thicknesses
2 the spring dynamometer, an apparatus for measuring force (dynamometer)
3 the lifting tackle (lifting blocks, set of pulleys, tackle, lifting block and tackle) for lifting heavy loads with less effort (with less power):
4 the pulley
5 the rope (tackle fall);
6 the gyroscope, an apparatus used in gyroscopy
7 the hydraulic press
8 the hydrometer
9 the gas syringe
10 the gas bulb for weighing air:
11 the clip (tube clip, tube clamp, screw clip);
12 the air pump bell-jar:
13 the cap;
14 the air pump plate:
15 the three-way cock;
16 the discharge tube
17 the oil-driven vacuum pump
18–21 apparatus (apparatuses) for the science of sound (for acoustics):
18 the mechanical wave machine
19 the labial pipe
20 the sound-emitter (loudspeaker or microphone)
21 the resonance pendulum;
22–41 apparatus (apparatuses) for the science of light (for optics),
22 the Reuter lamp:
23 the simple condenser;
24 the arc lamp:
25 the double condenser;
26 the spectral lamp
27 the optical bench:
28 the Reuter lamp
29 the stop (diaphragm)
30 the lens
31 the prism
32 the screen;
33 the plane mirror
34 the spectrometer:
35 the prism table
36 the prism
37 the adjusting screw
38 the graduated circle (divided circle)
39 the vernier
40 the collimator
41 the telescope;
42 the communicating tubes
43 the device for demonstrating capillarity:
44 the capillary tube;
45–85 apparatus (apparatuses) for the science of electricity:
45 the Faraday cage
46 the testing sphere:
47 the handle;
48 the Leyden jar:
49 the conducting rod
50 the discharging tongs;
51 the plate condenser:
52 the metal plate
53 the insulating plate;
54 the electrostatic generator (Wimshurst machine):
55 the Leyden jar
56 the strip of tin foil
57 the discharger (discharging rod);
58 the belt generator:
59 the driving roller
60 the driving belt
61 the conductor knob (spherical conductor);
62 the electroscope:
63 the screening
64 the insulator
65 the needle-holder
66 the needle;
67 the Bunsen cell:
68 the carbon rod (carbon stick)
69 the zinc cylinder;
70 the induction coil:
71 the contact-breaker (break)
72 the transformer
73 the spark gap;
74 the drum armature:
75 the shaft
76 the armature
77 the direct-current (D. C., *Am.* d. c.) slip rings;
78 the shuttle armature (rotor):
79 the shaft
80 the armature
81 the alternating-current (A. C., *Am.* a. c.) slip rings
82 the direct-current (D. C., *Am.* d. c.) slip rings;
83 the adjustable resistance (variable resistance):
84 the resistance
85 the sliding contact

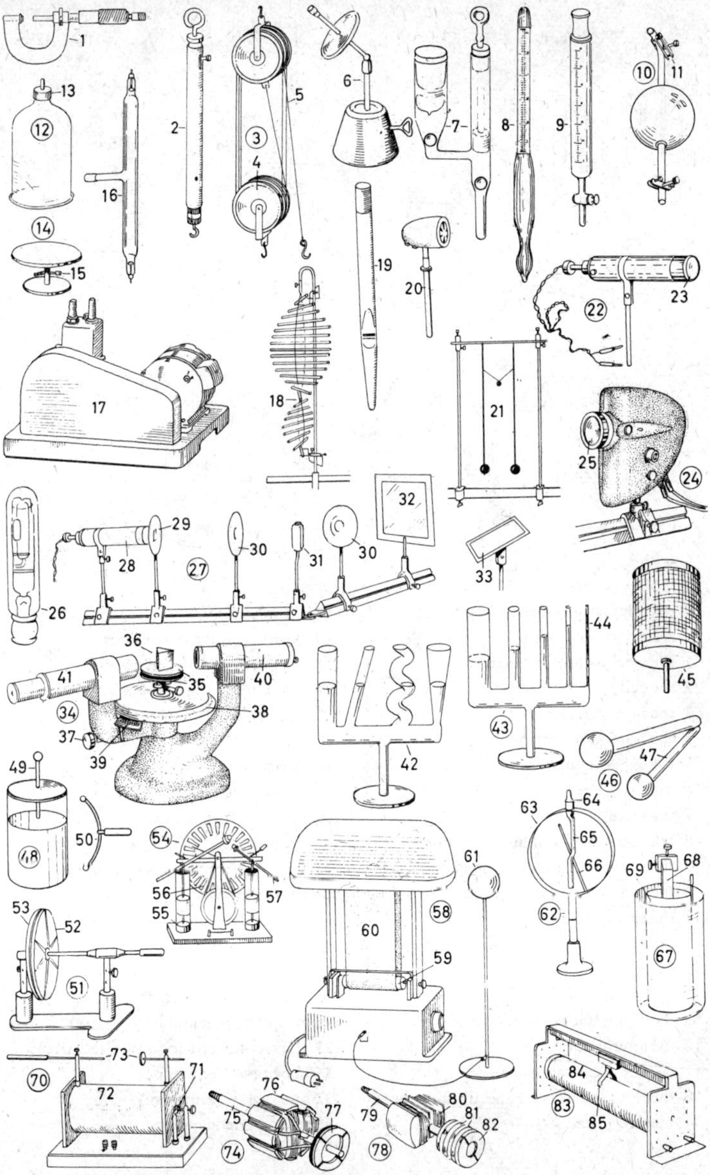
1
2
3
4
5
6
7
8
9
10
11
12
13
14
15
16
17
18
19
20
21
22
23
24
25
26
27
28
29
30
30
31
32
33
34
35
36
37
38
39
40
41
42
43
44
45
46
47
48
49
50
51
52
53
54
55
56
57
58
59
60
61
62
63
64
65
66
67
68
69
70
71
72
73
74
75
76
77
78
79
80
81
82
83
84
85

332 Appliances for Instruction in Physics II

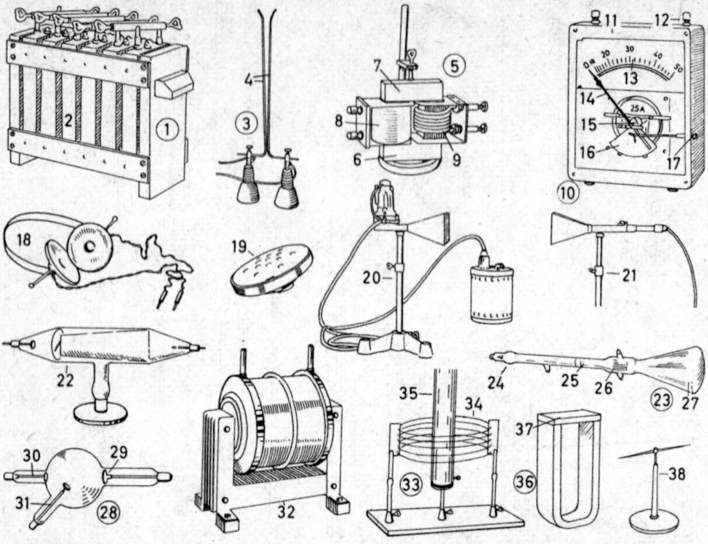

1–35 apparatus (apparatuses) for the science of electricity,

1 the steel accumulator battery:

2 the cell;

3 the horn arrester:

4 the horn gap electrodes;

5 the experimental transformer:

6 the core

7 the yoke

8 the secondary winding (secondary coil)

9 the primary winding (primary coil);

10 the moving-coil instrument:

11 the casing

12 the terminal

13 the scale

14 the index (pointer)

15 the meter with moving coil

16 the attenuator

17 the zero point adjuster;

18 the double earphone (headphone, head receiver, head set)

19 the microphone

20 the microwave transmitter

21 the microwave receiver

22 the cathode-ray tube for magnetic deflection

23 the Braun tube:

24 the cathode

25 the Wehnelt tube

26 the deflecting plates

27 the screen;

28 the roentgen tube (X-ray tube):

29 the cathode

30 the anode

31 the anti-cathode;

32 the high-tension transformer

33 the Tesla transformer:

34 the primary winding (primary)

35 the secondary winding (secondary);

36 the horseshoe magnet:

37 the keeper (armature)

38 the magnetic needle

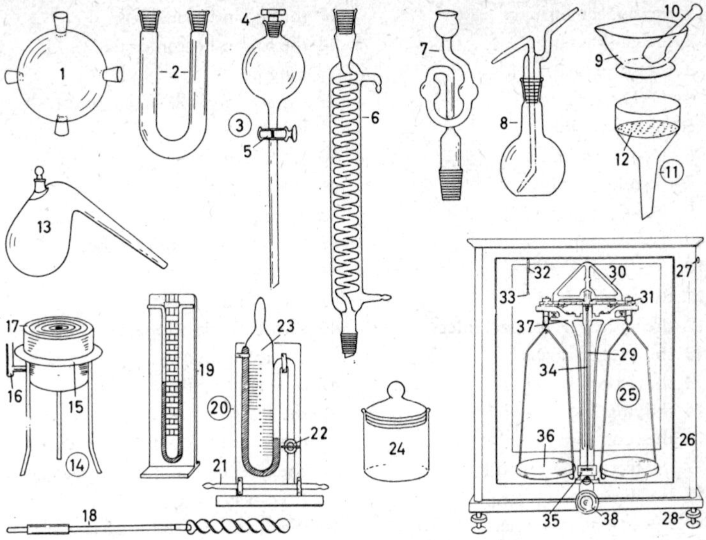

1 the Scheidt globe
2 the U-tube
3 the separating funnel:
4 the octagonal ground stopper
5 the tap (*Am.* faucet);
6 the coiled condenser
7 the safety tube (seal on the top of a fermenting apparatus)
8 the wash-bottle (washing bottle)
9 the mortar
10 the pestle (pounder)
11 the vacuum filter (suction filter, Büchner filter):
12 the filter sieve (sieve plate);
13 the retort
14 the water bath:
15 the tripod
16 the water gauge (constant level device)
17 the insertion rings;
18 the stirrer
19 the excess and low-pressure gauge (*Am.* gage; manometer)
20 the mirror manometer for measuring small pressures (vacuum gauge):
21 the suction tube
22 the tap (*Am.* faucet)
23 the sliding scale;
24 the weighing bottle (weighing jar)
25 the analytical balance:
26 the case
27 the raisable (raiseable) front pane
28 the three point support
29 the balance column
30 the balance beam
31 the slide rail
32 the slide-holder
33 the slide (sliding weight)
34 the pointer (index)
35 the graduated scale
36 the scale pan
37 the stop
38 the stop knob

1 the Bunsen burner:
2 the gas inlet pipe
3 the air regulator;
4 the Teclu burner:
5 the pipe union
6 the gas regulator
7 the tube
8 the air regulator;
9 the blowpipe:
10 the casing
11 the oxygen inlet
12 the hydrogen (or gas) inlet
13 the oxygen nozzle;
14 the tripod
15 the ring
16 the funnel
17 the baked-clay triangle
18 the wire net
19 the asbestos wire net
20 the beaker (heating beaker)
21 the burette for measuring liquids
22 the burette stand:
23 the burette clamp;
24 the graduated (calibrated) pipette
25 the plain pipette (pipette)
26 the graduated measuring glass or cylinder (graduated measure)
27 the stoppered graduated measuring glass
28 the volumetric flask
29 the evaporating basin (dish) of porcelain
30 the tube clip (tube clamp, screw clip)
31 the baked-clay (fireclay) crucible with lid
32 the crucible tongs
33 the clamp
34 the test tube
35 the test tube stand
36 the flat-bottomed flask:
37 the ground mouthpiece;
38 the round-bottomed flask with long neck
39 the conical flask (Erlenmeyer flask)
40 the filtering flask (vacuum flask)
41 the folded filter
42 the one-way cock
43 the calcium chloride tube:
44 the cock stopper;
45 the cylinder glass
46 the distillation apparatus (distilling apparatus):
47 the distilling flask
48 the condenser
49 the return tap (reflux tap, return cock, reflux cock), a two-way tap (two-way cock);
50 the distilling flask (Claisen flask)
51 the desiccator (exsiccator):
52 the glass bowl lid
53 the tap for evacuation
54 the desiccator (exsiccator) insert of porcelain;
55 the three-necked flask
56 the connecting piece (Y-piece)
57 the three-necked bottle
58 the gas-washing bottle (wash-bottle)
59 the Kipp apparatus:
60 the overflow flask
61 the substance container
62 the acid container
63 the gas outlet

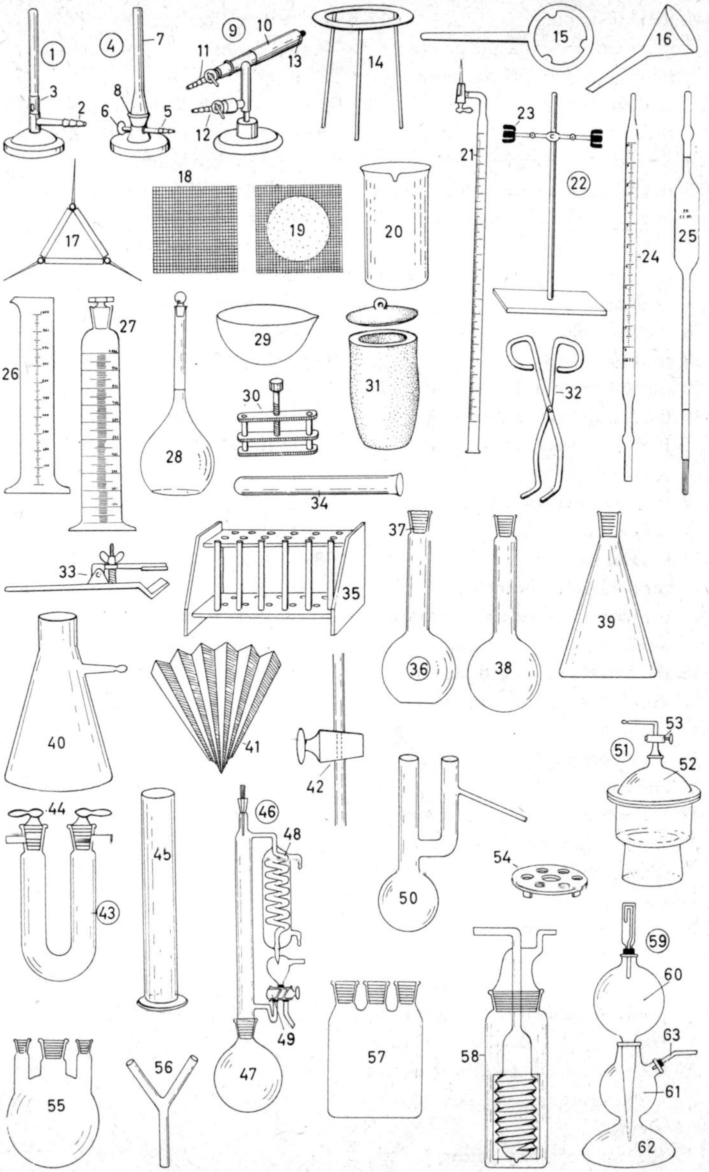
1
2
3
4
5
6
7
8
9
10
11
12
13
14
15
16
17
18
19
20
21
22
23
24
25
26
27
28
29
30
31
32
33
34
35
36
37
38
39
40
41
42
43
44
45
46
47
48
49
50
51
52
53
54
55
56
57
58
59
60
61
62
63

1 the totem pole:
2 the totem, a carved and painted, figurative, or symbolic, representation;
3 the plains Indian
4 the mustang, a prairie horse
5 the lasso, a long throwing rope of raw hide with running noose
6 the pipe of peace
7 the wigwam (tepee, teepee, *sim.* wickiup):
8 the tent pole
9 the smoke flap;
10 the squaw, an Indian woman
11 the Indian chief, a Red Indian, a Red Man (Redskin, *Am. pop.* copperskin):
12 the head dress (war bonnet), a feather decoration
13 the war paint
14 the necklace of bear claws
15 the scalp (hair and skin cut from an enemy's skull), a trophy
16 the tomahawk, a battle axe (war axe, *Am.* battle ax, war ax)
17 the leggings
18 the moccasin, a shoe of raw hide and bast;
19 the canoe of the forest Indians
20 the pyramid surmounted by a Maya temple, a pyramid-temple
21 the mummy
22 the quipu (knotted cords, knotted record of the Incas)
23 the Indio (Indian of Central and South America); *here:* highland Indian:
24 the poncho, a blanket with slit for the head used as armless, cloak-like wrap;
25 the Indian of the tropical forest:
26 the blowpipe (blowgun, blowtube);
27 the quiver
28 the blow gun dart:
29 the point of the blow gun dart
30 the shrunken head, a trophy;
31 the bola (bolas), a missile, and entangling, device:
32 the leather-covered stone, or metal, ball;
33 the pile dwelling (pile house, lake dwelling)
34 the Duk-duk dancer, member of a men's secret society
35 the outrigger canoe (canoe with outrigger):
36 the outrigger;
37 the aboriginal (aborigine, native) Australian:
38 the loin cloth of men's hair
39 the boomerang, a missile weapon
40 the spear thrower with spears

1
2
3
4
5
6
7
8
9
10
11
12
13
14
15
16
17
18
19
20
21
22
23
24
25
26
27
28
29
30
31
32
33
34
35
36
37
38
39
40

1 the Eskimo
2 the sledge dog *(Am.* sled dog), an arctic dog (husky)
3 the dog-sledge *(Am.* dog-sled)
4 the igloo, a dome-shaped snow hut:
5 the block of snow
6 the entrance tunnel;
7 the blubber lamp
8 the spear thrower (throwing board)
9 the lance
10 the harpoon
11 the skin float
12 the kayak, a light one-man canoe:
13 the skin-covered wood, or bone, framework
14 the paddle;
15 the reindeer harness *(Am.* reindeer rig):
16 the reindeer
17 the Ostiak
18 the passenger sledge *(Am.* passenger sled);
19 the yurt, a dwelling tent of the western and central Asiatic nomadic tribes:
20 the felt covering
21 the smoke outlet;
22 the Kirghiz:
23 the sheepskin cap;
24 the shaman:
25 the decorative fringe
26 the frame drum;
27 the Tibetan:
28 the flint-lock with props used as bayonets
29 the prayer wheel
30 the felt boots;
31 the house boat (sampan)
32 the junk:
33 the mat sail;
34 the ricksha (rickshaw, jinricksha, jinrikisha)
35 the ricksha (jinricksha) coolie or cooly
36 the Chinese lantern
37 the samurai:
38 the padded armour *(Am.* padded armor);
39 the geisha:
40 the kimono
41 the obi
42 the fan;
43 the coolie (cooly)
44 the creese (crease, kris), a Malay dagger
45 the snake-charmer:
46 the turban
47 the flute
48 the dancing snake

1
2
3
4
5
6
7
8
9
10
11
12
13
14
15
16
17
18
19
20
21
22
23
24
25
26
27
28
29
30
31
32
33
34
35
36
37
38
39
40
41
42
43
44
45
46
47
48

1 the camel caravan:
2 the riding animal
3 the pack animal;
4 the oasis:
5 the grove of palm trees;
6 the Bedouin (Beduin, Bedawi, Bedawee, Bedawy):
7 the burnous (burnouse, barnous, bernouse);
8 the Masai warrior:
9 the style of hair dressing
10 the shield
11 the painted ox-hide
12 the long-bladed spear;
13 the negro (black, *coll.* darkey, darky, *contempt.* nigger):
14 the dance drum;
15 the throwing knife
16 the wooden mask
17 the figure of an ancestor
18 the slit gong [sometimes used for signalling]:
19 the drumstick;
20 the dug-out, a boat made by hollowing out a tree trunk
21 the negro hut
22 the negress:
23 the lip plug;
24 the grinding stone
25 the Herero (Ovaherero) woman:
26 the leather cap
27 the calabash (gourd);
28 the beehive-shaped hut
29 the bushman:
30 the ear peg
31 the loin cloth
32 the bow
33 the knobkerry (knobkeerie, *Am.* kiri), a club with round knobbed end;
34 the bushman woman, making fire by twirling a stick
35 the wind break
36 the Zulu in dancing finery:
37 the dancing-stick
38 the leg ring;
39 the war horn of ivory
40 the string of amulets and gambling bones
41 the pigmy *(in Afrika :* negrillo; *in Asia and Oceania :* negrito):
42 the magic pipe for the exorcism of evil spirits;
43 the fetish

1
2
3
4
5
6
7
8
9
10
11
12
13
14
15
16
17
18
19
20
21
22
23
24
25
26
27
28
29
30
31
32
33
34
35
36
37
38
39
40
41
42
43

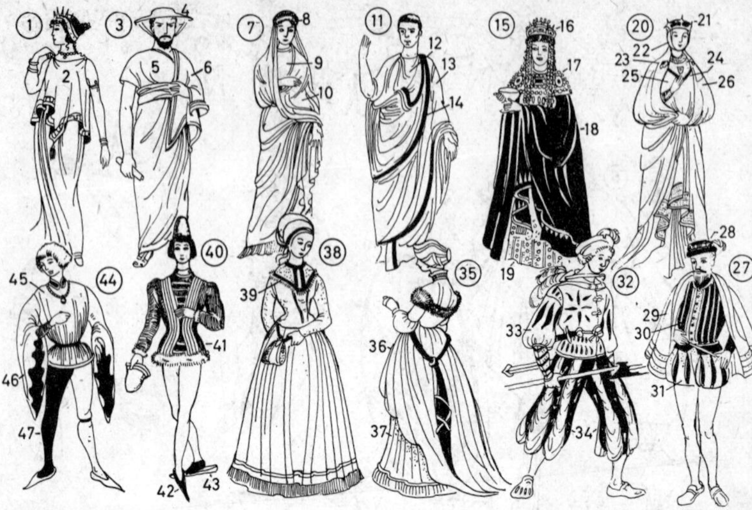

1 Greek woman:
2 the peplos;
3 Greek man:
4 the petasos (Thessalian hat)
5 the chiton, a linen gown worn as undergarment
6 the himation, a woollen (*Am.* woolen) upper garment;
7 Roman woman:
8 the forehead toupet (toupee)
9 the stola
10 the palla, a coloured (*Am.* colored) cloak;
11 Roman man:
12 the tunic
13 the toga
14 the purple border;
15 Byzantine empress:
16 the pearl diadem
17 the pendant ornaments
18 the purple cloak
19 the gown;
20 German princess [13th cent.]:
21 the diadem
22 the wimple
23 the tassel
24 the cloak cord
25 the girdled robe
26 the cloak;
27 German in Spanish style dress [about 1575]:
28 the cap
29 the short cape
30 the padded doublet (peascod)
31 the padded trunkhose;
32 landsknecht [about 1530]:
33 the slashed doublet
34 the baggy breeches (slops);
35 woman of Basle [about 1525]:
36 the gown
37 the petticoat;
38 woman of Nuremberg [about 1500]:
39 the wide collar;
40 Burgundian [15th cent.]:
41 the short doublet

42 the cracowes
43 the poulaines;
44 young nobleman [about 1400]:
45 the short jerkin
46 the scalloped sleeves
47 the parti-coloured (*Am.* parti-colored) tights or hose;
48 Augsburg patrician lady [about 1575]:
49 the puffed sleeves
50 the sleeveless gown;
51 French lady [about 1600]:
52 the ruff
53 the corseted waist (wasp waist);
54 gentleman [about 1650]:
55 the Swedish hat ('cavalier' hat)
56 the falling collar
57 the white linen lining
58 the bucket-topped boots;
59 lady [about 1650]:
60 the puffed sleeves; *later* gigot sleeves, leg-of-mutton sleeves;
61 gentleman [about 1700]:
62 the three-cornered hat (Kevenhuller)
63 the dress sword;
64 lady [about 1700]:
65 the lace bonnet (fontange, commode)
66 the lace-trimmed cloak
67 the silver embroidery;
68 lady [about 1875]:
69 the drapery bunched at the back (bustle);
70 lady [about 1858]:
71 the bonnet
72 the crinoline;
73 Biedermeier gentleman [about 1845]:
74 the high collar (choker)
75 the embroidered waistcoat (*Am.* vest)
76 the frock-coat;
77 the tie-wig:
78 the bow of the tie-wig;
79 ladies in court dress [about 1780]:
80 the train
81 the high head-dress
82 the hair ornaments
83 the paniered skirt

339 The Zoological Gardens (Zoo)

1–15 the house for beasts of prey [interior],
1 the cage for beasts of prey:
2 the iron bars
3 the tree for climbing and sharpening claws
4 the sliding drawer or tray
5 the air-conditioning installation;
6 the beast of prey (predacious animal, raptorial animal, predatory animal, wild animal)
7 the food pail (food bucket)
8 the keeper (keeper of the wild animals)
9 the water basin
10 the safety barrier
11 the water gutter (for deodorant)
12 the hospital and operating cage:
13 the sliding door for operations
14 the pulley for lifting slides
15 the sliding door;
16 the outdoor (outside) enclosure:
17 the natural rock
18 the waterfilled dyke
19 the ramped wall
20 the animals on show; *here:* a pride of lions
21 the zoo visitor
22 the warning notice;
23 the aviary, a large bird cage
24 the giraffe house; *sim.* elephant house, monkey house
25 the outdoor cage or enclosure (summer cage)
26 the aquarium:
27 the water-inflow pipe
28 the aeration system
29 the magnetic valve
30 the shut-off (stop) valve
31 the silt collector
32 the mixing valve
33 the mixing vessel
34 the water meter
35 the thermostat
36 the double sheet of glass
37 the water basin;
38 the combined vivarium and aquarium:
39 the glass case
40 the fresh-air inlet
41 the air outlet (ventilation)
42 the heating from beneath the cage;
43 the vivarium:
44 the explanatory notice
45 the tropical landscape garden (model of a climatic zone)

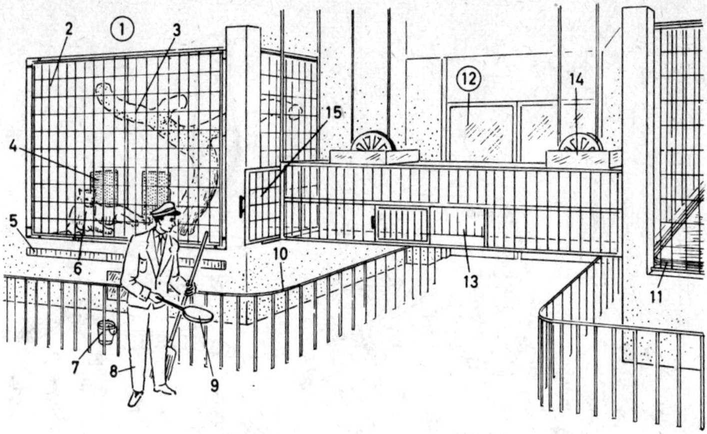
1
2
3
4
5
6
7
8
9
10
11
12
13
14
15

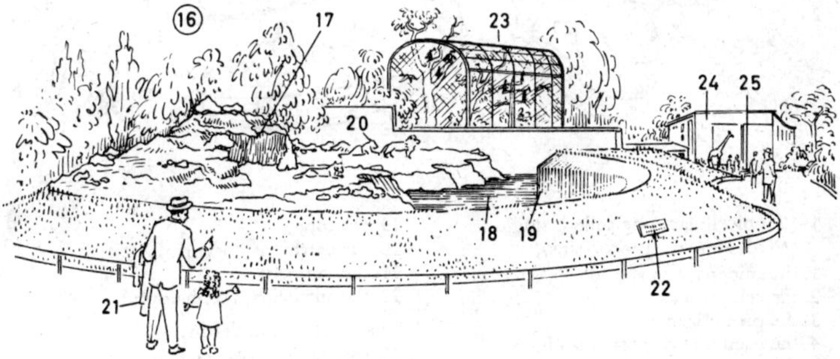
16
17
18
19
20
21
22
23
24
25

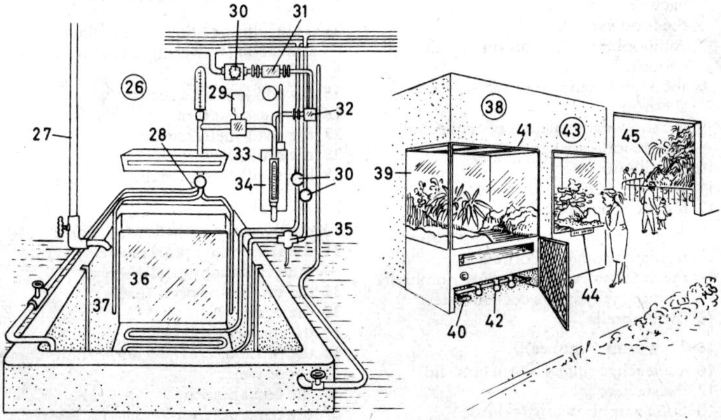
26
27
28
29
30
31
32
33
34
35
36
37
38
39
40
41
42
43
44
45

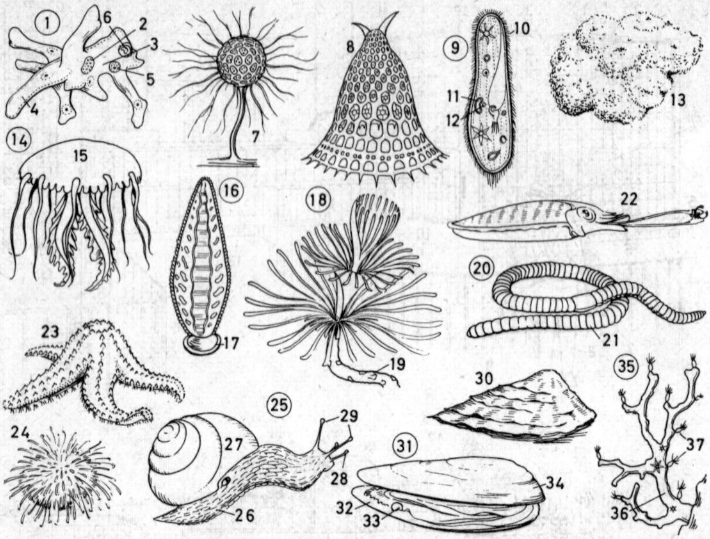

1–12 unicellular (one-celled, single-celled) animals (protozoans),
1 the amoeba, a rhizopod:
2 the cell nucleus
3 the protoplasm
4 the pseudopod (pseudopodium)
5 the contractile and pulsating excretory vacuole
6 the food vacuole;
7 Actinophrys sol, a sun animalcule (heliozoon)
8 the radiolarian; *here:* the siliceous skeleton
9 the slipper animalcule, a Paramecium (ciliate infusorian):
10 the cilium
11 the macronucleus (meganucleus)
12 the micronucleus;

13–37 multicellular animals (Metazoa):
13 the bath sponge, a Porifera
14 the medusa, a discomedusa (umbrella medusa, jellyfish), a coelenterate:
15 the umbrella;

16–21 worms (Vermes):
16 the leech, a ringed worm (annelid):
17 the sucker;
18 Spirographis, a bristle-worm:
19 the tube;
20 the earthworm (worm):
21 the segment;
22 the cuttlefish, a cephalopod

23 and **24** echinoderms:
23 the starfish (sea star)
24 the sea urchin (sea hedgehog);

25–34 Mollusca (mollusks, molluscs, *also:* Conchylia, testaceous and crustaceous animals),
25 the edible snail, a snail:
26 the muscular foot
27 the snail shell (conch)
28 the stalked eye
29 the snail's horn (snail's tentacle);

30–34 mussels:
30 the oyster; the shell: *Am.* shuck
31 the fresh-water pearl mussel (river mussel, swan mussel):
32 the mother-of-pearl (nacre)
33 the pearl
34 the mussel shell;
35 the precious coral, an anthozoon (coral zoophyte):
36 the coral branch
37 the coral polyp

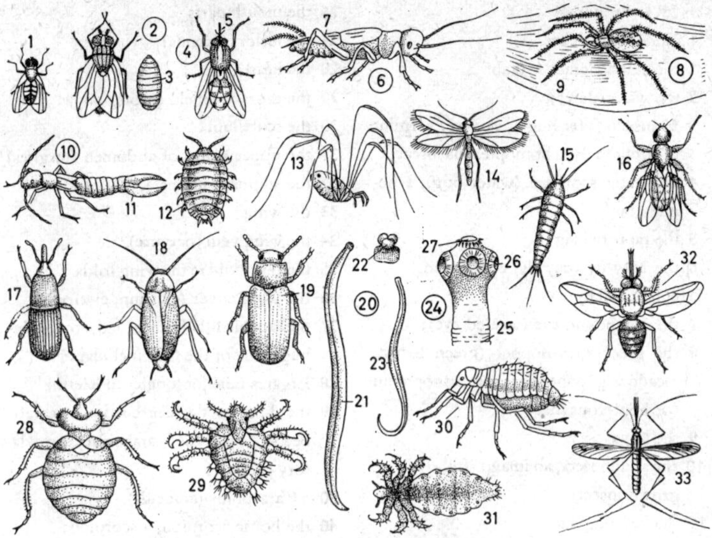

1–13 house insects:
1 the lesser house fly
2 the common house fly:
3 the pupa;
4 the stable fly (biting house fly):
5 the trichotomous antenna;
6 the cricket (house cricket):
7 the wing with stridulating apparatus;
8 the house spider:
9 the spider's web;
10 the earwig (Dermaptera):
11 the caudal pincers;
12 the wood louse (sow bug), a segmented crustacean
13 the harvester (harvestman, harvest spider);
14 and 15 textile pests:
14 the clothes moth
15 the silver fish (sugar mite, *Am.* slicker), an insect with bristle tail;
16–19 food pests:
16 the cheese fly
17 the grain weevil
18 the cockroach (black beetle)
19 the meal beetle (meal worm beetle, flour beetle);
20–31 parasites of man,
20 the round worm (maw worm, Ascaris):
21 the female
22 the head
23 the male;
24 the tapeworm (cestodes), a flatworm (platyhelminth):
25 the head (scolex), a sucker (suctorial organ, organ of attachment)
26 the sucker
27 the crown of hooks;
28–33 vermin:
28 the bug (bed bug, *Am.* chinch)
29 the crab louse
30 the common flea
31 the body louse (clothes louse);
32 the tsetse fly (tsetse, Glossina morsitans)
33 the malaria mosquito (Anopheles)

1–23 arthropods,
1 and **2** crustaceans,
1 the mitten crab, a crab
2 the water-slater;
3–23 insects (*Am.* bugs); *noxious:* vermin:
3 the dragon fly, a homopterous insect
4 the water scorpion (water bug), a hemipteran:
5 the raptorial leg;
6 the May fly (day fly, ephemerid, ephemeral fly):
7 the compound eye (faceted eye);
8 the green grasshopper (green locust, meadow grasshopper), an orthopteran (orthopterous insect):
9 the larva
10 the adult insect, an imago (full-grown insect)
11 the jumping leg;
12 the caddis fly (spring fly, water moth), a neuropteran
13 the aphis (green fly), a plant louse:
14 the wingless aphis
15 the winged aphis;
16–20 dipterous insects (dipterans, Diptera),
16 the gnat (mosquito), a culex:
17 the sucking proboscis;
18 the blue bottle (blow fly, flesh fly), a fly:
19 the maggot (larva)
20 the pupa;
21–23 Hymenoptera,
21 and **22** the ant:
21 the winged female (queen ant)
22 the worker;
23 the humble bee (bumble bee);
24–39 beetles (Coleoptera),
24–38 polyphagous beetles,
24 the stag beetle, a lamellicorn beetle:
25 the mandibles ('antlers')
26 the mouth parts
27 the feeler (antenna)
28 the head
29 the thoracic shield (prothorax)
30 the scutellum
31 the upper plates of abdomen (tergites)
32 the stigmas (stigmata, spiracles)
33 the wing
34 the wing vein (nervure)
35 the place where the wing folds
36 the wing cover (elytrum, elytron);
37 the ladybird (ladyclock, ladycow, ladybug), one of the Coccinellidae
38 Ergates faber, a longicorn beetle;
39 the dung beetle (dor beetle), a scarab beetle (one of the Scarabeidae), a predatory beetle;
40–47 arachnids (araneids),
40 the house scorpion, a scorpion:
41 the chelicera (claw)
42 the maxillary feeler (maxillary antenna)
43 the tail sting;
44–46 spiders:
44 the European tick (dog tick), a tick
45 the garden spider (cross spider), an orb-spinner:
46 the spinneret;
47 the cobweb (spider's web, spider web);
48–56 butterflies,
48 the mulberry-feeding silk moth (common silkworm moth), a silk moth:
49 the eggs (ova)
50 the silkworm
51 the cocoon;
52 the swallowtail, a butterfly:
53 the feeler (antenna)
54 the eyespot;
55 the privet hawk-moth, a sphinx (hawk-moth):
56 the proboscis

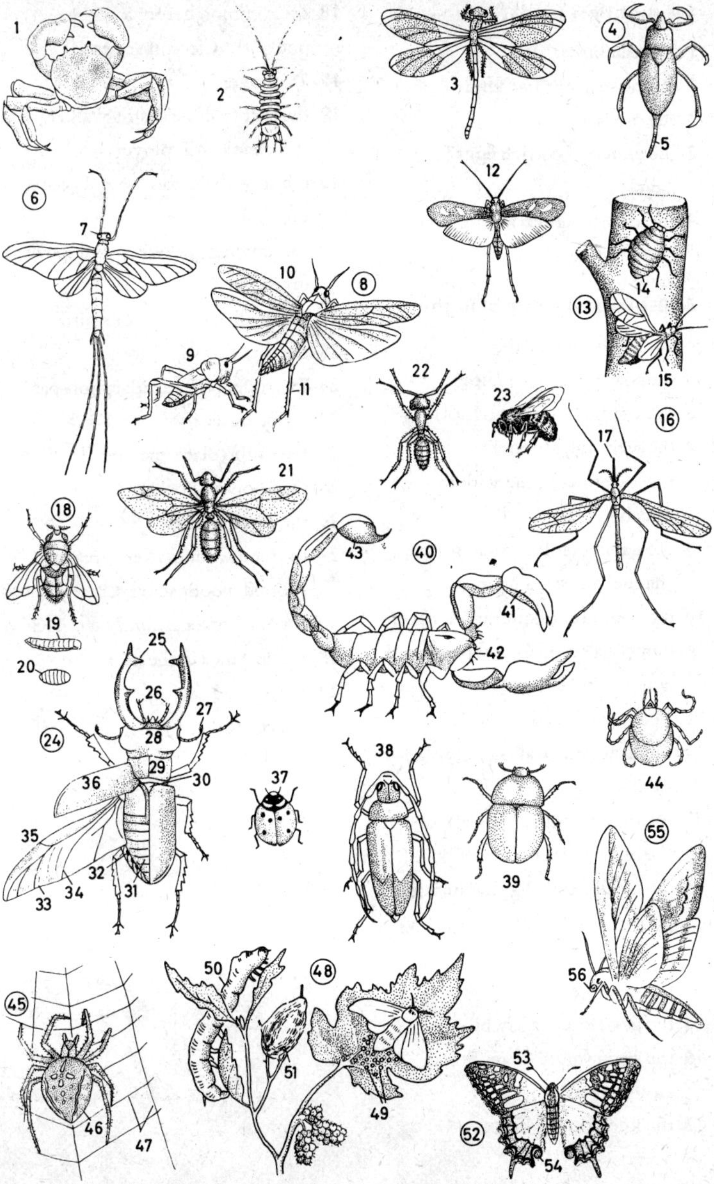
1
2
3
4
5
6
7
8
9
10
11
12
13
14
15
16
17
18
19
20
21
22
23
24
25
26
27
28
29
30
31
32
33
34
35
36
37
38
39
40
41
42
43
44
45
46
47
48
49
50
51
52
53
54
55
56

1-4 flightless birds,

1–3 ratite birds:

1 the cassowary; *sim.* emu

2 the ostrich

3 the clutch of ostrich eggs [12 to 14 eggs];

4 the king penguin, a penguin (Apenodytes);

5-30 birds capable of flight,

5–10 webfooted birds,

5 the rosy pelican, a pelican:

6 the webbed foot (web foot)

7 the web (membrane)

8 the lower mandible with the pouch;

9 the gannet (solan, solan goose, channel goose), a gannet

10 the common cormorant, a cormorant (Phalacrocorax) with spread wings, displaying;

11–14 long-winged birds:

11 the tern (sea swallow) diving for food

12 the fulmar (fulmar petrel)

13 the black guillemot, an auk

14 the black-headed gull (laughing gull, sea gull, mew, mire crow), a gull;

15–17 anserine birds:

15 the goosander, a sawbill

16 the swan (mute swan, Polish swan), a swan:

17 the knob on the bill;

18 the common heron, a heron, one of the Ciconiiformes

19–21 plovers:

19 the stilt (stilt bird, stilt-walker, stilt shank, stilt plover)

20 the coot (bald coot), a rail (water rail, rallus)

21 the lapwing (peewit, pewit, pewet, green plover);

22 the quail, a gallinaceous bird

23 the turtle dove, a pigeon

24–29 rollers (Coraciidae, non-passerine birds):

24 the swift (black martin)

25 the hoopoe (hoopoo):

26 the erectile crest;

27 the pied woodpecker (greater spotted woodpecker, a woodpecker; *related :* wryneck:

28 the entrance to the nest

29 the nesting cavity;

30 the cuckoo

1
2
3
4
5
6
7
8
9
10
11
12
13
14
15
16
17
18
19
20
21
22
23
24
25
26
27
28
29
30

1, 3, 4, 5, 7, 9 song-birds:

1 the goldfinch, a finch

2 the bee-eater

3 the redstart (star finch), one of the Turdidae

4 the blue tit (*fam.* tomtit, nun) a tit (titmouse), a resident bird (non-migratory bird)

5 the bullfinch

6 the roller (European roller)

7 the golden oriole, a bird of passage (migratory bird)

8 the kingfisher (*poet.* halcyon)

9 the white wagtail, a wagtail

10 the chaffinch

1
2
3
4
5
6
7
8
9
10
S. Vogel

1 the sulphur-crested cockatoo, a parrot
2 the blue and yellow macaw (Ara ararauna)
3 the blue bird of paradise
4 the sappho, a colibri (humming-bird)
5 the cardinal bird (cardinal grosbeak)
6 the toucan, a climber (climbing bird, scansorial bird)

1
2
3
4
5
6
S. Vogel

1–20 song-birds (singing-birds, songsters),

1–3 Corvidae (corvine birds, crows):

1 the jay (jay bird), a jay

2 the rook, a crow

3 the magpie;

4 the starling (pastor, shepherd bird)

5 the house-sparrow

6–8 Fringillidae (finches),

6 and **7** buntings:

6 the yellow-hammer (yellow-bunting; *dial.* yellow ham)

7 the ortolan (ortolan bunting);

8 the siskin (aberdevine), a siskin;

9 the great titmouse (great tit, ox-eye), a titmouse

10 the golden-crested wren (goldcrest); *sim.:* firecrest, a goldcrest

11 the nuthatch (*dial.* nutjobber)

12 the wren (jenny wren, kitty wren)

13–17 Turdidae (thrushes):

13 the blackbird

14 the nightingale (*poet.* Philomel, Philomela)

15 the robin (redbreast, robin redbreast)

16 the song thrush (*poet. and dial.* throstle, mavis)

17 the thrush-nightingale (sprosser);

18 and **19** Alaudidae (larks):

18 the wood lark; *sim.:* skylark

19 the crested lark (tufted lark);

20 the barn-swallow (chimney-swallow), a swallow

1–19 diurnal birds of prey,

1–4 falcons:

1 the merlin

2 the peregrine falcon (peregrine, *Am.* duck-hawk):

3 the 'trousers' (thigh feathers, thigh plumage)

4 the tarsus;

5–9 eagles,

5 the white-tailed eagle (sea-eagle, erne):

6 the hooked beak

7 the claw (talon)

8 the tail;

9 the common buzzard;

10–13 Accipiters (hawks):

10 the goshawk (*Scot.* gos)

11 the kite (glede)

12 the sparrow hawk (sparhawk)

13 the marsh harrier (moor buzzard, moor harrier, moor hawk);

14–19 nocturnal birds of prey (owls):

14 the long-eared owl

15 the eagle-owl (great horned owl):

16 the plumicorn (ear-tuft, horn);

17 the barn owl (white owl, silver owl, yellow owl, church owl, screech owl, *dial.* hobby owl):

18 the facial disk or disc (feathers radiating round the eyes);

19 the little owl (sparrow owl)

1
2
3
4
5
6
7
8
9
10
11

1-11 Lepidoptera,

1-6 butterflies (diurnal Lepidoptera):

1 the red admiral
2 the peacock butterfly
3 the orange-tip butterfly
4 the brimstone butterfly
5 the Camberwell beauty (mourning cloak)
6 the large blue butterfly (lycaenid butterfly);

7-11 moths (nocturnal Lepidoptera):

7 the common tiger-moth
8 the ilia underwing
9 the death's-head hawk-moth, a hawk-moth (sphinx):
10 the caterpillar
11 the pupa

349

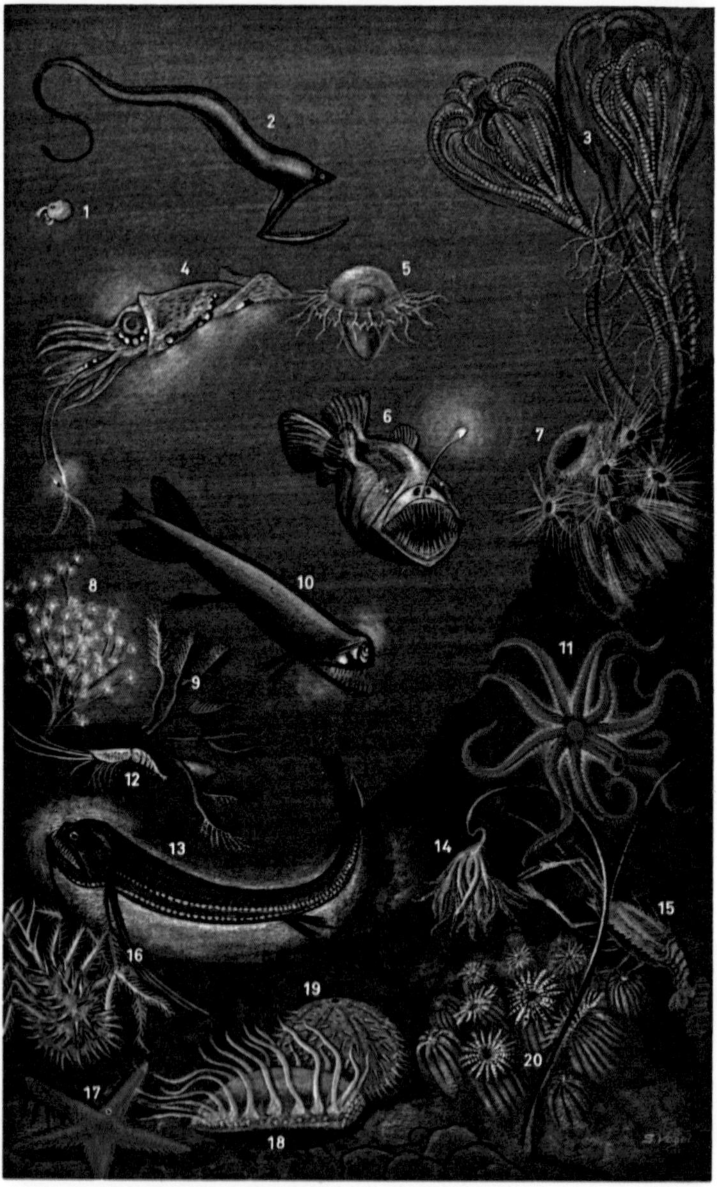
1
2
3
4
5
6
7
8
9
10
11
12
13
14
15
16
17
18
19
20

1 Gigantocypris agassizi (giant cypris, giant ostracod)
2 Macropharynx longicaudatus (pelican eel)
3 Pentacrinus (larva of feather star), a sea lily, an echinoderm
4 Thaumatolampas diadema ('wonder lamp'), a squid [luminescent]
5 Atolla, a deep-sea medusa, a coelenterate
6 Melanocetes, an angler fish (one of the Pediculati) [luminescent]
7 Lophocalyx philippensis, a glass sponge
8 Mopsea, a sea-fan [colony; luminescent]
9 Hydrallmania, a hydroid polyp, a polyp, a coelenterate [colony]
10 Malacosteus indicus, one of the Stomiatidae [luminescent]
11 Brisinga endecacnemos, an ophiuroid echinoderm, an echinoderm [luminescent only when stimulated]
12 Pasiphaea, a deep-sea prawn
13 Echiostoma, one of the Stomiatidae, a fish [luminescent]
14 Umbellula encrinus, a sea pen, a coelenterate [colony]
15 Pentacheles, a deep-sea prawn
16 Lithodes, a deep-sea crab
17 Archaster, a starfish, an echinoderm
18 Oneirophanta, a sea cucumber (sea gherkin), an echinoderm
19 Palaeopneustes niasicus, a sea hedgehog (sea urchin), an echinoderm
20 Chitonactis, a sea anemone (Actinia), a coelenterate

1-17 fish,

1 the man-eater (blue shark, requin), a shark:
2 the nose (snout)
3 the gill slit;
4 the carp, a mirror carp or king carp:
5 the gill cover (operculum)
6 the dorsal fin
7 the pectoral fin (breast-fin)
8 the pelvic fin
9 the anal fin
10 the caudal fin
11 the mirror scale;
12 the sheat fish (wels):
13 the barbel;
14 the common herring
15 the brook trout, a trout
16 the common pike
17 the fresh-water eel
18 the sea horse (Hippocampus):
19 the Lophobranchia;

20-26 amphibians (amphibia),

20–22 newts (efts),
20 the great water newt (warty newt), a water newt:
21 the dorsal crest;
22 the spotted salamander, a salamander; (*other species:* the giant salamander; the hellbender);
23–26 anurans (tailless amphibians, batrachians):
23 the toad (common toad, *Am. coll.* hoptoad), a toad
24 the tree frog (arboreal frog):
25 the vocal sac (croaking sac)
26 the adhesive disk or disc;

27-41 reptiles,

27 and 31–37 lizards (Lacertidae):
27 the sand lizard
28 the hawk's-bill (hawk's-bill turtle):
29 the back shield (carapace);
30 the basilisk
31 the monitor (varanus), a varan
32 the green iguana, an iguana
33 the chameleon, one of the Chamaeleontidae (Rhiptoglossa):
34 the prehensile foot
35 the prehensile tail;
36 the wall gecko, a gecko
37 the slow worm (blind worm);
38–41 snakes (*esp. when large and, or, venomous:* serpents),
38 the ring snake (ringed snake, grass snake, water snake):
39 the ring (collar);
40 and 41 vipers:
40 the common viper (adder), a poisonous viper
41 the asp

1
2
3
4
5
6
7
8
9
10
11
12
13
14
15
16
17
18
19
20
21
22
23
24
25
26
27
28
29
30
31
32
33
34
35
36
37
38
39
40
41

1 the duck-bill or platypus (duck-mole, water- mole), a monotreme (egg-laying animal)

2 and **3** marsupials (pouch-bearing animals):

2 the North American opossum, a didelphic marsupial

3 the giant red kangaroo, a kangaroo;

4–7 insectivores (insect-eaters, insect-eating animals):

4 the mole

5 the hedgehog:

6 the spine;

7 the shrew (shrewmouse);

8 the nine-banded armadillo

9 the long-eared bat (flitter mouse), a placental flying animal (one of the Chiroptera), a bat

10 the pangolin (scaly ant-eater), a scaly animal

11 the two-toed sloth (unau)

12–19 rodents:

12 the guinea pig (Brazilian cavy)

13 the porcupine

14 the beaver (Castor)

15 the jerboa

16 the hamster

17 the water vole

18 the marmot (Alpine marmot, *Am.* ground hog, whistle pig)

19 the squirrel;

20–31 ungulates (hoofed animals),

20 the African elephant, an animal with a trunk (a proboscid):

21 the trunk (elongated proboscis)

22 the tusk;

23 the manatee (manati, manatin, lamantin), one of the Sirenia

24 the Australian dugong (Halicore, sea cow), a dugong

25–27 odd-toed ungulates:

25 the African two-horned rhinoceros, a nasicorn

26 the Brazilian tapir, a tapir

27 the zebra;

28–31 even-toed ungulates,

28–30 ruminants (cud-chewing animals):

28 the llama

29 the two-humped camel (Bactrian camel)

30 the guanaco;

31 the hippopotamus

1
2
3
4
5
6
7
8
9
10
11
12
13
14
15
16
17
18
19
20
21
22
23
24
25
26
27
28
29
30
31

1–10 ungulates (hoofed animals):
1 the European elk (*Am.* moose)
2 the wapiti (*Am.* elk)
3 the chamois (Alpine goat)
4 the giraffe
5 the blackbuck (antelope)
6 the mouflon (wild sheep)
7 the ibex (bouquetin, steinbock)
8 the domesticated buffalo
9 the American bison
10 the musk-ox;
11–17 beasts of prey (rapacious animals, raptorial animals, carnivores),
11–13 Canidae:
11 the jackal
12 the red fox (common European fox)
13 the wolf;
14–16 martens:
14 the stone marten (*other species :* beech marten)
15 the sable
16 the weasel;
17 the sea otter;
18–22 seals (pinnipeds):
18 the ursine seal (fur seal, sea bear)
19 the common seal (sea calf)
20 the walrus (morse):
21 the moustache
22 the fang;
23–29 whales:
23 the bottle-nosed dolphin (Tursiops)
24 the common dolphin
25 the sperm whale (spermaceti whale, cachalot), a toothed whale:
26 the blow hole (spout hole)
27 the dorsal fin
28 the flipper
29 the tail-fluke

1
2
3
4
5
6
7
8
9
10
11
12
13
14
15
16
17
18
19
20
21
22
23
24
25
26
27
28
29

1–11 beasts of prey (raptorial animals, carnivores):
1 the striped hyena (Hyaena), a hyena
2–8 cats,
2 the lion:
3 the mane (lion's mane)
4 the paw;
5 the tiger
6 the leopard
7 the cheetah (hunting leopard)
8 the lynx;
9–11 bears:
9 the racoon (coon)
10 the brown bear
11 the polar bear (white bear);
12–16 primates,
12 and **13** monkeys:
12 the rhesus monkey (Indian macaque)
13 the baboon;
14–16 apes (man-like apes, anthropoids):
14 the chimpanzee
15 the orang utan (orang outan)
16 the gorilla

1
2
3
4
5
6
7
8
9
10
11
12
13
14
15
16

1 the tree:
2 the bole (tree trunk, trunk)
3 the crown of the tree
4 the top of the tree (tree top)
5 the branch; *a main branch :* bough (limb)
6 the twig;
7 the bole [section]:
8 the bark (rind)
9 the inner fibrous bark
10 the cambium (cambium ring)
11 the medullary rays (vascular rays, pith rays)
12 the sapwood (alburnum)
13 the heartwood (duramen)
14 the medulla (vascular cylinder, pith cylinder);
15 the plant,
16–18 the root:
16 the main root
17 the side root
18 the root hair;
19–25 the shoot (sprout):
19 the leaf
20 the stalk
21 the side shoot
22 the terminal bud
23 the flower
24 the flower bud
25 the axil with the axillary bud;
26 the leaf:
27 the leaf stalk (petiole)
28 the leaf blade (lamina)
29 the venation (leaf veins, leaf nerves, leaf ribs)
30 the leaf midrib;
31–38 forms of leaves:
31 linear
32 lanceolate
33 orbicular (orbiculate)
34 acerose (acerous, needle-shaped)
35 cordate
36 ovate
37 sagittate
38 reniform;
39–42 compound leaves:
39 digitate (digitated, quinquefoliate)
40 pinnatifid
41 abruptly pinnate
42 odd pinnate;
43–50 forms of leaf margins:
43 entire
44 serrate (toothed)
45 doubly serrate
46 crenate (scalloped)
47 dentate
48 sinuate (sinuous)
49 ciliate (ciliated):
50 the cilium;
51 the flower:
52 the flower stalk (scape, flower stem)
53 the receptacle (thorus, thalamus)
54 the ovary
55 the style
56 the stigma
57 the stamen
58 the sepal; *all the sepals :* calyx
59 the petal; *all the petals :* corolla;
60 ovary and stamen [section]:
61 the wall of the ovary
62 the cavity of the ovary
63 the ovule
64 the embryo sac
65 the pollen
66 the pollen tube;
67–77 inflorescences:
67 the spike
68 the raceme
69 the panicle
70 the cyme
71 the fleshy spike
72 the umbel
73 the capitulum (head)
74 the discoid flower head
75 the globose flower head (pear-shaped flower head)
76 the bostryx (helicoid cyme)
77 the cincinnus (scorpioid cyme);
78–82 roots:
78 the adventitious root
79 the tuber
80 the adventitious roots (aerial roots)
81 the root thorns
82 the pneumatophore;
83–85 the blade of grass:
83 the leaf sheath
84 the ligule (ligula)
85 the blade;
86 the embryo (germ):
87 the seed leaf (seed lobe, cotyledon)
88 the radicle
89 the hypocotyl
90 the leaf bud (plumule);
91–102 fruits,
91–96 dehiscent fruits:
91 the follicle
92 the two-suture legume
93 the three-suture legume
94 the schizocarp seed vessel (schizocarp seed capsule)
95 the pyxidium (circumscissile seed vessel or capsule)
96 the poricidal capsule;
97–102 indehiscent fruits:
97 the berry
98 the nut
99 the stone fruit (drupe)
100 the collective nut fruit
101 the collective stone fruit (collective drupe)
102 the pome

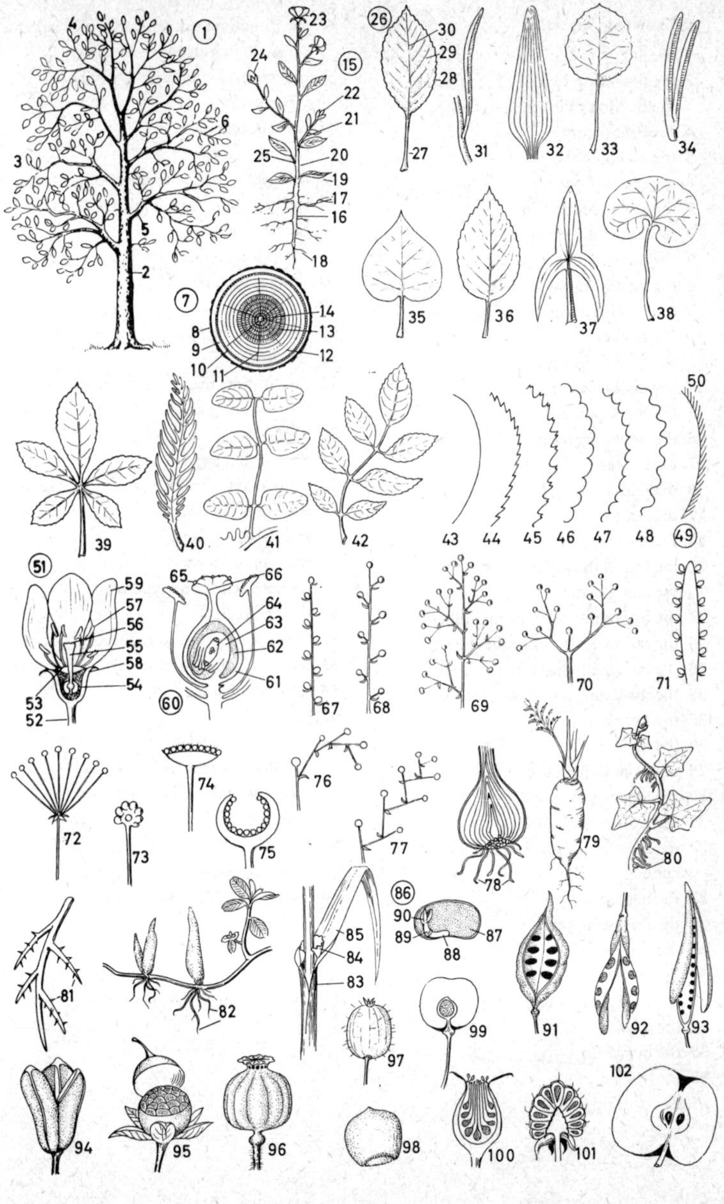
1
2
3
4
5
6
7
8
9
10
11
12
13
14
15
16
17
18
19
20
21
22
23
24
25
26
27
28
29
30
31
32
33
34
35
36
37
38
39
40
41
42
43
44
45
46
47
48
49
50
51
52
53
54
55
56
57
58
59
60
61
62
63
64
65
66
67
68
69
70
71
72
73
74
75
76
77
78
79
80
81
82
83
84
85
86
87
88
89
90
91
92
93
94
95
96
97
98
99
100
101
102

1–73 deciduous trees,
1 the oak:
2 the flowering twig (twig in flower)
3 the fruiting twig (twig in fruit)
4 the fruit (acorn)
5 the cup (cupule)
6 the female flower
7 the bract (bractea)
8 the male inflorescence;
9 the birch:
10 the flowering twig (twig with catkins)
11 the fruiting twig
12 the samara
13 the female flower
14 the male flower;
15 the black poplar:
16 the flowering twig
17 the flower
18 the fruiting twig
19 the fruit
20 the seed
21 the leaf of the aspen
22 the fructification
23 the leaf of the white poplar (abele);
24 the sallow (goat willow):
25 the twig with the flower buds
26 the male catkin with single flower
27 the twig in leaf
28 the fruit
29 the osier twig in leaf;
30 the alder (howler, aller):
31 the fruiting twig
32 the flowering twig with last year's cones;
33 the beech:
34 the flowering twig
35 the flower
36 the fruiting twig
37 the fruit (beech nut, mast);
38 the ash:
39 the flowering twig
40 the flower
41 the fruiting twig;
42 the mountain ash (rowan tree, Fouler's service, cock-drunks, hen-drunks, quickbeam, witchwood, witchen, white ash):
43 the inflorescence
44 the fructification
45 the fruit [longitudinal section];
46 the lime (lime tree, linden, linden tree):
47 the fruiting twig
48 the inflorescence;
49 the elm (elm tree):
50 the fruiting twig
51 the flowering twig
52 the flower;
53 the Norway maple (maple tree):
54 the flowering twig
55 the flower
56 the fruiting twig
57 the maple seed with wing (winged seed);
58 the horse chestnut (chestnut, chestnut tree, *Am.* buckeye):
59 the twig with young fruit
60 the seed (chestnut, conker)
61 the ripe fruit
62 the flower [longitudinal section];
63 the hornbeam (hardbeam):
64 the fruiting twig
65 the seed
66 the flowering twig;
67 the plane (western plane tree, *Am.* button tree, button wood, button ball):
68 the leaf
69 the fructification and the fruit;
70 the locust tree (false acacia, common robinia):
71 the flowering twig
72 part of the fructification
73 the stipule with bracts (bracteae)

1
4
♀
2
5
♂
4
3
6
7
8
9
12
♀
11
10
♂
13
14
15
19
♀
17
♂
16
18
20
19
♀
21
22
26
24
♂
30
31
23
25
27
26
♀
29
28
33
37
♀
37
36
40
32
♀
♂
35
♂
34
35
♀
38
41
42
45
47
46
49
39
44
43
48
50
52
51
55
53
63
70
65
54
64
66
♀
♂
71
58
59
56
57
67
60
61
62
69
68
72
73

1–71 coniferous trees (cone-bearing trees),
1 the fir (fir tree, silver fir):
2 the fir cone (fir strobilus), a fruit cone
3 the axis
4 the female flower cone
5 the bract scale
6 the sprig of male flowers
7 the stamen
8 the cone scale
9 the seed with wing (winged seed)
10 the seed [longitudinal section]
11 the fir needle (needle);
12 the spruce (spruce fir, Norway spruce):
13 the fruit cone (spruce cone)
14 the cone scale
15 the seed
16 the female flower cone
17 the male inflorescence
18 the stamen
19 the spruce needle;
20 the pine (Scots pine, pine tree, *coll., but incorrect* Scotch fir, Scots fir):
21 the dwarf pine
22 the female flower cone
23 the bundle of two leaves of young shoot
24 the male inflorescence
25 the new year's shoot
26 the fruit cone (pine cone)
27 the cone scale
28 the seed
29 the fruit cone of the Swiss stone pine (stone pine, cembra pine)
30 the fruit cone of the Weymouth pine (white pine)
31 the young shoot [cross section];
32 the larch (larch tree):
33 the flowering twig
34 the scale of the female flower cone
35 the anther
36 the twig with larch cone (fruit cone)
37 the seed
38 the cone scale;
39 the tree of life (arbor vitae, Thuja):
40 the fruiting twig
41 the fruit cone
42 the scale
43 the twig with reproductive shoots
44 the male shoot
45 the scale with pollen sacs
46 the female shoot;
47 the juniper:
48 the female shoot [longitudinal section]
49 the male shoot
50 the scale with pollen sacs
51 the fruiting twig
52 the juniper berry
53 the fruit [cross section]
54 the seed;
55 the stone pine:
56 the male shoot
57 the fruit cone (stone-pine cone) with seed [longitudinal section];
58 the common cypress (cypress, cypress tree):
59 the fruiting twig
60 the seed;
61 the yew (yew tree):
62 the reproductive shoots
63 the fruiting twig
64 the fruit [longitudinal section];
65 the cedar of Lebanon:
66 the fruiting twig
67 the fruit scale
68 the reproductive shoots;
69 Wellingtonia (mammoth tree):
70 the fruiting twig
71 the seed

1
2
3
5
4
8
9
10
6
11
7
6
12
13
19
14
15
16
17
18
20
26
23
25
24
31
30
33
35
34
36
38
32
37
37
21
22
29
27
28
55
57
56
60
47
59
42
41
40
51
52
53
58
54
52
39
45
44
48
49
50
43
46
64
61
70
66
67
69
63
64
65
70
62
68
71

1 the Forsythia:
2 the ovary and the stamen
3 the leaf;
4 the yellow-flowered jessamin(e) or jasmin(e):
5 the flower [longitudinal section] with style, ovary, and stamens (*rare :* stamina);
6 the privet:
7 the flower
8 the fructification;
9 the fragrant (sweet-scented) mock orange (*pop., but err.* syringa)
10 the common guelder rose (snowball tree):
11 the flower (blossom)
12 the fruits;
13 the oleander (rosebay, rose laurel):
14 the flower [longitudinal section];
15 the red magnolia:
16 the leaf;
17 the japonica (Japanese quince):
18 the fruit;
19 the common (evergreen) box-tree:
20 the female flower
21 the male flower
22 the fruit [longitudinal section];
23 the Weigela (Weigelia)
24 the yucca [part of inflorescence]:
25 the leaf;
26 the dog-rose:
27 the fruit;
28 the corchorus (Kerria):
29 the fruit;
30 the cornel bush (dogwood):
31 the flower
32 the fruit (cornel cherry,cornel berry);
33 the gale (sweet gale, boy myrtle, Dutch myrtle)

1
2
3
4
5
6
7
8
9
10
11
12
13
14
15
16
17
18
19
20
21
22
23
24
25
26
27
28
29
30
31
32
33

1 the common tulip tree (tulip poplar, saddle tree, whitewood):
2 the carpels
3 the stamen
4 the fruit;
5 the hyssop:
6 the flower [from above]
7 the flower
8 the calyx with fruit;
9 the holly:
10 the hermaphrodite flower (androgynous flower)
11 the male flower
12 the fruit with stones exposed;
13 the honeysuckle (woodbine, woodbind):
14 the flower buds
15 the flower [cut open];
16 the Virginia creeper:
17 the open flower
18 the fructification (fruits)
19 the fruit [longitudinal section];
20 the common broom:
21 the flower with the petals removed
22 the young pod;
23 the spiraea:
24 the flower [longitudinal section]
25 the fruit
26 the stamen;
27 the blackthorn (sloe):
28 the leaves
29 the fruits;
30 the one-pistil (one-style, one-stylus) hawthorn (whitethorn, *pop.* the May):
31 the fruit (haw);
32 the laburnum:
33 the raceme
34 the fruits;
35 the common elder (*Scot.* bourtree, bountree):
36 the elder flowers, flower cyme
37 the elderberries

1
2
3
4
5
6
7
8
9
10
11
12
13
14
15
16
17
18
19
20
21
22
23
24
25
26
27
28
29
30
31
32
33
34
35
36
37

359 Meadow and Hedgerow Flowers (Field Flowers) I

1 the round-leaved (rotundifoliate, rotundifolious) saxifrage:
2 the leaf
3 the flower
4 the fruit;
5 the common anemone:
6 the flower [longitudinal section]
7 the fruit;
8 the meadow buttercup (meadow crowfoot, crowfoot, *also called* butterflower, gold-cup, king-cup):
9 the root-leaf
10 the fruit;
11 the meadow ladies'-smock (cuckoo flower):
12 the basilar leaf
13 the fruit;
14 the harebell (hairbell, bluebell, bell flower, campanula):
15 the root-leaf
16 the flower [longitudinal section]
17 the fruit;
18 the ivy-leaved ale-hoof (ground ivy):
19 the flower [longitudinal section]
20 the flower [from above];
21 the stonecrop
22 the speedwell:
23 the flower
24 the fruit
25 the seed;
26 the pennycress:
27 the dehiscent capsule
28 the seed;
29 the field scabious:
30 the root-leaf
31 the ray floret
32 the disk (or disc) floret
33 the involucral calyx with awns
34 the ovary with awns
35 the fruit;
36 the lesser celandine (pilewort):
37 the fruit
38 the leaf axil with bulbil;
39 the annual meadow grass:
40 the flower
41 the spikelet [from the side]
42 the spikelet [from above]
43 the caryopsis (indehiscent fruit);
44 the tuft of grass (clump of grass, tussock)
45 the comfrey:
46 the flower [longitudinal section]
47 the fruit

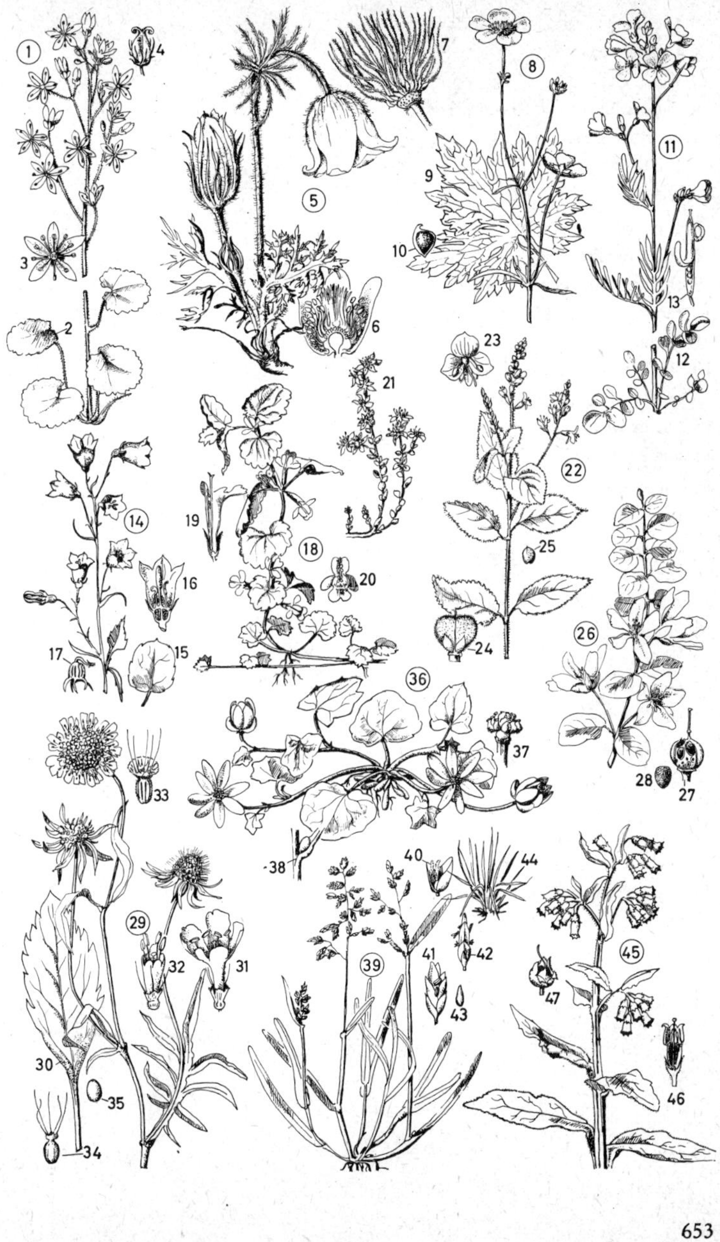
1
4
7
8
11
5
9
10
3
13
2
6
23
12
21
22
14
19
18
20
16
25
17
15
24
26
36
37
28
27
33
38
40
44
45
29
32
31
41
42
39
47
43
30
46
35
34

1 the daisy (*Am.* English daisy):
2 the flower
3 the fruit;
4 the white ox-eye (ox-eye daisy, marguerite):
5 the flower
6 the fruit;
7 the large Astrantia
8 the cowslip
9 the mullein (great mullein, high taper, shepherd's-club, Aaron's rod)
10 the bistort (snake weed; *pop.* snake root, adder's wort):
11 the flower;
12 the knapweed
13 the common wild mallow:
14 the fruit;
15 the yarrow (milfoil)
16 the self-heal (Prunella)
17 the common bird's-foot trefoil
18 equisetum (horse-tail, scouring rush) [a shoot]:
19 the cone;
20 the English catch-fly
21 the ragged robin
22 the birth-wort:
23 the flower;
24 the meadow crane's-bill
25 the wild chicory (succory)
26 the common yellow toad-flax (butter-and-eggs)
27 the lady's-slipper (Venus's-slipper, *Am.* moccasin flower)
28 the orchis, an orchid

1
2
3
4
5
6
7
8
9
10
11
12
13
14
15
16
17
18
19
20
21
22
23
24
25
26
27
28

361 Forest, Marsh (Swamp, Bog), and Heath (Moor), Plants

1 the wind flower (wood anemone)
2 the lily of the valley
3 the cat's-foot (mountain everlasting, mountain cudweed); *sim.* immortelle
4 the Turk's-cap (Turk's-cap lily)
5 the goat's-beard
6 the ramson
7 the lungwort
8 the larkspur
9 the orpine (orpin, live-long, livelong)
10 the spurge-laurel (Daphne)
11 the touch-me-not (yellow balsam)
12 the club-moss
13 the butterwort, a carnivorous plant
14 the sundew; *sim.* Venus's fly trap
15 the bearberry (bear's bilberry)
16 the polypod fern; *sim.* shield fern, brake
17 the hair moss, a moss
18 the cotton grass
19 the heather (ling, heath); *sim.* bell heather (cross-leaved heath)
20 the commen rock-rose
21 the marsh rosemary
22 the sweet sedge
23 the bilberry (whortleberry; *Scot.* blaeberry, *Am.* huckleberry); *sim.* cranberry (craneberry), moss berry, crakeberry (crowberry)

1
2
3
4
5
6
7
8
9
10
11
12
13
14
15
16
17
18
19
20
21
22
23

1–13 Alpine plants,
1 the Alpine rose (rusty-leaved rhododendron):
2 the flowering stem;
3 the Alpine Soldanella (Alpine snowbell):
4 the unfolded corolla
5 the seed capsule with the style;
6 the yellow wormwood:
7 the inflorescence;
8 the auricularia
9 the edelweiss:
10 the forms of flower
11 the fruit with the pappus tuft
12 the section of a flower head (capitulum);
13 the stemless gentian (common Gentianella);
14–57 aquatic plants,
14 the white water lily:
15 the leaf
16 the flower;
17 the Amazon (giant, royal) water lily (Victoria regia):
18 the leaf
19 the underside of the leaf
20 the flower;
21 the reed mace (cat's-tail, bulrush, reed spike, ditch reed, club rush):
22 the male part of the spike (*Am.* cob)
23 the male flower
24 the female part
25 the female flower;
26 the forget-me-not:
27 the flowering stem
28 the flower [section];
29 the frogbit
30 the water cress:
31 the stalk with flowers and immature fruit
32 the flower
33 the pod with seed
34 two seeds;
35 the duckweed (duck-meat, duck's-meat):
36 the plant in flower
37 the flower
38 the fruit;
39 the flowering rush:
40 the flower umbel
41 the leaves
42 the fruit;
43 the green alga
44 the water plantain:
45 the leaf
46 the flower panicle
47 the single flower;
48 the sea tangle, a brown alga:
49 the thallus (leafy plant body)
50 the holdfast;
51 arrowhead:
52 the forms of leaves
53 the inflorescence with male flowers [at the top] and female flowers [below];
54 the eel grass (grass wrack, sea grass):
55 the inflorescence;
56 the Canadian water weed:
57 the flower

1
2
3
4
5
6
7
8
9
10
11
12
13
14
15
16
17
18
19
20
21
22
23
24
25
26
27
28
29
30
31
32
33
34
35
36
37
38
39
40
41
42
43
44
45
46
47
48
49
50
51
52
53
54
55
56
57

1 the aconite (monk's-hood, wolf's-bane)
2 the foxglove (Digitalis)
3 the meadow saffron (naked lady, naked boys)
4 the common hemlock (spotted hemlock)
5 the black nightshade (common nightshade)
6 the henbane
7 the deadly nightshade (belladonna, dwale), one of the Solanaceae
8 the thorn apple (stramony, *Am.* stink weed, Jamestown weed, Jimson weed, Jimpson weed)
9 the cuckoo-pint (lords-and-ladies, common arum, wild arum, wake-robin)
10–13 poisonous fungi (toadstools):
10 the fly agaric (fly amanita), an agaric
11 the death-cup (bulbous agaric, poisonous agaric)
12 Boletus satanus
13 Lactarius torminosus

363

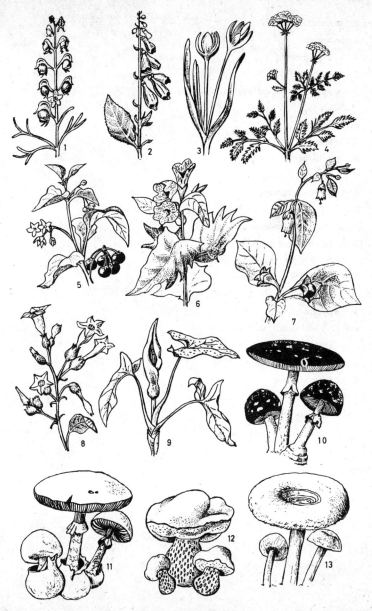

364 Medicinal Plants

1 the chamomile (camomile)
2 the arnica
3 the peppermint
4 the wormwood
5 the valerian (*fam.* cat's valerian, all-heal)
6 the fennel
7 the lavender
8 the coltsfoot
9 the tansy
10 the common centaury
11 the ribwort (rib grass, ribwort plantain, narrow-leaved plantain)
12 the common marsh mallow
13 the black alder (alder buckthorn)
14 the castor-oil plant (Palma Christi)
15 the opium poppy
16 the senna (cassia); *the dried leaflets :* senna leaves
17 the cinchona (chinchona)
18 the camphor tree
19 the betel tree (betel nut tree):
20 the betel nut

1
2
3
4
5
6
7
8
9
10
11
12
13
14
15
16
17
18
19
20

365 Edible Fungi (Esculent Fungi)

1 the field mushroom (common mushroom):
2 the interwoven hyphae (mycelium) with fruiting body (mushroom)
3 the mushroom [longitudinal section]
4 the cap (pileus) with gills
5 the velum (veil)
6 the gill [section]
7 the basidia [on the gill with basidiospores]
8 the germinating spores;
9 the truffle:
10 the truffle [external view]
11 the truffle [section]
12 interior showing the asci containing spores [section]
13 two asci with the spores;
14 the chanterelle
15 the cèpe (cep, chestnut boletus)
16 the edible boletus (edible pore mushroom):
17 the layer of tubes (spongy lining)
18 the stem;
19 the egg-shaped puffball
20 the flask-shaped puffball
21 Boletus luteus (ringed boletus)
22 the rough-stemmed boletus
23 the edible agaric
24 the scaly urchin
25 the turban-top (edible helvella, saddle fungus)
26 the morel (edible morel, common morel)
27 the conical morel (bell morel)
28 the honey agaric
29 the green agaric
30 the parasol mushroom
31 the urchin of the woods
32 the yellow clavaria (goat's-beard)
33 Agaricus (Pholiota) mutabilis

1
2
3
4
5
6
7
8
9
10
11
12
13
14
15
16
17
18
19
20
21
22
23
24
25
26
27
28
29
30
31
32
33

1 the coffee tree (coffee plant):
2 the fruiting stem
3 the flowering stem
4 the flower
5 the fruit (cherry) with the two beans [longitudinal section]
6 the coffee bean; *when processed:* coffee;
7 the tea plant (tea shrub, tea bush, tea tree):
8 the flowering twig
9 the tea leaf; *when processed:* tea
10 the fruit;
11 the maté plant (Paraguay tea, yerba de maté):
12 the flowering twig with the hermaphrodite flowers (androgynous flowers)
13 the male flower
14 the hermaphrodite (androgynous) flower
15 the fruit;
16 the cocoa tree (cacao tree):
17 the branch with flowers and fruits
18 the flower [longitudinal section]
19 the seeds (cocoa beans); *when processed:* cocoa, cocoa powder
20 the seed [longitudinal section]
21 the embryo;
22 the cinnamon tree:
23 the flowering stem
24 the fruit
25 the cinnamon bark; *when crushed:* cinnamon;
26 the clove tree:
27 the flowering stem
28 the bud; *when dried:* clove
29 the fruit (mother of cloves);
30 the nutmeg tree:
31 the flowering stem
32 the female flower [longitudinal section]
33 the ripe fruit
34 the mace, a seed with slashed seed-covering (arillode mace)
35 the seed (kernel) [cross section]; *when dried:* nutmeg;
36 the pepper plant:
37 the fruiting stem
38 the inflorescence
39 the fruit [longitudinal section] with the seed (peppercorn); *when ground:* pepper;
40 the Virginian tobacco plant (common tobacco):
41 the flowering stem
42 the flower
43 the tobacco leaf; *when cured:* tobacco
44 the ripe fruit capsule
45 the seed;
46 the vanilla plant:
47 the flowering stem
48 the vanilla pod; *when cured:* the stick of vanilla;
49 the pistachio tree (pistacia):
50 the flowering stem with the female flowers
51 the nut (pistachio nut);
52 the sugar cane:
53 the plant in bloom
54 the panicle
55 the flower

1
2
3
4
5
6
7
8
9
10
11
12
13
14
15
16
17
18
19
20
21
22
23
24
25
26
27
28
29
30
31
32
33
34
35
36
37
38
39
40
41
42
43
44
45
46
47
48
49
50
51
52
53
54
55

1 the rape (*rare :* cole seed):
2 the basal leaf
3 the flower [longitudinal section]
4 the ripe pod (siliqua)
5 the oleiferous seed;
6 the flax (flax plant, *Scotch* lint):
7 the flower stalk (flower stem)
8 the seed capsule;
9 the hemp:
10 the fruiting female plant (carl hemp, carl)
11 the female inflorescence
12 the flower
13 the male inflorescence (*male plant :* fimble, fimble hemp)
14 the fruit
15 the seed (hemp seed);
16 the cotton plant (cotton):
17 the flower
18 the boll
19 the lint (lint hairs) [cotton];
20 the kapok tree (silk-cotton tree):
21 the pod
22 the sprig of blossoms
23 the seed
24 the seed [longitudinal section];
25 the jute plant (jute):
26 the flowering stem
27 the flower
28 the fruit;
29 the olive tree (olive):
30 the flowering spray
31 the flower
32 the fruit;
33 the rubber tree (India rubber tree):
34 the stem with fruits
35 the fig
36 the flower;
37 the gutta-percha tree:
38 the flowering stem
39 the flower
40 the fruit;
41 the pea nut (ground nut, monkey nut, ground pea):
42 the flowering stem
43 the root with fruits
44 the nut [longitudinal section];
45 the sesame plant (simsim, gingelly, benniseed):
46 the stem with flowers and fruit
47 the flower [iongitudinal section];
48 the coconut tree:
49 the inflorescence
50 the female flower
51 the male flower [longitudinal section]
52 the fruit [longitudinal section]
53 the coconut (coker nut);
54 the oil palm:
55 the male flower spike (spadix) with the flower
56 the cluster of fruits
57 the seed with the germinating holes;
58 the sago palm (sago tree):
59 the fruit;
60 the bamboo:
61 the spray of leaves
62 the flowers
63 the length of cane with joints;
64 the papyrus plant:
65 the flower tuft
66 the flower

1
2
3
4
5
5
6
7
8
9
10
11
12
13
14
15
16
17
18
19
20
21
22
23
24
25
26
27
28
29
30
31
32
33
34
35
36
37
38
39
40
41
42
43
44
45
46
47
48
49
50
51
52
53
54
55
56
57
58
59
60
61
62
63
64
65
66

1 the date palm (date tree, date):
2 the fruiting palm
3 the palm leaf
4 the male spadix
5 the male flower
6 the female spadix
7 the female flower
8 a stalk from a date cluster
9 the date
10 the date kernel (seed);
11 the fig:
12 the twig with multiple fruits (pseudocarps, sorosis)
13 the fig with flowers [longitudinal section]
14 the female flower
15 the male flower;
16 the pomegranate:
17 the flowering twig
18 the flower [longitudinal sections, corolla removed]
19 the fruit
20 the seed (kernel) [longitudinal section]
21 the seed [cross section]
22 the embryo (germ);
23 the lemon; *sim.* tangerine (mandarin), orange, grapefruit, pomelo (shaddock):
24 the flowering twig;
25 the orange flower [longitudinal section]
26 the fruit
27 the orange [cross section]
28 the banana plant:
29 the crown
30 the pseudostem (false stem) with the leaf sheaths
31 the inflorescence with young fruits
32 the bunch (cluster) of fruit
33 the banana
34 the banana flower
35 the banana leaf [diagram];
36 the almond:
37 the flowering twig
38 the fruiting twig
39 the fruit
40 the shell with the seed (almond);
41 the carob (algarroba, locust):
42 the twig with female flowers
43 the female flower
44 the male flower
45 the fruit
46 the fruit pod [cross section]
47 the seed;
48 the edible chestnut (sweet chestnut):
49 the flowering twig
50 the female inflorescence
51 the male flower
52 the burr (cupule) with the seeds [chestnuts, nuts];
53 the Brazil nut:
54 the flowering twig
55 the leaf
56 the flower [from above]
57 the flower [longitudinal section]
58 the opened seed vessel with the seed
59 the Brazil nut [cross section]
60 the nut [longitudinal section];
61 the pineapple (pine, ananas):
62 the pseudocarp with the leaf rosette
63 the flower
64 the ananas flower
65 the flower [longitudinal section]

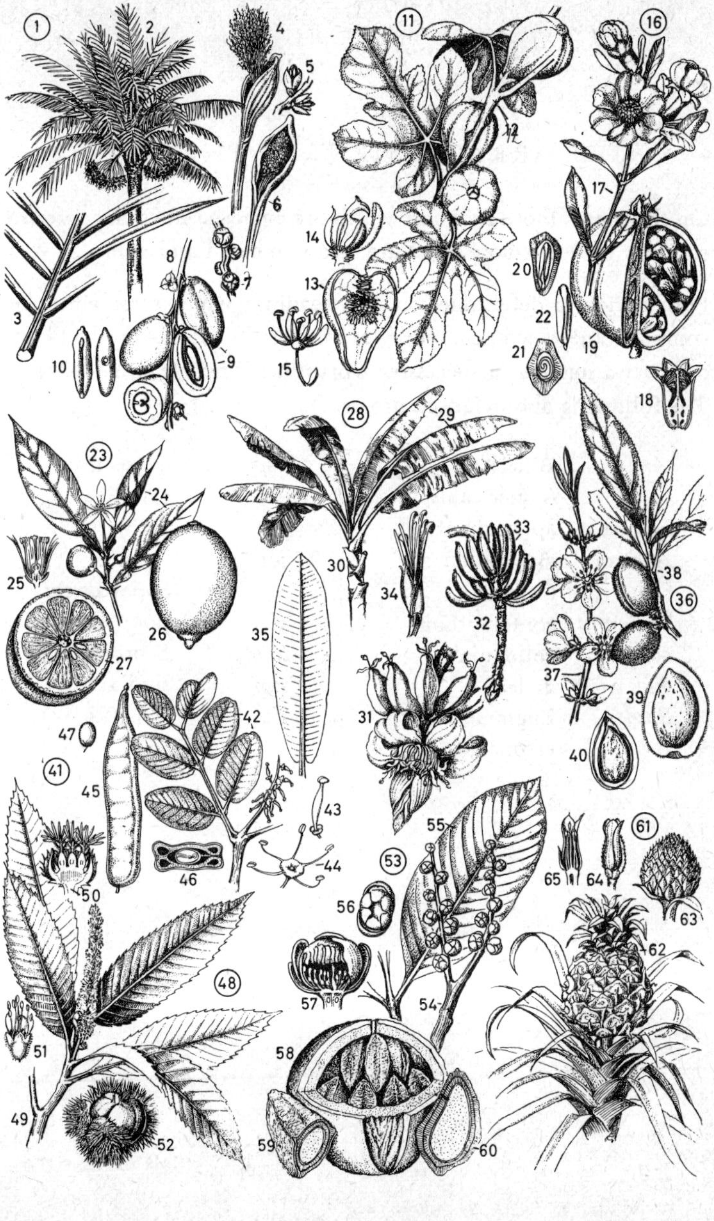
1
2
3
4
5
6
7
8
9
10
11
12
13
14
15
16
17
18
19
20
21
22
23
24
25
26
27
28
29
30
31
32
33
34
35
36
37
38
39
40
41
42
43
44
45
46
47
48
49
50
51
52
53
54
55
56
57
58
59
60
61
62
63
64
65

THE ARRANGEMENT OF THE BOOK

On the plates those numbers which are enclosed in circles refer to complex objects whose parts are also numbered and named.

Punctuation is determined by the headings which refer either to complex objects whose numbers are enclosed in circles on the plates or cover a number of successive words in the text (e. g. 17—24). The following abbreviations are used:

Am.	American (Americanism)
approx.	approximative
Austral.	Australian
Can.	Canadian
contempt.	contemptuous
coll.	colloquial
dial.	dialect
Engl.	England
err.	erroneous
esp.	especially
fam.	familiar
form.	formerly
joc.	jocular
opp.	opportunely
pop.	popular
Scot.	Scottish
sim.	similar
sl.	slang

THE ARRANGEMENT OF THE ENGLISH INDEX

The numbers in heavy type refer to the plate numbers, which are given at the top outer edge of each page.

To avoid repetition of the headwords a tilde (~) has been used; it stands for the whole of the preceding headword, or for that part of it which is followed by a point (·); when a tilde refers to a hyphened headword, only the part of the word preceding the hyphen is meant.

Americanisms are marked with an asterisk(*).

The alphabetical order ignores prepositions such as *of*, *with*, *from*, *under*, and the conjunction *and*, etc. (thus *bridge over railway* is arranged alphabetically as *bridge railway*), but takes into account the second parts of compound words such as *man-of-war*, *built-in*, *hide-and-seek*.

The following abbreviations are used in the index:

Agric.	Agriculture
Anat.	Anatomy
app.	apparatus
Arch.	Architecture
Astr.	Astronomy
Bak.	Bakery
Bot.	Botany
Box.	Boxing
Broadc.	Broadcasting
Build.	Building
Chem.	Chemistry
Cloth.	Clothing
Comm.	Commerce
Danc.	Dancing
Educ.	Education
El.	Electricity
Fenc.	Fencing
Fish.	Fishing
Footb.	Football
f.	for
fr.	from
furn.	furniture
Geol.	Geology
Geom.	Geometry
Gymn.	Gymnastics
Her.	Heraldry
Hunt.	Hunting
Hyg.	Hygiene
instr.	instrument
Just.	Justice
Knitt.	Knitting
loc.	locomotive
mach.	machine
Math.	Mathematics
Mech.	Mechanics
Med.	Medicine
Met.	Meteorology
Mineral.	Mineralogy
Mus.	Music
Mythol.	Mythology
mus. instr.	musical instrument
n.	noun
Nav.	Navigation
newsp.	newspaper
Opt.	Optics
Phot.	Photography
Print.	Printing
Railw.	Railway
rept.	reptile
Skat.	Skating
Sledg.	Sledging
Spinn.	Spinning
subst.	substance
Tech.	Technics
teleph.	telephone
Text.	Textile
T.V.	Television
Typ.	Typography
typewr.	typewriter
w.	with
Weav.	Weaving
Wrestl.	Wrestling
Zool.	Zoology

A

A.A. gun **222** 35, **223** 44
Aaron's rod **360** 9
abacus *[Art]* **316** 20
~ *[School]* **249** 38
abattoir **252** 51
abature **86** 8
abbey **314** 1–12
abbreviated title **178** 44
abdomen **18** 35–37
abdominal aorta **20** 16
~ muscle **20** 43, 44
abele **355** 23
aberdevine **346** 8
A-bomb **1** 47
aborigine **335** 37
about-sledge **132** 24
abruptly pinnate **354** 41
abscissa **329** 9
abscisse **329** 9
abseiling **282** 29–34
absorbent cotton* **28** 9
~ diaper **30** 6
absorption **212** 61
~ plant **139** 28
abstract **304** 33
~ number **326** 3
abutment *[Arch.]* **210** 28, **212** 80, **318** 20
acacia **54** 11
accelerator **185** 39
accent of pronunciation **325** 30–35
~ of stress **325** 30-35
acceptance **242** 12, 23
access manhole **254** 26
accessories **111** 31-59
accessory shoe **111** 21
acciaccatura **300** 29
accident **253** 58–69
~ on ice **17** 28–33
~ victim **253** 68
accidental **299** 51–59
Accipiters **347** 10–13
accolade **310** 66
accomodation bureau **200** 28
~ road **65** 12
~ train **203** 1
accompanist **298** 1
accordeon **303** 36
accordion **303** 36
accountant **238** 37
account book **238** 52
accounting machine **238** 60, **240** 42
accounts department **238** 37–80, **256** 27
account sheet **238** 62, 67
accused **248** 29
acerose **354** 34
acerous **354** 34
acetylene cylinder **135** 60
~ welding **135** 29–64
achaenocarp **60** 23
achene **60** 23
achievement *[Her.]* **246** 1–6
Achilles' tendon **20** 48
acid container **334** 62
acidifying apparatus **77** 27
acidometer **192** 44
acid solution **176** 4
acolyte **312** 45
aconite **363** 1
acorn **355** 4
acrobat **290** 47, **298** 9
acrobatic cycling **287** 31
~ dive **268** 41–46
~ diver **268** 5
acroter(ium) **316** 34
a. c. slip ring* **331** 81
act **290** 25, **298** 11, 15
acting area· **296** 3
~ lamp **297** 14
Actinia **349** 20
Actinophrys sol **340** 7
action **178** 3
~ check head **304** 27
~ of keys **304** 22–39
~ lever **304** 32
active carbon **255** 58
~ game **258** 23
actor **292** 28, **297** 37
actress **292** 27, **297** 38
acute accent **325** 30
~ angle **328** 10
~-angled triangle **328** 28
ad *[fam.]* **325** 51+52
Adam's apple **21** 13
adaption goggles **29** 46
adder **350** 40
adder's wort **360** 10
adding mechanism **256** 9
addition **326** 23
additional brake cock **206** 51
additive mixture of colours **320** 10
additives **167** 25
address **232** 37, **239** 4
addressee **232** 37, **239** 5
addressing machine **239** 37
addressograph **239** 37
A-deck **218** 28–30
adhesion engine **205** 1
~ motor rail coach **209** 1
adhesive disk **350** 26
~ plaster **17** 7
~ tape **23** 54, **238** 79
adjacent angle **328** 14
adjoining house **53** 23
adjunct* **250** 3
adjustable bar **68** 29
~ bow **68** 14
~ comb **158** 26
adjustable fence **128** 10
~ head rest **204** 35
~ knob **144** 22
~ nozzle **227** 45
~ nut **136** 33
~ pipe wrench **119** 57
~ proscenium **297** 22
~ resistance **331** 83
~ rulers **173** 37
~ spanner **119** 51, **192** 3
~ stamp **238** 41
~ table top **29** 15
~ wrench **119** 51
adjuster **176** 19, 22
adjusting device **306** 7
~ equipment **141** 56–59
~ knob **11** 41
~ lever **68** 39
~ rod **104** 31
~ screw **114** 79, **136** 105, **144** 46
~ spindle **221** 39
adjustment plate **142** 7
administration **212** 24
~ building **292** 4
~ of justice **248**
admiral *[Zool.]* **348** 1
admiral's cabin **213** 27
admirer **261** 22
admission ticket **296** 11
adolescent valley **13** 54
adult insect **342** 10
~ scale insect **81** 36
advance-booking office **256** 26
advance signal **199** 38
advancing cylinder **138** 39
adventitious root **354** 78, 80
advertisement **325** 52
~ pillar **253** 21
~ postmark **231** 50
advertising space **252** 14
~ text **178** 39
~ van **189** 9
advocate **248** 30
adze **126** 12
aerated water **47** 41
aeration system **339** 28
aerial **234** 21
~ cableway **209** 15–38
~ connection plate **236** 3
~ contact wire frog **193** 30
~ lead **223** 13
~ lead-in **218** 4
~ line **206** 2
~ photogrammetry
aerial root **354** 80, **15** 63–66
aerobatic figure **271** 17
aerodrome **230** 1
aero engine **227**
aerolite **7** 29
aeronautical radio navigation service **230** 22–53
aeroplane **225, 226**
aero-tow flight **271** 7
Afghan *[dog]* **71** 23
A flat major **300** 12
A flat minor **300** 15
Africa **14** 35–38, **15** 14
African elephant **351** 20
~ hemp **56** 9
after-burner **226** 14, **227** 44
~-burner turbojet power unit **227** 42
~ castle **213** 23
~ deck **218** 32
~ holds **218** 49
~noon dress **32** 28
~-shave lotion **104** 14
~ stay **270** 47
agaric **363** 11, **365** 28, 29
Agaricus mutabilis **365** 33
age **309**
ageing pit **151** 6
agency **256** 24
agent *[broker]* **243** 5
~* *[ticket ~]* **200** 39
aggregate **113** 36, **114** 26
~ fruit **60** 28
agitator motor **172** 5
agricultural machine **67, 68**
~ product **69** 1–45
agriculture **65**
Agulhas Current **15** 37
aid **17**
aileron **228** 46
~ rod **228** 40
aim **86** 34
aiming grip **90** 58
~ telescope* **15** 48, **87** 29
air **184** 75
~ adjusting screw **183** 60
~ blast **133** 6, 61
~-blast circuit-breaker **146** 34, **147** 51–62
~-blower **148** 15
~ brush **121** 12, **171** 51
~ compression chamber **227** 16
~ compression stage **227** 20, 35

air compressor **191** 26, **206** 17, **227** 6
~ compressor switch **206** 37
~-conditioning installation **339** 5
~-conditioning system **186** 22–24
~ container manometer **206** 47, 48
~ control cable **182** 30
~-cooling louvre **183** 14
aircraft **222** 29, 30, 50, 51, 74, **225**, **226**
~ aerial unit **226** 44
~ antenna unit **226** 44
~ cargo hatch **226** 35
~-carrier **222** 65–77
~ clock **228** 8
~ compass **228** 11
~ complement **226** 38–41
~ control **228**
~ control surfaces **228** 39 – 47
~ crane **222** 29
~ crew **226** 38–41
~ elevator* **222** 67, 74
~ engine **227**
~ engine nacelle **226** 6, 49
~ flying-controls system **228** 39–47
~ hangar **222** 30
~ instrument board **228** 3–16
~ instrument panel **228** 3–16
~ kitchen **226** 43
~ lift **222** 67, 74
~ navigation light **226** 46
~ passenger compartment **226** 45, 68
~ reactor **225** 71
~ receiver **230** 25
~ storage position **222** 50
~ tail-wheel **225** 8
~-towed take-off **271** 7
~ transmitter **230** 27
~ wing unit **228** 45
~ wireless operator **226** 40
air·crew* **226** 38–41
~ current **9** 25–29
~ cushion **23** 28
~ door **137** 16
~drome* **230** 1
~ duct **97** 59, **133** 5
~ duct handle **97** 60
~ feed pipe **140** 28
~ field* **230** 1
~ filter **93** 18, **184** 17
~ foam **255** 64
~-fuel-mixture **227** 36
air gun **258** 3
~-heater **133** 2
~-heating chamber **140** 29
~ hose **185** 36
~-impeller blade **183** 19
~ injector **40** 58
~ inlet **255** 60
~-inlet duct **47** 3
~-inlet valve **138** 50
~ intake **227** 2, 21
~ intake duct **47** 3
~ intake stage **227** 34
~ jet **183** 59
~-jet base **140** 62
~-knife **168** 31, 34, 35
~ layer **1** 32
~ letter* **232** 18
~ liner **226** 30
~ lock **137** 16
~ mail box* **231** 28
~-mail label **232** 32
~-mail letter **232** 18
~-mail posting box **231** 28
~-mail stamp *[U.S.A.]* **232** 19
~ man* **226** 38
~ mattress **266** 36
~ navigation aid **230** 22–38
~ outlet **162** 29, **186** 23, **339** 41
~ outlet duct **166** 30
~ outlet pipe **166** 30
~ outlet slot **187** 20
~ outlet valve **224** 24
~ passage **315** 4
~ passenger **226** 31
~ pipe **190** 29
airplane* **225** **226**
~ radio operator* **226** 40
airport **230**
~ administration office **230** 5
~ freight hangar **230** 21
~ meteorological station **230** 8
~ operational control **230** 5
~ radio beacon **230** 12 + 18
~ repair hangar **230** 9
~ restaurant **230** 5
~ terminal building **230** 5
air pre-heater **133** 58, **146** 11
~ pump **175** 6
~ pump bell-jar **331** 12
~ pump column **190** 27
~ pump plate **331** 14
~-purifier **51** 29
~ radio **230** 22-53
~ refuelling **226** 25
air-regulating screw **183** 60
~ regulator **334** 3, 8
~ separator **153** 24
~ shaft **1** 33, **92** 20
airscrew **226** 10
~-driven aeroplane **226** 1–8
~ power unit **227** 1, 8
~ reduction gear **227** 39
airship **226** 65
~ anchor mast **226** 66
~ envelope **226** 74
~-mooring mast **226** 66
~ pilot post **226** 69
~ propeller **226** 78
~ screw **226** 78
~ stern **226** 79
~ tail unit **226** 80–83
air sifter **153** 24
~ space **75** 50
airspeed indicator **228** 16
~ meter* **228** 16
air suction filter **206** 20
~ supply **168** 36
~ tanker **226** 26
~ temperature **267** 8
~ thermometer **228** 14
~ top *[toy]* **258** 25
~ traffic control procedure **230** 22–38
~ tube **76** 23, **224** 21
~ valve **180** 31,
~ vessel **254** 17, 50
airway **137** 25
air whistle lever **206** 50
aisle *[church]* **311** 27, **316** 63, **317** 2
~ *[forest]* **84** 1
à-jour-work **101** 27
akene **60** 23
Akropolis **316** 1–7
alarm *[clock]* **107** 41
~ bell **107** 42, **262** 41
~ clock **107** 41, **112** 19
Alaudidae **346** 18 + 19
alb **314** 38
Albania **14** 1
album **112** 52
~ cover **112** 53
albumen **75** 51
albuminous substance **75** 52
album leaf **112** 54
alburnum **115** 85, **354** 12
~ side **149** 43
alcohol **52** 32, **98** 56–59
~ container **28** 44
alcoholic liquor **98** 56–59
alcohol tap **28** 45
Alcor **5** 29
Aldebaran **5** 25
alder **355** 30
~ buckthorn **364** 13
~-fen peat **13** 18
ale-hoof **359** 18
Alençon lace **101** 30
alfalfa **70** 9
~ grass **130** 26
alga **362** 43, 48
algarroba **368** 41
algebra **327** 4 + 5
algebraic symbol **326** 9, **327** 5
alighting board **78** 49
aligning mark **323** 58
alignment guide **240** 13
alinement guide* **240** 13
alining mark* **323** 58
alison **63** 17
alkali cellulose **163** 7
~ and rinsing water casing **166** 4
alkylation **139** 31
~ plant **139** 31
aller **355** 30
alley **252** 40, **287** 2
~way* **252** 40
all-heal *[fam.]* **364** 5
all-in wrestling **281** 11 + 12
allotment **252** 68
all-purpose· excavator* **196** 1
~ table **44** 3
~ tank wagon **208** 13
~ tractor **67** 1
all-round-view·cabin **221** 5
~ windscreen **183** 43
all-steel body **185** 1
alluvial deposit **211** 52
all-weather roof **196** 38
~-wing model **271** 40
almond **45** 50, **368** 36, 40
almonds **46** 41
alms **311** 64
~ basket* **311** 63
~ box **311** 61
aloe **56** 13
alpenstock **282** 35
alphabetical flag **245** 22–28
alphabetic-numerical keyboard **241** 44
alpha particle emission **1** 10
~ radiation **1** 10
alpine climbing **282** 1–56
Alpine goat **352** 3
~ hut **282** 1
~ jacket **282** 7
~ marmot **351** 18
~ plant **362** 1–13
~ rose **362** 1
~ snowbell **362** 3
~ Soldanella **362** 3

Alsatian *[dog]* **71** 31
alsike (clover) **70** 3
Altair **5** 9
altar **311** 7, 37, **316** 48, 69
~ bell **313** 47
~ bells **313** 43
~ candle **311** 10, 41
~ carpet **311** 6
~ cloth **311** 9, 51
~ fire **311** 44
~ picture **311** 15
~ piece **311** 42
~ rails **311** 32
~ step **311** 8
alternating-current slip ring **331** 81
alternator **146** 23, **147** 26
altimeter **228** 6, 9
altitude **328** 27
alto clef **299** 12
alto-cumulus·castellanus **8** 16
~ cloud **8** 15
~ floccus **8** 16
alto-stratus· cloud **8** 8
~ praecipitans **8** 9
alto trombone **302** 46
alum **104** 22
aluminum* see aluminium
aluminium coin **244** 1–28
alyssum **63** 17
A major **300** 4
amalgam **27** 17
amaranth **62** 21
Amaranthus **62** 21
Amaryllis **56** 8
amateur camera **294** 24
~ gardener **55** 24
~ observation telescope **108** 44
~ photographer **257** 43
~ rider **272** 49
Amazon water lily **362** 17
amble **73** 40
ambulance **255** 19
~ attendant **255** 21
~ car **255** 19
~ station **200** 54, **291** 61
ambulatory **311** 35
ambush shed **86** 51
America **14** 29–34, **15** 12 + 13
American bison **352** 9
~ buggy **179** 49
~ football **275** 28–30
~ Organ **304** 43
~ softball **275** 39–54
amice **314** 40
A minor **300** 1
ammonia **164** 24
~-evaporator **261** 48
~ solution **52** 31
~-washer **148** 34
ammonia-water waste pipe **148** 35
ammonium sulphate solution **164** 26
ammunition **223** 72
amoeba **340** 1
amoretto **257** 20
amorino **257** 20
amount of bill **242** 18
~ of moisture **10** 23
~ to be paid **256** 8
amphibian *[Zool.]* **350** 20–26
~ *[aircraft]* **225** 32
amphitheater* **296** 17
amphora **309** 10
amplifier **236** 7, 16, **292** 59, **295** 20
~ rack **293** 9
~ valve **235** 15, 17
amplifying device **306** 42
ampoule **26** 32
ampulla **26** 32
amulet **337** 40
amusement machine **260** 48
anaesthesimeter **28** 37
anaesthetist **28** 30
anaesthetizer **28** 34-41
anaesthetizing apparatus **28** 34–41
anaglyph **322** 33
anal fin **350** 9
analytical balance **333** 25
anamorphic lens **294** 37
anamorphoscope **294** 43
anamorphote front lens **294** 43
anamorphous lens **294** 37
ananas **368** 61
~ flower **368** 64
ancestor **337** 17
'ancestor stone' **309** 6
anchor **217** 75, 76
anchorage **210** 40, **211** 13
anchor cable **213** 18, **217** 74, **218** 45
~ chain **210** 19, **218** 45
~ gear **218** 44–46
~ hawser **213** 18
~ mast **226** 66
androgynous flower **358** 10, **366** 14
Andromeda **5** 24
anemometer **10** 27, **230** 19
anemone *[Bot.]* **359** 5, **361** 1
anemophilous plant **61** 44–51
aneroid **10** 8
~ barometer **10** 8
~ box **10** 6
aneroid chamber **10** 6
anesthetist **28** 30
anesthetizer **28** 34–41
anesthetizing apparatus **28** 34–41
angel **311** 54
~ cake* **97** 44
angle *[Geom.]* **328** 1–23
~ *[iron]* **136** 1
~ brace **116** 57
~ of departure **87** 75
~ of descent **87** 78
~dozer **196** 28
~ drive **91** 25
~ of elevation **87** 76
~ handpiece **27** 15
~ hinge **134** 58
~ iron **136** 1
angler **89** 7
~ fish **349** 6
angle ring **141** 66
~ screwdriver **192** 30
~ shears **119** 2
~ stitch **102** 8
~ symbol **327** 23
~ tie **116** 57
~ tower **310** 14
angling **89** 7–12
Angora cat **74** 17
angular point **328** 1
~ reamer **119** 10
animal **74, 351–353**
~ awaiting slaughter **94** 2
~cule **340** 7, 9
~ glue **127** 39
~ on show **339** 20
~ trainer **290** 52
ankle gaiter **283** 57
~-sock **33** 64
annelid **340** 16
annex **53** 1
announcer **298** 2
annual clock **107** 45
~ fair **291** 1–67
~ meadow grass **359** 39
~ ring **84** 23
annuent muscle **20** 34, **21** 1
annuity **243** 11–19
annular kiln **151** 19
annulus **328** 57
anode **332** 30
~ rod **172** 2
Anopheles **341** 33
anorthic crystal system **330** 26
anserine bird **343** 15–17
ant **342** 21 + 22
Antarctic **15** 18
~ Current **15** 44
~ Drift **15** 44
~ Ocean **15** 22
antarctic sea **90** 37
ant-eater **351** 10
antechamber **184** 66
antelope **352** 5
antenna *[aerial]* **235** 4
~ *[Zool.]* **82** 3, **342** 27
~ switch **235** 3
anther **60** 45, **61** 10, **356** 35
anthozoon **340** 35
anthropoid *n.* **353** 14 – 16
anti-aircraft· defence **222** 35
~ gun **223** 44
anti-cathode **332** 31
~cline **12** 16
~cyclone **9** 6
~-dazzle light **185** 17
~-dazzle shield **205** 62
~-distortion magnet **236** 26
~-friction bearing **136** 67
antique shop **253** 57
anti-roll bar **184** 13
antiseptic **104** 16
anti-set-off spray **175** 10
~-skid tread **189** 13
anti-syphon trap **119** 41
antlers **88** 5–11, 29–31
anuran **350** 23–26
anus **22** 62
anvil *[smith]* **119** 19, **132** 16, **133** 21
~ *[Anat.]* **19** 61
~ bed **133** 29
~ block **133** 21
~ block insert **133** 22
~ body **132** 17
~ chisel **132** 29
~ cutter **132** 29
~ face **132** 19
~ fuller **132** 28-30
~ hardy **132** 28–30
~ plate **132** 19
~ tool **132** 28–30
aorta **20** 10, **22** 54
aortic arch **20** 10
~ valve **22** 49
apache girl **289** 9
apartment hotel* **252** 49
~ house* **53** 12, **252** 49
ape **353** 14–16
Apenodytes **343** 4
aperture diaphragm knob **109** 5
~ f. radio-isotopes **1** 44
apex **87** 77
aphid **82** 38, 39
aphis **342** 13–15
apiarist **78** 57
apiary **78** 56
apiculture **78**
Apocalypse **307** 50
Apollo **308** 15

apostrophe **325** 22
apparatus **331** 22-41, 45-85, **332** 1–35
appendix **22** 18
apple **60** 56
~ blossom **60** 54
~ blossom weevil **81** 10
~ core **60** 59
~ flower **60** 54
~ grub **60** 64
~ of love **59** 12
~ pip **60** 60
~ quince **60** 49
~ skin **60** 57
~ stalk **60** 61
~ tree **60** 51
~ twig **60** 52
appliance **331**, **332**
~ plug **120** 24
~ room **255** 1
appoggiatura **300** 28
appointment book **200** 10
apprentice **238** 44
approach **16** 16, **283** 9, **310** 34
~-radar set **230** 10
~ f. trucks* **202** 9
approximately equal **327** 17
apricot **61** 35
~ blossom **61** 33, 34
~ flower **61** 34
~ leaf **61** 36
~ tree **61** 33–36
~ twig **61** 33
apron *[Cloth.]* **32** 17
~ *[Tech.]* **67** 42, **142** 16
'apron' *[Spinn.]* **157** 16
~ pocket **32** 18
~ string **32** 24
apse **316** 64, **317** 5
aquarelle **44** 19
aquarium **339** 26
Aquarius **6** 42
aquatic plant **362** 14–57
aquatics **269**, **270**
aquatic sports **269**, **270**
aquatint **323** 14–24
aqueduct **316** 53
aquifer **12** 22, **254** 2
Aquila **5** 9
Aquilegia **62** 10
Ara ararauna **345** 2
arabesque **288** 9
Arabian capital **319** 18
Arabic numeral **326** 2
~ script **324** 2
~ writing **324** 2
arachnid **342** 40–47
araneid **342** 40–47
Araucaria **56** 16
arbor* see arbour
arboreal frog **350** 24
arbor vitae **312** 29, **356** 39
arbour **257** 17
arbour(ed) walk **54** 5
arc *[Geom.]* **328** 53
~ *[Tech.]* **135** 7, **295** 42
arcading **317** 8, 10,
arch *[Arch.]* **114** 6, **210** 12, **318** 19–37
~ *[foot]* **21** 61
~ *[lyre]* **301** 15
Archaster **349** 17
arch bridge **210** 41
~ crown **210** 44
arched bridge **210** 12
~ span **210** 16
~ tomb recess **312** 63
archer **287** 37
Archer **5** 37, **6** 40
archery **287** 37–47
Archimedean drill **129** 22
architect **292** 43
architect's plan **144** 57
architrave **316** 18
archives **292** 5
archivolt **317** 25
arch springer **210** 42
~way **266** 52, **319** 3
arcing horn **146** 47, **147** 61
arc lamp **171** 24, **331** 24
arcosolium **312** 63
arc-shaped screen **294** 49
arctic dog **336** 2
Arctic Ocean **15** 21
Arcturus **5** 30
area **9** 5, 6
~ of deposition **11** 47
~ letter box **200** 52
~ mail **231** 38
~ to be operated **28** 25
~ of precipitation **9** 30
arena **287** 58, **290** 21
~ entrance **290** 11
~-type stage **296** 1–4
areola **18** 29
Ares **308** 9
argent *[Her.]* **246** 25
Argentina **14** 32
Argentine Republic **14** 32
Argo **5** 45
Aries **6** 32
arillode mace **366** 34
arista **69** 12
arithmetic **326** 1–26, **327**
arithmetical operation **326** 23–26
~ series **327** 11
arm *[Anat.]* **18** 43–48, **19** 12–14
~ *[horse]* **73** 21
arm *[Tech.]* **220** 53, **221** 2
~ *[Geom.]* **328** 7
~ *[weapon]* **87** 2
armadillo **351** 8
arm armour **310** 47
armature *[magnet]* **233** 55, **331** 80
~ *[device]* **322** 25
~ lever **233** 56
~ support **322** 24
armband **255** 22
~ bandage **17** 1
~chair **47** 57
Armenian script **324** 3
arm-hold **281** 15
~let **38** 23, **251** 11
~-lock **281** 11
armor(ed) * see armour(ed)
armorial bearings **246** 1–6
~ shield of locality **244** 14
armoring * see armouring
armory *[Her.]* **246** 1–36
~* *[Gymn.]* **279** 1–48
armour **308** 11
armoured ship **222** 31–64
armpit **18** 26
~ hair **18** 27
arm prosthesis **23** 49
~-rest **47** 60, **203** 47
arms *[Her.]* **246** 1–6
arms bending upwards **278** 6
arm sling **17** 2
arms-raising sideways **278** 8
arm-stretching upwards **278** 5
arnica **364** 2
arpeggio **300** 36 + 37
arrangement **259** 37
arrangement of rollers **141** 75
arrest **248** 1
arrested person **248** 5
arrester **205** 24
~ wire **222** 71
arresting gear* **222** 71
arrest warrant **248** 4
arrière-bras **310** 47
arrival and departure lines **199** 14
~ indicator **201** 26
~ schedule* **200** 19
~ timetable **200** 19
arrow **287** 41, **308** 28
~ head **287** 42, **309** 4
~head *[Bot.]* **362** 51
~ point **287** 42
~ shaft **287** 43
~ stem **287** 43
arrow tip **287** 42
~-type wing aircraft **225** 27
art **315–319**
~ album **47** 54
~ of Asia Minor **315** 37
~ of the Assyrians **315** 29–36
~ of the Baroque **318** 1–8
~ of dancing **288** 29–41
~ director **292** 43
Artemis **308** 12
arteria* *[road]* **16** 83
arterial avenue **252** 32
~ blood **20** 12
~ road **16** 17
artery *[Anat.]* **20** 1
~ *[road]* **252** 32
~ forceps **28** 55
~ tweezers **28** 55
Artesian well **12** 26
art of fencing **277** 1–66
~ glazier **122** 8
arthropod **342** 1–23
artichoke **59** 41
article *[object]* **129** 19
~ *[newsp.]* **325** 40
articulate *n.* **342**
articulated diesel train **207** 37 + 38
~ locomotive **205** 39
artificial arm **23** 49
~ bait **89** 36–43
~ breathing device* **17** 27
~ falls* **257** 9
~ firmament **6** 13
~ flower **36** 36
~ fly **89** 36
~ honeycomb **78** 42
~ horizon **228** 4
~ ice rink **284** 3
~ leg **23** 48
~ limb **23** 48–50
~ maggot **89** 38
~ respiration **17** 24–27
~ shrimp **89** 37
~ silk **163** 27
~ ski jump *[bill]* **283** 7
~ sponge **112** 16
~ sun **24** 17
~ waterfall **257** 9
~ waves **25** 3
artiodactyl **74** 9
artist **321** 2
artiste **291** 25–28, **298** 19
artistes' agent **290** 18
artistic dance **288** 29–41
artist's hat **36** 9
Art Nouveau style **318** 18
art of the Persians **315** 21–28

avalanche gallery **286** 3
avant-bras **310** 47
Ave bead **313** 30
avenging goddess **308** 51
avenue **262** 11
~ * **252** 32
aviary **339** 23
aviation gasoline **139** 37
~ ground **230** 1
~ spirit **139** 37
awl **123** 27, 32, 33, **124** 9
awn **69** 12
awner **67** 48
awning **39** 71, **79** 42, **213** 15, **216** 59
~crutch **213** 14
~ spar **216** 61
~ stanchion **216** 60
ax* see axe
axe **64** 20, **85** 13, **115** 73, **150** 38
axil *[Bot.]* **354** 25
axillary bud **354** 25
axis *[Bot.]* **356** 3
~ *[Geom.]* **108** 10, **329** 2, 3, 23, 24
~ of abscissae **329** 2
~ of anticline **12** 17
~ of coordinates **329** 2 + 3
~ of ordinates **329** 3
~ of parabola **329** 17
~ of symmetry **328** 25, **330** 4
~ of syncline **12** 19
axle **131** 11, **180** 76
~ * **183** 13
~ arms **131** 13
~ bearing **204** 66, **205** 10
~-pressure equalizer **206** 11
~ shaft **204** 64
~ suspension spring **204** 68
~ tree **131** 11
~-tree bed bolster **131** 6
azalea **56** 12
azimuth **218** 6
azure **246** 28, **320** 6

B

babe in arms **30** 26
babies' clothes **31** 16
~ wear **31** 1–60
baboon **353** 13
babouche **48** 34
baby **30** 26
~ bathtub* **30** 25
~ buggy* **258** 30
~ bus **188** 1
~ car **183** 41
~ carriage **258** 30
~ doll **50** 4
baby enema syringe **23** 59
~ equipment **30**
~ hygiene **30**
Babylonian art **315** 19 + 20
~ frieze **315** 19
baby powder **30** 38
~ rabbit **74** 18
baby's bath **30** 25
~ bonnet **31** 21
~ bootee **31** 18
~ bottle **30** 46
baby scales **30** 28
baby's cap **31** 21
~ coat **31** 20
~ cot **30** 11
~ crib* **30** 11, **49** 2
~ dressing table **30** 1
~ jacket **31** 20
~ nail-scissors **30** 45
~ rattle **30** 42
~ rompers **31** 19
~ shoe **100** 14
~ socks **30** 16
~ vest **31** 17
baby-walker* **49** 3
Bacchante **308** 35
Bacchic staff **308** 33
Bacchus **308** 32
back *[body]* **18** 22–25
~ *[knife]* **46** 56
~ *[windmill]* **91** 2
~ *[Sports]* **268** 50, **276** 58
back•band **72** 19
~-bend **278** 28, **298** 12
~board **275** 32
~-bone **19** 2–5
~ of book **178** 41
~ brush **51** 26
~ building **53** 1
~ of chair **47** 58
~ check **304** 27
~-cloth **297** 10
~-comb **38** 13, **103** 36
~ corner pin **287** 14
~-door **53** 15
~-drop **297** 10
~ fat **95** 40
~ filling **212** 7
~ garden **39** 57
~ gauge **177** 17, **178** 6
~ground **292** 33
~ of hand **21** 83
~-hand stroke **276** 20
~ of head **18** 2
backing *[linen]* **102** 67
~ *[Tech.]* **254** 29
~ gauze **178** 20
~ material **177** 33
~ mull **178** 20
back of knee **18** 51
~ margin **178** 55
~ pad **72** 17, 31
~-pedal brake **180** 63
~ player **276** 43
back pressure valve **135** 34
~ rest **159** 37
~ row pins **287** 13
~-scouring valve **211** 61
~ seat **183** 8, **185** 57
~ shield **350** 29
~side **18** 40
~sight leaf **87** 67
~sight slide **87** 69
~ spacer **240** 22
~ spin **264** 4
~ square **127** 15, **145** 35
~-stage loudspeaker **294** 44
~stay **214** 19
~stiched seam **101** 1
~ stop **304** 31
~ strap **99** 42
~ stroke **268** 36
~ tooth **21** 35
~ trouser pocket **34** 33
~ vault **279** 49
~ weight **224** 26
~ wheel **179** 17
~ wheel brake linkage **182** 15
~ wheel swinging arm **182** 5
~yard **53** 1–49
bacon **96** 11, 26, 27
~-slicer **96** 19
Bactrian camel **351** 29
badge **247** 24, **280** 59
~ f. masked ball **289** 34
badger **88** 48
~-baiter **71** 33
~ dog **71** 33
badgerer **71** 33
badger-hair softener **121** 20
bad land* **65** 1
badminton **276** 36
bad visibility landing **230** 22–38
baffle board **234** 50,
bag *[band~]* **37** 10
~ *[paper~]* **98** 48, 49
~ *[bagpipe]* **301** 9
~ *[booty]* **86** 38
~ of cement **113** 43
baggage* **200** 21
~ car * **203** 11
~ elevator* **201** 62
~ man* **200** 17, **259** 17
~ net* **203** 42
~ rack* **203** 42, **204** 33
baggy breeches **338** 34
bag net **89** 14
~pipe **301** 8
~ f. rods **269** 64
bag of letter mail **203** 22
~ of parcels mail **203** 23
~ of rolls **97** 3
bags **34** 10
bag wig **35** 4
bailey **310** 2
bails **275** 55
bait **83** 1, **86** 21
~ can **89** 18
~ tin **89** 18
baked-clay• crucible **334** 31
~ triangle **334** 17
bakehouse **97** 57–80
bakelite pad **159** 64
baker-boy beret **36** 55
baker's boy **97** 1
~ cap **97** 34
~ oven **97** 61
~ scraper **42** 51
~ shop **253** 52
~ shovel **97** 66
bakery **97**
baking-dish **42** 40
~-sheet **42** 53
~-tin **42** 40
balalaika **303** 28
Balances **5** 19, **6** 38
balance *[scales]* **98** 12
~ *[watch]* **107** 24
~ beam **333** 30
~ book **238** 64
~ bridge **210** 61
~ column **221** 33, **333** 29
~ rail **301** 39
~ spring **107** 25
~ weight **212** 76, **221** 38, **238** 39
~ wheel **102** 17
balancing act **290** 44
~ exercise **279** 41
~ form **279** 40
~ pole **279** 42, **290** 42
balata **121** 44
balcony *[house]* **39** 18, **262** 23
~* *[Theatre]* **296** 18
~ apartment **39** 72–76
~ door **48** 22
~ flat **39** 72–76
~ flower box **39** 20
baldachin **312** 49
baldaquin **312** 49
bald head **35** 22
~ part **35** 21
~ pate **35** 22
bale **202** 12
~-breaker **156** 7
baleen bone **37** 19
bale gauge **221** 29
~ of goods **221** 34
~ of perlon staple **164** 62
~ of rayon staple **163** 34
~ of straw **65** 29, **202** 29, **273** 40
baling press **163** 33

bar screen **153** 5
~ of staples **240** 40
~ stool **259** 53
~tender* **259** 62, **260** 8
~ trio **259** 44
barysphere **11** 5
basal leaf **367** 2
~ pinacoid **330** 20
bascule **210** 62
~ bridge **210** 61
base *[mach.]* **172** 11, **177** 25
~ *[Math.]* **327** 1,6, **328** 27, **329** 35
~ *[Her.]* **246** 22 + 23
~ * **198** 36
~ bag **275** 51
baseball *[ball]* **275** 54
~ *[game]* **275** 39–54
~ bat **275** 52
~ field **275** 39–45
~ park* **275** 39–45
baseboard **111** 9, **112** 33, **118** 21, **285** 14
~ swivel catch **171** 8
base concrete **197** 45
~ line **276** 3 to 10, 52
~ log **85** 9
~ of machine **162** 15
~man **275** 50
basement **39** 1
~ stairs **118** 16
~ wall **118** 1
~ window **39** 27, **113** 3
base paper **168** 32
~-paver **196** 31
~ plate **10** 14, **141** 51, **160** 34, **198** 36
~ plate screw **198** 38
~ wall of house **39** 17
basher **36** 22
basic material **163** 1
~ position **278** 1
basidiospore **365** 7
basidium **365** 7
basilar leaf **359** 12
basilica **316** 61
basilisk *[Zool.]* **350** 30
~ *[Mythol.]* **307** 34
basin **51** 52–68, **217** 33, **311** 3
basinet **310** 61
basin shower **104** 37
~ stand **26** 24
basket **130** 11, 16, **275** 33
~ ball **275** 31–38
~ ball court **275** 34-36
~ baller **275** 37
~ ball player **275** 37
~ cord **226** 59
~ crib on wheels **30** 32
~-maker **130** 33
~-maker's plane **130** 39
~-making **130** 1–40
basket ring **226** 58
~ of rolls **97** 2
~ rope **226** 59
basketry **130** 1–40
basket weave **165** 11
~-work **130** 1–40
bas relief **322** 33
bass **302** 23
~ belly bridge **304** 13
~ bridge **304** 13
~ button **303** 43
~ clarinet **302** 34
~ clef **299** 11
~ drum **302** 55, **303** 47
bassinet on wheels **30** 32
bassoon **302** 28
basso relievo **322** 33
bass register **303** 44
~ stop **303** 44
~ string **303** 24, **304** 12
~ stud **303** 43
~ tone control **234** 44
~ trombone **302** 46
~ tuba **302** 44
~ viol **301** 23
~ violin **302** 16
bast **130** 29
bastard title **178** 44
bast binding **57** 35
~ hat **36** 8
basting thread **102** 52
bast shoe **100** 7, **117** 75
bat **351** 9
batch **81** 2, 30
bateau **210** 18
~ bridge **210** 17
bath **25** 6
~* **51** 1–28
Bath chair **23** 51
bath crystals **51** 25
bather **267** 30
bathing beach **267**
~-cap **267** 29, 44
~-gown **267** 25
~ platform **267** 9
~-shoes **267** 23
~-suit **267** 26
~-trunks **267** 27
~-wrap **267** 25
bath lid **172** 30
~-mat **51** 21, **262** 49
~ mit **51** 7
batholith **11** 29
bathrobe* **33** 6, **48** 56
bathroom **51** 1–28, **262** 40
~ cabinet **51** 82
~ mirror **51** 52
~ scales **51** 1
~ stool **51** 2
baths **25** 1–6, **268** 1–32
bath salts **51** 25
~ slipper **51** 20, **100** 48
~ soap **51** 11
bath sponge *[Zool.]* **340** 13
~ sponge **51** 12
~ thermometer **30** 21, **51** 8
~ towel **25** 17, **51** 23
~ water **51** 9
bathysphere **11** 5
baton *[conductor]* **296** 27
~ *[Sports]* **280** 15
~ *[Police]* **248** 10
~-changing **280** 14
~-exchange area **280** 16
~ roll **97** 38
batrachian **350** 23–26
batsman **275** 46, 59
batsman's lines **275** 40
bat's wing **307** 4
battement **288** 7
batten gauge **117** 18
battens **117** 17, **217** 59, **297** 13
batter's box **275** 41
battery **138** 56, **185** 33, **192** 38
~ bow* **108** 24
~ box **192** 41
~ case **111** 50, **183** 22
~ cell tester **192** 46
~-charger **192** 42–45
~ leg **108** 24
~ locomotive **138** 46
~ master switch **228** 27
~ railcar **206** 58
~ room **223** 40
~ stand **185** 34
~ terminal **192** 39
batting crease **275** 57
~ side **275** 46, 59
battle axe **335** 16
~ cruiser **222** 26
~dore **258** 45
~field **16** 93
~ment **310** 6, 7
~ship **213** 51–60, **222** 31
battue **86** 34–39
baulk **65** 3, **115** 87
Bauta stone **309** 18
Bavarian leathers **31** 50
bay *[lake]* **13** 7
~ *[barn]* **64** 42
~ *[window]* **115** 59
bayadere **289** 25
bay antler **88** 7
B-deck **218** 32–42
B/E **242** 12
beach **13** 35–44, **267**
~ attendant **267** 34
~-bag **267** 24
~-ball **267** 18
~ debris **13** 29
~-guard **267** 1
~-hat **36** 57, **267** 20
~-jacket **267** 21
~ lagoon **13** 44
~ mattress **267** 17
beach rubble **13** 29
~ sandal **100** 34
~ -shoes **267** 23
~-suit **267** 19
~ tent **267** 45
~-trousers **267** 22
~-wear **267** 19–23
beacon **16** 10, 49, **230** 12, 18
bead **50** 20
~ *[abacus]* **249** 39
~ *[rosary]* **313** 29, 30
~ *[antlers]* **88** 30
~ -and-dartmoulding **316** 38
~ buoy **219** 55
beading kammer **119** 46
~ iron **119** 9, 47
~ machine **119** 21
~ swage **119** 46
beagle **272** 63
beak *[Tech.]* **26** 54, **132** 18
~ *[Skat.]* **284** 22
beaker *[cup]* **49** 29
~ *[Chem.]* **334** 20
beak iron **132** 11, 18
beam *[Tech.]* **114** 57
~ *[Weav.]* **158** 41, **159** 48
~ *[antlers]* **88** 11
~ balance **97** 77
~ bearing roller **158** 58
~ bleaching plant **161** 40
~ compass(es) **119** 44, **144** 13
~ flange **158** 30, **159** 49, **160** 26
~ head **116** 33
beaming machine **158** 22
beam of light **219** 58
~ of roof **116** 29
~ ruffle **159** 60
~ trammel* **119** 44, **144** 13
bean *[plant]* **59** 8, **70** 15
~ *[coffee]* **366** 5
~ blossom **59** 9
~ flower **59** 9
~ plant **59** 8
~ pole **55** 28
~ stalk **59** 10
~ stem **59** 10
~ stick **55** 28
bear **353** 9–11
~berry **361** 15
~ claw **335** 14
beard **35**
~ *[animal]* **88** 73
~ *[Bot.]* **69** 12
Bear Driver **5** 30
bearer **312** 40, 43, 46
~ certificate of shares **243** 11
bearing *n.* **116** 83, **136** 67
~ plate ***219** 30

bicycle panniers **181** 19
~ pedal **180** 78
~ pump **180** 48
~ rack **253** 43
~ saddle **180** 22
~ speedometer **180** 33
~ stand **253** 43
~ trailer **181** 20
bidet **51** 51
Biedermeier dress **289** 22
~ gentleman **338** 73
~ sofa **318** 17
~ style **318** 17
bier **312** 41
bifocal glass **108** 11
Big Dipper* **5** 29
big dipper **291** 39
bight **13** 7
big toe **21** 52
~ top **290** 1
bijouterie **38** 1–33
bike **180** 1
bilberry **361** 23
bile duct **22** 37 + 38
bilge blocks **217** 37
~ keel **217** 44
~ strake **217** 43
bill *[poster]* **253** 22
~ *[~ of exchange]* **242** 12
~* *[invoice]* **238** 50, **256** 7
~* *[note]* **244** 29–39, **256** 6
~ *[bird]* **88** 84
~board* **113** 45, **145** 45
~ clause **242** 17
billet *[Hunt.]* **272** 64
bill of exchange **242** 12
~ of fare **260** 21
~hook **85** 30
billiard ball **264** 1
~ clock **264** 17
~ cloth covering **264** 15
~ player **264** 8
~ room **264** 7–19
billiards **264**
~ w. pockets **264** 7
billiard stroke **264** 2–6
~ table **264** 14
bill of lading **221** 25
billowy cloud **8** 1
bill stamp **242** 24
Billy* **248** 10
billy-cock **36** 7
bi-motor aircraft **226** 3
bin **80** 32, **196** 45, **253** 46
binary stars **5** 29
bind *n.* *[Mus.]* **300** 41
binder *[book~]* **177** 2
~ *[cigar]* **105** 6
binder *[office]* **238** 13
~ *[app.]* **65** 33
~ *[baby]* **30** 44
~ injector **196** 53
~ jet **196** 53
bindery* **177** 1–38
binding *[book]* **178** 40–42
~ *[trimming]* **102** 5
~ *[ski]* **283** 45–50
~ locking place **165** 28
~ machine **177** 39
bindweed **63** 26
bing **137** 9
binocular inclined twin tube **110** 18
~ microscope **110** 9
binoculars **108** 37
biplane **225** 7
biprism **330** 22
bipyramid **330** 18
birch **257** 40, **355** 9
~ broom **52** 78, **53** 45
~ rod **25** 13
~ twig **25** 13
bird **343–347**
~ bath **54** 15
~ cage **339** 23
~ capable of flight **343** 5–30
~-foot **70** 11
~ house **54** 14
~ of paradise **345** 3
~ of passage **344** 7
~ of prey **347**
bird's body **307** 57
~ claws **307** 61
~-foot **70** 11
~-foot trefoil **360** 17
~-mouth **85** 20
~ talons **307** 61
~ wing **36** 52
bird table **54** 14
biretta **314** 36
birth *[advertisement]* **325** 51
birth-wort **360** 22
biscuit **97** 42
~ barrel **45** 35
bisector **328** 30
bishop *[Church]* **314** 43
~ *[chess]* **265** 10
bishop's crook **314** 48
bison **309** 9, **352** 9
bistort **360** 10
bit *[tool]* **129** 16, **139** 20
~ *[key]* **134** 47
~ *[horse]* **72** 52
bitch **74** 16
~ fox **88** 42
bitter cherry **61** 5
bitumen **139** 47
~ blowing plant **139** 58
~-heater **196** 46
~ layer **196** 58
~ oxidation **139** 58
~ plant **139** 35
bituminous layer **196** 58
~ road **196** 55
black *[colour]* **320** 13
~ *[negro]* **337** 13
Black *[roulette]* **263** 21
black alder **364** 13
~ arches moth **82** 17
~ beetle **341** 18
~berry **60** 29
~bird **346** 13
black-board· **249** 2
~ cloth **249** 5
~ frame **249** 3
~ sponge **249** 4
black bread **97** 26
blackbuck **352** 5
~cock **86** 11, **88** 66
black draughtsman **265** 19
Black Friar **314** 19
black game **88** 66
~ grouse **88** 66
~-headed gull **343** 14
~jack* **248** 10
~ key **304** 5
~-letter **325** 3
~ level clamp **236** 12
~-line block **323** 2
~ martin **343** 24
Black Monk **314** 13
black nightshade **363** 5
~ pieces **265** 5
~ poplar **355** 15
~ salsify **59** 35
blacksmith **132**
blacksmith's tongs **132** 1–4
~ workshop **132** 1–42
black square **265** 3
~thorn **358** 27
~ tuxedo bow tie* **34** 64
bladder *[Med.]* **22** 33, 78
~ *[Zool.]* **350** 25
blade *[axe, etc.]* **46** 54, **115** 62, **196** 21, **282** 41
~ *[Bot.]* **69** 20, **354** 85
~bone **95** 22, 30
~ of the foresight **87** 72
~ of grass **354** 83–85
~-slewing gear **196** 22
blaeberry **361** 23
blaid a chiestera **287** 51
blancmange powder **98** 50
blank *[metal]* **244** 43
~* *[form]* **232** 6–15
blanket **30** 7, **48** 51
~ of snow **286** 20
blanking tool **134** 61
blank sheet **174** 24, **175** 23
~sheet pile **174** 24
blast chamber **227** 60–63
~-deflector **229** 30
blasted rock **150** 4
blaster **150** 25
blast furnace **140** 1
~-furnace plant **140** 1–19
~-furnace shaft **140** 7
~ head **147** 55
blasting cartridge **150** 27
~ position **140** 50
blast main **140** 61, **141** 2
blastoderm **75** 54
blastodisc **75** 54
blast pipe **205** 25
blazonry **246** 1–36
bleaching **163** 21
~ plant **161** 31
bleach vat **161** 47
bleeding-heart **62** 5
~-out **94** 15
blending chest **168** 1
blimp *[Film]* **292** 48
blind *n.* **39** 71
blind alley **252** 40
~ arcading **317** 10
blinder(s)* *[horse]* **72** 26, **272** 42
blind landing **230** 22–38
~man's buff **50** 5
~ person's glasses **108** 21
~ spot **21** 50
~ worm **350** 37
blinker *[light]* **186** 27, **193** 20
~* **16** 49
~ *[horse]* **72** 26
blister **222** 58
block *[piece]* **119** 18, **322** 27
~ *[tackle]* **216** 49
~ *[Print.]* **172** 31
~ *[organ]* **305** 20
~ of apartments* **39** 77–81
~ of balcony flats **39** 72–76
~ brake **136** 95
~ calendar **238** 2
~-etching machine **172** 23
~ of flats **39** 77–81, **252** 49
~ flute **301** 7
blocking oscillator **236** 28
block instrument **199** 62
~ line **139** 6
~-making **172** 23–30
~ mountains **12** 4–11
~ mounting **172** 34

book-keeping department **238** 37–80
~-keeping machine **238** 60
~ kiosk **200** 26
~marker **178** 70, 71
~ plate **178** 51
~ section **177** 12
~seller's shop (store*) **253** 3
~-sewing machine **178** 16
~ shelf **250** 12, **314** 12
~shop **253** 3
~stall **206** 26
~stand* **200** 26
~ stock **250** 11
~store* **253** 3
~ of tickets **201** 55
~ tray **178** 23
~ uncased **178** 23
boom **114** 36, **193** 44, **210** 49, **292** 21
boomerang **335** 39
boom fore sail **215** 12
boot *[shoe]* **99** 38–55, **100** 8
~ *[car]* **185** 23
~ *[organ pipe]* **305** 17
~black* **200** 11
Boötes **5** 30
booth **251** 23, **291** 44
~* **231** 24
boot-jack **52** 47
~lace **99** 47
~-lid **185** 7
~-lid handle **186** 26
~ lock **186** 25
~maker **99** 23
~maker's workshop **99** 1–37
boots **259** 17
boot strap* **99** 42
~-stretcher **100** 16
~string* **99** 47
~ tree **100** 16
border *[rim]* **43** 26, **55** 20, **130** 17
~ *[Theatre]* **297** 12
~ bed **55** 18
~ check **247** 12
~ of concrete-slab **55** 20
bordered white moth **82** 28
border w. perennials **55** 22
~ shears **58** 24
~ zone **6** 49
bore **87** 40, **136** 84
boreal climate **9** 56
bore axis **87** 38
borecole **59** 34
borehole **12** 25, **139** 19, **150** 12
bore surface **87** 39
boring machine **192** 52
borrower's ticket **250** 25
bosk **257** 4
bosket **257** 4
bosom **18** 30
boss *[Arch.]* **317** 32
~ *[shield]* **310** 58
bostryx **354** 76
bosun* **216** 57
botanical gardens **252** 57
botany **354**
bottle **93** 40, **260** 16
~ *[Chem.]* **334** 57, 58
~ basket **45** 52, **80** 34
~-blowing machine **155** 12
~ bobbin **160** 4
~-brush **41** 25
~-capping plant **77** 13 – 22
~ cellar **80** 31
~-cleaning machine **93** 31
~-closing machine **93** 32
~ compartment **42** 10
~ conveyor belt **77** 20
~ cork **80** 29
~ crown cork **93** 43
bottled beer **93** 40
~wine **98** 60–64
bottle extractor **77** 17
~-filling machine **93** 32
~-filling plant **77** 13 – 22
~-holder **77** 16
~-label **93** 42
~ of liquid disinfectant **27** 22
~-nosed dolphin **352** 23
~-opener **46** 47
~ oven **154** 3
~ shelf **259** 64
~-washing machine **77** 13
~-washing plant **77** 13–22
~ of whisk(e)y **47** 44
~ of wine **260** 43
bottling apparatus **80** 26
~ the wine **80** 25
bottom **114** 56, **212** 30, **254** 11
~ *[body]* **18** 40, **30** 39
~ *[shoe]* **99** 50–54
~ bracket bearing axle **180** 42
~ chord **116** 73, **210** 49
~ clip **112** 7
~ cross **130** 21
~ die **132** 30, **133** 15, 28, **244** 41
~ discharge **140** 30
~ discharge tunnel **212** 62
~ film box **295** 27
~ fork **180** 20
~ member **116** 73
bottoming **196** 60
bottom mould **132** 30
~ nipper **156** 65
~ outlet **254** 34
~ platen **177** 29
~ plating **217** 45
~ press plate **128** 57
~ road **137** 38, **138** 11
~ rod **89** 22
~ roller **157** 10
~ rope **90** 9
~ shaft wheel **159** 55
~ sheet **48** 9
~ shutter **114** 54
~ slide **143** 39
~ stone **91** 23
~ swage **132** 30, **133** 15
~ tank **217** 35
~ water outlet valve **254** 31
~ weight **90** 10
bough **354** 5
boulder* **65** 9
boules player **287** 22
boundary ba(u)lk **65** 3
~ layer control **225** 55
~ ridge **65** 3
~ stone **65** 2
bountree **358** 35
bouquet **313** 17
bouquetin **352** 7
bourdon strings **301** 31
bourgeois **170** 26
bourtree **358** 35
bovine animal **74** 1
bow *[curve, etc.]* **134** 45
~ *[violin]* **302** 12
~* *[glasses]* **108** 16
~ *[ship]* **217** 71–73
~ *[Sports]* **287** 38
~ *[rower]* **269** 13
~ *[watch]* **107** 10
~ back **287** 39
Bowden cable **181** 41
bow doors **222** 10
bowel **22** 14–22
bow elevation **222** 65
bower *[pergola]* **257** 17
bow gin **87** 48
bowed instrument **302** 1–27
bowl **26** 62, **42** 31, **54** 15, **262** 31
~ *[spoon]* **46** 63
bowler **36** 7
bowl fitting **45** 31
bowler hat **36** 7
~ w. incised ornaments **309** 11
bowline **213** 35
bowling alley* **287** 2
~ crease **275** 56
~ the hoop **258** 20
bowl lid **105** 37
bowlodrome* **287** 2
bowls **287** 21
~* **287** 1
bowl of sand **312** 36
bow·man **287** 37
~ oarsman **269** 13
bows *[ship]* **218** 43
bow saw **85** 39, **115** 61, **127** 8
~sprit **213** 20, **214** 1
~ stay **270** 48
~ stay jumper strut **270** 49
~-string **287** 40
~-string girder **210** 36
~string girder bridge **210** 35
~-tie **33** 44
~ trap **87** 48
~ tube **223** 50
~ wave **218** 71
box *[receptacle]* **52** 55, **98** 79, **257** 65, **321** 10
~ *[stable]* **76** 7, **272** 2
~ *[Gymn.]* **279** 43
~ camera **111** 1
~ cart **64** 53
~ of cigars **105** 1
boxer *[Sports]* **281** 22
~ *[dog]* **71** 10
box fall **86** 20
~ feeder **151** 7
~ freight car* **208** 4, 34
~ goods wagon **208** 4
~ horse **279** 43
boxing **281** 18–46
~ glove **281** 23
~ match **281** 18–46
~ ring **281** 32
~-ring ropes **281** 33
~ transport **208** 14
box office **295** 2
~-plate pile **212** 6
~ pleat **32** 10
~ of punches **106** 30
~ room **40** 20
~ seat **51** 24
~ spanner **192** 10
~ trap **86** 20
~-tree **357** 19
~-type fuselage **225** 46
boy **45** 3, **259** 18
~ myrtle **357** 33
boys' clothing **31** 1–61
boy scout **266** 40
~-scouts' rally **266** 40–52
boy's leather shorts **31** 50
~ Lederhosen **31** 50
~ sleeper* **31** 14
~ sleeping-suit **31** 14
~ suit **31** 53
boys' wear **31** 1–61

boy's windjacket **31** 46
bra **33** 14, 15, **267** 28
brace *[tool]* **127** 22
~ *[Arch.]* **115** 27, 54, **116**
~ *[ship]* **214** 67
brace bits **127** 16–18
bracelet **38** 5, 18, 21, 23
braces **31** 52, **33** 47
brachial biceps **20** 37
~ plexus **20** 27
~ triceps **20** 38
brachio radialis **20** 39
bracing **210** 11
~ cable **210** 38
bracket *[Tech.]* **111** 41, **119** 26, 29, **180** 77, **258** 39
~ *[Skat.]* **284** 18
~ *[Script]* **325** 24, 25
~-change-bracket **284** 20
~ clock **107** 47
~ crane **145** 16
~ table **27** 16
bract(ea) **355** 7, 73
bracteate **244** 4
bract scale **356** 5
bradawl **99** 63
braid *[hair]* **35** 30
~ *[Cloth.]* **102** 6
braided belt **37** 13
~ coat **179** 23
~ collar **179** 22
~ sleeve **179** 24
Braille **325** 15
brain **19** 42
brake *[Techn.]* **136** 95–105, **179** 16, **185** 40
~ *[windmill]* **91** 8
~ *[vehicle]* **179** 2, 33, **189** 2
~ *[Bot.]* **361** 16
~ actuated by trailer **189** 43
~ air cock **206** 26
~ arm **180** 66
~-arm cone **180** 67
~ axle **136** 97
~ back plate **186** 50
~ band **136** 103
~ block **131** 19. **136** 98, **179** 16
~ cable **182** 14
~ casing **180** 70
~ cheek **136** 98
~ cone **180** 71
~ cylinder **204** 5
~ cylinder manometer **206** 49
~ handle **131** 4
~ lever **182** 13, **193** 38
~-lifter **206** 14
~ lining **136** 104, **186** 51
~ magnet **136** 100
~man's cabin **208** 7
~ motor **206** 13
brake pedal **185** 40
~ pipe manometer **206** 46
~ pressure gauge **205** 52
~ pulley **136** 96
~ roller mill **91** 57
~ shaft **131** 18, **136** 97
~ shoe **131** 19, **136** 98, **179** 16, **186** 51
brakesman **285** 8
brake spring pliers **192** 28
~ strap **136** 103
~ weight **136** 101
braking block **114** 40
~ figure **284** 22
~ shoe **114** 40
bramble **60** 29
~berry **60** 29
branch *[tree]* **354** 5
~ *[Tech.]* **255** 33
~ *[antlers]* **88** 31
~ line **16** 23
~ men **255** 34
~ of parabola **329** 15
brandy **98** 59
~ glass **46** 88
brass **134** 60
brassart **310** 47
brassie **276** 69
brassière **33** 14, 15, **267** 28
brass wind instruments **302** 39–48
~ winds **302** 39–48
Braun cathode-ray tube **230** 49
~ splint **23** 43
~ tube **332** 23
brayer **323** 12
Brazil **14** 33
Brazilian cavy **351** 12
~ cigar **105** 2
~ formation **274** 27
~ tapir **351** 26
Brazil nut **368** 53, 59
~ Stream **15** 35
bread **97** 22–28
~ basket **46** 20
~-bin **41** 6
~ corn **69** 1–37
~ crust **97** 23
breadery* **97** 1–56
bread-knife **41** 54
~ mould **97** 80
~ shelf **97** 29
~-slicing machine **41** 78
breadth indicator **149** 7
~ scale **149** 5
break *[vehicle]* **179** 2, 33
~ *[El.]* **331** 71
breakdown crane **189** 53
~ lorry **189** 52, **255** 47
~ trailer **189** 54
breakdown van **208** 33
breaker *[mach.]* **148** 7
~ *[El.]* **331** 71
breaking through **274** 63
break valve **206** 22
~ water **212** 16, **222** 46
breast *[body]* **18** 28–30
~ beam **159** 46
~-beam board **159** 16
~bone **19** 8, **95** 27
~ collar **72** 28
~ collar ring **72** 27
~ drill **134** 29
~-fin **350** 7
~ harness **72** 26–36
~plate **310** 46
~ pocket **34** 8, 19
~ rail **115** 56
~ roll **168** 10
~ roller **162** 5
breasts **18** 28 + 29
breast spot **88** 71, 74
~ stroke **268** 33
~ of veal **95** 4
~ weight **224** 25
~ wheel **91** 37
breather **147** 10
~ tube **40** 51
breathing· apparatus **255** 39
~ device* **17** 27
~ tube **267** 39
breeches **34** 22, 27, **282** 8
~ buoy **224** 51
breeder reactor **3** 20–23
breeding apparatus **89** 59
~ comb **78** 46
~ jar **89** 56
~ of poultry **75** 1–46
~ tank **89** 61
breeds of dogs **71**
bretzel **97** 48
breve **299** 14
~ rest **299** 22
breviary **314** 18
brevier **170** 25
brewer **92** 32
brewer's dray **93** 36
brewery **92, 93**
brewhouse* **92** 25–36
brewing house **92** 25–36
~ process **92** 25–36
brick **151**
~ clay **151** 2
~ edging **79** 39
~ field **151**
~ kiln **151** 19
~layer **113** 18
~layer's hammer **113** 53
~layer's tool **113** 50–57
~ machine **151** 11
~ paving **118** 7
bricks **50** 13
brick wall **64** 13, **113** 8, **118** 29
~work base **118** 15
~works **16** 89, **151**
~yard **151**
bridal bouquet **313** 17
~ couple **313** 14 + 15
~ cushion **313** 20
~ veil **313** 19
~ wreath **313** 18
bride **313** 14
~groom **313** 15
bride's bouquet **313** 17
bridge **210**
~ *[glasses]* **108** 15
~ *[mus.instr.]* **301** 17, **303** 4
~ *[Wrestl.]* **281** 8
~ beam **210** 20
~ bearing **210** 33
~ deck **218** 12–18
~ floor **210** 2
~ flooring **210** 21
~ girder **210** 20
~ lattice work **210** 48–54
~ leaf **210** 62
~ member **210** 17
~ over motorway **197** 32
~ pier **210** 15, 46
~ pile **210** 46
~ portal **210** 25
~ railing **210** 10
~ over railway **16** 22, 40
~ under railway **16** 42, 44
~ strut **210** 43
~ tower **210** 25
~ of violin **302** 5
bridle **72** 7–13, 25, **90** 14
~ path **12** 46
~ tape **304** 36
~ wire **304** 35
brief case **238** 36
briefs **33** 20, 57
brig **215** 17
bright **9** 21
brightener **292** 52
bright light* **185** 17
brig schooner **215** 14
brillantine **104** 10
brilliant **38** 26
~ *[Typ.]* **170** 20
brim **36** 15
~stone butterfly **348** 4
brine pipe **262** 4
briquette box **52** 57
Brisinga endecacnemos **349** 11
brisket **95** 23, 25, 26
~ of beef **95** 23
bristle **52** 23, **88** 52
~-bearing animal **74** 9
bristles **35** 23
bristle tail **341** 15
~-worm **340** 18

bristly beard **35** 23
~ hair **35** 10
broaching tap **93** 22
broach roof **116** 24
broad ax* **131** 32
~ axe **115** 70, **131** 32
~-brimmed hat **36** 17
broadcast **234** 1–20
broadcasting **234**, **235**
broad chisel **150** 37
~cloth coat* **32** 42
~ jump* **280** 29–32
~ tool **150** 37
brocade hat **36** 34
brock **88** 48
broderie anglaise **101** 11
brogue **100** 23
broiled sausage **291** 34
~-sausage stand **291** 32
broiler* **291** 33
broken pottery **154** 21
~-stone layer **194** 13
broker **243** 4
brokers' counter **243** 3
bronchus **22** 5
Bronze Age **309** 21–40
~ axe **309** 23
~ dagger **309** 22
~ knife **309** 31
~ pin **309** 29
~ spearhead **309** 21
~ trumpet **301** 1
brooch **38** 17, 22, **309** 27
brood cell **78** 31
~ chamber **78** 46
brooder **75** 28
~ house **75** 27
broody hen **75** 17
brook **13** 8, **16** 80
~ trout **350** 15
broom *[sweeping]* **40** 36
~ *[Bot.]* **358** 20
~ cupboard **52** 15
~ head **52** 22
~stick **40** 37, **52** 21
broth cube **98** 27
brougham **179** 3
brow antler **88** 6
~ band **72** 9
brown **320** 5
~ alga **362** 48
~ bear **353** 10
~-tail moth **81** 28
brow point **88** 6
~sing **86** 13
~ snag **88** 6
~ tine **88** 6
'brush **51** 76, **52** 16, **321** 6, 7, 8, 9
brush * *[forest]* **16** 15, **84** 5
~ *[fox]* **88** 47
~ f. applying polish **52** 41
brushing boot **272** 44
brush wood **16** 15, **84** 5
Brussels lace **101** 18
~ sprouts **59** 30
bubble-car **183** 41
buck *[animal]* **74** 18, **88** 28
~ *[Gymn.]* **279** 19
~ *[saw ~]* **53** 6
~ *[dandy]* **289** 33
buckers* **84** 20
bucket *[pail]* **52** 50
~ *[Tech.]* **153** 3, **196** 5, **221** 65
~ *[mill]* **91** 36
~ arm **196** 4
~ chain **211** 57, **221** 63
~ conveyor **221** 64
~ dredger **221** 63–68
~ elevator **197** 24
~ elevator feed **196** 49
~ tooth **196** 6
~-topped boot **338** 58
~ yoke **76** 11
buck·eye* **355** 58
~ of fallow deer **88** 40
~hound **272** 63
bucking saw **115** 14
buckle **37** 14, **249** 44
buckled shoe **100** 37
buckle machine **178** 8
buckler **310** 57
buckling strap **249** 43
buckram **102** 67
buckskin shoe **100** 2
buckwheat **70** 20
bud **57** 23, 26, **62** 16
~ capital **315** 14
Buddhistic sacred building **319** 21
budding **57** 30
~ knife **57** 31
buffalo **352** 8
~ horns **246** 34
buffer **209** 50
~ stop **199** 40
buffet **45** 57, **260** 1–11
buffoon **289** 38, 69
buff pad **127** 11
bug **341** 28, **342** 3–23
buggy **179** 48, 49
builder's hoist **113** 31
~ lift **113** 31
~ trough **117** 22
building **252** 19, 45
~ brick **151** 20
~ elevator ***113** 31
~ glazier **122** 8
~ a house **113** 1–49
~ lot* **113, 114**
~ plan **144** 57
~ site **113, 114**
building site latrine **113** 49
~ slip **217** 11–26
~ timber **115** 10, 83–96
built-in· balcony **53** 17
~ bath **51** 5
~ motor **157** 2
built-on motor **157** 33
built piece **296** 32
built-up wall **117** 39
bulb *[Bot.]* **57** 28
~ *[El.]* **120** 56, 57
~ flash light **111** 49
~-headed probe **28** 46
bulbiferous plant **69** 38
bulbil **359** 38
bulbous agaric **363** 11
~ plant **69** 38
bulb psychrometer **10** 32
~ thermometer **10** 33, 34
Bulgaria **14** 3
bulge **282** 14
~ of forehead **18** 5
bulk goods wharf **220** 44–53
~head **114** 17, **212** 5, **222** 54
~ material **196** 12
bulky goods **202** 23
bull **74** 1, **287** 67
Bull **5** 25, **6** 33
bull calf **74** 1
~ capital **315** 28
~ column **315** 23
~ dog **71** 1
bulldozer **196** 28, **198** 16
~ blade **196** 29
bullet **87** 55
~ barrel **87** 26
~-shaped fuselage **225** 44
~-shaped shade **47** 51
bull·fight **287** 57
~finch **344** 5
bullock **74** 1
bull ring **287** 58
bull's body **307** 48
bull set **322** 14
bull's-eye **318** 2
bull terrier **71** 16
bulrush **362** 21
bulwark **217** 64
bumble bee **342** 23
bump *[eminence]* **18** 4
bumper **185** 13
~ car **291** 63
~ guard **186** 37
~ steel **159** 44
~ steel spindle **159** 45
bumping post* **199** 40
bun *[roll]* **97** 49
~ *[hair]* **35** 29
bunch of currants **60** 11
~ of fruit **368** 32
~ of grapes **80** 6
~ pink **62** 6
bundle of brushwood **211** 53
~ of firewood **52** 61
~ of serpents **308** 52
~ of straw **76** 9
~ of twigs **84** 17
bung **126** 28
~ hole **126** 29
~ hole borer **126** 1
bunker *[storage]* **148** 3, 20, 22
~ *[golf]* **276** 61
bunkering tanker **220** 23
bunker wall **199** 45
bunks **262** 34
Bunsen burner **334** 1
~ cell **331** 67
bunting *[cloth]* **245** 3
~ *[flags]* **216** 37
~ *[Zool.]* **346** 6+7
buntline **214** 71
buoy **219**
buoyant body **212** 34
buoy bell **219** 50
~ chain **219** 47
~ rope **90** 3
~ stone **219** 48
~ whistle **219** 45
burden **74** 5
bureau* *[office]* **238** 1–36
~ *[desk]* **238** 12
~ lamp* **238** 23
~ telephone* **238** 24
burette **334** 21
~ clamp **334** 23
~ stand **334** 22
burgee **245** 22
burgonet **310** 60
Burgundian **338** 40
~ cross **313** 54
burial **312** 34–41
~ ground **312** 21–41
~ place **312** 62
burin **170** 33, **323** 5
burlap* **124** 24
burlesque dance **288** 35
burner **41** 36, **227** 44
~ jet **40** 60
burnet **70** 28
burning-gas connection **135** 52
~ zone **153** 15
burnisher **154** 19, **323** 17
burnishing box **106** 47
~ brush **106** 48
~ machine **106** 43
burnous(e) **337** 7
burn-out **229** 40, 43
burr *[Tech.]* **88** 5, 29
~ *[Bot.]* **368** 52
burrow **86** 26
~ hole **86** 27

burrowing passage
60 63
burying ground*
312 21–42
~ place **312** 23
bus **188** 1–16
~bar **146** 29
~ garage **199** 8
bush *[Bot.]* **55** 13, 19
~ *[socket]* **111** 32
bushed chain* **180** 36
bushing insulator
147 12
bushman **337** 29
~ woman **337** 34
bush of peacock's
feathers **246** 36
~ rose **55** 13
business area **252** 33
~ communication
239 1–12
~ letter **239** 1–12
~ office **238–241**
~ premises **252** 15
~ section* **252** 33
~-shirt **31** 55
~ street **252** 32
~ suit* **34** 2, 4
busk **33** 17
bus station **199** 5
bust *[breast]* **18** 30
~ *[Her.]* **246** 11
bustle **338** 69
bus trailer **188** 3
~ w. trailer **188** 2
butcher **96** 9
butcher's deck **90** 30
~ findings* **96** 29–35
~ hook **94** 16
~ knife **96** 32
~ shop **96** 1–28
~ tool **96** 29–35
butt *[cask]* **55** 4,
64 15
~ *[rifle]* **87** 3
~ *[Knitt.]* **160** 60
~ *[meat]* **95** 50
butter **98** 22
~-and-eggs *[Bot.]*
360 26
~ brush **97** 70
~ churn **77** 30
~cup *[Bot.]* **359** 8
~ dish **46** 36
~flower **359** 8
butterfly **342** 48–56,
348
~ collection **47** 34
~ nut **136** 40, **180** 29
~ stroke **268** 34
~ valve **183** 61
butter knife **46** 73
~milk tank **77** 12
~-packing machine
77 31
~-shaping machine
77 31
~wort **361** 13
buttock of beef **95** 14
buttocks **18** 40, **30** 39
button *[Cloth.]* **34** 6,
37 27
button *[Tech.]* **120** 2,
147 6
~ *[sabre]* **277** 41, 59
~ *[watch]* **107** 14
~ *[oar]* **269** 36
~ ball* **355** 67
~-fastening **37** 17
buttonhole **34** 7
~ of myrtle **313** 21
~ scissors **102** 66
~ stitch **101** 6
buttonholing **101** 6
button shoe **100** 9
~ tab **31** 15
~ tree* **355** 67
~-through dress **32** 8
~ wood* **355** 67
butt plate **87** 14
buttress *[Arch.]*
317 27+28
~ *[tree]* **85** 22
buyer **253** 12
buzzard **347** 9
buzzer **206** 45
buzz saw* **114** 19,
128 5, **149** 2, 20,
21, 45
buzz saw blade* **128** 6
By Air Mail **232** 32
~ Express **232** 31
by-pass **252** 3
~-pass line **199** 34
~-product **164** 13
byre **76** 17–38
by-street **253** 7
Byzantine art
316 72–75
~ empress **338** 15

C

cab **179** 26
~* **253** 35
cabaret **298** 1–3
~ performer **298** 2
~ singer **298** 3
cabbage **59** 32
~ head **59** 32
~ plant **59** 28–34
~ white butterfly
81 47, 48
cabby **179** 32
cab-driver **179** 32
~-driver* **253** 37
~ guard **189** 19
~ horse **179** 28
cabin *[dressing~]*
25 4, **268** 1
~ *[ship]* **218** 13, 29
~ *[cable railw.]*
209 20
~ * *[house]* **39** 84–86
~ boy **216** 55
~ car **183** 41
~ colony* **39** 54–57,
252 69
cabinet **26** 19
~ drier **166** 19
~-maker **127** 45
~-maker's workshop
127 1–65
cabinet respirator **24** 8
~ washing machine
166 12
cabin pulley system
209 66
~ scooter **183** 6
~ superstructure
270 8
~ trunk **200** 6,
201 12
~ vehicle **183** 41–52
cable **125** 19, **209**
~ anchorage **210** 26
~ box **147** 33
~-braced bridge
210 37
~ car* **16** 67,
209 13, 15–24
~ cellar **146** 21
~ chain **218** 45
~ crane berth
217 11–18
~ drum **255** 55
~ ferry **211** 1
~ guide **197** 7
~ of loading winch
85 4
~ pole **229** 31
~ railway **209** 15–38
~ release **111** 42
~ shears **120** 49
~ shoe **184** 6
~ slipway **217** 11–18
~ terminal **147** 33
~ thimble **184** 6
~ tunnel **146** 20
~way **16** 67,
209 15–38
~way support **209** 76
~ winch **189** 28
cabman **179** 32
caboose* **218** 37
cabotage* **216** 38
cab passenger*
253 38
~ protector **189** 19
cabriole **288** 16
cabriolet **179** 29
cab stand* **253** 35
cacao tree **366** 16
cachalot **352** 25
caddie **276** 64
caddis fly **342** 12
caduceus **308** 25
caecum **22** 17
café **261** 1–26
~ customer **261** 24
~ table **261** 11
cafeteria **260** 45–54
cage *[crane, etc.]*
137 18, 19, **145** 11,
256 46
~ *[zoo]* **339** 25
~ f. beasts of prey
339 1
~ caravan **290** 62
caisson **217** 28
cake *[Bak.]* **97**, **261** 4
~ *[Tech.]* **163** 18,
19–27
~ box **97** 4
~ -brush **42** 59
cake-finishing **163** 22
~ mold* **42** 48+49
~ mould **42** 48+49
~ plate **45** 26, **97** 36
~ shovel **45** 28
~ slice **45** 28
~ of soap **30** 22
~ -tin **42** 48+49
~ tongs **45** 36, **97** 8
calabash **337** 27
calash **179** 35
calcaneal tendon
20 48
calcaneum **19** 27
calcareous slate stone
323 57
calcium chloride tube
334 43
calcographer **323** 44
calculating frame
249 38
~ machine **240** 42
~ punch **241** 45–51
calculation **327** 6
calculator **240** 42
~ clearance **240** 54
calculus **327** 13+14
calendar **238** 2
calender **166** 25,
168 21, 23,,
~ operator **166** 28
~ roll **166** 26
~ roller
156 20, 37, 59
calf *[leg]* **18** 53
~ *[animal]* **74** 1,
95 1–13
caliber* **87** 40
calibrated pipette
334 24
calibre **87** 40,
~ gauge **142** 52
California Current
15 39
caliper **23** 45
~ gauge **142** 49
calipers **322** 3
calking chisel **132** 37
~ tool **132** 37
call-box **231** 24
call box* **233** 1
caller **233** 4
calling card* **43** 22
~ game **87** 43–47
~ lamp **233** 6
Calliope **308** 68
calliper gauge
142 49
call lamp **296** 52
~ f. luring game
87 43–47
callosity **73** 27
calm *n.* **9** 11
~-zone **9** 46+47
calyx *[Bot.]* **60** 8, 22,
354 58, **359** 33
~ *[Med.]* **22** 30
~ leaf **60** 44
cam **160** 14, **182** 45,
184 60
Camberwell beauty
348 5

cambium **354** 10
~ ring **354** 10
cam box **160** 13
cambré **288** 15
cam controller **193** 35
~ for raising the needles **160** 59
came *n.* **122** 13
camel **351** 29
~-back girder* **210** 36
~ caravan **337** 1
Camenae **308** 59–75
cameo brooch **38** 22
camera **111** 1–27, **292** 23, **294** 1–35
~ f. astrophotography **6** 3
~ baseboard **171** 13
~ w. bellows **111** 2
~ cable **237** 2
~ carriage **171** 14 **171** 12
~ crane **292** 49
~ frame **171** 4
~ frame adjustment **171** 10
~ housing door **294** 18
~ man **292** 41
~ microscope **110** 19
~ operator **237** 3, **292** 42
~ precision drive **171** 12
cami-knickers **33** 13
cam f. lifting or lowering the cylinder **175** 3
camomile **364** 1
cam-operated controls **206** 8
camp **266** 4–52, **290** 61
campanile **316** 65
campanula **359** 14
camp archway **266** 52
~ bed **266** 7
~-chair **266** 11
camphor tree **364** 18
camping **266**
~-ground **266** 4–52
~ trailer **183** 36
camporee* **266** 40-52
camp-stool **266** 14
~ stove **266** 19
~-table **266** 5
cam shaft **159** 56
~ shaft wheel **159** 55
can *n.* **54** 17, **191** 22
Canada **14** 29
Canadian canoe **269** 3
~ water weed **362** 56
canal **16** 57, **212** 15–28
~ *[meatus]* **19** 34, 58
~ bottom **212** 30
~ entrance **212** 15 +16
canals of Mars **7** 15
canard aircraft **225** 36
canard model **271** 42
~ nose **225** 38
Canaries Current **15** 41
can of beer* **93** 39
~ buoy **219** 52
cancel **232** 39
~ button **305** 41
cancellation **231** 40
cancelling lever **240** 44
Cancer **6** 35
candelabra **44** 24, **312** 56
candies* **98** 75–86
candle **47** 24, **78** 66, **311** 10, 41
~ flame **47** 26
~ stick **44** 24, **46** 16, **47** 27, **312** 56
candy store* **253** 19
cane *[sugar]* **366** 52
~ *[stick]* **43** 15
~ back **43** 23
~ basket **258** 33
~ pen **324** 23
~ pram **258** 30
~ seat **43** 23
can-holder **156** 36
Canidae **352** 11–13
canine tooth **21** 17
Canis Major **5** 14
~ Minor **5** 15
canister stopper **305** 35
canned* see tinned
cannery **220** 9
cannon **73** 23
~ billiards **264** 7
~ bone **73** 23
cannula **26** 31
canoe **269** 3, 4, 54–66 **335** 19, 35
canoeist **269** 55
canoe stern **270** 13
canon *[Mus.]* **300** 46–48
cañon **13** 45
canonical **311** 22
cañon river **13** 51
canon table **311** 38
can-opener* **266** 18
canopy *[baldachin]* **50** 9, **311** 21, **312** 49
~ *[building]* **39** 67
~ *[parachute]* **228** 49
~-bearer **312** 46
~ of heaven **6** 1
cant *[banking]* **197** 30
canteen *[room]* **114** 45
~* *[bottle]* **266** 41
canter **73** 42
cant hook **84** 19
cantilever crane **217** 29
~ leaf spring **183** 45
~ roof bar **138** 26
~ saddle **181** 48
canting *[skiing]* **283** 34
cantle **72** 39
cantus mensuratus **299** 4
canvas **269** 56, **321** 21
~ cover(ing) **189** 15
~ hull **269** 58
canyon **13** 45
~ river **13** 51
cap *[headwear]* **36**, **247** 3
~ *[cover]* **78** 39, **239** 24
~ *[fungus]* **365** 4
~ *[Geol.]* **12** 30
~ *[letter]* **170** 1
~ *[mus. instr.]* **305** 31
capa **287** 60
capacitance **234** 26
capacity plate **145** 6
~ test **273** 33
caparison **310** 74
cap and bells **289** 39
cape **34** 35, **104** 5
cape* **103** 26
capeador **287** 59
Capella **5** 27
capelline bandage **17** 3
caper **98** 42
capercaillie **88** 72
capercailzie **88** 72
capillarity **331** 43
capillary tubes **331** 44
capital *[Art]* **315**, **316** 20–25, **319** 18
~ *[letter]* **170** 14
~ letter **170** 1, **324** 16
~ ship **222** 31–64
capitulum **63** 14, **354** 73, **362** 12
cap-lamp **138** 55
capon **74** 21, **98** 6
cappa magna **314** 51
cap peak **36** 25
capped blossom **81** 11
~ cell **78** 32
cap ribbon **31** 33
Capricorn(us) **5** 36, **6** 41
capriole **72** 5, **288** 16
capro lactam **164** 28
~ lactam oil **164** 25
cap-sleeve **32** 32
capstan **161** 43, **212** 22
capsule *[cork]* **93** 44
~ *[Bot.]* **354** 95
captain **219** 22
Captain of Prince's Guards **289** 67
captain's cabin **218** 13, **223** 46
~ bridge **222** 45
caption* *[Film]* **294** 33, 35
captive model **271** 62
cap-type insulator **147** 54
car *[motor-~]* **185**
~ *[lift]* **256** 46
~ *[coach, etc.]* **185**, **204**, **208**
car air-conditioning **186** 22
carambole **264** 7
caramel **98** 77
carapace **350** 29
car ashtray **186** 19
carat mark **38** 30
caravan *[camels]* **337** 1
~ *[circus]* **202** 26, **290** 34, 62
~ *[trailer]* **266** 4
caravel **213** 27–43, **215** 37
caravelle **215** 37
caraway roll **97** 56
~ stick **97** 56
car barn* **252** 17
carbine **86** 30, **87** 1
car body* **185** 1–58
carbon **295** 40
~ crater **295** 44
~ disulphide injector **83** 4
~-holder **295** 43
carbonic acid container **28** 35
~ disulphide **163** 8
carbon paper **238** 68
~ rod **331** 68
~ stick **331** 68
~-stick lamp **173** 20
~ tissue **176** 25
~ tissue transfer machine **176** 23
carborundum disc **27** 38
~ wheel **27** 39
carboy **202** 14
car brake **186** 50–54
carburetor* **183** 53–69
carburetted water-gas plant **148** 25+26
carburetter **182** 31, **183** 53-69, **184** 2
~ body **183** 54
~ engine **184** 1–36
~ float **183** 65
~ air lever **182** 22
~ tickler **183** 63
carcass **113** 1-49
car chassis **185** 1–58
~ clock **186** 15
card *[post~, etc.]* **43** 22, **232** 4, 5, **238** 72, **312** 59
~ *[Spinn.]* **156** 34
Cardan joint **185** 53
~ shaft **185** 52
car dashboard **186** 1–21
cardboard **321** 22
~ case **87** 50
~ distance piece **323** 37
card can **156** 35
~ delivery **241** 42
~ feed **241** 41, 49, 53
~-holder **240** 11

cardigan **32** 41
cardinal *[Church]* **314** 49
~ bird **345** 5
~ grosbeak **345** 5
~ number **326** 5
cardinal's cross **313** 59
card index **26** 5, **238** 71
~-index cabinet **238** 5, **250** 22
~-index drawer **238** 6, 70
~-index guide card **238** 73
carding engine **156** 34
card magazine **241** 56
car documents **253** 66
~ door **185** 4
card punch **241** 40, 48
cards **265** 36
card-sorter **241** 52
car dump **252** 70
~ dumper* **208** 22
card unit **241** 36
caretaker **53** 28
car ferry **16** 47, **211** 10
cargo **218** 67
~ barge **211** 25
~ boat **216** 1
~ boom **216** 3
~-checker **221** 27
~ hatch **226** 35
~ hook **221** 16
~ ship **216** 1
Carina **5** 46
car instrument panel **186** 1–21
~ jack **191** 30, **192** 47, 66
carl **367** 10
~ hemp **367** 10
carload* **202** 53
Carlovingian minuscule **324** 18
car maintenance **191**
~ mascot **190** 35
~ mechanic **191** 10, **192** 65
carnation **62** 6, 7
carnival **289**
~ decoration **289** 60
~ float **289** 57
~ parade **289** 57–70
~ prince **289** 58
~ princess **289** 61
~ procession **289** 57–70
~ queen **289** 61
~ truck* **289** 57
carnivores **352** 11–17, **353** 1–11
carnivorous plant **361** 13
carob **368** 41
Caroline (or Carolingian) minuscule **324** 18
carom billiards* **264** 7
carosserie **185** 1–58
carotid artery **20** 1
carousal (carousel or carrousel)* **291** 2
carp **350** 4
carpal bone **19** 15
~ joint **21** 76
car park **252** 27
carpel **358** 2
carpenter **115**
carpenter's findings* **115** 60–82
~ hammer **115** 74
~ hat **115** 13
~ pencil **115** 77
~ tool **115** 20, 60-82
~ workshop **115** 4
~ yard **115** 1–59
carpet **47** 61, **48** 32, 33
~-beater **52** 19
~-beating bar **53** 46
~ brush **52** 60
~ runner **48** 32
~-sweeper **52** 9
carport* **252** 62
carpus **21** 76, **73** 22
car radio* **186** 17
carriage *[vehicle]* **179** 1–54, **203**
~ *[Tech.]* **143** 39, **160** 39, **171** 14, **240** 2–17
~ catch **171** 15
~-cleaner **201** 14
~ drive **171** 11
~ and four **257** 54
~ horse **179** 28
~ release **240** 2
~ step **179** 13
~ and wagon examiner **201** 36
carriageway **16** 99, **253** 34
carrier *[bicycle]* **180** 44
~ *[postman]** **231** 47
~ *[porter]** **201** 32
~ *[carter]* **202** 16
~ *[Mech.]* **68** 33
~ aircraft **226** 23
~ arrangement **226** 22–24
~ bicycle **181** 15
~ equipment **237** 33
carrier's cart **202** 18
carrion beetle **81** 45
carrion flower **56** 15
carrom billiards **264** 7
carrot **59** 17, 18
carrousel* **291** 2
car rug* **48** 55, **201** 8
carryall* **86** 3
carrying axle **205** 35
~ bar **141** 16
~ cable **114** 37, **193** 40, **209** 27, 49
carrying-cable·anchorage **209** 59
~ bearing shoe **209** 33
~ brake **209** 71
~ shoe **209** 58
~ support shoe **209** 79
carrying tensioning weight **209** 41
carrying grip **17** 22
~ and haulage cable (or rope) **209** 21
~ saddle **74** 4
~ strap **249** 45
car slings **221** 11
~ springing system **185** 24–29
~-steering mechanism **186** 39–49
~ suspension system **185** 24–29
cart **64** 29, 33, 53
carte crossing **277** 49
carter **202** 16
cart f. game **86** 39
~ horse **202** 17
cartilage **19** 11
carton **75** 36
cartoon *[design]* **321** 43
~ *[newsp.]* **325** 48
cartouche **318** 7
~ work **318** 8
cartridge **87** 49, 54
~ chamber **87** 15
~ clip **87** 19
~ fuse **120** 35
~ hoist **223** 71
~ magazine **87** 17
~ pouch **247** 7
cartrunk* **187** 5
cart track **84** 3
~-weighing machine **145** 88
~ wheel *[cart]* **131** 26
~ wheel *[Gymn.]* **278** 30
~wright **131** 25
car tyre **185** 31
caruncle **74** 22
carved column **315** 18
carvel **213** 27–43, **215** 37
~-built boat **269** 9
~ planking **270** 22
carver **322** 28
carvers **42** 65
car vibration damper **209** 55
carving **309** 7
~ fork **42** 65, **46** 70
~ knife **42** 65, **46** 69
car-washing compressor machine **191** 25
~ wireless **186** 17
~ wrap* **201** 8
caryatid **316** 36
caryopsis **359** 43
cascade **257** 9
case **143** 34, **201** 9
~ *[book]* **178** 40
~ cabinet **169** 4
cased book **178** 30
case-making machine **177** 43
casement curtain **52** 53
case room **169**, **170**
~ stand **169** 2
cash book **238** 58
~ box **238** 55
~ desk **263** 2, **291** 7
cashier **242** 2, **256** 1
cash-on-delivery form **232** 8
~ register **256** 2, **260** 17
~-report pad **238** 54
casing **10** 43, **136** 77
~ head **139** 53
~ cover **136** 78
~ head **139** 53
~-in machine **178** 25
casino **262** 8, **263** 1
~ entrance-card **263** 14
cask **80** 37, **126** 24
~-adzing machine **126** 37
~ body **126** 25
casket* **312** 35, 51
cask-filler **93** 29
~-filling machine **93** 29
~-maker **126** 16
~-making machine **126** 34–38
~ stave **126** 21
cassia **364** 16
Cassiopeia **5** 33
cassock **314** 33
cassowary **343** 1
castanet **303** 46
caster *[wheel]* **29** 12
cast glass **122** 6
casting **141** 37
casting aperture **172** 17
~ box **141** 25
~ chamber **172** 18
~ crew* **141** 13
~ ladle **140** 41
~ ladle lip **140** 42
~ machine **169** 32–45
~ mechanism **169** 25
~ mould **172** 22
~ net **89** 6
~ off a loop **160** 66
~ rod **89** 23
~ team **141** 13
cast in situ concrete wall **114** 7
~-iron box **120** 17
~-iron pipe **39** 14
castle **252** 54, **310** 1
~ chapel **310** 29
~ garden **252** 55
~ gate **310** 22
~ nut **136** 24, 75
~ ruin **80** 20
cast letters **169** 44
castle wall **315** 31
cast line **169** 27
Castor *[Astr.]* **5** 28
castor *[wheel]* **29** 12, **145** 81
~ *[horse]* **73** 27
Castor *[Zool.]* **351** 14
castor-oil plant **364** 14

cast single letter **169** 44
casual clothes **33** 7
~ suit **32** 58
cat **74** 17, **353** 2–8
catacomb **312** 62
catafalque **312** 52
catalog* see catalogue
catalogue **250** 21
~ room **250** 18
catalytic cracker **139** 63
~ hydrogenation of phenol **164** 16
~ reformer **139** 64
catapult *[aircraft]* **222** 28, 49, 73
~ *[sling]* **258** 9
cataract **11** 45
catch *[device]* **136** 27
~-as-catch-can style **281** 11+12
catcher *[Sports]* **275** 47, **279** 16
catcher's area **275** 44
~ mitt **275** 47
catch-fly **360** 20
catching game **298** 22
~ stick **261** 30
catchment area **12** 24
catchup **46** 43
cat cracker **139** 63
caterpillar **81**, **82** 20
~ grinder **167** 18
~ lamp **58** 20
~ motor lorry **189** 36
~ mounting **196** 3
~ scraper **196** 16
~ track **189** 37
~ truck **196** 3
catgut string **276** 29, **303** 6
cathedral **252** 37, **317** 1–13
catheter **26** 53
cathetus **328** 32
cathode **172** 3
~-ray discharge head **109** 2
~-ray tube **332** 22
Catholic church **311** 31–65
~ clergy **314** 32–58
catkin **61** 39, 45
cat-o'-nine tails **124** 18
cat's-foot **361** 3
~-tail **362** 21
~ tongue **98** 84
catsup* **46** 43
cat's valerian **364** 5
~ whisker **234** 31
cattle **74** 1+2
~ boat **216** 40
~ lorry **189** 8
~man* **76** 10
~ pen **202** 7
~ ramp **202** 1
~ shed **76** 17–38
~ van **189** 8
~ yard **252** 51
catwalk **90** 42, **292** 53, **296** 29
caucus* **251** 1–15
caudal fin **350** 10
~ pincers **341** 11
cauliflower **59** 31
~ cloud **8** 1
caulking chisel **132** 37
~tool **132** 37
caustic soda **163** 3, **164** 10
cautery **26** 48, **27** 45
~ burner **26** 48
~ cords **26** 49
'cavalier hat' **338** 55
cavalry standard **245** 13
cave **13** 79, **16** 85
~ painting **309** 9
cavern **13** 79
cavetto **318** 50
~ vault **318** 49
caviar knife **46** 81
caving riddle **68** 65
~ screen **68** 65
~ spout **67** 52
cavity of mouth **21** 14–37
~ of ovary **354** 62
cavy **351** 12
C clef **299** 13
cedar of Lebanon **356** 65
cedilla **325** 33
ceiling **118**, **217** 60
~ hook **255** 15
~ joist **114** 5, **116** 54
ceiling panelling **234** 17
~ plaster **118** 59, 72
~ shower **51** 15
~ slat **48** 37
celandine **359** 36
celeriac **59** 27
celestial chart **5** 1–35
~ equator **5** 3
~ globe **308** 73
~ pole **5** 1
cell *[convent]* **314** 4
~ *[bee]* **78** 26–30
~ *[Tech.]* **332** 2
cella **316** 51
cellar *[basement]* **39** 1
~ *[Tech.]* **146** 21
~ door **53** 2
cellarer's assistant **80** 35
cellar foreman **93** 24
~man **80** 39
~ steps **53** 3, **113** 4
~ window **39** 27, **113** 3
cell nucleus **340** 2
cello **302** 16
cellular chimney brick **151** 28
~ vest **33** 49
celluloid ball **276** 42
cellulose sheet **163** 2
Celtic silver coin **309** 37
cembalo **301** 45
cembra pine **356** 29
cement **295** 24
~ *[tooth]* **21** 29
~ floor **53** 68
~ grinding mill **152** 14
~ guiding kerb **197** 38
~ hopper **197** 25
~ packing plant **152** 18
~ paving **118** 14
~ pipe **196** 62
~ silo **114** 30, **152** 17, **197** 25
~ tube **196** 62
~ works **152**
cemetery **16** 106, **312** 21-41
~ chapel **312** 28
censer **313** 37
cent **244** 33
Centaur *[Myth.]* **307** 52
~ *[stars]* **5** 39
Centaurea **63** 1
Centaurus **5** 39
centaury **364** 10
centavo **244** 23
center* see centre
center bank to port* **219** 63
centering magnet **236** 24
~ rod **110** 35
centesimal balance **145** 88
centesimo **244** 20
centime **244** 15, 16
centimeter* see centimetre
centimetre scale **249** 68
céntimo **244** 22
central* *n.* **233** 1–17
Central America **14** 31
central area of town **252** 33
~ control panel **173** 10
~ corridor **203** 45
~ effacer **240** 53
Central European dance **288** 41
central gangway **203** 45, **213** 46
~ heating furnace **40** 57
~ heating installation **40** 38–81
centralised building **316** 55
central ovary **61** 14
centrally-planned building **316** 55
central nave **316** 62, **317** 1
~ reserve **197** 37
~ signal box **199** 16
~ station **252** 30
~ tower **317** 6
centre *[Geom.]* **328** 26, 43
centre *[player]* **274** 19, **276** 57
~ angle **328** 55
~ band **276** 14
~ bit **127** 18
~ board **270** 10
~-board yacht **270** 6–10
~ bolt **186** 47
~ of curvature **328** 23
~ entrance **204** 55
~ flag **274** 46
~ forward **274** 19
~ girder **217** 50
~ half **274** 15
~ line **276** 8 to 9
~ mark **276** 11
~ of old town **252** 34–45
~ parting **35** 19
~ pole **131** 14
~ punch **134** 68, **145** 32
~ service line **276** 8 to 9
~ strake **217** 52
~ of symmetry **330** 3
centrifugal cleaner **168** 4
~ cream-heater **77** 25
~ drive **173** 34
~ force **4** 51
~ governor **184** 41
~ pump **161** 72, **254** 44, **255** 8
~ regulator **184** 41
centripetal force **4** 52
centrosphere **11** 5
cep **365** 15
cèpe **365** 15
cephalopod **340** 22
Cerberus **307** 29
cereal-dressing **83** 13–16
cereals **69** 1–37, **98** 35–39
cerebellum **19** 45, **20** 23
cerebrum **19** 42, **20** 22
ceremonial vestments **314** 49
certificate of posting book **231** 11
cervical muscle **21** 12
~ vertebra(e) **19** 2
cesspit emptier **195** 25
cesta **287** 53
cestodes **341** 24
Cetus **5** 11
C flat major **300** 15
chaffinch **344** 10
chain **31** 61, **38** 33, **76** 31, **273** 20
~-adjuster **180** 39, **181** 53
~ f. automatic guiding **68** 13
~ of barges **211** 22
~ barrier **253** 29
~ bracelet **38** 18
~ conveyor **168** 39

chain cover **181** 51
~ curtain **133** 55
~ cutter moulding machine **115** 17
~drive **180** 35–42
chaîné **288** 19
chain of egg insulators **234** 22
~ ferry **211** 1
~ of flowers **289** 17
~ gripper **174** 11
~ guard **180** 37, **181** 51
~ guard inspection plug **182** 56
~ insulator **147** 54
~ link **181** 32
~ of locks **212** 17–25
~ mail **310** 63
~ mortiser **128** 29
~ parts **181** 28
~ pull and handle **51** 45
~ reaction **1** 18–21, 22–30
~ saw **115** 14
~ stay **180** 20
~ stitch **101** 2
~ stop **218** 46
~ transmission **180** 35–39
~ wheel **180** 35
chair **44** 9, **47** 18, **49** 27
~ back **29** 23, **104** 29
~ car* **204** 49
~ commode **23** 25
~ grip **17** 21
~-hoist **209** 16–18, **283** 1
~ leg **44** 14
~-lift **209** 16–18, **283** 1
chairman **251** 1
~ of board of directors **243** 15
~ of executive (managing) committee **243** 16
chair o'plane **291** 4
~ worker **155** 16
chaise **179** 54
~ longue **29** 21
chaitya **319** 28
~ hall **319** 27
chalaza **75** 52
chalcographist **323** 44
chalcography **323** 14–24
chalice **311** 13, **313** 44
~ veil **314** 41
chalk **102** 82, **249** 6
~ crayon **321** 5
~ method **323** 14–24
~ pencil **321** 5
~ sketch **321** 4
Chamaeleontidae **350** 33
chamber *[room, etc.]* **315** 2, 3, 5
chamber *[Tech.]* **94** 16–18, **184** 26, **227** 60–63
'chamber' *[pot]* **30** 17
chamber lock **16** 58
~maid* **45** 54, **48** 48
~-pot **30** 17
~ wall **254** 25
chameleon **350** 33
chamfer **136** 60
chamfering hammer **119** 48
chamfrain **310** 84
chamfron **310** 84
chamois **352** 3
~ leather **52** 28, **190** 25
chamomile **364** 1
chamotte slab **135** 43
champagne **98** 63
~ bucket **259** 59
~-cooler **259** 59
~ cork **259** 58
~ glass **46** 85+86
chancel **311** 1, 36, **317** 4
~ chair **311** 5
chandelier **259** 21
change gears box **142** 7
~ lever **142** 10, **199** 58
changement **288** 13
change-over switch **206** 33, **233** 12
changer spindle **306** 33
change wheel **157** 40
changing the baby('s napkin) **30** 37
~ room **268** 3
channel *[water]* **316** 54
~ *[Tech.]* **136** 7, **140** 34
~ *[Television]* **237** 36
~-cutter **99** 18
~ goose **343** 9
~ iron **136** 7
channelling file **106** 51
channel marks **219** 43–58
~ section **185** 60
~ switch **236** 4
chanson singer **298** 3
chanter **301** 10
chanterelle **365** 14
chantlate **116** 31
chap *[jaw]* **71** 32
chapel **16** 61, **312** 12
chaplet hair style **35** 31
~ of plaited hair **35** 32
chapter **107** 3
~ heading **178** 60
char **52** 52
char-à-banc **179** 33
character dance **288** 35
character dancer **288** 36
~ mask **289** 33
characteristic *n.* **327** 6
charcoal pencil **321** 16
charge **87** 51, 57
charger **87** 19, **192** 42–45
charging apparatus **111** 55
~ gallery **140** 4
~ mast **188** 11
~ mouth **140** 44
~ platform **140** 4
~ pole **188** 11
~ position **140** 48, 49
~ skip **140** 2
Charioteer **5** 27
charity postage stamp **232** 21
~ surtax **232** 23
Charles's Wain **5** 29
Charleston choke cymbals **303** 50
charlock **63** 18, 21
chart **5** 1–35, **144** 15, **219** 13
~ room **218** 14
~ section **219** 13
charwoman **52** 52
chase *[Hunt.]* **86**
~ *[type]* **175** 38
'chase *[Sports]* **272** 23–29
'chaser **272** 24
chasing **87** 28
~ hammer **106** 42
chasm **282** 2
chassis-frame construction **185** 59
~-less construction **185** 1
~ sheet* **141** 70
chasuble **314** 39
Cheap Jack **291** 64
~ John **291** 64
check* *[invoice]* **238** 50
~ *[ticket]* **145** 84
~* **296** 7
~ *[piano]* **304** 27
~ clock **145** 85
checker* **265** 18
~-board* **265** 17
checkered ornament* **317** 14
checkers* **265** 17–19
check felt **304** 28
~ girl* **296** 6
checking instrument **77** 19
~ office* **200** 27
~ shop **145** 1–45
~ table **145** 37
check loudspeaker **234** 5
~ mate **265** 15
~ rail **198** 54
~rein **272** 41
checkroom* **200** 27, **296** 5
checkroomgirl* **296** 6
~ hall* **296** 5–11
check tail **304** 31
~ wire **304** 29
cheek *[face]* **18** 9
~ *[rifle]* **87** 4
~bone **18** 8, **19** 37
~ brake **136** 95
~ piece **72** 8
~ straps **72** 8
cheese *[food]* **98** 5
~ *[Text.]* **161** 52
~ dish **46** 35
~ dish cover **45** 63
~ fly **341** 16
~ frame **161** 54
~-head screw **136** 34
~ knife **46** 72
~-press **77** 39
~ stick* **45** 61
~ straw **45** 61
cheetah **353** 7
chef **204** 23
~ de partie **263** 3
chelicera **342** 41
Chelsea bun **97** 49
chemical plant **3** 38
chemicals **112** 10
chemical wood pulp **167** 1–10
chemise **31** 4, **33** 11
chemistry **333, 334**
chemist's shop **253** 28
chemosphere **4** 15
chequered ornament **317** 14
chequers* **265** 17–19
cheroot **105** 4
cherry *[fruit]* **61** 5, **357** 32
~ *[mach.]* **106** 7
~ blossom **61** 3
~ flower **61** 3
~ fruit fly **81** 18
~ gall wasp **82** 33
~ leaf **61** 2
~ stone **61** 7
~ tree **61** 1–18
~ twig **61** 1
chess **265** 1–16
chessboard **47** 48, **265** 1
~ square **265** 2
chess clock **265** 16
~man **265** 1, 4
~ player **261** 17
~ position **265** 7
~ table **47** 47
chest *[breast]* **18** 28–30, **19** 8–11
~ *[mus. instr.]* **303** 2, 15
~ band **278** 45
~-developer **278** 50
~-expander **278** 50
~ grip **17** 37
chestnut *[Bot.]* **355** 58, 60, **368** 52
~ *[horse]* **73** 27
chestnut boletus **365** 15

chestnut tree **355** 58
chestpiece **26** 15
chevron ornament **317** 16
chew **105** 23
chewing tobacco **105** 23
chianti **98** 61
chibouk **105** 32
chibouque **105** 32
chick **75** 33
~ box **75** 40
chicken **74** 19–26, **75** 20
~ ladder **75** 4
~ run* **75** 18
~ yard* **75** 18
chick hopper **75** 38
~ pea **70** 19
~ trough **75** 34
chicory **360** 25
~ plant **59** 40
chief *[Her.]* **246** 18 + 19
~ camera man **292** 41
~ clerk **238** 1
~ inspector **145** 44
~ judge **248** 20
~ respectionist **259** 7
~ star **5** 9
chignon **35** 29
child **45** 3+4, **50** 3
~ in arms **30** 26
~ carrier seat **180** 21
children's clothing **31**
~ games **258** 1–59
~ nurse **30** 9, **258** 12
~ playground **258**
~ play room **49** 1–29
~ wear **31**
child's bicycle **181** 13
~ bike* **181** 13
~ boot **31** 45
~ buttocks **30** 39
~ chair **49** 27
child under school age **49** 26
child's coat **31** 37
~ cot **49** 2
~ cycle **181** 13
~ dress **31** 22
~ frock **31** 22
~ grave **312** 30
~ hat **31** 38
~ milk-beaker **49** 29
~ overcoat **31** 37
~ rattle **30** 42
~ seat **180** 21
~ shoe **100** 9
~ stool **50** 11
~ table **49** 28
~ tricycle **258** 59
Chile **14** 34
chilled iron roller **168** 24
chimaera **307** 16
chimbre **126** 30
chimera **307** 16
chimney **40** 5, **113** 21, **146** 15, **205** 22
~ *[rock]* **282** 9
~ base **145** 47
chimney bond **113** 66
~ brick **151** 28
~ cleaner* **40** 31
~ cooler **145** 60
~ flashing **117** 14
~ hood **132** 6
~ piece **259** 24
~pot* **36** 20
~ shaft **145** 46
~ stack **145** 48
~-swallow **346** 20
~ sweep **40** 31
~ top **145** 49
chimpanzee **353** 14
chin **18** 15
China **14** 48, 49
china cupboard **41** 1
China-ink attachment **144** 41
china painter **154** 17
China rose **62** 15
~ rush string **130** 27
chinch* **341** 28
chinchona **364** 17
chine bone **22** 59
Chinese art **319** 1–6
~ lantern **55** 15, **336** 36
~ notable **289** 29
~ script **324** 5
~ shadow show **298** 28
chinook wind soaring **271** 23
chin rest **302** 8
chip *[shavings]* **130** 12
~ *[jetton]* **263** 12
~ basket **130** 11
~ container **164** 40
~-extractor opening **128** 17
~ hat **36** 57
chipper motor **149** 57
chipping hammer **135** 25, 57
chippings **150** 23, **197** 51
~-spreader **196** 41
chips *[shavings]* **127** 47, **129** 26
chiropodist **25** 19
Chiroptera **351** 9
chisel **115** 71, **127**, **132** 37, **150** 37
chitarrone **303** 1
chiton **338** 5
Chitonactis **349** 20
chivalry **310**
chives **59** 22
chlorine **164** 7
chock **141** 56, **189** 51, **286** 2
chocolate **98** 78
~ box **98** 79
~ liqueur **98** 83
chocolates **98** 80
choir *[Arch.]* **311** 36, **317** 4
~ organ **305** 5
~ stalls **311** 34
choker **338** 74
choke tube **183** 68
chopped wood **53** 8
chopper *[tool]* **96** 46
~ * *[ticket collector]* **200** 25
~ *[scissors]* **177** 16
chopping block **53** 9, **64** 18
~ board **41** 57, **96** 45
~ hoe **66** 32
choral poetry and dance *[symbol]* **308** 70
~ vestments **314** 32
chord *[Tech.]* **210** 48, 49
~ *[Geom.]* **328** 51
~ *[Mus.]* **300** 16–18
~ of the seventh **300** 18
chorus **296** 21
~ girl **298** 7
chow(-chow) **71** 21
christening **313** 1
~ dress **313** 8
~ robe **313** 8
~ veil **313** 9
Christian baptism **313** 1
~ crosses **313** 49–66
christiania **283** 32
Christian monogram **313** 61
christie **283** 32
Christmas cake **97** 6
christy **283** 32
chromatic scale **299** 49
chromo-board **168** 31
chromolithographic print **323** 28
chrysalis **81** 4, 43, **82** 13
Chrysanthemum **63** 7
chuck **127** 24, **129** 6, 10, **240** 71
~ key **142** 39
~ rib **95** 19
~ slot **142** 36
~ spindle **128** 23
chulo **287** 59
church **311–313**
~ banner **312** 44
~ bell **312** 9
~ clock **312** 7
~ door **312** 16
~-goer **311** 29, **312** 17
~ organ **305** 1–52
~ owl **347** 17
~ pew **311** 28
~ porch **312** 16
~ roof **312** 11
~ spire **312** 6
~ tower **312** 2
~ w. two towers **16** 53
~ window **311** 16
churchyard **312** 21–41
~ gate **312** 19
~ wall **312** 18
churn **76** 34, **77** 2
~ conveyor **77** 3
chute *[Tech.]* **67** 41, **221** 66
~ *[slide, etc.]* **258** 36, **291** 40
~ *[Sledg.]* **285** 11
~ *[parachute]* **228** 48
ciborium **313** 46
cicatricle **75** 55
cicatricula **75** 55
cicatricule **75** 55
Ciconiiformes **343** 18
C. I. D. officer **248** 3
cigar **105** 2
~-box **47** 33
~ case **105** 11
~ and cigarette boy **259** 49
~-cutter **105** 10
cigarette **105** 14, 15
~-box **47** 32
~ case **105** 12
~-holder **105** 17
~-lighter **186** 20
~ machine **105** 18
~ packet **105** 13
~ paper **105** 19
~ seller **291** 51
~ tip **105** 15
~ tray **259** 50
cigar-holder **105** 9
~ scissors **105** 8
ciliate(d) **354** 49
ciliate infusorian **340** 9
cilium **340** 10, **354** 50
cinchona **364** 17
cincinnus **354** 77
cinder oval* **280** 5
~ track **280** 5
cinema **295** 1
~ box office **295** 2
~ car **204** 24
~-goer **295** 5
~ gong **295** 22
~ projector **295** 26
~ stage **295** 8
~ ticket **295** 3
cinerary urn **309** 38
cingulum **314** 20
cinnamon **98** 44
~ bark **366** 25
~ tree **366** 22
cinquefoil **317** 40
cipher *[letter]* **170** 1
~ *[0]* **263** 18
circle **275** 12, **280** 44, 47
~ *[Math.]* **328** 42
~ *[Gymn.]* **279** 12
~ of feathers **276** 38
circling crossing **277** 51
circuit-breaker **120** 18, **147** 51–62
~ diagram **147** 8
circular adjustment **15** 62
~ medallion **322** 36
~ place* **252** 12
~ plane **329** 39
~ saw **128** 5, **143** 46, **149** 45

clothes-basket **53** 41
~-brush **52** 66
~-drying place **53** 35–42
~ hanger **256** 31
~-line **40** 23, **53** 36
~-line post **53** 38
~ louse **341** 31
~ moth **341** 14
~-peg **53** 42
~-peg bag **53** 40
~-pin **53** 42, **260** 14
~-pin bag **53** 40
~-prop **53** 37
~-rack **43** 1, **52** 69, **260** 12
~ section **259** 30
cloth-finishing **162**
~ gaiter **100** 31
~ hat **36** 1
clothing accessories **37**
~ requisites **37**
Clotho **308** 53
cloth-printing machine **162** 53
~ operative **162** 65
cloth roller **159** 20
~-shearing machine **162** 42
~ spat **100** 31
~ take-up motion **159** 19
~ take-up roller **159** 47
~ temple **159** 13
cloud **8** 1–19
~ chamber **2** 24
~ chamber photograph **2** 26
~ chamber track **2** 27
cloudiness **9** 20–24
cloudless **9** 20
cloud soaring **271** 15
cloudy **9** 23
clout **116** 94
~ iron **131** 12
~ nail **117** 96
cloven-hoofed animal **74** 9
clover **70** 1–5
clove tree **366** 26
clown **289** 69, **290** 23, 24
club *[Sports]* **276** 69, 70
~ * *[baton]* **248** 10
~ flag **274** 34
~ house **269** 23
~-moss **361** 12
~ rush **130** 28, **362** 21
clubs *[cards]* **265** 38+42
club's flag **269** 25
club-swinging **278** 31
clump of grass **359** 44
clumping machine **99** 24
cluster **368** 32
~ of blossoms **60** 15
~ of eggs **81** 2
~ of flowers **60** 15
cluster of fruits **367** 56
~ of grapes **80** 6
~ of stars **5** 26
clutch **181** 36, **185** 41
~ gear **207** 2
~ hub **186** 60
~ lever **181** 36
~ of ostrich eggs **343** 3
~ pedal **185** 41, **207** 23
clyburn **119** 51
C major **300** 1
C major scale **299** 47
C minor **300** 11
C minor scale **299** 48
coach *[vehicle]* **179**, **204** 1
~ *[Sports]* **269** 20
~ body **179** 5, **204** 4
~ box **179** 8
~ coupling **203** 35–39
~ door **179** 11
~ horse **179** 28
~ kitchen **204** 21
~man **179** 32
~ roof **179** 14
~ top **179** 14
~ wheel **204** 62
~ window **179** 10
~work **185** 1–58
~work sheet **141** 70
coal **164** 1
~-box **41** 46, **52** 55
~-breaker **148** 7
~ bunker **146** 2, **148** 3, **199** 44
~ carbonization **148** 10–12
~ chute **220** 50
~ chute crane **220** 66–68
~ conveyor **146** 1, 3
~-crusher **146** 4, **148** 9
~-crushing plant **148** 9
~-cutting machine **138** 41
~ depot **220** 48
~ distributor **220** 68
~ face **137** 39, **138** 12
~ gas **148** 1–46
~-grinder **146** 4
~ haulage **148** 1–9
~-hod **52** 56
coaling crane **199** 43
~ plant **199** 42
~ station **220** 49–51
coal lorry **253** 26
~man **253** 27
~ measures **137** 21
~ mill **146** 4, **152** 12
~ mine **137** 1–40
~-mixer **148** 9
~-mixing plant **148** 9
~ plough **138** 38, 40
~-processing **148** 10–12
coal pulverising plant **152** 12
~ seam **137** 22, **138** 22
~ separation plant **137** 8
~ separator **152** 11
~shovel **41** 47
~ storage **148** 3
~ store **152** 13
~ trimmer **220** 68
~ truck **148** 1
~ tub **137** 29
~ water-heater **51** 3
~ wharf **220** 46–53
~ winding **137** 14
coarse altimeter **228** 9
~ breaker **153** 6
~ cut **132** 35
~ cut sausage **96** 17
~ hackle **125** 4, 7
~ sieve **77** 36
coast **13** 25-31, 35-44
coastal craft **216** 38
~ fishery **90** 24–29
~ submarine **222** 18
~ trade **216** 38
coaster *[ship]* **216** 38
~ *[Sports]* **285** 12
~ brake **180** 63
coasting *[Sports]* **285** 11+12
~ motorship **216** 38
~ path **285** 11
~ slide **285** 11
coat *[Cloth.]* **31** 20, **32** 36, **34** 36
~ *[Her.]* **246** 1–6
~ of arms **246** 10
~ button **34** 50
~ collar **34** 49
~-dress **32** 8
coated paper **168** 37
coat hook peg **43** 3
coating *[paint]* **118** 5
~ *[Tech.]* **138** 32
coat-of-arms **246** 1–6
~ peg **260** 14
~ pocket **34** 37, 51
~ rack **43** 1
~-tail **34** 58
cob **69** 36
~* **362** 22
cobalt tele-radiation apparatus **2** 28
cobbler **99** 23
cobbler's boy **99** 13
~ knife **99** 60
~ stand **99** 27
~ thread **99** 19
~ wax **99** 16
cob nut **61** 49
~web **342** 47
Coccinellidae **342** 37
coccygeal vertebrae **19** 5
coccyx **19** 5, **22** 60
cochlea **19** 63
cock *[Zool.]* **74** 21, **75** 9, **86** 11
cock *[bay]* **65** 37
cockade **247** 4
cockatoo **345** 1
cockatrice **307** 34
cockchafer **82** 1
~ larva **82** 12
cock-drunks **355** 42
cockerel **74** 21
cocker spaniel **71** 42
cock fight **258** 40
cocking lever **111** 14
cockle **63** 6
cock pigeon **74** 33
cockpit **269** 8, **270** 7
cockroach **341** 18
cockscomb **74** 22
cock's feather **36** 42
cocksfoot grass **70** 25
cockshead **70** 10
cock's head **307** 35
~-head **70** 10
~ plume **36** 42
~ tail **74** 25
cock stopper **334** 44
cock's tread(le) **75** 54
cocktail cabinet **47** 39
~ dress **32** 28
~ glass **47** 43, **259** 56
~ set **47** 40–43
~-shaker **259** 61
cock of the woods **88** 72
cocoa **98** 66
~ bean **366** 19
~ jug **45** 32
~ tree **366** 16
coconut **367** 53
~ fat **98** 23
~ tree **367** 48
cocoon **81** 4, **82** 21, **342** 51
cocotte **289** 37
code **245** 29
cod end **90** 22
C. O. D. form **232** 8
codilla **125** 7
cod line **90** 23
codling moth **60** 62
coefficient **327** 4
coelenterate **340** 14, **349** 9, 14, 20
coelostat **6** 15–18
coffee **98** 67
~ bean **366** 6
~ cosy **45** 41
~ cup **45** 7
~ filter **41** 64
~ garden **261** 27–44
~-grinder **41** 62
~-grinder, el. **98** 69
~house **261** 1–26
~-maker* **41** 64
~-mill **41** 62
~-mill, el. **98** 69
~ plant **366** 1
~ pot **45** 12–17
~-roaster **98** 70
~ set **45** 7–21, **261** 18
~ spoon **45** 11

coffee-strainer **42** 44, **45** 25
~ substitute **98** 65
~ tree **366** 1
~ urn **261** 2
coffer dam **216** 29
coffin **312** 35, 51
~-bearer **312** 40
cog *[Tech.]* **91** 9
~ *[ship]* **213** 18–26
cognac **98** 59
cog wheel **136** 80–94
~wheel railway **209** 4+5
coiffeuse **103** 28
coiffure **35** 27–38
coil **332** 8, 9
~ assembly **235** 18
coiled condenser **333** 6
~ filament **120** 58
coiler top **156** 62
coiling drum **141** 69
coil oil cooler **206** 19
~ spring **185** 26, **187** 24
coin **244** 1–28
coinage *[money]* **244** 1–28
coin box **233** 2
~ bracelet **38** 5
coincidence-setting device **110** 33
coin collection **47** 38
~ image **244** 12
coining die **244** 40+41
coin slot **260** 50
~ stamp **244** 40+41
coke **139** 45
~ bunker **148** 20
~ bunker railway **148** 23
~ crane bridge **148** 21
~-firing system **40** 38
~-grading plant **148** 22
~-heating system **40** 38
~-loading plant **148** 24
~-oven plant **148** 17–24
~ plant **148** 17–24, **164** 2
~-processing **148** 17–24
~-quenching plant **148** 17
~-quenching tower **148** 17
~-quenching truck **148** 18
coker nut **367** 53
coke-sorting plant **148** 22
~ storage **148** 20
~-transporting unit **148** 19
colander **42** 47
cold air current **9** 29
cold-air store **94** 16–18
~ supply **92** 20
cold blast main **140** 16
~ chisel **132** 37
~ front **8** 13, **9** 27
~-house **79** 33
~ rolling mill **141** 67
~ saw **143** 46
~-start device **184** 45
cold-storage chamber **94** 16–18
~ house **220** 40
~ room **218** 50
cold vulcanization **191** 24
~-water bath **25** 14
~-water entry **3** 9
~-wave lotion **103** 31
Coleoptera **342** 24–39
coleopter aircraft **225** 70
colibri **345** 4
collapsible boat **269** 54–66
~ hood **179** 52, **187** 14
~ table **204** 38
~ top **187** 14
collar *[Cloth.]* **33** 37, 40, 55
~ *[coin]* **244** 42
~ *[shoe]* **100** 46
~ *[dog]* **71** 13
~ *[horse]* **72** 15
~ *[rept.]* **350** 39
~ *[stag]* **88** 27
~ *[Tech.]* **136** 31
~ awl **123** 33
~ badge **247** 5
~ beam **116** 35, 38, 70
~-beam roof **116** 34
~ bolt **136** 30
~ bone **19** 6
~-button* **33** 61
collared amphora **309** 12
~ beef **96** 22
collar harness **72** 7–25
~-headed bolt **136** 30
~-stiffener **37** 19
~ stud **33** 61
collecting bin **197** 23
~ box **257** 65
~ jar **10** 39
~ trough **93** 9
~ vessel **10** 39
~ well **254** 4
collection **47** 34–38
~ bag **311** 63
~ box **257** 65
~ of photos **47** 37
~ plate **311** 63
~ fr. post box **231** 31
collective consignment **202** 4
~ drupe **354** 101
~ nut fruit **354** 100
collective shipment **202** 4
~ stone fruit **354** 101
collector *[official]* **200** 25
~ *[El.]* **193** 15-19
colliery **137** 1–40
collimator **330** 30, **331** 40
collision **253** 58–69
cologne* **103** 20
Cologne **103** 20
~ water* **103** 20
colon *[Anat.]* **22** 19, 20, 21
~ *[punctuation]* **325** 17
colonnade **262** 9, **316** 67
colophony **302** 11
color* see colour
Colorado beetle **81** 52
colored* see coloured
colors* *[ship]* **216** 37
colour **320**
~ box **321** 10
coloured cloak **338** 10
~ crayon **50** 24
~ glass **135** 27
~ light **320** 10
~ pencil **50** 24
colour filter **111** 48
~ medium **292** 38
~ print **323** 28
~ ribbon **240** 14
colours of racing stud **272** 57
colposcope **110** 11
colt **74** 2
colter **67** 26, **68** 10, 11
coltsfoot **364** 8
Columbian **170** 30
columbine **62** 10
Columbine **289** 27
column *[Art]* **315**, **316** 8–34
~ *[Tech.]* **143** 26, **170** 50, **221** 1
~ *[Print.]* **178** 65, **325** 47
~ base **316** 28–31
~ heading **325** 46
~ indicator **240** 61
~ line **325** 43
~-setting indicator **240** 45
~ shaft **316** 26
~ sleeve **143** 26
comb *[brush]* **51** 77
~ *[cock]* **74** 22
~ *[Spinn.]* **156** 67
combed material **156** 72
comber **156** 56, 63
~ draw box **156** 60
comb foundation **78** 43
~ f. haircutting **104** 3
combinable two-seat chair **209** 18
combination **96** 36
~ brake **189** 43
~ compasses **144** 28
~ consignment **202** 4
~ furniture **47** 53
~ lever **205** 30
~ pliers **120** 53
~ shipment **202** 4
combinative game **265** 1–16
combine* **68** 48
combined filter and petrol tap **182** 32
~ grip **279** 56
~ sewer **194** 36
~ wardrobe **48** 40
combine harvester **68** 48
combing cylinder **156** 68
combustion chamber **146** 6, **184** 26, **227** 17, **229** 22
~ chamber cooling jacket **227** 63, **229** 23
~ gas valve **135** 53
comedy *[symbol]* **308** 61
~ act **290** 25
~ number **290** 25
comestible **46** 38
comet **7** 25
comet's head **7** 26
~ nucleus **7** 25
~ tail **7** 27
~ train **7** 27
comfortable* **48** 11
comforter *[baby]* **30** 51
~* *[quilt]* **48** 11
comfort station* **194** 20
comfrey **359** 45
comic mask **308** 62
comma **325** 18
commanding officer* **223** 46
commercial advertisement **325** 52
~ aircraft **226** 30
~ motor vehicle **189** 1–13
commère **298** 2
commissaries* **201** 48
commissary* **218** 51
commissionaire **256** 44, **296** 10
committee **251** 1+2
~ member **251** 2
~ table **251** 3
commode **23** 25, **48** 2
~ *[hat]* **338** 65
common anchor* **217** 76
~ bean **59** 8
~ brick **113** 58
~ buckwheat **70** 20
~ chord **300** 16 + 17

copper skin* **335** 11
~ sulfate* **330** 26
copy block **238** 17
~-board **171** 21
~ book **249** 46
~-holder **171** 22, 39
~-holder frame **171** 20
copying apparatus **241** 13
~ camera **171** 1
~ glass plate **171** 50
copy milling machine **128** 22
coquille **277** 57
Coraciidae **343** 24-29
coral branch **340** 36
~ polyp **340** 37
~ reef **13** 32
~ zoophyte **340** 35
cor anglais **302** 38
corchorus **357** 28
cord **125** 18, **280** 55
cordate **354** 35
corded ware **309** 10
cord-grip pendant **44** 22
cording **202** 13
cordon **55** 1, 2, 17, 29
cord of wood **84** 24
core *[Bot.]* **60** 36, 59
~ *[Earth]* **11** 5
~ *[Tech.]* **141** 29, **147** 17, **332** 6
~ *[bullet]* **87** 56
~ bit **139** 20
~-print impression **141** 28
Corinthian column **316** 10
~ helmet **308** 19
cork **80** 29
~ ball **275** 18, **276** 37
~ belt **268** 19
~ compressor **80** 28
~ float **89** 52, **268** 32
corking machine **80** 27
cork jacket **224** 58
~ life belt **224** 58
~ ring **268** 19
~screw **46** 46
~screw staircase **118** 76
~ sock **99** 8
~ sole **100** 36
~ tip **105** 15
cormorant **343** 10
corn **69** 1–37
~* **69** 31
~ camomile **63** 8
~ chamomile **63** 8
~ cob **69** 36
~ cockle **63** 6
~-dressing **83** 13–16
cornea **21** 47
~ microscope **109** 14
cornel berry **357** 32
~ bush **357** 30
~ cherry **357** 32
corner *[Geom.]* **329** 33
~ *[Footb.]* **274** 10, 58
~ *[balma]* **265** 27
~ area **274** 10
~ bench **260** 38, **262** 32
~ board **41** 33
~ bottom slate **117** 77
~ brace **115** 26
~ bulkhead fitting **43** 24
~ chisel **127** 65, **322** 19
~ flag **274** 10
~ kick **274** 58
~ of mouth **21** 19
~ pin **287** 11
~ seat **204** 42
~ shop **253** 40
~ stile **115** 52
~ store* **253** 40
~ strut **115** 52
~ stud **115** 52
~ tower **310** 14
cornet **302** 43
cornett **301** 12
corn·field **65** 19
~ flower **63** 1
~ husker **91** 52
cornice **39** 9, **115** 34, **282** 14, **316** 11–14
corn leaf **69** 19
~ marigold **63** 7
~ mill **91** 45–67
corno **302** 41
corn-polisher **91** 56
~-polishing machine **91** 56
~ poppy **63** 2
~ rick **65** 27
~ salad **59** 38
~ sheaf **65** 23
~ spurrey **70** 12
~ stack **65** 27
~ stem **69** 5
~ thistle **63** 32
cornucopia **308** 39
corolla **354** 59, **362** 4
corona **7** 22
Corona Borealis **5** 31
corona of sun **7** 22
coronet *[crown]* **246** 43, 44, 45
~ *[jewellery]* **38** 6
~ *[horse]* **73** 25
corps de ballet **288** 29
corpse **312** 54
corpus callosum **19** 44
~ cavernosum and spongiosum **22** 67
correction button **256** 4
corresponding angle **328** 12
corrida **287** 57
corrugated asbestos-cement roofing **117** 90–103
~ paper **83** 25
~ paper band **83** 24
~ sheet **117** 98
corseted waist **338** 53
corvette **222** 13
Corvidae **346** 1–3
corvine bird **346** 1–3
cosmetics trolley **103** 4
cosmic particle **4** 27
~ radiation **4** 27–34
~ ray particle **4** 27
cosmotron **2** 49
Cossack cap **36** 4
costal cartilage **19** 11
coster **253** 11
costermonger **253** 11
costume **32** 1, 58
~-designer **296** 38
~ jacket **32** 2
~ skirt **32** 4
cosy **45** 41, 51
cot **30** 11, **49** 2
~* **266** 7
cottage* **39** 84–86
cotton *[Bot.]* **367** 16, 19
~ *[wool]* **30** 50
~ bale **156** 3
~ bandage **23** 55
~ boll **156** 1
~ disk **77** 37
~ grass **361** 18
Cotton's Patent knitting machine **160** 18
cotton line **90** 29
~ plant **367** 16
~-spinning mill **156, 157**
~ waste **192** 69
~-wool **28** 9, **30** 50
~-wool roll **27** 25
cotyledon **354** 87
couch *[sofa]* **47** 46, **48** 53, **124** 21
~ *[Bot.]* **63** 30
~ covering **124** 26
~ grass **63** 30
couching stitch **101** 8
couch f. massage **24** 4
couchman **168** 47
couch roll **48** 54
coudière **310** 48
coulee* **13** 45
coulter **67** 12, 26, **68** 10, 11
counsel **248** 30
counselor-at-law* **248** 30
counter *[table]* **96** 1, **242, 260** 1–11, **261** 1
~ *[Tech.]* **2** 21, **240** 43
~ *[ship]* **222** 77
~ *[shoe]* **99** 39
~ *[Skat.]* **284** 19
~ *[letter]* **170** 41
~ *[jetton]* **263** 12
~ *[School]* **249** 39
~ f. brokers **243** 3
~ clerk **231** 10
~ envelope **2** 20
counter drawer **231** 16
~ gear assembly **254** 55
~-jump **284** 6
~poise **212** 76
counters **254** 59
counter·sink **127** 16
~-spin stroke **264** 6
countersunk head **136** 44
~-head bolt **136** 26
counter top **242** 9
~weight **114** 33, **212** 76
counting bead **249** 39
~ detector tube **2** 19
~ frame **249** 38
~ out **281** 38
country road* **197** 28
~ seat **16** 94
count's coronet **246** 45
coupé *[vehicle]* **179** 3, **187** 10, 13
~ *[Railw.]* **204** 27
couple **259** 46, **288** 44+45
~ of dancers **259** 46
coupled axle **205** 36
~ sleeper **198** 45
couple of lovers **257** 44
coupler **305** 48
coupling **133** 37, **189** 48
~ bolt **198** 46
~ device **189** 48
~ hook **117** 64
~ link **203** 35
~ screw **203** 36
~ spindle **141** 53
~ unit **189** 32
coupon **243** 18
~ sheet **243** 17
courbette **72** 6
course *[Arch.]* **113** 63, 64, 67, 68
~ *[windmill]* **91** 21
~ *[Sports]* **272** 1–35, **283** 19
~-counter **160** 43
~ judges' box **272** 35
~ of outer station **4** 55
~ of river **211** 9
~ of rocket **4** 44
~-transmitter **230** 11
court *[yard]* **53** 1–49
~ *[Just.]* **248** 19
~ *[Sports]* **276** 1
court doctor **248** 37
~ dress **338** 79
courting couple **257** 44
Court of Justice **248** 18
~ of Law **248** 18
court room **248** 19
~ shoe **100** 40
courtyard **53** 1–49
~ wall **53** 25
coute **310** 48

cover [*lid*] **45** 63
~ [*tyre*] **180** 30
~ [*Text.*] **161** 5
~ [*table*] **46** 3–12
covered [*sky*] **9** 24
~ bridge **145** 52
~ chaise **179** 54
~ goods wagon **208** 4
~ market **252** 50
~ storage reservoir **254** 13
~ wagon **208** 34
~ walk **54** 5
~ way **39** 73
covering **147** 39
~ board **79** 9
~ a frame **130** 22–24
~ ground **323** 56
~ shutter **79** 9
cover slide **2** 32
coving **318** 10
cow **74** 1, **76** 18
~boy **289** 31
~ calf **74** 1
~-catcher **205** 34
~ chain **76** 31
~ droppings **76** 22
~ dung **76** 22
~hand* **289** 31
~hide whip **124** 18
~ horn **76** 38
~ house **76** 17–38
cowl **314** 16
cowling **185** 47
Cowper's gland **22** 75
cowshed **76** 17–38
cowslip **360** 8
cox **269** 11
~comb **289** 33
coxswain **224** 38, **269** 11
~less four **269** 9
coxswain's seat **269** 27
Crab **6** 35
crab [*Zool.*] **342** 1
~ [*Tech.*] **140** 3, **145** 2, 56, **217** 14
~ guard **196** 10
~ louse **341** 29
~-traversing gear **145** 4
crack **52** 67, **282** 4
cracker* [*rusk*] **97** 43
~ [*firework*] **289** 50
cracking plant **139** 33
crack shot **290** 38
cracowes **338** 42
cradle [*baby*] **50** 15
~ [*teleph.*] **233** 29
~ [*gun*] **223** 69
~ [*tool*] **323** 19
craft [*air~*]* **225**
crakeberry **361** 23
cramp **114** 58, **115** 66
~ iron **114** 58
crampon **283** 51
~ strap **282** 48
cranberry **361** 23
Crane **5** 42
crane [*Tech.*] **145** 1-19, **189** 53, **221** 1–7
crane arm **145** 17
~berry **361** 23
~ boom **192** 62
~ bridge **145** 7, **148** 21
~ cable **217** 13
~ camera **292** 19
~ chain **133** 33, **161** 59
~ column **192** 61
~ dolly **292** 19
~-driver **145** 12
~-driver's cabin **114** 35, **217** 16, **221** 40
~ frame **221** 41
~ girder **145** 7
~ gully and cesspit emptier **195** 25
~ hoist **140** 54
~ hook **133** 34, **221** 21
~ jib **145** 17
~ lorry **189** 52
~man **145** 12
~ navvy **196** 1
~-operated ladle **140** 53
~-operator **145** 12
~ portal **221** 7
~ rail **145** 14
~ rope **145** 8
crane's-bill **360** 24
crane slipway **217** 23–26
~ track **114** 27, **217** 24
~ truck* **255** 47
~ wagon **208** 37
cranium **19** 30–41
crank **145** 23, **162** 52, **180** 41, **323** 33
~ axle **85** 28
crankcase scavenging **181** 49
~ ventilation **184** 20
crank-connecting arm **159** 52
~ drive **212** 53
cranked wing **225** 20
crank handle **162** 52, **197** 18
~ shaft **159** 50, **184** 56
~ shaft wheel **159** 51
crannog(e) **309** 15
crap game* (or craps, crap shooting) **265** 29
crash helmet **190** 18, **273** 3, **285** 16
crate **202** 19
crater [*volcano*] **11** 16
~ [*carbon*] **295** 44
craw **74** 20
crawfish net* **89** 15
crawl(ing) **268** 38
crayfish net **89** 15
crayon **50** 24, **321** 5, **323** 26
~ method **323** 14–24
crazy pavement **54** 22
~ paving **54** 22
cream [*milk*] **97** 11
~ [*cosmetic*] **51** 70, **103** 11
~ cake **97** 35
~-cheese machine **77** 41
~-cooler **77** 26
creamer* **261** 21
cream-heater **77** 25
~ jug **45** 19, **261** 21
~-maker **42** 38
~-maturing vat **77** 28
~-pitcher* **261** 21
~ puff **97** 50
~ roll **97** 12
~-separator **77** 24
~-server **261** 21
crease [*fold*] **34** 12
~ [*Cricket*] **275** 56, 57
~ [*dagger*] **336** 44
~ of trousers **34** 12
creek* **13** 8, 13, **16** 80
creel **89** 9, **157** 28, 41
creeper **55** 5, **59** 8
~-type truck* **189** 36
creeping wheat grass **63** 30
~ thistle **63** 32
creese **336** 44
crenate **354** 46
crenel **310** 18
crenellated battlements **310** 6
crenellations **310** 6
crepe bandage **23** 47
~ paper **51** 31
~ rubber sole **100** 3
crescendo **300** 49
~ roller **305** 49
Crescent **245** 19
crescent [*moon*] **7** 3, 7
~ * [*croissant*] **97** 41
crescentic dune **13** 40
crescent-shaped· knife **123** 7
~ roll **97** 41
crescent wing **225** 68
~-wing aircraft **225** 67
cress **362** 30
crest [*animal*] **73** 12, **74** 22, **350** 21
~ [*Her.*] **246** 1, 11, 30–36
~ coronet **246** 12
~ crown **246** 12
crested helmet **308** 10
~lark **346** 19
crevasse **12** 50, **282** 24
crew* **84** 20, **141** 13
~ haircut* **35** 10
crib **30** 11, 32, **49** 2
cricket [*Zool.*] **341** 6
~ [*Sports*] **275** 55–61
~ bat **275** 60
~-cap **31** 58
~ shirt **31** 49
crier **291** 8
criminal investigation department **247** 21–24
~ records office **247** 21
criminals' photograph register **247** 22
crimping the tow **164** 59
crimson clover **70** 4
crinoline **338** 72
cripple **257** 55
crisp bread **97** 21
criss-cross stitch **102** 9
croaking sac **350** 25
crockery board **41** 18
~ cloth **41** 16
crocket **317** 38
crocodile **298** 26
croisé derrière **288** 8
croissant **97** 41
cro' jack yard **215** 25
cromorne **301** 6
crook of arm **18** 44
~ handle **43** 14
crooner **298** 3
crop [*harvest*] **65** 35–43
~ [*hen*] **74** 20
croquet **275** 62–67
~ ball **275** 67
~ mallet **275** 66
~ player **275** 65
crosier **314** 48
cross [*symbol*] **5** 44, **313** 49–66
~ [*hybrid*] **74** 8
~ ancrée **313** 63
~ arm **146** 37
~ arms* **10** 29
~ bar **44** 13, **76** 14, **131** 3
~ beam **76** 14
~-bearer **312** 43
~ bond **113** 65
~ botonée **313** 65
~ chisel **132** 37
cross-country· path **16** 102
~ race **273** 33, **280** 23
~ racer **283** 30
~ tyre **189** 12
cross crossletted **313** 62
~ w. cups **10** 29
~ cut [*mine*] **137** 35, 36
cross-cut· chisel **134** 19
~ circular saw **149** 45
~ saw **85** 34, 38, **115** 14
cross-cutting **128** 10
cross fall **196** 57
~ feed bar **177** 59
~-fold knife **178** 12
~ gear **295** 38
~-grain timber **115** 92
~ grip **279** 55

cross-hair diopter* **87** 31+32
~ hairs* **87** 32
~ handle **263** 32,
~ hatching **323** 54
~head **133** 26, **205** 27
~-head bollard **212** 14
~ heading **325** 46
crossing *[road, etc.]* **198** 67–78, **253** 9
~ *[Fenc.]* **277** 48–52
~ of blades **277** 48
~ of cords **113** 70
~ of a glacier **282** 23–25
~ at grade* **16** 26, **198** 67–78
~ of legs during jump **288** 13
~ watchman* **198** 70
crossjack sail **215** 26
~ yard **215** 25
cross of Jerusalem **313** 64
cross-leaved heath **361** 19
crosslet **313** 62
cross-line screen **171** 35
~ of Lorraine **313** 56
~ measure drift **137** 35
~ on the tomb **312** 25
crossover **199** 31
cross-over pipe **147** 28
cross pall **313** 55
Cross of the Passion **313** 49
cross piece *[Tech.]* **114** 57, 61, **217** 15
~ piece *[foil]* **277** 56
~ potent **313** 64
~ roads **253** 9
~-section **283** 42
cross-section· of a concrete road **197** 43–46
~ of bituminous road **196** 55
~ of bridge **210** 1
~ of street **194**
cross-shaped bollard **212** 13
~ slide **142** 23, **143** 2, 44
~- slide handwheel **142** 15
~ spider **342** 45
~ stitch **101** 5
~ street **253** 7
~ strut **114** 67
~ tie **116** 30, **210** 6
~ tree **214** 51, 53
~ wires **87** 32
cross-wound· cheese **157** 58, **161** 52, 54
~ cone **158** 8, **157** 58, **161** 52, 54
~ frame **161** 54
crotchet **299** 17
~ rest **299** 25
crouch **281** 9, 26
crouched burial **309** 17
~ jump **268** 14
crouching **278** 23, **281** 26
croup(e) *[horse]* **73** 31
~ *[vaulting horse]* **279** 36
~ dock **72** 34
~ loop **72** 34
~ pommel **279** 38
~ strap **72** 32
croupier **263** 4
croupier's rake **263** 5
croupon strap **72** 32
crow **346** 1–3
~bar **150** 32
~berry **361** 23
crowd **251** 8
~ actor **292** 29
crowfoot **359** 8
crown *[diadem]* **246** 37, 38, 42–46
~ *[vault]* **318** 39
~ *[tooth]* **27** 31
~ *[watch]* **107** 14
~ block **139** 3
~ of Charlemagne **246** 38
~ cork **93** 43
~-cork bottle-opener **46** 47
~ of feathers **276** 38
~ of head **18** 1
~ of Holy Roman Empire **246** 38
~ of hooks **341** 27
~ of orange blossom **313** 18
~ of rank **246** 43–45
~ piece **72** 10
~ platform **139** 2
~ of tree **354** 3
crow quill **301** 53
crow's-nest *[boat]* **90** 39
croze **126** 30
crozer **126** 30
croze saw **126** 23
crozier **314** 48
crozing machine **126** 38
crucible **106** 9, **334** 31
~ tongs **106** 10, **334** 32
crucifer **312** 43
crucifix *[cross]* **311** 40, **313** 32, **314** 6
~ *[Gymn.]* **279** 48
crude-gas main **148** 13
~ iron outlet **140** 11
~ oil **139**
~-oil product **139** 36–47
~-oil production **139** 48–55
cruet stand **260** 22
cruiser **222** 21–30
~ stern **270** 14
~ combustion chamber cooling jacket **227** 61
crumb **97** 22
~ brush **45** 58, **52** 70
~ set **45** 58+59
~ tray **45** 59
crunch **98** 85
crupper **73** 31
~ dock **72** 34
~ loop **72** 34
~ strap **72** 32
crusader **310** 72
crush hat **36** 20
crushed grapes **80** 14, 15
~ limestone **153** 10
~ stone **150** 24
~ stone aggregate **153** 11
crushing the grain **91** 57
~ ring **67** 6
crush room **296** 12+13
crust **97** 23, 24
crustacean **341** 12, **342** 1+2
crustaceous animal **340** 25–34
crusta petrosa **21** 29
crutch **213** 14
Crux **5** 44
crux ansata **313** 57
cryptogear* **136** 92
crystal *[Mineral.]* **234** 30, **330**
~ * *[watch]* **107** 7
~ centre **330** 3
~ combination **330** 1–26
~ cone **78** 21
~ form **330** 1–26
~ glass **46** 86
crystalline lens **21** 48
crystallography **330**
crystallometry **330** 27–33
crystal receiver **234** 21–34
C sharp major **300** 8
C sharp minor **300** 5
'C'spanner **192** 2
cubby-hole **186** 21
cube **98** 26, 27, **329** 30, **330** 2, 16
~-root **327** 2
~ sugar **98** 53
cubic crystal system **330** 1–17
cubicle **25** 4, **268** 1
cubic meter (or metre*) of wood **84** 24
cuckoo **343** 30
~ clock **107** 54
~ flower **359** 11
~-pint **363** 9
cucumber **59** 13
cud-chewing animal **351** 28–30
cuddie **74** 3
cuddly toy **49** 5
cuddy **74** 3
cudweed **361** 3
cue **264** 9
~ ball **264** 11
~ rest **264** 19
~ tip **264** 10
cuff **33** 38, 53
~-link **33** 60
cuffs **248** 9
cuirass **310** 46
cuissart **310** 52
cuisse **310** 52
cul-de-sac **252** 40
culex **342** 16
cullender **42** 47
cultivation of land **65** 1–46
cultivator **58** 17, **68** 31, **79** 21
~* **68** 45
culture *[Hyg.]* **25**
~ *[Biology]* **93** 15-18
cumulo-nimbus cloud **8** 17
cumulus **8** 1
~ cloud **8** 1, **271** 16
~ congestus **8** 2
cuneiform script **324** 8
cup **45** 7, **266** 41
~ *[Bot.]* **355** 5
~-bearer **310** 69
cupboard **48** 40
~ shelf **48** 41
cup of coffee **261** 19
cupid **257** 20
Cupid **308** 26
Cupid's dart **308** 28
cupola *[Art]* **316** 58
~ *[Tech.]* **141** 1
~ furnace **141** 1
cupping glass **26** 56
~ instrument **26** 56
cupule **355** 5, **368** 52
curb **53** 21, **194** 8
~ bit **72** 13
~ chain **72** 12
~ roof **116** 18
~stone **53** 22, **194** 9
Curculionidae **81** 49
cure **29** 21-25
curette **26** 60, **28** 58
curing floor **92** 15
curl **35** 3
curled horsehair **124** 11
curler *[hair]* **103** 35
~ *[Sports]* **284** 43
curling **284** 42
~ irons **103** 38
~ stone **284** 44
~ tongs **103** 38
curly greens **59** 34
~ hair **35** 17
~ kale **59** 34
~ tail **74** 12

danger area **2** 50
danseuse **288** 31
Daphne **361** 10
darkey **337** 13
darkness **4** 26
darkroom **112** 1–61
darkroom lamp **112** 18
dark slide **171** 5
darky **337** 13
darner **102** 57
darning arm **102** 26
~ ball **102** 63
~ egg **102** 63
~ last **102** 63
~ mushroom **102** 64
~ needle **102** 57
~ stitch **101** 17
~ wool **102** 51
~ yarn **102** 51
dart **78** 10, **287** 64
dash **325** 23
~board **186** 1–21
~-light lever **186** 8
date *[time]* **239** 6
~ *[rendezvous]* **257** 44
~ *[Bot.]* **368** 1
~ book* **200** 10
~ cluster **368** 8
~ of issue **242** 14
~ kernel **368** 10
~ of letter **239** 6
~ of maturity **242** 16
~ palm **368** 1
~ of payment **242** 16
~ punch **201** 56
~ stamp *[postmark]* **232** 39
~ stamp *[office]* **238** 41
~ tree **368** 1
daughter boat **224** 44
davit **216** 45, **218** 20,
day clock **107** 45
~ cream **103** 11
~ fly **342** 6
~light signal **201** 35
~-nursery **49**
~-service diesel train **207** 37
~ sheet **238** 66
day's takings **256** 10
daytime layer **4** 18
d. c. slip ring* **331** 77
dead body **312** 54
~ bolt **134** 39
~ branch of river **211** 17
~ centre **129** 8
~-end station **199** 1
~ end street **252** 40
~ house **312** 21
deadly nightshade **363** 7
dead man **312** 54
~-man's button (or handle) **206** 35
dead wood **270** 15
de-aerator **147** 16
de-airing· brick machine **151** 11
~ pug **154** 7
dealer **243** 7
death *[advertisement]* **325** 51
~ *[Hunt.]* **272** 59
~-cup **363** 11
~ mask **44** 31
death's-head hawk-moth **348** 9
debenture **243** 11–19
debris **13** 29
decade *[rosary]* **313** 30
decanter **46** 48, **260** 32
decathlon competitor **280** 56
decatizing machine **162** 49
~ roller **162** 50
deceased **312** 54
deciduous forest **16** 4
~ tree **355** 1–73
~ wood **16** 4
decimal bar **240** 49
~ fraction **326** 20, 21
~ point **326** 20
deck **210** 20, **218**, **269** 57
~ beam **217** 54
~ brake* **222** 71
~ cargo **220** 55
~-chair **54** 10, **216** 54
~ hand **297** 46
~ house **218** 34
~ load **220** 55
~ plan **222** 48
~ plating **217** 53
~ space **218** 28
~ tennis **267** 31
declination axis **6** 6, **109** 22
~ circle **109** 23
décolletage lowcut **32** 26
decorated bowl **309** 11
decoration **38** 1
decorative fillet **183** 16
~ fringe **336** 25
~ vencer **127** 34
decorator* **121** 35
decorator's hammer* **121** 39
decoy bird **86** 48
decoyed bird **86** 50
decoy-shooting **86** 47–52
decrescendo **300** 50
dedication **178** 50
deep-etched parts **172** 36
~-freezer show case **98** 3
~-freezing compartment **42** 4
~ fryer **97** 69
~ hull **225** 34
~ keel **221** 55
~-loading small lorry **189** 6
~ plate **46** 5
~ pool **268** 23
deep-sea· crab **349** 16
~ descent **4** 9
deep-sea
~ diving **224** 13–19
~ fauna **349**
~ fish **349**
~ fishery **90** 1–23
~ medusa **349** 5
~ platform **11** 10
~ prawn **349** 12
deep-well **254** 4
deer **88** 1–27
~hound **272** 63
~skin shoe **100** 2
~-stalker **86** 1
~-stalking **86** 1–8
defence **274** 12+13
defendant **248** 29
defender **277** 21
defending counsel **248** 30
defensive position **281** 8
defile **16** 84
deflecting coil **236** 25
~ plate **332** 26
~ roller **295** 29
~ wall **286** 2
deflorate flower **60** 55
defroster hose **185** 35
~ louvre **186** 11
degree *[Math.]* **327** 2
~ *[Mus.]* **299** 46
~ of root **327** 2
dehiscent fruit **354** 91–96
deity **307** 23
delicatessen shop **98** 1–87
~ store* **98** 1–87
delivery *[machine]* **177** 53, **178** 35
~ bed **29** 5
~ bicycle **181** 15
~ blower **175** 33
~ board **177** 51, **241** 9
~ box **178** 15
~ cart **202** 18
~ chute **67** 41
~ cylinder **174** 20
~ hose **255** 31
~ jaw **241** 10
~ motor lorry **189** 1
~ pile board **174** 10
~ pipe **254** 16, 52
~ roller **156** 32, **157** 59, **176** 32
~ room **29** 1
~ table **175** 31
~ to folder **175** 53
~ truck* **189** 1
~ van **189** 7
Delphinium **62** 13
delta **13** 1
~ aircraft **225** 53
~ connection **147** 21
~-shaped fuselage **225** 57
~ tail unit **225** 56
~-type aircraft **225** 29
delta wing **225** 30, 54
~-wing aircraft **225** 29
deltoid **328** 38
~ muscle **20** 35
de luxe limousine **187** 9
demesne **16** 94
demi-goat **246** 32
~john **202** 14
~-mondaine **289** 37
~-rep **289** 37
demisemiquaver **299** 20
~ rest **299** 28
demodulator **237** 35
demon **307** 58
den **47** 1–61
Deneb **5** 23
Denmark **14** 4, **245** 17
denominator **326** 15
dent **36** 13
dental bridge **27** 29
~ chair **27** 3
~ engine **27** 12–15
~ pulp **21** 32
~ surgeon **27** 1
~ treatment **27** 2
~ unit **27** 6
dentate **354** 47
dent corn **69** 31
dentifrice **51** 58, 59
dentils **316** 14
dentine **21** 31
denting arrangement **165** 6
~ f. weaver **165** 4
dentist **27** 1
dentist's assistant **27** 26
denture **27** 28
deodorant **51** 29
department **242** 1-11, **247** 18+19
departmental store **256**
department manager **256** 60
~ store **252** 18
departure indicator **201** 25
~ lines **199** 14
~ schedule* **200** 20
~ timetable **200** 20
deposit *[Geol.]* **11** 26, 31
~ counter **242** 7
deposition **11** 47
deposits *[Geol.]* **13** 69
depot **252** 17
~* **200**
depression **9** 5
~ adjustment* **184** 16
depth **6** 50, **137** 12 to 13
~ of focus **11** 34
~ gauge **134** 54, **142** 48

derailment guard **209** 75
derby* *[hat]* **36** 7
Derby brogue **100** 2
~ casual **100** 13
~ tie **100** 1
derivation **327** 13
Dermaptera **341** 10
derrick **12** 33, **139** 1, 48, **216** 3
descant viol **301** 23
descending branch of the aorta **20** 16
~ arpeggio **300** 37
~ climber **282** 31
~ colon **22** 21
~ line **224** 17
~-line weight **224** 18
descent indicator **228** 13
desert belt **9** 54
~ zone **9** 54
deshabille **48** 16
desiccator **334** 51
~ insert **334** 54
designation of series **244** 36
designer **144** 9, **296** 37, 38
designing engineer **144** 23
desk **47** 11, **238** 12, **249** 27, **293** 23
~ chair **47** 18
~ clerk* **259** 7
~ lamp **47** 17, **238** 23
~ microphone **234** 8
~ pad **238** 65
~ scale **200** 41
~ telephone **47** 12, **238** 24
dessert plate **46** 6
destination board **201** 24
~ plate **201** 34
destroyer **222** 14, 16, 17
desulfurization* **163** 20
desulphurizing **163** 20
detachable collar **33** 37
~ piece **303** 71
~ snow plough **286** 8
~ stanchion **208** 8
detached houce **39** 1–53
detaching roller **156** 71
detachment **247** 1–8
detective **248** 3, **263** 16
detective's badge **247** 24
detector **234** 29–32
detent screw **29** 10
detergent **41** 29
~ casing **166** 4
determinant triangle **110** 36
detonating rammer **196** 26
detonator cap **87** 58
detritus **12** 45
deuteropyramid **330** 20
Devanagari **324** 9
developer **278** 49, 50
developing dish **112** 36
~ slot **241** 20
~ tank **112** 1, 13
development **293** 15-18
développé **288** 8
deviation card **228** 12
~ table **228** 12
device *[Tech.]* **335** 31
devil **289** 14, **298** 27
devil's grandmother **298** 24
~ wheel **291** 46
de-waxing plant **139** 34
dew claw **88** 23, 57
~lap **74** 24
dexter **246** 18, 20, 22
D. F. aerial **218** 5
D. F. loop **218** 5
D flat major **300** 13
3D-grouping **235** 22+23
diabolo **258** 24, **298** 22
diadem **38** 6, **338** 21
diaeresis **325** 34
diagonal **328** 33
~ brace **113** 88, **114** 51
diagonal board **114** 63
~ bracing **114** 14
~ cable **210** 38
~-cable anchorage **210** 40
~-cable bridge **210** 37
~ carvel planking **270** 25
~ dip-shear action **178** 3
~ stay **113** 25, 88
~ tie **116** 30
diagram **144** 15
diagrammatic map **200** 33
dial *[watch]* **107** 2
~ *[teleph.]* **233** 18, **241** 34
~ balance **98** 12
~ bench gage* **145** 38–43
~ indicator **145** 42
dialogue tape **293** 13
~ track **293** 13
dial piece **107** 2
~ plate **107** 2
diameter **328** 45
~of fabric **160** 16
~ of spiral nebula **6** 46
diamond *[stone]* **38** 26
~ *[baseball]* **275** 39
~ *[Typ.]* **170** 21
~ bit **139** 20
~ crossing **199** 32
~ disc **27** 38
~ formation **287** 8
~ glass-cutter **122** 25
~ horseshoe* **296** 18
~ necklace **38** 8
~ necklet **38** 8
~ ring **38** 24
~ wheel **27** 39
diamonds *[cards]* **265** 41+45
Diana **308** 12
diapason bass **305** 31–33
diaper **30** 6
diaphragm *[Med.]* **22** 9, 26, **27** 36
~ *[Tech.]* **10** 52, **331** 29
~ blade **111** 45
diaphragmatic shutter **111** 44
diaphragm leaf **111** 45
~ knapsack sprayer **83** 31
~ shutter **111** 44
diapositive projector **295** 25
diary **238** 31
diaulos **301** 3
dibber **57** 7, **58** 2
dibble **57** 7, **58** 2
dibbler **67** 18
~ star **67** 19
dice **265** 31
~ box **265** 30
~ game **265** 29
dicing **265** 29
dick(e)y seats **187** 12
dictaphone **241** 24
dictating machine **241** 24
didelphic marsupial **351** 2
die **106** 15, **151** 13, **244** 40+41
~ hammer **85** 43
~ head **136** 55
dieresis* **325** 34
diesel compressor **196** 39
diesel electric· drive **218** 58-64
~ power transmission **207** 6
~ railcar* **201** 27
~ ship drive **218** 58–64
diesel engine **184** 37–80
~ goods traction rail-car **207** 39
diesel hydraulic· long-distance railcar train **207** 29
~ power transmission **207** 3
diesel mechanical· light-alloy (or light-metal) railcar **207** 28
~ power transmission **207** 1
~ rail omnibus **207** 25
diesel observation railcar **207** 40
~ oil **139** 43
~ railcar **207** 28-40
~ rail coach **207** 28–40
~ railway vehicle **207** 1–43
~ traction railcar **207** 39
~ train **207** 37+38
die-sinking machine* **128** 22
~ stock **120** 48
~ wrench **134** 27
differential *[Math.]* **327** 13,14
differential *[Tech.]* **184** 36, **185** 50
~ gear **185** 50
~ housing **189** 27
~ quotient **327** 13
diffuser **294** 5
digester **167** 2
digger **312** 22
digging fork **58** 5, **66** 30
digit **326** 3
Digitalis **363** 2
digitate(d) **354** 39
dihedral angle **225** 45
dike **211** 32
~ batter **211** 40
~ drainage lock **211** 34
~ drainage sluice **211** 34
~-keeper **211** 46
~-keeper's cottage **211** 45
~ ledge **211** 38
~ ramp **211** 47
~ reeve **211** 46
~ slope **211** 40
~ summit **211** 39
~ top **211** 39
diligence **179** 39
dimension **144** 17
~ line **144** 58
dim light* **185** 17
dimmer* **186** 3
dimple in chin **18** 16
~ at the corner of mouth **18** 14
dimswitch* **186** 3
diminuendo **300** 50
dinar **244** 28
diner* *[car]* **204** 17
~ headwaiter* **204** 44
dining car **204** 17
~ car headwaiter **204** 44
~ chair **204** 45
~ compartment **204** 18, 52

doll's kitchen **49** 7
~ kitchen range **49** 8
~ pram **49** 12
~ room **49** 9
~ tableware **49** 11
dolly *[tool]* **53** 73
~ *[camera]* **237** 4, **292** 19
~ operator **292** 24
dolmen **309** 16
dolphin *[Zool.]* **308** 31
~ *[harbour]* **220** 37
dolphin's tail **307** 25
dolphin stroke **268** 35
domain **16** 94
dome *[Arch.]* **319** 21
~ *[Tech.]* **195** 37, **205** 12, **216** 11
~ cover **40** 48
domed roof **116** 25
domestic animal **74**
~ ass **74** 3
~ cat **74** 17
~ dog **74** 16
~ duck **74** 35
~ fowl **74** 19–26
~ goose **74** 34
~ help **45** 54
~ pig **74** 9
~ pigeon **64** 10, **74** 33
~ rabbit **74** 18
~ servant **45** 54
dome system **316** 72+73
dominant seventh **300** 18
Dominican **314** 19
domino *[fancy dress]* **289** 15
~ brick **265** 34
dominoes **265** 33
domino piece **265** 34
donjon **310** 4
donkey **74** 3
~-riding **257** 45
donor **29** 27
door **43** 30, **109** 3, **204** 28, **312** 16
~-bolt **53** 66
~ button **120** 2
~ catch **75** 26
~ chain **43** 32
~ handle **179** 12, **185** 5
~-lifting mechanism **133** 60
~ lock **75** 26, **185** 6
~man **256** 44
~ mat **43** 34
~ of object chamber **109** 3
~ opening **52** 68
~ scraper **118** 25
~ shelf **42** 8
~steps **39** 66
~way **53** 19
~ window **185** 20
~yard* **39** 57, **53**
dor beetle **342** 39
Doric column **316** 8
~ temple **316** 1
dormer **40** 7, **310** 11
~ window **40** 7, **116** 6, 23, **318** 4
dorsal crest **350** 21
~ fin *[Zool.]* **350** 6, **352** 27
~ fin *[aircr.]* **228** 41
~ stabilizer **228** 41
~ vertebra(e) **19** 3
dosimeter **2** 8–23
dosser **64** 40
dot *[Mus.]* **299** 9
~ wheel **102** 62
double aulos **301** 3
~ backward somersault **268** 43
~-barrel gun **87** 33
~ bass **302** 23
~ bassoon **302** 28
~ bed **48** 3–15, **259** 38
~ berth **262** 34
~ bevel shoulder notch **116** 91
~-bladed paddle **269** 39
~ bollard **212** 11
~ bottom **217** 57
~-bottom tank **218** 68
~-breasted suit **34** 4
~ cable suspension railway **209** 30
~ card* **232** 4
~ chair **209** 17
~ claw **78** 8
~ clock **265** 16
~-column type area **178** 64
~-concave lens **108** 2
~ condenser **331** 25
~ contraoctave **300** 62
~-convex lens **108** 7
~ cradle **209** 68
~ cross stitch **101** 5
~-decker **188** 6
double-decker· bus **188** 6
~ luggage van **208** 39
~ passenger coach **204** 60
~ wagon **208** 31
doubled sliver **157** 12
~ yarn **157** 60
double earphone **332** 18
~-ended spanner **191** 15, **192** 1
~-end stern **270** 14
~ flat **299** 54
~ fortissimo **300** 60
~-handed rod **89** 22
~ helical spur wheel **136** 85
~ hook **89** 32, **145** 10
double horizontal cordon **55** 17
~-image rangefinder **110** 30
~ incline* **202** 49
~ ladder **121** 4
~ lath **117** 43
~ leg-lock **281** 12
double letter **170** 6
~-light window **39** 22
~ overarm stroke **268** 38
~ oxer **272** 33
~ pianissimo **300** 57
~-pointed needle **124** 10
~ quotation marks **325** 26
~ rack **209** 11
~ rewind **168** 43
~ rip **160** 23
~ -roller mill **91** 57
~ room **29** 8–20, **259** 27–38
~ rose **62** 17
~ row **265** 25
doubles **276** 2 to 3
double seater **269** 61
~ set of doors **259** 27
~ scutcher **156** 14
~ seat **34** 32
doubles game **276** 2 to 3
double-shaft trough mixer **151** 10
~ row radial engine **227** 1
~ sharp **299** 52
~ shawm **301** 3
double sheet of glass **339** 36
~ shoulder stand **279** 29
~ six **265** 35
~ sleeper **198** 88
~ spacer **240** 23
~ spiral brooch **309** 30
~ stand **99** 27
~ star **5** 29
doublet *[Cloth.]* **338** 30, 33, 41
double thigh rappel **282** 33
~-three **284** 16
~ tie **116** 50
~ tooth **21** 35
~-track main line **199** 20
~-tube frame **181** 9
~ tyre **189** 33
~ wash basin **259** 32
~ wheel **189** 33
~- wire overhead line **188** 16
doubling **293** 25–29
~ frame **157** 57
~ of slivers **157** 5
doubly serrate **354** 45
douche **23** 46, **25** 1
dough brake **97** 78
~ machine **97** 74
~nut **97** 7
~ scales **97** 77
~-scraper **42** 51
Douze dernier **263** 27
~ milieu **263** 26
~ premier **263** 25
dove **74** 33
~cot(e) **64** 8
~tail halving **116** 89
dowel hole **115** 22
~ maker **128** 42
down gate **141** 22
down-hill· racing **283** 18
~ running **283** 17
~ ski **283** 36
down pipe **40** 10, **140** 56
~-pull **283** 49
~ quilt **48** 11
~stream end **212** 17
down·town* **252** 33
~town ticket office* **256** 24
~ tube **180** 17
donwy mildew **81** 20
D-pfennig **244** 7
drachma **244** 39
drachmai **244** 39
Draco **5** 32
draft **165** 4, **242** 12
~ animal* **202** 17
~ beam* **68** 18, 30
~ board **162** 7
~ chain* **68** 23
~ clause **242** 17
~-door * **41** 44
drafter* **202** 17
draft-free window* **204** 58
~ horse* **202** 17
drafting machine **144** 16
~ roller **157** 22
draft numerals* **217** 70
~ of selvedge threads **165** 20
draftsman **144** 9
draftsman's overall **144** 24
draft pad **321** 35
~ of threads **165** 21
drag *[Hunt.]* **272** 64
dragée **23** 13
drageoir **23** 12
drag hook* **72** 14, **255** 49
~ hunt **272** 58–64
~line excavator **113** 81
~ link **186** 44
~ nozzle **211** 59
Dragon **5** 32
dragon **307** 1
~ of Apocalypse **307** 50
~ figure head **213** 16

E

echinoderm
340 23+24, **349** 3
Echinops **56** 14
echinus **316** 21
Echiostoma **349** 13
echo **219** 41
~ receiver **219** 42
~ sounder **219** 38
~ studio **293** 19
~ studio loudspeaker **293** 20
~ studio microphone **293** 21
ecliptic **5** 2
eddy **7** 21
edelweiss **362** 9
edge *[Geom.]* **329** 32
~ *[knife]* **46** 57
~ *[lace]* **37** 3
~ *[cello]* **302** 25
~ board **113** 73, 74
~-to-edge cardigan **32** 41
~ of hat brim **36** 16
~ of layer **13** 21
~ runner mill **151** 8
~-trimmer **58** 33
edging *[Cloth.]* **32** 7, **102** 6
~ *[lath]* **43** 26
~ iron **244** 44
~ tool **123** 9
edible agaric **365** 23
~ boletus **365** 16
~ chestnut **368** 48
~ fungus **365**
~ morel **365** 26
~ pore mushroom **365** 16
~ snail **340** 25
editing *[Film]* **293** 30–34
~ room **292** 3
edition binding **178**
editor *[Film]* **293** 24, 31
editorial (article) **325** 40
educational picture **250** 8
eelgrass **362** 54
~worm **81** 51
effacer **240** 44
effect of earthquake **11** 45–54
~ loudspeaker **294** 51
E flat major **300** 11
E flat minor **300** 14
eft **350** 20–22
egg *[Med.]* **22** 84
~ *[hen]* **75** 47
~-and-dart cyma **316** 42
~ batch **81** 2, 30
~ box **75** 36
~ carton **75** 36
~ cosy **45** 39
~ cup **45** 38
~ gallery **82** 23
~-grader **75** 39
~ insulator **234** 22
egg integument **75** 48
~ lamp **75** 46
~-laying animal **351** 1
~-laying hole **81** 12
~-rack **42** 9
~-shapedpuffball **365** 19
~shell **75** 48
~-slicer **41** 86
~-sorting machine **75** 39
~ spoon **45** 40
~-tester **75** 46
~-testing lamp **75** 46
~-timer **42** 46
~-weigher **75** 39
~-whisk **42** 55
Egypt **14** 35
Egyptian *[Typ.]* **325** 8
~ art **315** 1–18
~ cross **313** 57
~ hieroglyphs **324** 1
~ sphinx **315** 11
~ writing stamp **324** 22
eiderdown quilt **48** 11
eight *[boat]* **269** 10
~ *[Skat.]* **284** 13
~-faced polygon **330** 17
~-faced polyhedron **330** 6
eighth note* **299** 18
Einstein tower **6** 15–20
Eire **14** 10
elastic *n.* **33** 22, 24
~ bandage **23** 47
~ inset **33** 24
~-sided boot **100** 26
~ top **33** 22, 65
~ washer **136** 32
E-layer **4** 17
elbow *[arm]* **18** 45
~ *[horse]* **73** 20
~ lever **28** 43
~-operated tap **28** 43
elderberry **358** 37
~ flower **358** 36
election **251** 16–30
~ meeting **251** 1–15
~ official **251** 17
~ placard **251** 12, 13
~ regulations **251** 25
~ speaker **251** 5
~ supervisor **251** 28
electoral meeting **251** 1–15
~ register **251** 18
elector's hat **246** 41
electors' meeting **251** 1–15
electric air pump **23** 36
electrically controlled organ **305** 36–52
~ driven portable apparatus **173** 26
~ operated signal box **199** 64
electrical musical instrument **306** 11
electric arc **135** 7
~ precipitation plant **146** 13
~ arc welding **135** 1-28
~ bell **312** 9
~ blanket **48** 51
~ bulb **24** 10, **120** 56
~ bus **188** 8–16
~ cable **29** 34
~ car **291** 63
~ church bell **312** 9
~ clippers **104** 33
~ clock **107** 37
~ cooker **42** 26
~ dividing and moulding mashine **97** 64
~ dough mashine **97** 4
~ drill **115** 21
~ flex **29** 34
~ generator **204** 6
~ hand lamp **138** 57, 58
~ heating **169** 45
electrician **120** 1, **290** 4, **292** 37, **297** 20
electrician's scissors **120** 45
~ knife **120** 63
electric ice-cream machine **261** 47
~ iron **166** 33
electricity **331** 45–85, **332** 1–35
~ cable **194** 25
~ meter **43** 18
~ transmission line **16** 113
electric grinding machine **149** 51
~ locomotive **206** 1
electric locomotive·driver **206** 28
~ driver's assistant **206** 30
~ driver's cab **206** 27
~ driver's cabin **206** 27
~ driver's seat **206** 29
~ shed **199** 18
electric lungs **17** 27
~ mine locomotive **137** 28
~ motor **40** 59, **128** 25, **173** 11
~ motor room **218** 58
~ planing machine **149** 56
~ platform truck **201** 29
~ power cable **229** 35
~ print dryer **112** 44
~ rail coach **206** 55
~ razor **51** 79
~ revolution-counter **207** 15
electric saucepan **42** 15
~ saw **96** 40
~ shears **104** 33
~ shunting locomotive **206** 59
~ starter **227** 55
~ stove **42** 26
~ three-car train **206** 60
~ torch **120** 26
~ tractor **202** 2
~ tractor trailer **202** 3
~ truck **202** 38
~ truck trailer **202** 39
electrified main line **199** 25
electro blocks **145** 18
~cardiogram **24** 16
~cardiograph **24** 15
electrode **135** 20
~-holder **135** 5, 23
electro-dynamic loudspeaker **235** 22
~ gyro **188** 8
~lethaler **94** 6
electrolytic bath **172** 1
electro·magnet **233** 54
~motor **40** 59
electron **1** 3, 7, **4** 33
~-controlled slow-motion camera **294** 28
electronic calculating punch **241** 45–51
~ calculator **241** 45
~ flash unit **111** 54
~ map **230** 50
~ pads **24** 13
~ punched-card sorting machine **241** 52
~ shell **1** 4
electron microscope **109** 1
~ orbit **1** 4, 8
electro pulley blocks **145** 18
~scope **331** 62
~static generator **331** 54
~static microphone **237** 5
~-turbo-generator **3** 32
~typer **172** 4
~ typing **172**
element **1** 22, **120** 35
~ *[Math.]* **327** 11
elementary geometry **328** 1–58
elephant **351** 20
~ house **339** 24
elevated* *n.* **252** 4
~ goal **275** 33
~ railway **252** 4

elevated water tank **79** 2, **199** 48
elevating motor **223** 66
~ spindle **223** 67
elevation *[ship]* **222** 65
~ lock nut **155** 5
elevator *[mach.]* **67** 51, **145** 70, **169** 22
~ *[aircr.]* **226** 82, **228** 44
~ *[lift]* **151** 5, **256** 45
~ boy* **256** 47
~ bucket **145** 71
~ car* **256** 46
~ man* **256** 47
~ platform* **220** 66
~ potato-digger **67** 38
~ push-pull rod **228** 36, 39
~ runner* **256** 47
~ scoop **145** 71
~ shaft* **256** 51
eleven *[Footb.]* **274** 11–21
elk **352** 1
~* **352** 2
ellipse **329** 22
ellipsis **325** 29
ellipsoid of revolution **329** 42
elm **355** 49
~ tree **355** 49
elocutionist **298** 3
elytron **82** 10, **342** 36
elytrum **342** 36
E major **300** 5
embankment **16** 104
embossing platen **177** 29
~ stick **154** 20
embrace **201** 61
embroidery **50** 30 **101** 11, 31
embryo *[Bot.]* **69** 16, **354** 86, **366** 21
~ plant **69** 14
~ sac **354** 64
emcee* **234** 9
emergency bandage **17** 1–13
~ belly band **72** 23
~ brake **204** 36, **209** 71
~ brake valve **205** 59
~ bridge **210** 17
~ cable **209** 47
~-cable tensioning mechanism **209** 48
~ exit **290** 33, **295** 7
~ ladder **138** 33
~ landing runway **230** 3
~ light **295** 6
~ splint **17** 10
~ stretcher **17** 23
~ tender **255** 53
~ tourniquet **17** 15
emery paper **129** 25
~ wheel **134** 34
eminence *[hill]* **13** 66
~ *[Med.]* **18** 4
E minor **300** 2
emission of waves **230** 42
empennage **226** 80–83
emphasized line **239** 10
Empire style **318** 16
~ table **318** 16
employed foot **284** 10
employee **238** 1
empress **338** 15
emptying cock **40** 65
~ faucet* **40** 65
~ of post box **231** 31
~ system **195** 2
empty tubs return **138** 7
emu **343** 1
enamel *[tooth]* **21** 30
enamel remover* **103** 13
encaustum **21** 30
enchasing hammer **106** 42
enclosure **339** 16
encyclopaedia **250** 17
encyclopedia* **250** 17
end *[knife]* **46** 55
~ *[Geom.]* **328** 17, 18
~ crust **97** 24
~ dumping truck* **195** 12
~ dump truck* **196** 7
endemic bird **344**
end-grain block **323** 1
~-grain timber **115** 92
endive **59** 39
~* **59** 40
endless cableway **209** 19
~ chain **149** 33
~ elevator* **164** 36
~ ropeway **209** 15–24
~ track **189** 37
end man **282** 28
~ moraine **12** 55
endorsee **242** 26
endorsement **242** 25
endorser **242** 27
end paper **178** 49
~-piece **303** 4
~ plate **157** 26
~ stage **4** 56
~-tip lorry **196** 7
~ tipper **196** 7
endurance race **273** 11–15
end vice **127** 44
~ wall **211** 35
enema **30** 20
~ syringe **23** 59
engaged column **317** 35
engagement *[Fenc.]* **277** 48
~ calendar **238** 31
engaging dog **149** 35
engine **139** 11, **184**, **205** 1
~ arm **27** 13
engine block **184** 25
~ bonnet **185** 8
~ car **207** 30
~ compartment **207** 31
~ cooling system **183** 17
~ crew **203** 9+10
~-driver **203** 9
~-driver's timetable **205** 54
engineer **144** 23
~* **203** 9
engineering **211**
engineer's cab* **201** 63
engine hood* **185** 8
engine in inclined position **187** 25
~ lifting eye bolt **192** 32
~ line **199** 12, 21
~ nacelle **226** 6
~ oil container **191** 14
~ room **145** 67, **216** 26, 27, **223** 33 **255** 1
~ room superstructure **216** 25
~ room telegraph **219** 20
~ shed **199** 6
~ shed turntable roads **199** 9
~ spur **199** 12
~ staff **203** 9+10
~ superstructure **221** 46
~ workshop **217** 8
English *[Typ.]* **170** 29
~ asphodel **70** 13
~ bond **113** 62
~ buggy **179** 48
~ catch-fly **360** 20
~ daisy* **360** 1
~ handwriting **325** 10
~ horn **302** 38
~ Royal Crown **246** 42
~ setter **71** 41
~ type of park **257** 41–69
engraver **323** 44
engraving *[ring]* **38** 29
~ *[method]* **172** 23–30
~ ball **106** 34
enlargement **112** 51
~ frame **112** 34
enlarger **112** 28
enrockment **211** 51
ensign of head of state **245** 14
~ staff **218** 31
entablature **316** 52
entangling device **335** 31
entertainment car **204** 24
entire *[Bot.]* **354** 43
entrance *[door]* **39** 65
~ *[bridge]* **210** 54
~ *[hive]* **78** 48
~ and exit **290** 19
~ gateway **316** 7
~ hall **43** 1-34
~ hatch **226** 34
~ steps **226** 33
~ to the nest **343** 28
~ tower **319** 24
~ tunnel **336** 6
entrechat (quatre) **288** 13
entry* **43** 1–34
~ stamp **238** 57
envelope *[letter]* **239** 13
~ *[airship]* **226** 74
~ flap **232** 26, **239** 14
~ window **239** 16
epaulet(te) **247** 6
épée **277** 40, 62
~ fencer **277** 39
~ fencing **277** 39–43
~ play **277** 39–43
ephemerid **342** 6
epicentral region **11** 38
epicentre **11** 33
epi-condenser **110** 14
epicontinental sea **15** 26
epicyclic gear **136** 92
epidemic signal **245** 25
epididymis **22** 73
epiglottis **19** 51
epimanikion **314** 28
episcopal ring **314** 47
epistle side **311** 47
epistyle **316** 18
epitaph **312** 14
epitrachelion **314** 27
equalizing magnet **236** 26
equation **327** 4, 5, 9
equator **5** 3
Equator **15** 1
equatorial climate **9** 53
Equatorial Counter Current **15** 33
equestrian **290** 26
equestrianism **72** 1–6
equilateral triangle **328** 26
equilibrist **290** 48, **298** 16
equinoctial *n.* **5** 3
equinox **5** 6+7
equipment of deep-see diver **224** 20–30
~ shed **220** 12
equisetum **360** 18
equitation **72** 1–6
erase cut-out button **306** 25
eraser **144** 56, **171** 55
~ shield **240** 32
~ switch **241** 27

erasing knife **144** 56, **171** 55
Erato **308** 63
erectile crest **343** 26
erection of roof **115** 8
~ shop **145** 1–45, **217** 4
~ spring **193** 18
Ergates faber **342** 38
ergot **69** 4
Ericaceae **56** 12
Eridanus **5** 12
Erinys **308** 51
Erlenmeyer flask **334** 39
erne **347** 5
Eros **308** 26
erosion **211** 5
erotic poetry *[symbol]* **308** 63
errand boy **238** 8
error lever **240** 62
ersatz coffee **98** 65
erupting cloud of gas **7** 23
escalator **256** 22
escape hood **97** 59
escapement *[watch]* **107** 22+23
escape wheel **107** 22
escapologist **291** 28
escort **261** 22
~ vessel **222** 13
escudo **244** 23
esculent fungus **365**
escutcheon **246** 1–6
Eskimo **336** 1
~ dog **71** 22
esophagus **19** 49, **22** 23
espada **287** 65
espalier **55** 16, 17
~ fruit tree **55** 1, 2, 16, 17, 29
esparto grass **130** 26
espresso bar **261** 45–51
~ machine **42** 17, **261** 50
esquire **310** 68
estate **16** 94
estrangler disk **183** 61
e''-string **302** 9
etched zinc plate **172** 33
etching **176** 1, **323** 14–24
~ bath **172** 24, **176** 6, **323** 51
~ ground **323** 55
~ needle **323** 16
ether bottle **28** 38
Ethiopia **14** 36
ethmoid (bone) **19** 39
ethnology **335–337**
ethyl-alcohol tank **229** 6
Etruscan art **316** 49–52
~ temple **316** 49
eucharistic vestments **314** 37
Euclidean geometry **328** 1–58
euphonium **302** 44
Eurasia **15** 15+16
Europe **14** 1–26, **15** 15
European elk **352** 1
~ fox **352** 12
~ roller **344** 6
~ tick **342** 44
Eustachian canal (or tube) **19** 65
Euterpe **308** 65
evaporating basin **334** 29
~ dish **334** 29
evaporator **42** 3
evening dress **32** 25
~ dress vest* **34** 59
~ gown **32** 25
~ hat **36** 34
~ primrose **56** 3
~ sandal **100** 44
~ shoe **100** 32
~ suit **34** 57, 61
even number **326** 11
event *[Sports]* **280**
even-toed ungulate **351** 28–31
ever-burning light **311** 44
~lasting *n.* **361** 3
evolution **327** 2
ewe **74** 13
examination chair **26** 25
~ couch **26** 6
~ of passport **247** 14 + 15
~ wagon **206** 57
excavator *[mach.]* **113** 81, **150** 13, **151** 3, **153** 2, 3
~ * *[worker]* **113** 76
~ bucket **153** 3
excess gauge **333** 19
~ water conduit **254** 23
exchange *[Teleph.]* **233** 1–17
~ *[Comm.]* **243**
~ counter **242** 1
~ line **233** 32
Exchange list **243** 8
~ usher **243** 9
exclamation mark **325** 21
~ point* **325** 21
excrement **76** 22
excretory vacuole **340** 5
excursion boat **216** 45–66, **269** 1
~ steamer **220** 18
~ vehicle **179** 33
~ vessel **216** 36
executive producer **292** 26
exercise **278** 1-23
~ book **249** 30
~ of classical dancing **288** 1–50
exhalation **17** 26
exhaust **185** 64
~ box **182** 8
~ of combustion gases **227** 24
~ cone **227** 33
~ gas deflector **229** 30
~ gases **184** 76, **227** 11
~ gas shaft hood **226** 72
~ manifold **184** 62
~ port **184** 74
~ tail pipe **185** 64
~ tube **120** 59
~ tubing **120** 59
~ turbine **227** 10
~ turbine-driven supercharger **227** 8
~ valve **184** 29, **227** 18
exhibition hall **252** 6
~ grounds **252** 5
exhibitor's projection unit **295** 26
exit **64** 9, **295** 7
ex libris **178** 51
extinct volcano **11** 25, 28
exosphere **4** 14
exotic bird **345**
~ dancer **298** 14
~ woman **289** 30
expander *[Sports]* **278** 50
~ *[tool]* **119** 58
~ exercise **278** 43
~ roller **161** 14
expanding comb **158** 56
~ file f. sorting letters **238** 53
expansion joint **197** 39 + 40
~ tank **40** 24
experimental transformer **332** 5
expert **248** 36
expiration **17** 26
explanatory notice **339** 44
exponent **327** 1
export beer **93** 45
exposition building* **252** 6
~ grounds* **252** 5
exposure-counter **111** 19
~ meter **111** 38
~ regulator **173** 22
~ scale **111** 11
~ slot **241** 19
~ switch **241** 21
~ timer **112** 32, **241** 16
Express **232** 31
express-delivery letter **232** 34
~ diesel locomotive **207** 41
~-mail label **232** 31
expression mark **300** 55-61
express tender locomotive **205** 38
~ train passenger coach **204** 1
expulsion of exhaust gases **227** 37
exquisite *[dandy]* **289** 33
ex-service man **257** 55
exsiccator **334** 51
~ insert **334** 54
ex-soldier **257** 55
extended front **196** 10
extendible upholstered seat **204** 41
extension **205** 33
~ apparatus **23** 41
~ arm **144** 35
~ cord **120** 20
~ cord socket **120** 22
~ divider* **144** 28
~ ladder **255** 14
~ piece **83** 35
extensor carpi radialis longus **20** 56
~ digitorum **20** 63
~ digitorum communis **20** 57
exterior angle **328** 26
~ construction set **292** 7
~ of horse **73** 1–38
~ shooting **292** 18
external calipers **129** 18
~ ear **19** 56–58
~ limit gauge **142** 49
~ plaster **117** 38
~ rendering **117** 38
~ toothing **136** 94
extinguisher **255** 61
extinguishing work **255** 1–46
extra *n.* **292** 29
~ *[newspaper]* **253** 45
extraction forceps **27** 48
~ of heat **1** 28
~ of phenols **164** 3
~ of root **327** 2
~ of tar **164** 3
~ of wort **92** 22–36
extractor **166** 40
~ lid **162** 18
extrados **318** 26
extra sail **270** 39
extremity **18** 43–54
extrusion press **154** 7
eye *[Anat.]* **18** 7, **21** 38–51
~ *[Arch.]* **316** 75
~ *[catheter]* **26** 25
eye *[Tech.]* **37** 24, **102** 58

feeding cup **29** 20
~-in of roving **157** 15
~ passage **76** 33
~ place **86** 28
~ plate **160** 6
~ roller **149** 4
~ site **81** 50
~ station **177** 55
~ trough **76** 43
feed opening **133** 54, **196** 52
~pawl **241** 3
~ pedal **207** 22
~-pipe **141** 33
~ plate **102** 32
~ point **102** 31
~ roller **149** 13, **241** 15
~ scale **149** 8
~ shaft **142** 33
~ slide **240** 39
~ spring **87** 18
~ table **177** 49, 57, **178** 34
~ tap **40** 65
~ trip **142** 18
~ trough **86** 28
~ valve **205** 20
feed-water· tank **146** 17
~ cleaner **205** 29
~ pre-heater **205** 23
~ pump **205** 9
feeler *[Zool.]* **82** 3, **342** 27
~ gauge **134** 62
feller **84** 27
fellies **131** 29
felling axe **85** 13
~ wedge **85** 24
~ of wood **84** 15–34
felloes **131** 29
felt **168** 49
~ blanket **162** 56
~ boot **336** 30
~ buffing wheel **134** 32
~ casual **100** 11
~ cloche **36** 33
~ cloth **323** 42
~-covered buck **166** 37
~ covering **336** 20
~ damper **304** 37
~-drier **168** 18–20
~ guide roll **168** 15
~ hat **36** 7, 19
~ shoe **100** 11
~ sock **99** 6
~ underlining **117** 62
~ wad **87** 52
female bee **78** 1
~ dancing partner **288** 45
~ fish **89** 66
~ flower **61** 38
~ flower cone **356** 4
~ grape-gatherer **80** 9
female moth **82** 30
~ part **362** 24
~ partner **288** 45
~ roe **88** 34
~ secretary **238** 10
~ shoot **356** 46
~ spadix **368**6
~ vocalist **296** 23
~ voter **251** 22
femoral artery **20** 19
~ biceps **20** 61
~ nerve **20** 31
femur **19** 22
fence **128** 4, 8, 20, **272** 28
fencer **277** 17+18
fencer's salute **277** 32
fencing **277** 1–66
~ breeches **277** 30
~ clothes **277** 29+30
~ cut **277** 1–14
~ distance **277** 23, 24
~ equipment **277** 25–31
~ glove **277** 26
~ instructor **277** 15
~ jacket **277** 29
~ master **277** 15
~ shoe **277** 31
~ terrain **277** 16
~ weapon **277** 53-66
fender **84** 33, **205** 34, **221** 50
~ dolphins **217** 32
~ side* **187** 21
~ skid **85** 10
fennel **364** 6
fen peat **13** 18
fermata **300** 42
fermentation of beer **93** 20–28
~ cellarer **93** 14
~ of wort **93** 12–19
fermenting cabinet **97** 57
~ vessel **93** 12
fern **361** 16
ferrel **43** 16
ferret **86** 24
ferreter **86** 25
ferreting **86** 23
ferris wheel **291** 37
ferrite rod· aerial **235** 5
~ antenna control **234** 43
ferroconcrete ceiling **114** 8
~ construction **114** 1–89
~ frame **114** 2
~ skeleton structure **114** 1
ferrule **43** 16, **282** 36
ferry **16** 12, **211**
~ boat **211** 11, **216** 16, **220** 24
~ bridge **216** 16
~ deck **216** 18
~ landing stage **211** 7
~man **211** 2
~man's house **211** 45
ferry rope **211** 3
fertilizer **65** 14
fescue (grass) **70** 24
fess point **246** 17
festoon **289** 5, **317** 54
fetish **337** 43
fetlock **73** 24, 25
feuilleton **325** 50
f-hole **302** 6
fiacre **179** 26
fiber* see fibre
fibre **162** 43
~ of visual nerve **78** 23
fibrous bark **354** 9
fibula **19** 24
fiddle **302** 1
~ bow **302** 12
fiddler **259** 45
fiddlestick **302** 12
fiddle string **302** 9
field *[land]* **65** 4, 19
~ *[Footb.]* **274** 1
~ *[horses]* **272** 14
~ barn **65** 26
~ base **275** 42
~ of beet **65** 46
~ bindweed **63** 26
fielder **275** 61
field event **280**
~ flower **359**, **360**
~ glass **86** 6, **108** 37-44
~ guard **65** 13
~ hockey* **275** 9–18
fielding side **275** 50, 58
field jump **283** 22
~ mangel **70** 21
~ mushroom **365** 1
~ pests **81** 37–55
~ poppy **63** 2
~ produce **69**
~ railway **16** 90, **196** 23
fields **65** 17
field scabious **359** 29
fieldsman **275** 61
field storage tank **139** 22
~ team **275** 8
~ work **65** 1–46
fifth *[Mus.]* **300** 23
~ *[Fenc.]* **277** 38
fight **287** 57
fighting ship **222**, **223**
figure *[Art]* **321** 38, **322** 7
~ *[number]* **107** 3
~ *[Skat.]* **284** 13–20
~ of eight **284** 13
~ fr. fable (or legend) and myth **307**
~ of figure-skating **284** 13–20
~ skate **284** 31
~-skater **284** 4
~-skating **284** 4–24
~ of three **284** 15
filagree work **101** 30
filament bulb **120** 56
~ lamp **120** 56
~ rayon yarn **163** 1–34
filbert **61** 49
file *[office]* **238** 4, 9, **248** 21
~ *[tool]* **134** 3, 8, 22
~ of letters **238** 15
filer **238** 4, 53
file w. records **238** 9
file-stabling machine **240** 37
filet **101** 22
filigree work **38** 16, **101** 30
filing block **132** 28
~ cabinet **238** 3
~ case **238** 13
~ machine **134** 1
~ margin **239** 2
~ pin **106** 22
filler *[cigar]* **105** 7
~ hoist **196** 51
~ opening **196** 52
~ rod **135** 39
fillet *[meat]* **95** 24
~ *[lath]* **115** 45, **118** 57, 67
~ of beef **95** 24, **96** 20
~ of pork **95** 44
filling *[Tech.]* **254** 29
~ *[tooth]* **27** 33
~ *[cigar]* **105** 7
~ appendix **226** 55
~ cloth **124** 25
~ compound **147** 38
~ hole **192** 40
~ machine **77** 21, **124** 1
~ pit **145** 72
~ plant **77** 13–22
~ rod **1** 39
~ sleeve **226** 55
~ sleeve cord **226** 57
~ sleeve line **226** 57
~ station **190** 1
fillister **127** 59
~-head screw **136** 34
filly **74** 2
film **292–295**
~ archives **292** 5
~ break contact **295** 30
~ camera **292** 47, **294** 1–35
~ cement **295** 24
~ clip **112** 6, 8
~-cooling turbo-blower **295** 34
~-counter **294** 26
~-cutter **293** 31
~-developing machine **293** 15
~ director **292** 40
~ dosimeter **2** 8
~ extra **292** 29
~ gate **295** 34
~-goer **295** 5

fissure **11** 52
~ bur **27** 42
fist **18** 84
'fist ball' **276** 52–58
fitted body **185** 61
~ coat **32** 52
fitter **119** 23, **134** 7
fitter's trolley **192** 67
fitting **119** 38, 40
~ mark **323** 58
~-out quay **217** 5-9
~ parts **119** 33–67
~ room **256** 32
~ tool **119** 33–67
~ yard **115** 1–59
fivefold cross **313** 66
five-four time **299** 43
~-lift waterless piston gasometer **148** 56
~-line octave **300** 70
~-masted bark (or barque) **215** 32–34
~-mast full-rigged ship **215** 35
~-metre platform **268** 8
~-section waterless piston gasometer **148** 56
~-sided polygon **330** 9
~-times accented octave **300** 70
~-times marked octave **300** 70
fixed furnace **140** 22
~ star **5** 9–48
~ undercarriage **225** 5
fixing bearings **230** 22, 26
~ tank **112** 3
fizz **98** 63
flacon **48** 27
flag *[banner]* **14, 245**
~ *[Bot.]* **62** 8
~ cloth **245** 3, 11
~ of Council of Europe **245** 4
~pole **245** 7
~ signal **218** 9
~staff **245** 1, 7
~ stick **276** 68
~stone paving **118** 26
flail **66** 27
~ handle **66** 29
~ helve **66** 29
~ staff **66** 29
flaked length of hose **255** 54
flame **47** 26
flames of resurrection **307** 10
flame tube **227** 60-63
flan *[cake]* **45** 27, **97** 15
~ *[metal]* **244** 43
flancards **310** 86
flanchards **310** 86
flange **204** 63, **271** 50
~ ring **141** 66
flanging beading **119** 21
flank *[Anat.]* **18** 32, **88** 26, **95** 2
~ *[Arch.]* **114** 6
~ vault **279** 51
flannel diaper* **30** 5
~ napkin **30** 5
flannels **34** 3
flannel square **30** 5
flap *[envelope]* **232** 26, **239** 14
~ *[saddle]* **72** 40, 47
~ *[Fish.]* **90** 21
~ *[aircr.]* **228** 47, **229** 26
~ hinge **134** 7, 57
~jack* **97** 7
~ pantile **117** 60
~ valve **227** 14
flare brush **103** 37
flare fat **95** 45
flash bulb **111** 53
~ contact **111** 46
~ gun **111** 49–59
flashing **117** 14
~ light **255** 6
flash lamp **111** 49–59
flash-light· *[torch]* **120** 26
~ *[Phot.]* **111** 49–59
flashlight* *[blinker]* **193** 20, **255** 6 **186** 8
~ lever* **186** 8
flash plug **227** 43
~ stick **111** 57
~ tube **111** 58
~ unit **111** 49–59
flask **273** 10, **334**
~-shaped puffball **365** 20
flat *[house]* **39** 74
~ *[Mus.]* **299** 53
~* *[Nav.]* **219** 62, 72
~ *[set piece]* **296** 31
~ arch **318** 28
~ bar **136** 10
~ beach **13** 35-44
flat-bed offset· machine **174** 38
~ proofing press **174** 38
flat belt **156** 49
~-bottomed flask **334** 36
~ bridge **210** 30
~ brush **121** 19, **321** 6
~ cake **97** 30
~ chisel **134** 18
~ cleaner **156** 44
~ coast **13** 35–44
~ course **272** 10
~ crown **36** 24
~ file **134** 23
~-glass manufacture **155** 1–11
~-knitting machine **160** 35
flat net **89** 17
~ plate **46** 4
~-plate keel **217** 46
~ pliers **134** 70
~ race **272** 1–29
~ racing **272** 1–29
~ rasp **99** 22
~ rib **95** 21
~ roof **39** 75, 77
flats *[Spinn.]* **156** 45
flat scorper **323** 7
~ seam **102** 4
flat's heating system **44** 16
flat stitch work **101** 10
flattening-out **114** 9
flat tile **117** 46
~-trained fruit tree **55** 1, 2, 16, 17, 29
~ vane **91** 40
~ware drawer* **41** 9
~worm **341** 24
flauto piccolo **302** 30
flax **367** 6
~ plant **367** 6
flea **341** 30
fleecy cloud **8** 14, 15
fleet destroyer **222** 16
flensing deck **90** 32
~ knife **90** 61
flesh *[Bot.]* **60** 24, **61** 6
~ brush **51** 26
~-coloured clover **70** 4
~ fly **342** 18
fleshy spike **354** 71
fleur-de-lis **246** 13
flew **71** 32
flex **120** 23
flexible arm **47** 50
~ conduit **120** 43
~ cord **120** 23
~ metal hose **52** 4
flexor carpi· radialis **20** 40
~ ulnaris **20** 58
flickers* **295** 1
flicks **295** 1
flies *[Theatre]* **297** 1-60
~ *[trousers]* **34** 30
flight into the atmosphere **4** 38–47
~ board **78** 49
~ deck **222** 69–74
~ of duck **86** 41
~ engineer **226** 41
~less bird **343** 1–4
~ of locks **212** 17–25
~ ticket office **230** 5
flint **41** 88, **105** 30
~ axe **309** 1
~ corn **69** 31
~-lock **336** 28
flipper **267** 41, **352** 28
flitch of bacon **96** 11
flitter mouse **351** 9
flivver* **183** 41
float *[cork, etc.]* **89** 4, 52, **119** 60, **212** 34
~ *[aeroplane]* **225** 33
~ *[level]* **113** 56
~ *[Theatre]* **297** 26
~ bowl* **183** 66
~ chamber **183** 66
floater *[volley]* **276** 51
floating bridge **16** 46
~ crane **221** 37–46
~ dredger **211** 56
~ dry dock **217** 31–40
~ ice **90** 35
~ quill **89** 51
~ ribs **19** 10
~ rope **90** 4
~ tube **89** 54
float needle **183** 67
~ shaft **212** 35
~ valve **183** 69
flong **172** 7
flood bank **211** 32
~ bed **211** 41
~ dam **211** 32
~ damage **211** 5
~ dike embankment **211** 32
~gate **212** 77, **217** 28
flooding valve **223** 20
flood·lamp **112** 61
~light **138** 34, **199** 46
~ protection **211** 33
floor *[room]* **118**
~ *[Film]* **292** 26–61
~ *[mine]* **138** 21
~ acrobat **298** 9
~ board **115** 36
~ contact **231** 25
floored *n.* **281** 36
floor-filling **115** 44, **118** 69
~ indicator **256** 49
~ lamp **47** 49
~ plate **217** 56
~-polish **52** 37
~-polisher **52** 9, 13
~-polishing cloth **52** 36
~ panel **185** 46
~ socket **120** 31
~ tank **217** 35
~walker* **256** 33
~ wax **52** 37
~ work **292** 26–61
floppy hat **36** 9
florin **244** 19, 37
florist's **253** 24
~ kiosk **200** 48
flounce **30** 34, **32** 30
flour **91** 28, **97** 18+19
flour beetle **341** 19
~ bin **97** 73
~ mill **91** 45–67
~ milling machine **91** 57-67
~-mixer **91** 64
~-mixing machine **91** 64

foot valve **40** 49, **254** 6
~ winch **145** 21
fop **289** 33
forage crop **70** 1–28
~ frame **131** 5
~ ladder **131** 5, 23
~ plant **70** 1–28
forced flower **79** 24
~ landing runway **230** 3
forceps **26** 40, **27** 48, **28** 50, 55, 57, **29** 53
force of wind **9** 10
forcing bed **79** 16
~ house **79** 4
fore-and-aft· gangway **216** 24
~ line **222** 52
~ sails **214** 20–31
~ schooner **215** 18
forearm *[man]* **18** 46
~ *[horse]* **73** 21
fore·bay **212** 39
~-blade **67** 20
~carriage **68** 14–19
~castle **218** 43
~-clamp **283** 45
~course **213** 41
~ deck **218** 42
foredge margin **178** 57
fore-edge margin **178** 57
~finger **21** 65
~ flank **95** 16
~foot **73** 22–26
~ grip **87** 13
~ hammer **132** 23
~ hand **73** 18-27
~-hand stroke **276** 21
forehead **18** 4+5, **73** 3
~ mirror **26** 4
~ toupet **338** 8
fore-hearth **141** 5
foreign exchange counter **242** 10
~ postage **232** 40
fore knuckle **95** 8
~leg **88** 25
~lock **73** 2
~, main and mizzen stay **214** 10
~, main and mizzen topmast stay **214** 11
~, main and mizzen topgallant stay **214** 12
~ and main royal stay **214** 13
foreman **84** 30, **201** 39, **202** 40
foremast **213** 42, **214** 2–4, **215** 21
forensic specialist **248** 36
fore nuckle **95** 5
~-paw **71** 6
~ plan **90** 30
~ rib **95** 19, 21
~ royal sail **214** 60
~ royal yard **214** 37
fore· sail **213** 41, **214** 55
~sight **87** 71
~skin **22** 70
forest **84** 1–34
forestage **297** 25
forest cart track **84** 3
~ labourer **84** 18
~ pest **82**
~ plant **361**
~ protection **83** 46
~ road **84** 3
~ section **84** 2
forestry **84, 85**
~ office **16** 3
fore-tightener **283** 45
~top **214** 50
~ topgallant mast **214** 4
~ topgallant sail **213** 52, **214** 58, 59
~ topmast **214** 3
~ topmast cross tree **214** 51
~ topmast staysail **214** 20
~ topsail **214** 56, 57
~ yard **214** 32
forge **132** 1–42, **134** 4
forged piece **132** 21
forget-me-not **362** 26
forge tongs **132** 2
forging furnace **133** 1, 52
~ manipulator **133** 49
~ press **133** 23, 48
fork **46** 58, **66** 11, **150** 33
~ *[Med.]* **22** 64
~ *[harness]* **72** 29
~ *[game]* **88** 68
~ blade **180** 12
~ carriage **202** 21
~ cover **183** 24
forked mortice (or mortise) **116** 85
~ tenon **116** 85
~ tongue **307** 6
~ twig **57** 13
fork lift **202** 20, **221** 12
~ truck **202** 20, **221** 12
form *[postal ~]* **232** 6–15
~ *[Typ.]* **323** 32
~ *[Gymn.]* **279** 40
formation of loop **160** 65
forme *[Typ.]* **175** 36, **323** 32
~ *[hat]* **36** 31
~ bed **174** 41, **175** 17
forming iron **119** 16
form register **249** 13
~ room **249** 1
~ f. sample cubes **114** 84
formwork **114** 11, 54–76
Forsythia **357** 1
forte *[Mus.]* **300** 58
~ pedal **304** 8
forte-piano **300** 61
fortissimo **300** 59
~ possibile **300** 60
fortress **16** 74, **310** 1
Fortuna **308** 37
fortune-teller **291** 36
forward *n.* **268** 51, **274** 17–21, **287** 27
~ bridge-building **208** 37
~ grand circle **279** 12
~ holds **218** 65
~ hydroplane **223** 51
forwarding container **202** 25
forward jack **218** 48
~ lunge **278** 19
foss(e) **310** 37
fossette **18** 16
fossula **18** 16
foster mother **75** 28
fouetté **288** 25
foul *[Footb.]* **274** 51
Fouler's service **355** 42
foundation **118** 2, **194** 14
~ base **118** 3
~ garment **33** 23
~ plan **144** 63
~ trench **113** 69–82
founder **141** 8
foundry **141**
foundryman **141** 8
~ team **141** 13
fountain **54** 20, **257** 21, **316** 68
~ pen **239** 19
~ pen holder **239** 30
'fountain-pen' monitor **2** 15
fountain pen· nib **239** 20
~ rim **257** 25
~ stand **47** 13
fountain syringe **23** 46
four-channel magnetic-sound reproducing unit **295** 50
four-cycle* **184** 1
~-cycle diesel engine* **184** 37
~-cycle motor* **182** 61
fourdrinier section **168** 10-13
~ wire **168** 13
four-eight time **299** 33
~-engined aircraft **226** 7
~-faced polyhedron **330** 1
~-family house **39** 69–71
~-figure number **326** 3
~-four time **299** 34
~-in-hand **257** 54
~-leaf clover **70** 5
~-leaved clover **70** 5
~-light window **39** 86
four-line octave **300** 69
~-masted barque **215** 29
~-masted full-rigged ship **215** 31
~-masted ship **215** 28–31
~-master **215** 28–31
~-mast fore and aft schooner **215** 28
~-mast ship **215** 28–31
~-oared gig **269** 26–33
~-pin plug **120** 9
~-pole plug **120** 9
~-roller draw-frame **157** 9
~-seater motor cabin **183** 50
~-stroke carburettor engine **184** 1
~-stroke diesel engine **184** 37
fourth *[Mus.]* **300** 22
four-tier letter tray **238** 25
~-times accented octave **300** 69
~-times marked octave **300** 69
~-two time **299** 35
fourty-eight-faced polyhedron **330** 13
four-wheel drive **189** 11
fowl **74** 19–36
~ tally **75** 43
fox **88** 42, **352** 12
~ droppings **272** 64
~glove **363** 2
~hound **272** 63
~tail grass **70** 27
~ terrier **71** 15
~trot **288** 43
foyer **296** 12+13
fraction *[Math.]* **326** 10, 15, 16
fractional quantity **326** 10
fractionating column **139** 26
fraction inverted **326** 16
fracto-cumulus cloud **8** 12
~-stratus cloud **8** 11
fractured leg **17** 11
frail **122** 9
frame *[picture, etc.]* **48** 17, **85** 40, **160** 33
~ *[Spinn.]* **157** 1, 34, 57
~ *[hand-setting]* **169** 3
~ *[ship]* **217** 55, **270** 20
~ *[hotbed]* **79** 16

fruit surface eating tortrix moth **81** 9
~ tart **45** 27
~ tree **55** 1, 2, 16, 17, 29
~ tree spraying machine **83** 42
~ twig **368** 38
frustum of cone **329** 45
frying-pan **41** 84, **42** 41
~ sausage **96** 23
fry tank **89** 57
F sharp· major **300** 7
~ minor **300** 4
fuchsia **56** 3
fudge **98** 81
fuel **1** 39
~ cock **228** 32
~ contents gauge **228** 21
fuel feed· control **227** 57, **228** 32
~-pipe **229** 15
~ pump **184** 40
fuel-filler neck **229** 12
~ filter **184** 42
~ injection nozzle **227** 28
~ injection pump **187** 28, **228** 24
~ injection pump feed pedal **207** 22
~ inlet valve **227** 14
~ intake **227** 9
~ jet **227** 28, 59
~ lead **227** 13
~ level visual indicator **228** 26
~ manifold **227** 13
~ nozzle **227** 59
~ oil **40** 50, **139** 42
~ of pile **1** 39
~ pipe **227** 56, **229** 11
~ piping **227** 13
~ pipes from tank **229** 33
~ pressure gauge **228** 20
~ pump **184** 9, **229** 14
~ tank **226** 47, **229** 6
~ tank section **229** 6–11
~ tender **205** 68
full beard **35** 14
~-bottomed wig **35** 2
~- cone indicator **158** 7
~ cop **156** 2
~-dress wig **35** 2
fuller **132** 28–30
full gallop **73** 43+44
~-grown insect **342** 10
~ width hub brake **182** 27
~-jacket ball **87** 55
~-jacket bullet **87** 55
full-jacket projectile **87** 55
~-length bath **51** 5
~ moon **7** 5
~ Nelson **281** 10
~-rigged mast **215** 16
~-rigged ship **215** 24–27, 31, 35
~ stop **325** 16
fulmar (petrel) **343** 12
Fumariaceae **62** 5
fumigating apparatus **83** 38
~ candle **47** 28
fumigation chamber **83** 21
~ pastil(le) **47** 28
~ plant **83** 10
funeral **312** 34–41
funerary candle **312** 55
~ temple **315** 7
~ vessel **309** 34
fungus **363** 10–13, **365**
funicular (railway) **209** 12
~ railway coach **209** 13
funnel **10** 38, 44, **41** 89, **333** 3
~ *[ship]* **218** 1
~ capping **222** 40
~-forming machine **119** 22
~ marking **218** 2
~-shaped cavity **13** 71
~-shaped fissure **11** 49
fur **32** 49
~ bonnet **32** 46
~ cap **32** 46, **36** 4
~ coat **32** 49, **34** 65
~ collar **32** 53, **34** 68
~ cuff **32** 53
~ hat **32** 46
~ jacket **32** 44, 45
~ lining **34** 66
furnace **97** 58, **141** 1, **146** 6
~ bed(ding) **40** 66
~-charger **140** 24
~man **141** 7
~ pot **155** 22
~ room **40**
~ thermometer **40** 64
furniture *[room]* **43** 23, **44** 25
~ *[printing]* **175** 40
~ *[Typ.]* **169** 8
~ polish **127** 12
~-polishing cloth **52** 45
~ truck* **189** 41
~ van **189** 41
~ van trailer **189** 42
furred game **86** 35
furrier's shop **253** 1
furrier store* **253** 1
furring **34** 66
furrow *[field]* **65** 8
~ *[mill]* **91** 17
furrow-closer **67** 13
~ slice **65** 8
~ wheel **68** 16
~-width adjuster **68** 28
fur scarf **32** 48
~ seal **352** 18
~ trapper **289** 8
~ trimming **32** 53
Fury **308** 51
fuse **120** 35, **150** 28, **235** 12
~ body **120** 38
~ box **159** 23
~ cap **120** 37
~ cartridge **120** 35
~ contact **120** 39
~ element **120** 35
fuselage **225**
fuse link **120** 35
~ pliers **192** 22+23
fusible element **120** 35

G

gable **39** 15, **116** 5
~ end **39** 15, **117** 25
~ roof **116** 1
~ slate **117** 80
gaff *[Fish.]* **89** 12
gaffer* **292** 37
gaff-rigged sloop **215** 6
~sail **215** 1
~ topsail **214** 31
gag (bit) **72** 53
gage* see gauge
gage f. pressure* **77** 18
~ f. temperature* **77** 18
gaging rod* **126** 2
gaillardia **62** 19
gain control **236** 12
Gainsborough hat **36** 39
gaiter **100** 30, 31
gaits of horse **73** 39–44
galactic system **6** 47
Galaxy **5** 35
gale **357** 33
galingale **56** 17
galinsoga **63** 31
gall *[on leaf]* **82** 34
~ bladder **22** 11, 36
~ caused by wooly aphid **81** 33
gallery *[church]* **311** 25
~ *[platform]* **1** 42
~ *[theatre]* **296** 16
~ under bark **82** 23+24
galley *[ship]* **213** 44–50
~ *[Typ.]* **169** 12, 44
~ convict **213** 48
~ slave **213** 48
~ of slugs **169** 27
gall midge **81** 40
gallinaceous bird **343** 22
gallooned coat **179** 23
~ collar **179** 22
~ sleeve **179** 24
gallop **73** 42, 44
gall wasp **82** 33, 35
galosh **100** 27
galvanometer **11** 44
gamba **301** 23
gambling game **263** 1–33
~ hall **263** 1
~ spot* **263** 1
~ table **263** 8
gambrel **94** 11
~ roof **116** 18
game *[Zool.]* **88**
~ *[play]* **258** 1-59, **274-276**
~ of ball **258** 42
~ of boules **287** 21
~ cart **86** 18
~ of chance **263** 1–33
~ of chess **261** 17
~ of the devil **258** 24
~ of draughts **265** 17–19
~ of marbles **258** 56
~ path **86** 16
~ of skill **258** 24
~ of tag (or tig, or touch) **258** 23
gamma radiation **1** 12, 17
~-ray treatment **29** 48–55
gamut **299** 47–50
gander **74** 34
gang boarding **40** 3
ganger **198** 30
gang foreman **198** 30
~ mill* **149** 10, 16
~ plank* **216** 24, 34
gangway **40** 3, **140** 37, **201** 47, **204** 7, **216** 24, 34
gangwayed corridor compartment coach **204** 1
gangway plate **203** 33
gannet **343** 9
gantry **146** 31, **199** 17, **220** 52, **221** 7, **292** 53
~ crane **217** 20
~ support **209** 24
gap gage* **142** 49
garage **39** 32, **190** 32, **252** 62
~ approach **39** 52
~ compartment **190** 33
~ man* **190** 10
garbage **253** 48
~ basket **253** 46
~ can* **41** 11, **53** 32, **195** 2
garboard strake **217** 45
garde de bras **310** 48

garden **39** 57, 58, **54**, **79**
~ bench **54** 18
~ café **261** 27–44
~ cart **58** 30
~ chair **39** 49, **54** 7,
gardener **54** 23, **79** 20
garden fence **55** 10
~ flower **62**
~ frame **79** 16
~ furniture **54** 3
~ gravel **261** 43
~ hand* **79** 50
~ hand syringe **58** 8
~ hose **39** 42, **58** 37
gardening tool **58** 1–29
garden ladder **55** 8
~ lamp **39** 38
~ pansy **62** 2
~ parasol **54** 9
~ path **55** 23
~ pests **81**
~ plot **55** 1–31
~ pond **54** 19
~ produce **79** 43
~ shears **58** 14
~ shed **55** 3
~ shovel **79** 14
~ spider **342** 45
~-sprinkler **58** 40
~ strawberry **60** 16
~ suburb **16** 28
~ swing **54** 25
~ table **39** 50
~ tool **58**
~ trowel **58** 13
~ truck **58** 30
~ umbrella **39** 48
~ wall **39** 37
gargoyle **317** 30
garland **289** 17, **317** 54
garneto **330** 7
garret **40** 1–29
~ window **116** 8
garter* **33** 19, 63
~ belt* **33** 18
garth **314** 2
gas **148**
~ *[petrol]* **139** 38, **190**
~ bag **226** 75
~ bulb **331** 10
~ burner **41** 36, **133** 3, 53
~ cap **12** 30
~ cartridge **83** 39
~ cell **226** 75
~ circulattion unit **83** 22
cloud **7** 23
~-cock **41** 37
~ compressor **148** 49
~ conduit*
~ **119** 24–30
consumers' pipe-
~ line **148** 53+54
~-cooker **41** 35
~ de-poisoning plant **148** 41
gas-discharge valve **111** 58
~ duct **146** 12
~ engine locomotive **207** 45
gaseous nebula **6** 51
gas escape **53** 50
~-distributing plant **148** 47–55
~-extractor **148** 30
~-fitter **119** 23
~-heating apparatus **119** 65-67
~-heating chamber **140** 27
~ holder **148** 56–64
~ hose **135** 35
~-igniter **41** 87
~ inlet **133** 7, **334** 12
~ inlet pipe **334** 2
~ installation **148** 55
gaskin **73** 36
gas-lighter **41** 87
~ main **148** 47, **194** 26, 33, 34
~ main cock **148** 52
~ manufacture **148** 1–46
~ mask **83** 19
~ mask filter **255** 57
~ meter **43** 21, **119** 28, **148** 50, 51
~ oil **139** 40
gasoline* **139** 38, **190**
~ injector* **187** 27
~ level gage* **186** 14
~ motor* **184** 1
~ stove* **266** 19
~ tank* **182** 28, **185** 65
gasometer **148** 56–64
gas outlet **334** 63
gasper* **105** 14
gas pipe **119** 24–30, **133** 59, **140** 17
~ pipe network **148** 53+54
~-pipe tongs **119** 56
~ plant **148**
~ pliers **119** 55, **134** 72
~ pressure main **148** 53+54
~ production **148** 1–46
~ purification **148** 28–46
~-purifier **135** 33
~ radiator **119** 67
~-range* **41** 35
~ regulator **334** 6
~-ring **41** 36
~-separation plan **139** 62
~ separator **139** 21
~ service pipe **148** 53+ 54
~ space **148** 58
~ steam generator **227** 58
~ storage **148** 46
gas-stove **41** 35
~ syringe **331** 9
~ tank **216** 10
~ tank* **148** 56–64
~-tap **41** 37
gastric tube **26** 9
gastrocnemius head **20** 62
gas turbine locomotive **207** 44
~ vent **216** 12
~-washing bottle **334** 58
~ water heater **119** 66
~ water tank **148** 37
~ water truck **148** 39
~ welder **135** 38
~ welding **135** 29–64
~ works **148**
gate **212** 55, **252** 39, **312** 19
~ barrier **198** 68
gated automatic gain control **236** 12
gate house **310** 22
~ keeper **145** 87, **198** 70
gatekeeper's box **198** 72
~ cabin **198** 72
gateman* **200** 25
gate valve **212** 53–56
gateway **319** 11
gathering table **177** 36
gaucho **289** 31
gauge **147** 11, **186** 14, **228** 19, 20, 21
~ rail chair **198** 14
gauging rod **126** 2
gauntlet **277** 35, **310** 50
~ cuff **37** 7
gauze **28** 11, **177** 33, **178** 20
~ clamp **294** 3
~ cover **181** 6
~ diaper* **30** 6
~-holder **178** 19
~ square **30** 6
G clef **299** 10
gear **68** 73, **136** 92, **137** 5
~* **161** 17
~ box **129** 4, **133** 36, **142** 2, **157** 2
~ box flange **186** 57
~ box mounting **186** 62
~ case **142** 2, **157** 39
~-change rod **185** 45
geared-down shaft **186** 56
~ rack **212** 69
gearing **107** 19–21, **197** 11, **222** 63
gear lever **182** 36, **186** 9
~ rack **221** 3
~ rim **221** 6
~ ring **221** 6
gear room **222** 62
gears **186** 55–62
~* **136** 80–94
gear selector **207** 12
~ shift* **183** 27
~ twist grip **181** 35
~ wheel **136** 80-94, **161** 17
gecko **350** 36
Geiger counter **2** 19
~-Müller counter **29** 48
~ survey meter **2** 19
~ tube **29** 50
geisha **336** 39
gelatine *[Theatre]* **297** 49
~ roller **323** 12
gelder **74** 2
gelding **74** 2
gelly *[Theatre]* **297** 49
Gemini **5** 28, **6** 34
general merchandise store* **98** 1–87
~ offices **217** 1
~ practitioner **26** 12
~-purpose table **44** 3
~ store* **98** 1–87
generating plant **152** 19
~ station **146** 1–28
generation of heat **1** 16
Genoa jib **270** 35
genouillière **310** 53
gentian **362** 13
Gentianella **362** 13
gentleman **338** 54, 61
~ rider **272** 49
gentleman's shoe **100** 2
~ umbrella **43** 13
gentlemen's hat-shop **36** 1–26
~ underclothing **33** 35–65
~ wear **34**
~ wear department **256** 12
gentle slope **13** 58
gent's bicycle **180** 1
geodesic instrument **110** 30–38
geodesy **15** 46–62
geodetic instrument **110** 30–38
~ surveying **15** 46–62
geographical latitude **15** 2
~ longitude **15** 4
~ pole **15** 3
geography **11–13**
geology **12** 1–33
geometrical series **327** 12
~ symbol **327** 21–24
geometry **328, 329**
Georgian script **324** 4
geranium **56** 1
germ **354** 86, **368** 22
German dance **288** 41
~ Federal Republic **244** 7, 27, **245** 14

German flute **302** 31
~ handwriting **325** 11
germanium **234** 30
German mark **244** 7
~ pointer **71** 40
~ princess **338** 20
~ print **325** 3
~ terrier **71** 37
~ text **325** 1
Germany **14** 5
germinal disk **75** 54
~ vesicle **75** 55
germinating barley **92** 11
~ hole **367** 57
~ spore **365** 8
germination of barley **92** 8–12
~ box **92** 8
Gesneriaceae **56** 7
gesso **322** 29
geyser *[Geol.]* **11** 21
~ *[app.]* **119** 66
geyserite terraces **11** 23
G flat major **300** 14
gherkin **98** 29
ghost train **291** 5
Giant **307** 37
giant **291** 20, **307** 37, **308** 45
~ cypris **349** 1
~ figure **289** 63
~ ostracod **349** 1
~ salamander **350** 22
giant's stride **258** 41
giant stride **258** 41
~ waterlily **362** 17
~ wheel **291** 37
gib **136** 72, **215** 2
~ crane **217** 31
~-headed key **136** 72
gig *[vehicle]* **179** 34
~ *[boat]* **269** 26–33
Gigantocypris Agassizi **349** 1
gilded stern **213** 55-57
gilder **177** 2
gilder's brush **121** 23
gilding **177** 1
~ press **177** 4
~ tool **177** 3
gill *[Zool.]* **74** 24
~ *[Bot.]* **365** 6
~ cover **350** 5
~ slit **350** 3
gilly-flower **62** 7
gimbals **219** 27
gimlet **115** 65, **127** 19
gimp **314** 23
gimping **101** 28
~ needle **101** 29
gimp needle **123** 30
~ pin **124** 6
gingelly **367** 45
gingerbread **97** 5
gin glass **46** 90
gipsy moth **81** 1
~ woman **289** 36
giraffe **352** 4
~ house **339** 24
girder **136** 3–7, **145** 7, **210**
~ bridge **210** 30, 35
girdle **33** 16, **314** 20, 29
girdled robe **338** 25
girl **45** 4, **298** 7
~ assistant **290** 39
~ at counter **261** 7
girls' clothing **31** 1–61
girl's coat **31** 37
~ Dirndl dress **31** 36
girls' hair styles **35** 27–38
girl's hat **31** 38
~ jacket **31** 40
~ night dress **31** 1
~ night gown **31** 1
~ nightie **31** 1
~ nighty **31** 1
~ pinafore **31** 48
~ shoe **100** 23
~ ski trousers **31** 44
~ slacks **31** 41
~ spotted blouse **31** 60
girl student* **250** 10
girl's vest **31** 4
girls' wear **31** 1–60
girl's wind-jacket **31** 42
girth **72** 18
glacier **12** 49
~ covered with névé **282** 23
~ ice **12** 48–56
~ snout **12** 51
~ stream **12** 52
glade **16** 2, 112
gladiolus **62** 11
gland *[Anat.]* **21** 9, 10, 11
~ *[Tech.]* **218** 54
~ of head **21** 1–13
glans penis **22** 69
glare screen **292** 51
glass *[material]* **122** 5, 6, **155**
~ *[objects]* **46** 82–86, 87–91, **108** 31, 37, **296** 9
~ bead **50** 20
~ of beer **260** 27
~-blower **155** 13
~-blower's tongs **155** 20
~-blowing **155** 13–15
~ bowl lid **334** 52
~ bulb **120** 57
~ case **339** 39
~ chamber-pot **30** 17
~-cloth **41** 14
~-cutter **122** 25+26
~ cylinder **10** 40, **26** 30, **93** 27
~-drawing machine **155** 7
~ dropper **26** 44
glasses **108** 12–14
~ case **108** 25
~ and hearing aid **108** 22
glasses finisher **155** 16
glass funnel **112** 14
~ globe **99** 25
~ holder **122** 9
~ lid **42** 23
glass-maker's bench **155** 21
~ chair **155** 21
~ stool **155** 21
glass manufacture **155**
~ melt **155** 8
~ pane **173** 15, 18
~ observation panel **40** 62
~ of orangeade **261** 35
~ paper **129** 25, **181** 7
~ reflector **180** 86
~ rod **89** 24
~ roller **163** 16
~ roof **28** 27, **79** 5
~-roof car **207** 40
~-roofed well **252** 22, **256** 11
~ sand **323** 48
~ sheet **155** 11
~ shelf **259** 65
~ slide **26** 3
~ sponge **349** 7
~ stopper **112** 11
~ top **173** 36
~-towel **41** 14
~ tube **26** 46, **234** 29
~ veranda **261** 32
~ wall **260** 45
~ware **155** 16–21
~ window **161** 2
~ wool insulation **229** 9
glauke **244** 1
glazier **122** 8
glazier's beam compass **122** 22
~ diamond glass-cutter **122** 25
~ hammer **122** 18
~ lath **122** 21
~ pincers **122** 19
~ square **122** 20
~ workshop **122** 1
glazing **321** 42
~ machine **154** 16
glede **347** 11
glen **13** 52
glider *[pilot]* **271** 29
~ *[plane]* **271** 28
~ hangar **271** 39
~ launching methods **271** 1-12
~ pilot **271** 29
~-pilot pupil **271** 30
~ type **271** 24–27
gliding **271** 1–23
~ club **271** 39
~ field* **271** 38
~ flight **271** 18
~ plane **271** 28
~ ring **282** 42
~ site **271** 38
gliding ski **283** 29
~ step **288** 18
glima **281** 14
glissade **288** 18
globe *[Earth]* **249** 14
~ *[glass]* **333** 1
~ lamp **259** 4
~-shaped tree **257** 12
~ stop valve **254** 48
~ thistle **56** 14
globose flower head **354** 75
globular acacia **54** 11
Glossina morsitans **341** 32
glossy paint **121** 10
glove **135** 4
~ compartment* **186** 21
~ w. cross **314** 57
~ drawer **43** 7
~ stand **256** 20
glower plug **184** 64, **207**
~ plug control device **207** 17
gloxinia **56** 7
glue **127** 39
~-dispenser **238** 45
glueing machine **178** 31
~ section **177** 41
glue pot **127** 39, **177** 15, **231** 5
~ rollers **178** 27, 33
~ spreader **128** 54
~ tank **177** 46, **178** 32
~ well **127** 38
glume **69** 11
gluteal muscle **20** 60
glycerine **52** 33, **103** 22
G major **300** 2
G minor **300** 10
gnat **342** 16
goaf packed with dirt **137** 40
goal **274** 2, **275** 1, 13, 24
~ area **274** 4, **275** 3
goaler* **248** 14
goalie **274** 11, **284** 36
~keeper **274** 11, **284** 36
goal kick **274** 41
~ line **274** 3, **275** 2, 11, 21, 34
~ post **274** 37
Goat **5** 36, **6** 41
goat **74** 14
goatee (beard) **35** 9
goat pen **64** 47
goat's beard **74** 15
~-beard *[Bot.]* **361** 5, **365** 32
~ foot **308** 42
~ head **307** 18
goat willow **355** 24
gob packed with dirt **137** 40
gobbler **74** 28

Gobelin tapestry **47** 45
go-cart **49** 3
god of commerce **308** 21
goddess of arts **308** 17
~ of chance **308** 37
~ of destiny **308** 53–58
~ of fortune **308** 37
~ of hunting **308** 12
~ of science **308** 17
~ of victory **308** 43
Godet roller **163** 16
god of light **308** 15
~ of love **308** 26
godparents **313** 12
god of roads **308** 21
God's acre **312** 21–41
god of sea **308** 29
~ of war **308** 9
~ of wine **308** 32
goggles **24** 18, **135** 58
going about **270** 52–54
gold *[Her.]* **246** 24
~ blocking press **177** 26
~ coin **244** 1–28
~crest **346** 10
~ crown **27** 31
~-cup **359** 8
golden-crested wren **346** 10
~ oriole **344** 7
goldfinch **344** 1
~fish pond **257** 57
~ foil **177** 5
~ leaf **177** 5
~-leaf cutting pad **177** 6
~-leaf knife **177** 7
~ nib **239** 20
~-scales **107** 59
gold and silver· scales **106** 35
~ smith **106**
gold·smith **106** 19
~ tip **105** 15
~ wire **106** 3
golf **276** 59–71
~ bag **276** 65
~ ball **276** 71
~ club **276** 69+70
~ course **276** 59–62
golfer **276** 63
golfing outfit **34** 20
golf links **276** 59–62
~ shoe **100** 25
golosh **100** 27
gondola car* **208** 2, 6
gonfalon **245** 12
gong **281** 43
goniometer **330** 27, 28
goods **202** 33
~ clerk **202** 34
~ delivery service **202** 18
~ locomotive **208** 1
~ porter **202** 37
~ shed **202** 8, 31
goods-shed foreman **202** 34
goods-shed platform **202** 10
goods shelf **98** 14
~ station **202**
~ train steam locomotive **208** 1
~ van **202** 6
~ vehicle **207** 39
~ wagon **208** 2–34
goosander **343** 15
goose **74** 34
gooseberry **60** 9
~ blossom **60** 6
~ bush **60** 1
~ flower **60** 6
~ twig **60** 2
goose feather **324** 26
~-foot **63** 25
~gog **60** 9
~neck *[tube]* **47** 50
gorge **13** 52
~ hook **89** 44
gorgerin **316** 22
gorget **310** 43
Gorgon **308** 49
gorilla **353** 16
gos **347** 10
goshawk **347** 10
go-side **142** 50
gosling **74** 34
gospel side **311** 48
gossip *[woman]* **53** 29
Gothic art **317** 22–41
~ cathedral **317** 22
~ church **317** 22
~ pier **317** 34
~ structural system **317** 27–35
~ type **325** 1
gouache colour **321** 17
gouge **129** 15, **322** 17, **323** 6
gourd **337** 27
governess **257** 27
government loan **243** 11–19
governor *[Tech.]* **184** 41, **219** 33
~-tester **192** 59
G. P. **26** 12
grab **145** 57
~ bucket **145** 57
grace *[Mus.]* **300** 28–38
~ note **300** 28–38
grade* *[report]* **249** 54
~ crossing* **198** 67–78
graded coke bunker **148** 22
grade mark **94** 14
~ room* **249** 1
grader ploughshare **196** 21
grading plansifter **91** 59
graduated arc **219** 2
~ circle **330** 32, **331** 38
graduated fence slide rail **128** 9
~ limb **219** 2
~ measure **112** 35, **334** 26
~ measuring glass (or cylinder) **334** 26
~ pipette **334** 24
~ scale **109** 25, **128** 10, **333** 35
~ thimble **142** 55
Graeco-Roman· Mythology **308**
~ wrestling **281** 7-10
graffito drawing **321** 41
graft **57** 37
grafting **57** 30–42
~ knife **58** 26
grain **69** 1–37, **91** 45
~-cleaner **91** 45–56
~ collector **68** 66
~ conveyor **68** 64
~-elevator **221** 56-58
~ husker **91** 52
graining disk **173** 28
~ machine **173** 29
~ marble **173** 32
~ table **173** 30
grain of maize **69** 37
~-polisher **91** 56
~-polishing machine **91** 56
~ weevil **341** 17
~-weighing machine **91** 46
grand *n. [piano]* **304** 40
~ circle **279** 12
grandee **289** 26
grandfather clock **107** 32
grandfather's cap **36** 5
grand jeté en tournant **288** 24
grand·ma **258** 14
~mother **258** 14
~ piano **304** 40
~stand **272** 7, **274** 31
~ total key **240** 64
granny **258** 14
granulated sugar **98** 55
granulating the corn (or grain) **91** 57
granulation **323** 47
grape·fruit **368** 23
~-gatherer **80** 9
~ juice **80** 45
~ moth **81** 22
~ press **80** 16, 42
grapes **80** 6
grape-vine* **80** 3-6
graph **29** 16, **144** 15
graphic art **323**
~ studio **323** 27–64
graphite **3** 18
~ pile **1** 31–46
~ stick **239** 36
~ vane **229** 27
grapnel **213** 11
grapple **213** 11
grappling beam **213** 11
grasp on horizontal bar **279** 53–56
grass **354** 83–85, **359** 44
~ court **276** 1
~hopper **342** 8
~ lot **39** 76, **257** 36
~ plot **39** 76, **257** 36
~ skirt **289** 18
~ snake **350** 38
~ wrack **362** 54
grate **68** 60
grater **41** 85
grate type cooler **152** 9
graticule **87** 31, 32
~-adjuster **87** 30
~ systems **87** 31
grating **25** 5, **191** 11, **194** 24, **254** 11
~ machine **41** 79
~ of slats **262** 48
grave *n. [tomb]* **312** 23
~ *[accent]* **325** 31
~ accent **325** 31
~-digger **312** 22
gravel bottoming **196** 60
~ packing in front of chamber **254** 37
~ path **55** 23, **257** 18
~ terrace **13** 64
grave mound **312** 24
graver **107** 28, **170** 33, **323** 5
grave·stone **312** 26
~yard **16** 106, **312** 21–41
graving dock **217** 27–30
~ tool **323** 20
gravity filter plant **254** 9
~ mixer **113** 33
gravure ink **176** 17
gravy boat **46** 17
~ ladle **46** 18
gray scale* **320** 15
grazing **86** 13
grease compressor **191** 4
~ gun **191** 17, **192** 50
~ gun nipple **191** 18
~ nipple **136** 79
~ paint stick **296** 46
Great Bear **5** 29
~ Britain **14** 9, **244** 37, **245** 15
great cattle **74** 1+2
~coat **34** 48, 65
Great Dane **71** 34
~ Dipper* **5** 29
~ Dog **5** 14
Greater Bear **5** 29
greater than **327** 19
great horned owl **347** 14
~ octave **300** 64

great organ **305** 1
~ tit **346** 9
~ toe **21** 52
~-toe flexor **20** 49
greave **310** 54
Greece **14** 8, **244** 39
Greek art **316** 1-48
~ cross **313** 50
~ lace **101** 30
~ man **338** 3
~ ornamentation **316** 38–43
~-Orthodox church **252** 2
~ point **101** 30
~ script **324** 15
~ theatre **316** 44
~ vase **316** 37
~ woman **338** 1
green **320** 8
~ agaric **365** 29
~ alga **362** 43
~ baize covering **264** 15
~ brick **151** 16
~-cloth covering **264** 15
~ fly **342** 13
~gage **61** 24
~house **79** 33
~ locust **342** 8
~ malt **92** 11
~-malt turner **92** 9
~ oak tortrix **82** 43
~ plover **343** 21
~ spelt **69** 25
green-stuff· cutter **75** 41
~ silage **75** 19
~ silo **75** 19
greeting **239** 8
grenade **90** 53
grey hen **88** 66
~hound **71** 24
~ scale **320** 15
grid **68** 60, **291** 33
~ *[Theatre]* **297** 4
~ bars **156** 26
griddle cake **97** 30
gridiron* *[Sports]* **275** 21-27
grief stem **139** 13
griffin **307** 11
griffin's claws **307** 13
grill **291** 33
grille **166** 27, **185** 12
grilled sausage **291** 34
grinder shaft **167** 17
grinding cylinder **154** 1
~ disk **323** 46
~-dust extractor **143** 15
~ machine **134** 31, **141** 39, **143** 7, 10
~-roller bearing **156** 41
~ stone **337** 24
~ wheel **143** 11.
~-wheel head **143** 8
grip *[grasp]* **17** 37, 38, **279** 53-56
grip *[bag]** **201** 7
~ hand* **297** 46
~ on horizontal bar **279** 53–56
gripper carriage **174** 11
gripping arm **2** 47
grip·sack* **201** 7
~-testing dumb-bell **278** 49
grist **92** 24
~mill* **91** 45–67
grit filter **145** 50
~ guard **141** 35
grits-cleaner **91** 60
grit-spreader **195** 5,16
~-spreading attachment **195** 17
grits-reducing roller **91** 61
groats-cleaner **91** 60
~-reducing roller **91** 61
grocer **98** 41
grocer's **98** 1–87
~ assistant **98** 13
~ shop **98**
~ store* **98** 1–87
groceteria* **98** 1–87
groin **18** 38
groined vault **318** 42
groom *[stableman]* **179** 27
~ *[bridegroom]* **313** 15
groove *[body]* **18** 12
~ *[Tech.]* **141** 54
grooved bowl **287** 24
~ pin **136** 38
groove milling tool **143** 16
groover **99** 66
grooving **149** 14
~ tool **129** 24
groschen **244** 13
grotto **257** 1
ground **219** 62, 72
~ avalanche **286** 1
~ clearance **189** 5
grounded plate* **233** 52
ground floor **39** 2, **113** 7
~-floor brick wall **118** 29
~-glass screen **294** 8
~ hog* **351** 18
~ ivy **359** 18
~ mouthpiece **334** 4, 37
~ plan **144** 63
groundsel **63** 12
ground stopper **333** 4
~ water **12** 21
ground-water· level **254** 42, 63
~ stream **254** 3
ground work **278** 24–30
~-wrestling **281** 8, 9, 11
group **241** 40–61, **287** 25
groupe **288** 29
grouping of stars **5** 9–48
group of machines **241** 40–61
~ of players **287** 25
~ selector **233** 38
~ of stages **292** 10
grouse **88** 66, 69, 72
grove **337** 5
groved rod **122** 13
grove of urns **312** 31
growler **179** 26
groyne **13** 37, **211** 19
~ head **211** 20
grub **60** 64, **81** 54, **82** 12
grubber **68** 31
Grus **5** 42
G sharp minor **300** 6
g-string **302** 9
guanaco **351** 30
guard *[protection]* **161** 11
~ *[Railw.]* **201** 54, **203** 13, 17
~ *[watchman]* **310** 9
~ *[Techn.]* **128** 28
~ *[Fenc.]* **277** 43, 57, 64
~ plate **303** 18
~ rail **84** 8, **114** 43, **158** 31
guard's compartment **201** 57
guard tower **310** 17
gudgeon wrist (pin) **184** 71
guelder rose **357** 10
guests at table **259** 40-43
guide *[Tech.]* **133** 13
~ arm **234** 32
~ bar **157** 17, **158** 38, **160** 28
~ cable **2** 30
~ card **238** 73
~-card tab **238** 74
~ column **133** 30
~ groove **212** 75
~ pin **134** 41
~ rail **2** 37, **6** 11, **158** 3, **256** 54
~ rib **133** 40
~ roll **141** 65
~ roller **128** 44, **141** 65, **158** 47, **162** 5
~ roll for paper **168** 20
~ rope **226** 63
~ f. shaft **159** 3
guiding cross **298** 30
~ cross piece **68** 12
~ groove **283** 38, **301** 41
~ handle **173** 27
~ kerb **197** 38
~ pin **301** 40
guiding rod **196** 27
~ roller **149** 13
guillemot **343** 13
guilloche pattern **244** 38
guillotine *[paper-cutter]* **178** 1
~ *[plumber]* **119** 15
guinea fowl **74** 27
~-hen **74** 27
~ pig **351** 12
guitar **303** 12, 73
gulden **244** 19
gules *[Her.]* **246** 27
Gulf Stream **15** 30
gull **343** 14
gullet **18** 19, **19** 49, **22** 23, 40, **88** 12
gull wing **225** 20
'gull-wing' door **187** 30
gully *[drain]* **39** 14, **194** 22
~ *[Geol.]* **12** 44
~ drain **253** 49
~-emptier **195** 25
~ hole **253** 49
gum **21** 15
gummed tape **238** 79
gun *[rifle]* **86** 4, **87** 1–40
~ *[hunter]* **86** 1
~ barrel **90** 56, **223** 68
~ cradle **223** 69
~ dog **86** 7
~man **290** 38
gunnel **269** 30
gunner **90** 43
gun openings **213** 59
~ port **213** 60
gunter gaff **270** 46
gun turret **222** 24, 41
gunwale **269** 30
gutta-percha tree **367** 37
gutter **117** 28, 92, **194** 7
~ bracket **117** 32
~ f. deodorand **339** 11
guttering **40** 9
gutter pipe **117** 29
~ tile **117** 59
guy-rope **266** 30
gym **279** 1–56
~ belt **278** 46
~ clothes **278** 44–48
~ instructor **279** 39
gymkhana **273** 32
gym leader **279** 32
~ mat **279** 13
gymnasium **279** 1–48
gymnast **279** 31
~ on apparatus **279** 31
gymnastic lesson **279** 1–48
gymnastics **278, 279**
~ w. apparatus **279** 1–56
~ on bar **279** 11 + 12

head beam **177** 21
~ of bed **48** 3
~ of cabbage **59** 32
~ clerk **238** 1
~ croupier **263** 6
~ of department **256** 60
~ dress **335** 12
header *[Footb.]* **274** 56
~ bond **113** 60
~ course **113** 64
head frame **137** 6
~ gear *[harness]* **72** 7–13, 25
~gear *[hats]* **36**
~ of Gorgon **308** 50
~ guard* **203** 13
heading **239** 8, **325** 38
~ chisel **127** 63
~ of letter **239** 3
head·lamp **185** 17
~less screw **136** 46
~ of lettuce **59** 36
headlight **181** 40, **185** 17
~ beam setter **192** 58
head·line **21** 73, **325** 42
~ lock ring **180** 11
~ margin **178** 56
~master **249** 23
~ of Medusa **308** 50
~ muscle **20** 50
~phone **332** 18
~phones **29** 17
~piece *[harness]* **72** 7–11
~piece *[Arch.]* **318** 12
~ pin **287** 12
~ post **115** 53, **118** 54
~race **91** 41
~ receiver **29** 17, **332** 18
~-rest **17** 13, **47** 59, **104** 30
~ rope **90** 7, 17
~ rules **325** 41
~ set **233** 13, **332** 18
~ shield **135** 16
~ stake **119** 17
~stall **72** 7–11
~stand **278** 27
headstock **142** 2, **157** 39
~ spindle **142** 20
head·stone **312** 26
~ strap **72** 10
~ string **298** 31
~ tube **180** 14
~waiter **260** 30
~way structure **212** 44
~wear **36**
~ wheel **91** 7
heald **159** 27
~ eye **159** 28
~ shaft **159** 4
health resort **262** 1–49
heap of branchwood (or brushwood) **84** 16
~ cloud **8** 1, 2
~ of earth **79** 15
~ of snow **286** 24
hearing aid **108** 22
heart *[Anat.]* **20** 14, **22**
~ *[wood]* **149** 41
~ line **21** 74
~ point **246** 17
hearts *[cards]* **265** 40 + 44
~ease **62** 2
heart's-ease **62** 2
heartwood **115** 84, **354** 13
~ plank **115** 93
~ side **149** 40
he-ass **74** 3
heat colours **320** 16
heater plug **184** 64
~ plug control device **207** 17
heat-exchanger **3** 7, **152** 6, **184** 51
heath *[moor]* **16** 5
~ *[Bot.]* **361** 19
~ bird **88** 66
~ cock **88** 66
heather **361** 19
heath hen **88** 66
~land **16** 5
~ plant **361**
heating **339** 42
~ beaker **334** 20
~ blanket **48** 51
~ chamber **92** 19
~ element **173** 3
~ gas **148** 1–46
~ pad **23** 52
~ pipe **79** 8
~ pressure gauge **205** 45
~ system **92** 19
~ tension gauge **206** 41
heat regulator **204** 40
heavens **6** 1, **308** 46
heavy concrete **114** 72
~ dressing axe **150** 38
~-duty boot **100** 21
~-faced letters **170** 2, 9
~ gymnastics **279** 1–56
~ lift cargo ship **216** 1
~ lift derrick **216** 2
~ lorry **196** 7
~-oil engine **184** 37–80
~ sabre **277** 46
~ truck* **196** 7
~ warship **222** 18–64
Hebraic script **324** 7
Hebrew script **324** 7
heckelphone **302** 38
heckler *[meeting]* **251** 15
heckling **125** 1–7
~ bench **125** 3
hectometre post **198** 83
hedge **16** 98, **257** 37
~-clipper **58** 14
~hog **351** 5
~ mustard **63** 16
~row flower **359**, **360**
~ shears **58** 14
heel *[Anat.]* **21** 63
~ *[shoe]* **99** 54, 56
~ bone **19** 27
~-clamp **284** 25
~-glazing iron **99** 64
~ grip **283** 56
~ iron **99** 57
~-parer **99** 61
~ protector **100** 18
heels raised **278** 7
heel string **20** 48
'Heidelberg' *[machine]* **175** 29
heifer **74** 1
height-adjustment handle **44** 5
~ of cone **329** 44
~ gauge **145** 29
~-index level **110** 33
~-measuring **26** 21
~ scale **149** 9
~-to-paper **170** 44
helical gearing **136** 87
~ gear wheels **186** 59
~ spring **52** 76, **185** 26
~ spur wheel **136** 87
helicoid cyme **354** 76
helicopter **83** 47
~ landing field **230** 15
~ platform **222** 6
heliozoon **340** 7
helium nucleus **1** 10
~ tank **229** 7
hellbender **350** 22
hell hound **307** 29
helm *[ship]* **213** 13
~ *[Her.]* **246** 4, 7–9
helmet **138** 54, **264** 4 **285** 16, **310** 39–42
~ affrontée with open visor **246** 9
~ w. bars **246** 8
~ bowl **310** 39
~ plume **308** 18
helmsman **219** 18, **224** 39
helmsman's grating **219** 17
help* **45** 54
helper **17** 20
helter-skelter **291** 40
helve **132** 27
helvella **365** 25
hem **102** 2
hematite* **106** 49
hemicycle **328** 46
hemidemisemi-quaver **299** 21
~ rest **299** 29
hemihedron **330** 24
hemipteran **342** 4
hemi·pyramid **330** 24
~sphere **5** 1–35
hem line **256** 37
~-line marker **256** 40
hemlock **363** 4
hemming **102** 11
hemp **125** 6, **367** 9
~ fibre **125** 20
~hard **125** 7
~ seed **367** 15
~ shoe **117** 75
~ tow **125** 7
hemstitch **101** 14, **102** 10
hen **74** 19, **75** 20
~bane **363** 6
~ drunks **355** 42
~ house **75** 13
Henri Quatre beard **35** 8
hen's egg **75** 47
hepatic duct **22** 37
Hera **308** 5
herald of gods **308** 21
heraldic arms **246** 1-6
~ colour **246** 24–29
heraldry **246** 1–36
Hercules **5** 21
herd of deer **86** 15
Herdsman **5** 30
Herero woman **337** 25
here we go round the mulberry bush **258** 29
herma **316** 35
hermaphrodite flower **358** 10, **366** 14
hermes **316** 35
Hermes **308** 21
hero **292** 28
heroine **292** 27
heron **86** 46, **343** 18
heron's feather **36** 35
herring **350** 14
~-bone **283** 27
~ gear **136** 85
~ stitch **101** 9
~ driftnet **90** 2-10
hessian **124** 24
Hessian fly **81** 40
hexagon **330** 15
hexagonal biprism **330** 22
~ crystal system **330** 20–22
~ headed bolt **136** 13
~ nut **136** 18
~ prism **330** 21
hexahedron **330** 2
hexakis-octahedron **330** 13
hexoctahedron **330** 13
H. F. amplifier valve **235** 15
H. F. first stage **236** 2

hub **131** 27, **180** 26, **181** 43
~ barrel **180** 69
hubble-bubble **105** 39
hub body **180** 69
~ brake **182** 12 27
~ cap **185** 14, **189** 24
~ shell **180** 69
~ sprocket **180** 38
huckleberry* **361** 23
hula-hula girl **289** 16
hull **217** 25, **222** 3, **226** 73
~ of airship **226** 73
~ shape **270** 1–10
human body **18** 1–54, **307** 53
~ head **307** 21
humble bee **342** 23
hum eliminator **236** 19
humerus **19** 12
hummeller **67** 48, **68** 68
humming-bird **345** 4
~-top **49** 24
hummock **13** 42
humour **21** 46
hump **202** 49
humped fuselage **225** 47
humus covering **196** 64
hundred **326** 3
Hungarian red pepper **59** 42
Hungary **14** 25
hunt **272** 23–29, 58 -64
hunter **272** 24, 58
Hunter **5** 13
hunting binoculars **108** 38
~ cap **272** 50
~ dog **71** 40–43
~ equipment **87**
~ horn **87** 60, **272** 60
~ w. hounds **272** 58–64
~ implements **87** 41–48
~ knife **87** 41, 42
~ preserves **86** 1–8
~ rabbits **86** 23
~ screen **86** 9
~ trophy **262** 26
~ weapon **87**
hunt servant **272** 59
huntsman **272** 58
huntsman's hat **86** 5
~ suit **86** 2
hurdle **272** 27, **280** 12
hurdler **280** 11
hurdle race **272** 23–29, **280** 11+12
hurdy-gurdy **301** 25
'hurling' **287** 48
'hurling ball' **287** 49
hurst **91** 20
husk **61** 50, **69** 33
husking machine **91** 52
husky **71** 22, **336** 2
hut **113** 48, **282** 1
Hyaena **353** 1
hybrid **74** 8
hydra of Lerna **307** 32
Hydrallmania **349** 9
hydrant **255** 35
~ key **255** 27
hydrated lime **153** 27
~ lime silo **153** 26
hydrator **153** 21
hydraulic braking **183** 49
~ car jack **191** 2
~ engineering **212**
~ forging press **133** 23
~ lift **297** 33
~ mechanical articulated diesel train **207** 37+ 38
~ moulding press **172** 8
~ press **192** 54, **297** 53, **331** 7
~ press pump **172** 12
~ system **133** 24
~ three-way tipper **189** 18
hydro·carbon gas **139** 41
~chlorid acid **52** 35
~desulphurization plant **139** 65
~-extracting **163** 23
~extractor **162** 14, **166** 18
~former **139** 64
~fining plant **139** 65
~genation **164** 16
hydrogen balloon **10** 60
~-cooler **147** 27
~ cyanide **83** 20, 21
~ inlet **164** 15, **334** 12
~ peroxide tank **229** 19
hydroid polyp **349** 9
hydro·meter **192** 43, **331** 8
~pathic **262** 8
~plane *[aircr.]* **273** 48
~plane *[boat]* **223** 26, 51
~plane control **223** 42
~stabilizer **225** 63
~xylamine inlet **164** 21
hyena **353** 1
hygiene **30**
hygro·graph **10** 54
~meter **10** 23, 32, **166** 10, **171** 59
Hymenoptera **342** 21–23
hymn board **311** 24
~ book **311** 30
hyoid bone **22** 2
hyperbola **329** 26
hypha **365** 2
hyphen **325** 28
hypocotyl **354** 89
hypodermic (syringe) **26** 28, **27** 54
~ needle **26** 31
hypophysis cerebri **19** 43
hypostasis **26** 7
hypotenuse **328** 32
hypotrachelium **316** 22
hypsographic curve **11** 6-12
hypsometrical curve **11** 6–12
hyssop **358** 5

I

ibex **352** 7
ice axe **282** 17, 38
~ bag **23** 29
~berg **90** 34
~ boat **284** 47+ 48
~ bomb **261** 34
~-box **262** 35
~breaker **210** 29, **222** 5
~-breaking bows **222** 8
~ bridge **282** 25
~-climber **282** 16, 27
~-climbing **282** 15-22
ice-cream **261** 46
ice-cream·bar **261** 45-51
~ cornet **291** 31
~ dish **261** 37
~ freezer **97** 31
~ machine **97** 31, **261** 47
~ man **291** 30
~ spoon **261** 39
ice-crystal· cloud **8** 6
~ haze cloud **8** 7
ice cube **260** 44
~ dance **284** 8
~ drift **90** 35
~ field **90** 36
~ floe **90** 35
~ guard **210** 14
~ hockey **284** 35–41
ice-hockey· player **284** 35
~ skate **284** 28
~ stick **284** 37+38
Iceland **14** 11
Icelandic glima **281** 14
ice·maker **97** 31
~ pail **260** 42
~ piton **282** 54
~ raft **90** 35
~ ridge **282** 22
ice rink **284** 3
~ runner **284** 47
~-sailing **284** 46
~ scooter* **284** 47+48
~ skate **284** 25–32
~ skid **284** 47
~ slope **282** 15
~-sport **284** 1–48
~ stadium **284** 1
~ step **282** 18
~-tray **42** 6
~ yacht **284** 47+48
icicle **286** 21
icing sugar **98** 54
icosahedron **330** 11
icositetrahedron **330** 12
icy ground **286** 19
~ surface **286** 19
identical equation **327** 5
identically equal to **327** 16
identification tally **75** 43
~ mark **221** 35
identity **327** 16
idling control knob **207** 19
~ vent **183** 58
idol **309** 8, 20
igloo **336** 4
igniter **184** 64
~ plug **227** 43
ignition **227** 4, 15
~ cable **184** 5
~ cable pole **229** 31
~ coil **184** 8
~ key **182** 11, **186** 13
~ keyhole **207** 18
~ switch **186** 12, **228** 28
iguana **350** 32
ileum **22** 16
iliac artery **20** 17
~ vein **20** 18
ilia underwing **348** 8
ilium **19** 18
illuminated circuit diagram **147** 8
~ milk balance **77** 5
illuminating mirror **15** 59
illusionist **298** 20
illustrated paper **47** 10
I. L. S.· course-transmitter **230** 11
~ glide-path transmitter **230** 14
~ middle marker **230** 13
imaginary number **326** 14
imago **342** 10
imbricated ornament **317** 15
imitating part **300** 47
imitation of animal calls **87** 43–47

immersion heater **41** 83
~ roller **158** 42
immortelle **361** 3
impact crusher **150** 20
~ mill wheel **91** 39
Impair **263** 23
imparipinnate leaf **61** 40
impeller wing wheel **212** 52
imperial *[beard]* **35** 16
~ roof **116** 25
impermeable bed (or layer, or stratum) **12** 23
impervious bed (or layer, or stratum) **12** 23
implement **155** 18
impost **318** 21
impounded lake **212** 57
impregnating agent sprayer **83** 34–37
~ chamber **161** 32
impression cylinder **174** 19, **175** 2, 44, **176** 20, 29
~ handle **323** 34
~ of model **141** 27
~ of pattern **141** 27
~ of seal **232** 27
~ tray **27** 56
imprint **178** 48, **325** 39
imprinted stamp **232** 3
improper fraction **326** 16, 18
impulse cam **233** 21
~ contacts **233** 23
~ microphone* (or mike) **219** 39
~ mill wheel **91** 39
~-transmitting cable **237** 18
impure clay **151** 2
incandescent bulb **120** 56
~ lamp **120** 56
incense boat **313** 41
~ spoon **313** 42
inch tape **102** 73
incident-light micro-scope **110** 13
incisor **21** 16, 34
inclined approach **202** 1
~ elevator **148** 8
~ eyepiece tube **110** 12
~ fold **12** 13
~ hoist **148** 8, **150** 16
~ Otto engine **187** 25
~ ramp **202** 1
~ tube **110** 3
inclinometer* **228** 5
increase in air volume **227** 23
incubator **75** 30
incus **19** 61
indehiscent fruit **354** 97–102, **359** 43
indentation **170** 16
indention **170** 16
independent broker **243** 5
index *[Math.]* **327** 1
~ bar **192** 4
~ cabinet drawer **250** 23
~ card **238** 72
~ lever **107** 26
~ mirror and horizon glass **219** 6
~ of root **327** 2
~ scale **241** 26
India **14** 46
Indian *[America]* **335** 11, 23, 25
~ art **319** 19–28
~ chief **335** 11
~ club **278** 32
~ club exercise **278** 31
~ corn **69** 31
~ cress **56** 4
~ god **319** 19
~ ink **144** 55
~-ink attachment **144** 41
~-ink rubber **144** 54
~ macaque **353** 12
~ Ocean **15** 23
~ pagoda **319** 21
~ rose **62** 15
~ steel style **324** 21
~ of tropical forest **335** 25
~ woman **335** 10
india rubber **249** 52
India rubber tree **367** 33
indication of pace (or tempo) **300** 48
indicator **228** 3, 4, 5, 10
~ board **259** 5
~ lamp **157** 8, **180** 47
~ light **259** 6
indictment **248** 28
indigenous birds **344**
Indio **335** 23
indirect-light lamp **112** 60
Indonesia **14** 53
indoor clothing **33**
~ display window **256** 13
~ gymnastics **278** 49 + 50, **279** 1-56
~ handball **275** 1–8
~ plant **56**
~ swimming pool **25** 1–5
~ track **273** 1
indoor wear **33** 1-34
induced draught fan **146** 14
inductance **234** 25
induction coil **11** 44, **184** 8, **331** 70
~ elbow **184** 15
~ pipe **182** 9
industrial *n.* **243** 11–19
~ district **252** 58
~ motor vehicle **189** 14–50
industry bond **243** 11–19
inescutcheon **246** 17
infant **30** 26, **49** 26
~ to be baptized **313** 7
infant's outfit **31** 16
inferior purlin **114** 3, **117** 40
~ vena cava **20** 15, **22** 57
infield **275** 39
infighting **281** 27
infiltration water drain **211** 37
infinitesimal calculus **327** 13 + 14
infinity *[Math.]* **327** 15
inflatable animal **267** 33
inflation appendix **226** 55
~ neck* **226** 55
~ sleeve **226** 55
inflator **180** 48
inflected curve **329** 13
inflection **299** 51–55
inflorescence **61** 39, **354** 67–77
informal wear **34** 1
information bureau* **200** 29
~ office **200** 29
~ official **200** 49
infra-red radiation **4** 25
infusorian **340** 9
in-goal **275** 22
ingot **140** 32, **141** 43
~ chariot **141** 44
~ mould **140** 31
inhalant **23** 55
inhalation **17** 25
~ cure **262** 6 + 7
~ of oxygen **24** 19
inhalatorium **262** 6
inhaler **23** 33
inhaling apparatus **23** 33
initial **37** 4
~ letter **170** 1
~ position **277** 32
injection nozzle **184** 39
~ pump **184** 38
~ valve **184** 39
injector head **229** 21
injured person **253** 68
ink barrel **239** 21
~ blot **249** 47
~ bottle **144** 55
~ duct **175** 65, **176** 16
inker **174** 5, 18, 27, **233** 58
ink feed button **241** 7
~ fountain **174** 6, 34, 39, **175** 57
inking ball **323** 22
~ duct **175** 65
~ roller **175** 18, 27
~ unit **175** 19, 28, 50, 57
ink pad **238** 20
~ recorder **233** 58
~ reservoir **239** 21
~ ribbon **239** 39
~ ribbon feeder **239** 50
~ roller **174** 5, **175** 7
~ slab **175** 8
~ table **175** 8
~ unit **174** 34, 39
~ well **249** 29
inlaid border **302** 26
~ work **47** 48
inland postage **232** 40
inlet **145** 66
~ ballvalve **119** 63
~ pipe **254** 19
~ port **184** 73
~ valve **184** 29
inn **260** 1–29
inner bailey **310** 2
~ ear **19** 62–65
~ harbour **220** 26
~ jamb **113** 11
~ jib **214** 21
~ keel **269** 50
~ lining **269** 31
~ margin **178** 55
~ planking **270** 26
~ pocket **34** 19
~ race **136** 70
~ sole **99** 51
~ string **118** 45
~ title **178** 45
~ top rail **131** 20
~ tube **180** 30
input coil assembly **235** 18
~ selector **306** 18
inquiry office **200** 29
inscribed circle **328** 31
inscription **244** 11, **312** 14
insect **342** 3–23
~ collection **47** 35
~-eater **351** 4–7
~-eating animal **351** 4–7
~ eye **78** 20–24
insecticidal dust **83** 48
~ gas **83** 41
insecticide-dusting **83** 46
~-sprayer **58** 8

insectivore **351** 4-7
insert **161** 60
inserted ceiling **118** 61
~ eye **57** 34
~ floor **115** 43
inserting section **177** 40
insertion ring **333** 17
insert f. snow **10** 41
inset pocket **32** 59
inshore fishery **90** 24–29
inside calipers* **129** 23
~ forward **274** 18
~ keel **269** 50
~ left **274** 18
~ margin **178** 55
~ pocket **34** 19
~ right **274** 20
insole *[shoe]* **99** 51
~ *[sock]* **99** 4
inspection glass **190** 4, **239** 23
~ hole **141** 4
~ lamp **191** 20
~ manhole **254** 51
~ panel **51** 6, **158** 50
~ pit **191** 27, **199** 50
~ trolley* **208** 42
~ window **171** 60
inspector **201** 39
inspiration **17** 25
installation **40** 38–81
instalment office **256** 27
instantaneous gas water heater **119** 66
~ shutter **111** 44
instep **21** 61
institute f. tropical diseases (or tropical medicine) **220** 3
instruction **249** 1–31
instructor **279** 39
instrument *[tool]* **26** 26-62, **28**, **109**, **110**
~ *[Mus.]* **301–306**
instrumental music *[symbol]* **308** 65
instrument board* **186** 1-21
~ box **10** 62, **144** 10
~ cabinet **26** 18, **27** 23
~ case **2** 5, 22
instrumented satellite **4** 48, 53
instrument landing **230** 22–38
~ landing system course-transmitter **230** 11
instrument f. measuring· angles **15** 52–62
~ atmospheric pressure **10** 1–18
instrument f. microscopy **110** 1–23
~ panel **77** 18, **183** 25 **186** 1–21, **207** 11
~ section **229** 3–5
~ stand **161** 55
~ table **27** 24, **28** 12
~ trolley **26** 20
insulated handles **120** 54
~ jumper **234** 28
insulating conduit **120** 44
~ contact **193** 28
~ plate **117** 44, **331** 53
~ tape **120** 34
~ tube **120** 44
insulation **40** 72
~-stripping pliers **120** 51
insulator **234** 22, **331** 64
insured registered letter **232** 25, 35
intaglio printing **176**
~-printing method **323** 14–24
~-printing process **323** 14–24
intake **183** 62, **227** 2, 21
~ airway **138** 10
~ chamber **212** 40
integer **326** 10
integral **327** 14
~ collar **136** 31
~ constant **327** 14
~ sign **327** 14
integrating meter **29** 49
integration **327** 14
integrator **29** 49
intensity coil **184** 8
interchangeable filter **112** 18
~ lens **111** 25
~ mount **48** 18, **112** 46+47
interest **327** 7
~ coupon **243** 18
~ formula **327** 7
interference comparator **110** 29
~ inverter **236** 13
interferometer **110** 25
interior angle **328** 26
~ work **292** 26–61
interleaving paper feeder **175** 11
interlinear space **170** 5
interlocking board **199** 66
intermediate drill **143** 32
~ floor **115** 43, **118** 68
~ frame **157** 27
intermediate-frequency·amplifier valve **235** 15
~ filter **235** 18
~ transformer **235** 15
intermediate gear lever **142** 3
~ house **79** 32
~ landing **118** 52–62
~ layer **11** 3
~ mast **209** 29
~ screen-viewer **109** 7
~ support **209** 29
~ tank **220** 60
interment **312** 34–41
intermission* **249** 65
intermittent jet tube **226** 21
~ kiln **154** 3
~ pulse-jet tube **227** 12
intern* **28** 29
internal calipers **129** 23
~ combustion engine **184**
~-combustion punner **196** 26
~ ear **19** 62–65
~ electrode **2** 3
~ organ **22** 1–57
~ toothing **136** 93
interne* **28** 29
interrogation point* **325** 20
intersection **253** 9
~ of curve **329** 12
interstellar craft **4** 57
~ flight **4** 48–58
interurban coach **204** 53
interval **300** 19, 20-27
~ selector **306** 39
intestinal tube **26** 9
intestine **22** 14–22
intrados **318** 25
intrusion **11** 30
intrusive rock **11** 29
inundation area **211** 41
invalid carriage **181** 22
~ chair **23** 51
~ tricycle **181** 22
Inverness **179** 32
invertebrates **340**
inverted bowl fitting **45** 31
~ mordent **300** 34
~ pleat **32** 5
inverter **236** 13
investigation department **247** 21–24
investigator* **263** 16
invoice **238** 50
involucral calyx **359** 33
involution **327** 1
involving **327** 1
ion chamber **2** 2, 17
Ionic column **316** 9
ionization chamber **2** 2, 17
ionosphere **4** 13
ion trap magnet **236** 17
Irak **14** 45
Iran **14** 44
Iraq **14** 45
Ireland **14** 10, **244** 37
iris *[Anat.]* **21** 42
~ *[Bot.]* **62** 8
Iris **62** 8
iron *[metal]* **136**, **141** 11
~ *[stirrup]* **72** 43
~ *[Golf]* **276** 70
Iron Age **309** 21–40
iron band **156** 5
~ bar **339** 2
~ bridge **16** 56
ironer **166** 25, 32
iron foundry **141**
~ frame **304** 2
~-headed hammer **322** 16
~ heel-protector **99** 57
ironing **166** 31
iron in-gate **140** 34
ironing-board **52** 72, **166** 29, 34
~ woman **166** 32
iron key **309** 32
~ last **99** 27
~ lung **24** 8
~ pyrites **330** 8
~ rake **58** 3
~ sleeker **99** 30
~ square **115** 78
~ stove **52** 64
~ tap-hole **140** 11
~ weight **141** 18
~ wire **136** 12
~ works **140**
irradiation chair **24** 11
~ lamp **24** 17
~ table **2** 36
irregular curve **144** 49
~ quadrilateral **328** 39
irrigator **23** 46
isander **268** 42
ischium **19** 19
Islam(it)ic art **319** 12–18
island **13** 6
~ superstructure **222** 68
islet **211** 4
isobar **9** 1
isobaric line **9** 1
isocheim **9** 42
isohel **9** 44
isohyet **9** 45
isolated farm **16** 101
isolating switch **206** 6
isometric crystal system **330** 1–17

isosceles triangle 328 27
isoseismal 11 37
isothere 9 43
isotherm 9 40
isotope-separating plant 3 39
Israel 14 39
issue 232 21
issuing bank 244 30
~ counter 250 20
Italian foil 277 53
~ mocha machine 261 50
italic letters 170 7
italics 170 7
Italy 14 12, 244 20
item-counter 239 52
itinerant trader 291 51
ivory ball 264 1
~ key 304 4
~ statuette 309 8
ivy 359 18

J

jack [Tech.] 191 2, 30, 233 7, 255 12
~ [mus. instr.] 301 50, 304 30
~ [game] 287 23
~ [toy] 49 14
jackal 352 11
jackanapes 289 33
jackass 74 3
jacket [Cloth.] 32 2, 36, 34 5
~ [Tech.] 67 56
~ base 67 56
~ button 34 6
~ collar 34 15
~ crown 27 31
~ flap 178 38
~ lining 34 18
jack-in-a-box 289 56
jacking pier 210 66
jack-in-the-box 289 56
~ plane 127 53
~-pudding 289 69
~ rafter 116 61, 63
~ spur 72 50, 51
~ staff 218 47
Jacobin 314 19
~ cap 36 2
Jacob's ladder 216 14
Jacquard stocking 33 34
jai alai 287 51
jailer* 248 14
jam 98 51, 52
jamb [roof] 116 47
~ [leg armour] 310 54
~ [window] 115 32
jambart 310 54
jambe 310 54
jambeau 310 54
jamboree 266 40–52
Jamestown weed* 363 8
jam nut 136 28
janitor 53 28
~* 145 87, 256 44
Janus 308 47
~ head 308 48
Japan 14 50, 245 20
Japanese art 319 7–11
~ quince 357 17
~ script 324 6
japonica 357 17
jar 41 66, 78 63
jasmin(e) 357 4
javelin 280 54
~-thrower 280 52
~-throwing 280 52–55
jaw [Anat.] 18 17 19 35
~ [Tech.] 135 24
~bone 18 17
~ trap 87 48
jay (bird) 346 1
jazz band 289 2
~ band player 289 3
~ band instrument 303 47–78
~ guitar 303 73
~ percussion instrument 303 47-54
~ player 289 3
~ tomtom 303 49
~ trumpet 303 65
J-box 161 33
J-box inspection window 161 35
jeans 32 57, 266 12
jeep 195 3
jejunum 22 15
jelly-bag cap 36 2
~fish 340 14
jenny-ass 74 3
~ wren 346 12
jerboa 351 15
jerk 281 4
jerkin 338 45
jerkwater train* 203 1
jerry* 198 20
jessamin(e) 357 4
jesses 86 45
jester 289 69
jet 94 18, 184 65
jeté 288 21
~ passé 288 23
jet exhaust 226 11
~ needle 183 55
~ nozzle 195 33
~-propelled model 271 63
~ switch 171 52
~-tester 192 51
jetton 263 12
jetty 211 19, 220 32
jet of water 257 22
jewel 38 1–33
~-case 38 11
~-casket 38 11
jewelled tiara 38 6
jewellery 38 1–33
~ department 256 62
jewelry 38 1–33
jib [Tech.] 114 36, 145 17, 221 2, 27
~ boom 213 51
~ header rig 270 31, 36, 38, 43
~ stay 214 14
~ topsail 270 30
jig 161 12
jigger [yacht] 215 34
~ [Text.] 161 12
~ sheet 214 69
jig-saw puzzle 50 14
Jim(p)son weed* 363 8
jingle tambourine 303 45
jinricksha 336 34
~ coolie (or cooly) 336 35
jinrikisha 336 34
jiu jitsu 281 15–17
jobber 243 7
job carriage* 179 26
jockey 272 56
~ dress 272 57
join [roof] 117 94
joiner 127 45
joiner's bench 127 40–44
~ tool 127 10-31
~ workshop 127 1–65
joint 116 84-98, 144 31, 37, 197 39 + 40
~ bar* 198 43
~-cutter 197 16
~-cutting knife 197 17
jointed fishing rod 89 20-23
joint knife 197 17
~ platter* 46 26
~ vice 106 34
joist 136 6
~ shuttering 114 12
joker 289 69
jolly boat 270 6–10
Jordan 14 42
journal [newsp.] 47 8
~ [Tech.] 136 61
~ bearing 136 67
~ bearing* 205 10
~ box* 204 66
~ sheet 238 66
journeyman blacksmith 132 13
~ shoemaker 99 1
joust 310 71
joystick 228 35
judge [Just.] 281 39
~ [Sports] 248 20, 22
judges' box 272 19
~ stand 283 13
judo 281 15-17
jug 30 24
juggler 298 17
jugular vein 20 2
juice 80 45
~-extractor 42 39
ju jitsu (or jutsu) 281 15-17
jump [jumping] 268 13, 288 12, 21
~ [obstacle] 272 31
jumper [Sports] 280 29, 36, 38
~ [Cloth.] 32 12
~ [Tech.] 234 28
jumping 280 29–55
~* 258 53
~ bar 280 37
~ cracker 289 52
~ hill 283 7
~ hoop 290 58
~ jack 49 14
~ leg 342 11
~ net 224 40, 290 14
~ pit 280 31
~ post 279 22, 280 40
~ rope 279 23
~ rope* 258 54
~ sheet 255 18
~ ski 283 41
jump turn 283 21
junction 313 31
~ sign 197 50
~ signal box 199 24
junior 238 8
juniper 356 47
~ berry 356 52
junk [boat] 336 32
~ shop 253 54
~ stall 291 60
Juno 308 5
Jupiter [Myth.] 308 1
~ [planet] 6 27
juror 248 23
juryman 248 23
just n. 310 71
justice 248
jute 367 25
~ plant 367 25
~ serving 147 49
~ wrapping 156 4

K

Kaffir lily 56 8
kail 59 34
kale 59 34
kaleidoscope 50 19
kamelaukion 314 31
Kandahar binding 283 45–50
kangaroo 351 3
kapok 124 23
~ tree 367 20
karabiner 282 56
karst cave 13 79
~ formation 13 71–83
kayak 269 4, 336 12
Keel 5 46
keel 217 22, 269 32, 50, 270 3

keel blocks 217 36
~ in position 217 22
~ plate 217 46
keelson 217 50
keel yacht 270 1-4, 5
keep *n.* 310 4
keeper *[zoo]* 339 8
~ *[Tech.]* 332 37
~ of wild animals 339 8
keeping the balance (or equilibrium) 279 41
~ of fowls 75 1-46
keg 89 63
kelly 139 13
kelson 217 50, 269 50
kennel 64 23
kerb 53 21, 194 8, 210 3
~stone 53 22, 194 9
kerchief 266 47
kerf 85 20, 138 45
kernel 61 8, 69 13
kernelled fruit 61
kerosene* 139 39
~ lamp* 76 16
kerosine 139 39
ketch 215 9, 270 41–44
ketchup 46 43
kettle 41 73
~ cart 309 36
kettledrum 302 57
~ skin 302 58
~ vellum 302 58
Kevenhuller 338 62
key *[f. lock]* 134 44
~ *[rivet]* 136 71+72
~ *[Build.]* 118 71
~ *[mus. instr.]* 302 35, 304 4, 5, 305 8
~ *[telephone]* 233 12
~ *[typewr.]* 240 26
~ *[Mus.]* 300 1–15
keyboard 169 37, 240 25, 301 28, 304 4+5
~ instrument 304 1
keyed instrument 304 1
keyhole 134 40
~ saw 115 63, 127 27
key lever 301 38, 49
~ rack 259 3
keys 301 28
key seat 136 83
keyshelf 233 10
key slot 136 83
keysmith vice 134 24
key·stone 318 23
~ way 136 64, 83
kibble 138 29
kick 274 53, 58
~-back fingers 128 16
kicking-sack 30 31
kick-off 274 11–21
~ stand 180 34
kickstarter 181 50, 182 35
~ turn 283 31
kidney 22 28, 30+31
~ dish 26 62
~-shaped bowl 26 62
~ vetch 70 6
kid's bike* 181 13
kiln 151 19
~ charge 153 14
~-charger 153 13
~ drying chamber 149 46
~ shell 153 17
kilometer* see kilometre
kilometre board 211 44
~ post 198 82
kimono 48 56, 336 40
kindergarten 50
~ teacher 50 1
kindling 53 8
~ wood 52 61
king *[chess]* 265 8
~ *[skittles]* 287 12
~ carp 350 4
~-cup 359 8
~fisher 344 8
~ penguin 343 4
~-post roof truss 116 42
king's chamber 315 2
~ tomb 315 1
kiosk 200 26, 46, 47, 48
Kipp apparatus 334 59
Kirghiz 336 22
kiri* 337 33
Kirschner beater 156 25
kiss 201 60
kit *[tools]* 87 61–64
~ *[mus. instr.]* 310 20
~-bag 266 22
kitchen 41, 42
~ cabinet 41 8
~ car 204 51
~ chair 41 52
~ clock 42 19, 107 50
~ cupboard 41 8
~ department 302 49–59
~ garden 55
~ implement 42 1–60
~-knife 41 56
~ machine 42 1–60
~ range 41 39
~ scales 41 59
~ table 41 53
~ utensil 42 1–66
~ waste 41 34
~ window curtain 41 13
kite *[Zool.]* 347 11
~ *[paper~]* 258 50
~ *[Geom.]* 328 38
~ cord 258 52
~- flying 258 49
kite's tail 258 51
kite string 258 52
kitten 74 17
kitty wren 346 12
Kletterschuh 282 51
knapping hammer 137 2
knapsack 86 3, 266 42
knapweed 70 10, 360 12
kneading arm 97 75
~ machine 42 30
~ pan 97 76
~ table 97 71
~ trough 97 72
knee *[Anat.]* 18 50
~ bend 278 15
~ bending 278 15
~ breeches 34 22
~cap *[Anat.[* 19 23, 73 33
~ cop *[armour]* 310 53
~ full-bending 278 15
~ grip 182 53
~lever 102 14, 304 45
kneeling desk 314 9
knee pad 275 15, 285 17
~ pan 73 33
~ piece 310 53
~-raising 278 4
~ roll 72 48
knees full bend 278 13, 15
knee-sock 31 39
~ strap 99 15
~ swell 304 45
~ swing 279 11
knickerbockers 34 22
knickers 33 13, 21
knife 46 50, 69, 178 3
~ beam 177 19, 178 2
~ folding machine 178 8
~ and fork 46 7
~ rest 46 11
~-thrower 290 37
knight *[Chivalry]* 310 67
~ *[chess]* 265 11
knighting 310 66
knight's armour 310 38–65
~ coronet 246 43
~ mate position 265 15
Knight Templar 310 73
knitted band 36 45
~ fabric 160 48
~ hat 36 53
~ waistband 34 25
knittie* 32 12
knitting action 160 51
~ factory 160 1–66
~ head 160 21
~ machine 160 1, 23, 35
~ mill 160
knob 45 14, 234 41–45
~ on the bill 343 17
knobkeerie 337 33
knobkerry 337 33
knockout 281 36
~ blow 281 36
knot *[cord]* 33 46, 117 68
~ *[hair]* 35 29
~ *[measure]* 9 12–19
~-borer 128 39
~-boring machine 128 39
~-driller 128 39
knotted cords 335 22
~ record 335 22
~ work 101 21
knotter 168 9
knot of tie 33 46
knotting point 125 29
knuckle 21 82
knurling iron 244 44
K. O. 281 36
K. O.'d opponent 281 36
kohlrabi 59 26
Kollergang 167 11
konimeter 110 23
Korea 14 51, 52
kris 336 44
krona 244 25
krone 244 24, 26
krum(m)horn 301 6
Kuro Shio 15 31
Kursaal 262 8

L

label 201 5, 232
~ f. air mail 232 32
~ f. express mail 232 31
labelling machine 93 33
label f. partly insured registered mail 232 33
~ f. registered insured mail 232 28
~ f. reserved seat 204 34
labial pipe 331 19
laboratory 6 20
~ dish 168 2
labourer 113 19
Labrador Current 15 40
laburnum 358 32
labyrinth *[Anat.]* 19 62
~ *[maze]* 257 5
laccolite 11 30
laccolith 11 30
lace 101 18
~ bonnet 338 65
~ collar 37 6
~ cuff 37 7

lace flounce **30** 34
~ frill **30** 34
Lacertidae
350 27, 31–37
lace top **33** 29
~-trimmed cloak
338 66
~ work **101** 30
Lachesis **308** 55
lachrimal bone **19** 40
lacing **33** 25
lackey **179** 20
~ moth **81** 13
lackey's dress **179** 21
lacquered work **319** 6
lacqueur remover*
103 13
lacrimal bone **19** 40
Lactarius torminosus
363 13
lacustrine building
309 15
lad **45** 3
ladder **40** 15, **216** 14,
255 9, **279** 4
~ *[cart]* **131** 20+21
~ hook **117** 15, 69
~ mechanism **255** 11
~-mender **102** 61
~ operator **255** 13
~ post **131** 20
~ scaffold **113** 86–89
~ work **255** 1–46
laddie **45** 3
ladies' hairdresser's
salon **103** 1–34
~ hair style **35** 27-38
~-smock
359 11
~ underclothing
33 1–34
~ wear **32**
~ wear department
256 28
ladle **41** 5, **53** 64,
140 12
~-shaped thermom-
eter **92** 36
~ truck **140** 12
lad's duffle-coat **31** 57
lady **338** 59, 64, 68,
70, 79
~ assistant **28** 28
~bird **342** 37
~bug **342** 37
~ cashier **256** 1,
260 46
~ clock **342** 37
~cow **342** 37
~ customer **256** 16
~-dog **74** 16
~finger **70** 6
~ librarian **250** 14
~ purchaser **256** 16
lady's bag **37** 10
~ bicycle **181** 8
~ chemise **33** 11
~ cycle **181** 8
~-fingers **70** 6
~ hand bag **37** 10
~ hat **36** 48
~ maid **48** 48
lady's pyjamas **33** 3
~ shoe **100** 44
~-slipper *[Bot.]*
360 27
~ stocking **33** 32
~ umbrella **43** 12
lady surgeon **28** 28
lady's vest **33** 11
lagoon **13** 33, 44
lake **13** 3
~ dwelling **309** 15,
335 33
lamantin **351** 23
lamb **74** 13
lambrequin **246** 3
lamb's-tail **61** 45
lambs' tongues **59** 38
lamellar diaphragm
2 33
lamellicorn beetle
342 24
lamina **69** 20, **354** 28
laminated spring
185 25
lamp **28** 26, **44** 7,
253 16
~ arm **171** 23
~ bracket **180** 6
~ cap w. thread
120 60
~-house **112** 29, 56,
295 39–44
lampion **289** 4
lamp post **75** 12,
253 17
~-shade **47** 52
~ shelf **224** 42
~ signal **147** 3,
233 6
~ signalling
switchboard **233** 5
lam rod **159** 54
Lancashire asphodel
70 13
lance *[weapon]* **287** 62,
310 81, **336** 9
~ *[app.]* **83** 34
lanceolate **354** 32
lance rest **310** 80
lancet **28** 49
land *[rifle]* **87** 37
~ aircraft **225** 32
landau **179** 36
landaulette **179** 36
land end of groyne
13 38
landing **118** 34–41
~ beam **118** 34, 55
~ bumper **226** 70
~ craft **222** 9
~ deck **222** 69
~ field **230** 15
~ gearlever
228 29
~ marker* **230** 12
~ net **89** 10
~ pier **220** 17
~ runway **222** 70,
230 3
~ signal **230** 12
~ skid **225** 9, 43,
271 33
landing sled* **225** 9
~-slope **283** 11
~ stage **220** 17, 33,
269 19
~ step **118** 19
land·plane **225** 32
~ practice **268** 20
~ roller **67** 9
landscape **13** 1–13,
47 6
~ architect* **54** 23
~ garden **339** 45
~ gardener **54** 23
~ park **257** 41–69
landside **68** 5
landsknecht **338** 32
land-surveying
15 46–62
~ wheel **68** 15, 26
lane *[Sports]* **280** 5
~ *[forest]* **84** 1
languid **305** 28
lansquenet drum
289 70
lantern *[lamp]* **76** 1,
179 9
~ *[Arch.]* **317** 45
~ cupola **318** 3
~ tower **219** 57
lap *[overlapping]*
117 100
~ *[tape]* **147** 46,
156 64
~-counting apparatus
280 19
lapel **34** 16, 54
lap-holder **156** 48
~-judge **273** 6
lappet **74** 23
lapping plate **119** 4
lap ready f. combing
156 58
~ machine **156** 14
~ rest **156** 15
~-riveting **136** 54
~ robe* **48** 55,
201 8
~-turner **156** 19
~wing **343** 21
larboard **221** 49
larch **356** 32
~ cone **356** 36
~ tree **356** 32
lard **96** 5
large Astrantia **360** 7
large-capacity· cabin
209 52
~ tram and trailer
193 1
~ van **189** 39
large city **252** 1–70
~ compartment
204 25
~ container **208** 26
~ dividers **144** 34
~ hand screw **127** 36
~ Host **313** 34
~ rock **150** 8
~ suitcase* **200** 6,
201 12
~ town **252** 1–70
lark **346** 18, 19
larkspur **62** 13, **361** 8
larmier **88** 14
larva **60** 64, **81** 29,
46, 53, **82** 12, 44, 47,
342 19
~ of feather star **349** 3
larval chamber **82** 368
~ gallery **82** 24
laryngeal mirror **26** 61
laryngoscope **26** 61
larynx **22** 2+3
lashings **213** 32
lass **45** 4
lassie **45** 4
lasso **335** 5
last *n.* **99** 10, 27
~-hook **99** 11
~ man **282** 28
~ quarter **7** 6
latch **102** 34
~ needle
160 12, 27, 61
Lateen sail **213** 29,
215 3
~ yard **213** 30
lateral adjustment
143 45
~ guide **240** 6
~ ligament **22** 34
~ lock nut **15** 57
~ lunge **278** 20
~ moraine **12** 53
~ stay **193** 45
Late Stone Age
309 10–20
lath **117** 26, 43
~ axe **117** 21
lathe **129** 1, **142** 1
~ accessory
142 35–42
~ base **142** 12
~ bed **129** 2, **142** 31
lather **104** 27
lathering dish **104** 23
lathe stand **142** 12
lathing **118** 71
Latin *[type]* **325** 4, 5, 6
~ capital **324** 16
~ cross **313** 49
~ handwriting
325 12
latissimus of the back
20 59
~ dorsi **20** 59
latitude **15** 6
latrine **266** 39
lattice barrier **198** 68
~ bridge **210** 47
~ feeder **156** 8
~ girder **145** 7
~ mast **209** 31,
222 7
~ tube **6** 2
~ work **210** 48–54
laughing gas cylinder
28 34
~ gull **343** 14
launch *[take-off]*
271 1, 4
~ *[boat]* **216** 20
launching **229** 28–31
launder **141** 3

letterpress printing **175**
~ printing method **323** 1–13
~ rotary printing press **175** 41
letter punch **238** 80
~ rack **259** 2
~ scales **231** 22
~ seal **232** 27
~ slot **203** 20, **231** 27
~ sorting frame **231** 37
~ tray **238** 25
lettuce **59** 36
~ leaf **59** 37
levade **72** 4
levee **13** 9
~* **16** 104, **211** 49
level *[surface]* **13** 77
~ *[Geodesy]* **15** 48
~ *[Building]* **113** 55
~ area **7** 11
~ crossing **16** 26, **198** 67–78, **201** 20
~ layer **118** 39
levelling **15** 46
~ beam **197** 3
~ staff **15** 47
level road **137** 34
lever **142, 144** 14
leverage **119** 43
leveret **88** 59
lever f. raising and lowering **157** 42
~ set hand-operated calculator **240** 42
~-stopper **93** 41
~-top collar stud **33** 61
lewis bolt **136** 41
Leyden jar **331** 48, 55
L. F. transformer **235** 2
Liberia **14** 37
liberty cap **36** 2
~ horses **290** 30+31
Libra **5** 19, **6** 38
librarian **250** 14, 19
library **250** 11–25
~ ticket **250** 25
~ user **250** 24
license number* **186** 34
~ plate* **185** 43, **186** 31
lich house **312** 21
licker-in roller **156** 53
lid **45** 13, **208** 18
lidded ashtray **203** 46
~ inkstand **249** 63
lido **268** 1–32
~ deck **218** 22
liege lord **310** 67
lierne vault **318** 44
life-belt **224** 45, 58
~boat **218** 19
~ buoy **216** 63, **224** 45
~-guard *[person]* **267** 1
life guard *[locomotive]* **205** 34
~-guard station **267** 46
~ jacket **224** 57
~ line *[band]* **21** 72
~ line *[rope]* **224** 49, **267** 2
~ mortar **224** 52+53
~-preserver* **224** 58
~ rope **224** 49
~-saver **17** 36
~-saving service at sea **224**
lift **209** 15, **214** 47, **256** 45, **297** 34
~boy **256** 47
~ chair **209** 16
~ controls **256** 48
~ drop hammer* **133** 16
lifter *[Sports]* **281** 1
~ rail **157** 30
lifting blocks **331** 3
~ block and tackle **331** 3
~ chain **133** 39
~ device **221** 13
~ door **133** 56
~ gear **145** 3
~ height **210** 70
~ hook **85** 31
~ motor **143** 27
~ plan **165** 4
~ plant **297** 50
~ platform **1** 42
~ ramp **191** 3
~ rope **224** 11, **256** 52
~ screw **212** 36
~ span **210** 68
~ spindle **212** 36
~ tackle **216** 4, **331** 3
~ truck **145** 27
~ a wreck **224** 9–12
lift operator **297** 59
~ platform **220** 66, **221** 70
~ room **39** 83
~ shaft **256** 51
ligature *[letters]* **170** 6
~ of blood vessel **17** 14–17
~-holding forceps **28** 50
light *n.* **47** 24, **219** 58, **256** 23
~-alloy passenger coach **203** 34
~ alloy prop **138** 25
~-alloy railcar **207** 28
~ aluminium construction **207** 25
~ and bell buoy **219** 49
~ button **120** 2
~ diesel locomotive **196** 24
~-faced letter **170** 8
lighter *[device]* **105** 29
~ *[ship]* **220** 20, 22
~ *[person]* **292** 37
light four **269** 9
~ gun **222** 34
~house **16** 8
lighting aperture **316** 75
~ gas **148** 1–46
~ plot **297** 3
~ rail **292** 53
~ technician **290** 4
light literature **325** 50
~-metal passenger coach **203** 34
~-metal railcar **207** 28
lightning protector earth connection **234** 24
light overcoat **34** 52
~ railway **16** 90, **196** 23
~-railway track **149** 26
~ sabre **277** 34, 63
~ shaft **6** 17
~ship **16** 13, **219** 56
~ switch **181** 38
~-vessel **219** 56
~ visor **2** 34
~ warship **222** 14–17
light-weight picture camera **294** 22
~ slab **118** 58
~ suitcase **259** 15
light and whistle buoy **219** 43
ligula **354** 84
ligule **69** 22, **354** 84
Liliaceae **56** 13
lily **62** 12
~ of the valley **361** 2
limb *[Anat.]* **18** 43–54
~ *[tree]* **354** 5
~ *[Tech.]* **219** 2
~ *[sun]* **7** 22
lime *[Bot.]* **355** 46
~ brush **121** 24
~ bunker **140** 55
~ crusher **153** 18
~ kiln **16** 86, **153** 12
~light flap* **296** 1
~ slaking plant **153** 21
~stone **153** 10
~ tree **355** 46
~ works **153**
limit gauge **142** 49
limousine **187** 1, 9
linch pin **131** 24
linden **355** 46
~ tree **355** 46
line *[Typ., etc.]* **170** 4, **249** 35, **299** 45
~ *[Geom.]* **328** 1–23
~ *[Railw.]* **198**
~ *[cord]* **89** 29, **125** 18
~ *[harness]* **72** 25, 33
linear **354** 31
line of azimuth **87** 74
~ block **172** 35
~ dancers **298** 6
~ diagram of the card **156** 51
~ of equal atmospheric pressure **9** 1
~ furrow **18** 11
~ of fault **12** 5
~ fisher **89** 7
~ fishing **89** 7–12
~ of flight **4** 49
~ of geographical latitude **15** 2
~ of geographical longitude **15** 4
~ of hand **21** 72–74
~ of head **21** 73
~ of heart **21** 74
~ inspection car* **208** 38
~ inspection trolley **208** 38
~ inspector **198** 73
~ of latitude **15** 2
~ of life **21** 72
~ of longitude **15** 4
linen **33** 1–34, **48** 42, **256** 57
~ button **37** 26
~ compartment **259** 31
~ cupboard **48** 40
~ goods **256** 57
~ gown **338** 5
~ initials **37** 4
~ lining **338** 57
~ monogram **37** 4
~ sheet **48** 9
~ shelf **48** 41
~ stencil **37** 5
~-tester **171** 25
line-of-battle-ship **213** 51–60
~ oscillator **236** 29
liner *[ship]* **216** 32
liners *[tool]* **121** 21
lines *[Theatre]* **297** 8
line schedule* **200** 32
~-setting composing machine **169** 19
linesman **274** 23, 47
linesman's flag **274** 48
line space gauge **240** 5
~ lever **240** 30, 67
~ plunger **240** 31
line of terrestrial latitude **15** 2
~ of terrestrial longitude **15** 4
~ timetable **200** 32
~ of type **169** 15
ling **361** 19
lining *[cloth]* **34** 18, **99** 43, **102** 69
~ *[brake]* **136** 104
~ *[Bot.]* **365** 17
~ board **114** 18, **118** 56

link **107** 11, **181** 29–31, 32
linkage **182** 15, **185** 27
link bracelet **38** 21
links *[Golf]* **276** 59-62
lino **121** 42
linoleum **121** 42
~ knife **121** 46
~ lining **121** 43
~ putty **121** 45
linotype **169** 19
~ matrix **169** 29
lint **367** 6, 19
lintel **113** 9
lint hairs **367** 19
Lion **5** 17, **6** 36
lion **353** 2
~ *[symbol of railway]* **201** 64
lion's body **307** 14, 22
~ head **307** 17
~ mane **353** 3
lip *[Anat.]* **21** 14, 26
~ *[organ]* **305** 26, 27
~ plug **337** 23
~stick **103** 19
~-synchronist **293** 27
~-synchronization **293** 25–29
~-synchronization studio **293** 25
~-synking **293** 25–29
~ of vulva **22** 87
liquefied petroleum gas (LPG) **139** 36
liqueur **98** 58
~ decanter **46** 48
~ glass **46** 89
liqueurs **98** 83
liquid-column barometer **10** 1
~-fuel rocket **227** 49, **229** 1
~-gas tanker **216** 9
liquid-manure· cart **64** 56
~ channel **76** 45
~ drain **76** 44
~ gully **76** 45
~ gutter **76** 21, 45
~ pit **64** 54
~ pump **64** 55
~ scoop **58** 42
~ tank **64** 57
liquid seal **148** 60
liquor circulation pipe **161** 71
lira **244** 20
list *[enumeration]* **98** 73, **231** 26
~ *[Weav.]* **159** 11, **165** 24
lister* **68** 31
list of postal rates **231** 26
literature **325** 50
litho chalk **323** 26
~ crayon **323** 26
Lithodes **349** 16
lithographer **323** 45
lithographic press **323** 60
~ stone **323** 57
lithography **323** 25+26
lithosphere **4** 1, **11** 1
litter **75** 29, **76** 12, **253** 46
~ bin **39** 63
Little Bear **5** 34
~ Dipper* **5** 34
~ Dog **5** 15
little finger **21** 68
~ one **30** 26
~ owl **347** 19
liturgical vessels **313** 33–48
~ vestments **314** 25–58
live-bait fish **89** 35
~long **361** 9
~-long **361** 9
liver **22** 10, 34+35
~ paste **96** 16
livery **179** 21
~ servant **179** 20
livestock **76**
living room **44**
lizard **350** 27, 31–37
llama **351** 28
load **74** 5
~ of dung **65** 15
load hook **145** 10, **255** 49
loading aperture **1** 38
~ bridge **220** 52
~ channel **195** 14
~ dock **202** 28
~ door **166** 8
~ driveway **202** 9
~ gauge **202** 27
~ net **221** 14
~ officer **221** 8
~ pipe **221** 58
~ platform **202** 10, 24
~ shelf **77** 14
~ side **1** 37
~ skip **113** 35
~ surface **208** 30
~ vent **195** 14
~ of vessel **221** 1–36
~ well **208** 30
~ wharf **221** 10
~ yard **16** 91
load of pollen **78** 3
~ ring **226** 58
~ rope **145** 59
loaf **97** 22–27
loam **151** 2
~ seal **254** 39
lobby **296** 12+13
lobe of the ear **19** 57
~ of liver **22** 35
~ of lung **22** 7
lobster fork **46** 79
lobule **195** 7
local advertisement postmark **231** 50
~ bond **243** 11–19
~ bye-laws **257** 29
~ postage **232** 40
~ precipitation **8** 19
local railway **16** 25, **199** 19
~ railwaystation **199** 4
~ train* **203** 1
location *[Film]* **292** 1
~ shooting **292** 18
loch **13** 3
lock **134** 35, **212** 20
lockable hamper **52** 58
lock case **134** 36
~ chamber **212** 20
~-chamber gate **212** 32
locked-up forme **175** 36
locket pendant **38** 14
lock gate **212** 18
locking device **127** 23
~ lever **2** 40, **199** 58
~ mechanism **145** 24+25
~ pin **210** 60, **228** 56
~ stopper **140** 30
~ washer **136** 32
lock nut **136** 28, **180** 54
~ pick **134** 10
~ saw **115** 63
locksmith **134** 7
locksmith's shop **134** 1–34
locksmith vice **134** 24
loco **203** 2
locomotive **138** 46+47, **205** 1, **206** 1, **207** 41
~ brake cylinder manometer **206** 49
~ coupling **206** 23
~-driver **203** 9
~ driving gear **205** 2–37
~ pilot* **205** 34
~ shed **199** 6
locust **368** 41
~ tree **355** 70
lodge **145** 83
loft **39** 4, **40** 1–29
log *[wood]* **84** 22
~ *[Nav.]* **219** 31
~ *[Math.]* **327** 6
logarithm **327** 6
logarithmic calculation **327** 6
logarithm sign **327** 6
log cabin **262** 25
~-cleansing **149** 36
~ conveyor **149** 32
loggia **53** 17
logging* **84** 15–34
log house **262** 25
~ register **219** 34
~ ship **219** 32
~ stock yard **149** 30
~ truck **149** 27
~ yard **149** 30
loin *[Anat.]* **18** 24
~ *[meat]* **95** 3, 46
loin cloth **335** 38, **337** 31
loins **18** 24, **73** 30
lollipop **257** 59
Lombardy poplar **257** 53
London hammer **127** 14
long barrow **309** 16
~-bladed spear **337** 12
~ bow **287** 38
long-distance· bus **188** 2
~ cyclist **273** 14
~ cyclist's bicycle **273** 15
~ gas main **194** 33
~ lorry w. trailer **189** 44
~ race **273** 11–15, **280** 17–19
~ railcar train **207** 29
~ road-train **189** 44
~ runner **280** 17
long-eared· bat **351** 9
~ owl **347** 14
long fly and forward roll **278** 25
long-handled· brush* **52** 20
~ hammer **201** 37
~ scrub brush* **52** 25
longicorn beetle **342** 38
longitude **15** 7
longitudinal bulkhead **222** 56
~ frame **270** 24
~ girder **210** 7, 35
~ joint **197** 39
~ slide **142** 24, **143** 4
~ strength **217** 41–53
~ web **210** 7
long jump **280** 29–32
~-jumper **280** 29
~ line **90** 28
~-line fishing **90** 28+29
~ loaf **97** 25
~ log **115** 2
~ mirror **43** 5
~ moustache **35** 18
~-nosed pliers **192** 24
~ pants **33** 58
~ pipe **105** 35
~-playing switch **306** 37
~ pole **278** 36
~-pole exercise **278** 35
~ primer **170** 27
~shoreman* **221** 23
~ sleeve **32** 14
~ trousers **34** 10
~ wave **4** 20
~-wave range **234** 39
~-winged bird **343** 11–14
~ wood **115** 2

M

machine f. chipless machining **133** 1-61
~ drum **302** 57
~ f. etching blocks **172** 23
~ fell **102** 4
~ housing **196** 2
~ f. making bottles **155** 12
~ f. multiplying **240** 55
~ part **136**
machinery **261** 48
~ and apparatus for pest control **83** 1–48
~ room **223** 2
machine-starting handle **156** 17
~-stitched seam **102** 1–12
~ f. subtracting **240** 55
~ tap **143** 32
~ tool **142, 143**
machinist* **113** 32
mackerel cloud **8** 14
mackintosh **34** 39
macramé work **101** 21
macronucleus **340** 11
Macropharynx longicaudatus **349** 2
Madeira cake **97** 10
madonna lily **62** 12
Maenad **308** 35
Mae West **268** 18
magazine *[journal]* **47** 9, **102** 71
~ *[Tech.]* **87** 17, **169** 21
~ creel **158** 25
~ rack **47** 7
~ racks **250** 15
~ rifle **87** 2
~ spring **87** 18
~ stand **47** 7
maggot **60** 64, **81** 41, **342** 19
~ hole **60** 65
~-like larva **78** 28
magic eye **234** 48
magician **298** 18
magic pipe **337** 42
magmatism **11** 29–31
magnet **106** 32, **136** 100, **332** 36
magnetic-barrel calculating machine **241** 35
~ brake **136** 100
~ chuck **143** 12
~ compass **219** 23
~ needle **332** 38
~ recording disk **241** 25
~-sound camera **293** 2
~ soundhead **295** 51
~-sound reproducing unit **295** 50
magnetic sound-scanner **295** 50
~ tape recorder **234** 1
~ valve **339** 29
magnifier **108** 31–34
~ adjustment **294** 12
magnifying glass **108** 31–34
~ glass w. handle **108** 31
~ lens **26** 34, **170** 34
magnolia **357** 15
magpie **346** 3
maharaja **289** 28
maid **45** 54
maiden trip **216** 36
~ voyage **216** 36
maid's apron **45** 55
~ cap **45** 56
mail *[Post]* **231** 35
~ bag* **231** 48
~ belt* **231** 36
~ box* **231** 31, 35
~-carrier* **231** 47
mailcoach **179** 39, 53
~ driver **179** 40
mail collection bag* **231** 32
~ compartment* **207** 33
~ conveyer belt* **231** 36
mailing clerk* **231** 39
mail·man* **231** 47
~-sorting frame* **231** 37
main *n.* **148** 47, 53 + 54, **194** 26, 27, 29, 30
~ air pipe manometer **206** 46
~ altar **311** 37
~ arterial road **197** 32–50
~ artery **252** 32
~ beam **115** 38, **116** 66
~ business street **252** 32
~ cable **210** 24
~ carrying rope **228** 52
~ catalogue **250** 21
~ chassis ***226** 48
~ combustion chamber **227** 62
~course **213** 33
~ deck **218** 32–42
~ dike **211** 32
~ distributing pipe **40** 71
~ dome **316** 72
~ drive **209** 63
~ driving pulley **156** 50
~ engine **218** 63
~ engine room **218** 62
~ fairway **219** 68
~ floor* **39** 2, **113** 7
main gate conveyor **138** 15
~ gateway **315** 34
~ generator **207** 7
~ girder **145** 7, **210** 7
~ ground gear* **226** 48
main landing· beam **118** 66
~ gear **226** 48
~ undercarriage **226** 48
main line **199** 20
~ line railway **16** 21
~ market **252** 50
~mast **213** 40, **215** 22
~ outlet road **252** 1
~ portal **315** 34
~ post **91** 34
~ post office **252** 19
~ producer **148** 16
~ pump **254** 15
~ ring **228** 53
~ road **197** 28
~ rocket-stage **229** 37
~ roll bearing **141** 55
~ root **354** 16
main royal· sail **214** 66
~ staysail **214** 26
~ yard **214** 43
main·sail **213** 33, **215** 11, **270** 28
~ screw **141** 57
~ shaft **137** 14
~spring **107** 17
~ station **252** 30
~ stay **214** 10
~ steam piping **223** 7
~ stem **88** 11
mains transformer **235** 1
main street **252** 32, **253** 8
~ swing-tree **131** 8
~ switch **43** 19, **206** 4
~-switch hand release lever **206** 53
~ switch tower* **199** 16
maintenance shop **199** 6+7
main tent **290** 1
~ through-line **199** 35
~ top **214** 52
main topgallant· mast **214** 7
~ sail **213** 53
~ staysail **214** 25
main topmast **214** 6
main topmast· cross tree **214** 53
~ staysail **214** 24
main topsail **214** 62, 63
~ transformer **206** 7
main trunk **88** 11
~ truss **210** 5
~ web **210** 7
~yard **213** 37, **214** 38
maize **69** 31
~ cob **69** 36
~ kernel **69** 37
major chord **300** 16
~ key **300** 1–15
~ ninth **300** 27
~ road **253** 8
~ second **300** 20
~ seventh **300** 25
~ sixth **300** 24
~ third **300** 21
majuscule **170** 11
maker's badge **182** 20
make-up **103** 15
make-up· artist **292** 36, **296** 47
~ expert **292** 36
~ galley **169** 12
~ man **296** 47
~ smock **296** 44
~ table **296** 45
Malacosteus indicus **349** 10
malamute **71** 22
malaria mosquito **341** 33
Malay dagger **336** 44
male *[stag]* **88** 4
~ bee **78** 5
~ catkin **61** 45, **355** 26
~ fish **89** 66
~ flower **61** 39
~ flower spike **367** 55
~ inflorescence **61** 39
~ moth **82** 29
~ partner **288** 44
~ part of spike **362** 22
~ shoot **356** 44
~ spadix **368** 4
~ vocalist **296** 22
malleable iron pipe fitting **119** 40
malleolus **21** 59, 60
mallet **115** 67, **132** 39, **275** 66, **322** 21
Mallet-type locomotive **205** 39
malleus **19** 61
mallow **364** 12
malt-cleaner **92** 21
~-cleaning machine **92** 21
Maltese cross gear **295** 38
malthouse **92**
malting **92** 1–21
malt kiln **92** 13–20
~man **92** 12
~ mill **92** 22
maltster **92** 12
malt-turner **92** 16
mamilla **18** 28
mammae **18** 28 + 29
mammal **351–353**

mixing drum **113** 34, **196** 15
~ machine **42** 34, **97** 79
~ panel **292** 55
~ pot **164** 53
~ set **47** 40–43
~ of sound tracks **293** 22–24
~ tool **261** 49
~ unit **196** 15
~ valve **339** 32
~ vessel **339** 33
mixture of colours **320** 10, 12
~ control lever **228** 31
~ throttle **183** 61
Mizar **5** 29
mizen mast **214** 8+9
mizzen **213** 29
~ mast **214** 8+9, **215** 30, 33, **270** 34, 42
~-masted sailing boat **215** 9+10
~ sail **270** 33, 41
~ staysail **214** 27
~ top **214** 54
~ topgallant sail **213** 54
~ topgallant staysail **214** 29
~ topmast **214** 9
~ topmast staysail **214** 28
μ-meson **4** 32
μ-mesotron **4** 32
moat **252** 38, **310** 37
mobile car jack **192** 66
~ diesel compressor **196** 39
~ platform **29** 44
moccasin **100** 42, **335** 18
~ flower* **360** 27
mocha cup **261** 51
~-grinder **41** 63
~ machine **42** 17, **261** 50
~ mill **41** 63
~ percolator **42** 17
~ urn **42** 17
mock orange **357** 9
model of atom **1** 1–4
~ of climatic zone **339** 45
modeler* see modeller
model framework **271** 44
~ glider construction **271** 40–63
modeling* see modelling
model of isotope **1** 5–8
modeller **322** 6
~ in clay **322** 6
modelling board **50** 23, **322** 34
~ clay **322** 31
~ loop **322** 11
~ material **50** 22
~ spatula **322** 10
modelling stand **322** 9
~ substance **322** 8
model skid **271** 45
moderator **1** 26, 34
modern dance **288** 41
modified rib weave **165** 19
modillions **316** 14
modulator **237** 36, 37
module **126** 33
Moirai **308** 53–58
moiré ribbon **36** 41
moistener **238** 78
moistening sponge **238** 78
molar *n.* **21** 18, 35
mold* see mould
molded* see moulded
molder* see moulde
moldery* **141** 25–32
molding* see moulding
mole *[canal]* **212** 15, **220** 32
~ *[Zool.]* **351** 4
~-trap **58** 43, **83** 8
mollusc **340** 25–34
Mollusca **340** 25–34
mollusk **340** 25–34
molten glass **155** 8
monastery **16** 63, **314** 1–12
~ cell **314** 4
monastic habit **314** 14–16
money **244**
~ compartment **256** 6
~ letter* **232** 25
~ order **232** 12
~ rake **263** 5
~ tray **200** 37
monitor *[Zool.]* **350** 31
~ *[ship]* **222** 64
~ *[water gun]* **255** 66
~ *[dosimeter]* **2** 15
~ for transmitted picture **237** 27
monitoring apparatus **237** 19
~ console **293** 30
~ desk **293** 30
~ loudspeaker **234** 5
~ receiver **237** 31
~ room **237** 31–34
monk **314** 3
monkey *[Zool.]* **353** 12+13
~ *[ram]* **221** 60
~ island **218** 4–11
~ wrench **119** 52, **192** 9
monk's cell **314** 4
~ frock **314** 8
~-hood *[Bot.]* **363** 1
monocable ropeway **209** 15–24
monoceros **307** 7
mono·chlorobenzene **164** 9
~chromator **110** 28
monocle **108** 27
monoclinic crystal system **330** 24, 25
monocoque construction **185** 1
monocular field glass **108** 42
~ microscope **110** 1
mono·gram **37** 4
~plane **225** 1
~symmetric crystal system **330** 24, 25
~treme **351** 1
monotype **169** 32–45
~ caster **169** 39
~ keyboard **169** 32
~ standard composing machine **169** 32
monster **307** 47
monstrance **312** 48, **313** 33
monthly *n.* **47** 9
~ rose **62** 15
monument **16** 92, **257** 10
monumental gateway **315** 9
monument pedestal **257** 11
moon *[satellite]* **6** 24, **7** 1–12
~ *[finger]* **21** 81
~ crater **7** 12
moon's limb **7** 24
~ orbit **7** 1
~ phases **7** 2–7
moor **16** 5
~ buzzard **347** 13
~ harrier **347** 13
~ hawk **347** 13
~land **16** 5
mooring gear **226** 67
moor plant **361**
moose* **352** 1
mop **52** 11
~ board **118** 21
moped **181** 33
Mopsea **349** 8
moraine **12** 53–55
mordent **300** 33
morel **365** 26, 27
morion **310** 60
morning coat **34** 55
morris **265** 18
morse *[Zool.]* **352** 20
Morse alphabet **233** 62
~ code **233** 62
~ cone **143** 29
~ key **233** 64
morse lamps **218** 7
Morse printer **233** 54–63
~ receiver **233** 54–63
~ telegraph sytsem **233** 52–64
mortar *[tool]* **27** 52, **333** 9
mortar *[gun]* **224** 52+53
~ bed **118** 27
~ pan **113** 39
~ trough **113** 20, 39, 84
~ tub **113** 39
mortgage debenture **243** 11–19
mortice **115** 54, **134** 35
mortise **115** 54
~ axe **115** 72
~ chain **128** 30
~ chisel **127** 63
~ gauge **127** 20
~ lock **134** 35
mortising machine **115** 17
mortuary *n.* **312** 21
mosaic *n.* **321** 37
~ figure **321** 38
~ game **50** 18
~ tesserae **321** 39
mosque **319** 12
mosquito **341** 33, **342** 16
moss **361** 17
~ berry **361** 23
moth **82, 341** 14, **342** 48, 55, **348**
mother *[wife]* **45** 2
~ *[deer]* **88** 1, 34
~ of cloves **366** 29
~-of-pearl **340** 32
motif **181** 42, **321** 27
motion **159** 19
~-picture camera* **294** 1
~ work **107** 14–17
motor **76** 27, **128** 25, **161** 18, **182** 1, 21, 61
~ air pump **206** 17
~ automatic safety switch **254** 46
~ base plate **157** 36
~ bicycle **182**
~boat **269** 2
~boat landing stage **211** 7
~ f. brake-lifter **206** 13
~ bus **188** 5
~ cabin **183** 41, 50
motor-car, motorcar **185, 207** 30
~ boot **187** 5
~ carrier unit **208** 31
~ implement **192**
~ race **273** 34–45
~ repair tool **192**
~-tow launch **271** 1
~ type **187** 1–30
motor chain saw **85** 44
motorcycle **182**
~ battery **182** 54
~ boots **190** 19
~ carburettor **183** 53–69

motorcycle combination **182** 60
~ dual seat **182** 55
~ driving mirror **190** 14
~ gymkhana **273** 32
~ headlight **182** 10
~ race **273** 24–28
~ ramp **191** 33
~ and sidecar **182** 60
~ stand **182** 38
~ tool box **182** 41
motorcyclist **190** 15, **253** 68
motor-driven air pump **190** 27
~ ferry **211** 6
motoring goggles **190** 17
motorist **187** 6, **253** 65
motorised dusting machine **83** 43
~ spraying machine **83** 43
~ traffic patrol **247** 19
~ vaporising machine **83** 43
motor launch **216** 20, **269** 2
motorless aerobatics **271** 17
~ flight **271** 10
~ model glider **271** 40–58
~ stunt flying **271** 17
motor lifeboat **224** 31–43
~ lorry **189** 14–50
~man* **193** 21
~ passenger ship **216** 33
~ pump **255** 8
~ railcar* **201** 27, **209** 1
~ rail coach **209** 1
~ room **223** 28
~ scooter **183** 17–35
motorship **218**
~ f. cabotage* **216** 38
motor snow plough **195** 30
~ spirit **139** 38
~ sport **273** 24–50
~ truck **189** 14–50
~ truck f. refuse collection **195** 1
~ turntable ladder **255** 9
~ vehicle **189** 1–13
~ ventilator **206** 16
~ ventilator switch **206** 34
motorway **16** 16, **197** 32–50
~ approach **197** 36
~ exit **197** 36
~ under bridge **197** 33
mouflon **352** 6
mould *[Tech.]* **140** 36, **155** 23, **198** 29
~ *[earth]* **79** 15
~board **68** 4
moulder **141** 30
moulding box **141** 19, 25
~ machine **97** 64, **115** 17
~ sand **141** 26
~ shop **141** 25–32
mould loft **217** 3
mound **312** 24, **319** 21
mount **89** 43, **112** 47
mountain **12** 4–20
~ ash **355** 42
~ building **12** 4–20
~ climate **9** 56
~-climbing **282** 1–56
~ cock **88** 72
~ cudweed **361** 3
mountaineer **282** 6
mountaineering **282** 1-56
~ boot **282** 49
~ equipment **282** 35-56
~ party **282** 26–28
mountaineer's cap **36** 26
mountain everlasting **361** 3
~ hut **282** 1
~ pass **12** 47
~ railway **209**
~ range **12** 39
~ ridge **12** 36
~ saddle **12** 42
~side **12** 43
~ slope **12** 37
~ station **209** 57
~ top **12** 40
mourning cloak **348** 5
~ hat **36** 46
~ veil **312** 39
mouse **52** 74
~ trap **83** 9
moustache *[beard]* **35** 12, 18, 26
~ *[Zool.]* **352** 21
mouth *[Anat.]* **18** 13
~ *[organ pipe]* **305** 25
~ *[river]* **13** 1
~-binder **301** 5
~-blowing **155** 13–15
~-blown goblet **155** 17
~ lamp **27** 44
~ mirror **27** 43
~ organ **303** 35
~ parts **342** 26
~piece **302** 29, 36, **303** 33, 72
~-rinsing basin **51** 64
~ wash **51** 60
move *[chess]* **265** 6
movement *[Fenc.]* **277** 20
~ *[watch]* **107** 14–26
~ weight **107** 35
moves of pieces **265** 14
movie projector* **295** 26
movies* **295** 1
movie theater* **295** 1
moving bridge **210** 55–70
~-coil instrument **332** 10
~ picture camera* **294** 1
~ staircase **256** 22
~ van* **189** 41
mower **67** 27
mowing machine **67** 27
mucilage-dispenser* **238** 45
muck-spreader **67** 7
mud **262** 39
~ bath **262** 37–49
~ collector **205** 28
~ cone **11** 51
mudguard **180** 13, 43, **185** 3
~ side **187** 21
mud hose **139** 12
~ layer **13** 15
~ pump **139** 15
~ trap **194** 23
~ tub **262** 38
muff **32** 47
muffle furnace **134** 20
muffler **182** 8
~* **182** 42, **185** 62
mug **260** 6, **266** 41
,Mühle' **265** 23–25
mule *[Zool.]* **74** 8
~ *[shoe]* **48** 34, **100** 48
muleta **287** 66
mull-applying section **177** 42
~-holder **178** 19
mullein **360** 9
mullion **39** 35
mullioned window **39** 86
mullions **317** 41
multi-bucket excavator **151** 3
~-bucket ladder dredger **211** 56
~cellular animal **340** 13–37
~-channel stereo-sound reproduction **295** 45
~-colour rotogravure press **176** 27, 35
~-deck partitioned wagon **208** 28
~-engined turboprop **226** 12
~-light fitting **259** 21
~-light pendant fitting **45** 30
multiple drying machine **163** 31
~ sound-reproducing unit **294** 52
multiple unit-car* **207** 29
multiplicand **326** 25
multiplication **326** 25
~ key **240** 66
~ sign **326** 25
multiplier **326** 25
multiplying **326** 25
multi-point **119** 66
~-purpose cupboard **44** 25
~-purpose wagon **208** 32
~-roller plant **141** 74
multi-stage· air compressor **227** 27
~ rocket **229** 34
~ satellite rocket **4** 56
multi-stor(e)y· block of flats **39** 77–81,
~ building **39** 82 **252** 13
~ garage **252** 62
multi-tool holder **143** 3
mum **45** 2
mummy *[mother]* **45** 2
~ *[embalmed body]* **335** 21
municipal bond **243** 11–19
~ gardener **257** 68
~ hall **252** 7
~ park **252** 10
~ ward **252** 16
mural *n.* **321** 40
~ crown **246** 46, **308** 38
~ painting **321** 40
muriatic acid **52** 35
Musagetes **308** 15
muscle **20** 34–36
~ of head **21** 1–13
muscular foot **340** 26
~ system **20** 34–64
Muse **308** 59–75
Muses' steed **307** 26
musette **301** 8
museum **252** 21
mushroom **365** 2, 3
music *[sheet, etc.]* **44** 33, 34, **306** 9
musical apparatus **306** 1–10
~ box **306** 1
~ clown **290** 23
~ instrument **301–306**
~ interval **300** 20–27
~ notation **299, 300**
musica mensurata **299** 4
music hall **298** 4–8
musician **53** 24
music light **44** 38
~-recording studio **292** 14
~ rest **305** 36
~ room **44**
~ shelf **44** 26

music stand **44** 30
~ stool **44** 35
~ tape **293** 13
~ track **293** 13
musk-ox **352** 10
muslin lap **147** 46
~ square **30** 6
mussel **340** 30–34
~ shell **340** 34
mustang **335** 4
mustard *[Bot.]* **63** 16
~ *[spice]* **98** 28
mute *n.* **302** 10, **303** 68
~ swan **343** 16
mutton **74** 13
mutule **316** 13
muzzle *[animal]* **71** 4, **73** 6–10, **88** 45
~ *[dog]* **71** 27
mycelium **365** 2
myrtle **56** 11, **313** 21
~ wreath **313** 18
mythological animal **307** 1–61
~ being **307** 1–61
mythology **308**

N

nacelle **226** 76, 77
nacre **340** 32
nail **136** 49
~ *[finger]* **21** 80
~ bag **117** 72
~ box **99** 17
~ brush **51** 67
~-cleaner **103** 8
~ enamel* **103** 12
~ file **103** 7
~ of flag **245** 8
nailing *[boot]* **99** 33
~ *[stapling]* **240** 41
nail lacqueur* **103** 12
~ polish **103** 12
~-scissors **30** 45, **103** 5
~ varnish **103** 12
naked boys **363** 3
~ lady **363** 3
name **239** 15
~ of plant **57** 4
~-plate **113** 47, **181** 18, **270** 16
~ of street **253** 2
names of stars **5** 9–48
nanny **30** 9, **258** 34
Nansen sledge **285** 1
nape band **36** 38
~ of neck **18** 21
naphta **139**
naphthalene-washer **148** 32
napkin *[serviette]* **23** 63, **46** 9
~ *[diaper]* **30** 6
~ ring **46** 10
Narcissus **62** 3
narcissus **62** 4
narghile(h) **105** 39
narrow-film· camera **294** 24
~ cinema projector **295** 52
~ scanner **237** 22
narrow-gage railroad track* **149** 26
narrow-gauge· locomotive **196** 24
~ tramway **151** 4
narrow-necked amphora **309** 12
~ pass **16** 84
~-tape recorder **293** 7
nasal bone **19** 41
~ cavity **19** 53
nasicorn **351** 25
nasturtium **56** 4
natatorium* **25** 2
natatory* **25** 2
national coat-of-arms **244** 12
~ colors* **245** 15–21
~ colours **245** 15–21
~-costume jacket **34** 26
~ dance **288** 39
~ flag **245** 15–21
Nationalist China **14** 49
nationality sign **186** 33
native **335** 37
natural *[accidental]* **299** 47, 55
~ gardens **257** 41–69
~ gas **12** 30
~ history collection **47** 34–36
~ honeycomb **78** 60
~ rock **339** 17
~ scale **299** 47
~ sponge **112** 15
~ stone **194** 12
nautical mark **219** 43–76
naval cap **36** 23
nave *[Art]* **316** 62, **317** 1
~ *[Tech.]* **131** 27
~ plate **185** 14
navel **18** 34
navigable channel **211** 21
navigating bridge **218** 12–18
~ bridge superstructure **216** 23
navigation **219**
~ light **226** 46
navigraph* **228** 7
navvy **113** 76, **150** 13, **198** 20
~ excavator **153** 2
navy yard* **217** 1–40
near beer* **93** 40
Near East **14** 39–45
near wheeler **179** 47
nebula **6** 44–46
neck *[Anat.]* **18** 19-21
neck *[vaulting horse]* **279** 34
~ *[Tech.]* **136** 62, **229** 12, 13, **269** 37
~ *[mus. instr.]* **303** 7
~ *[peninsula]* **13** 5
~ brush **104** 18
~ cushion **48** 54
~ duster **104** 18
neckerchief **37** 9, **266** 47
neck flap **255** 38, **277** 28
~ grasp **278** 7
~ guard **255** 38, **277** 28, **310** 83
~lace **38** 8, 12, **309** 25
~let **38** 8
~line **32** 40
~ pommel **279** 37
~ ring **309** 26
~ strap **72** 30
~-tie **33** 45
~ of veal **95** 3
~ of violin **302** 2
nectary of leaf **61** 18
needle *[Tech., etc.]* **102** 55–57, **136** 74, **160** 53, **331** 66
~ *[Bot.]* **356** 11
~ bar **102** 29
~ bed **160** 55
~ butt **160** 60
~ clamp screw **102** 30
~craft **101**
~ cylinder **160** 8, 11
needled half-lap **156** 70
needle-holder **26** 37, **331** 65
~ hook **160** 64
~ jet **183** 56
~-made lace **101** 30
~ roller bearing **136** 73, **182** 49
~-shaped **354** 34
~ thread **102** 21
~ tricks **160** 15
~work **50** 30, **101**
negative *n.* **112** 41
~ carbon **295** 41
~-carrier **112** 30
~ cyanotype machine **241** 13
~ direction **329** 7
~-holder **112** 30
~ number **326** 8
~ sign **326** 8
négligé **48** 16
negress **337** 22
negrillo **337** 41
negrito **337** 41
negro **337** 13
~ hut **337** 21
neighbor* see neighbour
neighbour **259** 41
neighbouring house **53** 23
nematode **81** 51
Neo-Classic style **318** 15
neolithic period **309** 10–20
neon lamp **194** 19
Neptune *[Myth.]* **308** 29
~ *[planet]* **6** 30
Neptune's horse **307** 44
Nereid **307** 23
nerve *[Anat.]* **20** 28–33
~ *[Bot.]* **354** 29
~ fibre **21** 33
nervous system **20** 22–33
nervure **342** 34
nest **343** 28
nesting box **75** 6
~ cavity **343** 29
Net **5** 48
net *n.* **89, 90** 8
~ adjuster **276** 14
~ background **101** 16
~-cutter **223** 52
~ factory **220** 8
~ fishing **89** 1–6, 13–19
Netherlands **14** 14, **244** 19
nether millstone **91** 23
net knot **125** 29
~-making **125** 24
~ player **276** 48
~ post **276** 15
N. E. Trades **9** 48
net stocking **33** 33, **289** 10
~ strap **276** 14
netting **101** 22
~ loop **101** 23
~ needle **101** 26, **125** 28
~ thread **101** 24, **125** 26
nettle **63** 33
net wing **90** 16
network *[main]* **148** 53+54
~ of meridians **15** 1–7
~ of parallels **15** 1–7
neumatic notation **299** 1–4
neumes **299** 1
neums **299** 1
neuropteran **342** 12
neutral corner **281** 34
~ point **147** 22
neutron **1** 2, 6, **4** 30
névé **12** 48, **282** 23
newborn child **30** 26
~ baby **29** 6
newel **118** 78
~ post **118** 43
Newfoundland dog **71** 39
new moon **7** 2
news·agent* **201** 19
~boy **253** 44
~ in brief **325** 53
~dealer* **201** 19

newsmonger **53** 29
newspaper **325** 37
~ boy **253** 44
~ heading **325** 38
~-holder **261** 26
~ man **253** 44, **281** 45
~ packet **232** 24
~ photograph **325** 44
~ rack **47** 7, **261** 8
~ reader **261** 24
~-seller **253** 44
~ shelf **261** 8
~ stand **47** 7
~ wrapper **232** 24
news-reel camera **294** 23
~ studio **234** 7–12
~ trolley **201** 17
~vender **201** 19
~vendor **201** 19 **253** 44
newt **350** 20–22
new year's shoot **356** 25
New Zealand **14** 28
~ Zealand clover **70** 2
next-door house **53** 23
nib *[pen, etc.]* **144** 43, **239** 18, **249** 59
~ *[tile]* **117** 51
niblick **276** 70
niche **48** 39, **212** 70
nick *[Typ.]* **170** 47
nickel coin **244** 1–28
~-in-the-slot machine* **260** 48
~ steel pendulum **107** 39
nigger **337** 13
night cap **36** 2
~ clouds **4** 36
~ commode **23** 25, **48** 2
~ cream **103** 11
~dress **31** 1, **33** 1, **48** 16
~ glass **108** 38
~-gown **31** 1, **33** 1
night-gown· frill **33** 2
~ lace **33** 2
~ top **31** 2
nightie **31** 1, **33** 1
nightingale **346** 14
night layer **4** 19
~ life-buoy **216** 63
~-luminous cloud **4** 36
~robe* **33** 1
~shade **363** 5
~shirt **33** 50
~stick* **248** 10
~ stool **23** 25
~ table **48** 2
nighty **31** 1
Nike **308** 43
nimbo-stratus cloud **8** 10
nimbus cloud **8** 10
Nine *[Muses]* **308** 59–75
nine-eight time **299** 41
~-four time **299** 42
~-men's morris* **265** 18
~-penny morris **265** 18
ninepins **287** 1
~ alley **287** 2
~ yard **287** 2
ninth *[Mus.]* **300** 27
nippers **28** 57, **99** 35
nipping section **177** 42
nipple *[teat]* **18** 28
~* **30** 48
nitrous oxide cylinder **28** 34
nix **307** 23
nixie **307** 23
nixy **307** 23
nobleman **338** 44
nock **287** 45
nocturnal birds of prey **347** 14–19
~ Lepidoptera **348** 7–11
~ moth **82** 14
node **69** 7
nogging piece **115** 55
Noir **263** 21
nominal value **232** 22+23
~ value of share **243** 12
non-migratory bird **344** 4
nonpareil **170** 23
non-passerine bird **343** 24–29
~-plus-ultra **170** 19
~-printing parts **172** 36
~-professional wrestler **281** 7
~-skid chain **286** 9
~-slip tread **189** 13
~-smoker **203** 29
~-smoking compartment **203** 29
~-spherical hollow mirror **295** 39
~-storage heater **27** 27, **119** 66
~-swimmers' pool **268** 21
~-terminating decimal **326** 22
~-terminating decimal fraction **326** 21
~-toothed artery forceps **28** 55
~-toothed forceps **26** 35
noodle machine **97** 78
noose **335** 5
no-parking sign **253** 18
Norfolk Island Pine **56** 16
normal fault **12** 7
North America **14** 29+30, **15** 12
~ Atlantic Current **15** 30
~-East trade winds **9** 48
~ Equatorial Current **15** 32
Northern Crown **5** 31
~ heavens **5** 1–35
~ hemisphere **5** 1–35
~ Ireland **244** 37
northern light **4** 35
~ sky **5** 1–35
north light **116** 21
North pole **15** 3
~ sea **15** 26
north star **5** 1, 34
Norway **14** 15, **244** 26
~ maple **355** 53
~ spruce **356** 12
nose **18** 10
~ band **72** 7
~ wheel **225** 49
~ wheel release lever **228** 33
~wheel ground gear* **226** 36
nosing **118** 20
nostril **73** 7
notable *n.* **289** 29
notation *[Mus.]* **299**, **300**
~ of chess game **265** 6
notch *[Tech., etc.]* **85** 20, **87** 66, **287** 45
~ *[Geol.]* **13** 30
~* **16** 84
notched-stamp pottery **309** 35
note *[foot~]* **178** 62
~ *[Mus.]* **299** 5–9
~ *[money]* **244** 29–39
~ bar **299** 8
~ crook **299** 7
~ head **299** 5
~ hook **299** 7
~ pad **238** 17
~ paper **239** 1
~ stem **299** 6
~ tail **299** 6
not-go side **142** 51
notice **231** 26
~ board **145** 45, **267** 6, 7
nought **263** 18
~ key **240** 65
novelty department· sales assistant **256** 63
~ salesclerk* **256** 63
~ salesgirl **256** 63
~ saleslady **256** 63
nozzle **52** 3, **83** 33, 36
~ tip **135** 54
~ pump **211** 62
N-truss bridge **210** 47
nuclear fission **1** 13-17, **4** 28
~ physicist **1** 40
~ propulsion **223** 6–10
~ reactor **1** 31–46
~ submarine **223** 1
nucleus of galatic system **6** 47
~ of spiral nebula **6** 44
nude *n.* **321** 32
~ life model **321** 32
~ model **321** 32
nugget **244** 1
number **326** 1–22
~ board **272** 6
~ girl **298** 8
~ key **256** 3
~ plate **185** 43, **186** 31, **204** 29
~ plate lighting **186** 37
~ of postal area **232** 38
~ tab **259** 10
~ tag **259** 10
~ of winning horse **272** 22
numen **308** 47
numeral **326** 1, 2
~ pennants **245** 33+34
numerator **326** 15
nun *[sister]* **314** 22
~ *[Zool.]* **344** 4
~ of nursing order **29** 18
nurse **23** 23, **30** 9
~maid **49** 1
nurser* **30** 46
nursery *[child]* **30** 1–52
~ (garden) **79**
~ gardener **79** 20
~ maid **49** 1
~ school **50**
nurse's cap **30** 10
~ uniform **50** 2
nursing **30**
~ the baby **30** 30
~ bottle* **30** 46
~ mother **30** 30
~ sister **29** 18
nut *[Bot.]* **61** 37–51, **354** 98
~ *[Tech.]* **136**, **180** 53
~ *[violin]* **302** 13
~-crackers **46** 49
~ crunch **98** 85
~hatch **346** 11
~jobber **346** 11
~meg tree **366** 30
~ tree **61** 37–43
~-tree twig **61** 37
Nydam boat **213** 1–6
nylon-6 manufacture **164** 1–62
~ stocking **33** 32
nymph *[Myth.]* **307** 23

O

oak **355** 1
oar **269** 14, 35–38
~ blade **269** 38
~lock* **269** 29, 41
~ shaft **269** 35
oarsman **257** 52, **269** 12
oarsman's seat **269** 28
~ thwart **269** 28
oasis **337** 4
oath **248** 31
oats **69** 27
obelisk **315** 10
Oberwerk **305** 2
obi **336** 41
object chamber handle **109** 4
objective *n.* **110** 5
~ slide changer **110** 16
object stage **110** 6
~ stage adjustment **109** 6
~-teaching **249** 17
oblianus abdominis **20** 43
oblique crystal system **330** 24, 25
~ randing **130** 3
~ scarf joint **116** 88
oblong cake **97** 45
oboe **302** 38
~ da caccia **302** 38
~ d'amore **302** 38
observation car **207** 40
~ hole **93** 16
~ panel **42** 27
~ platform **226** 71
~ ship **9** 7
~ telescope **108** 44, **330** 31
~ window **224** 23, **234** 4
observatory **6** 2–11
observing aperture **6** 9, **295** 15
~ position **6** 10
obstacle **272** 25, **280** 21+22
obstetrical forceps **28** 59
obstetrician **29** 3
obtuse angle **328** 11
~-angled triangle **328** 30
obverse **244** 8
ocarina **303** 32
occasional postmark **231** 51
occipital bone **19** 32
~ muscle **21** 2
occluded front **9** 25
ocean **15** 19–26
~ current **15** 27, 28, 30–45
~ depth **4** 10
~-going liner **216** 32
ocean going seaplane* **226** 30
~-going tug **221** 47–50
oceanic deeps **11** 12
Oceanid **307** 23
ocean ship **216** 13
~ steamship **216** 32
~ tanker **216** 22
ocellate spot **74** 32
ocellus **74** 32, **78** 2
octagonal ground stopper **333** 4
octahedron **330** 6, 10, 13, 14, 16
Octans **5** 43
Octant **5** 43
octave **300** 26, 62–70
~ sign **300** 44+45
octogon **330** 17
ocular **6** 3
odalisque **289** 41
odd number **326** 12
~ pinnate **354** 42
~-toed ungulate **351** 25–27
odometer* **186** 7
Oertz rudder **217** 66+67
oesophagus **19** 49, **22** 23
off-end framing **158** 14
off-the-peg dress **256** 29
offering **311** 64
office **231** 1–30, **238**, **239**
~ *[train]* **204** 20
~ apprentice **238** 44
~ block **252** 15
~ boy **238** 8
~ chair **238** 34
~ duplicator **241** 1
~ machine **240** 1-71, **241** 1-61
~ paste **238** 46
officer **219** 19, **221** 8
officer's cabin **218** 21, **223** 47
officer of the watch **216** 65
official at counter **242** 8
~ list **243** 8
official's electric hand lamp **138** 58
offset **57** 27, 29
~ machine **174** 1, 38
~ press **174** 1
~ printing **174**
~ printing machine **174** 1
~ process **173**
~ proofing press **174** 38
~ sheet-fed press **174** 33
offshoot **57** 17
offside **274** 57
off-the-road tire* **67** 2, **189** 12
off wheeler **179** 47
ogee arch **318** 36
ogre **307** 37
O.H.V. single-cylinder motor **182** 21
oil *[salad~]* **98** 24
~ *[petroleum]* **139**
~ bottle **46** 42
~ brake switch **206** 4
~ burner **40** 58–60
~-burning system **40** 44–60
~ cabinet **190** 11
~ can **102** 48
~-circulating pump **146** 45
~ colour **321** 11
~ conservator **146** 42, **147** 9
~ container **191** 14
~ cooler **146** 46, **206** 19
~ dip-stick **184** 18
~ drilling **139** 1–20
~-driven vacuum pump **331** 17
~ engine **184** 37–80
oiler **107** 31
~ clip **180** 62
oil-filler pipe **184** 47
~-filler sleeve **186** 58
~ filter **184** 48
~-firing system **40** 44–60
~ fuel tank **216** 28, **218** 70, **223** 37
~ furnace **40** 57
~ gauge **40** 54
~-heating system **40** 44–60
~ injection pump **228** 25
~ level gauge **147** 11
~ level pipe **40** 53
~ manometer **149** 15
~ f. massage **24** 6
~-painted dado **121** 5
~ painting **47** 6
~ palm **367** 54
~ pan **184** 49
~ pressure gauge **149** 15, **207** 14, **228** 17
~ production **139** 48–55
~ pump **184** 22, **190** 12
~ pump shaft **184** 21
~ refinery **139** 56–67
~ refining **139** 21–35
oils **224** 54–56
oil scraper ring **184** 80
oilskin coat **224** 56
~ jacket **224** 55
oil·skins **224** 54–56
~ stand **191** 31
~stone **323** 21
~ sump **184** 23
~ switch **206** 4
~ tank **40** 44, **182** 34
oil temperature gauge **228** 19
~ trough **143** 6
~ wharf **220** 59–62
ointment **26** 10
~ tin **26** 10
old English **325** 1
Old Glory* **245** 18
old style **325** 4
~ town **252** 34–45
~ valley **13** 56
'old woman's tooth' **127** 60
oleander **357** 13
oleiferous seed **367** 5
olive **367** 29
~ oil **98** 24
~-pointed probe **28** 46
~-shaped ear nib **26** 16
~ tree **367** 29
Olympian god **308** 1
Olympic flag **245** 5
omnibus **179** 37, **188**
omni-directional radio beacon **230** 18
~-range radio beacon **230** 18
Onagraceae **56** 3
on-and-off switch **306** 27
once accented octave **300** 66
~-marked octave **300** 66
one-and-a-half plane* **225** 4
~-axle railbus luggage trailer **207** 27
~-berth cabin **218** 41
~-celled animal **340** 1–12
~-channel sound **293** 23
~-color offset machine* **174** 1
~-cut finishing drill **143** 32
~-direction traction car **193** 8
~-hand snatch **281** 2
~-horse carriage **179** 29
~-horse vehicle **179** 18
Oneirophanta **349** 18
one-line octave **300** 66
one-man· canoe **336** 12
~ crosscut saw **85** 38
~ motor chain saw **85** 44
one-mast support **209** 23
~-metre board **268** 10
~-piece collar-stud **33** 61

one-seeded fruit **60** 23
~-sided snow plough **195** 30
~-side print **323** 27
~-tower support **209** 23
~-way cock **334** 42
~-way plough **68** 20
~-way ticket* **200** 36
on-guard position **277** 43
onion **59** 24
onsetter **138** 5
~ skin **59** 25
opaque glass **122** 5
open-air· cure **29** 21–25
~ inhalatorium **262** 6
~ meeting **257** 48
~ pool **268** 1-32
~ rest cure **262** 12–14
~ theater* **257** 6
~ veranda **29** 21–25
open-cast excavation locomotive **206** 56
opencast working **150** 1
open compartment **204** 56
~ fire **259** 25
~ flue pipe **305** 23-30, 31-33
~ freezer **96** 2
~ goods wagon **208** 2, 21
opening **117** 24
~ f. cleaning purposes **93** 21
~ joint **144** 32
~ f. lift **297** 32
~ position **265** 1
~ f. stairs **115** 46
~ f. washing material **166** 14
open-line pole **233** 66
~-necked shirt **266** 8
~ platform **203** 31
~-platform coach **203** 26
~ string **303** 24
~ visor **246** 9
~ well **269** 8
~-width scouring machine **162** 8
~ wood **305** 31–33
~work **101** 27
opera glass **108** 40
~ hat **36** 20
~ house **252** 20
operating bridge **298** 37
~ cap **28** 18
~ desk **176** 39
~ handle **240** 51
~ glove **28** 20
~ gown **28** 21
~ lamp **27** 18, **28** 26
~ lever **128** 38, **197** 12, **239** 42
~ mask **28** 19
operating overall **28** 21
~ platform **298** 37
~ position **140** 50
~ room **28** 1-45
~ sister **28** 16
~ surgeon **28** 17
~ table **28** 4, 23
~ theatre **28** 1–45
operation area **28** 25
operative's platform **162** 23
operator **135** 1, 38, **233** 16, **255** 13
~* **136** 100
~ brake* **136** 100
operator's cabin **145** 11
~ platform **162** 23
operculum **350** 5
ophiuroid echinoderm **349** 11
ophthalmometer **109** 15
ophthalmic instrument **109** 11–15
ophthalmoscope **26** 33
opium poppy **364** 15
opossum **351** 2
opponent **281** 24, 36
opposed-cylinder engine **182** 6
optical bench **331** 27
~ instrument **109, 110**
~ measuring instrument **110** 24–29
~ plummet **110** 34
~ system **108** 9
optician **108**
optic nerve **21** 51, **78** 24
or *[Her.]* **246** 24
orach(e) **63** 24
orale **314** 55
orange *[Bot.]* **368** 27
~ *[colour]* **320** 7
orangeade **261** 35
orange flower **368** 25
~-peel **98** 11
orangery **257** 3
orange-tip butterfly **348** 3
orang (o)utan **353** 15
orator **257** 49
orbicular **354** 33
orbicularis oculi **21** 5
~ oris **21** 8
orbiculate **354** 33
orbit **1** 4, 8, **5** 2
~ of sun **5** 2
orbspinner **342** 45
orchard **16** 108
orchestra *[band]* **296** 25
~ *[Greek Theatre]* **316** 47
~ *[seat]* **296** 19
~ chair* **296** 19
orchestral instrument **302** 1–62
orchestra pit **296** 24
~ seat* **296** 19
~ stall **296** 19
orchestrion **291** 38
orchid **360** 28
orchis **360** 28
order *[religous]* **314**
~ *[Comm.]* **232** 12, **242** 19
~ on bill **242** 19
ordinal *n.* **326** 6
~ number **326** 6
ordinary grip **279** 53
ordinate **329** 10
ordinates' intersection of curve **329** 22
ore deposit **11** 31
~ transport wagon **208** 19
öre **244** 24
organ *[Anat.]* **22** 1–57
~ *[Mus.]* **53** 26, **305** 1–52
~ of attachment **341** 25
~ case **305** 1–5
~ casework **305** 1–5
~ console **305** 36–52
~ of equilibrium **19** 56–65
~-grinder **53** 27
~ of hearing **19** 56–65
organistrum **301** 25
organ pipe **305** 17–35
oriental slave **289** 41
~ woman **289** 41
orifice of stomach **22** 41
origin **11** 32, **329** 4
original sum invested **327** 7
origin of earthquake **11** 32
~ of ordinates **329** 4
oriole **344** 7
Orion **5** 13
~ nebula **6** 51
ornament *[Art, etc.]* **38** 4, **317** 14–16, **338** 17
~ *[Mus.]* **300** 28–38
ornamental band **316** 38
~ bush **257** 14
~ flower bed **257** 39
~ hub cap **185** 14
~ park **257** 1–40
~ shrub **54** 4, **257** 14, **357, 358**
~ stitch **101** 3
~ tree **357, 358**
~ waistcoat **34** 42
ornamentation **316** 38–43
ornamented column **315** 18
Ornithopoda **70** 11
orographic lift **271** 13
orpin(e) **361** 9
orrery **6** 12–14
orthopaedic instep support **99** 29
~ shoe **99** 34
orthopedic instep support **99** 29
~ shoe **99** 34
ortho-pinacoid **330** 25
orthopteran **342** 8
orthopterous insect **342** 8
orthorhombic pyramid **330** 23
ortolan **346** 7
~ bunting **346** 7
oscillator **236** 5
~ coil assembly **235** 18
~ valve **235** 16
oscillatory circuit **234** 25–28
~ circuit coil **234** 25
oscillograph **237** 32
osier stick **130** 14
~ twig **130** 14, **355** 29
osseous framework **19** 1-29
ossicles **19** 61
Ostiak **336** 17
ostrich **343** 2
~ egg **343** 3
~ plumes **246** 30
os uteri **22** 85
ottava alta **300** 44
~ bassa **300** 45
~ sopra **300** 44
~ sotto **300** 45
otter board **90** 13
Otto engine **187** 25
~ motor **184** 1–36
outboard float **225** 64
~ motor **269** 7, **273** 49
~ motorboat **269** 6
~ tail fin **225** 15
out counter **250** 20
outdoor cage **339** 25
~ enclosure **339** 16
~ filming ground **292** 1
~ inhalatorium **262** 6
~ rest cure **262** 12-14
~ shooting **292** 18
~ substation **146** 29–35
outer bailey **310** 31
~ case **166** 7
~ casing **162** 17
~ container **161** 47
~ cover **180** 30
~ gate **310** 32
~ hall **269** 58
~ home signal **199** 41
~ keel **269** 32
~ moat **310** 33
~ race **136** 69
~ skin **217** 41–46, **269** 33,48

outer station **4** 54
~ string **118** 44
~ top rail **131** 2
~ wall **116** 32, **117** 37, **310** 15
~-wing turbine **226** 20
outfall **13** 1
~ arm **13** 2
~ ditch **211** 36
outfeed roller **128** 43
outfit box **99** 17
out for a ride **257** 42
outlet **162** 29, **186** 23 **334** 63
~* *[El.]* **120** 5
~ control valve **254** 30
~ chute **140** 38
~ cock **172** 27
~ faucet* **166** 16
~ pipe **176** 38, **254** 21
~ road **252** 1
~ structure **212** 44
~ terminal of the heating system **44** 16
~ tunnel **212** 62
out-look tower **16** 68, **252** 52
output stage **236** 28
~ transformer **235** 2
~ tube* **235** 13
~ valve **235** 13
outrig **269** 42
outrigged rowlock **269** 41
outrigger **269** 9–16, **335** 36
~ canoe **335** 35
outside board **115** 96
~ covering **226** 74
~ cut-at-head **277** 37
~ girder **210** 9
~ hood iron **187** 15
~ keel **269** 32
~ left **274** 17
~ margin **178** 57
~ plank **270** 19
outsider **272** 16
outside right **274** 21
~ staircase **315** 33
~ string **118** 44
~ thermometer **228** 14
~ wall **117** 37
outskirts of the town **252** 31
outsole **99** 50
Ovaherero woman **337** 25
oval table **204** 46
~-tube frame **181** 46
~ winch **161** 6
~ wing **225** 23
ovary *[Anat.]* **22** 83
~ *[Bot.]* **60** 40, **354** 54, 60
ovary with awns **359** 34
ovate **354** 36
oven **41** 38, **97** 57–63
overall **28** 21, **32** 19, **50** 2, **144** 24
overalls* **28** 21
over-and-under rifle-shotgun **87** 33
overburden *[Tech.]* **137** 20, **150** 2
overcast *[sky]* **9** 24
overcoat **32** 52, **34** 48, 52
overfall **91** 43
overfeed **162** 26
overflow **51** 66, **212** 60
~ basin **257** 23
~ flask **334** 60
~ pipe **40** 69, **51** 18, **254** 20, 33
overfold **12** 15
over grip **279** 53
overhead camshaft **182** 46, **187** 26
~ conductor **146** 32
~ contact wire **188** 16, **206** 2
~ contact wire frog **193** 30
~ lighting battens **297** 13
~ line **188** 16, **206** 2
overhead line· pylon **146** 36
~ tension **206** 42
~ tower **146** 36
overhead monorail **145** 53
~ inclined Otto engine **187** 25
~ planer **128** 11
~ support **29** 33
~ travelling crane **217** 20
operating crank **182** 43
overhead-valve· operating crank **182** 43
~ single-cylinder motor **138** 53 **182** 12
overhead-wire examination wagon **206** 57
overland timber haulage **85** 1–6
overload circuit-breaker **120** 18
overman's yardstick **138** 53
overpass* **197** 32
oversea airplane* **226** 30
overshoe **100** 27
overshot bucket wheel **91** 35
oversite **118** 13
overthrust fold **12** 15
ovoscope **75** 46
ovule **60** 39, **61** 14, **354** 63
ovum **22** 84
Owen's bottle-blowing machine **155** 12
owl **244** 1, **347** 14–19
owl-glass **289** 38
ox *[Zool.]* **74** 1, **95** 14–37
~-bow lake **16** 75
oxer **272** 33
ox-eye **360** 4
~-eye daisy **63** 7, **360** 4
~-hide **337** 11
oxidation **164** 19
oxidiser **227** 51
ox-stomach scraper **96** 34
~ team **65** 16
oxy-acetylene welding **135** 29–64
~-acetylene equipment **135** 29
oxydation **164** 19
oxygen cylinder **255** 20
~ capsule **47** 42
~ connection **135** 51
~ container **229** 8
~ cylinder **28** 36, **135** 32, 61, **196** 40
~ distributor **229** 17
~-filler neck **229** 13
~ hose **135** 36
~ meter **24** 20
~ nozzle **334** 13
~ pump **229** 16
~ respirator **24** 19
~ tank **229** 8
~ valve **135** 50
~ welder **135** 62
oyster **340** 30
~ fork **46** 80

P

pabouch(e) **48** 34
pace **73** 40
~maker **273** 11
pacemaker's machine **273** 12
~ motorcycle **273** 12
Pacific Ocean **15** 19
pack *[load]* **74** 5
~ *[hounds]* **86** 33, **272** 62
~* *[packet]* **105** 13
package* **231** 3
~-washing **164** 48
pack animal **337** 3
~ass **74** 3
~ of cigarettes* **105** 13
packet **23** 12, **105** 13, **232** 24
~ of blue **53** 58
pack of hounds **272** 62
packing counter **256** 14
~ plant **153** 28
~ roll **204** 54
~ shed **220** 10
~ f. whole body **23** 19
packsack* **266** 22
pack saddle **74** 4
pad **23** 39, **30** 2, **72**, **88** 46, **284** 40
padded armour **336** 38
~ doublet **338** 30
~ trunkhose **338** 31
~ wall **287** 5
padding material **124** 23
paddle **269** 34, 39
paddling **269** 1–66
~ pool **39** 44, **258** 10
paddock **272** 4
pad·lock **40** 21, **53** 4
~ saddle **72** 45–49
~ saw **115** 63, **127** 27
~-saw handle **127** 28
page *[boy]* **259** 18
~ *[book]* **178** 53
~ boy **259** 18
~-boy style **35** 35
~ cord **169** 16
~ number **178** 63 **243** 14
pagoda **319** 1
pail **52** 50
paillette **38** 1
pailoo **319** 3
pailou **319** 3
pailow **319** 3
pail f. used dressings **26** 23
paint **121** 10
~-box **50** 31, **321** 10
Painter **5** 47
painter **121** 2, 28, **321** 2
painter's ladder **121** 4
~ room **296** 29–42
~ stencil **121** 25
painting-book **50** 25
~ gun **83** 34–37
~ spatula **321** 15
~ studio **321**
~ surface **321** 22
~ table **321** 25
~ utensil **321** 6–19
~ wall **121** 1–28
paint pail **121** 27
~ spray **121** 12
~-sprayer **83** 34–37
Pair **263** 20
pair **42** 65, **257** 44
~ of carvers **42** 65
~ of dancers **259** 46, **288** 44+45
pairing *[basket-making]* **130** 1
~ season **86** 9–12
pair of lovers **257** 44
~-oar **269** 15
~ of pincers **99** 35
pairs *[Skat.]* **284** 7

pair-skating **284** 7
~ of steps **52** 1
pajamas* seepyjamas
Pakistan **14** 47
palace **16** 96, **252** 54, **317** 47
~ buildings **315** 29
~ garden **252** 55
~ gardens **257** 1–40
Palace of Sargon **315** 29
palaeolithic period **309** 1–9
Palaeopneustes niasicus **349** 19
palatine tonsil **21** 23
paleolithic pepori **309** 1–9
palet **177** 3
palette **321** 28
~ dipper **321** 29
~ knife **321** 14
paling **39** 53, **55** 10, **115** 96
palisade **310** 36
pall *[cloth]* **312** 53
~ *[pallium]* **314** 56
~ *[Her.]* **313** 55
palla *[cloak]* **338** 10
pallet **305** 10
pallets *[watch]* **107** 23
pallette **310** 45
pallium **314** 56
palm *[Bot.]* **368** 2
~ *[hand]* **21** 71
~ *[horn]* **88** 41
Palma Christi **364** 14
palmate antlers **88** 40
palm column **315** 17
palmette capital **315** 25
palm of hand **21** 71
palm leaf *[Bot.]* **368** 3
~ leaf *[ornament]* **316** 41
~-leaf capital **315** 25
pamphlet **251** 9
Pan **308** 40
pan *[trough, etc.]* **41** 70, **115** 59
~ *[Anat.]* **73** 33
Panama hat **36** 6
pancreas **22** 44
Pandean pipes **301** 2
pandore **301** 21
pane *[glass]* **122** 16
~ *[hammer]* **66** 22, **132** 26
~ of glass **57** 10, **122** 16
panel **40** 67, **115** 59, **124** 27
panelled mirror **259** 66
panelling **260** 37
panel rotary switch **120** 11
~ saw **115** 60
pangolin **351** 10
panicle **354** 69, **366** 54
paniculate phlox **62** 14
paniered skirt **338** 83
pan-lid **41** 71
pannier **64** 40
~ bag **190** 21
panorama film **294** 45–52
panoramic screen **294** 49
~ sound-recording **294** 45
Pan-pipes **301** 2, **308** 41
Pan's pipes **301** 2
pansy **62** 2
panther's skin **308** 34
panties **33** 20
pantile **117** 54
pantiled roof **117** 53
pantograph *[instr.]* **15** 65, **170** 58
~ *[conductor]* **193** 15–19, **206** 3
~-carrier **170** 53
~ current-collector **193** 15–19
pantry **204** 19, **218** 38
pants **33** 56
papal cross **313** 60
Papaver **63** 2
paper **51** 31, **167**, **168**, **175** 43
~-bag **98** 48 + 49
~ ball **289** 55
~ chain **289** 5
~ chase **272** 58–64
~ clip **238** 42
~ cup **201** 50
~-cutter **178** 1
~ cutting machine **178** 1
~ delivery **175** 14
~-fastener **238** 43
~ feed **175** 14, **240** 15
~ feeder **175** 11
~ feed release **240** 16
~ guide roll **240** 8
~ hanger **121**
~ hanger's hammer **121** 39
~ hanger's trestle **121** 41
~ hanging **121** 29–41
~ hat **289** 45
~-holder **51** 30, **240** 8
~ kite **258** 50
~ knife **238** 47
~ lantern **55** 15, **289** 4
~ machine **168** 6
~ manufacture **167**, **168**
~ money **244** 29–39
~ plate **201** 51
~-reel **175** 46
~ reel holder **176** 40
~ release **240** 58
~ rest **240** 9
~ ribbon **169** 34
~ roll **240** 56
~ scissors **238** 76
paper serpent **291** 14
~-stapling machine **240** 36
~ stock preparation **167** 24–27
~ streamer **289** 66
~ strip **240** 57
~ tape **233** 61, **240** 57
~ tower **169** 33
~ web **168** 19
~ weight **238** 30
papilionaceous flower **59** 1
papoosh **48** 34
pap plate **30** 18
pappus tuft **362** 11
paprika **59** 42
papyrus column **315** 15
~ plant **367** 64
para **244** 28
parabola **329** 14
parabolic arch **318** 29
~ girder **210** 36
~ mirror **6** 4, **230** 40
~ radar mirror **230** 52
~ reflector **6** 4
parachute **228** 48
~ bag **228** 51
~ canopy **228** 49
~ harness **228** 54
parachute rigging line **228** 50
~ rip cord **228** 55
parachuter's harness* **228** 54
parachutist's harness **228** 54
parade **289** 57–70
~ ground **252** 47
paraffin **139** 39, 46
~ lamp **99** 26
~ lantern **76** 16
~ oil **139** 39
~ wax **139** 46
paragon **170** 31
paragraph-indention **170** 16
Paraguay tea **366** 11
parallel *n.* **15** 2, **327** 21, **328** 4
~ bars **279** 27
~ brake levers **182** 26
~ christiania **283** 32
parallelepiped **329** 36
parallel guide **144** 8
parallelism **327** 21
parallel keys **300** 1-15
~ of latitude **15** 2
parallelogram **328** 33–36
parallel swing **283** 32
~ vice **134** 12
Paramecium **340** 9
parapet **39** 19, **310** 21
~ walk **310** 20
parasite **341**
~ of man **341** 20–31
parasol **32** 34
~ mushroom **365** 30
~-wing aircraft **225** 21
Parcae **308** 53–58
parcel **231** 3, **200** 2
~ counter **231** 1
~ form **232** 15
parcels label **200** 3
~ office **200** 1
parcel-weighing machine **231** 2
parclose **311** 32
parent aircraft **226** 23
'parent-child' aircraft **226** 22
'parent-child' arrangement **226** 22–24
parentheses (or parenthesis) **325** 24, 25
parent plant **57** 15
parents **45** 1 + 2
parietal bone **19** 31
parietales **56** 2
paring chisel **127** 65
parish church **252** 28
parison **155** 15
park **16** 97, **257**
~ bench **257** 16
~ entrance **257** 32
~ gate **257** 31
parking ground **252** 27
~ light **185** 17
~ lot* **252** 27
~ meter **253** 51
~ place **252** 27
park keeper **257** 30, 68
~ life **257** 41–69
~ path **257** 38
~ pond **257** 50
~ railings **257** 33
~ regulations **257** 29
parlor* **39** 70, **44**, **103** 1–34
~ car * **204** 49
parlour **39** 70
parotid gland **21** 9
parquet* **296** 19
~ floor **118** 74
parrot **345** 1
parry **277** 21
~ of fifth **277** 38
~ of tierce **277** 22
parsley **59** 19
parson **311** 22
parsonage **312** 20
part **136**, **233** 47
parterre *[beds]* **257** 39
~* *[Theatre]* **296** 19
Parthenon **316** 1
participant in procession **312** 50
parti-coloured hose **338** 47
~ tights **338** 47
parting *[hair]* **35** 13, 19
~-off tool **142** 45
~ tool **129** 24, **323** 9
partition **114** 25

partitioned plate-tray **260** 54
~ wall **114** 25
partly bald head **35** 20
~ insured registered letter **232** 35
partner **259** 42, **288** 44
partridge **88** 70
~ call **87** 47
part of roof **116** 1–26
party **259** 40–43
~ wall **53** 25
pas de chat **288** 17
~ de trois **288** 31–34
Pasiphaea **349** 12
pass *[defile]* **12** 47
~ *[calibre]* **141** 63
~ *[Footb.]* **274** 61
passage **53** 19, **319** 4
~way **53** 19
Passe **263** 19
passegarde **310** 44
passenger **187** 7, **201** 3, **216** 52, **226** 31
~ aircraft **226** 30
~ cabin **209** 28, 52
~ cable railway **209** 15–38
~ car **209** 28
~ car* **203** 26
~ and cargo motor-ship **218** 1–71
~ coach **203** 26, **204** 1
~ and commercial motor vehicle **189** 2
~ ferry **16** 60, **211** 1
~ and freight boat (or vessel) **218** 1–71
~ gondola **226** 68
~ lift **256** 45
~ liner **216** 32
~ motor vehicle **187**
~ nacelle **226** 68
~ quay **220** 16
~ ship **216** 33
~ sled* **336** 18
~ sledge **336** 18
~ steamer **216** 32
~ train **201** 27, **203** 1
passenger train·engine **203** 2
~ locomotive **203** 2
~ luggage van **203** 11
passé-position **288** 15
passerine *n.* **346**
pass guard **310** 44
passiflora **56** 2
passing the ball along the ground **274** 61
~ place **212** 27
~ precipitations **8** 19
passion flower **56** 2
pass key* **134** 10
passport **247** 14, **259** 13
~ check **247** 14+15
paste *[meat]* **96** 16
paste *[soldering]* **135** 45
~ *[tooth]* **51** 58
~ *[plastic]* **240** 34
pasteboard distance piece **323** 37
~-brush **50** 27, **121** 37
~ foods **98** 32–34
pastel pencil **321** 19
paste pot **50** 26, **231** 5
pastern **73** 25
~ joint **73** 24
paste-work **50** 28
pastor *[clergy]* **311** 22
~ *[Zool.]* **346** 4
pastoral staff **314** 48
pastry cook **97** 33
~-cutter **42** 62
~ wheel **42** 50
patch **181** 4, 5, **289** 24
~ pocket **32** 3
pate *[head]* **35** 22
patella **19** 23
paten **311** 12
patent anchor **217** 75
~ key **180** 50
~-leather strap **203** 14
~ log **219** 31
~ valve **180** 31
paternoster bead **313** 29
~ lift **164** 36
path **16** 102, **257** 18
~ border **257** 37
~ of the sun **5** 2
patient **26** 17, **27** 2, **262** 7, 18
patients' bed **29** 8
~ table **29** 14
patriarchal cross **313** 58
patrician lady **338** 48
patrol car **248** 2
~man* **247** 1
~ wagon* **248** 2
patter **113** 57
pattern **102** 68, **121** 25, **170** 55
~ book **102** 72
~-holder **171** 29
~ repeat **165** 12
~ sheet **102** 72
~ table **170** 56
patty **97** 13
pauldron **310** 44
pause **300** 42
~ sign **300** 42
paved footpath **194** 6
pavement **39** 60, **194** 6, **212** 1
~* **210** 2, **253** 34
~ concrete **197** 43
~ snow plough **195** 4
paver *[worker]* **194** 16
~ *[tool]* **194** 17
pavilion **246** 14, **262** 15
~ roof **116** 22
paving **118** 14, 26
~ brick **151** 27
~ sett **194** 12
pavior **194** 16
paviour **194** 16
pavise **310** 56
Pavo **5** 41
paw **88** 50, **353** 4
pawl **107** 18, **145** 25
pawn **265** 13
payee **242** 19
paying-in counter **231** 19
pea **59** 1, **70** 19
~ blossom **59** 2
peach **61** 31
~ blossom **61** 27
~ flower **61** 27
~ leaf **61** 32
~ tree **61** 26–32
Peacock **5** 41
peacock **74** 30
~ butterfly **348** 2
peacock's feather **74** 31
pea flower **59** 2
~hen **74** 30
peak **11** 6
~ pendant **214** 49
pea nut **367** 41
~ plant **59** 1
pear **60** 33
~ blossom **60** 38
~ flower **60** 38
pearl **340** 33
~ *[Typ.]* **170** 22
~-barley **98** 35
~ diadem **338** 16
~ hen **74** 27
~ necklace **38** 12
pear pip **60** 37
~ quince **60** 50
~ seed **60** 37
~-shaped flower head **354** 75
~ stalk **60** 34
~ tree **60** 31
~ twig **60** 32
~ twig in flower **60** 32
peascod **338** 30
peat bed **13** 20, 22
~ dust **79** 31
pea tendril **59** 4
peat moss* **79** 31
~-moss litter **75** 29
pectoral cross **314** 52
~ fin **350** 7
~ muscle **20** 36
pectoris major **20** 36
pedal **274**, 5, **180** 40, 78, **185** 39-41, **302** 62
~ ball-race **180** 59
~ car **258** 2
~ frame **180** 83
~ harp **302** 60
~ key **305** 51, 52
~ lever **156** 28
~ mechanism **303** 54
~ pin **180** 81
~ pipe **305** 3
~ rod **304** 42
pedal roller **156** 27
~ spindle **180** 60
~ tower **305** 4
peddler* **253** 11
pedestal **290** 55
~ mat **51** 34
pedestrian **253** 32
~ crossing **194** 3, **253** 33
Pediculati **349** 6
pedicure **25** 18
pediment **316** 3, **317** 49
pedlar **53** 30, **253** 53
peduncle **61** 4
peek-a-boo **258** 1
peel **97** 66
peeling iron **85** 25
~ knife **85** 42
peen **132** 26
peep hole **43** 31, **248** 15
peewit **343** 21
peg **118** 11, **260** 13, 14, **303** 11
Pegasus *[Myth.]* **307** 26
~ *[Astr.]* **5** 10
peg box **302** 20, **303** 10
~-box cheek **303** 19
pein **132** 26
~ ***66** 22
Pekinese spaniel **71** 20
Pekin(g)ese **71** 20
pekin(g)ese dog **71** 20
pelargonium **56** 1
pelican **343** 5
~ eel **349** 2
pelota **287** 51
~ player **287** 52
pelvic fin **350** 8
pelvis **19** 18–21, **22** 31
pen *[writing]* **239** 19
~ *[play~]* **49** 4
~ *[enclosure]* **202** 7
penalty area **274** 5
~ corner **275** 6
~ spot **274** 6
pencil *[writing]* **239** 31, **249** 60
~ *[Geom.]* **328** 19
~ attachment **144** 29, 42
~ box **249** 66
~ cap **239** 34
~-holder **239** 34 **249** 61
~ india rubber **144** 53
~ lead **239** 36
~ point **239** 33
~ of rays **328** 19
~ rubber **144** 53
~-sharpener **240** 68
~-sharpening machine **240** 69
~ shield **249** 62
pendant *[jewellery]* **31** 61, **38** 14, 32
~ *[pennant]* **245** 22
~ fitting **45** 30

piano *[soft]* **300** 55
~ action **304** 2–18
~ case **304** 6
~forte **304** 1
~ hammer **304** 3
~ lesson **44** 32-37
~ mechanism **304** 2–18
~ pedal **304** 8+9
~ teacher **44** 37
piazza* **39** 18
pica **170** 28
picador **287** 61
piccolo **302** 30
pick **138** 52, **150** 31, **282** 39, **301** 19
pick-a-back· aircraft **226** 22
~ fight **258** 44
pick-counter **159** 2
picker **159** 64
~ head **177** 48
picking bowl **159** 67
~ cam **159** 66
~ -machine **124** 1, 2
~ stick **159** 17
~ stick buffer **159** 65
~ stick return spring **159** 68
~-up bearings **230** 22
pickled cucumber **98** 29
pick f. plucking **301** 19
pickpocket **291** 16
pick-up **306** 35
picnic case **266** 21
~ stove **266** 19
Pictor **5** 47
picture **311** 15
~-book **50** 16
~ camera **292** 47, **294** 22
~ caption **325** 45
~ of Christ **311** 15
~ frame **48** 17
~ gate **295** 31, 34
~ hat **36** 39
~ house **295** 1
~ light **44** 38
~ line adjustment **295** 29
~ monitor **237** 26
~ in outline **321** 4
~ palace **295** 1
~ paper **47** 10
~ postcard **232** 5
~-printing machine **293** 17
~ projection **293** 33
pictures **295** 1
picture of saint **314** 7
~ signal **237** 24
~-sound camera **294** 23
~-sound-printing machine **293** 16
~ tube **236** 1
~ writing **324** 1
pie* **97** 16
piece *[part, etc.]* **30** 22, **95**, **260** 44, **310** 53, 54, 88
~ *[games]* **265**
~ *[Theatre]* **297** 35
~ of cloth **162** 51
~ of combination furniture **47** 25
~ of furniture **44** 25
~ of ice **260** 44
~ of meat **86** 43
~ of scenery **297** 35
pieces of meat **95**
piece of soap **30** 22
~ of type **170** 38
~ of wood **52** 62
~ work **155** 16–21
pied woodpecker **343** 27
pier *[landing stage]* **16** 59, **220** 17
~ *[bridge]* **210** 32
~ *[Art]* **317** 34
piercing saw **106** 11
piercing-saw· blade **106** 13
~ frame **106** 12
pierrette **289** 12
pierrot **289** 19
pig *[pork]* **74** 9, **88** 51, **95** 38–54
~ *[iron]* **140** 39
~-bristle scraper **96** 34
~-casting machine **140** 33–43
~ creep door **76** 46
pigeon **64** 10, **74** 33, **343** 23
~ hole **231** 21, **259** 2
~ house **64** 8
piggin **126** 9
piggy back* **226** 22
pig-iron **141** 11
pig-iron· ladle **140** 12, 20, 41
~ outlet **140** 11
piglet **74** 9, **76** 40
~ creep **76** 39
pigmy **337** 41
pig's ear **74** 11
~-ear *[pastry]* **97** 52
~ head **95** 43
~ liver **96** 28
~ snout **74** 10
pigsties **76** 39-47
pigsty **76** 39–47
pigtail *[wig]* **35** 6
~ *[tobacco]* **105** 22
~ tress **35** 30
~ wig **35** 5
pig trough **76** 43
pike *[Zool.]* **350** 16
~ dive **268** 41
pilaster **317** 46
~ strip **317** 11
pile *[stake]* **211** 18
~ *[heap]* **177** 37, **221** 36
~ *[reactor]* **1** 31–46
~ of boards **115** 1
pile of branchwood **84** 16
~ of bricks **113** 40
~ of brushwood **84** 16
~ carpet **47** 61
~-driven well **254** 60
~-driver **221** 59–62
~ dwelling **309** 15, **335** 33
~ feed **174** 36
~ foundation **211** 8
~ house **335** 33
~ of linen **48** 42
~ of logs **64** 16, **84** 24
~ of plates **260** 11
~ of sheets of paper **168** 48
~ of unprinted sheets **174** 24
pileus **365** 4
pile wall **114** 17 **212** 5
~ of wood **53** 31
~wort **359** 36
piling **114** 17
pill **23** 9
pillar **13** 82
~ crane **221** 1–7
~ stand **2** 29
~ tap **119** 36
pill box **23** 8
pillion **183** 32, **190** 20
~-rider's foot-rest **182** 57
~ seat **183** 32, **190** 20
pillow **48** 6
~ lace **101** 18
~ slip **48** 7
pilot *[aircr.]* **226** 38
~ *[Tech.]* **183** 57
~ *[piano]* **304** 33
~ balloon **28** 40
~ jet **183** 57
~ lamp **207** 21
~ required signal **245** 23
pilot's cabin **228** 1–38
~ cockpit **226** 37, **228** 1–38
~ seat **228** 1
pilot wire **304** 34
pimpernel **63** 27
pin **102** 78, **136** 19, 29, **303** 11
pinacoid **330** 20, 24, 25, 26
pinafore **31** 48, **32** 17
~ dress **32** 11
~ slip **31** 34
pince-nez **108** 28
pincers **127** 21, **130** 37
pinchbar* **150** 32
pinchers **134** 73
pin cushion **102** 77
pine *[fir]* **356** 20
~ *[ananas]* **368** 61
~apple **368** 61
~apple gall **82** 40
~ beauty moth **82** 46
pine cone **356** 26
~ forest **16** 1
~ hawk moth **82** 27
~ looper **82** 31
~ moth **82** 28
~ tree **356** 20
~ weevil **82** 41
~ wood **16** 1
ping-pong **276** 39–42
ping-pong· ball **276** 42
~ bat **276** 40
~ player **276** 39
pin groove **136** 47
~ head **102** 79
pinion *[Tech.]* **136** 90, **210** 64
~ *[bird]* **88** 76
pink *[Bot.]* **62** 7
~ *[colour]* **320** 4
pinnacle **317** 29
pinnate **354** 41, 42
pinnatifid **354** 40
pinned barrel **306** 2
pinning **240** 41
pinniped *n.* **352** 18–22
pinny **32** 17
pin slit **136** 47
~ slot **136** 47
~ spanner **192** 7
~ tumbler cylinder **134** 48
Piorry's wooden stethoscope **26** 26
pip *[Bot.]* **60** 60
~ *[dice]* **265** 32
pipe *[conduit]* **119** 24–30, **140** 13, 17
~ *[organ]* **305** 17–35
~ *[smoking]* **105** 32–39
~ *[Mus.]* **301** 3
~ bend **53** 51
~ bowl **105** 36
~ bridge **220** 59
~-cleaner **105** 43
~ clip **117** 31
~ connection **203** 35–39
~-cutter **119** 54
~ elbow **53** 51
~-fitter **119** 23
~ knee **53** 51
~line **119** 30, **139** 56, **212** 41
~ of one stop **305** 19
~ of peace **335** 6
pipes *[organ]* **301** 57
pipe-scraper **105** 41
~ stem **105** 38
~ still **139** 25, 32
pipette **26** 44, **334** 24
pipe union **334** 5
~ vice **119** 12
~ vise* **119** 12
~ wrench **119** 56
piping *[pipes]* **227** 13
~ *[braid]* **102** 6

pirate **289** 43
pirn **159** 7, 30
~-holder **159** 33
pirouette **284** 12, **288** 27
Pisces **6** 43
pisciculturist **89** 65
pissabed **63** 13
pistachio nut **366** 51
~ tree **366** 49
piste **277** 16
~ fencing **277** 15–43
pistil **61** 13, **69** 34
pistol **248** 7
~ grip **87** 6
~ holster **247** 8
~-type handle **89** 25
piston **148** 59, **184** 54, **239** 22
~ aero engine **227** 1
~-edge packing **148** 60
~ knapsack sprayer **83** 34–37
~ pen **239** 19
~ ring **184** 79, 80
~ ring fitting tool **192** 13
~ rod **205** 33
~ sprayer **83** 34–37
pit *[mine]* **137** 1–40
~ *[Agr.]* **64** 11, 12
~ *[Theatre]* **296** 19
~* *[Exchange]* **243** 1
~ *[Sports]* **273** 41, **280** 31
~ bank circulation hall **137** 7
~-bottom **137** 27, **138** 1
pitch *[Tech.]* **136** 58
pitched roof **39** 5
pitcher **30** 24, **309** 35
~ ***42** 45
~ *[Baseb.]* **275** 53
pitching **194** 13
~ plate **275** 43
~ rubber **275** 43
pitch of rivets **136** 58
pith cylinder **354** 14
pit-head gear **137** 5
~ house **79** 33
pith ray **354** 11
pit hydrant **255** 25
~man* **243** 5
Pitman shaft **186** 42
pit mechanic **273** 43
piton **282** 52, 54
pituitary gland **19** 43
pivot bearing **91** 10
~-buffing machine **107** 57
~ drive **210** 59
pivoted lamp-arm **171** 23
~ saddle **182** 19
~ spring **193** 19
pivoting bearing **221** 62
pivot pier **210** 58
pix* **295** 1
placard **98** 2, **253** 22
~ advertising bargains **256** 65
place **252** 43
~ card **46** 13
~ for clamps **64** 11
~ of coinage **244** 9
~ of issue **242** 13
placing of hands **276** 49, 50, 51
place of meteorological observation **9** 7
~ of mintage **244** 9
placental flying animal **351** 9+10
place of observation **9** 7
~ of payment **242** 15, 22
~ f. pits **64** 11
~ of registration **186** 35
~ where the wing folds **342** 35
plain pipette **334** 25
~ segment **156** 69
~song notation **299** 2+3
~ tile **117** 6, 46
~-tile double-lap roofing **117** 2
~-turning slide **142** 24
~ weave interlacing **165** 1
~ web girder **210** 30
~ white ball **264** 11
plains Indian **335** 3
plait **35** 30
plaited belt **37** 13
~ bun **97** 53
plaiting device **162** 30, 35
plan *[Arch.]* **144** 62
~ *[ship]* **222** 48
planche **277** 16
plane *[tool]* **115** 64, **127** 52–61
~ *[aircr.]* **225**, **226**
~ *[Geom., etc.]* **329** 31, **330** 5
~ *[Bot.]* **355** 67
~ carried by another aircraft **226** 24
~ curve **329** 12
~ geometry **328** 1–58
~ iron **127** 57
~ mirror **331** 33
planer **143** 41
plane stock **127** 58
~ surface *[lens]* **108** 6
~ surface *[Geom.]* **328** 24–58
~ of symmetry **330** 5
~ table **128** 13
planet **6** 22-31, **7** 13-18
plane-table micrometer **110** 38
planetarium **6** 12–14
planetary gear **136** 92
~ system **6** 21–31
plane tree **355** 67
~ triangle **328** 26–32
plan-filing cabinet **144** 27
~ of game **263** 9
planing machine **143** 41
~ shed **149** 29
~ shop **149** 1–59
~ slide **143** 45
~ table **143** 42
planishing hammer **132** 31
planisphere **5** 1–35
plank **115** 91
~ cut **323** 4
~ fence **113** 44
planking *[Build., etc.]* **113** 44, **115** 9
~ *[boat]* **270** 19–26
plank platform **113** 28
~ roadway **113** 79
~-wood block **323** 2
plano-concave lens **108** 1
~-convex lens **108** 5
planographic printing process **323** 25+26
plansifter **91** 58
plant *[Bot.]* **354** 15
~ *[works, etc.]* **140** 1–19, **146**, **147**
plantain **70** 10, **364** 11
plantation **84** 10+11, 12
~ protection **83** 46
plant body **362** 49
~ bowl **44** 18
~ disease **81** 20
~ in bloom **366** 53
~ in flower **60** 17, **362** 36
~ in fruit **60** 17
planting stick **57** 7, **58** 2
plant label **57** 4
~ louse **342** 13
~-marker **57** 4
~ in pot **79** 25
plant protection **83**
~ tub **79** 47, **312** 61
~ used f. industrial purposes **367**
plaque **322** 38
plaster *[coating]* **117** 38, **118** 59, 60 **321** 42
~ *[Med.]* **17** 7, **23** 54
~ cast **322** 4
plasterer **113** 83
plaster floor **53** 68
plastering **113** 83–91
plaster key **118** 71
~ model **322** 4
~ mould **154** 15
~-of-Paris bandage **26** 8, **29** 25
plastic art **322** 32
plastic ball **264** 1
~ curtain **51** 19
plasticine **50** 22
plastic material **29** 55
~ paste **240** 34
~ rain cape **34** 35
~ stiffener **37** 19
~ substance **322** 8
plate *[Tech.]* **136** 91
~ *[Phot.]* **112** 41
~ *[dish]* **46** 3–6
plateau **13** 46
~ climate **9** 56
plate armour **310** 65
'plate' brooch **309** 30
plate clamp **173** 33
~ clock **107** 49
~ condenser **331** 51
~ cylinder **174** 8, **175** 51, 60
~ dinner* **260** 54
~ feed **239** 44
~ of food **260** 17
~ girder bridge **210** 30
~-heater **77** 8
~layer **198** 20
~layers' railcar crane **208** 36
~ lunch* **260** 54
~-mark **38** 30, **112** 46
~ mill* **141** 67
platen *[Typ.]* **175** 13, 15, **177** 29, **323** 31
~ *[typewr.]* **240** 10
~ machine **175** 13, 29, **323** 29
~-turning knob **240** 17
plate rack **172** 28
~-receiver **239** 38
~ rod **172** 3
~ shears **119** 1
~ showing model number **182** 51
~ showing type number **182** 51
~ f. sweet course* **46** 6
~-warmer **46** 45
~-whirler **173** 1
platform *[elevated surface]* **1** 42, **139** 2
~ *[Railw.]* **201**
~ f. artiste **290** 5
~ clock **201** 53
~ edge **201** 21
~ indicator **200** 18
~ loudspeaker **201** 28
~ mail box* **201** 46
~ pillar box **201** 46
~ post box **201** 46
~ railing **113** 24
~ refreshment stall **201** 48
~ roofing **201** 1
~ scale **221** 32
~ seat **201** 43
~ stairway **201** 2

platform telephone kiosk **201** 44
~-ticket machine **200** 22
~ tip **145** 73
~ truck **202** 38
~ tunnel **201** 2
~ underpass* **201** 2
platinum-iridium electrode **27** 46
~ tube **29** 52
platoon* **247** 1—8
platter **46** 26, 33
platyhelminth **341** 24
platypus **351** 1
play **277** 1–66
playback button **306** 22
~ head **293** 4
player *[Theatre]* **297** 37
~ *[Mus.]* **289** 3
~ *[Sports]* **274** 11–21, **276** 16
player's line **275** 45
playgoer **296** 8
playing cards **265** 36
~ at catch **258** 23
~ field **261** 31
~ the races* **272** 8
~ at touch **258** 23
play-pen **49** 4
~-room **49** 1–29
~suit **31** 5, 9
~things **49** 5–29
pleasure boat **216** 36, **269** 1
~ garden **54**
~ steamer **216** 45–66, **220** 18
pleat **32** 5
pleated skirt **31** 34, **32** 33
pleat held by stitching **102** 3
pleating **32** 33
plectrum **301** 19, 53
~ guitar **303** 20, 27
pledget **28** 8
Pleiad(e)s **5** 26
pleiobar **9** 2
plié **288** 6
pliers **119** 55
Plimsoll **100** 24
plinth **316** 31
Plough **5** 29
plough **65** 6, **68** 1–34
~ beam **68** 9
~ body **68** 4–8
~ share **68** 7, **309** 33
plover **343** 19–21
plow* see plough
plow bottom* **68** 4–8
~ neck* **68** 3
~ tail* **68** 3
plug *[El.]* **52** 7, **120**, **192** 56, **233** 9
~ *[bait]* **89** 39
~ *[chew]* **105** 23
~ and body **134** 49
~-cock **119** 27
~ drill **143** 32
plug gauge **142** 52
plugging sand **150** 29
plug hat* **36** 20
~ lever **51** 65
~ point **120** 5
~ tap **134** 64
~ tester **192** 56
~-type cut-out* **120** 35
plum **61** 20
plumage **347** 3
plumb-bob **113** 50
plumber **119** 13
plumb bob* **219** 35
plumbing gland **147** 40
plumb line **113** 71
plume *[helmet]* **308** 18, **310** 78
~ *[mill]* **91** 41
~ of peacock's feathers **246** 36
plumicorn **347** 16
plum leaf **61** 21
plummet **110** 34
plum stone **61** 23
~ tree **61** 19–23
plumule **354** 90
plunge **268** 29
plunger *[compasses]* **144** 39
~ *[syringe]* **26** 29
~ *[Tech.]* **139** 50
~ *[typewr.]* **240** 31
plus-fours **34** 22
plus-minus lever **240** 60
~ sign **326** 23
Pluto **6** 31
plutonic magmatism **11** 29–31
~ rock **11** 29
plutonium **1** 48, **3** 40, 41, 42
plywood **127** 34+35
~ frame **271** 48
π-meson **4** 31
π-mesotron **4** 31
pneumatic axle car jack **191** 30
~ brake cylinder **204** 5
~ bumping bag* **226** 70
~ chisel **141** 40
~-dispatch postage stamp **232** 30
~ drill **138** 49
~ grinder **141** 39
~ grinding machine **141** 39
~ letter **232** 29
~ power hammer **133** 8
~ printing-down frame **173** 13
~ rammer **141** 31
~ sanding gear **205** 19
~ tyre **180** 30
pneumatophore **354** 82
poacher **86** 29
P. O. boxes **231** 7
pochette **301** 20
pocket **31** 10, **32** 59
~ clip **2** 18, **239** 25
~ dosimeter **2** 15
~ fiddle **301** 20
~ flap **34** 9
~ grinder **167** 14
~ handkerchief **31** 8
~-knife **266** 17
~ pencil-sharpener **240** 68
~ spittoon **23** 32
~ timetable **200** 44
~ torch **120** 26
~ train schedule* **200** 44
~ trimming **32** 53
~ watch **107** 9
pod *[seed vessel]* **63** 11, 20, 23, **70** 8, 16
~ auger **126** 1
~ corn **69** 31
'Poets' horse' **307** 26
point *[Geom.]* **328** 1–23, 1
~ *[tool]* **322** 15
~ *[tip]* **36** 3
~ *[ice axe]* **282** 37
~ *[antlers]* **88** 10
~ *[Railw.]* **198** 47
~* *[halt]* **16** 27
~* *[report]* **249** 54
~ of blow gun dart **335** 29
~ of contact **328** 49
~ drive **198** 66
pointe danseuse **288** 31
pointed arch **318** 31
pointe d'arrêt **277** 41
pointed beard **35** 8, 9
~ tree **257** 19
pointer *[index]* **10** 9, 26
~ *[stick]* **249** 22
~ *[dog]* **71** 40, 43
pointe shoe **288** 34
point of hock **73** 37
~ of hough **73** 37
~ of inflection **329** 21
~ of inflexion **329** 21
pointing **117** 55
point of intersection **328** 1
~ lace **101** 30
~ lock **198** 59
~ paper design **165** 4
~-protector **249** 62
points of horse **73** 1–38
point of shoulder and chest (or breast) **73** 19
points lamp **198** 64
~ lever **199** 58
~ signal lamp **193** 29
~ tongue **193** 33
~ trough **198** 65
poison foam apparatus **83** 44
poison gas atomiser **83** 40
~gland **78** 14
poisonous agaric **363** 11
~ fungus **363** 10–13
~ plant **363**
~ viper **350** 40
poison sac **78** 13
poitrel **310** 85
poker *[tool]* **40** 41, **41** 49
Poland **14** 17
polar axis **6** 5
~ bear **353** 11
~ cap of Mars **7** 14
~ circles **15** 11
~ climate **9** 57+58
polaris **5** 1, 34
polar light **4** 35
~ wind **9** 51
pole *[Geogr.]* **15** 3
~ *[shaft]* **72** 21, **179** 19, 30
~ *[sea mark]* **219** 75, 76
~ *[Sports]* **279** 8, **280** 39
~-climbing **279** 7
~ horse **179** 46
~ of horse-gear **64** 59
~ jump **280** 38–41
~-jumper **280** 38
~ star **5** 1, 34
~ vault **280** 38–41
~ wagon **84** 15
police **247**
~ alarm **253** 14
~ car* **253** 58
~ constable **247** 1
~ detachment **247** 1–8
~ detective **248** 3
~ dog **71** 31, **248** 8
~ force **247** 1-8, 9–11
police identification mark **186** 32
~ number **186** 32
police-man **247** 1, 11, **248** 6, **253** 64
~man's uniform **247** 2
~ officer **248** 6
~ telephon cable **194** 35
~ van **253** 58
polish **127** 12
polishing brush **52** 14, 42, **106** 45
~ head **107** 57
~ lathe **107** 57
~ machine **106** 43
~ mop **106** 45
~ steel **106** 52
polish rod **139** 54
Polish swan **343** 16
polje **13** 72
pollard-cleaner **91** 60
~ reducing roller **91** 61

poll card with registration number **251** 19
~ clerk **251** 26
pollen **354** 65
~-basket **78** 6
~ sac **356** 45
~ tube **354** 66
polling booth **251** 23
~ box **251** 23
~ number **251** 19
~ station **251** 16
Pollux **5** 28
polo **287** 26
~ cycle player **287** 30
~ neck **32** 13
~ player **287** 27
~ stick **287** 28
polyamide chip **164** 39
polyanthus narcissus
polygon **328** 40
polyhedron **330**
Polyhymnia **308** 67
polymerization **164** 54
~ in autoclave **164** 33
Polymnia **308** 67
polyp **340** 37, **349** 9
polyphagous beetle **342** 24–38
polypod fern **361** 16
Pom *[coll.]* **71** 19
pome **354** 102
pomegranate **368** 16
pomelo **368** 23
Pomeranian (dog) **71** 19
pomes **60** 31–61
pomiferous fruit **60** 31–61
pommel **72** 38, 46, **279** 37
pommer **301** 13
Pomoideae **60** 31–61
pompom **100** 47
pompon **100** 47
~ dahlia **62** 23
poncho **335** 24
pond **16** 79, **54** 19, **257** 50
pons **19** 46
pontic **27** 32
pontifex maximus **314** 54
pontifical ring **314** 47
~ vestments **314** 54
pontoon **210** 18, **221** 45
~ bridge **16** 46, **210** 17
pony-tail hair-style **31** 62
poodle **71** 14
pool *[Swimming]* **268** 1–32
~ *[Roulette]* **263** 11
~room* **264** 7–19
poop **218** 33
poor-box **311** 61
~ man's weather glass **63** 27
popcorn **69** 31
Pope **314** 54
Pope's ring of investiture **314** 58
pop hole **75** 3, 31
poplar **257** 53, **355** 23
poplin coat **32** 42
poppet valve* **184** 57
popping crease **275** 57
poppy **63** 2
~ blossom **63** 4
~ capsule **63** 5
~ flower **63** 4
~ head **63** 5
~ roll **97** 55
~ seed **63** 5
~ stick **97** 55
popular musical instrument **303** 1–66
porcelain insulator **233** 67
~ manufacture **154**
~ painter **154** 17
~ pontic **27** 32
~ tooth **27** 32
~ vase **319** 5
porch *[tent]* **266** 34
~ *[entrance]* **312** 16, 24
~ roof **39** 67
porcupine **351** 13
pore mushroom **365** 16
poricidal capsule **354** 96
Porifera **340** 13
pork **74** 9, **95** 38–54
~-fat cutter **96** 41
~ loin **95** 46
~ spare rib **95** 47
~ trotters **96** 24
porous layer **12** 29
port *[harbour]* **220**
~ *[~hole]* **216** 21
~ *[side]* **221** 49
~ *[Tech.]* **184** 73, 74
portable forge **134** 4
~ motor pump **255** 52
~ organ **301** 56
~ paint box **296** 34
~ radio* **266** 10
~ railway **16** 90
~ tape-recorder **306** 13
~ wireless **266** 10
portal *[bridge]* **210** 54
~ crane **198** 15
~ figure **315** 36
~ ornament **315** 35
~ support **217** 12
~ vein **22** 39
portamento **300** 52
portando **300** 52
portato **300** 52
porta triumphalis **316** 59
port bit **72** 52
portcullis **310** 24
porter *[janitor]* **53** 28, **145** 87, **256** 44
~ *[luggage~]* **201** 32
porterhouse* **95** 17
~ steak* **95** 17, **96** 20
porter's lodge **145** 83
porters' room **201** 45
portfolio **238** 36
port hole **216** 21
portico **262** 9, **316** 56
port light **218** 15
~ mouth **72** 52
portrait watermark **244** 31
ports *[ship]* **215** 27
port side **221** 49
Portugal **14** 18, **244** 23
Posaune **305** 17–22
Poseidon **308** 29
position **140** 48–51
positional game **265** 1–16
position of the hands **276** 49, 50, 51
~ of team **274** 1
positive *[Phot.]* **112** 9
~ carbon **295** 40
~ direction **329** 6
~ engraving **323** 3
~ number **326** 7
~ organ **301** 56
~ sign **326** 7
post *[Post]* **203** 18, **231, 232**
~ *[timber]* **80** 7, **84** 25, **116** 40, 81
postage book **238** 48
postage meter·machine **231** 46
~ stamp **232** 17
postage stamp **232** 3, 40, **239** 46
~-stamp book **238** 49
postal card* **232** 2
~ card w. view* **232** 5
~ check **232** 10, 11
postal check· f. cash payment **232** 11
~ envelope **232** 10
~ f. transferring* **232** 11
postal cheque **232** 11
~ cheque envelope **232** 10
~ compartment **207** 33
~ form **232** 6–15
~ franking machine **231** 46
~ meter stamp **232** 17
~ note* **232** 12
~ order **232** 12
~ parcel **231** 3
post boy **179** 40
~card **232** 2, 4, 5
~ crown **27** 34
poster **98** 2, **251** 12, 13, **256** 25
poste-restante letter **231** 21
posterior **18** 40
~ ruga **18** 41
poster pillar **253** 21
post horn **179** 41
~ horse **179** 43
postil(l)ion **179** 40
postil(l)ion's horn **179** 41
post·man **231** 47
~man's bag **231** 48
~mark **232** 39
~master's office **231** 23
~ office **231** 1–30
post-office· box **231** 8
~ employee **231** 39
~ motorcycle **231** 33
~ official **231** 39
~ receipt **232** 9
post-paid stamp **232** 3, 17
~ synchronizing **293** 25–29
~ synking **293** 25–29
~ windmill **91** 31
pot **41** 70
~-hat **36** 7
potassium permanganate tank **229** 18
potato **69** 38, 40
~ basket **66** 38
~ beetle **81** 52
~ berry **69** 43
~ clamp **64** 12
~ delivery spout **67** 14
~-digger **68** 41
~ dish **46** 31
~ foliage **69** 41
~ fork **66** 8
~-harvester **67** 38
~ hoe **66** 6
~ hopper **67** 15
~-masher **41** 3
~-peeler **41** 55
~ pit **64** 12
~ plant **69** 38
~-planter **67** 11
~-planting trug **66** 26
~-raiser **67** 38
~ rake **66** 24
~ scoop **67** 43
~ spoon **46** 75
~-spinner **68** 41
~ tuber **69** 40
potcher **167** 7
pot f. cotton-wool **30** 49
pot hat **36** 7
~ plant **79** 25
potted plant **79** 25
potter's wares **291** 66
pottery **291** 66
~ stand **291** 64–66
pottice *[fam.]* **30** 17
potting table **79** 12
pouch-bearing animal **351** 2+3
~-shaped pod **63** 11
pouf **48** 31
pouffe **48** 31
poulaines **338** 43
poulard **98** 7

Q

quick lunch* **260** 45–54
~-lunch restaurant **602** 45–54
~-motion camera **294** 30
quicksilver column **10** 2
quid **105** 23
quiff **31** 7
quill **89** 49, **324** 26
~ float **89** 48
quillons **277** 56
quilt **30** 33, **48** 11
~ cover **48** 12
quilting seam **101** 1
quince **60** 49, 50
~ leaf **60** 47
~ tree **60** 46
quinquefoliate **354** 39
quinte *[Fenc.]* **277** 38
quintuple cross **313** 66
quipu **335** 22
quirle **42** 58
quitch **63** 30
~ grass **63** 30
quiver **287** 46, **308** 13, **335** 27
quoin **175** 39
quoit **261** 29, **267** 32, **291** 47
quoits **261** 28, **267** 31
quotation mark **325** 26
quotient **326** 26

R

rabbet plane **127** 59
rabbit **88** 65
~ fence **84** 7
rabbit's earth **86** 26
race *[Sports]* **269** 1–18, **272**, **273**
~ *[mill]* **136** 69, 70
~ *[Tech.]* **136** 69, 70
~ board **159** 42
~ committee **273** 4
racecourse **272** 1–35
~ f. flat race **272** 10
~ f. steeplechasing **272** 23
racehorse **272** 14
raceme **354** 68, **358** 33
racer *[competitor]* **273** 2, 8, 14
~ *[vehicle]* **273** 16, 38
racer's shirt **273** 9
racers' pavilion **273** 7
raceway* **91** 44
racing bicycle **273** 15, 16
~ boat **269** 9–16. **273** 46–50
~ car **187** 19–30, **273** 38
~ cycle **273** 16
~ cyclist **273** 8
~ dive **268** 29
~ driver **273** 39
~-eight **269** 10
~ handlebars **273** 18
~ keel-yacht **270** 5
racing machine **273** 16, 27
~ motorboat **269** 6
~ motorcycle **273** 29
~ motorcyclist **273** 25
~ number **280** 18
~ plunge **268** 29
~ saddle **273** 17
~ sculler **269** 16
~ shell* **269** 16
~ skate **284** 29
~ ski **283** 40
~ sledge **285** 11
~ toe cap **273** 21
~ track **273** 34
rack *[clothes~]* **43** 1,
~ *[shelf]* **262** 16
~ *[Tech.]* **209** 9, 11, **221** 3, **253** 43, **301** 51
rack-and-pinion· railway **209** 7–11
~ winch **145** 21
rack f. conditioning the paper **174** 32
racket *[tennis]* **276** 27
~ *[snowshoe]* **286** 13
~ handle **276** 28
~ press **276** 30
rack f. furniture **169** 8
~ f. glasses **262** 16
~ head **156** 16
racking apparatus **93** 29
~ back **113** 61
~ back the beer **93** 20–28
rack mountain railway **209** 4+5
~ railroad car* **209** 5
~ railway **209** 4+5
rack railway· coach **209** 5
~ locomotive **209** 4
rack wagon **64** 44
racoon **353** 9
racquet **276** 27
radar connection **4** 23
~-controlled blind landing **230** 34
~ display unit **219** 11
~ image **219** 13
~ map **230** 51
~ mast **223** 15, 16
~ mirror **230** 52
~ receiver **230** 46
~ scanner **218** 8, **230** 4, 40
~scope **230** 48
~ sounding **10** 61
~ transmitter **230** 35, 45
~ unit **219** 9–13, **222** 75
radial artery **20** 21
~ bearing **136** 67
~ brick **151** 25
~ drilling machine **143** 23
~ nerve **20** 28
~ side of hand **21** 69
radiant-heat bath cabinet **24** 9
~ heater **119** 65
radiation lamp **27** 20
~-measuring instrument **2** 1–23
~ meter **2** 1–23
~-monitoring instrument **2** 1–23
~ shield **2** 31
~ shielding **2** 31
~ of waves **230** 42
radiator *[heating]* **40** 76
~ *[motorcar]* **185** 9
~ bonnet **286** 10
~ brush **121** 16
~ cap **185** 10
~ grille **185** 12
~ hood* **286** 10
~ mascot **187** 3
~ rib **40** 77
~ shutter **286** 11
~ shutter opening **286** 11
radical *n.* **327** 2
~ leaf **359** 9
~ quantity **327** 2
~ sign **327** 2
radicle **354** 88
radio *[Broadc.]* **234**, **235**
~ *[air~]* **230**
~* *[set]* **234** 35, **235** 1–23, **306** 46
~active cobalt **29** 55
~ announcer **234** 9
~ beacon **230** 12, 18
~ cabin* **218** 12, **223** 14
~ cabinet* **234** 36
~ casting* **234** 1–20
~ communicator* **234** 9
~ detecting and ranging apparatus **219** 9–13
radio direction· finder station **230** 20
~ indicator **228** 10
radio-equipped patrol car **248** 2
radiogram **44** 28, 29, **306** 45
radio·grapher **29** 38
~-isotope **1** 36, 44
radiolarian **340** 8
radio location· service **230** 22–33
~ system **230** 22–33
radiologist **29** 45
radio navigation service **230** 22–53
~ play studio **234** 7–12
~ receiver **234** 35
~ reception **234** 21–50
radioscopy **29** 39
radio set **234** 35
~ signal **230** 12
~-sonde **10** 59
radio-sounding apparatus **10** 59
~ stage **234** 14
~ station concert hall **234** 13–17
~ set **306** 46
~ therapy **29** 30–38
~ tower* **16** 33
~ transmission **234** 1–20
radish **59** 15, 16, 20
radium container **29** 52
~ cupboard **29** 51
~-packing table **29** 54
~ therapy **29** 48–55
~ treatment **29** 48–55
radius *[Geom.]* **328** 47
~ *[Anat.]* **19** 13
~ *[windmill]* **91** 2
~ of curvature **328** 22
raffia **130** 29
~ binding **57** 35
raffle **289** 11
rafia **130** 29
raft **266** 2
~ channel **269** 60
~ chute **269** 60
rafter **116** 28, 36, **117** 19
~ cornice **39** 9
~ head **116** 45, **117** 41
~ roof **116** 27
rag *[bolt]* **136** 41
ragamuffin **53** 11
rag boiler **167** 21
~ bolt **136** 41
ragged robin **360** 21
rag halfstuff **167** 21
raglan **34** 41
rail *[bar]* **2** 37, **160** 45 **198** 32, **209** 10
~ *[Zool.]* **343** 20
~ bicycle **208** 42
~ bottom **198** 35
~bus **207** 25, 27
~bus trailer **207** 26
~car **201** 27, **208** 35
~car train **207** 29
~ cycle **208** 42
~ drainage system **194** 32
~ fish-plate **198** 43
~ foot **198** 35
~ guard **205** 34
~ head **198** 33
railing **113** 89, **257** 34
rail joint **198** 42
~ level **198** 31
~ motorcycle **208** 42
~ omnibus **207** 25
railroad* see railway
rail/road bus **208** 45
railroad car* **216** 19
~ car cleaner* **201** 14
~ depot* **16** 41
~ laborer* **198** 20
~ mail car* **203** 19

railroad omnibus **208** 45
railroad policeman* **201** 22
~ postmark* **231** 52
~ schedule* **200** 50
~ shop* **199** 7
~V-dump car* **208** 22
~ vehicle* **203–208**
rail and road vehicle **208** 35–47
rail scotch **202** 52
~ spindle **157** 50
~ tongs **198** 21
~ truck **150** 14
railway bridge **16** 42
~-building **198** 1–31
~ cap **203** 15
~ construction **198** 1–31
~ embankment **198** 22
~ engine **205** 1
~ foreman's office **199** 55
~ grounds **199**
~ guide **200** 50
~ kilometre post **198** 82
~ line **198**
~ milepost **198** 82
~-owned container **202** 25
~ policeman **201** 22
~ post **203** 18
~ postmark **231** 52
~ post official **203** 21
~ premises **199**
~ repair shops **199** 6+7
~ station **16** 41, **199** 4
~ station hall **200**
~-supplied container **202** 25
~ terminus **252** 30
~ ticket **200** 36, **203** 48
~ timetable **200** 50
~ truck **208** 2–34
~ van **208** 2–34
~ vehicle **203–208**
~ viaduct **16** 42
~ wagon **208** 2–34
~ worker **198** 20
rail web **198** 34
rain **8** 18, **9** 32
~ belt **9** 53, 55
~-cape **31** 25, **34** 35
~ cloud **8** 10
~-coat **32** 42, **34** 39
~ collector **10** 39
~-deflector **10** 45
~ gage* **10** 37
~ gauge **10** 37
~ measure **10** 40
~ pipe **117** 29
~storm* **9** 37
~ streak **8** 9
rain-water· butt **64** 15
~ downpipe **39** 13
~ head **39** 12
raised beach **11** 54
~ side **189** 17
raisin **98** 8
raising apparatus* **89** 59
~ the arms **278** 3
~ jar* **89** 56
~ of the leg **278** 6
~ of poultry* **75** 1–46
~ ship **224** 9
~ of stock* **76**
~ tank* **89** 61
~ a wreck **224** 9–12
rake **40** 42, **66** 31
~ arm **67** 30
~ tine **67** 23
rallus **343** 20
rally **266** 40–52
~* **251** 1-15
Ram **6** 32
ram *[Zool.]* **74** 13
~ *[Tech.]* **133** 10, **143** 53, **221** 60
~ *[column]* **297** 60
rambler **55** 5
~ rose **55** 12
ram framework **221** 59
~-jet **227** 44
ram-jet· aeroplanes **226** 19–21
~ barrel-shaped aircraft **226** 19
~ tube **227** 19
ramie hat **36** 8
rammed concrete **113** 1
rammer **124** 14, **221** 60
ramming weight **221** 60
ramp *[approach]* **114** 41, **202** 1
~ *[stairs]* **118** 30
~ *[loading impl.]* **85** 5
rampart **252** 35
ramson **361** 6
ram-type snow plough **208** 44
randing **130** 3, 4
range *[mountains]* **12** 39
~ *[distance]* **86** 15
~ *[shooting ~]* **291** 58
~ *[kitchen]* **41** 39
~-finder **111** 40, **222** 36, 37
ranger* **84** 35
range selector **2** 4, 23
Ranunculaceae **62** 13
rapacious animal **352** 11–17
rapid-fire gun* **223** 45
~ interurban coach **204** 53
~-motion camera **294** 30
~ photometer **110** 26
~ water-heater **27** 27
rappel **282** 32, 33, 34
rapping iron **130** 36
raptorial animal **339** 6, **352** 11–17, **353** 1–11
~ leg **342** 5
Raschel fabric **160** 29
~ warp-knitting machine **160** 23
rasp *[Bot.]* **60** 28
~ *[Tech.]* **127** 30
raspberry **60** 28
~ blossom **60** 26
~ bush **60** 25
~ flower **60** 26
ratan **130** 32
~ cane **97** 80
rat-catcher **83** 18
ratchet **127** 23, **145** 24+25
~ f. inclining the top **171** 32
~ stop **142** 56
~ wheel **145** 24
rate **231** 26
~ of climb indicator **228** 13
~ of descent indicator **228** 13
~ of interest **327** 7
ratite bird **343** 1–3
rattan **130** 32
~ cane **97** 80
rattle **30** 42, **289** 40
rat trap **83** 7
ravine **13** 52
raw-gas· main **148** 13
~ pre-cooler **148** 28
~ primary condenser **148** 28
~ secondary condenser **148** 33
~ secondary cooler **148** 33
raw grinding mill and drier **152** 4
~ hemp **125** 1
Rawlplug drill **120** 55
raw material **152** 1, **163** 1–12, **167** 25
~ material intake **152** 1
~ material store **152** 3
~ meal silo **152** 5
~ stone **322** 5
~ tobacco **83** 11
~ water **254** 4
ray *[Phys.]* **29**
~ *[Geom.]* **328** 20
~ floret **359** 31
rayon manufacture* **163** 1–34
~ staple **163** 1–34
~ stocking **33** 32
~ yarn **163** 27
razor **51** 71, 79, **104** 25
~ blade **51** 72
razor blade· hone **51** 73
~ sharpener **51** 73
razor strop **104** 24
reach *[cart]* **131** 14
~ gate **212** 31
reaction chamber **227** 60–63
~ pile **1** 31–46
~-propulsion jet **226** 29
reactor **3** 1–23, **223** 9, **225** 71
~ cycle **3** 24–42
~ liquid **3** 14
~ tank **3** 25
reader *[person]* **298** 40
~ *[book]* **249** 31
reading board **249** 15
~ eyepiece **110** 32
~ lamp **48** 1
~ matter **201** 18
~ meter **239** 51
~ microscope **109** 26
~ room **250** 13
~ room supervisor **250** 14
~ tachometer* **159** 2, **207** 15
ready-to-wear dress* **256** 29
real **244** 22
reamer **134** 25
reanimation **17** 24–27
reaping hook **58** 28, **66** 25
rear axle **185** 51
~ break pedal **182** 16
~ boarding door **193** 12
~ bumper **186** 36
~ diesel-engine bus **188** 5
~-dump truck* **196** 7
~ engine **188** 5
~-engined bus **188** 5
~ fender* **180** 43
~ forage ladder **131** 23
~ hub sprocket **180** 38
rearing jar **89** 56
~ of livestock **76**
~ of poultry **75** 1–46
rear lamp **186** 29
~ license plate* **186** 31
~ light **180** 46, **182** 18, **186** 29
~ light indicator lamp **180** 47, **181** 44
~ mudguard **180** 43
~ nacelle **226** 77
~ number plate **186** 31
~ part of car **186** 25–38
~ quarter vent **185** 22
~ reflector **180** 45
~ seat **183** 8
~ side-panel **185** 2
~ sprocket wheel **180** 38
~ view mirror **185** 38

remedy **26** 11, **28** 7
remnants of planet **6** 26
remote-control· apparatus **207** 41
~ of elevation **15** 54
~ of lateral movement **15** 56
~ panel **306** 44
remote-controlled· model **271** 60
~ point **198** 58
~ switch **198** 58
remote-control tongs **2** 47
~-heated building **3** 37
~-reading thermometer **166** 9
removable base **111** 26
~ seat **189** 3
removal van **189** 41
removing bark **85** 25
Renaissance church **317** 42
~ Latin **325** 4
~ palace **317** 47
~ Roman **325** 4
renal calyx **22** 30
~ pelvis **22** 31
rendering **117** 38, **118** 6
rendezvous **257** 44
reniform **354** 38
repair kit **181** 1
~ kit box **18** 12
~ pit **192** 63
~ quay **217** 10
~ shed **199** 6+7
~ shop **199** 6+7
~ tool **192** 6
repeat switch **306** 38
repeater *[rifle]* **87** 2
~ *[flag]* **245** 30—32
~ compass **219** 29
repeating decimal fraction **326** 21
~ rifle **87** 2
repeat mark **300** 43
reply coupon **232** 20
~-paid postcard **232** 4
report *[school]* **249** 53
reporter **248** 39, **281** 45
~ camera **294** 23
representation **335** 2
~ of wind **9** 9–19
reproducer **306** 2
reproducing camera **171** 1
reproduction of talkies* **237** 21
reproductive shoot **356** 43, 62, 68
reptile **350** 27–41
requin **350** 1
requisite **105**
rerebrace **310** 47
reredos **311** 42
rescue **17** 28–33
rescuer **17** 29
rescue work **255** 1–46
research laboratory **292** 9
reserve **274** 45
reservoir **212** 39, **239** 28, **254** 18
~ rock **12** 29
resetting button **120** 19
resident bird **344** 4
residential area* **252** 11, 59
~ district* **252** 59
~ section* **252** 11, 59
resilient clutch **207** 10
resin **302** 11
resistance **331** 84
resistor **147** 56, **206** 21
~* **129** 3
resonance box **303** 26
~ pendulum **331** 21
resonator **303** 78
resort **262** 1–49
respirator **17** 27
respiratory apparatus **17** 27
rest *[support]* **47** 60
~ *[teleph.]* **233** 29
~ *[Mus.]* **299** 22–29
restaurant **260**
~ car **204** 17
~ compartment **204** 18,52
rest cure **29** 21–25
resting rail **301** 42
restraining spring **233** 57
rest room **25** 15
result **326** 23
~-effacer **240** 52
~ register **240** 48
resuscitation apparatus **17** 27
~ equipment **255** 20
resuscitator **17** 27
retailer **98** 41
retaining lock **16** 69
~ wall for stowage **138** 17
reticella lace **101** 30
reticulated screen **171** 35
~ vault **318** 45
Reticulum **5** 48
retina **21** 49
retinoscope **109** 12
retort **333** 13
~-charging **148** 10
~-feeding **148** 10
~ furnace **148** 11
~ furnace house **148** 10–12
retouching desk **171** 28
~ tool **171** 51
retractable undercarriage **225** 51
retrievable rope **271** 5
retrieving **86** 36
~ winch **271** 6
return **40** 79, 80
~ chute **287** 16
~ cock **334** 49
~ conveyor **68** 64
~ pipe **40** 56
~ tap **334** 49
~ ticket **203** 48
Reuter lamp **331** 22, 28
rev-counter **207** 15
reveal **115** 10, 31
revel **113** 10, 31
revenue stamp **105** 21
reverberatory furnace **133** 1
reverse dive **268** 42
~ face **244** 10
~ grip **279** 54
~ shaft **142** 34
reversible warp-faced cord **165** 27
reversing **283** 31
~ light **186** 38
~ resistor **206** 21
~ rheostat **206** 21
~ screw **205** 58
revo-counter **228** 18
révoltade **288** 25
revolution-counter **159** 2, **207** 15
~ of moon **7** 1
~ regulator **106** 46
revolutions-per-minute indicator **228** 18
revolving die hammer **85** 43
~ disk **263** 31
~ dome **6** 8
~ flat card **156** 34
~ head **128** 26
~ nosepiece **110** 5
~ punch **123** 13
~ stage **297** 31
~ table **141** 36
~ table type shot **141** 34
~ tool box **143** 3
revue girl **298** 7
~ star **298** 4
~ theatre **298** 4–8
reward **86** 43
re-wind button **306** 24
re-winding **164** 50
re-winding· desk **295** 23
~ knob **111** 23
rewind plates **293** 32
rheostat **206** 21
~ f. control of light **171** 46
rhesus monkey **353** 12
rhinoceros **351** 25
Rhiptoglossa **350** 33
rhizome **60** 18
rhizopod **340** 1
rhododendron **362** 1
rhomb **328** 35
rhombic crystal system **330** 23
~ dodecahedron **330** 7
rhombohedron **330** 22
rhomboid **328** 36
rhombus **328** 35
Rhön wheel **287** 54
rib *[Anat.]* **19** 9, 10
~ *[Bot.]* **354** 29
~ *[Tech.]* **118** 36
~ *[ship]* **217** 55, **269** 49
ribbed vault **318** 43
ribbon **36** 41, **240** 14
~ cylinder **169** 35
~ of pigtail **35** 7
~ spool **240** 18
~ switch **240** 29
Ribes **60** 1-15
rib grass **364** 11
rib of violin **302** 4
ribwort (plantain) **364** 11
rice **69** 29, **98** 38
~ grain **69** 30
ricksha **336** 34
~ coolie **336** 35
rickshaw **336** 34
riddle **79** 13
ride *[riding]* **257** 42
~ *[forest]* **84** 1
rider **257** 42
ridge *[mountain]* **12** 36, **13** 60
~ *[roof]* **116** 2, **117** 93
~ board **116** 48
~ capping piece **117** 99
~ course **117** 47, 79
~-course tile **117** 4
~ cross **312** 10
~ of hills **13** 60
~ hook **117** 65
~ plough **68** 1
~ purlin **116** 43
~ roof **116** 1
~ tent **266** 27
~ tile **117** 3, 52
~ turret **116** 14
ridging hoe **66** 4
~ plough **68** 1
riding animal **337** 2
~ boot **272** 54
~ breeches **34** 27
~ cap **272** 50
~ horse **272** 47
~ jacket **272** 52
~ position **278** 14
~ saddle **72** 37–49
~ track **257** 41
~ whip **272** 53
riffler **127** 31, **168** 8
~ file **127** 31
rifle *[gun]* **86** 30, **87** 1–40

rifle *[barrel]* **87** 36
~ butt **87** 3
rifled gun barrel **87** 34
rifle range **291** 58
~-shotgun **87** 33
rifling **87** 36
riftvalley **12** 11
rig **214** 1–72
Rigel **5** 13
rigging *[sailing ship]* **214** 1–72, **226** 53, 56
~ line **228** 50
right *[Her.]* **246** 18, 20, 22
~ angle **328** 9, 32
~-angled triangle **328** 32
~ back **274** 13
~ cylinder **329** 38
~ full back **274** 13
~ half **274** 16
~ half-back **274** 16
~-hand projector **295** 14
~ leg forwards **278** 3
~ pedal **304** 8
rigid axle **183** 47
~ dirigible **226** 65
rim **130** 17, **180** 28, **185** 30
~ of gear wheel **136** 88, **180** 74
~ of lenses **108** 14
~less spectacles **108** 18
rind **354** 8
ring *[jewellery, etc.]* **38** 20, 24, 28, **107** 10, **350** 39
~ *[Geom.]* **328** 57
~ *[Sports]* **272** 5, **281** 32, **290** 21
~-a-ring-a-roses **258** 29
~ attendant **290** 27
~ cake **45** 29
ringed boletus **365** 21
~ snake **350** 38
~ worm **340** 16
ring entrance **290** 11
~ fence **290** 22
~ finger **21** 67
~ frame **157** 34
~ gauge **106** 25
~ horn **132** 22
~ of investiture **314** 58
ringlet **35** 2
ring master **290** 31
~ net **90** 25
~ pipe **140** 46
~-rounding tool **106** 26
rings *[Gymn.]* **279** 47
ring size gauge **106** 27
~ snake **350** 38
ring spanner **191** 16
~ spindle **157** 45
~ spinning frame **157** 34
rings of Saturn **7** 17
ring stand **48** 25
~ and traveller **157** 51
rink **284** 3
rinsing bath **262** 47
~ pipe **173** 6
~ sink **41** 20
~ tank **112** 2
~ water **41** 21
~ water casing **166** 4
rip cord **226** 54, **228** 55
~ panel **226** 54
ripper **196** 20
ripping chisel **322** 19
ripple **13** 41
~ marks **13** 41
riprap **211** 55
riser *[iron foundry]* **141** 23
~ *[stairs]* **118** 33, 48
rising gas pipe **119** 24
~ ground **13** 66
Rising Sun **245** 20
rising table **241** 4
ritual cart **309** 36
~ procession **312** 42–50
river *[stream]* **13** 61, **16** 45, **211**
~ *[tool]* **126** 11
~ arm **13** 2
~ bed **13** 68
~ bend **211** 42
~ branch* **13** 2
~ course **211** 42
~ dam **211** 49
~ engineering **211**
River Eridanus **5** 12
river ferry **211** 10
~ islet **211** 4
~ landscape **13** 1–13
~ mouth **13** 1
~ mussel **340** 31
~ outfall **13** 1
~ pier **210** 32
~ regulation **211** 31
~ tug **211** 23
~ valley **13** 57–70
~ works **211**
rivet **136** 55–58, **181** 31
~ head **136** 55
riveting **136** 54
~ hammer **134** 17
~ stand **107** 62
rivet point **136** 57
~ shank **136** 56
riving hammer **85** 26
~ knife **128** 7
road **194** 10, **253** 34
~ bridge **16** 55
~-building machine **197** 1
~-cleaner's barrow **195** 7
road clearance **189** 5
~ construction **197**
~ embankment **197** 35
~ engineering **197**
~-grader **196** 19
~ machine **196** 1-54
~-making **197**
~-making machine **196** 1–54
~-metal spreading machine **196** 31
~plow* **196** 20
~ race **273** 8–10
~ racer *[person]* **273** 8
~ racer *[vehicle]* **273** 16
~-racing bicycle **273** 16
~ roller **196** 36, 37, **197** 19
~-scarifier **196** 20
roadster *[bicycle]* **180** 1
~ *[motorcar]* **187** 11
road surface **212** 1
~ surfacing **210** 2
~-sweeper *[person]* **195** 8, **253** 47
~-sweeper *[mach.]* **195** 6, 12
~-sweeper's barrow **195** 7
~-sweeping machine **195** 12
~ trailer **208** 40
~way **194** 10, **210** 2, **253** 34
~ wheel **68** 40
roaring **86** 12
roasting drum **98** 71
roast meat **46** 27
robe **248** 27
~* **48** 55, 56
robes **311** 22, **313** 4
robin *[Zool.]* **346** 15
~ *[Bot.]* **360** 21
robinia **355** 70
robin redbreast **346** 15
Rob Roy **269** 4
rocaille **318** 13
rochet **314** 50
rock **13** 28, **307** 38
~ bit **139** 20
~ climber **282** 6
~-climbing **282** 2–14
~ drill **150** 11
rocker *[tool]* **323** 19
~ *[lever]* **182** 44
~ arm **184** 58
~ bearing **221** 62
~ switch **120** 4
rockery **39** 40, **54** 1
rocket **224** 53, **227** 46, 49, **229**, **289** 54
~ apparatus **224** 52+53
~ assembly tower **229** 32
rocket car **187** 18
~ combustion chamber **227** 60–63, **229** 22
~ control operating mechanism **229** 3
~-driven car **187** 18
~-driven model **271** 61
~ flight **229**
~ head **229** 2–5
~-launching **229** 28–31
~-launching platform **229** 29
~ motor **229** 12–24
~ nose **229** 2
~ power unit **229** 12–24
~ propulsion charge **227** 47
~ propulsive charge **227** 47
~ ready for launching **229** 28
~-stage **229** 36, 37
~ steering vane **229** 27
~ tail section **229** 12–27
rock face **150** 3, 15, **282** 3
~ garden **39** 40, **54** 1
rocking-duck **49** 15
~-horse **49** 13
~-seat **49** 15
~ tablet **305** 39
~ tool **323** 19
rock layer **13** 78
~ painting **309** 9
~ pile **150** 4
~ piton **282** 55
~ technique **282** 2–14
~ terrace **13** 47, 63
~ tomb **315** 38
~ wall **282** 3
Rococo ornament **318** 13
~ period **318** 9-13
~ wall **318** 9
rod **1** 39, **158** 54, **159** 54, **228** 36
rodent *n.* **351** 12–19
~ trap **83** 7–9
rod fisher **89** 7
~ fishing **89** 7–12
~ rest **89** 11
roe *[deer]* **88** 28–39
~ *[fish eggs]* **89** 66, 67
~ antlers **262** 27
~buck **88** 28
~ call **87** 43
~ deer **88** 28-39
roentgen apparatus **29** 39
~ film **2** 10, 13
~-like radiation **1** 17
~ therapy **29** 30–38
rogue **289** 38

roll *[bread]* **46** 21, **97** 37–40
~ *[cushion]* **48** 54
~ *[saddle]* **72** 48
~ *[Tech.]* **141** 49+50
~ basket **46** 20
~ of clay **322** 8
~ of cloth **256** 59
~ of crepe paper **104** 4
rolled-asphalt drying and mixing plant **196** 48
~ ham **96** 27
~ steel joist **136** 6
~ oats **98** 37
~ steel section **136** 3–7
roller *[Tech.]* **175** 7, **212** 65, **240** 10
~ *[Zool.]* **343** 24–29, **344** 6
~ bearings **223** 64
~ bit* **139** 20
~ chain **180** 36
~ dam **212** 65–72
~ guide **197** 4
~ hoist **113** 91
~-holder **174** 31
~ indicator **305** 37
~ lift **113** 91
~ postmark **231** 49
~ printing machine **162** 53
~ rail **202** 42
~ skate **287** 35
~ skate hockey **287** 33
~ skater **287** 34
~ skating **287** 33
~ squeegee **112** 37
~ stamp **231** 43
~-straightening machine **141** 72
~ table **141** 45
~ top **212** 66
~-type blotter **238** 19
~ weir **212** 65–72
rollfilm-winder **111** 4
roll front **238** 7
~-front cabinet **238** 5
~ of gauze **28** 11
~ of gauze bandage **17** 9
~ of gummed tape **238** 78
~ housing **141** 52
rolling chock **217** 44
~ mill **141**
~-mill case **141** 68
~-pin **42** 54, **97** 67
~ plant **151** 9
roll of material **256** 59
~ of matting **79** 6
~ of paper **175** 43
roll of postage stamps **231** 18
~ of steril bandage **28** 10
~ stand **141** 51–55
~ standard **141** 52
~ top **231** 15
Roman *[Typ.]* **325** 4
~ art **316** 53–60
roman capital letter **170** 11
Roman capitals **324** 16
~ Catholic church **311** 31–65
~ Catholic clergy **314** 32–58
Romanesque art **317** 1–21
~ cathedral **317** 1–13
~ church **317** 1–13
~ ornament **317** 14–16
~ vaulting system **317** 17
Roman lace **101** 30
~ man **338** 11
~ metal pen **324** 25
~ mythology **308**
~ numeral **326** 1
~ point **101** 30
roman small letter **170** 12
~ warship **213** 9-12
~ woman **338** 7
rompers **31** 19
roof *[house]* **40**, **116**, **117**
~ *[coach, etc.]* **179** 14, **183** 9
~ *[mine]* **138** 20
~ boarding **117** 61
~ cornice **40** 11
~ course **117** 78
~ disconnecting switch **206** 6
~ door **187** 30
roofed platform **199** 3
roof finish **40** 1
~ hook **40** 6
roofing **40** 1
~ felt **117** 62
~ tack **136** 53
roof ladder **40** 4, **117** 63
~ lock **183** 11
~ of mouth **21** 20
~ paper* **117** 62
~-slating **117** 76-82
~ stay **183** 10
~ timberwork **116** 27–83
~ trestle **117** 66
~ truss **115** 7, **116**
~ window **64** 50
rook *[Zool.]* **346** 2
~ *[chess]* **265** 12
room **45**, **48**, **259** 27–38
~ clerk* **259** 7
~ w. distorting mirrors **291** 55
roomette* **204** 15
room exit **39** 83
rooming house* **262** 22
room key **259** 9
~ number **259** 10
~ f. storing books **250** 11
~ telephone **259** 34
~ thermometer **23** 26
~ thermostat **40** 78
~ w. two beds **29** 8–20
~ waiter **259** 33
rooster* **74** 21, **75** 9
root *[Bot.]* **354** 16–18, 78–82
~ *[beet]* **69** 45
~ *[tooth]* **21** 36
~ *[Math.]* **327** 2, 3
~-cleaner **67** 33
~ crop **69** 38–45
~ crotch **85** 22
~ of curve **329** 12
~-cutter **67** 33
~ of dock **73** 34
rooter plow* **196** 20
root gall **81** 27
~ hairs **69** 18, **354** 18
~-leaf **359** 9, 15, 30
~ louse **81** 26
~ stock **60** 18
~ of tail **73** 34
~ thorn **354** 81
rope **125** 18, 19, **209** 21, **282** 13, 26-28
~ block **145** 20
~-climbing **279** 6
~ core **125** 23
roped crossing of a glacier **282** 23–25
~ party **282** 26–28
rope ferry **211** 1
~ heart **125** 23
~ ladder **216** 14, **290** 8
~maker **125**
ropemaker's spinning machine **125** 8
~ workshop **125** 1–18
rope-pulley hoist **113** 91
~-pulley lift **113** 91
ropes *[Box.]* **281** 33
rope sandal **100** 7
~ start* **271** 4
~-steering **285** 6
~ top **125** 16
~ walk **125** 1–18
ropeway **209** 15–24
~ gondola **209** 52
~ support **209** 76
rope yard **125** 1–18
roping **202** 13
rosace *[stovepipe]* **53** 52
rosary **313** 28, **314** 21
rose *[Bot.]* **55** 12, 13, 21, **62** 15, **361** 20
rose *[mus. instr.]* **301** 22, **303** 5
~ *[antlers]* **88** 5
~ *[shower]* **79** 28, **104** 38
~bay **357** 13
~bud **62** 16
~ bush **55** 13
~ laurel **357** 13
~ standard **55** 21
~ thorn **62** 18
~ tree **55** 21
rosette *[badge]* **289** 34
rose window **317** 23
rosin **302** 11
rostrum **250** 4, **251** 6
'rotaprint' sheet-fed machine **174** 33
rotary battery **159** 5
~ blower **141** 34
~ column sleeve **143** 26
~ counting mechanism **240** 43
~ cutter **177** 58
~ digester **167** 21
~ grab crane **148** 5
~ kiln **152** 8
~ line switch **233** 33
~ magazine **159** 5
~ magnet **233** 48
~ milling machine **162** 1
~-piston gas meter **148** 45
~-piston water meter **254** 53
~ press **162** 38
~ printing machine **175** 41
~ ratchet **233** 46
~ sand-spreader **195** 18
~ switch **120** 10, 11
~ swivel **139** 9
~ table **139** 14
~ veneer lathe **128** 52
~ wheel **68** 42
~ wing aircraft **226** 28
rotatable directional antenna **235** 5
rotating armour **223** 58-60
~ brush **162** 46
~ cage **162** 17
~ cylinder **166** 2
~ prism **200** 42
~ radar scanner **230** 40
~ shuttle **102** 38
~ table **177** 36
~ turret **143** 3
rotational mirror tower **230** 53
rotator **219** 32
rotogravure **176**
~ cylinder **176** 2
~ press **176** 27, 35
~ printing unit **176** 14

rotor-plane **226** 28
~ wheel **180** 9
~ wing **226** 29
rotunda **199** 6
Rouge **263** 24
rough *[Golf]* **276** 60
~ draft **321** 4
~ file **132** 35
~-grinding the corn (or grain) **91** 57
~ lumber* **115** 83
~-stemmed boletus **365** 22
~-turning tool **142** 43
~ wood **129** 21
roulette *[tool]* **123** 14, **323** 18
~ *[game]* **263**
~ *[table]* **263** 10
~ ball **263** 33
~ bowl **263** 29
~ plan **263** 9, 17
~ player **263** 15
~ table **263** 8, 17
~ wheel **263** 28
round *[rung]* **40** 17
~ *[canon]* **300** 46–48
~about traffic (flow) **252** 12
~ arch **318** 27
~ awl **123** 26
~ axe **126** 8
~ bar **136** 8
~-bar steel **114** 80
~ bed **54** 6
~ of beef **95** 14
~-bottomed flask **334** 38
~ bracket **325** 24
~ brush **121** 15, **321** 8
~ cage **290** 49
~ cake tin **42** 48
~ dance **258** 29
rounded end **136** 20, 48
~ stern **213** 25
rounders **275** 39–54
round game **258** 4
~-headed graver **323** 20
~-headed screw **136** 34
~house* **199** 6
~house track* **199** 9
rounding to **270** 52
round knife **123** 6
~ loaf **97** 26
~ mallet **124** 15
~ neck **32** 40
~ neckline **32** 40
~-nose pliers **120** 50
~ nut **136** 33
~ parentheses (or parenthesis) **325** 24
~ punch **134** 69
~ set hammer **132** 32
~ shave **126** 13
roundsman* **247** 1
round-tapered wing **225** 18
~ top of mountain **12** 35
~ tree **55** 16, **257** 12
~-trip ticket* **201** 55, **203** 48
~ trunk **115** 83
~ window **317** 12
~ wood **115** 35
~ worm **341** 20
route number **193** 22
~ plate **193** 23, **201** 34
router **128** 22
~ bit **128** 24
~ cutter **128** 24
route timekeeper **193** 37
rover **266** 40
roving **157** 29
rowan tree **355** 42
rowboat* **257** 51, **269** 9–15
row of books **47** 5
rowen* **65** 35-43
rower **269** 12
rowing **269** 1–66
~ barge **213** 1–6
~ boat **257** 51, **269** 9–15
~ instructor **269** 20
~ practice **269** 20-22
~ slave **213** 48
row of leaves **316** 25
~lock **269** 29, 41
~ of needles **160** 46, 47
~ of ports **215** 27
~ of pumps **190** 13
~ of seats **290** 15
royal game **265** 1–16
~ sail **214** 60
~ stay **214** 13
rubber *[india ~]* **249** 52
~ *[Baseb.]* **275** 43
~* *[boot]* **100** 27
~ animal **30** 41, **267** 33
~ arm bandage **23** 4
~ band **238** 75
~ bandage **23** 4
~ bath **30** 25
~ bladder **274** 52
~ blanket **162** 56
~-blanket cylinder **174** 18
~ block **180** 85
~ boot *[horse]* **272** 45
~ brush **52** 43
~-bulb blower **23** 3
~ cap **26** 45, **30** 48
~ cement **181** 3
~ compound **157** 11
~-covered cylinder **176** 20
~ cylinder **174** 9
~-driven model **271** 59
rubber expander **278** 50
~-foam sock **99** 7
~ heel **99** 56
~ hot-water bottle **23** 27
rubberised hair **124** 23
rubber ledge **264** 16
~ mallet **192** 17
~ operating glove **28** 20
~ nosing **43** 29
~ packing roll **204** 54
~ panties **30** 15
~ pedal **180** 78
~ printing blanket **174** 42
~ puncture roller **24** 5
~ ring **41** 68, **267** 32
~ roller **176** 25
rubbers* **100** 5
rubber sheet **30** 4, **171** 41
~ shoe **28** 22, **100** 5
~ solution **181** 3, **323** 49
~-sprung bogie **193** 5
~ square **30** 4
~ stamp **238** 22
~ stud **180** 84
~ suspension bogie **193** 5
~ syringe **30** 20
~ thread **271** 59
~ tire* **30** 36
~ tread **180** 85
~ tree **367** 33
~ truncheon **248** 10
~ tyre **30** 36
~ water-bottle **266** 16
~-wheeled farm-cart **64** 33
rubbing strake **221** 48
rubbish basket **253** 46
rubble **13** 29
ruche **37** 18
ruching* **37** 18
Rückpositiv **305** 5
rucksack **266** 42
~ f. hull **269** 65
rudder *[ship, etc.]* **223** 25, **269** 26, 51–53
~ *[aircr.]* **228** 42
~ bar **228** 37
~ blade **217** 66, **269** 53
~ pedal **228** 38
~ post **217** 67
~ stock **217** 65
~ yoke **269** 51
ruff **289** 20, **338** 52
ruffle *[ruche]* **37** 18
~ *[Tech.]* **159** 60
rug **48** 55
ruga **18** 41
rugby **275** 19–27
~ ball **275** 20
~ football **275** 19-27
rugger **275** 19-27
ruin **16** 72, **80** 20
ruins **80** 20
rule of three **327** 8-10
rule-of-three sum **327** 8-10
ruler **249** 67
ruling up table **173** 35
rum **98** 57
Rumania **14** 19
rumble seat* **185** 57, **187** 12
ruminant *n.* **351** 28-30
rummer **46** 87
rump *[Anat.]* **73** 31, **88** 20
~ *[meat]* **95** 35
~ bone **22** 59
~ piece **310** 88
~ steak **96** 20
run **285** 11
runabout* **183** 41
runch **63** 21
run-down **283** 9
~-down tower **283** 8
rune **324** 19
rung **40** 17, **279** 2
runic script **324** 19
runner *[Sports]* **280** 6
~ *[rail, etc.]* **92** 10, **225** 43, **285** 3
~ *[Foundry]* **141** 22
~ *[millstone]* **91** 22
~ *[carpet]* **48** 32
~ *[Bot.]* **57** 16, **60** 20
~ stone **167** 12
running **280** 1–28
~ chain **92** 17
~ gate **141** 22
~-line lever **199** 61
~ noose **335** 5
~ race **280** 1–28
~ rigging **214** 67–71, **226** 56
~ scroll **316** 39
~ shoe **280** 26
~ shorts **31** 13
~ surface **283** 37
~ through-vault **279** 44
~ title **178** 66
~-track sign **198** 79–86
~ twist **268** 44
~ vest **31** 12
~ wheel **209** 7
run-up board **287** 19
runway **84** 32, **230** 2, **287** 16
~* **86** 16
rush **130** 27, 28
rusk **97** 43
Russian cigarette **105** 16
~ cross **313** 51
~ Orthodox priest **314** 25
~ script **324** 20
rustication **317** 51
rustic work **317** 51
rusty-leaved rhododendron **362** 1

rutting mane **88** 27
~ season **86** 9–12
rye flour **97** 19
~ grass **63** 29

S

sabbaton **310** 55
saber* see sabre
sable *[Zool.]* **352** 15
~ *[Her.]* **246** 26
sabre **277** 34, 46, 63
~ fencer **277** 33
~ fencing **277** 33–38
~ glove **277** 35
~ helmet **277** 36
~ mask **277** 36
~ play **277** 33–38
sabreur **277** 33
sac *[Zool.]* **350** 25
~ *[Bot.]* **356** 45
sack **91** 66
~ barrow **202** 15
~ coat* **34** 2
~ of corn **83** 16
~-filling plant **91** 67
sacking **91** 67
sack race **258** 7
~ f. soot **40** 34
~ truck **202** 15
~-weighing plant **91** 67
sacrament **313** 24
sacramental wine **313** 27
sacrarium **311** 36
sacred building **319** 21
~ song *[symbol]* **308** 67
~ vessels **313** 33-48
~ vestments **314** 37
sacrificial bowl **308** 6
sacristan **311** 26, 62
sacristy **312** 13
~ door **311** 18
sacrum **19** 21, **22** 59
saddle *[horse]* **72** 17, 31, 37–49
~ *[bench]* **126** 22
~ *[vaulting horse]* **279** 35
~back roof **116** 1
~ bag **266** 23
~ blanket **72** 44
~-bottomed wagon **208** 23
~ bow **72** 38
~ bracket **183** 31
~ cloth **272** 17
~ cover **182** 19
~ fungus **365** 25
~ grip **183** 33
~ horse **272** 47
~ post **126** 19
~ post head **126** 20
saddler **123** 16
~* **272** 47
saddle roof **116** 1
saddler's hammer **123** 5
~ needle **123** 28–33
sadler's roulette **123** 14
~ tracing wheel **123** 14
~ treadle sewing machine **123** 23
~ workshop **123** 1–33
saddlery **123** 1–33
saddle seat **72** 37
~ springs **180** 23
safety belt **30** 12
~ catch **2** 40, **87** 8, 25
~ chain **38** 19, **119** 32
~ contact **206** 35
~ curtain **297** 24
~ dam **220** 62
~ device **178** 5
~ door chain **43** 32
~ glass lid **42** 23
~ hat **150** 10
~ helmet **150** 10, **183** 40
~ key **134** 52
~ net **290** 14
~ nut **180** 64
~-pin **37** 25, **102** 60
~ platform **139** 4
~ razor **51** 71
~ stop device **162** 19
safety strap **30** 12
~ switch **42** 25, **254** 46, **294** 9
~ tube **333** 7
~ valve **40** 70, **205** 3
safe vault **242** 4
saffron **363** 3
saggar **154** 2
Sagittarius **5** 37, **6** 40
sagittate **354** 37
sago **98** 39
~ palm **367** 58
~ tree **367** 58
sail *[boat]* **214, 215, 270, 284** 34
~ *[basket]* **130** 6
~ axle **91** 5
~boat* **215** 6–8, 9+10, **270** 1-10
~ f. folding boat **269** 62
sailing **270** 1–60
~ boat **270** 1–10
~ dinghy **270** 6–10
~ regatta **270** 51–60
~ ship **214, 215**
~ skate **284** 30
~ vessel **215**
~ before the wind **270** 56–58
sailor-blouse **31** 29
~-cap **31** 32
~-collar **31** 30
~-knot **31** 31
sailor's knot **125** 29
sailor-suit **31** 28
~ tie **31** 31
sailplaning **271** 1–23
sail top **91** 6
sainfoin **70** 10
saint **311** 46, **314** 7
St. Andrew's cross **313** 54
St. Anthony's cross **313** 53
St. Bernard (dog) **71** 38
saintfoin **70** 10
St. Peter's cross **313** 52
salad bowl **46** 23
salade **310** 61
salad fork **46** 68
~ oil **98** 24
~ plant **59** 36–42
~-server **46** 24
~ set **46** 24
~ spoon **46** 67
salamander **350** 22
salame **96** 13
salami **96** 13
sal-ammoniac block **119** 7
sales assistent **256** 18
sales·clerk* **98** 13 **256** 18, 63
~ counter **256** 42, 61
~girl* **98** 31 **256** 18, 63
~lady **256** 18, 63
~-lady* **98** 31
~woman **98** 31, **256** 18
salicional **305** 23–30
salient **310** 16
salina **16** 32, **262** 1–7
~ attendant **262** 5
saliva ejector **27** 8
sallow **355** 24
saloon *[motorcar]* **187** 8
~ *[Railw.]* **204** 50
~* *[inn]* **260** 1–29
~ car **204** 49
~ w. sliding roof **187** 8
salt **98** 40
Salta **265** 20
~ piece **265** 21
salted almond **45** 50
~ roll **97** 54
~ stick **97** 54
saltier **313** 54
saltire **313** 54
salt pot **45** 37
~ refinery **262** 1-7
~ shaker **45** 37
~ sticks* **45** 61
~ straws **45** 61
~ works **16** 32
salutation **239** 8
salvage inspector **224** 15
~ vessel **224** 5–8
~ of wrecks **224**
Salvation Army·band **257** 61
~ cadet **257** 63
~ soldier **257** 62
salvationist **257** 62
samara **355** 12
samovar **45** 49
sampan **336** 31
sample **231** 17
~ container **231** 17
~ of frames **122** 2
sample of frame wood **122** 2
~ saggar **154** 2
~ scoop **98** 72
~ seggar **154** 2
sampling of the beer **93** 10
samurai **336** 37
Sanctissimum **313** 33
sanctuary **311** 36
Sanctus bells **313** 43
sand **16** 6, **41** 27
sandal **100** 29, **266** 13
sand bag **211** 50, **279** 24
~ ballast **226** 61
~bed **118** 8
~ box **205** 14
~ bucket **258** 27
~-castle **267** 35
~-deflecting blade **195** 19
~ deposit **211** 52
sander control **193** 36, **206** 40
~ control lever **207** 20
sand-feeder **199** 54
~ glass **107** 48
sanding apparatus **195** 17
~ belt **128** 47
~ gear **205** 19, **206** 15
sanding gear· control **193** 36, **206** 40
~ control lever **207** 20
sanding machine **195** 17
~ pad **128** 48
~ shoe **128** 48
~ table **128** 49
sand lizard **350** 27
~ lorry **195** 16
~lot* **258** 26
~ pail **258** 27
~ paper **129** 25, **181** 7
~ pipe **141** 33
~ pit **258** 26
~-pump dredger **211** 59
~ spade **258** 28
~-spinner **195** 18
~-spreader **195** 5, 18
~ track **273** 24
~-track race **273** 24–28
~ tube **205** 15
sandwich **46** 37, 39
~ fork **46** 76
~ f. mid-morning break **249** 65
~ loaf **97** 27
~man on stilts **291** 49
sanitary napkin **23** 63
~ towel **23** 63
sanitation **195**
San-José scale **81** 35
Sanscrit **324** 9
sanserif (print) **325** 7
sap *[wood]* **115** 85
sapling **84** 10+11

selector shaft 233 43
selenium 234 30
~ rectifier 236 14
~ vapour rectifier 295 18
self-centering chuck 142 38
~-cocking gun 87 23
self-contained house 39 1–53
~ tractor 67 1
self-cooker 262 36
~-defence 281 15–17
~-defense* 281 15–17
~-discharger 208 17
~-discharging van 208 24
~-feeder 67 45, 75 8
~-feed hopper 75 8
~-heal 360 16
~-locking catch 75 26
~-recording barometer 10 4
~-recording rain gauge 10 42
~- recording thermometer 10 19
~-rescue 17 33
~-service snack bar 260 45-54
~-starter 227 26
~-timer 111 24, 37
~-timing release 111 37
~-watering trough 64 30
~-winding wrist watch 107 1
seller 253 5
selvage to selvage 102 7
~ tape 102 54
selvedge 159 11, 165 24
~ to selvedge 102 7
~ tape 102 54
semaphore type direction indicator 189 46
semi-automatic machine 143 1
~-balloon tyre 181 10
~-bold letter 170 3
semibreve 299 15
~ rest 299 23
semicircle 328 46
semi-circular arch 317 19, 318 27
~ steering wheel 183 52
semicircumference 328 46
semicolon 325 19
semi-detached house 39 69–71
~-dome 316 73
~-high wing monoplane* 225 19
seminal vesicle 22 77
semiquaver 299 19
~ rest 299 27
semi-rotary pump 212 47–52
semolina 98 36
sempstress 102 75
send a letter to my love 258 4
sender 232 36
sender's address 239 15
~ name 239 15
Sendzimir rolling mill 141 67
senna 364 16
~ leaves 364 16
sensitive altimeter 228 9
~ element 10 22
~ section 78 22
sepal 60 44, 354 58
separating funnel 333 3
~ tank 148 36+37
separation point 4 46
~ of the rockets 229 39-42
separator 167 5
~ check flap 68 63
~ pump 148 29
septum musculare ventriculorum cordis 22 52
sepulchral monument 312 26
sequestrum forceps 28 52
serial number of bond 243 13
series [Math.] 327 11, 12
~ compressors 227 27
~ of pig moulds 140 35
~ resistance 236 8
~ topographic camera 15 63
Serpens 5 20
Serpent 5 20
serpent [Zool.] 350 38–41
~ [mus. instr.] 301 12
~ foot 307 39
serpentine [Skat.] 284 14
serpent's body 307 2
~ tail 307 31
serrate 354 44
serratus anterior 20 42
serum 26 32
servant 179 20
server [impl.] 45 24, 97 32
~ [Sports] 276 16, 45
~ [Church] 311 52
service [Sports] 276 17
~ area 276 44
~ bell plate 259 28
~ brake* 182 16, 185 40
~ bridge 212 72
service court 276 12
~ gangway 212 72
~ hatch 248 16
~ line 276 6 to 7
~ pipe 148 53+54
~ reservoir 254 18
serviette 46 9
~ ring 46 10
serving the ball 276 50+51
~ hatch 45 62
~ spoon 46 74
~ tray 261 14
~ trolley 46 32
sesame plant 367 45
sesquiplane 225 4
set [assortment] 46 24, 286 26, 297 35
~ [Film, etc.] 237 10, 292 33
~ [Bot.] 57 20
seta 359 33
set of bells 286 26
~ of carvers 46 69+70
~ collar 136 31
~-designer 296 37
~ of filters 172 6
~ of flags 245 22–34
~ of floodlights 199 46
~ hammer 132 31
~ head 136 55
~ of hooks 89 34
setiferous animal 74 9
set of machines 241 40–61
~ of mathematical instruments 144 28–48
~ of pearls 38 12
~ piece 296 30, 297 47
~ of points 199 15
~ of pulleys 216 4, 331 3
~ of rollers 141 49+50
~ of rolls 141 49+50
~ of saw blades 149 3
~ screw 111 35
~ of spindles 125 8
S. E. Trades 9 49
set square 144 5
~ of stones 91 21
~ of taut strings 276 29
sett 194 12
set table 46
~ of teeth 21 16–18
settee-bed 47 46
setter 71 41
~-combination 305 46
setting [jewellery] 38 25
~ [scene] 296 2
~ back 113 61
~ lever 240 46
~ lotion 103 29
~ mechanism 240 47
~ of offshoots 57 18
setting rule 169 14
~ stick 169 13
settling tank 252 65
seven-headed dragon 307 50
seventh [Mus.] 300 25
~ [chord] 300 18
seven-unit day-service diesel train 207 37
~-yard line 275 10
sewage disposal works 252 64
~ farm 252 66
~ lorry 195 34
~ purification works 252 64
~ treatment works 262 64
~ waters 194 36
~ works 252 64
sewer 194 36
sewing [book] 177 34
~ awl 99 62, 123 32
~ box 102 74
~ clip 124 7
~ cord 177 10
~ frame 177 9
~ machine 102 14–47
~ machine [electr.] 102 14-40
sewing machine cabinet 102 13
~ case 102 49
~ cover 102 40
~ light 102 47
~ needle 102 55, 56
sewing needle holder 178 21
~ saddle 178 24
~ silk 102 50
~ table 102 46
~ tape 177 10
~ thread 102 21
~ wax 99 16
sewn book 177 32
sextant 219 1
sexton 311 26, 62
sexual organs [female] 22 79–88
~ organs [male] 22 66–77
sgraffito drawing 321 41
shackle 185 24
~ insulator 234 23
shaddock 368 23
shade [shield] 276 35
~* [shutter] 39 28
~* [Theatre] 297 24
~ guide* 39 29
shader 79 6
shadow puppets 298 28
~ roll 272 43
~ show 298 28
shaft [column] 317 35
~ [thill] 72 21, 179 19, 30
~ [screw] 136 59

shaft *[Weav.]* **159** 4
~ bracket **218** 53
~ chain **72** 20
~ circuit f. empty tubs **138** 3
~ furnace **140** 1
~ hood **226** 72
~ horse **179** 28
~ kiln **153** 12
~ landing **137** 27, **138** 1
~ f. selvedge **165** 20
~ sinking **138** 27
~ trunk **218** 56
~ tunnel **218** 56
shaker *[cocktail~]* **47** 40, **259** 61
~ *[Tech.]* **67** 46
~ shaft **67** 53
shake without turn **300** 31
shako **247** 3
shale* **323** 57
shallot **305** 18
shallow bog **13** 14
~-bowled champagne glass **46** 86
~ ground **219** 62, 72
~ pool **268** 21
shallows **219** 62, 72
~ limit **16** 9
shallow water **219** 62, 72
shaman **336** 24
shambles **94** 11–15
shammy **52** 28
shampoo **104** 15
shamrock **70** 1
shank *[Anat.]* **18** 52
~ *[meat]* **95** 14, 33
~ *[screw]* **136** 15, **141** 24
~ *[shoe]* **99** 53
~-end mill **143** 17
shape gauge **155** 19
shaper* **143** 52
shaping hammer **106** 41
~ machine **128** 22, **143** 52
'shard' **154** 21
share *[plough]* **68** 7
~ *[security]* **243** 11-19
~ of stock* **243** 18
~ warrant **243** 11
shark **350** 1
sharp *[Mus.]* **299** 51
~* *[expert]* **248** 36
sharpening steel **96** 30
sharpers' marks **247** 25
shave *[tool]* **126** 13, 14+15
~ *[beard]* **35** 25
shaving *[beard]* **104** 11
~ *[wood]* **115** 80
~ brush **104** 35
~ cream **51** 70
~ dish **104** 23
~-horse **126** 18
~ mirror **51** 81
shavings **127** 47, **129** 26
~ container **240** 72
shaving soap **51** 69, **104** 21
shawl collar **32** 20
shawm **301** 13
sheaf **65** 23
~ tie band **65** 24
shearing blade **162** 44
~ cylinder **162** 44
shears **119** 2
she-ass **74** 3
sheat fish **350** 12
sheath **69** 9, 21
sheathing board **114** 76
~ of supports **114** 73
sheath-knife **266** 46
shed *[hut]* **53** 47, **113** 48
~ *[Weav.]* **159** 40
shedding tappet **159** 57
shed f. electric locomotives **199** 18
~ entrance **221** 30
~ foreman **221** 22
she-dog **74** 16
shed platform **202** 24
sheep **74** 13
~ dog **71** 31
~ pen **64** 47
sheep's fescue **70** 24
sheepskin cap **336** 23
sheeps-wool quilt **48** 11
sheer·strake **217** 41
~wale **217** 41
sheet **48** 9, **141** 70, **214** 68, **239** 21
~ bronze **309** 34
~ cloud **8** 3, 4, 8, 9, 10
~-counter **175** 54, **241** 8
~ feed board **174** 22
~-feeder **174** 3, **175** 5
~ feed mechanism **174** 23
~ feed table **178** 9
~ glass **122** 5
~-glass manufacture **155** 1-11
sheeting-carrier **114** 78
~ support **114** 86
sheet-lightning **9** 39
~-metal casing **183** 34
~ of lined paper **249** 40
~ of writing paper **239** 1
~ pile **174** 2
~-pile bulkhead **114** 17, **212** 5
~ piling **114** 17
~ of postage stamps **231** 14
~ roller **106** 1
~ steel **141** 70
sheet-steel casing **181** 47
sheet wall **114** 17, **212** 5
~ writer **241** 32
~ of yarn **158** 55
she-fox **88** 42
shelf **250** 12, 15
~ *[shallows]* **219** 62, 72
~ f. bottles **260** 10
~ f. glasses **260** 9
~ f. magazines **250** 15
shell *[egg]* **75** 48
~ *[foil]* **277** 57
~* *[boat]* **269** 16, 63
~-built boat **269** 9
~ hoist **223** 70
~-like structure **11** 1–5
~ membrane **75** 49
~ plating **217** 41–46
~ trumpet **307** 41
shelter **193** 7
shepherd bird **346** 4
shepherd's-clock **70** 28
~-club **360** 9
~ flute **301** 2
~ god **308** 40
~-purse **63** 9
shield *[protection]* **3** 1, **135** 26
~ *[Her.]* **246** 5
~ *[wild boar]* **88** 55
~ *[chivalry]* **310** 57
~* *[badge]* **247** 24
~-budding **57** 30
~ fern **361** 16
shielding **236** 23
shield(ing) against radiation **3** 1
shield volcano **11** 13
shifting gauge **145** 30
~ keel **270** 10
~ spanner **119** 53
shift key **240** 26
~ lock **240** 27
shilling **244** 13, 37
shin *[meat]* **95** 28
~ bone **19** 25
shingle **117** 48
shingled hair **35** 34
shinny **275** 9–18
shin pad **274** 30, **284** 40
shinty **275** 9–18
ship **214–216, 218, 222, 223, 226** 65
~* **226**
Ship Argo **5** 45
ship·building **217**
~-building hangar **217** 3+4
~ chamber **212** 33
~ channel **211** 21
~ under construction **217** 26
~ drive **218** 58-64
~ elevator* **212** 29-38
shiplapped lumber* **115** 88
ship lift **212** 29-38
~ of the line **213** 51–60
~ run aground **224** 47
ship's kitchen **218** 37
~ library **218** 25
~ parts **217** 41–58
ship screw **217** 69
~ siren **218** 3
ship·wreck **224** 47
~wrecked man **224** 46
~yard **217** 1–40
shirt **33** 36, 39, 41
~ blouse **32** 6
~ bosom* **33** 42
~ button **33** 52
~ collar **33** 51
~ front **33** 42
~ sleeve **33** 43
~waist* **32** 6, **33** 9
Shiva **319** 19
shoal **219** 62, 72
shoat* **74** 9, **76** 40
shock *[Agr.]* **65** 21, 22
~-absorber **185** 29
shoe **100**
~ *[Tech.]* **114** 50
~ *[windmill]* **91** 14
~black **200** 11
~ brake **136** 95
~ brush **52** 40–43
~ buckle **100** 38
~-button hook **100** 10
~ clasp **38** 10
~-cleaner **200** 11
shoe-cleaning· cupboard **52** 26
~ foot rest * **200** 12
~ stool **200** 12
shoeing hammer **132** 42
shoe·horn **100** 17, 19
~ knife **99** 60
~maker **99** 23
shoemaker's apprentice **99** 13
~ globe **99** 25
~ stool **99** 14
~ workshop **99** 1-37
shoe ornament **38** 10
~-polish **52** 38
shoeshine* **52** 38
~ boy* **200** 11
shoeshining cupboard* **52** 26
~ stool* **200** 12
shoe sock **99** 4
~ sole **99** 50+51
~-stretcher **52** 46, **99** 20
~string* **99** 47
~-tree **52** 46
shoot *[Bot.]* **57** 37, **354** 19–25
~ *[preserves]* **86** 1–8
~ *[Sledg.]* **285** 11
~* *[slide]* **286** 17

shooting *[hunting]* **86** 1–52
~ *[Film]* **292** 26-61
~ brake **189** 2
~ cutting **57** 24
~ distance **86** 15
~ gallery **291** 58
~ fr. high stand **86** 14–17
~ hut **86** 51
~ in rutting season **86** 9–12
~ script **292** 45
~ shelter **86** 51
~ stand **86** 14
~ star **7** 28
~-stick **86** 10
shop **98, 127** 1-65
~ assistant **98** 31, **256** 18
~ counter **79** 44
~keeper **98** 41
~ mincer **96** 4
shopper **253** 12
shopping bag **52** 48, **253** 13
shop traveller **145** 1
~ walker **256** 33
~ window **98** 1
shore **13** 4
short cape **338** 29
~-distance racer **273** 8
~ doublet **338** 41
shortening* **98** 23
shorthand **325** 13
~ note-book **238** 11
~ typist **238** 10
~ writer **238** 10
short jerkin **338** 45
~ line **90** 29
~ moustache **35** 26
~ pace **72** 2
~ pants **33** 56
~ pipe **105** 33
~-range light **185** 17
~ rifle **86** 30
shorts **31** 54, **266** 9
short sleeve **32** 32
~-stroke planing machine **143** 52
~ title **178** 44
~ wave **4** 22
short-wave· apparatus **24** 12
~ range **234** 37
~ therapy **24** 12
~ transmitter **10** 62
shot **89** 47
~ *[weight]* **280** 46
shote* **74** 9, **76** 40
shot·firer **150** 25
~ gun **86** 4, **87** 33
~ number **292** 35
shoulder *[Anat.]* **18** 22
~ *[street)** **197** 47
~ *[meat]* **95** 5, 9
~ *[Geol.]* **12** 41
~ *[Tech.]* **269** 46
~ *[letter]* **170** 40
~ bag **249** 69
shoulder blade **18** 23, **19** 7, **73** 18
~ camera **294** 22
shouldered arch **318** 33
~ bucket **309** 34
shoulder girdle **19** 6+7
~ height *[letter]* **170** 45
~ iron **40** 33
~-length hair **35** 27
~ pad **102** 80, **275** 30
~ stand **278** 29
~-strap **33** 12, **249** 45, 70
shovel *[coal ~]* **40** 43
~ *[excavator]* **196** 1
~ *[deer]** **88** 40
~-type excavator **196** 1
~* **113** 82
show **298** 29–40
~case **98** 3, **249** 18
shower *[rain]* **8** 19, **9** 37
~ *[bath]* **268** 2
~ bath **25** 1, **268** 2
~ cabinet **51** 14
~ rose **104** 38
showers **25** 1
shower tray **51** 17
show of goods **98** 1
~ jumping **272** 31-34
~man **291** 10
~man's caravan **202** 26
~ pipe **305** 1-3
~ window **98** 1, **253** 41
shredder **96** 39
shredding **163** 6
shrew **351** 7
~mouse **351** 7
shroud **214** 16
shrub **54** 4
shrubbery **84** 5
shrub-sprayer **58** 8
shrunken head **335** 30
shuck* **340** 30
shunting engine **202** 46
~ locomotive **202** 46, **206** 59
~ platform **220** 49
~ yard **202** 44–54
shutter **111** 44
~ catch **39** 31
shuttering **114** 11, 54–76
~ strut **114** 13
shutter opening **145** 64, **286** 11
~ release **111** 5
~ setting scale **111** 12
~-type dark slide **171** 5
~ f. ventilation **93** 4
shut-off valve **339** 30
shuttle *[Weav.]* **159** 25
~ *[game]* **258** 46
~ aerial ropeway* **209** 25
~ armature **331** 78
~ box **159** 9
~ car* **209** 28
~cock **258** 45, 46, **276** 37
~ eye **159** 29
Siamese script **324** 10
sickle **58** 28, 29, **66** 25
~-shaped tail **74** 25
sick-nursing **23, 24**
side *[body]* **18** 32
~ *[Tech.]* **136** 2, **318** 40
~ *[Geom.]* **328** 26
~ *[spectacles]* **108** 16
~ altar **311** 45
~ armour **222** 57, **223** 60
~ of bacon **96** 11
~ of bed **48** 5
~ board *[planking]* **118** 10
sideboard *[cupboard]* **45** 42, 57, **46** 44
sideboards *[beard]* **35** 24
side building **53** 1
~ buntline **213** 36
~-burns* **35** 24
sidecar **182** 60, **183** 3
~ body **182** 62
~ bumper **182** 63
side cargo battens **217** 59
sidecar wheel **182** 64
~ windscreen **182** 66
side-comb **103** 36
~ corridor **204** 10
~ cutting pliers **192** 15
~ discharger **208** 19
~ drop-cloth **297** 11
~ drum **302** 51, **303** 48
~ drums **303** 57
~ elevation **144** 61
~ entrance **312** 15, **317** 13
~ of excavation **113** 72
~ of fourth **277** 12
~ frame **160** 20
~ gate **64** 2
~ girder **217** 49
~ light **182** 65, **218** 15
~ line **275** 9, **276** 2 to 3, 4 to 5
~ log **85** 11
~ nacelle **226** 76
~ note **178** 68
~ parting **35** 13
~ plank **131** 16
~-plate **45** 9, **181** 30, **212** 67
~-plate unit **181** 30 + 31
side platform **202** 24
~ pocket **34** 14
~ port **216** 43
~ rail **40** 16
~rite **7** 29
~ root **354** 17
~ rudder **213** 6
~ shoot **60** 20, **354** 21
~-show **291** 24
~ shutter **114** 55
~ snow-sweeper **195** 15
~-step **179** 13, **283** 24
~ stop **196** 34, 44
~ of storage bin **196** 35
~ strake **217** 42
~ street **194** 2, **253** 7
~ stringer **217** 47
~ stroke **268** 37
~ support position *[Gymn.]* **278** 18
~ swivel door **208** 3
~ tank **217** 34
~ of third **277** 11
~ trappings **72** 16
~ unit **195** 15
~ valve **184** 1–36
~-valve single-cylinder four-stroke motor **182** 61
~ vault **279** 51
~ view **144** 61
~ viewfinder **294** 17
~ of violin **302** 4
~walk* **39** 60, **194** 6, **195** 4
~ways lunge **278** 20
~ wall **212** 80
~-whiskers **35** 11, 24
siding *[track]* **199** 27, 29
sidings *[yard]* **202** 44–54
Siemens electric low-shaft furnace **140** 44–47
~ open hearth furnace **140** 20-29
sieve **77** 34–36
~ plate **333** 12
sifter **42** 52, **91** 26
sight *[scope]* **87** 29
~ graticule **87** 31, 32
sighting arrangement **87** 65
sights *[gun]* **87** 65, **90** 57
sight-scale division **87** 68
~seeing car* **179** 33
~ testing chart **26** 1
sign **6** 21-31, 32-43, **326** 15, 23, **327** 16
~ of accentuation **300** 40
signal *[Railway]* **199** 37-39, 41

signal *[index card]* **238** 74
~ bell **198** 69
~ box **16** 24, **199** 56, 64
~ f. customs officer **245** 37
~ disk **201** 41
~ f. doctor **245** 27
~ flag **201** 40, **245** 22–34
~ gantry **199** 17
~ halyards **218** 10
~ hooter **255** 7
~ horn **198** 10, **255** 7
signaling* see signalling **218** 7
signal knob **199** 65
~ lamp **224** 41, **241** 47
~ lever **199** 59
signalling lamp **218** 7
~ whistle **203** 16
signal·man **198** 70
~ mast **220** 5
~ plant **199** 56-72
~ stick **201** 40
signature *[hand-written]* **239** 12
~ *[book]* **177** 37
~ of chairman **243** 15
~ mark **178** 69
signboard **79** 41, **113** 45
sign of division **326** 15
~ raising a note **299** 51+52
signet ring **38** 28
sign of identity **327** 16
~ of increase in length **299** 9
~ of relative intensity **300** 55–61
~ lowering a note **299** 53+54
~ of parallelism **327** 21
~ of planet **6** 21–31
~ post **16** 110
~ raising a note **299** 51, 52, 56, 57
~ of similarity **327** 22
~ of zodiac **6** 32–43
sikhara **319** 26
sikra **319** 26
silencer **182** 8, 42, **185** 62
~ f. noise abatment* **182** 42
siliceous skeleton **340** 8
siliqua **63** 20, **367** 4
silk band **36** 41
~ blouse **272** 57
~ cap **272** 57
~-cotton tree **367** 20
silk hat **36** 20, 48
~ moth **342** 48
~ ribbon **36** 41
~ stocking **33** 32
~ suture **28** 51
silkworm **342** 50
~ moth **342** 48
sill *[window]* **113** 12
~ *[Geol.]* **11** 31
~ *[boat]* **269** 59
~ rail **115** 56
silo **64** 45
~ bin **220** 45
silver *[Her.]* **246** 25
~ coin **244** 1–28
~ disk **10** 49
~-disk pyrheliometer **10** 48
~ embroidery **338** 67
~ fir **356** 1
~ fish **341** 15
~ owl **347** 17
~ screen* **295** 11
~side **95** 34
~ thaw* **286** 19
~ware drawer* **41** 9
~ wire **106** 3
similarity **327** 22
similar to **327** 22
simple condenser **331** 23
~ equation **327** 4
~ eye **78** 2
~ interest formula **327** 7
~ mortice **116** 84
~ mortise **116** 84
~ proportion **327** 8—10
~ tie **116** 49
simsim **367** 45
simultaneous equation **327** 4
Sinaic script **324** 13
Sinaitic script **324** 13
singer **296** 22
singing-bird **346** 1–20
single-axle trailer **189** 35
~-bed cabin **218** 41
~ box **76** 7
~-breasted suit **34** 13
~ cabin **218** 41
~ cell **248** 11
~-celled animal **340** 1–12
~-colour offset machine **174** 1, 14
~ consignments **202** 4
~-cut cow grass **70** 1
~-cylinder engine **181** 49
~-cylinder four-stroke motor **182** 61
~-decker **188** 5
~-decker bus **188** 5
single-engined aircraft **226** 1
single-engined propeller-turbine aircraft **226** 9
~ flower **355** 26, **362** 47
~-handed fishing rod **89** 20
~-letter composing machine **169** 32-45
~-masted sailing boat **215** 6–8
~ paddle **269** 34
~-picture counter **294** 14
~ quotation mark **325** 27
singles **276** 4 to 5
single sculler **269** 16
~-seater folding boat **269** 54
singles game **276** 4 to 5
single skiff **269** 18
~-slide carburetter **183** 53–69
~-stem fruit tree **55** 2
single-track main line **199** 26
single window **39** 23
~ yarn **125** 21
sinister *[Her.]* **246** 19, 21, 23
sink *[kitchen]* **41** 17, 22
sinker *[lead]* **89** 46+47
~* *[doughnut]* **97** 7
sink hole **13** 71
sinking bucket **138** 29
~ kibble **138** 29
sinking **138** 27
~ platform **138** 31
~ team **138** 36
sinningia **56** 7
sinter terraces **11** 23
sinuate **354** 48
sinuous **354** 48
siphon **47** 41
~ barometer **10** 1
~ bottle **47** 41
~-tube **10** 47
sire **74** 2
Siren **307** 58
siren *[Techn.]* **145** 69, **218** 3, **255** 4
Sirenia **351** 23
Sirius **5** 14
sirloin **95** 17
sisal mat **44** 15
siskin **346** 8
sissonne **288** 26
sister *[Hospital]* **29** 18
sit-down bath **51** 50
site **113, 114**
~ office **113** 48
sitting hen **75** 17
~ room **44**
situla **309** 34
Siva **319** 19
six-day· race **273** 2–7
~ racer **273** 2
six-eight time **299** 36
~-engined aircraft **226** 8
six-faced polyhedron **330** 2
~-four time **299** 37
~-sided polygon **330** 15
sixth *[Mus.]* **300** 24
size *[dimension]* **274** 24
~ *[glue]* **121** 31, **158** 44
~ box **158** 45
sized yarn **158** 57
size of field **274** 24
~ of types **170** 18
sizing machine **158** 40
~ plansifter **91** 59
skate **284** 25–32
~ blade hollow moulding **284** 26
~ key **284** 27
skater **284** 4
skate-sailing **284** 33
~ f. skate-sailing **284** 30
skating **284** 1–32
~ boot **284** 31
~ jump **284** 6
~ rink **284** 3
~ step **283** 28
skein **161** 29
~-carrier **161** 27–30
~ dyeing machine **161** 20
skeleton **19** 1–29
~ key **134** 10
~ sledge **285** 18
~ structure **114** 1
skene **316** 45
skep *[hive]* **78** 52
sketch **321** 4
~ block* **321** 35
~ f. costume **296** 39+40
sketching block **321** 35
~ easel **321** 26
skewer **123** 28
skew notch **116** 90
ski *[Sports]* **283** 35-41
~* *[aircr.]* **271** 33
skiagraphy **29** 39
skiascope **109** 12
ski-binding **283** 45–50
~ boot **283** 55-57
~ crampon **283** 51
skid **225** 6
~ mark **253** 62
skier **283** 30
~ leaning forward **283** 18
skiff **269** 18
ski-hoist **209** 15, **283** 2
~ hut **283** 6
skiing **283** 1–34
~ boot **283** 55–57
~ cap **36** 26
~ outfit **283** 35–58
~ trousers **31** 44

slops **338** 34
slot *[slit]* **136** 47
~ *[Hunt.]* **86** 8
~ *[organ]* **305** 30
~ f. insertion **169** 48
~ forging furnace **133** 1
sloth **351** 11
slot machine **253** 50, **260** 48
~ milling tool **143** 16
~ mortiser **128** 32
slotted board **2** 45
~ wing **225** 58
slot f. weft feeler **159** 32
slouch hat **36** 9
slowing-down layer of graphite **1** 26
slow-motion camera **294** 28
slow-running· air jet **183** 59
~ vent **183** 58
slow train **203** 1
~ worm **350** 37
slubber tenter **157** 24
slubbing bobbin **157** 23
~ frame **157** 19
slub-catching device **158** 13
sludge bucket **195** 27
~ cone **11** 51
sludger **195** 25
'slug' of clay **154** 9, 10
sluice **212** 77
~ dam **212** 73–80
~ gate **212** 77
~-gate house **212** 42, 63
~ valve **212** 53–56
~-valve house **212** 42, 63
~way **212** 56, 62
~ weir **212** 73–80
slumber robe* **48** 56
small arm **87** 2
~ of back **18** 25
~ bus **188** 1
~ of butt **87** 7
~ cabbage white butterfly **81** 48
~ cabin **209** 20
~ cabin cableway **209** 19
~ capital **170** 14
~ cart **53** 49, **209** 19
~ car cableway **209** 19
~-cattle pen **202** 7
~ child **49** 26
~ cigar **105** 3
~ ermine **81** 5
~ garden **55** 1–31
~ holding **64** 1–60
~ Host **313** 46
~ intestine **22** 14–16
~ lamp **26** 51
~ letter **170** 12
~ lorry **189** 1–13
~ mask **289** 13
small moth **60** 62
~ moth's caterpillar **60** 64
~ octave **300** 65
~ parcel **231** 6
~ platform lorry **189** 10
~ punching ball **281** 20
small-shot·barrels **87** 27
~ cartridge **87** 49
~ charge **87** 51
~ round **87** 49
small soft hat **36** 28
~ sugar basin **261** 20
~ tart **45** 10
~ town **252** 1–70
~ van **189** 1–13
smash **276** 34
smash-up **253** 58–69
smelter **141** 7
smelting furnace **141** 1, **172** 19
~ head **164** 41
~ operations **141** 1–12
~ section **140** 8
smith **132** 10
smith's assistant **132** 13
~ hammer **132** 15
smithy **132** 1–42
~ chimney **132** 5
~ fire **132** 5
~ hearth **132** 5
smock windmill **91** 29
smoke *[cigarette]* **105** 14
~ box door **205** 26
~ cloud **4** 4
~-consumer **47** 30
smoked meat **96** 12
smoke flap **335** 9
~ hood **132** 6
smokeless powder **87** 53
smoke outlet **199** 11, **205** 22, **336** 21
smoker *[Railw.]* **203** 27
smoker's companion *[fam.]* **105** 40
smokers' requisite **105** 40
smoke stack **145** 48
~ stack cap **222** 40
~ tube **205** 8
smoking-cap **36** 5
~ chamber **96** 47
~ compartment **203** 27
~-jacket **34** 47, **47** 56
~ requisite **105**
~ table **47** 21
smoother **121** 38
smoothing blade **196** 18
~ brush **121** 13
~ choke **236** 19
smoothing hammer **132** 31
~ plane **127** 52
~ screed **197** 14
~-shaven face **35** 25
smuggled goods **247** 17
smuggler **247** 16
snack bar **260** 45–54
snag* **88** 10
snail **340** 25
snail shell **340** 27
snail's horn **340** 29
~ tentacle **340** 29
snaithe **66** 16
snake **350** 38–41
~ brooch **309** 28
~-charmer **336** 45
~ root **360** 10
snakeskin shoe **100** 33
snake weed **360** 10
snap *[button]* **37** 20
~ bean* **59** 8
~-fastener **37** 20
~ gage* **142** 49
~ hammer **132** 12
~ head die **132** 12
~ lid **23** 17
~link **282** 56
snapping beetle **81** 37
snap set **132** 12
snare drum **302** 51, **303** 48
snatch **281** 2
sneaker* **278** 48
snipe **88** 83
snippet **102** 81
snips **119** 1
~ f. cutting holes **119** 33
snorkel **223** 11, **267** 39
snort **223** 11
snout **74** 10, **88** 53, **350** 2
snow **9** 34
snowball **286** 15
~ fight **286** 14
~ tree **357** 10
snow·bell **362** 3
snow-blowing machine **195** 21
~ bridge **282** 25
~ chain **286** 9
snow-clearing· machine **208** 43
~ machinery **195** 1-40
snow cornice **282** 21
~drift **286** 5
~drop **62** 1
~fall **8** 18, **286** 4
~ fence **286** 6
~flower **62** 1
~ goggles **282** 19
~ guard **40** 8
~ guard hook **117** 16
~-handling equipment **195** 1–40
~ hut **336** 4
~ and ice climbing **282** 15-22
~-loader **195** 13
snow-loading lorry **195** 13
~-loading truck* **195** 13
~man **286** 12
~ paling **286** 6
~ plough *[mach.]* **195** 1–40
~-plough *[skiing]* **283** 20
~plow* **195** 1–40, **283** 20
~ push **286** 23
~ scooter **286** 16
~shoe **286** 13
~ shovel **286** 23
~ slope **282** 15
~ sport **285** 5–20
~storm **286** 4
~ vent **195** 24
snubber* **185** 29
snuff **105** 24
~ box **105** 24
snuffers **47** 29
soaking pit **141** 41
~ pit crane **141** 42
~ tank **153** 23
~ tub **130** 13
soap **30** 22
~-box orator **257** 49
~ dish **30** 22, **104** 34
~-dish recess **51** 10
~-powder **53** 55
soaring **271** 1–23
~ field* **271** 38
~ flight **271** 10
~ instructor **271** 29
~ pilot **271** 29
~ site **271** 38
soccer **274** 1
social class *[bees]* **78** 1, 4+5
sock *[stocking]* **31** 39, 56, **33** 62, 64, 65
socket **120** 5, **235**
~ f. accessories **111** 21
sock-suspender **33** 63
~ top **33** 65
soda **41** 28
~ water **47** 41, **98** 87
sodium **3** 19
~ chloride **164** 13
~ graphite reactor **3** 17–19
sofa **318** 17
~-bed **47** 46
~ cushion **44** 2
soffit *[roof]* **117** 27
soft animal **49** 5-29
~ball **275** 39–54
~ broom **52** 20
~ collar **33** 37
~ corn **69** 31
softener **121** 20
soft felt hat **36** 19
~ fruit **60** 1–30
softies* **48** 34
soft-lead core **87** 56
~ money **244** 29–39
~ palate **21** 21
~ pedal **304** 9
~ roe **89** 66

speaking membrane **200** 38
~-tube appliance **198** 76
~ window membrane **200** 38
spear* *[Nav.]* **219** 74
~-head **309** 2
~ thrower **335** 40, **336** 9
special bib tap **119** 35
~ bicycle **181** 15
~ camera **294** 28–35
~-delivery letter **232** 34
~ drilling machine **170** 49
~ issue **232** 21
specialist **26** 12, **248** 36
special postmark **231** 51
~ vessel **216** 40
specie **244** 1–28
specimen **26** 3, **249** 18
specs *[glasses]* **108** 12–24
~ *[Skat.]* **284** 21
'spectacle' brooch **309** 30
spectacle case **108** 25
~ frame **108** 14–16
~ glass **108** 13
~ lens **108** 13
spectacles **108** 12–24
spectator **291** 29
spectator's seat **296** 28
spectators' stand **274** 31
spectral analysis **6** 20
~ lamp **331** 26
spectrometer **331** 34
spectrum **320** 14
speed·boat **269** 6
~ change lever **142** 6
~ frame **157** 19
~ gauge **206** 54
~ indicator* **206** 54
~ jumping **272** 31–34
speedometer **180** 33, **186** 7
~* **206** 54
speed regulator **241** 12
~ roller skating **287** 33
~-skater **284** 24
~-skating **284** 23
~ switch **306** 36
~way* **16** 16
~well **359** 22
spelt **69** 24
spencer **215** 1
spermaceti whale **352** 25
spermatic duct **22** 74
sperm whale **352** 25
sphenoidal sinus **19** 54
sphenoid bone **19** 38
sphere **7** 19, **329** 41
~ conductor **331** 61
sphincter of anus **22** 63
Sphinx *[Myth.]* **307** 20
~ *[Art]* **315** 11
sphinx *[Zool.]* **342** 55, **348** 9
sphygmograph **29** 19
sphygmomanometer **23** 1
Spica **5** 18
spice biscuit **97** 5
~ rack **41** 10
spicula **70** 23
spider **341** 8, **342** 44–46
spider's web **341** 9, **342** 47
spigot hole **126** 27
spike *[shoe]* **280** 27, **282** 10, 37
~ *[bolt]* **94** 5
~ *[Bot.]* **69** 2, **354** 67
spikelet **69** 3, 10, **359** 41
spikes **280** 26
spillway **212** 60
spin *[billiards]* **264** 5
spinach **59** 29
spinal cord **19** 48
~ marrow **20** 25
spindle **142** 20, **180** 80, **308** 54
~ catch **157** 49
~ drive **157** 31
~ shaft **157** 46
~ wharve **157** 48
spine *[Anat.]* **19** 2–5
~ *[Zool.]* **351** 6
~ *[thorn]* **62** 18
~ of book **178** 41
spinet **301** 45
spinnaker **270** 39
~ boom **270** 40
spinner *[fish]* **89** 40
spinneret **342** 46
spinner gritter system **89** 45
~-type potato-digger **68** 41
spinning bath **163** 15
~ box **163** 17
~ device **157** 51
~ head **164** 41
~ jet **163** 14, **164** 42
~ machine **125** 8
~ pump **163** 13
~ reel **89** 27
~ rod **89** 20
~ top **258** 18
~ the top **258** 17
~ tower **164** 43
spiracles **342** 32
spiraea **358** 23
spiral *[Skat.]* **284** 8
~ arm **6** 45
~-chute in staple pit **137** 33
~ gasometer **148** 61
~ guide rails **148** 63
~ lead **89** 46
~-meander ware **309** 13
spiral mixer **261** 49
~ nebula **6** 44–46
~ oil cooler **206** 19
~-ornamented bowl **309** 13
~ separator **91** 51
~ spring **283** 50
~ staircase **118** 76
~ toothing **136** 90+91
spire **312** 6
spirit *[alcohol]* **98** 56–59
~ *[fuel]* **52** 32
~ *[Myth.]* **307** 55
~ blowlamp **120** 32
~ lamp **27** 57
spirits of salt **52** 35
spirit stove **266** 19
Spirographis **340** 18
spit **96** 48
~ rod **158** 54
spittoon **23** 16, 32
~ dodger **27** 7
Spitz **71** 19
splash board **179** 6
~ dodger **221** 47
splasher **269** 56
splash form **187** 19
~ guard **161** 22
splatter sieve **323** 24
spleen *[Anat.]* **22** 12, 27
splenius **20** 51
splice-grafting **57** 39
splint **17** 10, 12
~ bone **19** 24
splinter **131** 15
~ bar **131** 15
~ screen **222** 42
split guiding drum **158** 10
~ nucleus **1** 20
~ pin **136** 19, 76
splits **288** 22
split-tiled roof **117** 45
splitting hammer **85** 26
spoke **131** 28, **180** 27
~shave **126** 14, **127** 61
sponge **249** 4
~ cake **97** 14
~ string **249** 37
spongy lining **365** 17
sponson **222** 66, **225** 62
sponsor **313** 12
spool **295** 32
~* **102** 35
~ box **295** 27
~ of thread* **102** 20
spoon **45** 11, **46** 61, **266** 20
~ *[Golf]* **276** 69
~ bait **89** 41
~ bit **129** 16
~ chisel **322** 18
~-edged scraper **192** 16
spoon-shaped bow **270** 2
spoon-shaped rasp **99** 36
spoor **86** 8
spore **365** 13
sport **269, 270, 273, 283–285, 287**
~ boat **269** 9–16, **273** 46–50
~ fencing **277** 15–43
~ fishing **89**
sporting dog **71** 40–43
~ gun **87** 1–40
~ rifle **87** 1–40
~ single **269** 54
~ sledge **285** 11
~ weapon **87** 1–40
sports bicycle **181** 8
~ bike **181** 8
~ cap **36** 18
~ car **187** 11
~ coat **34** 2, 21, 41
~ deck **218** 22
~ handlebar **181** 12
~ jacket **31** 40
~man **86** 1
~ model **182** 59
~ news **325** 49
~-racing car **187** 19-30
~ shirt **31** 49, **33** 39
~ shoe **100** 22
~ stadium **252** 53
spot **21** 50
~ *[Film]* **292** 52
~ bar lamps **297** 16
~ light **171** 49
~-light printing arc lamp **173** 20
spotlight(s) **292** 52, **297** 16, 21, 48
~ flap **296** 1
spot remover* **53** 56
spotted hemlock **363** 4
spot white ball **264** 13
spout *[pot]* **45** 15
~ *[whale]* **90** 51
~ hole **352** 26
spray *[atomizer]* **48** 28, **121** 12
~ *[Bot.]* **367** 30
sprayer **83** 34–37
~ f. disinfection **94** 17
spray gun **121** 12, **175** 34, **191** 19, 21
~ head **104** 38
spraying apparatus **27** 9
~ machine **83** 43
~ tube **94** 18
~ liquid **83** 37
spray of leaves **367** 61
~ outlet **83** 6
~ screen **269** 56
~ tank **83** 32
spread-eagle **284** 5
~ fences **272** 33
spreading box **67** 8
~ flap **196** 42
~ roller **128** 55

sprig *[nail]* **122** 29
~ *[Bot.]* **356** 6
~ bit **99** 63
~ of blossoms **367** 22
~ pin **122** 29
~ wire **122** 28
spring *[water]* **16** 82
~ *[meat]* **95** 41
~ *[Tech.]* **10** 10, **185** 25, 26, **187** 24
~board **279** 17, 25, **290** 36
~board acrobat **290** 35
~ bolt **134** 37
spring bow· compasses **144** 38
~ dividers **144** 44
spring buffer **209** 50
~ bumper **209** 50
~ clip **41** 67, **42** 48
~ clip fastener **181** 29
~-clip pirn-holder **159** 33
~-contact switch **233** 7
~-damper **183** 46, **185** 29
~ developer **278** 50
~ dynamometer **331** 2
springer *[Arch.]* **318** 22
spring expander **278** 50
~ fly **342** 12
~-grip dumb-bell **278** 49
springing system **185** 24–29
spring mattress **52** 75
~ rail **304** 39
~-regulating device **10** 15
~ set teeth **127** 6
~ support **10** 13
~ tongue **193** 33
~ washer **136** 32, **198** 39
spring-water· collecting chamber **254** 24
~ pump **64** 25
sprinkler **79** 19, **195** 39
sprinklers **297** 6
sprinkler system **297** 6
sprinkling box **23** 60
~ can* **54** 17, **79** 26
~ device **195** 39
~ truck* **195** 36, 40
sprinter **273** 8, **280** 6
sprinting **280** 1–28
spritsail **213** 43, **215** 5
sprocket **180** 74
~ piece **116** 31
~ wheel **180** 38
sprosser **346** 17
sprout **354** 19–25
sprouting cutting **57** 24
sprouts **59** 30
spruce **356** 12
~ cone **356** 13
~ fir **356** 12
~ gall aphid **82** 38
~ needle **356** 19
sprue* **141** 22
sprung seat **67** 3, **68** 38
spud **69** 40
spun yarn **125** 17
spur *[cock, etc.]* **72** 50+51, **74** 26, **88** 82
~ *[tree]* **85** 22
~* *[Railw.]* **16** 25
~ gear **207** 9
spurge-laurel **361** 10
spur line* **16** 25
spurr(e)y **70** 12
spurt **273** 2
spur vein **73** 28
~ wheel **136** 80, 85
~ wheel gear **207** 9
Sputnik **4** 48
sputum container **23** 32
~ mug **23** 16
spy hole **248** 15
squab **74** 33
squad car* **248** 2
square *[Geom.]* **328** 33, **329** 31
~ *[chessboard]* **265** 3
~ *[instr.]* **127** 15
~ *[cloth]* **30** 4, 5, 6
~ *[scarf]* **37** 9
~ beard **35** 15
~ bracket **325** 25
squared plank **149** 1
square-faced hammer **137** 2
~ fore sail **215** 13
~ fuselage **225** 46
~ head **136** 37
~-head bolt **136** 37
~ iron **136** 9
~ mallet **127** 9
~ mesh **90** 19
~ notation **299** 3
~ parentheses (or parenthesis) **325** 25
~ root **327** 3
~ sail **214** 55–66
~ stern **270** 17
~ stock* **136** 9
~ tapered wing **225** 13
~ thread **142** 32
squash* **59** 23
~ hat **36** 9
squatting **278** 23
squaw **335** 10
squeaker **74** 33
squeegee **112** 37, **162** 61
squeezer **42** 42
squeeze roller **158** 43
squid **349** 4
squire-at-arms **310** 68
squirrel **351** 19
squirt oiler **102** 48
stabilization plant **139** 29
stabilizer **139** 29
~* **226** 81
stabilizing fin **229** 25, **273** 50
~ nose undercarriage **226** 36
~ surface **226** 80+81
stable **76** 1–16, **272** 1
~ boy **76** 10, **290** 27
~ door **64** 49
~ dung **65** 15
~ fly **341** 4
~ lantern **64** 37, **76** 1
~man **179** 27
~ window **64** 48
stabling **64** 47
staccato **300** 54
stack *[chimney]* **145** 48
~ *[goods]* **221** 36
~ *[rock]* **13** 25
~ *[pile]* **64** 16, 17
~ armour **223** 61
stacker truck **151** 18
stack of firewood **64** 17
stacking table **241** 43
stack of linen **48** 42
~ of logs **64** 16, **84** 24
~ of planks **149** 1
~ of plates **260** 11
~ room **250** 11
~ of wood **53** 31
stadium **284** 1
staff *[crew]* **203** 9+10
~ *[stick]* **278** 38, **308** 25
~ *[Mus.]* **299** 45+46
~ exercise **278** 37
stag **88** 4
~* **352** 2
~ beetle **342** 24
~ call **87** 46
stage *[Theatre]* **296** 14
~ *[platform]* **268** 7
~ *[rocket]* **229** 36, 37
~ bridge **297** 34
~ coach **179** 37, 39, 53
~ directions **297** 41
~ director **297** 30
~ floor **296** 3
~ frame **298** 39
~ hand **292** 24, **297** 46
~ horizon **297** 9
~ w. machinery **297** 1–60
~ manager **297** 30, 45
~ manager's desk **297** 29
~ work **292** 26–61
staghound **272** 63
stagnant water **211** 17
stain **127** 12
stained glass **311** 17
stain-remover **53** 56
stair carpet **43** 27
stircase **39** 72
~ bolt **118** 46
staircase construction **118**
~ cover board **113** 22
~ exit **39** 83
~ landing **118** 23
~ locks **212** 17–25
~ without well hole **118** 42–44
~ window **39** 81
stair rod **43** 28
~ runner **43** 27
stairs **40** 25, **118**
~ lamp **43** 24
stairway **161** 37
~* **39** 72
stake *[post, etc.]* **80** 7, **84** 25, **130** 6, **131** 10
~ *[Roulette]* **263** 13
~ brace **131** 22
~ net **89** 14
stalactic structure **13** 80+81
stalactite **13** 80
~ cavern **13** 79
~ vaulting **319** 17
stalagmite **13** 81
stalk **69** 6, **354** 20
~ w. flowers and immature fruit **362** 31
stalked eye **340** 28
stalker **86** 1
stalking **86** 1–8
stall *[shed]* **76** 7
~ *[Theatre]* **296** 19
~ box **272** 2
stallion **74** 2
stalls **272** 1
stamen **354** 57, **356** 18
stamp *[instr.]* **169** 7, **231** 42–44
~ *[postage]* **232** 3, 21, 30, 40
~ *[postmark]* **232** 17, 39
~ booklet **231** 12
~ cancelling **231** 45
stamped matrix **170** 37
stamper **141** 32
stamp folio **231** 13
stamping **231** 40
~ arm **239** 41
~ machine **231** 45
~ table *[Tech.]* **172** 10
~ table *[Post]* **231** 41
stamp rack **238** 21
stamps position **231** 9
stance **276** 20, 21
stanching blood **17** 14–17
stanchion **131** 10
~ brace **131** 22
stand *[support, etc.]* **99** 27, **111** 31, **130** 10
~ *[frame]* **102** 41
~ *[Gymn.]* **279** 29, 30
standard *[pole]* **114** 47, 59

U

V

W

ZUR EINRICHTUNG DES REGISTERS

Die fetten Zahlen sind die Tafelnummern, die im Bilderteil *oben* auf den Seiten angegeben sind.

Im Register wurden ~ als Unterführungen verwendet, die entweder für das ganze vorangegangene Wort stehen oder für einen Teil des Wortes, der dann durch einen Punkt (·) abgegrenzt worden ist.

Um dem Benutzer das Suchen zu erleichtern, wurden, soweit es nötig erschien, kursiv gesetzte Hinweise auf den Verwendungsbereich des Wortes gegeben.

Ärmel **32** 14, 16, 32, **34** 17
~, gepuffter **338** 60
~aufschlag **33** 53
~chen **31** 23
~puffe **338** 49
~weste **34** 23
armenisch **324** 3
Arm·feile **132** 35
~flosser **349** 6
~geflecht **20** 27
~hebel **281** 15
Armierung **114** 54–76
Armierungseisen **114** 23
Arm·kachel **310** 48
~lehne **47** 60
~leuchter **44** 24
~manschette **23** 4
~muskel **20** 37, 38 54, 55
~prothese **23** 49
~reif **38** 15, 16
~schiene **310** 47
~schlinge **17** 2
~schlüssel **281** 11
~spange **38** 23
~speichenmuskel **20** 39
~stütze **203** 47
~tragetuch **17** 2
~verband **17** 1
Arnika **364** 2
Aronsstab **363** 9
Arpeggio **300** 36, 37
Arretierstift **134** 51
Arretierter **248** 5
Arretierung **67** 61, **333** 37
Arretierungsknopf **333** 38
Arretspitze **277** 41
Artemis **308** 12
Arterie **20** 1
Arterienpinzette **28** 55
Artikel *[Zeitung]* **325** 40
Artillerie **222** 32,33 34
Artischocke **59** 41
Artisten·stand **290** 5
~vermittler **290** 18
Artistik **298** 9–22
Arznei **28** 7
~flasche **26** 11
Arzt **26**
Ärztezelt **273** 44
Arzt·mantel **26** 13
~rufsignal **245** 27
A-Saite **302** 9
Asbest·anzug **255** 46
~drahtnetz **334** 19
~schürze **135** 3
~untersatz **42** 16
Asche **307** 10
~abscheider **145** 50
~fangscheibe **173** 21
Aschen·abzug **146** 8
~bahn **280** 5
~becher **47** 31
~kasten **41** 45, **67** 57
Aschen·kugel **260** 5
~tür **40** 39
~urne **309** 38
Ascher **47** 31
Aschkasten **67** 57, **205** 6
~bodenklappe **205** 7
Aschkuchen **97** 44
As-Dur **300** 12
Äser **88** 13
Asien **14** 39–45, **15** 16
as-Moll **300** 15
Aspergill **313** 48
Asphalt·auslauf **196** 54
~bahn **287** 2
~decke **196** 58
~mischtrommel **196** 50
~papier **147** 48
Aspirateur **91** 48
Aspirationspsychrometer **10** 32
Aspisviper **350** 41
Assaut **277** 17 u 18
Assel **341** 12
assemblé **288** 14
Assistent **28** 29
Assistentin **27** 26, **28** 28, **290** 39
Assistenz·arzt **28** 29
~ärztin **28** 28
Ast **354** 5
~anker **84** 26
Ästeaxt **85** 13
Asteroid **6** 26
Ast·gabel **57** 13
~hippe **58** 23
~lochbohrmaschine **128** 39
~reisighaufen **84** 16
Astrofotografie **6** 3
Astronom **6** 10
Astronomie **5–7**
Ast·schere **58** 6
~schneider **58** 6
Äsung **86** 13
Asymptote **329** 29
Atelier **321** 1–43
~aufnahme **292** 26–61
~fenster **321** 1
~mikrophon **292** 31
~sekretärin **292** 39
~staffelei **321** 3
~tonbox **292** 54
~wohnung **39** 74
Atem·beutel **28** 39
~gerät **17** 27
~loch **352** 26
~öffnung **342** 32
~schutzgerät **255** 39
~wurzel **354** 82
Athena **308** 17
Athene **308** 17
Ätherflasche **28** 38
Athlet **280** 56
Äthiopien **14** 36
Äthylalkoholtank **229** 6
Atlant **316** 36
Atlant. Ozean **15** 20
Atlas **308** 45
Atmosphäre **4**
Atmung, künstliche **17** 24–27
Atoll **13** 32
Atolla **349** 5
Atom **1 – 3**
~antrieb **223** 6–10
~bombe **1** 47
~brennstoff **3** 3
~brennstoffstab **3** 17
~flugzeug **225** 71
~kern **1** 1 u. 2, 9, 13 15, 19, 21, 24, 25
~meiler **1** 31–46
~ofen **1** 31-46
~physiker **1** 40
~reaktor **1** 31–46, **3** 1–23
Atom-U-Boot **223** 1
Atrium **316** 66
Atropos **308** 57
Attika **316** 60
Attitude **288** 10
Attribut **308** 2–4
Atümesser **190** 28
Ätzbad **323** 51
Atzel *[Perücke]* **35** 2
Atzel *[Vogel]* **346** 3
Ätzen **176** 1
Ätz·flüssigkeit **176** 4
~grund **323** 55
~maschine **172** 23
~trog **172** 24, **176** 6
Auditorium **250** 2
Aue **13** 62
Auerbachsprung **268** 42
Auerhahn **88** 72
Aufbahrung **312** 51–61
Aufbau **185** 1–58, **222** 68
Aufdoppelmaschine **99** 24
Auffahrt **16** 16
~rampe **202** 1
Auffang·blech **161** 15
~gefäß **10** 38, 44
~schale **191** 32
Aufgabekasten **113** 35
Aufgabenheft **249** 30
Aufgabe·raum **276** 44
~stempel **232** 39
Aufgang **161** 37, **218** 24, **290** 20
Aufgeber **276** 45
aufgehüpft **288** 12
Aufgriff **279** 53
Aufhalte·kette **72** 20
~ring **72** 27
Aufhänge·bügel **94** 16
~kette **68** 17
~vorrichtung **161** 27
Aufhängevorrichtung, kardanische **219** 27
Aufheller **292** 52
Aufkadung **211** 33
Aufklebeadresse **231** 4
Auflagenzähler **241** 8
Auflager **116** 83, **210** 33, **301** 42
~balken **208** 9
~bock **115** 18
Auflagetisch **77** 14
Auflauf- u. Abreißbremse **189** 43
~walze **161** 16
Auflegematratze **48** 10
Auflegen **160** 64
Auflicht·kondensor **110** 14
~mikroskop **110** 13
Auflösungszeichen **299** 55
Aufmaschnadel **102** 61
Aufnahme·becherwerk **196** 49, **197** 24
~bogenlampe **171** 24
~halle **292** 26–61
~kammer **109** 10
~leiter **292** 44
~optik **294** 2
~taste **306** 21
Aufnähnadel **123** 32
Aufputzdrehschalter **120** 10
Aufreiber **127** 16
Aufreißer **196** 20
Aufrichtfeder **193** 18
Aufriß **144** 60
Aufrollmaschine **168** 43
Aufruf **251** 14
Aufsatz *[Gerät]* **333** 7
~seite **303** 74
Aufschiebling **116** 31
Aufschiebseite **138** 2
Aufschlag *[Ball]* **276** 17
~*[Kleidung]* **34** 16
~feld **276** 12
~linie **276** 6–7
Aufschleppe **90** 33
Aufschnitt *[Mus.]* **305** 25
~maschine **96** 19
Aufschwung **279** 46
Aufsicht **250** 14
Aufsichtsbeamter **201** 39
Aufsitz·platz **290** 12
~stange **75** 14
Aufspann·platte **143** 37
~tisch **143** 20
Aufsprechkopf **293** 3
Aufsprung **280** 35
~bahn **283** 11
Aufsteck·fuß **111** 41
~schiene **111** 56
Aufsteck·schuh **111** 21
Aufstellung **274** 25
Aufstieg **283** 24–27
Aufstoßgerät **177** 41
Auftakt **300** 39
Auftragbürste **52** 41
Auftragetablett **261** 14

C

Dreieck, rechtwinkliges **328** 32
~, spitzwinkliges **328** 28
~, stumpfwinkliges **328** 30
~flügel **225** 54
~flugzeug **225** 53
~hut **338** 62
~schaltung **147** 21
~tuch **17** 2
Dreieckszeichen **327** 24
Dreier **284** 15
Dreifach·bildkamera **294** 47
~bildprojektor **294** 48
~-Seitenleitwerk **225** 48
~steckdose **120** 14
~stecker **120** 16
Drei·fuß **333** 15, **334** 14
~gespann, russisches **179** 45
~halbetakt **299** 40
Dreihals·flasche **334** 57
~kolben **334** 55
Dreikanalverfahren **294** 38
Dreikant·feile **127** 26
~maßstab **144** 51
~prisma **329** 37
~schaber **192** 16
Dreiklang **300** 16 u. 17
Dreimaster **215** 18–27, **338** 62
Dreimast·-Gaffelschoner **215** 18
~-Marssegelschoner **215** 20
~-Toppsegelschoner **215** 19
Drei·meterbrett **268** 9
~motorenflugzeug **226** 5
~paßbogen **318** 32
~punktaufhängung **234** 13
~punktauflage **333** 28
Dreirad **258** 59
~kabinenroller **183** 6
~kehrmaschine **195** 6
~lieferwagen **189** 1
~-Walze **196** 36
Drei·satzrechnung **327** 8–10
~schlitz **316** 15
~seitenkipper **189** 18
~spitz **58** 18, **338** 62
~sprung **280** 33–35
~stufenschalter **23** 53
~tastaggregat **306** 36 u. 37
Dreiviertel·takt **299** 39
~tonerhöhung **299** 57
~tonerniedrigung **299** 59
Dreiwegehahn **331** 15
Dreiweg·steckdose **120** 14
~stecker **120** 16
Drei·zack **129** 11, **308** 30
~zehnmeterlinie **275** 4
~zinkgrubber **58** 17
Drellüberzug **48** 10
Drempel **116** 47
Dresch·flegel **66** 27
~korb **68** 59
~maschine **67** 44
~trommel **68** 57
Dreß **272** 57
Dresseur **290** 31
Dribbeln **274** 63
Dribbling **274** 63
Drillbohrer **129** 22
Drilling **87** 23
~haken **89** 33
Drillings·panzerdrehturm **223** 57
~turm **222** 27, **223** 57
Drill·maschine **67** 24
~schar **67** 26
Driver **276** 69
Drogerie **253** 23
Drohne **78** 5
Drohnenzelle **78** 36
Drop **276** 50
Drops **98** 76
Droschke **179** 26
Drossel **346** 13–17
~grube **18** 20
~vogel **344** 3
~vögel **346** 13–17
Druck·absteller **175** 32
~abweiser **229** 30
~ansteller **175** 32
~anstieg **227** 22
~anzeiger **161** 56
~arm **239** 41
~ausgleicheinrichtung **206** 11
~behälter **164** 33
~bogenhängevorrichtung **174** 32
~einstellung **174** 44
~element **172** 32
Drücken **281** 6
Drucker **323** 35
Druckerei **323** 27–64
Druck·feder **169** 41
~form **323** 32
~fundament **174** 41
~gaskesselwagen **208** 15
~gasschalter **206** 4
~hebel **239** 42, **323** 61
~kessel **297** 55
~kissen **239** 40
Druckkissen *[mediz.]* **23** 39
Druckknopf **37** 20, **239** 27, **305** 46
~auslöser **111** 5
~tafel **176** 28
Druck·körper **223** 21
~lager **218** 57, **223** 4
~leitung **297** 54, **254** 16, 49, **255** 31
Druckluft·anschluß **147** 53
~behälter **147** 51
~bremszylinder **204** 5
~manometer **207** 16
~schlauch **138** 44
~schnellschalter **146** 34, **147** 51–62
Druck-Luftschraube **226** 2
Druck·luftzufuhr **138** 44
~messer **206** 46, 47, 48, 49
~minderventil **135** 31
~papier **174** 2
Druckplatte *[Bau]* **118** 38
~ *[Druckerei]* **173** 9, **239** 43
Druck·plattenkörnmaschine **173** 29
~presse **297** 53
~pressenanlage **297** 50
~prüfer **190** 28
~punktabzug **87** 11
~randversteller **241** 6
~reduzierer **135** 31
~regler **323** 38
Druckrohr **212** 50
~leitung **212** 41
Druckrolle **141** 64
Drucksache *[Post]* **232** 16
~ zu ermäßigter Gebühr **232** 24
Druck·säule **297** 60
~schablone **162** 62
~schmiernippel **136** 79
~schraube **141** 57
~schrauber **226** 1
~spindel **145** 75
~spüler **119** 39
~stab **304** 16
~stock **239** 46
~taste **199** 70, **234** 47
~tiegel **175** 15
~tisch **162** 63, **323** 41
~träger **174** 8
~tuch **174** 9
~verband **17** 17
~wächter **254** 47
~ware **162** 57
~wasserreaktor **3** 24, **223** 9
Druck·werk **176** 27,36
~zylinder **174** 19, **175** 2, 44, 59, **176** 33
Drüse **22** 75
D-Saite **302** 9
D-Schicht **4** 16
Dschiu-Dschitsu **281** 15-17
Dschunke **336** 32
Dübel **197** 46
~loch **115** 22, 23
Ducht **269** 28
~weger **269** 31
Duckdalben **220** 37
Dückdalben **220** 37
Dudelsack **301** 8
Dufflecoat **34** 36, **256** 21
Dukduk-Tänzer **335** 34
Duktorwalze **175** 64
Dülfersitz **282** 34
Dult **291** 1–66
Düne **13** 39
Dung **65** 15
Düngemergel **153** 10
Dünger **65** 14
~streuer **67** 7
~wagen **64** 53
Dung·haufen **64** 51
~karren **64** 46
~platte **64** 52
~wagen **64** 53
Dunkelkammer **112** 1–61
~lampe **112** 18
Dunkelnebel **6** 49
Dünndarm **22** 14–16
Duole **300** 38
Duo-Walzwerk **141** 48
Durchbruch **274** 63
~arbeit **101** 14, 27
Durch·flußöffnung **212** 56
~führungsisolator **147** 12, 35
~gang **319** 4
Durchgangs·bahnhof **199** 36
~dose **120** 15
Durch·laß **16** 44
~lauferhitzer **119** 66
Durchleuchtungs·-gerät **29** 39
~kontrolleinrichtung **77** 19
~schirm **29** 41
~tisch **29** 42
Durch·lüftungsanlage **339** 28
~messer **328** 45
~reiche **45** 62
Durchschlag *[Küchengerät]* **42** 47
~ *[Werkzeug]* **134** 69
Durch·schläger **134** 69
~schuß **170** 5
~stoßen **160** 63
~suchung **247** 9

Durch·wurf **79** 13
~ziehkurbel **323** 33
~ziehnadel **102** 59
~zug **101** 17
~zugwalze **157** 18
Durdreiklang **300** 16
Dürnitz **310** 30
Dürrfleisch **96** 12
Durtonart **300** 1–15
Duschanlage **25** 1
Dusche **104** 37, **268** 2
Dusch·kabine **51** 14
~nische **51** 14
Düse **171** 53, **227** 45
~, konische **227** 48
Düsen·boden **140** 62
~hebel **171** 52
~kopf **104** 38
~nadel **183** 55
~pumpe **211** 62
~schanzkleid **221** 51
~ventil **147** 29
Dynamo **180** 8, **204** 22
Dynamometer **331** 2
Dynastarter **183** 26
D-Zug-Wagen **204** 1

E

Eau de Cologne **103** 20
Ebenholztaste **304** 5
Eber **74** 9
~esche **355** 42
E-Brief **232** 35
échappé **288** 11
Echinodermen **340** 23 u. 24
Echinopsis **56** 14
Echinus **316** 21
Echiostoma **349** 13
Echo **219** 41
~empfänger **219** 42
~lot **219** 38
Echsen **350** 27 u. 31–37
Eck·ball **274** 58
~bank **260** 38, **261** 10, **262** 32
~brett **41** 33
Ecke **329** 33
~ *[Sport]* **275** 7, **281** 34
Ecken·kragen **33** 55
~steher **249** 19
Ecker **355** 37
~ *[Kartenspiel]* **265** 42
Eck·fahne **274** 10
~feld **274** 10
~fußstein **117** 77
~kegel **287** 11
~laden **253** 40
~leuchte **43** 24
~platz **204** 42
~stein **265** 41
~stiel **115** 52
~stoß **274** 58
~turm **310** 14
Eckzahn **21** 17
Edel·auge **57** 23
~falter **342** 52
~fasan **88** 77
~fink **344** 10
~hirsch **88** 4
~kastanie **368** 48
~koralle **340** 45
~mann **338** 44
~raute **362** 6
~reis **57** 37
~rose **62** 15
~stein **38** 26
~tanne **356** 1
~tier **88** 1
~weiß **362** 9
~wild **88** 1–27
E-Dur **300** 5
Effektdämpfer **303** 68
Effekten **243** 21–19
~börse **243** 1–10
~händler **243** 7
~makler **243** 4
~schalter **242** 6
Effektlautsprecher **294** 51
Effetstoß **264** 5
Effilierschere **103** 39
Egge **68** 35
Eggenteller **68** 36
Egyptienne **325** 8
Ehe·bett **48** 3–15
~ring **313** 16
~wappen **246** 10–13
Ehren·preis **359** 22
~tor **319** 3
Ei **75** 47, **78** 26, **81** 15, **342** 49
~ *[Gewicht]* **221** 20
~ablage **81** 2
Eibe **356** 61
Eibisch **364** 12
Eiche **355** 1
Eichel **355** 4
~ *[Kartenspiel]* **265** 42
~ *[mediz.]* **22** 69
~habicht **346** 1
~häher **346** 1
~zerstäuber **83** 36
Eichen·gallwespe **82** 33
~wickler **82** 43
Eichhörnchen **351** 19
Eier·becher **45** 38
~bovist **365** 19
~kette **234** 22
~lampe **75** 46
~leiste **42** 9
~löffel **45** 40
~prüfer **75** 46
~schale **75** 48
~sortiermaschine **75** 39
~spiegel **75** 46
~stabkyma **316** 42
~stock **22** 83
~teiler **41** 86
~uhr **42** 46
~versandkasten **75** 36
~waage **75** 39
Eierwärmer **45** 39
eiförmig **354** 36
Eigelb **75** 57
Eigentumszeichen **37** 4
Ei·hülle **75** 48
~klar **75** 51
Eilbrief **232** 34
Ei·leger **351** 1
~leiter **22** 81
Eimer **30** 52, **121** 11, **216** 56
~bagger **221** 63–68
~kette **211** 57, **221** 63
~kettenbagger **211** 56
~leiter **221** 64
Ein·achsenanhänger **189** 35
~achsergepäckanhänger **207** 27
~achsgrubenheber **191** 30
~atmung **17** 25
~back **97** 46
Einband **178** 40–42
~decke **112** 53, **178** 40
Einbaum **213** 7, **337** 20
Einbau·stück **141** 56
~tachometer **181** 39
Ein·bettkabine **218** 41
~bindeahle **123** 33
~blattdruck **323** 27
~decker **225** 1
~docken **217** 38–40
Eineinhalbmaster **215** 9 u. 10, **270** 33–36
Einer **269** 16, 18
~stelle **326** 3
Einfachkondensor **331** 23
Einfahrt **64** 1
~ *[Hafen]* **212** 15 u. 16
Ein·fahrvorsignal **199** 41
~fallbaum **86** 47
~familienhaus **39** 1-53
~farben-Offsetmaschine **174** 1, 14
Einfassung *[Beet]* **55** 20
~*[Schmuck]* **38** 25
~ *[Schneiderei]* **102** 5
~ *[Stuhl]* **44** 12
Einfriedung **39** 53
Einführ·lineal **177** 59
~tisch **178** 34
Einführungs·buchse **147** 40
~isolator **206** 5
Einfüll·maschine **93** 32
~öffnung **96** 42, **192** 40
Einfüllstutzen **40** 47, **184** 47, **186** 58
Eingang **194** 20, **290** 19
Eingangs·luke **226** 34
~tor **319** 24
~treppe **39** 66
~tunnel **336** 6
~- und Oszillatorspulensatz **235** 18
~wähler **306** 18
Eingießende **140** 33
Einglas **108** 27
Einguß **141** 22
~rinne **140** 21
Einhand·rute **89** 20
~stoßsäge **85** 38
Ein·hängeöse **146** 48
~heit, zahnärztliche **27** 6
~heitenzeiger **169** 36
~holtasche **52** 48
~horn **246** 16, **307** 7
~kammer-Wäschetrockenapparat **166** 19
Einkaufs·netz **52** 71
~tasche **52** 48, **253** 13
Einklang **300** 19
Einlage *[Musikinstrument]* **302** 26
~ *[Schuh]* **105** 7
~blatt **112** 54
Einlaß·karte **296** 11
~schlitz **184** 73
~ventil **184** 29, **227** 14
Einlauf·apparat **23** 46
~stutzen **39** 12, **117** 30
~walze **241** 15
Einlege·arbeit **47** 48
~keil **136** 71
~lampe **171** 48
~ring **333** 17
~sohle **99** 4
~vorbau **155** 2
Ein·lieferungsschein **232** 9
~lochen **276** 66
~machglas **41** 69
Einmann·boot **336** 12
~-Motorkettensäge **85** 44
~sessel **209** 16
Ein·master **215** 6–8
~maststütze **209** 23
~meterbrett **268** 10
~motorenflugzeug **226** 1
~ödhof **16** 101
~reiher **34** 13
~reißhaken **255** 15
~-Richtungs-Triebwagen **193** 8
~rollinie **275** 10
Einsatz **161** 60, **263** 13
~aufhängung **161** 42
~verschraubung **161** 43
~zirkel **144** 28

Elektronenröhre **234** 48
Elektro·omnibus **188** 8–16
~schaltanlage **162** 58
~schaltkasten **162** 25
~schleifapparat **173** 26
~schweißer **135** 1
~schweißung **135** 1–28
Elektroskop **331** 62
Elektro·tagebaulok **206** 56
~triebwagen **206** 55
~triebzug **206** 60
~turbogenerator **3** 32
~verschiebelok **206** 59
~zähler **43** 18
~zug **145** 18
Element **1** 22, **40** 77
Elementarfigur **284** 13–20
Elevationswinkel **87** 76
Elevator **67** 51, **91** 47, **145** 70.
Elf **274** 11–21
Elfenbein·kugel **264** 1
~statuette **309** 8
~taste **304** 4
Elfenschuh **62** 10
Elfmeterpunkt **274** 6
Ellbogen **18** 45, **73** 20
Elle **19** 14
Ellen·bogen **18** 45
~beuger **20** 58
~griff **279** 55
~nerv **20** 29
~rand **21** 70
Ellipse **329** 22, 25
Ellok **206** 1
~beimann **206** 30
~führer **206** 28
~führersitz **206** 29
~führerstand **206** 27
~schuppen **199** 18
Elster **346** 3
Eltern **45** 1 u. 2
E-Maschinenraum **218** 58, **223** 28
Embryo **368** 22
~sack **354** 64
Emd **65** 35–43
e-Moll **300** 2
E-Motor **218** 59
Empfänger **230** 28, 29, **232** 37, **239** 5
Empfangs·antenne **234** 21
~chef **256** 33, **259** 7
~gebäude **199** 2, **201** 16
~gerät **234** 35
~raum **259** 1–27
Empire·stil **318** 16
~tisch **318** 16
Empore **311** 25
Endbildfenster **109** 8
Ende *[Geweih]* **88** 10, 31
~ *[Rest]* **96** 57
End·einstieg **204** 59
~gestell **158** 14
Endivie **59** 39
End·knospe **354** 22
~linie **275** 34
~maß **142** 47
~moräne **12** 55
Endoskop **26** 14
Endportal **210** 54
Endpunkt **328** 17
~, krummer **328** 18
End·scheibenleitwerk **225** 15
~stück **97** 24
~stufe **4** 56
~verriegelung **210** 60
~verstärkerröhre **235** 13
Energie·erzeugung **3** 40–42
~erzeugungsanlage **152** 19
Engel **311** 54
Engerling **82** 12
Engländer *[Zange]* **119** 53
Englisches Fräulein **314** 22
Entbindungs·bett **29** 5
~zimmer **29** 1
Ente **74** 35
~ *[Segelflugzeug]* **271** 42
Enten·flugzeug **225** 36
~hals **225** 38
~jagd **86** 40
~küken **74** 35
~modell **271** 42
Enterbalken **213** 11
Enterich **74** 35
Entfernungs·einstellung **111** 13
~messer **111** 40, **222** 36, 37
Entfesselungskünstler **291** 28
entflohen **288** 11
Entfrosterschlauch **185** 35
Entgaser **146** 16
Entgasungsanlage **148** 10–12
Entgiftungsanlage **148** 41
Entgleisungsschutz **209** 75
Entgranner **67** 48, **68** 68
Entlader **331** 50, 57
Entladetür **148** 12
Entladungsrohr **331** 16
Entleerungsschieber **254** 31
Entlüfter **254** 27
Entlüftung **51** 49, **147** 10, **339** 41
Entlüftungs·haube **145** 51
~hutze **226** 72
~kappe **40** 52
~leitung **40** 51
~rohr **161** 34
~schacht **194** 31
Entnahmehahn **166** 16
Entparaffinierung **139** 34
Entrahmungs-separator **77** 24
entrechat **288** 13
Entrinden **85** 32, 42
Entsäuerung **163** 19
Entschlackung **199** 51
Entschwefelung **163** 20
Entstaubung **153** 20
Entstaubungsanlage **124** 1, **152** 7, **231** 34
Entwässerungs·graben **65** 45, **211** 36
~rinne **196** 63
Entwesung **83** 17
Entwickler·schale **112** 36
~tank **112** 1
Entwicklungs·dose **112** 13
~tank **112** 1
~zange **112** 38
Entwurf **321** 43
Entzerrlinse **294** 43
Entzerrungsmagnet **236** 26
Enzian **362** 13
Epimanikion **314** 28
Enzyklopädie **250** 17
Epistelseite **311** 48
Epistyl **316** 18
Epitaph **312** 14
Epitrachelion **314** 27
Epizentralgebiet **11** 38
Epizentrum **11** 33
Eppich **59** 27
Epsis **56** 14
Erato **308** 63
Erbse **59** 7
Erbsen·blüte **59** 2
~pflanze **59** 1
~ranke **59** 4
Erd·apfel **69** 38
~arbeiter **113** 76
~aushub **113** 78
Erdbeben **11** 32–38
~herd **11** 32
~kunde **11** 32–38
~messer **11** 39
~welle **11** 36
~wirkung **11** 45–54
Erd·beere **60** 21
~beerpflanze **60** 16
~birne **69** 38
Erde **4** 1–10, **6** 24, **7** 8, **15** 1–7
Erde, kompostierte **79** 15
Erd·eule **81** 42
~fink **346** 8
~floh **81** 39
~gas **12** 30
Erdgeschoß **39** 2, **113** 7
~mauerwerk **118** 29
Erd·haufen **79** 15
~haus **79** 33
~hobel **196** 33
~jagd **86** 23
~karte **15** 10–45, **249** 20
~kern **11** 5
~kröte **350** 23
~kruste **4** 1, **11** 5
~kugel **7** 8
~messung **15** 46–62
~mond **6** 24
~nuß **367** 41
~oberfläche **11** 6–12
Erdöl **12** 31, **139**
~bohrung **4** 6, **139** 1–20
~erzeugnis **139** 36–47
~förderung **139** 48–55
~gewinnung **139** 48–55
~lagerstätte **12** 27
~leitung **139** 56
~produkt **139** 36–47
~raffinerie **139** 56–68
~verarbeitung **139** 21–35
Erd·pol **15** 3
~rauchgewächs **62** 5
~raupe **81** 44
~reich **118** 9
~riese **84** 32
~rutsch **11** 46
~satellit **4** 49
~schaufel **79** 14
~schäufelchen **58** 13
~sieb **79** 13
~spalte **11** 52
~teil **15** 12–18
~wall **272** 25
Erfrischungs·bude **291** 3
~kiosk **257** 58
Ergebnis **326** 23
Erhitzer **77** 8
Erhöhungs·winkel **87** 76
~zeichen **299** 51 u. 52
Erika **361** 19
Erinnye **308** 51
Erinnys **308** 51
Erkennungs·dienst **247** 21
~nummer **186** 32
Erläuterungstafel **339** 44
Erle **355** 30
Erlenbruchtorf **13** 18

Erlenmeyerkolben **334** 39
Erlenzeisig **346** 8
Erneuerungsschein **243** 19
Erniedrigung **299** 54
Erniedrigungszeichen **299** 53 u. 54
Ernte **65** 19–24
~maschine **68** 41
~wagen **64** 44
Eros **308** 26
Erpel **74** 35
Ersatz·rad **185** 54
~schlauchreifen **273** 23
~spieler **274** 45
Erstarrung **164** 43
Erste Hilfe **17**
Erstkläßler **249** 9
Ertrinkender **17** 34–38
Eruptionskanal **11** 17
Erve **70** 19
Erwartungsstellung **281** 9
Erwerbsgartenbau **79** 1–51
Erzieherin **257** 27
Erz·lagerstätte **11** 31
~transportwagen **208** 19
E-Saite **302** 9
Esche **355** 38
E-Schicht **4** 17
escudo **244** 23
Es-Dur **300** 11
Esel **74** 3
~hengst **74** 8
~reiten **257** 45
Eselsrücken **202** 49
Eskimo **336** 1
~hund **71** 22
es-Moll **300** 14
Espada **287** 65
Esparsette **70** 10
Espartogras **130** 26
Espe **355** 21
Esper **70** 10
Espresso·bar **261** 45–51
~maschine **42** 17, **261** 50
Esse **40** 5, **132** 5, **145** 46
Essen·kehrer **40** 31
~schieber **30** 19
Essig **98** 25
~flasche **46** 42
~gurke **98** 29
Eß·besteck **46** 7, **266** 20
~löffel **46** 61
~teller **46** 4
~tisch **45** 5, **46** 1
~zimmer **45**
Estrich **53** 68, **118** 39, 40
Etagen·geschäft **253** 1
~heizung **44** 16
Etagentrockner **163** 31
Etikett **93** 42
Etikettiermaschine **93** 33
Etui **105** 11, 12
Eule **347** 14–19
Eulenspiegel **289** 38
Eumenide **308** 51
Eurasien **15** 15 u. 16
Europa **14** 1–26, **15** 15
~flagge **245** 4
~karte **249** 21
~-Union **245** 4
Eustachische Röhre **19** 65
Euter **76** 19
Euterpe **308** 65
Evangelienseite **311** 47
Ever **215** 9
Ewer **215** 9
Ewige Lampe **311** 44
Ewiges Licht **311** 44
Exercice **288** 1–10
Exhaustor **128** 50
Exkrement **76** 22
Exlibris **178** 51
Exosphäre **4** 14
Exotin **289** 30
Expander **278** 50
~übung **278** 43
Expansions·gefäß **40** 24
~kamm **158** 26
Experimental-Brutreaktor **3** 19
Experimentier-transformator **332** 5
Explosions·motoren **184**
~ramme **196** 26
~schutz **135** 34
Exponent **327** 1
Expreßgut **200** 2
~abfertigung **200** 1
~anhänger **200** 3
~annahme u. -abgabe **200** 1
Exsikkator **334** 51
Exsikkatoreneinsatz **334** 54
Exterieur **72** 1–38
Extrablatt **253** 45
Extraktionszange **27** 48
Extraktor **164** 37
Extremität **82** 6–8
Extremthermometer **10** 57 u. 58
Exzenter **159** 57, **182** 47
~rolle **159** 67
~scheibe **172** 5
~tritthebel **159** 58
~welle **159** 56
~wellenzahnrad **159** 55
E-Zettel **232** 33

F

Fabel **307**
~tiere **307** 1–61
~wesen **307** 1–61
Fabrik **16** 37, **145**
~lokomotive **205** 69
~nummer **180** 51
~schmiede **133**
~schornstein **145** 46
~sirene **145** 69
~trawler **216** 6
Facette **27** 35, **38** 27, **78** 20
Facetten·auge **78** 20–24, **342** 7
~schliff **38** 27
Fach **115** 59, **159** 40
~arzt **26** 12
Facher **162** 35
Fächer **336** 42
~ *[Wild]* **88** 75
~besen **54** 16
~gewölbe **318** 46
~- u. Einstreichmaschine **177** 40
Fachkreuzspulen **157** 58
Fachwerk **64** 4
~balken **64** 4
~binder **116** 78
~brücke **210** 47
~haus **64** 3, **252** 48
~knoten **210** 52
~stütze **209** 77
~wand **115** 48
Fackel **308** 36
Faden **157** 53, **160** 17, 36
~absaugung **157** 44
~aufwicklung **164** 44
~auge **159** 28, 29
~band **163** 28
~buchheftmaschine **178** 16
~einzug **165** 5, 20, 21
~fühler **159** 14
~führer **160** 3, 37, 38, 54
~führerhaltestange **160** 2
~führungshebel **102** 23
~geflecht **365** 2
~haken **102** 22
~kops **178** 18
~kräuselung **164** 59
~kreuz **87** 32
~scheibe **158** 30
~spanner **102** 24, **160** 5
~spule **178** 18
~trenner **157** 43
~trocknung **164** 58
~wurm **81** 51
~zähler **171** 25
Fagott **302** 28
Fähe **88** 42
Fahne **245** 7–11
Fahnen **245**
~band **245** 9
~nagel **245** 8
~schaft **245** 7
~spitze **245** 10
~tuch **245** 11
Fahrbahn **194** 10, **253** 34
~breite **197** 49
~übergang **210** 2
Fährboot **211** 11
Fahrdamm **194** 10
Fährdeck **216** 18
Fahrdraht **193** 43, **206** 2
~aufhängung **193** 39
~grubenlokomotive **138** 47
~lok **138** 47, **206** 1
~spannungsmesser **206** 42
~strommesser **206** 43
Fähre **211** 10
Fahrende **291** 25–28
Fahrer **187** 6, **193** 21, **272** 37
~haus **189** 40, **196** 11
~hausschutz **189** 19
~kabine **189** 40
~sitz **185** 55
Fahrgast **187** 7, **216** 52, **253** 38
~anlage **220** 16
~gondel **226** 68
~kabine **209** 28, 52
Fahrgestell **114** 32, **146** 41
~rahmen **185** 60
Fahrgrube **145** 78
Fährhaus **211** 45
Fahr·kabine **256** 46
~karte **200** 36, **203** 48
Fahrkarten·ausgabe **200** 34
~druckmaschine **200** 40
~knipszange **201** 56
~schalter **200** 35
~verkäufer **200** 39
Fahr·leitung **206** 2
~leitungsuntersuchungswagen **206** 57
Fährmann **211** 2
Fahr·motor **206** 10, **207** 8
~motorenzugkraftmesser **206** 44
~plan **200** 32
~plantrommel **200** 16
~preisanzeiger **253** 36
Fahrrad **180–181**
~anhänger **181** 20
~antrieb **180** 35–42

Fahrrad·gepäcktasche **181** 19
~gestell **180** 14–20
~glocke **180** 4
~kippständer **180** 34
~klingel **180** 4
~lampe **180** 7
~nummer **180** 51
~pedal **180** 78
~pumpe **180** 48
~rahmen **180** 14–20
~sattel **180** 22
~schloß **180** 49
~ständer **253** 43
~tachometer **180** 33
Fahrrinne **211** 21
Fahrschalter **193** 35
~handrad **206** 31
Fahr·scheinheft **201** 55
~schiene **92** 4
Fähr·schiff **216** 16
~seil **211** 3
Fahrstand **193** 34
Fährsteg **211** 7
Fahr·stock **138** 53
~straße **199** 71
~straßenhebel **199** 61
Fahrstuhl **220** 66, **256** 46
~führer **256** 47
Fahrt, große **216** 1
~, kleine **216** 38
~, mittlere **216** 13
Fährte **86** 8
Fahrten·kieljacht **270** 1–4
~messer **266** 46
Fahrtmesser **228** 16
Fahrtrichtungs·änderung **270** 52–54
~anzeiger **186** 27, **201** 23
~schalter **206** 33
~wender **205** 58
~zeiger **189** 46
Fahrwasser·bezeichnung **219** 59–76
~mitte **219** 73
~zeichen **219** 43–58
Fahrweg **16** 99
Fahrwerk **225** 5, 51
~betätigung **228** 29
Fahrzeituhr **193** 37
Fahrzeug **179** 1–54
~halle **255** 1
~papiere **253** 66
~rampe **202** 1
Fäkalienwagen **195** 34
Faksimileunterschrift **244** 34
Faktor *[Math.]* **326** 25
Faktur **238** 50
Falke **347** 1–4
Falken·beize **86** 42–46
~haube **86** 44
Falkenier **86** 42
Falken·jagd **86** 42–46
~jäger **86** 42
~kappe **86** 44
~männchen **86** 46
Falkner **86** 42
Falknerei **86** 42–46
Fällaxt **85** 13
Fallbrücke **310** 25
Falle **83** 9
~ *[Schloß]* **134** 37
~ *[Webr]* **212** 77
Falleitung **254** 21
Fallen **12** 3
Fällen **84** 27, **85** 19
Fallgatter **310** 24
Fällkeil **85** 24
Fall·kerb(e) **85** 20
~klappe **295** 16
~nestgestell **75** 5
~reep **216** 34
~richtung **12** 3
~rohr **40** 10, **51** 44, **140** 56
Fallschirm **228**
~aufziehleine **228** 55
~fangleine **228** 50
~kappe **228** 49
~verpackungssack **228** 51
Fall·schnecke **142** 18
~streifen **8** 9
~tür **40** 13
~winkel **87** 78
Faltboote **269** 54–66
Faltboot·einer **296** 54
~fahrer **269** 55
~gerüst **269** 66
~segel **269** 62
~zweier **269** 61
Falte **32** 38, **102** 1
~, liegende **12** 15
~, schiefe **12** 13
~, stehende **12** 12
~, überkippte **12** 14
Falten·balg **201** 47, **204** 7
~balgübergang **188** 4
~filter **334** 41
~gebirge **12** 12–20
~trägerrock **31** 34
~wurf **321** 33
Falter **342** 48–56
Falthocker **266** 14
Faltigron **361** 6
Faltrian **361** 6
Falt·stuhl **266** 11
~tisch **266** 5
Falz **178** 54
~abpreßgerät **177** 42
~apparat **175** 55, **176** 37
~eisen **123** 24
~messer **178** 12
~pfanne **117** 59
~tasche **178** 10
~trichter **175** 53
Falzung **178** 13
Falzzange **99** 67
Familie **45** 1–4
Familien·anzeige **325** 51
~begräbnis **312** 27
~grab **312** 27
Famulus **250** 7
Fang **71** 3, **88** 45, **347** 7
~boot **90** 38–43, 46
Fangen **258** 23
Fanger **304** 27
Fänger **275** 47
Fangerdraht **304** 29
Fänger·handschuh **275** 47
~linie **275** 44
~partei **275** 50
Fangerpilz **304** 28
Fang·gerät **335** 31
~gürtel **83** 24
~jagden **86** 19–27
~kettstuhl **160** 23
~leine **228** 50, **255** 45
~partei **275** 58
~reifen **261** 29
~schuß **86** 17
~spiel **258** 23, **298** 22
~stab **261** 30
Fanon **314** 55
Fanone **314** 55
Faraday-Käfig **331** 45
Farb·ansatzbehälter **161** 70
~auffangblech **161** 15
~auftragwalze **175** 18, 27, 61
~badbehälter **161** 63
Farbband **239** 39, **240** 14
~einsteller **240** 29
~schieber **239** 50
~spule **240** 18
Farbdruck **323** 28
Farbe **320**
Färbe·apparat **161** 21–26, 58
~haspel **161** 1
~maschine **161** 12
~mittel **103** 32
Färben **161**
Färbetrog **161** 19
Farb·filter **111** 48
~gebungsknopf **241** 7
~glashalter **110** 4
~hebewalze **175** 63
~kasten **175** 65, **176** 16
~kübel **121** 27
Farbmischung, additive **320** 10
~, subtraktive **320** 12
Farbmittelzerstäuber **83** 34–37
Farbmuster·behälter **161** 21
~entnahmeöffnung **161** 67
Farb·papier **238** 68
~puder **52** 44
~pulver **121** 9
~scheibe **297** 49
~spritzapparat **171** 51
~stift **50** 24
Farbmuster·stoffzusatzleitung **161** 66
~stück **161** 7
~tube **321** 11
~verreibzylinder **175** 62
~walze **174** 5, 15, 40, **239** 47
~wanne **161** 8
~werk **174** 6, 15, 34, 39, **175** 19, 28, 50, 57
Farn **361** 16
~kraut **361** 16
farthing **244** 37
Fasan **88** 77
Fasanenfeder **36** 56
Faschiermaschine **96** 39
Faschine **211** 53
Fasching **289**
Faschings·prinzessin **289** 61
~wagen **289** 57
~zug **289** 57–70
Fase **136** 60
Faser **125** 20
~bandetagentrockner **163** 31
Faß **80** 23, **126** 24
~aushobelmaschine **126** 37
~band **126** 26
~binder **126** 16
~boden **126** 30
~daube **126** 21
Fassen **93** 20–28
Faß·fabrikationsmaschine **126** 34-38
~füller **93** 29
~haken **117** 23
~keller **80** 21
~krösemaschine **126** 38
Fäßler **126** 16
Fasson·hammer **106** 41
~lehre **155** 19
~leinen **124** 25
Faß·reif **126** 26
~rumpf **126** 25
~schaber **126** 13
~stab **126** 21
Fassung **254** 24–39
Faß·zange **29** 53
~zieher **126** 4
~zug **126** 4
Fastnacht **289**
Faul·baum **364** 13
~tier **351** 11
Fauna **349**
Faunus **308** 40
Faust **18** 48
~ *[Werkzeug]* **119** 17
~abwehr **274** 40
Faustball **276** 52–58
~spiel **276** 52–58
Fäustel **137** 1, **150** 35
Fausten **274** 40
Faust·hammer **132** 15
~kampf **281** 18–46

Flügel·hut **308** 23
~kopf **91** 6
~mauer **210** 28, **211** 35
~mutter **136** 40, **180** 29, **183** 13
~nagel **282** 47
~pedal **304** 41
~rad **201** 64, **212** 52
~radpumpe **212** 47–52
~radwasserzähler **254** 53
~roß **307** 26
~schiene **198** 56
~schuh **308** 22
~stab **308** 25
~stürmer **274** 17
~tang **362** 48
~turbine **226** 20
~welle **91** 5
Flug·figur **271** 17
~funk **230**
~funknavigation **230** 22–53
~gast **226** 31
~geschwindigkeitsmesser **228** 16
Flughafen **230**
~empfangsgebäude **230** 5
~frachthalle **230** 21
~funkbefeuerung **230** 12 u. 18
~restaurant **230** 5
~verwaltung **230** 5
~werftanlage **230** 9
~wetterstation **230** 8
Flug·höhe **4** 38
~leitung **230** 5
~loch **78** 48
~navigationseinrichtung **230** 22–38
~passagier **226** 31
~platz **230** 1
~postbrief **232** 18
~postbriefkasten **231** 28
~postmarke **232** 19
~scheinschalter **230** 5
~schlag **276** 33
~schleppstart **271** 7
~sicherungssystem **230** 22–38
Flugzeug **226** 21, 27, **230** 36
~anpeilung **230** 26
~antennenanlage **226** 44
~armaturenbrett **228** 3–16
~aufzug **222** 67, 74
~besatzung **226** 38–41
~empfänger **230** 25
~führer **226** 39
~führerkanzel **226** 37
~führersitz **228**
~halle **230** 6
~kolbenmotor **227** 1
~kran **222** 51
Flugzeug·kompaß **228** 11
~kran **222** 29
~küche **226** 43
~ladeluke **226** 35
~leitwerk **228** 39–47
~motoren **227**
~motorgondel **226** 6, 49
~passagierraum **226** 45
~positionslicht **226** 46
~reaktor **225** 71
~schlepp **271** 7
~schneekufe **225** 9
~schuppen **222** 30
~schwimmer **225** 33
~sender **230** 27
~-Sender-Empfänger **230** 31
~sporn **225** 6
~spornrad **225** 8
~steuerung **228**
~steuerwerk **228** 39–47
~träger **222** 65–77
~tragfläche **228** 45
Flugzeugtypen **225–226**
Fluidkompaß **219** 23
Flur **43** 1–34
~*[Feld]* **65** 17
~*[Sport]* **275** 34–36
~garderobe **43** 1
~hüter **65** 13
~wächter **65** 13
Fluß **13** 61, **16** 76, **211**
~aal **350** 17
~arm **13** 2, **211** 17
~aue **13** 62
~bau **211**
~bett **13** 68
~damm **211** 49
~ Eridanus **5** 12
~fähre **211** 10
Flüssiggastanker **216** 9
Flüssigkeits·barometer **10** 1
~getriebe **207** 4
~rakete **227** 49, **229** 1
Fluß·insel **211** 4
~kanalisierung **211** 31
~karpfen **350** 4
~krümmung **211** 42
~landschaft **13** 1–13
~lauf **211** 42
~mündung **13** 1
~nixe **307** 23
~perlmuschel **340** 31
~regulierung **211** 31
~schleppdampfer **211** 23
~tal **13** 57–70
~ufer **211** 5
~versickerung **13** 73
~wels **350** 12
Flußwindung **13** 11, **211** 42
Flüstertüte **269** 21
Fluter **211** 36
Flut·grenze **13** 35
~klappe **223** 20
~lichtanlage **199** 46
~welle **11** 53
Flyer **157** 27
~flügel **157** 25
Flyerin **157** 24
Flyer·lunte **157** 29
~spule **157** 23
~streckwerk **157** 22
f-Moll **300** 12
Fock·mast **213** 42, **214** 2, **215** 21
~rah **214** 32
~segel **213** 41, **214** 55
Fohlen **74** 2
Föhnsegeln **271** 23
Föhre **356** 20
Folie **10** 61
Follikel **22** 84
Fön **103** 30
Fond **185** 57
~fenster **185** 22
Fondsbörse **243** 1–10
Fondseitenteil **185** 2
Fontäne **257** 22
Fontur **160** 21
Football **275** 28–30
~spiel **275** 28–30
~spieler **275** 28
Förder·band **113** 77, **163** 32, **220** 39
~eimer **211** 58
~korb **137** 18, 19
~maschine **137** 3
~schacht **137** 14
~seil **137** 4
~sohle **137** 26
~strecke **137** 38, **138** 11
~turm **137** 5, **139** 48
~wagen **137** 18, 29, **138** 48
~werk **68** 55
Forelle **350** 15
Forellen·bach **89** 8
~wasser **89** 8
Forke **66** 7, 11
Forleule **82** 46
Form **198** 29
~, geschlossene **175** 36
~arbeit **155** 13–15
~brett **169** 10
Formel **327** 5
Former **141** 30
Formerei **141** 25–32
Formkasten **141** 19, 25
Formling **154** 9
Form·obstbäume **55** 1, 2, 16, 17, 29
~sand **141** 26
Formulare **232** 6–15
Formzylinder **175** 51
Forschungslaboratorium **292** 9
Forst **84** 1–34
~amt **16** 3
Förster **84** 35
Forst·garten **84** 6
~schädlinge **82**
Forstwirtschaft **84–85**
Forsythie **357** 1
forte **300** 58
~piano **300** 61
Fortepiano **304** 1
Fortführungspunkt **325** 29
fortissimo **300** 59
~ possibile **300** 60
Fortuna **308** 37
Foto **112** 45
~album **47** 14, **112** 52
~apparate **111** 1–27
~aufnahmelampe **112** 59
Fotograf **112** 20
Fotografie **111–112**
~ **47** 15, **112** 45
~, dreidimensionale **111** 27
Foto·grammetrie **15** 63–66
~karton **112** 47
~kopie **241** 23
~kopiergerät **241** 18
~labor **112** 1–61
~papier **112** 24
~platte **112** 41
~reproduktion **171**
~sammlung **47** 37
~ständer **112** 50
~thek **47** 37
~topographie **15** 63–66
~zelle **178** 5, **295** 49
~zubehör **111** 31–59
fouetté **288** 25
Foul **274** 51
Fox **71** 15
~terrier **71** 15
~trott **288** 43
Foyer **296** 12 u. 13
Fracht·brief **202** 35
~- Fahrgast-Schiff **216** 33, **218** 1–71
~fuhrmann **202** 16
~gut **202** 33
~gutannahme **202** 32
~kahn **211** 25, **220** 20
~wagen **202** 18
Frack **34** 57
~hemd **33** 41
~kragen **33** 55
~schleife **34** 60
~schoß **34** 58
Fragezeichen **325** 20
Fraktionierturm **139** 26
Frakto·kumulus **8** 12
~stratus **8** 11
Fraktur **325** 3
franc **244** 15, 16, 17, 18

Füllung **27** 33
Füllungsfußhebel **207** 22
Fund **309** 1–40
Fundament·graben **113** 75
~streifen **118** 2
~vorsprung **118** 3
Fundgegenstände, vorgeschichtl. **309** 1–40
Fünfeck **330** 9
Fünfmast·bark **215** 32–34
~vollschiff **215** 35
Fünf·meterplattform **268** 8
~paß **317** 40
~uhrtee **259** 44–46
~vierteltakt **299** 43
Funk·bake **228** 10, **230** 12
~befeuerung **230** 12 u. 18
Funken·fänger **205** 24
~horn **146** 47, **147** 61
~induktor **331** 70
~mariechen **289** 67
~strecke **147** 62, **331** 73
Funk·ermittlung **230** 34
~feuer **230** 12
~messung **230** 34
~peilerrahmenantenne **218** 5
~raum **218** 12, **223** 14
~sprechgerät **255** 41
~streife **248** 2
~streifenwagen **248** 2
~turm **16** 33
~zeichen **230** 12
Fürbug **310** 85
Furche **22** 25, **65** 8
Furchen·rad **68** 16
~wal **90** 44
Furie **308** 51
Furnier **127** 34, **128** 53
~bock **127** 32
~presse **127** 32
~schälmaschine **128** 52
~schnellpresse **128** 56
Fürstenhut **246** 40
Fürstin **338** 20
Fusa **299** 18
Fuß **18** 54, **19** 26–29, **21** 52–63
~ *[Orgel]* **305** 23
~abstreicher **261** 44
~abstreifer **118** 25
Fußball **274** 52
~elf **274** 11–21
Fußballer **274** 11–21
Fußball·feld **274** 1
~mannschaft **274** 11–21
Fußball·schuh **274** 29
~spiel **274** 1–63
~spieler **274** 11–21
~tor **274** 2
Fuß·bank **44** 36
~boden **118**
~bodensteckdose **120** 31
~bremse **173** 12, **182** 16, **185** 40
~brett **287** 56
~ende **48** 4
Fußgänger **253** 32
~überweg **194** 3, **253** 33
Fuß·gebinde **117** 76
~hebel **144** 14, **185** 39–41
~kasten **181** 23
~kissen **47** 20
~kontakt **27** 12, **133** 46
~leiste **121** 34, **259** 52
~linie **117** 81
~luftpumpe **192** 49
~maschine **303** 54
~maß **99** 12
~matte **43** 34
~muskel **20** 49
~note **178** 62
~pferd *[Segelschiff]* **214** 46
~pfette **116** 44, **117** 40
~pflege **25** 18
~pfleger **25** 19
~platte **114** 50, **283** 48, **322** 23
~position **288** 1–5
~rampenleuchte **297** 26
~raste **182** 37
~richter **276** 25
~ring **75** 42
~rücken **21** 61
~sack **286** 27
~schalter **52** 10
~schalthebel **182** 36
~schemel **44** 36
~sohle **21** 62
~sprung **268** 13
~steg **178** 58
~steuerhebel **133** 11
~stück **177** 25
~stütze **104** 32, **179** 7, **204** 43
~teil **29** 11, **48** 4
Fußtritt *[Orgel]* **305** 48
~ *[Wagen]* **179** 13
~hebel **177** 18
Fuß·ventil **254** 6
~verband **17** 4
~weg **16** 43
~winde **145** 21
~wurzelknochen **19** 26
Futter *[Kleidung]* **34** 18, 43
Futteral **201** 10
Futter·apparat **75** 8
~automat **75** 8
Futter·bau **70** 1–28
~brett **118** 56
~dämpfer **67** 55
~eimer **339** 7
Fütterer **75** 8
Futter·gang **76** 33
~haus **54** 14
~klee **70** 1
~krippe **76** 3
~messer **66** 34
~napf **71** 36
~pflanzen **70**
~rinne **76** 32
~rübe **70** 21
~rübenmiete **64** 12
~schneidemaschine **75** 41
~schneider **75** 41
~silo **64** 45
~speicher **64** 45
~stampfer **66** 34
~stelle **86** 28
~stoff **102** 69
~tisch **75** 22, **76** 32
~trog **76** 43
~wicke **70** 18

G

Gabel **46** 58
~ *[Telefon]* **233** 29
~ *[Wagen]* **72** 29, **179** 30
~deichsel **179** 30
~flinte **336** 28
~häkelei **101** 28
~heuwender **67** 29
~kopf **180** 11
~kreuz **313** 55
~mücke **341** 33
~schaft **180** 10
~schaftrohr **180** 10
~scheide **180** 12
~schleuder **258** 9
~schlüssel **191** 15
~stapler **202** 20, **221** 12
~verkleidung **183** 24
~weihe **347** 11
Gaff **89** 12
Gaffel **214** 45
~geer **214** 70
~segel **215** 1
~stander **214** 49
~toppsegel **214** 31
Gagel **357** 33
Gaillardie **62** 19
Galanterie·degen **338** 63
~warenabteilung **256** 62
Galaxis **5** 35
Galeere **213** 44 - 50
Galeeren·sklave **213** 48
~sträfling **213** 48
Galerie **1** 42, **296** 16
Galette **163** 16
Galgen **220** 67, **292** 21
~mikrophon **293** 28
Gallapfel **82** 34
Galle **82** 34
Gallen·blase **22** 11, 36
~blasengang **22** 38
~gang **22** 37 u. 38
Gall·mücke **81** 40
~wespe **82** 33
Galopp **73** 43 u. 44
~rennen **272** 1–29
Galosche **100** 27
Galvanoplastik **172**
Galvanoplastiker **172** 4
Gamasche **272** 44, **283** 57, **335** 17
Gamaschenhose **31** 27
Gambe **301** 23
Gamma·strahlung **1** 12, 17
~strahlenbehandlung **29** 48–55
Gams **352** 3
~wurz **63** 13
Ganasche **73** 11
Gang **39** 73, **311** 27
~ *[Fechten]* **277** 17 u. 18
~art **73** 39–44
~einstellung **181** 35
~gewicht **107** 35
~regler **107** 24–26
~schaltung **207** 4
~wähler **207** 12
Ganner **343** 15
Gans **74** 34
Gänse·blümchen **360** 1
~feder **324** 26
~fuß **63** 25
~füßchen **325** 26
~fußschar **68** 34
~kresse **63** 9
Ganser **74** 34
Gänserich **74** 34
Gänse·säger **343** 15
~vögel **343** 15–17
Gantelet **310** 50
Ganter **74** 34
Ganz·holz **115** 87
~packung **23** 19
ganzrandig **354** 43
Ganzstahlkarosserie **185** 1
Garage **39** 32, 79, **190** 32
Garageneinfahrt **39** 52
Gäraufsatz **333** 7
Garbe **65** 23
Gärbottich **93** 12
Garderobe **296** 5
~ *[Möbel]* **43** 1
Garderoben·frau **296** 6
~halle **296** 5–11
~marke **296** 7
~nummer **296** 7
~spiegel **43** 5
~ständer **260** 12
~stange **48** 45
~tisch **43** 6
Garderobiere **296** 6
Gardine **48** 21

Grab·stätte **312** 23, **319** 16
~stein **312** 26
~stelle **312** 23
~stichel **129** 24, **323** 20
~zahn **196** 6
Gradbogen **219** 2
Gradier·wärter **262** 5
~werk **16** 32, **262** 1
Gradnetz **15** 1–7
Grafenkrone **246** 45
Granatapfel **368** 16
Granate **90** 53
Granaten-Rumpf **225** 44
Granatoeder **330** 7
Grande **289** 26
Granierstahl **323** 19
Granne **69** 12
Graphit **3** 18
~meiler **1** 31–46
~mine **239** 36
Gras **130** 26
~ *[Spielkarte]* **265** 43
~büschel **359** 44
Grasen **265** 43
Gras·halm **354** 83–85
~hüpfer **342** 8
~mähmaschine **67** 27
Grat **282** 22
~ *[Dach]* **116** 12
Grätenschritt **283** 27
Gräting **219** 17
Grätsche **279** 20
Grätschen **278** 2
Grätsch·fahrt **283** 20
~stellung **278** 2
Grat·sparren **116** 62
~ziegel **117** 8
Grauleiter **320** 15
Graupe **98** 35
Graupeln **9** 35
Graureiher **343** 18
Gravier·kugel **106** 34
~nadel **323** 16
Gravis **325** 31
Gravur **38** 29
Greif **307** 11, **347** 1–24
~arm **2** 47
Greifenklaue **307** 13
Greifer **145** 57, **149** 35, **169** 22
~brücke **148** 21
~drehkran **148** 5
~system **174** 20
~wagen **174** 11
Greif·spiel **258** 23
~werkzeug **23** 50
~zange **2** 44, **29** 53, **323** 50
~zirkel **129** 18
Greiskraut **63** 12
Grendel **68** 9
Grenz·horizont **13** 21
~kontrolle **247** 12
~lehrdorn **142** 52
Grenz·lehre **142** 49
~rain **65** 3
~schichtzaun **225** 55
~stein **65** 2
~übertrittsausweis **247** 14
Gretchen·frisur **35** 31
~gewand **338** 37
Greyhound **71** 24
Griebs **60** 59
Grieche **338** 3
Griechenland **14** 8
Griechin **338** 1
griechisch **324** 15
Grieß **98** 36
Griessäule **68** 8
Grieß- u. Dunstauflösestuhl **91** 61
~- u. Dunstputzmaschine **91** 60
Grießung **91** 57
Grießwärtel **310** 75
Griff **37** 11, **134** 45, **180** 3, **249** 56
~ *[Sport]* **279** 53–56
~art **279** 53–56
~brett **302** 22, **303** 8
Griffel **249** 57
~ *[Fruchtknoten]* **60** 42, **354** 55
~kasten **249** 66
Griff·loch **302** 33, **303** 34
~saite **303** 24
~stange **160** 22, **277** 56
Grillapparat **42** 29
Grille **341** 6
Grimmdarm **22** 19-21
Grindel **68** 9
Grob·brecher **153** 6
~hechel **125** 4
~kreiselbrecher **150** 19
~schmied **132** 10
~sieb **77** 36
Grönländer **269** 4
Groom **179** 27
Groschen **244** 13
Groß·abteil **204** 56
~bagger **151** 3
~baum **214** 44
~behälter **208** 26
~binder **126** 16
~-Bramsaling **214** 53
~bramsegel **213** 53
~-Bramstagsegel **214** 25
~bramstenge **214** 7
Groß·britannien **14** 9
~buchstabe **170** 11
größer als **327** 19
Großer Bär **5** 29
~ Hund **5** 14
~ Ozean **15** 19
~ Wagen **5** 29
Groß·hirn **19** 42, **20** 22
~kabine **209** 52
Groß·kaffeemaschine **261** 2
~kern **340** 11
~kopf **81** 1
~markthalle **252** 50
~-Marssaling **214** 52
~marsstenge **214** 6
~mast **213** 40, **214** 5, **215** 22
~maul **349** 10, 13
~mutter **258** 14
~-Oberbramrah **214** 42
~-Oberbramsegel **214** 65
~-Obermarsrah **214** 40
~-Obermarssegel **214** 63
~rah **213** 37, **214** 38
Großraum **204** 25
~kabine **209** 52
~lastwagen **189** 39
~lore **150** 14
~-Straßenbahnzug **193** 1
Groß-Royal·rah **214** 43
~segel **214** 66
~stagsegel **214** 26
Groß·schneefräse **195** 21
~segel **213** 33, **214** 61, **215** 11, **270** 28
~specht **343** 27
~stadt **252** 1–70
~stenge **214** 6
~-Stengestagsegel **214** 24
~tanker **216** 22
~topp **214** 5–6
~-Unterbramrah **214** 41
~-Unterbramsegel **214** 64
~-Untermarsrah **214** 39
~-Untermarssegel **214** 62
~vatermütze **36** 5
~vieh **74** 1 u. 2
Grotesk **325** 7
Groteske **288** 35
Groteskschrift **325** 7
Grotte **257** 1
Grubber **68** 31
Grübchen **18** 16
Grube **312** 34
~ *[Bergwerk]* **137** 1–40
Gruben·betrieb **137** 3–11, 14–40
~geräte **138** 37–53
~helm **138** 54
~lampe **138** 57 u. 58
~lokomotive **137** 28, **138** 46 u. 47
~lüfter **137** 10
~maschine **138** 37–53
~ventilator **137** 10
Gruben·wagen **137** 29
~wasser **137** 30
~zug **137** 28 u. 29
Grummet **65** 35–43
grün **246** 29, **320** 8
Grün *[Golf]* **276** 62
~ *[Spielkarte]* **265** 43
~alge **362** 43
~anlage **252** 10
Grund·ablaß **212** 62, **254** 34
~birne **69** 38
~blatt **359** 9
~brett **112** 33
Gründel **68** 9
Grund·figur **284** 13–20
~fläche **329** 35, 39
~gewicht **90** 10, **224** 18
~hobel **127** 60
Grundierpinsel **321** 9
Grundlinie *[Ballspiel]* **276** 3–10
~ *[Mathematik]* **328** 27
Grund·platte **134** 36, **141** 51, **160** 34
~rahmen **162** 15
~rechnungsart **326** 23–26
~riß **144** 63
~rute **89** 22
~spieler **276** 43
~stellung **277** 32, **278** 1
~strecke **137** 38, **138** 11
~tau **90** 18, **224** 17
~teller **46** 3
Gründung **211** 8
Grundwasser **12** 21
~spiegel **254** 1, 42, 63
~strom **254** 3
Grund·werk **167** 28
~wert **327** 7
~zahl **326** 5, **327** 2, 6
Grün·fläche **39** 76, **257** 36
~futterschneider **75** 41
~futtersilo **75** 19
~kern **69** 25
~kohl **59** 34
Grünling **365** 29
Grünmalz **92** 11
~wender **92** 9
Grünstreifen **197** 37
Gruppenwähler **233** 38
Grus **5** 42
Gruß **277** 32
G-Saite **302** 9
G-Schlüssel **299** 10
γ-Strahlung **1** 17
Guanako **351** 30
Guaschfarbe **321** 17
Guckloch **43** 31, **248** 15
Gugelhupf **97** 44

Hohl·spiegel **6** 4, **108** 36, **111** 52
~stützisolator **147** 54
~tier **340** 14, **349** 5, 9, 14, 20
~vene **20** 9, 15, **22** 53, 57
~weg **16** 84
Höhrrohr **26** 26
Holder **358** 35
Holder·beere **358** 37
~blüte **358** 36
~busch **358** 35
Holländer **167** 27
~karren **145** 80
Höllennatter **350** 40
Holler **358** 35
~beere **358** 37
~blüte **358** 36
Holm **40** 16
~ *[Barren]* **279** 28
~ *[Segelflugzeug]* **271** 53
~ *[Rudersport]* **269** 35
Holoeder **330** 2
Holunder **358** 35
~beere **358** 37
~blüte **358** 36
~busch **358** 35
Holz **84** 1–34
~abfuhrweg **84** 3
~apfelbaum **60** 51
~auflage **149** 52
~bande **284** 41
~bearbeitungsmaschinen **128** 1–59
~bildhauer **322** 28
~birnbaum **60** 31
~blasinstrumente **302** 28–38
~block **322** 27
~bock **342** 44
~bottich **91** 27
~brücke **210** 45
~bündel **52** 61
~deckel **53** 54
~drehbank **129** 1
~druckwalze **156** 32
~einschlag **84** 15–34
~einspannvorrichtung **128** 31, 36
~ äller **84** 27
~faserplatte **321** 24
~fassung **239** 32
~feile **127** 29
~fender **213** 26
~feuer **266** 50
~fuhre **84** 15
~fuhrwerk **84** 15
~gehäuse **234** 36
~gewinde **136** 45
~gewindeschneiden **129** 14
Holzhacker **53** 10
~ *[Vogel]* **343** 27
Holz·hafen **220** 56 u. 57
~hammer **119** 14, **124** 15, **322** 21
~harmonika **303** 61
Holz·hauer **84** 27
~haufen **53** 31
~haus **39** 84-86
~keil **116** 96
~keule **275** 60
~klammer **112** 8
~klotz **53** 7, **64** 19
~korb **52** 63
~lager **220** 57
~lagerhalle **220** 56
~leitplanke **197** 38
~maske **337** 16
~miete **64** 17
~model **42** 63, **323** 2
~nagel **99** 17, **116** 92
~paneel **260** 37
~pantoffel **53** 63
~platte **321** 23
~platz **149** 30
~rand **249** 33
~raspel **127** 30
~rechen **58** 4
~reifen **126** 7
~riese **85** 7
~sandale **100** 6
~schaufel **91** 24
~scheit **52** 62
~schläger **276** 69
~schliff **167** 14–20
~schneidekunst **323** 1–13
~schnitt **323** 1–13
~schnitzel **167** 1
~schraube **117** 101, **127** 48, **136** 43
~schuh **100** 6
~span **129** 26
~stab **303** 62
~stapel **64** 16
~stativ **292** 23
~steckling **57** 25
~stethoskop **26** 26
~stich **323** 1
Holzstock **323** 1
~ *[Hauklotz]* **64** 18
Holz·stoß **53** 31, **84** 24
~transportwagen **208** 20
~treppe **40** 25
~trockner **149** 46
~turm **6** 16
~unterschuh **338** 43
~verbände **116**
~verbindungen **116** 84–98
~verkleidung **10** 51
~verschlag **25** 9, **40** 19
~wanne **262** 38
~ware **129** 19
~weg **84** 3
~zahn **91** 9
~zaun **39** 53
~zellstoff **167** 1–10
Honig **78** 33, 62, 63
~, türk. **291** 18
~behälter **78** 62
~biene **78** 1–25
Honig·glas **78** 63
~grube **61** 18
~kuchen **97** 5
~magen **78** 18
~raum **78** 45
~schleuder **78** 61
~wabe **78** 45
~zelle **78** 33
Honmaschine **192** 53
Hopfen·anpflanzung **16** 114
~garten **16** 114
~kessel **92** 35
Hordenblech **83** 23
Hörer **233** 30
Horizont **228** 4
Horizontal·bohrwerk **143** 33
~isolierung **118** 4
~seismograph **11** 39
~steuergenerator **236** 29
~stoß **264** 2
Horizont·hügel **292** 13
~kreisel **228** 4
Hörkopf **293** 4
Horn **307** 8
~ *[Werkzeug]* **119** 16, **132** 18
~ *[Musikinstrument]* **302** 41
~brille **108** 12
Hörnchen *[Gebäck]* **97** 41
~ *[Werkzeug]* **132** 28
Hörner·blitzableiter **332** 3
~elektrode **332** 4
~schlitten **285** 2
Hornhaut **21** 47
~mikroskop **109** 14
Horn·klee **360** 17
~tier **74** 1
Hör·saal **250** 2
~-Seh-Gerät **108** 22
~spielstudio **234** 7–12
Horst **12** 10
Hortnerin **50** 1
Höschen **33** 21
~ *[Biene]* **78** 3
Hose **34** 10, 56
~ *[Pferd]* **73** 36
~ *[Vogel]* **347** 3
~, kniefreie **31** 54
Hosen·bein **34** 11
~boden **34** 34
~boje **224** 51
~bügel **48** 46
~bund **34** 28
~knopf **34** 29, **37** 27
~latz **31** 51
~schlitz **34** 30
~spanner **48** 46
~tasche **34** 31
~träger **33** 47
Hostie **313** 26
Hostien·schachtel **311** 11
~teller **311** 12
Hotel **259**
~bar **259** 51
~boy **259** 18
~diele **259** 44–46
~diener **200** 17
~direktor **259** 19
~gast **259** 14
~halle **259** 18–26
~marke **201** 6
~page **259** 18
~rechnung **259** 11
~restaurant **259** 20
~- u. Zimmernachweis **200** 28
~zimmer **259** 27–38
Hourdi(s) **151** 26
~stein **151** 26
Hub·bandfeile **134** 3
~brücke **210** 65
Hubel **154** 10
Hub·höhe **210** 70
~karren **145** 27
~kette **133** 39
~magnet **233** 49
~motor **143** 27
~schrauber **83** 47
~schrauberlandeplatz **230** 15
~spindel **212** 36
~stapler **151** 18
~teil **233** 47
~tor **212** 31, 38
~turm **210** 66
~vorrichtung **221** 13
~werk **145** 3
Huckepackflugzeug **226** 22
Huf **73** 26
~eisenbogen **318** 30
~eisenmagnet **332** 36
~hammer **132** 42
~lattich **364** 8
~nagelnotenschrift **299** 2
~raspel **132** 41
~schmiedehammer **132** 38
Hüft·bein **19** 18
~blutader **20** 18
Hüfte **18** 33, **73** 32
Hüft·former **33** 16
~griff **17** 38
~gürtel **33** 18
~halter **33** 18
Huftiere **352** 1–10, 20–31
Hüft·nerv **20** 30
~schlagader **20** 17
~stütz **278** 9
Hügel **13** 66
Huhn **74** 19–26
Hühner·auslauf **75** 18
~ei **75** 47
~einschlupf **75** 3
~farm **75**
~habicht **347** 10
~haltung **75** 1–46
~haus **75** 13
~hof **75** 18

Hühner·hund **71** 41
~leiter **75** 4
~myrte **63** 27
~nest **75** 6
~ring **75** 42
~stall **75** 13
~steige **75** 4
~stiege **75** 4
~vogel **343** 22
~zucht **75** 1–46
Hülle **201** 10, **239** 13
Hüllkelch **359** 33
Hülse **59** 6, **354** 92
Hülsen·früchte
59 1-11
~kasten **159** 21
~kopf **87** 16
~mais **69** 31
Hülsstrauch **358** 9
Humboldtstrom **15** 42
Humerale **314** 40
Hummel **342** 23
Hummergabel **46** 79
Humusandeckung
196 64
Hund **71**, **74** 16
Hunde·abteil **203** 12
~artige **352** 11–13
~bürste **71** 28
~garnitur **71** 27–30
~halsband **71** 13
~haus **64** 23
~hütte **64** 23
~kamm **71** 29
~leib **307** 30
~leine **71** 30
~meute **86** 33,
272 62
~rassen **71**
Hunderterstelle
326 3
Hundert·meterstein
198 83
~satz **327** 7
Hundertstel **326** 20
Hunde·schlitten
336 3
~schwanz **71** 12
Hündin **74** 16
Hunds·kamille **63** 8
~kopf **93** 23
~lattich **63** 13
~quecke **63** 30
~rose **357** 26
Hünengrab **309** 16
Hunger·blume **63** 1
~korn **69** 4
Hunter **272** 24
Hupenknopf **182** 24
186 4
Hüpfspiel **258** 13
Hürde **272** 27,
280 12
Hürden·lauf
280 11 u. 12
~läufer **280** 11
Hut **36** 7, 17, 19
~ *[Böttcher]* **126** 36
~ *[Pilz]* **365** 4
~, thessalischer
338 4
~ablage **43** 4
Hut·band **36** 14
~bord **43** 4
Hütegeschäft **36** 1–26
Hut·form **36** 32
~geschäft **36** 1–26
~haken **260** 13
~kopf **36** 12
~laden **36** 1–26
~macherin **36** 30
~nadel **36** 50
~putz **36** 49
~rand **36** 16
~salon **36** 27–57
~schachtel **201** 11
~ständer **36** 51
Hütte **282** 1
~ *[Schiff]* **218** 33
Hüttenjagd **86** 47–52
Hutze **226** 72
Hyäne **353** 1
Hydra **307** 32
~ *[Sternbild]* **5** 16
Hydrallmania **349** 9
Hydrant **255** 35
Hydrantenschlüssel
255 27
Hydratsilo **153** 26
Hydraulik **133** 24
Hydreidpolyp **349** 9
Hydrierung **164** 16
Hydrofiner **139** 65
Hydroformer **139** 64
Hydroxylamin-
zuleitung **164** 21
Hygrograph **10** 54
Hygrometer **10** 23,
25 10, **166** 10
Hyperbel **329** 26
Hypotenuse **328** 32
Hypothekenpfand-
brief **243** 11–19
Hypotrachelion
316 22
Hypozentrum
11 32, 33

I

identisch **327** 16
Identität **327** 5
Identitätszeichen
327 16
Idol **309** 20
Igel **351** 5
~kopf **35** 10
~wulst **316** 21
Iglu **336** 4
Ikarier **298** 21
Ikosaeder **330** 11
Ikositetraeder **330** 12
Ilge **62** 12
Illusionist **298** 20
ILS-Gleitwegsender
230 14
ILS-Haupteinflug-
zeichen **230** 13
ILS-Kurssender
230 11
Illuminator **110** 20
Illustrierte **47** 10
Imago **342** 10
Imker **78** 57
Imme **78** 1–25
Impair **263** 23
Imprägnierkufe
161 32
Imprägnierungs-
mittelzerstäuber
83 34–37
Impressum **325** 39
Impuls·erzeuger
237 17
~trennstufe **236** 15
Indexskala **241** 26
Indianer **335** 25
~frau **335** 10
~häuptling **335** 11
Indien **14** 46
Indio **335** 23
Indirektstrahler
112 60
Indischer Ozean
15 23
Indonesien **14** 53
Indossament **242** 25
Indossant **242** 27
Indossat **242** 26
Indossatar **242** 26
Induktionsspule
11 44
Induktor **331** 70
Industrie·gelände
252 58
~hafen **139** 68
~obligation
243 11–19
~pflanzen **367**
In-Fässer-Bringen
93 20–28
Infinitesimalrechnung
327 13 u. 14
Influenzmaschine
331 54
Inful **314** 46
Ingenieur **144** 23
Inhaberaktie **243** 11
Inhalation **262** 7
Inhalations·gerät
23 33
~kur **262** 6 u. 7
Inhalatorium **262** 6
Inhalierflüssigkeit
23 35
Initial **170** 1
Injektionsspritze
26 28, **27** 54
Inkarnatklee **70** 4
Inkreis **328** 31
Inlett **48** 8
Innen·auslage **257** 13
~elektrode **2** 3
~kiel **269** 50
~plattform **204** 9
~ring **136** 70
~sohle **99** 51
~stadt **252** 33
~sturm **274** 18, 19, 20
~stürmer **274** 18, 20
~tasche **34** 19
~taster **129** 23
~titel **178** 45
~trommel **166** 3
~verzahnung **136** 93
Insekten **342** 3-24
~auge **78** 20-24
~fresser **351** 4-7
~sammlung **47** 35
Insel **13** 6
~ *[Schiff]* **211** 4,
222 68
~*[Straße]* **253** 30
~lampe **190** 30
Inserat **325** 51 u. 52
Inspizient **297** 30
Inspizientenstand
297 29
Installateur **119** 23
Installation **119** 33-67
Instrumente, ärztliche
26 26-62
~, chirurgische
28 46-59
~, geodät. **110** 30-38
~, meteorolog. **10**
~, sterile **28** 14
~, topograph.
110 30-38
Instrumenten·gehäuse
2 5, 22
~kasten **10** 62
~-Lande-System-
Kurssender **230** 11
~platte **27** 16
~schrank **27** 23
~teil **229** 3-5
~tisch **26** 20, **27** 24,
28 12
Intarsia **47** 48
Integral **327** 14
~zeichen **327** 14
Integrand **327** 14
Integration **327** 14
Integrationskonstante
327 14
Interferenzkomperator
110 29
Interferometer **110** 25
Intergrator **29** 49
Integriergerät **29** 49
Intervall **300** 20-27
Intrusion **11** 30
Invalide **257** 55
Ionenfallenmagnet
236 17
Ionisationskammer
2 2, 17
Ionosphäre **4** 13
Irak **14** 45
Iran **14** 44
Iris **21** 42
~ *[Pflanze]* **62** 8
Irland **14** 10
Irrgarten **257** 5
Irrigator **23** 46
Ischiasnerv **20** 30
Island **14** 11
Isobare **9** 1, 2, 3
Isobathe **16** 11
Isochimene **9** 42
Isohelie **9** 44
Isohyete **9** 45
Isohypse **16** 62
Isolator **331** 64
~kette **234** 22

Kithara **301** 14, **308** 71
Kitt **122** 17
Kittelschürze **50** 2
Kittmesser **122** 27
Kitz **88** 39
Kitzler **22** 88
Klamm **13** 52
Klammer **53** 42, **112** 8, **116** 97
~, eckige **325** 25
~, runde **325** 24
~beutel **53** 40
~fuß **350** 34
~gewicht **112** 7
Klammernstab **240** 40
Klammer·sack **53** 40
~schlittschuh **284** 25
Klampfe **303** 12
Klangfilter **306** 40
~schaltung **306** 40
Klangregister **306** 26
Klapp·aschenbecher **203** 46
~bett **262** 33
~brücke **203** 33, **210** 61
~dach **183** 9
~deckel **23** 17, **53** 33, **120** 15
Klappe **22** 46, **239** 14, **302** 35
Klappen·kasten **259** 5
~mann **292** 34
~schrank **233** 5
~text **178** 39
~ventil **227** 14
Klapper **30** 42, **289** 40
~mohn **63** 2
~storch **64** 7
Klapp·fenster **75** 2
~gelenk **298** 33
~gitter **203** 32
~hut **36** 20
~kamera **111** 2
~laden **39** 30
~lüftung **79** 10
~mütze **31** 47
~sitz **185** 55, **204** 11
~tintenfaß **249** 63
~tisch **266** 5
~tischchen **204** 38
~verdeck **179** 52
~vorrichtung **224** 32
~wehr **212** 65–72
Kläranlage **252** 64
Klarinette **302** 34
Klasse **249** 1
Klassen·buch **249** 13
~schrank **249** 25
~zimmer **249** 1
Klassieranlage **153** 8
Klassizismus **318** 15
Klatsche **83** 2
Klatsch·mohn **63** 2
~weib **53** 29
Klaue **307** 3, **308** 13
~ *[techn.]* **169** 48
Klauen·fassung **38** 25
~schote **70** 11
Klaviatur **301** 28, **303** 40, **304** 4 u. 5
Klavichord **301** 36
~mechanik **301** 37
Klavier **44** 32, **304** 1
~bank **44** 35
~gehäuse **304** 6
~hammer **304** 3
~lampe **44** 38
~lehrerin **44** 37
~mechanik **304** 2–18
~pedal **304** 8 u. 9
~saite **304** 7
~schüler **44** 34
~spiel **44** 34
~spieler **298** 1
~stunde **44** 32–37
~tasten **304** 4 u. 5
~unterricht **44** 32–37
Klavizimbel **301** 45
Klebarbeit **50** 28
Klebebindung **177** 39
Klebezettel für Eilsendung **232** 31
~ für Einschreibsendung **232** 33
~ für Luftpostsendung **232** 32
~ für Wertsendung **232** 28
Kleb·rolle **238** 78
~streifen **238** 79
Klecks **249** 47
Klee **70** 1, 2, 6, 9, 10
Kleeblatt **70** 5
~bogen **318** 32
~kreuz **313** 65
Klee·blüte **70** 7
~karre **66** 39
~sämaschine **66** 39
Kleiber **346** 11
Kleid **32** 8, **338** 25
Kleidchen **31** 22
Kleider·ablage **43** 1, **296** 5
~abteil **259** 30
~bürste **52** 66
~falte **32** 38
~haken **43** 3, **260** 14
~laus **341** 31
~leiste **52** 69
~moden **338**
~motte **341** 14
~netz **181** 11
~schrank **48** 40
~schürze **32** 19
~schutz **102** 43, **181** 11
~ständer **260** 12
~stange **256** 31
Kleidungszubehör **37**
Klein·auto **183** 41
~automat **120** 18
~bahn **16** 25, **199** 19
~bahnhof **199** 4
~behälter **202** 25
~bildkamera **111** 18
~bildfilm **112** 21
Klein·bildpatrone **112** 26
~buchstabe **170** 12
~bus **188** 1
kleiner als **327** 20
Kleiner Bär **5** 34
~ Hund **5** 15
~ Wagen **5** 34
Klein·garten **55** 1–31
~gärtner **55** 24
~hirn **19** 45
~kabine **209** 20
~kabinenbahn **209** 19
~kampfschiff **222** 11–13
~kern **340** 12
~kind **49** 26
~kunstbühne **298** 1–3
~lastwagen **189** 1–13
Kleinod **246** 1, 11, 30–36
Klein·offset-Stapeldrucker **174** 33
~omnibus **188** 1
~pritschenwagen **189** 10
~schmetterling **60** 62
~sieb **77** 35
~sprengwagen **195** 3
~stadt **252** 1–70
Kleinstkind **30** 26
Klein·teile-Sortimentkasten **192** 35
~tierpferch **202** 7
~transporter **189** 1–13
~vieh **74** 18–37
~wagen **183** 41
Kleister **121** 30
~bürste **121** 37
~pinsel **50** 27
~topf **50** 26, **121** 29, **231** 5
Klemmbacke **241** 5
Klemme **334** 33
Klemmer **334** 33
~ *[Brille]* **108** 28
Klemm·feder **159** 33
~lupe **107** 70
~platte **198** 40
~ring **142** 40
~schlittschuh **284** 25
~schraube **111** 35
~vorrichtung **2** 43
~walzenpaar **158** 39
Klempner **119** 13
Kleriker **314** 25–58
Klerus **314** 32–58
Kletter·baum **339** 3
~bohne **59** 8
~haken **282** 55
~hammer **282** 52
~hose **282** 8
Kletterjacke **282** 7
Klettern **282** 2–14
Kletter·pflanze **59** 8
~rose **55** 12
~schluß **282** 29
~schuh **282** 51
~seil **282** 13, **279** 5
~seilhangeln **279** 6
~stange **279** 8
~tau **279** 5
~tauhangeln **279** 6
~technik **282** 2–14
~vogel **345** 6
~weste **282** 7
~wurzel **354** 80
Klicker **258** 57
Kliff **13** 28
Klima **9** 53–58
~anlage **186** 22–24, **339** 5
~karte **9** 40–58
~kunde **9**
~landschaft **339** 45
~schaubild **339** 45
Klinge **46** 54, **277** 58
Klingel·beutel **311** 63
~tafel **259** 28
~taster **120** 2
Klingenschärfer **51** 73
Klinke **233** 7
Klinkenfeld **233** 8
Klinker·beplankung **270** 19–21
~einer **269** 18
~kühler **152** 9
~lager **152** 10
Klinknagel **270** 21
Klinopinakoid **330** 24
Klio **308** 59
Klipp **239** 25
~dachs **351** 24
Klippe **13** 25
Klipper **215** 36
Klipp·schliefer **351** 24
~vorrichtung **67** 59
Klips **38** 9
~schraube **38** 3
Klischee **172** 31
~ätzmaschine **172** 23
~facette **172** 37
~fuß **172** 34
~herstellung **172**
~holz **172** 34
Klischniggakt **298** 13
Klistier **23** 46
~apparat **23** 46
~spritze **30** 20
Klivie **56** 8
Kloakentier **351** 1
Klöbeisen **126** 11
Kloben **53** 39, **64** 19
Klopfeisen **130** 36
Klöpfel **127** 9, **150** 36

Krumm·schere 119 33
~stab 314 48
Krümmungs·halbmesser 328 22
~mittelpunkt 328 23
Kruppe 73 31
Krüppelwalm 116 17
~dach 116 16
Kruste 97 23
Krustentiere 342 1 u. 2
Kruzifix 311 40, 313 32, 314 6
Kübel 79 47, 312 61
~helm 246 7
~pflanze 79 46
Kubikwurzel 327 2
Kübler 126 16
Kubusspiel 50 13
Küche 41, 42
Kuchen 97 45
Küchenabfall 41 34
Kuchen·blech 42 53
~büfett 261 1
~bürste 42 59
~formen 42 48 u. 49
Küchen·gardine 41 13
~geräte 42 1–66
Kuchenheber 45 28
Küchenherd 41 39
~, elektr. 42 26
Küchen·maschinen 42 1–66
~meister 204 23
~messer 41 56
Kuchenplatte 45 26
Küchenschabe 341 18
Kuchen·schachtel 97 4
~schaufel 45 28
Küchen·schrank 41 8
~stuhl 41 52
Kuchenteller 45 9
Küchen·tisch 41 53
~tuch 41 14–16
~uhr 42 19, 107 50
~waage 41 59
~wagen 204 51
Kuchenzange 45 36, 97 8
Küchenzwiebel 59 24
Küchlein 75 33
Kuckuck 343 30
Kuckucks·knecht 343 25
~küster 343 25
~lichtnelke 360 21
~uhr 107 54
Kufe 271 33, 284 47, 285 3
Kufengleiter 286 16
Küfer 80 39, 126 16
~setzhammer 126 32
Kugel 180 56, 329 41
~ *[Fleischteil]* 95 36
~ *[Sport]* 280 46, 287 3
~akazie 54 11
~baum 257 12
Kugel·fang 287 4
~fangkasten 173 31
~fräser 106 7
~gasspeicher 148 64
~gelenk 111 33
~hantel 281 3
~kocher 167 21
~kopfnadel 309 29
~kuppe 136 48
~kupplung 181 21
~lager 136 67
~lauf 87 26
~leuchte 259 4
~manipulator 2 38
~mühle 153 25, 154 1
~ring 180 68
~rinne 287 16
~robinie 54 11
~rücklauf 287 16
~schreiber 239 26
~schlagapparat 40 32
~speicher 148 64
~spitze 26 47
~stoßen 280 45–47
~stoßer 280 45
~tank 139 67
~umlauflenkung 186 39
Kuh 74 1, 76 18
~blume 63 13
~fladen 76 22
~fuß 192 6
~horn 76 38
~kette 76 31
Kühl·anlage 96 2
~apparat 93 6
Kuhlattich 63 13
Kühle 93 6
Kühler 139 27, 164 5, 334 48
~ *[Auto]* 185 9
~attrappe 185 12
~figur 187 3
~haube 286 10
~haubenfenster 286 11
~verschluß 185 10
Kühl·flüssigkeit 184 69
~haus 94 16–18, 220 40
~kamin 145 61
~kessel 42 3
~körper 77 38
~mittelzuführung 142 25
~platte 96 3
~raum 94 16–18, 218 50
~rippe 187 29
~rohr 1 35, 93 13, 25
~schiff 93 1
~schiffträger 93 2
~schlitz 183 14
~schrank 42 1
~truhe 98 74
~turm 145 60
~vitrine 98 3
~wagen 208 27
Kühlwalze 164 27
Kühlwasser·ableitung 93 8
~anschlußstutzen 184 11
~austritt 3 29
~eintritt 3 28
~leitung 146 27
~pumpe 184 43
~rücklauf 3 11
~schlange 3 27
~schlauch 185 11
~temperaturanzeiger 207 13
~zuleitung 93 8
Kuh·magd 76 17
~mist 76 22
~schelle 359 5
~stall 64 47, 76 17–38
Küken 75 33
~aufzuchtstall 75 27
~heim 75 27
~napf 75 38
~tränke 75 37
~trog 75 34
~versandschachtel 75 40
Kukumer 59 13
Kukuruz 69 31
Külbel 155 15
Kuli 336 43
Kulisse 237 10, 292 33
Kulorohr 120 43
Kultivator 68 31
Kultur 84 9
~beutel 266 26
~haus 79 4
Kultwagen 309 36
Kümmelstange 97 56
Kümmerling 59 13
Kummet 72 15
~kissen 123 1
Kummetstock 123 4
Kumpel 137 1 u. 2
Kumpf 66 20
Kumt 72 15
~kissen 123 1
~stock 123 4
Kumulus 8 1
~wolke 271 16
Kunde 256 55
Kundin 98 45, 256 15
Kunst 315–319
~, ägypt. 315 1–18
~, altchristliche 316 61–71
~, babylonische 315 19–20
~, byzantinische 316 72–75
~, chinesische 319 1–6
~ der Assyrer 315 29–36
~ der Perser 315 21–28
~ der Renaissance 317 42–54
~ des Barocks 318 1–8
Kunst des Rokokos 318 9–13
~, etruskische 316 49–52
~, got. 317 22–41
~, graphische 323
~, griech. 316 1–48
~, ind. 319 19–28
~, islam. 319 12–18
~, japan. 319 7–11
~, kleinasiatische 315 37
~, roman. 317 1–21
~, röm. 316 53–60
~arm 23 49
~bein 23 48
~dünger 65 14
~flugfigur 271 17
~lauf 284 4–22
~läufer 284 4
~laufschlittschuh 284 31
Künstler 321 2
~hut 36 9
Künstlerin 298 3
Künstlerkopf 35 17
Kunst·maler 321 2
~mappe 47 54
~radfahren 287 31
~reiter 290 26
~schütze 290 38
~schwamm 112 16
~seide 163 1–34
~seidefabrikation 163 1–34
~springen 268 41–46
~springer 268 5
Kunststoff·förderband 138 15
~griff 135 23
~kugel 264 1
~polsterbank 203 40
~stäbchen 37 19
~trinkhalm 261 36
Kunst·tanz 288 29–41
~wabe 78 42
Kupee 187 10
Kupfer·anode 172 2
~druckpresse 323 36
~platte 323 53
~stecher 323 44
~stich 323 14–24
~zylinder 176 2, 24
Kupolofen 141 1
Kupon 243 18
~bogen 243 17
Kuppel 6 8, 316 58
~, feststehende 6 12
~achse 205 36
~bau 319 21
~ofen 141 1
~schraube 198 46
~schwelle 198 45, 88

Liege·halle **29** 21–25
~kur **29** 21–25, **262** 12–14
Liegende **138** 21
Liege·polster **29** 36
~sitz **204** 48
~sofa **48** 53
~stufe **25** 8
~stuhl **29** 21, **39** 47, **262** 13
~stütz **278** 16
~terrasse **39** 75
~wagen **204** 48
~wiese **39** 46, **262** 12
Lieschen **69** 33
Lift **256** 45
~boy **256** 47
~sessel **209** 16
Ligatur **170** 6
~führer **28** 50
Ligusterschwärmer **342** 55
Likör **98** 58
~karaffe **46** 48
~schale **46** 89
Liliaceae **56** 13
Lilie **62** 12, **246** 13
Liliengewächs **56** 13
Liliputaner **291** 22
Limonaden·glas **261** 16
~flasche **261** 15
Limone **368** 23
Limousine **187** 1, 8
Linde **355** 46
Linden·gewächs **56** 9
~holzgeflechteinlage **99** 9
Lindwurm **307** 1
lineal **354** 31
Lineal **144** 8, **177** 95, **249** 67
~einrichtung **173** 37
Linie **249** 35, **328** 1–23
Linien·blatt **249** 40
~fahrt **216** 32
~omnibus **188** 7
~richter **274** 23, 47
~schiff **213** 51–60
~schild **193** 23
~stichel **323** 5
Links·außen **274** 17
~maschine **295** 13
Linoleum **121** 42
~kitt **121** 45
~messer **121** 46
~unterlage **121** 43
Linotypematrize **169** 29
Linse *[Auge]* **21** 48
~ *[Optik]* **111** 10, **294** 43, **331** 30
~, sphär. **108** 1–8
Linsensystem **108** 9
Lintwurm **307** 1
Lippe **21** 26
Lippenmikrophon **255** 41
Lippenpfeife **331** 19
~ *[Orgel]* **305** 23–30, 31–33
Lippen·scheibe **337** 23
~stift **103** 19
lira **244** 20, 21
Lisene **317** 11
Lisse **131** 22
Litewka **216** 58
Litfaßsäule **253** 21
Lithodes **349** 16
Lithograph **323** 45
Lithographie **323** 25 u. 26
Litho·kreide **323** 26
~stein **323** 25, 57
Litze **125** 17, 22, **159** 27
Litzen·auge **159** 28, 29
~band **304** 36
Livree **179** 21
LKW **189** 14–50
LKW-Waage **145** 88
Loch **132** 20, **276** 67
~beitel **127** 63
~einsatz **41** 77
~eisen **119** 45, **123** 25, **132** 34
Locher **238** 80
Loch·feile **134** 22
~flagge **276** 68
~hammer **132** 33
~karte **241** 61
~kartenmaschinen **241** 35–61
~kranz **233** 27
~lehre **134** 63
~löffel **42** 61
~platte **134** 11
~rundmutter **136** 33
~säge **115** 63, **127** 27
~schere **119** 33
~stanze **134** 30
~stecher **101** 12
~stern **67** 19
~stickerei **101** 11
~- u. Datumprägezange **201** 56
~zange **123** 13
~ziegel **151** 21 u. 22
~zirkel **129** 23
Locke **35** 3
~ *[Jagd]* **87** 45
Locken·haar **35** 33
~kopf **35** 17
~perücke **35** 2
~wickel **103** 35
Lock·geräte **87** 43-47
~jagd **87** 43–47
~vogel **86** 48
~wellbürste **103** 37
Löffel **46** 61, **153** 3
~ *[Hase]* **88** 61
~bagger **113** 81, **153** 2
~bohrer **129** 16
~bug **270** 2
~gans **343** 5
Löffel·raspel **99** 36
~schaber **192** 16
Log **219** 31
Logarithmenrechnung **327** 6
Logarithmieren **327** 6
Logarithmierzeichen **327** 6
Logarithmus **327** 6
Logenschließer **296** 12
Logge **219** 31
Logger **90** 1
Loggia **39** 18, **53** 17
~tür **39** 21
Log·propeller **219** 32
~uhr **219** 34
Loh·eisen **85** 25
~löffel **85** 25
Lohnkutsche **179** 26
Lohrinde **84** 29
Lok **198** 6
Lokal **261** 27–44
~bahn **199** 19
~bahnhof **199** 4
Lok·aufstellgleis **199** 12
~bremszylinder **206** 49
~führer **203** 9
~führerhaus **205** 51
~heizer **203** 10
~kupplungsbügel **206** 23
~nummer **203** 6
Lokomotive **208** 44
~, elektrische **206** 1
Lokomotiv·achse **207** 1–10
~führer **203** 9
~heizer **203** 10
~kessel **205** 2–37
~personal **203** 9 u. 10
Lok·personal **203** 9 u. 10
~schuppen **199** 6
~schuppengleis **199** 9
~triebwerk **205** 2–37
~verkehrsgleis **199** 21
Lolch **63** 29
Long-Grip-Zange **192** 24
Looping **271** 17
Lophocalyx philippensis **349** 7
Lorbeerbaum **312** 60
Lore **196** 25
Lorgnon **108** 30
Lösch·anlage **153** 21
~blatt **249** 50
~boot **255** 65
Löscher **238** 19
Lösch·betrieb **221** 1–36
~fahrzeug **255** 5
~gerät **255** 63
~hebel **240** 44, 52, 54
Lösch·kammer **147** 55
~schalter **241** 27
~silo **153** 23
~trupp **255** 34
~turm **148** 17
~übung **255** 1–46
~wagen **148** 18
Loser **88** 16
Lösung **3** 26
~ *[Mathematik]* **327** 10
Losverkäufer **260** 20
Lot **113** 50, 71, **219** 35–42
~, opt. **110** 34
Löt·borax **106** 40
~gerät **119** 5–8
Lothringer Kreuz **313** 56
Lötkolben **106** 39, **119** 6, 50
Lotkörper **219** 36
Lötlampe **119** 49
Lotleine **219** 37
Lötmittel **106** 36
Lotossäule **315** 13
Löt·pistole **106** 14
~scheibe **106** 17
Lotsen·boot **216** 15
~rufsignal **245** 23
Löt·stange **106** 38
~stein **119** 7
~stelle **120** 61
Lotte **80** 13
Lötwasser **119** 8
Louisdor **244** 5
Louis-seize-Stil **318** 14
Löwe **353** 2
~ *[Sternbild]* **5** 17, **6** 36
Löwen·kopf **307** 17
~leib **307** 14
~mähne **353** 3
~rudel **339** 20
~rumpf **307** 22
~zahn **63** 13
Luchs **353** 8
Luffaschwamm **51** 13
Luft·ablaßschraube **23** 2
~abwehr-Schnellfeuergeschütz **223** 44
~abzug **339** 41
~akrobat **290** 7
~ansaugefilter **206** 20
~ansaugkanal **47** 3
~ansaugung **227** 34
~auslaßventil **224** 24
~austritt **186** 23
~austrittkieme **187** 20
~bad **268** 4
~ballon **291** 13
~behälter **206** 48
~bildmessung **15** 63–66
Luftbürsten-Streich·-anlage **168** 31
~maschine **168** 34

Noten·ständer **44** 30
~system **299** 45 u. 46
~wert **299** 14–21
Not·fahrte **138** 33
~gurt **72** 23
Notiz·block **238** 17
~zettel **238** 18
Not·landebahn **230** 3
~leiter **138** 33
~sitz **187** 12
~verband **17** 1–13
Nougat **98** 81
Nudel **98** 34
~holz **42** 54, **97** 67
~maschine **97** 78
Nugat **98** 81
Nullenzirkel **144** 38
Null·isotherme **9** 41
~meridian **15** 5
~punkt **147** 22
~punkteinstellung **2** 7, **332** 17
~taste **240** 65
Numerierschläge l **85** 43
Numerus **327** 6
Nummer **272** 22
Nummern·girl **298** 8
~kasten **259** 5
~schalter **233** 18
~schild **186** 31, **256** 10
~schildbeleuchtung **186** 37
~tafel **185** 43, **204** 29, **311** 24
Nurflügelmodell **271** 40
Nürnbergerin **338** 38
Nurse **30** 9, **258** 12
Nuß **354** 98, **368** 60
~ *[Fleisch]* **95** 52
~ *[Schloß]* **134** 43
Nußbaum **61** 37–43
~zweig **61** 37
Nüsse **61**
Nuß·häher **346** 1
~knacker **46** 49
~stück **95** 11
Nüster **73** 7
Nut **126** 30, **136** 83
Nuten·fräser **143** 16
~zylinder **158** 10, **177** 47
Nut·keil **136** 71 u. 72
~riemen **118** 74
Nutsche **333** 11
Nutz·fahrzeug **207** 39
~garten **55**
Nydamschiff **213** 1–6

O

Oase **337** 4
Obelisk **315** 10
Ober **259** 47, **260** 30
Oberarm **18** 43
~bein **19** 12
~knochen **19** 12
~schiene **310** 47
Ober·bauch **18** 35
~beton **197** 43
~check **272** 41
~deckomnibus **188** 6
~eisen **166** 36
~faden **102** 21
~feldwebelwohnraum **223** 48
Oberflächen·kondensator **146** 24
~prüfgerät **110** 27
~punkt **11** 33
~vorwärmer **205** 23
~welle **11** 36
Oberfräse **128** 22
Oberfräs·maschine **128** 22
~- und Bohrmaschine **128** 22
Ober·geschoß **39** 3, **113** 14
~gesenk **132** 36, **133** 42
~gurt **116** 74, 80, **210** 48
~haupt **212** 25
~hemd **33** 36
~kasten **141** 20
~kellner **260** 30
~kiefer **19** 36, **21** 27
~kieferbein **19** 36
~labium **305** 27
~lager **128** 21
~leder **99** 55
~leintuch **48** 12
~leitung **206** 2
~leitungsomnibus **188** 12, **252** 23
Oberlicht **28** 27, **39** 35
~band **116** 21
Oberlippe **21** 14, **73** 8
~ *[Orgel]* **305** 27
Ober·lippenrinne **18** 12
~messer **177** 19
~rohr **180** 16
Obers **97** 11, **261** 5
Oberschale **95** 13, 37, 54
Oberschenkel **18** 49
~bein **19** 22
~hose **338** 31
Oberschere **193** 16
Oberspannungs·-durchführung **146** 43
~wicklung **147** 15
Oberstein **91** 22
Oberstempel **244** 40
Ober·tasse **45** 7
~walze **141** 49
~werk **305** 2
~zange **156** 66
~zylinder **157** 11
Obi **336** 41
Objektgleittisch **110** 6
Objektiv **110** 5, **111** 10–14, 25, **112** 58
~revolver **110** 5
Objekt·schleuse **109** 3
~tischverstellung **109** 6
Oblate **313** 26
Obligation **243** 11–19
Oboe **302** 38
Observatorium **6** 2–11
Obstbaum **55** 30
~rückenspritze **83** 34–37
~schutz **83** 24–45
~-Zweiradkarrenspritze **83** 42
Obst·garten **16** 108, **55** 1–31
~händler **253** 11
~hochstamm **55** 30
~kern **60** 60
~konserve **98** 16
~korb **202** 11
~kuchen **45** 27
~messer **46** 71
~pflücker **58** 7
~schädlinge **81** 1–19
~schale **46** 40
~stand **291** 53
~torte **97** 16
~verkäufer **253** 11
~wagen **253** 10
Obus **188** 12, **252** 23
Occhiarbeit **101** 19
Ochse **74** 1, **94** 2
Ochsen·auge **318** 2
~gespann **65** 16
~treiber **5** 30
~ziemer **124** 18
Octans **5** 43
Odaliske **289** 41
Oertz-Ruder **217** 66 u. 67
Ofen **260** 34
~ *[techn.]* **140** 1, **153** 12
~aufgabe **153** 13
~bank **260** 36
~füllung **153** 14
~kachel **260** 35
~krücke **40** 42
~mantel **153** 17
~raum **140** 23
~rohr **41** 50, **53** 50
~schirm **52** 65
Office **204** 20
Offizier **216** 65
Offiziers·kajüte **218** 21
~wohnraum **223** 47
Öffnungsfrüchte **354** 91–96
Offset·druck **174**
~kopie **173**
~maschine **174** 1
Öhmd **65** 35–43
Ohr **18** 18, **19** 56–58, 62–64, **71** 2
Öhr **85** 18
Ohren·fledermaus **351** 9
~höhler **341** 10
~klappe **286** 28
~klips **38** 2
~kriecher **341** 10
~schützer **286** 28
~sessel **47** 57
~spiegel **26** 59
~spritze **26** 58
~stück **26** 16
Ohr·gehänge **38** 7
~klips **38** 2
~läppchen **19** 57
Öhrling **341** 10
Ohr·muschel **19** 56
~pflock **337** 30
~ring **38** 7
~speicheldrüse **21** 9
~wurm **341** 10
Okarina **303** 32
Okkiarbeit **101** 19
Okklusion **9** 25
Ökonom **64** 21
Ökonomie **64** 1–60
Oktaeder **330** 6, 14, 16
Oktant **5** 43
Oktave **300** 26, 66–70
Oktavzeichen **300** 44 u. 45
Oktogon **330** 17
Okular **6** 3, **26** 52, **110** 2
~mikrometer **145** 43
Okulation **57** 30
Okulieren **57** 31
Okuliermesser **57** 31
Öl **98** 24
~ablaßschraube **184** 24
~abstreifring **184** 80
~ausdehnungsgefäß **146** 42, **147** 9
Ölb **343** 16
Öl·bar **191** 31
~baum **367** 29
~behälter **40** 44
~beutel **224** 48
~bild **47** 6
~brenner **40** 58–60
Öldruck·bremse **183** 49
~manometer **149** 15, **207** 14
~messer **149** 15
Oleander **357** 13
Öleinfüllstutzen **184** 47, **186** 58
Öler **180** 65
~klipp **180** 62
Öl·feuerung **40** 44–60
~filter **184** 48
~flasche **46** 42, **191** 14
~hafen **139** 68, **220** 59–62
~heizungskessel **40** 57
Olivenbaum **367** 29

P

Pontonbrücke **210** 17
Pony·franse **35** 36
~frisur **35** 35
Pope **314** 25
Popelinemantel
32 42
Porenkapsel **354** 96
Porree **59** 21
Portal **217** 11,
221 7, 30, **297** 22
~bekleidung **315** 35
~figur **315** 36
~helling **217** 11–18
~kran **198** 15
~stütze **217** 12
Portativ **301** 56
portato **300** 52
Portenband **215** 27
Portier **256** 44,
259 1
Portikus **316** 56
Portionierer **96** 55,
97 32
Portobuch **238** 48
Porträtwasserzeichen
244 31
Portugal **14** 18
Porzellan·herstellung
154
~isolator **233** 67
~maler **154** 17
~scherbe **154** 21
~vase **319** 5
~zahn **27** 32
Posaune **302** 46
Posaunen·stange
302 47
~zug **302** 47
Pose **89** 48
Poseidon **308** 29
Position, 1. bis 5
288 1–5
Positions·licht
226 46
~spiel **265** 1-16
Positiv **112** 9
~kohle **295** 40
~schnitt **323** 3
Possenreißer **289** 38
Post **231, 232**
~ablage **259** 2
~abteil **207** 33
~angestellter **231** 39
~anweisung **232** 12
~auftragskarte
232 7
~automat **231** 29
~beamter **231** 39
~bote **231** 47
~buch **231** 9
~einlieferungsbuch
231 11
~einlieferungsschein
232 9
~fach **231** 8, **259** 2
~formulare **232** 6-15
~freistempel **232** 17
~freistempler **231** 46
~horn **179** 41
Postillion **179** 40
Postillon **179** 40
Post·kabel **194** 28
~karte **232** 2, 4
~krad **231** 33
~kraftrad **231** 33
~kutsche **179** 39, 53
~kutscher **179** 40
~leitzahl **232** 38
~nachnahmekarte
232 8
~paket **231** 3
~pferd **179** 43
~quittung **232** 9
~scheckbrief
232 10
~schließfach **231** 8
~stempel **232** 39
~tasche **231** 48
~überweisungs-
scheck **232** 11
~wagen **179** 39
Postwertzeichen
232 40
~schalter **231** 9
Potenz **327** 1
Potenzieren **327** 1
Potenz·rechnung
327 1
~wert **327** 1
Pottwal **352** 25
Poularde **98** 7
Präge·presse **177** 26
~ring **244** 42
~stempel
244 40 u. 41
~tiegel **177** 29
~tisch **172** 10
~zange **201** 56
Prahm **221** 45
Praktikabel **292** 20
Praliné **98** 80
Praline **98** 80
Pralleiste **304** 39
Praller **300** 33
Prall·hang **13** 57
~triller **300** 33
Prante **88** 46, 50
Präparation **164** 57
Prärieindianer
335 3
Präsentkorb **289** 11
Präsenzbibliothek
250 17
Präzisions·meßwerk-
zeug **145** 38–43
~-Radaranfluggerät
230 10
~radargerät **230** 38
~uhr **107** 37
~wasserwaage
145 39
Prediger **311** 22
~mönch **314** 19
Predigtstuhl **319** 15
Preis·angabe **190** 6
~liste **98** 73
~schild **256** 19
~tafel **79** 43
Prell·bock **199** 40
~klotz **159** 44
~polster **287** 5
Prellstein **53** 22
préparation **288** 28
Presbyterium **311** 36
Preß·balken **178** 4
~bieten **80** 44
~boden **128** 57
~deckel **128** 58
~druckskala **178** 7
Presse **154** 12,
163 12
~, hydraul. **192** 54,
331 7
Presse·foto **325** 44
~fotograf **281** 46
Preßeinrichtung
177 18, 50
Pressen·partie
168 14–17
~schleifer **167** 14
Pressetisch **248** 40
Presseur **176** 29
Preß·gewicht **160** 32
~holzplatte **321** 24
Pressionshaken
156 16
Preß·kanal **65** 34
~kasten **167** 16
~korb **80** 43
Preßluft·druck-
anzeiger **228** 15
~flasche **223** 31
~hahn **138** 50
~meißel **141** 40
~reifen **180** 30
~sandstreuer **205** 19
~schlauch **169** 38,
191 6
~schleifmaschine
141 39
~stampfer **141** 31
Preß·platte **177** 24,
323 31
~pumpe, hydraul.
172 12
~spindel **128** 59
~stoffgehäuse **234** 36
~stroh **65** 29
~walze **156** 20,
162 41
~zylinder **167** 15
Pricke **219** 74
Priester **311** 49,
312 47,
314 25, 32, 47
Prim *[Fechtsport]*
277 1–2
~ *[Musik]* **300** 19
Primaballerina **288** 31
Primär·luftgebläse
152 11
~spule **332** 34
~wicklung **147** 15
Prime **300** 19
Primel **360** 8
Primhieb **277** 1–2
Primoballerino
288 32
Primzahl **326** 13
Prinzengarde **289** 68
Prinzipal **305** 31–33
Prinz Karneval
289 58
Priquemaschine
123 15
Prisma **145** 31,
329 34, **331** 31, 36
~, hexagonales
330 21, 22
~, monoklines
330 24
~führung **170** 54
Prismentisch **331** 35
Pritsche *[Bau]* **114** 41
~ *[Sattel]* **72** 45–49
~ *[Schlaggerät]*
289 48
Pritschen·anhänger
208 46
~wagen **189** 14
~wagen-Frontlenker
189 25
Privat·dedektiv
263 16
~dozent **250** 3
~jacht **216** 20
Probe **296** 20
~abzug **323** 43
~druck **323** 43
~entnahme **93** 10
~kapsel **154** 2
~kugel **331** 46
~würfelform **114** 84
Probier·glas **334** 34
~schaufel **98** 72
Produkt **326** 25
Produktionsleiter
292 26
Professional **281** 22
Professor **250** 3
Profile **136, 283** 43
Profil·gummisohle
99 37
~rahmen **185** 60
~stahl **141** 73
Programm **296** 13
~heft **296** 13
Projektionen
144 59–63
Projektions·gerät
6 14
~öffnung **295** 15
~wand **295** 11
~zeichenspiegel
110 7
Projektor **112** 55,
294 42
~objektiv **295** 35
Promenade **218** 27
Promenadendeck
218 22–27
Propeller **226** 10
~flugzeug **226** 1–8
~kasten **161** 25
~pumpe **212** 47–52
~schutz **221** 54
~triebwerk **227** 1, 8
~turbine **227** 38
~-Turbinenflugzeug
226 9–12
Proportionszirkel
322 2
Propyläen **316** 7
Proskenium **316** 46

Q

Quinte **300** 23
Quinten·gang **300** 1–15
~parade **277** 38
Quintole **300** 38
Quipu **335** 22
Quirl **42** 58, **129** 9
Quitte **60** 49, **357** 17
Quitten·baum **60** 46
~blatt **60** 47
Quittung **238** 51
Quotient **326** 26

R

Rabatte **55** 18
Rabe **346** 1–3
Rabenvogel **346** 1–3
Rachegöttin **308** 51
Rachen **21** 14–37
~höhle **21** 24
~lehre **142** 49
Rackenvögel **343** 24–29
Racket **276** 27
~rahmen **276** 30
~schaft **276** 28
Rad **131** 26, **181** 1, 26–32
~ *[Fahrrad]* **180, 181**
~ *[Puter]* **74** 29
Radar **219** 9–14
~anfluggerät **230** 10
~antenne **218** 8
~bild **219** 12, 13
~blindlandung **230** 34
~empfänger **219** 11, **230** 46
~gerät **219** 9–14, **222** 75, **230** 38
~karte **230** 51
~mast **219** 10
~parabolspiegel **230** 52
~richtspiegel **230** 40
~rundsichtgerät **230** 37, 39
~sender **230** 35, 45
~sichtgerät **230** 48
~stenge **223** 15, 16
~verbindung **4** 23
Radball **287** 29
~spieler **287** 30
Rad·bolzen **185** 32
~bremse **91** 8
~bremszylinder **186** 52
Räder·kasten **142** 7
~werk **107** 19–21
Radfahrer **253** 31
Radi **59** 16
Radial·bohrmaschine **143** 23
~ziegel **151** 25
Radiator **119** 67
Radier·gummi **249** 52
~messer **144** 56, **171** 55
~nadel **323** 16
Radierschablone **240** 32
Radieschen **59** 15
Radikand **327** 2
Radio **234**
~apparat **44** 29
~bühne **234** 14
~sonde **10** 59
Radium·packtisch **29** 54
~schrank **29** 51
~therapie **29** 48–55
~träger **29** 52
Radius **328** 47
~feile **134** 22
Radizieren **327** 2
Rad·kappe **185** 14
~kappenschlüssel **192** 26
~kranz **131** 29
~leier **301** 25
~lenker **198** 54
~mutter **183** 13
~netzspinne **342** 45
~profil **189** 13
~prüfhammer **201** 37
~reifen **131** 30
~reifen- und Radscheiben-Walzwerk **141** 61
~rennbahn **273** 1
~rennfahrer **273** 8
~satz **204** 62–64
~scheibenwalzwerk **141** 61
~schlagen **278** 30
~schlepper **85** 1
~speiche **131** 28
~sport **273**
~stand **189** 4
~steuerung **285** 6
~weber **342** 45
~welle **91** 5
~zierkappe **185** 14
Raffiabast **130** 29
Raffinade **98** 55
Raffinerie **139** 56–68
~lagertank **139** 24
Raglan **34** 41
Rähm **115** 58, **116** 39
Rahmen **68** 32, **78** 40, **99** 52, **160** 33
~bau **185** 59
~holz **114** 64, 74
~rohr **180** 16, 17
~trommel **336** 26
~unterbau **199** 49
~werk **318** 11
Rähmholz **115** 58
Rahm·kreiselerhitzer **77** 25
~kühler **77** 26
~reifer **77** 28
Rahsegel **213** 21, 33, **214** 55–66
Raife **341** 11
Raigras **63** 29
Rain **65** 3
~farn **364** 9
~weide **357** 6
Rakel **162** 61
~einstellung **176** 19
Rakelmesser **176** 18, 34
Rakenvögel **343** 24–29
Rakete **4** 44, 45–47, **224** 53, **227** 49, **229**
Raketen **229**
~apparat **224** 52 u. 53
~brennkammer **227** 60–63, **229** 22
~flug **229**
~flugbahn **229** 44
~hauptstufe **229** 37
~modell **271** 61
~montageturm **229** 32
~motor **229** 12–24
~nase **229** 2
~ruder **229** 27
~schwanzteil **229** 12–27
~spitze **229** 2–5
~start **229** 28–31
~starttisch **229** 29
~steuerbedienungsgerät **229** 3
~stufen **229** 39, 42
~treibsatz **227** 47
~triebwerk **229** 12–24
~vorstufe **229** 36
~wagen **187** 18
Rakett **276** 27
~rahmen **276** 30
~schaft **276** 28
Ralle **343** 20
Rambate **213** 49
Ramiebasthut **36** 8
Ramm·bär **221** 60
~brunnen **254** 60
Ramme **194** 17, **196** 26, **221** 59–62
Ramm·gerüst **221** 59
~gewicht **221** 60
Rammler **74** 18, **88** 59
Ramm·spitze **254** 61
~sporn **213** 9
Rampe **221** 10
~ *[Theater]* **297** 25
Rampen·dekoration **256** 67
~kontrolle **77** 4
~leuchte **297** 26
~licht **297** 26
Rand **159** 11, **239** 2
Rand·balken **114** 3
~beet **55** 18
~bemerkung **178** 68
~bogen **271** 49
Rändel·backe **244** 44
~eisen **244** 43
~rad **111** 30
Randich **70** 21
Rand·inschrift **244** 11
~kluft **282** 2
~löser **240** 28
~meer **15** 26
~messer **99** 65
Rand·platte **217** 48
~steller **240** 7
~stellerskala **240** 7
~träger **210** 9
~versteller **241** 6
~wasser **12** 32
~zone **6** 49
Rang **296** 16, 17, 18
Range **53** 11
Rangier·bahnhof **202** 44–54
~gleis **202** 50
~heber **192** 66
~hügel **202** 49
~lokomotive **202** 46
~meister **202** 48
~stellwerk **202** 47
Rangkrone **246** 43–45
Ranke **60** 30
Ranschel **286** 17
Ranscheln **286** 18
Ranzen **249** 41
~deckel **249** 42
Rappen *[Münze]* **244** 15
Rapport **165** 12
Rapputz **118** 6
Raps **367** 1
Rapünzchen **59** 38
Rapunze **59** 38
Rapunzel **59** 38
Rapunzlein **59** 38
Raschel·maschine **160** 23
~ware **160** 29
Rasen **54** 21, **257** 36
~bankett **196** 56
~besen **54** 16
~fläche **257** 36
~mäher **58** 34
~mähmaschine **58** 34
~randschere **58** 24
~randstecher **58** 33
~schere **58** 24
~sprenger **39** 43, **58** 41
~streifen **197** 37
Rasierapparat **51** 71
Rasieren **104** 11
Rasier·klinge **51** 72
~krem **51** 70
~messer **104** 25
~paste **51** 70
~pinsel **104** 35
~seife **51** 69, **104** 21
~spiegel **51** 81
~wasser **104** 14
Raspel **99** 22, **127** 30, **132** 41
Rassel **30** 42, **289** 40
Raste **87** 70
Raster **171** 35
~punkt **172** 32
Rasur **35** 25
Rateau **263** 5
Rathaus **252** 41
Ratsche **289** 47
Rätsche **289** 47
Ratten·falle **83** 7
~schwanz **127** 31
Raubbein **342** 5
Räuber **60** 20

Riesen·rad **291** 37
~umschwung **279** 12
~welle **279** 12
Riester **99** 49
Riesweg **84** 32
Riet **159** 10
Riet·einzug **165** 6
~kamm **159** 10
Riff **13** 32
~bildner **340** 35
Riffelfeile **106** 51
Riffelung **149** 14
Riffelwalze **159** 47
Rikscha **336** 34
~kuli **336** 35
Rillenzieher **58** 32
Rind **74** 1, **95** 14–37
Rinde **115** 86, **354** 8
Rinden·bürste **58** 21, **83** 30
~gewinnung **85** 25
~koralle **349** 8
~kratzer **58** 16, **83** 29
~schäler **85** 25
~schälmesser **85** 32
Rinder·brust **95** 23
~filet **95** 24
~stall **64** 47
~star **346** 4
~talg **96** 6
Rinds·haut **337** 11
~roulade **96** 22
~talg **96** 6
Ring **38** 20, **313** 16
~ *[Börse]* **243** 3
~ *[Boxsport]* **281** 32
~ *[Turngerät]* **279** 47
~anker **115** 34
~bank **157** 54
~bankantrieb **157** 42
~einfassung **79** 37
Ringel·krebs **341** 12
~natter **350** 38
~reigen **258** 29
~schwänzchen **74** 12
~spiel **291** 2
~spinner **81** 13
~wurm **340** 16
Ringen **281** 7–14
Ringer **281** 7
Ring·finger **21** 67
~flügelflugzeug **225** 70
~graben **310** 37
~horn **132** 22
~kampf **281** 7–14
~kämpfer **281** 7
~leitung **140** 46
~maß **106** 27
~matte **281** 13
~mauer **252** 34, **310** 15
~muskel **21** 5, 8
~ofen **151** 19
~pinsel **121** 15
~richter **281** 37
~riegel **106** 26
~schlüssel **191** 16
Ring·spinnmaschine **157** 34, 45
~ständer **48** 25
~stiftzahn **27** 34
~stock **106** 25
~tennis **267** 31
~wade **90** 25, 26
Rinne **40** 9
Rinnenbügel **117** 32
Rinnstein **194** 7
Rippe **19** 9, 10
~ *[techn.]* **118** 36, **271** 54
Rippelmarke **13** 41
Rippenknorpel **19** 11
Rips **165** 13
Risa **314** 30
Risalit **317** 43
Rispe **354** 69
Rispengras **359** 39
Riß *[Bauzeichn.]* **144** 59–63
~auge **99** 66
~messer **99** 18
Rist **21** 61
~griff **279** 53
Ritter **310** 67
~ *[Falter]* **342** 52
~burg **310** 1
~dach **117** 50
~rüstung **310** 38–65
~schlag **310** 66
~schloß **310** 1
~sporn **62** 13
Rittertum **310**
Ritterwesen **310**
Ritzel **136** 90
Ritzer **324** 21
Rizinus **364** 14
Roadster **187** 11
Roastbeef **95** 17
Robben **352** 18–22
Robe **248** 27
Robinie **355** 70
Rocaille **318** 13
Rochett **314** 50
Rochetum **314** 50
Rock **34** 5
~futter **34** 18
~knopf **34** 6
~kragen **34** 15
~längenmesser **256** 40
~runder **256** 40
Rodehacke **58** 10
Rodel **285** 11
~bahn **285** 11
Rodeln **285** 11 u. 12
Rodel·schlitten **285** 11
~sport **285** 11 u. 12
Rödelung **114** 66
Rodemaschine **67** 38
Roder **68** 41
Rodler **285** 12
Rogen **89** 67
Roggen **69** 1
~ähre **69** 2
~feld **65** 19
~mehl **97** 19
~rose **63** 6
Roggen-Weizen-Brot **97** 25
Rogner **89** 66
Roh·bau **113** 1–49
~bramme **141** 43
Roheisen **140** 39
~abfluß **140** 11
~pfanne **140** 12, 20, 41
Rohgas·leitung **148** 13
~nachkühler **148** 33
~vorkühler **148** 28
Rohhanf **125** 1
Rohling **129** 21, **151** 16
Rohmaterial **163** 1–12
~lager **152** 3
Roh·mehlsilo **152** 5
~ölverarbeitung **139** 21–35
~papierrolle **168** 32
Rohr **180** 60
~, spanisches **130** 32
~abschneider **119** 54
~biegevorrichtung **120** 33
~biegezange **120** 47
Röhre **340** 19
~ *[Pferd]* **73** 23
Röhren, kommunizierende **331** 42
~kessel **146** 5
~laus **342** 13
~ofen **139** 25, 32
~schicht **365** 17
Rohr·feder **324** 23
~geflecht **44** 10
~knie **53** 51
~kolben **362** 21
~kolbenschilf **130** 27
~lehne **43** 23
~leitung **156** 11, **212** 41
~muffe **120** 41
~postbrief **232** 29
~postmarke **232** 30
~rahmen **181** 9, 46, **183** 29
~satz **222** 15
~schelle **117** 31, **119** 26
~schleuder **168** 4
~schmiedezange **120** 51
~schraubstock **119** 12
~sitz **43** 23
Rohrung **118** 71
Rohr·verbindung **119** 40
~weihe **347** 13
~wiege **223** 69
~zange **119** 56
Roh·stahlblock **141** 43
~stein **322** 5
Rohstoff **152** 1, **167** 25
Rohstoffe, textile **163, 164**
Roh·tabakballen **83** 11
~ton **151** 2
~wasser **254** 4
Rokoko·frisur **338** 81
~ornament **318** 13
~wand **318** 9
Rolladen **39** 28
~aussteller **39** 29
~schrank **238** 5
Rollapparat **121** 6, **168** 22
Rollbahn **77** 3
~ *[Ruderboot]* **269** 45
~gleis **149** 26
Rollbett **29** 8
Rolle **29** 12, **85** 4, **331** 4
~ *[Turnübung]* **278** 25
Rollen·block **139** 55
~boden **297** 4
~bohrer **139** 20
~führung **197** 4
~hacke **66** 36
~heft **297** 44
~kette **180** 36
~kopf **216** 5
~kranz **223** 64
~lager **157** 47
~quetscher **112** 37
~richtmaschine **141** 72
~schneider **168** 28
~stromabnehmer **188** 14
~tabak **105** 22
Roller **258** 8
~ *[Motorroller]* **183** 1–40
~anhänger **183** 36
~armaturenbrett **183** 25
~beiwagen **183** 3
~fahrer **183** 38
~kindersitz **183** 30
~mobil **183** 41
~rad **183** 35
~seitenwagen **183** 3
~sitzbank **183** 2
~- u. Motorradvergaser **183** 53–69
Roll·filmtransport **111** 4
~führerwagen **202** 18
~gabelschlüssel **119** 51, **192** 3
~gang **141** 45
~gitter **231** 15
~kragen **32** 13
~kugel **239** 29
~kunstlauf **287** 33
~kutscher **202** 16
~matte **79** 6

Schwamm *[Tier]* **81** 2, **340** 13
~faden **249** 37
~spinner **81** 1
~tier **340** 13
Schwan **257** 46, **343** 16
~ *[Sternbild]* **5** 23
Schwanen·blume **362** 39
~hals **87** 48
~häuschen **257** 47
Schwanz **71** 12, **73** 38, **88** 19, 47, 49
~flosse **350** 10, **352** 29
~stachel **342** 43
~stern **7** 25
~stück **95** 34
Schwärmer **82** 27, **342** 55, **348** 9
Schwarmnetz **78** 54
Schwarte *[Holz]* **115** 96, **149** 39
~ *[Wild]* **88** 56
Schwarten·holz **149** 37
~schälmaschine **149** 49
Schwartling **115** 96
schwarz **246** 26, **320** 13
Schwarz·amsel **346** 13
~beere **361** 23, **363** 7
~binder **126** 16
~brot **97** 26
~deckenfertiger **196** 43
~dorn **358** 27
Schwarzes Brett **145** 45
Schwarz·pulver **87** 53
~steuerung **236** 12
~wälderuhr **107** 54
~wild **88** 51
~wurz **70** 13, **359** 45
~wurzel **59** 35
Schwebe·bahn **209** 15–29
~balken **279** 42
~bank **279** 40
~baum **279** 42
~kante **279** 40
~reck **279** 45
~stange **279** 40
Schweden **14** 20
~klee **70** 3
~reuter **65** 38
Schwefelkohlenstoff **163** 8
~injektor **83** 4
Schwefel·kopf **105** 27
~puder **103** 18
~reinigung **148** 40
~säurezusetzung **164** 23
Schweif **73** 38
~riemen **72** 34
~rübe **73** 34
~säge **126** 3
~stern **7** 25
Schwein **74** 9, **95** 38–54
Schweine·fett **96** 5
~filet **95** 44
~kamm **95** 47
~koben **76** 41
~kotelett **95** 46
~schmalz **96** 5
~stall **64** 47, **76** 39–47
~trog **76** 43
Schweins·kopf **95** 43
~leber **96** 28
Schweinsohr **74** 11
~ *[Gebäck]* **97** 52
Schweinsrüssel **74** 10
Schweiß·aggregat **135** 15
~blatt **33** 31
~brenner **135** 37, 49, 64
~draht **135** 6, 22
Schweißer **135**
~brille **135** 58
~handschuh **135** 4
~schutzhandschuh **135** 28
Schweiß·hund **71** 25
~kabel **135** 12
~mundstück **135** 54
~paste **135** 45
~raupe **135** 8
~riemen **71** 30
~stab **135** 6, 39
~tisch **135** 19, 40
~transformator **135** 11
~trupp **198** 27
~umformer **135** 15
~umspanner **135** 11
~vorhang **135** 18
~zange **135** 5
~zelt **135** 17
Schweiz **14** 21
Schweizerbügel **79** 27
Schweizer Riegel **274** 26
Schwelchboden **92** 13–20
Schwelle **115** 49, **198** 89
Schwellen·rost **114** 39
~schraube **198** 38
~transportwagen **198** 23
~transportzug **198** 25
~verlegegerät **198** 19
~zubringer **198** 24
Schweller **304** 45
Schwellkörper **22** 67
Schwemmkegel **13** 9
Schwenk·arm **27** 21
~bug **116** 57
Schwenker **292** 42
~ *[Glas]* **34** 55
Schwenk·getriebe **221** 4
~kappe **102** 27
~kran **145** 16, **195** 26
~schiebetür **207** 35
~ventil **119** 37
Schwer·athletik **281**
~beschädigtenabteil **203** 28
~beton **114** 72
~gutbaum **216** 3
~gut-Frachtschiff **216** 1
~lastwagen **196** 7
~ölmotoren **184** 37–80
Schwert *[Segelschiff]* **215** 7, **270** 10
~ *[techn.]* **178** 29
~blume **62** 8
Schwertel **62** 11
Schwert·jacht **270** 6–10
~kämpfer **287** 65
~leite **310** 66
~lilie **62** 8
~schlucker **291** 26
Schwestern·häubchen **30** 10
~haube **30** 10
Schwibbogen **317** 28
Schwiele **73** 27
Schwimm·anlage **268** 1–32
~anstalt **268** 1–32
~anzug **267** 42
~arten **268** 33–40
Schwimmatratze **267** 17
Schwimm·bad **218** 23, **268** 1–32
~bagger **211** 56
~bahn **268** 31
~balken **335** 36
~bassin **268** 21–23
~becken **25** 2, **268** 21–23
~dock **217** 31–40
Schwimmeister **268** 16
Schwimmen **268** 17
Schwimmer *[Angelsport]* **89** 4, 52
~ *[techn.]* **93** 13, **119** 60, **211** 12, **212** 34
~becken **268** 23
~gehäuse **183** 66
~kugel **119** 60
~nadel **183** 67
~schacht **212** 35
Schwimm·flosse **267** 41
~fuß **343** 6
~gürtel **268** 19
~haut **74** 36, **343** 7
Schwimm·hose **267** 43
~kappe **267** 29, 44
~kissen **268** 18
~kran **221** 37–46
~lage **268** 33–40
~lehrer **268** 16
~natter **350** 38
~schüler **268** 17
~sport **268**
~stil **268** 33–40
~tier **267** 33
~unterricht **268** 16–20
~weste **224** 57
Schwing·achse **182** 5
~arm **185** 27
Schwinge **88** 76, **307** 15
Schwingel **70** 24
Schwinger **281** 28
Schwing·hebel **181** 24, **184** 58
~kreisspule **234** 25
~pflug **68** 24, 27
~sattel **68** 38, **181** 48, **182** 19
~sieb **153** 9
~sitz **68** 38
Schwingungs·-dämpfer **171** 17, **185** 29, **209** 55
~kreis **234** 25–28
~verdichter **198** 17
Schwung·hebel **182** 44
~rad **102** 44, **159** 15
~radregulator **219** 33
~scheibe **173** 34, **184** 34
Schwurhand **248** 33
Scorpius **5** 38, **6** 39
Scotchterrier **71** 17
Script **292** 45
~girl **292** 39
Sech **68** 10
Sechs·achteltakt **299** 36
~eck **330** 15
~flächner **330** 2
~kantmutter **136** 18
~kantschraube **136** 13
~kantstiftschlüssel **192** 29
~motorenflugzeug **226** 8
~tagefahrer **273** 2
~tagerennen **273** 2–7
~vierteltakt **299** 37
Sechzehntel·note **299** 19
~pause **299** 27
Sedimentgestein **12** 1
See **13** 3, 26
~adler **347** 5
~anemone **349** 20
~bäderschiff **216** 36
~bär **352** 18
~beben **11** 53
~drache **213** 13–17

Stoßzunge **304** 30
Straf·ecke **275** 6
~gefangener **248** 12
Sträfling **213** 48
Straf·raum **274** 5
~raummarke **274** 6
~satz **244** 32
Strahl **328** 20
~, infraroter **4** 25
~, ultravioletter **4** 24
Strahlen·bündel **328** 19
~kranz **313** 36
~schutz **29** 43
~schutzkopf **2** 31
~schutzmeßgerät **2** 1
~tierchen **340** 8
Strähler **129** 14
Strahlflugzeug **4** 38
Strahling **340** 8
Strahl·kopf **109** 2
~pumpe **205** 42
~rohr **255** 33
~tier **340** 8
~triebwerk **227** 41
~turbine **227** 30
~turbinenantrieb **225** 70
Strahlung, kosmische **4** 27–34
~, röntgenähnliche **1** 17, 29
Strahlungs·kessel **146** 5
~meßgerät **2** 1–23, **29** 48
~schutzrohr **10** 35
Strampel·höschen **31** 19
~sack **30** 31
Strand **11** 54, **13** 35–44
~anzug **267** 19
~bad **267**
~burg **267** 35
~ebene **13** 35–44
~geröll **13** 29
~hafer **16** 7
~hose **267** 22
~hut **36** 57, **267** 20
~jacke **267** 21
~kanal **13** 34
~kleidung **267** 19–23
~korb **267** 36
~reiter **343** 19
~schuh **100** 34, **267** 23
~see **13** 44
~tasche **267** 24
~terrasse **11** 54
~wall **13** 35
~wärter **267** 34
~weizen **63** 30
~zelt **267** 45
Strang **72** 22, 35, **154** 8, **161** 29
~aufdrehmaschine **124** 1
Strang·färbeapparat **161** 20
~presse **151** 11, **154** 7
Straße **39** 61, **194** 1
~ I. Ordnung **16** 83
~ II. Ordnung **16** 36
~ III. Ordnung **16** 30
Straßenaufreißer **196** 20
Straßenbahn **193**
~anhänger **193** 6
~anhängewagen **193** 6
~beiwagen **193** 6
~depot **252** 17
~fahrgast **193** 3
~haltestelle **193** 4
~insel **193** 4
~liniennummer **193** 22
~schaffner **193** 11
~triebwagen **193** 8
~weiche **193** 25
Straßenbau **196, 197**
~maschine **196** 1–54, **197** 1
Straßen·brücke **16** 55
~damm **197** 35
~decke **212** 1
~ecke **194** 5, **253** 15
~einlauf **194** 22
~fahrer **273** 8
~händler **253** 5
~hobel **196** 19
~kehrer **195** 8, **253** 47
~kehrmaschine **195** 12
~kehrwagen **195** 7
~kind **53** 11
~kreuzung **253** 9
~lampe **39** 62, **194** 19, **253** 16
~laterne **39** 62, **194** 19, **253** 16
~leuchte **39** 62, **194** 19, **253** 16
~musikant **53** 24
~name **253** 2
~passant **253** 32
~pflaster **194** 11
~querschnitt **194**
~reinigung **195**
~reinigungsmaschinen **195** 1–40
~reinigungswagen **286** 7
~rennen **273** 8–10
~renner **273** 16
~roller **208** 40
~sänger **53** 24
~-Schienen-Omnibus **208** 45
~schild **253** 2
~schmutz **253** 48
~schuh **100** 20
~senkkasten **194** 22
~spreng-, -kehr- u. -waschwagen **195** 31
Straßen·transport **85** 1–6
~überfahrt **16** 40
~walze **196** 36, **197** 19
Stratokumulus **8** 3
Stratoliner **226** 30
Stratosphäre **4** 12
Stratosphären·ballon **4** 41
~verkehrsflugzeug **226** 30
Stratovulkan **11** 15
Stratus **8** 4
Strauch **357, 358**
~besen **64** 39
Sträucherspritze **58** 8
Strauß **343** 2
Straußen·feder **246** 30
~gelege **343** 3
Straußvögel **343** 1–3
Streb **137** 39, **138** 12
Strebe **115** 27, 54, **116** 58, 69, 82, **271** 34, **285** 4
~bogen **317** 28
~pfeiler **317** 27
~werk **317** 27 u. 28
Streb·fördermittel **138** 15
~kappe **138** 26
Streckapparat **23** 41
Strecke *[Geometrie]* **328** 16
~ *[Jagd]* **86** 38
~ *[Spinnerei]* **157** 1
Strecken·abzweigung **199** 23
~band **157** 21
~block **199** 62
~bund **231** 38
~fördermittel **138** 15
~geher **198** 73
~kanne **157** 20
~kennzeichen **198** 79–86
~prüfwagen **208** 38
~schneeschleuder **208** 43
~wärter **198** 73
~wickel **156** 58
Strecker **278** 50
~schicht **113** 64
~verband **113** 60
Streck·gewicht **23** 42
~partie **168** 42
~stütz **278** 16
~walze **157** 13
~werk **156** 60, **157** 14, 21, 22
~werkabdeckung **157** 7
~zwirnerei **164** 46
Streich·balken **115** 40
~baum **159** 37
~blech **68** 4
~bürste **121** 1
~dalben **217** 32
Streichen **12** 2
Streichholz **105** 26
~schachtel **105** 25
Streich·holzständer **260** 24
~instrumente **302** 1–27
~maß **127** 20
~pfahl **212** 9
~rad **301** 26
~riemen **104** 24
~stange **113** 26
Streifband **232** 24
~sendung **232** 24
Streife **247** 19
Streifen·aufleger **177** 42
~hyäne **353** 1
Streif·kappe **272** 45
~stange **158** 38
Streitaxt **335** 16
Streu **75** 29, **76** 12
Streu·büchse **30** 38
~dose **23** 60
~gabel **76** 13
~kasten **67** 8
~klappe **196** 42
~scheibe **292** 38
~schutz **141** 35
Strich **325** 23
~ätzung **172** 35
~einteilung **30** 47
~punkt **325** 19
Strick **125** 18
~bund **34** 25, **36** 45
Strickerei **160**
Strick·holz **125** 27
~leiter **216** 14, **290** 8
~maschine **160** 35
~mütze **36** 53
~strumpf **258** 16
Striegel **72** 54
Stringer **217** 47
Strippe **99** 42
Stripperkran **141** 42
Stroh **130** 30
~ballen **65** 29, **202** 29, **273** 40
~besen **52** 78
~borte **36** 37
~bündel **76** 9
~dach **64** 35
~einfall **65** 31
~einlage **99** 5
~feile **132** 35
~fiedel **303** 61
~gabel **76** 13
~hut **36** 6, 22, 39
~leittrommel **68** 61
~matte **79** 6
~miete **65** 28
~presse **65** 30, **67** 54, **68** 71
~schuh **100** 7
~schütte **76** 12
~schüttler **68** 62
~seil **65** 24
~trinkhalm **261** 36
~zuführung **68** 70
Strom **16** 45
Stromabnehmer **206** 3, 55
~stange **188** 13
~ventil **206** 38

Strom·fähre **211** 10
~insel **211** 4
~kabel **29** 34
~leiter **147** 43
~leitung **194** 25
~messer **206** 43
~pfeiler **210** 32
~sammler **192** 38
~schiene **146** 29
~schlauch **211** 9
~spule **332** 8
~stoßflügel **233** 21
~stoßkontakt **233** 23
~strich **211** 9
Strömung **211** 9
Strömungs·getriebe **207** 4
~verlauf **211** 9
~weiser **211** 43
Strom·wandler **147** 58
~zuführung **145** 15
~zuleitungskabel **229** 35
Strumpf **33** 32
~fabrik **160** 1–66
~halter **33** 19
~hose **338** 47
~warenabteilung **256** 17
~wirker **346** 8
Stubben **84** 14
Stuben·fliege **341** 1, 2
~wagen **30** 32
Stück **162** 51
~, dickes **95** 50
Stückgut **202** 4
~schnellverkehrswagen **202** 6
~schuppen **220** 28
~waage **202** 36
Student **250** 9
Studenten·blume **62** 4, 20
~nelke **62** 6
Studentin **250** 10
Studie **321** 36
Studierzimmer **47** 1–61
Studio **234** 7, 12, **237** 1–11, **321** 1-43
~schauspieler **237** 11
~scheinwerfer **237** 9
Stufe **40** 27
Stufen·boot **273** 48
~dach **319** 2
~pyramide **315** 22, **335** 20
~rad **136** 80
~rakete **229** 3
~trennung **229** 39–42
~turm **315** 32
~volant **32** 30
Stuhl **44** 9
~bein **44** 14
~bohrer **126** 1
~schlitten **286** 29
Stulpe **37** 7, **100** 46
Stulpenstiefel **338** 58
Stülper **78** 52
Stülpkorb **78** 52
Stummel **186** 54
Stumpen **105** 4
Stumpftonne **219** 52
Stunden·achse **6** 5, **109** 20
~kreis **109** 21
~plan **249** 26
~rad **107** 38
~zeiger **107** 5
Stupa **319** 21, 28
Stupsbürste **121** 13
Sturm **274** 17–21
~ball **220** 6, **267** 4
Stürmer **268** 51, **287** 27
~reihe **274** 17–21
Sturmhaken **53** 48
Sturmhaube **282** 20
~ *[Ritterrüstung]* **310** 60
Sturm·hut **363** 1
~laterne **76** 16
~laufbock **279** 26
~laufbrett **279** 25
~warnung **220** 6
Sturz **283** 4
Stürze **302** 37
Sturz·haube **285** 16
~helm **273** 3, **275** 29, **285** 16
~kappe **285** 16
Stürzner **119** 13
Sturzriegel **115** 57
Stute **74** 2, 8
Stutzbart **35** 15
Stütze **157** 42, **217** 12
Stutzen **39** 12, **117** 30, **120** 59
~ *[Gewehr]* **86** 30
~ *[Strumpf]* **274** 54
Stützen·fundament **209** 81
~galgen **209** 80
~schuh **209** 79
~schalung **114** 11, 73
Stutzer **289** 33
Stütz·isolator **193** 46
~lager **91** 10
Stutzperücke **35** 2
Stütz·rad **68** 26, **189** 34
~rolle **255** 50
~schwimmer **225** 64
~stange **290** 13
~strebe **193** 45
~verband **17** 10
~weite **210** 34
~zylinder **223** 62
Stylobat **316** 32
Subkontraoktave **300** 62
Sublimatschale **28** 31
Substanzbehälter **334** 61
Subtrahend **326** 24
Subtrahieren **326** 24
Subtraktion **326** 24
Subvulkan **11** 20
Sucher **111** 6, **294** 8
~ausblick **111** 17
~einblick **111** 16
~fenster **294** 25
~fernrohr **109** 19
~objektiv **111** 17
~schacht **111** 16
Suchjagd **86** 1–8
Südamerika **14** 32-34, **15** 13
Süd·äquatorialstrom **15** 34
~früchte **368**
Südliches Dreieck **5** 40
~ Eismeer **15** 22
~ Kreuz **5** 44
Süd·licht **4** 35
Sudprozeß **92** 25-36
Süd·ostpassat **9** 49
~weinglas **46** 84
~wester **224** 54
Sulfidierung **163** 9
Sulky **272** 39
Süllrand **269** 59
Summand **326** 23
Summe **326** 23
Summen·taste **240** 64
~zähler **239** 51
Summer **206** 45
Sumpf·pflanzen **362**
~porst **361** 21
~sohle **137** 12–13
~weihe **347** 13
Super-Autovertikal-Reproduktionskamera **171** 33
Superpelliceum **314** 34
Suppen·kelle **46** 14
~knochen **96** 8
~löffel **46** 61
~schöpflöffel **46** 14
~schüssel **46** 15
~teller **46** 5
~würfel **98** 26
~würze **98** 30
Supplementwinkel **328** 14
Support **142** 22, **143** 4
Suppositorium **23** 7
Supraporte **318** 12
Süß·kirsche **61** 5
~klee **70** 10
~rahmbutterungsanlage **77** 31
Süßwaren **98** 75–86
~laden **253** 19
Symbol **6** 21–31
Symmetrie·achse **328** 25, **330** 4
~ebene **330** 5
~zentrum **330** 3
Synagoge **252** 29
Synchronisation **293** 25–29
Synchronisierungs·-einrichtung **147** 32
~atelier **293** 25
Synchron·klappe **292** 35
~kupplungsnabe **186** 60
~motor **293** 12
~regisseur **293** 26
~sprecherin **293** 27
Synklinale **12** 18
Synkope **300** 39–45
Syrien **14** 43
Syrinx **301** 2
Szene **297** 36

T

Tabak **105** 20
~ballen **83** 11
~blatt **366** 43
~pflanze **366** 40
~waren **105**
~warenkiosk **200** 47
Tabelle **144** 3
Tabelliermaschine **241** 55
Tabernakel **311** 39
Tableau **263** 9
Tablett **45** 60, **260** 19, **261** 14
Tablette **23** 11
Tablettenröhrchen **23** 10
Tabulator·einrichtung **240** 21
~löscher **240** 3
Tacho·graph **205** 56
~meter **175** 54, **181** 33, 39, **186** 7
Täcks **99** 17
Tafel **249** 32
~ *[Tisch]* **46**
~berg **13** 59
~glaserzeugung **155** 1–11
~lappen **249** 5
~leim **127** 39
~leuchter **46** 16
~pfosten **249** 3
~schere **119** 15
~schmuck **46** 19
~schwamm **249** 4, 36
~tuch **46** 2
~wasser **98** 87
Tagebau **150** 1
Tages·anlage **137** 3–11
~betrieb **137** 3–11
~karte **260** 21
~kasse **256** 2
~krem **103** 11
~lichtfilmentwickelmaschine **293** 15
~reisezug **207** 37
~stempel **232** 39
~umsatz **256** 10
~zeitung **47** 8
Tagetes **62** 20

Tag·falter **348** 1–6
~pfauenauge **348** 2
~raubvögel **347** 1-24
~undnachtgleiche **5** 6 u. 7
Taifunrad **291** 46
Taille **18** 31
~, geschnürte **338** 53
Taillenmantel **32** 52
Tailleur **32** 1
Tailor **32** 1
~made **32** 8
Takelung **214** 1–72, **270** 38, 43
Takt **299** 30–44
~art **299** 30–44
~geber **237** 17
~messer **304** 19
~stock **296** 27
~strich **299** 44
Talar **248** 27, **313** 4, **314** 33
Talaue **13** 62
Taler **244** 6
Talform **13** 52–56
Talg **96** 6
Tal·gletscher **12** 49
~grund **13** 67
Talje **216** 4, 48
Taljenläufer **216** 50
Tal·landschaft **13** 57–70
~lehne **13** 65
Tallymann **221** 27
Talon **243** 19
Tal·schi **283** 26
~sohle **13** 67
~sperre **212** 57-64
~station **209** 39
~stationsbahnsteig **209** 51
~tempel **315** 8
Tambour *[Architektur]* **317** 44
~ *[Spinnerei]* **156** 43
~rost **156** 55
Tamburin **258** 47, **303** 30, 45
~spiel **258** 45
Tamper **1** 50
Tampon **323** 22
Tamul **324** 11
tamulisch **324** 11
Tändelschürze **32** 23
Tandem **179** 50
~modell **271** 43
Tang **362** 48
Tangens **328** 32
Tangente *[Geometrie]* **328** 48
~ *[Musikinstrumente]* **301** 43
Tank *[Gefäß]* **3** 2, **185** 65, **216** 30
~bodenventil **40** 49
~boot **220** 23
~decke **217** 51
~deckelöffner **192** 26
~einfüllstutzen **186** 30
Tanker **216** 22
~brücke **216** 24
Tank·insel **190** 13
~löschfahrzeug **255** 51
~löschwagen **255** 51
~pumpe **190** 2
~rahmen **181** 46
~randplatte **217** 48
~säule **190** 2
~stelle **190**
Tankstellen·beleuchtung **190** 8
~dach **190** 7
Tankwart **190** 10
~raum **190** 9
Tankzuleitung **229** 33
Tanne **356** 1
Tannen·nadel **356** 11
~zapfen **356** 2
Tanz **288**
~, klassischer **288** 29–34
~, moderner **288** 41
~ für drei **288** 31–34
Tanzen **259** 46
Tänzerin **288** 40
~, indische **289** 25
Tanz·groteske **288** 35
~gruppe **288** 29
~knopf **258** 18
~kunst **288** 29–41
~orchester **289** 2
~paar **259** 46, **288** 44 u. 45
~partner **288** 44
~partnerin **288** 45
~platz **316** 47
~pantomime **288** 37
~raum **204** 25
~rock **288** 33
~schmuck **337** 36
~schuh **100** 32, **288** 34
~stock **337** 37
~trommel **337** 14
~truppe **298** 6
~übung **288** 1–10
~wagen **204** 24
Tapete **121** 32
Tapeten·bahn **121** 36
~kleister **121** 30
~leiste **121** 33
Tapezier·bock **121** 41
~hammer **121** 39
Tapezieren **121** 29–41
Tapezierer **121**
Tapir **351** 26
Tasche **31** 10, **32** 59, **37** 10
~ *[Schiff]* **213** 57
~, aufgesetzte **32** 3
Täschelkraut **63** 9
Taschen·besatz **32** 53
~dieb **291** 16
~dosimeter **2** 15
Taschen·fahrplan **200** 44
~geige **301** 20
~klappe **34** 9
~klemme **2** 18
~lampe **120** 26
~lampenbatterie **120** 27
~messer **266** 17
~schirm **43** 10
~tuch **31** 8, **37** 2
~uhr **107** 9
Tasse **45** 7, **261** 19
Tassel **338** 23
Tasso **119** 20
Tastatur **169** 37, **241** 33, 44, **304** 4 u. 5, **306** 12
Taste **240** 26, **301** 38, 49, **304** 4, 5, **305** 8, 40
Tasten·feld **240** 25, **241** 33
~instrument **304** 1
~mechanik **304** 22–39
Taster **169** 32
Tast·fühlerkontakt **159** 31
~zirkel **129** 18, **322** 3
Taterkorn **70** 20
Tätowierung **289** 44
Tatze **353** 4
Tatzelwurm **307** 1
Tau *[Seil]* **125** 19, **224** 50, **279** 5
Taube **64** 10, **74** 33, **343** 23
Tauben·schlag **64** 8
~skabiose **359** 29
Täuberich **74** 33
Taubgerste **63** 28
Tauchbrille **267** 38
Tauchen **268** 39
Taucher **135** 46, **224** 13–19
~anzug **224** 27
~ausrüstung **224** 20–30
~boot **224** 13
~helm **224** 22
~leiter **224** 16
~schuh **224** 30
Tauch·flosse **267** 41
~huhn **343** 13
~sieder **41** 83
~versuch **4** 9
~walze **158** 42
~zelle **223** 19
Taufe **313** 1
Tauf·becken **311** 3, **313** 11
~kapelle **313** 2
~kleidchen **313** 8
Täufling **313** 7
Tauf·schleier **313** 9
~stein **311** 2, **313** 10
Tauhangeln **279** 6
Taukreuz **313** 53
Taurus **5** 25, **6** 33
Tausenderstelle **326** 3
Tausend·güldenkraut **364** 10
~schön **62** 2, 21
Tausendstel **326** 20
Tau·wurm **340** 20
~ziehen **258** 35
Taxameter **253** 36
Taxe **253** 35
Taxi **253** 35
~chauffeur **253** 37
~fahrer **253** 37
~schofför **253** 37
~stand **253** 35
Tazette **62** 4
Techniker **1** 41, **144** 23
Teckel **71** 33
Teclubrenner **334** 4
Teddybär **49** 5
Tee **98** 68
~blatt **366** 9
~-Ei **41** 81
~haube **45** 51
~kanne **45** 47
~kessel **45** 49
~löffel **45** 11
~maschine **45** 49
Teenager **261** 23
Teer·abscheider **148** 31
~destillation **164** 4
~-Gaswasser-Pumpe **148** 29
~kessel **196** 47
~spritzmaschine **196** 46
~- u. Bitumenkocher **196** 46
~- u. Phenolgewinnung **164** 3
~vorbehälter **148** 36
~vorlage **148** 12
~wagen **148** 38
Tee·seiher **42** 43, **45** 48
~sieb **42** 43, **45** 48
~strauch **366** 7
~wagen **45** 53
~wärmer **45** 51
Teich **16** 79, **54** 19, **257** 50
~karpfen **350** 4
Teig·rad **42** 50
~rädchen **42** 50
~schaber **42** 51
~teilmaschine **97** 64
~waage **97** 77
~waren **98** 32-34
Teilbaum **160** 25
Teilen **326** 26
Teiler **326** 26
Teil·flach **330** 24
~gelesekamm **158** 56
~kamm **158** 56
~kreis **109** 25, **330** 32, **331** 38
~nehmer **233** 31

V